Lecture Notes in Artificial Intelligence 7003

Subseries of Lecture Notes in Computer Science

LNAI Series Editors

Randy Goebel
University of Alberta, Edmonton, Canada
Yuzuru Tanaka
Hokkaido University, Sapporo, Japan
Wolfgang Wahlster
DFKI and Saarland University, Saarbrücken, Germany

LNAI Founding Series Editor

Joerg Siekmann
DFKI and Saarland University, Saarbrücken, Germany

Hepu Deng   Duoqian Miao   Jingsheng Lei
Fu Lee Wang (Eds.)

Artificial Intelligence and Computational Intelligence

Third International Conference, AICI 2011
Taiyuan, China, September 24-25, 2011
Proceedings, Part II

 Springer

Series Editors

Randy Goebel, University of Alberta, Edmonton, Canada
Jörg Siekmann, University of Saarland, Saarbrücken, Germany
Wolfgang Wahlster, DFKI and University of Saarland, Saarbrücken, Germany

Volume Editors

Hepu Deng
RMIT University, School of Business Information Technology
City Campus, 124 La Trobe Street, Melbourne, VIC 3000, Australia
E-mail: hepu.deng@rmit.edu.au

Duoqian Miao
Tongji University, School of Electronics and Information
Shanghai 201804, China
E-mail: miaoduoqian@163.com

Jingsheng Lei
Shanghai University of Electronic Power
School of Computer and Information Engineering
Shanghai 200090, China
E-mail: jshlei@126.com

Fu Lee Wang
Caritas Institute of Higher Education, Department of Business Administration
18 Chui Ling Road, Tseung Kwan O, Hong Kong, China
E-mail: pwang@cihe.edu.hk

ISSN 0302-9743   e-ISSN 1611-3349
ISBN 978-3-642-23886-4   ISBN 978-3-642-23887-1 (eBook)
DOI 10.1007/978-3-642-23887-1
Springer Heidelberg Dordrecht London New York

Library of Congress Control Number: 2011936133

CR Subject Classification (1998): I.2, H.3-4, F.1, I.4-5, J.3, K.4.4, D.2

LNCS Sublibrary: SL 7 – Artificial Intelligence

Typesetting: Camera-ready by author, data conversion by Scientific Publishing Services, Chennai, India

Printed on acid-free paper

Springer is part of Springer Science+Business Media (www.springer.com)

Preface

The 2011 International Conference on Artificial Intelligence and Computational Intelligence (AICI 2011) was held during September 24–25, 2011 in Taiyuan, China. AICI 2011 received 1,073 submissions from 20 countries and regions. After rigorous reviews, 265 high-quality papers were selected for publication in the AICI 2011 proceedings. The acceptance rate was 24%.

The aim of AICI 2011 was to bring together researchers working in many different areas of artificial intelligence and computational intelligence to foster the exchange of new ideas and promote international collaborations. In addition to the large number of submitted papers and invited sessions, there were several internationally well-known keynote speakers.

On behalf of the Organizing Committee, we thank Taiyuan University of Technology for its sponsorship and logistics support. We also thank the members of the Organizing Committee and the Program Committee for their hard work. We are very grateful to the keynote speakers, session chairs, reviewers, and student helpers. Last but not least, we thank all the authors and participants for their great contributions that made this conference possible.

September 2011

Hepu Deng
Duoqian Miao
Jingsheng Lei
Fu Lee Wang

Preface

Organization

Organizing Committee

General Co-chairs

Wendong Zhang	Taiyuan University of Technology, China
Qing Li	City University of Hong Kong, Hong Kong

Program Committee Co-chairs

Hepu Deng	RMIT University, Australia
Duoqian Miao	Tongji University, China

Steering Committee Chair

Jingsheng Lei	Shanghai University of Electric Power, China

Local Arrangements Co-chairs

Fu Duan	Taiyuan University of Technology, China
Dengao Li	Taiyuan University of Technology, China

Proceedings Co-chairs

Fu Lee Wang	Caritas Institute of Higher Education, Hong Kong
Ting Jin	Fudan University, China

Sponsorship Chair

Zhiyu Zhou	Zhejiang Sci-Tech University, China

Program Committee

Adi Prananto	Swinburne University of Technology, Australia
Adil Bagirov	University of Ballarat, Australia
Ahmad Abareshi	RMIT University, Australia
Alemayehu Molla	RMIT University, Australia
Andrew Stranier	University of Ballarat, Australia
Andy Song	RMIT University, Australia
An-Feng Liu	Central South University, China
Arthur Tatnall	Victoria University, Australia
Bae Hyeon	Pusan National University, Korea
Baoding Liu	Tsinghua University, China
Carmine Sellitto	Victoria University, Australia
Caroline Chan	Deakin University, Australia
CheolPark Soon	Chonbuk National University, Korea
Chowdhury Morshed	Deakin University, Australia
Chung-Hsing Yeh	Monash University, Australia
Chunqiao Tao	South China University, China
Costa Marly	Federal University of Amazonas, Brazil
Craig Parker	Deakin University, Australia
Daowen Qiu	Zhong Shan University, China
Dat Tran	University of Canberra, Australia
Dengsheng Zhang	Monash University, Australia
Edmonds Lau	Swinburne University of Technology, Australia
Elspeth McKay	RMIT University, Australia
Eng Chew	University of Technology Sydney, Australia
Feilong Cao	China Jiliang University, China
Ferry Jie	RMIT University, Australia
Furutani Hiroshi	University of Miyazaki, Japan
Gour Karmakar	Monash University, Australia
Guojun Lu	Monash University, Australia
Heping Pan	University of Ballarat, Australia
Hossein Zadeh	RMIT University, Australia
Ian Sadler	Victoria University, Australia
Irene Zhang	Victoria University, Australia
Jamie Mustard	Deakin University, Australia
Jeff Ang Charles	Darwin University, Australia
Jennie Carroll	RMIT University, Australia
Jenny Zhang	RMIT University, Australia
Jian Zhou T.	Tsinghua University, China
Jingqiang Wang	South China University, China
Jinjun Chen	Swinburne University of Technology, Australia
Joarder Kamruzzaman	Monash University, Australia
Kaile Su	Beijing University, China
Kankana Chakrabaty	University of New England, Australia

Table of Contents – Part II

Heuristic Searching Methods

Immune Computation

Information Security

Information Theory

Intelligent Control

Intelligent Image Processing

Intelligent Information Fusion

Intelligent Information Retrieval

Intelligent Signal Processing

Knowledge Representation

Machine Learning

A Novel Artificial Bee Colony Algorithm Based on Attraction Pheromone for the Multidimensional Knapsack Problems

Hongkai Wei[1], Junzhong Ji[1], Yufang Qin[1], Yamin Wang[2], and Chunnian Liu[1]

[1] College of Computer Science and Technology, Beijing University of Technology
Beijing Municipal Key Laboratory of Multimedia and Intelligent Software Technology
Beijing 100124, China
[2] College of Computer Science, Liaocheng University
Liaocheng 252059, China
weihongkai010101@163.com

Abstract. In this paper, we propose a novel artificial bee colony(ABC) algorithm for the multidimensional knapsack problems, which introduces the attraction pheromone and presents a transition strategy based on the attraction pheromone. In our algorithm, the scout generates a food source according to the transition strategy and replaces the abandoned food source by comparison with the corresponding elite food source, while the employed bee and onlooker modify the repair operator using the transition strategy in the determination of the neighborhood of a food source. Experimental results show that our approach performs better in the quality of solutions, the convergence speed and the time performance than traditional ABC algorithm.

Keywords: Artificial bee colony algorithm, multidimensional knapsack problems, attraction pheromone, transition strategy.

1 Introduction

The objective of MKP is to find a subset of objects whose total profit can be maximized while satisfying a set of knapsack constraints. The MKP can be expressed as follows [1]: Given n objects and a set of resource constraints $B=\{b_1,b_2,...,b_m\}$, the optimization goal is:

$$\text{Max} \sum_{j=1}^{n} C_j x_j$$

$$\text{s.t.} \quad \sum_{j=1}^{n} a_{ij} x_j \leq b_i, \forall i \in \{1,2,\cdots,m\}$$

$$x_j \in \{0,1\}, j \in \{1,2,\cdots,n\}. \tag{1}$$

where x_j is the decision variable associated with an object j, and its value is set to 1 if j is selected, otherwise is 0. a_{ij} represents the required amount of a resource i by the

H. Deng et al. (Eds.): AICI 2011, Part II, LNAI 7003, pp. 1–10, 2011.

object j, b_i is the available quantity of the resource i, and C_j is the utility value of the object j. For the MKP, C_j, a_{ij}, b_i are nonnegative.

There are many practical problems which can be formulated as a MKP, e.g., the capital budgeting problem, the cargo loading, the processor allocation in distributed systems, and the project selection. Therefore, more and more people do the research for solving the MKP recently. In general, the algorithms include two kinds of methods to solve the MKP, exact and heuristic methods [2]. The exact method is used to employ some typical search techniques, such as Enumeration algorithm, Branch and Bound method and Approximate Dynamic programming, etc. However, this method can be only applied to some small-scaled MKP for high computation complexity. The heuristic method is proposed by simulating the natural phenomena and human thinking process. It includes many new techniques, e.g., Genetic algorithm [3], Particle swarm optimization [4] and Ant Colony Optimization algorithm [5], etc. In 2010, Shyam Sundar, Alok Singh and André Rossi [6] proposed an artificial bee colony (ABC) algorithm belonging to heuristic methods for solving MKP, which has already obtained good results. However, some problems are still existed such as large iteration number and blindness of searching food sources. To overcome the above shortcomings, we introduce the attraction pheromone and a transition strategy based on this pheromone. Applying this strategy, scouts reform their behavior in searching food source, while employed bees and onlookers modify the repair operator in the way determining the neighborhood of a food source. Experimental results show that our algorithm can speed up the convergence speed and obtain better solutions.

2   Artificial Bee Colony Algorithm

Artificial bee colony (ABC) algorithm is a meta-heuristic search technique inspired by the foraging behavior of real honey bees. This algorithm is proposed by Karaboga in 2005[7] and its performance are better than or similar to other population-based algorithms such as genetic algorithm, particle swarm optimization algorithm and so on [8]. In ABC algorithm, each food source represents a feasible solution of the problem and the amount of nectar of a food source represents the fitness of the solution. The artificial bee colony consists of three types of bees: employed bees, onlookers and scouts. In ABC algorithm, each employed bee is associated with a food source. The employed bees are responsible for bringing loads of nectar from their food sources to the hive sharing information about these food sources by dancing with onlookers. Onlookers are those bees waiting in the dance area of the hive for employed bees to share information about their food sources. Scouts are responsible for discovering new food sources. The artificial bee colony algorithm for MKP (ABC_MKP) is described in [6].Specially in ABC_MKP algorithm, the food source in the neighborhood of a particular food source i is determined by selecting another food source j (different from i) randomly. A maximum of two distinct objects from j but not present in i are selected randomly to insert solution i, which makes solution i infeasible. When i and j are identical, we call the situation collision. If a collision occurs, different approaches are taken for the employed bee and onlooker bee. If there is no collision, a repair operator is proposed for converting infeasible solution into a feasible one. The repair operator consists of a DROP PHASE and an ADD PHASE, and in these two phases, objects are dropped and added on the basis of their pseudo-utility ratios. In addition, ABC_MKP algorithm uses the local search in 1-1 exchange and 2-1 exchange ways to improve the solution quality.

3   ABC Algorithm Based on Attraction Pheromone for MKP

In this section we present the ABC algorithm based on Attraction Pheromone for MKP (ABCAP_MKP). It mainly contains two parts. Firstly, we introduce the attraction pheromone and propose the transition strategy based on this pheromone. Then, the novel ABC algorithm for MKP is presented in detail.

3.1   The Transition Strategy Based on Attraction Pheromone

In nature, honey bees mainly communicate with each other by behavior communication and chemistry communication [9]. However, in traditional artificial bee colony algorithm, honey bees only dance (behavior communication) to exchange information. For complying with the fact in nature and the basic idea of ABC, it is necessary and reasonable to add chemistry communication besides behavior communication to enhance the cooperation among honey bees. In the chemistry communication, the real honey bees usually use with bee attraction pheromone. More specifically, we assume each bee move to a solution and deposit the attraction pheromone on every object of this solution. Other bees perceive the presence of attraction pheromone and tend to select the objects where the pheromone intensity is higher. Through this mechanism, bees are able to search food sources in a more effective way.

In the searching process of our algorithm, honey bees calculate the transition probability according to the attraction pheromone and the heuristic information of MKP. The transition probability P can be defined as follows:

$$P_j = \frac{\varsigma_j^{\alpha} \times \eta_j^{\beta}}{\sum_t \varsigma_j^{\alpha} \times \eta_j^{\beta}}.$$

(2)

where ς_j and η_j represent the attraction pheromone and the local heuristic information of the object j, α and β represent the weight of ς_j and η_j separately. The selecting ratio for bees is obtained by (2) if the object t belongs to the candidate set with constraints met; otherwise, the ratio is set to 0. In (2), it can be seen that the probability of selecting an object is determined by the tradeoff between pseudo-utility and attraction pheromone intensity.

In (2), the local heuristic information of MKP can be defined as follows:

$$\eta_j = \frac{C_j}{\frac{1}{m} \sum_{i=1}^{m} \delta_{ij}}.$$

(3)

where δ_{ij} is the average consumption of resources for the object j, i.e., the ratio between the consumption of resources and the remained resources for j. We can see from (3), the more profit the object j provides, the greater the η_j is; meanwhile, the less average resources the object j consumes, the greater the η_j is.

The attraction pheromone of each object in (2) is set to a constant quantity in the initialization. That is, $\varsigma_j(0)= 1/\sum_{j=1}^{n}C_j$, $j=1,...,n$. In an iteration, when employed bees and onlookers have finished their work after a time internal $\Box r$, the attraction pheromone intensity of each object is updated. The formula of updating attraction pheromone intensity is defined as follows:

$$\varsigma_j(r+\Delta r) = \rho \times \varsigma_j(r) + \sum_{l=1}^{FoodNumber} \Delta\varsigma_j^l(r,r+\Delta r) + \sum_{t=1}\Delta\varsigma_{tj} \ . \tag{4}$$

Therein, $0 < \rho \leq 1$ is a surplus coefficient; $\varsigma_j(r)$ is the pheromone intensity of the object j at time r; $\Delta\varsigma_j^l(r,r+\Delta r)$ represents the pheromone trail that l^{th} bee deposited on the object j, and it is set to $o_l/\sum_{j=1}^{n}C_j$ if the object j is present in the solution l where o_l represents the profit of solution l, otherwise it is set to 0; t is an object related with the object j; $\Delta\varsigma_{tj}$ represents the pheromone effect between the object t and the object j, it can be quantized by (5):

$$\Delta\varsigma_{tj} = \begin{cases} \dfrac{f_{t,j}+1}{K+1} \times \Delta\varsigma_t, & f_{t,j} > 0 \\ 0, & f_{t,j} = 0 \end{cases} . \tag{5}$$

where K is the number of elite food sources selected from $FoodNumber$ food sources, $f_{t,j}$ represents the frequency of the object t and the object j appearing in the solution set together.

We can see from (4) that three factors determine the update of attraction pheromone intensity together. The first factor is the volatility strategy of pheromone, which can prevent the pheromone intensity from cumulating too fast and weaken the impact of history pheromone. The second factor is the reward based on object [10]. When the objects occur in the solution set with more frequency, the pheromone intensity of these objects will be increased more. The last factor is the reward based on pairs of objects [11]. In a pair of objects like an object t and an object j, the occurrence for t will increase the pheromone intensity of j. By this way, it is more reasonable to reflect the pheromone intensity of each object.

3.2   ABCAP_MKP Algorithm

The main features in our ABCAP_MKP algorithm are described below:

The reformed behavior of the scouts: The scouts mainly reform their behavior in two aspects.

1) In the initialization process, the scout selects objects one by one according to P with all the knapsack constraints satisfied.

2) Instead of the control parameter *limit*, the k elite food sources set are given. For each food source in the k elite food sources set, a scout relatively generates a new food source by P and computes the nectar amount of the new food source. By the comparison of the nectar amount between the new food source and the corresponding food source in the k elite food sources set, the food source with higher nectar amount is remained.

The modified repair operator in the determination of the neighborhood of a food source: We modify the repair operator by regarding the probability P as the basis of DROP PHASE and ADD PHASE. In the DROP PHASE, with probability p_d, the objects of a food source are dropped in the increasing order of their transition probabilities, otherwise the objects of the food source are dropped randomly. The process of dropping objects is repeated until the infeasible solution becomes feasible. In the ADD PHASE, objects not present in a food source are sorted in decreasing order according to their transition probabilities. Without violating all constraints, each sorted unselected object is checked one by one whether it can be added to the food source. Until all the unselected objects are checked, this process is end.

No the local search: Experimental results show that local search may not improve the profit of solution effectively but cost much time. Furthermore, it is difficult to control where the iteration happened for the local search in the iteration process. For these reasons, we do not apply the local search in our algorithm.

As a summary, the main steps of ABCAP_MKP algorithm are described in Algorithm.1.

```
Algorithm 1.The ABCAP_MKP algorithm
begin
  The scouts initialize Foods randomly.
  repeat
  For i=1: FoodNumber do:
    {An employed bee moves to Foods(i) and determines a
     neighborhood of this food source with the modified
     repair operator and gets the neighbor sol_i ;
     Foods(i)= Select(Foods(i),sol_i);}
  For j=1: FoodNumber do:
   {t=BinaryTournamentSelect(Foods);
    An onlooker moves to Foods(t) and determines a
    neighborhood  of this food source with the modified
    repair operator and gets the neighbor sol_t ;
    Foods(t)= Select(Foods(t),sol_t);}
  Select  FoodsK,  update  the  attraction  pheromone
  according to (4) and get P;
  The scouts reform their behavior by comparison with
  FoodsK.
  until a termination condition is met.
end.
```

Therein, *FoodNumber* represents the number of food sources; *Foods* represents the set of food sources; *FoodsK* represents the K elite food sources set selected from *Foods*. *Select()* returns the food source with higher nectar amount by comparing two food sources; *BinaryTournamentSelect()* is to select two food sources randomly from *Foods* and return the position of the food source with higher nectar amount in probability b_t or choose the other one in 1- b_t (b_t is a number in the range [0,1]).

4 Experiment Results

A series of experiments have been conducted to validate the performance of ABCAP_MKP. In these experiments, benchmark instances of MKP from OR-Library are used. ABCAP_MKP algorithm has been executed on a Windows XP based 2.00 GHz Intel Core system with 1G RAM, which is programmed by MATLAB. Parameter values are chosen empirically, that is *FoodNumber*=200, K=50, α= 1, β= 5, ρ= 0.7, b_t =0.9, p_d=0.3. In the following, we compare our algorithm with the original ABC_MKP algorithm in different ways and every algorithm terminates in 50 iterations and runs for 50 trials on each instance in the follows.

4.1 Effect of Two Features in ABCAP_MKP Algorithm

This section aims to investigate the improvements made by the behavior of scouts and modified repair operator in the determination of the neighborhood of a food source.

Table 1. Comparison of two algorithms on 20 instances of MKP

Instances	ABC_MKP		ABCAP1_MKP	
	Max	*Avg*	*Max*	*Avg*
5.100-00	24233	24043.46	**24381**	24339.28
5.100-01	**24274**	24212.48	**24274**	24274.00
5.100-02	23538	23476.66	23538	23538.00
5.100-03	23440	23193.64	23489	23455.25
5.100-04	23939	23734.04	**23991**	23947.66
5.100-05	**24613**	24513.52	**24613**	24589.54
5.100-06	**25591**	25269.12	**25591**	25528.00
5.100-07	23335	23238.70	**23410**	23395.45
5.100-08	**24216**	23983.30	**24216**	24182.00
5.100-09	**24411**	24270.65	**24411**	24384.73
10.100-00	22937	22660.44	**23064**	23005.50
10.100-01	22731	22413.92	22731	22673.00
10.100-02	21741	21593.60	**22131**	22006.46
10.100-03	22314	22113.58	22667	22537.29
10.100-04	22614	22305.44	22654	22552.40
10.100-05	22408	22187.62	22593	22552.70
10.100-06	21731	21565.08	**21875**	21803.90
10.100-07	22362	22163.22	22551	22545.60
10.100-08	22385	22094.96	22393	22337.30
10.100-09	22698	22335.12	**22702**	22582.50

The two main features used in ABCAP_MKP are separately compared with the original ABC_MKP algorithm. We call the ABCAP_MKP algorithm with the reformed behavior of the scouts as the ABCAP1_MKP algorithm, and the ABCAP_MKP algorithm employing the modified repair operator in the determination of the neighborhood of a food source as ABCAP2_MKP algorithm. ABCAP1_MKP algorithm and ABCAP2_MKP algorithm are compared with ABC_MKP algorithm in experiment 1 and experiment 2. The results are respectively shown in Table 1 and Table 2. In these Tables, *Max* represents the best result found by each method within 50 iterations; *Avg* represents the average solution quality running for 50 trials.

Table 1 shows that ABCAP1_MKP algorithm finds best result for 12 instances, whereas ABC_MKP algorithm only finds best result for 5 instances. In case of average results, ABCAP1_MKP performs better than ABC_MKP algorithm. Table 1 demonstrates ABCAP1_MKP has better solution quality and improves the effectiveness of algorithm significantly at the same time. The reasons for this are mainly that on one hand, scouts generate solutions in heuristic method based on attraction pheromone, which can improve the quality of solutions; on the other hand, each scout makes the decision by comparing the associated food source with the corresponding food source in K elite food sources, which can keep good solutions effectively.

Table 2 shows that ABCAP2_MKP algorithm finds 9 best results out of 20 instances on different scale, which is better than ABC_MKP algorithm. In case of average

Table 2. Comparison of two algorithms on 20 instances of MKP

Instances	ABC_MKP		ABCAP2_MKP	
	Max	*Avg*	*Max*	*Avg*
5.100-00	24233	24043.46	**24381**	24262.04
5.100-01	**24274**	24212.48	**24274**	24250.72
5.100-02	23538	23476.66	23538	23529.96
5.100-03	23440	23193.64	23440	23355.22
5.100-04	23939	23734.04	23959	23922.16
5.100-05	**24613**	24513.52	**24613**	24554.46
5.100-06	**25591**	25269.12	**25591**	25509.08
5.100-07	23335	23238.70	**23410**	23311.56
5.100-08	**24216**	23983.30	**24216**	24145.00
5.100-09	**24411**	24270.65	**24411**	24328.54
10.100-00	22937	22660.44	23055	22871.78
10.100-01	22731	22413.92	22753	22570.50
10.100-02	21741	21593.60	**22131**	21875.80
10.100-03	22314	22113.58	22589	22392.76
10.100-04	22614	22305.44	22654	22511.00
10.100-05	22408	22187.62	22582	22370.86
10.100-06	21731	21565.08	21799	21667.00
10.100-07	22362	22163.22	22551	22366.04
10.100-08	22385	22094.96	22393	22280.32
10.100-09	22698	22335.12	**22702**	22468.50

results, ABCAP2_MKP algorithm is better than ABC_MKP. The experimental results on test problems presented by Table 2 show that ABCAP2_MKP algorithm outperforms ABC_MKP in the solution quality and effectiveness. With respect to the results of Table 2, the reason is that modified repair operator, through taking the update of attraction pheromone into account, enhances the local search ability of employed bees and onlookers.

The above experiments show that through improving the behavior of scout and modifying the repair operator based on attraction pheromone, it can help ABC algorithm obtain more optimal results and improve the quality of solutions.

4.2   The Overall Performance

In this section, we evaluate the overall performance of ABCAP_MKP algorithm in comparison of ABC_MKP algorithm for 20 instances on different scale.

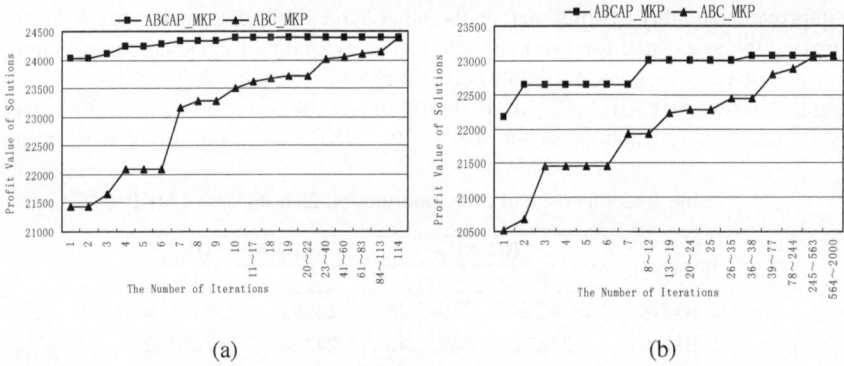

(a)   (b)

Fig. 1. The convergence curve of two algorithms on the MKP instances.(a) The instance of 5.100-00 and (b) The instance of 10.100-00.

Fig. 1 shows the convergence of ABCAP_MKP algorithm for different scaled instances which selecting the instances of 5.100-00 and 10.100-00 as the representatives. In Fig. 1 (a), ABCAP_MKP algorithm finds the best result 24381 at the 10th iteration which performs better than ABC_MKP algorithm. In Fig. 1 (b), ABC_MKP algorithm is unable to find ideal optimal result, whereas ABCAP_MKP algorithm finds the best result 23064 at the 36th iteration. From the experimental results, we can see that ABCAP_MKP algorithm performs better than ABC_MKP algorithm in terms of convergence.

Finally, we compare ABCAP_MKP with ABC_MKP in aspects of solution quality and time performance. In Table 3, *Best Known* represents the ideal optimal result for each instance; *Best* represents the best result found by each algorithm running for 50 trials; *Num* represents the least iterations achieving *Best* within the limit of 50 iterations. Obviously, ABCAP_MKP algorithm hits the optimal solutions for 19 instances out of 20 instances of different benchmark set, which is better than ABC_MKP algorithm. ABCAP_MKP algorithm needs less iteration to achieve *Best Known* than ABC_MKP algorithm.

Table 3. Comparison of two algorithms on 20 instances of MKP

Instances	Best Known	ABC_MKP		ABCAP_MKP	
		Best	*Num*	*Best*	*Num*
5.100-00	24381	24233	49	**24381**	10
5.100-01	24274	**24274**	20	24274	5
5.100-02	23551	23538	29	**23551**	5
5.100-03	23534	23440	32	**23534**	32
5.100-04	23991	23959	33	**23991**	14
5.100-05	24613	**24613**	27	24613	5
5.100-06	25591	**25591**	37	25591	11
5.100-07	23410	23335	48	**23410**	8
5.100-08	24216	**24216**	34	24216	19
5.100-09	24411	**24411**	41	24411	9
10.100-00	23064	22871	27	**23064**	36
10.100-01	22801	22731	47	**22801**	18
10.100-02	22131	21741	37	**22131**	10
10.100-03	22772	22314	50	**22772**	38
10.100-04	22751	22614	43	22697	49
10.100-05	22777	22408	30	**22777**	40
10.100-06	21875	21731	25	**21875**	16
10.100-07	22635	22362	43	**22635**	48
10.100-08	22511	22385	42	**22511**	40
10.100-09	22702	22698	41	**22702**	9

With the same time complexity, we can see ABCAP _MKP algorithm has been significantly improved in aspects of the solution quality, time performance and convergence. That is mainly owing to the introduction of attraction pheromone. The pheromone can strengthen the collaborations among bees in ABC algorithm and speed up the global convergence. Based on the transition strategy, scouts reform their behavior to accelerate the convergence; meanwhile, employed bees and onlookers enhance their local search ability effectively by modifying the repair operator.

5   Conclusion

In this paper, we propose an artificial bee colony algorithm for MKP based on attraction pheromone (ABCAP_MKP). The attraction pheromone is introduced for enhancing the cooperation among honey bees. By means of the transition strategy based on the attraction pheromone, scouts reform their behavior, and simultaneously the employed bees and onlookers modify the repair operator in the determination of the neighborhood of a food source. Compared with the original ABC_MKP algorithm, our approach has demonstrated competitive results in aspects of the solution quality, convergence and time performance. Our future research is to extend our approach in other representative combinational optimization problems.

Acknowledgments. This work is supported by the Beijing Natural Science Foundation (4102010).

References

1. Ji, J., Huang, Z., Liu, C., Liu, X., Zhong, N.: An ant colony optimization algorithm for solving the multidimensional knapsack problems. In: IEEE/WIC/ACM International Conference on Intelligent Agent Technology, pp. 10–16 (2007)
2. Freville, A.: The multidimensional 0-1 knapsack problem:an overview. European Journal of Operational Research 155, 1–21 (2004)
3. Chu, P.C., Beasley, J.E.: A genetic algorithm for the multidimensional knapsack problem. Journal of Heuristics 4, 63–86 (1998)
4. Kong, M., Tian, P.: Apply the particle swarm optimization to the multidimensional knapsack problem. In: Rutkowski, L., Tadeusiewicz, R., Zadeh, L.A., Żurada, J.M. (eds.) ICAISC 2006. LNCS (LNAI), vol. 4029, pp. 1140–1149. Springer, Heidelberg (2006)
5. Junzhong, J., Zhen, H., Chunnian, L.: Ant colony optimization algorithm based on mutation and pheromone diffusion for the multidimensional knapsack problems. Computer Research and Development 46, 644–654 (2009)
6. Sundar, S., Singh, A., Rossi, A.: An artificial bee colony algorithm for the 0–1 multidimensional knapsack problem. CCIS, vol. 94, pp. 141–151 (2010)
7. Karaboga, D.: An idea based on honey bee swarm for numerical optimization,Technical Report TR06,Computer Engineering Department, Erciyes University,Turkey (2005)
8. Karaboga, D., Akay, B.: A comparative study of artifical bee colony algorithm. Applied Mathematics and Computation 214, 108–132 (2009)
9. Wu, y.: The behavior of honey bees. Bulletin of Biology 36 (2001)
10. Leguizamon, G., Michalewicz, Z.: A new version of ant system for subset prolems. In: Proceedings of the 1999 Congress on Evolutionary Compution (CEC 1999), vol. 2, pp. 1458–1464 (1999)
11. Alaya, I., Solnon, C., Ghedira, K.: Ant algorithm for the multidimensional knapsack problem. Technique et Science Informatiques 26, 371–390 (2007)

Intelligence Optimization in Parameter Identification of the Border Irrigation Model

Jianwen Li, Xihuan Sun, Juanjuan Ma, Xianghong Guo, and Jingling Li

College of Water Conservation Science and Engineering,
Taiyuan University of Technology, 030024, Taiyuan, China
Ljw_zxh@163.com, sunxihuan@tyut.edu.cn, mjjsxty@163.com,
xianghong7920@126.com, lijingling33@163.com

Abstract. With the aim of estimating infiltration properties of surface irrigation and further saving water efficiently, a zero-inertia model was adopted for simulating the surface flow of border irrigation. The parameters identification of the model has been derived from hybrid volume balance model coupling artificial neural networks and numerical inversion approaches including differential evolution. With some special treatments to the advance and/or recession fronts of surface flow as its kinematical boundary, the discretization and/or the further linearization of zero-inertia model have been solved through the Newton-Raphson method and the pursuit algorithm. The validations of the identification of parameters and/or the model were verified by comparing the simulated data with measured and/or recorded data for advance or recession phase of border irrigation. The result shows that the optimization algorithm and/or model are appropriate and accurate.

Keywords: zero-inertia model, numerical inversion, model parameterization, differential evolution, border irrigation.

1 Introduction

With the farmland irrigation has occupied 62% of total water consumption in China, where agricultural consumption is up to 74.7%, the water shortage and unprofitable loss are increasingly urgent. With regard to popular surface irrigation methods, border irrigation is still the most commonly used, which is conditioned by a series of interrelated parameters: surface slope, size of the border, hydraulic properties of the soil and field roughness coefficient, [1]. Field roughness (or so-called Manning roughness n) and infiltration properties are often difficult to evaluate because of spatial-temporal variability and test conditions. As a result of poor estimates of them, the improper design and management of irrigation systems, particularly surface irrigation, produce excess water loss as deep percolation and runoff as concern of pollution source, [2]. The simulation of irrigation flow on infiltrating surfaces has many hydrological applications as to the study of overland flow, soil erosion and conservation, surface irrigation and contaminant transportation, [3].

H. Deng et al. (Eds.): AICI 2011, Part II, LNAI 7003, pp. 11–18, 2011.
© Springer-Verlag Berlin Heidelberg 2011

Estimation methods to identify the infiltration parameters satisfy the mass conservation principle in some form, which means that water applied into the border is either flow on the surface or infiltration into the soil. Given the changes in inlet and surface volume overtime, it becomes possible to infer the infiltration over time, [4]. There are many methods published on the estimation of the irrigation parameters, which can be classified into direct in situ measuring methods and indirect ones such as indoor testing combined with empirically or statistically calculating. Curve-fitting software and/or inverse modeling are indirect methods in some way. Differential Evolution (DE) is an easy and efficient heuristic algorithm for intelligence computation and/or model optimization, which is introduced by Storn and Price, [5].

In the present study, DE is adopted for the identification of Manning roughness and infiltration parameters of border irrigation model, and verified its feasibility by comparing the simulated results with the measured data.

2   Zero-Inertia Model of Border Irrigation

2.1   The Governing Equation

For border irrigation, the surface flow mechanistic model can be represented by the mass balance and the momentum balance equations known as Saint-Venant equations, after modification to include infiltration, with the following forms:

$$\frac{\partial A}{\partial t}+\frac{\partial Q}{\partial x}+B\frac{\partial Z}{\partial t}=0, \quad \frac{1}{g}\frac{\partial v}{\partial t}+\frac{v}{g}\frac{\partial v}{\partial x}+\frac{\partial y}{\partial x}=S_0-S_f+\frac{v}{2gy}\frac{\partial Z}{\partial t}. \tag{1}$$

where x is the distance along the border length in m; t is the irrigation start time in s; y is the flow depth in m; A and Q are the cross-sectional area in m^2 and discharge rate in $m^3\ s^{-1}$ of the border respectively; Z is the cumulative infiltration depth in m; K is the soil infiltration coefficient in $m\ min^{-\alpha}$; α is the infiltrion exponent; S_0 is the longitudinal slope of border; S_f is the friction slope.

As the flow velocities in border irrigation are usually small, Strelkoff and Katopodes therefore simplified the full hydrodynamic equations by neglecting the inertial terms in the Saint-Venant equations, [6]. If the inertia terms are neglected, (1) becomes:

$$\frac{\partial A}{\partial t}+\frac{\partial Q}{\partial x}+B\frac{\partial Z}{\partial t}=0, \quad \frac{\partial y}{\partial x}=S_0-S_f. \tag{2}$$

Models based on (2) are known as zero-inertia models, which are parabolic, rather than hyperbolic, and numerical solutions of the equation for these models are less complex than the full hydrodynamic models. Therefore, it requires less computer time to simulate an irrigation event than a hydrodynamic model.

The cumulative infiltration depth, Z can be calculated by the Kostiakov's formula as $Z=K\tau^\alpha$ with $0<\alpha<1$, where τ is the opportunity time in s during which the soil intake surface water as infiltration; K and α are empirical parameters.

The friction slope S_f can be computed as follows:

$$S_f = Q^2 n^2 / \rho_1 A^{\rho_2}, \tag{3}$$

where n is the field roughness which can be determined by a empirical formula according to field situation and/or some specific inverse model, and ρ_1, ρ_2 are shape factors which are empirically valued as 1.0,10/3 respectively.

2.2 The Definite Conditions

Initial Conditions. There is no infiltration and surface flow advance before and/or at the beginning of irrigation. Given that the border inflow advance distance be δx_1 for the first time step δt, the corresponding mass and momentum balance equations can be inferred out, by which, δx_1 and the wetted cross-sectional area at the border header A_0 are to be simultaneously solved out and then substituted into the next time step computation as initial conditions, [7].

Boundary Conditions. For border irrigation, there are the fixed boundaries at the head and/or the end of border, the advance front and/or the recession fronts of surface flow may be treated as the moving boundaries, detailed as follows:

$$\begin{cases} at\ x=0: A=0\ \ Q_0=0\ \ for\ t=0,\ \ Q=Q_0+\delta Q_0\ \ for\ 0<t\leq t_1, Q=0\ for\ t_1<t\leq t_2\ ; \\ at\ x=x_r: A=0\ \ \partial A/\partial x=0\ for\ t_2<t\leq t_4\ ;\ \ at\ x=x_a: A=0\ \ Q=0\ \ for\ 0<t\leq t_3; \\ at\ x=L: Q=0\ \ \ for\ t_3<t\leq t_4. \end{cases} \quad (4)$$

where δQ_0 is the inflow variation at border inlet in $m^3\ s^{-1}$; t_1 is the cutoff time at border inlet in s; t_2 is depletion finishing time at border head in s; t_3 the advance front's reaching time of border end; t_4, border depleting finishing time in s; x_a is the advance front position in m; x_r the receding front position in m; L is the border length in m.

During actual computation, given that Q be the discharge per unit width in $m^2 s^{-1}$, A is to be the surface flow depth in m.

3 Numerical Solution of Zero-Inertia Model

3.1 Discretization Scheme

Based on the surface flow nature, the irrigation event was divided into two phases in the previous study: advance phase and receding phase. The dividing point was the cutoff time t_1 at border head. But if the flow did not come to border end at that time t_1, there is still jacking rhomboid at advance front in fact, just with a slower velocity. So, in the present study, it is proposed that the dividing point be selected at t_3, the time when advance front has arrived at border end.

Fig.1 demonstrates the present spatial temporal dissection scheme. Rhomboid is superior to rectangle for the advance surface flow computation. Thus rhomboid was selected for advance phase computation, and rectangle for receding phase. Before the dividing time t_3, rhomboid is adopted except that the first grid after cutoff is rectangle and the second is same as the first grid before t_1 called half-advance grid. If cutoff began after the flow had reached border end, the format shall be completely same scheme as usual. If the surface flow at first grid has finished depletion, above-mentioned computing grids may shift backward one grid together. After the time t_3, rectangle shall be adopted for all the grids. Such scheme accords with the seal-fraction technique popularized in North China area.

For every computing grid block, its variations within time increment δt are also shown in Fig.1, in which the indices for left and right boundary in the two blocks of adjacent time sketch of dissection grids scheme step are denoted by the subscripts J, M and L, R respectively.

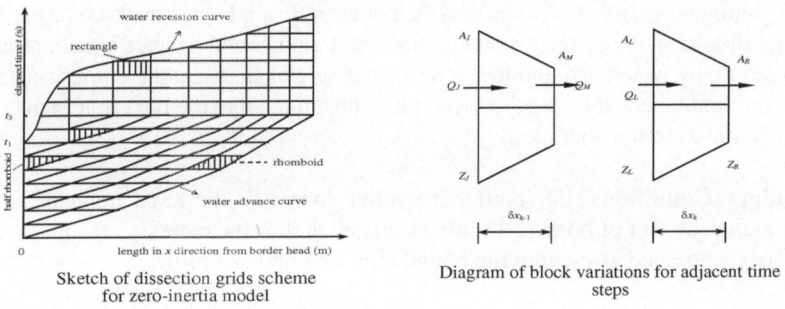

Sketch of dissection grids scheme for zero-inertia model

Diagram of block variations for adjacent time steps

Fig. 1. Discretizing schematic diagram for simulating model of border irrigation

3.2 Method and/or Algorithm

To approximate the governing equations and conditions with the Newton-Raphson method and the finite-difference format, one set of new variables are defined as follows:

$$\begin{cases} A_L = A_J + \delta A_L, A_R = A_M + \delta A_R, Q_L = Q_J + \delta Q_L, Q_R = Q_M + \delta Q_R \ (1 \le k \le N); \\ A_L = A_M + \delta A_L, Q_L = Q_M + \delta Q_L \ (k = 1); \quad \delta x_N = \delta x_{N-1} + \delta \delta. \end{cases} \tag{5}$$

where k is the computing grid index; N the number of grids computing at time step δt. The new variables δA_L, δA_R, δQ_L, δQ_R and $\delta \delta$ are related to the unknowns A_L, A_R, Q_L, Q_R and δx_N. Meanwhile A_J, A_M, Q_J, Q_M and δx_{N-1} for last time step are the known.

Noted that difference between rectangle and rhomboid grids is that the variable in rhomboid with J and/or M as its subscripts stands for the value of fore grid at previous time step, and in rectangle, it means the value of the present grid at previous time step. With the assumption of $y = \delta_1 A^{\delta_2}$, where δ_1, δ_2 are empirical shape factors which may be valued as 1.0, the definite conditions can be rewritten into the similar forms with corresponding treatment as rectangle and/or (half-) rhomboid grids.

The governing equations were discretized using a control volume of moving cells, by procedures reported in literatures [6]. Later, the discrtized equations were linearized according to the Newton-Raphson procedure, [7]. Thus, for all the computing grids, one set of similar linear equations can be derived and unified into matrix form as follows:

where the spatial increment X means $\delta \delta$ before advancing at the border end, and correspondingly δA_N after that time; and the first row stands for the left boundary at the border inlet. Assumed that there are linear relationships between Q and A for all computing grids, the linear equations can be iteratively solved by the Gaussian elimination technique (also named pursuit algorithm).

$$
\begin{bmatrix}
-S_1 & 1 \\
A_1 & B_1 & C_1 & D_1 \\
E_1 & F_1 & G_1 & H_1 \\
& & A_2 & B_2 & C_2 & D_2 \\
& & E_2 & F_2 & G_2 & H_2 \\
& & & & \ddots & & \ddots \\
& & & & & \ddots & & \ddots \\
& & & & A_{N-1} & B_{N-1} & C_{N-1} & D_{N-1} \\
& & & & E_{N-1} & F_{N-1} & G_{N-1} & H_{N-1} \\
& & & & & & A_N & B_N & C_N & D_N \\
& & & & & & E_N & F_N & G_N & H_N \\
& & & & & & & & -S_{N+1} & 1
\end{bmatrix}
\begin{bmatrix}
\delta A_0 \\
\delta Q_0 \\
\delta A_1 \\
\delta Q_1 \\
\delta A_2 \\
\delta Q_2 \\
\vdots \\
\vdots \\
\delta A_{N-1} \\
\delta Q_{N-1} \\
\delta A_N \\
X
\end{bmatrix}
=
\begin{bmatrix}
M_1 \\
U_1 \\
V_1 \\
U_2 \\
V_2 \\
\vdots \\
\vdots \\
U_{N-1} \\
V_{N-1} \\
U_N \\
V_N \\
M_{N+1}
\end{bmatrix}
\tag{6}
$$

With the grids divided at equal time step, uniform infiltration may be assumed which means $Z_L=Z_J$, $Z_R=Z_M$. Given that a grid with $A<5\%A_0$ during recession phase solution, it may be considered up to its termination.

With the solution of the area A and the flux Q for each computing grid, new coefficients matrix for next time step can be obtained by substituting them into as the known , this kind procedures of computation are to be repeated till the recession termination.

4   Parameter Identification

Normally, the infiltration parameters K and α, are figured from double ring infiltrating data with least square method (LSM), and field roughness n is often identified empirically and/or by inverse modeling.

As to the model validation, some parameters of certain border measured in situ are needed to be input such as length L and width B of the border and field longitudinal slope S_0.

4.1   Intelligent Computation of Differential Evolution (DE)

DE is known as heuristics for few assumptions about the problem being optimized and large search-spaces for solutions, and is a simple but powerful population based stochastic function intelligent optimization meanwhile [8]. The searching ability of DE scheme adopted in the present paper is accredited to parent selection, differential mutation, crossover and greedy decision.

Selection: All the individuals in the population have the same chance to generate candidate individuals. For each individual X_i, three other individuals are randomly selected from current population such that the four individuals are different from each other.

Mutation: A mutated individual V_i is generated with the three individuals randomly chosen by Selection as follows:

$$
V_i = X_{r1} + F \cdot (X_{r2} - X_{r3}) \quad i=1,2,\cdots,NP.
\tag{7}
$$

where r_1, r_2 and r_3 are chosen randomly from the interval [0, NP-1] and are different from the running index i. F is a positive real and constant factor usually less than 1.0, which controls the amplification of the differential variation.

Crossover: A trial vector T_i is formed by recombination of the elements of X_i and V_i one by one as follows:

$$t_{i,j} = \begin{cases} v_{ij} & \text{if } r \leq CR \text{ or } j = sn \\ x_{ij} & \text{otherwise} \end{cases} \quad j = 1, 2, \cdots, D . \tag{8}$$

where t_{ij} is the jth element/parameter of the trial individual T_i, $r \in [0, 1]$ is a uniformly random number, $CR \in [0,1]$ is a real number to control the ratio of selection between of the parent and mutated vector, and sn is an index randomly chosen to ensure that at least one element of V_i will be inherited

Decision: Greedy selection between the trial vector T_i and X_i is applied and the one with better objective value will be promoted to the next generation.

The crucial idea behind DE is a scheme for generating trial parameter vectors which can be illustrated as Fig.4

The choice of DE parameters such as differential weight F, crossover probability CR and population size NP can have a large impact onto optimization performance. Selecting the DE parameters that yield good performance has been the aim of much research. More advanced DE variants are also being developed with a popular research trend being to perturb or adapt the DE parameters during optimization.

4.2   Identification of Parameters K, α and n

For present study, the identifications of K, α and n were performed by a software SIPAR_ID, which is for estimating these parameters with a hybrid model combing volume balance approach with artificial neural networks for simulating the surface irrigation advance phase. SIPAR_ID has main window designed for input the basic data obtained in a field evaluation, [9].

In the present study, DE parameters are adopted the default settings of SIPAR_ID for identifying such parameters as K, α and n of the zero-inertia model.

The method was verified by comparing the calculated data as some results of parameters optimization with the in situ measured data of some border irrigation advance phase. The optimized parameters were further input into the zero-inertia model for validation by comparing the simulated advance and/or recession curves with the measured data of certain border irrigations.

5   Results and Discussion

In the present study, the experimental irrigation events data for two borders in Jiamakou irrigation district of Shanxi province were used to identify the parameters K, α and n of zero-inertia model for border irrigation through SIPAR_ID. Such parameters for the two borders named separately as Ru's clay border 1[#] and Zhongze loam border were identified by SIPAR_ID after the needed data such as advance data, S_0, B and inflow hydrograph being inputted. The objective function was just defined as to minimize the difference between observed and simulated advance distances. The results of SIPAR_ID running for the two verifying borders are shown in Table 1, which illustrated good indexes for advance distance.

Table 1. Parameters identifying results of some irrigating borders

Border name	Border specification			Identified parameters			Performance indexes		
/index	L(m)	B(m)	S_0	K	α	n	R^2	RMSE	%Error
Ru's clay 1#	176	4.9	0.0027	0.020	0.810	0.151	0.998	1.95	3.26
Zhongze loam	142	4.9	0.0029	0.015	0.818	0.117	0.997	2.69	7.42

The identified parameters of certain border were inputted into the zero-inertia computation program to valid the border irrigation model, the results of the two simulating borders were shown as Fig.2

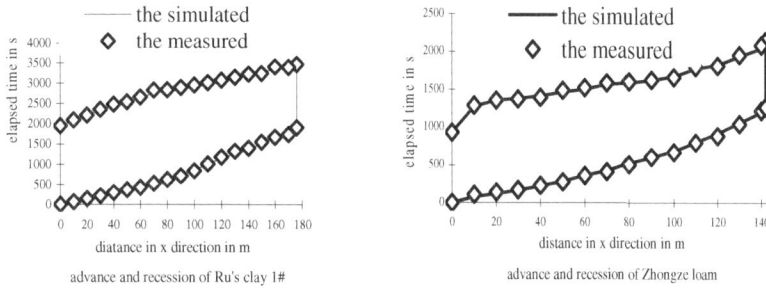

Fig. 2. Comparison of the simulated with the measured results for two irrigation borders

The results show that DE algorithm is easy and efficient to identify the parameters for irrigation mathematical model, the developed zero-inertia model for border irrigation is accurate and adequate enough for actual applications.

The numerical inversion procedure of the border irrigation model can be further improved by inseting the DE algorithm into its optimization procedure for parameter identification. The infiltration and redistribution of soil water, always physically demonstrated by Richards' equation, are greatly influenced by the soil hydraulic parameters, which can also be intelligently identified by the heuristic DE algorithm.

6   Conclusion

The paper presented a zero inertia model to simulate the border irrigation surface flow and adopted the special software with some intelligence computation approaches such as DE algorithm to identify parameters of soil infiltration and field roughness for the model. The results show that the present zero inertia model is accurate and adequate for the border irrigation simulation and the DE algorithm is also to be easy and efficient for intelligent optimization in irrigation systems.

Acknowledgment. The present study is supported by the 2nd Water Resources Assessment and General Planning Program of Shanxi Province. The present author is grateful to Mr. Yanfeng Li for some computer programming and experimental data arranging and to Mr. Rodríguez, J.A. for kindly providing the software SIPAR_ID and supporting materials.

References

1. Galbiati, G.L., Savi, F.: Effectiveness of Border Irrigation: A Case Study. J. Agric. Engng. Res. 66, 157–167 (1997)
2. Foroud, N., George, E.S., Entz, T.: Determination of Infiltration Rate from Border Irrigation Advance and Recession Trajectories. J. Agricultural Water Management 30, 133–142 (1996)
3. Gandol, C., Savi, F.: A Mathematical Model for the Coupled Simulation of Surface Runoff and Infiltration. J. Agric. Engng Res. 75, 49–55 (2000)
4. Clemmens, A.J., Eisenhauer, D. E., Maheshwari, B. L.: Infiltration and Roughness Equations for Surface Irrigation: How Form Influences Estimation. In: ASAE Annual Meeting, California (2001)
5. Storn, R., Price, K.: Differential Evolution – a Simple and Efficient Heuristic for Global Optimization over Continuous Spaces. J. Glob. Optim. 11, 341–359 (1997)
6. Strelkoff, T., Katopodes, N.D.: Border Irrigation Hydraulics with Zero-inertia. J. Irrig. Drain Div. ASCE 103, 325–342 (1977)
7. Yuanhua Li, C.: Theory and Techniques of Water-saving Irrigation. Wuhan University of Hydropower Press, Wuhan (1999) (in Chinese)
8. Mayer, D.G., Kinghorn, B.P., Archer, A.A.: Differential Evolution – an Easy and Efficient Evolutionary Algorithm for Model Optimization. J. Agricultural Systems 83, 315–328 (2005)
9. Rodríguez, J.A., Martos, J.C.: SIPAR_ID: Freeware for Surface Irrigation Parameter Identification. J. Environmental Modelling & Software 25, 1487–1488 (2010)

A Multi-MetaHeuristic Combined ACS-TSP System

Liang Meng and Lijuan Wang

Dept. of Computer Science, Taiyuan University of Technology, Taiyuan, China
browsertimes@126.com

Abstract. This paper presents a Multi-MetaHeuristic combined Ant Colony System (ACS)-Travelling Salesman Problem(TSP) algorithm for solving the TSP. We introduce genetic algorithm in ACS-TSP to search solutions space for dealing with the early stagnation problem of the traveling salesman problem. Moreover, we present a new strategy of Minimum Spanning Tree (MST) coupled with Nearest Neighbor(NN) to construct a initial tour for improving TSP thus obtaining good solutions quickly. According to our simulation results, the new algorithm can provide a significantly improvement for obtaining a global optimum solution or a near global optimum solution in large TSPs.

Keywords: ACS-TSP, Genetic Algorithm, Minimum Spanning Tree, Nearest Neighbor.

1 Introduction

The Ant System(AS)[1][5] was first developed by Dorigo and his colleagues and later a more promising method known as Ant Colony System(ACS)[6] was also developed. The ant colony system have been applied successfully in many applications such as Travelling Salesman Problem(TSP) [3], quadratic assignment problem[9], data mining[8], space-planning[4], job-shop scheduling and other applications[2][7].

Though the ACS-TSP algorithm[6] produced better results on many TSPs compared to some genetic algorithms(GA), simulated annealing(SA), and evolutionary programming (EP) [10], it still needs to cope with two kinds of problems: one is early stagnation, another is convergent time. Early stagnation is one phenomenon where pheromone intensities of few arcs become so high that the ants will always construct the corresponding tour again and again, making further tour improvements impossible. The goal of this paper is to combine other metaheuristic to cope with above problems.

The remainder of this paper is organized as follows: in the next section we present the basic idea and structure of the ant colony system algorithm. In section 3, methods which combines ACS with other metaheuristics are shown. In section 4, the computational study is described and results are reported. In section 5, we make a conclusion for this paper.

2 The Ant Colony System for TSP

The Ant Colony System has been inspired by the behavior of real ant colonies, in particular, by their foraging behavior. Ants deposit pheromone on the ground and

H. Deng et al. (Eds.): AICI 2011, Part II, LNAI 7003, pp. 19–25, 2011.

communicate with each other via pheromones. An ant's tendency to choose a specific path is positively correlated to the intensity of a found trail. The pheromone trail evaporates over time, i.e., it loses intensity if no more pheromone is laid down by other ants. If many ants choose a certain path and lay down pheromones, the intensity of the trails increases and thus this trail attracts more and more ants.

As for TSP, ACS works as follows: m ants are initially positioned on n cities randomly. Each ant builds a complete tour by choosing the cities according to a probabilistic state transition rule. While building its tour, an ant also modifies the amount of pheromone on the visited edges by applying the local updating rule. Once all ants have completed their tours a global updating rule is applied. The ACS algorithm is illustrated in Figure 1. In the following we discuss the state transition rule, the local updating rule, and the global updating rule.

Initialize;
Loop
   Each ant is positioned on a starting node;
   Loop
   Each ant applies a state transition rule to incrementally build a solution;
      And a local pheromone updating rule;
   Until all ants have built a complete solution
   A global pheromone updating rule is applied;
Until End_condition

Fig. 1. The ACS algorithm

2.1 The State Transition Rule

Let k be ant whose task is to make a tour: visit all the cities and return to the starting one. Associated to k there is the list $J_k(r)$ of cities still to be visited, where r is the current city. An ant k situated in city r moves to city s using the following rule, called pseudo-random proportional action choice rule (or state transition rule):

$$s = \begin{cases} \arg\max_{u \in J_k(r)} \left\{ [\tau(r,u)] \cdot [\eta(r,u)]^{\beta} \right\} & \textit{if} \quad q \leq q_0 \quad (\exp\textit{loitation}) \cdot \\ s, & \textit{otherwise} \quad (\textit{biased} \exp\textit{loration}) \end{cases} \quad (1)$$

Where $\tau(r,u)$ is the amount of pheromone trail on edge. $\eta(r,u)$ is a heuristic function which is the inverse of the distance between cities r and u, β is a parameter which weighs the relative importance of pheromone trail ants, q is a value chosen randomly with uniform probability in [0,1], $q_0(0 \leq q_0 \leq 1)$ is a parameter, and s is a random variable selected according to the distribution given by Equation.(2) which gives the probability with which an ant in city r chooses the city s to move to.

$$P_k(r,s) = \begin{cases} \dfrac{[\tau(r,u)] \cdot [\mu(r,u)]^\beta}{\sum_{u \in J_k(r)} [\tau(r,u)] \cdot [\mu(r,u)]^\beta} & if \quad s \in J_k(r) \\ 0 & otherwise \end{cases} \qquad (2)$$

2.2 The Local Updating Rule

While building a solution of the TSP, ants visit edges and change their amount of pheromone trail by applying the following local updating rule:

$$\tau(r,s) \leftarrow (1-\rho) \cdot \tau(r,s) + \rho \cdot \Delta\tau(r,s) \qquad (3)$$

Where $\rho(0 < \rho < 1)$ is the pheromone decay parameter. $\Delta\tau(r,s) = (n*Lnn)^{-1}$ is the initial pheromone level, where Lnn is the tour length produced by the nearest neighbor heuristic and n is the number of nodes.

2.3 The Global Updating Rule

Global Updating is performed after all ants have completed their tours. The pheromone amount is updated by applying the following global updating rule:

$$\tau(r,s) \leftarrow (1-\alpha) \cdot \tau(r,s) + \alpha \cdot \Delta\tau(r,s)$$

$$where \quad \Delta\tau(r,s) = \begin{cases} (L_{gb})^{-1} & ,if \ (r,s) \in global\_best\_tour \\ 0 & ,otherwise \end{cases} \qquad (4)$$

$0 < \alpha < 1$ is the pheromone decay parameter, and L_{gb} is the length of the globally best tour from the beginning of the trail.

3 The Proposed Approach

This paper combines genetic algorithm (GA) to search solutions space to avoid early stagnation and so as to obtain global minimum for solving the TSP problem, moreover, applies minimum spanning tree(MST) to construct initial tour to improve algorithm efficiency.

3.1 Combination with GA

The performance of ACS can be enhanced by allowing only the best ant to update the trails in every cycle, but too early exclusion of other potential ant can lead to early stagnation of the search, so we introduce genetic algorithm to ACS to dispose the problems of early stagnation of the search.

The genetic algorithm (GA)[11] is an optimization and search technique based on the principles of genetics and natural selection, was developed by John Holland and his colleagues at the university of Michigan. In general, the GA operates on the concept of the gene operation, which comprises three important procedures: reproduction, crossover and mutation. These gene operations use only the primitive operations such as copying, swapping and flipping genes. Utilizing the GA to solving the optimization problem has many advantages. First, the GA comprises both exploitation and exploration in its operation, which is different from optimization methods such as the gradient descent method that comprises only exploitation. Second, not only linear and nonlinear programming but also integer programming can be solved by utilizing GA.

To avoid sub-optimum and improve search solution space, we apply a two-phase strategy during global updating phase. In the first phase, after all ants have completed their tours, we choose three representative tours among all ant tours, one is the best tour, second one is the medium tour, third one is the worst tour. To these three tours, apply the Genetic Algorithm crossover operator to offspring three other tours. In the second phase, apply the best tour and GA-produced three other tours to globally update the pheromones of edges by the following global updating rule in equation (5).

$$\tau(r,s) \leftarrow (1-\alpha) \cdot \tau(r,s) + \alpha \cdot \Delta\tau(r,s)$$

$$where \quad \Delta\tau(r,s) = \begin{cases} (L_{tour})^{-1} & ,if\,(r,s) \in this\_tour \\ 0 & ,otherwise \end{cases} \quad (5)$$

By using the above method, we can illustrate the improved ACS-TSP algorithm in Figure 2.

```
Initialize
Loop
    Each ant is positioned on a starting node
    Loop
        Each ant applies a state transition rule to incrementally build a solution;
        And a local pheromone updating rule;
    Until all ants have built a complete solution
    Select three other tours based on GA crossover operator
            from representative tours;
    Globally update the pheromones using the four specific tours;
Until  End_condition
```

Fig. 2. The improved ACS-TSP algorithm

3.2   Traveling Salesman Tour Constructing Approach

Conventionally, Nearest Neighbor (NN) method has usually been adopted to construct a traveling salesman tour, but such a method can lead to severe mistakes. On the other hand, the Minimum Spanning Tree(MST) problem is to find a spanning tree of a graph with minimal total cost, and can be quickly identified by the well-known algorithm of Krushal and Prim. An optimal tour normally contains between 70 and 80 percent of the edges of a minimum spanning tree, Edges that belong to a Minimum Spanning Tree (MST) stand a good chance of also belonging to an optimal tour.

Based on the above phenomenon, we apply a new strategy of MST coupled with NN to construct an initial tour. According to the specific TSP problem, we construct its corresponding MST tree, form the candidate edge sets which belongs to the MST tree. Because MST is an n-tree, whose nodes may have degree greater than 2, we choose the longest path from the offspring node to ancestor node as the starting route to guarantee the property of degree 2 of node except the two degree 1 ends. Then we identify one end of the starting route as the new starting node, choose the next node based on the following strategy:

1) exist one edge which has not been visited from candidate edge sets, this edge connect the new starting node.

2) if above method does not succeed, chooses the nearest node which has not been visited as the next node based on NN method.

At initial stage, We utilize the above mentioned approach to increase a little amount of pheromone trail strength at the ants searching paths and thus reduce the convergent time, Fig 3 represents the initial tour construction procedure.

Procedure Constructing Initial Tour
   produce MST tree based on TSP problem;
   form the candidate edge sets from the MST tree;
   choose the longest path from the MST tree and
       ensure degree 2 of node except the two ends;
   choose one end as the new starting node;
   Do
     choose the next node based on the following two strategy;
     1)exist one edge which has not been visited from candidate edge sets,
       this edge connect the new starting node;
     2)if above method does not succeed, chooses the nearest node which has not
       been visited as the next node based on NN method;
     the next node is identified as the new starting node;
   while (there are node which has not been visited)
   form the Initial Tour
End Constructing Initial Tour

Fig. 3. The improved ACS-TSP algorithm

4   Experiment Results

In order to demonstrate the performance of our proposed approach, we conduct some computer simulations on a PC Pentium III. In all the experiments of this section we set parameter values as follows: q_0 =0.9, ρ =0.5, α =1, β =2, computer simulation runs=50. Moreover, we have used a population of 20 ants in our experiments, experimented with a280, att532, rat783, u1060, fl1400, rl1889 benchmark problems to compare the performance of our proposed method with Dorigo's ACS-TSP. Notably, all our sample problem instances have been taken from the library TSPLIB, which is a publicly available set of TSP. Fig. 4 shows the comparison of tour length that ACS-TSP and improved approach using rl1889 benchmark problems. Table 1 summarizes the comparisons of tour length of ACS-TSP and our improved approach with 3-opt local search using different TSP benchmark problems. It is observed that TSP combined with Genetic Algorithm and Minimum Spanning Tree provides a significantly improvement for obtaining a global optimum solution or a near global optimum solution.

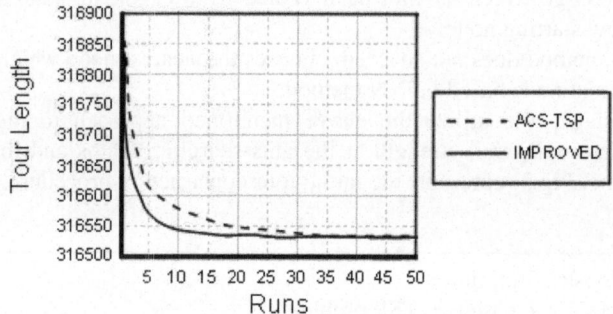

Fig. 4. Comparison of tour length for ACS-TSP and improved approach using rl1889 benchmark problem

Table 1. Comparison of Tour Length for ACS+TSP+LS with our Improved Approach+LS Using Six Different TSP Benchmark Problems

dataset	optimal	ACS+TSP+ls		Improved+ls	
		result	time(s)	result	time(s)
a280	2579	2579	0.875	2579	0.290
att532	27686	27752	3.490	27686	26.320
rat783	8806	8872	4.614	8806	26.338
u1060	224094	229522	6.819	224094	423.983
fl1400	20127	20611	10.301	20127	16.574
rl1889	316536	327420	14.675	316536	459.066

5 Conclusion

This paper presents a Multi-MetaHeuristic combined ACS-TSP algorithm for solving the TSP(traveling salesman problem). We introduce genetic algorithm in ACS-TSP to search solutions space for solving the early stagnation problem of the traveling salesman problem. In addition, we present a new strategy of MST coupled with NN to construct an initial tour for improving TSPs thus obtaining good solutions quickly. According to our simulation results, the new algorithm can provide a significantly improvement for obtaining a global optimum solution or a near global optimum solution in large TSPs.

Acknowledgments. The author would like to thank the Shanxi Natural Science Council of Republic of China for financially supporting this research under grant number NSC 2010011023-2.

References

1. Colori, A., Dorigo, M., Maniezzo, V.: Distributed optimization by ant colonies. In: Varela, F., Bourgine, P. (eds.) First Eur. Conference Artificial life, pp. 134–142 (1991)
2. Blum, C.: Ant colony optimization: Introduction and recent trends. Physics of Life Reviews 2, 353–373 (2005)
3. Hseuh-Fu, R., Shan, N.-P.: A new Hybrid heuristic approach for solving large traveling salesman problem. Information Sciences 166, 67–81 (2004)
4. Bland, J.A.: Space-planning by ant colony optimization. International Journal of Computer Applications in Technology 12(6), 320–328 (1999)
5. Dorigo, M., Maniezzo, V., Colorni, A.: Ant System: optimization by a colony of cooperating agents. IEEE Transactions on Systems, Man, and Cybernetics—Part B: Cybernetics 26(1), 29–41 (1996)
6. Dorigo, M., Gambardella, L.M.: Ant colony system: a cooperative learning approach to the traveling salesman problem. IEEE Transactions on Evolutionary Computation 1(1), 53–66 (1997)
7. Dorigo, M., Caro, G.D., Gambardella, L.M.: Ant algorithms for discrete optimization. Artificial Life 5(2), 137–172 (1999)
8. Parpinelli, R.S., Lopes, H.S., Freitas, A.A.: Data mining with an ant colony optimization algorithm. IEEE Transactions on Evolutionary Computation 6(4), 321–332 (2002)
9. Maniezzo, V., Colorni, A.: The ant system applied to the quadratic assignment problem. IEEE Transactions on Knowledge and Data Engineering 11(5), 769–778 (1999)
10. Bonabeau, E., Dorigo, M., Theraulaz, G.: Swarm Intelligence: From Natural to Artificial Systems. Oxford University Press, New York (1999)
11. Holland, J.H.: Adaptation in Natural and Artificial Systems. The University of Michigan Press, Ann Arbor (1975)

Indoor Positioning Data Obstacle Avoidance and Visualization Framework Based on A* Algorithm[*]

Ming Yang[1] and Ruonan Rao[2]

[1] School of Software, Shanghai Jiao Tong University, Shanghai, China
[2] School of Software, Shanghai Jiao Tong University, Shanghai, China
YM_SJTU@sjtu.edu.cn, rao-ruonan@cs.sjtu.edu.cn

Abstract. Currently the research on the map visualization and GIS visualization is relatively mature. But in the indoor environment, Indoor positioning system requires monitoring the location which is on vector map of positioning data and display positioning data trajectory. At the same time, Indoor positioning environment is complex, and has many obstacles such as walls. The connection between two positioning data point which are in the trajectory of positioning data always pass through the obstacles. To solve this problem, in this paper, we combine A* map routing algorithm and vector map visualization technology to propose a Obstacle Avoidance And Visualization Method of indoor positioning data trajectory which is on the vector map. And we introduce an indoor positioning data Obstacle Avoidance And Visualization Framework based on the method. The implementation of the framework is also discussed.

Keywords: Vector map, Visualization, Indoor Positioning Data, Obstacle, A* Algorithm.

1 Introduction

Map visualization and GIS visualization is two important part of the geographic study [1]. Map visualization focused on the visual expression and communication of geographic information, biased in favor of theory and application level. GIS Visualization is focused on the geological data model and structure design, vector data visualization, real-time dynamic processing, biased in favor of the technical level.

From the above analysis, the current research on map visualization and GIS visualization has been very mature. But in the indoor environment, Indoor positioning system requires monitoring the location which is on vector map of positioning data and display positioning data trajectory. At the same time, indoor positioning environment is complicated, and has many obstacles such as walls. The connection between two positioning data point which are in the trajectory of positioning data always pass through the obstacles.

To solve this problem, in this paper, we combine A* map routing algorithm and vector map visualization technology to propose a Obstacle Avoidance And Visualization Method of indoor positioning data trajectory which is on the vector

* This paper is supported by the medical engineering (science) cross research foundation project of Shanghai Jiao Tong University under Grant NO.YG2009MS21.

H. Deng et al. (Eds.): AICI 2011, Part II, LNAI 7003, pp. 26–33, 2011.

map. And we introduce an indoor positioning data Obstacle Avoidance And Visualization Framework (IPOAF) based on the method. The implementation of the framework is also discussed. The framework is now used in the actual project that shows its feasibility and effectiveness.

2   Related Work

The indoor positioning data IPOAF in this paper mainly related to DWG vector map visualization which supports by AutoCAD, environmental modeling, heuristic search technology and other key technologies.

2.1   Access DWG Graphic File with DWGDirect.Net

Vector map used in this project is the DWG drawing file. DWG file is binary format, contains five types of data, Character, single-byte type, double-byte integer, four-byte integer and floating point numbers stored in IEEE standard (Double precision floating point) [2].

Figure 1 is the data model of DWG files in DWGDirect.net. Other types tables of the figure include the view of tables, text tables, line form, size form, user coordinate system table, registration application form and so on. Figures in upper left corner of the box corresponding to the number of items.

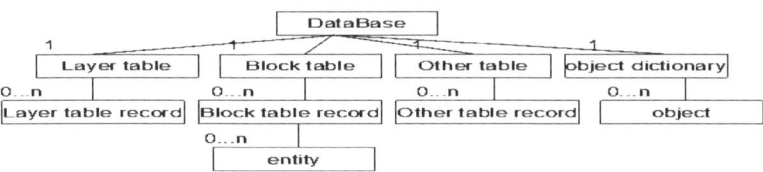

Fig. 1. The data model of DWG files in DWGDirect.net

2.2   Environment Modeling Method

The methods commonly uses in environmental modeling: Grid method [3] is proposed by Howden in1968. The method divides the robot's work environment into a series of grid cell with binary information. The obstacles get the same location and size in the workspace. And in the process of robot motion, the obstacles do not change the location and size.

2.3   Heuristic Search Technology

The basic problem in this Search algorithm is how to avoid obstacles. There are many types heuristic search algorithm proposed at home and abroad [4], e.g. A* algorithm, a single object routing algorithm, hierarchical path finding and route re-calculation and so on.

3   Vector Map Visualization and A* Algorithm

3.1   Vector Map Visualization

Vector maps can be viewed as a collection which forms by point, line, surface geometry of these three objects and their attribute data. This introduction the concepts of map vector library and map database. Map vector library is a set of graphics descriptive data, and saves the map geometry data. Map database is a set of descriptive data, and saves attribute data of each types of map geometry object.

We begin the data visualization based on the vector graphics data. The data render process is a pipeline operation process [5]. The process is divided into a number of relatively independent of the composition unit to complete the visual task.

The data visualization model is a pipeline operation process [6], and formed by data object and processing object (Figure 2). Data object is the data collection of visualization network process, there are four main components: DataBase (datasource object), DataSet(the expression of data in memory), Geometry(identifiable object of graphics porcessor), GrahicsSystem(rendering output image), The basic graphic elements of the vector map are modeled as a datasource object. Processing objects are: Access(data access control), Fileter, Mapper, Render and Display(display terminal).

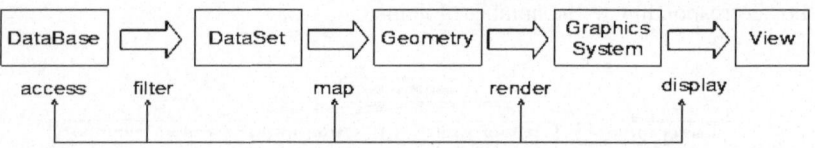

Fig. 2. Data visualization process

3.2   Indoor Environment Obstacles Model Generation with Gird Method

Based on the datasource object--DataBase, we generate the indoor environment obstacles model in the memory with grid method.

The definition of Obstacle model: we read a variety of vector graphics objects in the DataBase object from memory, and convert these vector graphics objects' map coordinates points into screen coordinates points, and then mark these screen coordinates of these points as obstacles.

Indoor positioning data' two-dimensional workspace (screen) are divided with the same size grids, the size of the grid subjects to the screen pixel. If a grid does not contain any obstacles, we call it free grid, on the contrary, we call it obstacle grid.

Identification method of grid: Cartesian coordinate method. We defines upper-left corner of the screen is the first origin of the coordinate grid, the right level for the x-axis positive direction, straight down for the y-axis positive direction, each grid interval corresponds to a unit length in the coordinate, that is, a pixel screen.

After positioning data path information is discretized, trajectory of positioning data is broken down into individual movements, the individual movements are recorded in each grid. Information on the movement of each grid provided the direction of positioning data movement. The direction of this grid is defined as the eight directions: Front, rear, left, right, right front, right rear, left rear, left front.

3.3 Indoor Positioning Obstacle Avoidance and Visualization Algorithm – A* Algorithm

Based on the above-mentioned obstacle model, the trajectory of indoor positioning data do the obstacle avoidance and visualization on the vector map through A* algorithm.

The evaluation function of A* algorithm designs in the subject:

Set h(n)=the actual price of the minimum cost path between node n and destination node(over all possible destination node and all possible paths)

Set g (n) = the cost of a minimum cost path which is from the start node n0 to node n.

Then f (n) = g (n) + h (n) the cost of the minimum cost path which is from n0 to the destination node and go through node n.

For each node n, set $\hat{h}(n)$ (heuristic factor) is an estimated of h(n), and $\hat{g}(n)$ (Depth factor) is the cost of the minimum cost path which found by A*. In the A* algorithm, the evaluation function $\hat{f}$ is an estimated of f function. This estimate can be given by:

$$\hat{f}(n) = \hat{g}(n) + \hat{h}(n) \tag{1}$$

This definition includes $\hat{g}(n) \geq g(n)$. For the estimated $\hat{h}(n)$ of h(n), it depends on the heuristic information of the problem areas, called h as the evaluation function.

The A* algorithm in this paper is a ordered search algorithm. To the common ordered search, it always chooses the smallest f value of the node as an extension node.

The design of A* algorithm in this paper:

1. Generate a search graph G which only contains a node-- n0, and put n0 in OPEN list.
2. Generate a CLOSED list, it is initialized to empty.
3. If OPEN is empty, then fail quit
4. If OPEN is not empty, select the first node in OPEN, move it from OPEN into CLOSED, and call it n0
5. If n is target node, along G, find a path from the pointers of n to the pointers of n0, return the solution and success quit (this pointer define a search tree which is built in step 7)
6. If n is not target node, expand node n, generate its successor node collection---M; in G, the ancestors of n cannot fit in M. put nodes in G and make them to be the successor of n.
7. Build a pointer to point n based on each members what is not in G from M, add the members of M into OPEN. To the each other member --m of M, if So far to find the best path to reach m throngh n, then put its pointer point to n.

For each member who already in CLOSED of M, redirect each successor that it fit in G, so that they follow the best path pointing to their ancestors.

8.   According to increasing f value, resort OPEN

9.   Return to step 3.

4   Indoor Positioning Data IPOAF Based on A* Algorithm

4.1   Framework Architecture

Based on the method described in the previous section, this paper design a indoor positioning data IOOAF based on A* algorithm. Mainly composed of three modules: Vector map visualization module, positioning data real-time visualization module, and historical path playback module.

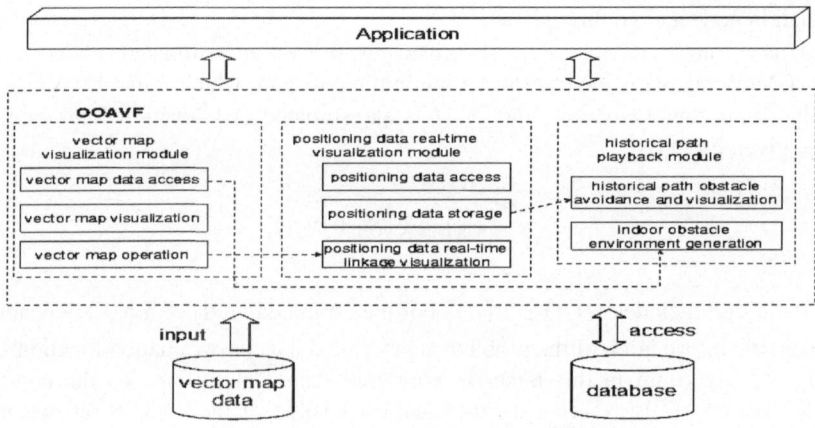

Fig. 3. Indoor positioning data IPOAF

4.2   Vector Map Visualization Module

Vector map visualization module mainly composed of three modules: DWG vector map file read sub-module, vector map visualization sub-module, the operation of vector map sub-module.

Vector map read sub-module: the DWGClass class of IPOAF which call the class library of DWGdirect.net read DWG vector map file into the memory and storage the vector map object into Database Services and Geometry Objects.

In the class library of DWGdirect.net, DWG file represents by a instance of OdDbDatabase Class in memory. Each instance of OdDbDatabase Class stands for a simple database, it formed by nine symbol table and one object dictionary.

There are multiple records in each symbol table and object dictionary. For example: BlockTable includes multiple BlockTableRecord, BlockTableRecord includes the data of entity such as line curve, map block. The common entity storage in the record of MODEL_SPACE block table; storage layer'information are recorded in the layer table; Dimension Styles table, layer table, line table and text style table are all used to storage corresponding table record. According to OdDbDatabase, we can access to the entity data in DWG conveniently through using the class function of DWGDirect.Geometry package.

Vector map visualization sub-module: we call the classes of DWGDirect. GraphicsSystem package by IPOAF' DWGClass class to render vector map, and instantiated DWGDirect.GraphicsSystem.View class as the display object of vector graphics.

The operation of vector map sub-module mainly achieve the DWG vector map' functions of zoomin, zoomout, shifting, roaming, reset. Vector map of roaming refers to move the vector map display object view to the position which a indoor positioning point presents as a mid-point of screen.

We realize the zoomin of vector Map through ZoomIn function which encapsulates by DWGclass of IPOAF. ZoomOut function realizes vector map zoomout. ControlScale function realizes the control of the zoom ratio.

The vector shifting and roaming function all are realized by calling the dolly function of DWGClass class, but there is an important different: the different coordinate values as parameters. The parameters for shifting function are the distant of dragging the map; the parameters of roaming function are the distant of current positioning data point and the center of screen. The backToini function by DWGClass encapsulating realizes the reset of the view.

4.3   Positioning Data Real-Time Visualization Module

Indoor positioning data real-time visualization module mainly composed of three sub-modules: positioning data access, positioning data storage, and positioning data real-time linkage visualization.

In the positioning data access and storage sub-modules, IPOAF receive indoor positioning data, and analysis the data according to custom communication format. Then we can get tag number, X coordinate, Y coordinates of indoor positioning data, and store them to the database.

In PosData Package of IPOAF, the PosData class is responsible for receiving positioning data; the PosDataCollection class is defining the collection of positioning data. Message class receives the information of positioning data what come from the server. OperateData class is responsible for subscribing service, subscribing message, canceling subscription and closing connection.

In the positioning data real-time linkage visualization module, there are two types visualization: single object positioning visualization and multiple object positioning visualization.

To realize real-time linkage visualization of positioning data and vector map, first of all, we must convert vector map coordinate to screen coordinate, and this process is handled by visualization class of PosDataClass package. Because the positioning data object' coordinate are map coordinate, the fromWorldtoEye function of visualization class is responsible for the conversion, and then realizing display by producing a pictureBox.

Secondly, the framework uses four layer architecture to real-time linkage visualization of positioning data and vector map. First layer, vector map visualization object--view; Second layer, the collection of vector map points--nodegrips, The coordinates of each map point is coordinates properties of the PosData object; Third layer, the collection of screen points--controlpoints is producing by nodegrips. Forth layer, pictureBox control layer.

4.4 Historical Path Playback Module

The historical path playback module mainly composed of two sub-modules: indoor obstacle environment generation and historical path' obstacle avoidance and visualization.

In this module, the Map class of IPOAF' AStar package is responsible for obstacle environment modeling to the Database which come from the memory, the model is a matrix also stored in memory, the content of the matrix formed by the digits 0 or 1. 0 represents free girds, and 1 represents obstacle grids.

Based on the obstacles model, historical path processes obstacle avoidance and visualization. AStar package is responsible for the whole process of the algorithm. As the node class of A* algorithm search tree, StarNode represent storage G value (the actual cost of initial node to n node), H value (the actual price of the minimum cost path between node n and destination node), F value (the cost of the minimum cost path which is from n0 to the destination node and go through node n). StarNodeCollection class is responsible the sort of F value, and operate the nodes which appear in the search process. AStar class is responsible for the calculation of G and H values and the recursive process of A*. The trajectory which A* returns finally stores in the AStar. Path object of StarNodeCollection class.

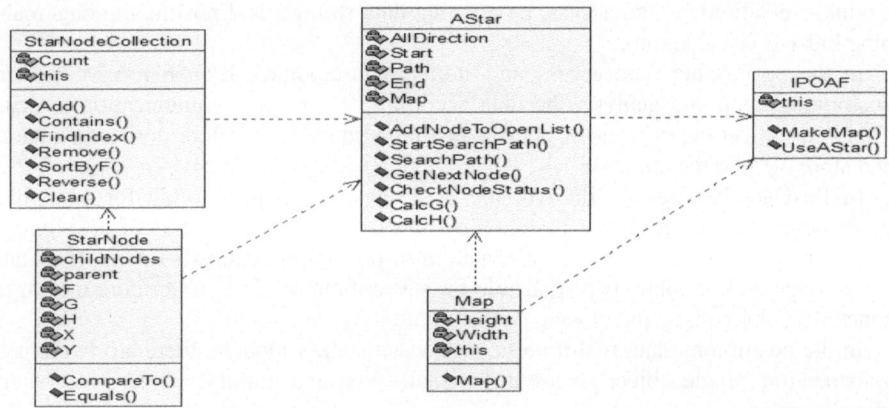

Fig. 4. The class diagram of AStar package in IPOAF

5 Framework Implementation

Under the guidance of the above theory, we develop a prototype of indoor positioning data IPOAF based on A*, and apply it in the actual projects. The implementation environment of the framework as shown in Table 1.

Table 1. The implementation environment of framework

Technology	Realization
Presentation layer	GDI+
Vector map operation	DWGDirect.net
Obstacle avoidance algorithm	A*
database	SQL Server 2005
Vector map file	DWG file

6 Conclusions and Future Work

Indoor positioning environment is complicated, and has many obstacles such as walls. The connection between two positioning data point which are in the trajectory of positioning data always pass through the obstacles. To solve this problem, in this paper, we combine A* map routing algorithm and vector map visualization technology to propose an Obstacle Avoidance And Visualization Method of indoor positioning data trajectory which is on the vector map. And we introduce an indoor positioning data Obstacle Avoidance And Visualization Framework (IPOAF) based on the method. The implementation of the framework is also discussed.

In our future work, we are going to further realize the real-time visualization of indoor positioning data trajectory.

References

1. Gao, J.: Visualization in Geo-Spatial Data. Engineering of Surveying and Mapping 9(3), 1–7 (2000)
2. Wan, M.-m., Gu, J.-w.: Exploring the Data Storage Format of AutoCAD DWG File. Journal of Engineering Graphics 1, 34–36 (2004)
3. Koren, Y., Borenstein, J.: Potential field methods and their inherent limitations for mobile robot navigation. In: Proceedings of the 1991 IEEE International Conference on Robotics and Automation, Sacramento, California, pp. 1398–1404 (1991)
4. Mero, L.: A Heuristic Search Algorithm with Modifiable Estimate. Artificial Intelligence 23, 1–13 (1984)
5. Zhu, M.x., Wu, Q.s., Rao, N.: Optimal pipeline decomposition and adaptive network mapping to support distributed remote visualization. Journal of Parallel and Distributed Computing 67, 947–956 (2007)
6. Brodlie, S.S.: Gaining understanding of multivariate and multidimensional data through visualization. Computers & Graphics 28, 311–325 (2004)

Power Mean Based Crossover Rate Adaptive Differential Evolution

Jie Li, Wujie Zhu, Mengjun Zhou, and Hua Wang

School of Computer & Information, Hefei University of Technology
Hefei 230009, China
{lijie_62,hfbozhu}@163.com,
zmjhfut@126.com, wang1984hua@sohu.com

Abstract. Crossover rate (CR) is a key parameter affecting the operation of differential evolution (DE). According to the different status appear in CR adaptive process, the present paper employs power mean averaging operators to improve the value of CR in appropriate chance and propose a Power Mean based Crossover Rate Adaptive Differential Evolution (PMCRADE). The performance of PMCRADE is evaluated on a set of benchmark problems and is compared with conventional and state-of-the-art DE variants. The results show that PMCRADE is better than, or at least comparable to, the compared DE variants in terms of convergence speed and reliability.

Keywords: Differential evolution (DE), power mean, crossover rate (CR), adaptive, optimization.

1 Introduction

Differential evolution (DE) algorithm, proposed by Storn and Price in 1995[1], is a population-based heuristic search technique for solving nonlinear and non-differentiable global optimization problems. Mainly for the sake of its effectiveness and reliability, DE has been successfully applied in diverse fields such as economy, communication, and control systems. The crucial parameters that affect the performance of DE are the population size (NP), crossover rate (CR) and scale factor (F). Choosing suitable value of CR is a problem dependent task and there is no fixed setting that is suitable for various problems or even at different evolution stages of a single problem [2]. In order to avoid time-consuming trial-and-error parameter tuning process, many different CR adaptive schemes have been presented. By analyzing different status appear in CR adaptive process, the present paper proposed a novel CR adaptive scheme based on power mean averaging operators. The value of CR in adaptive process is more conducive to improve DE performance, while the adaptive capability maintaining. Through this scheme to improve on JADE, a novel DE algorithm, namely Power Mean based Crossover Rate Adaptive Differential Evolution (PMCRADE), is proposed.

H. Deng et al. (Eds.): AICI 2011, Part II, LNAI 7003, pp. 34–41, 2011.

2   JADE-Adaptive Differential Evolution with Optional External Archive

The original DE algorithm follows the general procedure of an evolutionary algorithm (EA). The initial population, NP individuals, is randomly generated in search space according to a uniform distribution. After initialization, DE enters a loop of evolutionary operations: mutation, crossover, and selection. In order to classify the different variants of DE, the notation DE/x/y/z can be used. For example, DE/rand/1/bin, which used frequently in practice, denote implementing DE/rand/1 mutation operator and binominal crossover scheme.

JADE is a new DE variant, recently proposed by J. Zhang and A. Sanderson[2], which obtains very competitive results when solving some unconstrained benchmark problems and real-world problems. The new mutation operator employed in JADE is called "DE/current-to-$p$best/1(with/without archive)". In this paper, we only consider the variant of JADE without external archive and still denote it as JADE. In this way, the mutation vector is generated in the following manner:

$$v_{i,g} = x_{i,g} + F_{i,g} \cdot (x^p_{best,g} - x_{i,g} + x_{r1,g} - x_{r2,g}) . \tag{1}$$

where $x^p_{best,g}$ is randomly chosen as one of the top $100p\%$ individuals in the current population with $p \square (0, 1]$, and indices $r1$ and $r2$ are mutually exclusive integers randomly chosen from the range $[1, NP]$, which should also be different from the current trial vector's index i. $F_{i,g}$ is the scale factor that is associated with x_i and is regenerated at each generation g by the adaptive process introduced as follows:

$$F_{i,g} = randc_i(\mu_{F,g}, 0.1) . \tag{2}$$

where

$$\mu_{F,g} = (1-c) \cdot \mu_{F,g-1} + c \cdot mean_L(S_{F,g-1}) . \tag{3}$$

where $randc_i(\mu_{F,g}, 0.1)$ denotes the Cauchy distribution with location parameter $\mu_{F,g}$ and scale parameter 0.1; c is a constant in$[0,1]$; $S_{F,g-1}$ is the set of all successful scale factors $F_{i,g-1}$ at generation $g-1$, and $mean_L(\cdot)$ is the Lehmer mean, i.e.

$$mean_L(S_F) = \frac{\sum_{F \in S_F} F^2}{\sum_{F \in S_F} F} . \tag{4}$$

JADE adopts binominal crossover operator. At each generation g, for each target vector x_i, the crossover rate $CR_{i,g}$ is independently generated as follows:

$$CR_{i,g} = randn_i(\mu_{CR,g}, 0.1) . \tag{5}$$

where

$$\mu_{CR,g} = (1-c) \times \mu_{CR,g-1} + c \times mean_A(S_{CR,g-1}) . \tag{6}$$

where $\text{randn}_i(\mu_{CR,g}, 0.1)$ denotes the normal distribution of mean μ_{CR} and standard deviation 0.1; c is the same constant presented in (3); $S_{CR,g-1}$ is the set of all successful crossover rates $CR_{i,g-1}$ at generation $g-1$; and $\text{mean}_A(\cdot)$ is the usual arithmetic mean operation.

3 Proposed Algorithm

If *pow* is a non-zero real number, we can define the power mean with exponent *pow* of the positive real numbers $x_1, \ldots, x_n$ as:

$$\text{mean}_{pow}(x_1, \ldots x_n) = \left(\frac{1}{n} \cdot \sum_{i=1}^{n} x_i^{pow} \right)^{1/pow}. \tag{7}$$

Arithmetic mean is a special power mean with exponent 1, and power mean is an increasing function of exponent, so power mean with exponent greater than 1 is not less than arithmetic mean.

The improving strategy based on power mean averaging operators is to consider those different status that appear in the CR adaptive process and to collect successful CR data by employing power mean averaging operators, so as to make CR falls within reasonable range while possesses relatively greater value. As a bigger CR can not only accelerate the convergence speed of DE[3] but also can make DE more efficient for handling non-separable and multi-modal problems[4], therefore, an adaptive and relatively bigger CR is helpful to improve the performance of DE.

The good CR parameter value usually falls within a narrow range, with which adaptive DE can perform consistently well on a complex problem[5]. On the contrary, the successful CR parameter values spread more widely, which indicates that CR in chaos or the problem relatively has loose restrictions on CR. In order to maintain the adaptive capability of CR and increase its value in a reasonable manner, both cases should be treated with different ways. First, the standard deviation of successful CR can be used to distinguish the above two cases. When the standard deviation of successful CR is no more than the threshold σ, the successful CR values are concentrated; when the difference of the standard deviation exceeds the threshold, it is believed that the successful CR spreads widely. When successful CR is concentrated, its value is relatively reasonable, and the value should be maintained to prevent CR separating from the optimal range. Under this situation, power mean with exponent 1, i. e. arithmetic mean can be used to collect information of successful CR. When the values of successful CR spreading widely, it indicates that CR in chaos or the objective function relatively has loose restrictions on CR. In this case, big CR values can be emphasized or the value of CR can be increased to improve the performance of DE. Under this situation, we replace the arithmetic mean in (6) with the power mean with exponent 2. Specific operations are as the following:

$$\mu_{CR} = (1-c) \cdot \mu_{CR} + c \cdot \text{mean}_{pow}(S_{CR}). \tag{8}$$

where

$$pow = \begin{cases} 2, & \text{if } std(S_{CR}) > \sigma. \\ 1, & \text{if } std(S_{CR}) \leq \sigma. \end{cases} \tag{9}$$

JADE does not make a distinction between the two statuses mentioned above. In order to improve the performance of JADE, we adopt power mean averaging operators based crossover rate adaptive strategy. The proposed algorithm, namely Power Mean based Crossover Rate Adaptive Differential Evolution (PMCRADE), is a modified version of JADE. To make the description clearer, the complete pseudocode of the PMCRADE is given in Fig. 1.

01: Initialize the population P randomly
02: Evaluate the fitness for each individual in P
03: Set $\mu_{CR} = 0.5$; $\mu_F = 0.5$; g = 1 .
04: For g = 2 to G
05:     $S_F = \phi$; $S_{CR} = \phi$.
06:     For i = 1 to NP
07:         Generate $F_{i,g} = \text{randc}_i(\mu_{F,g}, 0.1)$; $CR_{i,g} = \text{randn}_i(\mu_{CR,g}, 0.1)$.
08:         Randomly choose $x_{best,g}^p$ as one of the $100p\%$ best vectors
09:         Randomly choose $x_{r1,g} \neq x_{r2,g} \neq x_{i,g}$ from current population P
10:         $v_{i,g} = x_{i,g} + F_{i,g} \cdot (x_{best,g}^p - x_{i,g} + x_{r1,g} - x_{r2,g})$.
11:         Generate $j_{rand} = \text{randint}(1,D)$
12:         For $j = 1$ to D
13:             If $j = j_{rand}$ or rand(0,1)$< CR_{i,g}$
14:                 $u_{i,j,g} = v_{i,j,g}$.
15:             Else
16:                 $u_{i,j,g} = x_{i,j,g}$.
17:             End If
18:         End For
19:         If $f(x_{i,g}) \leq f(u_{i,g})$
20:             $x_{i,g+1} = x_{i,g}$.
21:         Else
22:             $x_{i,g+1} = u_{i,g}$; $CR_{i,g} \rightarrow S_{CR}$; $F_{i,g} \rightarrow S_F$.
23:         End If
24:     End For
25:     If $std(S_{CR}) > \sigma$
26:         $\mu_{CR} = (1-c) \cdot \mu_{CR} + c \cdot \text{mean}_{pow=2}(S_{CR})$.
27:     Else
28:         $\mu_{CR} = (1-c) \cdot \mu_{CR} + c \cdot \text{mean}_{pow=1}(S_{CR})$.
29:     End If
30:     $\mu_F = (1-c) \cdot \mu_F + c \cdot \text{mean}_L(S_F)$.
31: End For

Fig. 1. Pseudocode of PMCRADE

4 Experimental Studies

4.1 Experimental Setup

In order to present the performance of new algorithm objectively, PMCRADE is compared with JADE[2] and the conventional DE/rand/1/bin[3] to minimize a set of 10 scalable benchmark functions(see Table 1)[6]. All functions have an optimal value $f^*=0$, some different characteristics are briefly summarized as follows. f_1-f_4 are continuous unimodal functions. f_5 is a discontinuous step function, and f_6 is a noisy quartic function. f_7- f_{10} are multimodal and the number of their local minima increases exponentially with the problem dimension. In addition, f_7 is the only bound-constrained function investigated in this paper.

In all simulations, the parameters of three algorithms are set to be fixed for fair comparison. We set the population size NP to be 100 and function dimension D=30. JADE and PMCRADE follow the parameter settings in [2], p=0.05 and c=0.1, except that the new parameter σ for PMCRADE is set to be 0.07. The parameters of DE/rand/1/bin are set to be F=0.5 and CR=0.9, as used or recommended in [3], [7]. All results reported in this section are obtained based on 50 independent runs, and do not run many 50 runs to pick the best run.

Table 1. Test functions of dimension D

Test Functions	Initial Range
$f_1(x)=\sum_{i=1}^{D} x_i^2$.	$[-100, 100]^D$
$f_2(x)=\sum_{i=1}^{D}\lvert x_i\rvert+\prod_{i=1}^{D}\lvert x_i\rvert$.	$[-10, 10]^D$
$f_3(x)=\sum_{i=1}^{D}(\sum_{j=1}^{i}x_j)^2$.	$[-100, 100]^D$
$f_4(x)=\max_i \left\{\lvert x_i\rvert, 1\le i\le D\right\}$.	$[-100, 100]^D$
$f_5(x)=\sum_{i=1}^{D-1}(\lfloor x_{i+0.5}\rfloor)^2$.	$[-100, 100]^D$
$f_6(x)=\sum_{i=1}^{D}x_i^4+random[0,1)$.	$[-1.28, 1.28]^D$
$f_7(x)=\sum_{i=1}^{D}(-x_i\sin(\sqrt{\lvert x_i\rvert}))+418.9829\times D$.	$[-500, 500]^D$
$f_8(x)=\sum_{i=1}^{D}(x_i^2-10\cos(2\pi x_i)+10)$.	$[-5.12, 5.12]^D$
$f_9(x)=-20\exp(-0.2\sqrt{\frac{1}{D}\sum_{i=1}^{D}x_i^2})-\exp(\frac{1}{D}\sum_{i=1}^{D}\cos(2\pi x_i))+20+\exp(1)$.	$[-32, 32]^D$
$f_{10}(x)=\frac{1}{4000}\sum_{i=1}^{D}x_i^2-\prod_{i=1}^{D}\cos(\frac{x_i}{\sqrt{i}})+1$.	$[-600, 600]^D$

4.2 Experimental Results and Discussions

Experimental results in terms of average final fitness and related standard deviation are given in Table 2; the number of successful runs (out of 50) that converges to sufficient accuracy and the corresponding mean number of function evaluations (FESS) are given in Table 3. An experiment is considered as successful if the best solution is found with sufficient accuracy: 10^{-2} for the noisy function f_6 and 10^{-8} for all others. FESS and the number of successful runs are useful to compare the convergence speed (in successful runs) and the reliability of different algorithms, respectively. The best and second best algorithms are highlighted in **boldface** and *italic*, respectively.

For the convenience of demonstration, we plot the convergence graph for f_4 and f_{10} in Fig 2 and 3. Note that in these graphs we plot the curves of median values (instead of the mean values reported in the tables), because these curves provide more information when an algorithm may lead to false convergence occasionally.

Important observations about the convergence speed and reliability of different algorithms in this study can be made from the results presented in Tables 2-3 and Figures 2-3.

Table 2. Average and the standard deviation of the final fitness for 50 runs

Function	G	PMCRADE	JADE	DE/rand/1/bin
f_1	1500	**7.7e-70(2.0e-69)**	*9.2e-58(6.5e-57)*	1.8e-13(1.0e-13)
f_2	2000	**1.8e-50(3.3e-50)**	*7.9e-28(5.6e-27)*	2.9e-09(1.8e-09)
f_3	5000	**4.8e-62(1.7e-61)**	*2.7e-61(1.7e-60)*	9.7e-11(1.6e-10)
f_4	5000	**1.8e-23(1.3e-22)**	*3.3e-07(1.3e-07)*	2.5e-02(7.6e-02)
f_5	100	**7.0e-01(9.9e-01)**	*2.6e+00(1.3e+00)*	4.8e+03(1.3e+03)
f_6	3000	**5.6e-04(2.3e-04)**	*6.3e-04(2.6e-04)*	4.9e-03(1.3e-03)
f_7	1000	**2.4e+00(1.7e+01)**	**2.4e+00(1.7e+01)**	*5.7e+03(1.4e+03)*
f_8	1000	**6.5e-07(1.0e-06)**	*1.1e-04(4.8e-05)*	1.9e+02(1.3e+01)
f_9	500	**1.0e-11(7.5e-12)**	*9.2e-10(7.6e-10)*	1.5e-01(4.5e-02)
f_{10}	500	*3.0e-04(1.5e-03)*	**1.5e-07(7.4e-07)**	2.7e-01 (1.5e-01)

Table 3. Number of runs (out of 50) that converged to sufficient accuracy and the corresponding mean number of function evaluations

Function	G	PMCRADE	JADE	DE/rand/1/bin
f_1	1500	**2.54e+04(50)**	*2.90e+04(50)*	1.09e+05(50)
f_2	2000	**4.11e+04(50)**	*5.21e+04(50)*	1.89e+05(50)
f_3	5000	**9.20e+04(50)**	*9.52e+04(50)*	4.25e+05(50)
f_4	5000	**1.54e+05(50)**	NaN(0)	*3.50e+05(7)*
f_5	100	**9.82e+03(29)**	*9.85e+03(2)*	NaN(0)
f_6	3000	**2.38e+04(50)**	*3.02e+04(50)*	1.50e+05(50)
f_7	1000	**8.87e+04(49)**	*NaN(0)*	*NaN(0)*
f_8	1000	**9.96e+04(1)**	*NaN(0)*	*NaN(0)*
f_9	500	**3.84e+04(50)**	*4.50e+04(50)*	NaN(0)
f_{10}	500	**2.70e+04(0.96)**	*3.28e+04(0.96)*	NaN(0.00)

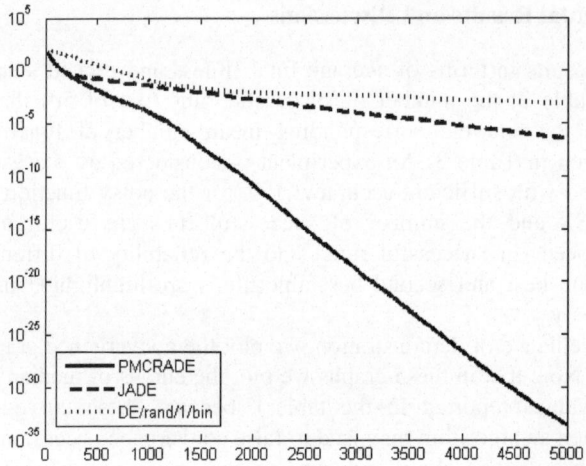

Fig. 2. Convergence graph for test function f_4. The horizontal axis is the number of generations, and the vertical axis is the median of function values over 50 independent runs.

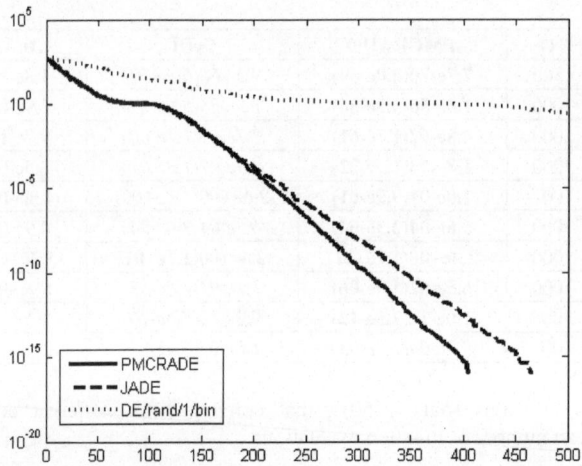

Fig. 3. Convergence graph for test function f_{10}. The horizontal axis is the number of generations, and the vertical axis is the median of function values over 50 independent runs.

In Table 2, the overall performance of PMCRADE is better than JADE and DE/rand/1/bin. PMCRADE gets the best average final fitness for the optimization of f_1-f_9. Only in the case of f_{10}, JADE performs best. In Table 3, PMCRADE converges most rapidly for the set of problems f_1-f_{10} in successful runs. For reliability, the number of successful runs (out of 50) of PMCRADE is also better than or equals to JADE and DE/rand/1/bin.

Especially, the results of PMCRADE for f_1, f_2, f_4, f_8 and f_9 have great advantages compared with JADE and DE/rand/1/bin. Where f_1, f_2, and f_4 are unimodal functions, the results of these functions depend mainly on the convergence speed. f_8 and f_9 are multimodal functions, PMCRADE good in the performance of these functions validate its capability to solute multimodal and non-separable problems.

Therefore, for this preliminary study we can conclude that PMCRADE is a very promising enhanced version of JADE, which is able to speed the convergence of JADE when its reliability maintained.

5 Conclusions

The present paper, through analyzing different status appearing in the process of CR adaptation, proposes an improving strategy based on power mean averaging operators. Relying on the improvement on JADE with such strategy, the improved algorithm demonstrates faster convergence speed and higher reliability in simulation results, which testifies the feasibility and effectiveness of the new algorithm. However, as the computation of the new algorithm is slightly higher than JADE, the following research is to focus on more simple and more effective CR adaptive strategy design and the actual application of the algorithm.

References

1. Storn, R., Price, K.V.: Differential evolution: A simple and efficient adaptive scheme for global optimization over continuous spaces, ICSI, USA, Tech. Rep. TR-95-012 (1995), http://icsi.berkeley.edu/~storn/litera.html
2. Zhang, J., Sanderson, A.C.: JADE: Adaptive differential evolution with optional external archive. IEEE Trans. Evol. Comput. 13(5), 945–958 (2009)
3. Storn, R., Price, K.: Differential evolution—A simple and efficient heuristic for global optimization over continuous spaces. J. Global Optim. 11(4), 341–359 (1997)
4. Ronkkonen, J., Kukkonen, S., Price, K.V.: Real parameter optimization with differential evolution. In: Proc. of the 2005 IEEE Congr. on Evol. Comput., vol. 1, pp. 506–513 (2005)
5. Qin, A.K., Suganthan, P.N.: Self-adaptive differential evolution algorithm for numerical optimization. In: Proc. of the 2005 IEEE Congr. on Evol. Comput., vol. 2, pp. 1785–1791 (2005)
6. Yao, X., Liu, Y., Lin, G.: Evolutionary programming made faster. IEEE Trans. Evol. Comput. 3(2), 82–102 (1999)
7. Vesterstroem, J., Thomsen, R.: A comparative study of differential evolution, particle swarm optimization, and evolutionary algorithms on numerical benchmark problems. In: Proc. of the 2004 IEEE Congr. on Evol. Comput., vol. 2, pp. 1980–1987 (2004)

Multi-objective Path Planning for Space Exploration Robot Based on Chaos Immune Particle Swarm Optimization Algorithm

Wei Hao and Shiyin Qin

School of Automation Science and Electrical Engineering
Beihang University, Beijing, China
haowei_1980@asee.buaa.edu.cn, qsy@buaa.edu.cn

Abstract. Multi-objective path planning for mobile robot in complex environments is a challenging issue in space exploration. In order to improve the efficiency and quality of the multi-objective path planning, a chaos immune particle swarm optimization (CIPSO) algorithm is proposed in this paper, which combines chaos and PSO with immune network theory so as to enhance the searching speed of path planning for mobile robot and insure the safety of space exploration. Simulation results show that the CIPSO has well performance for path planning and obstacle avoidance.

Keywords: path planning, chaos, particle swarm optimization, immune network.

1 Introduction

With the rapid development of space technology, human will have more and more chances to finish the tasks such as building international space station, servicing satellites and space exploration in outer space. However, it is very dangers and difficult for people to do by themselves. So, using robots to substitute human and to accomplish these work has a significant meaning [1].Nowadays, there are a lot of work which includes theory and practice of space robots have been done by many countries and research centers in the world. Space robots have been successfully applied in satellite release, maintenance, space station construction and so on. Therefore, space robots will take the place of astronauts to implement the outer space activities, which can greatly decrease the labor intensity and risks of the astronauts.

Path planning for mobile robots is aimed at finding an obstacle-free path from a starting position to a specified goal position under some certain constraints [2-3]. The approach used for path planning can be divided into traditional methods and intelligent methods. The traditional methods include road maps (Voronoi diagrams and visibility graphs), grids [4-5], and artificial potential fields [6]. In recent years, with the advent of artificial intelligence, some methods inspired by neural phenomena have been proposed to solve the problem on path planning. Hong Qu and Yang, S.X. [7] presents a modified pulse-coupled neural network model for real-time collision-free path planning. The proposed model is applied to produce collision-free paths for a mobile robot to solve a maze-type problem, to circumvent concave U-shaped obstacles, and to track a moving target in an environment. The results show that the effectiveness and

H. Deng et al. (Eds.): AICI 2011, Part II, LNAI 7003, pp. 42–52, 2011.
© Springer-Verlag Berlin Heidelberg 2011

efficiency of this approach is very well. Tewolde, G.S. and Weihua Sheng [8] present genetic algorithm and ant colony optimization to solve tool path for automated manufacturing problem. From comparing the results of two methods, they get pros and cons of each method. Masehian, E. and Sedighizadeh, D. [9] propose an original method which combines particle swarm optimization and probabilistic roadmap method for robot motion planning. The PSO and PRM are combined by joining new PSO particles as auxiliary nodes in the node group generated by the PRM and the results show that this method is useful for finding the shortest path.

Some of these approaches which are used global methods to search the possible paths in the workspace are good for dealing with simple environment, but not fit for the complex environment. Consequently, in this paper we proposed a new method named chaos immune particle swarm optimization (CIPSO) algorithm to improve the accuracy and efficiency of the mobile robot path planning. The simulation results indicate that mobile robots can get an optimized path in the complex environment. The remainder of this paper is organized as follows: Section 2 gives a brief overview of chaos theory, particle swarm optimization and immune network algorithm. In Section 3, we present the framework and steps of chaos immune particle swarm optimization (CIPSO) algorithm. Simulation results of mobile robot path planning are given in Section 4. Finally, conclusions are drawn in Section 5.

2   Background

2.1   Chaos Theory

Chaos [10] is a kind of relative common phenomenon existing in nonlinear systems, which is a kind of random behavior between rules showed by completely deterministic system without additional random factors. Professor Edward Lorenz was working on the problem of weather prediction for a long time, and from the phenomenon of weather he found the butterfly effect known as just a small change in the initial conditions can making enormous change of the system. This discovery led Lorenz to find the new theory what eventually came to be known as chaos theory. Chaos movement has some unique properties such as inner stochastic, sensitive to initial conditions, ergodic and regularity.

Usually, chaos optimization process [11] includes two stages: firstly, through inspecting every point passed successively, better points will be as the current best; secondly, we use the current best points as the center; last, around the current best points, we add some small chaos perturbations to search the best points until satisfying the termination criterion.

2.2   Immune Network Theory

According to the biological immune system, Jerne [12] proposed a theory of immune particular network firstly in 1974. The theory states that the immune system is an interacting network of lymphocytes and molecules that have B-cells. These B-cells bind not only to things that are foreign to the vertebrate, but also to other B-cells within the system. Therefore, the immune system is seen as a network, with the components connected to each other by B-cells interactions. Jerne presented the B-cells interaction in immune network system by a differential equation demonstrated in (1)

$$A_i = \sum_{j=1}^{M} (1 - D_{i,j}) + \sum_{k=1}^{n} (1 - D_{i,k}) - \sum_{k=1}^{n} D_{i,k} \tag{1}$$

where M denotes the number of antigen. n is the number of B-cells. $D_{i,j}$ is the Eucliden distance between antigen j and B-cells i. $D_{i,k}$ is the Eucliden distance between B-cells i and B-cells j.

At present, two artificial immune network models presented by Timmis and de Casto respectively are popular to be researched. Timmis[13] presents Resource Limited Artificial Immune System (RLAIS) based on Artificial Recognition Ball (ARB). This model introduces the concept of an ARB which is a representation of the identical B cells. Though making the similar ARB get together, RLAIS can be used for data mining analysis. de Castro L. N. [14] proposes the adaptation of an immune network model to solve multimodal function optimization problems. The simulation results show the performance of the algorithm is very well.

2.3 Particle Swarm Optimization

Particle swarm optimization (PSO) [15] is a computational method based on stochastic optimization technique attributed to Russell Eberhart and James Kennedy in 1995, inspired by simulating the movement of organisms in a bird flock or fish school. From the research results, we know that even though birds will change direction, decentralize and aggregation abruptly in the course of flying, a bird flock always keep consistency and safe distance between them. When the population searches for some objects, everyone will change its position and velocity according to its own and other information.

The steps of PSO are as follows [16]:

(1) Initialization
Code the problem which needs to be solved and generate random positions and velocities of population particles.

(2) Evaluation
Design the fitness function and calculate the fitness value of each particle according to the problem.

(3) Comparison
Compared fitness of each particle with its best fitness value of previous, the better one would be the new position. After that, compared fitness of each particle with its best fitness value of the whole population, the better one would be the new position.

(4) Evolution
Calculate new velocity and position of each particle on the basis of (2) and (3).

$$v_{id}(t+1) = v_{id}(t) + c_1 r_1 (p_{id}(t) - x_{id}(t)) + c_2 r_2 (p_{gd}(t) - x_{id}(t)) \tag{2}$$

$$x_{id}(t+1) = v_{id}(t+1) + x_{id}(t) \tag{3}$$

where $1 \leq i \leq N$, $1 \leq d \leq D$, t is the current iteration, c_1, c_2 are adjusting coefficient, r_1, r_2 are random coefficient between 0 and 1.

(5) Stop criterion
If the fitness value or a maximum number of iterations is achieved, stop the project. Then, returning to step 2.

3   Chaos Immune Particle Swarm Optimization Algorithm for Multi-objective Path Planning

Algorithm mainly consists of six parts: individual coding, generation of initial population, fitness function, and generation of new population, immune network adjusting and ending criterion. How to design every part is a key point of solving the problem successfully.

3.1   Environment Model

Environment model is using mathematic method to represent the circumstance of mobile robot and how to describe it is very important for the speed and efficiency of path planning. Nowadays, the most popular method of environment model is topological graph and geometric map. Topological graph map [18] is using nodes and lines to indicate the important position points and galleries. It is simple and convenience not only for behavior planning, but also for using graph searching algorithms. The efficiency of topological graph is higher on account of lower requirement of store space and running time. However, the disadvantage of this method is complex establishment processing. Geometric map is a very useful modeling method which is setting up the relationship between environment and geometric graph and it is used widely because of accurate and concise expression.

In this paper, we adopt geometric map to indicate the environment as Figure 1. Global scene is shown as rectangular coordinates system, and barriers in the circumstance are some irregular polygons. At same time, point coordinate of irregular polygons to be represented the barriers.

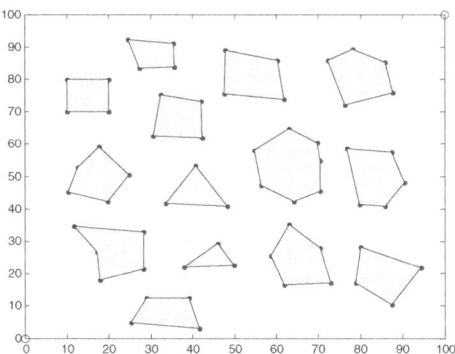

Fig. 1. The sketch map of barriers

3.2   Method of Path Coding

Nowadays, the common way to indicate the path is binary coding. However, for complicated optimization problem, the length of binary coding would be increase greatly and the efficiency of algorithm would be decrease. So, we adopt coded-decimal notation to express the path. Firstly, the total number of peak points of barriers is n and coding these points at counter-clockwise direction. Then, the path of mobile robot is represented as a decimal string and the number in the decimal string indicates the points of barriers which are mobile robot passed.

3.3 Initial Population

At first iteration, population Q will be generated stochastically as the group of initial antibodies A_b by using chaotic operator shown as (4).

$$x_{n+1} = \mu x_n (1 - x_n) \tag{4}$$

where x is chaos variable, $0 < x_n < 1$, n is iterations, μ is controls parameter. When $\mu=4$, system is in the state of chaos.

3.4 Multi-objective Function

Suppose that there are n robots and O_m (m=1, 2, …L) barriers in the workspace. S_i is the start point of robot i (i=1, 2,…, n) and G_i is the ending point. The multi-objective function of mobile robot is shown as (5):

$$F(P^*) = \min[\omega_1 f_1(P) + \omega_2 f_2(P) + \omega_3 f_3(P)] \tag{5}$$

where $f_1(P)$, $f_2(P)$, $f_3(P)$ represent the length, smoothness and safe of path respectively, ω_1, ω_2, ω_3,is accommodation coefficient and $\sum_{i=1}^{3} \omega_i = 1$.

(1) Length of path f_1 (P):

$$f_1(P) = \sum_{i=1}^{M-1} d(P_{ij}, P_{i(j+1)}) \tag{6}$$

where M is node points of path, $d(P_{ij}, P_{i(j+1)})$ indicates the distant between P_i and P_{i+1}.

(2) Smoothness of path f_2 (P):

$$f_2(P) = \frac{\sum_{j=2}^{n-1} \alpha_{ij} + k \times \pi/2}{n-2}, \quad n>2 \tag{7}$$

where α_{ij} represents the angle between $P_{i(j-1)}P_{ij}$ and $P_{ij}P_{i(j+1)}$; k is punishment factor; if n=2, the path is line from start point to end point.

(3) Danger of path f_3 (P):

$$f_3(P) = \begin{cases} 1/m & No\ crossover \\ 1/m + w & Having\ crossover \end{cases} \tag{8}$$

where m is the shortest distance between path and barriers; w is punishment factor.

3.5 Generation of New Population

(1) According to the fitness function, antibodies were divided into part A and part B equally.

(2) For the part A, the following steps are carried out:
a. Low frequency mutation

$$\alpha_m^* = T \times \alpha_m \tag{9}$$

where $T \in (0,1)$ is low mutation rate.
b. Antibodies recombination

α_m^* is used to replace the old ones.

(3) For the part B, the following steps are carried out:
a. High frequency mutation

$$c_m^* = c_m - p(c_m - A_g) \tag{10}$$

where $p = \{p_i^m, m = (0,1,\dots,n)\}$ is high frequency mutation rate.

b. Antibodies recombination

c_m^* is used to replace the old ones.

3.6 Immune Network Adjusting

On the basis of immune network theory, the course of immune network adjusting includes calculating the degree of stimulated antibodies, network suppression and updating network.

(1) Calculating the extent of stimulated antibodies
In the whole immune network, the extent of every antibody will calculated by (11)

$$A_i = \alpha_1 \sum_{j=1}^{M} (1 - D_{ij}) + \alpha_2 \sum_{k=1}^{n} (1 - D_{ik}) - \alpha_3 \sum_{j=1}^{M} D_{ik} + \beta_1 \sum_{j=1}^{n} (1 - D_{il}) \tag{11}$$

where M denotes the number of antigen. n is the number B-cells. $D_{i,j}$ is the Eucliden distance between antigen j and B-cells i. $D_{i,k}$ is the Eucliden distance between B-cells i and B-cells j. $D_{i,l}$ is the Eucliden distance between B-cells i and T-cells l. α and β are constants and $\sum_{i=1}^{3} \alpha_i = 1$, $\beta \in (0,1)$. $(1-D_{i,j})$, $(1-D_{i,k})$, $(1-D_{i,l})$ denotes the affinity between B-cells and other antigens.

(2) Network suppression
We will delete the antibodies which A_i is lower than threshold value X to improve the speed of algorithm. The retained antibodies are called memory cells.

(3) Updating network
N antibodies which are optimized by PSO algorithm would be putted into immune network. These antibodies will be combined with memory cells to compose the new population.
Executing (1)-(3) until stopping criterion satisfied

3.7 The Framework of Algorithm

The main steps of CIPSO algorithm for robot path planning are shown as follows:
Step1: Environment model;
Using method presented by A to describe the workspace of mobile robot.

Step2: Initial population;
Firstly, coding path of mobile robot according to B and C; then, setting up some parameters such as initial population Q, low mutation rate T, high mutation rate p, network suppression threshold X and stopping criterion.
Step3: Calculating fitness function;

$$f_{ij} = \frac{1}{F(P^*) + 1} \tag{12}$$

Step4: Generation new population by E;
Step5: Adjusting the immune network by F;
Step6: Stopping criterion;
Repeating step3-5 until satisfied the stopping criterion.
The flowchart of CIPSO algorithm shown as follows:

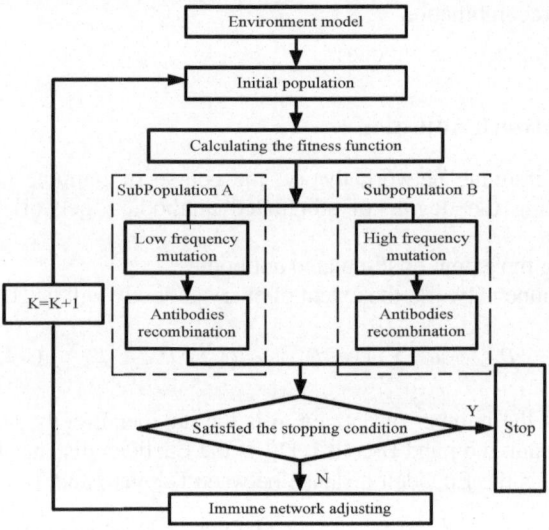

Fig. 2. The flowchart of CIPSO algorithm

4   Simulation

In this section, we suppose the test field of wheeled mobile robot is 300x300, start point is [0, 0] and stop point is [300, 300]. Then, we set the initial population Q=50, low mutation rate T=0.3, high mutation rate p=0.8, network suppression threshold X=0.5 and stopping criterion is iteration generation=200. Finally, in order to compare the performance of the algorithm, we adopt three algorithms which are CIPSO, GA and Immune-GA to solve the path planning problem at three different circumstances. For each instance, the algorithms are run for 20 times and the average is taken. Programs were coded with MATLAB 7.1 and run in the personal computer of Core i3 2.27 GHz.

Figure 3, 4 and 5 indicate path planning results of three algorithms respectively in the environment which have different barriers. In the graph, blue line presents CIPSO algorithm, red line presents Immune-GA and green line presents GA.

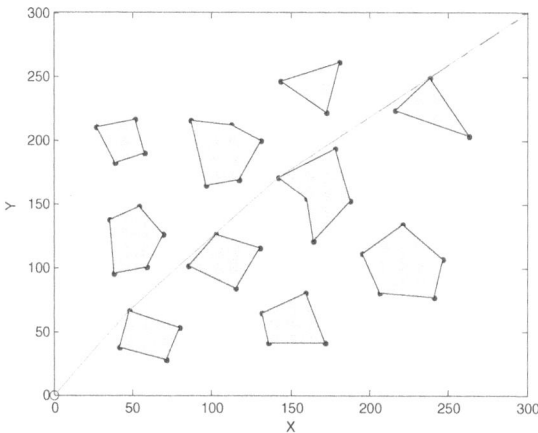

Fig. 3. The path planning results of three algorithms in the environment which includes 10 barriers

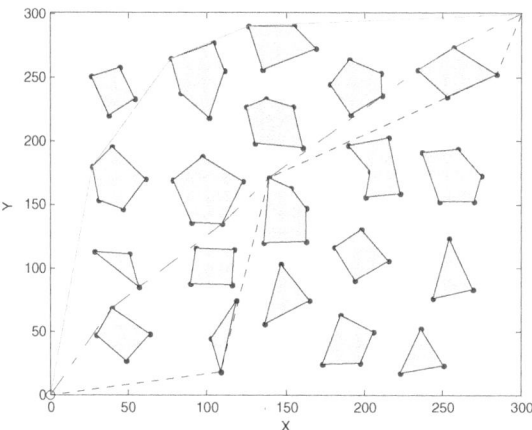

Fig. 4. The path planning results of three algorithms in the environment which includes 20 barriers

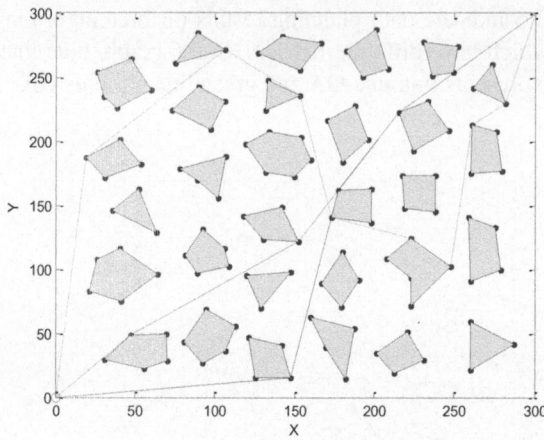

Fig. 5. The path planning results of three algorithms in the environment which includes 30 barriers

Table1, 2 and 3 include parameters such as evolution criterion, running time and length of path at different conditions.

Table 1. Path planning parameters in the 10 barriers environment

Barriers	Algorithm	Evolution criterion	Time	Length of path
10	CIPSO	16	2.89	426.2
	Immune-GA	19	3.09	426.2
	GA	24	3.05	426.2

Table 2. Path planning parameters in the 20 barriers environment

Barriers	Algorithm	Evolution criterion	Time	Length of path
20	CIPSO	50	3.79	433.2
	Immune-GA	64	4.16	472.1
	GA	83	4.28	545.3

Table 3. Path planning parameters in the 30 barriers environment

Barriers	Algorithm	Evolution criterion	Time	Length of path
	CIPSO	60	4.26	439.6
30	Immune-GA	75	4.96	506.3
	GA	89	5.65	735.8

From Figure 3 and Table 1, we can see that the green line, red line and blue line coincide. It represents that three algorithms can get the shortest path at same time in the simple environment. However, the evolution criterion and time of CIPSO is minimized. For complex environment which includes more barriers, we know that the performance of CIPSO is better than other algorithms just like Figure 4, 5 and Table 2, 3.

5 Conclusions

In this paper, a novel chaos immune particle swarm optimization algorithm is proposed. The CIPSO algorithm combines chaos theory and PSO with immune network theory to improve the efficiency of mobile robot path planning. Finally, the simulation results demonstrate that the ability of CIPSO to solve mobile robot problem in complex environment is better than GA and Immune-GA.

Acknowledgment. This work is partially supported by the National Natural Science Foundation of China (No.60875072) and International Cooperation Project (No.2007DFA11530).

References

1. Gao, Y.: Multi-robot Cooperation Based on Biological Immune System. Zhejiang University (2007)
2. Regele, R., Levi, P.: Cooperative Multi-Robot Path Planning by Heuristic Priority Adjustment. In: Proceedings of IEEE/RSJ International Conference on Intelligent Robots and Systems, pp. 5954–5959. IEEE Press, Beijing (2006)
3. Chen, J., Li, L.R.: Path Planning Protocol for Collaborative Multi-robot Systems. In: Proceedings IEEE International Symposium on Computational Intelligence in Robotics and Automation, pp. 721–726. IEEE Press, Espoo (2005)
4. Guo, S., Dai, L., Ouyang, Y.: The Research and Simulation on the path planning based on the Improved Grid Model. In: IEEE International Conference on Artificial Intelligence and Computational Intelligence, pp. 318–321. IEEE Press, Shanghai (2009)
5. Willms, A.R., Yang, S.X.: An efficient dynamic system for real-time robot-path planning. IEEE Transactions on Systems, Man, and Cybernetics, Part B: Cybernetics 36(4), 755–766 (2009)

6. Arambula Cosío, F., Padilla Castañeda, M.A.: Autonomous robot navigation using adaptive potential fields. Mathematical and Computer Modelling 40(9), 1141–1156 (2004)

7. Hong, Q., Yang, S.X., Willms, A.R., Zhang, Y.: Real-Time Robot Path Planning Based on a Modified Pulse-Coupled Neural Network Model. IEEE Transactions on Neural Networks 20(11), 1724–1739 (2009)

8. Tewolde, G.S., Sheng, W.: Robot Path Integration in Manufacturing Processes: Genetic Algorithm Versus Ant Colony Optimization. IEEE Transactions on Systems, Man and Cybernetics, Part A: Systems and Humans 38(2), 278–287 (2008)

9. Masehian, E., Sedighizadeh, D.: A multi-objective PSO-based algorithm for robot path planning. In: IEEE International Conference on Industrial Technology, pp. 465–470. IEEE Press, Tehran (2010)

10. Ren, W., Wang, Q., Wei, L., Zhang, L.: A Kind of Adaptive Immune Genetic Algorithm Based on Chaos and Its Application. In: Proceedings of the 8th World Congress on Intelligent Control and Automation, pp. 5018–5021. IEEE Press, Jinan (2010)

11. Zhao, Q.: Improved chaos optimization algorithm and its application. Automation and Instrumentation (3), 90–92 (2006)

12. Jerne, N.K.: Towards a network theorem of the immune system. Annual Immunology 125C, 373–389 (1974)

13. Timmis, J., Neal, M.: A resource limited artificial immune system for data analysis. Knowledge Based Systems 14(3), 121–130 (2001)

14. de Castro, L.N., Timmis, J.: An artificial immune network for multimodal function optimization. In: Proceedings of IEEE Congress on Evolutionary Computation, pp. 674–699. IEEE Press, Canterbury (2002)

15. Kennedy, J., Eberhart, R.: Particle swarm optimization. In: Proceedings of IEEE International Conference on Neural Networks, vol. 4, pp. 1942–1948. IEEE Press, Washington, DC (1995)

16. Sadeghpour, M., Salarieh, H., Vossoughi, G., Alasty, A.: Multi-variable control of chaos using PSO-based minimum entropy control. Commun. Nonlinear Sci. Numer. Simulat. 16, 2397–2404 (2011)

A Distributed Surveillance Model
for Network Security Inspired by Immunology

Caiming Liu[1], Run Chen[2], Yan Zhang[3,*], Luxin Xiao[4], Chao Chen[5], and Jin Yang[1]

[1] Laboratory of Intelligent Information Processing and Application, Leshan Normal University,
614004 Leshan, China
[2] School of Computer Science, Sichuan University, 610065 Chengdu, China
[3] School of Computer Science, Leshan Normal University, 614004 Leshan, China
[4] Teaching Affairs Office, Leshan Normal University, 614004 Leshan, China
[5] School of Computer Science, Sichuan University of Science & Engineering, 643000
Zigong, China
liucaiming@gmail.com, zhangyan_201016@163.com

Abstract. In the interest of surveying global attacks distributing in the networks, a distributed surveillance model for network security inspired by human immunity is proposed. The proposed model consists of attack detection agent, forensics sub-model, alarm sub-model and risk assessment sub-model. Through simulating immune mechanisms, a detection agent performs self-adaptation and self-learning to generate excellent detection elements and reach the target of attacks recognition. Local agents detect attacks independently and share the learning achievement with the other agents through communication. The sub-models realize the surveying process of evidence extraction, alarms configuration and quantitative risk assessment. Theoretical analysis shows that the proposed model effectively adapts the local network environment and globally improves the surveillance ability of network security.

Keywords: Immunology, Network Security Threat, Distributed Surveillance, Network Attack Detection.

1 Introduction

Network attacks are severely harmful to the computer networks. They threaten the confidentiality, integrity and controllability of the networks [1]. They cause many serious problems of network security. How to monitor the network security threat and its influence to the networks became a research focus. The surveillance of network security aims at this. Presently, researchers have presented Intrusion Detection System (IDS) [2] to detect network attacks. However, IDS only discovers attacks according to its attacks signature library which is static. Meanwhile, it can not provide the influence of attacks and network security situation to the network administrator. The surveillance technology of network security is to detect network attacks, gather the attacks evidence and form the status of networks. It is useful to establish active and positive defense strategy of network security.

---

* Corresponding author.

H. Deng et al. (Eds.): AICI 2011, Part II, LNAI 7003, pp. 53–60, 2011.
© Springer-Verlag Berlin Heidelberg 2011

Through simulating the excellent mechanisms of Biological Immune System (BIS), researchers established Artificial Immune System (AIS) [3-5]. AIS was applied to many research fields and acquired effective achievements [6-8]. It has attracted much attention of researchers in recent years [9-12]. It has the excellent attributes of distributed and parallel treatment, diversity, self-organization, self-adaptation, robustness, and etc [10]. These attributes make AIS being good at resolving complicated computation problems. Forrest and other researchers [13, 14] proposed computer immunology and used it to revolve computer security problems. Because the problems found in an information security system are quite similar to those encountered in a BIS [10], AIS is broadly applied to resolve the problems of information system security. Especially, during the last years, it has been used to detect network intrusions by many scholars [15-17] and its effects are outstanding.

In this paper, the principles in AIS are used for reference to resolve the problems of network security surveillance. A surveillance model for network security is proposed. In the rest of this paper, the following is described. First, the architecture of the proposed model is established. Second, simulation mechanism for network traffic is discussed. Third, attacks detection agent and its communication mechanism are presented. Finally, alarm, forensics and risk assessment sub-models are established.

2   Proposed Model

2.1   Architecture of the Proposed Model

The architecture of the proposed model is shown in Fig. 1. In the local network, the proposed model is made up of immune detection agent, forensics sub-model, alarm sub-model, risk assessment sub-model and attack library. The detection agent is

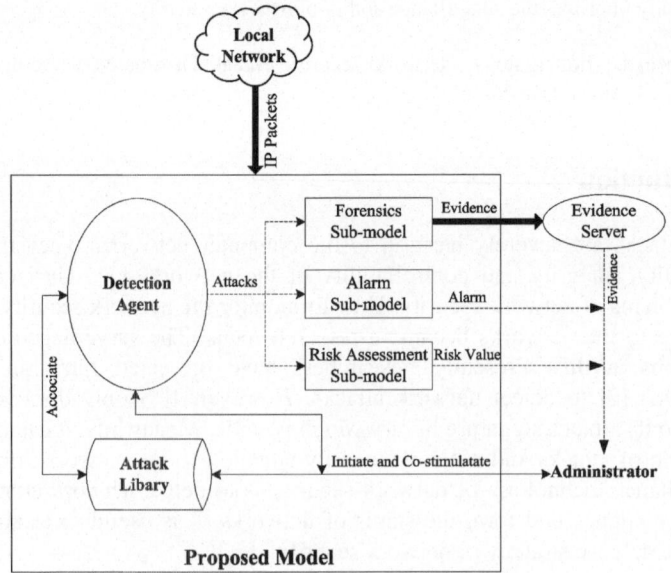

Fig. 1. Architecture of the Proposed Model

deployed in the local network by pass. It captures network traffics. Through simulating the excellent mechanisms in AIS, it classifies the IP packets into normal ones and abnormal ones (network attacks). The forensics sub-model takes charge of gathering evidence in the spot when network attacks being detected. It sends the evidence to the evidence server safely. The alarm sub-model collects the behavior information and the attribute information of network attacks and encapsulates them into alarm information. Afterwards, it sends the alarm information to the network administrator. The risk assessment sub-model gathers the attacks detection data and evaluates the quantitative risk value of the local network. The administrator can watch the risk in real-time. The attack library contains the information of network attacks. The attack information comes from the detection agent or is initiated by the administrator.

2.2 Information Simulation

Network IP packets contain some signature information and content. The signature information identifies network packets and denotes the main characteristics of network packets. It consists of the important fields of the packet head which includes source IP address, target IP address, protocol type, and etc. The main signature information is extracted to be switched to binary character string whose size is l. The signature information is simulated as antigens. Let the antigen set be Ag which is shown in Eq. (1).

$$Ag = \{ag | ag \in U, |ag| = l, ag = GetSig(packet)\} \tag{1}$$

Where, $U = \{0,1\}^l$, l is a nature number, $GetSig()$ is an extracting function of packet signature and its return value is diverted to binary string, $packet$ is the network IP packets which were captured.

To simulate the normal and abnormal antigens in BIS, let the self set and the non-self set be S and N, respectively. They denote the signature information of normal and abnormal packets separately. They consist of binary strings. S and N meet the condition that $S, N \in Ag$, $S \cup N = Ag, S \cap N = \varnothing$.

2.3 Detection Agent for Network Attacks

1) Definition

Detectors simulate immune cells in BIS to imitate the specificity recognition mechanism. They are used to recognize network attacks. Let the detector set be $D = \{\langle gene, age, count, type, attackID \rangle | gene \in U, age, count, type, attackID \in N\}$, where, $gene$ is the detector's gene, it is the key signature information which discovers network traffic packets contain attacks or not, N is a nature number set, $count$ is the sum of antigens matched by the detector, age is the life generations of the detector, $type$ denotes the type of the detector, $attackID$ is the serial number of the corresponding attack, it expresses the type number of the detector.

According to the evolution stages of detectors, detectors are classified into immature detectors, mature detectors and memory detectors. Let them be D_I, D_M and D_R, respectively. Immature detectors (D_I) simulate the initial stage of immune cells in BIS. They are newly generated detectors. They are generated by memory detectors through the way of cross, mutation and recombination, or randomly. Mature detectors (D_M) simulate the medium stage of immune cells in BIS. They are evolved to by immature ones. Its domain count adds by 1 when it detects an antigen. Memory detectors (D_R) simulate the highest evolution stage of immune cells in BIS. They are evolved to by immature ones or switched to by the administrator with the signature information of a known network attack. A memory detector contains the accurate signature which can recognize network attacks.

2) Self-tolerance

New immature detectors may recognize self elements (Normal IP packets). They can not be used to detect network attacks directly. They must accept the process of the self-tolerance. They evolve to mature ones after they succeed to pass the self-tolerance. If an immature one is matched by a self cell in a special period time, it fails to accept self-tolerance. Let the function of the self-tolerance be $f_{tolerance}()$ which is shown in Eq. (2).

$$f_{tolerance}(D_I) = \left\{ d \mid d \in D_I, d.age \geq \alpha, \forall s \in S \wedge f_{match}(d,s) = 0 \right\} \tag{2}$$

Where, α is a threshold of an immature detector's tolerance period, $f_{match}()$ is a match function, it returns 0 when d doesn't match s, otherwise it returns 1.

3) Detection

Let the attack library set be A which is shown in Eq. (3).

$$A = \left\{ \langle attackID, name, content, count \rangle \mid \forall d \in D_R, attackID = \\ d.attackID, attackID, count \in N, name, content \in ASCII \right\} \tag{3}$$

Where, $attackID$ is the sequence number of the attack, it is equal to $attackID$ of the corresponding memory detector, $name$ is the attack name, $content$ is the description of the attack, $ASCII$ is the ASCII character set.

Every memory detector is related to an attack. The memory detector uses its gene to capture antigens. Once its gene matches an antigen, the proposed model queries the corresponding attack information of the memory detector in the attack library and sends alarm information to the network administrator.

Let $D_{R\_detect}(t)$ be the memory detectors which recognize harmful antigens at the moment t. $D_{R\_detect}(t)$ is shown in Eq. (4).

$$D_{R\_detect}(t) = \left\{ d \mid \forall d \in D_R(t), \exists ag \in Ag(t), f_{match}(d,ag) = 1 \right\} \tag{4}$$

Where, $D_R(t)$ and $Ag(t)$ denote the memory detector set and the antigen set at the moment t, respectively.

2.4 Communication of Detection Agents

Each local detection agent generates excellent learning achievements (memory detectors). In a local detection agent, detectors detect and accept the training of the input antigens. With the mechanisms of self-adaptation and self-learning, antigens can train some enough excellent detectors to recognize mutated, even new unknown security threats. These good detectors which own the accurate detection ability to recognize harmful antigens and are good at adapting local network environment are new memory detectors. However, it takes the cost of much resource and time to generate new memory detectors. The other detection agents are not necessary to consume some cost to train the same memory detectors. Therefore, the learning achievements in a local agent need to be shared with the other agents to improve the global detection ability. The communication process is shown in Fig. 2.

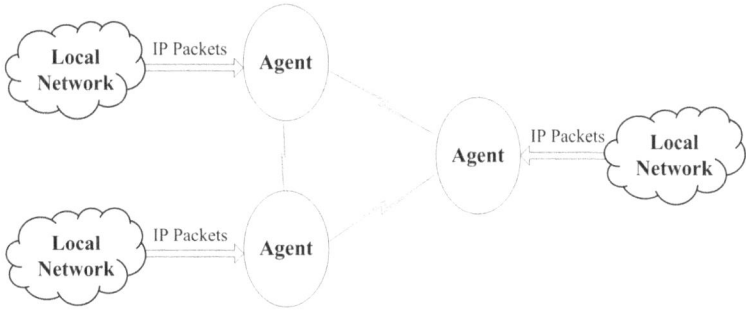

Fig. 2. Communication of Detection Agents

2.5 Sub-model of Alarm

When a harmful antigen is detected, the information of the corresponding network attack is extracted to form alarms which are sent to the administrator. Let the alarm information set be *Alarm* . The production process of alarm is described in Eq. (5).

$$Alarm = \{\langle ID, attackName, attackCount\rangle | ID \in N, \forall d \in D_{R\_detect}(t) \land \exists a \in$$
$$A \land d.attackID = a.attackID, attackName = a.name, attackCount = a.count\} \tag{5}$$

Where, *ID* is the sequence number of the alarm information, *attackName* is the name of the detected attack, *attackCount* is the sum of the attack times.

2.6 Sub-model of Forensics

The forensics sub-model collects the attack behavior information and sends it to the evidence server which is deployed independently and safely. Once a harmful antigen is detected by a memory detector in the detection agent, the evidence of network attacks is in the spot. The signature information of its corresponding network packet will be extracted to be the attack evidence. The signature information consists of source IP address, target IP address, attack time, and etc. Also, the immediate status information of the target system which suffers network attacks will be collected, which includes CPU status, CPU usage, network traffic speed, and etc. All the former information forms the real-time data of the attack behavior. Let it be *attackFlash* which is packed into the evidence which is defined as *Evidence* that is shown in Eq. (6).

$$Evidence = Encrypt(Hash(attackFlash), Key_{evi}) + Encrypt(attackFlash, Key_{evi}) \qquad (6)$$

Where, Key_{evi} is the public key provided by the evidence server.

2.7 Sub-model of Risk Assessment

Based on the intensity of network attacks, the harmfulness value of network attacks and the importance value of information assets attacked by attacks are used to compute the quantitative risk value. Let the harmfulness value of a security threat be h_i (i is the ID number of the security threat). Let the importance value of an information asset be v_j (j is the ID number of the information asset). The risk value r of the local network is shown in Eq. (7).

$$r = 1 - \cfrac{1}{1 + \ln\left(\sum_{j=1}^{m}\sum_{i=1}^{n} v_j \left(h_i \left(Count\left(d_I.attackID = i\right) + Count\left(d_M.attackID = i\right)\right)\right) + 1\right)} \qquad (7)$$

Where, m and n are the sum of information assets and the attacks respectively, $d_I \in D_I$, $d_M \in D_M$, the function $Count()$ counts the sum of detectors according to the condition in accordance with its parameter.

3 Discussion

The proposed model uses dynamical detection strategy to overcome the weakness of the static library in the traditional IDS. Meanwhile, it can adapt the real network environment. The dynamical detection is reflected by the evolution of detectors. The generation process of immature, mature and memory detectors embodies the evolution stages of detectors. The immature detectors meet the recognition diversity of intrusion detection. The mature detectors are evolved to by immature ones. The activated mature detectors are co-stimulated by the administrator and evolves to memory ones. Therefore, the attacks detection process depending on the detectors is dynamical. At the same time, the self cells train the immature detectors. The antigens which come from the real network behavior train the mature detectors. They meet the request of the environment adaptation and change according to the change of the real network environment.

4   Conclusion

To resolve the problems confronted by network security surveillance, a distributed surveillance model for network security inspired by human immunity is proposed in this paper. The detection ability of the proposed model is adaptive to the local network environment. Meanwhile, detection agents share the learning achievements with each other to improve the global detection ability in the whole computer networks. According to the detection result of network attacks, the surveillance of alarm, forensics and risk assessment are realized. The proposed model is useful to be clear about the network security situation to the administrator.

Acknowledgments. This work is supported by the Scientific Research Fund of Sichuan Provincial Education Department (No. 10ZC106) and the Scientific Research Fund of Leshan Normal University (No. Z1065).

References

1. Li, T.: An Introduction to Computer Network Security. Publishing House of Electronics Industry, Beijing (2004)
2. Denning, D.E.: An intrusion detection model. IEEE Transaction on Software Engineering 13, 222–232 (1987)
3. De Castro, L.N., Timmis, J.I.: Artificial Immune Systems: A Novel Computational Intelligence Approach. Springer, London (2002)
4. Hofmeyr, S.A., Forrest, S.: Architecture for an Artificial Immune System. Evolutionary Computation 8, 443–473 (2000)
5. Hofmeyr, S.A., Forrest, S.: Immunity by design: An artificial immune system. In: Genetic Evolutionary Computation Conf., San Francisco, CA, pp. 1289–1296 (1999)
6. Timmis, J., Neal, M., Hunt, J.: An artificial immune system for data analysis. Biosystems 55, 143–150 (2000)
7. Dasgupta, D.: An Artificial Immune System as a Multi-Agent Decision Support System. In: IEEE International Conference on Systems, Man and Cybernetics (SMC), San Diego (1998)
8. Hunt, J., Cooke, D.: An adaptative, distributed learning system based on immune system. In: IEEE International Conference on Systems, Vancouver, Canada (1995)
9. Mo, H.W., Zuo, X.Q.: Artificial Immune System. Science Press, Beijing (2009)
10. Li, T.: Computer immunology. Publishing House of Electronics Industry, Beijing (2004)
11. Jiao, L.C., Du, H.F.: Development and Prospect of the Artificial Immune System. Acta Electronica Sinica 31, 1540–1548 (2003)
12. Xiao, R.B., Wang, L.: Artificial immune system: principle, models, analysis and perspectives. Chinese Journal of Computers 25, 1281–1293 (2002)
13. Forrest, S., Hofmeyr, S.A., Somayaji, A.: Computer immunology. Communications of the ACM 40, 88–96 (1997)
14. Forrest, S., Perelson, A.S.: Self-nonself discrimination in a computer. In: IEEE Symposium on Security and Privacy, pp. 202–213. Oakland, CA (1994)

15. Harmer, P.K., Williams, P.D., et al.: An artificial immune system architecture for computer security applications. IEEE Transaction on Evolutionary Computation 6, 252–280 (2002)
16. Dasgupta, D.: An immunity-based technique to characterize intrusions in computer networks. IEEE Transactions on Evolutionary Computation 6, 281–291 (2002)
17. Kim, J., Bentley, P.J.: An evaluation of negative selection in an artificial immune system for network intrusion detection. In: The Genetic and Evolutionary Computation Conference (2001)

A Fault Model Centered Modeling Framework for Self-healing Computing Systems

Wei Lu[1], Yian Zhu[1], Chunyan Ma[1], and Longmei Zhang[2]

[1] Department of Software and Microelectronics, Northwestern Polytechnical University,
Xi'an, 710072, China
[2] Department of Electronics Information, Northwestern Polytechnical University,
Xi'an, 710072, China
{luweinpu,zhuya,machunyan}@nwpu.edu.cn, longmei.zhang@gmail.com

Abstract. As the computing systems become more and more complex, new technology and approach are desired to construct the system, so as to make them more reliable or self-healable. A modeling framework to generating self-healing system is proposed in this paper. The model framework consists of function model, fault model, self-healing model, model composition mechanism for integration of the function model and the self-healing model, as well as a code generation platform that supports automated generation of self-healing enabled software systems. The framework has the advantages of the following aspects: 1) The functional components of target system and the self-healing components for the target system can be modeled respectively under the framework; 2) The functional models and the self-healing models can be coupled through fault model; 3) The self-healability of the target system can be analyzed at he model level; 4) The modeling framework is platform-independent.

Keywords: computing systems, model, self-healing, framework.

1 Introduction

Large scale computing and information systems are a vital and integral part of today's society. Many modern IT systems are to such a degree critical for essential infrastructure, and sometimes for human life, that no downtime is actually acceptable. As the development of computer and network, typical present-day computing systems are more and more complex so that they are becoming increasingly difficult to execute robustly. Computing systems have reached a level of complexity where the human effort required to get the systems up and running and keeping them operational is getting out of hand. When computer systems operate abnormally, detecting and resolving the problem requires much time and effort, even some time it is impossible. An increasingly significant requisite for computing systems is the ability to handle resource variability, ever-changing user needs and system faults. This new requisite poses new challenges for computing systems designers and developers. Self-healing approach attempt to enable computing systems to automatically discover, diagnose,

H. Deng et al. (Eds.): AICI 2011, Part II, LNAI 7003, pp. 61–68, 2011.

and repair (or at least mitigate) faults without human intervention, thus it is a potential approach to resolve the problem.

In recent years, research of self-healing has been given a considerable attention to construct target system reliable. Several approaches have been proposed to develop self-healing system, including component-based, Architecture-based, and log-based approaches. These approaches have been used to developed software systems so as to make the systems more reliable or self-healable for some faults. As more and more researchers and engineers attempt to use self-healing approaches to develop computing systems in area such as deep-space exploring and environment monitoring where manual repairing is not feasible or difficult when anomalies occur, how to model a self-healing system and how to evaluate the self-healability of the system we have constructed become the important issues need to be resolved.

This paper proposed a modeling framework to generating the ability of self-healing. This remainder of the paper is organized as follows: Section 2 is devoted to an in-depth analysis of related works. Section 3 describes requirements for self-healing system. In Section 4, we describe our modeling framework for self-healing system. Finally, Section 5 presents our conclusions and future works.

2 Related Works

Currently, the architecture of self-healing systems and the technologies for implementing a self-healing system have been researched from diverse views and some engineers have been trying to make use of the self-healing mechanism to resolve special problems they encountered in various field [1].

Jeffrey O.Kephart et. al. view self-healing as the most important characteristic of an autonomic computing system. They depict the process of self-healing as the system to detect, diagnose, and repair localized problems resulting from bugs or failures in software and hardware[2]. To achieve autonomic computing, they has suggested a reference model which sometime called the MAPE-K(Monitor, Analyze, Plan, Execute, Knowledge) model[3]. This model is being referenced by more and more researchers to achieve a self-healing system.

SHADOWS (Self-healing Approach to Designing Complex Software Systems)[4] was a three-year EU IST STREP project started in Jun 2006 which aimed at developing technologies that augment large software systems with a sort of immune response against contingencies that can occur at design-time or runtime. The project proposes an automatic or semi-automatic detection and repair of possibly problematic behavior in its early design and development stages[5].

Emil Vassev proposed an Autonomic System Specification Language (ASSL) for describing autonomic systems[6]. The Autonomic System Specification Language (ASSL) is a declarative specification language for autonomic system with well defined semantics including modern programming language concepts and constructs like inheritance, modularity, type system and high abstract expressiveness. This language addresses the problem of formal specification and code generation of autonomic systems within a framework. Emil Vassev presented concrete results on the use of ASSL to specify a self-healing behavior model for NASA swarm-based exploration missions and to generate an application skeleton of the same.

Other researchers devote to design self-healing mechanisms for specific issues in their respective areas and implement specific systems with self-healing characteristics.

Most of the current researches in self-healing areas are directed at the system architecture and implementing technologies for specific self-healing mechanisms. But for a general system, how to model it so as to make the system with some self-healing characteristics and how to evaluate the self-healability of the system are two important problems reserved to be resolved.

3   Requirements for Self-healing Systems

At present, there is not an accurate or strict definition that is consensus-based for self-healing system or for self-healability of a system. Most of the depictions about self-healing system or self-healability appeared in relative literatures and reports are conceptive and qualitative.

Ghosh et al define self-healing as the property that enables a system to perceive that it is not operating correctly and, without (or with) human intervention, make the necessary adjustments to restore itself to normalcy[1]. Huebscher et. al. view self-healing as a property of an autonomic computing system and depict it as the capability of a system to detect, diagnose problems and to fix the problems if possible[7]. Gorla et. al. indicate that designing for self-healing should aim to make the system support four main phases as failure prediction or detection, fault diagnosis or localization, fault isolation or failure recovery, and validation[8]. Furthermore, they proposed some guidelines for enhancing self-healing capabilities of software systems during the design phase. Laster et. al. think that Self-Healing denotes the system ability to examine find, diagnose and react to system malfunctions. They describe the process of self-healing as a closed loop cycle composed of four stages which are monitoring, error detecting and diagnosing , error analyzing and repair operation selecting, repair operation executing[9].

According to literatures and reports delivered in public, for a system to be self-healing, it must be able to detect the faults occurrences, identify their causes, diagnose or localize the faults, isolate or repair the faults, and validate the repairs. We can divide the process of self-healing into two phases mainly. The first phase is the faults detection. The second phase is the system response. Different views have been proposed about respective tasks in every phase. We think that system monitor and faults diagnose should be the main tasks in faults detection phase and faults repair should be the main task in system response phase. But there is no a consensus-based view about the method and process for faults repair up to the present.

Through the discussion about the requirements for self-healing above, we can summarize that a self-healing system should be composed of two parts which are function part and self-healing part. The function part comprise function components which realize the system's functional requirements and the self-healing part comprise self-healing components which fulfill the self-healing process such as monitoring, diagnosing and repairing etc. So the structure of self-healing system can be depicted as an integrator composed of the function components and the self-healing components. We can illustrate the structure of self-healing system using figure 1.

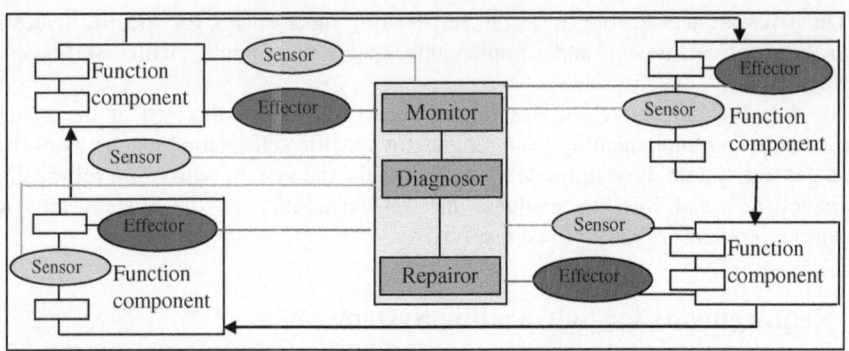

Fig. 1. The structure of self-healing system

In figure 1, the function part and the self-healing part are weaved tightly together through sensors and effectors. Sensors, often called probes or gauges, collect information about the function component and the environment in which the function component run. Effectors carry out changes to the function component.

According to the structure of self-healing system in figure 1, two problems should be resolved before we can achieve a self-healing system. The first problem we should encounter in system design phase is how to model the system especially the self-healing part so that make it with self-healing characteristics. The second problem we should encounter in system implementation phase is how to manage the degree of coupling between the function components and the self-healing components.

The problem about how to manage the degree of coupling between function components and self-healing components is out of this paper. We will discuss the first problem primarily in remainder of this paper.

4   The Modeling Framework

If we want to model or implement a self-healing system directly based on its structure depicted in figure 1, we will soon fall into chaos because we have to consider the self-healing part when we focus on the function part. How many sensors and effectors will be needed and where to deploy them are all problems that we should resolve before we can implement the self-healing part. All the issues about self-healing part will distract us from designing function part so we will soon find that the system are becoming more and more complex as more and more self-healing components tangled with the function components. Even we implement the system finally through our iterative hard work, how to evaluate the self-healability or self-healing degree of the system will be a crucial problem we have to consider.

We think that the function part and the self-healing part of the system should be modeled respectively. When the model of self-healing part was separated from the function model, the sensors and effectors will be removed from the function model so we can fix our attention on the function part. But when we finish the function model, how to set the sensors and effectors and redeploy them to the system or in other words how to joint the self-healing model to the function model so as to provide the system with some self-healing characteristic will be the key problem should be resolved. We propose a modeling framework to resolve the problem so as to facilitate the development of self-healing software systems. A fault model was used as the ligaments in our framework to keep the associations between the function model and the self-healing model.

In literature [10], we indicated that the self-healability of a computing system should be relative to the fault model of the system. We view the definition of self-healability of a computing system we proposed in literature [10] as the theoretical basis for the modeling framework.

The framework consists of a function model, a fault model, a self-healing model, a model composition mechanism for integration of the function model and the self-healing model, as well as a code generation platform that supports automated generation of self-healing enabled software systems. Figure 2 illustrates a conceptual architecture of the framework.

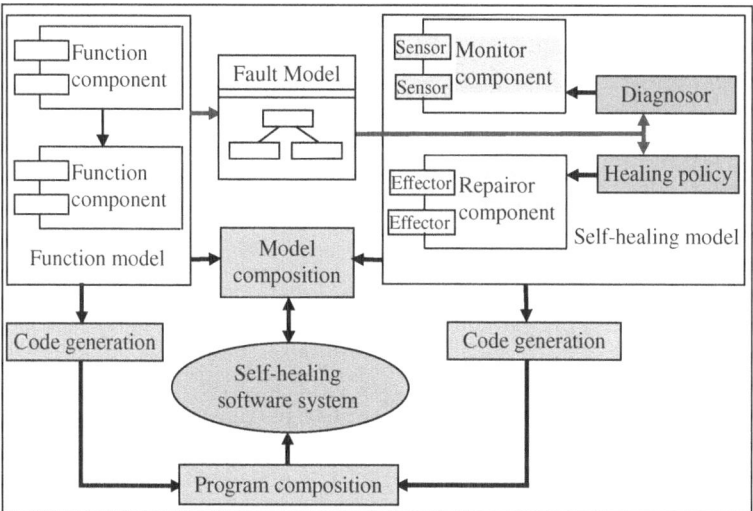

Fig. 2. Self-healing system modeling framework

The aim of this framework is to integrate various existing software techniques with Model Driven Architecture (MDA) approaches, with the intent to provide a united platform to enable self-healing software systems to be engineered and implemented from model specifications. Many technologies, methods and support tools have been proposed for function modeling so we will only discuss the other part in the framework.

4.1 Fault Model

We define the basic fault noted as symbol f as the minimal event unit that result in system abnormity. We note the set of all the possible basic faults as symbol Σ_f, so

$\Sigma_f = \{f_1, f_2, \ldots f_n\}$. We can divide the Σ_f to some mutually exclusive subsets according to their types. We define each subset of Σ_f as a macro-fault noted as F.

The macro-faults can also be classified according to their types. We can go on the classifying until we achieve a tree structure about the faults. Figure 3 illustrates the tree structure of faults model. All leaf nodes in the tree are basic faults and other nodes are macro-faults. Once we have constructed a tree structure of the system faults, the objective of self-healing modeling is how to support the fault model that is how to diagnose and repair every fault in the faults model. Furthermore, we can analyze the self-healability of the system after the self-healing model being finished through the faults model. We have discussed the relationship between self-healability and faults model in literature[10].

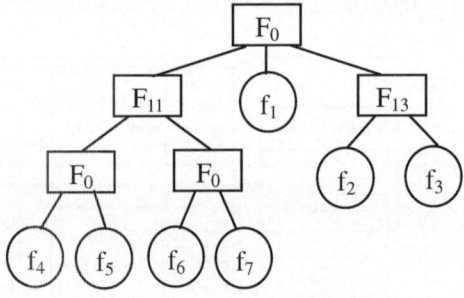

Fig. 3. The tree-based fault model

4.2 Self-healing Model

The self-healing model for software system can be constructed based on the fault model. A software fault (basic fault or macro-fault) can be detected by the diagnostician through the information collected by one or more monitors and repaired by the repairer through one or more effectors. Similarly, preventive effectors can be taken when the occurrence of faults is predicted. The self-healability of the system can by analyzed through the degree of the faults model supported by the self-healing model.

4.3 Model Composition

A self-healing model is described as a set of abstract constructs that are instantiated when it is associated with the base system models. In this way, the self-healing feature is kept separate from the base functionality of the software system. The decomposition of the base functionality and the self-healing feature improves modularity and re-usability of the self-healing modules. The main advantage of this approach is that it allows developing and maintaining the self-healing models independently from the base model. Furthermore, self-healing models can be applied to all levels in the software system hierarchy. Besides, according to different requirements for systems to be self-healing, we can construct different self-healing models to support the fault model in different degrees.

Deploying a self-healing model to the function model is done by model composition techniques. Typically, model composition involves merging two or more models to obtain a single integrated model.

Aspect-Oriented Modeling is a promising research area that supports model composition. Self-healing models can be specified as crosscutting aspects that are embedded in the base models.

Model weaving is another approach for model composition, wherein the relationships between the models are captured in a weaving model. A weaving model is one that specifies different kinds of mappings between model elements. By adopting this approach, a separate weaving model is created that explicitly specifies the links between base models and self-healing models. All three kinds of models (i.e., base, self-healing and weaving models) will be fed to a weaver engine and composed into a single integrated model.

4.4   Code Generation and Program Composition

The self-healing models are specified in a platform-independent manner. To support a complete self-healing application, a family of code generators needs to be employed for transforming platform-independent models into platform-specific code, each describing how the self-healing features are implemented on a different platform.

The base and self-healing models are translated into platform-specific implementations by their own code generators, respectively. The base code is then augmented with the self-healing instrumentation by using program composition techniques. As a result, a complete self-healing enabled software system is constructed and directly mapped to the representation of the composed self-healing enabled software model, upon which model-based analysis can be performed for system verification and validation.

5   Conclusions and Future Works

In this paper we show a generic framework for modeling self-healing software systems. A tree-based fault model is used in the framework to keep the association between function model and self-healing model of the system. We can model the self-healing part of the system based on the fault model so the function part and the self-healing part of the system can be modeled respectively under the framework. Furthermore, we can analyze the self-healability of the system through how the self-healing model can support the fault model when we implement the system. The framework can also be used to analyze the self-healability of legacy systems. Under our modeling framework, Self-healing is achieved by transforming the self-healing models into platform-specific implementation, which is then composed with the base module to form an integrated software system that provides failure resolutions to mitigate the effect of software faults. With the progress of AOM, we expect that the self-healing code framework can be build automatically through the self-healing model.

There are still a few open tasks that should be done. Currently we are focusing on developing the method to modeling the system faults based on tree structure. Model composition is another important technology we are investigating all along.

Acknowledgment. This work is partially supported by Aviation Science Fund #2010ZD53047 to Lu Wei.

References

[1] Ghosh, D., Sharman, R., Raghav Rao, H., Upadhyaya, S.: Self-healing systems – survey and synthesis. Decision Support Systems 42, 2164–2185 (2007)

[2] Kephart, J.O., Chess, D.M.: The vision of autonomic computing. Computer 36, 41–50 (2003)

[3] IBM, An architectural blueprint for autonomic computing, IBM (2003)

[4] Shehory, O.: SHADOWS: Self-healing complex software systems. In: 23rd IEEE/ACM International Conference on Automated Software Engineering - Workshops, ASE Workshops 2008, pp. 71–76 (2008)

[5] Jung, G., Margaria, T., Wagner, C., Bakera, M.: Formalizing a Methodology for Design- and Runtime Self-Healing. In: 2010 Seventh IEEE International Conference and Workshops on Engineering of Autonomic and Autonomous Systems (EASe), pp. 106–115 (2010)

[6] Vassev, E., Paquet, J.: ASSL - Autonomic System Specification Language. In: 31st IEEE Software Engineering Workshop, SEW 2007, pp. 300–309 (2007)

[7] Huebscher, M.C., McCann, J.A.: A survey of autonomic computing—degrees, models, and applications. ACM Comput. Surv. 40, 1–28 (2008)

[8] Gorla, A.: Towards design for self-healing. In: Fourth International Workshop on Software quality assurance: in conjunction with the 6th ESEC/FSE Joint Meeting, Dubrovnik, Croatia, pp. 86–89 (2007)

[9] Laster, S.S., Olatunji, A.O.: Autonomic Computing: Towards a Self-Healing System. In: Proceedings of the Spring 2007 American Society for Engineering Education Illinois-Indiana Section Conference (2007)

[10] Lu, W., Zhu, Y., Zhang, L.: Further exploring understanding of self-healability of computing system using discrete-event model. Xibei Gongye Daxue Xuebao/Journal of Northwestern Polytechnical University 28, 962–967 (2010)

Research of Immune Intrusion Detection Algorithm Based on Semi-supervised Clustering

Xiaowei Wang

Modern Education Technology Center, Physical Education College of Zhengzhou University,
Yinhe street 2,450052, Zhengzhou, China
xiaowei6702340@163.com

Abstract. Traditional immune intrusion detection algorithms need lots of labeled training data. However, it is difficult to obtain sufficient labeled data in real situation. In this paper we present a semi-supervised clustering based immune intrusion detection algorithm called SCIID, which can improve the quality of antibodies constantly and enhance the detection rate. Experimental results show that SCIID can get the classes of most unlabeled data in the case of only having a few labeled data, and it can also discover new types of attacks. The detection rate of SCIID is higher than that of simply immune-based approach with the same number of training data.

Keywords: semi-supervised clustering, immune, intrusion detection.

1   Introduction

Traditional intrusion detection algorithm [1~2] based on Immune mechanism is a kind of supervised learning algorithm, which requires adequate training data to generate a detection model that has good generalization performance. However, it is difficult and costly to obtain sufficient labeled data as training set in network environment. The learning methods of non-supervised [3] group the data according to the similarity between the data, overcoming the deficiencies of supervised learning method which need a large amount of labeled data. However, the detection accuracy of unsupervised detection algorithm is significantly lower than that of supervised intrusion detection method. In real applications, it is possible to obtain a small amount of labeled data, therefore, the semi-supervised learning technology is being widely used in the field of intrusion detection [4~5] that using a small amount of labeled data to lead the cluster process.

Semi-supervised learning is a framework of machine learning, and it is a way of learning between supervised learning and semi-supervised learning, in which the training set consists of labeled samples and unlabeled samples together, and it is usually composed of a small number of labeled samples and a large amount of unlabeled samples [6~7]. The main objective of semi-supervised clustering algorithm is to use a small amount of labeled samples to guide the clustering process to improve the quality of clustering. In immune-based approach, the quality of the initial

H. Deng et al. (Eds.): AICI 2011, Part II, LNAI 7003, pp. 69–74, 2011.

antibodies is very important, and it should be able to cover most nonselfs but not match the selfs. If the scale of antibody is not enough, most invasions will not be identified, which will be treated as normal samples to be released. However, the quality of the antibody depends on the number of training samples, while in network environment, it is difficult to get enough labeled data as the training set, so in this article we combined the semi-supervised clustering method with the immune based method, which used a small amount of labeled sample to get the categories of most unlabeled data, and it can improve the quality of antibodies constantly to improve the detection rates.

2   Relevant Definition

Define 1. Antigen and Antibody

Let Ag stand for the set of antigen and Ab stand for the set of antibody. An antigen or antibody is shown with a real coordinates M=$<m_1,m_2,m_3,...,m_L>$, which is a point in a real space of L dimension, $M \in S^L \subset R^L$, in which ,S is shape space and L is its dimension, $m_i(i=1 \sim L)$ are all real data. The presentation way of antigen is the same as antibody.

Define 2. Affinity between antigen and antibody

Suppose the coordinate of antigen Ag_i is given as $<Ag_{i1},Ag_{i2},...,Ag_{iL}>$ and the coordinate of antibody Ab_j is given as $<Ab_{j1}, Ab_{j2},..., Ab_{jL}>$, then the affinity between Ag_i and Ab_j is expressed as formula (1)

$$\text{Affi}(Ag_i,Ab_j) = 1 - D_{Ag_i - Ab_j} = 1 - \sqrt{\sum_{n=1}^{L}(Ag_{in} - Ab_{jn})^2} \tag{1}$$

Here, $D_{Ag_i-Ab_j}$ stand for the Euclidean distance between antigen and antibody, from which we can find that the shorter of the distance, the larger of the affinity. Where Ag_{in} and Ab_{jn} represent respectively the sample of antigen and antibody, which has L attributes.

Define 3. Cluster Center and Recognition Radius of self cluster

Suppose Self(i)=$(S_{i1}, S_{i2}, ..., S_{im})$ represent the cluster of the ith self set, which has m self samples, whose cluster center Sc(i) can be represented as :

$$Sc(i) = \{ Sc_{ik} = \sum_{i=1}^{m} X_{ik} / m \mid k = 1,2,3,...,L \} \tag{2}$$

In which, X_{ik} represent the kth attribute of sample X_i, while Sc_{ik} represent the value of the kth attribute of the cluster center.

   The recognition radius of self cluster is the average value of the distance between all vectors of the cluster, the formula is as follows:

$$R(Sc_i) = \sum_{i,j=1}^{m} D_{S_i - S_j} \Big/ m \tag{3}$$

In which, S_i and S_j are two vectors of self cluster.

Define 4. Recognition Radius of antibody

The recognition radius of the ith antibody can be derived from the cluster center and recognition radius of self cluster, the formula is represented as formula (4):

$$Ab_i.radious = \min\{D_{Ab_i - Sc_j} - R(Sc_j) \mid j = 1,2,..,s\} \tag{4}$$

Here, s stands for the number of the cluster of self set.

3   Semi-supervised Clustering Based Immune Intrusion Detection Algorithm (SCIID)

3.1   Algorithm thought

SCIID algorithm included three stages, in the initial stage, it first clustered self samples and accessed the center and the radius of the self clusters, where the cluster centers were the geometric center of all samples in the cluster, and the recognition radius of the cluster was the average distance between all samples of the cluster. Then the initial antibodies were generated through cloning and expansion according to the distance between non-selfs and the cluster center of selfs of training data set. Finally, we calculated the recognition radius of each antibody according to formula (4) which was equivalent to negative selection, thus the antibody production process completed.

In intrusion detection phase, when a new antigen arrived, we calculated the distance between the new antigen and antibody and the distance between the new antigen and the cluster centers of selfs, the new antigen would enter the corresponding cluster that identified it, and the corresponding class label would be marked as the class labels of the cluster. Thus it had been realized that using a small amount of labeled data to obtain the class tags of most other data, and at the same time we can update both the identification radius and the center of the antibodies. For some antigens, if it was not identified through the way of above, then we can consider using the method of K-nearest neighbor, which is a way of vote by which the class of the antigen could be confirmed. If the category of the antigen was still not determined after being voted, a new category would be generated, whether it was normal or intrusion was decided by the user, and at the same time it should produce the corresponding antibody that can recognize the new cluster.

In antibody update phase, if the number exceeded a threshold of antibodies after a period of time, we could remove the antibodies that lack of participation in identifying recently in order to ensure that the size of antibody population was within the controllable range.

3.2   Algorithm Description

Input: Training sample set $T=T_{self}\cup T_{nonself}$, which has been labeled; U, which is an unlabeled sample set. New coming antigen x.
Output: the class label of $x\in U$, whether it is normal or intrusion.

Step1: cluster the self samples of $T_{self}=\{S_1,S_2,...,S_m\}$, obtain the s clusters of self sets.

Step2: computer the center Sc_i and its recognition radius of each cluster of self according to formula (2), (3).

Step3: for each $NS_j\in T_{nonself}$,

　　　Compute the distance between NS_j and the cluster center of self, $D=D_{NSj-Sci}$

　　　Clone-mute according to the distance D, obtain a certain number of antibodies.

Step4: compute the recognition radius of the antibodies according to formula (4).

Step5: compute the distance $D=D_{x-Sci}$ and $D=D_{x-Abj}$,

　　　if $D<R(Sc_i)$, then the label of x is marked as normal;

　　　if $D<Abj.radious$, then the label of x is marked as intrusion;

　　　Let x into corresponding cluster, update the center and radius of the cluster;

　　　goto step 8.

Step6: call K-nearest neighbor algorithm, obtain the class label of x according to the vote mechanism, goto step8;

Step7: generate a new class, generate the antibody that can recognize the antigen; goto step 8;

Step8: repeat step 5~7, until unknown sample set U is empty.

Step1~Step4 is the antibody generation phase, while step5~step8 is the intrusion detection phase. In SCIID algorithm, during detection we increased the vote method to determine the class label of the antigen that was not recognized initially. Thus the recognition probability of the antigen was magnified, and at the same time, the new class could also be found.

4   Simulation Experiment and Results Analysis

The dataset KDD99 [8] was used as experimental data sets , which is composed of a large number of real data of network connections which is normal or attack, Each connection is a 42-dimensional vector, the former 41-dimension of which represent the characteristics of the connection and the final dimension represent the category of the connection.

　　The aim of the experiment was to compare the detection accuracy and the fault detection rate of the SCIID algorithm and the simple immune-based algorithm under the same circumstances of using the same number of labeled samples. Suppose N stands for the total number of the samples to be detected, which include N_{normal} normal samples and $N_{intrusion}$ intrusion samples, N_{right} stands for the number of intrusion samples that have been detected rightly, and $N_{normal-intrusion}$ stand for the number of normal samples that have been detected as intrusion samples wrongly, the definition of the detection rate and false detection rate are as follows:

Detection Rate= $N_{right}/N_{intrusion}$

False Detection Rate= $N_{normal-intrusion}/N_{normal}$

At the beginning of the algorithm, 10,000 network data records was randomly selected from the KDD99 data set, 200 of which were marked as the initial training sample set, which included positive samples and negative samples. For comparison, the same method of antibody production process was used in the two algorithms, and the difference was that it added the voting mechanism in SCIID algorithm. The K is set to 50 in the K-nearest neighbor algorithm, which was called during the detection process. The test results was obtained from the the average of the results that run the algorithm 10 times. Table 1 showed the detection rate and false positive rate of the SCIID algorithm, and it was compared with a simple immune-based algorithm. The results were shown in Fig 1, the upper two curves were the detection rate of two algorithms, and the below two curves were the false detection rate of two algorithms.

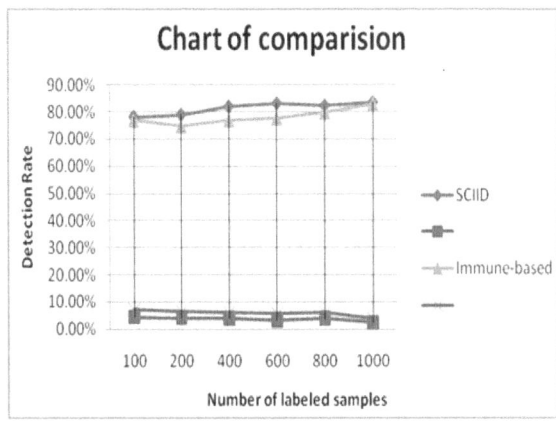

Fig. 1. The chart of comparisons between SCIID and Immune-based algorithm

As can be seen from Fig 1, when the number of labeled samples was not enough, the self clusters can't complete cover all the selfs, so the generated antibody was single, which would bring about the lower detection rate. At the same time, the possibility of the antibody fitting self was larger, which would make the false detection rate higher. With the increase of the number of labeled samples, the coverage area of self cluster became large. This would make the antibody type diversity, and make the quality of the antibodies higher, which could reflect the current network status. Thus the detection rate would increase, and at the same time, the generated antibodies were less likely to fit the selfs, which will make the false detection rate lower than before.

The voting mechanism was added in SCIID algorithm when the label of the new antigens was temporarily unable to determine, which increased the probability of new antigens to be identified, so the detection rate was higher than that of in a simple algorithm based on immunity. Meanwhile, it had been realized that using a small amount of labeled data to guide the classification process so as to improve the detection rate of the algorithm.

References

1. Junqwon, K., Bentley, P.J.: Towards an Artificial Immune System for Network Intrusion Detection: an Investigation of Clonal Selection with a Negative selection Operator. In: Proceedings of the Congress on Evolutionary Computation (CEC-2001), pp. 1244–1252. IEEE Press, Seoul (2001)
2. Dipankar, D., Fabio, G.: An immunity-based technique to characterize intrusions in computer networks. IEEE Transactions on Evolutionary Computation 6(3), 1081–1088 (2002)
3. Li, K.-L., Cao, Z., et al.: Some Developments on Semi-Supervised Clustering. Pattern Recognition and Artificial Intelligence 22(5), 735–742 (2009) (in Chinese)
4. Zhong, S.: Semi-supervised model based document Clustering: A comparative study. Machine Learning 65(1), 3–29 (2006)
5. Wagstaff, K., Cardie, C., Rogers, S., et al.: Constrained K-means Clustering with Background Knowledge. In: Proceedings of International Conference on Machine Learning, San Francisco, USA (2001)
6. Chapelle, O., Scholkopf, B., Zien, A.: Semi-supervised learning. MIT Press, Mass (2006)
7. Zhou, Z.H., Li, M.: Semi-Supervised Regression with Co-Training Style Algorithms. IEEE Transactions on Knowledge and Data Engineering 19(11), 1479–1493 (2007)
8. http://kdd.ics.uci.edu/databases/kddcup99/

Robust Digital Image Watermarking in DWT-SVD Domain

Mingli Zhang, Qiang Zhang[*], and Changjun Zhou

Key Laboratory of Advanced Design and Intelligent Computing
(Dalian university) Ministry of Education, Dalian, 116622, China
zhangq@dlu.edu.cn

Abstract. Digital multimedia content protection has increasingly become an important issue. Because image watermarking is identified as a major technology used in copyright protection, a key requirement for image watermarking is the development of its imperceptibility and robustness. To meet this requirement, a novel robust image watermarking scheme based on discrete wavelet transform (DWT), singular value decomposition (SVD), and chaotic mixtures is proposed in this paper, In this method, the singular values of the encrypt watermark are embedded on the singular values of the important inscribed circle domain of normalized cover image's DWT sub-bands. Experimental results illustrate that this approach is robust to a wide range of attacks, especially geometrical attacks.

Keywords: We would like to encourage you to list your keywords in this section.

1 Introduction

With the popularity of Internet and the quick development of multimedia technology, the chances of using multimedia data are rapidly growing. As a result, intellectual property rights protection of digital media has become an urgent issue. Digital watermarking has numerous applications in a variety of areas, such as the widely application on copyright protection, authentication, secret communication, measurement [1, 2] and so on.

Watermarking (data hiding) [3, 4, 5] is a process of embedding data into a multimedia element such as an element of an image, audio or video file, which is for security purposes, and this embedded data must be capable of extracting, or detectable in the original file. The watermark structure, embedding algorithm, and extraction, or detection, algorithm consist of the watermarking algorithm. The pixel domain or a transform domain is used to embed the watermark. In multimedia applications, embedded watermarks should be invisible, robust, and high capacity [6]. Based on the type of information needed by the detector, the watermarking schemes are classified into non-blind schemes, semi-blind schemes, and blind schemes.

---

[*] Corresponding author.

H. Deng et al. (Eds.): AICI 2011, Part II, LNAI 7003, pp. 75–84, 2011.

According to the domain that the watermark is inserted, two categories are classified: spatial-domain and transform-domain. A straightforward Watermarking method is embedding the watermark into the spatial-domain component of the original image. It has the advantages of low complexity and easy implementation. Whereas the spatial-domain methods are generally fragile to image-processing operations; Embedding the watermark by modulating the magnitude of coefficients in a transform domain is a representative transform domain techniques, such as discrete cosine transform(DCT), discrete wavelet transform (DWT), and singular value decomposition (SVD)[7, 8]. The transform-domain methods' have much better information embedding capability and robustness against many common attacks compare to spatial-domain watermarking methods, but with high computation cost.

As the DWT has excellent spatial-frequency localization properties, it is quite suitable to identify watermark can be imperceptibly embedded areas in the cover image. SVD is one of the most useful tools of linear algebra with several applications in image compression [9, 10, 11, 12, 13, 14], watermarking [15, 16, 17], and other signal processing fields. Because the SVD has the merit that slight variations of singular values do not affect the visual perception of the cover image, which apply to the watermark embedding procedure, many image-watermarking techniques [18, 19, 20, 21] combining these two transform methods have been proposed, to achieve better transparency and robustness.

Image normalization has been used in computer vision for pattern recognition for a long time. The normalized image is obtained form a geometric transformation procedure, thus it is invariant to any affine distortions of the image. This will make the watermark much more robust when the cover image undergoes general affine geometric attacks.

Chaotic system is a deterministic nonlinear system. It possesses a wide variety of characteristics, such as a periodic, high sensitivity to initial conditions and system parameters, random-like behaviors. As chaotic systems can improve the security of encryption systems, prior to the binary watermark pattern's embedding, it is mapped to a noise like binary pattern using a chaotic mixing method to increase the security of the proposed scheme.

In this paper, we distill an important circular domain of the normalized cover-image to embed watermark. This watermarking scheme is good at handle general affine geometric attacks. A mixed chaotic sequence is used to encrypt the watermark beforehand. This study uses a hybrid DWT-SVD-based watermarking scheme that decomposes the important circular domain to yield better performance. After decomposing the important circular domain into four sub-bands by one-level DWT, SVD was applied to the intermediate frequency sub-bands and encrypted watermark. To meet the imperceptibility and robustness requirements, embedding the singular values of the encrypted watermark into the singular values of the aforementioned sub-bands. The main properties of this work can be identified as follows:1) Good at counteracting RST attacks. 2) Needs less SVD computation, comparing to most existing DWT- SVD-based algorithms.

In the field of image watermarking, the DWT has received considerable attention. The similarity of data structure with respect to the resolution and available decomposition at any level are the most distinct advantages of DWT. In two-dimensional DWT, each level of decomposition produces four bands of data denoted by LL, HL, LH, and HH, where LH, HL, and HH represent the finest scale wavelet coefficients. The DWT can be implemented as a multistage transformation, the LL sub-bands can further be decomposed to obtain another level of decomposition. This process is continued until the desired number of levels determined by the application is reached.

In the respect of image processing, an image can be viewed as a matrix with nonnegative scalar entries. The decomposition of an image A, size $m \times m$, is given by $A = USV^T$, where U and V are orthogonal matrices, $U^TU = I, V^TV = I$, and $S = diag(\lambda_i)$ a diagonal matrix is called singular values of A. The columns of U are called the left singular vectors of A, and the columns of V are called the right singular vectors of A. This decomposition is known the singular value decomposition of A, and can be written as

$$A = \lambda_1 U_1 V_1^T + \lambda_2 U_2 V_2^T + \ldots + \lambda_i U_i V_i^T$$

Where i is the rank of matrix A.

In SVD-based watermarking, several approaches are possible. There are two main merits to apply SVD method in the digital-watermarking scheme:1) When a small perturbation is added to an image, large variation of its singular values does not occur. 2) Singular values represent intrinsic algebraic image properties [22].

Because there are invalid-keys and quasi invalid-keys in the Logistic-Map, the chaotic sequences wouldn't be obtained. In order to conquer this defect, in this paper, we use the mixed optic bistable system and Logistic system to implement the binary watermark encryption to increase the security of the proposed scheme. Where, the mixed optic bistable system and Logistic system are well-known to us. Now, we introduce them generally.

1) Mixed optic bistable system
mixed optic bistable system is defined as Eq. (1):

$$x_{n+1} = A\sin^2(x_n - x_b) \tag{1}$$

Where, the A, x_B are all parameters, $x_0 \in (0,1)$, the system is in chaotic state under the certain value of A and x_B, where we choose $A = 4$ and $x_B = 2.5$.

2) Logistic system
Logistic map is an model chaotic map, it's described as follow:

$$x_{j+1} = \mu x_j(1 - x_j) \tag{2}$$

Under the condition that $3.5699456\cdots < \mu \le 4$ the system is in chaotic state. $x_0 \in (0,1)$.

2   Proposed DWT-SVD Watermarking Scheme

Fig. 1 is the block diagram the chaotic watermark [23].

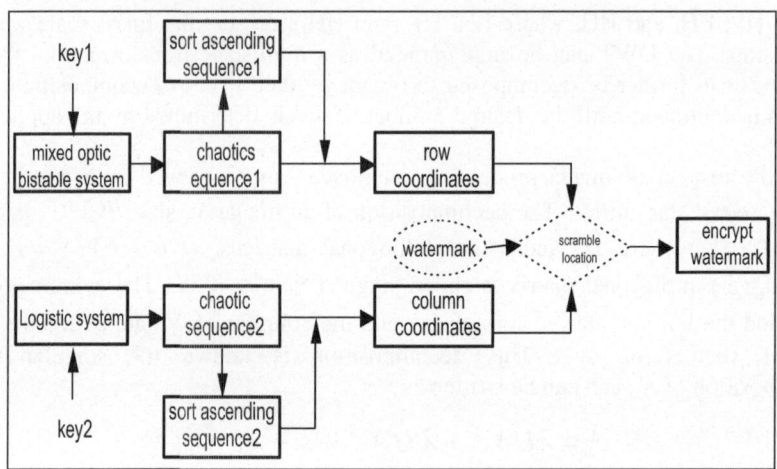

Fig. 1. Block diagram for the watermark encryption

The example of the proposed watermark encrypted scheme is given here, where $\mu = 3.9$, $key_1 = 0.3$ and $key_2 = 0.6$.

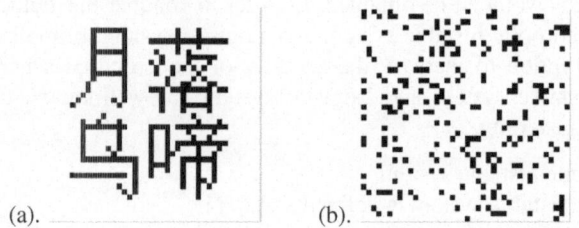

(a).   (b).

Fig. 2. The original watermark (a) and the encrypt watermark (b)

(a).   (b).   (c).

Fig. 3. (a)Cover image. (b)the important inscribed circle domain of normalized image (c) Watermarked image(PSNR=37. 64)

The proposed DWT-SVD watermarking scheme is formulated as following.

1) Watermark embedding

Assume the cover image A (Fig. 3. (a)) is 512×512 gray image, and the encrypt watermark (Fig. 2. (b)) is 40×40 binary image. The process of embedding watermark can be expressed as given here:

1) Treat the original cover image A with image normalization [24], then obtain an important inscribed circle domain B of the normalized image.

2) Decompose the inscribed circle domain B into four sub-bands (i.e., LL, LH, HL, and HH) with the help of one-level Haar DWT.

3) Apply SVD to LH and HL sub-bands and watermark, i.e.,

$$A^k = U^k S^k V^{kT}, \quad k = 1, 2$$
$$A_w = U_w S_w V_w \tag{3}$$

where k represent one of two sub-bands, w represent the watermark.

4) Divide the S_w into two parts: $S_w = S_w^1 + S_w^2$, where S_w^k denotes half of the S_w^k.

5) After modifying the singular values in HL and LH sub-bands with half of the ones of the watermark image, apply SVD to them respectively, i.e.,

$$S^k + \lambda S_w^k = U_{w^*}^k S_{w^*}^k V_{w^*}^{kT} \quad k = 1, 2. \tag{4}$$

where λ denotes the scale factor, which control the insert strength of the watermark.

6) Achieve the two sets of modified DWT coefficients, i.e.,

$$A^{*k} = U^k S_{w^*}^k V^{kT}, \quad k = 1, 2. \tag{5}$$

7) Use two sets of modified DWT coefficients and two sets of unmodified DWT coefficients performing the inverse DWT to obtain the inscribed circle domain watermarked, then add the remainder domain of the normalized image . After inverse normalization of the normalized watermarked image, we'll get the watermarked image.

2) Watermark extraction:

1) Treat the watermarked image with image normalization to achieve an important inscribed circle domain B_w^* of the normalized image.

2) Using one-level Haar DWT, decompose the watermarked (possibly attacked) normalized inscribed circle domain B_w^* into four sub-bands: LL, LH, HL, and HH.

3) Apply SVD to the LH and HL sub-bands,

$$A_W^{*k} = U^{*k} S_W^{*k} V^{*kT}, \quad k = 1, 2. \tag{6}$$

where k denotes the LH and HL sub-bands.

4)   Extract half of the watermark singular values from each sub-band:

$$S_w^{*k} = (S_W^{*k} - S^k)/\lambda, \quad k = 1, 2. \tag{7}$$

5)   Construct the two visual watermarks using the singular vectors:

$$W^{*k} = U_w S_w^{*k} V_w^{kT}, \quad k = 1, 2. \tag{8}$$

6)   Combine the results of Step 5 to obtain the embedded encrypt watermark: $W^* = W^{*1} + W^{*2}$. Then we inverse the encrypt watermark to obtain the watermark.

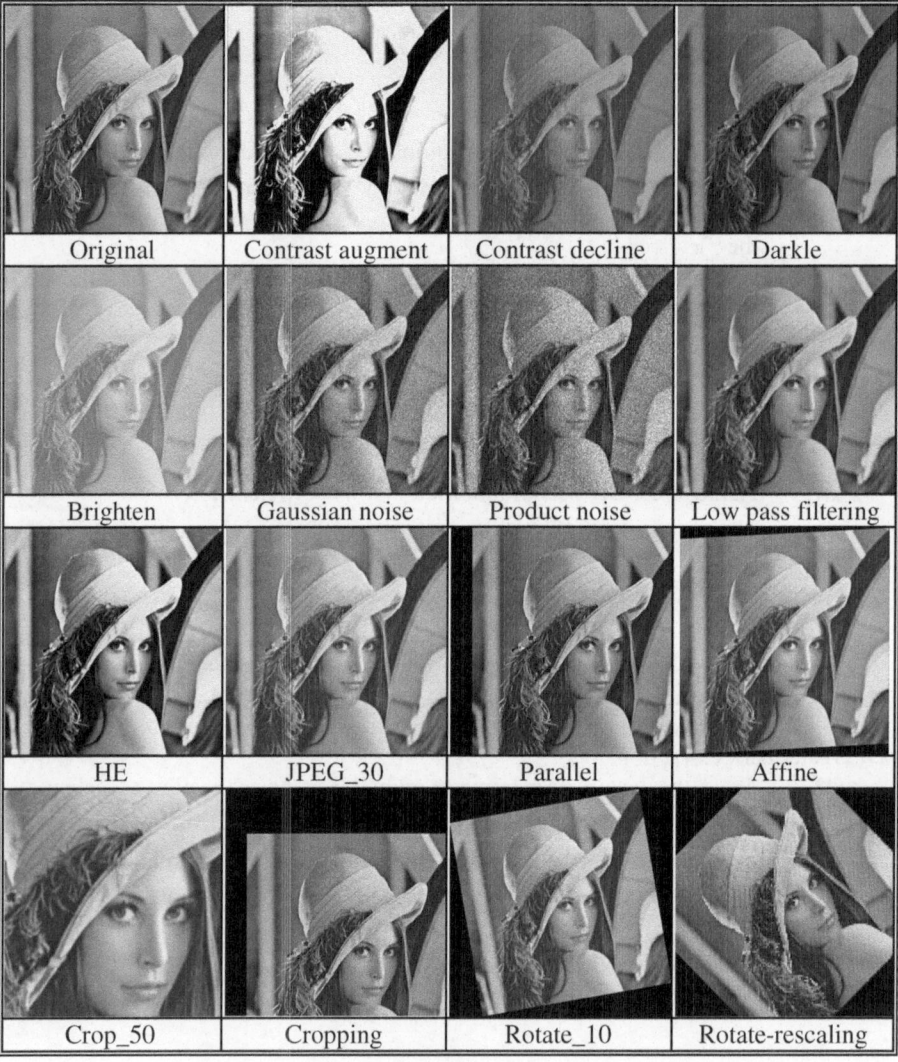

Fig. 4. The original and attacked watermarked images

3   Experimental Results

Fig. 3. (a) show the 512×512 gray scale cover image Lena, Fig. 2 show the 40×40 original binary watermark (Fig. 2. (a)) and the encrypt binary watermark (Fig. 2. (b)). Fig. 3. (c) illuminates the watermarked image. In the experiments, the scaling factor is 0.25 . The high perceptual quality of the watermarked image can be preserved using the proposed approach.

The peak signal-to noise ratio (PSNR) was used to evaluate the robustness of the proposed approach, and the degree of linear relationship between the original and extracted watermarks were estimate by Pearson's correlation coefficient. The DWT-SVD based watermarking scheme was tested based on five kinds of attacks with Matlab : 1) geometrical attack: cropping (CR), rotation(RO), rescaling(RE) and affine transformation(AT), parallel(PA);2) noising attack: Gaussian noise (GN), product noise(PN); 3) denoising attack: Low pass filtering (LF); 4) format compression attack: JPEG compression; 5) image processing attack: histogram equalization(HE), contrast adjustment(CA) and luminance enhance(LE).

Table 1. Construct watermarks (Extracted watermarks obtained from ours and L&T[25])

ORIGINAL		CONTRAST AUGMENT		CONTRAST DECLINE		DARKLE	

0.9993	0.9995	0.9901	0.9812	0.9863	0.9804	0.9789	0.9812
Brighten		Gaussian noise		Product noise		Low pass filtering	

0.9982	0.9885	0.9955	0.9620	0.9822	0.9768	0.9943	0.9870
HE		JPEG_30		Parallel		Affine	

0.9886	0.9901	0.9981	0.9840	0.9801	0.9875	0.9879	0.9220
Crop_50		Cropping		Rotate_10		Rotate-rescaling	
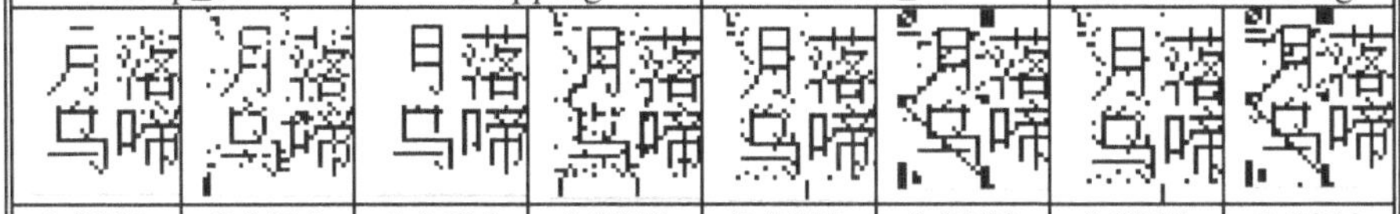							
0.9801	0.9210	0.9606	0.9280	0.9592	0.9050	0.9399	0.9312

Table 2. The Pearson's correlation coefficient between suffering rotate-rescaling constructed watermarks and original watermark

(λ, θ)	(0.5, 30)	(0.5, 45)	(0.5, 60)	(0.5, 90)
NC	0.9213	0.9332	0.9298	0.9243

We compare our results with those obtained form a DWT-SVD-based watermarking method [25], setting the adjustment strategy of scale factors the same as our aforementioned experiment. The original and attacked images are presented in Fig. 4. together with the tools used for the attacks.

Table 1 Lay out the constructed watermarks form the watermarked image and attacked ones. The numbers below the images is Pearson's correlation coefficient.

Table. 2 indicates the Pearson's correlation coefficient, where λ and θ denote rescaling multiple and rotating degree respectively. By studying the experimental results, we can see the proposed scheme not only significantly preeminence in resisting all kinds of attacks especially the synchronous geometrical attacks, but also has high perceptual quality in restore watermark.

Table 3. Compare of efficiency for G&E[20], L&T[25], and our algorithm(Unit: seconds)

	G&E[20]	**L&T[25]**	**OURS**
DWT_SVD embedding	2.4541	1.5938	1.6219
DWT_SVD extraction	1.7541	0.5938	0.4219

Where we obtain the values in the Table. 3 by running the three watermarked methods on a personal computer, which is Intel Core 2 Duo Processors rated at 2.70 GHz, with 2 GB main memory.

To testify the efficiency of our approach, we compare our method with two of the others, DWT_SVD extraction was revealed on un-attacked watermarked based on the three methods. It is clearly detecting our method's advantage on efficiency.

4 Conclusion

In this paper, the observation about the proposed novel watermarking scheme based on DWT and SVD can be summarized as follows: 1) The technique adequately calculates the features about spatial-frequency localization of DWT and SVD efficiently, which are intrinsic algebraic properties of an image. 2) The scheme's robust resisting all kinds of geometrical attacks is elevation with the help of image normalization. 3) The chaotic mixtures system is used to pretreatment watermark image, which security much excellent than using single chaotic system.

Experiment results of the proposed method unfold the eximious result in imperceptibility, and the significant improvement in robustness under geometrical attacks. But the process of watermark extraction need the singular values of the original cover image's DWT sub-bands, U_w and V_w^k of the watermark, that will preclude practicality of the watermarking. Further work of appending blindness watermark extraction into this approach is in progress.

Acknowledgment. The work is supported by the National Science Foundation Postdoctoral (No. 20100471451), High School Excellent Talents Support Plan in Liaoning Province (No. LR201003), Scientific Research Projects in Liaoning Province (No. LS2010179).

References

1. Sang, J., Alam, M.S.: Fragility and robustness of binary-phase-only-filter-based fragile/semifragile digital image watermarking. IEEE Trans. Instrum. Meas. 57(3), 595–606 (2008)
2. Wu, H.-T., Cheung, Y.-M.: Reversible watermarking by modulationand security enhancement. IEEE Trans. Instrum. Meas. 59(1), 221–228 (2010)
3. Cox, I.J., Miller, M.L., Bloom, J.A.: Digital Watermarking. Morgan Kaufmann Publishers, San Francisco (2002)
4. Podilchuk, C.I., Delp, E.J.: Digital Watermarking: Algorithms and Applications. IEEE Signal Processing Magazine, 33–46 (July 2001)
5. Lin, E.T., Eskicioglu, A.M., Lagendijk, R.L., Delp, E.J.: Advances in Digital Video Content Protection. Proceedings of the IEEE, Special Issue on Advances in Video Coding and Delivery (2004)
6. Hartung, F., Kutter, M.: Multimedia Watermarking Techniques. Proceedings of the IEEE 87(7), 1079–1107 (1999)
7. Liu, R., Tan, T.: An SVD-based watermarking scheme for protecting rightful ownership. IEEE Trans. Multimedia 4(1), 121–128 (2002)
8. Nikolaidis, A., Pitas, I.: Asymptotically optimal detection for additive watermarking in the DCT and DWT domains. IEEE Trans. Image Process. 12(5), 563–571 (2003)
9. Andrews, H.C., Patterson, C.L.: Singular Value Decomposition (SVD) Image Coding. IEEE Transactions on Communications 24(4), 425–432 (1976)
10. Garguir, N.: Comparative Performance of SVD and Adaptive Cosine Transform in Coding Images. IEEE Transactions on Communications 27(8), 1230–1234 (1979)
11. O'Leary, D.P., Peleg, S.: Digital Image Compression by Outer Product Expansion. IEEE Transactions on Communications 31(3), 441–444 (1983)
12. Yang, J.F., Lu, C.L.: Combined Techniques of Singular Value Decomposition and Vector Quantization. IEEE Transactions on Image Processing 4(8), 1141–1146 (1995)
13. Waldemar, P., Ramstad, T.A.: Hybrid KLT-SVD Image Compression. In: 1997 IEEE International Conference on Acoustics, Speech and Signal Processing, Munich, Germany, April 21-24, vol. 4, pp. 2713–2716 (1997)
14. Aase, S.O., Husoy, J.H., Waldemar, P.: A Critique of SVD-Based Image Coding Systems. In: 1999 IEEE International Symposium on Circuits and Systems VLSI, Orlando, FL, vol. 4, pp. 13–16 (May 1999)
15. Gorodetski, V.I., Popyack, L.J., Samoilov, V., Skormin, V.A.: SVD-based Approach to Transparent Embedding Data into Digital Images. In: International Workshop on Mathematical Methods, Models and Architectures for Computer Network Security (MMM-ACNS 2001), St. Petersbug, Russia, May 21-23 (2001)

16. Chandra, D.V.S.: Digital Image Watermarking Using Singular Value Decomposition. In: Proceedings of 45th IEEE Midwest Symposium on Circuits and Systems, Tulsa, OK, pp. 264–267 (August 2002)
17. Liu, R., Tan, T.: A SVD-Based Watermarking Scheme for Protecting Rightful Ownership. IEEE Transactions on Multimedia 4(1), 121–128 (2002)
18. Aslantas, V., Dogan, L.A., Ozturk, S.: DWT-SVD based image water-marking using particle swarm optimizer. In: Proc. IEEE Int. Conf. Multi-media Expo, Hannover, Germany, pp. 241–244 (2008)
19. Bhatnagar, G., Raman, B.: A new robust reference watermarking scheme based on DWT-SVD. Compute. Standards Interfaces 31(5), 1002–1013 (2009)
20. Ganic, E., Eskicioglu, A.M.: Robust DWT-SVD domain image water-marking: Embedding data in all frequencies. In: Proc. Workshop Multime-dia Security, Magdeburg, Germany, pp. 166–174 (2004)
21. Li, Q., Yuan, C.,, Y.: -Z. Zhong, "Adaptive DWT-SVD domain image watermarking using human visual model. In: Proc. 9th Int. Conf. Adv. Commun. Technol., Gangwon-Do, South Korea, pp. 1947–1951 (2007)
22. Liu, R., Tan, T.: An SVD-based watermarking scheme for protecting rightful ownership. IEEE Trans. Multimedia 4(1), 121–128 (2002)
23. Xue, X., Qiang, Z., et al.: A Digital Image Encryption Algorithm Based on DNA Sequence and Multi-Chaotic Maps. IEEE Neural Network World (2008)
24. Son, Y.H., You, B.J., Oh, S.R., et al.: Affine-invariant image normalization for Log-Polar Images using momentums. In: Proceedings of the 2002 International Conference on Control, Automation, and Systems, Gyeongju, Korea, pp. 1140–1145 (2003)
25. Lai, C.-C., Tsai, C.-C.: Digital Image Watermarking Using Discrete Wavelet Transform and Singular Value Decomposition. IEEE Transactions on Instrumentation and Measurement (May 22, 2010)

An Algorithm of Task Scheduling in Survivability

Liangxun Shuo[1], Jinhui Zhao[1], Lijie Yin[1], and Xuehui Wang[2]

[1] Network Information Security Laboratory, Shijiazhuang University of Economics,
Shijiazhuang, China
Shuolx@sjzue.edu.cn
[2] Foundation Department, Shijiazhuang Vocational College of Industry and Commerce,
Shijiazhuang, China
Wangxh9977@126.com

Abstract. The task scheduling of real-time tasks request is an important component of survivability system. In survivability system, how to schedule real-time tasks to meet the needs of various services at different levels is one of the important topics in survivability research. A task scheduling algorithm is proposed based on optimization decision theory of variable fuzzy set, which apply optimization model of variable fuzzy set to assess the priority of each task, and take relative membership degree as priority to schedule task. Taking FIFO scheduling algorithm as the benchmark, the performance of proposed algorithm is analyzed from two aspects: weighted guarantee ratio and differentiated guarantee ratio.

Keywords: task scheduling, survivability, variable fuzzy set, critical services.

1 Introduction

Survivability represents the new direction of network security. Maintaining the survival ability of system has become the core target of a new generation network security. The technology of survivability is not to build a completely secure system, which believed that the system can be compromised, the accidents are unavoidable and the key mission is to adopt the reasonable measures to keep continued operation of critical services and to minimize the negative effects. It emphasizes the ability to provide continuation of critical services in the event of attack, failure or accident. The task scheduling of real-time tasks request is an important component of survivability system. In survivability system, how to schedule real-time tasks to meet the needs of various services at different levels is one of the important topics in survivability research.

In the search on task scheduling of real-time system, the scheduling algorithm, based on priority, is the most studied, such as earliest deadline first (EDL), rate-monotonic (RM), least slack first (LSF), highest value first (HVF), and so on. In these algorithms, the calculation of priority is based on a key feature of the services, for example, deadline, waiting time, important degree of mission, etc. Studies [1, 2] show it is far from enough to calculate the priority on a single feature of services. Huang etc

H. Deng et al. (Eds.): AICI 2011, Part II, LNAI 7003, pp. 85–92, 2011.
© Springer-Verlag Berlin Heidelberg 2011

[3] propose a mechanism called criticalness-deadline first (CDF) that has greatly improved the comprehensive performance of dispatch system compared with the algorithm of single features. An algorithm called priority table design (PTD) has presented in references [4], which designs priority list according with deadline and free time to improve the success rate of service scheduling. In references [5], an algorithm of deadline value density first (DVDF) was used to schedule tasks, which took deadline and density of value into account to design priority list.

Through the above analysis, we can see that those algorithms don't too suitable for survivability system. Firstly, they did not consider the survivability of system. Secondly, because some parameters in scheduling process are constantly changing, fixed value limit the dynamics and flexibility of task scheduling. This paper introduces index of system survivability, and employs optimization model of variable fuzzy set to study task priority.

We would like to draw your attention to the fact that it is not possible to modify a paper in any way, once it has been published. This applies to both the printed book and the online version of the publication. Every detail, including the order of the names of the authors, should be checked before the paper is sent to the Volume Editors.

2 Optimal Decision Theory of Variable Fuzzy Set

2.1 Calculation of Relative Membership Degree

In the process of fuzzy decision-making, index includes two types: qualitative and quantitative. Assume these are n samples, which include m_1 quantitative indexes. If x_{ij} is the eigenvalue of i quantitative index in j sample, the relative membership degree of x_{ij} can be calculated as following:

The type of bigger – more emergency:

$$r_{ij} = \frac{x_{ij}}{x_{i\max}}. \tag{1}$$

Where i=1,2,…,m_1, j=1,2,…,n.

The type of smaller – more emergency:

$$r_{ij} = \begin{cases} \dfrac{x_{i\min}}{x_{ij}} & , x_{i\min} \neq 0 \\[2mm] 1 - \dfrac{x_{ij}}{x_{i\max}} & x_{i\min} = 0 \end{cases}. \tag{2}$$

The matrix of relative membership degree for quantitative index can be get:

$$R_{m_1 \times n} = \begin{bmatrix} r_{11} & r_{12} & \cdots & r_{1n} \\ r_{21} & r_{22} & \cdots & r_{2n} \\ \cdots & \cdots & \cdots & \cdots \\ r_{m_1 1} & r_{m_1 2} & \cdots & r_{m_1 n} \end{bmatrix}. \tag{3}$$

The relative membership degree of qualitative indexes can be calculated as following steps.

Assume decision sets of basic unit as:

$$D = \{d_1, \ d_2, \cdots, \ d_n\} . \tag{4}$$

Where n is the number of decision.

A vector of relative membership degree for c_i index in basic unit is as:

$$_i r = \{_i r_1, _i r_2, \cdots, _i r_n\} . \tag{5}$$

Where, $i = 1,2,\ldots, m_2$, m_2 is a number of qualitative index.

Sorted the qualitative comments of decision set, compared the importance of binary for d_k and d_l in decision set and selecting the sorting scale for the qualitative importance ($_i e_{kl}$) in set (0, 0.5, 1).

$$\begin{cases} _i e_{kl} = 1, _i e_{lk} = 0 & , \ d_k > d_l \\ _i e_{kl} = 0, _i e_{lk} = 1 & , \ d_l < d_k \\ _i e_{kl} = _i e_{lk} = 0.5 & , \ d_k = d_l \end{cases} . \tag{6}$$

Analysis above equation(6), $_i e_{kl} + _i e_{lk} = 1$, $_i e_{kk} = _i e_{ll} = 0.5$. The sorting scale matrix of the qualitative importance is consistently

$$_i E = \begin{bmatrix} _i e_{11} & _i e_{12} & \cdots & _i e_{1n} \\ _i e_{21} & _i e_{22} & \cdots & _i e_{2n} \\ \cdots & \cdots & \cdots & \cdots \\ _i e_{n1} & _i e_{n2} & \cdots & _i e_{nn} \end{bmatrix} = (_i e_{kl}) . \tag{7}$$

Where $k = 1,2,\ldots,n$; $l = 1,2,\ldots,n$; and

$$\begin{cases} _i e_{kl} = 0 & , _i e_{hk} > _i e_{hl} \\ _i e_{kl} = 1 & , _i e_{hk} < _i e_{hl} \\ _i e_{kl} = 0.5 & , _i e_{hk} = _i e_{hl} = 0.5 \end{cases} .$$

The sums of each line in $_iE$ are arranged from largest to smallest. The order of importance in sort consistency condition can get.

$$_iD' = \{_id_1',_id_2',\cdots,_id_n'\} \ . \tag{8}$$

The relative membership degree of importance can be calculated:

$$_ir_j = \frac{(1-_ia_{1j})}{_ia_{1j}}, \ 0.5 \leq_i a_{1j} \leq 1 \ . \tag{9}$$

Where $_ia_{1j}$ is the quantitative scale of importance between $_id_1'$ and $_id_j'$ in index c_i .

So the matrix of relative membership degree for qualitative index is as following:

$$R_{m_2 \times n} = \begin{bmatrix} r_{11} & r_{12} & \cdots & r_{1n} \\ r_{21} & r_{22} & \cdots & r_{2n} \\ \cdots & \cdots & \cdots & \cdots \\ r_{m_2 1} & r_{m_2 2} & \cdots & r_{m_2 n} \end{bmatrix} \ . \tag{10}$$

The relative membership degree matrix of all indexes can be got by combination equation (3) and equation (10).

$$R_{m \times n} = \begin{bmatrix} r_{11} & r_{12} & \cdots & r_{1n} \\ r_{21} & r_{22} & \cdots & r_{2n} \\ \cdots & \cdots & \cdots & \cdots \\ r_{m1} & r_{m2} & \cdots & r_{mn} \end{bmatrix} \ . \tag{11}$$

Where: m is the number of all indexes.

2.2 Fuzzy Optimal Decision

Applying variable fuzzy recognition model, to calculate optimal membership degree:

$$u_j = \frac{1}{1 + \left\{ \dfrac{\sum\limits_{i=1}^{m}[w_i(r_{ij}-1)]^p}{\sum\limits_{i=1}^{m}(w_i r_{ij})^p} \right\}^{\frac{a}{p}}} \ . \tag{12}$$

Where u_j refers optimal membership degree, a to optimal model rules parameter, w_i to index weight, m to recognizing indexes number, p to distance parameter and p=1 is Hamming distance, and p=2 is Euclidean distance.

2.3 An Algorithm of Task Scheduling Based on Variable Fuzzy Set Decision (VF_TS)

In the search on priority tasks scheduling, firstly, we must specify the characteristic parameters of mission. Because the significance, deadline, free time and remaining lifetime of tasks are importance parameters in tasks scheduling, these parameters are used to study the priority of tasks based on decision theory of variable fuzzy set. Deadline (d) presents that the request must be completed before this time. Free time (a) means how long has the request been waiting for. Left lifetime (l) indicates how long must the request be completed. $l = d - a$. Significance expresses the importance degree of the request, compared with other tasks.

The algorithm of task scheduling (VF_TS), based on decision theory of variable fuzzy set, can be described as following:

a) To calculated respectively the relative membership degree of d, a and l.

b) Qualitative indexes were divided into 5 comments sets. Mood operator of mission-critical = {crucial (L_1), every importance (L_2), importance (L_3), average (L_4), least important (L_5)}. According to the processing of relative membership degree of qualitative indexes, the linear relation of mood operator, quantitative scale and degree of relative membership of mission-critical is shown in table 1.

Table 1. Linear Relation of Mood Operator, Quantitative Scale and Degree of Relative Membership

Mood operator	L_1	L_2	L_3	L_4	L_5
Quantitative Scale	0.50	0.60	0.70	0.80	0.90
Degree of relative membership	1.000	0.667	0.429	0.250	0.111

c) To determine the weights of various factors. Because the key feature of survivability system is continuously provide key services in the event of attack, fault or accident, the weight of mission-critical has relatively high proportion. In order to timely response non-critical task, the weights are divided into three groups. Task management adapts different groups according to different survival situations.

d) The membership degree is token as priority scheduling, which is calculated for each task by equation (12).

3 Experiment and Analysis

In order to verify the performance of this algorithm, we take the first in fist service (FIFS) as reference, and analysis and validate the performance of proposed algorithm from two aspects: weighted guarantee ratio (WGR) and differentiated guarantee ratio (DGR). In the simulation experiments, the set of task composed by 50 missions, whose parameters are generated by the following rules:

a) The task execution time (C_i) selects in 0~600 unit time at random, and obeys the uniform distribution.

b) The task arrival time $T_i = N * C_i / \rho$, where N is the total number of tasks in task set, ρ is the survivability of system.

c) The deadline $D_i = 2(C_i + T_i)$.

d) The task scheduling time (Δt) is optionally generated in 0 ~ 6 units, and obeys the uniform distribution.

e) The quantitative scale of mission critical is selected in table 1 at random, and obeys the uniform distribution.

3.1   Weighted Guarantee Ratio (WGR)

The weighted guarantee ratio refers to completion situation of different type tasks within the deadline time, which reflects the capacity of survivability system to provide key services. The equation is

$$WGR = 100 * \frac{T_C^l}{T_S^l} \% \cdot \tag{13}$$

Where: l is the type of mission critical, which is shown in table 1; T_C^l is total number of l type tasks completed; T_S^l is total number of l type tasks received.

Because tasks are first come and first serve in the algorithm of FIFS, the weighted guarantee ratios of different type task are basic same. In the algorithm of VF_TS, the weights of indexes are adapted, so the weighted guarantee ratios appear difference. In the processing of experiment, weights include three groups. As show in Fig.1, when survivability of system is more than 80 percent, the weight of mission-critical is small. Therefore, completion rates of various type tasks are plan difference; the weight of mission-critical is larger when survivability of system is between 80 percent and 50 percent, we can see the gaps of completion rates increase; when survivability of system is less than 50 percent the completion rates of average and least important tasks sharply decline and reach zero, but the completion rates of crucial task keeps above 92 percent and every importance task's is also above 81 percent. Analysis show that

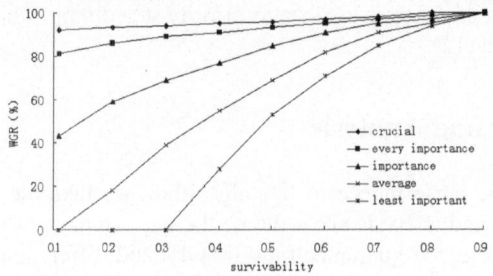

Fig. 1. Weighted Guarantee Ratio

proposed algorithm can meet the needs of survivability system, which can deprived of the resources of non-critical tasks to ensure the operation of mission-critical in less survivability.

3.2   Differentiated Guarantee Ratio (DGR)

In experiments, we contrast and analyze the performances of FIFS and VF_TS by DGR at ρ =0.5 and ρ =0.2, as show in Fig.2.

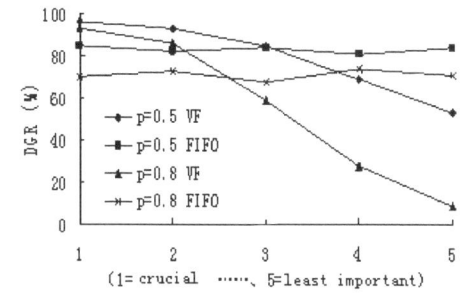

Fig. 2. Differentiated Guarantee Ratio

Because the algorithm of FIFS does not distinguish services type, the completion rates of various type services are basic same in two survivability situations. The algorithm of VF_TS not only distinguishes the task types, but also applies different weight group according to system survivability. The system, whose task scheduling employed proposed algorithm, uses different strategies for different service to guarantee the completion rate of key services.

4   Conclusions

How to enhance the survivability of key services has become an important research content in survivability system. A new algorithm was proposed from survivability, based optimization model of variable fuzzy set. The performance of VF_TS algorithm was compared with FIFS algorithm through WGR and DGR. The results of experiments show that the VF_TS algorithm can provide the guarantee of survivability for critical services. Especially in less survivability of system, the performance can gracefully and effectively improve the survivability of the overall system.

Acknowledgment. The authors would like to acknowledge Shijiazhuang University of Economics in support with the initial fund of scientific research to pursue our Ph.D Degee.

References

1. Burns, A., Prasad, D., Bondavalli, A., et al.: The Meaning and Role of Value in Scheduling Flexible Real Time Systems. Journal of Systems Architecture 325, 305–325 (2000)
2. Lu, C.Y., Stankovic, J.A.: Design and Evaluation of a Feedback Control EDF Seheduling Algorithm. In: Proeeedings of the 20th IEEE Real-Time Systems Symposium, pp. 55–66. IEEE Computer Society, Phoenix (1999)
3. Huang, J., Stankovic, J., Towesly, D., et al.: Experimental Evaluation of Real-time Transaction processing. In: Proceedings of the 10th IEEE Real-Time Systems Symposium, pp. 144–153. IEEE Computer Society, Santa Monica (1989)
4. Hong, J., Hongan, W., Qiang, W.: An Integrated Design Method of Task Priority. Journal of Software 14(3), 376–382 (2003)
5. Yongyan, W., Qiang, W., Hong, W.: A Real-Time Scheduling Algorithm Based on Priority Table and Its Implementation. Journal of Software 15(3), 360–370 (2004)
6. Cheng, S.C., Shiau, D.F., Huang, Y.M., et al.: Dynamic hard-real-time scheduling using genetic algorithm for multiprocessor task with resource and timing constraints. Expert Systems with Applications 36(1), 852–860 (2009)
7. Gong, Y., Zhang, Z.-z., Huang, X.-k.: Task allocation and scheduling algorithm based on dynamic dual-directional priority. Journal of Computer Applications 29(4), 1131–1134 (2009)
8. Yue, G., Yuzhuo, W.: The Task Distribution and Scheduling of the Parallel Delivery System. In: 2007 International Conference on Net work and parallel Computing Workshops. IEEE Computer Society, Dalian (2007)
9. Liang, S.-s., Wu, J.-j., Zhang, J.-c.: CCTD:A Scheduling Algorithm under Communication Constraints for Fork-Join Task Graphs. Computer Science 6 (2009)

A Generic Construction for Proxy Signature Scheme

Guoyan Zhang⋆

School of Computer Science and Technology, Shandong University, Jinan 250100,
China
guoyanzhang@sdu.edu.cn

Abstract. In proxy signature, the original signer can delegate his signature power to the proxy signer. Due to the extensive application of proxy signature, some schemes have been presented, but there is not a general model for proxy signature scheme, especially for the scheme with good properties. In this paper, we give the first generic model and security model for proxy-protected anonymous proxy signature, in which only the proxy signer can sign the messages for the original signer. Finally, we give one concrete scheme according to the model as example.

Keywords: Proxy Signature Scheme, Proxy Protected, Anonymous, Proxy Signer.

1 Introduction

The need of delegation of cryptographic operation leads to the introduction of proxy cryptography. M.Mambo, K.Usuda and E.Okamoto first invented the notion of proxy signature [1] in 1996, in which the original signer can delegate his signature capability to any reliable person called proxy signer. Since the introduction, proxy signature scheme has been extensively developed [2,3,4,5]. Depending on whether the original signer can generate the same proxy signature as the proxy signers do, there are two kinds of proxy signature schemes [1], namely, the proxy-unprotected scheme and the proxy-protected one;

Because we can't always trust a person, the drawback of delegation is important in proxy cryptography. There is not a more efficient method to solve the problem. In this paper, we introduce a model which is implicit delegation, it is to say, the verifier needn't check the validity of delegation, because, if the signature power of a proxy signer is revoked, he can not get valid signature. Further in our model, the channel between the original signer and the proxy signer needn't be secure and authenticated.

⋆ This work is Supported by the National Natural Science Foundation of China(No.60873232), Open Research Fund from Key Laboratory of Computer Network and Information Integration In Southeast University, Ministry of Education, China(No. K93-9-2010-10), Shandong Natural Science Foundation(No.Y2008A22) and Shandong Postdoctoral Special Fund for Innovative Research(No.200902022).

H. Deng et al. (Eds.): AICI 2011, Part II, LNAI 7003, pp. 93–100, 2011.

1.1   Our Contributions

In this paper, we give a generic proxy-protected anonymous proxy signature followed with the security model. Our model not only captures all the properties introduced by Lee et al., but also we also give a corresponding security model which makes the schemes have precise security guarantee. Especially, in our model, the verifier needn't verify the validity of the public key of delegated signer. Furthermore, the original signer can also run cryptographic operations as the delegated signer does, but he cannot impersonation any delegated signer. This model not only protects the privacy of the delegated signer, but also the one of the original signer. This is the first generic model satisfying the above properties in literature. Finally, we give a concrete proxy signature schemes as example.

2   Preliminaries

Definition 1. An identity-based encryption scheme (IBE) is specified by four randomized algorithms: Setup (IBE_{Gen}), Extract$(IBE_{Extract})$, Encrypt, Decrypt:

Setup: takes a security parameter k and returns system parameters *params* and master secret key MSK. The system parameters include a description of a finite message space $\mathcal{M}$, and a description of a finite ciphertext space $\mathcal{C}$. Intuitively, the system parameters will be publicly knew, while the master secret key will be knew only to the Private Key Generator (PKG).

Extract: takes as input *params*, master secret key, and an arbitrary $ID \in \{0,1\}^*$, and returns a private key d. Here ID is an arbitrary string that will be used as a public key, and d is the corresponding private decryption key. The Extract algorithm extracts a private key from the given public key.

Encrypt: takes as input *params*, ID, and $m \in \mathcal{M}$. It returns a ciphertext $c \in \mathcal{C}$.

Decrypt: takes as input *params*, $c \in \mathcal{C}$, and a private key d. It returns $m \in \mathcal{M}$. These algorithms must satisfy the standard consistency constraint, namely when d is the private key generated by algorithm Extract when it is given ID as the public key, then $\forall m \in \mathcal{M}$: $Decrypt(params, c, d) = m$, where $c = Encrypt(params, ID, m)$.

Definition 2. A hash function $H \leftarrow H(k)$ is collision resistant if for all PPT algorithms A, the advantage

$$Adv_A^{CR}(k) = Pr[H(x) = H(y) \wedge x \neq y | (x, y)$$

$$\leftarrow A(k, H) \wedge H \leftarrow H(k)].$$

is negligible as a function of the security parameter k.

Decisional Bilinear Diffie-Hellman (DBDH) Assumption: Let G, G_T is bilinear groups of degree of p, and g is the generator of G, $e : G \times G \longrightarrow G_T$

is the bilinear map. Given the tuple (g, g^a, g^b, g^c), there is no PPT algorithm A can distinguish $e(g, g)^{abc}$ from a random element $Z \in G_T$ with more than a negligible advantage. The advantage of A is

$$Adv_A^{DBDH}(k) = |Pr[1 \leftarrow A(g, g^a, g^b, g^c, T)|T \leftarrow e(g, g)^{abc} \wedge a, b, c \leftarrow Z_p^*]$$

$$-Pr[1 \leftarrow A(g, g^a, g^b, g^c, T)|T \leftarrow G_T \wedge a, b, c \leftarrow Z_p^*]|.$$

3   Our Generic Model and Attack Model

We first give the generic model, and in next subsection, we give the attack model.

3.1   Our Generic Model

Definition 3. A proxy-protected anonymous proxy signature (PPAPS) scheme also includes five algorithms as follows:

-Setup: Given the security parameter 1^k, the original signer runs the probability generation algorithm IBE_{Gen} to get the master secret key SK_O as his secret key and the master public parameter PK_O as his public key.

-Delegation Algorithm: The delegation algorithm includes two phases: user secret key generation and the partial proxy private key derivation.

1. **Secret Key Generation:** Taken the public parameter PK_O as input, the proxy signer randomly picks a secret key SK_P and computes the corresponding public key PK_P. Following, he chooses an existential unforgeable signature scheme $S = (Gen_{sign}, Sign, Verify)$, and computes the signature δ for the public key PK_P. Finally, he sends (δ, PK_P) with the verifying public key to the original signer.

2. **Partial Proxy Private Key Derivation:** Assuming the proxy time is t. Given the tuple (δ, PK_P), the public key PK_O, the secret key SK_O and the proxy time t, the original signer first checks the validity of the public key PK_P and of the signature δ, if either invalid, he aborts. Otherwise, he runs the private key extraction algorithm $IBE_{Extract}$ of IBE, and gets the partial proxy private key SK_{pp}. Then he sends SK_{pp} to the delegatee.

-Sign: Taken the public key PK_O and PK_P, the proxy time t, the secret key SK_P, the partial proxy private key SK_{pp} and the message M, the proxy signer runs the probabilistic scheme to return the signature C on message M.

-Verify: Receiving the signature C, the verifier can verify the validity of the signature C. If $verify(C, PK_O, PK_P, M, t) = 1$, he outputs 1, otherwise outputs *invalid*.

Remark 1.(Proxy-Protected). From the above model, we can see the original signer cannot run the cryptographic operations imitating the proxy signer, because he doesn't know the secret key corresponding to the public key of the proxy signer. Of course, the original signer can choose different public key whose corresponding secret key is knew to him instead of the proxy signer, but the proxy signer can publish his partial proxy private key to delate him.

Remark 2.(Anonymous). In our model, any third party can not identify the identity of the proxy signer only from the public information, but the proxy signer can not deny he has run the cryptographic operation, because the signature for the public key is sent to the original signer, and if the signature scheme used is existential unforgeable, the original signer can revoke the identity of the proxy signer in dispute.

Remark 3.(Privacy-Protected). In fact, the public key is not combined with the identity and any third party cannot identify the accurate identity of the proxy signer. In other words, the model ensures the anonymity of the delegation. Furthermore, if the original signer chooses a key pair (PK_P, SK_P), then he can run any cryptographic operations using the public key which also protects the privacy of the original signer.

3.2   The Attack Model

In our notion, we consider all potential actions of the adversary. There are two types of adversaries: the Type I adversary presents the outside adversaries who aren't delegated, the Type II adversary presents the proxy signer.

Definition 4. A proxy-protected anonymous proxy signature($PPAPS$) scheme is existential unforgeable against adaptive chosen message attack if no probabilistic polynomial time bound adversary has non-negligible advantage in either Game 1 or Game 2.

Game 1

1. This game for Type I adversary. Taken a security parameter 1^k, the challenger runs the Setup algorithm to get the original signer's secret key SK_O and the original signer's public key PK_O, and he gives PK_O to the adversary, keeping SK_O secret.
2. The adversary can request two oracles: Partial-Proxy-Private-Key-Oracle and Signature-Oracle.

   -Partial-Proxy-Private-Key-Oracle: On receiving the oracle$< PK_P, SK_P, t_i, \delta = Sign(PK_P) >$:

   (a) The challenger checks the validity of the public key and the signature δ, if either invalid, he aborts. Otherwise, he searches the PartialProxyPrivateKeyList for a tuple $< PK_P, SK_{PP}, t_i >$, if exists, he sends SK_{PP} to the adversary.

   (b) Otherwise, the challenger runs the Partial-Proxy-Private-Key-Derivation algorithm to get SK_{PP}, and adds the tuple $< PK_P, SK_{PP}, t_i >$ to the PartialProxyPrivateKeyList. He sends SK_{PP} to the adversary.

   -Signature-oracles: On receiving the oracle
   $< PK_P, SK_P, m_i, t_i >$:

   (a) The challenger checks the validity of the public key, if invalid, he aborts. Otherwise, he searches the PartialProxyPrivateKeyList for a tuple $< PK_P, SK_{PP}, t_i >$, if exists, he signs m_i using SK_{PP} and SK_P in the normal way. And he sends the signature σ_i to the adversary.

(b) Otherwise, the challenger runs the Partial-Proxy-Private-Key-Derivation algorithm to get SK_{PP}, and adds the tuple $< PK_P, SK_{PP}, t_i >$ to the PartialProxyPrivateKeyList. He signs m_i using SK_{PP} and SK_P as the above step. And he sends the signature σ_i to the adversary.

At the end of the game, the adversary outputs $< PK_{p^*}, C^*, m^*, t^* >$, where PK_{p^*} is the challenger public key, C^* is the signature on message m^*, t^* is proxy time. The adversary wins the game if he has never request the partial proxy private key oracle on a tuple $< PK_{P^*}, SK_{P^*}, t_i^* >$ and the signature oracle $< PK_p^*, SK_p^*, m^*, t^* >$.

Game 2

1. This game for Type II adversary. Taken a security parameter 1^k, the challenger runs the Setup algorithm to get the original signer's secret key SK_O and the original signer's public key PK_O, and he gives $< PK_O, SK_O >$ to the adversary.

2. The adversary can request one oracle: signature oracle.

   -Signature-oracle: On receiving the oracle
   $< PK_P, SK_P, m_i, t_i >$:

   (a) The challenger checks the validity of the public key, if invalid, he aborts. Otherwise, he searches the PartialProxyPrivateKeyList for a tuple $< PK_P, SK_{PP}, t_i >$, if exists, he signs the message m_i using SK_{PP} and SK_P. And he sends the signature σ_i to the adversary.

   (b) Otherwise, the challenger runs the Partial-Proxy-Private-Key-Derivation algorithm to get SK_{PP}, and adds the tuple $< PK_P, SK_{PP}, t_i >$ to the PartialProxyPrivateKeyList. He signs the message m_i using SK_{PP} and SK_P. And he sends the signature σ_i to the adversary.

   At the end of the game, the adversary outputs $(PK_{p^*}, C^*, m^*, t^*)$, where PK_{p^*} is the challenger public key, C^* is the signature on message m^*, t^* is proxy time. The adversary wins the game if he has never asked the signature oracle on $< PK_{p^*}, SK_{p^*}, m^*, t^* >$.

4   The Proxy-Protected Proxy Signature

4.1   The Construction

Setup: The original signer O chooses groups G, G_T of prime order q and a generator $P \in G$. There is also a bilinear map $e : G \times G \to G_T$. He chooses $H_1 : \{0,1\}^* \to G_T$ and $H_2 : \{0,1\}^* \to Z_q^*$. He randomly picks $s \in Z_q^*$ as his secret key, and computes $Q = sP$ as his public key. Then the public parameter is :

$$PK_O = (G, G_T, q, P, H_1, H_2, e, Q).$$

His secret key

$$SK_O = s.$$

Delegation Algorithm

1. **Secret Key Generation:** The proxy signer picks $x \in Z_q^*$ and computes $PK_P = (X, Y) = (xP, xQ)$ as his public key. He runs Gen_{sign} of a secure signature scheme $S = (Gen_{sign}, Sign, Very)$ to get the signature key pair (sk, vk), and he runs $Sign$ to get the signature δ on (X, Y). Finally he sends $((X, Y), \delta, vk)$ to the original signer O.
2. **Partial Proxy Private Key Derivation:** On receiving (PK_P, δ, vk), the original signer verifies the validity of the public key and the signature for the public key by the two equations:

$$e(X, Q) = e(Y, P), Very(\delta, PK_P, vk) = 1.$$

If either equation doesn't hold, he outputs invalid. Otherwise, if the proxy time is t, he computes

$$W = H_1(X, Y, t), SK_{PP} = sW,$$

and sends them to the proxy signer P.

Proxy Signature: The proxy signer P picks $k \in Z_q^*$ and computes

$$r = e(P, P)^k, c = H_2(m\|r), U = cxSK_{PP} + kP.$$

The proxy signature is (c, U, m).

Verification: Anyone can verify the validity of the proxy signature. The verifier computes

$$W = H_1(X, Y, t), r' = e(cW, Y)^{-1}e(U, P).$$

He checks whether $c = H_2(m\|r')$. If the condition holds, the signature is valid.

4.2 Security Analysis

Theorem 1. The proxy-protected anonymous proxy signature scheme is existential unforgeable against Type I adversary assuming the computational Diffi-Hellman(CDH) problem is hard in Gap Diffi-Hellman group.

Proof: If A is the Type I adversary, then we can construct a scheme B who can solve the computational Diffi-Hellman(CDH) problem by running A. Given the computational Diffi-Hellman(CDH) problem instance (G, G_T, P, aP, bP, e), and G, G_T is the group of degree of q. B simulates the attack environment of A until he solves CDH problem.

Setup: B sets $Q = aP$ as his public key, and $s = a$ as his secret key unknew to him. He chooses two hash functions: $H_1 : \{0, 1\}^* \to G_T$ and $H_2 : \{0, 1\}^* \to Z_q^*$. Then the public parameter is $(G, G_T, q, P, Q, e, H_1, H_2)$.

Then B can respond the queries of A as following:

-Partial-Proxy-Private-Key-Query: On receiving the oracle $< PK_P = (X, Y), SK_P, t, \delta, vk >$:

B checks the validity of the public key (X, Y) and the signature δ by the equations: $e(X, Q) = e(Y, P), Very(\delta, PK_P, vk) = 1$. If either invalid, he aborts. Otherwise, he searches the PartialProxyPrivateKeyList for a tuple $< PK_P, t, SK_{PP} >$. If exits, he returns SK_{PP} as answer. Else, he defines $W = H_1(X, Y, t) = c_1 P$ and sets $SK_{PP} = sH_1(X, Y, t) = ac_1 P = c_1 Q$. B adds $< PK_P, t, c_1, W = c_1 P >$ and $< PK_P, t, SK_{PP} >$ respectively into H_1 list and PartialProxyPrivateKeyList.

-Signature-Query: On receiving the oracle $< PK_P = (X, Y), SK_P, t, m >$:

B checks the validity of the public key, if invalid, he aborts. Otherwise, he searches H_1 list for a tuple $< PK_P, t, c_1, W = c_1 P >$, if doesn't exist, he defines $W = H_1(X, Y, t) = c_1 P$. He randomly picks $c \in Z_q^*, U \in G_1$ and computes $r = e(U, P)e(W, Y)^{-c}$, then he defines $c = H_2(m \| r)$ and adds $(m \| r, c)$ into H_2 list. Return (r, c, U) as answer.

Eventually, we apply the forking lemma by running A, we obtain a machine C who outputs two tuples (r, W, c, U) and (r, W', c', U') given the different values $(W = c_1 bP, W' = c_1' bP)$ for $H_1(X, Y, t)$ and different values c, c' for $H_2(m \| r)$. Because the two tuples are all valid signature for message m, we can get the following equations:

$$U = cSK_P sW + kP = cSK_P ac_1 bP + kP,$$

$$U' = c'SK_P sW' + kP = c'SK_P ac_1' bP + kP.$$

Then

$$U - U' = cc_1 SK_P abP - c'c_1' SK_P abP$$

$$= (cc_1 - c'c_1')SK_P abP,$$

$$abP = (U - U')(cc_1 - c'c_1')^{-1} SK_P^{-1}.$$

Theorem 2. The proxy-protected anonymous proxy signature scheme is existential unforgeable against Type II adversary assuming the computational Diffi-Hellman(CDH) problem is hard in Gap Diffi-Hellman group.

Proof: If A is the Type II adversary, then we can construct a scheme B who can solve the computational Diffi-Hellman(CDH) problem by running A. Given the computational Diffi-Hellman(CDH) problem instance (G, G_T, P, aP, bP, e), and G, G_T is the group of degree of q. B simulates the attack environment of A until he solves CDH problem.

Setup: B randomly chooses $s \in Z_q^*$ as his secret key and computes $Q = sP$ as his public key. He chooses two hash functions: $H_1 : \{0, 1\}^* \to G_T$ and $H_2 : \{0, 1\}^* \to Z_q^*$. Then the public parameter is $(G, G_T, q, P, Q, e, H_1, H_2)$. He guesses that the public key that A forges the signature is PK_{P*} and sets $PK_{P*} = (aP, saP)$ whose corresponding secret key is not knew by B. B sends s to A.

-Signature-Query: On receiving the oracle $< PK_P = (X, Y), SK_P, t, m >$:

B checks the validity of the public key, if invalid, he aborts. Otherwise, he searches H_1 list for a tuple $< PK_P, t, c_1, W = c_1 P >$, if doesn't exist, he defines

$W = H_1(X, Y, t) = c_1 P$. He randomly picks $c \in Z_q^*, U \in G_1$ and computes $r = e(U, P)e(W, Y)^{(-c)}$, then he defines $c = H_2(m\|r)$ and adds $(m\|r, c)$ into H_2 list. Return (r, c, U) as answer.

Eventually, we apply the forking lemma by running A, we obtain a machine C who outputs two tuples (r, W, c, U) and (r, W', c', U') given the different values $(W = c_1 bP, W' = c_1' bP)$ for $H_1(X, Y, t)$ and different values c, c' for $H_2(m\|r)$. Because the two tuples are all valid signature for message m, we can get the following equations:

$$U = casW + kP = csac_1 bP + kP,$$

$$U' = c'saW' + kP = c'sac_1' bP + kP.$$

Then

$$U - U' = cc_1 sabP - c'c_1' sabP$$

$$= (cc_1 - c'c_1')sabP,$$

$$abP = (U - U')(cc_1 - c'c_1')^{-1} s_P^{-1}.$$

5   Conclusion

In this paper, we first give a generic proxy-protected proxy signature followed with the security model. In our model, the verifier needn't verify the validity of the public key of proxy signer and the original signer can not run any cryptographic operations imitating the proxy signer. This is the first generic model satisfying the above properties in literature. Finally, we give a concrete proxy signature schemes as examples.

References

1. Mambo, M., Usuda, K., Okamoto, E.: Proxy Signature: Delegation of the Power to Sign Messages. IEICE Trans., Fundations E79-A(9), 1338–1353 (1996)
2. Hang, H.F., Chang, C.C.: A novel efficient (t, n) threshold proxy signature scheme. Inform. Sci. 176(10), 1338–1349 (2006)
3. Hsu, C.L., Tsai, K.Y., Tsai, P.L.: Cryptanalysis and improvement of nonrepudiable threshold multi-proxy multi-signature scheme with shared verification. Inform. Sci. 177(2), 543–549 (2006)
4. Mambo, M., Usuda, K., Okamoto, E.: Proxy signatures for delegating signing operation. In: Proceedings of the 3rd ACM Conference on Computer and Communications Security (CCS), New Delhi, India, pp. 48–57 (1996)
5. Zhou, Y., Cao, Z.-F., Chai, Z.: An Efficient Proxy-Protected Signature Scheme Based on Factoring. In: Chen, G., Pan, Y., Guo, M., Lu, J. (eds.) ISPA-WS 2005. LNCS, vol. 3759, pp. 332–341. Springer, Heidelberg (2005)

Secure Negotiation Approach for Share-Secret-Key of Kerberos Service

Lai-Cheng Cao[*]

School of Computer and Communication
Lanzhou University of Technology
Lanzhou 730050, China
caolch@lut.cn

Abstract. The generation and distribution of the shared secret-key in Kerberos protocol are a security infrastructure. In order to enhance the security of distributed applications based on Kerberos protocol, a scheme of the shared secret-key negotiation was put forward. The shared secret-key could be generated and distributed by the Diffie-Hellman algorithm. Negotiation parameters of communicating parties were protected by opposite party's public key to encrypt. The distribution of the public key and privacy key adopted ECC (Elliptic Curve Cryptography); there was a computational advantage to using ECC with a shorter key length than RSA. Security analysis shows that this scheme has high security and can resist Man-in-the-Middle attack.

Keywords: The shared secret-key, Kerberos protocol, Diffie-Hellman algorithm, ECC (Elliptic Curve Cryptography).

1 Introduction

Kerberos is a widely-adopted network authentication protocol based on symmetric cryptography system. By exploiting a shared secret-key, Kerberos ensures the confidentiality and integrity for a session. But, Kerberos has some inherent security flaws, such as undeniability, difficulty in key exchange, inability to fulfill digital signature and authentication. The paper [1] extends an ideal functionality for symmetric and public-key encryption proposed in previous work by a mechanism for key derivation. Ke Jia etc [2] propose the public key encryption algorithm based on braid groups to improve Kerberos protocol. Liu ke-long etc [3] present an improved way using Yaksha security system of ElGamal Public Key algorithm based on the original protocol framework to overcome the Kerberos' limitations. All these methods have extended public key algorithm based on RSA, but ECC (Elliptic Curve Cryptography) uses a considerably smaller key size compared to RSA. Furthermore, for equal key lengths, the computational effort required for ECC and RSA is comparable [4]. Thus, there is a computational advantage to using ECC with a shorter key length than RSA. In this paper, we put forward scheme to carry out network

---

[*] This work is supported by the National Natural Science Foundation of China under Grant No. 60972078; the Gansu Provincial Natural Science Foundation of China under Grant No. 0916RJZA015.

authentication based on ECC, the shared secret-key of users and server can be generated by the Diffie-Hellman algorithm. This method has high security and can resist Man-in-the-Middle attack.

The remainder of this work is organized as follows. In section 2 we describe Kerberos protocol. In Section 3 we present private key and public key of users and server distributing method based on ECC. In section 4 point out a scheme to generate the shared secret-key of users and server by the Diffie-Hellman algorithm. In section 5 we finish security analysis about our method. The conclusion is presented in section 6.

2   The Kerberos Protocol

In the distributed environment, in order to protect user information and server resources, we require that client systems authenticate themselves to the server, but trust the client system concerning the identity of its user. We describe the Kerberos protocol [5-7] (as shown in Fig. 1); it includes the gateway, Authentication Server (*AS*), Ticket-granting Server (*TGS*), web server. Authentication Server keeps a database containing the secret-keys of the users and the router and TGS. The client and the Server can communicate each other based on TCP/IP protocol.

- *Client*: Requires gaining access to Web server in the distributed environment.
- *AS*: Authenticates servers to the client.
- *TGS*: Grants service-granting ticket to the client.
- *Web server*: Stores resource and data for the web users.

If the client requests to access Web server, this server will authenticate the client. Similarly, if Web server requests to access client, this client authenticates web server.

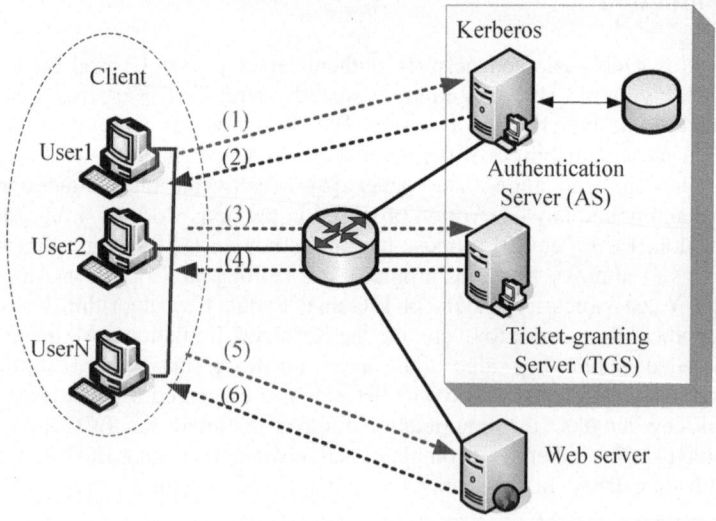

Fig. 1. The architecture about the Kerberos protocol

1) Authentication service exchange to obtain ticket-granting ticket

Message (1): Client requests ticket-granting ticket (corresponding to (1) in Fig. 1):

$$C \rightarrow AS : Options \parallel ID_c \parallel \mathrm{Re}\, alm_c \parallel ID_{tgs} \parallel Times \parallel Nonce_1$$

Message (2): AS returns ticket-granting ticket (corresponding to (2) in Fig. 1):

$$AS \rightarrow C : \mathrm{Re}\, alm_c \parallel ID_c \parallel Ticket_{tgs} \parallel E_{K_c}(K_{c,tgs} \parallel Times \parallel Nonce_1 \parallel \mathrm{Re}\, alm_{tgs} \parallel ID_{tgs})$$

where, $Ticket_{tgs} = E_{K_{tgs}}(Flags \parallel K_{c,tgs} \parallel \mathrm{Re}\, alm_c \parallel ID_c \parallel AD_c \parallel Times)$, the symbols are showed in Table1.

Table 1. Symbols of message (1) and message (2)

Symbol	Meaning
C	Client
AS	Authentication server
$Options$	Used to request that certain flags be set in the returned ticket
ID_c	Tells AS identity of user from this client
$Realm_c$	Tells AS realm of user from this client
ID_{tgs}	Tells AS identity of TGS that user requests access
$Times$	Used by the client to request to the time settings in the ticket, it consists the desired start time, the requested expiration time and the requested renew expiration time
$Nonce_1$	A random value that client produces to be repeated in message (2) to assure that the response is fresh and has not been replayed by an attacker
$Ticket_{tgs}$	Ticket to be used by client to access TGS
K_c	Encryption is based on client's password, enabling AS and user to verify password, and protecting contents of message (2)
$K_{c,tgs}$	Copy of session key accessible to client created by AS to permit secure exchange between client and TGS without requiring to share a permanent key
$Realm_{tgs}$	Tells client realm of TGS
K_{tgs}	Ticket is encrypted with key known only to AS and TGS, to prevent tampering
AD_c	Prevents use of ticket from client other than one that initially requested the ticket
$E(\ )$	Encryption function based on Rijndael encryption algorithm of AES

2) Ticket-granting service exchange to obtain service-granting ticket

Message (3): Client requests service-granting ticket (corresponding to (3) in Fig. 1): $C \rightarrow TGS : Options \parallel ID_{ws} \parallel Times \parallel Nonce_2 \parallel Ticket_{tgs} \parallel Authenticator_c$

where, $Authentica\, tor_c = E_{K_{c,tgs}}(ID_c \parallel \mathrm{Re}\, alm_c \parallel TS_1)$

Message (4): TGS returns service-granting ticket (corresponding to (4) in Fig. 1): $TGS \rightarrow C : Realm_c \parallel ID_c \parallel Ticket_{ws} \parallel E_{K_{c,tgs}}(K_{c,ws} \parallel Times \parallel Nonce_2 \parallel Realm_{ws} \parallel ID_{ws})$

where, $Ticket_{ws} = E_{K_{ws}}(Flags \parallel K_{c,ws} \parallel \mathrm{Re}\, alm_c \parallel ID_c \parallel AD_c \parallel Times)$, the symbols are showed in Table 2.

3) Client/Localserver authentication exchange to obtain service

Message (5): Client requests service (corresponding to (5) in Fig. 1):

$$C \rightarrow WS : Options \parallel Ticket_{ws} \parallel Authentica\, tor_c$$

where, $Ticket_{ws} = E_{K_{ws}}(Flags \parallel K_{c,ws} \parallel \mathrm{Re}\, alm_c \parallel ID_c \parallel AD_c \parallel Times)$

$$Authentica\,tor_c = E_{K_{c,ws}} (ID_c \parallel \text{Re}\,alm_c \parallel TS_2 \parallel Subkey \parallel Seq\#)$$

Message (6): Optional authentication of Web server to client (corresponding to (6) in Fig. 1): $WS \rightarrow C : E_{K_{c,ws}} (TS_2 \parallel Subkey \parallel Seq\#)$, the symbols are showed in Table 3.

Table 2. Symbols of message (3) and message (4)

Symbol	Meaning
ID_{ws}	Tells TGS identity of Web server
$Nonce_2$	A random value that client produces to be repeated in message (4) to assure that the response is fresh and has not been replayed by an attacker
$Authenticator_c$	Client transmits an authenticator, which includes the ID and address of client's user and a timestamp
$Ticket_{ws}$	Ticket to be used by client to access Web server
$K_{c,ws}$	Copy of session key accessible to client created by TGS to permit secure exchange between client and Web server without requiring to share a permanent key
K_{ws}	Ticket is encrypted with key known only to TGS and Web server, to prevent tampering
$Realm_{ws}$	Tells client realm of Web server
TS_1	Informs TGS of time this authenticator was generated

Table 3. Symbols of message (5) and message (6)

Symbol	Meaning
WS	Web server
TS_2	Informs Web server of time this authenticator was generated
$Subkey$	The client's choice for an encryption key to be used to protect this specific application session. If this field is omitted, the session key uses the ticket ($K_{c,s}$)
$Seq\#$	An optional field that specifies the starting sequence number to be used by Web server for messages sent to the client during this session. Message may be sequence number to detect replays

3 Distributing the Key Based on ECC

For a prime curve over Z_p: $y^2 \bmod p = (x^3 + ax + b)\bmod p$

First a large integer q, which is either a prime number p or an integer of the form 2^m and elliptic curve parameters a and b. This defines the elliptic group of points $E_q(a,b)$. Next, pick a base point $G=(x_1,y_1)$ in $E_q(a,b)$ whose order is a very large value n. The order n of a point G on an elliptic curve the smallest positive integer n such that $nG=0$. $E_q(a,b)$ and G are parameters of the cryptosystem known to all participants.

1) Distributing public key and private key of AS

Authentication Server selects an integer n_A less than n. This is Authentication Server's private key. Authentication Server then generates a public key $P_A = n_A \times G$, the public key is a point in $E_q(a,b)$.

2) Distributing public key and private key of TGS and Web server

Authentication Server selects two integer $n_T < n$ and $n_S < n$. They are TGS and Web server's private key. Authentication Server then generates their public key $P_T = n_T \times G$ and $P_S = n_S \times G$.

3) Distributing public key and private key of users

Authentication Server selects n integer $n_{u1} < n$, $n_{u2} < n$ ... $n_{uN} < n$. They are users' private key. Authentication Server then generates their public key $P_{u1} = n_{u1} \times G$, $P_{u2} = n_{u2} \times G$ ... $P_{uN} = n_{uN} \times G$.

4 Distributing Shared Secret-Key by Diffie-Hellman Algorithm

The Diffie-Hellman algorithm depends for its effectiveness on the difficulty of computing discrete logarithms. First, we define a primitive root α of the large prime number p.

1) Generating shared secret-key of AS and TGS

AS selects a random integer $X_A < q$ and computers $Y_A = \alpha^{X_A} \bmod q$, AS encodes Y_A as a point Z_A and chooses a random positive integer k to encrypt Z_A by TGS's public key P_T and sends this ciphertext C_A to TGS. C_A consists of the pair of points: $C_A = \{kG, Z_A + kP_T\}$. Similarly, TGS independently selects a random integer $X_T < q$ and computers $Y_T = \alpha^{X_T} \bmod q$, AS encodes Y_T as a point Z_T and chooses a random positive integer k to encrypt Z_T by AS's public key P_A and sends this ciphertext $C_T = \{kG, Z_T + kP_A\}$ to AS.

AS obtains Z_T from decrypted C_T by its own private key n_A. To decrypt C_T, AS multiplies the first point in the pair by AS's private key n_A and subtracts the result from the second point: $Z_T + kP_A - n_A(kG) = Z_T + k(n_A G) - n_A(kG) = Z_T$, thus AS gets Y_T. By the same token, TGS gets Y_A.

AS computers the shared secret-key $K_{A-T} = (Y_T)^{X_A} \bmod q$ and TGS computers the shared secret-key as $K_{A-T} = (Y_A)^{X_T} \bmod q$. These two calculations generate identical result:

$$
\begin{aligned}
K_{A-T} &= (Y_T)^{X_A} \bmod q \\
&= (\alpha^{X_T} \bmod q)^{X_A} \bmod q \\
&= (\alpha^{X_T})^{X_A} \bmod q \\
&= (\alpha^{X_T X_A}) \bmod q \\
&= (\alpha^{X_A})^{X_T} \bmod q \\
&= (\alpha^{X_A} \bmod q)^{X_T} \bmod q \\
&= (Y_A)^{X_T} \bmod q
\end{aligned}
$$

2) Generating shared secret-key of AS and Web server(users)

Using same method and *1)*, AS produces the shared secret-key K_{A-L} (AS and Web server), K_{A-U1} (AS and User1), K_{A-U2} (AS and User2), ..., K_{A-UN} (AS and UserN).

5 Security Analysis

The security of this algorithm of producing shared secret-key can be attributed to three factors:

1) The security of ECC

The security of ECC depends on the difficulty of to computer n_A given P_A and $n_A \times G$ (to computer n_T given P_T and $n_T \times G$, to computer n_S given P_S and $n_S \times G$, to computer n_{ul} given P_{ul} and $n_{ul} \times G$, etc), this is referred to as the elliptic curve logarithm problem. Table 4 compares various algorithms to depend on comparable key sizes for computational effort of cryptanalysis [4]. As can be found, ECC has a considerably smaller key size compared to RSA. Thus, it is more secure to use ECC with a shorter key length than RSA.

Table 4. Comparing between ECC and RSA/DSA

Symmetric Scheme (key size in bits)	ECC-Based Scheme (size of n in bits)	RSA/DSA (modulus size in bits)
56	112	512
80	160	1024
112	224	2048
128	256	3072
192	384	7680
256	512	15360

2) The security of Diffie-Hellman algorithm

In discrete logarithms $Y_A = \alpha^{X_A} \bmod q$, to computer X_A given Y_A and α and q is difficulty, thus attacker can not calculate confidential X_A of AS, confidential X_T of TGS, confidential X_L of Web server and confidential X_U of users, this is referred to as difficulty of computing discrete logarithms.

3) Resisting Man-in-the-Middle attack

The scheme is secure against a man-in-the-middle (a attacker) attack, if AS and TGS wish to generate shared secret-key, the attack proceeds as follows:

① Attacker prepares for the attack to produce two random integer $X_{M-A} < q$ and $X_{M-T} < q$, and then computers the corresponding $Y_{M-A} = \alpha^{X_{M-A}} \bmod q$ and $Y_{M-T} = \alpha^{X_{M-T}} \bmod q$.

② AS sends ciphertext C_A that includes Y_A and is encrypted by TGS's public key to TGS. Attacker intercepts C_A, but he can not obtain Y_A because he does not know TGS's private key n_T to decrypt C_A. Similarly, Attacker can intercept C_T, but he can not obtain Y_T.

③ Attacker can not imitate a man-in-the-middle to produce a pair shared secret-key K_{M-A} (shared secret-key of attacker and AS) with Y_A and K_{M-T} (shared secret-key of attacker and TGS) with Y_T.

④ Similarly, Attacker can not imitate a man-in-the-middle to attack the other user and server.

6 Conclusion

The shared secret-key negotiation is security core in the Kerberos protocol; it is also a hot research field of information security. In this paper, we adopt Diffie-Hellman algorithm to generate the shared secret-key, using ECC, man-in-the-middle attack can be resisted, and whole system shows high security.

References

1. Küsters, R., Tuengerthal, M.: Ideal Key Derivation and Encryption in Simulation-Based Security. In: Kiayias, A. (ed.) CT-RSA 2011. LNCS, vol. 6558, pp. 161–179. Springer, Heidelberg (2011)
2. Jia, K., Chen, X., Xu, G.: The improved public key encryption algorithm of Kerberos protocol based on braid groups. In: 2008 International Conference on Wireless Communications, Networking and Mobile Computing (WiCOM 2008), vol. 1, pp. 1–4 (2008)
3. Liu, K.-l., Qing, S.-h., Meng, Y.: An Improved Way on Kerberos Protocol Based on Public-Key Algorithms. Journal of Software 12(6), 872–877 (2001)
4. Jurisc, A., Menezes, A.: Elliptic Curve Cryptography. Dobb's Journal, 135–140 (April 1997)
5. Cao, L.-C.: Enhancing Distributed Web Security Based on Kerberos Authentication Service. In: Wang, F.L., Gong, Z., Luo, X., Lei, J. (eds.) Web Information Systems and Mining. LNCS, vol. 6318, pp. 171–178. Springer, Heidelberg (2010)
6. Rao, G.S.V.R.K.: Threats and security of Web services - a theoretical short study. In: Proceedings of IEEE International Symposium Communications and Information Technology, vol. 2(2), pp. 783–786 (2004)
7. Seixas, N., Fonseca, J., Vieira, M.: Looking at Web Security Vulnerabilities from the Programming Language Perspective: A Field Study. Software Reliability Engineering 1, 129–135 (2009)

Pulse Amplitude Modulation Time-Hopping Spread-Spectrum Based on Balance Gold Sequences[*]

Zhao-Xia Zhang[1,2] and Ming-Jiang Zhang[1]

[1] Department of Physics and Optoelectronics,
Taiyuan University of Technology, Tai Yuan, China
[2] State Key Laboratory of Millimeter Waves,
Southeast University, Nanjing 210096, China
zhangzhaoxia1@126.com

Abstract. To solve the problem that the spectrum spread rate is held in the clock period. A method based on the Balance Gold Sequences (BGS) is presented in Ultra-Wide Band communications. The theoretical bit error rate (BER) performance is deduced after building a mathematical model for the system. Computer simulation shows that the Balance Gold Sequences can obtain higher system capacity and superior performance over the Traditional Pseudorandom Code (TPNC) in additive noise and multi-user environments. Finally, the simulation results show that the high system capacity can be achieved in different multi-user interference (MUI).

Keywords: Balance Gold Sequences, Ultra-wide Band, Time-Hopping, Impulse Radio.

1 Introduction of UWB System

The UWB technique has been utilized for military radar technique so far. Recently, the technique has been paid much attention and debated by IEEE 801.15.3[1] for standardization. In this paper, a spread-spectrum (SS) [2-5] system is described in which the transmitted signal occupies an extremely large bandwidth even in the absence of data modulation.

Modulation of TH-SS impulse radio is accomplished through the time shifting of pulses. The key motivations for using TH-SS impulse radio are the ability to highly resolve multi-path and the availability of the technology to implement and generate UWB signals with relatively low complexity. This paper describes a modulation method that can be supported by current technology and presents receiver processing under additive white Gaussian noise channel condition.

[*] Project supported by open subject of the State Key Laboratory of Millimeter Waves(Grant No: K201108) and the young fund of Taiyuan University of Technology(Grant No:03010328) and the Doctor Fund of Taiyuan University of Technology(Grant No:03020723).

H. Deng et al. (Eds.): AICI 2011, CCIS 237, pp. 108–115, 2011.

2   Time-Hopping System Using Balance Gold Sequences

2.1   The Definition of Gold Sequences

Gold sequences have been proposed by Gold in 1967 and 1968. Gold codes can be generated by linearly combining two m-sequences with different offset in Galois field. Gold codes have three-valued autocorrelation and cross-correlation function with values $\{-1, -t(r), t(r) - 2\}$, where

$$t(r) = \begin{cases} 2^{(r+1)/2} + 1 & for\,odd\ \ r \\ 2^{(r+2)/2} + 1 & for\,even\ \ r \end{cases} \tag{1}$$

Where r is the degree of polynomials.

The generation of Gold codes is very simple. Using two preferred m-sequence generators of degree r, with a fixed non-zero seed in the first generator, 2r Gold codes are obtained by changing the seed of the second generator from 0 to 2r-1. Another Gold sequence can obtained by setting all zero to the first generator, which is the second m-sequence itself. In total, 2r+1 Gold codes are available. The software for Gold code generators has been written intuitively using the theory above. One of the methods of generating gold sequences is shown in Fig.1.

Where $F_1(x)$ and $F_2(x)$ are two polynomials respectively.

2.2   The Generation of Balance Gold Sequences

In this paper, we use balance gold sequences (BGS) [6] as time-hopping code. In the spectrum spread communications, the spectrum spread rate is held in the clock period, and the sequence length of address code depends on the quotient of clock rate with information rate. So, the application of the balance gold sequences (BGS) is limited in the practical engineering. The balance gold sequence has wider application with the method. It can be used as time-hopping (TH) code of spread spectrum and meets the particular requirements of some spread spectrum communications systems over traditional pseudorandom code (TPNC).

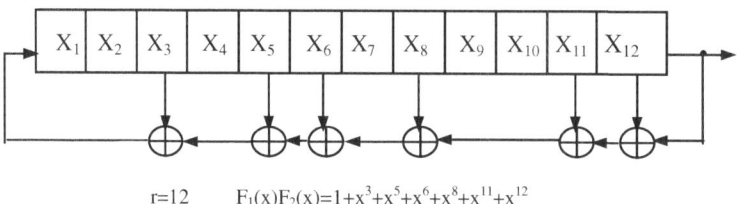

r=12 $F_1(x)F_2(x)=1+x^3+x^5+x^6+x^8+x^{11}+x^{12}$

Fig. 1. Simplified model of generation Gold sequences of serial type

2.3 The Model of the Transmitter Signal

A typical TH format of the nth impulse radio transmitter output signal $s_{tr}^{(n)}(t)$ [7] is:

$$s_{tr}^{(n)}(t) = \sum_{n=-\infty}^{\infty} \sqrt{E_{tx}^{(n)}} \, p_0(t - jT_s - c_j^{(n)}T_c) \tag{2}$$

Where $\sqrt{E_{tx}^{(n)}}$ is the transmitted power of a pulse. $p_0(t)$ is the transmitted pulse waveform. T_s is the pulse repetition duration. T_c is the chip duration.

2.4 Random/Pseudorandom Time-Hopping

To eliminate catastrophic collisions in multiple accessing, each link uses a distinct pulse-shift pattern $c_j^{(n)}$ called a TH sequence. These hopping sequences $c_j^{(n)}$ are pseudorandom with the period N_p, with each element an integer in the range $0 \le c_j^{(n)} \le N_h$. Therefore the TH sequences provides an additional time shift to each pulse in the pulse train, with the jth monocycle undergoing an added shift of $c_j^{(n)}T_c$, which are discrete values between 0 and N_hT_c. In this paper, we consider replacing $c_j^{(n)}$ with balance gold sequences (BGS).

In this model, the UWB pulse denoted by $p_0(t)$ is assumed to include the differential effects in the transmitter and receiver antenna systems. A typical pulse employed in [8-9] is the second derivative of a Gaussian pulse given by:

$$p_0(t) = \left[1 - 4\pi\left(\frac{r}{T_M}\right)\right]\exp\left[-2\pi\left(\frac{t}{T_M}\right)^2\right] \tag{3}$$

2.5 Receiver Signal Processing

In the receiver, for simplicity, we assume that the multi-path components arrives at the same integer multiple of a minimum path resolution time. Assuming the minimum path resolution time T_M, the received waveform can be expressed as follows:

$$r(t) = \sum_{n=1}^{N_u} \sum_{j=-\infty}^{j=\infty} \sqrt{E_{RX}^{(n)}} \, p_0\left(t - jT_s - c_j^{(n)}T_c - \tau^{(n)}\right) + n(t) \tag{4}$$

Where $\sqrt{E_{Rx}^{(n)}}$ is the receiver power of each pulse. $\tau^{(n)}$ is the transmitted delay, and $n(t) \sim N(0,1)$ is the additive white Gaussian noise. N_u is the number of transmitters.

Assuming the model is symmetrical, thus we can only analyze one effective link. Assuming the referenced receiver is coming from the signal of the first transmitter and the reference receiver is completely synchronous with the first transmitter, we can rewrite the received signal as follows:

$$r(t) = r_u(t) + r_{mui}(t) + n(t) \tag{5}$$

here $r_u(t)$ and $r_{mui}(t)$ denote respectively the useful signal and multi-user interference (MUI) of the transmitter input. $r_u(t)$ and $r_{mui}(t)$ can be of the form as follows:

$$r_u(t) = \sum_{j-0}^{N_s-1} \sqrt{E_{RX}^{(1)}} \, p_0(t - jT_s - c_j^{(1)}T_c)$$

(6)

$$r_{mui}(t) = \sum_{n=2}^{N_u} \sum_{j=-\infty}^{\infty} \sqrt{E_{RX}^{(n)}} \, p_0(t - jT_s - c_j^{(n)}T_c - \tau^{(n)})$$

(7)

Where N_s is the number of pulses of each bit.

Where $t \in [0, T_b]$, under the circumstances of soft decision detection ,the output of the receiver can be shown as follows:

$$Z = \int_0^{T_b} r(t)m(t)dt$$

(8)

Where $m(t)$ is the relative mask, and can be written as follows:

$$m(t) = \sum_{j=0}^{N_s-1} p_0(t - jT_s - c_j^{(1)}T_c)$$

(9)

Here, we use the detection of maximum likelihood (ML) rule, and this means the comparison between the Z inferred from equation (8) and threshold 0. ML detection rule can be written as follows:

$$\begin{cases} Z > 0 \Rightarrow \hat{b} = 0 \\ Z < 0 \Rightarrow \hat{b} = 1 \end{cases}$$

(10)

Where $\hat{b}$ represents the estimated bit. Combine equation (5) with equation (8), we can obtain equation (11) as follows:

$$Z = Z_u + Z_{mui} + Z_n$$

(11)

Where Z_u, Z_{mui} and Z_n represents the useful signal, MUI noise and the additive noise of the receiver output respectively.

2.6 Signal Noise Ratio (SNR) of the Receiver

In the hypothesis of standard Gaussian approximation (SGA), $Z_{mui} \sim N(0, \sigma_{mui}^2)$ and $Z_n \sim N(0, \sigma_n^2)$. Bit error rate can be written as follows:

$$\text{Pr}_b = \frac{1}{2} erfc\left(\sqrt{SNR}\right)$$

(12)

$$SNR = \frac{E_b}{\sigma_n^2 + \sigma_{mui}^2} \tag{13}$$

Where E_b is the power of the useful signals.

$$
\begin{aligned}
E_b &= (Z_u)^2 \\
&= \left(\sqrt{E_{RX}^{(1)}} \sum_{j=0}^{N_s-1} \int_{jT+c_j^{(1)}T_c}^{jT+c_j^{(1)}T+T_c} p_0(t - jT_s - c_j^{(1)}T_c) p_0(t - jT_s - c_j^{(n)}T_c) dt \right)^2 \\
&= E_{Rx}^{(1)} N_s^2 (\int_0^{T_c} p_0(t) p_0(t) dt)^2 \\
&= E_{Rz}^{(1)} N_s^2
\end{aligned}
\tag{14}
$$

The variance σ_n^2 of the additive noise which is the binary pulse amplitude modulation (PAM) receiver output can be expressed as follows:

$$\sigma_n^2 = N_s \frac{N_0}{2} \tag{15}$$

The variance σ_{mui}^2 of the MUI which is the binary PAM receiver output can be expressed as follows:

$$\sigma_{mui}^2 = \frac{N_s}{T_s} \sigma_M^2 \sum_{n=2}^{N_u} E_{Rx}^{(n)} \tag{16}$$

Where $\sigma_M^2 = \int_{-T_M}^{T_M} R_0^2(\tau) d\tau$, $R_0(\varepsilon)$ is the auto-relation function of the pulse waveform $p_0(t)$. Thus SNR_n and SIR can be shown as follows:

$$SNR_n = \frac{E_b}{\sigma_n^2} = \frac{E_{Rx}^{(1)} N_s^2}{N_s \frac{N_0}{2}} = 2 \frac{N_s E_{RX}^{(1)}}{N_0} = \frac{2E_b}{N_0} \tag{17}$$

$$SIR = \frac{E_b}{\sigma_{mui}^2} = \frac{E_{RX}^{(1)} N_s^2}{\frac{N_s}{T_s} \sigma_M^2 \sum_{n=2}^{N_u} E_{Rx}^{(n)}} = \frac{N_s T_s}{\sigma_M^2} \frac{E_{RX}^{(1)}}{\sum_{n=2}^{N_u} E_{RX}^{(n)}} \tag{18}$$

3   Results and Matlab Simulations

In this section, we present the performance of the proposed system by computer simulation. We assume the bit rate of system to be 55.55Mbps around and the channel to be additive Gaussian white noise channel. We use traditional pseudorandom code (TPNC) and the balance gold sequences (BGS) for comparison and present the BER performance in Fig.2-Fig.5. In Fig.2, we present the 2PAM BER performance under $N_s = 1$ by single user detection (SUD) scheme. Also, we present the 2PAM BER performance under $N_s = 3$ by SUD scheme in Fig.3. In these figures, we can observe that the proposed Gold-UWB system exhibits better performance than that of the traditional PAM-TH-UWB system. The results obtained using multi-user detection (MUD) of 12 users is presented in Fig.4. In Fig.5, the results obtained using MUD of 20 users is presented. In these figures, we observed that the proposed balance Gold-UWB system exhibits same BER performance both in SUD and MUD conditions, which is in accord with the theoretical results discussed in last section.

We consider the balance gold sequences (BGS) of length N=63 generated using preferred maximal length sequences having generator polynomials (211)8 and (217)8 to be used as spreading sequences. The method explained in this paper can as well be used with little modifications to evaluate performance of TH-UWB systems.

In Fig.2-Fig.5, N_s is the number of pulses per bit. T_c is the chip time[s]. f_c is the sampling frequency. N_p is the periodicity of the TH code.

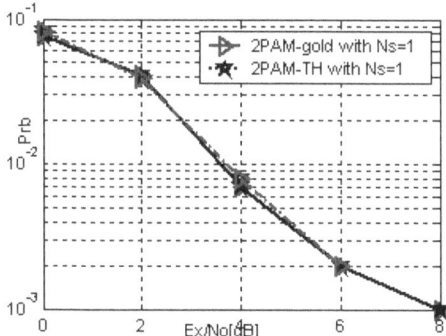

Fig. 2. Comparison of BER performance of BGS-UWB/2PAM, TPNC-UWB/2PAM, with SUD, Ns=1,Np=3000,Tc=1e-9, fc=5e10

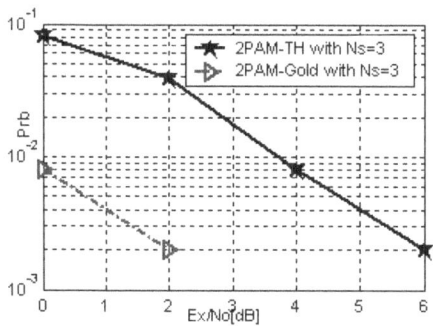

Fig. 3. Comparison of BER performance of BGS-UWB/2PAM, TPNC-UWB/2PAM, with SUD, Ns=3,Np=3000,Tc=1e-9, fc=5e10

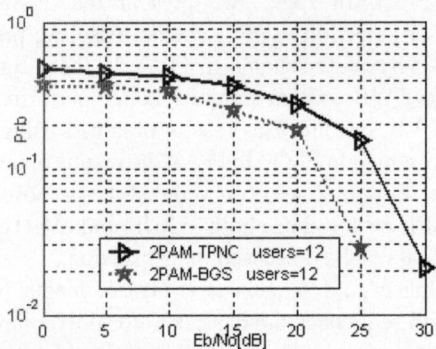

Fig. 4. Comparison of BER performance of BGS-UWB/2PAM, TPNC-UWB/2PAM, with MUD, Ns=3,Np=3000,Tc=5e-10, fc=5e10, users=12

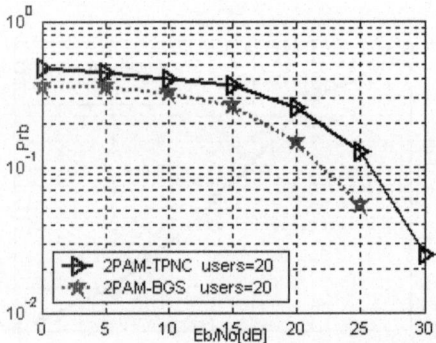

Fig. 5. Comparison of BER performance of BGS-UWB/2PAM, TPNC-UWB/2PAM, with MUD, Ns=3,Np=3000,Tc=3e-10, fc=5e10, users=20

4 Conclusions

In this paper, we proposed a balance Gold-UWB wireless communication system which can lower Bit error ratio than traditional TH-UWB system. By incorporating traditional TH-UWB scheme and enhanced balance gold spreading spectrum, we built a mathematical model for Gold-UWB wireless system. By presenting theoretical BER performance, we improved the proposed system performance. Throughout computer simulation, we showed that performance of the proposed is superior to the systems of conventional scheme and is compatible with the MUD system.

Furthermore, since the proposed system can obtain high performance with low computational complexity, we conclude that our scheme can be a good candidate for UWB communication system.

References

1. http://www.ieee802.org/15/pub/TG3.html
2. Scholtz, R.A.: The spread-spectrum concept. IEEE Trans. Commun. COM-25, 748–755 (1977)
3. Pickholtz, R.L., Schilling, D.L., Milstein, L.B.: Theory of spread-spectrum communications–A tutorial. IEEE Trans. Commun. COM-30, 855–884 (1982)
4. Simon, M.K., Omura, J.K., Scholtz, R.A., Levitt, B.K.: Spread Spectrum Communications Handbook revised ed. McGraw-Hill, New York (1994)
5. Petrson, R.L., Xiemer, R.E., Borth, D.E.: Introduction to Spread Spectrum Communications, 1st edn. Prentice Hall, Englewood Cliffs (1995)
6. Jianming, H., Zhiyong, S., Zheng, B.: Analysis of the statistic characteristics of the truncated balance Gold code. Systems Engineering and Electronics 28(5), 646–649 (2006)
7. De Benedetto, M.-G., Giancola, G.: Understanding Ultra Wide Band Radio Fundamentals. Publishing House of Electronics Industry, Beijing (2005)
8. Win, M., Scholtz, R.A.: Ultra-wide bandwidth time-hopping spread spectrum impulse radio for wireless multiple-access communications. IEEE Trans. Commun. 48(4), 679–691 (2000)
9. Scholtz, R.A.: Multiple access with time-hopping impulse modulation. In: Proc. MILCOM 1993, vol. 2, pp. 447–450 (1993)

Improving LD-aCELP's Gain Filter

Shuhong Wu and Gang Zhang

Taiyuan University of Technology
Taiyuan, Shanxi, China
shh_wu@163.com, tyzhgang@tom.com

Abstract. LD-aCELP algorithm has 2.5ms delay and speech coding rate is 8Kbit/s. The adaptive codebook and backward pitch detection is used. LD-aCELP depends on the Levinson-Durbin (L-D) algorithm to update gain filter coefficients. Because quantizer has not existed at optimizing gain filter, the quantization SNR can not be used to evaluate its performance. We use a new scheme to estimate SNR so that the gain predictor can be separately optimized with the quantizer. In this paper, using this scheme L-D method is replaced by three different methods which are the weighted L-S recursive filter, the finite memory recursive filter and the BP neural network, respectively. Experiments showing, they are all very effective to improve gain filter performance. The weighted L-S algorithm has the best effect, which is accordant with real speech coding. Its average segment SNR is higher than LD-aCELP about 0.720dB.

Keywords: LD-aCELP, weighted L-S, finite memory, SNR estimation, gain filter.

1 Introduction

In order to meet ITU requirement that the delay is less than 5ms and coding rate is 8Kbit/s. An 8Kbit/s LD-CELP coding algorithm is present. It is on the base of G.728 [1].The size of frame which is 5 samples in G.728 is extended to 20 samples, and the delay is 2.5ms. Because parametric update frame is same as G.728, the algorithm keeps the almost characters of G.728.Because introducing the adaptive codebook in codebook structure and backward pitch detection in codebook search, the algorithm is called LD-aCELP.

The adaptive codebook vector $\boldsymbol{u}_s$ and fixed codebook vector $\boldsymbol{y}_j$ are used to search the best excitation vectors.

$$\boldsymbol{u}_s = \{u_{s,0}, u_{s,1}, \cdots, u_{s,19}\} \quad s = 0,1,\cdots,N$$

$$\boldsymbol{y}_j = \{y_{j,0}, y_{j,1}, \cdots, y_{j,19}\} \quad j = 0,1,\cdots,M \ . \tag{1}$$

The input speech vector $s(n)$ consisted of 20 consecutive input samples is passed through perceptual weighting filter, resulting in the weighted speech vector $v(n)$, subtracts the zero-input response vector $r(n)$ from the weighted speech vector $v(n)$ to obtain the adaptive codebook search target vector $x(n)$.

H. Deng et al. (Eds.): AICI 2011, Part II, LNAI 7003, pp. 116–123, 2011.
© Springer-Verlag Berlin Heidelberg 2011

$$x(n) = v(n) - r(n).$$ (2)

$\hat{G}_i$, $\hat{g}_k$ is the quantized gain values of adaptive codebook and fixed codebook, respectively. The impulse response matrix function of weighted synthesis filter is H (z). Backward pitch detection is used for the recent excitation so as to obtain pitch period T. After it the exact research is done for adaptive codebook at smaller T range. The detail is described later.

For every adaptive codeword u_s in the range of searching, regards $\hat{G}_i u_s$ as adaptive excitation vectors of the current synthesis filter. Target vector $x(n)$ subtracts the filtered adaptive excitation $\hat{G}_i Hu_s$ to obtain the new target vector $x'(n)$ which is used fixed codebook search[2].

$$x'(n) = [x(n) - \hat{G}_i Hu_s] / \sigma(n).$$ (3)

Where $\sigma(n)$ is the backward gain prediction which is obtained by using the same method as G.728. The new target vector $x'(n)$ is used to search fixed codebook y_j and gain $\hat{g}_k$ until to obtain the best adaptive excitation $\hat{G}_i u_s$ and the best fixed codebook excitation $\sigma(n)\hat{g}_k y_j$, then the best excitation of synthesis filter will be get [3].

$$e(n) = \hat{G}_i u_s + \sigma(n)\hat{g}_k y_j.$$ (4)

Every input vector (20 samples) builds one adaptive period (called frames), LPC coefficients are updated once every frame. Adopting backward adaptive prediction technology [4], only excitation vector and gain index are transmitted to decoder, so there is buffering delay of only 20 samples, which is the 2.5ms delay to 8 KHz sampling rate.

2 SNR Estimation

LD-aCELP searches codebook according to the following equation [5].

$$D = \left\| x_a(n) - \hat{g} a_i Hu_s - \sigma(n)\hat{g}_k Hy_j \right\|^2.$$ (5)

let $x'(n) = [x_a(n) - \hat{g}a_i Hu_s]/\sigma(n)$,then

$$D_{min} = \sigma^2(n) \left\| x'(n) - g_i H(n) y_j \right\|^2.$$ (6)

Where, $\sigma(n)$ is the estimation value of excitation gain, $x'(n)$ is the target vector adjusted by $\sigma(n)$, $H(n)$ is the unit impulse respond of short-term predictor, g_i is gain codeword, and y_j is shape codevector. Therefore, the minimum of (6) equals the minimum follow.

$$\hat{D}_{min} = -2g_i P^T(n)y_j + g_i^2 E_j .$$ (7)

Where, $P(n)=H^T x'(n)$, $Ej= \| Hyj \|$. In (7), let $\partial \hat{D}_{min} / \partial g_j = 0$, we have the exact value of gain codeword.

$$g_j = [P^T(n)y_j]/E_j .$$ (8)

To understand easy, let y_j is normalized unit power. Then (6) can be written in another way

$$D_{min} = \left\| x(n) - G_j(n)H(n)y_j(n) \right\|^2 .$$ (9)

Where $x(n)= \sigma(n)x'(n)$ and $G_j(n)=g_j(n)\sigma(n)$ are the target vector and the exact value of excitation gain not adjusted by gain, respectively. The gain prediction residual error in logarithm domain is

$$\log_2 g_j(n) = \log_2 G_j(n) - \log_2 \sigma(n) .$$ (10)

Let $\hat{G}_j(n)$ denote the value of quantization $G_j(n)$[5]. Use $Q\{x\}$ to denote the quantization value of the signal $\{x\}$. Then

$$\log_2 \hat{G}_j(n) = Q\left\{\log_2 g_j(n)\right\} + \log_2 \sigma(n) .$$ (11)

When we choose the predictor, the signals are not quantized, so the true vales are used instead of the quantization value. Thus the system is in an optimal state all the time and the quantization SNR can not be used to evaluate predictor's performance. But we can estimate SNR so that the gain predictor can be separately optimized with the quantizer.

Let $\varepsilon(n) = G_j(n) - \sigma(n)$ is prediction residue, $G_j(n)$ is gain, then

$$\begin{aligned} g_j(n) &= G_j(n)/\sigma(n) \\ &= G_j(n)/[G_j(n) - \varepsilon_j(n)] \\ &= snr_j(n)/[snr_j(n) - 1] \end{aligned}$$ (12)

Where, $snr_j(n) = G_j(n)/\varepsilon(n)$ is the ratio of $G_j(n)$ to $\varepsilon(n)$ at time n, then

$$snr_j(n) = g_j(n)/[g_j(n) - 1] .$$ (13)

From the formula (13), it can be concluded that the more $g_j(n)$ closes to 1, the bigger $snr_j(n)$ devotes to $SNR_{av.}$ Let snr be an observation value of $snr_j(n)$, we can find out the all j of satisfying for $snr_j(n) \geq snr$. Suppose Δ is a level of SNR_{av} selected in advance,

that is $SNR = 10\lg N^{-1} \sum_{k=1}^{N} snr_j^2(k) \geq 20\lg|snr| \geq \Delta$ or $10^{\Delta/20} \leq |snr| = (1 - g_j(n)^{-1})^{-1}$.

If $g_j(n) > 1$, then $g_j(n) \leq (1-10^{-\Delta/20})^{-1}$ For example, let $\triangle = 20$dB, then $g_j(n) \leq 10/9$. If $g_j(n) < 1$, then $g_j(n) \leq (1+10^{-\Delta/20})^{-1}$ For example, let $\triangle = 20$dB, then $g_j(n) \geq 10/11$.

Having considered two kinds of algorithms, the prediction values $\sigma(n)$ of excitation gain is computed out with the formula $\log\sigma(n) = \sum_{i=1}^{p} p_i [\log\hat{\sigma}_e(n-i)] - g(n-i)] + g(n)$,

respectively. Where, the factor $\sigma_e(n)$ (or $\hat{G}_j(n)$) is replaced by $G_j(n)$ and $g_j(n) = G_j(n)/\sigma(n)$. Selecting a level Δ of SNR_{av}, the corresponding ranges are computed as follows.

$$(1+10^{-\Delta/20})^{-1} \leq g_j(n) \leq (1-10^{-\Delta/20})^{-1}. \tag{14}$$

The percentages of $g_j(n)$ satisfied (14) for two algorithm are computed, respectively. The one with bigger percentage is considered as better [4].

3 Gain Filter

Can be proved, suppose if model noise e_t is zero mean and white noise with same distribute, the estimate of the parameter of AR model is convergent to true value on the condition that mean square exists and probability is 1. Through proving of this problem, we can conclude increasing memory recursive formula and finite memory recursive formula.

3.1 Weighted L-S Algorithm

For p order AR model

$$Z(d,n) = H(d,n)\alpha(d,n) + V(d,n). \tag{15}$$

Where $H(d,n) = (\Phi^T(d) \quad \Phi^T(d+1) \quad \cdots \quad \Phi^T(n))^T$, $Z(d,n) = (x_d \quad x_{d+1} \quad \cdots \quad x_n)^T$,

$V(d,n) = (e_d(d,n) \quad e_{d+1}(d,n) \quad \cdots \quad e_n(d,n))^T$ and $P(d,n) = [H^T(d,n)H(d,n)]^{-1}$.

T shows transposition of vector or matrix. Vector $\Phi(t) = (x_{t-1},...,x_{t-p})^T$ is the last p samples, $\alpha(d,n) = (\alpha_1(d,n),...,\alpha_p(d,n))^T$ is the estimate of parameter based on sampling $x_d, x_{d+1},......, x_n$ from the dth sample, $e_t(d,n)$ is white noise with zero mean and variance σ^2.

So the corresponding increasing memory weighted L-S recursive filter formulas are get as follows.

Usually $\gamma_+(d,n)$ is called gain factor of model, $K_+(d,n)$ is called gain matrix, $\hat{e}_{n+1}(d,n)$ is prediction error. Initiate $\Phi^T(0)$ as zero matrix. And initiate $P(0,n) = \delta^{-1}I$,

$$P(d,n+1) = \frac{1}{\lambda}\left[I - K_+(d,n+1)\Phi^T(n+1)\right]P(d,n)$$

$$K_+(d,n+1) = P(d,n)\Phi(n+1)/\gamma_+(d,n+1)$$

$$\gamma_+(d,n+1) = \lambda + \Phi^T(n+1)P(d,n)\Phi(n+1) \tag{16}$$

$$\hat{e}_{n+1}(d,n) = x_{n+1} - \Phi^T(n+1)\hat{\alpha}(d,n)$$

$$\hat{\alpha}(d,n+1) = \hat{\alpha}(d,n) + K_+(d,n+1)\hat{e}_{n+1}(d,n).$$

where the typical value of δ is 0.01or less. $\lambda(0<\lambda<1)$ is the weight factor. Use inequality (14) to decide the capacity of the filter. λ is updated in order to choose the optimal weight factor. The optimal weight factor λ of Levinson-Durbin algorithm is 0.513941 when Δ=10dB. Table 1 is test result of weighted L-S filter when λ are set different value. As can be seen from this table, the optimal weight λ =0.955.

Table 1. 10 Order Weighted L-S Algorithm

Weight λ	Δ=10dB	Δ=20dB	Δ=40dB
0.91	0.554378	0.191413	0.0190882
0.92	0.558221	0.193125	0.0194521
0.93	0.561654	0.194247	0.0197729
0.94	0.56422	0.19510	0.019485
0.95	0.565663	0.195571	0.0196588
0.953	0.565995	0.195516	0.0198181
0.955	0.56604	0.195608	0.0197729
0.96	0.565841	0.195578	0.0196629
0.97	0.563937	0.194915	0.0198387

3.2 Finite Memory Algorithm

For increasing memory formulas (16), Let λ =1 to eliminate the effect of history data from $\hat{\alpha}(d,n+1)$. Finite memory formulas (17) are derived from increasing memory recursive formula. For every new sample data, finite memory algorithm deletes the effect of the oldest signals and maintains the fixed length. So we just need to conclude how to get $\hat{\alpha}(d+1,n+1)$ from $\hat{\alpha}(d,n+1)$.

The memory length is sample number of filter. The test of the memory length starts at 80 and adds 10 every time. Then have a fine adjustment around the former chose

$$P(d+1,n+1)=\left[I+K_{-}(d+1,n+1)\Phi^{T}(d)\right]P(d,n+1)$$

$$K_{-}(d+1,n+1)=P(d,n+1)\Phi(d)/\gamma_{-}(d+1,n+1)$$

$$\gamma_{-}(d+1,n+1)=1-\Phi^{T}(d)P(d,n+1)\Phi(d) \tag{17}$$

$$\hat{e}_{d}(d,n+1)=x_{d}-\Phi^{T}(d)\hat{\alpha}(d,n+1)$$

$$\hat{\alpha}(d+1,n+1)=\hat{\alpha}(d,n+1)-K_{-}(d+1,n+1)\hat{e}_{d}(d,n+1).$$

Length until the best value is obtained. Table 2 is test result of finite memory filter. As can be seen from this table, when memory length is 230, the algorithm's effect is the best.

Table 2. Finite Memory Algorithm

memory length	140	150	220	230	240
Δ=10dB	0.528022	0.531514	0.536312	0.536433	0.536165
Δ=20dB	0.180052	0.181601	0.182866	0.182855	0.182766
Δ=40dB	0.018206	0.0182605	0.0186121	0.0184918	0.018204

3.3 BP Neural Network Algorithm

In order to avoid the great differences among output variables, the input data of BP neural network are preprocessed with linearity normal scheme. To make up its structure, we use firstly one hidden layer which number of nodes should be as few as possible, and then increase by one node time and again until the effect is satisfied or increase another hidden layer. Its framework is denoted as *I-H-O* which indicates the input nodes *I*, the hidden nodes *H* and the output nodes *O*. In Table 3, several well BP network are listed out.

Table 3. BP Neural Network

BP structure	5-3-1	5-10-8-1	5-8-4-1	7-5-8-1	7-10-6-1
Δ=10dB	0.519069	0.531315	0.530974	0.531365	0.531214
Δ=20dB	0.177745	0.1803281	0.180293	0.179967	0.180240
Δ=40dB	0.0178848	0.0183704	0.0181708	0.0183385	0.0182479

4 Gain Quantization

4.1 Principles

Fig.1. is the Gain Quantization block scheme [4]. We sends the 3-bit index $I(n)$ got by quantizing $log_2 g_j(n)$ to decoder while decodes $I(n)$ to get the local quantized signal

$log_2 \hat{g}_j(n)$. Adding the gain estimation $log_2\sigma(n)$ can obtain the local rebuild signal $log_2 \hat{G}_j(n)$. This signal is input to a gain predictor in order to product the gain estimation $log_2\sigma(n)$ which is subtracted from the optimum gain value $log_2G_j(n)$ to have next prediction residual error $log_2g_j(n)$.

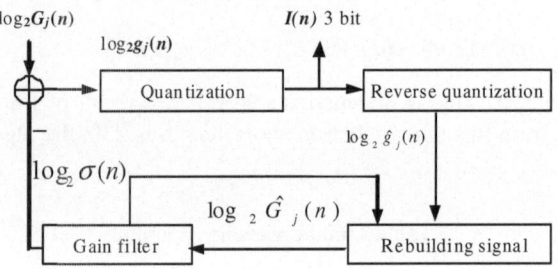

Fig. 1. Gain Quantization

4.2 Gain Quantization

Chinese speech data files are used as training data, which is from institute of acoustics, Chinese academy of sciences. They are sampled through telephone channels and contain the noise. There are 1600 sentences, including 800 male and 800 female utterances, the vocalization time is 417 minutes, and contain about 2 million vectors. Calculate these trained data to obtain the exact value of adaptive codebook gain G and fixed codebook gain g, respectively. We use the fixed quantized method to quantize the adaptive codebook gain, and adopt the iterative method to calculate optimum quantization value [6]. However, the fixed codebook gain is quantized by adaptive quantized method [7].

5 Experimental Result and Discussion

Our laboratory collects 30 utterances to be experimental data, including 15 male and 15 female utterances, and there are totally 15489 vectors. The test results are showed in table 4. From them, we can see the speech coding effect of three new filters is all better than LD-aCELP L-D method. And weighted L-S algorithm is the best. Its SNR is higher than LD-aCELP L-D method about 0.720dB. This result is absolutely accordant with (14) to evaluate filter.

With respect to the computing complexity, LD-aCELP L-D method is 10 divisions and 1750 additions or multiplications. Without window computing, weighted L-S algorithm takes only 2 divisions and 650 additions or multiplications, finite memory algorithm is double of weighted L-S algorithm and the 7-5-8-1structure of the BP network takes 220 divisions and 4640 additions or multiplications. Although BP network has complicate computation, average segment SNR is still higher than LD-aCELP about 0.16dB.

Table 4. Speech Coding Effect

Gain Filter Algorithm	LD-aCELP L-D method	Weighted L-S	Finite memory	7-5-8-1 BP Network
SNR	17.1272	17.8470	17.6466	17.2865

Acknowledgments. The paper is financed by Chinese National Natural Science Foundations (60772101).

References

1. CCITT, Recommendation G.728.: Coding of Speech at 16kbit/s Using Low-Delay Code Excited Linear Prediction. S. Geneva (1992)
2. Shuhong, W., Zhang, G.: 8Kbit/s Low Delay Speech Coding Algorithm with Adaptive Codebook. C. CCCM 1, 273–276 (2009)
3. Bao, C.-c.: Principles of Digital Speech Coding, pp. 175–176. Xidian University Press, Xi'an (2007)
4. Wang, Y., Huang, J.G., Li, F.: Fast Search Algorithm of Adaptive Code-book for Speech Coding. Computer Engineering and Applications 43(15), 69–71 (2007)
5. Xue, C.Y.: The optimization and choosing of the gain filter of the LD-CELP algorithm. Taiyuan University of Technology Master's Dissertation (2005)
6. Zhang, Q.G., Zhang, G.: The Optimal Gain Filter of LD-CELP. Journal of Electronics & Information Technology 28(8), 1533–1536 (2006)
7. Zhang, G., Xie, K.M., Zhang, X.Y., Huang Fu, L.Y.: Improving G.728's Hybrid Window and Excitation Gain. Journal of Electronics & Information Technology (6), 892–895 (2005)

Decidability on Dube's Self-similar Fractals

Qin Wang[1] and Lifeng Xi[2]

[1] Department of Computer Science, Zhejiang Wanli University,
Ningbo 315100, China
qinwang@126.com
[2] Institute of Mathematics, Zhejiang Wanli University, Ningbo 315100, China
xilifengningbo@yahoo.com

Abstract. Dube proved some undecidability on self-affine fractals. In this paper, we obtain the decidability for self-similar fractal of Dube's type. In fact, we prove that the following problems are decidable to test if the Hausdorff dimension of a given Dube's self-similar set is equal to its similarity dimension, and to test if a given Dube's self-similar set satisfies the strong separation condition.

Keywords: Decidability, fractal, self-similar set, dimension, strong separation condition.

1 Introduction

The decidability and undecidability related to Turing machine are very interesting topics in computability theory. We say that some problem is *decidable*, if there is an algorithm to answer "yes" or "no" to the problem for every possible input. Naturally, *undecidable* problem is a decision problem which no algorithm can decide.

There are *uncountably* many undecidable problems [5]:

Turing Halting Problem,

Post's Corresponding Problem (PCP),

Wang Tiling Problem, $\cdots$

1.1 IFS and Self-similar Set

Suppose that $\{f_i\}_{i=1}^n$ is a family of contractive self-mapping of Euclidean space R^m, where $f : \mathbf{R}^m \to \mathbf{R}^m$ is contractive, i.e., there exists $\lambda \in (0, 1)$ such that for all $x, y \in \mathbf{R}^m$,

$$|f(x) - f(y)| \le \lambda |x - y|.$$

We says that $\{f_i\}_{i=1}^n$ is an **iterated function system** (IFS). Let $F = \cup_{i=1}^n f_i(F)$ be the invariant set of IFS $\{f_i\}_{i=1}^n$ [4]. We say F satisfies the **strong separation condition** (SSC), if $f_i(F) \cap f_j(F) = \emptyset$ for any $i \ne j$.

For the mapping $S : \mathbf{R}^m \to \mathbf{R}^m$, if there exists $r \in (0, 1)$ such that for all $x, y \in \mathbf{R}^m$, $|S(x) - S(y)| = r|x - y|$, we call S a contractive similitude with its

H. Deng et al. (Eds.): AICI 2011, Part II, LNAI 7003, pp. 124–129, 2011.

ratio r. Given an IFS $\{S_i\}_{i=1}^n$, where S_i is a contractive similitude with ratio r_i, the **similarity dimension** s is defined to be the solution of the equation

$$(r_1)^s + \cdots + (r_n)^s = 1. \tag{1}$$

Then $E = \cup_{i=1}^n S_i(E)$ is called a **self-similar set**.

1.2 Dube's Undecidability on Self-affine Sets

In 1993-1994, by reducing Post's Corresponding Problem (PCP) to the given problem, Dube ([2,3]) discussed the undecidability of the problem on the invariant sets of iterated function systems. For example, Theorem 5 of [2] actually shows that given a self-affine fractal in the plane, it is *undecidable* to test if it satisfies SSC.

Fix an integer $d \geq 3$, let $u = a_1 \cdots a_{n_1}$ and $v = b_1 \cdots b_{n_2}$ be the words composed of the digits from $\{0, 1, \cdots, (d-2)\}$. Denote $|u|$, $|v|$ the lengths of u and v respectively.

The the affine mapping $A_{u,v} : \mathbf{R}^2 \to \mathbf{R}^2$ is defined by

$$A_{u,v} \begin{pmatrix} x \\ y \end{pmatrix} = \begin{pmatrix} \frac{1}{d^{|u|}} x \\ \frac{1}{d^{|v|}} y \end{pmatrix} + \begin{pmatrix} 0.a_1 \cdots a_{n_1} \\ 0.b_1 \cdots b_{n_2} \end{pmatrix}. \tag{2}$$

Here we use d-adic representation of real number, that means

$$x = x_0.x_1 x_2 \cdots = x_0 + x_1 d^{-1} + x_2 d^{-2} + \cdots.$$

Let E be the self-affine set generated by $\{A_{u_i,v_i}\}_{i=1}^k$. Then

$$E = \left\{ \begin{pmatrix} 0.u_{i_1} u_{i_2} \cdots \\ 0.v_{i_1} v_{i_2} \cdots \end{pmatrix} : 1 \leq i_t \leq k \; \forall \; t \right\}.$$

1.3 Dube's Self-similar Sets

In this paper, we consider the Dube's self-similar sets.

Fix an integer $d \geq 3$, let $u = a_1 \cdots a_n$ be a word composed of $\{0, 1, \cdots, (d-2)\}$. Given u, let S_u be the similitude defined by

$$S_u(x) = \frac{1}{d^{|u|}} x + 0.a_1 \cdots a_n = \frac{1}{d^n} x + 0.u. \tag{3}$$

Given words $u_1, \cdots, u_k$, a Dube's self-similar $E_{(u_1,\cdots,u_k)}$ is defined by $E_{(u_1,\cdots,u_k)} = \cup_{i=1}^k S_{u_i}(E_{(u_1,\cdots,u_k)})$. The similarity dimension of $E_{(u_1,\cdots,u_k)}$ is the solution of the function

$$\sum_{i=1}^k \left(\frac{1}{d}\right)^{s|u_i|} = 1.$$

In this paper, we prove the following theorem.

Theorem 1. Given word $u_1, \cdots, u_k$, the following problems on the self-similar set $E_{(u_1,\cdots,u_k)} = \cup_{i=1}^k \left[\frac{E_{(u_1,\cdots,u_k)}}{d^{|u|}} + 0.u_i\right]$ are decidable:

(i) if $E_{(u_1,\cdots,u_k)}$ satisfies the strong separation condition;
(ii) if the Hausdorff dimension of $E_{(u_1,\cdots,u_k)}$ is exactly the similarity dimension.

2   Preliminaries

Denote by $\dim_H$ and $\dim_S$ the Hausdorff dimension and the similarity dimension. As we known, it is difficult to check

$$SSC \text{ or } \dim_H E_{(u_1,\cdots,u_k)} < \dim_S E_{(u_1,\cdots,u_k)}$$

directly. In this section, we will give some conditions which are easy to check.

2.1   Key Lemma

By the techniques in [6], we have the following lemma.
Lemma 1. (i) $\dim_H E_{(u_1,\cdots,u_k)} < \dim_S E_{(u_1,\cdots,u_k)}$ if and only if there are two finite sequences $i_1 \cdots i_m, j_1 \cdots j_t$ with $i_1 \neq j_1$ such that

$$u_{i_1} u_{i_2} \cdots u_{i_m} = u_{j_1} u_{j_2} \cdots u_{j_t}.$$

(ii) $E_{(u_1,\cdots,u_k)}$ does not satisfy SSC if and only if there are two infinite sequences $i_1 i_2 \cdots, j_1 j_2 \cdots$ with $i_1 \neq j_1$ such that

$$u_{i_1} u_{i_2} \cdots = u_{j_1} u_{j_2} \cdots.$$

2.2   Directed Graph

Let $G = (\mathcal{V}, \mathcal{E})$ be a directed graph with vertex set $\mathcal{V}$ and directed-edge set $\mathcal{E}$. In this section, we will consider the following two decision problems.

Question (A): Given a directed graph G, for two different vertexes i and j in G, is there a directed path in G starting from i and ending at j?
Question (B): Given a directed graph G and a vertex i_0 in G, is there an infinity directed path in G starting from vertex i_0?

Lemma 2. Questions (A) and (B) are decidable.
proof. For Question (A), we give a *weighted graph* G' as follows. The vertex set of G' is $\mathcal{V}$, the edge set of G' is

$$\mathcal{E}' = \{e'_{(i,j)} : (i,j) \in \mathcal{V} \times \mathcal{V} \text{ with } i \neq j\},$$

and for every ordered pair (i,j) with $i \neq j$, there is a unique edge $e'_{(i,j)}$ from i to j with weight

$$w(i,j) = \begin{cases} 1 & \text{if there is an edge in } \mathcal{E} \text{ from } i \text{ to } j; \\ |\mathcal{V}| + 1 & \text{if there is no edge in } \mathcal{E} \text{ from } i \text{ to } j. \end{cases}$$

In the weighted graph G', given different vertexes i and j, the Dijkstra's algorithm [1] will obtain the shortest directed path with distance $c(i,j)$ starting from i and ending at j. Then there exists a directed path in G starting from i and ending at j if and only if the shortest distance $c(i,j) < |\mathcal{V}|$.

For Question (B), we write the adjacent matrix $A = (a_{i,j})_{i,j \in \mathcal{V}}$ defined by

$$a_{i,j} = \begin{cases} 1 \text{ if there is edge in } \mathcal{E} \text{ from } i \text{ to } j; \\ 0 \text{ if there is no edge in } \mathcal{E} \text{ from } i \text{ to } j. \end{cases}$$

Write $A^l = (a_{i,j}^{(l)})_{i,j \in \mathcal{V}}$. We conclude that there is an infinity path starting from i_0 if and only if there is a path of length $|\mathcal{V}|$ starting from i_0. In fact, if we have a path $e_1 e_2 \cdots e_{|\mathcal{V}|}$ of length $|\mathcal{V}|$ passing through the vertexes

$$i_0, i_1, \cdots, i_{|\mathcal{V}|} \text{ with } e_k \in \mathcal{E}_{i_{k-1}, i_k} \text{ for all } k,$$

then there are two indexes $k_1 < k_2$ such that $i_{k_1} = i_{k_2}$, i.e., two vertexes coincide. Therefore

$$e_1 \cdots e_{k_1} (e_{k_1+1} \cdots e_{k_2})(e_{k_1+1} \cdots e_{k_2})(e_{k_1+1} \cdots e_{k_2}) \cdots$$

is an infinity path starting from i_0. To test if there is a path of length $|\mathcal{V}|$ starting from i_0, we only need to check the sum $\sum_{j \in \mathcal{V}} a_{i_0, j}^{(|\mathcal{V}|)}$ of i_0-th row of $A^{|\mathcal{V}|}$. Then there is an infinity path starting from i_0 if and only if $\sum_{j \in \mathcal{V}} a_{i_0, j}^{(|\mathcal{V}|)} > 0$.   **Q.E.D.**

3   Directed Graph for Dube's Self-similar Sets

Fix the words $u_1, \cdots, u_k$, we will construct a directed graph. Before the construction, we give some notations as follows.

3.1   Notations

Given a word $u = a_1 \cdots a_n$ and an integer i with $1 \leq i \leq n$, let

$$u|_i = a_i \cdots a_n.$$

For $u = a_1 \cdots a_n$ and $v = b_1 \cdots b_m$, we denote $u \prec v$, if $u \neq v$ and

$$n < m \text{ and } a_i = b_i \text{ for all } i \leq n.$$

Consider the set of words

$$\Omega = \{u : u = (u_t)|_i \text{ for some } 1 \leq t \leq k \text{ and } i \leq |u_t|\}.$$

3.2   Directed Graph

We denote by $(u, v)(\in \Omega \times \{u_1, \cdots, u_k\})$ a vertex, if $u \in \Omega$, $v \in \{u_1, \cdots, u_k\}$, and

$$v \prec u, u \prec v \text{ or } v = u.$$

We say that a vertex (u, v) is an *initial point*, if

$$u \neq v \text{ and } u, v \in \{u_1, \cdots, u_k\}.$$

We say that a vertex (u, v) is a *terminate point*, if

$$u = v \in \{u_1, \cdots, u_k\}.$$

Given vertexes (u, v) and (u', v'), when $v \neq u$, i.e., (u, v) is not the terminate point, we have an edge from (u, v) to (u', v'), if

$$u' = \begin{cases} u\big|_{|u|-|v|} & \text{if } v \prec u, \\ v\big|_{|v|-|u|} & \text{if } u \prec v. \end{cases}$$

Given vertexes (u, v) and (u', v'), when $v = u$, i.e., (u, v) is a terminate point, we have an edge from (u, v) to (u', v'), if (u', v') is an initial point.

Then we have a directed graph G^*.

3.3   Proof of Theorem 1

In fact, Theorem 1 follows from Lemma 2 and the following proposition.

Proposition 1. (i) $\dim_H E_{(u_1, \cdots, u_k)} < \dim_S E_{(u_1, \cdots, u_k)}$ if and only if there is a directed path in G^* starting from an *initial point* and ending at a *terminate point*
(ii) $E_{(u_1, \cdots, u_k)}$ does not satisfy SSC if and only if there is an infinite path in G^* starting from an *initial point*.
proof. We only prove (i). By Lemma 1, suppose that there are two finite sequences $i_1 \cdots i_m, j_1 \cdots j_t$ with $i_1 \neq j_1$ such that

$$u_{i_1} u_{i_2} \cdots u_{i_m} = u_{j_1} u_{j_2} \cdots u_{j_t}.$$

Then (u_{i_1}, u_{j_1}) is an initial point with $i_1 \neq j_1$. Without loss of generality, we assume that

$$u_{i_1} \prec u_{j_1}.$$

Then $(u_{j_1}\big|_{|u_{j_1}|-|u_{i_1}|}, u_{i_2})$ is a vertex in G^* and there is an edge from (u_{i_1}, u_{j_1}) to $(u_{j_1}\big|_{|u_{j_1}|-|u_{i_1}|}, u_{i_2})$. Therefore, there is a finite path from an initial point to a terminate point as follows,

$$(u_{i_1}, u_{j_1}) \to (u_{j_1}\big|_{|u_{j_1}|-|u_{i_1}|}, u_{i_2}) \to \cdots \to (u_{j_t}, u_{j_t}),$$

here we assume that $|u_{j_t}| < |u_{i_m}|$. In the same way, we obtain the proof of the other direction.   **Q.E.D.**

Example 1. Fix $d = 5$. Set the words

$$u_1 = 0, u_2 = 01, u_3 = 11.$$

Then $\Omega = \{0, 01, 11, 1\}$ and the initial points are $(0, 01)$ and $(01, 0)$. We get an infinite path from $(0, 01)$

$$(0, 01) \to (1, 11) \to (1, 11) \to (1, 11) \to \cdots,$$

which implies $E_{(u_1,u_2,u_3)}$ does not satisfy SSC. On the other hand, there is no finite path starting from an initial point and ending at a terminate point, which implies that

$$\dim_H E_{(u_1,u_2,u_3)} = \dim_S E_{(u_1,u_2,u_3)}.$$

Compared Theorem 1 with Dube's result, we *fortunately* find that one-dimensional self-similar fractal seems to be much simpler than two-dimensional self-affine fractal.

Acknowledgment. The authors would like to thank professor Zhiying WEN for his helpful discussion. This work is supported by National Natural Science Foundation of China (No. 11071224) and Program for Excellent Talents in University of China.

References

1. Dijkstra, E.W.: A note on two problems in connexion with graphs. Numerische Mathematik 1, 269–271 (1959)
2. Dube, S.: Undecidable problems in fractal geometry. Complex Systems 7(6), 423–444 (1993)
3. Dube, S.: Fractal geometry, Turing machines and divide-and-conquer recurrences. RAIRO Inform. Théor. Appl. 28(3-4), 405–423 (1994)
4. Falconer, K.J.: Fractal geometry. Mathematical foundations and applications. John Wiley & Sons, Chichester (1990)
5. Sipser, M.: Introduction to the theory of computation. Course Technology (2005)
6. Wen, Z.Y.: Mathematical foundations of fractal geometry. Shanghai Scientific and Technological Education Publishing House (2000)

The Expression of Control Law for Zone Constraints Predictive Control

Xiling Zhang, Xionglin Luo, and Shubin Wang

Research Institute of Automation, China University of Petroleum
102249, Beijing, China
zhangxiling08@163.com, luoxl@cup.edu.cn, wsbwyy@126.com

Abstract. For the on-line optimization problem of constrained model predictive control, constraints are considered. However, these considered constraints may cause it become a nonlinear control problem even for the linear plant and model. Therefore, it is difficult to analyze the properties of constrained model predictive control. Based on the Newton control framework, for discrete-time state-space model of linear system, the control law of constrained predictive control is proposed. In this work the constraints are the zone constraints of input and output, and this control law is based on zone control. The state feedback form of presented control law is obtained, and the effect of constraints on control is discussed. Consequently, this proposed control law is applied into a second-order linear system, and simulation results demonstrated its effectiveness.

Keywords: State-space model, predictive control, constraint, control law.

1 Introduction

Model predictive control (MPC) has been widely used in process control of industry due to its characteristics of model prediction, receding optimization, feedback correction, and direct treatment of constraints especially (see [1-6]). Considering the constraints of input, output and/or other variables, MPC can be reduced to optimization problem of quadratic performance index with equality or inequality constraints, which is solved on-line to obtain the control law. The presence of constraints results in on-line optimization problem of constrained model predictive control is nonlinear, even though the plant and model are linear, so it is difficult to obtain the analytical solution of constrained model predictive control (CMPC). In [7-9] when the state of linear system was regarded as parameter, CMPC was expressed as a multi-parametric quadratic program (mp-QP). It was shown that the solution (control input) has a representation of a piecewise linear state feedback on a polyhedral partition of the state space. Then [10-16] developed mp-QP algorithm, but an analytical representation of CMPC hasn't been got. There is no report about the effect of constraints on control law yet.

In this article, based on Newton control framework, for discrete-time state-space model of linear system with the zone constraints of input and output, the control law

H. Deng et al. (Eds.): AICI 2011, Part II, LNAI 7003, pp. 130–140, 2011.
© Springer-Verlag Berlin Heidelberg 2011

of constrained predictive control based on zone control is deducted, and then the effect of constraints on control is discussed. Simulation results of control problem of a second-order linear system are used to show the effectiveness of the derivation and analysis.

2   MPC Law Based on Zone Control without Constraints

The discrete-time state-space model of linear system is

$$\begin{cases} \hat{x}(k+1|k) = G\hat{x}(k|k) + Hu(k) \\ \hat{y}(k|k) = C\hat{x}(k|k) \end{cases}, \tag{1}$$

where $\hat{x}(k+i|k) \in R^n$ is the predicted state vector at time $k+i$, $\hat{x}(k|k) = x(k)$ is the state vector at current time k; input vector $u(k) \in R^m$ is manipulated variable; output vector $y(k) \in R^r$ is controlled variable, $\hat{y}(k|k) = y(k)$ is the output vector at current time k; coefficient matrix $G \in R^{n \times n}, H \in R^{n \times m}, C \in R^{r \times n} \neq 0$.

The general form of performance index to be optimized in existing literatures is

$$\min \sum_{i=1}^{P} \left\| \hat{y}(k+i|k) - y_{sp}(k+i) \right\|_{Q(i)}^2 + \sum_{i=0}^{M-1} \left\| \Delta \hat{u}(k+i|k) \right\|_{R(i)}^2, \tag{2}$$

where $y_{sp}(k+i)$ is reference trajectory or set point of output; P and M are predictive horizon and control horizon respectively. In practical process control of industry, the constraints of manipulated and controlled variables are usually not strict to be at given values, but within a certain range. So we introduce two optimization variables α、β, as shown in Fig. 1, y is always within the constraint zone $[y_{min}, y_{max}]$ by the MPC controller based on zone control, and within the given expected zone $[\varepsilon_{min}, \varepsilon_{max}]$ as possible.

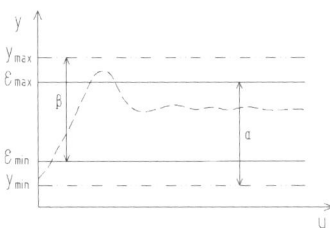

Fig. 1. MPC based on zone control

At time k the performance index (in [19]) to be optimized is

$$\min V(k) = \sum_{i=1}^{P} \left[\left\| \hat{y}(k+i|k) - \hat{\alpha}(k+i|k) \right\|_{Q_1(i)}^2 + \left\| \hat{y}(k+i|k) - \hat{\beta}(k+i|k) \right\|_{Q_2(i)}^2 \right] + \sum_{i=0}^{M-1} \left\| \Delta \hat{u}(k+i|k) \right\|_{R(i)}^2, \tag{3}$$

where $\hat{\alpha}(k+i|k) \in R^r, \hat{\beta}(k+i|k) \in R^r$ are predicted optimization variables introduced for zone control; $Q_1(i), Q_2(i) \geq 0, R(i) \geq 0$ are weight matrices of output and input respectively, and $\|\alpha\|_Q^2 = \alpha^T Q \alpha$. We assume that $M \leq P$, when $i \geq M$, $\Delta \hat{u}(k+i|k) = 0$.

Assuming that all of states are measurable, we adopt matrix and vector form to express the prediction of output:

$$\hat{Y}(k) = S_x x(k) + S_U \hat{U}(k) = Y_0(k) + S_U \hat{U}(k), \tag{4}$$

where $S_x = \begin{bmatrix} CG \\ CG^2 \\ \vdots \\ CG^P \end{bmatrix}, S_U = \begin{bmatrix} CH \\ CGH & CH \\ \vdots & \vdots & \ddots \\ CG^{M-1}H & CG^{M-2}H & \cdots & CH \\ CG^M H & CG^{M-1}H & \cdots & C(GH+H) \\ \vdots & \vdots & & \\ CG^{P-1}H & CG^{P-2}H & \cdots & C\sum_{i=0}^{P-M}G^i H \end{bmatrix}, \hat{U}(k) = \begin{bmatrix} \hat{u}(k|k) \\ \vdots \\ \hat{u}(k+M-1|k) \end{bmatrix}, Y_0(k) =$

$\begin{bmatrix} y_0(k+1) \\ \vdots \\ y_0(k+P) \end{bmatrix} = S_x x(k)$.

Let $\hat{\alpha}(k) = \begin{bmatrix} \hat{\alpha}(k+1|k) \\ \vdots \\ \hat{\alpha}(k+P|k) \end{bmatrix}, \hat{\beta}(k) = \begin{bmatrix} \hat{\beta}(k+1|k) \\ \vdots \\ \hat{\beta}(k+P|k) \end{bmatrix}, \hat{X}(k) = \begin{bmatrix} \hat{U}(k) \\ \hat{\alpha}(k) \\ \hat{\beta}(k) \end{bmatrix}, Q_1 = diag\{Q_1(1), Q_1(2), \ldots, Q_1(P)\}, Q_2 =$

$diag\{Q_2(1), Q_2(2), \ldots, Q_2(P)\}, R = diag\{R(0), R(1), \ldots, R(M-1)\}, f = \begin{bmatrix} -u(k-1)^T & 0_{1 \times m} & \cdots & 0_{1 \times m} \end{bmatrix}^T \in R^{mM},$

$F = \begin{bmatrix} I_m \\ -I_m & I_m \\ & -I_m & I_m \\ & & & \ddots \\ & & & -I_m & I_m \end{bmatrix} \in R^{mM \times mM}$, then

$$V(k) = \left\| \hat{Y}(k) - \hat{\alpha}(k) \right\|_{Q_1}^2 + \left\| \hat{Y}(k) - \hat{\beta}(k) \right\|_{Q_2}^2 + \left\| F\hat{U}(k) + f \right\|_R^2 = const + \hat{X}(k)^T \Phi \hat{X}(k) + 2\Theta^T \hat{X}(k), \tag{5}$$

where $\Phi = \begin{bmatrix} S_U^T(Q_1+Q_2)S_U + F^T RF & -S_U^T Q_1 & -S_U^T Q_2 \\ -Q_1 S_U & Q_1 & 0 \\ -Q_2 S_U & 0 & Q_2 \end{bmatrix}, \Theta = \Gamma Y_0(k) + \Psi f, \Gamma = \begin{bmatrix} S_U^T(Q_1+Q_2) \\ -Q_1 \\ -Q_2 \end{bmatrix}, \Psi = \begin{bmatrix} F^T R \\ 0 \\ 0 \end{bmatrix}$

$\in R^{mM+2rP}$, $const$ denotes constant, which has no impact on optimization computation, thus performance index function can be represented as: $J(k) = \hat{X}(k)^T \Phi \hat{X}(k) + 2\Theta^T \hat{X}(k)$.

The constraints of input and output:

$$u_{min} \leq u \leq u_{max}, y_{min} \leq y \leq y_{max}, \tag{6}$$

and the constraints of α, β :

$$y_{\min} \le \alpha \le \varepsilon_{\max}, \varepsilon_{\min} \le \beta \le y_{\max} , \tag{7}$$

can be represented as:

$$D_1\hat{X}(k) \le d_1, D_2\hat{X}(k) \le d_2, D_3\hat{X}(k) \le d_3, D_4\hat{X}(k) \le d_4 , \tag{8}$$

where $D_1 = \begin{bmatrix} I_{mM} & 0_{mM \times rP} & 0_{mM \times rP} \\ -I_{mM} & 0_{mM \times rP} & 0_{mM \times rP} \end{bmatrix}, D_2 = \begin{bmatrix} S_U & 0_{rP \times rP} & 0_{rP \times rP} \\ -S_U & 0_{rP \times rP} & 0_{rP \times rP} \end{bmatrix}, D_3 = \begin{bmatrix} 0_{rP \times mM} & I_{rP} & 0_{rP \times rP} \\ 0_{rP \times mM} & -I_{rP} & 0_{rP \times rP} \end{bmatrix},$

$D_4 = \begin{bmatrix} 0_{rP \times mM} & 0_{rP \times rP} & I_{rP} \\ 0_{rP \times mM} & 0_{rP \times rP} & -I_{rP} \end{bmatrix}, I$ is identity matrix, $d_1 = \begin{bmatrix} u_{\max}^T, \cdots, u_{\max}^T, -u_{\min}^T, \cdots, -u_{\min}^T \end{bmatrix}^T \in R^{2mM}, d_2$

$= \begin{bmatrix} y_{\max}^T - y_0(k+1)^T, \cdots, y_{\max}^T - y_0(k+P)^T, -y_{\min}^T + y_0(k+1)^T, \cdots, -y_{\min}^T + y_0(k+P)^T \end{bmatrix}^T \in R^{2rP}, d_3 = \begin{bmatrix} \varepsilon_{\max}^T, \end{bmatrix}$

$\cdots, \varepsilon_{\max}^T, -y_{\min}^T, \cdots - y_{\min}^T \end{bmatrix}^T \in R^{2rP}, d_4 = \begin{bmatrix} y_{\max}^T, \cdots, y_{\max}^T, -\varepsilon_{\min}^T, \cdots, -\varepsilon_{\min}^T \end{bmatrix}^T \in R^{2rP}, \varepsilon_{\max}$ and $\varepsilon_{\min}$ are the high and low limit of control zone respectively.

Then the constrained optimization problem of MPC based on control zone can be represented as a standard quadratic programming (QP) problem:

$$\min_{\hat{X}(k)} J(k) = \frac{1}{2}\hat{X}(k)^T 2\Phi\hat{X}(k) + 2\Theta^T \hat{X}(k)$$

$$s.t. \quad \begin{bmatrix} D_1 \\ D_2 \\ D_3 \\ D_4 \end{bmatrix} \hat{X}(k) \le \begin{bmatrix} d_1 \\ d_2 \\ d_3 \\ d_4 \end{bmatrix} . \tag{9}$$

Solving this QP can get the optimal solution of this problem $X^*(k)$, thus $U^*(k) = [I_{mM} \ 0_{mM \times rP} \ 0_{mM \times rP}]X^*(k)$. Let $L = [I_{mM} \ 0_{mM \times rP} \ 0_{mM \times rP}]$, then the analytical $U^*(k)$ without constraints is

$$U^*(k) = -L\Phi^{-1}\Gamma S_x x(k) - L\Phi^{-1}\Psi f . \tag{10}$$

At current time k, only the first move in $U^*(k)$ will be implemented, and the receding calculation of QP will be repeated at next time $k+1$, and therefore MPC law based on zone control is

$$u^*(k) = [I_m \ 0_{m \times (mM-m)}]U^*(k) = K_1 x(k) + K_2 u(k-1) . \tag{11}$$

In this solution, K_1 corresponds to a state feedback term, K_2 corresponds to the past control input term. K_1 and K_2 are functions of model and control parameters.

3   MPC Law Based on Zone Control with Constraints

If there are constraints, we need to solve (9). Assuming that at current time active constraints are denoted as

$$D_1\hat{X}(k) = d_1^a = U_b^a, D_2\hat{X}(k) = d_2^a = Y_b^a - Y_0^a = Y_b^a - S_x^a x(k), D_3\hat{X}(k) = d_3^a = \alpha_b^a, D_4\hat{X}(k) = d_4^a = \beta_b^a , \tag{12}$$

where the superscript a represents active constraints, and the subscript b represents constraint bound. Assuming that at current time k, the number of active constraints in (12) is n_x, n_y, n_α, n_β respectively. D_i^a, d_i^a consist of the rows of D_i, d_i corresponding to active constraints, $i=1,\dots,4$. $U_b^a, Y_b^a, \alpha_b^a, \beta_b^a$ represent active constraint bound of input, output, α, β respectively, which express high or low bounds, or equality constraints. These constraints can also be expressed as

$$A\hat{X}(k) = c_a, \tag{13}$$

where $A = \begin{bmatrix} D_1^a \\ D_2^a \\ D_3^a \\ D_4^a \end{bmatrix}, c_a = \begin{bmatrix} U_b^a \\ Y_b^a - S_x^a x(k) \\ \alpha_b^a \\ \beta_b^a \end{bmatrix}.$

The effect of constraints can be illustrated by a range and null-space decomposition of active constraints matrix A. Because A is ill-conditioned, we adopt QR factorization of A^T with column pivoting. Assuming that the rank of A is $n_r \leq mM+2rP$, then

$$A^T P_A = Q_A R_A = [Q_y \quad Q_z]\begin{bmatrix} R_y \\ 0 \end{bmatrix}, \tag{14}$$

where $P_A \in R^{(n_u+n_y+n_\alpha+n_\beta)\times(n_u+n_y+n_\alpha+n_\beta)}$ is got by interchange of the columns of the identity matrix of the same order. $Q_A \in R^{(mM+2rP)\times(mM+2rP)}$ is an orthogonal matrix satisfying $Q_A^T Q_A = I_{mM+2rP}$. $Q_y \in R^{(mM+2rP)\times n_r}, Q_z \in R^{(mM+2rP)\times(mM+2rP-n_r)}$ is obtained by a partition of the columns of Q_A. $R_y \in R^{n_r\times(n_u+n_y+n_\alpha+n_\beta)}$ is an upper triangular matrix.

Premultiplying both members of (14) by Q_A^T leads to

$$P_A^T A Q_y = R_y^T, A Q_z = 0, \tag{15}$$

hence Q_z corresponds to a basis for the null-space of A. So the full X space can be partitioned into range and null-space components as:

$$X = Q_y X_y + Q_z X_z, \tag{16}$$

where $X_y \in R^{n_r}, X_z \in R^{mM+2rP-n_r}$. The optimal solution of X can be computed separately in terms of these two components, which can be combined at last according to (16). It is observed that X_y is entirely determined by the current active constraints, thus the degree of freedom of input is $\lfloor m - n_r/M \rfloor$.

(1) Calculating X_y: By substitution of (13) in (16), we can obtain

$$AX = C_a = AQ_y X_y + AQ_z X_z = AQ_y X_y. \tag{17}$$

Premultiplying both members of (17) by P_A^T leads to

$$R_y^T X_y = P_A^T C_a. \tag{18}$$

If $n_r=n_x+n_y+n_\alpha+n_\beta$, that is, A is full row-rank, R_y^T is linear lower triangular matrix. The analytical solution of X_y can be (19), where $[B_y\ K_y\ W_y\ Z_y]$ corresponds to a partition of the columns of $R_y^{-T}P_A^T$. It should be noted that the feedback term $-K_yS_x^a x(k)$ will only

$$X_y = R_y^{-T}P_A^T C_a = [B_y\ K_y\ W_y\ Z_y]\begin{bmatrix} U_b^a \\ Y_b^a - S_x^a x(k) \\ \alpha_b^a \\ \beta_b^a \end{bmatrix} = B_y U_b^a + K_y\left[Y_b^a - S_x^a x(k)\right] + W_y\alpha_b^a + Z_y\beta_b^a \quad (19)$$

appear in the optimal solution if there exist active output constraints. If $n_r<n_x+n_y+n_\alpha+n_\beta$, R_y^T becomes a lower trapezoidal matrix, and (18) is over-determined, which corresponds to a disjointed active set in general. In this case we create the partitions:

$$R_y^T = \begin{bmatrix} R_u^T \\ R_l^T \end{bmatrix}, C_a = \begin{bmatrix} C_{au} \\ C_{al} \end{bmatrix}, \quad (20)$$

where $R_u^T \in R^{n_r \times n_r}$ corresponds to the upper triangular part of R_y, $R_l^T \in R^{(n_u+n_y+n_\alpha+n_\beta-n_r)\times n_r}$ is the remaining rectangular matrix, and $C_{au} \in R^{n_r}, C_{al} \in R^{n_u+n_y+n_\alpha+n_\beta-n_r}$ are corresponding partition of C_a. Thus we can solve the lower triangular equation $R_u^T X_y = P_A^T C_{au}$ to obtain X_y. Then the computed X_y can be replaced back in the remaining equations to check the feasibility of (18). If these equalities are compatible, then X_y can still be expressed in the form of (19), with $[B_y\ K_y\ W_y\ Z_y]$ corresponding to a partition of the columns of $R_u^{-T}P_A^T$.

(2) Calculating X_z: X_z can be found by adjusting the remaining degrees of freedom to minimize the objective, if there are any left. By substitution of (16) in (5), we can obtain

$$V(X_z) = constant + 2\Theta^T Q_z X_z + 2X_y^T Q_y^T \Phi Q_z X_z + X_z^T Q_z^T \Phi Q_z X_z. \quad (21)$$

Solving $\dfrac{\partial V(X_z)}{\partial X_z} = 0$ can give:

$$X_z = -(Q_z^T\Phi Q_z)^{-1}Q_z^T(\Theta+\Phi Q_y X_y). \quad (22)$$

Finally combining X_y and X_z according to (16) leads to

$$X = [-(I_{mM+2rP} - B\Phi)Q_y K_y S_x^a - B\Gamma S_x]x(k) - B\Psi f + (I_{mM+2rP} - B\Phi)Q_y B_y U_b^a$$
$$+ (I_{mM+2rP} - B\Phi)Q_y K_y Y_b^a + (I_{mM+2rP} - B\Phi)Q_y W_y\alpha_b^a + (I_{mM+2rP} - B\Phi)Q_y Z_y\beta_b^a, \quad (23)$$

where $B = Q_z(Q_z^T\Phi Q_z)^{-1}Q_z^T$. Then the analytical solution of $U(k)$ with constraints is

$$U(k) = [I_{mM}\quad 0_{mM\times rP}\quad 0_{mM\times rP}]X(k)$$
$$= [-L(I_{mM+2rP} - B\Phi)Q_y K_y S_x^a - LB\Gamma S_x]x(k) - LB\Psi f + L(I_{mM+2rP} - B\Phi)Q_y B_y U_b^a$$
$$+ L(I_{mM+2rP} - B\Phi)Q_y K_y Y_b^a + L(I_{mM+2rP} - B\Phi)Q_y W_y\alpha_b^a + L(I_{mM+2rP} - B\Phi)Q_y Z_y\beta_b^a \quad (24)$$

Therefore the MPC law based on zone control can be expressed as

$$u(k) = [I_m \quad 0_{m \times (mM-m)}]U(k) = K_1^a x(k) + K_2^a u(k-1) + d_u + d_y + d_\alpha + d_\beta . \tag{25}$$

Analogously to the case without constraints, K_1^a corresponds to a state feedback term, K_2^a corresponds to the past control input term. K_1^a and K_2^a are functions of model, control, and active constraints parameters. Comparing (25) with (11), it can be observed that the effect of the active output constraints is adding the active constraints term $-L(I_{mM+2rP} - B\Phi)Q_y K_y S_x^a$, replacing matrix Φ^{-1} by B, and introducing additional terms $d_u, d_y, d_\alpha, d_\beta$, which are functions of active constraint bound.

4 Simulation Example

Consider a second-order linear system (in[20])

$$y(t) = \frac{2}{s^2 + 3s + 2} u(t) , \tag{26}$$

sample the dynamics with $0.1s$ and obtain the state-space representation

$$x(k+1) = \begin{bmatrix} 0.7326 & -0.0861 \\ 0.1722 & 0.9909 \end{bmatrix} x(k) + \begin{bmatrix} 0.0609 \\ 0.0064 \end{bmatrix} u(k) .$$
$$y(k) = \begin{bmatrix} 0 & 1.4142 \end{bmatrix} x(k) \tag{27}$$

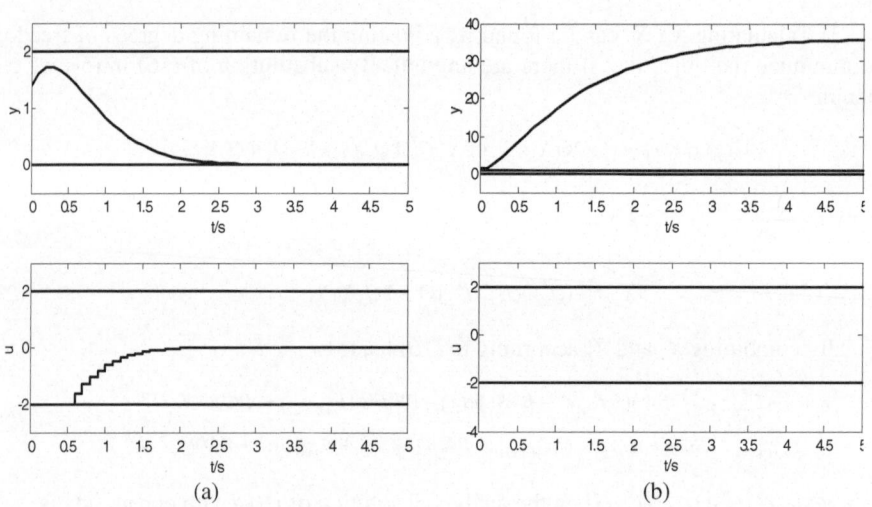

Fig. 2. Closed-loop response: (a) MPC based on zone control. (b) Matlab MPC Toolbox. The dashed lines are the limits of u, y (*solid line*).

The initial condition is $x(0)=[1,1]^T$, $u(0)=-2$. The task is to regulate the output to satisfy constraint $y \in [0,2]$ with the control input constraint $u \in [-2,2]$. To this aim, we design an MPC based on zone control controller previously, and the simulation compared with Matlab MPC Toolbox is shown in Fig.2.The results show that MPC based on zone control fulfills all the input and output constraints, the control action is efficient and in time, and the closed-loop response is fast.

Discuss the effect of input constraint $u \in [u_{min}, u_{max}]$. The output constraint $y \in [0,2]$ is fixed, with different input constraints: (a) $u \in [-\infty,+\infty]$,(b) $u \in [-2,0.5]$,(c) $u \in [-2,-1]$, the MPC controller based on zone control is designed and the closed- loop responses are shown in Fig.3 respectively. It can be seen that as the zone of input constraint becomes more restricted, the controller becomes less aggressive. The results of (a) are identical with Fig. 2. In (b) and (c), u reaches the high limit of control capacity i.e. constraint bound, causes y beyond the output constraint, and the response time is long.

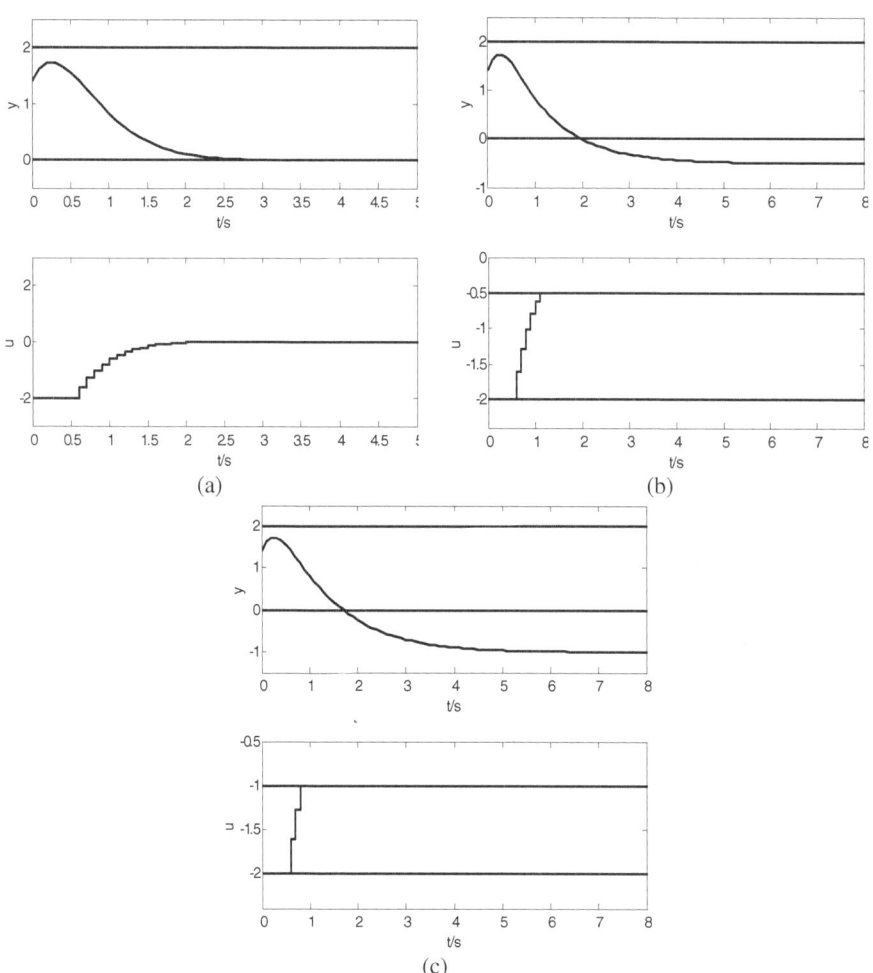

Fig. 3. Closed-loop response with different input constraint: (a) $u \in [-\infty,+\infty]$. (b) $u \in [-2,0.5]$. (c) $u \in [-2,-1]$. The dashed lines are the limits of u, y (*solid line*).

Discuss the effect of output constraint $y \in [y_{min}, y_{max}]$. The input constraint $u \in [-2,2]$ is fixed, with different output constraints: (a) $y \in [-2,2]$,(b) $y \in [0.5,2]$,(c) $y \in [1.5,2]$, the MPC controller based on zone control is designed and the closed-loop responses are shown in Fig. 4 respectively. It can be seen that as the zone of output constraint becomes more restricted, the controller becomes more aggressive. The zone of constraints of (a) is slack, and there is no need of controller action. In (b) and (c), u changes continually within the constraint zone, the output constraint is always satisfied, the response time is fast, and y is steady on the constraint bound in the end.

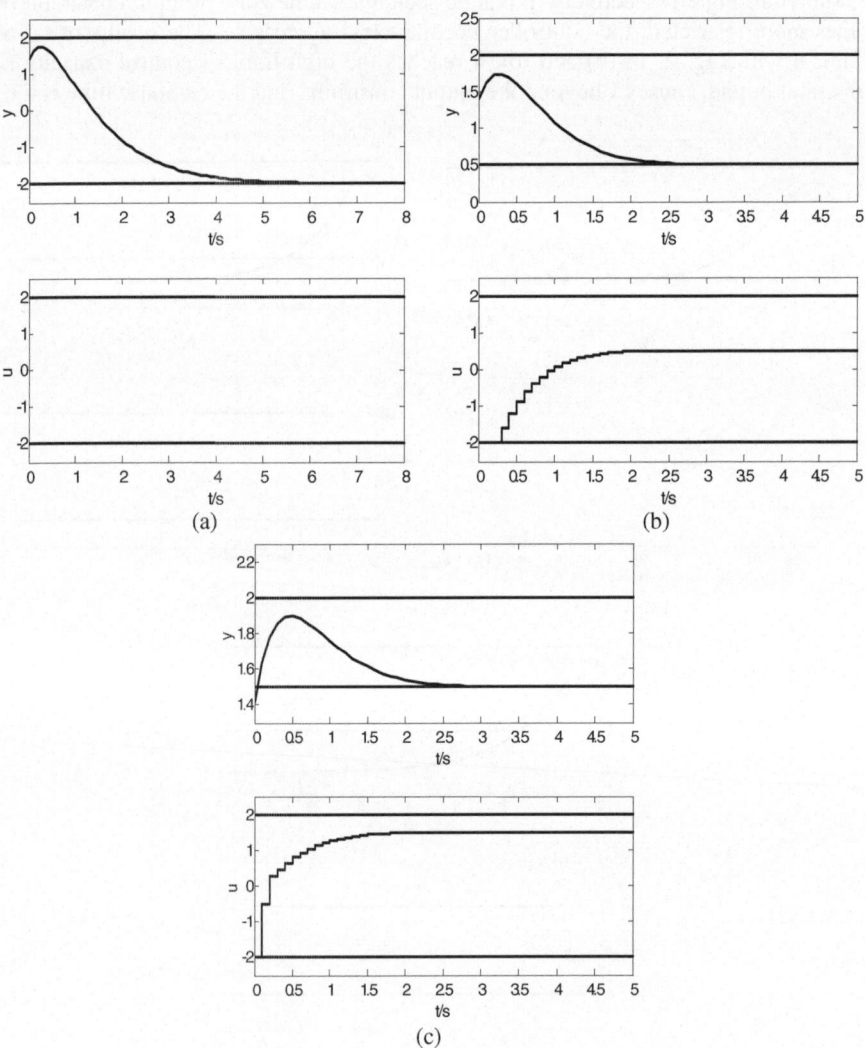

Fig. 4. Closed-loop response with different output constraint: (a) $y \in [-2,2]$. (b) $y \in [0.5,2]$. (c) $y \in [1.5,2]$. The dashed lines are the limits of u, y (*solid line*).

5   Conclusion

For the discrete-time state-space linear system with constraints of input and output, based on Newton control framework, we deduct the expression of MPC law based on zone control with and without constraints respectively, which can be expressed as a state-feedback form, and has an exhibition of the effect of constraints on that. The simulation results of a second-order linear system show that MPC law based on zone control has the advantage of fulfilling constraints as possible and excellent control performance compared with the general constrained MPC. Further more, the effects of constraints of input and output have been discussed.

Acknowledgment. This research was supported by the National Natural Science Foundation of China.

References

1. Abou-Jeyab, R.A., Gupta, Y.P., Gervais, J.R., Branchi, P.A., Woo, S.S.: Constrained multivariable control of a distillation column using a simplified model predictive control algorithm. Journal of Process Control 11(5), 509–517 (2001)
2. Piñón, S., Camacho, E.F., Kuchen, B., Peña, M.: Constrained predictive control of a greenhouse. Computers and Electronics in Agriculture 49(3), 317–329 (2005)
3. Perez, T., Goodwin, G.C.: Constrained predictive control of ship fin stabilizers to prevent dynamic stall. Control Engineering Practice 16(4), 482–494 (2008)
4. Gruber, J.K., Doll, M., Bordons, C.: Design and experimental validation of a constrained MPC for the air feed of a fuel cell. Control Engineering Practice 17(8), 874–885 (2009)
5. Maldonado, M., Desbiens, A., del Villar, R.: Potential use of model predictive control for optimizing the column flotation process. International Journal of Mineral Processing 93(1), 26–33 (2009)
6. Cristea, M.V., Agachi, S.P., Marinoiu, V.: Simulation and model predictive control of a UOP fluid catalytic cracking unit. Chemical Engineering and Processing 42(2), 67–91 (2003)
7. Bemporad, A., Morari, M., Dua, V., Pistikopoulos, E.N.: The explicit solution of model predictive control via multiparametric quadratic programming. In: Proceedings of the American Control Conference, Chicago, pp. 872–876 (2000)
8. Pistikopoulos, E.N., Dua, V., Bozinis, N.A., Bemporad, A., Morari, M.: On-line optimization via off-line parametric optimization tools. Computers & Chemical Engineering 24(2-7), 183–188 (2000)
9. Harrison, A.C., Qin, S.J.: Minimum variance performance map for constrained model predictive control. Journal of Process Control 19(7), 1199–1204 (2009)
10. Bemporad, A., Morari, M., Dua, V., Pistikopoulos, E.N.: The explicit linear quadratic regulator for constrained systems. Automatica 38(1), 3–20 (2002)
11. Johansen, T.A., Petersen, I., Slupphaug, O.: Explicit sub-optimal linear quadratic regulation with state and input constraints. Automatica 38(7), 1099–1111 (2002)
12. Seron, M., De Dona, J.A., Goodwin, G.C.: Global analytical model predictive control with input constraints. In: Proceedings of the 39th IEEE Conference on Decision and Control, Sydney, pp. 154–159 (2000)

13. Tøndel, P., Johansen, T.A., Bemporad, A.: An algorithm for multi-parametric quadratic programming and explicit MPC solutions. Automatica 39(3), 489–497 (2003)
14. Rossiter, J.A., Grieder, P.: Using interpolation to improve efficiency of multiparametric predictive control. Automatica 41(4), 637–643 (2005)
15. Grancharova, A., Johansen, T.A., Kocijan, J.: Explicit model predictive control of gas–liquid separation plant via orthogonal search tree partitioning. Computers & Chemical Engineering 28(12), 2481–2491 (2004)
16. Hegrenaes, Ø., Gravdahl, J.T., Tøndel, P.: Spacecraft attitude control using explicit model predictive control. Automatica 41(12), 2107–2114 (2005)
17. Li, W.C., Biegler, L.T.: Multistep, Newton-type control strategies for constrained nonlinear processes. Chemical Engineering Research and Design 67(10), 562–577 (1989)
18. de Oliveira, N.M.C., Biegler, L.T.: Constraint handing and stability properties of model predictive control. AIChE Journal 40(7), 1138–1155 (2004)
19. Feng, W., Qiping, Z., Han, Z., Fengmin, L.: A zone-control algorithm with unequal limits in the model predictive control. Computer and applied chemistry 22(5), 349–354 (2005)
20. Grieder, P., Borrelli, F., Torrisi, F., Morari, M.: Computation of the constrained infinite time linear quadratic regulator. Automatica 40(4), 701–708 (2004)

Research of Networked Control System Based on Fuzzy Immune PID Controller

Daogang Peng[1,2], Hao Zhang[1], Jiajun Lin[2], and Shenna Li[1]

[1] School of Electric Power and Automation Engineering,
Shanghai University of Electric Power, Shanghai 200090, China
[2] School of Information Science and Engineering,
East China University of Science and Technology, Shanghai 200237, China
jypdg@163.com, hzhangk@yahoo.com.cn, jjlin_ecust@126.com

Abstract. Networked control system has been a hotspot in the research fields of control theory and control engineering application at home and abroad. The simulation platform of real-time networked control system can be built by connecting the modules in TrueTime toolbox and the common modules in Simulink. Biological immune system has the properties of strong robustness and adaptability in the environment with lots of disturbance and uncertainty. The networked control system based on fuzzy immune PID controller is combined with immunological mechanism of biological, fuzzy logic and conventional PID controller. Through the simulation studies of changing parameters and increasing time delay show that the control method designed in this paper can get better control effectiveness with a better ability of robustness, adaptability and anti-interference.

Keywords: Networked control system, Immune PID Controller, Fuzzy Immune PID Controller, TrueTime toolbox.

1 Introduction

Networked control system has been a hotspot in the research fields of control theory and control engineering application at home and abroad in the late 1990s.The essence of the networked control system is that through the network, the messages of reference input, object output and control input exchange data between different components of networked control system, such as sensors, controllers and actuators and so on. Each node in the networked control system is connected to the network directly, so it has the advantages of resource sharing, fewer cables, easy to extend and maintain. The TrueTime toolbox is a simulation platform based on Matlab/Simulink for networked control system, which contains TrueTime Kernel module, TrueTime Network module, TrueTime Wireless Network Module, ttSendMsg module, ttGetMsg module and TrueTime Battery module. The corresponding real-time networked control system can be built by connecting the modules in TrueTime and the common modules in Simulink, which is an ideal platform for delay compensation algorithm of networked control system and scheduling algorithms of different resources.

H. Deng et al. (Eds.): AICI 2011, Part II, LNAI 7003, pp. 141–148, 2011.

Biological immune system has the properties of strong robustness and adaptability in the environment with lots of disturbance and uncertainty. The immune PID controller, a kind of nonlinear controllers, is designed by using the immunological mechanism of biological system for reference, and the fuzzy immune PID controller approaches to the immune PID controller by fuzzy reasoning logic. By the combination of biological immune principles and traditional PID controller, they can learn mutually from each other and improve the control performance of the system.

Taking the typical one-order inertia plant and second-order inertia plant in the process of industrial production for example, and using the TrueTime toolbox, the networked control system based on fuzzy immune PID controller had been designed in this paper, and the feasibility and effectiveness of the control scheme had been proved by the simulation studies.

2   The Fuzzy Immune PID Controller

Immunity is a characteristic physiological response of organisms. Biological immune system has the properties of strong robustness and adaptability in the environment with lots of disturbance and uncertainty. The non-self invasion (such as cells, viruses and varieties of pathogens) and mutated self-cells(such as cancer cells) can be identified accurately, responded appropriately and removed effectively. The organism body will be infected inevitably and leads to death if there's no protection of the immune system. Artificial immune system is an intelligent information processing system, which is developed by using the mechanisms of strong robustness and adaptability in the environment with lots of disturbance and uncertainty.

Biological immune system can product corresponding antibodies to protect against alien antigens. A series of reactions will be generated after the combination of antigens and antibodies, and then it destructs the antigens by phagocytosis or by producing special enzymes. Biological immune system consists of lymphocyte and antibody molecule, and the lymphocyte is composed of B cell produced by bone marrow and T cell produced by thymus(helper cell T_H and suppressor cell T_s). When the antigens invade body and is digested by peripheral cells, the information is passed to T cell (T_H and T_s) and it stimulates B cell, which produce antibodies to remove antigens. The T_H cell is more than T_s cells when there are a fairly larger number of antigens, so major B cell is produced. On the other side, the increasing T_s cell can inhibit the production of T_H cell along with the reduction of antigens, so the number of B cell is getting smaller. The immune feedback system will tend to equilibrium after a short time interval. The cooperation of suppressor mechanism and main feedback mechanism is finished by the rapid response to antigens and the steady immune system.

Though the immune system is quite complex, the adaptive ability to combat antigens is obvious. These intelligent behaviours provide a variety of academic reference and technical methods for science and engineering fields. The immune PID controller, a kind of nonlinear controllers, is designed by using the immunologicl mechanis for reference. By the combination of biological immune principles and traditional PID controller, they can learn mutually from each other and improve the control performance of the system.

The conventional PID controller takes consider of the past deviations, present deviation and future deviation. The disperse form of conventional PID controller is:

$$u(k) = u(k-1) + k_p(e(k) - e(k-1)) + k_i e(k) + k_d(e(k)$$
$$- 2e(k-1) + e(k-2))$$

(1)

Where k_p, k_i and k_d are coefficients of proportionality, integral and differential respectively. The proportional coefficient k_p can give response to the deviations between given value and the output, the integral coefficient k_i can eliminate static error, improve control precision and the static characteristics of system, and the function of differential coefficient is to reduce the overshoot, make the system tend to be steady quickly and improve the dynamic characteristics of the system. So just by adjusting the k_p, k_i and k_d, it can get an satisfied control effectiveness with a rapid, steady and accurate system.

The principle of immune PID controller based on biological immune feedback mechanism is as following: suppose k means generations, $\varepsilon(k)$ is the number of antigens, the output of T_H cell stimulated by antigens is $T_H(k)$, and the influence of B cell caused by T_S cell is $T_s(k)$, so the total stimulations received by B cell is:

$$S(k) = T_H(k) - T_s(k)$$

(2)

Where $T_H(k) = k_1\varepsilon(k)$, $T_s(k) = k_2 f(\Delta s(k))\varepsilon(k)$.

Suppose name the number of antigens $\varepsilon(k)$ as deviation $e(k)$ and name the total stimulations that received by B cell as the control input $u(k)$, then the feedback control rule is as follows:

$$u(k) = K(1 - \eta f(u(k), \Delta u(k)))e(k) = k_{p1}e(k)$$

(3)

Where $k_{p1} = K(1 - \eta f(u(k), \Delta u(k)))$, the control reaction velocity is $K = k_1$, the control stable effect is $\eta = k_2 / k_1$ and $f(\cdot)$ is a given nonlinear function.

Actually a nonlinear P control is described in formula (3), whose proportional coefficient $K^{'}$ is changed as the output is changed while the gain K is adjusted by its output. As the P control is not useful for second-order or higher order object, it can't eliminate control errors which is caused by noise and nonlinear interference, so immune PID control is proposed in formula (4).

$$u(k) = K\{1 - \eta f[\Delta u(k)]\}(1 + \frac{K_i}{z-1} + K_d \frac{z-1}{z})e(k)$$

(4)

Where, when $0 < \eta f[\Delta u(k)] \leq 1$, the immune PID control means negative feedback and when $1 < \eta f[\Delta u(k)]$, it means positive feedback. The upper limit of factor η keeps the system steady and the immune PID controller is equivalent traditional PID controller when $\eta = 0$.

The fuzzy immune PID controller approaches to the nonlinear function $f(\cdot)$ by fuzzy reasoning logic. Suppose every input variable is fuzzed by two fuzzy sets, which include positive P and negative N respectively. And the output variable is fuzzed by three fuzzy sets who are positive P, zero Z and negative N. Those all belong to degree functions that is defined in the entire range $(-\infty, +\infty)$. There are four rules in the fuzzy reasoning logic as follows:

1) If u is P and Δu is P then $f(u, \Delta u)$ is N   (1)
2) If u is P and Δu is N then $f(u, \Delta u)$ is Z   (1)
3) If u is N and Δu is P then $f(u, \Delta u)$ is Z   (1)
4) If u is N and Δu is N then $f(u, \Delta u)$ is P   (1)

The fuzzy logic AND operations of Zadeh are use in the above rules and the output $f(\cdot)$ of fuzzy controller is always obtained from defuzzification of mom.

3   Fuzzy Immune PID Networked Control System Based on TrueTime

The essence of the networked control system is that through the network, the messages of reference input, object output and control input exchange data between different components of networked control system, such as sensors, controllers and actuators and so on .These devices belong to the network nodes in the networked control system. Every node can execute several different tasks according to its own hardware configuration. The monitor computer receive data of the control layer through network, implement the optimized algorithm and download the optimized parameters to the related nodes of control layer in the field through the network too. Each node in the networked control system is connected to the network directly, so it has the advantages of resource sharing, fewer cables, easy to extend and maintain, etc.

The structure of networked control system based on fuzzy immune PID controller is shown in figure 1, where sensors are used to sample signals periodically from controlled objects on time driving and transmit them to the fuzzy immune PID controller through network communication channels, then controller calculates the control signals via fuzzy immune PID algorithm and transmit them to the actuators by network communication channels, finally the actuators control the controlled object in accordance with the results of fuzzy immune PID controller. The controllers and actuators use either time-driven mode or event-driven mode. The controller and actuator calculate and execute the latest date packet information in a steady time

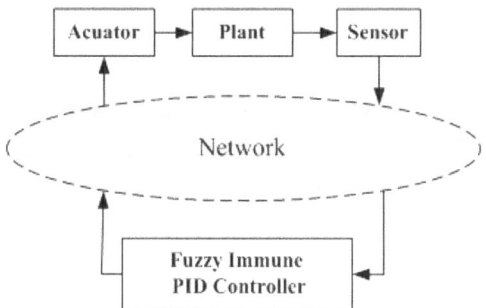

Fig. 1. The structure of fuzzy immune PID networked control system

interval when they are both time-driven mode. On the other side, when they both use event-driven mode, the controller calculates the new control variable when the controller received a date packet and the actuator doesn't work until it receives the date packet of control variable.

The TrueTime toolbox is a simulation platform based on Matlab/Simulink for networked control system, which is developed by Martin Ohlin, Dan Henriksson and Anton Cervin, etc of Sweden Lund University. There are six main modules in the TrueTime toolbox, namely TrueTime Kernel module, TrueTime Network module, TrueTime Wireless Network Module, ttSendMsg module, ttGetMsg module and TrueTime Battery module. The corresponding real-time networked control system can be built by connecting the modules in TrueTime and the common modules in Simulink. The dynamic process of networked control system, control task execution and co-simulation environment of network interaction can be built by the simulation module of simulink in the MATLAB. The simulation study of delay compensation algorithm of the networked control system and scheduling algorithms of different resources etc can be carried out.

The TrueTime Kernel module in the TrueTime box can be used to simulate nodes of networked control system, such as sensors, controllers and actuators etc. It has flexible real-time kernel, A/D and D/A converters, network sending and receiving interfaces etc. It also supports four kinds of task scheduling algorithms, such as fixed priority (prioFP), rate monotonic (prioRM), deadline monotonic (prioDM) and earliest deadline first (prioEDF). The TrueTime Network module uses event-driven mode, when the messages are read in or sent out, the module executes the task. The messages read in or sent out should contain the information about the sending and receiving computer nodes, user defined control signals or measured signal data, the total length of the message, real-time characteristic parameters such as priority, deadline and so on.

The simulation model of fuzzy immune PID control system based on TrueTime is consisted of a network module and a number of computer modules, where computer modules are used as nodes of network. A sensor node is periodic sampling from the controlled object, and through the network module, the samples will be sent to the controller node. The task of controller node is calculating the control signals and sending the results to actuator node, and the actuator node executes the control signals later. The sensor node is set to clock driven mode, and the controller node and actuator node are set to event-driven mode.

4 Simulation Studies

The network module simulates receiving and sending of data in accordance with the network module selected, which can provide six kinds of modes and network parameters, such as the number of network nodes, transmission rate and medium access control protocol (MAC) and so on, where MAC includes CSMA/CD (Ethernet), CSMA/AMP, Round Robin, FDMA, TDMA, and Switched Ethernet, etc. The network communication mode can be changed through setting the Network type in the TrueTime Network module, and this paper uses CSMA/CD (Ethernet).

Take the typical one-order inertia plant and second-order inertia plant in the process of industrial production as examples, whose transfer functions are as follows:

$$G_1(s) = \frac{1.25}{15s+1}, \quad G_2(s) = \frac{1.5}{(10s+1)^2}$$

In order to verify the robustness and adaptability of the control method, a comparison has been done when the time constant and proportional coefficient is changed. The parameters of fuzzy immune PID controller are as follows when the controlled object is one-order inertia: $K = 0.0012$, $\eta = 0.01$, $K_i = 0.15$, $K_d = 0.15$; And when the controlled object is second-order inertia the parameters are as follows: $K = 0.0009$, $\eta = 0.0012$, $K_i = 0.15$, $K_d = 0.15$. Figure 2 shows the simulation result of one-order inertia with the unit step input and figure 3 shows the simulation result of second-order inertia with the unit step input. Curve ① is the output response when parameters haven't been changed while curve ② is the output response when the time constant and proportional coefficients are increased to 20%. It can been seen from figure 2 and figure 3 that the fuzzy immune PID networked control system based on TrueTime has good control performance and the overshoot output is quite small. Better control quality can be obtained even the parameters are changed, so the system has a better ability of robustness and adaptability.

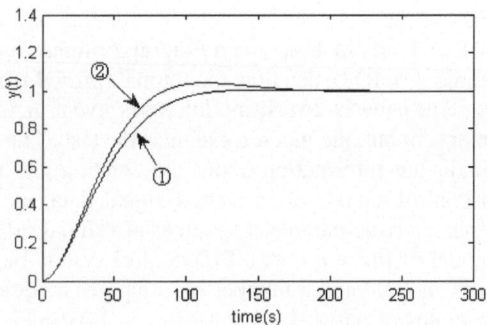

Fig. 2. The curves of one-order plant with step response

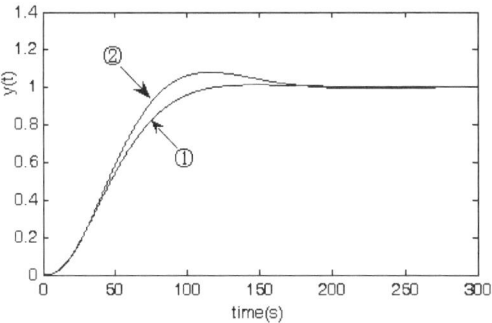

Fig. 3. The curves of second-order inertia with step response

For the date packet sent in the networked control system is usually short and the frequency of sending and receiving date is always high, the phenomenon of information collision and retransmission is caused inevitably for the limited broadband, which leads the delay of information transmission. Meanwhile, a larger overshoot and longer control period, which affect the control quality seriously during production and bring down the system stability greatly, is caused by the stochastic change of network delay and the influence of the time delay factors, such as network protocol and network load, etc. The delay time is changed by Transport Delay in the simulation model of networked control system based on TrueTime. Figure 4 shows the simulation result of second-order inertia plant after increasing network delay, where curve ① and curve ② are the output responses when network delays are 2s and 4s respectively. It can be seen that the system can keep steady and get better control effect after increasing certain network delay.

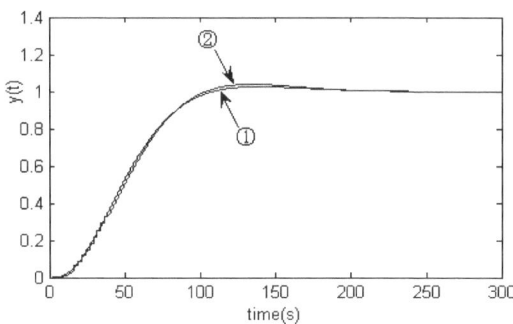

Fig. 4. The curve of second-order after increasing time delay

5 Conclusions

Networked control system has been a hotspot in the research fields of control theory and control engineering application at home and abroad. It has the advantages of fewer cables, easy to extend, high flexibility, resource sharing and remote controlling. The TrueTime toolbox is a simulation platform based on Matlab/Simulink for networked control system. The corresponding real-time networked control system can be built by connecting the modules in TrueTime and the common modules in Simulink, which can provide basis for the simulation study of delay compensation algorithm of the networked control system and scheduling algorithms of different resources. Immunity is a characteristic physiological response of organisms. The fuzzy immune PID controller, a kind of nonlinear controllers, is designed by using the immunological mechanism of biological system for reference. In this paper, taking the typical one-order inertia plant and second-order inertia plant in the process of industrial production for example, and using the TrueTime toolbox, the networked control system based on fuzzy immune PID controller has been designed. Through the simulation study of changing parameters and increasing time delay, it can see that the control method designed in this paper gets better control effect with a better ability of robustness, adaptability and anti-interference.

Acknowledgments. This work is supported by the State Key Program of National Natural Science Foundation of China (Grant No. 61034004) and Shanghai Science and Technology Commission Key Program (Grant No. 10250502000).

References

[1] Chen, B., Meng, C.M., Ge, B., et al.: Simulation Research on Networked Control System Based on Truetime. Control Engineering of China 15(5), 501–503 (2008)
[2] Sun, J.M., Deng, W., Li, L.P., et al.: Matlab based Simulation Platform for Networked Control System. Process Automation Instrumentation 31(3), 19–22 (2010)
[3] Peng, D.G., Zhang, H., Huang, C.H., et al.: Study of Immune PID Networked Control System Based on TrueTime. Journal of Network 6(6), 912–915 (2011)
[4] Yin, Y., Li, S.F., Wang, J.H.: Research on Adaptive Fuzzy PID Control Method For Networked Control Systems. Journal of Wuhan University of Technology 32(6), 144–148 (2010)
[5] Fei, C.G., Li, C.G., Zhang, Q.Z., et al.: Simulation of Adaptive DMC Algorithm in Networked Control Systems. Journal of System Simulation 20(1), 65–67 (2008)
[6] Dang, X.D., Zhang, Q.L.: Stability and PID control for networked control system. In: Proceedings of the 8th World Congress on Intelligent Control and Automation, Jinan, China, July 6-9, pp. 921–926 (2010)
[7] Zhao, Y.B., Liu, G.P., Rees, D.: Integrated predictive control and scheduling co-design for networked control systems. IET Control Theory Appl. 2(1), 7–15 (2008)

A New Type of Adaptive Neural Network Fuzzy Controller in the Double Inverted Pendulum System

Suying Zhang[1], Ran An[2], and Shuman Shao[1]

[1] School of Electrical Technology and Information Science,
Hebei University of Science and Technology, Shijiazhuang, China
[2] Electronic Information Department,
Yanjing Vocational and Technical College, Langfang, China
zhsy8985@sina.com, {ranan0,shaoshuman}@163.com

Abstract. A new type of adaptive neural network fuzzy controller based on the stability for the double inverted pendulum control problem is introduced. The method uses a fusion function to reduce the dimension of the system, reducing the number of input variables to solve the fuzzy rule explosion problem. In order to optimize and amend the front-part and later-part parameter of Takagi-Sugeno fuzzy model, a mixed algorithm of backward propagation (BP) and least square method (LSE) algorithm are used. Using the collected original input and output data to establish adaptive neural network fuzzy inference system (ANFIS), and to control the double inverted pendulum system. Simulation results show that the controller is better than the other controller.

Keywords: Double inverted pendulum, adaptive neural network-based fuzzy inference system, Takagi-Sugeno fuzzy model, fusion function.

1 Introduction

With the development of computer intelligence disciplines, the combination of fuzzy logic and neural network methods are concerned by more and more people. The advantages of fuzzy logic approach are logical and transparent and easy to combine a priori knowledge to the fuzzy rules, but its application has been greatly restricted for their features do not have the self-learning function. The advantages of artificial neural network is that it is good at adaptive learning network parameters, and has parallel processing and generalization, but it cannot express fuzzy language, in fact, like a black box, it is not a good expression of the human brain for the lack of transparency. Adaptive neural network-based fuzzy inference system ANFIS [1] can combine the two algorithm. The use of fuzzy logic "concept" abstraction and non-linear processing power and self-learning ability and arbitrary function approximation ability of neural networks, can make up their own deficiencies, making the system easy to express both human knowledge of fuzzy logic and neural networks of distributed information storage and the advantages of learning for modeling. This method provides an effective tool for control of the complex systems.

H. Deng et al. (Eds.): AICI 2011, Part II, LNAI 7003, pp. 149–157, 2011.
© Springer-Verlag Berlin Heidelberg 2011

Inverted pendulum system is a typical non-linear, higher-order, multivariable, strong coupling, unstable dynamic system[2]. For the multi-variable characteristics of inverted pendulum system, the use of fusion function [3] can reduce the dimension of input variables, so as to solve the question-"rule explosion problem." Fuzzy neural network are commonly used in non-linear, identification of unknown or non-deterministic system. In the nonlinear model of double inverted pendulum system[4], based on the fuzzy inference characteristics of Takagi-Sugeno, its combination with the neural network to construct adaptive fuzzy neural network learning system to achieve effective control of inverted pendulum.

2   The Mathematical Model of Inverted Pendulum System

Suppose no friction exists in the pendulum system. Then the dynamic equation of such a double inverted pendulum system can be obtained by Lagrange's equation of motion. The state equation and output equation of the double inverted pendulum is

$$\begin{cases} \dot{X} = AX + Bu \\ Y = CX \end{cases} \tag{1}$$

Here, $X = [x, \theta_1, \theta_2, \dot{x}, \dot{\theta_1}, \dot{\theta_2}]^T$ is the state vector. $Y = [x, \theta_1, \theta_2]^T$ is the output vector.

By calculated, the system is observable and controllable. But because the system has right half plane poles, it is natural unstable system.

3   ANFIS Based on the Fusion Function

3.1   The Design of the Fusion Function

For multi-variable nonlinear system, if the use of a conventional fuzzy controller, there will be a question "rule explosion problem" the input variable dimension control caused excessive number of rules increases exponentially [2][5]. In order to reduce the number of control rules, you can use fusion function to reduce the dimension of state variables. Combine the six state variables of double inverted pendulum system into integrated error E and integrated error rate EC by the use of fusion function. This approach not only reduces the number of control rules, but also conducive to learning and adjustment of the controller by using human experience to initialized weight fuzzy neural network. According to this method, the linear double inverted pendulum based on adaptive neural network fuzzy control system uses a state variable synthesis to reduce the variable dimension.

For synthesis state variables of double inverted pendulum system, state variable that represents the location is combined into a comprehensive error E through the specific weighting coefficient, and the state variable that represents the speed error is combined into a comprehensive error rate EC. E, EC as the two input variables of adaptive neural network fuzzy inference system, they represent.

$$E = k_1 x + k_2 \theta_1 + k_3 \theta_2 \tag{2}$$

$$EC = k_4 \dot{x} + k_5 \dot{\theta}_1 + k_6 \dot{\theta}_2 \tag{3}$$

Here, comprehensive coefficient K is

$$K = \begin{bmatrix} k_1 & k_2 & k_3 & k_4 & k_5 & k_6 \end{bmatrix} \tag{4}$$

By using linear optimal control theory, the state feedback factor of the system can be obtained, which can be integrated as a state variable synthesis of the initial value coefficient, then get the final comprehensive coefficient K through the optimization.

3.2 T-S Fuzzy Model for Fuzzy Systems

T-S model consists of the antecedent and subsequent network, the antecedent network matches the antecedent of fuzzy rules, the subsequent network used to generate the subsequent of fuzzy rules. For a MISO fuzzy systems ,which have input variables, one output variable, suppose the input variable is

$$x = [x_1, x_2, \cdots, x_n]^T \tag{5}$$

Each component are fuzzy linguistic variables.
  Suppose,

$$T(x_i) = \{A_i^1, A_i^2, \cdots, A_i^{m_i}\}, i = 1, 2, \cdots, n \tag{6}$$

It is defined in the domain of a fuzzy set on U_i. The corresponding membership function is

$$\mu_{A_i^j} (i = 1, 2, \cdots, n; j = 1, 2, \cdots, m_i) \tag{7}$$

T-S fuzzy rules the consequent is a linear combination of the input variables.

$$R_j : if \ x_1 \ is \ A_1^j \ and \ x_2 \ is \ A_2^j \ and \cdots and \ x_n \ is \ A_n^j \ then \ y_j = p_{j0} + p_{j1} x_1 + \cdots + p_{jn} x_n \tag{8}$$

Here, $j = 1, 2, \cdots, m; m \le \prod_{i=1}^{n} m_i$.

  If the input amount by a single point of fuzzy optimization method is fuzzy set, criterion for a given input x, seek for the fitness of each rule is

$$\alpha_j = \mu_{A_1^j}(x_1) \wedge \mu_{A_2^j}(x_2) \wedge \cdots \wedge \mu_{A_n^j}(x_n) \tag{9}$$

The total output of fuzzy system rules is the weighted average of the output.

$$y = \sum_{j=1}^{m} \alpha_j \cdot y_j / \sum_{j=1}^{m} \alpha_j \tag{10}$$

3.3 The Implementation of Adaptive Neural Network Fuzzy Control Algorithm Based on T-S Mode

The biggest characteristic of the adaptive neural network fuzzy inference system is based on data modeling method. The membership functions and fuzzy rules of the system is obtained by learning a large number of known data [6], but not based on experience or any given. Its advantage lies in it can use neural network learning mechanisms compensation fuzzy control system disadvantage[7].

In the process of establishing ANFIS system, first determine a parametric model structure, which combined input and output variables of the membership function and fuzzy rules .Then obtain a set of input and output data pairs, in accordance with certain combinations as ANFIS training algorithm data. Then use ANFIS function training the parameter of the front FIS model, adjusted membership function of error parameters in accordance with certain criteria, making the FIS model can continue to approach the given training data.

3.3.1 Selection of Sample Data

1) Based on the actual control needs for inverted pendulum system, largely determine the system state variables and control variables of domain.

2) Along the direction of each state variable of the double inverted pendulum, take a series of range permutation and combination, dividing point fuzzy BOX space. Then six dimensional state spaces in a series of state points is formed. Along the direction of each state variable of the double inverted pendulum, take a series of range permutation and combination, dividing point fuzzy BOX space. Then six dimensional state spaces in a series of state points is formed.

3) Fox the front of the BOX fuzzy space, with the above points for each discrete state space linearize the nonlinear model of inverted pendulum system. Select the appropriate LQR control parameters Q and R, and design a linear optimal controller to strike a state feedback matrix. After that the control points by taking state space as the output data points can be obtained.

3.3.2 Establishment of ANFIS Fuzzy Inference System

MATLAB fuzzy toolbox provides a main function of ANFIS as an auxiliary adaptive neural network fuzzy inference tools. The essence is borrow the more sophisticated neural network learning algorithm-back propagation algorithm and least squares algorithm, to learn a given set of input and output data sets and to adjust the parameters and structure of the neural fuzzy control system.

Fuzzy controller requires two types of adjustment-structural adjustment and parameter adjustment. Structural adjustment, including the number of variables, the domain partition of the input and output, variables of the number of rules and other adjustments. Once get a satisfactory structure, you need to adjust the parameters. Parameter adjustment, including the prerequisite set of parameters (nonlinear) and the conclusions set of parameters (linear) adjustment. Among them, the prerequisite set of parameters refers to the parameters of membership function, i.e. the slope, width, center $\{\alpha_i, \beta_i, \gamma_i\}$. And the conclusion set of parameters is the input and output parameters of Sugeno fuzzy linear model. As the network structure has been determined, the learning algorithm is really just learning the parameters of the controller, so you simply adjust the premise parameters and conclusions of the parameters. ANFIS model of the steps are as follows.

1) Determine the output and input variables membership functions. Bell-shaped membership function of the prototype is the probability distribution function and can better reflect reality. The system has good accuracy and simplicity, which uses bell-shaped membership function to represent the first i input membership functions.

$$\mu_{A_i}(x) = \frac{1}{1 + \left[\left(\dfrac{x - \gamma_i}{\alpha_i}\right)^2\right]^{\beta_i}} \tag{21}$$

The choice of the initial membership function covers the range of variables, then the membership of each input variable parameter values have been determined and to adjust the three parameters you can easily change the membership function.

2) Adjust the parameters of ANFIS fuzzy model. In this paper, ANFIS learning methods integrated use of gradient descent learning method and least square method (LSE) to identify the parameters for the premise parameters using gradient descent method, the conclusion parameters using least squares method. The learning process of system is divided into prior to learn and reverse learning. By the least square method (LSE), the premise parameters are fixed and the conclusion parameters are revised. By reverse learning gradient descent method, fixed output layer parameters is changeless and along the direction of error decreases to adjust the parameters of self-optimizing for the input layer or the middle layer. According to the rate of return error to make the premise parameters and the shape of membership functions change. Such alternate to premise or conclusion parameters revisionist, until the entire samples of mean square error reach formulary accuracy requirement, and network approximation to modeling system for a high precision after several times training.

3) According to previous data obtained on the original input and output (Discrete state space sampling points ,and the corresponding control), using functions ANFIS in the MATLAB to complete the training process and get the fuzzy controller and train a new generation of fuzzy rules and membership functions.

4) Select initial membership function shown in Fig. 1. This paper adopts Sugeno fuzzy model identification methods and hybrid learning algorithm .By using the grid method to obtain the after training method of the system. Closing value of the error (Error Tolerance) is set to 0 and the training times (epoch) is set to 10. After identification of the modified membership function shown in Fig. 2.

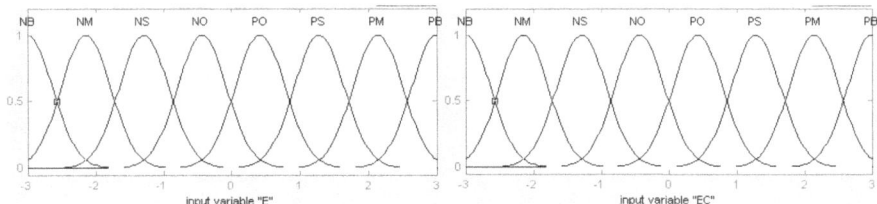

Fig. 1. Membership functions before training plans

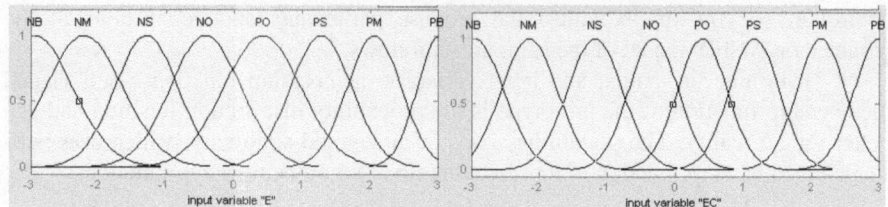

Fig. 2. Membership function after training plans

4   Simulink for Duuble Inverted Pendulum

Based on the above analysis, the first use of integrated coefficient of double inverted pendulum state variables were synthesized by comprehensive coefficient K.

In this article, double inverted pendulum system simulation model is Sugeno-type FIS model. The domain of input variables E ,EC and output variable U is $[-3 \quad 3]$. E, EC are respectively eight fuzzy sets{NB NM NS NO PO PS PM PB}. That there are eight membership function and the membership functions are Gaussmf. The controller is using the first-order linear output, and the output space is divided into 64 regions, a total of 64 fuzzy rules.

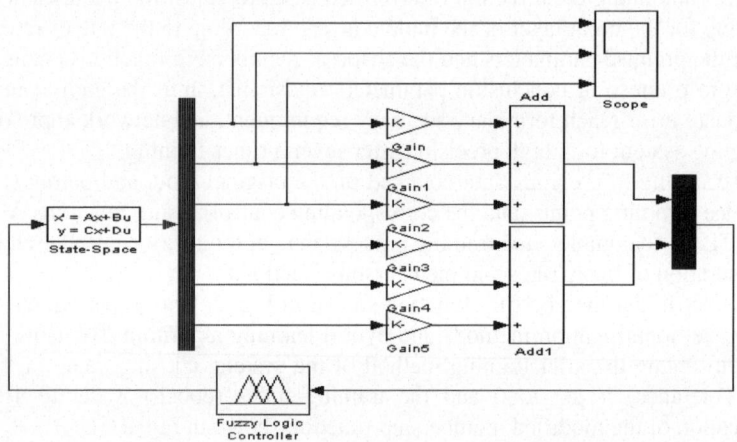

Fig. 3. Simulation model of double inverted pendulum based on ANFIS

In this simulation, the LQR controller is applied to the double inverted pendulum system to get input and output data. The sampling time is set to 0.01S.Select the 1000 sample data as the ANFIS controller training data. The simulink structure of inverted pendulum controller based on adaptive neural network simulation is showed as Fig. 3.

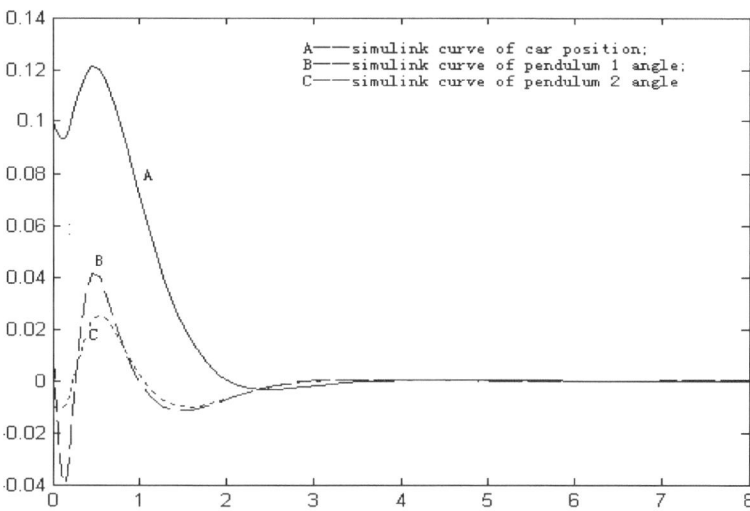

Fig. 4. The inverted pendulum simulation curve based on ANFIS

The inverted pendulum simulation curve based on ANFIS is shown as Fig. 4. In Fig.4, even if the initial position of the car father away from the equilibrium point, but can move to the balance within a short period of 3.5s.The simulation curve of pendulum can reach equilibrium within 3s.The simulation curve shows that fuzzy controller based on inverted pendulum is very good speed, while a very small overshoot.

Next, comparison of ANFIS and LQR controller performance in the double inverted pendulum simulation. The comparison simulation curve charts for car displace, the pendulum angle are respectively shown in Fig. 5, Fig. 6, Fig. 7.

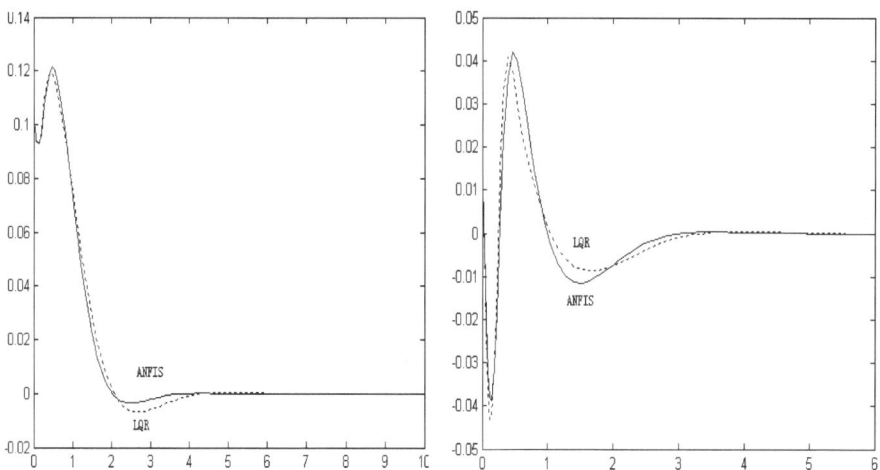

Fig. 5. Simulation curve of car displacement   **Fig. 6.** Simulation curve of pendulum 1 angle

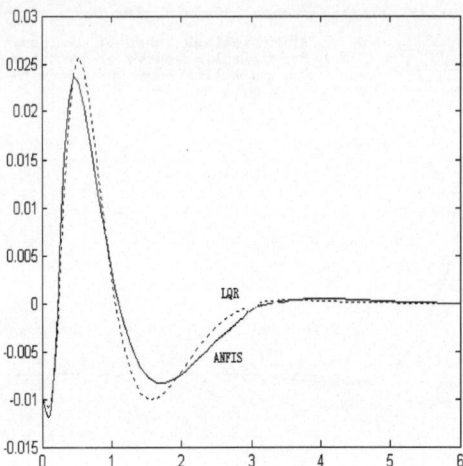

Fig. 7. Simulation curve of pendulum 2 angle

As is shown in Fig. 5, Fig. 6, Fig. 7, the double inverted pendulum simulation curve based on the ANFIS controller has better performance. The adaptive neural network fuzzy controller was not only significantly reduce overshoot and improve the control accuracy, but also significantly reduce the transition time

5   Conclusions

Inverted pendulum system is a typical non-linear, higher-order, multivariable, strong coupling and unstable dynamic system. For the multi-variable characteristics of Inverted pendulum system, the use of fusion function can reduce the dimension of input variables, so as to solve the question-"rule explosion problem". Fuzzy neural network are commonly used in non-linear, identification of unknown or non-deterministic system. In the nonlinear model of double inverted pendulum system, based on the fuzzy inference characteristics of Takagi-Sugeno, a mixed algorithm of backward propagation (BP) and least square method (LSE) algorithm are used to optimize and amend the front-part and later part parameter of Takagi-Sugeno fuzzy model .Based on objective input/output data get actual membership function, to avoid the conventional fuzzy control from a subjective optional membership function and fuzzy control rule the drawbacks. Simulation results show that, compared with the other controller, this controller was not only significantly reduce overshoot and improve the control accuracy, but also significantly reduce the transition time.

References

1. Roger Jang, J.-S.: ANFIS: Adaptive Neural Network based Fuzzy Inference System. IEEE Transactions on Systems, Man and Cybernetics 23(3), 665–685 (1993)
2. Gang, M., Zhang, S.: The design of the double inverted pendulum fuzzy controller based on fusion function. J. of Anhui University of Technology, 04-0413-04 (2008)

3. Huang, H.-P., Zhou, N.Q.: linear quadratic optimal control in the realization of the inverted pendulum system. Computer Measurement and Control 14(12), 1641–1642 (2006)
4. Yi, J., Yubazaki, N., Hirota, K.: A new fuzzy controller for stabilization of parallel-type double inverted pendulum system. Fuzzy Sets and Systema 126, 105–119 (2002)
5. Wai, R.-J., Chang, L.-J.: Stabilizing and Tracking Control of Nonlinear Dual-Axis Inverted-Pendulum System Using Fuzzy Neural Network. IEEE Transactions on Fuzzy Systems 14(1), 145–168 (2006)
6. Luo, Z.W., Fujii, S., Saitoh, Y., Muramatsu, E., Watanabe, K.: Feedback-error learning for explicit force control of a robot manipulator interacting with unknown dynamic environment. In: Proceedings of the IEEE International Conference on Robotics and Biomimetics 2004, pp. 262–267 (August 2004)
7. Magoulas, G.D., Plagianakos, V.P., Vrahatis, M.N.: Adaptive stepsize algorithms for on-line training of neural networks. Nonlinear Anal. 47, 3425–3430 (2001)

Adaptive Tracking Control for a Class of Perturbed Nonlinear Time-Delay Systems

Sheng-yu Wang[1], Geng Ji[1], and Xue-bing Hua[2]

[1] School of Mathematics and Information Engineering, Taizhou University, Linhai, China
[2] Advanced Manufacturing and Materials Technology Center,
Zhejiang Industry & Trade Vocational College, Wenzhou, China
zhwy601@163.com

Abstract. This paper addresses the adaptive neural tracking control problem for a class of nonlinear time delays systems. Radial basis function (RBF) neural networks are used to approximate unknown nonlinear functions, then the adaptive neural network controller is designed by using the dynamic surface control (DSC) technique and Lyapunov-Krasovskii functionals. The "explosion of complexity" problem has been eliminated by using DSC technique. Moreover, the proposed controller guarantees that all the signals in the closed-loop system are bounded and the system output converges to a small neighborhood of the desired reference signal. Finally, simulation results are used to demonstrate the effectiveness of the approach.

Keywords: Adaptive control, dynamic surface control, neural network, nonlinear time delay system.

1 Introduction

During the past decades, adaptive backstepping design [1] has received considerable attention using universal function approximators such as neural network [2], [3] or fuzzy systems [8], [9]. However, a drawback in the backstepping design procedure is the problem of "explosion of complexity", which is caused by the repeated differentiations of virtual controllers. Especially, the complexity of controller drastically grows as the order of the system increase. Recently, a dynamic surface control (DSC) technique was first proposed to solve the problem by introducing a first-order filtering of the synthesized virtual control law at each step of the backstepping design procedure in [4]. Based on adaptive backstepping control design framework, the authors in [5] incorporated DSC technique into neural network. Also, the adaptive neural network DSC method in [5] was extended to pure feedback systems in [6] and stochastic nonlinear systems in [7].

However, these proposed controllers contain a lot of adaptive parameters, so that learning time tends to became unacceptably long when these controllers are implemented. Fortunately, this problem was first solved in [8]. By the use of input-to-state stability theory and by combining traditional backstepping technique and T-S fuzzy systems, the robust adaptive fuzzy control scheme in [8] contained 2n adaptive parameters for the n-th order strict-feedback nonlinear system. Further improvement has

H. Deng et al. (Eds.): AICI 2011, Part II, LNAI 7003, pp. 158–165, 2011.

been given in [9], [10]. Unfortunately, due to the use of the traditional backstepping technique, these methods suffer from the problem of "explosion of complexity".

On the other hand, time delays are frequently encountered in real engineer systems. The control problem for time-delay strict-feedback systems has received more and more attention [10], [11]. Based on the above discussion, in this paper, the problem of output tracking is investigated for a class of nonlinear time delay systems via adaptive neural network control method. By using DSC technique, an adaptive neural network controller is proposed. Compared with the existing adaptive neural network or fuzzy control methods [8]-[10], the main feature of this paper is that the proposed controller can solve the "explosion of complexity" problem.

2 Problem Formulation

Consider a class of nonlinear time-delay systems described by

$$\dot{x}_i = f_i\left(\overline{x}_i(t)\right) + g_i\left(\overline{x}_i(t)\right) x_{i+1}(t) + h_i\left(\overline{x}_i(t-\tau_i)\right) + d_i(t, \overline{x}_i)$$
$$\dot{x}_n = f_n\left(\overline{x}_n(t)\right) + g_n\left(\overline{x}_n(t)\right) u + h_n\left(\overline{x}_n(t-\tau_n)\right) + d_n(t, \overline{x}_n) \qquad (1)$$
$$y = x_1(t)$$

where $1 \le i \le n-1$, $\overline{x}_i = [x_1, x_2, \cdots, x_i]^T \in R^i$, $\overline{x}_n = [x_1, x_2, \cdots, x_n]^T \in R^n$ and $u \in R$ are the state variables and the control input, respectively. $f_i(\cdot), g_i(\cdot)$ and $h_i(\cdot)$ are unknown smooth functions. $d_i(\cdot)$ are external disturbance uncertainties. τ_i are the unknown time delays of the states, and $\tau_{max} = \max\{\tau_i\}, i = 1, \cdots, n$. For $t \in [-\tau_{max}, 0]$, we have $\overline{x}_n(t) = \varphi(t)$, where $\varphi(t)$ is a known continuous initial state vector function. The main goal of this paper is to design an adaptive neural tracking controller for system (1) such that the system output y tracks a desired reference signal y_d while all signals in the closed-loop system remain bounded.

Assumption 1: The system states $\overline{x}_n(t)$ are all available for feedback, and the sizes of τ_i are upper bounded by unknown constants.

Assumption 2: The gain functions $g_i(\overline{x}_i)$ are unknown, but their signs are known, and there exist constants $g_{max} \ge g_{min} > 0$ such that $g_{min} \le |g_i(\overline{x}_i)| \le g_{max}$. Without loss generality, we will assume $0 < g_{min} \le g_i(\overline{x}_i)$, $i = 1, 2, \cdots, n$.

Assumption 3: The desired trajectory signal $y_d(t)$ is a sufficiently smooth function of t, and y_d and $\dot{y}_d$ are bounded.

Assumption 4: There exist positive unknown continuous functions $\rho_i(\overline{x}_i(t))$ such that

$$\left| d_i(t, \overline{x}_i) \right| \le \rho_i(\overline{x}_i(t)), \quad 1 \le i \le n.$$

To give Assumption 5, we first introduce the following coordinate transformation:

$$S_1 = x_1 - y_d, S_i = x_i - v_{if}, i = 2, \cdots, n \qquad (2)$$

where S_i and v_{if} denote the error surface vector and the virtual control laws through the first-order filters which will derive in the following control design procedure, respectively.

Assumption 5: The time delay function $h_i(\bar{x}_i(t))$ satisfies the following inequality:

$$\left|h_i\left(\bar{S}_i(t)+\bar{v}_{if}(t)\right)\right| \le \sum_{j=1}^{i}\left|S_i(t)\right| q_{ij}\left(\bar{S}_j(t)+\bar{v}_{if}(t)\right) \tag{3}$$

where $i = 1,\cdots,n$, $\bar{x}_i(t) = \bar{S}_i(t)+\bar{v}_{if}(t)$. $\bar{S}_i = [S_1,S_2,\cdots,S_i]^T$, $\bar{v}_{if} = \left[v_{1f},v_{2f},\cdots v_{if}\right]^T$ and $v_{1f} = y_d$. Also, $q_{ij}(\cdot)$ are unknown continuous functions.

Remark 1: A similar assumption, i.e., Assumption 3, has been made in [11], where the nonlinear functions $q_{ij}(\cdot)$ are assumed to be known. However, in this paper, Assumption 5 does not require $q_{ij}(\cdot)$ to be known functions.

3 Controller Design

In this section, we take the DSC technique to design an adaptive control instead of the traditional backstepping method.

Step i $(1 \le i \le n)$: Define the i-th error surface as $S_i = x_i - v_{if}$. Then

$$\dot{S}_i = f_i(\bar{x}_i)+g_i(\bar{x}_i)x_{i+1}+h_i(\bar{x}_i(t-\tau_i))+d_i(t,x)-\dot{v}_{if} \tag{4}$$

Choose the virtual (or actual) control as

$$v_i = -k_i S_i - \frac{\hat{\theta}_i}{2\eta_i^2} P_i^T(Z_i)P_i(Z_i)S_i \tag{5}$$

and the adaptation law as

$$\dot{\hat{\theta}}_i = \frac{\gamma_i}{2\eta_i^2} P_i^T(Z_i)P_i(Z_i)S_i^2 - \sigma_i\hat{\theta}_i \quad (i = 1,\cdots,n) \tag{6}$$

where η_i, γ_i and σ_i are positive design constants. k_i satisfies $k_i = k_{i0}+k_{i1}$, where $k_{i0} > 0$, $k_{i1} > 0$. $v_n = u$. $\hat{\theta}_i$ is the estimate of $\theta_i = g_{min}^{-1}\left\|W_i^*\right\|^2$, where W_i^* denotes the ideal constant weights of the neural network. $P_i(Z_i)$ is a basis function of the RBF neural network with $Z_i = [\bar{x}_i,v_{i-1f},v_{if},\dot{v}_{if}]^T$ being the input vector.

To avoid repeatedly differentiating virtual controllers, which leads to the so-called "explosion of complexity", in this paper, the DSC technique is employed to eliminate this problem. Introduce a first-order filter v_{i+1f}, let v_i pass through it with time constant ς_{i+1}, i.e.

$$\varsigma_{i+1}\dot{v}_{i+1f} + v_{i+1f} = v_i, \qquad v_{i+1f}(0) = v_i(0) \tag{7}$$

Define $y_{i+1} = v_{i+1f} - v_i = k_i S_i + \left(\hat{\theta}_i / 2\eta_i^2 \right) P_i^T (Z_i) P_i (Z_i) S_i + v_{i+1f}$,   we   have

$\dot{v}_{i+1f} = -y_{i+1} / \varsigma_{i+1}$ and

$$\dot{y}_{i+1} = -y_{i+1}/\varsigma_{i+1} + B_{i+1}\left(\overline{S}_{i+1}, y_2, \cdots, y_{i+1}, \hat{\theta}_1, \cdots, \hat{\theta}_i, y_d, \dot{y}_d \right) \tag{8}$$

where $B_{i+1}(\cdot)$ is a continuous function and has a maximum value M_{i+1} (please refer to [5], [11] for details).

4 Stability Analysis

Consider the following Lyapunov function

$$V = \frac{1}{2} \sum_{i=1}^{n} \left(V_{Q_i} + S_i^2 + \frac{g_{\min} \tilde{\theta}_i^2}{\gamma_i} \right) + \frac{1}{2} \sum_{i=1}^{n-1} y_{i+1}^2 \tag{9}$$

$$V_{Q_i} = \int_{t-\tau_i}^{t} Q_i \left(\overline{S}_i(\tau) + \overline{v}_{if}(\tau) \right) d\tau \tag{10}$$

where $\tilde{\theta}_i = \hat{\theta}_i - \theta_i$, $Q_i \left(\overline{S}_i(\tau) + \overline{v}_{if}(\tau) \right) = \sum_{j=1}^{i} S_i^2(\tau) q_{ij}^2 \left(\overline{S}_j(\tau) + \overline{v}_{jf}(\tau) \right)$

Assumption 6: For a given $\mu > 0$, there exists $V(0) \le \mu$.

Theorem 1: Under Assumptions 1-6, consider the nonlinear systems (1), the controller (5), and the adaptation laws (6), then for bounded initial conditions with $\hat{\theta}_i(0) \ge 0$, there exist $k_i, \eta_i, \gamma_i, \sigma_i$, and ς_j, $i = 1, \cdots, n, j = 2, \cdots, n$ such that all signals of the close-loop system are semiglobally uniformly bounded. Moreover, the output tracking error $y(t) - y_d(t)$ converges to a small neighborhood around zero by appropriately choosing design parameters.

Proof: First, for bounded initial conditions $\hat{\theta}_i(0) \ge 0$, it easily find that equation (6) implies $\hat{\theta}_i(t) \ge 0$ for $t \ge 0$. Then, we give the following inequalities

$$g_i\left(\overline{x}_i \right) S_i v_i \le -g_{\min} k_i S_i^2 - \frac{g_{\min} \hat{\theta}_i}{2\eta_i^2} P_i^T (Z_i) P_i (Z_i) S_i^2 \tag{11}$$

By using (11) and $x_{i+1} = S_{i+1} + y_{i+1} + v_i$, the time derivative of V is given as:

$$\dot{V} = \sum_{i=1}^{n} \left(\frac{1}{2} \dot{V}_{Q_i} + S_i \dot{S}_i + \frac{g_{\min} \tilde{\theta}_i \dot{\hat{\theta}}_i}{\gamma_i} \right) + \sum_{i=1}^{n-1} y_{i+1} \dot{y}_{i+1}$$

$$\le \sum_{i=1}^{n} \left(\frac{1}{2} \dot{V}_{Q_i} - g_{\min} k_i S_i^2 - \frac{g_{\min} \hat{\theta}_i}{2\eta_i^2} P_i^T (Z_i) P_i (Z_i) S_i^2 + S_i f_i \left(\overline{x}_i \right) + S_i h_i \left(\overline{x}_i (t - \tau_i) \right) \right.$$

$$\left. + S_i d_i(t,x) - S_i \dot{v}_{if} + \frac{g_{\min} \tilde{\theta}_i \dot{\hat{\theta}}_i}{\gamma_i} \right) + \sum_{i=1}^{n-1} \left(g_i \left(\overline{x}_i \right) S_i S_{i+1} + g_i \left(\overline{x}_i \right) S_i y_{i+1} - \frac{y_{i+1}^2}{\varsigma_{i+1}} + y_{i+1} B_{i+1} \right) \tag{12}$$

where $\dot{V}_{Q_i} = Q_i \left(\overline{S}_i(t) + \overline{v}_{if}(t) \right) - Q_i \left(\overline{S}_i(t-\tau_i) + \overline{v}_{if}(t-\tau_i) \right)$.

By Assumption 4-5 and triangular inequality, we obtain

$$S_i h_i \left(\overline{x}_i(t-\tau_i) \right) \le \frac{i}{2} S_i^2 + \frac{1}{2} S_i^2 (t-\tau_i) \sum_{j=1}^{i} q_{ij}^2 \left(\overline{S}_j(t-\tau_i) + \overline{v}_{if}(t-\tau_i) \right) \tag{13}$$

$$S_i d_i (t, \overline{x}_i) \le \frac{a_i^2}{2} + \frac{S_i^2 \rho_i^2 (\overline{x}_i)}{2a_i^2} \tag{14}$$

where a_i are positive design parameters.

Therefore,

$$\frac{1}{2} \dot{V}_{Q_i} + S_i h_i \left(\overline{x}_i(t-\tau_i) \right) \le \frac{i}{2} S_i^2 + \frac{1}{2} \sum_{j=1}^{i} S_i^2 (t) q_{ij}^2 \left(\overline{S}_j(t) + \overline{v}_{if}(t) \right) \tag{15}$$

Substituting (14) and (15) into (12) yields

$$\dot{V} \le \sum_{i=1}^{n} \left(-g_{\min} k_i S_i^2 - \frac{g_{\min} \hat{\theta}_i}{2\eta_i^2} P_i^T (Z_i) P_i(Z_i) S_i^2 + S_i F_i (Z_i) + \frac{g_{\min} \tilde{\theta}_i \dot{\hat{\theta}}_i}{\gamma_i} + \frac{a_i^2}{2} \right)$$

$$+ \sum_{i=1}^{n-1} \left(g_i \left(\overline{x}_i \right) S_i y_{i+1} - \frac{y_{i+1}^2}{\varsigma_{i+1}} + y_{i+1} B_{i+1} \right) \tag{16}$$

where $F_1(Z_1) = f_1 (x_1) + \frac{1}{2} S_1 + \frac{S_1 \rho_1^2 (x_1)}{2a_1^2} + \frac{1}{2} S_1 q_{11}^2 (S_1) - \dot{y}_d$ and

$$F_i(Z_i) = f_i (\overline{x}_i) + g_{i-1} (\overline{x}_{i-1}) S_{i-1} + \frac{i}{2} S_i + \frac{S_i \rho_i^2 (\overline{x}_i)}{2a_i^2}$$

$$+ \frac{1}{2} \sum_{j=1}^{i} S_i q_{ij}^2 \left(\overline{S}_j(t) + \overline{v}_{if}(t) \right) - \dot{v}_{if} \quad (i=2,\cdots,n)$$

By employing the RBF neural network to approximate the unknown function $F_i(Z_i)$, we get

$$F_i(Z_i) = W_i^{*T} P_i(Z_i) + \delta_i (Z_i) \tag{17}$$

where $Z_1 = [x_1, y_d, \dot{y}_d]^T \in \Omega_{Z1} \subset R^3$ and $Z_i = [\overline{x}_i, v_{i-1f}, v_{if}, \dot{v}_{if}]^T \in \Omega_{Zi} \subset R^{i+3}$, W_i^* denotes the ideal constant weights, and $\delta_i (Z_i)$ is the approximation error and satisfies $\left| \delta_i (Z_i) \right| \le \varepsilon_i$. Using triangular inequality, we get

$$S_i W_i^{*T} P_i(Z_i) \le \frac{g_{\min} \theta_i}{2\eta_i^2} P_i^T (Z_i) P_i(Z_i) S_i^2 + \frac{\eta_i^2}{2} \tag{18}$$

$$S_i \delta_i (Z_i) \le g_{\min} k_{i0} S_i^2 + \frac{\varepsilon_i^2}{4 g_{\min} k_{i0}} \tag{19}$$

Substituting (17) into (16) and using (6) (18) and (19), we have

$$\dot{V} \le \sum_{i=1}^{n}\left(-g_{\min}k_{i1}S_i^2 - \frac{g_{\min}\sigma_i\tilde{\theta}_i\hat{\theta}_i}{\gamma_i} + c_i\right) + \sum_{i=1}^{n-1}\left(g_i(\overline{x}_i)S_i y_{i+1} - \frac{y_{i+1}^2}{\varsigma_{i+1}} + y_{i+1}B_{i+1}\right) \tag{20}$$

where $c_i = \dfrac{a_i^2}{2} + \dfrac{\eta_i^2}{2} + \dfrac{\varepsilon_i^2}{4g_{\min}k_{i0}}$.

By the inequality $-\dfrac{g_{\min}\sigma_i\tilde{\theta}_i\hat{\theta}_i}{\gamma_i} \le -\dfrac{g_{\min}\sigma_i\tilde{\theta}_i^2}{2\gamma_i} + \dfrac{g_{\min}\sigma_i\theta_i^2}{2\gamma_i}$,

$$g_i(\overline{x}_i)S_i y_{i+1} \le S_i^2 + \frac{g_{\max}^2}{4}y_{i+1}^2 \quad \text{and} \quad y_{i+1}B_{i+1} \le |y_{i+1}B_{i+1}| \le \frac{y_{i+1}^2 B_{i+1}^2}{2\lambda} + \frac{\lambda}{2} \quad (\lambda > 0)$$

We have

$$\dot{V} \le -\sum_{i=1}^{n}\left(g_{\min}k_{i1}S_i^2 + \frac{g_{\min}\sigma_i\tilde{\theta}_i^2}{2\gamma_i}\right) + \sum_{i=1}^{n}\left(c_i + \frac{g_{\min}\sigma_i\theta_i^2}{2\gamma_i}\right)$$
$$+ \sum_{i=1}^{n-1}\left(S_i^2 + \frac{g_{\max}^2}{4}y_{i+1}^2 - \frac{y_{i+1}^2}{\varsigma_{i+1}} + \frac{y_{i+1}^2 B_{i+1}^2}{2\lambda} + \frac{\lambda}{2}\right) \tag{21}$$

Choose $g_{\min}k_{i1} - 1 = \alpha_0 > 0 \ (i = 1, \cdots, n-1)$, $g_{\min}k_{n1} = \alpha_0 > 0$.

Let $\dfrac{1}{\varsigma_{i+1}} = \dfrac{g_{\max}^2}{4} + \dfrac{M_{i+1}^2}{2\lambda} + \alpha_0$, $\dfrac{\sigma_i}{2} = \alpha_0$ and $C = \sum_{i=1}^{n}\left(c_i + \dfrac{g_{\min}\sigma_i\theta_i^2}{2\gamma_i}\right) + \dfrac{(n-1)\lambda}{2}$.

Then, we have

$$\dot{V} \le -\sum_{i=1}^{n}\alpha_0\left(S_i^2 + \frac{g_{\min}\tilde{\theta}_i^2}{\gamma_i}\right) - \sum_{i=1}^{n-1}\alpha_0 y_{i+1}^2 - \sum_{i=1}^{n-1}\left(1 - \frac{B_{i+1}^2}{M_{i+1}^2}\right)\frac{y_{i+1}^2 M_{i+1}^2}{2\lambda} + C$$
$$\le -\sum_{i=1}^{n}\alpha_0\left(S_i^2 + \frac{g_{\min}\tilde{\theta}_i^2}{\gamma_i}\right) - \sum_{i=1}^{n-1}\alpha_0 y_{i+1}^2 + C \le -\alpha_0\left(2V - \sum_{i=1}^{n}V_{Q_i}\right) + C \tag{22}$$

Inequality (22) implies $\dot{V} < 0$ on $V = \mu$ when $\alpha_0 > C\big/\left(2\mu - \sum_{i=1}^{n}V_{Q_i}\right)$. Thus, $V \le \mu$ is an invariant set, i.e., if $V(0) \le \mu$, then $V(t) \le \mu$ for all $t \ge 0$. Also, from (22), all error signals in the closed-loop system are semiglobally uniformly bounded in the compact set $\Pi = \left\{\overline{S}_n, y_2, \cdots, y_n, \overline{\hat{\theta}}_n \Big| \sum_{i=1}^{n}\left(S_i^2 + \dfrac{g_{\min}\tilde{\theta}_i^2}{\gamma_i}\right) + \sum_{i=1}^{n-1}y_{i+1}^2 \le \dfrac{C}{\alpha_0}\right\}$, where

$\overline{\hat{\theta}}_n = [\hat{\theta}_1, \cdots, \hat{\theta}_n]$. Moreover, by increasing the design parameter α_0 , i.e., adjusting $k_i, \eta_i, \gamma_i, \sigma_i$, and ς_j , $i = 1, \cdots, n$, $j = 2, \cdots, n$, the compact set Π can be kept arbitrarily small. Thus, the tracking error $S_1 = y - y_d$ converges to a small neighborhood around zero.

Remark 2: Compare with [12], we consider unknown virtual control coefficient, thus the system model in this paper is more general. The proposed method can avoid the controller singularity problem.

5   Simulation Example

Consider the following second-order nonlinear time-delay system [10]:

$$\begin{cases} \dot{x}_1 = x_1 e^{-0.5x_1} + \left(1 + x_1^2\right)x_2 + \sin\left(x_1(t-\tau_1)\right) + d_1(t, x_1) \\ \dot{x}_2 = x_1 x_2^2 + \left(3 + \cos\left(x_1\right)\right)u + x_1(t-\tau_2)x_2(t-\tau_2) + d_1(t, \overline{x}_2) \end{cases} \quad (23)$$

where $d_1(t, x_1) = 0.7x_1^2 \cos(1.5t), d_2(t, \overline{x}_2) = 0.5\left(x_1^2 + x_2^2\right)\sin t$, $\tau_1 = 1$ and $\tau_2 = 2$. Then $\tau_{\max} = 2$. The reference signal $y_d = \sin(0.5t) + 0.5\sin(1.5t)$.

We choose the initial conditions $\left[x_1(t), x_2(t)\right]^T = \left[0.1, -1\right]^T$, $-\tau_{\max} \le t \le 0$, $v_{2f}(0) = 0$ and $\left[\hat{\theta}_1(0), \hat{\theta}_2(0)\right]^T = \left[0, 0\right]^T$. In the simulation, design parameters are taken as follows: $k_1 = 10$, $k_2 = 8$, $\gamma_1 = \gamma_2 = 1$, $\eta_1 = 0.1$, $\eta_2 = 2$, $\sigma_1 = \sigma_2 = 0.2$, $\varsigma_2 = 0.005$. Neural network $W_1^{*T}P_1(Z_1)$ contains 125 nodes with centers evenly spaced in $[-2, 2] \times [-2, 2] \times [-2, 2]$, and widths being equal to 1. Neural network $W_2^{*T}P_2(Z_2)$ contains 3125 nodes with centers evenly spaced in $[-2, 2] \times [-2, 2] \times [-2, 2] \times [-2, 2] \times [-4, 4]$, and widths being equal to 2.

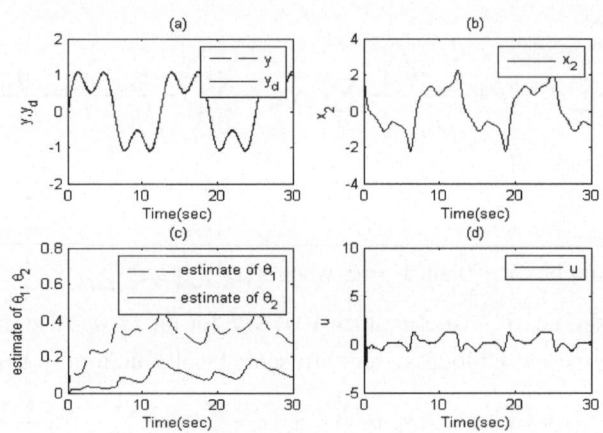

Fig. 1. Simulation results of system (23)

Fig. 1 shows the simulation results. Fig.1(a) shows the system output y and the reference signal y_d. Fig.1(b) shows the response of state variable x_2, Fig.1(c) shows the boundedness of adaptive parameters $\hat{\theta}_1$, $\hat{\theta}_2$, and Fig.1(d) displays the control input signal u. From the simulation results, it can clearly be seen that the proposed controller guarantees the boundedness of all signals in the closed-loop system, and also achieves the good tracking performance.

6   Conclusions

In this paper, by using appropriate Lyapunov-Krasovskii functionals and the dynamic surface control method, an adaptive neural network tracking control scheme has been presented for a class of perturbed nonlinear time-delay systems. The proposed adaptive neural network tracking controller guarantees the boundedness of all the signals in the closed-loop system, while the tracking error converges to a small neighborhood of the origin. In addition, the proposed controller contains less adaptive parameters, and its computation load is dramatically reduced. Simulation study has been conducted to show the effectiveness of the proposed scheme.

References

1. Krstic, M., Kanellakopoulos, I., Kokotovic, P.: Nonlinear and Adaptive Control Design. Wiley, New York (1995)
2. Ge, S.S., Wang, J.: Robust Adaptive Neural Control for a Class of Perturbed Strict Feedback Nonlinear Systems. IEEE Transactions on Neural Networks 13, 1409–1419 (2002)
3. Zhang, T.P., Ge, S.S.: Adaptive Neural Network Tracking Control of MIMO Nonlinear Systems with Unknown Dead Zones and Control Directions. IEEE Transactions on Neural Networks 20, 483–497 (2009)
4. Swaroop, D., Hedrick, J., Yip, P., Gerdes, J.: Dynamic Surface Control for a Class of Nonlinear Systems. IEEE Transactions on Automatic Control 45, 1893–1899 (2000)
5. Wang, D., Huang, J.: Neural Network-based Adaptive Dynamic Surface Control for a Class of Uncertain Nonlinear Systems in Strict-feedback Form. IEEE Transactions on Neural Networks 16, 195–202 (2005)
6. Zhang, T.P., Ge, S.S.: Adaptive Dynamic Surface Control of Nonlinear Systems with Unknown Dead Zone in Pure Feedback Form. Automatica 44, 1895–1903 (2008)
7. Chen, W.S., Jiao, L.C., Du, Z.B.: Output-feedback Adaptive Dynamic Surface Control of Stochastic Nonlinear Systems Using Neural Network. IET Control Theory and Applications 4, 3012–3021 (2010)
8. Yang, Y.S., Feng, G., Ren, J.S.: A Combined Backstepping and Small-gain Approach to Robust Adaptive Fuzzy Control for Strict-feedback Nonlinear Systems. IEEE Transactions on Systems, Man and Cybernetics, Part A: Systems and Humans 34, 406–420 (2004)
9. Chen, B., Liu, X.P., Liu, K.F., Lin, C.: Direct Adaptive Fuzzy Control of Nonlinear Strict-Feedback Systems. Automatica 45, 1530–1535 (2009)
10. Wang, M., Chen, B., Shi, P.: Adaptive Neural Control for a Class of Perturbed Strict-feedback Nonlinear Time-delay Systems. IEEE Transactions on Systems, Man, and Cybernetics, Part B: Cybernetics 38, 721–730 (2008)
11. Yoo, S.J., Park, J.B., Choi, Y.H.: Adaptive Dynamic Surface Control for Stabilization of Parametric Strict-feedback Nonlinear Systems with Unknown Time Delays. IEEE Transactions on Automatic Control 52, 2360–2365 (2007)
12. Ji, G., Hua, X.B.: Adaptive Dynamic Surface Control for Perturbed Nonlinear Time-delay Systems Using Neural Network. In: 2011 International Conference on Information Science and Technology, pp. 900–904 (2011)

Dual Fuzzy Neural Network Control in Civil Aviation Intelligent Landing System

Kaijun Xu[1], Guangming Zhang[1], and Yang Xu[2]

[1] Department of air navigation, School of flight technology
Civil aviation flight university of China, Guanghan, Sichuan, 618307, P.R. China
[2] Intelligent Control and Development Center,
Southwest Jiaotong University, Chengdu, Sichuan 610031, P.R. China
K_j_xu@163.com

Abstract. An intelligent landing system design using dual fuzzy neural network is proposed for research aircraft similar in configuration to civil aviation aircraft. The control law to track the pitch rate command is developed based on system theory. The controller architecture uses two fuzzy neural networks, which is capable of implementing fuzzy inference in general and neural network mechanism in particular. Neural network 1 with linear filters and back propagation through time learning algorithm is used to approximate the control law as system control part. The bounded signal requirement to develop the neural controller is circumvented using an off-line finite time training scheme in neural network 2 as system learning part, which provides the necessary stability and tracking performances. On-line learning scheme is implemented to compensate for uncertainties due to variation in aerodynamic coefficients, control surface failures and also variations in center of gravity position. The performance of the proposed control scheme is validated at different flight conditions. The disturbance rejection capability of the neural controller is analyzed in the presence of the realistic gust and sensor noises.

Keywords: intelligent landing system, dual fuzzy neural network, learning algorithm, civil aviation.

1 Introduction

Conventional landing control systems are designed using the linearized aircraft models at different equilibrium or trim conditions and the controller gains are scheduled to provide good performance in the complete operating flight envelope [1, 2]. However, it is difficult for the gain scheduling technique to provide the necessary tracking performance under severe uncertainty and fault conditions. Intelligent landing control schemes offer effective alternatives to overcome this difficulty. Intelligent control research is directed towards nonlinear systems with a special class of parametric uncertainty, which appear linearly with respect to known nonlinearities. Recently, neural networks have been explored for modeling and control of nonlinear systems due to their approximating capabilities and inherent adaptive features. Also,

H. Deng et al. (Eds.): AICI 2011, Part II, LNAI 7003, pp. 166–174, 2011.

from a practical perspective, massive parallelism and fast adaptability of neural network implementations provide more incentives for further investigation in problems involving systems with unknown uncertainties. The feasibility of applying neural network architectures for nonlinear system identification and control is first demonstrated through numerical simulation studies in [3], where the role of the neural networks is to learn some underlying relationship between the input–output data and also approximate the corresponding control law. Since then, a great deal of progress has been made both in theory and practice of neural network based nonlinear adaptive control system designs [4].

One of the areas to receive wide attention with respect to adaptive controller based neural network architectures is aircraft landing control system design. Modern day aircraft landing control systems are designed such that they can accommodate stringent flying quality requirements, parameter uncertainties, and component failures. In this context, an adaptive control scheme based on inversion of a linearized plant model is developed in [5], where the inversion errors are compensated through multilayer perceptron neural networks. The above method is proven to be effective in many applications including systems operating in highly nonlinear aerodynamic regime [5], systems with rapidly varying nonlinear dynamics [6, 7] and systems with high levels of uncertainties [8]. The most widely used flight control scheme based on neural networks is the feedback error-learning scheme [5]. In this scheme, the control architecture uses a conventional controller in the inner loop to stabilize the system dynamics, and the neural controller acts as an aid to the conventional controller for compensating any nonlinearities. Under severe modeling uncertainties, fault conditions and time varying nonlinear dynamics of the plant, the neural network is adapted on-line to ensure better tracking ability, provided the conventional controller in the inner loop satisfies the bounded signal requirements. Since the conventional controller is not designed for the new conditions, the control effort required by the feedback error-learning scheme is usually high when compared to the adaptive neural controllers [9].

The landing approach to civil aviation aircraft is generally considered one of the most demanding phases in human pilot control [2]. The combination of high workload, having to interpret the visual scene, timing the initiation of subsequent maneuvers and executing those maneuvers, all with the risks inherent to low-altitude flight, makes this process difficult to learn for new pilots. Real and/or simulated experience is indispensable to obtain and maintain landing skills, and performance feedback is thought to greatly improve learning efficiency [2, 10]. However, most pilots cannot explain what they look at or how they make their decisions and even training methods are not consistent.

The main contribution of the paper is the design of dual fuzzy neural control scheme that circumvents the above problems. A dual fuzzy neural networks controller (K.J XU et al, 2007) [11, 12] invariably includes two neural networks that have been trained to model of the aircraft control plant. The controller proposed in this paper is comprised of a fuzzy logic controller (FLC) in the feedback configuration (Zadeh, L.A., 1965) [13] and two dynamic neural networks in the forward path. A dynamic control network (DCN) is used to control the intelligent landing system, and a dynamic learning network (DLN) is employed to learn the weighting factor of the fuzzy logic. It is envisaged that the integration of fuzzy logic and neural network based-controller will encompass the merits of both technologies. The fuzzy logic controller, based on fuzzy set theory, provides a means for converting a linguistic control strategy into control action and offering a high level of computation. On the other hand, the ability of a dynamic recurrent network structure to model an arbitrary dynamic nonlinear system is incorporated to approximate the unknown nonlinear input–output relationship using a dynamic back propagation learning algorithm.

This paper is organized as follows. Section 2 deals with the definition of the problem and describes the aircraft landing approach procedure. Section 3 is devoted to description of intelligent landing system model. Section 4 describes the dual fuzzy neural network specifications and finally, Section 5 presents the simulations of the control scheme and conclusion comes from the last Section.

2   Aircraft Landing Approach Analysis

In a normal landing process, the pilot descends from cruising altitude to an altitude of approximately $1200\,ft$. The pilot then positions the aircraft so that the aircraft is on a heading towards the runway centerline. When the aircraft approaches the outer airport marker, which is about 4 nautical miles from the runway, the glide path signal is intercepted (as shown in Fig. 1). As the aircraft descends along the glide path its pitch, attitude, and speed must be controlled. The aircraft maintains a constant speed along the flight path. The descent rate is about $10\,ft/s$ and the pitch angle is between -51 and $+51$. Finally as the aircraft descends to $20-70\,ft$ the glide path control system is disengaged and a flare maneuver is executed. The vertical descent rate is decreased to $2\,ft/s$ so that the landing gear may be able to dissipate the energy of the impact at landing. The pitch angle of the aircraft is then adjusted to between 01 and 51 for most aircraft, which allows a soft touchdown on the runway surface.

The final approach to landing can be divided into two phases. In the first phase the pilot should maintain a constant descent which is generally about 3 degrees and keep the airplane aligned with the runway centerline. This phase will be referred to as the

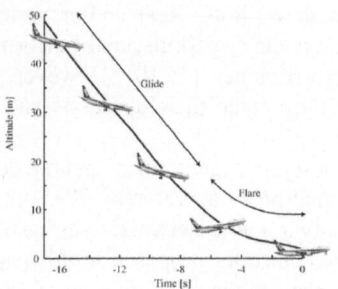

Fig. 1. Glide path and flare path

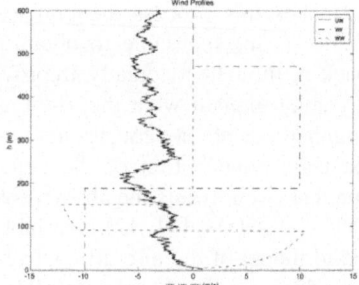

Fig. 2. Wind profiles during landing

'glide'. The second phase is the 'flare' (also called round out), where the pilot slowly pulls the column to make the aircraft pitch up in order to decrease the sink rate and land on the main landing gear first before the nose gear.

The aircraft is subjected to winds while flying this trajectory. The winds are a combination of Dryden turbulence along the x-body axis and deterministic winds in the other two axes (Fig. 2). The sharp step changes in the v_w (at 470 m and 190 m) and w_w (150m and 90 m) are particularly noticeable. These profiles represent a large horizontal and vertical wind shear respectively.

3   Description of the Intelligent Landing System

In this paper, we proposed the intelligent landing system using two fuzzy neural networks (Dual FNN). Two fuzzy neural networks with the same structure are considered. First, an FNN which to be designed as controller is obtained from one fuzzy neural network, the uncertainties compensation control uses ANFIS technique. Second, the learning FNN is obtained from neural learning model, the training data from plant can get the suitable control strategy in the learning part. Third, with the changes of the external environment, the learning part which has been training already, now it is used as controller on-line. The other neural network was to be regarded as controller, and now tuned into a learning part.

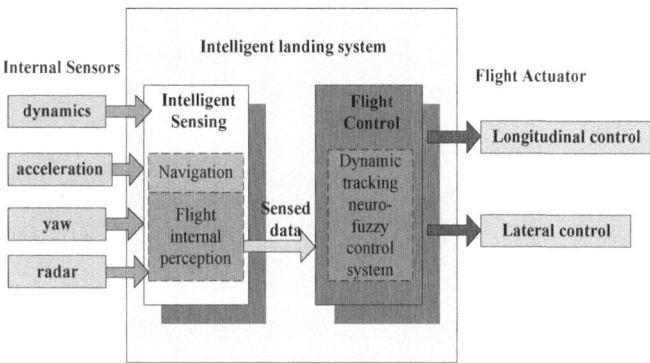

Fig. 3. Block-diagram of the intelligent landing system

Research on intelligent landing system mainly focused on control laws and the learning process that enhanced comfort and lowered fuel consumption by moderating the aircraft's accelerations. In the flight control part, we designed the dynamic tracking neuro-fuzzy control (DTNC) system which used the sensed data to control the aircraft.

The flight controller is comprised of the system identifier and two fuzzy neural networks. The system identifier inspect the control strategy which is not satisfied the real system after a while, it changes two fuzzy neural networks function. The learning neural network which has suitable strategy became to control the adaptive cruise control system. The former control network became to learning the new strategy. The identifier combines two parts: performance index and selector.

4   Description of the Dual Fuzzy Neural Network

4.1   Discussion of Dual Fuzzy Neural Network Control

Consider a nonlinear process given by:

$$\dot{x}_t = f(x_t, u_t) \tag{1}$$

Let us consider the following dynamic neural network to identify the nonlinear process Eq. (1):

$$\dot{\hat{x}}_t = A\hat{x}_t + W_t \phi(V_t \hat{x}_t) + U_t \tag{2}$$

$$\dot{x}_t = A x_t + W^0 \phi(V^0 x_t) + U_t - \mu_t \tag{3}$$

The identified nonlinear system Eq. (1) can also be written as:

$$\dot{x}_t = A x_t + W^* \phi(V^* x_t) + U_t - \tilde{f}_t \tag{4}$$

where $\tilde{f}_t$ is modeling error, v^* and w^* are set of weights chosen by the system identification agency.

Although the single fuzzy neural network Eq. (2) can identify any nonlinear process, the identification error is big if the network structure is not good for the steady state data from environment change. In general we cannot find the optimal network structure, but we can use two possible networks and select the best one by a proper switching algorithm.

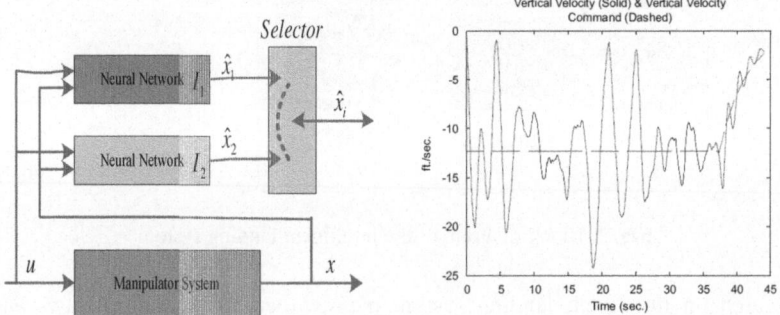

Fig. 4. The structure of DFNN control system   **Fig.5.** Aircraft vertical velocity and command

The structure of two fuzzy neural networks is shown in Fig. 4. The two fuzzy neural networks are presented:

$$\dot{\hat{x}}_\sigma = A_\sigma \hat{x}_\sigma + W_t^\sigma \phi_\sigma(V_t^\sigma \hat{x}_\sigma) + U_t \tag{5}$$

In each instant the identification error $\Delta_i (\Delta_i = \hat{x}_i - x, i = 1,2)$ which corresponds to each neural identifier I_i is calculated. We can define identification error performance index J_i for each neural identifier as:

$$J_i(t) = k_1 \Delta_i^2(t) + k_2 \int_0^t \Delta_i^2(\tau) d\tau \tag{6}$$

4.2   The Learning Algorithm

The neural network can be trained with the presence of a set of target examples or correct outputs, or with the presence of a mechanism that can provide corrections (a teacher), then the measure of error can be the sum of the squared errors as in the following:

$$e = \frac{1}{2} \sum_{i=1}^{N} (y_t(i) - y(i))^2 \tag{7}$$

The following recursive update mechanism for the sensitivity weights, w_s, is proposed:

$$z(i)^{(m+1)} = (w_S^{(m)}(i) \sum_{i=1}^{N} (w_S^{(m)})^2)(1 - \eta_{w_S} \bullet e \bullet S_N(i)) + \eta_{w_S} \bullet e \bullet x(i) \bullet S_N(i) \tag{8}$$

$$w_S^{(m+1)}(i) = \frac{z(i)^{(m+1)}}{\sum_{i=1}^{N} (z(i)^{(m+1)})^2} \tag{9}$$

Recall the measure of error with respect to the i-th neuron is given by:

$$e(q) = \frac{1}{2} \sum_{i=1}^{2N_r+1} (y_t(i) - y(i))^2 \tag{10}$$

$$y(k) = \frac{\sum_{i=1}^{N} \alpha_N(k) S_N(i)}{\sum_{i=1}^{N} S_N(i)} \tag{11}$$

$$w_\alpha^{m+1}(k) = w_\alpha^{(m)}(k) - \eta_{w_\alpha} \bullet \frac{\partial e(q)}{\partial w_\alpha(k)}$$

$$= w_\alpha^{(m)}(k) + \eta_{w_\alpha} \bullet (y_t(k) - y(k)) \frac{(S_N(i))^2}{\sum_{i=1}^{N} (S_N(i))^2} \tag{12}$$

$$\frac{\partial e(q)}{\partial y(k)} = -(y_t(k) - y(k)) \tag{13}$$

and the following equations are used to update the activation weights of k-th neuron:

$$w_\alpha^{m+1}(k) = w_\alpha^{(m)}(k) - \eta_{w_\alpha} \cdot \frac{\partial e(q)}{\partial y(k)} \cdot \frac{\partial y(k)}{\partial w_\alpha(k)}$$

$$= w_\alpha^{(m)}(k) - \eta_{w_\alpha} \cdot \frac{\partial e(q)}{\partial y(k)} \cdot \frac{(S_N(i))^2}{\sum_{i=1}^{N}(S_N(i))^2} \tag{14}$$

5   Simulation of Control Scheme and Conclusions

Suppose that the aircraft starts the initial states of the intelligent landing system as follows: the flight height is $500\,ft$, the horizontal position before touching the ground is $9240\,ft$, the flight angle is $-3°$, and the speed of the aircraft is $234.7\,ft/s$. Successful touchdown landing conditions are defined as follows:

(I) $-3 \le \dot{h}_{TD} \le -1(ft/s)$

(II) $-300 \le x_{TD}(T) \le 1000(ft)$

(III) $200 \le V_{TD}(T) \le 270(ft/s)$

(IV) $-10 \le \theta_{TD}(T) \le 5(\deg)$

where T is the time at touchdown, $\dot{h}_{TD}$ is vertical speed, x_{TD} is the horizontal position, V_{TD} is the horizontal speed, and θ_{TD} is the pitch angle.

As a final test of the simulation of the proposed control scheme, the neural controller is used for tracking a desired pitch rate in the presence of nonlinearities. The MATLAB™ based program that incorporates the nonlinear variation of force and moment coefficients is used for this purpose. For the safe landing of an aircraft using dual fuzzy neural network, we can get the results from using different wind turbulence speeds. The dual fuzzy neural network controller which we proposed can successfully guide an aircraft flying through $0-60\,ft/s$. Figs. 5–7 show the results from using the dual fuzzy neural network controller.

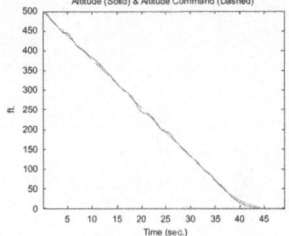

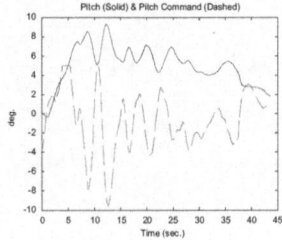

Fig. 6. Aircraft altitude and command   **Fig. 7.** Aircraft pitch and pitch command

Using intelligent landing flight path data, trajectory tracking of aircraft landing was simulated by the use of the dual fuzzy neural network. Since during trajectory tracking and learning, many of the atmospheric influencing factors are uncertain and changing rapidly, especially under severe weather conditions, dual fuzzy neural network control with the ability of learning appears to be one of the promising approaches. Even with these limited results due to limited data, this simulation approach by the use of the fuzzy adaptive network appears to be a promising approach

The adaptive neural fuzzy inference system has been shown to be very useful in many different areas where the data are vague and may be even linguistic. This is because of the combined advantages of both the linguistic representation ability of fuzzy sets and the learning ability of neural networks. Thus, at the beginning, the data can be represented approximately by fuzzy membership functions and these approximate representations can be improved or updated as more data become available. It should be noted that many useful systems such as in manufacturing or in control are vague and frequently need human experts to operate. These experts can only give data linguistically.

Acknowledgment. This work is supported by the National Natural Science Foundation of P.R. China (Grant No. 60875034). Also be supported by National Natural Science Foundation of the United Foundation of China Civil Aviation (Grant No. 60736046).

References

1. Zhao, Q., Jiang, J.: Reliable state feedback control system design against actuator failures. Automatica 34(10), 1267–1272 (1998)
2. Snell, S.A., Enns, D.F., Garrard, W.L.: Nonlinear control of a super-maneuverable aircraft. In: Proceeding AIAA Guidance Navigation and Control Conference, Washington, DC (August 1989); Paper AIAA-89-3486
3. Narendra, K.S., Parthasarathy, K.: Identification and control of dynamical systems using neural networks. IEEE Trans. Neural Netw. 1(1), 4–27 (1990)
4. Narendra, K.S., Mukhopadhyay, S.: Adaptive control of nonlinear multivariable systems using neural networks. Neural Netw. 7(5), 737–752 (1994)
5. Calise, A.J., Sharma, M., Corban, J.E.: An adaptive autopilot design for guided munitions. In: AIAA Guidance, Navigation, and Control Conference, AIAA, Reston, VA, vol. 3, pp. 1776–1785 (1998)
6. Leitner, J., Calise, A.J., Prasad, J.V.R.: A full authority helicopter adaptive neuro-controller. In: IEEE Aerospace Conference Proceedings, Int. Electrical and Electronics Engineers, NY, vol. 2, pp. 117–126 (1998)
7. Nardi, F., Rysdyk, R.T., Calise, A.J.: Neural network based adaptive control of a thrust vectored ducted fan. In: AIAA Guidance, Navigation, and Control Conference, AIAA Reston, VA, vol. 1, pp. 374–383 (1999)
8. McFarland, M.B., Calise, A.J.: Robust adaptive control of uncertain nonlinear systems using neural network. In: Proceedings of American Control Conference, American Automatic Control Council, Evanston, vol. 3, pp. 1996–2000 (1997)

9. Suresh, S., Omkar, S.N., Mani, V., Sundararajan, N.: Nonlinear adaptive neural controller for unstable aircraft. J. Guidance Control Dyn. 28(6), 1103–1111 (2005)
10. Lee, T., Kim, Y.: Nonlinear adaptive flight control using backstepping and neural networks controller. J. Guidance Control Dyn. 24(4), 675–682 (2001)
11. Xu, K.J., Zou, L., Lai, J.J., Xu, Y.: An application of Dual-Fuzzy Neural-Networks to Design of Adaptive Fuzzy Controllers. In: The 3rd International Conference on Natural Computation, ICNC 2007 (2007)
12. Xu, K.J., Lai, J.J., Li, X.B., Pan, X.D., Xu, Y.: Adjustment strategy for a dual-fuzzy-neuro controller using genetic algorithms -application to gas-fired water heater. In: 8th International FLINS Conference on Computational Intelligence in Decision and Control (2008)
13. Zadeh, L.A.: Fuzzy sets. Inf. Control 8, 338–353 (1965)

Coal Level Monitoring System of Coal Warehouses Based on CAN Field Bus

Xian-Min Ma[1] and Yuan-Yuan Yu[2]

[1] College of Electrical and Control Engineering
Xi'an University of Science &Technology
Xi'an, 710054, China
maxm@xust.edu.cn
[2] College of Electrical and Control Engineering
Xi'an University of Science &Technology
Xi'an, 710054, China
yu30152698@126.com

Abstract. A new method of monitoring the coal level in three coal warehouses is introduced in the paper. Coal bulk position in the coal bin is real-time detected by CCD cameras, and controlled by CAN field bus monitoring system which is composed of ARM7TDMI (-S) and SJA1000 hardware. The principle of monitoring coal level in the coal warehouse is discussed, the position algorithm of the coal level in coal bin is proposed, the system configuration is designed, and the alarm interface is given. The research shows that the coal level monitoring system for the coal warehouse is helpful to raise the real time detection performance and intellectualization of coal position monitor in coal warehouses as well.

Keywords: Coal level, Coal Warehouse, Monitoring System, Coal Position Algorithm, CAN field bus, ARM7TDMI (-S).

1 Introduction

The coal warehouse is a very important middle transportation link in the coal mine production system. Coal loading, unloading and the storage are all generally realized through the coal warehouse, regardless of the mine production transportation system on the ground or in the underground. In actual production, there are many accidents appeared frequently in the coal warehouses, because the coal warehouse is empty or full, and the shift process of the loading or unloading in these coal warehouses is not smoothly completed. So it is necessary to set up the real time monitoring system to detect the coal level in the coal warehouse in order to carry on the effective examination to the coal position in the coal bin and assure the normal operation of the all coal mine production system.

At present there are many methods to monitor the coal level in the coal bin. The majority of coal mine enterprise use the ultrasonic wave way, the electric capacity method or the heavy hammer type to examine the coal level in the coal warehouses in

H. Deng et al. (Eds.): AICI 2011, Part II, LNAI 7003, pp. 175–182, 2011.

the domestic coal mine. The ultrasonic wave method is high in equipment precision but it is very expensive. Moreover, the detecting head of ultrasonic wave sensor is often polluted by coal dust which creates the uncertainty of work and brings certain hidden danger accident. The electric capacity type measurement method easily is affected by coal environment, and the switching circuit is also very complex. Although the heavy hammer type has the merits of working reliably, the cost low, antijamming ability strong and so on, but the controlled process of electrical machinery is complex. On the other side, the localization is not accuracy even the gravity hammer may be buried in the material.

The modern coal mine production development needs to carry on the uninterrupted supervising the coal bulk position in the coal bins, and guarantees each production link safety highly and effective running[1]. It is urgently to develop a kind of working reliably monitoring system to detect the coal level in the coal bin. This paper proposed a new coal level monitoring system, which is composed of the CCD cameras, CAN field bus , ARM7TDMI(-S) and SJA1000 to real time monitor coal position in coal bin and to control conveyer belt direction real-time.

2   System Constitution

The proposed system structure is shown in Fig. 1.

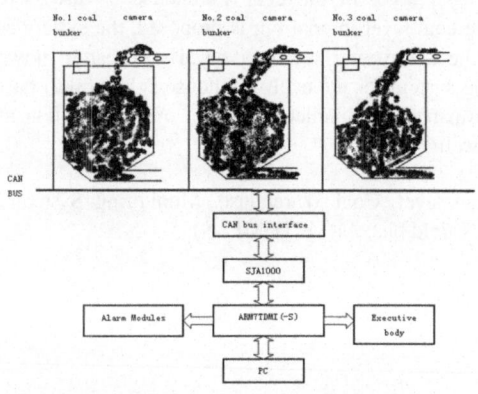

Fig. 1. The system constitution

The system consists of two parts of monitoring system and controlling system. The main task of the monitoring system is to track coal position of the coal bin in real-time. And the core of the control part is ARM7TDMI (-S) which controls the transport direction of the coal conveyor belt according to the receiving signal from PC.

There are three coal warehouses for shift working in turn, so three CCD cameras are used to monitoring the coal level for each other. Through the CAN bus, ARM controller disposes the correlate image and sends alarm signal, if the coal bin is full or empty. At the same time the host computer PC shows which coal bin is full or empty in order to can change the transportation direction of coal conveyer belt.

3   Coal Position Algorithm

The camera is installed at the top of the coal bunker to monitor the coal position of the coal bin real-time with a secondary light source, and the image signal transmits to the PC for processing through CAN bus and ARM7 so as to obtain the real time coal level image. The different coal level in the coal warehouse is illustrated in Fig.2.

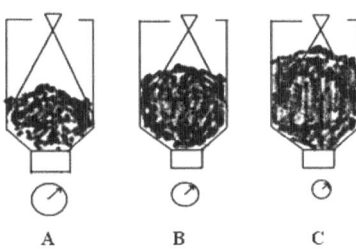

A   B   C

Fig. 2. The different coal level in the coal warehouse

Fig. 2 shows that the coal surface area is becoming smaller and smaller when the coal level height in the coal warehouse of A, B, C is approaching the CCD camera.

Supposed that the height of the coal warehouse of A,B,C is H_1,H_2,H_3,respectively, and the corresponding radius of the coal surface is R_1,R_2,R_3 respectively, at this point. The reposing angle of coal position is the maximum angle when the coal bulk of the coal bin is in the natural stable state. The reposing angle of coal block in the coal warehouse is generally 30 degrees, which is shown in the Fig.3.

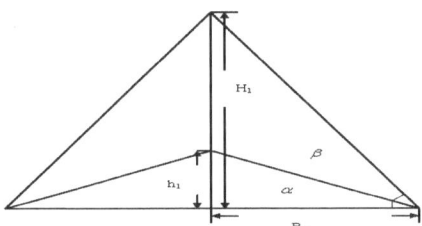

Fig. 3. The cross-section surface of the coal bin radius

As shown in Fig.3, the angle β is defined as the angle between boundaries of coal and light, and the coal reposing angle is α. If the ideal state of the reposing angle α is not changed, the similar isosceles triangle is formed in cross-section of different coal face with the continuous increasing of coal bulk. For example taking the cross section of first coal as shown above, the cross-section height of coal surface is h_1. Because of the reposing angle, the radius of coal surface area is R_1, if h_1 is formed. So the actual height between the highest positions of coal level and the input port of coal bin is H_1-h_1. If the highest point is located away from the coal bin input port, the reposing angle is derived as following:

$$\tan\alpha = h_1/R_1 \tag{1}$$

So the cross-section height of coal surface is deduced as:

$$h_1 = R_1 \tan\alpha \tag{2}$$

The angle between the light source and the coal bottom surface in the coal warehouse is can be expressed as follows:

$$\tan(\alpha+\beta) = H_1/R_1 \tag{3}$$

Wherefore the first coal bin level is deduced:

$$H_1 = R_1 \tan(\alpha+\beta) \tag{4}$$

In order to compute coal position h simple, the angle between the light source and the coal bottom surface in the coal warehouse is can also be transformed as follows:

$$\tan(\alpha+\beta) = (\tan\alpha + \tan\beta)/(1 - \tan\alpha\tan\beta) \tag{5}$$

Thus the highest point h of the coal position from the coal bin input port is described as follows:

$$h = H_1 - h_1 = R_1(\tan(\alpha+\beta) - \tan\alpha) \tag{6}$$

The simple equation of the highest point h can be expressed as:

$$h = R_1((\tan\alpha + \tan\beta)/(1 - \tan\alpha\tan\beta) - \tan\alpha) \tag{7}$$

If the surface area of the coal level in first coal bin is S_1 at this time, the corresponding radius R_1 of the coal surface is described as:

$$R_1 = \sqrt{S_1/\pi} \tag{8}$$

As long as the coal surface area S of any height or the radius in the coal bin is known, the height of coal level in the coal bin can be obtained from above formula. The circle of light source can be measured through the optical circle detection algorithm, and the adaptive threshold can be set up for processing the image. Sobel edge detection is used to detect the light boundary circle for the coal surface area S.

4   Hardware Design

According to the system performance requirement, the system hardware design is shown in Fig.4.

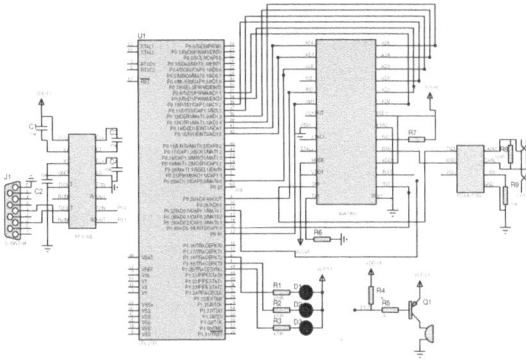

Fig. 4. Hardware circuit

In Fig.4 LPC2131 is a kind of ARM7TDMI (-S) [2] and connected to the CAN controller. In a large scale coal mine working site, there are many problems such as the monitoring points, distance and so on. Therefore the CAN field bus is fully used due to the better characteristics which are of the multi-master-slave mode, high transmission rate, and strong anti-interference. So the CAN field bus plays the role in the system. The coal level image data are acquired and transported to ARM7TDMI (-S) from the ports of the AD0-AD7 of SJA1000 to the pin P0.8-P0.15 of the LPC213 for data exchange. LPC2131 P0.22, P0.25, P0.31, P0.23, respectively, are connected to the SJA1000 ALE / AS, RD / E, WR, CS to achieve the function of reading, writing and chip selection. In order to achieve the interrupt and reset function the P0.30, P0.27 is respectively connected to the INT, RST pin in SJA1000, which can process the reading and writing in the SJA1000 via software simulation by timing, when LPC2131 is accessing SJA1000. SJA1000 mode pin are set in high level through the VCC, to make the SJA1000 working in internal model. The P0.0 and P0.1in the LPC are connected to the T2IN and R2OUT pins in the SP3232E that is connected to the serial port. Through the serial port interface, the received image data and controlled command are communicated between PC and ARM monitoring equipment. When the bunker is full or empty, the monitoring equipment sends the alarm signals and controls the direction of the conveyor belt. The alert flag is displayed in PC at the same time.

In this design, there are three coal bins to use load or unload the coal bulks. When the first coal bin is full, ARM controller issues the shift commands to the executing agencies through the CAN bus to control the transporting state of converter belt to the second coal bin. When the second bin is full, the converter belt must be transferred to the third coal bin in the same way. When the third coal bin is full, the transportation direction of coal conveyer belt is transferred to the first coal bin, which is now in empty. Loop control of conveyors state in the order of the first coal bin, the second coal bin and the third coal bin has characteristics of good real-time, versatility and high reliability.

The SJA1000 controller is widely used in general industrial environments. In this system, SJA1000 controller is connected between the ARM and CAN bus, and communicated each order with CAN communication protocol. At the same time, the enhanced CAN additional mode PeliCAN supports CAN2.0B protocols [3]. According to the system requirements, the CAN controller interface chip PCA82C250 is selected as the CAN bus connection interface.

5 Software Design

The module design method is used for system software design. According to the different function modeule, there are tree parts in the system software. The main program flow chart is shown in Fig.5.

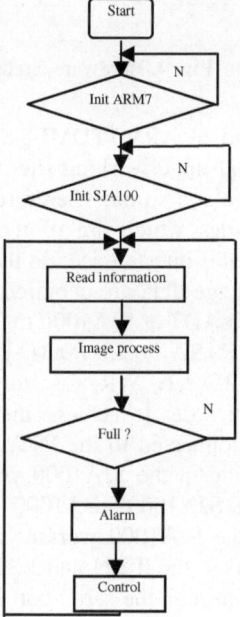

Fig. 5. The main program

Shown in Fig. 5, the task of the main program is to initialize the controller such as ARM7 and the SJA1000. Then the coal level image information in the coal warehouses is collected and transported to host computer PC through CAN bus and ARM7. The coal level image process is completed in PC. If the processed result is full, the PC gives the shift command and sends the alarm sign displayed in visual interface. The ARM7 controls the conveyor belt to next bin.

In this system, the data transportation function between host computer PC and ARM7 through CAN is very important for the real time monitoring the coal level in these three warehouses. The host computer PC is in master state and to control serial communication. And the ARM7 is in slave status with the asynchronous, half-duplex manner through communication cable 232. The data communication flow chart between host computer PC and slave ARM7 is show in Fig.6.

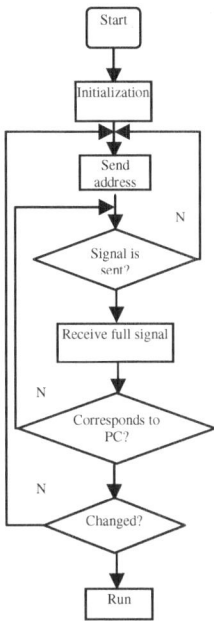

Fig. 6. The ARM7 serial communication with PC

As shown in Fig.6, the main task of the communication module is to set the baud rate, initialize serial communication. The address from the host computer is sent to the ARM7, and then the host computer PC checks whether the command signal has been sent out. If the command has been emitted, the host computer PC receives the signal from the ARM7 and then sends the signature signal to it. If the command has not been emitted, PC is waiting to receive the handshake signal. The ARM7 determines whether it is its own signature. If the communication is successful, the host computer PC issue commands to change the state of coal converter belt to next coal warehouse, and the ARM7 receives and executes the order.

The VB6.0 programming language is used to write the communication program, because this interface is very intuitive and the effective of human-computer interaction [4]. The visual interface created by VB is shown in Fig. 7.

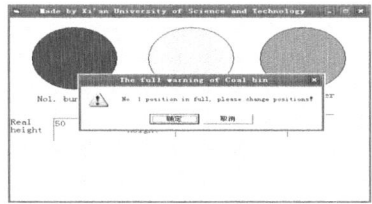

Fig. 7. The alarm sign when the first coal bin is full

When the coal bin is full, the warning window is pop up and the red alarm sign is displayed to ask for exchanging coal bin. At the same time, if the second coal bin is not full, the yellow sign shows the coal is loading. Meantime the green flag shows that the third coal bin has all been shipped out, so the coal conveyor belt can be transferred from full marked coal bin to the empty one. The intelligent monitoring coal level in three coal bins can be finished.

6 Conclusions

The new design for the intelligent monitoring and control of the coal level in the three coal warehouses is proposed in the paper. The embedded ARM chip is used as the main controller, the CAN bus is adopted to communicate data. The VB6.0 programming language is used to write the communication program. The primary research shows that the accurate communication between PC and ARM is achieved and the direction of coal conveyor belt control can be controlled. Thus the danger of full or empty coal bin is avoided.

References

1. Zhang, Y., Zhao, J.: Coal bin coal-bit auto-detection system. Coal Mine Machinery (7), 107–109 (2005)
2. Liu, Z., Gao, J., Guo, J., Zhang, S., Han, Y.: The application of can bus technology in bunker environmental monitoring system. Coal Mine Machinery (9), 153 (2009)
3. Ma, S., Lin, G., Zhao, Y.: The application of can bus in the video surveillance system. East China University of Technology Newspapers 29(2) (June 2006)
4. Huang, T., et al.: Serial communication adapter set design and implementation between can bus and the pc. Instrument Technique and Sensor (7), 35 (2004)

Networked Strong Tracking Filters With Noise Correlations and Bits Quantization

Xiaoliang Xu[1] and Quanbo Ge[2]

[1] School of Computer Science and Technology, Hangzhou Dianzi University
Hangzhou, P.R. China, 310018
xxl@hdu.edu.cn
[2] School of Automation, Hangzhou Dianzi University
Hangzhou, P.R. China, 310018
qbge@hdu.edu.cn

Abstract. We study the design of quantized Kalman filters with strong tracking ability for the single sensor system with the correlation between process and measurement noises and adaptive bits quantization in this paper. Firstly, we perfect the problem formulation for the quantized tracking system about the correlation between original process and measurement noises and the correlation matrixes between quantized error and original process and measurement noises. Both are clear innovation in our study. Secondly, based on this problem formulation, two direct quantized Kalman filters are presented by use of statistical modeling and augmented state modeling ways respectively. Finally, the strong tracking method which can deal with noise correlation is used to propose two quantized strong tracking filters, which can effectively reduce the modeling uncertainty and get the strong tracking ability to the state abrupt change.

Keywords: Sensor networks, adaptive bits quantization, noise correlation, Kalman filter, strong tracking filtering.

1 Introduction

Extensive application of sensor networks in many fields such as event detection, target tracking and state monitoring makes the design of networked filters suffer many new constraints and difficulties. Especially, the limited bandwidth of wireless sensor network is one of many important constraints [1,2]. In order to satisfy this limitation and time-variant dynamic bandwidth, there is one of good choice to adopt the adaptive bits quantization [3]. Accordingly, to design quantized filters or fusion estimators is becoming a popular research direction in sensor networks and data fusion fields [4].

Compared with the traditional researches, the design of networked filter will suffer many new difficulties and challenges. The essence is that the adaptive bits quantization operation which is random and nonlinear will induce a uncertain quantization error

H. Deng et al. (Eds.): AICI 2011, Part II, LNAI 7003, pp. 183–192, 2011.

(QE) [4,5]. As a result, how to accurately model or effectively deal with this noise becomes the key to design networked filter. For constructing the quantized Kalman filter with adaptive bits quantization scheme, there are some significative achievements recently such as [3-12]. Among them, the representative results are given by [7-12]. For the linear dynamic estimate system without noise correlation, the adaptive bits quantization scheme was used to get a quantized state estimate system in [7]. Meantime, the correlations between the QE and original process and measurement noises are neglected, namely the assumption of uncorrelated noise. Three different quantized information forms are considered and the quantized fusion estimators were proposed by use of statistical modeling way to the quantization error and approximative technique to the variance of quantization error. In [8-10], aiming at the nonlinear time-variant dynamic system, the quantized nonlinear fusion filters were studied for EKF, UKF and PF based on the similar assumption of uncorrelated noises and statistical modeling way to the QE. But, due to the inaccuracy of the statistical modeling way to the QE, augmented state modeling way was presented to improve state estimation accuracy [11]. Continuously, strong tracking scheme was introduced to deal with the uncertainty of both modeling ways to the quantization error in order to improve the state estimate in [12]. Besides, it also gets good strong tracking ability to state abrupt change because of the essence of strong tracking idea.

Although the above researches provided some useful algorithms to deal with the quantized filtering or quantized state estimation, there are some shortcomings because the assumption on uncorrelated noises is used and especially the correlations between the quantized error and original process and measurement noises are neglected. Accordingly, in order to extend the algorithm's range and improve the universal property, we study the design of quantized filters for single sensor system with the correlation between original process and measurement noises. The innovation is also to consider the correlations between the QE and original process and measurement noises and to formulate their correlation matrixes. Strong tracking filtering with noise correlation is introduced to design the quantized tracking filters based on two different modeling ways to the QE. As a result, their state estimate performances are fully improved and the strong tracking function is realized to the state abrupt change.

The rest of the paper is organized as follows. In section 2, the problem formulation is presented. Section 3 presents Kalman filter with statistical modeling to quantization error and noise correlations. Kalman filter with augmented state modeling for quantization error is designed in section 4. In section 5, quantized strong tracking filters with two different modeling ways to the QE are proposed. Section 6 is conclusion.

2 Problem Formulation

2.1 System Description

Consider a kind of target tracking system with following linear dynamic equations

$$x(k) = \boldsymbol{\Phi}(k,k-1)x(k-1) + \boldsymbol{\omega}(k,k-1) \tag{1}$$

$$z(k) = \boldsymbol{H}(k)x(k) + \boldsymbol{v}(k) \tag{2}$$

where $x(k) \in R^{n \times 1}$ is the state variable of the target; $\boldsymbol{\Phi}(k,k-1) \in R^{n \times n}$ is the system matrix from discrete time $k-1$ to k ; $z(k) \in R^{q \times 1}$ is the measurement at time k , and $\boldsymbol{H}(k) \in R^{q \times n}$ is the measurement matrix. process noise $\boldsymbol{\omega}(k,k-1) \in R^{n \times 1}$ and measurement noise $\boldsymbol{v}(k) \in R^{q \times 1}$ are both zero mean Gaussian white, and both of them have the following properties

$$\boldsymbol{E}\{\boldsymbol{\omega}(k,k-1)\} = \boldsymbol{0}, \boldsymbol{E}\{\boldsymbol{\omega}(k,k-1)\boldsymbol{\omega}^T(j,j-1)\} = \boldsymbol{Q}(k,k-1)\delta_{kj} \tag{3}$$

$$\boldsymbol{E}\{\boldsymbol{v}(k)\} = \boldsymbol{0}; \boldsymbol{E}\{\boldsymbol{v}(k)\boldsymbol{v}^T(j)\} = \boldsymbol{R}(k)\delta_{kj}, \ \boldsymbol{E}\{\boldsymbol{\omega}(k,k-1)\boldsymbol{v}^T(j)\} = \boldsymbol{S}(k)\delta_{kj} \tag{4}$$

where $Q(k,k-1)$ is non negative definite matrix.

Initial state $x(0)$ is independent with $\boldsymbol{\omega}(k,k-1)$ and $\boldsymbol{v}(k)$, and

$$\boldsymbol{E}\{x(0)\} = \hat{x}(0|0), \ \boldsymbol{E}\{[x(0) - \hat{x}(0|0)][x(0) - \hat{x}(0|0)]^T\} = \boldsymbol{P}(0|0) \tag{5}$$

2.2 Problem Formulation

Because the network bandwidth is limited and the digital transmission should be satisfied, generally the local sensor information such as original measurement [7,9], innovation[4,10] and local estimate should be quantized before they are sent to the fusion center. At present, we have several quantization strategies and the adaptive bits quantization method is popular for wireless sensor networks. Naturally, there are many works on state estimation or data fusion by use of the adaptive bits quantization when the local information is original sensor measurement. But, there is a common characteristic, namely some correlations relating to bits quantization error are neglected. Thereby, it is necessary to adequately consider these correlations in the design of quantized filter such that its estimation accuracy and stability can be further improved. As a result, we study the design of networked Kalman filter based on adaptive bits quantization and consideration of correlation on bits quantization error.

In this paper, the following assumptions are needful.

Assumption 1: Suppose the bandwidth is L bits, and the communication channel from local sensor to estimate center is perfect, namely no bit error.

Assumption 2: We assume all of components of measurement vector are bounded, namely $z(k,i) \in [\underline{D}(i), \overline{D}](i)(1 \le i \le q)$, $z(k,i)$ is the ith component of $z(k)$ and $\underline{D}(i) < \overline{D}(i)$.

According to above assumptions, we can get the following adaptive quantization strategy. In this adaptive quantization strategy, we consider that the available bandwidth is time-variant and each component of quantized message must be transmitted effectively. Thereby, in order to accord with the dynamic property of network bandwidth, it is necessary to adaptively assign the bandwidth to each component in term of the real-time situation, but not averagely. Then, the message $m(k) \in R^{q \times 1}$, which is the information after quantized, is

$$m(k) = H(k)x(k) + v(k) + n(k) \tag{6}$$

where $n(k) \in R^{q \times 1}$ is quantization error vector, and

$$n(k) = m(k) - z(k) \tag{7}$$

And, denote

$$\theta(k) = v(k) + n(k) \tag{8}$$

Thereby, we can get the quantized message equation from original measurement equation as follows

$$m(k) = H(k)x(k) + \theta(k) \tag{9}$$

After the quantized operation is done, we can find the following several noise correlations:

1) The first correlation between $\omega(k, k-1)$ and $v(k)$. It is directly from initial system description and denoted as $S(k)$.

2) The second is the correlation between $v(k)$ and $n(k)$ .Because $n(k)$ roots in $z(k)$, it is necessary that there is correlative between $v(k)$ and $n(k)$, and the correlation is denoted as $R_{n,v}(k)$.

3) The third correlation is $S_{\omega,n}(k)$ between $\omega(k, k-1)$ and $n(k)$ It is easily derived from 1) and 2).

Consequently, the issue to design quantized filters is changed to how to construct state estimators in terms of Eq. (1) and (9). Next, we discuss the design of networked state estimators by use of two different modeling ways to bits quantization error such as approximate covariance modeling and augmented state modeling ways. In many current works they generally suppose to neglect the noise correlations above-mentioned in order to simplify the design process of state estimator. As a result, what is different against the current works is that the cross-correlations on the quantization error should be considered in this paper.

3 Kalman Filter with Statistical Modeling to Quantization Error and Noise Correlations

3.1 Kalman Estimator with Approximate Covariance Modeling

The first way to model the quantization error is to look for its statistical property. According to [7], the covariance of $n(k)$ can be computed as

$$R_n(k) = diag[R_n(k,1), R_n(k,2), ..., R_n(k,q)] \tag{10}$$

where

$$R_n(k,r) \leq \frac{\Delta^2(k,r)}{4}, r = 1, 2, ..., q \tag{11}$$

$$\Delta(k,r) = \frac{\overline{D}(r) - \underline{D}(r)}{T(k,r) - 1}, T(k,r) = 2^{l(k,r)} \tag{12}$$

and $l(k,r)$ can be obtained from [7].

According to (4), (5), (6) and (9), we have

$$R_\theta(k) = E\{\theta(k)\theta^T(k)\} = R(k) + R_n(k) + R_{n,\upsilon}(k) + R_{n,\upsilon}^T(k) \tag{13}$$

$$S_{\omega,\theta}(k) = E\{\omega(k,k-1)[\upsilon(k) + n(k)]^T\} = E\{\omega(k,k-1)\upsilon^T(k)\} + E\{\omega(k,k-1)n^T(k)\}$$
$$= S(k) + S_{\omega,n}(k) \tag{14}$$

As a result, the optimal state estimator with quantized message can be obtained.

Theorem 1. The optimal quantized state estimator with approximate covariance modeling and noise correlations induced by bits quantization is as follows

$$\begin{cases} \hat{x}(k \mid k) = \hat{x}(k \mid k-1) + K(k)[m(k) - H(k)\hat{x}(k \mid k-1)] \\ P(k \mid k) = P(k \mid k-1) - K(k)[P(k \mid k-1)H^T(k) + S_{\omega,\theta}(k) \end{cases} \tag{15}$$

where

$$\begin{cases} \hat{x}(k \mid k-1) = \Phi(k,k-1)\hat{x}(k-1 \mid k-1) \\ P(k \mid k-1) = \Phi(k,k-1)P(k,k-1)\Phi^T(k,k-1) + Q(k,k-1) \end{cases} \tag{16}$$

$$K(k) = [P(k \mid k-1)H^T(k) + S_{\omega,\theta}(k)] \times [H(k)P(k,k-1)H^T(k)$$
$$+ H(k)S_{\omega,\theta}(k) + (H(k)S_{\omega,\theta}(k))^T + R_\theta(k)]^{-1} \tag{17}$$

So, the optimal quantized state estimate can be done.

3.2 Brief Analysis

The kernel of statistical modeling method to random bits quantization is to take the statistical property of quantized error vector and the Kalman filter with correlated noise is used to solve optimal networked state estimate. Although, we can describe the noise correlations induced by bits quantization, it is difficult to take the values of these noise correlations. A direct method is to tune them during the tracking process. Certainly, the statistical learning and neural network methods can be used to train these noise correlation matrixes.

4 Kalman Filter with Augmented State Modeling for Quantization Error

4.1 Kalman Filter with Augmented State Modeling

It is an available method to model the statistical property of bit quantization error in order to solve quantized state estimation. But, we find that in this method the accurate statistical property of the quantized error can not be taken because of random adaptive quantized strategy, and the magnitude of quantized error is unknown and it is difficult to estimate for processing center. For improving the accuracy of networked state estimation, it is necessary to look for novel processing scheme for the quantized error. Accordingly, we find that the combined estimation idea of parameter and state is useful. Namely, the quantization error $n(k)$ is taken to a component of systemic state vector. Thereby, state vector $x(k)$ is augmented to $x^*(k)$, namely

$$x^*(k) = [x^T(k), n^T(k)]^T \tag{18}$$

where $x^*(k) \in R^{(n+q) \times 1}$. The key for the augmented state scheme should re-model the quantized error vector to a Markova random process with time series form. Then, because of the random uncertainty of bits quantization, small disturbance should be considered for the modeling. As a result, we define

$$n(k) = n(k-1) + \omega_n(k, k-1) \tag{19}$$

where $\omega_n(k, k-1)$ is a zero mean Gauss white noise process with variance $Q_n(k, k-1)$

Then, the new system with augmented state modeling can be taken as

$$x^*(k) = \Phi^*(k, k-1)x^*(k-1) + \omega^*(k, k-1) \tag{20}$$

$$m(k) = H^*(k)x^*(k) + v(k) \tag{21}$$

where $H^*(k) = [H(k), I]$, and

$$\Phi^*(k, k-1) = [\Phi(k, k-1), 0_{n \times q}; 0_{q \times n}, I_{q \times q}] \quad \omega^*(k, k-1) = [\omega^T(k, k-1), \omega_n^T(k, k-1)]^T \tag{22}$$

where $\boldsymbol{\Phi}^*(k,k-1) \in \boldsymbol{R}^{(n+q)\times(n+q)}$ and $\boldsymbol{H}^*(k) \in \boldsymbol{R}^{q\times(n+q)}$, and $\boldsymbol{\omega}^*(k,k-1)) \in \boldsymbol{R}^{(n+q)\times 1}$ and $\boldsymbol{v}(k) \in \boldsymbol{R}^{q\times 1}$ are both dependent zero mean gauss white noise sequences, and

$$E\{\boldsymbol{\omega}^*(k,k-1)\} = E\{\boldsymbol{v}(k)\} = \boldsymbol{0} \,, \; E\{\boldsymbol{v}(k)\boldsymbol{v}^T(k)\} = \boldsymbol{R}(k) \qquad (23)$$

And, $\boldsymbol{\omega}(k,k-1)$ and $\boldsymbol{\omega}_n(k,k-1)$ are independent, so

$$\boldsymbol{Q}^*(k,k-1) = E\{\boldsymbol{\omega}^*(k,k-1)[\boldsymbol{\omega}^*(k,k-1)]^T\} \; = [\boldsymbol{Q}(k,k-1),\boldsymbol{0};\boldsymbol{0},\boldsymbol{Q}_n(k,k-1)] \qquad (24)$$

$$E\{\boldsymbol{\omega}^*(k,k-1)\boldsymbol{v}^T(k)\} = [\boldsymbol{S}(k);\boldsymbol{0}] = \boldsymbol{S}^*(k) \qquad (25)$$

where $\boldsymbol{S}^*(k) \in \boldsymbol{R}^{(n+q)\times q}$.

As a result, one can get the following algorithm.

Theorem 2. The networked state estimator with augmented state modeling for quantization error is as follows

$$\begin{cases} \hat{\boldsymbol{x}}^*(k \mid k-1) = \hat{\boldsymbol{x}}^*(k-1 \mid k-1) + \boldsymbol{K}^*(k)[\boldsymbol{m}(k) - \boldsymbol{H}^*(k)\hat{\boldsymbol{x}}^*(k \mid k-1)] \\ \boldsymbol{P}^*(k \mid k) = \boldsymbol{P}^*(k,k-1) - \boldsymbol{K}^*(k)[\boldsymbol{P}^*(k,k-1)[\boldsymbol{H}^*(k)]^T + \boldsymbol{S}^*(k) \end{cases} \qquad (26)$$

where

$$\begin{cases} \hat{\boldsymbol{x}}^*(k \mid k-1) = \boldsymbol{\Phi}^*(k,k-1)\hat{\boldsymbol{x}}^*(k-1 \mid k-1) \\ \boldsymbol{P}^*(k \mid k-1) = \boldsymbol{\Phi}^*(k,k-1)\boldsymbol{P}^*(k,k-1)[\boldsymbol{\Phi}^*(k,k-1)]^T + \boldsymbol{Q}^*(k,k-1) \end{cases} \qquad (27)$$

$$\boldsymbol{K}^*(k) = [\boldsymbol{P}^*(k \mid k-1)[\boldsymbol{H}^*(k)]^T + \boldsymbol{S}^*(k)] \times [\boldsymbol{H}^*(k)\boldsymbol{P}^*(k,k-1)[\boldsymbol{H}^*(k)]^T$$
$$+ \boldsymbol{H}^*(k)\boldsymbol{S}^*(k) + (\boldsymbol{H}^*(k)\boldsymbol{S}^*(k))^T + \boldsymbol{R}(k)]^{-1} \qquad (28)$$

where

$$\hat{\boldsymbol{x}}^*(k \mid k) = \begin{bmatrix} \hat{\boldsymbol{x}}^T(k \mid k) & \boldsymbol{n}^T(k \mid k) \end{bmatrix}^T \qquad (29)$$

$$\boldsymbol{P}^*(k \mid k) = \begin{bmatrix} \boldsymbol{P}_{xx}(k \mid k) & \boldsymbol{P}_{xn}(k \mid k) \\ \boldsymbol{P}_{nx}(k \mid k) & \boldsymbol{P}_{nn}(k \mid k) \end{bmatrix} \qquad (30)$$

Finally, $\hat{\boldsymbol{x}}(k \mid k)$ and $\boldsymbol{P}_{xx}(k \mid k)$ are needful for us to track the system state.

5   Strong Tracking Filters with Bits Quantization Error

Strong tracking idea was presented by Prof. D.H Zhou in Tsinghua University and its purpose is to deal with the model uncertainty including parameter uncertainty, model mismatching and state abrupt change and so on. The basic principle is to introduce a fading factor to reduce the influence of previous measurements to state estimation. Namely, for above two networked state estimators the computation formulas of one step state prediction covariance $P(k\mid k-1)$ in (16) and $P^*(k\mid k-1)$ in (27) should be respectively modified as

$$P(k\mid k-1)=\lambda(k)\boldsymbol{\Phi}(k,k-1)P(k,k-1)\boldsymbol{\Phi}^T(k,k-1)+Q(k,k-1) \qquad (31)$$

and

$$P^*(k\mid k-1)=\lambda^*(k)\boldsymbol{\Phi}^*(k,k-1)P^*(k,k-1)\boldsymbol{\Phi}^T(k,k-1)+Q^*(k,k-1) \qquad (32)$$

And, the residual errors or measurement innovations for two filters are respectively as follows

$$\gamma(k)=m(k)-H(k)\hat{x}(k\mid k-1)_,\ \gamma^*(k)=m(k)-H^*(k)\hat{x}^*(k\mid k-1) \qquad (33)$$

For the convenience, we denote

$$\begin{cases} \lambda^{\bullet}(k)\in\{\lambda(k),\lambda^*(k)\},\boldsymbol{\Phi}^{\bullet}(k,k-1)\in\{\boldsymbol{\Phi}(k,k-1),\boldsymbol{\Phi}^*(k,k-1)\} \\ Q^{\bullet}(k,k-1)\in\{Q(k,k-1),Q^*(k,k-1)\},H^{\bullet}(k)\in\{H(k),H^*(k)\} \\ R^{\bullet}(k)\in\{R_\theta(k),R(k)\},V_0^{\bullet}(k)\in\{V_0(k),V_0^*(k)\} \\ S^{\bullet}(k)\in\{S_{\omega,\theta}(k),S(k)\},J^{\bullet}(k)\in\{J(k),J^*(k)\} \\ P^{\bullet}(k\mid k)\in\{P(k\mid k),P^*(k\mid k)\},\gamma^{\bullet}(k)\in\{\gamma(k),\gamma^*(k)\} \end{cases} \qquad (34)$$

Then, the fading factor for the systems with correlated noises can be computed according to the following theorem.

Theorem 3: the fading factor $\lambda^{\bullet}(k)$ can be computed as follows

$$\lambda^{\bullet}(k)=\begin{cases} c(k), & c(k)>1 \\ 1, & c(k)\le 1 \end{cases} \qquad (35)$$

where $c(k)=tr[N^{\bullet}(k)]/tr[M^{\bullet}(k)]$, and

$$\begin{cases} N^{\bullet}(k)=V_0^{\bullet}(k)-\beta R^{\bullet}(k)-H^{\bullet}(k)[Q^{\bullet}(k,k-1) \\ \quad -J^{\bullet}(k-1)R^{\bullet}(k-1)(J^{\bullet}(k-1))^T]\times[H^{\bullet}(k-1)]^T \\ M^{\bullet}(k)=[\boldsymbol{\Phi}^{\bullet}(k,k-1)-J^{\bullet}(k-1)H^{\bullet}(k)]P^{\bullet}(k-1\mid k-1) \\ \quad \times[\boldsymbol{\Phi}^{\bullet}(k,k-1)-J^{\bullet}(k-1)H^{\bullet}(k-1)]\times[H^{\bullet}(k-1)]^T H^{\bullet}(k-1) \end{cases} \qquad (36)$$

$$J^{\bullet}(k)=S^{\bullet}(k)[R^{\bullet}(k)]^{-1} \qquad (37)$$

$$V_0^{\bullet}(k)=\begin{cases} \gamma^{\bullet}(k)[\gamma^{\bullet}(k)]^T, & k=1 \\ \dfrac{\left[\rho V_0^{\bullet}(k-1)+\gamma^{\bullet}(k)[\gamma^{\bullet}(k)]^T\right]}{1+\rho} & k>1 \end{cases} \qquad (38)$$

where the forgetting factor $0 < \rho \leq 1$ and is commonly chosen to 0.95. The softening factor β is equal or greater than 1 and the purpose is to smooth the state estimation. It can be set by experience. In this paper, it is chosen to $\beta = 1.5$.

6 Conclusions

In this paper the design of networked Kalman filters with limited bandwidth constraint is studied. It considers not only the correlation between process noise and measurement noise but also the correlations between quantized error and process and measurement noises. Thereby, they have the better universal property than the quantized filters in [11,12]. Certainly, there are still some opening issues such as the training of the correlations between the quantized error and process and measurement noises such neural network method and multisensor data fusion.

Acknowledgments. This work was partially supported by Natural Science Fund of China (Grant. 61002018, 60804064) and China Postdoctoral Science Foundation (Grant. 20100471727).

References

1. Arampatzis, T., Lygeros, J., Manesis, S.: A Survey of Applications of Wireless Sensors and Wireless Sensor Networks. In: Proceedings of the 2005 IEEE International Symposium on Mediterranean Conference on Control and Automation, pp. 719–724. IEEE Press, Cyprus (2005)
2. Luo, Z.: Universal Decentralized Estimation in a Bandwidth Constrained Sensor Network. IEEE Transactions on Information Theory 51(6), 2210–2219 (2005)
3. Xu, J., Li, J., Wu, J.: Convergence of Kalman Filter with Quantized Innovations. In: 11th International Conference on Control, Automation, Robotics and Vision, Singapore, December 7-10, pp. 1703–1708 (2010)
4. Ribeiro, A., Giannakis, G.B., Roumeliotis, S.I.: SOI-KF: Distributed Kalman filtering with low-cost communications using the sign of innovation. IEEE Transactions on Signal Processing 54(12), 4782–4795 (2006)
5. Mansouri, M., Snoussi, H., Richard, C.: A Nonlinear Estimation For Target Target Tracking In Wireless Sensor Networks Using Quantized Variational Filtering. In: 2009 International Conference on Signals, Circuits and Systems, Medenine, Tunisia, November 6-9, pp. 1–4 (2009)
6. Sun, S., Lin, J., Xie, L., Xiao, W.: Quantized Kalman Filtering. In: IEEE 22nd International Symposium on Intelligent Control, pp. 7–12. IEEE Press, USA (2007)
7. Wen, C., Ge, Q., Tang, X.: Kalman Filtering in a Bandwidth Constrained Sensor Network. Chinese Journal of Electronics 17(4), 713–718 (2009)
8. Xu, J., Li, J.: State estimation with quantised sensor information in wireless sensor networks. IET Signal Processing 5(1), 16–26 (2011)
9. Zhou, Y., Li, J., Wang, D.: Posterior Cramér–Rao Lower Bounds for Target Tracking in Sensor Networks with Quantized Range-Only Measurements. IEEE Signal Processing Letters 17(2), 157–160 (2010)

10. Zhou, Y., Li, J., Wang, D.: Unscented Kalman Filtering based quantized innovation fusion for target tracking in WSN with feedback. In: The 2009 International Conference on Machine Learning and Cybernetics, July 12-15, vol. 3, pp. 1457–1463. IEEE Press, China (2009)
11. Ge, Q., Xu, T.: Quantized State Estimation for Sensor Networks. In: Proceedings of the Ninth International Conference on Machine Learning and Cybernetics, July 11-13, pp. 3111–3116. IEEE Press, China (2010)
12. Xu, T., Ge, Q.: Strong Tracking Filter with Bandwidth Constraint for Sensor Networks. In: 2010 8th IEEE International Conference on Control and Automation, June 9-11, pp. 596–601. IEEE Press, China (2010)

Development of Control System for Automatic Mechanical Transmission of Battery Electric Bus

Hong-bo Liu, Yu-long Lei, Yu Zhang, Xiao-lin Zhang, and You-de Li

State Key Laboratory of Automotive Simulation and Control, Jilin University,
130022 Changchun, China
hbliu08@mails.jlu.edu.cn, leiyl@jlu.edu.cn, phoenix_zy@yahoo.cn,
zxl2257cn@yahoo.com.cn, auto_tsc@jlu.edu.cn

Abstract. Due to the advantages of high efficiency, zero emission and good drivability, the battery electric vehicles (BEVs) promise to be one of the best choices to replace the oil fueled vehicle. In this paper a solution for the development of a control system for AMT (Automatic Mechanical Transmission) equipped in battery electric bus is presented. The system is based on multi-layered architecture that includes two high-level layers and further subdivided into some low-lever layers. The standardized applications interfaces (API) are employed to implement the interlayer interaction. The modular design approach is used during the development process. The system is developed by C language and MATLAB/Simulink/Stateflow toolset and uses Real-Time Workshop tool to generated ANSI C source code. The system is reusable, extensible, and flexible. It is applied in the buses and on-road tests show its correctness, efficiency, reliability.

Keywords: Battery Electric Vehicle, AMT, Control System, Layered Architecture, Modular Design.

1 Introduction

With ever increasing concerns on energy shortage and environment protection, the development of the electric vehicles (EVs) has taken on an accelerated pace [1]. As a type of EVs, the BEVs, who feature high efficiency, low noise, zero emissions and easy drivability, can effectively resolve above problems caused by conventional vehicles. One of the most important applications of BEVs is the city buses. Relevant data shows that China's vehicle emissions accounts for 60% of urban air pollution, while the city bus exhaust emission pollution accounts for more than 40% of car exhaust pollution [2]. Therefore, the development of battery electric bus has great potential to solve urban environmental problems.

Nowadays, the microelectronic control technologies played the key role in automotive domain. In BEVs, many control systems existed. These systems accomplish the torque distribution, body control, safety management and dashboard display, etc. So, how to build a valid, reliable, efficient control system is one of most important issue during the development process. As one of kernel control systems of

H. Deng et al. (Eds.): AICI 2011, Part II, LNAI 7003, pp. 193–200, 2011.

BEVs, the AMT control system realizes gear shift control automatically, which affects the vehicle dynamic performance and fuel economy directly.

In this paper, a solution for the development of AMT control system in battery electric bus is presented. In section 2, the structure of BEVs with AMT is described; in section 3, we introduce the related works; in section 4, the multi-layer based system architecture is described; in section 5, the modular design method is presented; in section 6, the development process in MATLAB/Simulink/Stateflow environments is introduced and the on-road test data is analyzed. Conclusions are drawn on how this solution benefits the AMT control system development.

2 Structure of BEVs with AMT

The BEVs are a type of EVs, which are powered by electric motor that is fed by batteries. As shown in Fig.1, its structure is mainly consisted of rechargeable battery packs, electric motor, transmission, driver shaft and wheels. The chemical energy is stored in the battery packs, and then powers the motor. The torque generated from motor is transferred to driveshaft by transmission, and then turns the wheels.

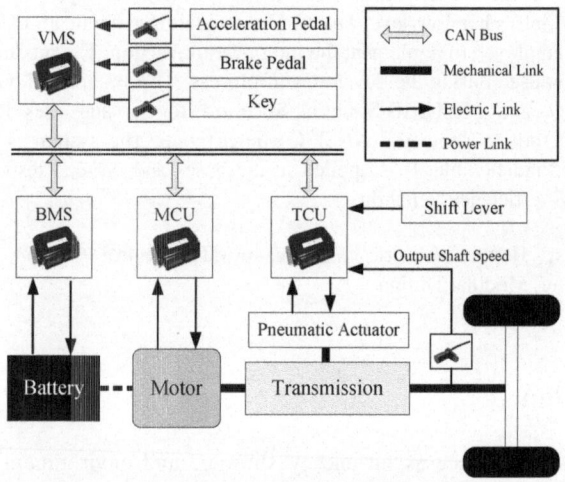

Fig. 1. Framework of AMT for battery electric bus

The BEVs are controlled by Multi-ECU jointly, as shown in Fig.1, including VMS (Vehicle Management System), BMS (Battery Management System), MCU (Motor Control Unit), ICU (Instrument Control Unit) and TCU (Transmission Control Unit). They control vehicle, battery, motor, dashboard, and transmission respectively.

The AMT system is the part of driveline, which is composed of the transmission, TCU, pneumatic actuators, and sensors. Compared with conventional vehicles, the clutch between the power source and transmission is removed since the induction motor's speed can be easily controlled.

The control system/software is the control center of AMT, which is a real-time system and runs in TCU. Its function can be mainly defined as information acquiring, shift strategy and actuators control. The "information acquiring" is the "eye" of system, which provides dependable information for other parts of system; the "shift strategy" is the "brain" of the system, which takes charge of shift-decision making and shift-timing control; the "actuator control" is the "arm" of the system, which executes gear shift operations automatically on the command of shift strategy function.

To realize the joint control, the ECUs are connected by high-speed CAN (Controller Area Network) bus and use SAE J1939 protocol to communicate with each other. By the CAN protocol, the information including control commands and sensor data is exchanged and shared easily, such as the data of brake pedal, acceleration pedal, motor speed and motor torque, etc. Other information is acquired directly by the sensors connected with TCU.

3   Related Work

In paper [3], a three-speed AMT is applied in BEV successfully. The necessity of employing multi-speed AMT system is analyzed, and the shift schedule is designed. Paper [4] developed a pneumatic AMT actuator for the pure electric garbage truck. The communication method based on CAN network is proposed.

In paper [5], the CAN network protocol based on SAE J1939 was established on electric city bus and an implementation method was put forward. In paper [6], on the basis of CAN network, the vehicleboard information system for pure electric vehicles (PEV) was developed to control and manage the electronic systems of PEV coordinately.

Paper [7] designed an abstraction layer structure based powertrain controller platform for electric vehicles. The CAN control network is adopted. The software is abstracted into three layers to ensure easy configuration. Each layer is divided into manageable sub-functions for further splitting.

4   Multi-layered Architecture

With the increasing of vehicle functional requirements, the complexity, size and cost of the automotive electric control software have grown accordingly. The AMT control system is an embedded real-time system. One of the goals of system development is to get a high cohesion and low coupling system with the features of reusability, extensibility, and flexibility.

We adopted multi-layer based architecture to design the system. As shown in Fig. 2, the system is divided into two high-level layers, i.e. basic drivers layer (BDL) and advanced control layer (ACL). Between the two layers, the standardized application interface (API) is used to accomplish the interlayer interaction. Within each layer the low-lever layers exist.

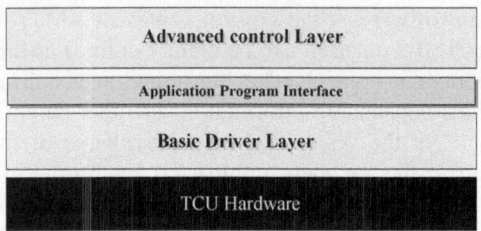

Fig. 2. Architecture of AMT control system

4.1 Basic Driver Layer (BDL)

The BDL is responsible for TCU onboard devices driving and the real-time OS kernel based task scheduling, as shown in Fig.3, which contains Microcontroller Abstraction Layer (MAL), TCU Abstraction Layer (TAL), System Services Layer (SSL), and Direct Drivers Layer (DDL).

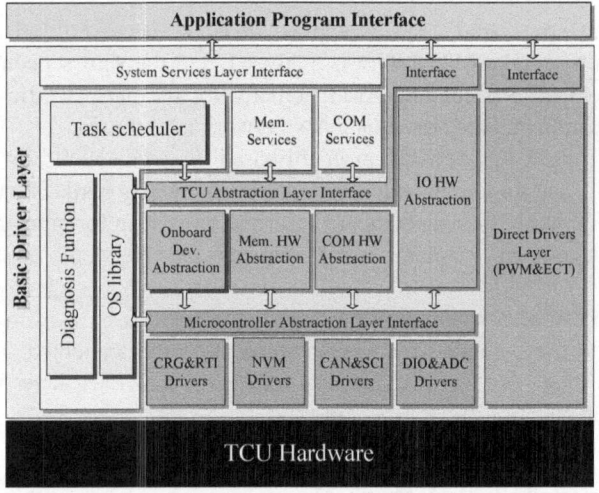

Fig. 3. Architecture of Basic Driver Layer

The purple section is the MAL. It is the lowest layer of the BDL, and makes higher layers independent of MCU (Micro Control Unit). It contains internal drivers, for example, DIO&ADC drivers, CAN&SCI drivers, FLASH&EEPROM Drivers and CRG&RTI drivers, which are software modules with direct access to the MCU internal peripherals and memory mapped MCU external devices.

The blue section is the TAL, which makes higher layers independent of TCU hardware layout. It interfaces and encapsulates the drivers of MAL, provides the abstraction of IO HW, communication HW and memory for system services layer. It also contains drivers for external devices, for instance, the watch dog and K-line driver. The API is offered for access to peripherals and devices regardless of their location and their connection to the MCU.

The yellow section is the SSL. It is the highest layer of BDL, and provides basic services for the upper-layer applications and other basic driver modules. It offers the Operation System functionality, memory services, communication services, and diagnosis functions.

The pink section is the DDL, which is a special layer. It fulfills the special functional and timing requirements for handling complex sensors and actuators. It implements complex sensor evaluation and actuator control with direct access to the MCU using interrupt and/or MCU peripherals, so it makes the system capable of high sensitivity and high-speed responsibility.

4.2 Applications Program Interface (API)

In order to make the advanced control layer independent from the mapping of special TCU, The standardized API is used, which provides the communication services to the ACL. As shown in Fig.2, not all API come from SSL interface, others in part come from the interfaces of TAL IO HW abstraction and DDL; this enables the system high-speed access and high-speed responsibility.

4.3 Advanced Control Layer (ACL)

The ACL is responsible for advanced shift strategy. Within the ACL, the architecture style changes from "layered" to "component style". As shown in Fig.4, there are 3 modules contained in ACL, which are Vehicle Information Input (VII), Advanced Control Strategy (ACS), and COM &Actuator Control (CAC). The VII module is the input of ACS, which gets data by calling API, after filtering and scale-conversion, and then transfers data to ACS; The ACS is the kernel module of control system, which takes charge of shift strategy and fault diagnosis; The CAC is the output of ACS, which receives the command of ACS, executes the gear-shifting by controlling the actuators and communication with VMS and MCU.

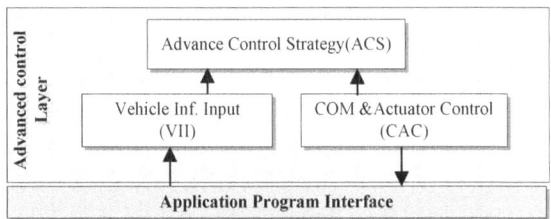

Fig. 4. Components of Advanced Control Layer

5 Modular Design of Control System

The modular design is an approach that subdivides a system into smaller modules that can be independently created and then used in different systems to drive multiple functionalities. Besides reduction in cost and flexibility in design, modularity offers other benefits such as augmentation by adding new solution by merely plugging in a new module, and exclusion [8].

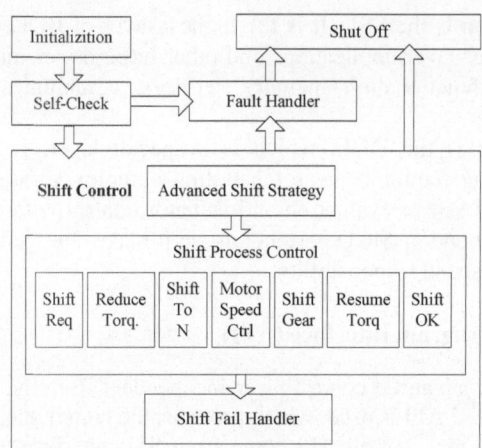

Fig. 5. Modular design of ACS model

The AMT control system is based on modular design approach. The system is subdivided into modules and sub-modules within each high/low level layer. For example, within sub layer of MAL, there are modules of "CRG Driver", "NVM Drivers", and "CAN Driver" etc exist.

The module of ACS is responsible for shift-decision making, shift gear timing control, vehicle state management, and fault handler etc. As shown in Fig.5, by using the modular design method, the module is divided into some sub-modules, such as "Initialization", "Self-Check", "Shift Control", "Fault Handler", and "Shut Off". Then, the sub-module of "Shift Control" is divided into low-level modules again. Each module takes charge of a sub-function; the execution sequence of each module is controlled by Simulink/Stateflow.

6 On-Road Test

The traditional manual programming way has the error-prone, un-maintainable and un-reusable etc shortcomings. To solve this problem, we use C language, MATLAB/Simulink/Stateflow and RTW (Real-Time Workshop) tools to develop the system.

The Simulink is a popularly used tool in MATLAB for model-based design, which provides graphical user interface for building hierarchical models. The RTW is an optional product of MATLAB which can generate ANSI C code from SIMULINK models. The Fig.6 shows the integration process of Simulink models with C code. On the one hand, the basic driver layer is coded by C language manually; on the other hand, the high-level advanced control layer is modeled in MATLAB/Simulink/Stateflow environment and then converted into ANSI C codes by RTW; finally, the two parts codes are integrated in Freescale CodeWarrior IDE.

The Stateflow is an interactive graphical design tool that works with Simulink software to model and simulate event-driven systems. In AMT control system, Stateflow is used to vehicle state management, shift-gear timing control etc.

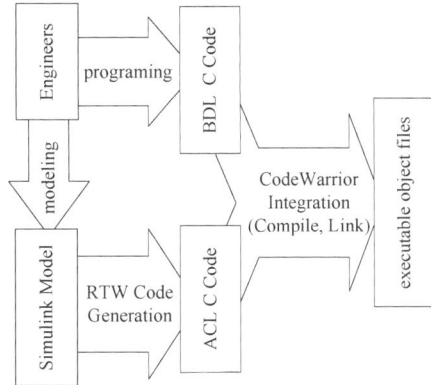

Fig. 6. Integration of Simulink models with C code

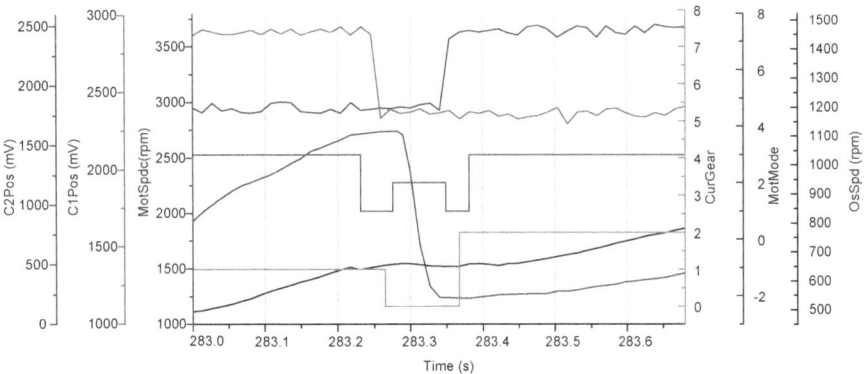

Fig. 7. On-road test results

The control system has been applied in the WanXiang battery electric bus. The Fig.7 shows on-road test results of shift process when shifting from gear 1 to 2. From the experiment curves, we can see the motor work mode, the motor rotor speed, cylinder position, output shaft speed and gear change processes. The definition of motor work mode is as follows: 1 - free mode, 2 - speed control mode, 3 - torque control mode. Shift time can reflect the comprehensive indicator of shift quality. Regardless of the shift requested time, the total shift time is only 0.89s, which is very fast and satisfied the driver requirements well.

7   Conclusion

The AMT is an integrated drivetrain system, which is based on the traditional manual gearbox, and has the advantages of low cost, good inheritance and easy manufacture. The battery electric buses equipped with AMT can realize gear shift automatically, improve fuel economy, reduces the driving fatigue, and increase passenger comfort.

This paper mainly focuses on the development of battery electric vehicles. It is also meaningful for the application of AMT system in other EVs, such as HEVs and FCEVs etc.

Acknowledgments. The authors would like to thank Technology development project of Jilin Province of China (No.20096008) for its support.

References

1. Chan, C.C.: The state of the art of the electric and hybrid vehicles. Proc. IEEE 90(2), 247–275 (2002)
2. Zhang, C., Mao, Y.-z.: Pure Electric Bus is the Direction of Development of Urban Public Transport. Advanced Materials Industry 8, 54–55 (2007)
3. Xi, J.-q., Xiong, G.-m., Zhang, Y.: Application of automatic manual transmission technology in pure electric bus. In: IEEE Vehicle Power and Propulsion Conference, VPPC (2008)
4. Xiong, G., Xi, J., Zhai, Y., Hu, Y., Yang, Y., Chen, H.: Development of Pneumatically Automatic Mechanical Transmission for a Pure Electric Garbage Truck. In: Proceedings IEEE International Conference on Industrial Technology, pp. 1108–1112 (2010)
5. Wang, D., Nan, J., Sun, F.: The application of CAN communication in distributed control system of electric city bus. In: IEEE Vehicle Power and Propulsion Conference, VPPC (2008)
6. Li, D., Chen, J., Huang, R., Cheng, X.: CAN network-based vehicleboard information systems for pure electric vehicles (PEV). Journal of Huazhong University of Science and Technology(Nature Science Edition) 36(2), 17–21 (2008)
7. Zhou, N., Xie, H., Yan, Y., Zhu, D.: Development of Powertrain Controller Platform for Electric Vehicles Based on Abstraction layer Structure. In: IEEE Vehicle Power and Propulsion Conference, VPPC (2008)
8. Meehan, J.S.: Supporting 'design for re-use' with modular design. Concurrent Engineering Research and Applications 15(2), 141–155 (2007)

A Deterministic Sensor Node Deployment Method with Target Coverage and Node Connectivity

Xiuming Guo[1], Chunjiang Zhao[2], Xinting Yang[2], and Chuanheng Sun[2]

[1] College of Information and Electrical Engineering,
China Agricultural University, Beijing,100083, China
[2] National Engineering Research Center for Information Technology in Agriculture
Beijing 100097, China
xiumingguo@gmail.com, {zhaocj,yangxt,sunch}@nercita.org.cn

Abstract. The paper proposes a deterministic node deployment method based on grid scan to achieve targets coverage and nodes connectivity. Target area is divided into girds from which the most suitable one is selected to place the next node. In the coverage phase, the grid where the sensor node can sense the most targets and have the best coverage level is selected to place the next sensor node. To make the sensor nodes connected, first, the sensor nodes are divided into connected groups, then, the grid where the relay node can connect the most groups and have the best connectivity level is selected to place the next relay node. Simulation experimental results show that the method can achieve target coverage with the least sensor nodes and sensor node connectivity to a great extent.

Keywords: WSNs (wireless sensor networks), deployment, coverage, connectivity, target monitor.

1 Introduction

In recent years, sensor networks have emerged as promising platforms for many applications, such as environmental monitoring, battlefield surveillance, and health care [1], [2]. The sensor node deployment is the first and very important step in WSNs. There are mainly two deployment ways including random deployment and deterministic deployment. The former simply scatters (for example, air drop) a sufficiently large number of sensors over the monitoring region with the expectation that the sensor nodes that survive the air drop will be able to adequately monitor the target region. This is usually adopted where human can not get in touch easily such as battlefields. However, when the place is easy for human to get in, the latter way can be chosen to deploy the sensor nodes manually.

Many researches have been done on coverage [3-5,7] and connectivity problems [6] in WSNs. References [8] and [9] discuss some deployment pattern and prove that the strip-based patterns are absolutely optimal to achieve both coverage and 1- or 2-connectivity. Yanli Cai et al. [10] organize the directions of sensors into a group of non- disjoint cover sets to extend the network lifetime in directional sensor networks.

H. Deng et al. (Eds.): AICI 2011, Part II, LNAI 7003, pp. 201–207, 2011.

Jie Wang and Ning Zhong [11] study minimum-cost sensor placement on a bounded 3D sensing field to monitor target points with several types of sensors with different sensing ranges and different costs. Xiaochun Xu and Sartaj Sahni [12] develop an integer linear programming formulation to find the minimum cost deployment of sensors that provides the desired coverage of a target point set and propose a greedy heuristic for the problem. Mihacla Cardei et al. [13] propose an efficient method to extend the sensor network life time by organizing the sensors into a maximal number of set covers that are activated successively. Chia-Pang Chen et al. [14] project a novel coverage-preserving algorithm that is able to prolong the lifetime and to maximize the coverage. Jing He et al.[15]introduce failure probability into target coverage problems, model the solution as the Maximum Reliability Sensor Covers (MRSC) problem and design a heuristic greedy algorithm that efficiently compute the maximal number of reliable sensor covers. Xingfa Shen et al. [16] propose a re-deployment which randomly places some sensors and then deploys some sensors manually to meet any k-covered rate in some regions according to application requirements.

Most of the researches mentioned aiming at targets' coverage and monitor are based on sensor nodes with big density that have been scattered in the interest area. However, in some cases such as fields with limited certain targets to be covered and monitored, deterministic deployment can use much fewer sensors to cut down cost greatly.

The paper proposes a simple deterministic deployment method which considers coverage and connectivity at the same time based on grid scan. The target area is divided into grids from which the most suitable one is selected to place the next node to cover targets or connect sensor nodes. In section 2, grid selection for sensors' placement to cover targets is developed. Section 3 shows how to add fewest relay nodes to connect the sensor nodes generated in section2. Simulation experimental results are presented in section 4. Conclusions and further work are showed in section 5.

2 Targets Coverage

To achieve targets coverage, placing a sensor node in each target point can get the best coverage level. However when the density of target points is large and the demanded coverage level is not very high, more than one targets can be sensed by a sensor node placed suitably. The binary coverage model is used to denote how a sensor node can sense a target.

2.1 Binary Coverage Model

The paper adapts binary coverage model. Equation (1) shows the binary sensor model [17][18] that expresses the coverage $c\left(s_i\right)$ of a target point p by the sensor s_i .When the distance between p and s_i $d(s_ip)$ is smaller than sensing radius r_s, s_i can sense p, otherwise can not.

$$c(s_i) = \begin{cases} 1, & if \ d(s_i, p) < r_s \\ 0, & otherwise \end{cases} \tag{1}$$

2.2 Coverage Algorithm

Target area is divided into square grids to denote positions of targets and sensor nodes. The smaller the grid size is, the more accurate the position is.

To cover the targets with the least nodes, the grid where the sensor can cover the most targets should be chosen first to place the next sensor node. Grid m should be chosen to place the next node in equation (2) where $s(i)$ denotes the sensor node amount sensed by the grid i. After a new grid has been chosen, the targets covered by the sensor placed at the grid should be taken away from the targets needed to be covered to prevent repetitive coverage.

$$m = \arg\max(s(i)) \tag{2}$$

When selecting the next grid, there may exist more than one grids that cover the same most targets, in this case, the grid with the shortest distance to the farthest target should be chosen in order to achieve better overall coverage. Grid n in Equation (3) should be chosen to place the next sensor node where G denotes the grid set that can cover the same most targets and T denotes the target set that can be covered by the sensor node at the grid i.

$$n = \arg\min_{i \in G} \max_{t \in T} (d(i,t)) \tag{3}$$

3 Sensor Nodes Connectivity

The sensor nodes for targets coverage may not connected, so relay nodes need be placed to connect sensor nodes so that data can be transmitted and gathered. First, sensor nodes are divided to connected groups. Then, the grid where relay node can connect the most groups is selected.

3.1 Sensor Nodes Grouping

Sensor node i and j can communicate with each other directly only when their distance $d(s_i, s_j)$ is smaller than the communication radius r_c which can be seen in equation (4). When two sensor nodes can communicate with each other, they are said to be a neighbor node of each other. The sensor node group is said to be connected when each of them has at least one neighbor in the group (equation (5)).

$$d_{ij} = \begin{cases} 1, & if \ d(s_i, s_j) < r_c \\ 0, & otherwise \end{cases} \tag{4}$$

Sensor nodes generated in the coverage phase may not be connected among which some sensor nodes are connected. No relay node is needed to be placed to connect sensor nodes in the same connected group. Relay nodes are only needed to be placed to connect the non-connected groups. The sensor nodes are divided into some connected groups neither of which is connected. Two sensor nodes group g_i and g_j are said to be connected if there exists at least one sensor node in g_i who has at least one neighbor in g_j. Otherwise they are said to be non-connected which can be seen in equation (6).

$$g_i = \begin{cases} 1, & if \ \forall x \in g_i \ \exists y \in g_i d(x,y) < r_c \\ 0, & otherwise \end{cases} \tag{5}$$

$$c_{ij} = \begin{cases} 1, & if \ \exists x \in g_i \ \exists y \in g_j d(x,y) < r_c \\ 0, & otherwise \end{cases} \tag{6}$$

3.2 Groups Connectivity

Target area is divided into square grids to denote positions of relay nodes and sensor nodes. In order to place the least relay nodes, the grid where a relay node can connect the most groups should be chosen to place the next relay node. The distance between a relay node r_i and group j is defined in equation (7). The relay node r_i is assumed to be connected with group j when $d_{rj} < r_c$. The sensor node with the nearest distance to the relay node in group j is said to be the communication node between r_i and group j.

$$d_{rj} = \min(d(r_i, s_k)) \quad s_k \in group \ j \tag{7}$$

After a new grid has been chosen, the sensor nodes in all the groups connected by the new relay node placed at the grid should be combined into one group. Looping continues until there does not exist a grid where sensor can connect more than one groups.

When choosing the grid to place the next relay node, there may exist more than one grids where the relay node can connect the same largest number of groups. In this case, the grid where the relay node is nearest to its furthest communication node should be chosen to place the next relay node to achieve the better overall connectivity. In equation (8), the set R denotes all the grids where relay nodes can connect the same largest number of groups, the set P is consisted of the communication nodes of the relay node r_i at each grid in R.

$$g_n = \arg \max_{r_i \in R} \min_{t \in P} (d(r_i, t)) \tag{8}$$

4 Experiment Results

Suppose in an area whose length and width are all 100 meters, 10 and 20 target points are generated randomly. The targets' coordinates are with the accuracy of 0.1 meter.

The sensor radius and communication radius are 20 meters and 40 meters respectively. The grid side is 0.1 meter.

Fig.1 and Fig.2 show the experiment results when the target number is 10 and 20 respectively. In (a) of Fig.1 and Fig.2, the blue circles denote the target points behind which the black numbers denote the target serial number. The green dots denote the sensor nodes in front of which the red numbers denote the order to place the sensor node to cover target points and the green circles denote the coverage domain of the sensor node.

In Fig.1 (b) and Fig.2 (b), the blue circles denote sensor nodes generated in (a), and the black numbers behind and in front of the blue circles denote the sensor node's serial number and its group number respectively. The * characters denote the relay nodes to connect groups, behind which the red numbers denote the order to place the relay node and the red circles and green circles denote the communication domain of the relay node.

In Fig.1 (a), sensor node 2 and sensor node 3 both can coverage two target points. However, sensor node 2 can achieve better coverage, that is, it can sense its two targets 2 and 5 more easily than sensor 3. So the grid at sensor 2 is selected to place the second sensor node. Likewise in Fig.2 (a), the grid at the sensor node 1 is selected to place the first sensor instead of the grid at the sensor node 2.

In the six sensor nodes placed for coverage in Fig.1 (a), none of them can communicate with one another. So they are divided into six groups, which can be seen in Fig.1 (b). When selecting grids to connect groups, relay node 1 can connect three groups including group 1, 4 and 6 and it has the better communication situation than the relay node placed at any other grid. After relay node 1 is placed, group 1, 4, 6 are connected and combined to group 1. Then there exist four groups needed to be connected, the grid at relay node 2 where relay node can connect the most groups and has the best communication situation, so it is chosen to place the second relay node to combined group 1 and group 2.

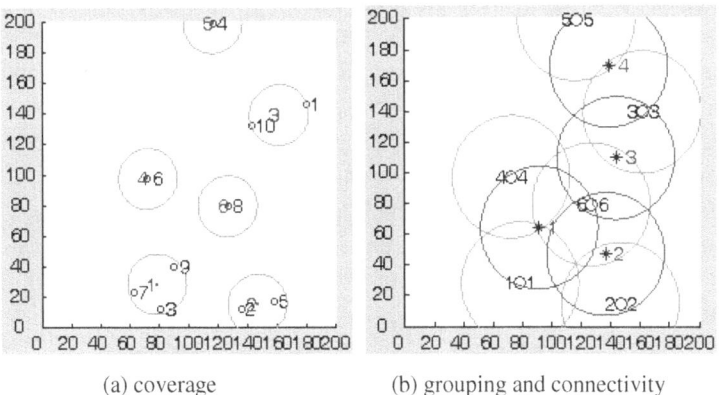

(a) coverage   (b) grouping and connectivity

Fig. 1. Coverage and connectivity(target number is 10)

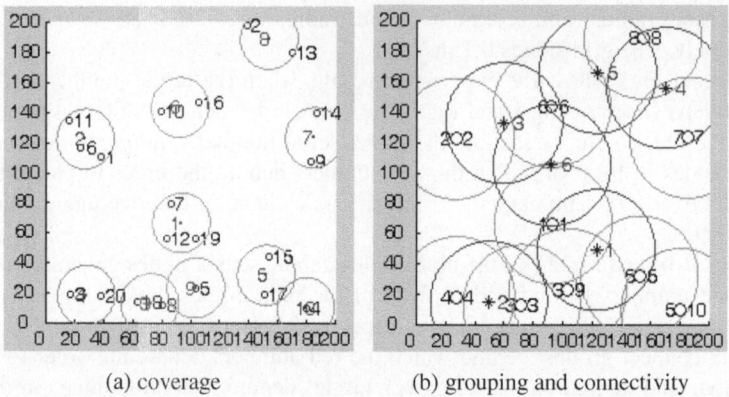

(a) coverage   (b) grouping and connectivity

Fig. 2. Coverage and connectivity (target number is 20)

5   Conclusions and Further Work

The paper proposes a simple and valid method to achieve target coverage and sensor node connectivity based on grid scan. The target area is divided into grids. It can achieve target coverage using the least sensor nodes and sensor node connectivity to a great extent.

In coverage phase, the grid where sensor node can cover the most target points and have the most coverage level is selected to placed the next sensor node, then the targets covered by the new sensor nodes are removed from the targets set waiting for coverage, and the next grid is selected to place the next sensor node until each target is covered.

The sensor nodes generated in the coverage phase may not be connected. They are divided into connected groups firstly in the connectivity phase, then the grid where a relay node can connect the most groups and has the best connectivity level is selected to place the next relay node, then the groups connected by the new relay node is combined to one group, select the next grid to place the new relay node until no more than one groups are connected.

There are still some shortages in the proposed method. Firstly, the paper adopts the binary model, in which the sensing result is either success or failure. It is not in accordance with the actual situation, introducing a probability model to the method is the future work. Secondly, sensor nodes may be still not connected after the connectivity algorithm, so researches on how to place sensor nodes to achieve overall connectivity need to be done.

Acknowledgment. The paper is supported partly by National Spark Program (2010GA6 00001).

References

1. Akyildiz, L., Su, W., Sankarasubramaniam, Y., Cayirci, E.: A survey on Sensor Networks. ACM Trans. Multimedia Computing, Comm. And Applications 40(8), 102–114 (2002)
2. Szewczyk, R., Mainwaring, A., Polastre, J., Anderson, J., Culler, D.: An Analysis of a Large Scale Habitat Monitoring Application. In: Proc. ACM Conf. Embedded Networked Sensor Systems, SenSys (2004)
3. Akyildiz, I.F., Su, W., Sankarasubramaniam, Y., Cayirci, E.: A Survey on Sensor Networks. IEEE Communications Magazine 40, 102–114 (2002)
4. Estrin, D., Govindan, R., Heidemann, J., Kumar, S.: Next Century Challenges: Scalable Corordination in Sensor Networks. In: Proceedings of MOBICOM (1999)
5. Mainwaring, A., Polastre, J., Szewczyk, R., Culler, D., Anderson, J.: Wireless Sensor Networks for Habitat Monitoring. In: Proceedings of ACM International Workshop on Wireless Sensor Networks and Applications (WSNA) (2002)
6. Zhang, C., Bai, X., Teng, J., Xuan, D., Jia, W.: Constructing Low- Connectivity and Full-Coverage Three Dimensional Sensor Networks. IEEE Journal on Selected Areas in Communications 28(7) (2010)
7. Yang, Z., Xu, B., Ye, S., Yang, B.: tk-coverage: Time-based K-Coverage for Energy Efficient Monitoring. In: International Conference on Parallel and Distributed Systems (2009)
8. Bai, X., Kumar, S., Xuan, D., Yun, Z., Lai, T.H.: Deploying Wireless Sensors to Achieve both Coverage and Connectivity. In: Poceedings of the 7th ACM International Symposium on Mobile and Hoc Networking and Computing (MobiHoc) (2006)
9. Sun, Y., Yu, Z., Ge, J., Lin, B., Yun, Z.: On Deploying Wireless Sensors to Achieve both Coverage and Connectivity. In: International Conference on Wireless Communications, Networking and Mobile Computing (2009)
10. Cai, Y., Lou, W., Li, M., Li, X.-Y.: Energy Efficient Target-Oriented Scheduling in Directional Sensor Networks. IEEE Transactions on Computers 58(9) (September 2009)
11. Wang, J., Zhong, N.: Efficient Point Coverage in Wireless Sensor Networks. Journal of Combinatorial Optimization 11(3) (2006)
12. Xu, X., Sahni, S.: Approximation Algorithms for Sensor Deployment. IEEE Transactions on Computers 56(12) (December 2007)
13. Cardei, M., Thai, M.T., Li, Y., Wu, W.: Energy-Efficient Target Coverage in Wireless Sensor Networks. In: Proc. IEEE INFOCOM (2005)
14. Chen, C.-P., Chuang, C.-L., Lin, T.-S., Liu, C.-W., Liao, K.-C., Shieh, J.-C., Jiang, J.-A.: A Novel Coverage-Preserving Algorithm with Energy Efficiency. Sensors, 568–571 (October 2009)
15. He, J., Xiong, N., Xiao, Y., Pan, Y.: A Reliable Energy Efficient Algorithm for Target Coverage in Wireless Sensor Networks. In: IEEE 30th International Conference on Systems Workshops (ICDCSW 2010), June 21-25 (2010)
16. Shen, X., Chen, J., Sun, Y.: Grid Scan: A Simple and Effective Approach for Coverage
17. Chakrabarty, K., Iyengar, S.S., Qi, H., Cho, E.: Grid Coverage for Surveillance and Target Location in Distributed Sensor Networks. IEEE Transactions on Computers 51, 1448–1453 (2002)
18. Chakrabarty, K., Iyengar, S.S., Qi, H., Cho, E.: Coding Theory Framework for Target Location in Distributed Sensor Networks. In: Proc. International Symposium on Information Technology: Coding and Computing, pp. 130–134

Optimal Switch in Constant-Speed Pumping Stations

Fulai Yao[1] and Hexu Sun[2]

[1] Institute of Automation, Hebei University of Technology, Tianjin, China
fulaiyao@yahoo.com.cn
[2] Institute of Automation, Hebei University of Technology, Tianjin, China
hxsun@hebut.edu.cn

Abstract. This paper presents a kind of optimal switch method for constant-speed pumping stations with the same model pumps, and gives the minimum total power consumption. There are many this kind pumping stations in industry and other areas. The optimal switch method is given for the changing total flow, and the optimal switch point is given. The conclusion can also be applied to the energy optimization of other general devices.

Keywords: optimal switch, constant-speed, pumping stations.

1 Introduction

In industry, water transfer exists in many areas, so that pumps which are used for water transfer have been widely used. According to statistics, the electricity consumption of pumps is 20-25% of the world's total electricity consumption. However, there still haven't optimal control methods which can accurately predict and control energy-saving effect in pumping stations [1].

2 The Characteristics of Constant-Speed Pump

The efficiency function of a centrifugal pump at rated speed n_0 is shown in Fig. 1.

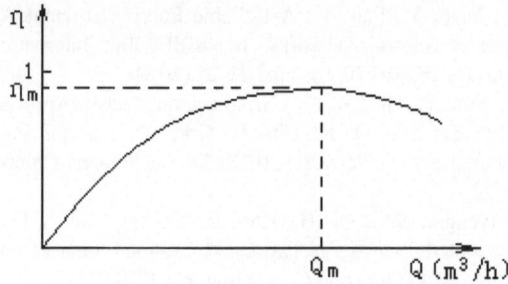

Fig. 1. The efficiency function of a centrifugal pump

H. Deng et al. (Eds.): AICI 2011, Part II, LNAI 7003, pp. 208–213, 2011.
© Springer-Verlag Berlin Heidelberg 2011

Fig.1, Q is flow (m³/hour), and η is the efficiency (%), Q_m is the flow at the maximum efficiency η_m. We have

$$\eta_m = \eta(Q_m) \tag{1}$$

The flow-head characteristic curve H(Q) of this centrifugal pump at speed n_0 is shown in Fig. 2.

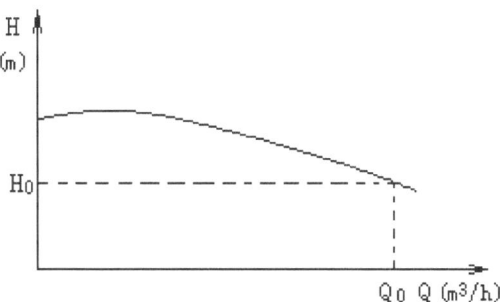

Fig. 2. The flow-head characteristic curve

Fig.2, Q is flow, and H is the head (m), H_0 is the head at flow Q_0. The pump's shaft power is P(Q) (kW), it can be expressed as

$$P(Q) = \frac{QH(Q)}{367\eta(Q)} \tag{2}$$

The flow capacity per unit power is V(Q) (m³/kWh), V(Q) is expressed as

$$V(Q) = \frac{Q}{P(Q)} = \frac{367\eta(Q)}{H(Q)} \tag{3}$$

When the pump is used to transfer water to the fixed height H_0, the maximum flow Q_{max} should be kept

$$Q_{max} \leq Q_0 \tag{4}$$

When P_e is the rated power of the motor that drives the pump, in order to avoid the motor overload, P should be kept

$$P \leq P_e \tag{5}$$

Namely,

$$Q_{max} \leq \frac{367\eta P_e}{H} \tag{6}$$

So we have

$$Q_{max} = \min(Q_0, \frac{367\eta P_e}{H})$$ (7)

We can draw the Q-V curve shown in Fig. 3.

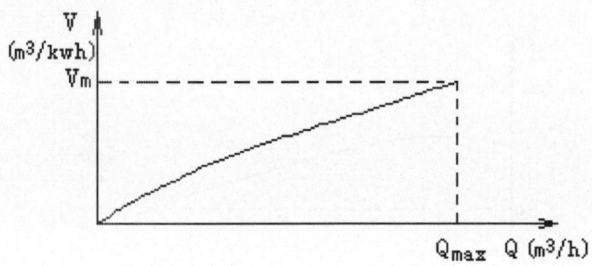

Fig. 3. The Q-V curve

Fig.3, V_m is the point of the Q-V curve at Q_{max}.

3 The Total Power Consumption of a Pumping Station

Suppose a pumping station has n units pumps, witch are running in parallel and the same model, and the pumping station is used to transfer water to the fixed height H_0, the total flow is Q_t, the ith pump's flow is Q_i, we have

$$Q_i \leq Q_{max}$$

$$Q_t = \sum_{i=1}^{n} Q_i$$ (8)

Suppose

$$\theta_i = \frac{Q_i}{Q_t}$$ (9)

Then

$$Q_i = \theta_i Q_t$$

$$\sum_{i=1}^{n} \theta_i = 1$$ (10)

All pump's speed are fixed and equal the rated speed n_0, the output head of the ith pump is $H(Q_i)$, we have

$$H(Q_i) \geq H_0 \tag{11}$$

The ith pump efficiency at the point $(Q_i, H(Q_i))$ is $\eta(Q_i)$, the ith pump's power is P_i, the total power consumption of the pumping station is

$$P_t = \sum_{i=1}^{n} P_i = \frac{Q_t}{367} \sum_{i=1}^{n} \theta_i \frac{H(\theta_i Q_t)}{\eta(\theta_i Q_t)} \tag{12}$$

where P_t is the total power consumption.

4 The Optimization Control of the Constant-Speed Pumping Station [1]

When each pump's flow is greater than zero, consider the minimization of the total power consumption

$$\min P_t$$
$$s.t. \quad \theta_i > 0, i = 1, 2, \dots n$$
$$\sum_{i=1}^{n} \theta_i = 1 \tag{13}$$
$$\theta_i Q_t \leq Q_{max}, i = 1, 2, \dots n$$

The optimal point is

$$\theta_1 = \theta_2 = \dots = \theta_k = \frac{1}{k} \tag{14}$$

The optimal control method is to keep

$$Q_1 = Q_2 = \dots = Q_k = \frac{Q_t}{k} \tag{15}$$

The minimal value of the total power consumption is

$$\min P_t = \frac{Q_t}{367} \frac{H(\frac{Q_t}{k})}{\eta(\frac{Q_t}{k})} \tag{16}$$

5 The Optimization Switch of the Constant-Speed Pumping Station

Suppose a pumping station has M unit pumps which are the same model, and the pumping station is used to transfer water to the fixed height H0, the total flow is Q_t, the ith pump's flow is Q_i, n-unit pumps are running, and the total power consumption is the minimum, we have

$$V_t(Q_t) = \frac{Q_t}{\min P_t} = \frac{367\eta(\frac{Q_t}{n})}{H(\frac{Q_t}{n})} \qquad (17)$$

$$n \leq M$$

$$\frac{Q_t}{n} \leq Q_{max}$$

When the total flow Q_t increases, we should decide the optimal switch point of n-unit run pumps and n+1 unit run pumps. When n-unit run pumps can not meet with the need of the total flow Qt, we should increase run-pump n to n+1. Similarly, when the total flow Q_t decreases, we should decide the optimal switch point of n-unit run pumps and n-1 unit run pumps. When the $V_t(Q_t)$ of n-unit run pumps is greater than the $V_t(Q_t)$ of n-1 unit run pumps, we should decreases run-pump n to n-1.

The Q-V curve is the same as the Q_t-V_t curve of n=1. We know every point (Q,V) of the Q-V curve, the (nQ,V) is the point of the Q_t-V_t curve of n>1, since we have

$$Q_t = nQ$$

$$V_t(Q_t) = \frac{367\eta(\frac{nQ}{n})}{H(\frac{nQ}{n})} = \frac{367\eta(Q)}{H(Q)} = \frac{Q}{P(Q)} = V(Q) \qquad (18)$$

The Q_t-V_t curve of n=1 is V_2 at Q_2, and is V_m at Q_{max}, the $(2Q_2,V_2)$ is a point of the Q_t-V_t curve of n=2, the $(2Q_{max},V_m)$ is another point of the Q_t-V_t curve of n=2, and so on. Then, we can get the Q_t-V_t curve of n=2 shown in Fig. 4. Similarly, the $(3Q_2,V_2)$ is a point of the Q_t-V_t curve of n=3, the $(3Q_{max},V_m)$ is another point of the Q_t-V_t curve of n=3, and so on. Then, we can get the Q_t-V_t curve of n=3 shown in Fig. 4.

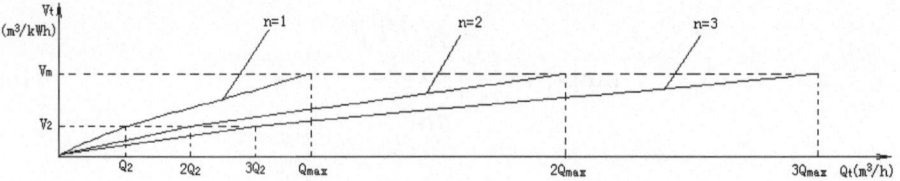

Fig. 4. The Q_t-V_t curve of n=1,2,3

The Q_{max} is the optimal switch point of n=1 and n=2, the $2Q_{max}$ is the optimal switch point of n=2 and n=3, the $3Q_{max}$ is the optimal switch point of n=3 and n=4. When the total flow $Q_t < Q_{max}$, the optimal run-unit is n=1; when $Q_{max} < Q_t < 2Q_{max}$, the optimal run-unit is n=2; when $2Q_{max} < Q_t < 3Q_{max}$, the optimal run-unit is n=3.

Similarly, when n>3, the Q_t-V_t (n=4,5...) curves and the corresponding optimal switch points can be obtained also.

Acknowledgments. To resolve the optimization problems of general devices, the authors conducted a long-term research [2-12]. The optimal method for pumping station presented in this article has been applied successfully to hundreds of occasions. The conclusion can also be applied to optimizations of fan, blowers, compressors, power transformers, manpower, animal force, locomotives, power generator, boilers, motors, and so on. The authors would like to thank Zhang Yanfang, Hebei Province Automation Company, Yao Bosheng, Beijing IAO Technology Development Company for all their valuable help and suggestions during the development and experiment of this theory..

References

1. Yao, F.L., Zhang, Y.F.: Electric Energy-saving Control Methods and practices. China Electric Power Press, Beijing (2009)
2. Yao, F.L., Zhang, Y.F.: Energy-saving Amount Calculation for Variable-speed Pumping Stations and System Design. Science Press, Beijing (1998)
3. Yao, F.L., Zhang, Y.F., Yao, B.S.: Study on water supply system of efficiency calculation. Control Engineering of China 6, 561–563 (2003)
4. Yao, F.L., Zhang, Y.F.: Electrical Automation Engineers Express Tutorial. China Machine Press, Beijing (2007)
5. Yao, F.L., Zhang, Y.F., Yao, B.S.: Using target-power theory design pumping stations. Journal of Irrigation and Drainage 22, 121–122 (2003)
6. Yao, F.L., Zhang, Y.F., Yao, B.S.: Determine the power consumption of the large-scale water transfer project. China Water Resources 2, 99–100 (2003)
7. Yao, F.L., Zhang, Y.F., Yao, B.S.: Significance of determination of object power waste for the large-scale water transfer projects. Advances in Science and Technology of Water Resources 23, 56–57 (2003)
8. Yao, F.L.: Study on energy-saving criterion of pump stations. Drainage and Irrigation Machinery 6, 37–39 (2004)
9. Yao, F.L., Hu, X.Y.: Reform variable-speed pumping station to maximize energy-saving effect on Ruian water work. Energy Conservation 2, 32–34 (2006)
10. Yao, F.L., Zhang, Y.F.: Mistakes in energy conservation of water supply. Electrotechnical Journal 2, 40–42 (2003)
11. Yao, F.L., Zhang, Y.F., Yao, B.S.: Calculation of energy-conservation ratio in pump station. Energy Engineering 6, 33–36 (2002)
12. Yao, F.L., Zhang, Y.F., Yao, B.S.: Finding electricity-saving potentiality of pump house using target-power technology. The World of Inverters 11, 56–59 (2002)

Grey Prediction Control in the Application of Networked Control Systems

XiaoQiang Wen and ZhiYi Sun

Dept of Electronics and Information Engineering,
Taiyuan University of Science and Technology, Taiyuan 030024, China
wenxiaoqiang2011@126.com, sunzhiyi@263.net

Abstract. Focusing on the influence made by the time-delay of networked control systems to the system performance and the problems that we are unable to obtain controlled object with all state information in industrial field, a new algorithm to compensate the bad effect caused by the network time-delay is proposed based on the grey prediction method to predict the output of the controlled object at future time. Finally simulate the algorithm by using the TRUETIME toolbox. The result demonstrates that the compensatory strategy in this paper can improve the system performance.

Keywords: Network control system, time-delay, grey prediction, delay compensation.

1 Introduction

In the network control system, as a result of the network existence, the network-induced delay has had many influences to the systems control performance, even possibly caused the system to be instability [1-3]. At present, extensive researches for the network-induced delay in the NCS have been carried out by many domestic and international scholars. References [4] proposed a kind of design algorithm which can construct control system stochastic controller and optimal state estimator for network delay in the control system, but the method only can be used when the network-induced delay is less than a sampling period, so it has certain limitations. References [5] used generalized predictive control theory in network control systems, but the method based on the traditional parameter model asked the model accuracy.

Grey prediction theory considers the uncertainty of the system, "partial information is known, the unknown part of the information", as the research object. It can correctly describe the operation behavioral of the system mainly through the development of some known information and extract useful information [6]. Grey prediction theory has the characteristics of few parameter identification, low online computation and strong robustness, and it can be better applied in the networked control systems. References [7] Supposed the delay of networked control system as a predictor target, made the gray model using prediction algorithm, compensated for the time delay by use of predictions results, but the network delay is random, and the prediction error prone to be large.

H. Deng et al. (Eds.): AICI 2011, Part II, LNAI 7003, pp. 214–220, 2011.
© Springer-Verlag Berlin Heidelberg 2011

In this paper, the predict controller is designed for the controlling system in which the full state information of the controlled object can not be gained and network has random time delay. It uses gray prediction algorithm to estimate the controlled object output value at future time, makes the compensation for the network delay and ensures the control performance of the system.

2 Description of the Networked Control System

In the networked control systems, sensors, controllers and actuators etc multiple nodes share channels via network connection. Due to the fact that bandwidth is limited and the change of network data flow is irregular in industrial field network, the packet collisions, network congestion etc phenomena inevitably exist, and they will lead to the emergence of network-induced delay [8]. Normally, the network-induced delay mainly consists of delay of packet waiting in line, information generated delay, transmission delay and the delay of data processing and calculation. And thanks to the gradual improvement of the processor speed of sensors, controller node, information produce delay and data processing calculation delay usually can be ignored.

In order to facilitate modeling system, make the assumptions as follows:

(1) The sensor and controller nodes use clock driver, actuator nodes use event driver. The controlled objects adopt the periodic sampling.

(2) Direct connection between the controller and sensor, there is no network. Delay exists only between the sensor and controller.

(3) The sampling signal of sensor has timestamp, controller can get the delay time of the sampling signal through contrast local clock to timestamp.

Control system diagram is shown below:

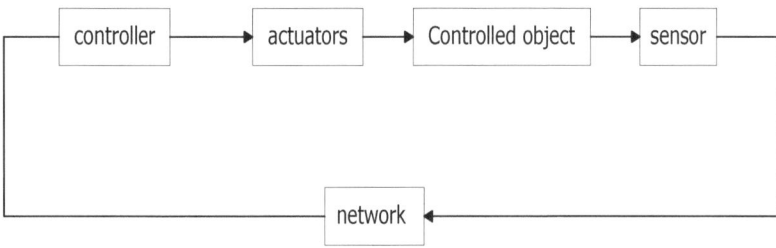

Fig. 1. Network control system composition diagram

Ignoring the noise in control system, we can obtain a controlled object state equation as follows:

$$\begin{cases} \dot{x}(t) = Ax(t) + Bu(t) \\ y(t) = Cx(t) \end{cases} \tag{1}$$

Consider that controller adopts discrete output feedback:

$$U(kh) = -KY(kh) \qquad k = 1,2\cdots \tag{2}$$

Where $X \in R^n$ is the state of an object, $U \in R^m$ is the controller output, $y \in R^p$ is the output of the controlled object, h is sampling period, and A, B, and C is optimum dimension matrix respectively.

3 Grey Prediction for the Design

The reason why the problems caused by the delay have an influence in system performance in networked control systems mainly lies in that the controller cannot timely get the real-time output of the controlled object. And we can forecast system behavior by using grey prediction control through the extraction of the system behavior data sequence, and search for the development rules, and according to the behavior trend of the system future actions, we can confirm the corresponding control decision-making to undertake beforehand control. According to this thought, we can design the optimal grey prediction to estimate the output of the controlled object at future time.

We consider $y^{(0)}(k)$ as the value of the controlled object's output at time k, Where $y^{(0)} = \{y^{(0)}(1), y^{(0)}(2), \cdots y^{(0)}(k)\}$, and 1-AGO sequence is created after once accumulation $y^{(1)} = \{y^{(1)}(1), y^{(1)}(2), \cdots y^{(1)}(k)\}$, Where $y^{(1)}(k) = \sum_{m=1}^{k} y^{(0)}(m)$.

The formula of the gray model background value is defined as:

$$z^{(1)}(k) = 0.5 y^{(1)}(k) + 0.5 y^{(1)}(k-1) \tag{3}$$

And then we can generate sequence $z^{(1)}$ which is close to sequence $y^{(1)}$

$$z^{(1)} = (z^{(1)}(2), z^{(1)}(3), \cdots z^{(1)}(k)) \tag{4}$$

Grey differential equation corresponding to the GM (1,1) model can be got as:

$$y^{(0)}(k) + az^{(1)}(k) = b \tag{5}$$

Where a is development coefficient and b is grey actuating quantity. The Parameters a, b can be derived by the least square method.

The time response sequence can be obtained when solution of grey differential equation is gained.

$$\hat{y}^{(1)}(k+1) = \left[y^{(0)}(1) - \frac{b}{a} \right] e^{-ak} + \frac{\mu}{a}, k = 0,1,2,\cdots n \tag{6}$$

Calculate the restore sequence and the prediction model of the controlled object output value is got as follows:

$$\hat{y}^{(0)}(k+1)=(1-e^{a})(y^{(0)}(1)-\frac{b}{a})e^{-ak}, k=1,2,\cdots n \qquad (7)$$

For the grey predict sequence asked the queue must be non negative, when using it we first determine whether $y^{(0)}{}_{min}$ is less than 0. If it is less than 0, then all the elements of the queue add $|y^{(0)}{}_{min}|$, then all the predicted results minus $|y^{(0)}{}_{min}|$ after the end of predicted.

4 Delay Compensation Method

Because of the network's existence, there must be network-induced delay inevitably [3]. Consider delay may be more than one sampling period, and assume τ_k as the network delay at time k, then controller can receive only $y(kh-\tau_k)$ or previous sampling period information at time k. In order to realize the compensation for the network delay, a buffer is set up in controller input, to save the N controlled object outputs value before this moment. Controller uses event-driven way to update buffer and uses time driving mode to send control signals to actuators.

And then discuss the two situations:

(1) Delay is less than one sampling period. In this case, the only signal which can reach controller in the interval of everyone sampling period is $y(kh-\tau_k)$. And it is shown in the diagram below.

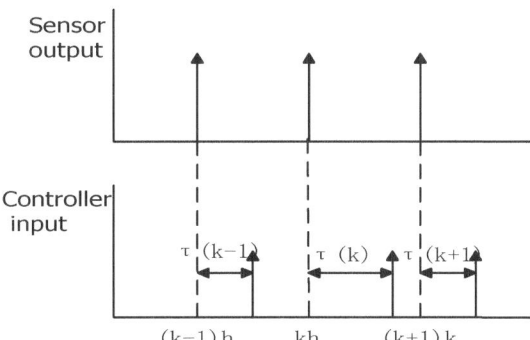

Fig. 2. Delay less than one sampling period signal transmission chart

At time k, controller contrasts timestamp information with local time to gain the present moment delay information, and we can use formula (7) to recurs the predicted output $\hat{y}(k)$ of the controlled object without delay, put the predicted value $\hat{y}(k)$ to the formula (2)and the control quantity which is after the compensation can be got.

(2) Delay more than one sampling period delay and delay interval less than one sampling period. In this case, the empty sampling and more signal may be arrive simultaneously at the controller in one sampling period of interval, there are shown below.

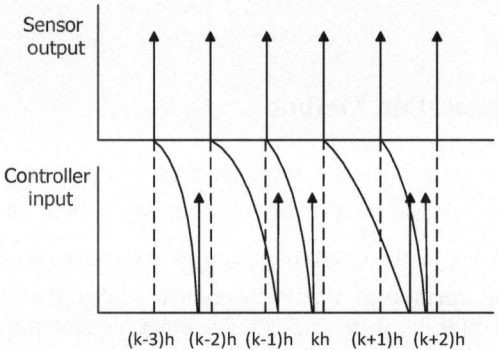

(k-3)h (k-2)h (k-1)h kh (k+1)h (k+2)h

Fig. 3. Delay more than one sampling period signal transmission chart

At time [(k -2)h ,(k -1)h], there is no new data input to controller and the data buffers cannot be updated, then the controller keeps sending control signals the last moment . At time [(k +1)h ,(k +2)h], there are multiple signal reaches the controller and the data buffers get updated, controller through comparing timestamp information, chooses the latest sampling signal as controller input.

5 Simulation

Consider the state equations of the controlled object as:

$$\begin{cases} \begin{bmatrix} \dot{x}_1 \\ \dot{x}_2 \end{bmatrix} = \begin{bmatrix} 0 & 1 \\ 0 & -1 \end{bmatrix} \begin{bmatrix} x_1 \\ x_2 \end{bmatrix} + \begin{bmatrix} 0 \\ 1000 \end{bmatrix} u \\ y = [1,0] \begin{bmatrix} x_1 \\ x_2 \end{bmatrix} \end{cases} \qquad (8)$$

We build a simulation model for networked control system and set network environment for CSMA/AMP (CAN) via the TRUETIME toolbox of MATLAB. Take T = 0.01 s for the sampling period and network time delay is set for the random time-delays between 0 - 2T.

Simulate the system under the condition without compensation mechanism, can get the simulation results as follows:

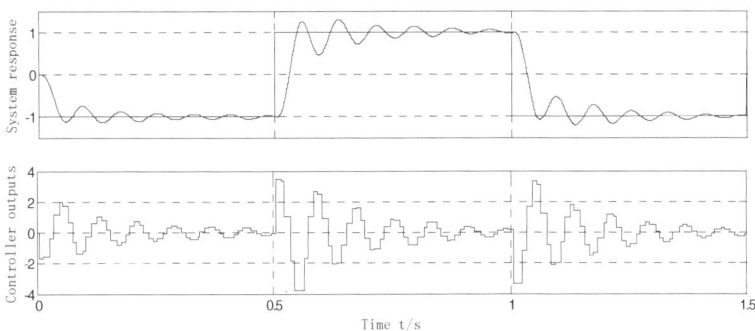

Fig. 4. No compensation mechanism controlled object and the controller outputs

Use the compensation algorithm which is proposed in this paper to compensate to the network delay. Draw the simulation results as follows:

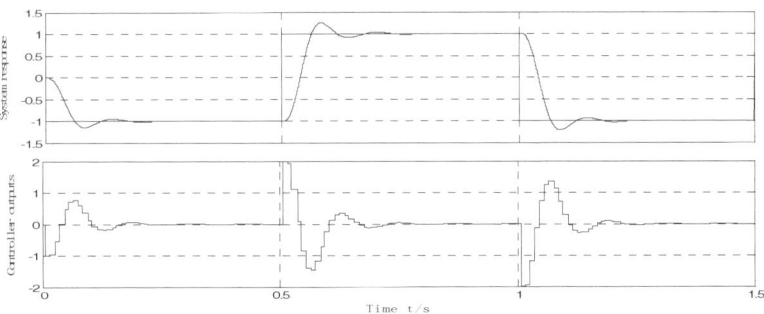

Fig. 5. With estimated compensation mechanism controlled object and the controller outputs

The three curves in the above figure are system reference input 、 the controlled object response and the controller output respectively. According to the simulation results we can see that because of the existence of the network delay, the system without compensation mechanism needs longer regulation time and has a larger shock, which explains that under the condition of the delay disturbance, the control algorithm without compensating already cannot satisfy the needs of the system performance. If the upper bound of the delay is determined, the control algorithm with estimated compensation mechanism proposed in this paper is adopted to reduce the system regulation time and can quickly be stable, which better overcomes the drawbacks brought by the network time delay to the system.

6 Conclusion

For a class of the network control system that the controlled object with all state information cannot be got, we design a gray predictor using a small amount of the system known information to estimate the system output at future time and to compensate for the system delay with the output feedback control. The simulation results indicate that the method proposed in this paper can compensate for the network delay effectively and improve the system performance.

References

1. Hespanha, J.P., Naghshtabrizi, P., Xu, Y.G.: A survey of recent results in network control systems. Proceedings of the IEEE 95(1), 138–172 (2007)
2. Montestruque, L.A., Antsaklis, P.J.: Stability of model-based networked control of networked systems with time-varying transmission times. IEEE Transaction Automatic Control 49(9), 1562–1572 (2004)
3. Rivera, M.G., Barreiro, A.: Analysis of networked control systems with drops and variable delays. Automatic 43(12), 2054–2059 (2007)
4. Nilsson, J., Bernhardsson, B., Wittenmark, B.: Stochastic analysis and control of real time systems with random time delays. Automatic 34(1), 57–64 (1998)
5. Wu, F., Chen, Z.-p.: The application of generalized predictive control theory in networked control system. Journal of Tian Jin University of Technology 26(1), 32–34 (2010)
6. Zhou, Z.J., Hu, C.H.: An effective hybrid approach based on grey and ARMA for forecasting gyro drift. Chaos, Solitons and Fractals 35(3), 525–529 (2008)
7. Li, X.-z., Sun, Q., Li, B.: Study of Network Control Systems Based on Optimal Grey Prediction. Micro Computer Information 3(26), 100–104 (2010)
8. Ahmet, O., Teoman, N., Emrah, P., Mutluer, O.: Control over imperfect networks: Model-based predictive networked control systems. IEEE Transactions on Industrial Electronics 58(3), 905–913 (2011)

Modeling and Chaos Control of Feedback-Type PWM DC/DC Converter

Feng Pan, Yang Du, and Zonghui Dong

Electronic Information Engineering College
Taiyuan University of Science and Technology
Taiyuan, PRC
paneng74@163.com

Abstract. In this paper, a discrete iterative model of feedback-type DC/DC converter is constructed using Laplace transform. The advantage of this model is proved comparing with state space average model. Self-adaptive control and parameter synchronization is applied to the chaos control of DC/DC converter. Simulation results show the effectiveness of this mathematical model and control method.

Keywords: modeling, chaos control, DC/DC converter, adaptive control, parameter synchronization.

1 Introduction

Since the concept of chaos control presented in 1990, it is researched by many academicians, some effective control methods is brought forward. Based on the principle, these control methods can be classified into feedback control method and non-feedback control method. Feedback control method include parameter perturbation resonance method, OGY method, OPF method, sequence variable feedback method, direct feedback method, proportion variable pulse feedback method, variable feedback control method, and so on. Non-feedback control method include neural networks, noise control method, periodic signal method, chaos signal synchronization method, artificial intelligent method, self-adaptive method, and so on.

Most of above methods can not be applied to chaos control of power electronics converter directly. At first, power electronics converter is time-varying switch circuit, the topology of converter is varied with the different switch state. According to the research of scholars, state space average model is not but discrete iterative model is more suitable for power electronics converter. That made the modeling analysis more difficult. Second, most control method can't be used to the chaos control of converter for the complexity and limitations of themselves [1][2].

In this paper, the discrete iterative model of feedback PWM DC/DC converter is conducted, and an adaptive synchronization method is presented for the chaos control of this model. Simulation results based MATLAB demonstrate the valid of this model and control method.

H. Deng et al. (Eds.): AICI 2011, Part II, LNAI 7003, pp. 221–226, 2011.
© Springer-Verlag Berlin Heidelberg 2011

2 Modeling and Analysis of DC/DC Converter

As well known, Buck converter is a switch circuit. It has two different states: current continuous mode and current interruption mode [3].

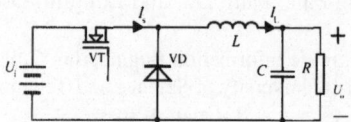

Fig. 1. Construction diagram of Buck converter

Fig. 1 is the construction diagram of Buck converter. Assuming current is continuous. There are two switch states in this mode: switch VT turn on and turn off. State space average method constructs the model according to the average turn-on time of switch.

Supposed the state equation of turn-on and turn-off of circuit as follow respectively:

$$\frac{dx(t)}{t} = A_1 x(t) + B_1 v_g, \quad v_0 = C_1^T x(t) \tag{1}$$

$$\frac{dx(t)}{t} = A_2 x(t) + B_2 v_g, \quad v_0 = C_2^T x(t) \tag{2}$$

Where A_1, B_1, A_2, and B_2 is the coefficient matrix of equation, C_1 and C_2 are row vectors, $x(t) = \begin{bmatrix} i_L \\ v_C \end{bmatrix}$ is the state variable of system.

Average (1) and (2), we can obtain the average equation as follow:

$$\frac{dx(t)}{t} = \left[(dA_1 + d'A_2)x(t) + (dB_1 + d'B_2)v_g \right] \tag{3}$$

$$v_0 = \left[dC_1^T + d'C_2^T \right] x(t)$$

Where d is the duty ratio of circuit. Add a perturbation into this equation, then

$$\frac{d(X + \hat{x})}{dt} = AX + BV_g + A\hat{x} + B\hat{v}_g + \left[(A_1 - A_2)X + (B_1 - B_2)V_g \right]\hat{d}$$

$$+ (A_1 - A_2)\hat{x}\hat{d} + (B_1 - B_2)\hat{v}_g\hat{d} \tag{4}$$

$$V_0 + \hat{v}_0 = C^T X + C^T \hat{x} + (C_1^T - C_2^T) \cdot X\hat{d} + (C_1^T - C_2^T)\hat{x}\hat{d}$$

Appling linearization and Laplace transform, we can get the transfer function of system:

$$G_{vd}(s) = \frac{\overset{\wedge}{v_0}(s)}{\hat{d}(s)} C^T (sI - A)^{-1} \left[(A_1 - A_2)X + (B_1 - B_2)V_g \right] + (C_1^T - C_2^T)X \tag{5}$$

Substitution the parameter of system into (5), then

$$G_{vd}(s) = \frac{\dfrac{U_i}{LC}}{s^2 + \dfrac{1}{RC}s + \dfrac{1}{LC}} \tag{6}$$

To verify the effectiveness of this model, select the parameters of circuit as follow: $R = 10 ohm$, $L = 10mH$, $C = 25\mu F$, $U_i = 20V$, then

$$G_{vd}(s) = \frac{80000000}{s^2 + 4000s + 4000000}$$

The simulation results are shown as Fig. 2 to Fig. 4.

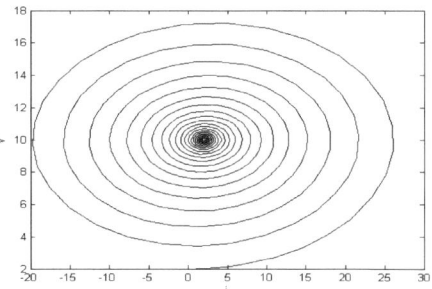

Fig. 2. Response curve of $i_L - v_C$

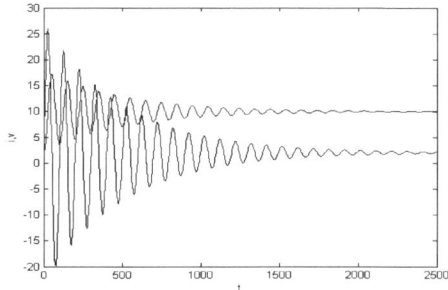

Fig. 3. Time response of state variables i_L and v_C

Fig. 2 and Fig. 3 show that the response of state variable based on state space average method is well. Further experience indicates that it is difficult for chaos to present in average model for the linearization processing. That means this average model can not embody the non-linearization characteristics of reality system. In fact, low-order discrete iterative model can be used as the ideal model [4][5].

3   Chaos Control Strategy

Many control methods can be applied to chaos control. Among these methods, self-adaptive control is used extensively recently for its simplicity and flexibility. We introduced a self-adaptive synchronization method in DC/DC converter.

The equation of feedback-type PWM Boost converter is:

$$x_{n+1} = \frac{V_i(I_{ref} - x_n)}{L} K_1 T \tag{7}$$

We select K as the bifurcation function, the target system is:

$$y_{n+1} = \frac{V_i(I_{ref} - y_n)}{L} K_2 T \tag{8}$$

The aim of self-adaptive synchronization control is to find a set of parameters that make the bifurcation functions of two system equivalency. $K_1 = K_2$, then these two system will be synchronized. That is:

$$\lim_{n\to\infty}|y_n - x_n| = 0 \tag{9}$$

Supposed the original states of these two systems are different, append followed iterative function as the control regulation:

$$K_{n+1} = K_n + u(t) \tag{10}$$

The error of system is $e_{n+1} = x_{n+1} - y_{n+1}$

As we know, chaos system is sensitive to original condition and slight disturbance. If an additional feedback is mixed when the synchronous error is small, these two systems will synchronize quickly. So we select:

$$u(t) = \begin{cases} 0, |e| > \delta \\ x - y, 0 < e < \delta \\ y - x, -\delta < e < 0 \end{cases} \tag{11}$$

Where $e = x - y$, δ is adjacent domain.

After some times iterative regulating, the synchronous error will be decreased; the response system will synchronize with target system.

4   Simulation Experiment of System

According to transform equation, bifurcation theory and Lyapunov Theorem, while $\left|\dfrac{di_{Ln+1}}{di_{Ln}}\right| < 1$, system will be steady. That means $-1 < \dfrac{V_i KT}{L} < 1$, select K as the bifurcation parameter $-\dfrac{L}{V_i T} < K < \dfrac{L}{V_i T}$.

Error signal $e_n = K(i_{ref} - i_n)$, regulation function of duty ratio is:

$$d_n = \begin{cases} 0, e_n \leq 0 \\ e_n, 0 < e_n < 1 \\ 1, e_n \geq 1 \end{cases}$$

The parameters of circuit: $V_i = 10V$, $V_0 = 50V$, $I_{ref} = 12A$, $T = 0.0006s$, $L = 0.006H$.

Derived from these parameters, the range of bifurcation parameter K is $-1 \leq K \leq 1$ while system is steady. System will bifurcate when K>1, then chaos occurs.

The simulation results are shown as below.

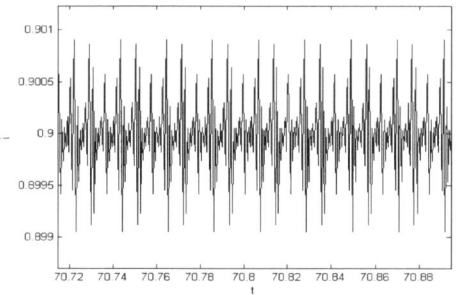

Fig. 4. The curve of i_{Ln+1} while K>1

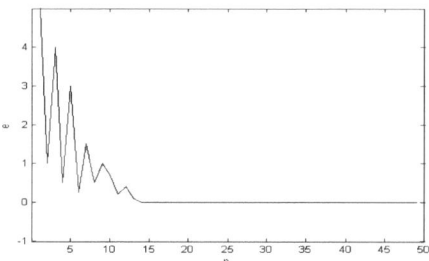

Fig. 5. The curve of system error

In evidence, system synchronizes with target system in limited times iterative, error comes to be zero little by little, and inductance current comes to be constant finally. Simulation results show that self-adaptive synchronization method can control the chaos in feedback-type PWM DC/DC converter.

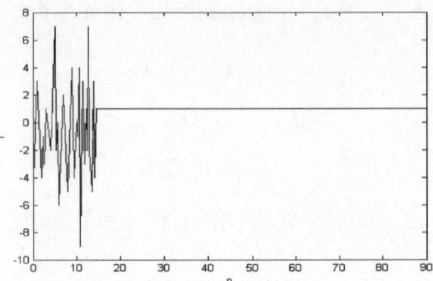

Fig. 6. The curve of inductance current

5 Conclusion

Because of the heavy nonlinear characteristics of power electronics device, many modeling method are not suitable for converter. A discrete iterative model of DC/DC converter is presented in this paper. Most of chaos control method can eliminate the chaos but system can not return the original state, chaos synchronization can do that. In this paper, a simple parameter self-adaptive method is applied to achieve synchronization of DC/DC converter, an unstability system return to the original state in a short time. Simulation results indicate the effectiveness of this method.

Acknowledgment. This paper is supported by Shanxi natural science fund (ID: 2010011024-3) and Shanxi graduate innovation project (ID: 20103097).

References

1. Qu, Y., Zhang, B.: The precise mathematical discrete model of buck converter in DCM and its analysis for bifurcation stability. Chinese Journal of Electronics 30(8), 1253–1256
2. Zhang, B., Li, P., Qi, Q.: Methods for Analyzing and Modeling Bifurcations and Chaos in DC-DC Converter. The Proceeding of CSEE 22(11), 81–86 (2002)
3. Fossas: Study of Chaos in the Buck Converter. IEEE Trans. on Circuit and System I (43), 13–25 (1996)
4. El Aroudi, A.: Quasi periodicity and Chaos in the DC-DC Buck-Boost Converter. International Journal of Bifurcation and Chaos 10(2), 359–371 (2000)
5. Tse, C.K.: Chaos from a Buck switching regulator operating in discontinuous mode. International Journal of Circuit Theory and Applications 22, 263–278 (1994)

Unsupervised Multiresolution Segmentation of SAR Imagery Based on Region-Based Hierarchical Model

Yan Zhang[1] and Yanwei Ju[2]

[1] Department of Applied Mathematics and Physics, the PLA University of Science and Technology, Nanjing, 2111101, China
[2] Nanjing Research Institute of Electronic Technology, Nanjing, 210039, China
zhangyan12073100@126.com

Abstract. This paper presents a novel method of unsupervised segmentation for synthetic aperture radar (SAR) images. Firstly, we define a generalized multiresolution likelihood ratio (GMLR), which classifies different kinds of signals more accurately than classical likelihood ratio by fusing more and different signal features. For our SAR image segmentation application, multiresolution stochastic structure inherent in SAR imagery is well captured by a set of multiscale autoregressive (MAR) models. Secondly, good parameter estimates of GMLR can be obtained by estimating several MMARP models using EM algorithm. Thirdly, considering the independence assumption of maximum likelihood estimation of parameter by EM algorithm and reduction of the segmentation time, we present the bootstrap sampling techniques applied above algorithm. Experimental results demonstrate that our algorithm performs fairly well.

Keywords: SAR images, MAR model, GMLR, EM algorithm.

1 Introduction

The segmentation of images is very important for the following processing. In the case of SAR imagery, speckle noise seriously degrades segmentation performances. Recently, many algorithms and Markov models, such as popular maximum posterior marginal (MPM) [1, 2], multiresolution Gaussian autoregressive (MGA) model [3], have been proposed; and some methods based on multiscale autoregressive (MAR) models, have also been present, such as scale-autoregressive model and mixture multiscale autoregressive (MMAR) model [4, 5]. However, as MGA model, in many (multiresolution) Markov models, spatial interaction parameters are selected experimentally. The MPM estimator as an alternative to MAP estimation minimizes the probability of classification error. However, it may only be approximately computed in a computationally expensive procedure similar to simulated annealing. Also, the MPM criterion doesn't consider the spatial placement of errors when distinguishing among the quality of segmentations. So the good segmentation performance of MGA model or MPM is difficult to get. An acceptable segmentation can be provided by MAR model, but the approach is not precise and is a supervised

H. Deng et al. (Eds.): AICI 2011, Part II, LNAI 7003, pp. 227–235, 2011.

segmentation method. The segmentation results of MMAR model is precise, however, parameter estimation of MMAR model is very time-consuming for it is actually a searching algorithm based on maximize likelihood frame.

In addition, in almost all statistical approaches, the image model is frequently based on the assumption of statistically independent image signals with different marginal probability distributions in each region. After the distributions are recovered from the mixed empirical signal distribution over the image [6]–[10], initial segmentation is performed by low-level pixel-wise classification. Approximation and classification of scalar data using a mixture of probability distributions are also widely used for data clustering in pattern recognition and applied statistics [9], [11], [12]. These statistical approaches are to maximize likelihood function, and a very important assumption is statistical independence of image signals. In fact, all the image signals are statistically dependent.

In this work, we both give and estimate the GMLR for segmentation in SAR imagery. GMLR has the advantage of classifying different signals more accurately than that of classical likelihood ratio by fusing more and different signal features. We model autoregressive predicted images of multiresolution sequence with several MMARP model that can capture the different types of image classification features. Each class is learned in an unsupervised fashion and contains the statistical intrinsic structure of its image features. To reduce the dependence effect of pixels in the images and redundancy of information connected to the choice of a small representative sample, bootstrap sampling technique is employed. Experimental results show segmentation algorithm proposed not only is precise and save time, but also is robust to speckle noise.

2   Multiresolution Likelihood Ratio (GMLR)

2.1   The Definition of GMLR

Considering more and different signal features (including image features), we define the following GMLR which can fuse more and different signal features better so that the GMLR can make more precise decision for classification and pattern recognition:

$$\lambda(x_1,\cdots,x_K) = \frac{\prod_{k=1}^{K} p_k(x_k|H_1)}{\prod_{k=1}^{K} p_k(x_k|H_0)} \tag{1}$$

where correspond to the hypotheses H_0 and H_1 that the considered portion of signal belongs to either a signal of type 0 or type 1, and that you may potentially consider more than just two types of signals. The dimensionality of vector $x_k = (x_{k1},\cdots,x_{kp})(k=1,\cdots,K)$ is p; although in some cases, such as RGB images, p can be larger than 1, in this paper, we only deal with scalar values; the K is the number of signal features; $p_k(x_k|\cdot)(k=1,\cdots,K)$ is probability density function (PDF) and each of them may be different types for describing different signal features.

We can make decision that signal feature x_k is from signal of type 0 when (1) is larger than some value, and reversely feature of signal x_k is from signal of type 1. When the $x_1,\ldots,x_K$ are dependent each other or $p(x_1,\cdots,x_K|H_1)$ is non-Gaussian distribution it is complicated to deal with $p(x_1,\cdots,x_K|H_1)$, therefore, we presented definition (1) from the point of view of fusion. But it is not really classical likelihood when $x_1,\ldots,x_K$ is dependent, so we call it generalized multiresolution likelihood ratio (GMLR). We can notice that the definition (1) degenerates to classical likelihood ratio when $K=1$.

2.2 GMLR of SAR Imagery

The starting point for our segmentation method development is a multiresolution sequence X_K, X_{K-1}, $\cdots$, X_0 of original SAR imagery Y_0, where X_K and X_0 correspond to the coarsest and finest resolution images, respectively. The detail can be found in [4]. As an example, Fig. 1 illustrates a multiresolution sequence of three SAR images, together with the quadtree mapping. The parent of node s is denoted by $s\overline{\gamma}$, and parent of node $s\overline{\gamma}$ is denoted by $s\overline{\gamma}^2$, and so on. We use the notation $X(s)$, $X(s\overline{\gamma})$ to indicate the pixel mapped to node s and $s\overline{\gamma}$ respectively. The scale (resolution) of node s is denoted by $k(s)$.

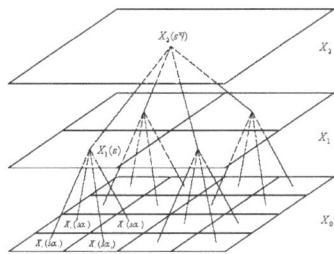

Fig. 1. Sequence of three multiresolution SAR images mapped onto quadtree

For SAR image segmentation, we address the segmentation by using the predicted values at each resolution under the MAR models as the input to the classification procedure, which can not only filter and reduce the possible effect generated by the presence of speckle of SAR images, but also captures the structure inherent in SAR imagery well and accuracy characterizes the evolution in scale of homogenous regions. So the GMLR of SAR imagery is defined as follows:

$$\lambda(x_0^p(s),\cdots,x_{K-2}^p(s\overline{\gamma}^{K-2})) = \frac{\displaystyle\prod_{k=0}^{K-2} p_k(x_k^p(s\overline{\gamma}^k)|H_1)}{\displaystyle\prod_{k=0}^{K-2} p_k(x_k^p(s\overline{\gamma}^k)|H_0)} \tag{2}$$

where $x_k^p(s\overline{\gamma}^k)$ is realization of predicted image $X_k^p(s\overline{\gamma}^k)$ at resolution k, which can be gotten by multiresolution autoregressive prediction $X_k^p(s\overline{\gamma}^k) = a_{k,1}X_{k+1}(s\overline{\gamma}^{k+1}) + \cdots + a_{k,F_k}X_{k+r_k}(s\overline{\gamma}^{k+r_k}) + b_k$, where $X_{k+1}(s\overline{\gamma}^{k+1}), \cdots,$ $X_{k+r_k}(s\overline{\gamma}^{k+r_k})$ are the multiresolution sequence. The order of the regression r_k associated with modeling $X_k^p(s\overline{\gamma}^k)$ from its ancestors will vary with the level $k \in \{0, 1, \cdots, K\}$ as defined by the function

$$r_k = \begin{cases} K-k & if \ K-R+1 \le k < K \\ R & if \ 0 \le k < K-R+1 \end{cases} \tag{3}$$

where the maximal regression order $R = 3$ because it is found that we can achieve a lower probability of misclassification and good tradeoff between modeling accuracy and computational efficiency. Such a definition ensures a maximal regression order at most equal to R and subject to the tree height.

3 Representative Criterion of Bootstrap Sampling

Since Efron [13] introduced a very general re-sampling procedure, called the Bootstrap model, to estimate the distributions of statistics based on independent observations, Many researches have applied a Bootstrap method in pattern classification [14]-[16] and showed that it was a powerful non-parametric technique to evaluate classifier's performance. Here we employ Bootstrap sampling technique to get representtive and robust bootstrap sample [17].

The criterion is chosen so that the sample would be representative only if each image grey level w_j occurs more than once into the Bootstrap sample. Since the sample size of each class $N_j's$ can be considered as independent Poisson random variables of parameter $n\pi_j$ (π_j is prior probability of each class), it must be subject to the condition $\sum_{j=1}^{2} n_j = n$ for two classes, where n_j is a realization of N_j. Let us evaluate the probability P_n defined as:

$$P_n = P(N_1 > 0, N_2 > 0) = \prod_{j=1}^{2}(1 - e^{-n\pi_j}) \tag{4}$$

Then, the representative criterion requires P_n tending to 1. The problem we propose to solve is to determine the value n of the n-size sample from which our Bootstrap sample would be representative and can be used robustly for parameter estimation [17].

The use of the sampling random model in image segmentation presents two advantages:

(i) The choice of independence pixel sample which would allows an estimation of the statistical parameters of the image in the best conditions of independence;

(ii) The reduction of redundancy of information connected to the choice of a small representative sample, allows a gain in a factor N/n in times of calculation.

4 Parameter Estimation for GMLR of SAR Imagery

Estimation of the parameters related to the GMLR is treated separately for each scale k. We can obtain the parameters of each scale k for GMLR (2) by estimating the model (5).

$$P(x_k^{p^*}(s\overline{\gamma}^k)\,|\,H_0,H_1) = w_1 p_k\left(x_k^{p^*}(s\overline{\gamma}^k)\,|\,H_0\right) + w_2 p_k\left(x_k^{p^*}(s\overline{\gamma}^k)\,|\,H_1\right), k = 0,\cdots,K-2 \;(5)$$

where w_1, w_2 denote the probability of the any pixel belonging to signal of type 0 or signal of type 1 at resolution k respectively, and $0 \le w_1, w_2 \le 1$, $w_1 + w_2 = 1$. $P(x_k^{p^*}(s\overline{\gamma}^k)\,|\,H_0,H_1)$ denotes weighted probability sum. The inputted feature $x_k^{p^*}(s\overline{\gamma}^k)$ is bootstrap sample of predicted image $X_k^P(s\overline{\gamma}^k)$. The $x_k^{p^*}(s\overline{\gamma}^k)$ can be gotten as follows: firstly, we obtain bootstrap image Y_0^* of original SAR image Y_0 using the method in [17]; secondly, we get bootstraping multiresolution sequence $X_0^*,\cdots,X_K^*$ of Y_0^* as in section 2.2; then we get predicted image $X_k^{p^*}(s\overline{\gamma}^k)$ as follows:

$$X_k^{p^*}(s\overline{\gamma}^k) = \sum_{i=1}^{p_k} a_{k,i} X_{k+i}^*(s\overline{\gamma}^{k+i}) + b_k \tag{6}$$

The order of the regression associated with modeling $X_{pk}^*(s\overline{\gamma}^k)$ from its ancestors will vary with the level $k \in \{0,1,\cdots,K\}$ as defined by function (3). The regression coefficients are obtained by a standard least squares estimation.

The parameters at resolution k of the GMLR for SAR imagery can be estimated via the MMARP model (5). If the probability density functions, $p_k(x_k^P(s\overline{\gamma}^k)\big|H_0)$ and $p_k(x_k^P(s\overline{\gamma}^k)\big|H_1)$, are Gaussian, the $p_k(x_k^{p^*}(s\overline{\gamma}^k)\big|H_0)$ and $p_k(x_k^{p^*}(s\overline{\gamma}^k)\big|H_1)$ in model (5) are also Gaussian distribution. The estimation of parameters is easily performed via expectation maximization (EM) algorithm [18, 19], and the resulting iterations for the EM algorithm are given by

$$w_g^{s^{(i)}} = \frac{w_g^{(i)} p_k(x_k^{p^*}(s\overline{\gamma}^k)\big|H_{g-1})}{w_1^{(i)} p_k(x_k^{p^*}(s\overline{\gamma}^k)\big|H_0) + w_2^{(i)} p_k(x_k^{p^*}(s\overline{\gamma}^k)\big|H_1)}, g = 1,2 \tag{7}$$

$$w_g^{(i+1)} = \frac{1}{N^2} \sum_{\{s\,|\,k(s)=k\}} w_g^{s^{(i)}}, g = 1,2 \tag{8}$$

$$u_g^{(i+1)} = \frac{\sum\limits_{\{slk(s)=k\}} w_g^{s^{(i)}} x_k^{p*}(s\overline{\gamma}^k)}{\sum\limits_{\{slk(s)=k\}} w_g^{s^{(i)}}}, g = 1,2 \tag{9}$$

$$\left[\sigma_g^2\right]^{(i+1)} = \frac{\sum\limits_{\{slk(s)=k\}} w_g^{s^{(i)}} [x_k^{p*}(s\overline{\gamma}^k) - u_g^{(i+1)}]^2}{\sum\limits_{\{slk(s)=k\}} w_g^{s^{(i)}}}, g = 1,2 \tag{10}$$

If the probability density functions, $p_k(x_k^p(s\overline{\gamma}^k)|H_0)$ and $p_k(x_k^p(s\overline{\gamma}^k)|H_1)$, are Rayleigh distribution with parameter b, the $p_k(x_k^{p*}(s\overline{\gamma}^k)|H_0)$ and $p_k(x_k^{p*}(s\overline{\gamma}^k)|H_1)$ in model (5) are also Rayleigh distribution. The resulting iterations for the EM algorithm are given by (7), (8) and the following equation (11):

$$\hat{b}^{(i+1)} = \sqrt{\frac{\sum\limits_{\{slk(s)=k\}} w_g^{s^{(i)}} x_k^{p*2}(s)}{2 \sum\limits_{\{slk(s)=k\}} w_g^{s^{(i)}}}} \tag{11}$$

The estimates of the parameters are then obtained by iterating above steps until convergence.

Obtaining the estimation of the GMLR, based on GMLR histogram of SAR imagery, we classify each individual pixel based on a test window of pixels surrounding the classified pixel. The classification of the original image pixel $Y_0(s)$ at node s, denoted as $C(s)$, can be obtained via the rule

$$C(s) = \begin{cases} H_1 & if \ \lambda(Y_0(s)) \geq \eta \\ H_0 & if \ \lambda(Y_0(s)) < \eta \end{cases} \tag{12}$$

where the threshold value η can be determined by detecting peak-valley of GMLR histogram of SAR imagery.

For clarity of outline, all above explanation is binary (M=2), however, the M-ary hypotheses (M>2) of GMLR also can be gotten, which is similar to pp.46-96 in [20]. And we give the experimental result when M=3 in next section.

5   Experimental Results and Analysis

We implemented our method and presented our results on a synthetic SAR imagery and three true SAR images (256×256)(the first row in Fig.3) using the pixels in square windows of 9×9 pixels to classify the central pixel. And we use a quadtree with $K = 4$ levels and maximal regression order $R = 3$ for the results presented here. Rayleigh distribution is used for the second and third images, and Gaussian for the first and fourth images. The number of classes for the fourth image is 3 and 2 for the others. In order to assure the bootstrap sample has representation, robustness, and the size of samples satisfy representative (4), we choose bootstrap sample size n=1024. The latter four rows in Fig.3 are segmentation results using classical mixture model, unsupervised MPM, MGA model and our approach respectively. Fig .1 is histograms of the original images (the first row) and the histograms of the predicted image at scale 0 (the second row), and the histograms of the latter show obvious peaks. From Fig.3, it is easy to see the segmentation using classical mixture model and MPM are very sensitive to speckle of SAR images. We can notice the edge of segmentation is not smooth and doesn't get precise segmentation in the bottom left corner of the synthetic SAR from the use of MGA model. It is obvious that a smoother and more precise segmentation resulting from the use of our approach is obtained, and our method is robust to speckle. We also list the CPU time for different methods applied to these images in Table 1, and our method needs the least computation time.

The reason for poor results of mixture model is that mixture model can't consider the dependence or Markov property of neighboring pixels; MPM estimator may only be approximately computed in a computationally expensive procedure similar to simulated annealing, and the MPM criterion doesn't consider the spatial placement of errors when distinguishing among the quality of segmentations. It is difficult to give appropriate parameters of the Gibbs distribution of the region process in MGA model, so the segmentation is not precise. And they are computationally complex.

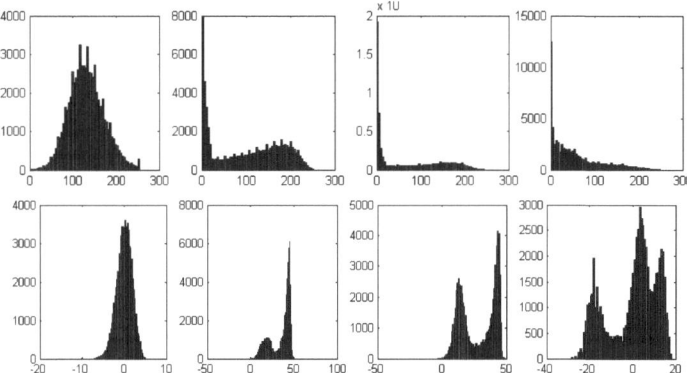

Fig. 2. Histograms of the four original images (the first row); histograms of the four predicted images at scale 0 (the second row)

We find our analysis and experiments results are identical that our approach is timesaving considerably and the segmentation is precise for the synthetic SAR imagery and the three true SAR images. All these show that our algorithm gives better results than the three methods in the quality of the segmentation and the computational costs.

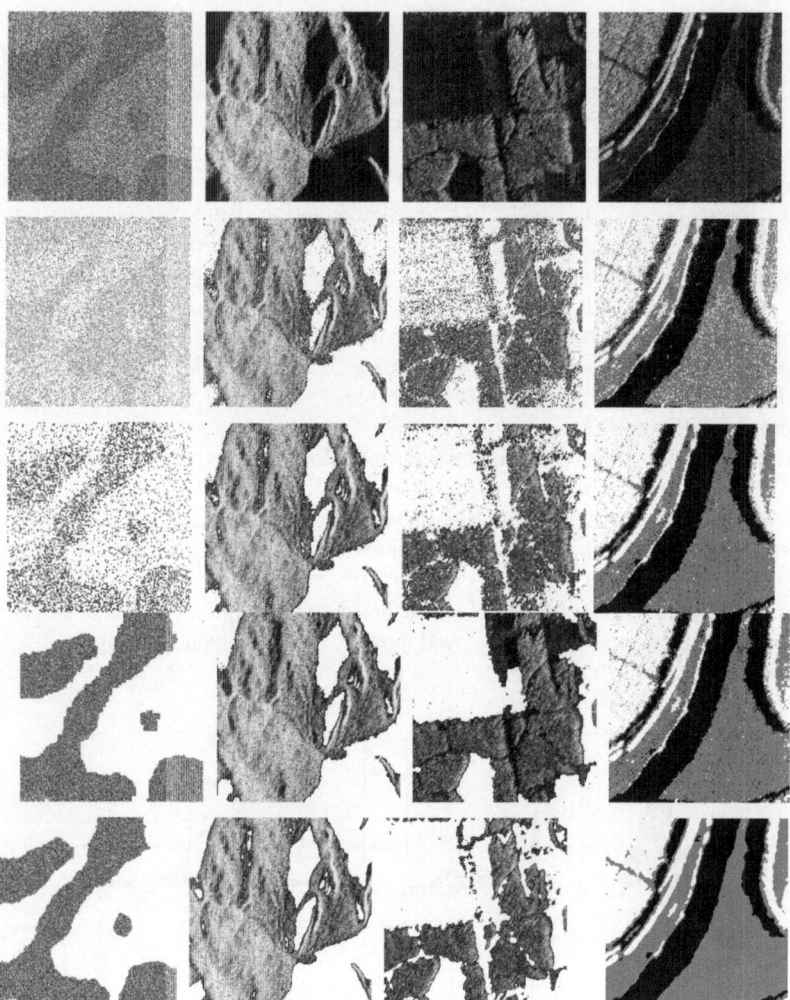

Fig. 3. Segmentation results. Original images (the first row). Segmentation based on classical mixture model (the second row); Segmentation based on unsupervised MPM (the third row); Segmentation using MGA model (the fourth row); Our approach (the fifth row, and the second and third images are segmentation results when PDF are Rayleigh distribution in GMLR).

Table 1. CPU time (sec.) for the classical mixture model, MPM, MGA model and our approach

image \ method	the synthetic SAR image	the first true SAR image	the second true SAR image	the third true SAR image
Classical mixture model	**109.8**	**60.3**	**51.2**	72.0
MPM	**205.2**	**180.5**	**110.7**	196.3
MGA model	**338.6**	**296.6**	**290.1**	318.9
Our approach	57.0	42.8	40.3	54.1

References

1. Marroquin, J., Mitter, S., Poggio, T.: Probabilistic solution of illposed problems in computation vision. Journal of the American Statistical Association 82(397), 76–89 (1987)
2. Yang, Y., Sun, H., He, C.: Supervised SAR Image MPM Segmentation Based on Region-Based Hierarchical Model. IEEE Trans. Geoscience and Remote Sensing Letters 3(4), 517–521 (2006)
3. Comer, M.L., Delp, E.J.: Segmentation of textured images using a multiresolution Gaussian autoregressive model. IEEE Trans. Image Processing 8(3), 408–420 (1999)
4. Kim, A., Krim, H.: Segmentation and compression of SAR imagery via hierarchical stochastic modeling. In: Proceedings of Geoscience and Remote Sensing Symposium, vol. 6, pp. 2635–2638 (2000)
5. Xianbin, W., Zheng, T.: Mixture multiscale autoregressive modelling of SAR imagery for segmentation. Electronics Letters 39(17), 1272–1274 (2003)
6. Glasbey, C.A.: An analysis of histogram-based thresholding algorithms, CVGIP: Graph. Models Image Process 55(6), 532–537 (1993)
7. Kittler, J., Illingworth, J.: Minimum error thresholding. Pattern Recognition 19(1), 41–47 (1986)
8. Otsu, N.: A threshold selection method from gray level histograms. IEEE Trans. Syst., Man, Cybern. SMC-9(1), 62–66 (1979)
9. Pal, N.R., Pal, S.K.: A review on image segmentation techniques. Pattern Recognition 26(9), 1277–1294 (1993)
10. Trier, O.D., Jain, A.: Goal-directed evaluation of binarization methods. IEEE Trans. Pattern Anal. Mach. Intell. 17(10), 1191–1201 (1995)
11. Dubes, R.C., Jain, A.K.: Random field models in image analysis. J. Appl. Stat. 16(2), 131–164 (1989)
12. Duda, R.O., Hart, P.E., Stork, D.G.: Pattern Classification. Wiley, New York (2001)
13. Efron, B.: Bootstrap methods: another look at the jackknife. Ann. Stat. 7(1), 1–26 (1979)
14. Koch, I., Marshall, G.: Bootstrap coverage plots for image segmentation. In: IEEE-ICPR, vol. 2, pp. 447–451 (1996)
15. Vijaya, S.V., Murty, M.N.: Bootstrapping for efficient handwritten digit recognition. Pattern Recognition 34(5), 1047–1056 (2001)
16. Jain, A.K., Dubes, R.C., Chen, C.C.: Bootstrapping techniques for error estimation. In: Proc. 8th International Conference on Pattern Recognition, Paris, pp. 330–332 (1986)
17. Zribi, M.: Non-parametric and unsupervised Bayesian classification with Bootstrap sampling. Image and Vision Computing 22(1), 1–8 (2004)
18. Dempster, A.P., Laird, N.M., Rubin, D.B.: Maximum likelihood estimation from incomplete data via the EM algorithm. Journal of the Royal Statistical Society, Series B 39, 1–38 (1977)
19. Gopal, S.S., Herbert, T.J.: Bayesian pixel classification using spatially variant finite mixtures and the generalized EM algorithm. IEEE Trans. Image Processing 17(7), 1014–1018 (1998)

A Video Vehicle Tracking Algorithm Based on Ploar Fourier Descriptor

Jian Wu, Zhi-ming Cui, Yue-hui Zhang, and Jian-ming Chen

The Institute of Intelligent Information Processing and Application,
Soochow University, Suzhou 215006, China
Jiangsu Yihe Technology Co., Ltd., Suzhou 215002, China
{jianwu,szzmcui,20104227055,jmchen}@suda.edu.cn

Abstract. Video-based vehicle tracking movement in the field of intelligent transportation is an important research question. This paper presents a video vehicle tracking algorithm based on polar Fourier descriptor according to the Fourier transform properties. This paper first gets the ideal vehicle for the target object and extract its contour by using background subtraction for the reason that the traffic monitoring video scenes are fixed and then gets the video frequency spectrum characteristics of the vehicle by implementing Discrete Fourier Transform to the image data in polar coordinates and then achieves the video vehicle tracking based on linear prediction and shape similarity measurement. Experimental results show that this algorithm's tracking accuracy is higher and time-consuming is less.

Keywords: Vehicle tracking, Fourier descriptors, shape recognition, linear prediction.

1 Introduction

Vehicle Tracking is within the moving target tracking's scope. With the development of computer technology and in-depth research, tacking technology is also increasingly update and its applications are gradually expanding. Moving target tracking refers to detecting, extracting, identifying and tracking moving object in the image sequence and understanding the behavior of moving objects [1]. Target tracking technology is usually used in areas such as the traffic junction, houses, car parks, public places and banks. Related technologies have also been widely used technology and they are mainly used in traffic control, vehicle abnormal behavior detection, intelligent vehicles, etc. The commonly used moving tracking algorithm can be divided into the following categories: Model-based tracking, Active Contour-based tracking, Region-based tracking and Feature-based tracking [2, 3]. Model-based tracking is used when it is needed to track the target's various parts' motion state in detail. In this case, we need to establish a priori model of moving target and then search the image sequence,

H. Deng et al. (Eds.): AICI 2011, Part II, LNAI 7003, pp. 236–245, 2011.

so that we achieve the purpose of tracking; Active Contour-based tracking is initialized with high profile and cannot enter the interested region's deep section; Region-based tracking is time-consuming which is particularly acute when global searching is needed; Feature-based tracking uses knowledge of target's feature information to identify the moving target which is different from Region-based tracking in that the former uses the whole target as the related object and the latter uses one or more local features.

The object's shape recognition is an important direction of pattern recognition which is widely used in image analysis, machine vision and object recognition and other application areas. Fourier descriptor is an important method to analyze and recognize object's shape which usually implements discrete Fourier transform to the contour data and retains a few of the previous coefficient. Due to coefficients' concentration to low frequency after Fourier transform, abandoning the majority coefficients behind will not affect the basic shape of the object features and then dimensions are reduced and data are compressed [4, 5]. Based on this, this paper presents a method based on Fourier descriptor in polar coordinates [6] to achieve video vehicle tracking. This paper first gets the ideal vehicle for the target object and extract its outline by using background subtraction for the reason that the traffic monitoring video scenes are fixed and then gets the video frequency spectrum characteristics of the vehicle by implementing Discrete Fourier Transform to the image data in polar coordinates and then achieves the video vehicle tracking based on linear prediction and shape similarity measure. Experiments show that this algorithm is rotation, translation and scale invariance, it can achieve a better vehicle tracking in traffic control, maintains a high tracking accuracy and time-consuming is significantly reduced when compared to other tracking algorithms.

2 Introduction

2.1 Extraction of Vehicle's Contour

The Fourier descriptor is Fourier transform coefficient of the boundary curve of object's shape which is the analysis results of the signal frequency domain from object boundary curve. In this paper, it is needed to extract the contour of vehicles first. As traffic monitoring is a unique video application, the camera angle is fixed, so the video background is relatively fixed, we have accumulated much experience in this area [7], so the accuracy of background extraction is ensured. Then, we get the binary image and extract the contours of the vehicle by the use of background subtraction method. As Figure 1 shows that picture (a) presents the original video frame, picture (b) presents the constructed video background, picture (c) presents the binary image of video frame obtained by subtracting the background, picture (d) presents the schematic diagram of the vehicle contour extraction.

(a) original video frame   (b) video background

(c) binary image   (d) contour extraction

Fig. 1. Video vehicle's contour schematic

2.2 Polar Fourier Transform

We set f (x, y) as a binary function of target shape, then its discrete Fourier transform is:

$$f(u,v) = \sum_{x=0}^{M-1} \sum_{y=0}^{N-1} f(x,y) * \exp[-j2\pi(\frac{ux}{M}+\frac{uy}{N})] \qquad (1)$$

Let $x = r\cos(\theta)$, $y = r\sin(\theta)$, $u = \rho\cos(\varphi)$, $v = \rho\sin(\varphi)$, put them into formula (1), and then we get the results of two-dimensional Fourier transform in polar coordinates:

$$PF(\rho,\psi) = \sum_{r} \sum_{i} f(r,\theta_i) * \exp[-j2\pi(\frac{r}{R}\rho+\frac{2\pi i}{T}\psi)] \qquad (2)$$

In formula (2), $0 \leq r \leq R$, $\theta_i = i(\dfrac{2\Pi}{T})(0 \leq i < T)$, $0 \leq \rho < R$, $0 \leq \varphi < T$. R is radial frequency's resolution and T is angular frequency's resolution. To calculate Fourier descriptors we need to make the boundary curve discrete, and then we get N discrete points between whom the spaces are equally. Then we use the formula to calculate the discrete Fourier transforming coefficients of those points $z(k)(k = 1,2,...,N-1)$ which are regarded as Fourier descriptors. According to the nature of the Fourier transform, Fourier descriptors are related to the scale, direction and location of the shape and the curve's starting point. So we need to normalize the Fourier transformation and using a normalized Fourier descriptor has the characteristics of rotation, translation and scale invariance to identify the shape of the object. Normalized descriptor is defined as $d(k)$.

$$d(k) = \frac{\|z(k)\|}{\|z(1)\|} \tag{3}$$

2.3 Vehicle's Contour's Similarity

By the use of normalized descriptor $d(k)$, we can calculate the degree of similarity between any two shapes i and j, and identify objects with the rotation, translation and scale invariance. As the frequency components of the Fourier transform are orthogonal to each other, we use Euclidean distance to calculate the shape difference between Fourier descriptors. As the following formula shows:

$$dis\,\tan ce = \sqrt{\sum_{k=2}^{M} \|d_i(k) - d_j(k)\|^2} \tag{4}$$

As the energy of the shape are mainly concentrated in low frequency, the high frequency component of Fourier transform is generally small and vulnerable to the interference from high frequency noise, generally we only use the low frequency of the normalized Fourier descriptors to calculate similarity differences between the shapes of objects. When distance = 0, the two shapes are completely similar to each other and if the distance is bigger, the greater the difference in the shape of the object is.

2.4 Tracking Based on Prediction

In the tracking process we can get the target trajectory, according to which we can predict the moving target's position in the next frame, then According to which we execute matching operation between the moving template and forecast regional. Finally we find the vehicles with smallest similar differences and reducing a large number of computation time of matching. We need to achieve the tracking of moving objects in Vehicles Contour matching based on prediction first, and then get the trajectory of moving object. Supposed that there is a moving object A, whose position in the current frame $f(n)$ is p_n, and its position in the previous frame f_{n-1} is p_{n-1}. Taken the current location of moving object region as a benchmark, expected size of moving object's matching area can be calculated by the Formula(5) and Formula(6):

$$rect.x = t.x + 2 \times (p_n.x - p_{n-1}.x) \qquad (5)$$

$$rect.y = t.y + 2 \times (p_n.y - p_{n-1}.y) \qquad (6)$$

In formula(5) and (6), x is predicted area's length and y is its width. $t.x$ is template's length and $t.y$ is template's width. $p_n.x$ 、 $p_n.y$ and $p_{n-1}.x$ 、 $p_{n-1}.y$ are two adjacent points in the trajectory.

3 Experimental Results and Analysis

The data of these experiments is provided by Jiangsu Yihe Technology Co., LTD. The company occupies more than 90% of traffic engineering field market in the city of Suzhou, since 2008, the company works together with our institute to research and develop in technology of traffic video analysis. This paper adopts the fixed cameras videos as objects which are uncalibration, these videos are selected in loop expressway of downtown and in the gateway of urban traffic. Development environment is Window Xp + OpenCv 2.1.

3.1 Extraction of Vehicle's Fourier Descriptors

As Figure 2 shows, select four small images of single vehicle in video frames, represent cars, SUVs, vans and trucks respectively to test the reasonable value of coefficient number of the Fourier descriptor.

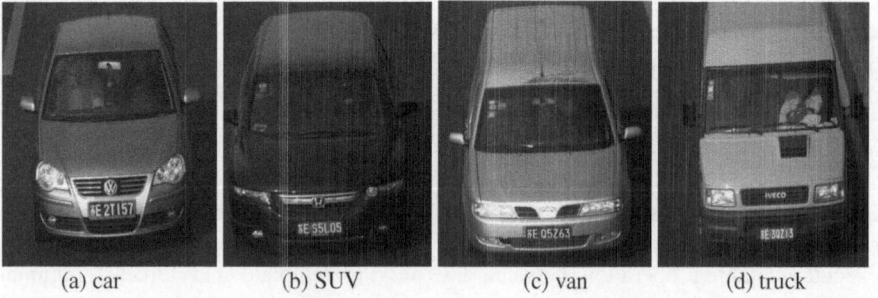

(a) car   (b) SUV   (c) van   (d) truck

Fig. 2. Examples of video vehicle

In Figure 2, we use Fourier transform in vehicle contours and the statistics result of the coefficient are as follows.

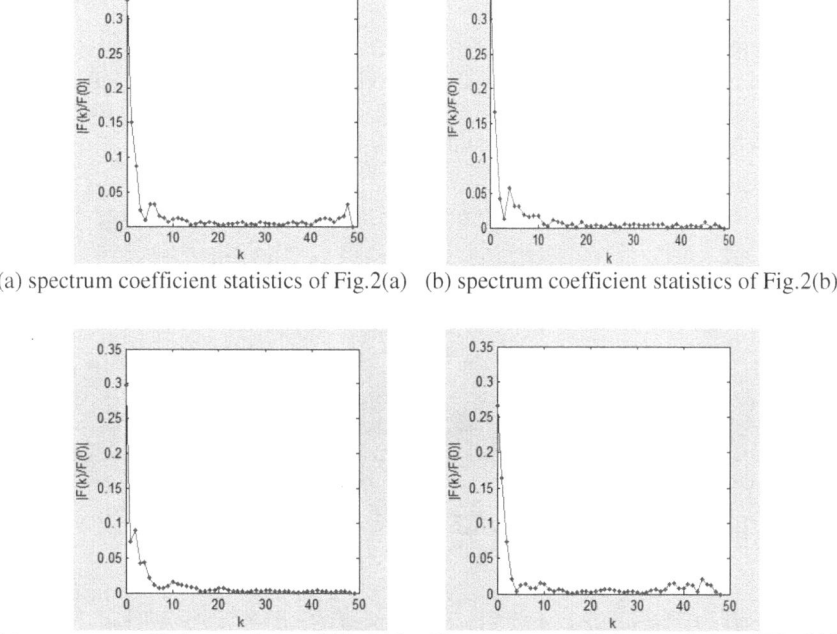

(a) spectrum coefficient statistics of Fig.2(a)   (b) spectrum coefficient statistics of Fig.2(b)

(c) spectrum coefficient statistics of Fig.2(c)   (d) spectrum coefficient statistics of Fig.2(d)

Fig. 3. Statistics of spectrum coefficient of vehicle contour

As it shows in Figure 3, as frequency increases, Fourier coefficient diminishes quickly, when the frequency more than 16, the Fourier coefficient can be neglected. Then we can extract first 16 Fourier coefficient as features to carry out the similarity calculation. The similar calculation results of four vehicles in figure 2 are shown in Table 1, the experiment results show that different type of vehicle exists similarity differences at different degree.

Table 1. Calculation of different vehicles in similarity differences

	Car1	Car2	Car3	Car4
Car1	0.0000000	0.0695213	0.0950621	0.1085350
Car2	0.0695213	0.0000000	0.0856331	0.1318020
Car3	0.0950621	0.0856331	0.0000000	0.1186350
Car4	0.1085350	0.1318020	0.118635	0.0000000

3.2 Vehicle Tracking Effect

In order to verify the effectiveness of tracking algorithm in this paper, the following consider straight vehicle tracking and turn vehicle tracking respectively, video collection rate is 25fps, video frame resolution is 320*240.

Straight Vehicle Tracking

Figure 4 is urban loop expressway traffic surveillance video vehicle tracking, Figure 4(a) and Figure 4(b) are single object tracking and multi-objective tracking schematics base on this paper's algorithm.

(a) single object tracking

(b) multi-objective tracking

Fig. 4. Straight vehicle tracking.

Turn Vehicle Tracking.

Figure 5 is the vehicle tracking of gateway video in urban, Figure 5(a) and Figure 5(b) are single object tracking and multi-objective tracking schematics base on this paper's algorithm.

(a) single object tracking

(b) multi-objective tracking

Fig. 5. Straight vehicle tracking

3.3 Tracking Performance Analysis

Evaluating tracking effect quality, generally consider tracking accuracy and tracking time-consuming. This paper selects three video in the loop expressway and gateway of urban to test. the tracking accuracy as shown in Table 2.

Table 2. Tracking accuracy

	Video 1	Video 2	Video 3
Actual vehicle number	27	78	102
Correct tracing number	26	76	100
Tracking accuracy	92.29%	97.44%	98.04%

From Table 2, we know that the whole tracking accuracy is good. With the increasing of vehicle number in video, our algorithm also can maintain good tracking accuracy. While ensuring the tracking accuracy, video real-time problem is also very important. Time-consuming calculation of three sections of video tracking is shown in Table 3.

Table 3. Time-consuming calculation of tracking

	Video 1 (seconds/frame)	Video 2 (seconds/frame)	Video 3 (seconds/frame)
Camshift Algorithm	0.0243s/p	0.0187s/p	0.0387s/p
Our Algorthm	0.0088s/p	0.0075s/p	0.0114s/p

This paper selects the Camshift algorithm which has been realized in OpenCV SDK. The time-consuming of three sections of traffic video using Camshift algorithm respectively are 0.0243 s/p, 0.0187 s/p and 0.0387 s/p, and the time-consuming of these sections of traffic video using our algorithm are 0.0088 s/p, 0.0075 s/p and 0.0114 s/p. We can see time-consuming decreased significantly and meet the requirements of real-time vehicle tracking very well.

4 Conclusions

According to the characteristics of Fourier transformation, this paper puts forward a method based on polar Fourier descriptor in video vehicle tracking. Through the analysis of the spectrum coefficient of video vehicle contour, linear prediction and similarity measurement of vehicle contour are well used in video vehicle object tracking. This algorithm has the invariance of rotation, translation and scale, which can well realize the vehicle traffic monitoring object tracking, and the tracking accuracy is higher, the tracking time-consuming is less. Traffic video vehicle trajectory contains rich feature information that reveals the structure, provides the clue of traffic events, and infers the correlation of moving vehicles. The next step of our work is to model the vehicle traffic behavior scenario for automatic detection of traffic events.

Acknowledgments. This research was partially supported by the Natural Science Foundation of China under grant No. 60970015, the 2009 Special Guiding Fund Project of Jiangsu Modern Service Industry (Software Industry) under grant No. [2009]332-64, the Applied Basic Research Project (Industry) of Suzhou City under grant No. SYJG0927 and SYG201032, and the Beforehand Research Foundation of Soochow University.

References

1. Wang, L., Hu, W., Tan, T.: Recent developments in human motion analysis. Pattern Recognition 36(3), 585–601 (2003)
2. Hou, Z., Han, C.: Review of vision tracking technology. Acta Automatic 4(32), 603–617 (2006)
3. Yang, G., Liu, H.: Review of vision tracking algorithm. Journal of Intelligent System 5(2), 95–105 (2010)

4. Wang, T., Liu, W., Sun, J., Zhang, H.: Fourier descriptor acceptor recognition the shape of an object. Journal of Computer Research and Development 39(12), 1714–1719 (2002)
5. Wang, X.-m., Wang, Y.-l., Niu, P.-h.: Based on adaptive background model gait detection and recognition. Computer Application and Research 23(11), 258–260 (2006)
6. Fan, C.-n., Chen, J.-k., Fu, D.-s.: A two-dimensional polar Fourier descriptive clauses in image retrieval application. Computer Engineering and Application 40(24), 77–79 (2004)
7. Xia, J., Wu, J., Chen, J., Cui, Z.: Based on adaptive on-line clustering background extraction. Computer Engineering 37(3), 169–171 (2011)

An Improved Biomimetic Image Processing Method

Chen Chen, Weijun Li[*], and Liang Chen

Lab of Artificial Neural Networks,
Institute of Semiconductors, Chinese Academy of Sciences,
Beijing, China
Tel.: +86 010 8230 4336
{eunicechen,wjli,achenliang}@semi.ac.cn

Abstract. Biomimetics is a rapidly developing discipline and has been suggested applicable in machine vision and image processing because human vision system has almost evolved to be perfect. Previously proposed BA+DRF method is a biomimetic image processing method which improves images quality effectively on the basis of the brightness adaption and disinhibitory properties of concentric receptive field (DRF). However, BA+DRF is not automatic and dynamic leading to the lack of practicability. This paper proposes an improved biomimetic image processing method, the parameterized LDRF method, to make BA+DRF method more adaptive and dynamic. Parameterized LDRF method constructed a parameterized logarithmic model to automatically enhance the image's global quality and constructed a model to dynamically adjust the gain factor which is used in improving the image's local quality. The experimental results have proved its ability of enhancing the image quality with keeping details. The improved biomimetic image processing method is applicable and automatic.

Keywords: Biomimetic, visual characteristics, logarithm, disinhibitory properties of concentric receptive field (DRF), parameterized dynamic, gain factor.

1 Introduction

Biomimetics is a rapidly developing discipline. More recently, biomimetics have been suggested applicable in machine vision systems, image processing, and data converters.

Human visual system is the most effective image processor and has almost evolved to be perfect. Therefore, visual characteristics and its application in image processing have aroused much interest among researchers. Since 1970 when *Robison* did his research on monkeys' visual neural system, scientists began to deeply study the physiology of visual mechanisms and explored new image processing methods on the basis of bionic vision [1]. For example, *Land E.H.* proposed image enhancement algorithm based on retinex theory [2-4] and *Zi Fang* applied vision bionics in the design of multi-waveband imaging guidance head [5]. Researches show that applying physiological visual mechanisms in image processing technology has efficiently improved speed and quality of image processing algorithms.

---

[*] Corresponding author.

H. Deng et al. (Eds.): AICI 2011, Part II, LNAI 7003, pp. 246–254, 2011.

In 2010, *Xiaoxian Jin* introduced BA+DRF method to imitate the brightness adaption feature of vision characteristics and the disinhibitory properties of retinal neuron receptive field [6, 11]. BA+DRF method can be used for image processing and produce better results. However, BA+DRF method has many numerical variables that require researchers to assign a value to each parameter for every image. Therefore, it is not able to improve images quality automatically and dynamically which results in lacking practicability.

In order to alleviate these problems, this paper proposes an improved biomimetic image processing method based on BA+DRF method. We constructed models for some parameters that are used in BA+DRF and named this method as Parameterized LDRF method that can apparently improve the practicability. In section 2, we review the visual characteristics and BA+DRF method. In section 3, we introduce the improved global image enhancement method that embeds a parameter model and present the experimental results. In section 4, a biomimetic local image enhancement method that includes a parameter model is demonstrated and the experimental results are shown. In section 5, we get to the conclusion of this parameterized LDRF method.

2   Visual Characteristic and BA+DRF Method

2.1   Visual Characteristic

Because digital images are displayed as a discrete set of intensities, the eye's ability to discriminate between different intensity levels is an important consideration in image processing technology. Experimental evidence indicates that subjective brightness is a logarithmic function of the light intensity incident on the eye. Fig. 1, a plot of light intensity versus subjective brightness, illustrates this characteristic. This non-linear brightness adaptation happened at the beginning of visual system. [7, 8]

In 1991, *Chaoyi Li*, [12, 13] discovered that there was a large range of disinhibitory region outside the classical receptive field, which is very insensitive, but acts as an important role in transmitting the large-area brightness and the brightness gradients (Fig. 2). Because the activity of this region can offset the antagonism between the peripheral region and the central region, it will also compensate the decline of the low frequency image components in the classical receptive field structure. Li gave a new model of Tri-Guassians (as in (1)) to imitate the disinhibitory properties of concentric receptive field (DRF).

$$G(x, y) = A_1 \exp(-\frac{x^2 + y^2}{2\sigma_1^2}) - A_2 \exp(-\frac{x^2 + y^2}{2\sigma_2^2}) + A_3 \exp(-\frac{x^2 + y^2}{2\sigma_3^2}) \tag{1}$$

Where A_1, A_2, A_3 denote the response intensity of the central, peripheral, and border region, $\sigma_1, \sigma_2, \sigma_3$ denote the corresponding range.

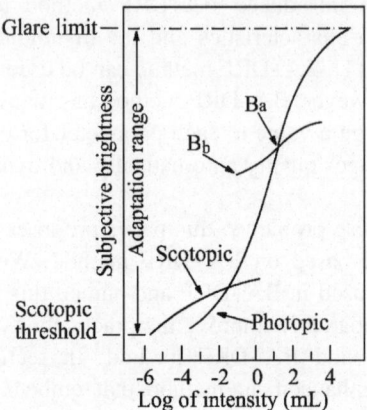

Fig. 1. Logarithm of intensity

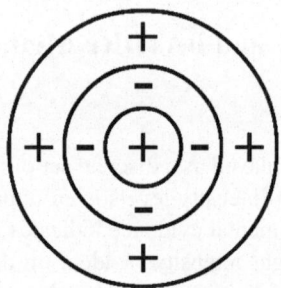

Fig. 2. Disinhibitory Properties of Concentric Receptive Field (DRF)

2.2 BA+DRF Method

BA+DRF method [6, 11] implements brightness adaptation function and DRF function in image enhancement. First, a global logarithmic transform (as in (2)) is carried out on the image. Second, the DRF Tri-Gaussians model combined with the bi-lateral gaussian filter (as in (3), (4), (5)) is used to enhance the local contrast of the image. When intensity of pixel is lighter than its neighbor's intensities which are perceived by human vision, the pixel's intensity value will be increased and when intensity of pixel is darker than its neighbor, the pixel's intensity value will be decreased. Finally, linear transformation is utilized to restore image.

$$I_g(x, y) = \log(I(x, y) + 1) / \log(256) \tag{2}$$

$$I_{lin}(x, y) = parak \bullet (I_g(x, y) - I_V(x, y)) + I_V(x, y) \tag{3}$$

$$I_V(x, y) = \sum_{i,j=-M}^{M} G_R G_V I_g(x_i, y_j) \bigg/ \sum_{i,j=-M}^{M} G_R G_V \qquad (4)$$

$$G_V(I_g(x, y), I_g(x_i, y_j)) = \exp(-\frac{(I_g(x, y) - I_g(x_i, y_j))^2}{2\sigma_V^2}) \qquad (5)$$

Where $parak$ is a gain factor and its value is positive constant.

$I(x, y)$ is the pixel value of the original image.

$I_g(x, y)$ is the pixel value of globally enhanced images.

$I_v(x, y)$ is the subjective intensity of pixel (x, y).

G_R represents the DRF Tri-Guassians model shown in (1)

G_v is the guassian function that computes similarity between center pixel value and its surrounding.

σ_v is the scale parameter to adjust decay rate of guassian function.

3   Parameterized Logarithmic Model in Global Enhancement and Experimental Results

Parameterized logarithmic model is the first step of parameterized LDRF method to globally enhance images contrast. Considering logarithm of intensity which has the fundamental of human vision system and each image condition, we compute images intensity by parameterized logarithmic model (as in (6)-(9))

$$I_g(x, y) = c(k) \bullet [\log(I(x, y) + k + 1) / \log(m(k)) - t(k)] \qquad (6)$$

$$m(k) = 256 + k \qquad (7)$$

$$t(k) = \log(k + 1) / \log(m(k)) \qquad (8)$$

$$c(k) = 1 / (1 - t(k)) \qquad (9)$$

Where $I(x, y)$ is the pixel value of the original image and $I_g(x, y)$ is the pixel value of the globally enhanced image. $m(k), t(k), c(k)$ are parameters that are used for adjusting pixels intensity range automatically according to the condition of images themselves. k is a parameter that depends on original image intensity condition. Here, we use threshold value (thresh) to determine k which is shown by the following law:

If {sum(histogram(1:k)) / sum(histogram(:)) <= thresh}
and {sum(histogram(1:k+1)) / sum(histogram(:)) > thresh},
the value of k is used in (6)-(9).

The parameterized logarithmic model can enhance the image automatically and adaptively to the image's own condition which is very useful in avoiding enhancing images too light. Based on the properties of the logarithmic function, the global non-linear transform of the image can efficiently boost the intensity of the dark area of the image, but will compress the dynamic range of the intensity that results in the lack of the image's details. The experimental results of global image enhancement are shown in Fig. 3 (b) to Fig. 6 (b). For example, comparing Fig. 3 (b) with Fig. 3 (a), the light contrast in the building's door part of images becomes larger, while the light contrast in the sky part of images becomes smaller. The same changing also happened in Fig. 4 (b) to Fig. 6 (b).

4   Parameterized DRF Model in Local Enhancement and Experimental Results

Parameterized DRF model is the second step of parameterized LDRF method which is to locally improve the quality of the image. After we studied statistical differencing [9] and Wallis statistical difference operator [10], we construct a model to compute gain factor *parak* which is just a constant in BA+DRF method. In the parameterized LDRF method, the model of *paraK* is presented in (10), (11), (12).

$$parak(x, y) = \frac{A_{max} * D_d}{A_{max} * D(x, y) + D_d} \tag{10}$$

$$D_{max} = \max\{D(x, y)\} \tag{11}$$

$$D_d = \frac{A_{min} * A_{max} * D_{max}}{A_{max} - A_{min}} \tag{12}$$

Where $parak(x, y)$ is a gain factor function and its value is positive.

$D(x, y)$ is a standard deviation that is calculated in the w*w field around the (x, y) pixel.

A_{min} , A_{max} is the smallest and largest values of gain factor, according to experience, the value are 1 and 3 and these values are applicable for most of images.

Equation (2) to (5) and (10) to (12) compose the parameterized DRF method. According to (10) (11) (12), we can improve the image quality more dependent on the local contrast information. If the local intensity contrast is larger, the gain factor will be smaller and if the local intensity contrast is smaller, the gain factor will be larger. In addition, (12) can limited gain factor in the range of $[A_{min}, A_{max}]$. Therefore, parameterized DRF model is able to improve image quality locally and dynamically.

Fig. 3. Building images, (a): Original image, (b): global enhanced image, (c): local enhanced image, (d): parak(x, y)

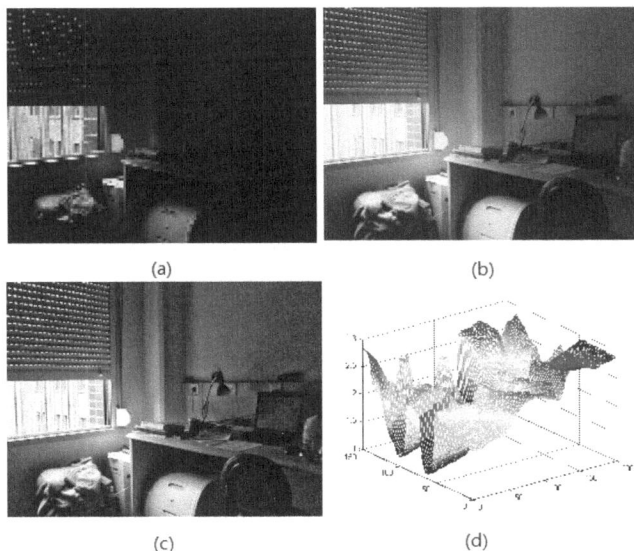

Fig. 4. Office images, (a): Original image, (b): global enhanced image, (c): local enhanced image, (d): parak(x, y)

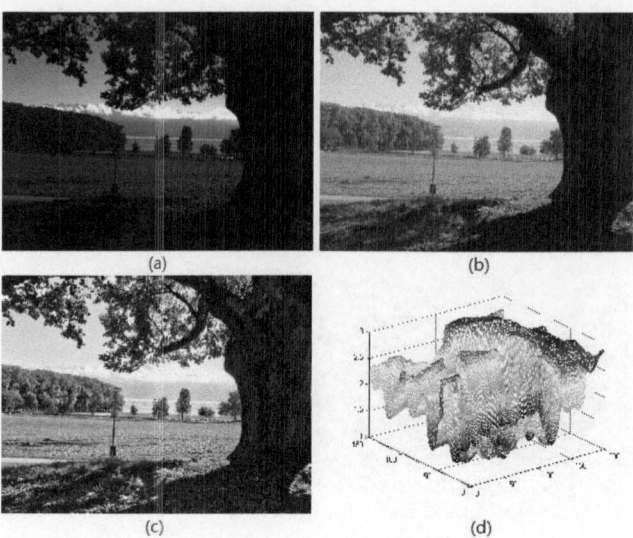

Fig. 5. Tree images, (a): Original image, (b): global enhanced image, (c): local enhanced image, (d): parak(x, y)

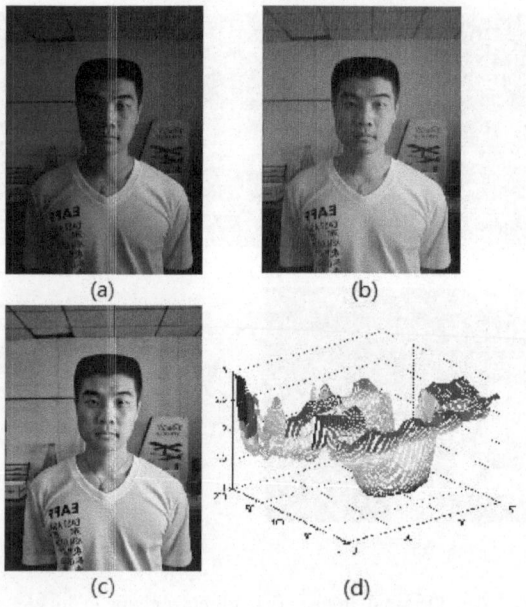

Fig. 6. Facial images, (a): Original image, (b): global enhanced image, (c): local enhanced image, (d): parak(x, y)

The combination of Parameterized Logarithmic model and Parameterized DRF model better imitates the varying response of human eye at large light deviation versus small light deviation. These two models compose the parameterized LDRF method. We used parameterized LDRF method to enhance four images. The experimental results are shown in Fig. 3 to Fig. 6. In Fig. 3 to Fig. 6, the image's quality is dynamically improved in the range of [1, 3]. When gain factor is equal to 1, it means that the local contrast of the image has no need to be boosted while the value is larger, the contrast of local field will be greater. When gain factor is larger than 3, the enhanced image will be too light to lose some intensity information. Fig. 3 (c), Fig. 4 (c), Fig. 5 (c), and Fig. 6 (c) give the value of gain factor $parak(x, y)$ of different images which show that various images is assigned with various gain factors and they correspond to the local region of images. Experimental results prove that parameterized LDRF method is able to enhance some area smoothly and other area sharply that is to mean this kind of biomimetic image enhancement method can improve image quality adaptively, automatically and dynamically.

5 Conclusion

This paper proposed an improved biomimetic image processing method based on the BA+DRF method to imitate brightness adaption and Disinhibitory Properties of Concentric Receptive. This improved biomimetic method, parameterized LDRF method, has constructed parameter models to make biomimetic method more adaptive, automatic and dynamic. The experimental results have proved its applicability and practicability.

Visual bionic is gradually developing from theoretical study to practical application. The research on biomimetic image processing method will be helpful both in bettering image processing technologies and in boosting the deeply understanding of human visual system. In the future, we will continue contribute our effort to study biomimetic image processing method and push it developing.

Acknowledgments. National Natural Science Foundation of China (No. 90920013) supported this work.

References

1. Wang, H.-m., Li, Y.-j., Zhang, K.: Application of bio-vision bionics on computer vision. Application Research of Computers 26(3), 1157–1159 (2009)
2. Kolb, H.: How the Retina Works. American Scientist 91(1) (2003)
3. Land, E.H.: The Retina Theory of Color Vision. Scientific American 237(6), 108–129 (1997)
4. Jobson, D.J., Rahman, Z., Woodell, G.A.: Properties and Performance of a Center / Surround Retinex. IEEE Transaction on Image Processing 6(3), 451–462 (1997)
5. Zi, F., Li, Y.-j., Zhao, D.-w., Zhang, K.: Vision Bionics and Its Application on Design of Multi-Wavehand Imaging Guidance Head. Control Technology 27(1), 55–56 (2008)
6. Jin, X., Li, W., Wang, S.: An algorithm for Biomimetic Image Enhancement Based on Human Visual Property. CAD&CG 22(3), 534–537 (2010)

7. Gonzalez, R.C., Woods, R.E.: Digital Image Processing, 2nd edn. Prentice Hall, Englewood Cliffs (2002); ISBN 978-7-121-04398-7

8. Pratt, W.K.: Digital Image Processing, 4th edn. Wiley, Chichester (2009); ISBN 978-7-111-28968-5

9. Rosenfeld, A.: Picture Processing by Computer. Academic Press, New York (1969)

10. Wallis, R.H.: An Approach for the Space Variant Restoration and Enhancement of Images. In: Proc. Symposium on Current Mathematical Problems in Image Science, Monterey, CA (November 1976)

11. Jin, X.: Study on Biomimetic Processing Method of Face Image. Institute of Semiconductors, Chinese Academey of Sciences, Beijing (2010)

12. Qiu, F., Li, C.: Mathematical Stimulation of Disinhibitory Properties of Concentric Receptive Field. Acta Biophysica Sinica 11(2), 214–220 (1995)

13. Li, C.Y., Pei, X., et al.: Role of the extensive area outside the x-cell receptive field in brightness information transmission. Vision Research 31(9), 1529–1540 (1991)

Research on the Principle of Homology-Continuity in Image Degradation

Liang Chen, Weijun Li[*], and Chen Chen

Lab of Artificial Neural Networks,
Institute of Semiconductors, Chinese Academy of Sciences,
Beijing, China
Tel.: 010 8230 4336
{achenliang,wjli,eunicechen}@semi.ac.cn

Abstract. Image restoration is the inverse process of image degradation. Based on the general imaging model to represent image degradation, various restoration algorithms have been designed. However, none of these algorithms have taken into account the inherent properties of Homology-Continuity in the image degradation process. Such neglect leads to the ill-posedness and detail loss that can not be completely overcome by the traditional image restoration. In this paper, according to the Principle of Homology-Continuity (PHC) proposed in High Dimensional Biomimetic Informatics, we will offer insight into image degradation process and discuss the advantages of the corresponding restoration algorithm.

Keywords: Image restoration, degradation process, general imaging model, the Principle of Homology-Continuity, High Dimensional Biomimetic Informatics.

1 Introduction

Image restoration technologies date from the 50's in the 20th century when space exploration projects were launched [1], and it has so far become a crucial part of digital image processing. Traditional image restoration methods are usually based on an objective imaging model to describe the image degradation process, and estimate the original image from the degraded one directly. The well-known Wiener Filtering [2], Tikhonov Regularization Method [4,5], ARMA Model Estimation [6,7] and Iterative Blind Deconvolution [8] are all derived from this idea. No matter whether they work in the spatial domain or the frequency domain, these approaches aimed directly at the original image, and extracted information merely from the single blurred image. However, they have ignored the inherent properties of the whole degradation process, and thus arouse two main problems in restoration: ill-posedness and non-unique solutions [9].

To conquer these hard-tackling problems, we turned the way of restoration. After in-depth study on the laws of image degradation, we have discovered the existence of

---

[*] Corresponding author.

H. Deng et al. (Eds.): AICI 2011, Part II, LNAI 7003, pp. 255–263, 2011.

Homology-Continuity properties in the degradation process, which are quite in conformity with subjective human perception. And thus we can form an entirely different way for restoration on the basis of the Principle of Homology-Continuity (PHC) [3,9].

In [12], Cao Yu proposed the concept of Signal-Noise Angle (SNA) to assess the definition of images. When she applied circular inverse deduction to locate the homologous points of given images, SNA is accordingly decreased as the iteration proceeded, which shows the experimental evidence of Homology-Continuity contained in "Blur — Clear" process. And Chen Yang has proposed another way of inverse deduction and a different biomimetic definition assessment metric in [13]. In both of their experiments, the advantages of PHC methods over traditional methods have been shown through contrast tests. PHC methods are mainly superior in the aspects of robustness to noise and less dependence of PSF estimation.

In this paper, we go on discussing the properties of Homology-Continuity existing in image degradation, and will give mathematical certification of its existence in detail. Based on the proofs, we offer insight into the real image degradation process and theoretical basis for the further algorithm designs.

2   Objective Imaging Model and the PHC Model

Fig. 1 shows a general continuous imaging model. To simplify the calculation, this process is usually modeled as a type of Linear Spatial-Invariant (LSI) System [1,10,14].

The degradation process can be formulated as following:

$$d(x, y) = \iint_{\infty} f(\xi, \eta) h(x - \xi, y - \eta) + n(x, y) = f(x, y) * h(x, y) + n(x, y) \qquad (1)$$

where the notation * denotes convolution, d denotes the degraded image, h denotes PSF, f denotes the original image, and n is the system noise.

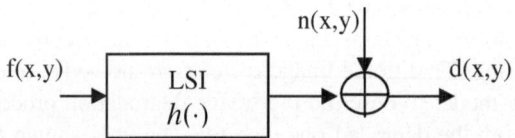

Fig. 1. Continuous Imaging Model

According to the later proofs, there exist Homology-Continuity properties between the original image and the degraded image. On the basis of PHC, it is a gradual change from the original image to the degraded one, so is the reversed process. Therefore, we can model the PHC restoration as following:

In the high dimensional space R^n (that is, a whole image can be denoted by a single point in the space), a point set containing all homologous patterns of one certain image is named A, the points corresponding to the blurred image and the clear image in set A are x and y respectively, and $\forall \varepsilon$, there definitely exists a set B that

$$B = \{x_1, x_2, x_3, \ldots, x_n \mid x_1 = x, x_2 = y, n \subset N,$$
$$\rho(x_m, x_{m+1}) < \varepsilon, \varepsilon > 0, n - 1 \geq m \geq 1, m \subset N\}, \quad (2)$$
$$B \supset A$$

where ρ is the distance between two points in the high dimensional space. We call this expression the PHC model of image restoration. Based on the PHC model, we can obtain the final clear image by sequentially locating a serial of homologous points in the high dimensional space, which has transformed restoration from directly solving the inverse problem of (2) to the inverse deduction of high-dimensional tracks.

3 The Homology-Continuity Properties of Continuous Signals Being Blurred

3.1 The Discussion of Homology-Continuity in One-Dimensional Case

To illustrate the Homology-Continuity properties in two-dimensional image signals' case, we first consider the situation of simple one-dimensional signals. Suppose the original signal be $f(x), x \in R$, which is continuous throughout its definitional domain (an original hypothesis).

Denote a general blurring function for unidimensional signals by $h(\tau, r)$, $-r < \tau < r$, which is finite-support and bivariate with respect to τ and r. Before we explore its effect on the original signal f, we constrain function $h(\tau, r)$ with a supposition that it is continuous with respect to τ and derivable with respect to r.

Then we get the blurred signal as below:

$$d(x, r) = \int_{-\infty}^{\infty} h(\tau, r) f(x - \tau) d\tau = \int_{-r}^{r} h(\tau, r) f(x - \tau) d\tau \quad (3)$$

Theorem 1, The general blurred signal

$$d(x, r) = \int_{-r}^{r} h(\tau, r) f(x - \tau) d\tau$$

is continuous and derivable with respect to r.

With **Theorem 1** proved, we can reasonably conclude that an arbitrary one-dimensional continuous signal is gradually changing when it is convoluted by a general blurring function whose support radius is also gradually increasing.

3.1.1 The Proof of Continuity
For $\forall \Delta r > 0, \Delta r \in R$,

$$\lim_{\Delta r \to 0} d(x, r + \Delta r) = \lim_{\Delta r \to 0} \int_{-r - \Delta r}^{r + \Delta r} h(\tau, r + \Delta r) f(x - \tau) d\tau$$
$$= \lim_{\Delta r \to 0} \int_{r}^{r + \Delta r} h(\tau, r + \Delta r) f(x - \tau) d\tau + \lim_{\Delta r \to 0} \int_{-r}^{r} h(\tau, r + \Delta r) f(x - \tau) d\tau + \lim_{\Delta r \to 0} \int_{-r - \Delta r}^{-r} h(\tau, r + \Delta r) f(x - \tau) d\tau$$
$$= \lim_{\Delta r \to 0} \int_{r}^{r + \Delta r} h(\tau, r + \Delta r) f(x - \tau) d\tau + \int_{-r}^{r} h(\tau, r) f(x - \tau) d\tau + \lim_{\Delta r \to 0} \int_{-r - \Delta r}^{-r} h(\tau, r + \Delta r) f(x - \tau) d\tau$$

Then we will prove

$$\lim_{\Delta r \to 0} \int_r^{r+\Delta r} h(\tau, r+\Delta r) f(x-\tau) d\tau = 0 \tag{4}$$

According to Cauchy–Schwarz inequality in L^2 space, we have

$$\left| \int_r^{r+\Delta r} h(\tau, r+\Delta r) f(x-\tau) d\tau \right| \le \sqrt{\int_r^{r+\Delta r} h^2(\tau, r+\Delta r) d\tau} \cdot \sqrt{\int_r^{r+\Delta r} f^2(x-\tau) d\tau} \tag{5}$$

Set $\lambda_1 = \sup_{\tau \in (r, r+\Delta r)} h^2(\tau, r+\Delta r), \lambda_2 = \sup_{\tau \in (r, r+\Delta r)} f^2(x-\tau)$, and (5) yields

$$\left| \int_r^{r+\Delta r} h(\tau, r+\Delta r) f(x-\tau) d\tau \right| \le \lambda_1 \lambda_2 \Delta r \tag{6}$$

For $\forall \xi \in R$, $\exists \Delta r$, that $\Delta r = \dfrac{\xi}{\lambda_1 \lambda_2}$, to let $\left| \int_r^{r+\Delta r} h(\tau, r+\Delta r) f(x-\tau) d\tau - 0 \right| \le \xi$, so we will obtain

$$\lim_{\Delta r \to 0} \int_r^{r+\Delta r} h(\tau, r+\Delta r) f(x-\tau) d\tau = 0 \tag{7}$$

And similarly we will have

$$\lim_{\Delta r \to 0} \int_{-r-\Delta r}^{-r} h(\tau, r+\Delta r) f(x-\tau) d\tau = 0 \tag{8}$$

Therefore, $\lim_{\Delta r \to 0} d(x, r+\Delta r) = \int_{-r}^r h(\tau, r) f(x-\tau) d\tau = d(x, y)$, and the continuity of $d(x, r)$ with respect to r is thus proven.

3.1.2 The Proof of Derivability

For $\lim_{\Delta r \to 0} \dfrac{d(x, r+\Delta r) - d(x, r)}{\Delta r}$

$$= \lim_{\Delta r \to 0} \frac{\int_{-r-\Delta r}^{r+\Delta r} h(\tau, r+\Delta r) f(x-\tau) d\tau}{\Delta r} - \lim_{\Delta r \to 0} \frac{\int_{-r}^r h(\tau, r) f(x-\tau) d\tau}{\Delta r}$$

$$= \lim_{\Delta r \to 0} \int_r^{r+\Delta r} \frac{h(\tau, r+\Delta r)}{\Delta r} f(x-\tau) d\tau + \int_{-r}^r \lim_{\Delta r \to 0} \frac{1}{\Delta r} [h(\tau, r+\Delta r) - h(\tau, r)] f(x-\tau) d\tau + \lim_{\Delta r \to 0} \int_{-r-\Delta r}^{-r} \frac{h(\tau, r+\Delta r)}{\Delta r} f(x-\tau) d\tau$$

$$= \lim_{\Delta r \to 0} \frac{1}{\Delta r} \int_r^{r+\Delta r} h(\tau, r+\Delta r) f(x-\tau) d\tau + \int_{-r}^r \frac{\partial h(\tau, r)}{\partial r} f(x-\tau) d\tau + \lim_{\Delta r \to 0} \frac{1}{\Delta r} \int_{-r-\Delta r}^{-r} h(\tau, r+\Delta r) f(x-\tau) d\tau$$

So we shall discuss the existence of the limits:

$$\lim_{\Delta r \to 0} \frac{1}{\Delta r} \int_r^{r+\Delta r} h(\tau, r+\Delta r) f(x-\tau) d\tau, \lim_{\Delta r \to 0} \frac{1}{\Delta r} \int_{-r-\Delta r}^{-r} h(\tau, r+\Delta r) f(x-\tau) d\tau \tag{9}$$

We have $h(\tau, r')$ and $f(x-\tau)$ continuous with respect to τ in h's support of τ, and thus it is easy to prove the continuity of their product in the support. According to the Integral Mid-Value Theorem,

$$\int_r^{r+\Delta r} h(\tau,r+\Delta r)f(x-\tau)=\Delta r \cdot h(\xi_1,r+\Delta r)f(x-\xi_1), \xi_1 \in (r,r+\Delta r)$$

$$\int_{-r-\Delta r}^{-r} h(\tau,r+\Delta r)f(x-\tau)=\Delta r \cdot h(\xi_2,r+\Delta r)f(x-\xi_2), \xi_2 \in (-r-\Delta r,-r)$$

(10)

Substitute (10) into (9):

$$\lim_{\Delta r \to 0}\frac{1}{\Delta r}\int_r^{r+\Delta r} h(\tau,r+\Delta r)f(x-\tau)=h(\xi_1,r+\Delta r)f(x-\xi_1), \xi_1 \in (r,r+\Delta r)$$

$$\lim_{\Delta r \to 0}\frac{1}{\Delta r}\int_{-r-\Delta r}^{-r} h(\tau,r+\Delta r)f(x-\tau)=h(\xi_2,r+\Delta r)f(x-\xi_2), \xi_2 \in (-r-\Delta r,-r)$$

(11)

Therefore, the existence of the limits in (9) get proved.

3.2 The Discussion of Homolog-Continuity in Two-Dimensional Case

In this subsection, we will extend the properties to the two-dimension signals. Similarly, we first generate a commonly used blurring function to convolute with the original two-dimensional continuous signal $f(x,y), x \in R, y \in R$, which is continuous throughout its definitional domain. But now the variables of blurring function h is increased to three: coordinates x, y and the support radius R. Suppose the area h acts on is approximately circular, and constrain h with an original hypothesis that it is continuous with respect to x, y and derivable with respect to R.

Since the blurring region is circular, we can formulate the blurred signal like:

$$d(x,y,R)=\int_{-\infty}^{\infty}\int_{-\infty}^{\infty}h(\tau,\xi)f(x-\tau,y-\xi)d\tau d\xi=\int_0^R\int_0^{2\pi}h(r\sin\theta,r\cos\theta,R)f(x-r\sin\theta,y-r\cos\theta)d\theta dr \quad (12)$$

(12) will be equivalently transformed if we use polar coordinates to denote f and h:

$$d(x,y,R)=\int_0^R\int_0^{2\pi}h(r,\theta,R)f(\rho-r,\omega-\theta)d\theta dr \quad (13)$$

Theorem 2, The general two-dimensional blurred signal

$$d(x,y,R)=\int_0^R\int_0^{2\pi}h(r,\theta,R)f(\rho-r,\omega-\theta)d\theta dr$$

is continuous and derivable with respect to r.

3.2.1 The Proof of Continuity

First, $\lim_{\Delta R \to 0}d(x,y,R+\Delta R)=\int_0^{2\pi}\lim_{\Delta R \to 0}\int_0^{R+\Delta R}h(r,\theta,R+\Delta R)f(\rho-r,\omega-\theta)drd\theta$

$=\int_0^{2\pi}\int_0^R\lim_{\Delta R \to 0}h(r,\theta,R+\Delta R)f(\rho-r,\omega-\theta)drd\theta+\int_0^{2\pi}\lim_{\Delta R \to 0}\int_R^{R+\Delta R}h(r,\theta,R+\Delta R)f(\rho-r,\omega-\theta)drd\theta$

$h(x,y,R)$ is presumed to be continuous with respect to R, so

$$\int_0^{2\pi}\int_0^R\lim_{\Delta R \to 0}h(r,\theta,R+\Delta R)f(\rho-r,\omega-\theta)drd\theta=\int_0^{2\pi}\int_0^R h(r\sin\theta,r\cos\theta,R)f(x-r\sin\theta,y-r\cos\theta)drd\theta$$

And we can verify

$$\lim_{\Delta R \to 0} \int_R^{R+\Delta R} h(r,\theta,R+\Delta R) f(\rho-r,\omega-\theta)dr = 0 \tag{14}$$

in the same way as the proof of **Theorem 1**. Finally,

$$\lim_{\Delta R \to 0} d(x,y,R+\Delta R) = \int_0^{2\pi} \int_0^R h(r,\theta,R) f(\rho-r,\omega-\theta)drd\theta = d(x,y,R)$$

3.2.2 The Proof of Derivablity

First, $\lim_{\Delta R \to 0} \dfrac{d(x,y,R+\Delta R) - d(x,y,R)}{\Delta R}$

$$= \int_0^{2\pi} \lim_{\Delta R \to 0} \int_R^{R+\Delta R} \frac{h(r,\theta,R+\Delta R)}{\Delta R} f(\rho-r,\omega-\theta)drd\theta + \int_0^{2\pi} \int_0^R \lim_{\Delta R \to 0} \frac{h(r,\theta,R+\Delta R) - h(r,\theta,R)}{\Delta R} f(\rho-r,\omega-\theta)drd\theta$$

The latter term of the equation above

$$\int_0^{2\pi} \int_0^R \lim_{\Delta R \to 0} \frac{h(r,\theta,R+\Delta R) - h(r,\theta,R)}{\Delta R} f(\rho-r,\omega-\theta)drd\theta$$

$$= \int_0^{2\pi} \int_0^R \frac{\partial h(r,\theta,R)}{\partial R} f(\rho-r,\omega-\theta)drd\theta = \int_0^{2\pi} f(\rho-\xi,\omega-\theta) \int_0^R \frac{\partial h(r,\theta,R)}{\partial R} drd\theta, \xi \in (0,R) \tag{15}$$

$h(x,y,R)$ and $f(x,y,R)$ are integrable with respect to ρ,ω and $h(x,y,R)$ is derivative with respect to R, so the value of (15) exists.

And the former term $\int_0^{2\pi} \lim_{\Delta R \to 0} \int_R^{R+\Delta R} \frac{h(r,\theta,R+\Delta R)}{\Delta R} f(\rho-r,\omega-\theta)drd\theta$ is mainly concerned with

the integral $\int_R^{R+\Delta R} \frac{h(r,\theta,R+\Delta R)}{\Delta R} f(\rho-r,\omega-\theta)dr$. Using the same method as the proof of

Theorem 1, we will verify the existence of its limit when $\Delta R \to 0$. Finally, the existence of the partial derivative of $d(x,y,R)$ with respect to R is proven.

4 The Homology-Continuity Properties of Discrete Image Signals Being Blurred

Discrete image signals are sampled from continuous image signals, amounting to a special case of the original continuous signals. Think of a finite-support continuous image signal $f(x,y), 0 < x < m, 0 < y < n$, where m and n are the width and height of this image respectively. When a blurring function $h(x,y,R)$ acts on $f(x,y)$ matching the conditions mentioned in 3.2, with d's radius increasing gradually, the blurred results $d(x,y,R)$ show their homology-continuity. For $\forall \varepsilon$, ε is above zero and small, we can find a distance ΔR ($\Delta R > 0$), to let $\forall R'(|R'-R| < \Delta R)$:
$\|d(x,y,R') - d(x,y,R)\| < \varepsilon$.

If we set a finite distance of $\Delta T = R_1 - R_2 (R_1 > R_2)$, and we want to move from $d(x,y,R_1)$ to $d(x,y,R_2)$, then we choose a tolerable distance ε_0 for every step forward, and for each value of $d(x,y,R_c)$ when $R_2 < R_c < R_1$, there exists a ΔR_c to let $\forall R_c' (\left| R_c' - R_c \right| < \Delta R_c)$: $\left\| d(x,y,R_c') - d(x,y,R_c) \right\| < \varepsilon_0$. We choose $\Delta R_0 = \inf_{R_2 < R_c < R_1} \Delta R_c$, and the set

$$Sc_{R_1 R_2} = \{ d(x,y,R_1), d(x,y,R_1 - \Delta R_c), d(x,y,R_1 - 2\Delta R_c), \ldots d(x,y,R_1 - n\Delta R_c), \ldots d(x,y,R_2) \}$$

will meet the PHC condition mentioned in (2).

Actually, when we sample $f(x,y)$ to obtain the discrete signal, the dimension of the original signal is decreased from infinity to finite N $(N = m \times n)$ dimension. Suppose the sampled discrete signal is $g_f(x,y)$, the horizontal sample interval is Δ_1 and the vertical sample interval Δ_2, and then we will get $g_f(x,y)$ as:

$$g_f(x,y) = c(n_1,n_2) f(x,y), c(n_1,n_2) = \sum_{n_1=-\infty}^{+\infty} \sum_{n_2=-\infty}^{+\infty} \delta(x - n_1 \Delta_1, y - n_2 \Delta_2) \tag{16}$$

Similarly, discrete blurred image can be represented as below:

$$g_d(x,y) = c(n_1,n_2) d(x,y), c(n_1,n_2) = \sum_{n_1=-\infty}^{+\infty} \sum_{n_2=-\infty}^{+\infty} \delta(x - n_1 \Delta_1, y - n_2 \Delta_2) \tag{17}$$

With the dimension of signal decreased, coordinates to measure the signal reduced accordingly, which means, the distance of two continuous signals in infinite dimensional space is always more than that of their discrete signals sampled in the finite dimensional space.

When we choose the same step of radius as the continuous signals, and for the same tolerable distance, we will surely find that

$$\left\| g_d(x,y,R_c + \Delta R_0) - g_d(x,y,R_c) \right\| \leq \left\| d(x,y,R_c + \Delta R_0) - d(x,y,R_c) \right\| < \varepsilon_0 \tag{18}$$

where $R_2 < R_c < R_1$. The set

$$Sd_{R_1 R_2} = \{ g_d(x,y,R_1), g_d(x,y,R_1 - \Delta R_c), g_d(x,y,R_1 - 2\Delta R_c), \ldots, g_d(x,y,R_1 - n\Delta R_c), \ldots, g_d(x,y,R_2) \}$$

will meet the PHC condition mentioned in (2).

Till now, we have found a definite discrete sequence to satisfy the PHC requirement mentioned in (2), which shows a line of homologous points between the point $g_d(x,y,R_1)$ representing the relatively blur form of the original image and the point $g_d(x,y,R_2)$ representing the relatively clear one. The conclusion can be used to guide the algorithm design.

5   Conclusion

With the Homology-Continuity properties demonstrated in the image degradation process, we will more reasonably suggest a new way for image restoration based on

PHC. Fig. 2 and 3 show the differences between the traditional methods and the method based on PHC. The major disadvantages of traditional methods are twofold compared with the PHC method: (1) the restoration is merely based on the information of the degraded image itself, but have not taken into account properties of the whole degradation process; (2) the restoration only contains a forward path, without making use of the backward paths that represent degradation. For the two shortcomings, there exist problems of ill-posedness and prior knowledge insufficiency in traditional image restoration. On the contrary, in PHC methods we realized the existence of Homology-Continuity contained in the degradation process and fully studied it to guide algorithm designs. In every iteration, we first find the backward path ("Clear—Blur") from the present image, and then locate the point representing relative clear image by inverse deduction ("Blur—Clear"). In this way, we guarantee the homology-continuity of points in every step forward, and thus overcome the ill-posedness that may lead to the restoration failure. On the other hand, the information we use is extracted from different backward paths at different time other than merely from the degraded image itself, so we can surely gain more priori information than traditional methods do, and conquer the problem of lacking prior knowledge in a great extent.

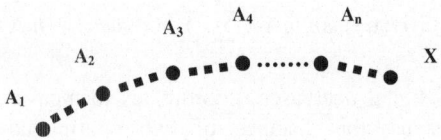

Fig. 2. Schematic diagram of traditional Inverse track (A_i: present image for every iteration, X: final result)

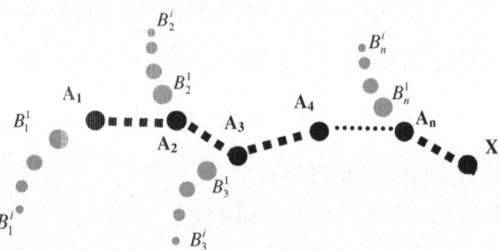

Fig. 3. Schematic diagram of PHC inverse track (A_i: present image, B_i^j: blurred from A_i, X: final result)

Beginning with the tentative experiments implemented in [12,13], we will explore more precise description of degradation process and more accurate high-dimensional point location for inverse deduction according to the proved theorems in the paper.

Acknowledgments. National Natural Science Foundation of China (No. 90920013) supported this work.

References

1. Banham, M.R., Katsaggelos, A.K.: Digital image restoration. IEEE Signal Processing Magazine, 24–41 (1997)
2. Gonzalez, R.C., Woods, R.E., Eddins, S.L.: Digital Image Processing, 2nd edn. Prentice-Hall, Englewood Cliffs (2002)
3. Wang, S.: Biomimetic(Topological) Pattern Recognition — A New Model of Pattern Recognition Theory and Its Applications. Chinese Journal of Electronics 30(10), 1417–1420 (2002)
4. Tikhonov, A.N., Arsenin, V.Y.: Solutions of Ill-Posed Problems. Wiley, New York (1977)
5. Katsaggelos, A.K., Biemond, J., Schafer, R.W., Mersereau, R.M.: A Regularized Iterative Image Restoration Algorithm. IEEE Trans. Acoust., Speech, Signal Proc. 39, 914–929 (1991)
6. Reeves, S.J., Mersereau, R.M.: Blur identification by the method of generalized cross-validation. IEEE Trans. Imuge Processing 1(3), 301–311 (1992)
7. Lagendijk, R.L., Biemond, J., Boekee, D.E.: Identification and restoration of noisy blurred images using the expectation-maximization algorithm. IEEE Trans. Acoust, Speech, Signal Processing 38(7) (July 1990)
8. Ayers, G.R., Dainty, J.C.: Iterative blind deconvolution method and its applications. Optics Letters 13(7), 547–549 (1988)
9. Wang, S.: First Step to Multi-Demensional Space Biomimetic Informatics. National Defence Industry Press, Beijing (2008)
10. Andrews, H.C., Hunt, B.R.: Digital Image Restoration. Prentice-Hall, Inc., New Jersey (1977)
11. Hansen, P.C., Nagy, J.G., O'Leary, D.P.: Deblurring Images: Matrices, Spectra, and Filtering, Fundam, vol. 3. SIAM, Philadelphia (2006)
12. Yu, C.: Study on Image Debluring Based on High-Dimensional Biomimetic Informatics. In: CAS. Institute of Semiconductor, Beijing (2007)
13. Yang, C.: Research on High-Dimensional Biomimetic Information Processing and Its Applications. In: CAS. Institute of Semiconductor, Beijing (2010)
14. Kundur, D., Hatzinakos, D.: Blind Image Deconvolution. IEEE Signal Processing Magazine 13(3), 43–64 (1996)

Multi-granularity Video Unusual Event Detection Based on Infinite Hidden Markov Models

Chunsheng Guo and Youhui Zou

College of Communication Engineering
Hangzhou Dianzi University
Hangzhou 310018, China
`guo.chsh@gmail.com, zouyouhui@tom.com`

Abstract. The multi-rate phenomenon of video unusual event is one of the factors to reduce the detection accuracy of video unusual event. Based on the infinite state Hidden Markov Model (iHMM), a multi-granularity detection algorithm for video unusual event is proposed. This algorithm first effectively extracts the feature sequence from the original data through subspace projection technique. Then the feature sequence is sampling at different time intervals to obtain the multi-rate feature sequences. And these multi-rate feature sequences can be used to construct the different time granularities model in the model training stage, and to find the video unusual event at different time granularities in the detection stage. In parameter learning of iHMM, the Beam sampling and EM is combined to improve the efficiency of the iteratively estimation. The experimental results using the surveillance data of vehicles forbidding section, show that the proposed method can be effectively detect unusual events in a complex outdoor scene.

Keywords: Unusual events detection, Independent Component Analysis (ICA), Multi-granularity, infinite Hidden Markov Model (iHMM).

1 Introduction

In recent years, video surveillance system is widely used in banks, supermarkets, car parks, residential areas, public transport and so on. The face of massive video surveillance data, how to effectively detect video unusual events is a key technology for intelligent video surveillance. Now, video unusual event detection has developed into a research hotspot in video surveillance.

Unusual event detection mainly includes methods based on moving targets detection and tracking and methods based on subspace. The method based on moving targets detection and tracking first extracts the speed, trajectory, acceleration and other objects features, then sets up model of features to realize unusual event detection. In the true scene, however, the difficulty of detecting and tracking the special object due to interference factor such as complex background, shelter and the moving multi-targets tends to restrict its practical application. The method based on subspace extracts features from whole scene which overcoming the disadvantage of the method based on moving targets detection and tracking.

H. Deng et al. (Eds.): AICI 2011, Part II, LNAI 7003, pp. 264–272, 2011.

It is difficult to get abnormal event sample which is incomplete event in video, a method based on statistic model is often used to solve this problem that it only builds statistic model of normal events, then we decide whether the event under test is an abnormal event by calculating approximate probability between the event under test and normal events model. There are commonly used the Gaussian mixture model (GMM), the hidden Markov model (HMM) and the infinite hidden Markov model (iHMM). In [1], GMM is used for detecting unusual events such as scream and knocks at the door of voices in the frequency; during the welding process unusual events are detected by HMM[2]; iHMM [3] also can detect unusual events in city traffic. GMM is HMM that the number of states is one; its complexity of modeling is low while the temporal dynamics of events is unaccounted for. In video unusual event detection based on HMM [2, 4-6] considers the temporal dynamics, but HMM is a parameterized model that its number of states should be specified. By the data iHMM [7] can determine optimal number, which conquers over-fit and under-fit from HMM model.

In order to reduce the processing data, the existing methods based on subspace sample time-interval of projection sequence and don't consider that different events have difference at different time granularities, so it is hard to distinguish events fit at their time granularities in video. For this reason, this article proposes multi-granularity video unusual event detection algorithm based on iHMM, it is most efficient in detecting unusual events at different time granularities.

2   Principle and Realization

The block diagram as shown in Fig.1, the upper half is the training section, and the lower half is the unusual events detecting section. In the training phase, by downsampling the image feature sequences after pretreatment in different time granularities we build iHMM expresses normal events of each group coefficient. In the detecting phase, unknown events mage feature sequences after pretreatment are input into the corresponding iHMM detecting unusual events. Finally we can estimate the image feature sequences are unusual events when one observation probability of iHMM is lower than the threshold value.

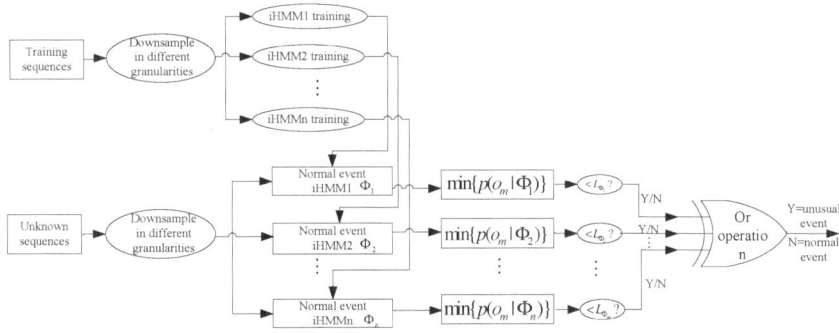

Fig. 1. The processing diagram of the algorithm

2.1 The Pretreatment of the Image Sequences

As shown in Fig. 2 the pretreatment of image feature sequences includes Independent Component Analysis (ICA), feature projection and Hodrick-Prescott (HP) filter. First, feature subspace of image sequences is obtained by training image sequences based on FastICA [8] algorithm. Then the training image sequences and unknown image sequences are projected into this feature subspace, and the projection coefficients are as image feature. Finally HP filter is used to enhance the adaptation of feature sequence to illumination change.

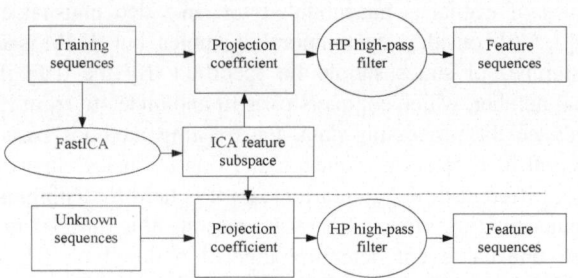

Fig. 2. The pretreatment of image sequences

There are m observed images $Z_i, i = 1, \cdots, m$, which can be regarded as the linear combination of n frames of independent basic images $X_i, i = 1, \cdots, n$ [9].

$$X = AZ \tag{1}$$

where $X = [x_1, x_2, \cdots, x_m]^T$, each row represents one frame of observed image. $Z = [z_1, z_2, \cdots, z_n]^T$, each row represents one frame of basic image, A is a mixing matrix.

ICA achieves the separation of independence image base through the separation matrix W, which can be expressed as

$$Y = WX = WAZ \tag{2}$$

where $Y = [y_1, y_2, \cdots, y_n]^T$, each row vector stands for the estimation of the images bases. And all row vector of matrix Y expand into a feature subspace. Let the image F_j is described as an column vector f_j line by line, that

$$f_j = b_{j,1} y_1 + b_{j,2} y_2 + \cdots + b_{j,n} y_n \tag{3}$$

where $b_j = [b_{j,1}, b_{j,2}, \cdots, b_{j,n}]^T$ is the projection coefficient in the feature subspace. For image F_j expressed by the projection coefficient b_j, it greatly reduces the burden of data in the subsequent treatment.

In outdoor scene, illumination change and shadow will cause volatility of projection coefficient b_j. Further it leads to the deterioration of the detection probability of unusual events. This paper adopts HP filter [10] to filter out fluctuations in the sequence of projection coefficients. HP filter assumes projection coefficient sequences $b_j(t)$ are the sum of fluctuate components and trend components of projection coefficient, ie $b_j(t) = b_j^c(t) + b_j^\tau(t)$, $t = 1, 2, \cdots, T$. Algorithm determines the trend components $b_j^\tau(t)$ by minimizing the objective function below,

$$\underset{b_j^\tau(t)\ t=1,2,\cdots,T}{\arg\min} \left\{ \sum_{t=1}^{T} [b_j(t) - b_j^\tau(t)]^2 + \lambda \sum_{t=2}^{T-1} \{ [b_j^\tau(t+1) - 2b_j^\tau(t) + b_j^\tau(t-1)] \}^2 \right\} \qquad (4)$$

where λ is a constant. Fluctuate components $b_j^c(t) = b_j(t) - b_j^\tau(t)$ can be used as stable feature vector in the following process.

2.2 iHMM Modeling and Unusual Events Detection

iHMM can automatically determine the optimal number of states, and overcome the shortcoming of HMM on the determination of the state number by empirical.

iHMM. iHMM can be expressed as Hierarchical Dirichlet process (HDP) [11]:

$$\beta \sim GEM(\gamma),\ \pi_k \mid \beta \sim DP(\alpha, \beta),\ \phi_k \sim H,\ s_t \mid s_{t-1} \sim Multinomial(\pi_{s_{t-1}}),$$
$$o_t \mid s_t \sim \Theta(\phi_{s_t}),\quad k = 1, 2, \cdots, \infty. \qquad (5)$$

DP is a nonparametric model and can automatically determine model order. HDP is a collection of several DP which sharing random measurement. The state transition probability $\pi_k \sim DP(\alpha, \beta)$ is controlled by a DP, where β is sharing basic measurement, α is precision parameter. Precision parameter determines the variability of basic measurement. β is also given by higher level of DP: $\beta \sim DP(\gamma, H)$, where H is global basic measurement and γ is its precision parameter. State $\phi_{k'}$ obeys the basic measurement H . $s_t \mid s_{t-1}$ represents the state transition from s_{t-1} -th state to s_t -th state, which is consistent with the polynomial distribution π_k . $\Theta(\phi_k)$ is corresponding to the output distribution of state ϕ_k .

Parameter Learning of iHMM. Parameter learning of iHMM includes two steps. The first step is to learn transition probability. Let the prior distribution and observed probability function to be Gaussian distribution that they are conjugate distribution. Then the state transition matrix is obtained by Beam sampling. The second step is to learn initial conditional probability distribution and state observed probability density function. In order to accurately describe observation data, state observed probability is assumed as GMM. So EM algorithm can be used to learn parameters.

By introducing an auxiliary variable u_t, Beam sampling [12] achieves the efficient estimation of the iHMM transition probability using the dynamic programming method to calculate the state trajectory posteriori probability and sampling the entire trajectory. Specific process is as follows:

Sampling u_t: knowing π, s_{t-1} and s_t, auxiliary variable u_t obeys the conditional distribution $u_t \sim Uniform(0, \pi_{s_{t-1}, s_t})$.

Sampling s_t: Giving auxiliary variable u_t, the whole state sequences sampling S is obtained by forward-backward filter. Then the state transition probability matrix can be determined. The posterior probability of u_t is

$$p(u_t \mid s_{t-1}, s_t, \pi) = \frac{\mathrm{II}(0 < u_t < \pi_{s_{t-1}, s_t})}{\pi_{s_{t-1}, s_t}}. \tag{6}$$

If $0 < u_t < \pi_{s_{t-1}, s_t}$, $\mathrm{II}(\bullet) = 1$, otherwise $\mathrm{II}(\bullet) = 0$. The Posterior probability is s_t

$$
\begin{aligned}
p(s_t \mid o_{1:t}, u_{1:t}) &\propto p(s_t, u_t, o_t \mid o_{1:t-1}, u_{1:t-1}) \\
&= p(o_t \mid s_t) \sum_{s_{t-1}: u_t < \pi_{s_{t-1}, s_t}} p(s_{t-1} \mid o_{1:t-1}, u_{1:t-1}).
\end{aligned} \tag{7}
$$

Known the state transition probability matrix of iHMM by Beam sampling, and supposed state observed probability function is GMM, then GMM parameters is estimated by EM algorithm. Under the condition of state q_i, the observation probability o is

$$b_{q_i}(o) = \sum_{m=1}^{M} \omega_{q_i, m} p(o \mid \mu_{q_i, m}, \Sigma_{q_i, m}), \quad i = 1, 2, \cdots k \tag{8}$$

where M is the number of mixed component in GMM. $\omega_{q_i, m}$ is the weight of m th Gaussian component. $p(o \mid \mu_{q_i, m}, \Sigma_{q_i, m})$ is Gaussian probability function with mean $\mu_{q_i, m}$ and covariance matrix $\Sigma_{q_i, m}$.

Similar to the traditional HMM parameter estimation [13], parameters can be calculated as follows:

$$
\begin{aligned}
&\bar{\pi}_i = \zeta_1(q_i), \quad \bar{\omega}_{q_i, n} = \frac{\sum_{t=1}^{T} \zeta_t(q_i, n)}{\sum_{t=1}^{T} \sum_{n=1}^{M} \zeta_t(q_i, n)}, \quad \bar{\mu}_{q_i, n} = \frac{\sum_{t=1}^{T} \zeta_t(q_i, n) \cdot o_t}{\sum_{t=1}^{T} \zeta_t(q_i, n)}, \\
&\bar{\Sigma}_{q_i, n} = \frac{\sum_{t=1}^{T} \zeta_t(q_i, n) \cdot (o_t - u_{q_i, n}) \cdot (o_t - u_{q_i, n})'}{\sum_{t=1}^{T} \zeta_t(q_i, n)}, \quad n = 1, 2, \cdots, M
\end{aligned} \tag{9}
$$

where $\zeta_t(q_i) = \sum_{j=1}^{K} \varepsilon_t(q_i, q_j)$ is the probability of state q_i at time t, $\varepsilon_t(q_i, q_j)$ is the probability of state transition from state q_i at time t to state q_j at time $t+1$.

Unusual Events Detection based on iHMM. After Beam sampling and EM estimation, the iHMM model for usual events is constructed. So the unusual events detection can be solved in classic HMM framework. If the likelihood of observed sequences correspond with the model is less than the given threshold, this observed sequences can be determined to be caused by the abnormal event.

2.3 Much Time Granularities Unusual Event Detection

To solve the multi-rate of video unusual events, model with different time granularities is used. It means that rapid unusual events require an unusual events detection model with small time granularities, and unusual events require an unusual events detection model with large time granularity. For the multi-rate problem, unusual events with different rates need to different time granularities model. In practice, the compromise between the calculation efficiency and calculation precision is often necessary.

The scheme of time granularity adopted in this paper is shown in Fig. 3. Each row represents the feature sequence along the time axis at different time intervals. The first row stands for the original sequence of image feature. From the top down, the time granularity becomes larger and larger in accordance with twice ratio.

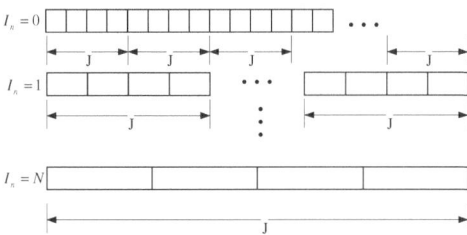

Fig. 3. The scheme of time granularity

In the training phase, the projection coefficients in different intervals are used to train the different time granularities detection model.

In the detection phase, the test sequences are sampled to form different time granularities sequences. And different time granularities sequences are respectively tested by the different time granularities detection model. At last, all test results are synthesized to get the final result through the logical OR operation.

3 Experimental Result and Analysis

In order to verify the efficiency of the proposed algorithm, a video surveillance data in a vehicle forbidding section is used. Fig. 4 below shows some sampling frame of data. In the experiments, hardware platform is the personal computer of Intel Core2 E7500 (2.93G), simulation platform is MATLAB R2008a.

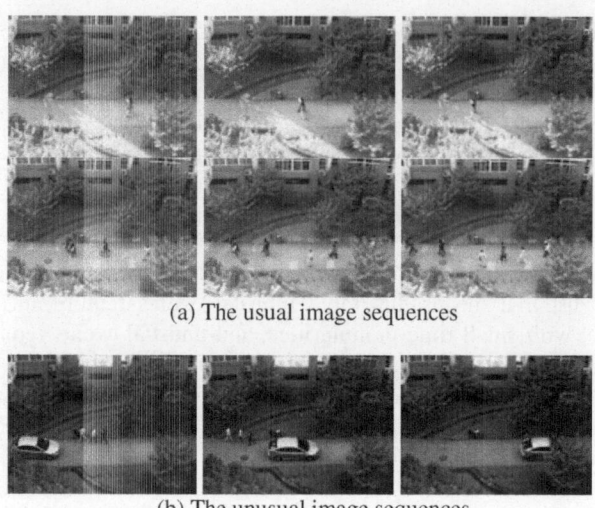

(a) The usual image sequences

(b) The unusual image sequences

Fig. 4. The different image sequences

3.1 Image Preprocessing

In image preprocessing, the training image sequences are decomposed into several independent image bases through FastICA algorithm. From Fig. 5 it can be seen that each image base includes responding information and each original image can be expressed as the linear combination of these image bases. In the experiment, 40 image bases are used, which can better reconstruct the original image.

Fig. 5. Some images bases

3.2 Unusual Events Detection Based on iHMM

Detection rate and error rate are used to evaluate the performance of the proposed algorithm, which defined as follows:

$$\text{Detection rate} = \frac{\text{the number of detecting unusual video section}}{\text{the total number of video section}}$$

$$\text{Error rate} = \frac{\text{the number of error detection} + \text{the number of miss detection}}{\text{the total number of video section}}$$

In Fig. 6, the test sequences with different state number are selected. It is obvious that the detection rate of the proposed algorithm is better than the conventional method of

HMM. And when the actual number of states is greater than or less than the settings in the method of HMM, the detection rate of HMM will decrease, showing the phenomenon of over-fitting or under-fitting.

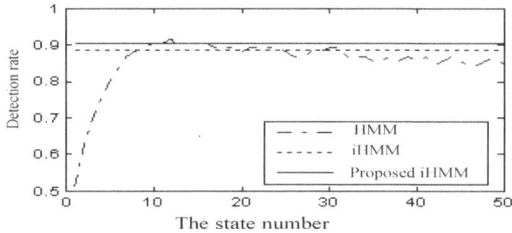

Fig. 6. A detection rate comparison for different algorithm

3.3 Multi-granularity Video Unusual Event Detection

Different rate events require different time granularities model. In preliminary experiments, 3 different time granularities mode are used to test the detect performance. Result of unusual events detection is shown in table 1. We can see from table, there are obvious differences in different time granularities. For the test data adopted in the experiment, the test model which the time granularity number is 3 obtains the best detection performance comparing with the remaining two cases. This model can improve the detection rate but the error rate is slight increase.

Table 1. Detection scheme comparison in different granularities

Different granularities	Detection rate	Error rate	Order of iHMM
$I_n=1$	0.8810	0.0233	6
$I_n=3$	0.9405	0.0272	6
$I_n=7$	0.9286	0.0259	10

4 Conclusion

According to the different rate events need different time granularities model in video unusual event detection. a multi-granularity detection algorithm for video unusual event based on iHMM is proposed. Result shows that this algorithm can effectively detect video unusual events in complex outdoor scene.

References

1. Atrey, P.K., Maddage, N.C., Kankanhali, M.S.: Audio based event detection for multimedia surveillance. In: International Conference on Acoustics, Speech and Signal Processing, Toulouse, France (2006)
2. Jager, M., Knoll, C., Hamprecht, F.A.: Weakly supervised learning of a classifier for unusual event detection. IEEE Transactions on Image Processing 17, 1700–1708 (2008)

3. Pruteanu-Malinici, I., Carin, L.: Infinite hidden Markov models for unusual-event detection in video. IEEE Transactions on Image Processing 17, 811–822 (2008)
4. Snoek, J., Honey, J., Stewart, L., Zemel, R.S.: Automated detection of unusual events on stairs. Image and Vision Computing 27, 153–166 (2009)
5. Jiang, F., Wu, Y., Katsa ggelos, A.K.: A Dynamic Hierarchical Clustering Method for Trajectory-Based Unusual Video Event Detection. IEEE Transactions on Image Processing 18, 907–913 (2009)
6. Zhong, H., Shi, J.B., Visontai, M.: Detecting unusual activity in video. In: Proceedings of the 2004 IEEE Computer Society Conference on Computer Vision and Pattern Recognition, vol. 2, pp. 819–826 (2004)
7. Beal, M.J., Ghahramani, Z., Rasmussen, C.E.: The infinite hidden Markov model. Advances in Neural Information Processing Systems 1, 577–584 (2002)
8. Oja, E., Hyvarinen, A.: A fast fixed-point algorithm for independent component analysis. Neural Computation 9, 1483–1492 (1997)
9. Hyvarinen, A., Oja, E.: Independent component analysis: algorithms and applications. Neural Networks 13, 411–430 (2000)
10. Schlicht, E.: Estimating the Smoothing Parameter in the So-Called Hodrick-Prescott Filter. Dept. Economics, U. Munich (2004)
11. Teh, Y.W., Jordan, M.I., Beal, M.J., Blei, D.M.: Hierarchical dirichlet processes. Journal of the American Statistical Association 101, 1566–1581 (2006)
12. Van Gael, J., Saatci, Y., Teh, Y.W., Ghahramani, Z.: Beam sampling for the infinite hidden Markov model. In: 25th International Conference on Machine Learning, Helsinki, Finland, pp. 1088–1095 (2008)
13. Rabiner, L.R.: Tutorial on hidden Markov models and selected applications in speech recognition. Proceedings of the IEEE 77, 257–286

An Algorithm of Color Image Mosaic Based on Fourier-Mellin Transform

Zhaoxia Fu[1,2] and Yan Han[1]

[1] Science and Technology on Electronic Test &
Measurement Laboratory and Key Laboratory of Instrumentation Science &
Dynamic Measurement(Ministry of Education),
Information and Communication Engineering Institute,
North University of China, Taiyuan, 030051, China
[2] Party School of Shanxi Provincial Committee of the C.P.C, Taiyuan, 030006, China
fzx2005@163.com, hanyan@nuc.edu.cn

Abstract. The article proposes an algorithm of color image mosaic based on Fourier-Mellin transform. The algorithm need not accurately control the motion of camera, and need not know the internal camera parameters and detect image feature. The algorithm firstly extracts a color parameter from two color images on the existence of rotation, scaling and translation transform, and then emendates them by Fourier-Mellin algorithm and phase correlation algorithm, finally completes image mosaic after compensating on rotation and proportion zoom. The experimental result indicates that registration precision of the algorithm can reach one pixel level.

Keywords: Fourier-Mellin transform, image mosaic, rotation, color parameter.

1 Introduction

Image registration is discovering the relations of relative position between the images by using their mutual scenery in the images to compare with and match. These images are obtained from different view angle and an identical scenery in the different time by using different detector. Its goal is eliminating inconsistence in the geometry between the preparative matching image and the reference image, including translation, rotation and scaling, and preparing for the next image processing. Image mosaic is that merges two or many images having overlap region with a big image. The precision of image registration is the most immediate influence on the success of image mosaic.

The methods of image registration may be approximately divided into two kinds ones, which are based on image feature and based on gray-level image. The registration method based on image feature need seek for a series of feature points, then establish feature points' corresponding relationships, and calculate their coordinate transform relations between these images preparing for mosaic. Its shortcoming lies in lacking the adaptability, and is only suitable to such images having the corresponding image feature, but some images do not possibly have such feature. Moreover the computation quantity is rather big, the algorithmic reliability and astringency may have certain problem. The method of image registration based on the gray-level image studied quite early. It takes the foundation of image registration by containing target area of the corresponding images and searching gray-level of pixels the area. It uses some

H. Deng et al. (Eds.): AICI 2011, Part II, LNAI 7003, pp. 273–279, 2011.

correlated measure to determine the corresponding pixels in two images, such as covariance or correlative coefficient's maximum value. In 1994, Q.S. Chen et al. proposed the method of image registration based on Fourier-Mellin transform [1-2] that is a kind of classical algorithm. It is by calculating the corresponding position of peak value from which uses inverse Fourier transform of power spectrum of two images to obtain, so as to seek their relative displacement; and by carrying on the logarithm-polar coordinate transform to scope spectrum of the images, i.e., obtains the relative rotation angle and the scale factor similar to the algorithm of calculating the relative displacement in the logarithm-polar coordinate space; thus realizes the image matching. The Fourier-Mellin transform algorithm need not detect image feature, and its request is not very high to photographer and photography condition. Moreover its computation speed is faster and it is strong practicability.

This article proposes one kind of color image mosaic algorithm based on Fourier-Mellin transform. The color image has rich color information. If we transform two color images preparing for mosaic to gray-level images, which use gray value to substitute for tricolor, will lose a large number of useful information. In the very big similar region, it will result in mismatch that the corresponding pixels' tricolor value can be possibly completely identical. Therefore we retain the character of tricolor, and separately pick up a corresponding color component to carry on mosaic in two images, the precision may achieve highly. The algorithm in this article firstly extracts a component in color components of R, G, B from color images, and gains the characteristics of rotation and proportion; secondly, uses the correlation function according to these characteristics to compute two images' parameters of rotation and scale transform in identical scene; then carries on the compensation in two images' rotation angle and zoom; finally, still uses the correlation function to determinate translation parameter. So it completes the entire image mosaic process. In following content, we firstly give the theory of image registration based on Fourier-Mellin transform, then give the algorithm process of panoramic image mosaic, finally carry on the mosaic experiment and the discussion.

2   The Principle of Image Registration Based on Fourier-Mellin Transform

2.1   Phase Correlation Theory [3]

Suppose two separate images f_1 and f_2 are relative in the spatial field only with displacement (x_0, y_0), i.e.,

$$f_1(x, y) = f_2(x - x_0, y - y_0) \tag{1}$$

The corresponding Fourier transforms F_1 and F_2 will be relative, i.e.,

$$F_2(\xi, \eta) = e^{-j2\pi(\xi x_0 + \eta y_0)} F_1(\xi, \eta) \tag{2}$$

The cross-power spectrum of two images f_1 and f_2 is

$$\frac{F_1(\xi, \eta) F_2^*(\xi, \eta)}{\left| F_1(\xi, \eta) F_2^*(\xi, \eta) \right|} = e^{-j2\pi(\xi x_0 + \eta y_0)} \tag{3}$$

Where F^* expresses the complex conjugate of F. Carry on the inverse Fourier transform to the formula (3), and produce function δ in the place (x_0, y_0). After measuring the location of the peak of the inverse Fourier transform of the cross-power spectrum phase about the formula (3), we will obtain the displacement (x_0, y_0) between two images.

2.2 Computing Relative Rotation Angle and Scale Factor [4] Using Fourier-Mellin Transform between Two Images

If two matching images are respectively f_1 and f_2, which f_2 is a replica of f_1 with displacement (x_0, y_0) and rotation angle θ_0, we have the following equation

$$f_2(x, y) = f_1[a(x\cos\theta_0 + y\sin\theta_0) - x_0, a(-x\sin\theta_0 + y\cos\theta_0) - y_0] \tag{4}$$

In the equation (4), a is scale factor of two images. According to the Fourier translation property and the Fourier rotation property, we get the following equation

$$F_2(\xi, \eta) = a^{-2}\left|F_1[a^{-1}(\xi\cos\theta_0 + \eta\sin\theta_0), a^{-1}(-\xi\sin\theta_0 + \eta\cos\theta_0)]\right|\exp\{-j\varphi_{f_2}(\xi, \eta)\} \tag{5}$$

In the equation (5), $\varphi_{f_2}(\xi, \eta)$ is the spectrum phase of f_2, whose value mainly depends on translation, rotation and scale, etc. Therefore, by taking module to the equation (5), we get their relation of the Fourier power spectrum, i.e.,

$$\left|F_2(\xi, \eta)\right| = a^{-2}\left|F_1[a^{-1}(\xi\cos\theta_0 + \eta\sin\theta_0), a^{-1}(-\xi\sin\theta_0 + \eta\cos\theta_0)]\right| \tag{6}$$

The equation (6) has invariable translation property, i.e., revolving an angle to a figure causes also the power spectrum to revolve a same angle, simultaneously the scale factor a changes power spectrum a^{-1} times. Another interesting property is that spectrum center $\xi = \eta = 0$ is invariable on rotation and scaling. So as to shift rotation and scale transform to translation form, we first carry on the polar coordinate transform to the frequency spectrum. The polar coordinate transform can turn the original coordinate (ξ, η) to (ρ, θ). Therefore, we get the next relations:

$$\begin{cases} a^{-1}(\xi\cos\theta_0 + \eta\sin\theta_0) = \dfrac{\rho}{a}\cos(\theta - \theta_0) \\ a^{-1}(-\xi\sin\theta_0 + \eta\cos\theta_0) = \dfrac{\rho}{a}\sin(\theta - \theta_0) \end{cases} \tag{7}$$

If make $S(\rho, \theta) = \left|F_2(\rho\cos\theta, \rho\sin\theta)\right|$ and $R(\rho, \theta) = \left|F_1(\rho\cos\theta, \rho\sin\theta)\right|$, the formula (8) may be gotten with the above deduction.

$$S(\rho, \theta) = a^{-2}R(\dfrac{\rho}{a}, \theta - \theta_0) \tag{8}$$

Therefore, the revolving difference is converted to the translation difference by the above polar coordinate transform. But scale factor's transform need also take the logarithmic transform to achieve. If make $\lambda = \log \rho$ and $k = \log a$, the formula (8) becomes

$$S_l(\log \rho, \theta) = a^{-2} R_l(\log \rho - \log a, \theta - \theta_0) \longrightarrow S_l(\lambda, \theta) = a^{-2} R_l(\lambda - k, \theta - \theta_0) \qquad (9)$$

In the formula (9), the expression with the subscript l is the one by logarithmic transform. So the formula (9) is called Fourier-Mellin transform, which R_l is called the Fourier-Mellin invariable descriptor of f_1. By the above transform, the factors of rotation and scale are similarly converted into translation form. Reusing the formula (2), (3) we may calculate the scale factor a and the rotation angle θ_0. According to a and θ_0, we carry on the inverse transform to f_2 and obtain f_3. Consequently we can calculate the displacement (x_0, y_0) between f_1 and f_3 with the formula (2), (3).

3 The Algorithm of Color Image Mosaic

The algorithm process of color image mosaic is as follows [5]:

a) Extract a color component f_1' and f_2' which respectively come from two image f_1 and f_2, carry on the Fourier transform to f_1' and f_2', and compute $F_1(\xi, \eta)$ and $F_2(\xi, \eta)$'s absolute value $|F_1(\xi, \eta)|$ and $|F_2(\xi, \eta)|$.

b) Make $|F_1(\xi, \eta)|$ and $|F_2(\xi, \eta)|$ pass the high-pass filter, for eliminating the low-frequency noise. And the filter can be used in the following function:

$$H(\xi, \eta) = (1.0 - X(\xi, \eta)) * (2.0 - X(\xi, \eta)) \qquad (10)$$

Where $X(\xi, \eta) = \cos(\pi \xi) \cos(\pi \eta)$, and $-0.5 \le \xi, \eta \le 0.5$.

c) Transform the filtered images to the logarithm-polar coordinate form, and calculate their cross-power spectrum. Carry on the inverse Fourier transform to the cross-power spectrum, and find out the location $(\log a, \theta_0)$ of the peak of the inverse Fourier transform of the cross-power spectrum phase, thus may get the rotation angle a and the scale factor θ_0.

d) Carry on the matching image f_2 to compensate on rotation and proportion zoom, consequently obtain the new image f_3. The new image f_3 and the original image f_1 are picked up a color component respectively. After calculating the cross-power spectrum, we can get the displacement (x_0, y_0).

e) Carry on splicing to two image f_1 and f_3. If we only adopt simply medial splicing in the overlap image region, the mosaic image could have possibly the quite obvious boundary or the color warp. The vision of the person is suitable with difficulty. Therefore, in the algorithm about the overlap image region, we use the method of image fusion to carry on fusion splicing. Nowadays the methods of color image fusion based on wavelet transform [6] and pyramid fusion technology [7] are applied widespreadly, and have better stability. Due to the length limits, this article will not give unnecessary description in details.

4   Experimental Result

The following content is applying this article's algorithm to carry on the experiment of image mosaic. Fig. 1 (a), (b) are original images, which (b) has a certain rotation and scaling to (a). Using the above improved algorithm of image mosaic to measure the rotation angle of (b) is 16.001 degrees, and the scale factor is 1.043. After compensating (b) on revolving and zooming, we obtain Fig. 2. We reuse the principle of phase correlation to get the displacement (322.792, 0.001), which is between Fig. 2 and Fig. 1 (a). Fig. 1 (a) and Fig. 2 are carried on splicing and fusion, then Fig. 3 is obtained.

(a) the size of 563×475 pixels   (b) the size of 640×617 pixels

Fig. 1. Original images

Fig. 2. The compensated image

Fig. 3. Mosaic result

Table 1. The comparison result of transform parameters

	Rotation angle (degree)	Scale factor	Translation (pixel)	Calculation (time/s)
Original value	16	1.000	(323,0)	26.238
Estimated value	16.001	1.043	(322.792,0.001)	

In order to confirm this algorithm's accuracy, transform parameters of Fig. 1(b) that are obtained from this algorithm compare with the ones designated in advance. The comparison result is shown in Table 1. We may see from Table 1 that the quite precise transform parameters can be obtained from this algorithm process.

5 Conclusion

This article proposes one kind of color image mosaic algorithm based on Fourier-Mellin transform. When the projective distortion is not very remarkable which is obtained from the camera's general movement, we carry on geometry matching with image characteristic of the overall frequency domain, and may obtain the quite satisfying panoramic image. This article has made a mass of mosaic experiments. In the experiments, this algorithm can not be applied there is a very serious situation in perspective distortion, and requests all the regions of the images to be spliced have the same rotation, scaling and displacement. Because the algorithm of Fourier-Mellin transform depends on its own invariable attribute and has its own limitation, it is not too sensitive to the degrees of rotation. But it has certain restriction to the scaling. If the scaling surpasses 1.8, it is very difficult to get the correct matching result under normal circumstances.

Acknowledgment. This work was supported in part by the National Natural Science Foundation of China (NSFC) under Grant No. 61071193.

References

1. Reddy, B.S., Chatterji, B.N.: An FFT based technique for translation, rotation and scale-invariant image registration. IEEE Trans. Image Processing 8(8), 1266 (1996)
2. Kan, C., Srinath, M.: Invariant character recognition with Zernike and orthogonal Fourier-Mellin moments. Pattern Recognition 35(1), 143–154 (2002)
3. Ma, J., Xu, K.-h., Tan, L.-y.: Extend-beacon tracking for deep space optical communication based on phase-correlation. Optics and Precision Engineering 14(3), 515–519 (2006)
4. Li, X.-M., Zhao, X.-P., Zheng, L., Hu, Z.-Y.: An image registration technique based on Fourier-Mellin transform and its extended applications. Chinese Journal of Computers 29(3), 466–472 (2006)
5. Derrode, S., Ghorbel, F.: Robust and efficient Fourier-Mellin transform approximations for gray-level image reconstruction and complete invariant description. Computer Vision and Image Understanding 83(1), 57–78 (2001)
6. Wang, Q., Feng, Y., Liu, G.-q.: The color image fusion algorithm using wavelet transform. Computer Simulation 22(11), 201–204 (2005)
7. Shum, H.-Y., Szeliski, R.: Construction of panoramic image mosaics with global and local alignment. International Journal of Computer Vision 36(2), 101–130 (2000)

Automatic Color Cast Detection Algorithm for Surveillance Video Sequence Based on Color Histogram Characteristic

Shurong Chen and Jinna Bi

College of Information Engineering,
Shanghai Maritime University, Shanghai, 200135, China
srchen@shmtu.edu.cn

Abstract. Color cast defect detection of video image is challenging and of great importance in the field of video quality evaluation, and one of the difficulties therein is how to distinguish a dominant color (caused by a predominant color, such as an image in which blue sky is a basic tone) from an inherent cast (image presenting a cast due to imaging device failure or taken in a special environment, such as underwater). By analyzing color histogram characteristics of different color spaces, in this paper, we propose a fast two-step automatic cast detection algorithm for an original surveillance video sequence. First a video image is detected in a RGB space; then, according to the color distribution of cast-frame in CIELAB color space, an improved clustering algorithm is employed to distinguish a dominant color from an inherent color cast; finally, the residual frames without clearly concentrated chroma histogram can be reevaluated using cast sensitive region to improve the accuracy and reliability. Experimental results show that the proposed algorithm can better correspond to people's subjective evaluation and achieve valid color cast quality prediction.

Keywords: Surveillance video, color cast, CIELAB color space, dominant color, cast sensitive area.

1 Introduction

The color cast quality metric of still image has long been concerned and applied to digital camera product line, biomedical and other fields to solve practical problems. With the rapid development of network and the extensive use of video communication technologies, image quality metric involving surveillance video sequence is becoming a new research hot topic. Video data analysis in the surveillance system indicates that the cast image will result in degradation and will make further image analysis and recognition difficult. Color cast is usually connected with the light color temperature, color rendering and optical properties of image acquisition equipment. As usual, color objects in different light conditions exists a color deviation. The human visual systems (HVS) can automatically adjust this deviation to a certain extent to eliminate the impact of different light conditions on color, and thus get correct perception of the true color, which is known as color

H. Deng et al. (Eds.): AICI 2011, Part II, LNAI 7003, pp. 280–287, 2011.

constancy. The digital cameras at the first end of monitoring system, however, do not have this adjustment ability, which is prone to video color cast.

Currently, many researches focus on color cast detection technology of still images, which mainly includes gray world model [1], white patch [2], prior knowledge, and edge detection method for color cast, wherein gray word model is inaccurate to monochromatic color image (e.g. sea or blue sky) or photos taken in too dark or bright environment, and white patch method depends on highlight or white area on the surface of object. Li and Jin determine the degree of color cast by calculating the ratio of average color cast D and the image central distance M at CIELAB space, namely, $k = D / M$, but they do not distinguish the dominant color and influence of dark conditions [3]. According to color distribution in a specific color space, F. Gasparini and R. Schettini classify images into different cast degrees and design a cast remover [4]. Cooper adopts an adaptive segmentation to identify cast images and estimate cast level, then correct color cast by altering image color of near neutral area [5]. Zheng applies color histogram characteristics to detect and correct image with color cast [6].

Video surveillance systems must adapt to different lighting conditions at complex environment and work in real time, therefore, the above cast detection algorithms about still images are not fully applicable. Generally, most of video quality metrics focus on overall impairment of video sequence and evaluate quality by calculating the mean square error (MSE) and peak signal noise ratio (PSNR), which is simple but fails to consider HVS characteristics. Some evaluation models introduce the features of visual attention and estimate local quality of video frame by identifying the region of interest. Aldo Maalouf et al. propose a no-reference color video quality metric based on HVS 3D wavelet transform [7]. Dusica Marijan proposes an image similarity algorithm for testing specific degradations in TV set by estimating the difference between the image to test and the reference one, which however is a full-reference intra-frame assessment scheme and does not fit cast detection for real time video [8]. In addition, video quality can be assessed by using the quality of each frame in the video sequence with different weights [9].

Therefore, we propose an automatic color cast detection algorithm based on color histogram for surveillance video sequences, which firstly analyzes histogram features in RGB space and color distribution in CIELAB space, then invokes frame edge pretreatment and improved k means clustering algorithm to determine cast frames and cast degree, finally   evaluate total original video sequence by a weighting method.

2   Algorithm Design

2.1   Algorithm Principle

Generally, acquisition and storage of video images from surveillance cameras are based on RGB space image. Many studies about still image demonstrate that histograms of normal color image uniformly distribute in three channels R, G, B, and the gray scale of pixels and quantity in each channel keep equalization, nevertheless, histograms of cast images are non-uniform and give rise to a large difference between gray scale and amount of pixels [6], which enables quickly performing initial color cast detection.

In RGB color space, the Euclidean distance between two points and the actual color distance are nonlinear, which can cause certain error between the calculated color distance and actual visual error perceived by human, hence, an appropriate color space needs to be chosen. In this paper, CIELAB color space is used, within which the calculated color difference most closely resembles human visual perception and better fits the detection and correction of tiny color casts [5].

The color cast of digital image is related to mean chroma value and chroma distribution characteristics. The chromaticity histogram of a polychrome image without cast illustrates a multimodal distribution in an ab-plane, as shown in Fig.1 (b); whereas a plain colored image indicates a single peak or several peaks in a limited region, as shown in fig.2 (b). The more concentrated and farther from the gray axis where the two-dimensional histogram of an image is, the stronger the color cast [3][4]; this feature can be used to calculate color cast strength in CIELAB space.

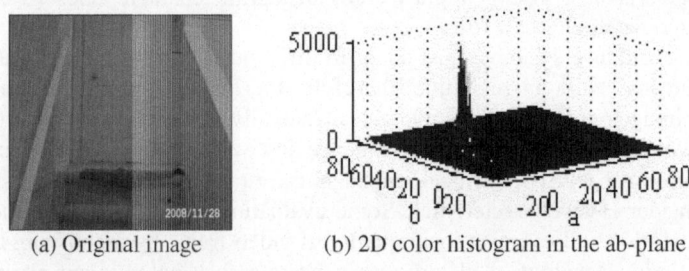

(a) Original image   (b) 2D color histogram in the ab-plane

Fig. 1. choroma histogram of normal ploychrome image in ab- plane

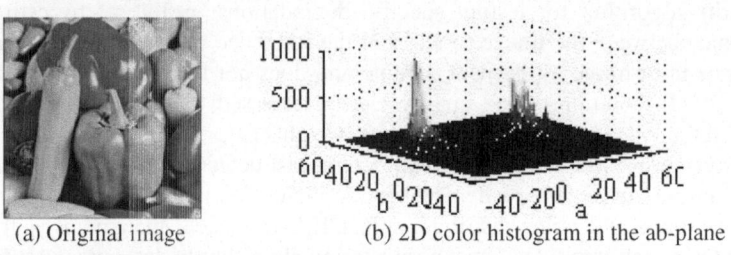

(a) Original image   (b) 2D color histogram in the ab-plane

Fig. 2. Chroma histogram of color cast image in ab- plane

For survey video images under different light environments, the content and background thereof have a great contrast, attached by more high frequency variations on the edge, causing the calculation of edge pixels prone to noise. Consequently, a color edge pretreatment is adopted, as shown in Fig.3: the color edge of an image is firstly extracted, followed by binarization and dilation to obtain a binary matrix of key areas; and subsequently a key-area image in RGB space is extracted and converted to CIELAB space, running the second detection algorithm.

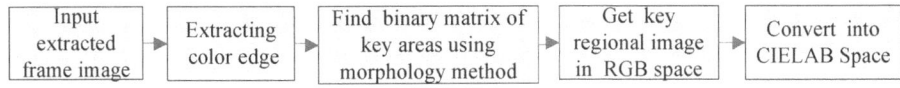

Fig. 3. Block diagram of pretreatment

In order to distinguish true color cast and dominant color, an improved k-means clustering based on maximum and minimum distance algorithm is employed for images with an intense color cast. The k-means clustering intelligently determines the best initial clustering centers, avoiding the initial clustering centers being too mutually close, thereby improving the accuracy of clustering. Fig. 4 (a) is a normal no-cast image with a bluish dominant color, wherein if the proportion of a clustered area is greater than 40%, it will be regarded as a dominant color (the black area, as shown in Fig.4 (b).

(a) Original image   (b) k-means clustered region

Fig. 4. Cluster analysis of image with dominant color

For not yet determined image after identifying dominant color, the cast sensitive area can be chosen in which chroma characteristic is similar and color value is less than the initial color radius r ($r = 6$). According to the characteristics that this area is more easily influenced by cast than texture details, a chroma analysis can be employed to evaluate whether cast exists or not. The r value can be adjusted self-adaptively to continuously reevaluate the sensitive areas to ensure the pixels of sensitive region reach 6%. What is retained in Fig.5 (b) is the sensitive area.

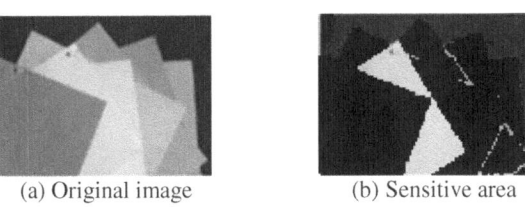

(a) Original image   (b) Sensitive area

Fig. 5. Characteristics analysis of cast sensitive area

2.2   Algorithm Flow

Video frames are extracted at a certain interval from a surveillance video sequence and detected using the proposed algorithm which is shown in Fig.6.

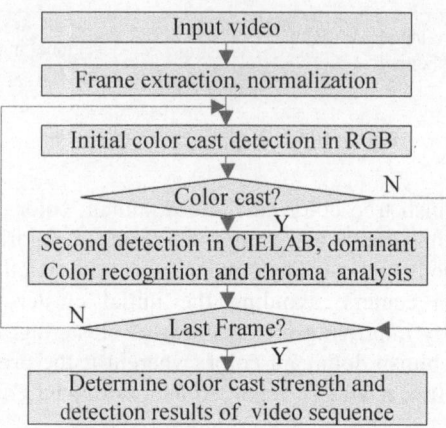

Fig. 6. Algorithm flow chart

The above algorithm can be summarized as follows:

Step 1: Initialization. According to the time span of surveillance video sequences and frame playback rate, set sampling interval, record frame number, and normalize the images to 320 * 240.

Step 2: Initial color cast detection. Color cast estimation of sample-frame can be quickly run in terms of the histogram characteristics described with mean μ_1 and variance σ_1 in RGB space. The following M, N indicate the number of pixels in each row and column respectively, and μ_p denotes mean value of one of three channels (R, G or B) in which p can be replaced by R, G or B as follows:

$$\mu_p = \frac{\sum\limits_{x=1}^{M}\sum\limits_{y=1}^{N} f(x,y)}{M \times N}, \tag{1}$$

Calculate channel mean u_R, u_G and u_B respectively using (1), and μ_1, σ_1 as below:

$$u_1 = (\mu_R + \mu_G + \mu_B)/3, \tag{2}$$

$$\sigma_1 = \sum_{p}(\mu_p - \mu_1)^2. \tag{3}$$

The variance of normal color image is relatively little, while the variance of cast image is large. According to a large number of frames test analysis, we set threshold σ_1 as 30. When value σ_1 is less than 30, the frame is regard as normal without cast; when greater than 30, proceed to step 3.

Step 3: Color edge preprocessing. The algorithm firstly find a binary matrix for the key areas of the frame to test, then pixels of frame in the RGB channel is multiplied by the binary matrix, thereby obtaining the key area image, which is then converted to a CIELAB color space.

Step 4:   Second color cast detection. The algorithm is run to distinguish dominant color and determine cast degree, as described in the following: select pixels with a brightness value less than 90 and greater than 25, and according to (4) and (5) calculate mean and variance of the histogram projection along the color axes a, b, wherein k = a, b

$$\mu_k = \int_k kF(a,b)dk, \tag{4}$$

$$\sigma_k^2 = \int_k (\mu_k - k)^2 F(a,b)dk, \tag{5}$$

In the ab-plane, the distance from the chroma histogram to the origin (a = 0, b = 0) of gray axis is defined by Euclidean distance as :

$$D = \mu - \sigma, \tag{6}$$

Wherein $\mu = \sqrt{\mu_a^2 + \mu_b^2}$, $\sigma = \sqrt{\sigma_a^2 + \sigma_b^2}$.

A proportion D_σ is introduced to calculate color cast strength,

$$D_\sigma = D/\sigma . \tag{7}$$

The greater D_σ is, the stronger the color cast. If $D_\sigma \square 1.5$ or $\mu \square 12$ and $D_\sigma \square 0.6$, go to step 5 to distinguish the dominant color; otherwise, go to step 6 to make a chroma analysis for the sensitive area of frame.

Step 5: Running the improved k-means clustering to identify image with dominant color. The algorithm combines with the maximum and the minimum distance algorithm, picking pixel points away from each other as the initial clustering centers to avoid falling into a local minimum. A key area of testing frame is divided into four blocks, and if a sub-block region is greater than a proportion of 40%, it would be regarded as a dominant color; otherwise a cast frame.

Step 6: Sensitive area analysis. Select a sensitive area for a frame with an intense color cast to make a chroma analysis as described in step 4. If the D_σ is greater than 0.2, a cast frame would be deemed existing; otherwise the frame is normal.

Step 7: Record test results and evaluate video sequence to determine whether color cast exists or not. Count cast frames (including cast frame number, color cast intensity, the dominant color or inherent color cast), estimate color cast degree of the overall video sequence based on the quality of single frame.

3   Experimental Results and Analysis

To verify the proposed two-step cast detection algorithm, we test 50 surveillance video clips (10-min length) which are shot at different scenarios (indoor, outside, intersection, and so on) under the different lighting conditions, with the resolution of 640×480, and the playback rate of 25 frames per sec. we use the weighted gray world, the weighted cast factor detection model, and the proposed method respectively, and the results are compared with the subjective judgments. In order to improve computing speed, we set sampling rate as one frame per 10 sec, moreover normalize the resolution of frame image to 320 ×240 and run programs on PC.

The following Fig.7 is cast detection results of 60 frames extracted from a surveillance video sequence, wherein the bigger D_σ value is, the greater the cast degree of frame. The frames with $D_\sigma=0$ mean no cast in the frame. The lager D_σ implies that the frame probably has a dominant color or a color cast. The result shows that there are 18 frames with larger color cast degree, wherein 13 frames true cast and 5 frames dominant color, in line with people's subjective tests.

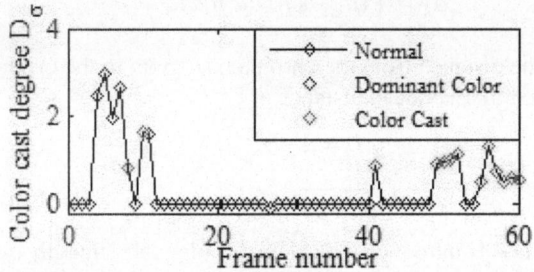

Fig. 7. Color cast test results of extracted frames

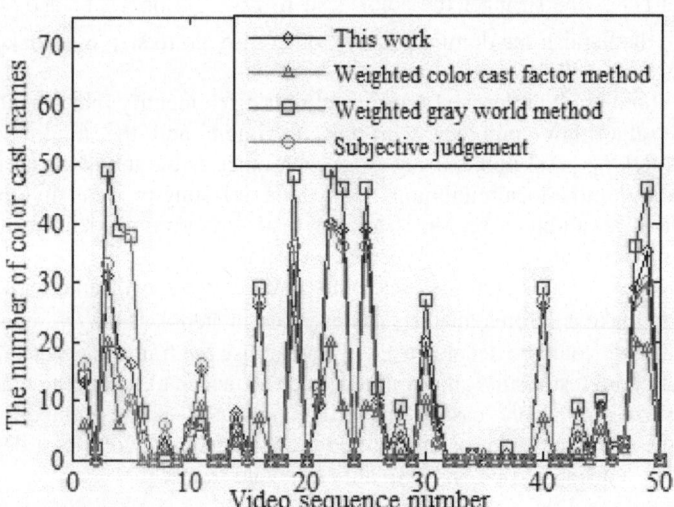

Fig. 8. Experimental results comparison of three algorithms

A surveillance video sequence with color cast can be detected by using weighted model based on cast evaluation of each frame. As shown in Fig.8, within 50 tested video sequences, subjective test shows 11 video with obvious color cast, however the weighted gray world detects 12 cast video, the weighted color cast factor algorithm detects 5 cast video, and the proposed algorithm detects 11 cast video. Experimental results indicate that the weighted world gray method tests more cast frames, mainly due to the algorithm deficiency of potentially regarding an image with single background as a cast image. The weighted cast factor detection method finds minimal amounts of cast frames owing to no distinguishment of dominant color from cast image. Although the running results of the proposed algorithm has a little gap with people's subjective judgment in a few frames, the overall color cast evaluation for a surveillance video complies with people's subjective feelings.

4   Conclusion

This paper presents an automatic cast detection algorithm based on color histogram characteristics for surveillance video sequences. First video sequences are detected in RGB space; then according to chromas distribution in CIELAB color space, calculate cast frames and cast degrees; lastly evaluate cast quality of the overall video. Experimental results show that the proposed algorithm can better match people's subjective evaluation. Our further research topics also include integrating inherent cast blocks detection of intra-frame into our model.

Acknowledgments. This research was supported by Science & Technology Program of Shanghai Maritime University (No.20110043).

References

1. Kawamura, H., Yonemura, S., Ohya, J., Matsuura, N.: Illuminant color estimation by hue categorization based on gray world assumption. In: Proceedings of the SPIE, vol. 7873, pp. 787312–787312-12 (2011)
2. Kim, S., Kim, W.J., Kim, S.D.: Automatic white balance based on adaptive feature selection with standard illuminants. In: ICIP, San Diego, California, pp. 485–488 (2008)
3. Li, F., Jin, H.: An approach of detecting image color cast based on image Semantic. In: IEEE Proceedings of 2004 International Conference on Machine Learning and Cybernetics, Shanghai, vol. 6, pp. 3932–3936 (2004)
4. Gasparini, F., Schettini, R.: Color balancing of digital photos using simple image statistics. Pattern Recognition Society 37, 1201–1217 (2003)
5. Cooper, T.J.: Color Cast Detection and Removal in Digital Images. United States Patent, USA (2002)
6. Zheng, J.h.: Automatic illuminations detection and color correction of image using chromatci histogram characters. Journal of Image and Graphics 8, 1001–1007 (2003)
7. Maalouf, A., Larabi, M.C.: A no-reference color video quality metric based on a 3D multi-spectral wavelet transform. In: 2010 2nd International Workshop on Quality of Multimedia Experience, pp. 11–16. IEEE Press, Trondheim (2010)
8. Marijan, D.: Automatic functional TV Set failure detection system. IEEE Transactions on Consumer Electronics 56, 125–133 (2010)
9. Chang, Q., Tong, Y.B., Zhan, Q.S.: Video quality assessing model based on single image quality with different weights. Journal of Beijing University of Aeronautics and Astronautics 33, 311–314 (2007)

Authentication System That Mobile Terminal Serves as a Key Carrier

Jianping Gong, Yajuan Xu, and Bingkai Liu

College of Information Engineering, Taiyuan University of Technology
030024 Taiyuan, China
gongjianping@tyut.edu.cn

Abstract. With the rapid development of information technology, the tradition-al way of user name + password authentication system to couldn't have far sa-tisfied the people's high quality requirements to the information security. People tend to look for a kind of data encryption techniques connecting mobile intelligent terminal with modern cryptography technology to meet the needs of people. This text completes the double factor authentication with PC software based on the routine use of the handheld mobile terminal (such as a handset) about how the carrying elements of authentication, achieves a new security au-thentication mechanism, improves the system safety and ease of use. at the same time ,the introduction of mobile phone key concept skillfully combines the mobile intelligent terminal and modern cryptography technology, provides a more secure authentication mechanism for the users who have a more important protection requirements to the files.

Keyword: Two-factor authentication Mobile Terminal Encryption Bluetooth communication.

1 Introduction

At present, many systems take the traditional way of the user name + password as identity authentication its security strength is not enough, and very easy to be broken. Using two-factor authentication is necessary, and is the basis of security encryption system, now most security products basically use the means of USB KEY+PIN code, namely only when both of material object's USB KEY and its corresponding PIN code are right ,it can enter into security encryption system. But they all require an additional investment and extra to carry along with, that is neither convenient nor economical. Achieving the PC-side software authentication by mobile handheld devices (such as handset) is not only to enhanced individual document private security, also has simultaneously given brings more convenient personally. The research based on mobile handsets two-factor authentication system is extremely essential.

2 Working Principle

Adopting the elements of mobile handheld devices of bearing authentication must get the Bluetooth communications' support to facilitate the authentication information

H. Deng et al. (Eds.): AICI 2011, Part II, LNAI 7003, pp. 288–295, 2011.

charged with computers and simultaneously the safer reliable authentication mechanism for the users who have more important protection requirements to private documents.

The system requires authentication module installed on the phone side, and preserve the files to protect the relevant keys, the cipher text preserved by the software of PC side can restore the protected key under the handset key participation, thus completes the process of encryption and decryption protection and identity authentication. The handset key is passed by encryption protection to the PC side, and the random number would participate during the passing process each time in order to prevent replay vulnerabilities effectively.

2.1   Composition of Modules

The security design module of authentication mechanism is shown in Figure 1.Mobile terminal and PC side software are required to deploy the authentication module.

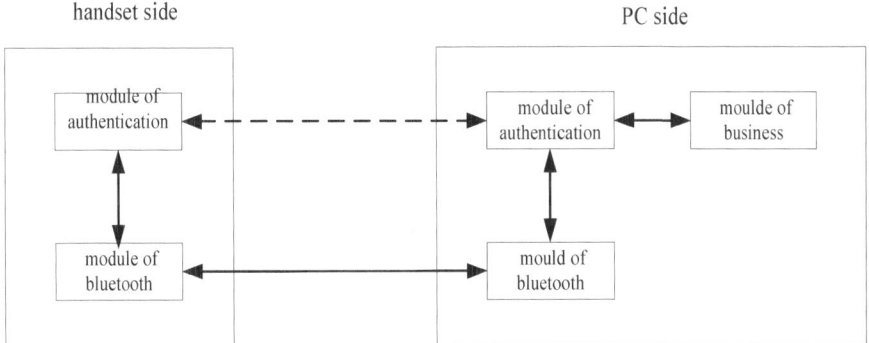

Fig. 1. Composition of Modules

Handset authentication module preserves the phone key (authentication keys' participants) to complete information exchange with PC authentication module. PC authentication module is responsible for obtaining the handset key and testing the connection status between PC and handset, and also has the function of informing service module whether opens or controls. The service module is responsible to open and close the local file encryption and decryption functions, and the local file encryption and decryption functions. Authentication key is preserved on the PC side by the means of cipher text.

2.2 Work Processes

1) Handset authentication module initiates remote business operation requests;

2) Bluetooth module of the PC side searches PC devices and connects with them ;

3) The parties complete matching the connection based on the password;

4) The handset authentication transmits the requests initiating the service operation to the PC side authentication module;

5) PC-side authentication module generates a random number and return it to the handset authentication module;

6) The handset authentication module requires the user to input the protected password of the handset key to decrypt the phone keys;

7) The handset authentication module conducts the relevant operation to encrypt the handset key under the PC-random number participation, and forms a temporary cipher text of handset key;

8) The handset authentication module returns a temporary cipher text of handset key back to the PC via Bluetooth module side;

9) PC-side authentication module conducts the operations to obtain plaintext file protection key after receiving the temporary cipher text of handset key;

10).PC-side authentication module pass the protected key to the business module;

11) The business modules use the key to complete authentication and encryption and decryption of files;

12) PC-side authentication module loopy checks whether the paired handset is connected, if disconnected, PC –side would notify services module to turn off file protection function.

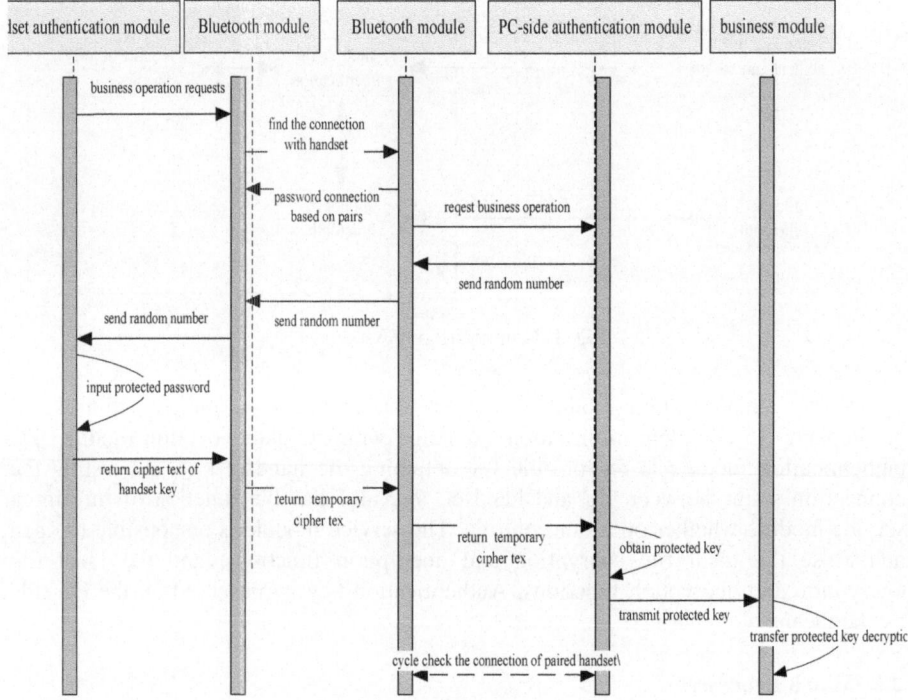

Fig. 2. Work Processes

2.3 Key Generation Processes

Handset authentication module and PC-side authentication module set up the same seed key. While initial installation. Generation process of protected key is divided into two steps, first, the PC-side obtains handset key, second , doing operations by handset key obtains the protected key.

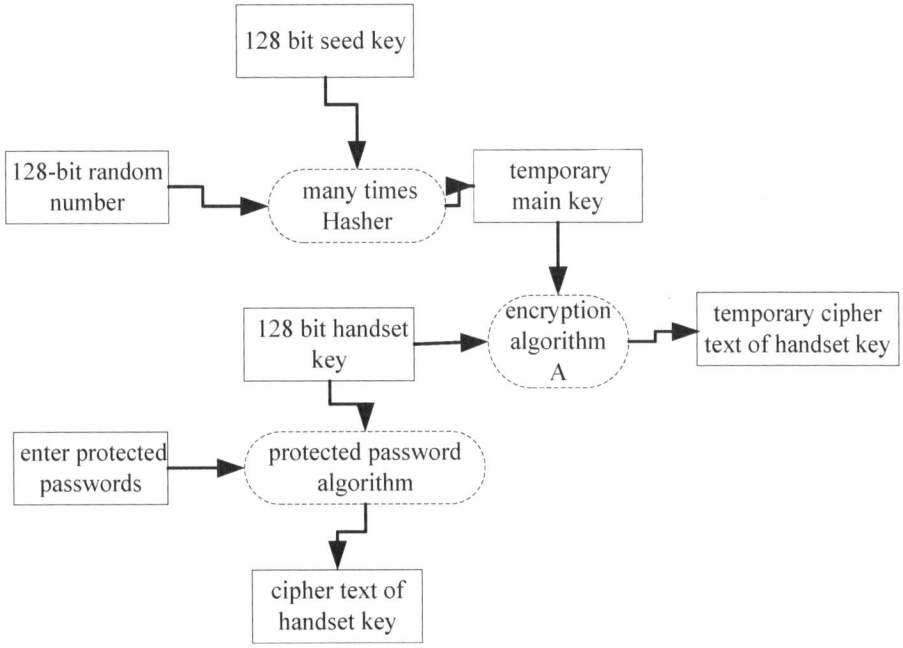

Fig. 3. Obtaining Handset Key Processes

1) 128-bit random number generated by PC side is sent to the handset side through authentication module;

2) The handset authentication module carries on the Hasher operation 128-bit seed key built in and the PC-128-bit random number to avoid duplication, each time the Hasher operation will join a packing value (each time fixedly), combine the many times' hasher results to form the temporary main key;

3) The handset authentication module generates 128-bit random number as the phone keys, requiring the user to enter protected passwords;

4) The handset key, after encrypting by the protected password, will preserve the handset key in the handset;

5) Form the temporary cipher text of handset key after the temporary main key encrypts procession to handset key;

6) Mobile phone key-side authentication module returns the temporary cipher text of handset key to the PC side.

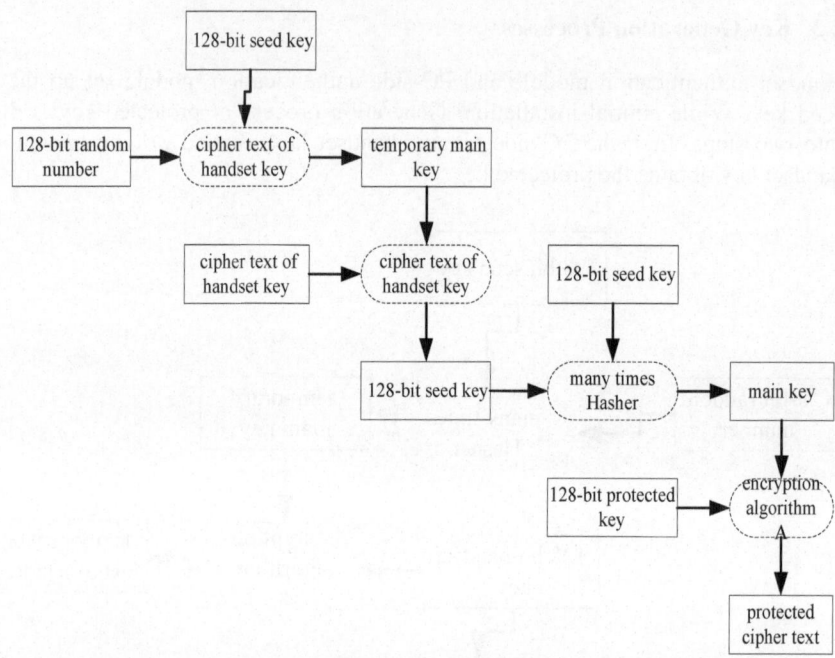

Fig. 4. Operating to Protected Key

1) PC-side authentication module carries on the Hasher operation between 128-bit seed key and 128 random number seed, the hash value ,in order to avoid duplication, fill adding a hash value (for each fixed) each time, combine the results of several Hash together to form a temporary main key;

2) The temporary main key decrypt the cipher text of handset key by the decryption algorithm A, to obtain 128-bit the plain text of handset key.

3) PC-side authentication module carries on the Hasher operation between 128-bit seed key and the 128-bit handset key, the hash value ,in order to avoid duplication, fill adding a hash value (for each fixed) each time, combine the results of several hash together to form a main key;

4) PC-side authentication module generates 128-bit random number as a protected key

5) Protected key cipher text is formed after the main key encrypts by the encryption algorithm A, and persevered to the local PC;

6) Destruct the 128 random numbers and handset key generated by the local
After key generation, PC-side only retains the cipher text of protected handset key the seed key, handset side preserves the handset key.

The passion of handset key has got the effective protection when the key generates in this way, so that it makes the protected key more secure and reliable.

2.4 File Encryption and Decryption Process

File encryption and decryption is divided into handset key obtaining, handset key decryption, file encryption and decryption. In which, the process of handset key which is similar to the process of the PC side obtaining handset key during the key generation

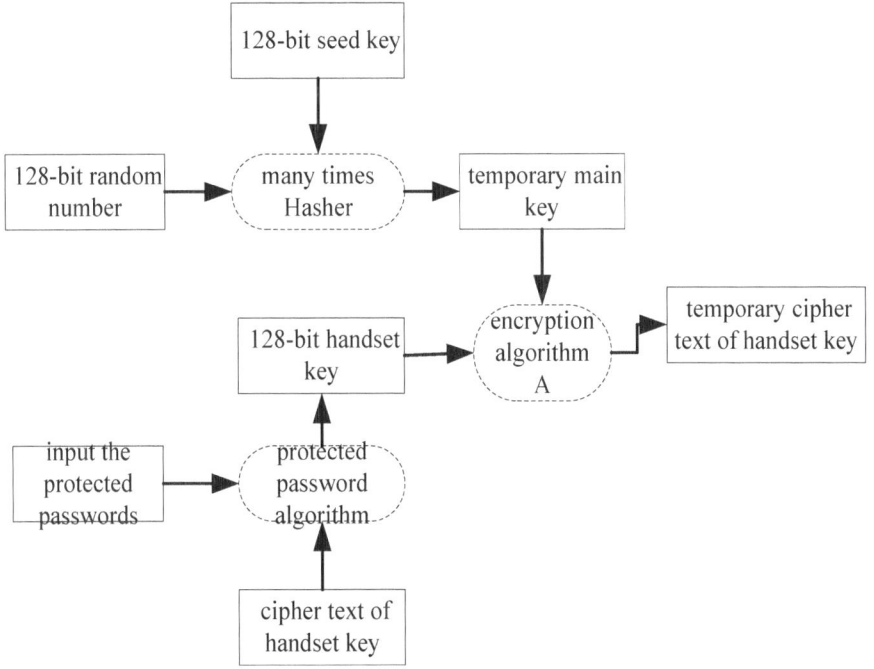

Fig. 5. Process of Handset Key

1) 128-bit random number generated by PC side is sent to the mobile terminal by authentication module;

2) The mobile terminal authentication module carries on the Hasher operation between 128-bit seed key and 128 random number seed, the hash value ,in order to avoid duplication, fill adding a hash value (for each fixed) each time, combine the results of several hash together to form a temporary main key;

3) The mobile terminal authentication module requires the user to input the protected password of handset key to decrypt the cipher text of handset key, so that we get handset key;

4) Form the temporary cipher text of handset key after the temporary main key encrypts procession to handset key;

5) The mobile terminal authentication module returns the temporarily cipher text to the PC side.

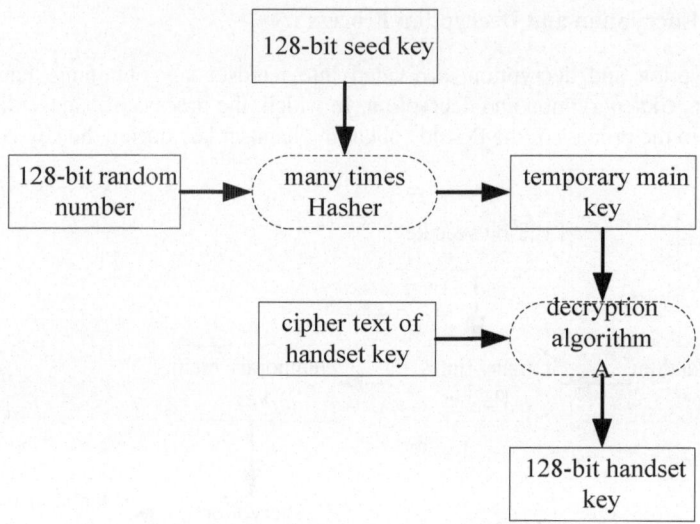

Fig. 6. Handset Key Decryption Process

PC-side authentication module carries on the Hasher operation between 128-bit seed key and 128 random number seed, the hash value ,in order to avoid duplication, fill adding a hash value (for each fixed) each time, combine the results of several hash together to form a temporary main key.The temporary main key decrypt the cipher text of handset key by the decryption algorithm A, to obtain 128-bit the plain text of handset key.

1) PC-side authentication module carries on the Hasher operation between 128-bit seed key and 128 bit handset key, the hash value ,in order to avoid duplication, fill adding a hash value (for each fixed) each time, combine the results of several hash together to form a main key;

2) The main key decrypts the cipher text of protected key by the decryption algorithm A to obtain the plain text of protected key;

3) The protected key decrypts the cipher text of protected file by the decryption algorithm B to obtain the plain text of protected file(or encrypt protected file to obtain the cipher text of protected file.);

4) Destruct the system memory of protected key built in when the business module is turned off Handset key must participate in the process of decryption, otherwise local file can't be encrypted and decrypted.

5) Security Analysis

The generation of secret cabinet key is more complex than simple authentication mechanisms, the handset key must participate in the process, and handset key is neither secret cabinet key nor the protected key of secret cabinet key (main key), during the key generation process, even if the third party obtains the handset key, it can't complete the decryption operations to secret cabinet. Secret cabinet key uses the main key to encrypt and protect while storing, doesn't worry about the key being stolen. But its shortcoming is that the handset key has no security protection during the transfer process.

3 System Implementation

The system includes two parts: PC-side authentication module and handset authentication module .PC-side authentication module can be realized based on windows platform, handset authentication module can complete the module functions based on the Android platform.

PC-side authentication module completes corresponding operation via the connection between Bluetooth equipment and handset establishment and data received from the mobile terminal. Its main missions includes: intercept the blue tooth connection, receive the orders from the handset side, and analyze the orders. This part of designs include three parts design : blue tooth part design, the instruction receive and the analysis, and the service module interaction. The instructions receive and the analysis is mainly to process the data received. This module mainly receives analyses and distributes the orders of handset side.

The design of handset side application programs mainly includes the two parts: design of the blue tooth part and design of the user operation interface. The development platform of handset side is Android 2.2 Platform, its development environment and compiler use Eclipse_Jee_4.5 and JDK1.6, and its application programs develop around the frame of the Android application procedure. The surface development completes via roiddraw-r1b16, it can design and produce the Android surface document (the xml document). This module uses the OutputStream and Input Stream of Bluetooth Socket class of the Android SDK to send and receive data.

4 Conclusion

The system of Two-factor authentication based on mobile handset not only saves the investment cost of users, but also greatly improves the ease of use, and improves authentication mechanism of different safety for different user groups. This authentication method can easily be used to opening authentication of the file cabinet, the entrance guard system, checking attendance system; even paying by the handset and so on.

References

1. Feng, G.: Network security principle and technology. Science Press, China (2003)
2. Feng, G., Pei, D.: Cryptography guide. Science Press, China (1999)
3. Chen, L.: Modern cryptography. Science Press, China (2002)
4. Lai, X., et al.: Computer cryptography and its application. National Defence Industry Press (July 2001)
5. Shi, Z., et al.: Computer network security tutorial. Tsinghua University Press, Beijing (2004)
6. Guo, D., et al.: Actual encryption and decryption Raiders. Tsinghua University Press, Beijing (2003)
7. IEEE802.15, Bluetooth communication standard protocol
8. Bluetooth Special Interest Group, Specification of the Bluetooth System Core
9. Bluetooth Special Interest Group, Specification of the Bluetooth System Profile

Research of 3D Stratum Model and Cutting Algorithm Based on DEMs-TEN

Rui-sheng Jia and Hong-mei Sun

College of Information Science & Engineering, Shandong University of Science
& Technology, Qingdao, China
jia.ruisheng@hotmail.com, shm0221@163.com

Abstract. 3D stratum modeling and its cutting algorithm is one of the hotspot in the field of 3D geological simulation. For the constructing demand of the 3D digital stratum, proposed a 3D mixed data model that composed by Multi-DEM and TEN models. The model uses the Multi-DEM to express the simple, regular, laminar 3D geologic body, uses TEN structure to express the complex, non-laminar geologic body, and then forms the 3D stratum model that has the coincident models and the uniform logic, and meets the need of the stratum 3D attributes calculation and 3D spatial analysis. Based on the mixed model DEMs-TEN, use the cutting plane to slice the stratum reconstruction model, and generate edges sequence and points sequence on the cutting plane, and then generate a closed contour by edges sequence and points sequence and determine included relation among the contour lines. Therefore with the above methods, carry Delaunay triangulation on closed contour, thus get a whole profile model. The slice sample indicates: the cutting algorithm has high rate.

Keywords: Stratum model, stratum slice, DEMs-TEN model, constraint surface.

1 Introduction

The 3D stratum modeling and cutting is one of the hotspot in 3D geological simulation field, scholars at home and abroad have done a large number of exploration on 3D geological modeling theory structure and realization methods in different application fields, and put forward their own data model and the modeling method to describe the 3D geological space, currently data model applied to 3D geological modeling of twenty or thirty kinds, and can dived 3D data model into three categories surface model, body model, mixed model and so on[1]. The mixed model always aims at the actual situation, and has the advantages of surface models and body models, and they make the mutual complementarities. Currently commonly used 3D mixed models are: TIN- CSG mixed model [2,4,5], Octree-TEN mixed model [3,4,6], TIN-Octree mixed modeling[7,8], Wire Frame-Block mixed model[9] and so on. Among this, the TIN-CSG model uses TIN model to express the terrain surface, uses CSG to express the regular structures entity, and currently it is the main form to modeling in digital cities; the Octree-TEN model is suitable for preserving the primitive sampled data, and has the ability to express the complex space topology relation, and expresses the target

H. Deng et al. (Eds.): AICI 2011, Part II, LNAI 7003, pp. 296–303, 2011.

space precisely. So combine the two models to descript the application model precisely in special field(such as geology, coal mine, oil and so on); the TIN-Octree model uses TIN to express the surface of space entity, and it mainly realizes the visualization and the expression of topology relation; uses Octree to express the internal structures of space entity, uses pointers to establish the relations between them; the Wire Frame-Block model uses Wire Frame model to express the target space outline, the stratum object or the excavation boundary, and uses Block model to fill the internal entity.

2   3D Stratum Model DEMs-TEN

Currently there are many technical methods for stratigraphic information detection, but the most direct and the most widely used method to obtain stratigraphic information is drilling method. According to the arrangement position of rock strata demarcation point in stratum borehole data, can determine the sequence of the stratum. And can treat the Multi-DEM by lithology in cross-classification processing, thus can form 3D stratigraphic framework, which divided by elements of lithology in 3D space. Also can introduce special body object to rich stratum content, last form complete meaning of 3D stratigraphic model. In the model of DEMs-TEN, DEMs consists of some adjacent triangles, so its basic geometrical element is triangle. TEN includes basic geometrical elements as follows: vertex, line segment, triangle, tetrahedron and so on. Use object-oriented ideas, and abstract the stratum entity to the following four basic elements: vertex, line segment, triangle, tetrahedron and so on. In Fig.1, shows the DEMs-TEN model based on UML.

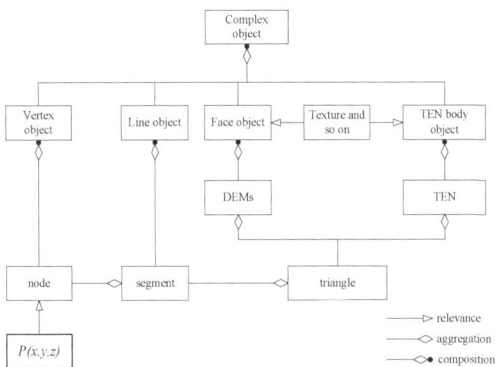

Fig. 1. 3D DEMs-TEN hybrid model based on UML

Fig.1 shows the corresponding relations between geometrical element and entity object. In order to establish the true 3D stratum model, it is necessary to design detailed data structure for the space position, attribute information and topological relation of the research object. The paper designed the data structure for the nodes, lines, triangles, and DEM, TEN, geologic body and so on based on TIN. The spending is considerable for establishing and maintaining data structure based on topological relation, and this brings a series of limitations and problems, such as, the data organization of the topological relation is complex, the data generation of the topological relation spends too much time and energy and only expresses part spatial relations, and the dynamic maintenance of topological data is difficult. Due to the complex topological relation, it is impossible to consider all the spatial relations when design the model, and always only consider the connecting relation, adjacency relation and included relation among elements of the model, and other relations can be obtained by the several relations' deduction. The description of the topological relation of the model in this paper mainly contains: (1)vertex-edge; (2)vertex-triangle; (3)vertex-tetrahedron; (4)edge-edge; (5)edge-triangle;(6)edge-tetrahedron;(7)triangle-tetrahedron. And the seven topological relations do not separately design the topological relation table, and directly put it in the corresponding data structure of the basic element, and other relations can be deduced by the actual situation.

3   The Stratum Cutting Algorithm Based on DEMs-TEN

In order to express and reappear the 3D geological profile of mining subsidence stratum, show details of the internal stratum and explain the spatial regularity of distribution of the stratum, so we need to do some research about how to construct the stratum 3D model and how to dissect them. On the basis of the analysis of the 3D mixed data model DEMs-TEN, use the cutting plane to slice the stratum reconstruction model, and generate edges sequence and points sequence on the cutting plane, and then generate a closed contour by edges sequence and points sequence and determine included relation among the contour lines. Therefore, with the above methods, carry Delaunay triangulation on closed contour, thus get a whole profile model.

3.1 Related Definition

Definition. Suppose the equation of cutting plane Ω is: $ax+bx+cz=0$, the cutting planeΩ will be divided into two spaces α ,β, $P(a,b,c)$ is the vector of the cutting plane, if suppose the space of α at the direction of the loathsome vector, for arbitrary space point $P(X,Y,Z)$, the distance from point P to cutting plane Ω, will be defined as: $Dist\ (P) =aX+bY+cZ+d$, therefore:

(1)when $Dist(P)>0$, point P is on the half space of α;
(2)when $Dist(P)=0$, point P is on the cutting plane;
(3)When $Dist(P)<0$, point P is on the half space of β.

Form section 2, the four faces of TEN tetrahedron, which constitute the stratum, are made up of the triangular patch, then calculate the distance of Dist from the vertex of triangular patch to the profile, if the values of the three Dist of triangular patch are greater or less than 0, then there are no intersections between triangular patch and cutting plane. If one value of Dist is greater than 0 and the other is less than 0, then the line segment AB that connected with these two points must be intersected with the cutting plane. The intersection will be obtained by the combination of equation of line and cutting plane-equation determined from vertex A(x1, y1, z1) and B(x2, y2, z2).

3.2 Cutting Model and Algorithm

The 3D stratum model and the cutting plane will product a boundary when cutting the stratum model, this boundary probably has many closed annular outlines, and the area which is made up of these annular outlines is the cutting plane. Carry Delaunay triangulation on those annular outlines, and then the cutting plane formed. To save the information of cutting plane, it is necessary to establish a data structure to save each edge, point and their topological relation:

```
class CEdgeVertex {
    double Coordinate_x, Coordinate_y, Coordinate_z;      //the coord of nodal;
    double Normal_x, Normal_y, Normal_z;           //the vector of nodal□
    CEdgeVertex *Next_ptr;      //the pointer for next;
    CVertexAttributeType VertexAttribute;           //user custom attributes;
};
class CEdge {
    CEdgeVertex *StartVertex_ptr;       //initial point of border;
    CEdgeVertex *EndVertex_ptr;                    //finish point of border□
    CEdge *Next_ptr;                       //the pointer to the next border;
    CEdgeAttributeType EdgeAttribute;   //user custom attributes;
};
```

Calculate the distance Dist from the three vertexes of triangular patch to the cutting plane, observe the six location relations between triangular patch and cutting plane, and modify the original model as following:

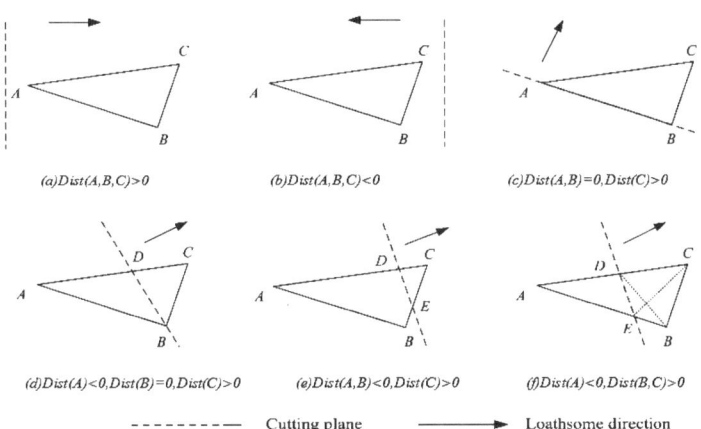

(a)Dist(A,B,C)>0   (b)Dist(A,B,C)<0   (c)Dist(A,B)=0,Dist(C)>0

(d)Dist(A)<0,Dist(B)=0,Dist(C)>0   (e)Dist(A,B)<0,Dist(C)>0   (f)Dist(A)<0,Dist(B,C)>0

- - - - - - - -   Cutting plane   ──────▶ Loathsome direction

Fig. 2. Location relationship between slice and triangular

(a)If all the distance Dist from the three vertexes of triangular patch to the cutting plane is greater than 0, then the triangular patch will be preserved in the original model. As Fig.2.(a) shows;

(b)If the distance Dist from the three vertexes of triangular patch to the cutting plane is less than 0, or the distance Dist from two vertexes of triangular patch to the cutting plane is less than 0 and the distance from another vertex of triangular patch to the cutting plane is equal to 0,then the triangular patch will be deleted from the original model. As Fig.2. (b) shows;

(c) If the distance Dist from two vertexes of triangular patch to the cutting plane is equal to 0, and the distance Dist from another vertex of triangular patch to the cutting plane is greater than 0, then the triangular patch will be preserved in the original model. As Fig.2. (c) shows;

(d) If one distance Dist is equal to 0, one distance Dist is less than 0, and one distance Dist is greater than 0. As Fig.2.(d) shows; then obtain the UCS of the intersection D, and put the information of the vertex B,D and the edge BD into the CEdgeVertex and CEdge structure, and separately form vertex linked list and edge linked list, replace vertex A of the original model by vertex D, replace $\triangle ABC$ by $\triangle DBC$;

(e) If two distance Dist is less than 0, and the other distance Dist is greater than 0, As Fig.2.(e) shows; then obtain UCS of the intersection D,E; put the information of vertex D,E and the edge DE into the CEdgeVertex and CEdge structure, and separately form vertex linked list and edge linked list, replace vertex A,B of the original model by vertex D, E; replace $\triangle ABC$ by $\triangle DBC$;

(f) If two distance Dist is greater than 0, and the other distance Dist is less than 0, As Fig.2.(f) shows; then obtain UCS of the intersection D,E; put the information of vertex D,E and the edge DE into the CEdgeVertex and CEdge structure, and separately form vertex linked list and edge linked list, the $\triangle ABC$ become quadrangle DEBC, and can divide the quadrangle into $\triangle DEB$ and $\triangle DBC$,or $\triangle DEC$ and $\triangle EBC$.

Dissection for the stratigraphic model, the algorithm is described as follows:

STEP 1: take the first triangular patch from triangular patchs that composed the stratigraphic model TEN, then assign it to the pointer CTriangle *Tri_ptr; (CTriangle has been defined in Section 2.

STEP 2: calculate the distance from each vertex of triangular patch Tri_ptr to the cutting plane: Dist(A),Dist(B),Dist(C);

STEP 3: For Dist (A), Dist (B) and Dist (C), modify the stratigraphic model according to the six location relations of triangular patch and cutting plane described in Fig.3. Write the information of the insection's coordinates and the edges into the CEdgeVertex and Cedge structure, then connected them into linked list Vertex_ptr and Edge_ptr;

STEP 4: modify Tri_ptr to make it point to the next adjacent triangular patch, if Tri_ptr is null, then go to STEP 5, else go to STEP 2;

STEP 5: return the insertion linked list Vertex_ptr and the formed edge linked list Edge_ptr of the cutting plane and triangular patch.

3.3   The Generation of Cutting Plane

In order to get the cutting plane, need to carry constrained Delaunay triangulation on generated polygon, this paper uses the mixed algorithm based on a combination of point insertion and polygon dissection, the algorithm is as follows:

Algorithm 1: constrained Delaunay triangulation based on a combination of point insertion and polygon dissection

STEP 1: initialize triangle linked list Tri_ptr=null, m=1;

STEP 2: determine the amount of points and the maximum value and the minimum value of x, y according to the point data linked list in the cutting plane, establish grid index for the point data. Formula (1) can calculate the length of ranks:

$$average = 4*sqrt((long)(maxx-minx)*(maxy-miny)/total\_v)/3 \qquad (1)$$

Formula (2) can calculate the number of rows and columns of grid:

$$\begin{cases} row = (int)((max\ y - min\ y)/average) + 1 \\ col = (int)((max\ x - min\ x)/average) + 1 \end{cases} \qquad (2)$$

Formula (3) can calculate the ranks location index of any point in the grid:

$$\begin{cases} m = (int)((point\ y - min\ y)/average) \\ n = (int)((point\ x - min\ x)/average) \end{cases} \qquad (3)$$

maxx, maxy, minx, miny are respectively the max abscissa, max ordinate, min abscissa, min abscissa, total_v is the total number of points. Pointx, pointy are the abscissa, ordinate of a point.

STEP 3: sort all the vertexes in every polygon linked list Profile_ptr[m] anticlockwise and save these vertexes in linked list Vertex_ptr, two adjacent vertexes create a constraint edge, put it into Edge_ptr and set a FLAG at the end of Edge_ptr;

STEP 4: make all of the edges in Edge_ptr as basic edges, use the maximum angle criterion to generate around triangles (refer to algorithm 2), update the data information of point, put the new edge into edge linked list Edge_ptr(that is insert a new edge after the FLAG at the end of Edge_ptr), put the new triangle into triangle linked list Tri_ptr, update the information of basic edge;

STEP 5: start from the next edge of FLAG(that is the first none-constrained edge) in edge linked list Edge_ptr, get it out and make it as a basic edge, apply the algorithm of maximum angle criterion toward left then generate a new triangulation network, update the data information of point, put the new edge into the edge linked list Edge_ptr, put the new triangle into the triangle linked list Tri_ptr, update the information of basic edge;

STEP 6: start from the next edge of FLAG in the edge linked list Edge_pt, for the none-constrained edge in around triangles, judge whether the edge intersect other edge that composed by the points around the edge.

STEP 7: m=m+1, repeat STEP 3, 4, 5, 6 until traverse all the polygons.

Algorithm 2: regard constrained edge as basic edge and generate around triangles

STEP 1: regard the constrained edge as the basic edge, determine the third point of the around triangle according to the start point and end point of the basic edge and its polygon .

STEP 2: according to maximum angle criterion, first, search the two eligible third points; if there is not the third point, then expand one grid and continue to search; if find the eligible third point, go to STEP 4, else go to STEP 3;

STEP 3: if still not find the eligible point even expand to all the points, that means this constrained edge is the outermost constrained boundary, and does not exist a left or right triangle, Edge_ptr=Edge_ptr->next, go to STEP 2;

STEP 4: put the triangle formed with the third point and the current edge into triangle linked list.

The process of generating a profile with this algorithm can be summarized as four steps.(1) Sort polygon's points anticlockwise;(2) Generate the grid index of point data;(3) Generate a triangulation network based on constrained edge;(4) Carry optimization on the triangulation network.

4   Simulation Example

The system program code uses C/C++ and IDL, and has been successfully applied in mining subsidence 3D visualization system--3D Subsidence, which developed independent. 3D stratum modeling data mainly come from random distribution of each drill data, take each drillhole as a record, each record includes drillhole coordinates and the depth and thickness of each stratum. In order to obtain ideal modeling effect, we use interpolation method to encrypt data point, then take the random distribution borehole data girding by stratum.

The screen shot of the working face subsidence stratum modeling and 3D visualization simulation results by 3D Subsidence system shown in Fig.3. The picture shows the effect drawing of subsidence stratum modelling, (a) is the 3D stratum effect drawing , (b) is the 3D stratum effect drawing with remote sensing map.

Fig.4. shows the slice of mining subsidence stratum; (a) is the slice that is perpendicular to the y-axis, (b) is the coexistence slice that is perpendicular to the x-axis and y-axis; (c) are the slices that are perpendicular to the y-axis; (d) are the slices that are perpendicular to the x-axis.

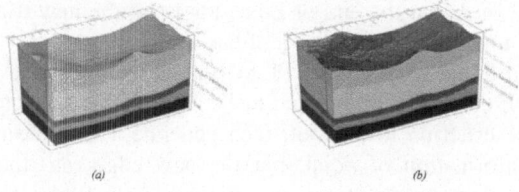

Fig. 3. Three-dimensional visualization of mining subsidence effect picture

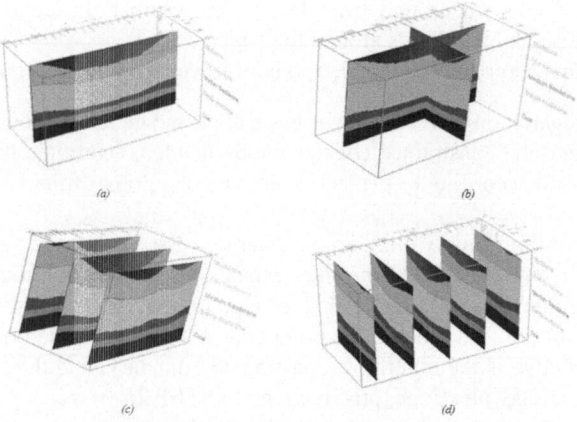

Fig. 4. Slices of subsidence stratum effect picture

5 Conclusions

(1) We make a classification, summarize, accumulation to the 3D geology phenomena, put forward multi-DEMs and mixed tetrahedron grid 3D stratum model (DEMs-TEN), the model uses multi-DEMs to structure the earth's surface and layer geology surfaces, and uses TEN to structure interlayer geologic-mass with the accurate express of face object.

(2) Based on the DEMs-TEN mixed model, we put forward a stratum cutting algorithm. The cutting algorithm creates slices by obtaining the internal information of DEMs-TEN mixed model, it makes technical staff convenient to check the geologic situation of internal stratum and provides detailed geological conditions to reveal the details of internal stratum and explain stratum space distribution law.

Acknowledgments. This work was supported by Research & Development Program of Shandong Educational Commission (No.J09LG54).

References

[1] Wu, L., Shi, W.: The geographic information system principle and algorithm, pp. 48–62. Science Press, Beijjing (2003)

[2] Sun, M., Chen, J., Zhang, X.: A 3DCM Data Model Based on Surface Partition. Acta Geodaetica et Cartographica Sinica 29(3), 257–265 (2000)

[3] Burford, D.J., Ger, L., Blake, E.H., et al.: A seismic modelling environment as a research and teaching tool for 3-D subsurface modelling. International Journal of Applied Earth Observation and Geoinformation 2(2), 69–77 (2000)

[4] Galera, C., Bennis, C., Moretti, I., et al.: Construction of coherent 3D geological blocks. Computers & Geosciences 29(8), 971–984 (2003)

[5] Wu, Q., Xu, H., Zou, X.: An effective method for 3D geological modeling with multi-source data integration. Computers & Geosciences 31(1), 35–43 (2005)

[6] Silvennoinen, H., Kozlovskaya, E.: 3D structure and physical properties of the Kuhmo Greenstone Belt (eastern Finland): Constraints from gravity modelling and seismic data and implications for the tectonic setting. Journal of Geodynamics 43(3), 358–373 (2007)

[7] Lan, H., Derek Martin, C., Lim, C.H.: RockFall analyst: A GIS extension for three-dimensional and spatially distributed rockfall hazard modeling. Computers & Geosciences 33(2), 262–279 (2007)

[8] Kaufmann, O., Martin, T.: 3D geological modelling from boreholes, cross-sections and geological maps, application over former natural gas storages in coal mines. Computers & Geosciences 34(3), 278–290 (2008)

[9] Calcagno, J.P., Chilès, G., Guillen, C.A.: Geological modelling from field data and geological knowledge: Part I. Modelling method coupling 3D potential-field interpolation and geological rules. Physics of the Earth and Planetary Interiors 171(1-4), 147–157 (2008)

Images Registration Based on Mutual Information and Nonsubsampled Contourlet Transform

Dandan Tian, Xian-bin Wen, Hai-xia Xu, and Ming Lei

Tianjin Key Laboratory of Intelligence Computing
and Novel Software Technology
Tianjin University of Technology, 300191, Tianjin, China
dandantianokok@163.com

Abstract. Aiming at the problem that how to improve the accuracy of image registration, this paper presents an approach for image registration based on mutual information and non-subsampled contourlet transform. First of all, the reference image and the floating image are decomposed with nonsubsampled contourlet transform. Secondly, register approximate component of the floating image from the highest level to the lowest level based mutual information. Finally, the new image is obtained. Experimental results on remote sensing images demonstrate that the presented method can improve the accuracy.

Keywords: Mutual information, registration, nonsubsampled contourlet transform.

1 Introduction

Image registration is the process of establishing point-by-point correspondence between two images obtained from a same scene. It is very important in image processing. Image registration can transform the images which are taken at different time, in different angles, or through two different sensors into the same coordinate system. In medical images, satellite remote sensing images, astronomical images, astronomical-borne SAR images, image mosaic, and many other areas of image processing, image registration is an important step. In astronomy research, in order to obtain a larger area of the astronomical view, the images got at different time will be spliced [1] [2]. Therefore, the image registration is needed.

In general, image registration methods could be divided into two categories: feature-based and intensity-based. The feature-based methods which use feature points, line and surface in the images often involve extraction of features to be matched. Consequently the performance of registration algorithm is affected by the feature extraction. As for some images, some important features may not commonly exist in both images, therefore, instead of extracting salient features, gradient information is used in several methods. However, gradient magnitudes may not be correlated due to different contrasts between images. On the contrary, intensity-based approaches use the intensity of whole images and find the mapping by optimizing

H. Deng et al. (Eds.): AICI 2011, Part II, LNAI 7003, pp. 304–311, 2011.

some criterion functions, the accuracy of these methods is not limited by the feature extraction. Among the existing intensity-based methods, mutual information (MI) is one of the most popular methods [3-7]. It has attracted more attention currently because of its advantages of measuring the similarity between images. However, it takes a long time to search the global registration transformation by optimizing MI similarity measure, which could not be used in real time system.

In this paper, we proposed image registration based on the nonsubsampled contourlet transform (NSCT) and mutual information(MI) to increase the efficiency and accuracy of entire registration procedure. This article is organized as follows. In section 2, we describe the principle of mutual information, and in section 3, we describe the principle of the nonsubsampled contourlet. An image registration procedure is presented in Section 4. Experimental results and discussion are presented in Section 5. Finally, conclusions are drawn in Section 6.

2   The Principle of Mutual Information

According to information theory, MI is a measurement of statistical correlation between two images, or the amount of information that one contains about the other. Assume A and B denote two images, their MI is defined as:

$$I(A,B) = H(A) + H(B) - H(A,B) \tag{1}$$

The items in the right hand of equation (1) are calculated respectively by

$$H(A) = \sum_a -P_A(a)\log P_A(a),$$

$$H(B) = \sum_a -P_B(b)\log P_B(b), \tag{2}$$

$$H(A,B) = \sum_a -P_{A,B}(a,b)\log P_{A,B}(a,b).$$

where $H(A)$ and $H(B)$ are the entropies of A and B, $H(A,B)$ is their joint entropy, $P_A(a)$ and $P_B(b)$ are the marginal probability mass functions, and $P_{A,B}(a,b)$ is the joint probability mass function, a and b denote two pixel values in A and B respectively. Suppose h is the joint histogram of this image pair, these probability mass functions can be computed by [4]

$$P_{A,B}(a,b) = \frac{h(a,b)}{\sum_{a,b} h(a,b)},$$

$$P_A(a) = \sum_b P_{A,B}(a,b),$$

$$P_B(a) = \sum_a P_{A,B}(a,b). \tag{3}$$

From the above formulas, we can see that the joint histogram h determines the MI between two images. Given the intensity information in A, essentially, $H(A,B)$ estimates the uncertainty of the intensity information and $I(A,B)$ estimates the decrease of uncertainty at the corresponding location in B. That is to say, MI can be used to measure the statistical dependency between two images or to predict information of B from A. The traditional MI based registration criterion shows that the two images should be registered when $I(A,B)$ is maximal.

3 The Principle of the Nonsubsampled Contourlet

3.1 Nonsubsampled Pyramid

The nonsubsampled contourlet transform (NSCT), which is a flexible multi-scale, multi-direction, and shift-invariant image decomposition [9]. The NSCT is based on a nonsubsampled pyramid structure and nonsubsampled directional filter banks. Fig. 1 indicates an example of the decomposition of the image implemented by NSP.

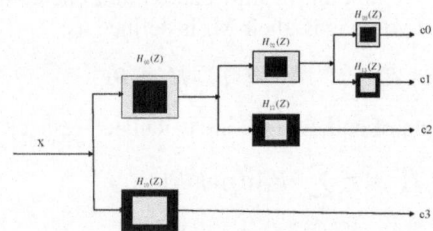

Fig. 1. An example of the decomposition of the image implemented by NSP

The nonsubsampled pyramid (NSP) frame in the NSCT is similar to the Laplace Transform of the image coding; both of them have the form of multi-resolution. The basic idea of the NSP transform is as follows. First of all, the low-resolution subband image is extracted from original image using the method of the low-pass filtering.

$$q[n] = \sum_{k \in Z^{\theta}} c[Mk] g[n-k]$$

(4)

Where $x(Mk)$ is the input original image, $h(nk)$ is the low-pass filter, $c(n)$ is the low-resolution subband.

$$c[n] = \sum_{k \in Z^{\theta}} x[Mk] h[n-k].$$

(5)

$$q[n] = \sum_{k \in Z^{\theta}} c[Mk] g[n-k]$$

(6)

$$d[n] = c[n] - q[n].\tag{7}$$

Where $c(Mk)$ is the subband image, $g(nk)$ is the corresponding high-pass filtering function, $q(n)$ is the reconstruction of image, $d(n)$ is the difference image.

3.2 Nonsubsampled Direction Filter Bank

Compared to other multi-resolution transform methods which decompose the images into the same directions at every level subband such as wavelet transform, NSCT can decompose the image into 2^p directions at each level subband, where the p is a different integer value. The ideal frequency response for a NSDFB is shown in Fig. 2.

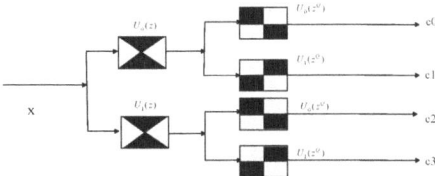

Fig. 2. An example of the decomposition of the image implemented by NSDFP

To obtain finer directional decomposition, we construct NSDFB by iterated this nonsubsampled filter banks. For the next level, we upsample all filters by a quincunx matrix given by:

$$Q = \begin{Bmatrix} 1 & 1 \\ 1 & -1 \end{Bmatrix}\tag{8}$$

The equivalent filters of this 2-level cascading NSDFB are given by:

$$
\begin{aligned}
y_0 &: U_0^{eq}(z) = U_0(z)U_0(z^Q) \\
y_1 &: U_1^{eq}(z) = U_0(z)U_1(z^Q) \\
y_2 &: U_2^{eq}(z) = U_1(z)U_0(z^Q) \\
y_3 &: U_3^{eq}(z) = U_1(z)U_1(z^Q)
\end{aligned}
\tag{9}
$$

We can see that the output y_0 in Fig. 2 corresponds to the direction "1" in Fig. 3, the output y_1 corresponds to the direction "2", the output y_2 corresponds to the direction "3" and the output y_3 corresponds to the direction "4". As a result of using the nonsubsampled directional filter banks, the transfer of the pixel in spatial domain corresponds to the movement of the coefficient in NSCT transform domain [9]; this character is known as shift-invariance.

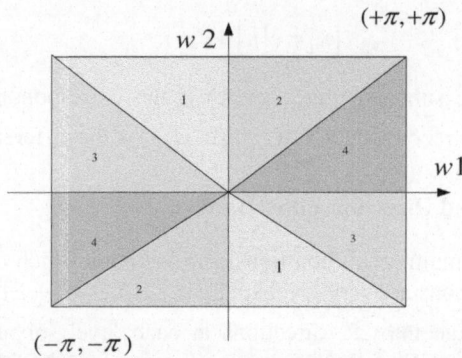

Fig. 3. Frequency divisions of a NSDFB

4   Image Registration Procedure

We suppose that $f_1(x, y)$ is the reference image, and $f_2(x, y)$ is the floating image. According to the method of image registration based on the mutual information and the principle of the contourlet transformation, the process of two image registration is as follows:

- Step 1: Both image $f_1(x, y)$ and $f_2(x, y)$ are decomposed with nonsubsampled contourlet transform. $LL_{f_1 j}$ and $LL_{f_2 j}$ is respectively the j level approximation of image $f_1(x, y)$ and $f_2(x, y)$.
- Step 2: Register approximate component of the highest level of image, and the meaning is to register $LL_{f_1 j}$ and $LL_{f_2 j}$ .The search strategy is Powell algorithm. The value I are calculated in every position of $LL_{f_1 j}$ and $LL_{f_2 j}$ .We can choose the coefficient (θ_N, x_N, y_N) when I is the maximum. $LL_{f_2 j}$ is rotated and translated.
- Step 3: Repeat iteration based on the registration results of prior level until that the process of registration image have done. So we can get the result (θ_0, x_0, y_0) and the new image.

5   The Results of Image Registration

According to the figure 4 and figure 5, image (a) and (b) are decomposed to 3 levels with nonsubsampled contourlet transform. Maxflat filters, which derived from 1-D using maximally flat mapping function with 4 vanishing moments, are used in nonsubsampled pyramid structure. Diamond maxflat filters obtained from a three stage ladder are used in the nonsubsampled direction filter bank. Then register approximate component of every level based MI and image (d) is obtained. The coefficient (θ_0, x_0, y_0) of figure 4 is (18, 64, 0), I is 1.353. We got image (c) from image registration based MI.The coefficient (θ_0, x_0, y_0) of figure 4 is (4,-20, 0) and I is 0.58886 .On the basis of figure 5, the coefficients (θ_0, x_0, y_0) of image (d) is (1,0,2), I is 1.1737. The coefficients (θ_0, x_0, y_0) of image (c) is $(1, 0, 2)$ and I is 1.1737.

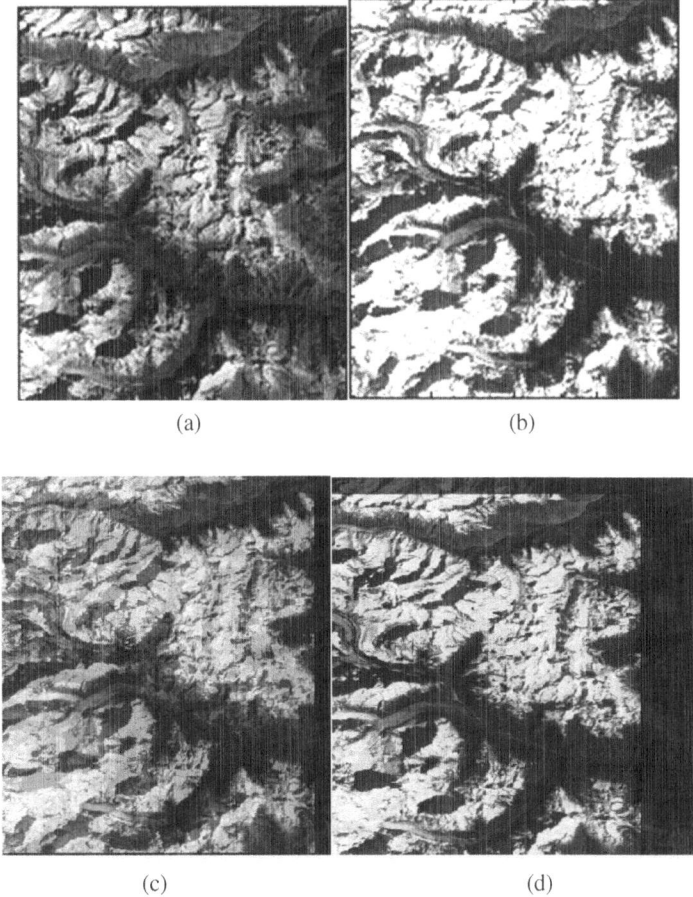

(a)   (b)

(c)   (d)

Fig. 4. (a) The reference image (b) the floating image (c) The resulting of image registration based MI (d) The resulting of image registration based MI and NSCT

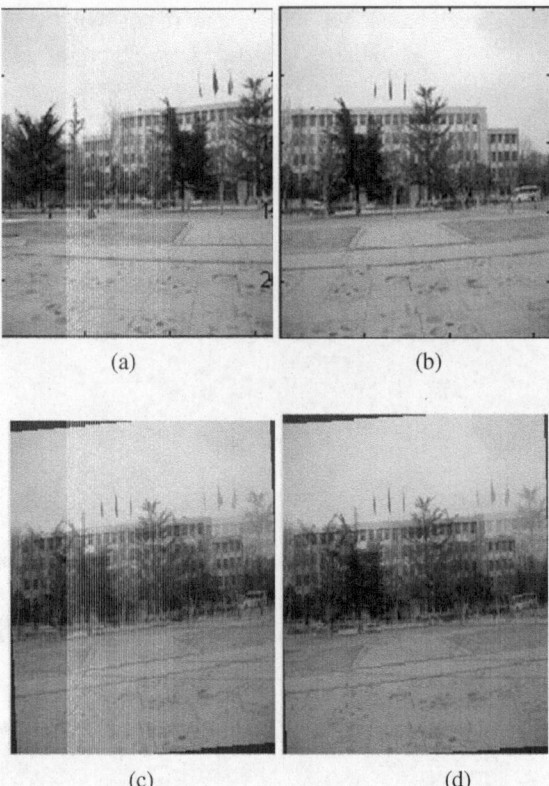

(a)   (b)

(c)   (d)

Fig. 5. (a) The reference image (b) the floating image (c) The resulting of image registration based MI (d) The resulting of image registration based MI and NSCT

6 Conclusion

In this paper, we have presented a new approach based on the nonsubsampled contourlet transform and MI to register images. The performance of the proposed registration algorithm based on NSCT and MI was demonstrated. The experimental results show that the registration accuracy is relatively high.

Acknowledgments. This work was supported by National 863 plans project (Grant No.2010AA12220107), National Natural Science Foundation of China (Grant No. 60872064), the Natural Science Foundation of Tianjin (Grant No. 08JCYBJC12300 and 08JCYBJC12200).

References

1. Starck, J.L., Murtagh, F.: Astronomical Image and Signal Processing-Looking at Noise Information and scale. Journal, IEEE Signal Processing Magazine, Astronomical image and signal processing 18, 30–40 (2001)

2. Christian, D.J., Pollacco, D.L.: The WASP Project and the Super WASP Cameras. Journal, Astronomic Nachrichten 327, 800–802 (2006)
3. Xu, P., Yao, D.: A study on medical image registration by mutual information with pyramid data structure. Computers in Biology and Medicine 37, 320–327 (2007)
4. Studholme, C., Hill, D.L.G., Hawks, D.: An overlap invariant entropy measure of 3D medical image alignment. Pattern Recognition 32, 71–86 (1999)
5. Pluim, P.W., Maintz, B., Viergever, M.A.: Image Registration by Maximization of Combined Mutual Information and Gradient Information. IEEE Transactions on Medical Imaging 19(8), 809–814 (2000)
6. Kim, Y.S., Lee, H., Ra, B.: Multi-sensor image registration based on intensity and edge orientation information. Pattern Recognition 41, 3356–3365 (2008)
7. Chen, H.M., Varshney, P.K., Arora, M.K.: Performance of mutual information similarity measure for registration of multitemporal remote sensing images. IEEE Tran. Geoscience and Remote Sensing 41(11), 2445–2454 (2003)
8. Cunha, A.L., Zhou, J.P., Do, M.N.: The Nonsubsampled Contourlet Transform: Theory, Design, and Applications. Journal, IEEE Transactions on Image Processing 15, 3089–3101 (2006)

Signal Reconstruction Based on Block Compressed Sensing

Liqing Sun, Xianbin Wen, Ming Lei, Haixia Xu,
Junxue Zhu, and Yali Wei

Tianjin Key Laboratory of Intelligence Computing and
Novel Software Technology
Tianjin University of Technology, 300191,
Tianjin, China
sunliqing1217@126.com

Abstract. Compressed sensing (CS) is a new area of signal processing for simultaneous signal sampling and compression. The CS principle can reduce the computation complexity at the encoder side and transmission costs, but has huge computation load at the decoder. In this paper, a simple block-based compressed sensing reconstruction for still images is proposed. Firstly, original image is divided into small blocks, and each block is sampled independently. Secondly, the image block is divided into flat and non-flat block, and processed with different ways. Finally, mean filter and an improvement total-variation (TV) method is sued to optimize image. Simulation results show that the proposed algorithm can effectively remove the blocking artifacts and reduce the computation complexity.

Keywords: Compressed sensing, blocking artifacts, OMP, TV.

1 Introduction

Recent years have seen significant interest in the paradigm of compressed sensing (CS). It builds upon the groundbreaking work by Candès and Donoho, who showed that under certain conditions, signals can be sampled at sub-Nyquist rates via linear projection onto a random basis while still enabling exact reconstruction of the original signals [1, 2]. CS is a new technique for simultaneous data sampling and compression.

However, most of existing works in CS remain at the theoretical study. As applied to 2D image, CS faces several challenges including a computationally expensive reconstruction process and huge memory required to store the random sampling operator [3]. So this algorithm is not suitable for real-time processing of large image. Recently Lu Gan have proposed Block compressed sensing theory [4], while using a block-based sampling will cause blocking artifacts. Later Fan Xiaowei using hard threshold in the contourlet domain and projection onto the convex set to reduce blocking artifacts [5]. According to the characteristics of CS, we classify the blocks into two types by contrasting their mean square error. We use different method to deal with Flat blocks and non-flat block in this paper.

H. Deng et al. (Eds.): AICI 2011, Part II, LNAI 7003, pp. 312–319, 2011.

This paper is organized as follow. An overview of compressive sensing is given in section 2. Section 3 describes improved block-based algorithm for compressing, and discusses de-blocking algorithm. Section 4 shows the algorithm description. The simulation results for still images are reported in section 5. Section 6 concludes with a discussion of conjectured directions of future inquiry.

2 Compressed Sensing

CS is used for natural signals. The signals combine two elements: sparsity and incoherence; the former is depending on the signals itself, and the latter is depending on the measuring systems. Consider a length-N, real valued signal f, we project it into a lower dimension:

$$y = \Phi f . \tag{1}$$

However, the reconstruction of f from y is generally ill-posed. If f has a sparse representation in a known transform domain Ψ (e.g., the DCT and the wavelet), then f can be well approximated using only K non-zero entries.

$$f = \Psi x \tag{2}$$

where Ψ is an $N \times N$ sparse matrix, and x is an $N \times 1$ sparse vector. Then we can get the following formula:

$$y = \Phi f = \Phi \Psi x = \Theta x \tag{3}$$

The signal f can be recovered from the inverse transform of (2) after getting x from the values of y and Θ by solving (3). Exact recovery is possible at the condition that x is sufficiently sparse, i.e., x can be represented by K non-zero components, so the number of unknowns is less than observations ($M > K$). In this case, we need to make sure the positions of the non-zero coefficients.

Two important problems in CS are: how to design Φ and what signal reconstruction algorithm should be chosen. The purpose of designing Φ is to use fewer observations to recover original signals. The ideal recovery procedure searches for x is to find the smallest l_0 norm consistent with the observed y.

$$\hat{x} = \min \| x \|_0 \ \ s.t. \ \ y = \Theta x \tag{4}$$

Recently, the signal reconstruction algorithms usually used are Basis Pursuit (BP), Matching Pursuit (MP), total-variation (TV) reconstruction, and so on. A popular class of sparse recovery algorithms is based on the idea of iterative greedy pursuit. The earliest ones include the matching pursuit (MP) and orthogonal matching pursuit (OMP). MP change (4) to (5):

$$\hat{x} = \min \| x \|_0 \ \ s.t. \ \ \| \Theta x - y \|_2^2 < \xi \tag{5}$$

where ξ is a small const. The basic idea of MP is to search the atom which best matches the signal from atom dictionary (i.e., Θ), calculate the signal residual, and then choose the atom which best matches the residual. Through the local optimization we can find the position of each non-zero coefficients. OMP search the non-zero coefficients in orthogonal directions in order to speed up the convergence rate.

3   Reconstruction Algorithm for Block CS

3.1   Block Compressed Sensing

An $N_1 \times N_2$ image is divided into small blocks with size of $n_1 \times n_2$ each. Let f_i represent the vectorized signal of the i-th block through raster scanning, $i =1$, $2... n$, and $n = N_1 N_2 / n_1 n_2$. We can get a $m \times 1$ sampled vector y_B through the following linear transformation:

$$y_B = \Phi_B f_i \tag{6}$$

where f_i is an $n_1 n_2 \times 1$ vector, Φ_B is an $m \times n_1 n_2$ measurement matrix, $m \ll n_1 n_2$.

Note that block CS is memory efficient as we just need to store a $m \times n_1 n_2$ Gaussian ensemble Φ_B, rather than a full $M \times N_1 N_2$ (i.e., $nm \times nn_1 n_2$)one. Small requires less memory in storage and faster implementation, while large offers better reconstruction performance [5]. The main advantages of block-based CS can be summarized as follow: (a) Measurement operator can be easily stored and implemented through a random under-sampled filter bank; (b) Block-based measurement is more advantageous for real-time applications as the encoder does not need to send the sampled data until the whole image is measured; (c) Since each block is processed independently, the initial solution can be easily obtained and the reconstruction process can be substantially speeded up [4].

3.2   Classify the Blocks

CS utilizes the characteristic that the signal is sparsity in some transform domain to reconstruct the signal, and the small coefficients can be ignored. At wavelet transform domain, small coefficients are in high frequency subbands, so the high frequency will be lost after reconstruction. Flat blocks contain little high frequency, so it will have high reconstruction precision; but non-flat blocks contain some texture (i.e. high frequency), the reconstruction precision will be lower than flat blocks. According to their different characteristics, we need to classify the blocks and deal with them in different ways.

We divide the image blocks into flat and non-flat blocks according to their variance. Suppose $f = \{ p_{m_1 m_2} \}$, the size is $N_1 \times N_2$, the mean value and mean square deviation of the full image can be calculate as follow [6]:

$$\mu = \frac{1}{N_1 \times N_2} \sum_{m_1 =1}^{N_1} \sum_{m_2 =1}^{N_2} p_{m_1 m_2} \tag{7}$$

$$\sigma^2 = \frac{1}{N_1 \times N_2} \sum_{m_1=1}^{N_1} \sum_{m_2=1}^{N_2} (p_{m_1 m_2} - \mu)^2 \tag{8}$$

where μ is the mean value, and σ^2 is the mean square deviation for the full image.

As to each block $f_i = \{b_{m_1 m_2}\}$ $i = 1, \ldots, n$; $n = N_1 N_2 / n_1 n_2$, the mean value and mean square deviation can be calculated as follow:

$$\mu_i = \frac{1}{n_1 \times n_2} \sum_{m_1=1}^{n_1} \sum_{m_2=1}^{n_2} b_{m_1 m_2} \tag{9}$$

$$\sigma_i^2 = \frac{1}{n_1 \times n_2} \sum_{m_1=1}^{n_1} \sum_{m_2=1}^{n_2} (b_{m_1 m_2} - \mu_i)^2 \tag{10}$$

where μ_i is the mean value, and σ_i^2 is the mean square deviation for each block.

Compare σ_i^2 with σ^2 as the following formula:

$$t_i = \begin{cases} 1 & \sigma_i^2 \geq \lambda \sigma^2 \\ 0 & \sigma_i^2 < \lambda \sigma^2 \end{cases} \tag{11}$$

If $t_i = 1$, the block is non-flat; and if $t_i = 0$, the block is flat.

The flat blocks contain little texture and high frequency, so K will be small, then use only a few observations and iterations can exact recovery the blocks. The non-flat blocks contain too much texture, the measurements and iterations should be more than the flat. In this way, we can reduce the false edges between non-flat blocks and the flat ones caused by the different reconstruction precision. The quality of the reconstruction is improved without increasing computational complexity.

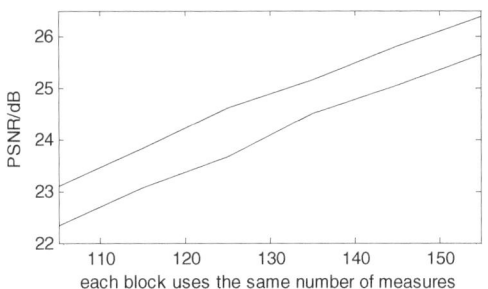

Fig. 1. The PSNR for Different Methods. The curve on the top is the PSNR for the proposed method, and the other is the PSNR for original method.

Fig.1 is the simulation result for the proposed method and original method when use the same measurements and iterations. The result show that deal with the two type blocks in different ways can improve the PSNR about 0.8dB.

3.3 Reduce the Blocking Effect

Although block classification can improve the image quality, there still remain some blocking artifacts. The false boundaries between non-flat blocks and the boundaries between flat blocks are not very obvious if there are enough measurements. But the false boundaries between non-flat blocks and flat blocks are especially obvious, so next we will focus on the de-blocking algorithm. We use meaning filter process the boundaries first, and then calculate minimized TV.

The sparsity of image gradient is judged by TV. The formula for TV is as follow:

$$TV(u) = \sum_{i,j} |[u(i+1, j) - u(i, j)]^2 + [u(i, j+1) - u(i, j)]^2| \qquad (12)$$

u is the original image. Calculate the minimized TV is to ensure that the D-values between close pixels are as small as possible. Minimized TV is calculated by (13):

$$Min_i \ TV(i) + \frac{\lambda}{2} \| i - u \|_2^2 \qquad (13)$$

i is the image after optimization, λ is a balanced parameter. We use the gradient descent algorithm to minimize the TV.

Before minimize the TV, add two adjacent Columns and rows to each block. A column or a row from adjacent blocks will participate in the calculation of minimized TV. Then every pixel in the border of the blocks will be calculated twice, and the D-values between adjacent pixels will be as small as possible, so blocking artifacts are weakened. Simulation result is in figure 2(b). For comparison, figure 2(a) is the result for dealing with each block alone. As we can see in Fig.2, minimized TV can eliminate the noise inside blocks, and the quality of image is improved.

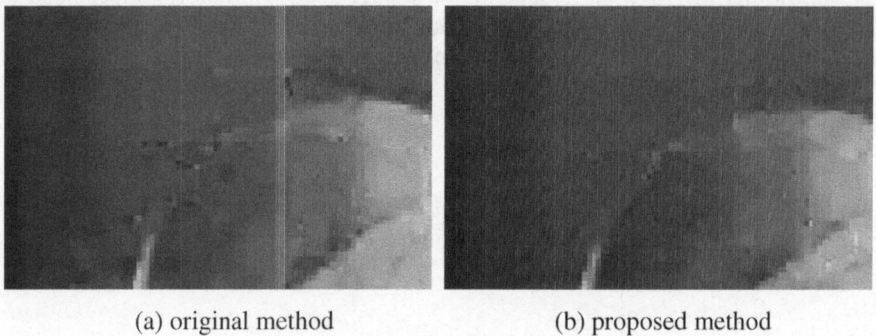

     (a) original method   (b) proposed method

Fig. 2. The Compare for Different Methods

4 Algorithm Description

The procedure for block CS in this article is as follow:

Step1: Divide the image f into small blocks with size of $n_1 \times n_2$ each, sign f_i ;

Step2: Compute σ_i^2 with σ^2, then divide the blocks into flat and non-flat blocks according to (11);

Step3: Projection. Choose Φ_{B1} ($m_1 \times n_1 n_2$) for flat blocks, and Φ_{B2} ($m_2 \times n_1 n_2$) for non-flat blocks, $m_1 < m_2$;

Step4: OMP for recovery:

Input: matrix Θ, sampled vector y, sparsity level K.

Initialization: residual $r_0 = y$, index set $\Lambda_0 = \varnothing$, and the iteration counter $t = 1$.

a)   Find the index λ_t that solves the easy optimization problem:

$$\lambda_t = \arg\max_{j=1,\dots,N} |\langle r_{t-1}, \varphi_j \rangle|$$

b)   Augment the index set and the matrix of chosen atoms, Θ_0 is an empty matrix:

$$\Lambda_t = \Lambda_{t-1} \cup \{\lambda_t\}; \Theta_t = [\Theta_{t-1}, \varphi_{\lambda_t}]$$

c)   Solve a least squares problem to obtain a new signal estimate:

$$\hat{x}_t = \arg\min_{\hat{x}} \| y - \Theta_t \hat{x} \|_2$$

d)   Update the residual $r_t = y - \Theta_t \hat{x}_t$, $t = t+1$; return to Step a if $t < K$.

Output: $\hat{x}$, The value of the estimate $\hat{x}$ in component λ_j equals the j-th component of $\hat{x}_t$, others are zeros.

Step5: Process the boundaries between non-flat blocks and flat blocks by meaning filtering.

Step6: Add the adjacent Columns and rows to each block, and then optimize each block by minimizing the total variation.

5   Simulation Results

Sparse matrix Ψ and measurement matrix Φ must be incoherent, a Gaussian measurement vector is incoherent with most sparse matrix [8], so in this paper we choose a Gaussian measurement vector as Φ, and the wavelet transform domain as Ψ; the signal reconstruction algorithm is OMP; the size of each block is 16×16.

Fig.3 shows the reconstructed results. The original algorithm uses m observations. In this paper, the scale of flat blocks and non-flat blocks is 1:1, and $m_1 + m_2 = 2m$. According to experiences, let $m_1 = m - 30$, $m_2 = m + 30$, and the number of iterations is $0.3 \times m$. Fig.3 is the result when $m/n = 0.4$. As we can see, the PSNR values of these images constructed by the new algorithm are improved by about 2.5~3dB with the same number of CS measurements. In figure (b), the non-flat blocks (e.g. the edge of the hat and the eyes) have low reconstruction accuracy, the boundaries of non-flat blocks and flat blocks are clear. In figure (c), the proposed algorithm eliminates the obvious noise in non-flat blocks, and the false boundaries are weakened.

The Fig.4 shows the reconstructed results for boat image. The proposed method improved 3.4dB. From the enlarged view we can see that the proposed method used in (e) has high-accuracy, and the blocking artifacts are weakened. Compared with the original algorithm, the flat blocks use fewer measurements and iterations, but there is not much change in the result of the reconstruction.

Fig. 3. Block CS Reconstruction ($m / n = 0.4$).From left to right :(a)lena; (b)original method (PSNR=22.1578); (c)the proposed method(PSNR=25.0346)

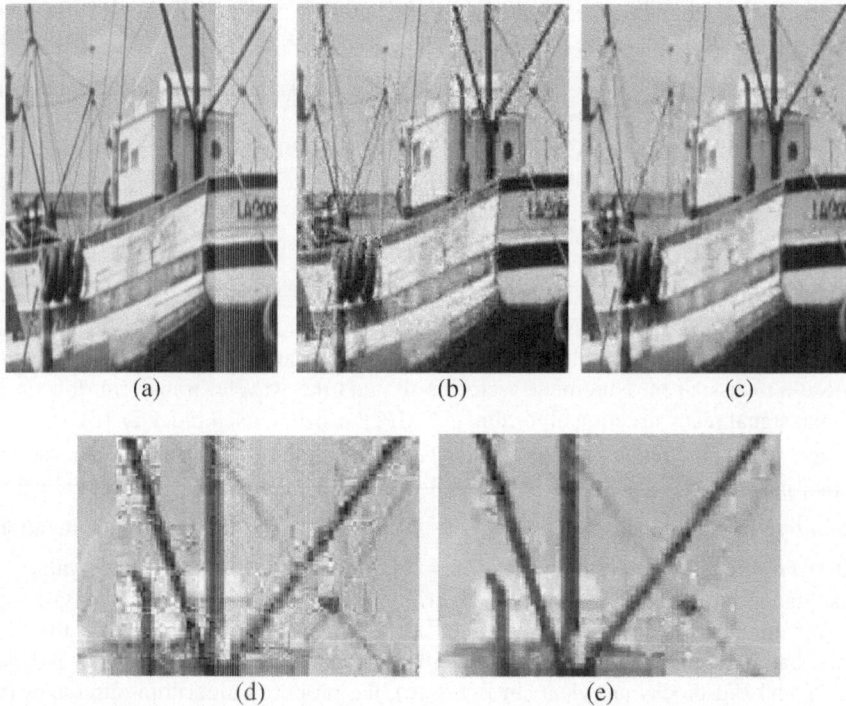

Fig. 4. Block CS Reconstruction ($m / n = 0.5$). (a)boat; (b)original method (PSNR=25.2477dB); (c)the proposed method(PSNR=28.6254dB), Figure (d) and (e) correspond to the mast part in (b) and (c).

6 Conclusions and Future Words

This paper has proposed a block compressed sensing reconstruction algorithm. We first divide the image blocks into flat and non-flat blocks, then deal with them in different ways. We use the mean filter and an improved TV method to optimize the image. This method removes the false boundaries between blocks and the noise in blocks, so improved the quality of image.

Block-based CS has great potential, however the relevant research still stay at the theoretical stage. The traditional de-blocking algorithms usually use post-processing methods, but CS utilizes the characteristic that the signal is sparsity in some transform domain; according to this feature, we can explore pre-processing algorithms, i.e., remove blocking effect at transform domain.

Acknowledgement. This work was supported by National 863 plans project (Grant No.2010AA12220107), National Natural Science Foundation of China (Grant No. 60872064), the Natural Science Foundation of Tianjin (Grant No. 08JCYBJC12300).

References

1. Candès, E.J.: Compressive sampling. In: Proceedings of the International Congress of Mathematicians, Madrid, Spain, pp. 1433–1452 (2006)
2. Donoho, D.L.: Compressed sensing. IEEE Trans. Inform. Theory 52, 1289–1306 (2006)
3. Mun, S., Fowler, J.E.: Block compressed sensing of images using directional transforms. In: IEEE International Conference on Image Processing, Cairo, Egypt, pp. 3021–3024 (November 2009)
4. Gan, L.: Block Compressed sensing of natural images. In: Proceedings of the International Conference on Digital Signal Processing, Cardiff, UK, pp. 403–406 (2007)
5. Fan, X.-w., Liu, Z., Liu, C.: Image reconstruction model using block compressed sensing. Computer Engineering and Applications 45(29), 153–155 (2009)
6. Zhang, X.-q., Gu, X.-d., Sun, H.-x.: Deblock Algorithm for Compressed Image Based on Adaptive Space Domain Filter. Computer Engineering 35(4) (February 2009)
7. Tropp, J.A., Gilbert, A.C.: Signal Recovery From Random Measurements Via Orthogonal Matching Pursuit. IEEE Transactions on Information Theory 53(12), 4655–4666 (2007)
8. Shi, G.-m., Liu, D.-h., Gao, D.-h.: Advances in Theory and Application of Compressed Sensing. Acta Electronica Sinica 37(5) (May 2009)

Image Segmentation Using the Multiphase Level Set in Multiple Color Spaces

Yonghong Zhang[1] and Yongqin Zhang[2]

[1] Practicing and Training Center, Shanghai Second Polytechnic University,
Shanghai 201209, P.R. China
[2] School of Information Engineering, North China University of Water Resources and Electric
Power, Zhengzhou 450011, P.R. China
{yonghongzhang,zyqwhu}@gmail.com

Abstract. The goal of image segmentation in imaging science is to solve the problem of partitioning an image into smaller disjoint homogeneous regions that share similar attributes. The novel technique of the multiphase level set based on principal component analysis (PCA) with adaptively selecting dominant factors for color image segmentation in color spaces is studied here. And simultaneously, the final segmentation is completed by a simple labeling scheme. Then the comparative study of the refined Chan-Vese method is done in multiple color spaces. The experimental results illustrate that the multiphase Chan-Vese algorithm with or without PCA has good segmentation results with fine adaptability in RGB, CIE XYZ, NTSC and YCbCr color spaces where the results of test image changes little. Nevertheless, the h1h2h3 color space, produce poor segmentation on the reliability and accuracy of a set of test images by performance analysis with evaluation indicators.

Keywords: Multiphase level set, principal component analysis, image segmentation, color space.

1 Introduction

The problem of segmenting images into coherent regions has been one of the foundational tasks in the field of image analysis, computer vision and system identification. And its aim is to partition a given image into its semantically significant sub-regions which contain distinct objects. The main goal of any image segmentation process consists in approaching a set of unconnected points that conform to certain characteristics including low-level and high-level approaches, such as color, texture, intensity, edge, spectrum, optical flow, gradient, velocity field, geometric properties, structure, or model. But standard approaches driven by low-level cues, such as texture, intensity, color and so forth, often fail in segmentation. To overcome this limitation, prior knowledge can be used to constrain the segmentation

H. Deng et al. (Eds.): AICI 2011, Part II, LNAI 7003, pp. 320–327, 2011.

process. So image segmentation needs to incorporate prior knowledge and to be flexible with respect to complicated shapes or topologies. It also needs to discriminate noise and textures (or structures). The accuracy of partition and efficiency in implementing these operations are two important criteria for evaluating an algorithm. Segmentation techniques can be divided in three categories, namely boundary-driven, region-driven, boundary and region-driven hybrid. Boundary-driven includes edge detectors, snakes/active contours [1,2], and active shape models. Deformable templates, statistical/clustering techniques, MRF-based techniques, and active appearance models, belong to region-driven. Active contours [3], graph-based techniques, and level set methods [4,5,6,7,8], fall into boundary and region-driven hybrid.

Here we present the common color spaces used in the image processing field. In this article we discuss multiphase level set with or without component analysis for color image segmentation in multiple color spaces. As level set algorithm is often used for grayscale image segmentation, we extend level set algorithm for vector image with or without PCA to partition color images. And then we comparatively study the performance of color image segmentation based on C-V method[9] with or without PCA which reduces the three dimensional images to two dimensional ones.

2   Basic Concepts and Techniques

2.1   Color Space

Color spaces, also called color models, can be expressed in many different ways, each with its advantages and drawbacks. Some representations are formulated to help humans select colors, and others are formulated to ease data processing in machines. And its choice depends on the priori knowledge and the specific applications, provide a rational method to sample, specify, order, manipulate and effectively display the object colors.

Each color space has its own property. RGB, whose information about the chromaticity (hue and saturation) and intensity components is dependent, is an additive color system based on tri-chromatic theory and nonlinear with visual perception. CIE is based on direct measurements of human color perception and it is a device independent color space. YIQ is often used for broadcasting, television, video and image compression schemes in communication. HSV and HSL based on lightness, hue and saturation components have been created for more convenient human interaction. As known to all, the range of pixel value with 8 bits depth in RGB color space is 0~255. Since the ranges of pixel values in different color spaces are often not the same, we may normalize some color space in accordance with RGB to compare segmentation results for convenience. Moreover, the normalized operation for different spaces is done before partitioning.

2.2 Review of the Multiphase Chan-Vese Model

Vese and Chan proposed active contour without edges [3] and its extension, i.e. the multiphase level set method [9] successively. The former method allows for triple junctions and other complex topologies through definitions of the partition, no vacuum and no overlap. The latter one with high computational cost, associates one level set function to each phase, and needs additional constraints to prevent vacuum and overlap. However, multiphase level set method needs more than one level set function to represent more than two segments. It is worth noting that more than two partitions and non-constant regions can be labeled using the multi-phase level set approach for image segmentation. The relation is that the level set algorithm with n level set functions can represent 2^n phases or segments.

Assume that the edges can be represented by one level set function ϕ, i.e. $C = \{(x, y) \mid \varphi(x, y) = 0\}$. Here u^+, u^- are C^1 functions on $\phi \geq 0$ and $\phi < 0$ respectively with an open set Ω. As in the 1-dimensional case, active contour model is to minimize the following energy minimization problem with respect to u^+, u^- and ϕ. So the corresponding level set variant with the steepest descent results is achieved in the following Euler-Lagrange equations:

$$\frac{\partial \phi}{\partial t} = \delta_\varepsilon(\phi)\left[\nabla\left(\frac{\nabla \phi}{|\nabla \phi|}\right) - \left|u^+ - u_0\right|^2 - \mu\left|\nabla u^+\right|^2 + \left|u^- - u_0\right|^2 + \mu\left|\nabla \mu^-\right|^2 \right] \tag{1}$$

Where $\partial / \partial \bar{n}$ represents the partial derivative in the normal direction $\bar{n}$ at the corresponding boundary. And the boundary condition of an implicit function $\phi = \phi(t, x, y)$ is $\partial \phi / \partial \bar{n} = 0$ on $\partial \Omega$.

And the object partition problem in 2-dimensional case can be solved using two level set functions without a priori knowledge about how many segments. And it is to minimize the general Mumford-Shah functional. By means of approximation, the associated Euler-Lagrange equations can be simplified to evolve ϕ_1 and ϕ_2 for each fixed t in a dynamic scheme with respect to u^{++}, u^{+-}, u^{-+} and u^{--} as follows:

$$\frac{\partial \phi_1}{\partial t} = \delta_\varepsilon(\phi_1)\left[\nabla\left(\frac{\nabla \phi_1}{|\nabla \phi_1|}\right) - \left|u^{++} - u_0\right|^2 H(\phi_2) \right.$$
$$-\mu\left|\nabla u^{++}\right|^2 H(\phi_2) - \left|u^{+-} - u_0\right|^2 (1 - H(\phi_2))$$
$$-\mu\left|\nabla u^{+-}\right|^2 (1 - H(\phi_2)) + \left|u^{-+} - u_0\right|^2 H(\phi_2)$$
$$+\mu\left|\nabla u^{-+}\right|^2 H(\phi_2) + \left|u^{--} - u_0\right|^2 (1 - H(\phi_2))$$
$$\left. +\mu\left|\nabla u^{--}\right|^2 (1 - H(\phi_2)) \right] \tag{2}$$

$$\frac{\partial \phi_2}{\partial t} = \delta_\varepsilon \left(\phi_2 \right) \left[\nu \nabla \left(\frac{\nabla \phi_2}{|\nabla \phi_2|} \right) - \left| u^{++} - u_0 \right|^2 H \left(\phi_1 \right) \right.$$

$$-\mu \left| \nabla u^{++} \right|^2 H \left(\phi_1 \right) + \left| u^{+-} - u_0 \right|^2 H \left(\phi_1 \right)$$

$$+\mu \left| \nabla u^{+-} \right|^2 H \left(\phi_1 \right) - \left| u^{-+} - u_0 \right|^2 \left(1 - H \left(\phi_1 \right) \right) \tag{3}$$

$$-\mu \left| \nabla u^{-+} \right|^2 H \left(1 - \left(\phi_1 \right) \right) + \left| u^{--} - u_0 \right|^2 \left(1 - H \left(\phi_1 \right) \right)$$

$$\left. +\mu \left| \nabla u^{--} \right|^2 \left(1 - H \left(\phi_1 \right) \right) \right]$$

3   Chen-Vese Method with Improvement

Principal component analysis (PCA) is a general method for modeling and segmenting such mixed data using a collection of subspaces. As a classical linear transform, it has been widely used in data analysis and compression [10,11]. This linear transform is based on the statistical representation of a random variable. The PCA involves the calculation of the eigenvalue decomposition of a data covariance matrix or singular value decomposition of a data matrix, usually after mean centering the data for each attribute. This mathematical procedure transforms a number of possibly correlated variables into a smaller number of uncorrelated variables called principal components. The first principal component accounts for as much of the variability in the data as possible, and each succeeding component accounts for as much of the remaining variability as possible. And now it is mostly used as a tool in exploratory data analysis to uncover unknown trends in the data and for making predictive models. The PCA that is founded on the multivariate analysis methods with eigenvectors, can be considered to reveal the internal structure of data in a way that explains the variance in the data. And it supplies the user with most informative viewpoint by reducing a higher-dimensional image to a lower-dimensional one.

The PCA, which is suitable for data sets in multiple dimensions, is a general method that reduces data dimensionality by performing a covariance analysis between factors. And it is closely related to factor analysis. Both of them can help reveal simpler patterns within complex set variables. These two methods seek to discover if much fewer variables called factors without much loss of information, can be used to express largely or entirely the observed variables. PCA on data provide a way to identify predominant factor expression patterns. When applied under different conditions, PCA will explore correlations between samples or elements. Finally, we come to the procedures of Chan-Vese method based on PCA for color image segmentation in color spaces.

Assume that a vector image $u_{0,i}(x, y, i)$ of size $P \times Q \times N$, is the ith channel of a color image on Ω, with $i = 1, \cdots, N$ channels. Each pixel location (x, y) is represented by an N channel vector $u_0(x, y)$ for $x = 1, 2, \cdots, P$ and $y = 1, 2, \cdots, Q$. Each channel component can be represented as $u_{0,i}, i = 1, 2, \cdots, N$. Then, the maximum-likelihood (ML) estimate of the mean is calculated as

$$\bar{u}_0 = \frac{1}{P \times Q} \sum_{x=1}^{P} \sum_{y=1}^{Q} u_0(x, y) \tag{4}$$

And the ML covariance matrix estimate by subtracting the mean value is

$$C_m = \frac{1}{P \times Q} \sum_{x=1}^{P} \sum_{y=1}^{Q} \left(u_0(x, y) - \bar{u}_0 \right) \left(u_0(x, y) - \bar{u}_0 \right)^T \tag{5}$$

Here C_m is $N \times N$ real and symmetric matrix. Then, this covariance matrix is used to solve for eigenvectors $v_i, i = 1, 2, \cdots, N$, corresponding to eigenvalues such that $\lambda_1 > \lambda_2 > \cdots > \lambda_N$.

After selecting appropriate components and forming a feature vector, the decorrelated color components can be written as

$$I_i(x, y) = v_i^T u_0(x, y), \quad i = 1, 2, \cdots, N \tag{6}$$

As a result of applying PCA, the data is projected along the directions where it varies most. And the variation of I_1 is selected as the more appropriate component than that of other channels. At last, color image segmentation is finished by using monochromatic Chen-Vese method for the derived new image dataset.

4   Implementation and Results

The main process of the color image segmentation based on multiphase Chan-Vese algorithm with PCA described in detail is illustrated in Fig.1. And it picks up relative components from the color image. To compare the performance of the multiphase level set in several color spaces, we ran test images selected from Berkeley Segmentation Dataset [12] in this experiment. Here the images we used were chosen as they contained areas of various performance indicators. As well as visually comparing the resulting images, we take performance indicators for each image as an objective measure of performance. The visual effects of color image segmentation using the multiphase level set with or without PCA are shown in Fig.2 and Fig.3 respectively.

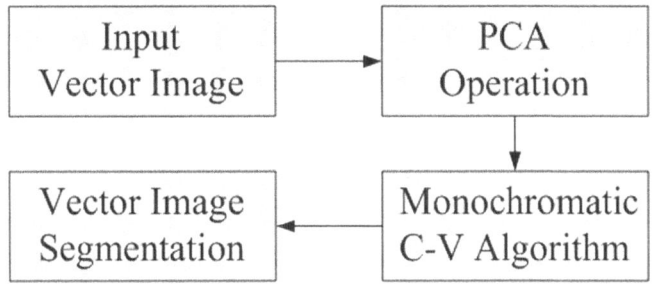

Fig. 1. Overview of PCA-based multiphase Chan-Vese Algorithm for color image segmentation

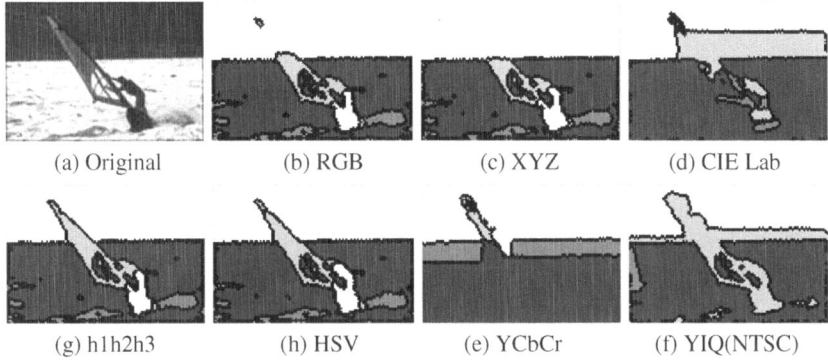

Fig. 2. Results of the multiphase level set for color image segmentation

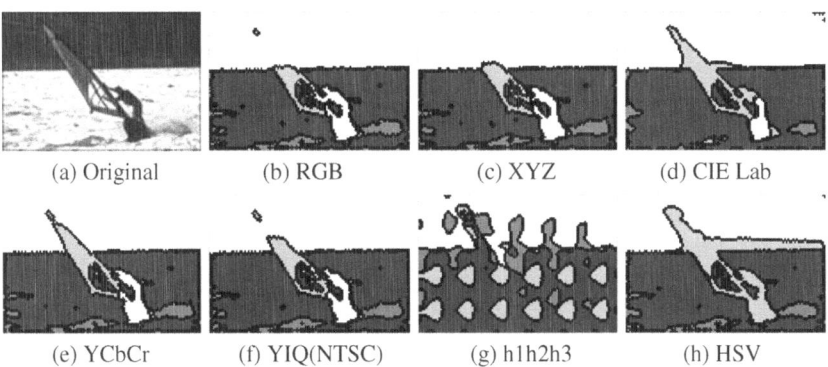

Fig. 3. Results of the multiphase level set with appropriate component for color image segmentation

Through experimental tests with a set of images, performance analysis with evaluation indexes shows that best results by the multiphase level set came from RGB, CIE XYZ, YCbCr and NTSC color spaces, where the results of test image changes little. However, the h1h2h3 color space leads to bad partition results. RGB space generally outperformed other color spaces when using multiphase Chan-Vese method. Moreover, the performance of color image segmentation is much better than that of standard gray conversion.

5 Conclusion

In this paper, the multiphase level set with or without PCA, which adaptively selects the dominant components from the color image in several color spaces, is reported to explain what color space is better for its segmentation. The experimental results prove the effectiveness of the multiphase Chan-Vese algorithm in RGB, CIE XYZ, and YCbCr color spaces, while the h1h2h3 color space, yields poor effects. The monochoromatic multiphase level set with principal component often bring out worse segmentation results in color spaces. Notice that the results using RGB are generally better than results obtained from other color spaces. However, the difference in quality between these color spaces, i.e. RGB, CIE XYZ, and YCbCr, is small. Moreover, the performance of color image segmentation is much better than that of standard gray conversion. The decision of image segmentation map quality with performance indicators introduced in this paper is quite subjective and relative. Like visually comparing the resulting images, we will take quantitative evaluation indices, such as Probabilistic Rand Index (PRI), Variation of Information (VI), Global Consistency Error (GCE), and boundary displacement error (BDE), to measure segmentation results [12]. Therefore, better results can be acquired by appropriately selecting some segmentation algorithm with or without PCA in proper color space.

References

1. Kass, M., Witkin, A., Terzopoulos, D.: Snakes: Active contour models. International Journal of Computer Vision 1(4), 321–331 (1987)
2. Caselles, V., Kimmel, R., Sapiro, G.: Geodesic Active Contours. International Journal of Computer Vision 22(1), 61–79 (1997)
3. Chan, T.F., Vese, L.A.: Active contours without edges. IEEE Transactions on Image Processing 10(2), 266–277 (2001)
4. Osher, S., Sethian, J.A.: Fronts Propagating with Curvature Dependent Speed: Algorithms Based on Hamilton-Jacobi Formulations. Journal of Computational Physics 79, 12–49 (1988)
5. Caselles, V., Catté, F., Coll, T., Dibos, F.: A Geometric Model for Active Contours. Numerische Mathematik 66, 1–31 (1993)
6. Paragios, N., Deriche, R.: Geodesic Active Regions and Level Set Methods for Supervised Texture Segmentation. International Journal of Computer Vision, 223–247 (2002)
7. Cremers, D., Osher, S.J., Soatto, S.: Kernel density estimation and intrinsic alignment for shape priors in level set segmentation. Int. J. of Computer Vision 69(3), 335–351 (2006)

8. Hajihashemi, M.R., El-Shenawee, M.: Shape Reconstruction Using the Level Set Method for Microwave Applications. IEEE Antennas and Wireless Propagation Letters 7, 92–96 (2008)

9. Vese, L.A., Chan, T.F.: Multiphase Level Set Framework for Image Segmentation Using the Mumford and Shah Model. International Journal of Computer Vision 50(3), 271–293 (2002)

10. Liu, K., Du, Q., Yang, H., et al.: Optical Flow and Principal Component Analysis-Based Motion Detection in Outdoor Videos. Eurasip Journal on Advances in Signal Processing, no 680623 (2010)

11. Celik, T.: Unsupervised Change Detection in Satellite Images Using Principal Component Analysis and k-Means Clustering. IEEE Geosciencs and Remote Sensing Letters 6(4), 772–776 (2009)

12. Martin, D., Fowlkes, C., Tal, D., Malik, J.: The Berkeley Segmentation Dataset and Benchmark (January 6, 2011), `http://www.eecs.berkeley.edu/Research/Projects/CS/vision/grouping/segbench/`

No-Reference Video Monitoring Image Blur Metric Based on Local Gradient Structure Similarity

Shurong Chen and Huijuan Jiao

College of Information Engineering, Shanghai Maritime University, Shanghai, 200135, China
srchen@shmtu.edu.cn

Abstract. No-Reference (NR) quality metric for monitoring video image is a challenging and meaningful research. In this paper, we propose a novel objective NR video blurriness metric for monitoring surveillance tapes based on human visual system (HVS) characteristics and the local structure similarity of gradient images. Firstly, according to the low-pass filter (LPF) characteristics of optical imaging system, we construct a reference frame image by passing an original (to be tested) frame through a LPF; secondly, weight the gradient images of reference frame and original frame respectively with contrast sensitivity function (CSF) of HVS, followed by extracting gradient information-rich blocks in the reference gradient image and then computing the local gradient structure similarity between the corresponding blocks of the original frame image and the reference one to assess the blurriness of single frame of original sequence; finally the blur quality of overall original video sequence is evaluated by employing a weighting method which calculates the quality of each frame with different weights. Experimental results show that the proposed metric model has a good correlation with subjective scores and achieves valid blurriness evaluation effects.

Keywords: Video quality metric, No-Reference, blur evaluation, HVS, gradient-based structure similarity.

1 Introduction

With the rapid development of network and video communication technology and wide application of video monitoring system, research on video monitoring image blur quality assessment has received more and more attentions nowadays. Generally, the objective video quality metrics are mainly classified into full-reference (FR), reduced-reference (RR) and no-reference (NR) techniques. FR and RR metrics require full or partial information on both sequences (i.e., the reference and the original sequences) which are complex and not suitable for real-time applications. Therefore, the no-reference video quality assessment metrics become the hot topics of the current research [1] [2] [3] [4].

Different application environment has different digital video quality assessment. Traditional methods mainly adopt mean squared error (MSE) and peak signal to noise

H. Deng et al. (Eds.): AICI 2011, Part II, LNAI 7003, pp. 328–335, 2011.

ratio(PSNR) which are simple but not concerned about human visual characters; Farias presents a no-reference video quality metric based on individual measurements of three artifacts: blockiness, blurriness, and noisiness and then develops a combination metric model [4], Yang et al. introduce a NR quality measure for networked video by extracting information from the compressed bit stream to assess degradation due to lost packets or bit error [2]. Furthermore, no-reference still image blur assessment metrics recently has been widely studied, such as image sharpness metrics based on the analysis of edge characters [5][6], and some new NR methods [7]. Some video quality metrics apply a still image quality assessment on a frame-by-frame basis where quality of each frame is evaluated independently, and finally overall quality of the video sequence is computed by performing time average, or a Minkowski summation of per-frame quality [3]; In addition, some NR video quality metrics introduce the model of visual attention, identify the interested region and percept the video quality. The structure similarity (SSIM) proposed by Wang evaluates image quality via calculation in scenario structure similarity between the original image and the reference one [8]. Dusica Marijan applies SSIM and compares the overlapped block similarity of both reference TV sequence and original one to estimate an original TV image blur and distortion artifacts [9]. Although SSIM is widely used due to simple computation and well performance, it also has some defects, e.g., requiring reference image, the structure information not reflecting image-edge texture details owing to just computing pixel correlation coefficients between the blocks of original and distortion image.

As video surveillance system works in real-time and the recorded contents momentarily vary, it is difficult to find a reference video sequence, and human visual system (HVS) has a very high sensitivity to edge texture. Therefore, we propose a modified NR video blur assessment method called NGVM. Firstly, we construct reference frame image by a low-pass filter in terms of features of optical imaging system, and compute the gradient information of original and reference frame which are afterwards weighted by contrast sensitivity function (CSF) [10]; then divide the gradient image into blocks on the basis of structure information to extract enriched blocks; lastly assess single frame blur quality using SSIM of local gradient blocks and then evaluate total original video sequence by a weighting method.

2   Algorithm Characteristics

2.1   NR Video Image Blur Characteristics Analysis

Sharp image has more detailed information (i.e., high frequency components) than blurred image, and the loss of high frequency components will result in the unsharpness of image edge or texture. Generally the optical imaging system is equivalent to a low-pass filter (LPF) [11]. The lower the cutoff frequency, the more blurry the image is. By using this feature, we can obtain the reference image frame by filtering the original frame with a low-pass filter, and then evaluate the original frame sharpness by computing the local structure similarity between the original frame image and the reference one. Obviously, the sharp image loses large numbers of high frequency components after passing a low-pass filter, and the structural similarity value is correspondingly lowered, and vice verse.

2.2 CSF Model of HVS

Many studies demonstrate that a structural similarity based on the gradient information reflects image-edge and texture details better than SSIM [12]. One of features of HVS, CSF model is directly bound up with image quality assessment due to indicating human eye sensitivity to different frequency components of image. Hence, we respectively obtain the gradient image of the original frame and reference one by using Sobel edge gradient operator, and then weight gradient image with CSF model. CSF is usually a spatial frequency function with a band pass filter property. CSF model in this algorithm is as follows [10]:

$$S_\alpha(u,v) = S(\omega)O(\omega), \tag{1}$$

Wherein,

$$S(\omega) = 1.5e^{-\sigma^2\omega^2/2} - e^{-2\sigma^2\omega^2}, \tag{2}$$

and $\sigma = 2$, $\omega = \dfrac{2\pi f}{60}$, $f = \sqrt{u^2 + v^2}$, and wherein u , v are the horizontal and vertical spatial frequencies, respectively, in cycles per degree(CPD);

$$O(\omega) = \frac{1 + e^{\beta(\omega-\omega_0)}\cos^4 2\theta}{1 + e^{\beta(\omega-\omega_0)}}, \tag{3}$$

Wherein, $\theta = \tan^{-1}(v/u)$, $\beta = 8$ and $f_0 = 11.13 cycle/degree$

Formula (2) highlights an image-edge coefficient in low frequency, and Formula (3) shows an image frequency response in a high frequency section. Normally the spatial frequency in human vision is approximate $0 \sim 60cpd$.

2.3 Blocking and Extracting Process of Gradient Image

We extract K blocks with abundant information from a gradient image, wherein K value directly impacts evaluation result and speed of algorithm. Suppose the gradient image g has a size of $N \times M$, and the minimum impartible block is defined as $n \times m$. By using the quadtree decomposition, we divide the image g_i into four regions, as shown in Fig.1(a), repeating the process until sub-image g_i cannot be divided, and then merge regions g_i , g_j $(i \neq j)$, where similar characteristics exist and find appropriate K value. Fig.1(b) is an extracted frame; Fig.1(c) is its gradient image; and Fig.1(d) shows information-rich gradient blocks marked in white areas after spitting and merging. Thereafter the structure similarity of K blocks between original gradient image and the referenced one will be computed to evaluate blur quality.

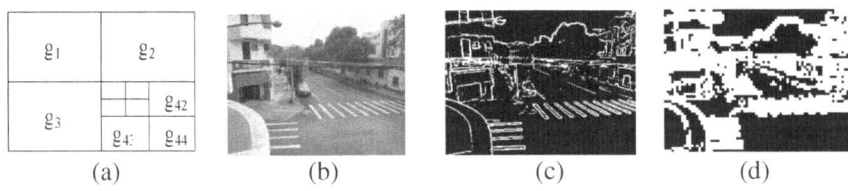

(a)   (b)   (c)   (d)

Fig. 1. Region-based splitting and results

3   NGVM Algorithm

The NVGM algorithm can be summarized as follows:

Step1: Initialization. Set a sampling interval to extract frames according to recorded surveillance video duration and frame playback rate, and normalize each frame to 320×240.

Step2: Build reference frames. Pass the extracted original frame f through a Gaussian low-pass filter of size 6×6, i.e., $f_r = LPF(f)$, and choose standard deviation $\sigma^2 = 3$ so as to better match imaging system features.

Step3: Determine gradient image of f_r and f separately. Convolve each pixels of image with two Sobel operators as shown in Fig.2 respectively, then find horizontal and vertical gradient vector G_H and G_V.

$$S_H = \begin{bmatrix} -1 & -2 & -1 \\ 0 & 0 & 0 \\ 1 & 2 & 1 \end{bmatrix} \quad S_V = \begin{bmatrix} -1 & 0 & 1 \\ -2 & 0 & 2 \\ -1 & 0 & 1 \end{bmatrix}$$

Fig. 2. Sobel operator templates

$$G_H = f(i, j) * S_H, \tag{4}$$

$$G_V = f(i, j) * S_V. \tag{5}$$

The amplitude of gradient vector can be formulated as follows:

$$grad = |G_H| + |G_V|. \tag{6}$$

With the above method, we can find gradient image of f_r and f and define them as $gradf_r$, $gradf$ respectively.

Step 4: Weight $gradf_r$ and $gradf$ with CSF. By considering the gradient image as a spatial frequency matrix and combining with the contrast sensitivity characteristic of HVS, we determine the weighted gradient of $gradf_r$ and $gradf$ by the following equation (7):

$$wgradf = gradf * S_\alpha, \quad wgradf_r = gradf_r * S_\alpha. \tag{7}$$

Step5: Extract K blocks with abundant structural information in $wgradf_r$. Define sd as the standard deviation of each selected region, thus the criterion of segmentation and extraction is:

$$sd \geq TN \tag{8}$$

Wherein $sd = \dfrac{1}{N \times M} \sqrt{\sum_{i=1}^{N} \sum_{j=1}^{M} [wgradf_r(i,j) - \mu_{mean}]^2}$ and $TN = \sqrt{\dfrac{\sum_{i=1}^{N} \sum_{j=1}^{M} f_r(i,j)}{N \times M}}$.

Therein, N and M is the number of rows and columns respectively, $wgradf_r(i,j)$ is weighted gradient amplitude of f_r, μ_{mean} is mean value of $wgradf_r$, the extracted K blocks in $wgradf_r$ marked with $\{x_i, i = 1,2,\cdots,K\}$, the corresponding blocks in $wgradf$ defined as $\{y_i, i = 1,2,\cdots,K\}$, and define minimum impartible block size as 4×4.

Step 6: Determine blur evaluation of extracted frame. Calculate gradient structure similarity (GSSIM) evaluation value of corresponding peer-blocks between $wgradf_r$ and $wgradf$, i.e. $gssim(x_i, y_i)$ of each block as follows:

$$gssim(x, y) = [l(x_i, y_i)]^\alpha \bullet [c(x_i, y_i)]^\beta \bullet [s(x_i, y_i)]^\gamma, \tag{9}$$

Wherein $l(x_i, y_i)$, $c(x_i, y_i)$, $s(x_i, y_i)$ are luminance, contrast, and structure similarity respectively, and α, β, γ refer to weight ratio, generally greater than 0, herein $\alpha = \beta = \gamma = 1$. The final blur assessment value for the original frame image is:

$$NGFM_i = \frac{1}{K} \sum_{i=1}^{K} gssim(x_i, y_i). \tag{10}$$

The higher the value, the more blurry the frame image is.

Step 7: Determine blur metric of the overall video sequence. Weight each frame image of the video sequence, such as (11), get the whole video evaluation VQ [13]:

$$VQ = \frac{\sum_{i=1}^{N} w_i NGFM_i}{\sum_{i=1}^{N} w_i}, \tag{11}$$

Wherein, N is the number of frames in the sequence, $NGFM_i$ is blur evaluation value of i-th frame, w_i denoting the weight of the i-th frame and is generally bounded in terms of the following formula (12):

$$w_i = \begin{cases} 3 & , \quad 0 < NGFM_i < 0.4 \\ 2 & , \quad 0.4 < NGFM_i < 0.6 \\ 1 & , \quad 0.6 < NGFM_i < 1 \end{cases} \tag{12}$$

On the basis of extensive test results and the VQ metric, we can classify blur evaluation of surveillance video sequence into three levels, namely, blur ($0.4 < VQ < 1$), acceptability ($0.25 < VQ < 0.4$), and sharpness ($0 < VQ < 0.25$).

4   Experimental Result and Analysis

To verify proposed NGVM algorithm, we test 20 surveillance video clips (5-min length) which are shot at different scenarios (indoor, outside, intersection, and so on), with the resolution of 720×576, the rate of 25 frames/s, and the playback rate of 25 frames per sec. In order to improve computing speed, we convert RGB color into gray scale and set the sampling rate as one frame per 5 sec, moreover normalize the frame image resolution to 320×240 and run test programs on PC.

We sample 60 frames from a video sequence and evaluate individually blur level using PSNR, GSSIM and the proposed NGVM, as shown in Fig.3, wherein PSNR values are normalized, and subjective judgments are represented by the horizontal dotted line. Results show that the number of blur frames by subjective prediction is 26 and the other three algorithm results are 30, 28, and 26, respectively. Since PSNR and GSSIM aim at overall blur evaluation of image which is not sensitive to the details, the blurriness evaluation value are larger, whereas proposed NGVM can better match subjective visual prediction due to extracting the information-rich blocks and computing local structural similarity.

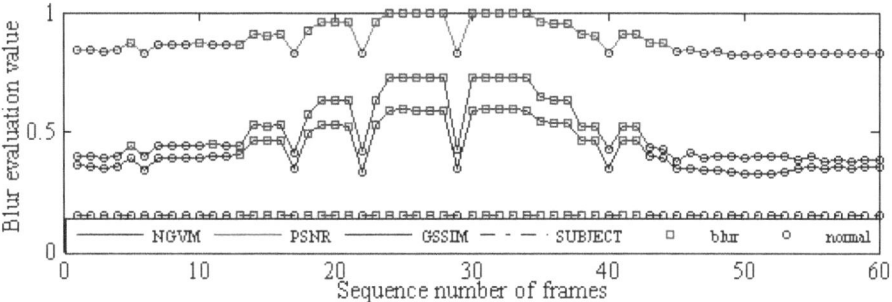

Fig. 3. Comparison of frame blur estimations

For 20 original monitoring video sequences, subjective judgment manifests 10 blurred, 6 acceptable, and 4 sharp, as shown in Fig.4; weighted PSNR picks 12 blurred, 2 sharp, and 6 acceptable; weighted GSSIM checks 12 blurred, 4 sharp, and 4 acceptable; however, NGVM detects 10 blurred, 5 sharp, and 5 acceptable. Obviously, the proposed algorithm can better correspond to human subjective visual perception for blur evaluation of video sequence.

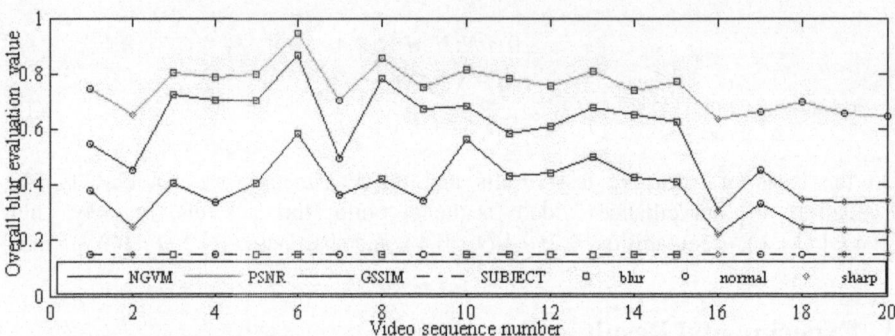

Fig. 4. Comparisons of video sequence blur evaluations

In order to objectively estimate the performance of three approaches, a subjective test is organized using DSCQS provided by ITU-R BT.500-11 to get subjective assessment of 20 video sequences [14]. We compute evaluation values of three algorithms using nonlinear regression model and compare with subjective scores based on mean absolute error (MAE), root mean square (RMS), and Pearson correlation coefficient, as listed in Table 1, therein MAE and RMS of NGVM are clearly less than that of the other two methods, and Pearson correlation coefficient indicates high accordance with subjective visual perception, thus NGVM has better performance than others.

Table 1. Objective Performance Metric of Three Algorithms

Approaches	Pearson	MAE	RMS
NGVM	0.9407	2.1965	2.7268
PSNR	0.8424	4.0108	4.9012
GSSIM	0.8813	3.7713	4.4266

5   Conclusion

In this paper, a novel NR video blurriness quality metric based on local gradient information structure similarity is proposed with an integrated visual attention model for a better simulation of the HVS response to blur distortion. Simulation results show that the proposed NGVM can achieve an increased correlation with the subjective measures and better perform blurriness evaluation for video surveillance images. This improvement results from the integration of CSF weighting and of structure similarity computation on local gradient image. Our further research topics also include integrating motion information metric into our model and considering performance effects of human eye perception for changeable video surveillance scenario.

Acknowledgments. This research was supported by Science & Technology Program of Shanghai Maritime University (No.20110043).

References

1. Eden, A.: No-reference estimation of the coding PSNR for H.264-coded sequences. IEEE Transactions on Consumer Electronics 53, 667–674 (2007)
2. Yang, F., Wan, S., Xie, Q., Wu, H.: No-reference quality assessment for networked video via primary analysis of bit stream. IEEE Transactions on Circuits and Systems for Video Technology 20, 1544–1554 (2010)
3. Maalouf, A., Larabi, M.C.: A No-reference color video quality metric based on a 3D multispectral wavelet transform. In: Second International Workshop on Quality of Multimedia Experience, QoMEX 2010 Financial Sponsors, Norway, pp. 11–16 (2010)
4. Farias, M.C.Q., Mitra, S.K.: No-reference video quality metric based on artifact measurements. In: Proceedings of ICIP, Italy, vol. 3, pp. 141–146 (2005)
5. Marziliano, P., Dufaux, F., Winkler, S., Ebrahimi, T.: Perceptual blur and ringing metrics: Applications to JPEG 2000. Signal Processing: Image Communication 19, 163–172 (2004)
6. Caviedes, J., Oberti, F.: A new sharpness metric based on local kurtosis, edge and energy information. Signal Processing: Image Communication 19, 147–161 (2004)
7. Ferzli, R., Karam, L.J.: A no-reference objective image sharpness metric based on the notion of Just Noticeable Blur (JNB). IEEE Transactions on Image Processing 18, 717–728 (2009)
8. Wang, Z., Bovik, A.C., Sheikh, H.R., Simoncelli, E.P.: Image quality assessment: from error visibility to structural similarity. IEEE Transactions on Image Processing 13, 600–612 (2004)
9. Marijn, D., Zlokolica, V., Teslic, N., Pekovic, V., Tekcan, T.: Automatic functional TV set failure detection system. IEEE Transaction Consumer Electronics 56, 125–133 (2010)
10. Miyahar, M., Kotani, K., Algazi, V.R.: Objective picture quality scale (PQS) for image coding. IEEE Transactions on Communications 46, 1215–1226 (1998)
11. Xie, X.F., Zhou, J., Wu, Q.Z.: No-reference quality index for image blur. Journal of Computer Applications 30, 921–924 (2010) (in Chinese)
12. Yang, C.L., Chen, G.H., Xie, S.L.: Gradient information based image quality assessment. ACTA ELECTRONIC SINICA 35, 1313–1317 (2007) (in Chinese)
13. Lu, G.Q., Li, J.L., Chen, Zhang, G.Y., Man, J.J.: Method of video quality assessment based on visual regions-of-interest. Computer Engineering 35, 217–219 (2009) (in Chinese)
14. ITU-R, RecommendationBT.500-11-2002.: Methodology for the subjective assessment of the quality of television pictures. International Telecommunication Union, Geneva, Switzerland (2002)

A Simple Semi-automatic Technique for 2D to 3D Video Conversion

Jun Chen, Jianhui Zhao[*], Xiaomao Wang, Chuanhe Huang, Erqian Dong,
Bingyu Chen, and Zhiyong Yuan

Computer School, Wuhan University, Wuhan, Hubei, 430072, PR China
jianhuizhao@whu.edu.cn

Abstract. 3D movies and 3D TV have become more and more popular, but
they may be hampered by the lack of 3D contents. One possible solution of this
problem is to convert the existing monocular videos into 3D versions. This
paper presents a semi-automatic technique for 2D to 3D video conversion. Our
method segments key frames first through interactive watershed algorithm, and
then the partitions are manually assigned with their corresponding depth values.
For non-key frames, we use interpolation approach to obtain initial contours of
the different partitions, and then adjust them with snake model. Based on the
computed depth image, the left view and the right view are generated through
rendering followed by hollows' filling, and the 3D image of each frame is
synthesized, and then the 3D video is integrated. Our approach can simplify the
operation of key frames, and improve the tracking accuracy of non-key frames.
Experimental results on a set of monocular movies have proved that our
algorithm is a practical technique for 2D to 3D conversion.

Keywords: 3D video, 2D to 3D conversion, DIBR, interactive watershed, snake
model, image segmentation.

1 Preface

3D video, also known as stereo video, can provide depth perception of the scenery
being observed, compared with the conventional 2D video. Such 3D depth perception
is observed with the help of certain 3D display systems which ensure that the user
sees a specific different view with each eye [1]. 3D video can come from the
capturing of stereoscopic camera or the conversion of 2D content to 3D. The former
method needs special equipments and a relative long production time, which cannot
satisfy with the requirements. The conversion method, on the other hand, can make
full use of the existing 2D videos.

There are a variety of formats for the 3D video, including conventional stereo
video (CSV), video plus depth, multi-view video plus depth, and layered depth video
[2]. Besides the conventional stereo video, a 3D video can be obtained through
rendering a 2D video and its corresponding depth images. The rendering process is
known as depth image based rendering (DIBR) [3]. Therefore, the generation of depth

---

[*] Corresponding author.

H. Deng et al. (Eds.): AICI 2011, Part II, LNAI 7003, pp. 336–343, 2011.

image is the key problem for the conversion of 2D video to its 3D format, and has received more and more attentions from the researchers recently together with the popularity of stereo videos.

The estimation algorithms of depth image usually fall into three categories: manual, semi-automatic and automatic. The manual method requires a lot of operations on pixels or regions of image, and is thus time-consuming and tedious. Thus more research work has been performed on semi-automatic and automatic methods. The automatic estimation algorithms rely on all kinds of depth cues [4], such as binocular disparity, motion [5], defocus, focus, edge [6], height [7], and so on. In Reference [5], the motion information between consecutive frames is utilized to help approximate the depth map of the scene. In Reference [6], the proposed algorithm utilizes the edge information to segment the image into object groups, and then a hypothesized depth gradient model and a cross bilateral filter are used to generate the depth maps efficiently. Reference [7] proposes a novel line tracing method and depth refinement filter to estimate depth information by the optimal use of relative height cue. Machine learning and fusing several depth cues [8, 9] have been more and more popular in this area to improve the performance of estimation algorithms. But the main shortage of the automatic methods is that the accuracy of generated depth maps still can't meet the demand.

Therefore, many semi-automatic depth estimation schemes have been presented, which combine both depth cues and manual operations [10-12]. These semi-automatic estimation methods usually need manual scribbles in key frames and then generate the depth images for non-key frames through motion tracking approaches. Of course, they have to find the acceptable balance between the complexity of manual operation and the accuracy of motion tracking.

In Reference [10], the proposed method uses a two-stage approach, where a depth estimation per-pixel is first done using a bilateral filter, after which the estimation is corrected in the second step through the block-based motion compensation from the previous frame. But the depth estimation in [10] often has some artifacts and only experiment results of the synthetically generated videos are presented. Reference [11] combines a diffusion scheme, which takes into account the local saliency and the local motion at each video location, coupled with a classification scheme that assigns depth information to image patches. But the estimation of the edges between objects is not very accurate. In Reference [12], an object-based approach is employed where objects with large depth differences are first segmented by semi-automatic tools and the depth values are assigned by inpainting techniques. It uses level set method for object tracking and the main problem is that level set method is slow for images with high resolution.

The overall framework of our method is based on the semi-automatic approach. That is to say, we first segment the key frames and then assign depth information to each segmented partition. All pixels in the same partition have the same depth value, which can help simplify the manual operations. Depth images of the non-key frames are automatically generated. And finally 3D video is obtained based on rendering and synthesis. Our method only needs a few scribbles on the key frames and the accuracy of automatic tracking is satisfying, which provides one way to convert the existing 2D videos into their 3D versions.

2 Concepts and Methods

2.1 Depth Image

The concept of "depth image" is from Depth Image Based Rendering (DIBR), which is one part of the project "Advanced 3D Television System Technologies" (ATTEST), an activity where industries, research centers and universities have joined forces to design a backwards-compatible, flexible and modular broadcast 3D-TV system [13].

Video   +   "Per-Pixel" Depth

Fig. 1. Original 2D video frame and corresponding depth image

In a depth image, the value (0-255) of any pixel shows how far that pixel is to the camera, while pixels with zero are the farthest. The real depth images obtained by the depth cameras with range sensors are pixel-wise, as shown in the right of Figure 1. In our method, every pixel within the same object is assumed to have the same depth value, which is one way to simplify the manual operation.

2.2 Watershed Segmentation

We adopt interactive watershed method in segmentation of key frames of video. The watershed method was first proposed by Meyer [14], and the algorithm is one kind of region growing algorithms. With several points set as the seeds, they overflow gradually as different regions, thus dividing the original image into different partitions. The main procedure can be grouped as the following three steps:

1. Mark each minimum with a distinct label, and initialize a set S with the labeled nodes.
2. Extract a node x of minimal altitude F from S, i.e. $F(x) = min\{F(y)|y$ in $S\}$. Attribute the label of x to each non-labeled node y adjacent to x, and insert y in S.
3. Repeat Step 2 until S is empty.

The interactive watershed method used in our algorithm is named as marker-controlled watershed, which is one major enhancement of the watershed transformation and consists in flooding the topographic surface from a previously defined set of markers.

As shown in Figure 2(a), interactive operations of watershed method are performed on the key frame, i.e. the person is marked as foreground, while the other region is marked as background. As illustrated in Figure 2(b), the segmented results are obtained from the marker-controlled watershed method, i.e. the region of the person has been successfully segmented as the foreground of the key frame. In this way, all the key frames of the 2D video are interactively processed.

(a)   (b)

Fig. 2. (a) The interactive operations of watershed method. (b) Segmentation result

2.3 Active Contour Model

The active contour model [15], also known as the snake method, is used to make contours in each frame to propagate close to the real edges of foreground objects in image. A snake is an energy-minimizing spline, which is guided by the external constraint forces and influenced by the image forces pulling it toward features such as lines and edges.

Representing the position of a snake parametrically by $v(s) = (x(s), y(s))$, we can write its energy function as

$$E^*_{snake} = \int_0^1 E_{snake}(v(s))ds = \int_0^1 E_{int}(v(s)) + E_{image}(v(s)) + E_{con}(v(s)ds \qquad (1)$$

E_{int} represents the internal energy of the spline due to bending and stretching, E_{image} gives rise to the image forces, and E_{con} gives rise to the external constraint forces [15]. As a closed curve, the original snake moves through the spatial domain of an image to minimize the energy function.

As shown in Figure 3(a), the edge of the segmented object is taken as the initial contour for snake method. After adjustment from the active contour model, the contour is close to the real edge of the person and becomes much smoother at the same time, as illustrated in Figure 3(b).

Fig. 3. (a) The initial contour for snake method. (b) The adjusted contour after snake method

3 Procedures

3.1 General Idea

First, the interactive watershed method is applied to divide two neighboring key frames from 2D video clip into different partitions and then depth value is manually assigned to each partition, in this way the depth image for each key frame is created. Depth images of non-key frames between these two key frames are automatically generated based on the partitions' determination with rough interpolation and fine adjustment of contours. Then the left view and the right view can be obtained through rendering and hollows' filling, and then be synthesized to form the 3D video.

The general idea can be divided into the following three concrete steps: key frame processing, non-key frame processing, and rendering & synthesizing.

3.2 Concrete Steps

3.2.1 Key Frame Processing

First, select one key frame from the 2D video, and apply the interactive watershed algorithm to divide the key frame into different partitions.

Second, manually assign one depth value to each of the partitions, thus forming a depth image of the key frame.

Third, select the other key frame which is several frames after the first key frame, and segment the second key frame similarly, during which the divided partitions should properly correspond between the two key frames.

3.2.2 Non-key Frame Processing

First, for each partition except for the background in both key frames, extract the same number of points with the same order along the contour of the segmented partition. Then the contours for that partition in the non-key frames can be linearly calculated with the help of interpolation method. Of course, the interpolated contour is only an approximation to the real edge of the partition.

Then use active contour model, i.e. snake method, to adjust the contour of each partition per non-key frame. Obviously, the contour is represented with a set of discrete points.

Based on the adjusted discrete points along the edge of each partition, the cubic Bezier curve fitting method is applied to obtain the continuous and complete contour.

At last, the depth image of each non-key frame can be generated automatically based on the contours of partitions and the manually assigned depth value for each partition in the corresponding key frames.

3.2.3 Rendering and Composition

As long as we have a monocular video and corresponding depth images for each frame of the video, we can calculate the positions of each pixel in the left view and the right view according to Equation (2) and Equation (3).

$$x_l = x_c + (t_x*f)/(2*Z) \tag{2}$$

$$x_r = x_c - (t_x*f)/(2*Z) \tag{3}$$

The meanings of the above equations can be illustrated in Figure 4. P is any point in 3D space, cl and cr are two virtual cameras (or corresponding to two virtual eyes), f is their focal length, Z (depth value) is the distance of P relative to the plane of two virtual cameras, tx is the distance between two virtual cameras, while (xl, y), (xc, y) and (xr, y) are the corresponding projections of P in the imaging plane.

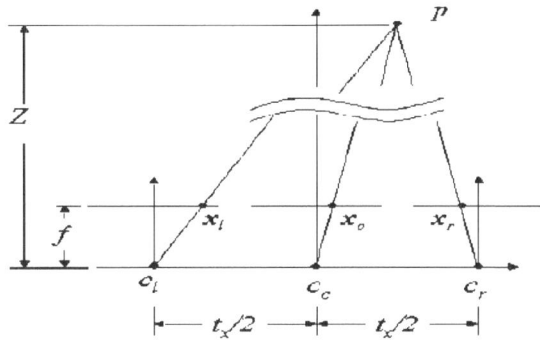

Fig. 4. The calculation of left view and right view

Some hollows may exist in the left view image or right view image, due to the fact that different partitions move with different distances because of their various depth values. We use the color of the nearest pixel to fill the hollows, i.e. for one pixel in the hollows, its nearest pixel outside the hollows is found and the corresponding color value is borrowed.

Finally, the left view image and the right view image are composed into a synthetic 3D image, and then the 3D frames are integrated into a synthetic 3D video. The generated 3D video can be displayed with certain equipment, such as the 3D TV set.

4 Experimental Results

We have implemented our proposed algorithm and then tested it with experiments on several 2D movies, as shown in Figure 5, Figure 6 and Figure 7.

Fig. 5. Experiment on Sample 1. (a) Left view. (b) Right view

Fig. 6. Experiment on Sample 2. (a) Left view. (b) Right view

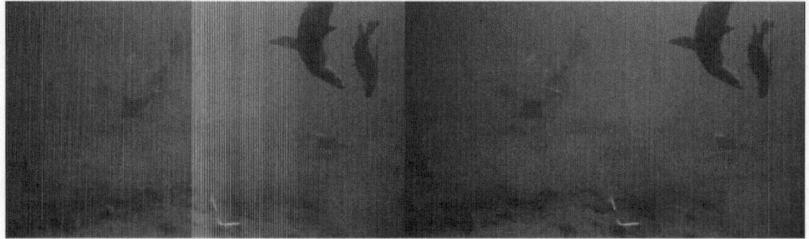

Fig. 7. Experiment on Sample 3. (a) Left view. (b) Right view

As illustrated above, we segment each video frame so that the objects (such as people, animals, et al.) are taken as the foregrounds and the rest is the background. Then the depth images are obtained according to the assigned depth values of the key frames. Based on the depth image, left view and right view are generated for the related frame.

5   Conclusion

From the experimental results displayed in 3D TV, it can be found that our method can achieve a good 3D effect with the help of manual operations to a certain limited extent. Our method is semi-automatic while very simple, only needs some operations to the key frames while the non-key frames can be processed automatically.

In our experiments we found that the contours in the non-key frames may not meet the real edges of objects, especially when the scene is very complex and in such case the snake method cannot work very well. We are trying other possible improvements on it, and currently our method is being tested with more sample videos.

References

[1] Konrad, J., Halle, M.: 3-D displays and signal processing: ananswer to 3-D ills? IEEE Signal Processing Magazine 24(6), 97–111 (2007)
[2] Smolic, A., Mueller, K., Merkle, P., Kauff, P., Wiegand, T.: An overview of available and emerging 3D video formats and depth enhanced stereo as efficient generic solution. In: Proceedings of the 27th conference on Picture Coding Symposium, pp. 389–392, Institute of Electrical and Electronics Engineers Inc. (2009)

[3] Fehn, C.: Depth-image-based rendering (DIBR), compression and transmission for a new approach on 3D-TV. In: Proceedings of the SPIE Stereoscopic Displays and Virtual Reality Systems XI, San Jose, CA, USA, pp. 93–104 (January 2004)

[4] Wei, Q.: Converting 2D to 3D: a survey. Information and Communication Theory Group. Delft University of Technology, The Netherlands (2005)

[5] Pourazad, M.T., Nasiopoulos, P., Ward, R.K.: An H.264-based scheme for 2D to 3D video conversion. IEEE Transactions on Consumer Electronics 55, 742–748 (2009)

[6] Cheng, C.-C., Li, C.-T., Chen, L.-G.: A novel 2D-to-3D conversion system using edge information. In: Proc. IEEE Int. Conf. Consumer Electronics, pp. 1739–1745 (August 2010)

[7] Jung, Y.J., Baik, A., Kim, J., Park, D.: A novel 2D-to-3D conversion technique based on relative height depth cue. In: Proc. of SPIE, vol. 7237, pp. 72371U-1–72371U -8 (January 2009)

[8] Cheng, C.-C., Li, C.-T., Huang, P.-S., Lin, T.-K., Tsai, Y.-M., Chen, L.-G.: A block-based 2D-to-3D conversion system with bilateral filter. In: Proc. IEEE Int. Conf. Consumer Electronics (2009)

[9] Kim, D., Min, D., Sohn, K.: A Stereoscopic video generation method using stereoscopic display characterization and motion analysis. IEEE Trans. on Broadcasting 54(2), 188–197 (2008)

[10] Varekamp, C., Barenbrug, B.: Improved depth propagation for 2d to 3d video conversion using key-frames. In: IETCVMP (2007)

[11] Guttmann, M., Wolf, L., Cohen-Or: Semi-automatic stereo extraction from video footage. In: ICCV, pp. 136–142 (2009)

[12] Ng, K.T., Zhu, Z.Y., Chan, S.C.: An approach to 2D-To-3D conversion for multiview displays. In: IEEE International Conference on Information, Communications and Signal Processing, pp. 1–5 (2009)

[13] Fehn, C., Atzpadin, N.: An advanced 3DTV concept providing interoperability and scalability for a wide range of multi-baseline geometries. In: Proceedings of International Conference on Image Processing, Atlanta, GA pp. 961–964 (2006)

[14] Beucher, S., Meyer, F.: The morphological approach to segmentation: The watershed transform. In: Dougherty, E.R. (ed.) Mathematical Morphology in Image Processing, vol. 12, pp. 433–481, Marcel Dekker, New York (1993)

[15] Kass, M., Witkin, A., Terzopoulos, D.: Snakes: Active contour models. In: Proc. First Int. Conf. Comput. Vision, London, pp. 321–331 (1987)

Variable-*p* Iteratively Weighted Algorithm for Image Reconstruction

Zhe Liu and Xiaoxian Zhen

School of Science, Northwestern Polytechnical University, Xi'an 710072, China
liuzhe@nwpu.edu.cn

Abstract. In this work, a novel variable-*p* iteratively weighted algorithm is proposed for image reconstruction. The proposed algorithm introduced a dynamically adjusting strategy for the variable *p* in the nonconvex $l_p(0<p<1)$ norm optimization problem, which can be solved via an iteratively reweighted algorithm. Thus, the image reconstruction procedure could start with the l_1 norm problem which is easy to implement, and approach the original l_0 norm problem during the iteration. Numerical experiments indicate that the proposed algorithm can reconstruct the images with fewer measurements than existing fixed-*p* algorithms.

Keywords: Compressed Sensing, image reconstruction, iteratively weighted, variable-*p*.

1 Introduction

Compressed Sensing, also known as compressive sampling or CS[1,2] , is a novel sensing/sampling framework, which indicates that a compressible signal or image can be accurately reconstructed with much fewer samples than conventional Nyquist sampling via solving an l_0 norm optimization problem. However, this problem is nonconvex and NP-hard. Chen, Donoho and Saunders[3] suggested replacing l_0 norm with l_1 norm, which makes a series of methods feasible. Recently, a ε -regularized iteratively weighted l_1 norm algorithm[4] is proposed, which is verified to have a good performance. However, the l_1 optimization problem usually requires much more measurements, which causes new challenges for images even with usual size. Then, Rick Chartrand asserted that exact reconstruction is possible by replacing the l_1 norm with $l_p(0<p<1)$ norm and it requires substantially fewer measurements[5]. Followed with that, iteratively weighted least square $l_p(0<p<1)$ norm algorithm is proposed[6], which produces the local minima of the objective. In practice, we are able to recover signals exactly, combined with theoretical results [5,7] that give circumstances which guarantees the local minima is also the unique, global minimum. Further research find that the behavior of the $l_p(0<p<1)$ algorithm is highly dependent on the parameter *p*. Therefore, Sergio D. Cabrerab proposed to vary the values of *p* as a function of the iteration in the affine scaling transformation (AST) algorithm[8]. Simulation experiments demonstrate that the variable- *p* AST algorithm takes advantages of the benefits of fixed-*p* approaches, when the *p*=0 or *p*=1.

H. Deng et al. (Eds.): AICI 2011, Part II, LNAI 7003, pp. 344–351, 2011.

Currently, most of the l_p(0<*p*<1) norm optimization algorithms are proposed for one-dimensional signals and images with a high sparseness. However, the reconstruction of common compressible images is still a challenge. In this work, we try to introduce the dynamically adjusting strategy of *p* parameter to improve the reconstruction performance of the iteratively weighted l_p(0<*p*<1) norm optimization, thus to achieve the purpose of exact reconstruction of common compressible images.

2   Image Reconstruction for Compressed Sensing

It is known that a compressible signal $s \in R^N$ can be reconstructed accurately from data $y = \Phi x = \Phi \Psi^T s$ under the condition Φ and Ψ is incoherent and $x = \{x_i\}_{i=1}^N$ is sparse. Where Φ is an $M \times N$ $(M \ll N)$ measurement matrix and $\Psi = [\psi_1, \psi_2, \cdots, \psi_N]$ is an orthogonal transform matrix satisfying $s = \sum_{i=1}^N x_i \psi_i = \Psi x$, ψ_i is the column vectors of matrix Ψ and $x_i = \langle s, \psi_i \rangle$, $i = 1, 2, \cdots, N$ is the projection coefficients.

Theoretically, signal *s* can be reconstructed by solving the following combinatorial optimization problem [1]

$$\min_x \|x\|_0 \qquad \text{s.t. } \Phi x = y \tag{1}$$

where $\|x\|_0 = |\{i : x_i \neq 0\}|$. This is a common sense approach which seeks the simplest explanations fitting the data. Unfortunately, this optimization problem is nonconvex and generally impossible to solve when the signal dimension is large, as its solution usually requires an intractable combinational search.

A general alternative approach is to consider the nonconvex problem which can actually be recast into a linear program as

$$\min_x \|x\|_1 \qquad \text{s.t. } \Phi x = y \tag{2}$$

where $\|x\|_1 = \sum_{i=1}^n |x_i|$. Surprisingly, the work in [3] has shown that the solutions to (1) and (2) are equivalent on condition that the measurement matrix Φ and transform matrix Ψ are incoherent. However, the computational complexity of the l_1 norm optimization problem is very high in general.

Then, Rick Chartrand asserted that exact reconstruction is still possible by replacing the l_1 norm with the norm l_p(0<*p*<1)

$$\min_x \|x\|_p^p \qquad \text{s.t. } \Phi x = y \tag{3}$$

which is nonconvex and intractable. However, the author demonstrated that such improvement can result in a much simpler task of finding a local minimum, thus to produce exact reconstruction of sparse signals with many fewer measurements than l_1 minimization.

However, the behavior of the $l_p(0<p<1)$ algorithm is highly dependent on the parameter p. Therefore, a dynamical adjustment strategy of p parameter can be introduced to improve the reconstruction performance.

3 Variable-p Iteratively Reweighted Algorithm

3.1 Iteratively Weighted l_p Norm Algorithm

Consider the weighted l_1 norm minimization problem:

$$\min_x \sum_{i=1}^n \omega_i |x_i| \qquad \text{s.t.} \quad \Phi x = y \qquad (4)$$

where $\omega_1, \omega_2, ..., \omega_n$ are positive weights which are computed from the solution of the previous iteration, that is $\omega_{k+1}(i) = |x_k(i)|^{-1}$. In order to provide stability and to ensure that a zero-valued component in x_k does not strictly prohibit a nonzero estimate at the next step, a parameter $\varepsilon > 0$ is introduced, and so the weights are computed as $\omega_{k+1}(i) = (|x_k(i)| + \varepsilon)^{-1}$.

For the parameter ε affects the weight coefficient, its selection influences the reconstruction effect directly. In general, ε should be slightly smaller than the expected nonzero magnitudes of x_0 [9]. A simple strategy is to set ε as a fixed positive, but it has several limitations since the solution changes all the way. This paper adopts a regularized adaptive selection of ε proposed in [4] and iteratively solves the $l_p(0<p<1)$ minimization problem in which the weights is computed as follows:

$$\omega_i = (|x_i| + \varepsilon)^{p/2-1} \qquad (5)$$

The proposed algorithm can be summarized to following steps:

Step1 : Initialize $W^{(0)}$, $p_k=1$ and set the iteration counter $k=0$, regularization parameter $\varepsilon = 1$;

Step2 : Solve the weighted $l_p(0<p<1)$ norm minimization problem iteratively:

$$x^{(k)} = \min_x \left\| W^{(k)} x \right\|_p^p \qquad \text{s.t.} \quad \Phi x = y \qquad (6)$$

Step3 : Update the weights according to (5) and also the variable p;

Step4 : Terminate on convergence or when k attains the maximum number of iterations K. Otherwise, increment k and go to step2.

3.2 Selection of Parameter p

The variable p method start with $p=1$ and then gradually move to $p=0$. A simple strategy is to vary p in a fixed number of iterations L. If more iteration is needed, p can remain at the value $p=0$. If convergence is reached before L iterations, the list of values of p used will end before $p=0$ [8]. The imperfection of this method is that it cannot select p adaptively in terms of different images. Therefore, another approach adjusts the p value using a gradient-like measure of the relative RMSE value, which is calculated as the difference between rRMSE and the rRMSE in the previous iteration:

$$p_k = p_{k-1} + \alpha \left(rMSRE_k - rMSRE_{k-1} \right) / rMSRE_{k-1}$$

$$\text{and} \quad rRMSE_k = \left\| x^{(k)} - x^{(k-1)} \right\|_2 / \left\| x^{(k-1)} \right\|_2$$

where $\alpha < 1$ is a scale factor and its selection has an important effect on the reconstruction algorithm. Fig.1 illustrates the reconstruction performance of standard image Lena with the change of α , from which we can see that $\alpha = 0.07$ is an optimal value. For simplicity, this paper chooses $\alpha = 0.07$ for all experiments, although it might not be the optimal parameter for other images.

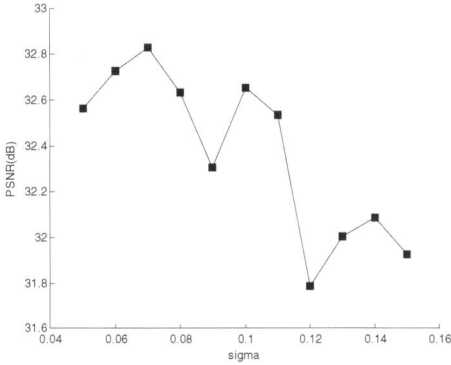

Fig. 1. Reconstruction performance with the change of scale factor

To verify that the gradient based measure is indeed superior to the linear based measure, we select several images for experiments and the results are listed in Tab.1. The peak signal-to-noise ratio (PSNR) of the gradient based measure is higher than that of linear based measure and the mean square error (MSE) is lower. Therefore, in this paper, we adopted the gradient based method to adjust the value p.

Table 1. Comparison of the two adjusting method of variable-p

Image	Linear based		Gradient based	
	PSNR/dB	MSE	PSNR/dB	MSE
House	33.95	26.16	34.69	22.09
Angiogram	31.48	46.22	31.87	42.24
MR-head	30.25	61.46	30.43	58.91
shepp	36.16	15.73	36.24	15.45
Lena	33.14	31.58	33.27	30.61

4 Numerical Experiments and Analysis

For most images are not strictly sparse, but compressible, we perform wavelet transform before all reconstruction. Therefore, in the following experiments the wavelet transform matrix is selected as the transform matrix and partial Fourier matrix is chosen as the measurement matrix $\Phi_{M \times N}$.

4.1 Reconstruction Effect Comparison

The first experiment is to verify that the reconstruction performance of the variable-p iteratively weighted algorithm is better than the fixed-p algorithms. To facilitate the comparison, we select a natural image *house* and a medical image *MR-head* of size 256×256 and set the maximum iteration number to 10, measurements $M=128$.

The original *house* and *MR-head* images as well as their reconstructed versions are illustrated in Fig.2 and Fig.3, respectively. For the fixed-p algorithm, the value of p is set to 0.25, 0.5, 0.75 and 1, respectively.

From the results, we can observe the reconstruction based on the proposed algorithm is visually superior to those based on fixed-p algorithm at all values of p. Otherwise, from the perspective of PSNR, the variable-p algorithm outperforms the fixed-p algorithms by 1.14-5.48 dB for the image *house*, and 0.33-2.51 dB for the image *MR-head*.

(a) Original image   (b) $p=0.25$, *PSNR*=29.21   (c) p=0.5, *PSNR*=31.67

(d) $p=0.75$, *PSNR*=33.24   (e) p=1, *PSNR*=33.55   (f) variable-p, *PSNR*=34.69

Fig. 2. Reconstructions of image house

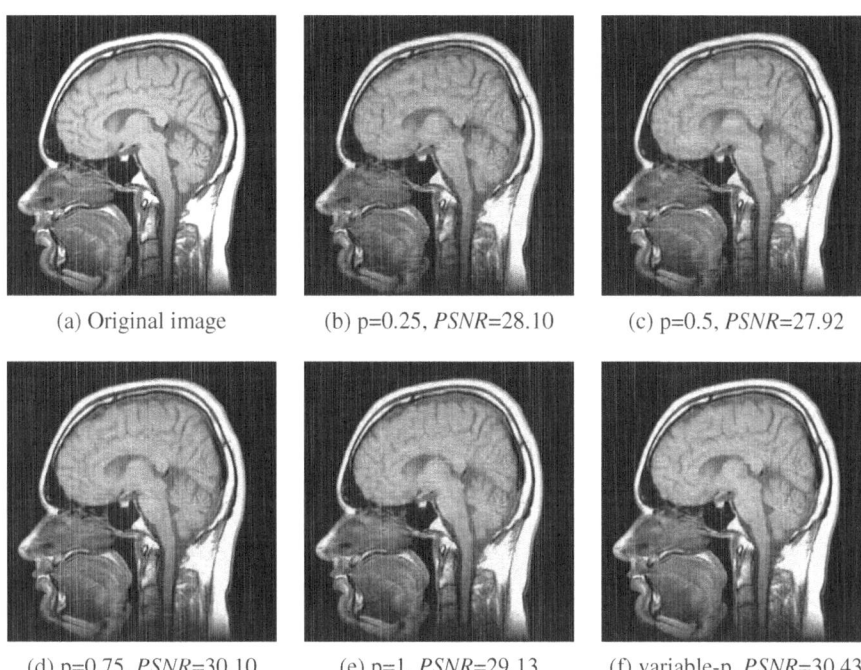

(a) Original image   (b) p=0.25, *PSNR*=28.10   (c) p=0.5, *PSNR*=27.92

(d) p=0.75, *PSNR*=30.10   (e) p=1, *PSNR*=29.13   (f) variable-p, *PSNR*=30.43

Fig. 3. Reconstructions of MR image

Table 2. Reconstruction performance of different algorithms

Images	Algorithms	PSNR/dB	MSE	TIME/s
barbara	p=0.25	29.31	76.14	197.45
	p=0.5	31.00	51.68	197.44
	p=0.75	31.74	43.53	196.97
	p=1	31.45	46.59	196.56
	variable-p	32.41	37.34	197.56
Lena	p=0.25	29.21	77.99	197.98
	p=0.5	31.48	46.21	196.89
	p=0.75	32.61	35.63	195.95
	p=1	31.72	43.77	194.47
	variable-p	33.27	30.61	197.47
shepp	p=0.25	30.73	54.91	187.23
	p=0.5	.33.79	27.14	187.48
	p=0.75	34.73	21.86	187.87
	p=1	34.02	25.78	188.84
	variable-p	36.24	15.45	192.21
MR-head	p=0.25	28.10	100.66	194.17
	p=0.5	27.92	104.96	191.67
	p=0.75	30.10	63.50	193.92
	p=1	29.13	79.37	192.70
	variable-p	30.43	58.91	194.41

To have a comprehensive quantitative comparison of the proposed algorithm and the fixed-p algorithm performance, we apply them on four 256×256 images (Barbara, Lena, MR-head, Shepp), and list the experimental results in Tab.2.

From the results, we can see that the PSNR results of the proposed algorithm is higher than that of the fixed-p algorithms for all four images at different p, while the MSE results of the proposed algorithm is lower than that of the fixed-p algorithms for all four images at different p. Furthermore, the time needed for different experiments is nearly the same, which means the proposed algorithm doesn't introduce notable computation burden.

In conclusion, the proposed variable-p algorithm outperforms the fixed-p algorithms in both PSNR and MSE measurements without losing the computational efficiency.

4.2   Performance with the Change of Measurements

The purpose of the following experiments is to show that the variable-p algorithm requires fewer measurements than the fixed-p algorithms to obtain the same reconstruction performance which is quantitated by PSNR, thus, fewer iterations are needed using the proposed algorithm to achieve the same PSNR.

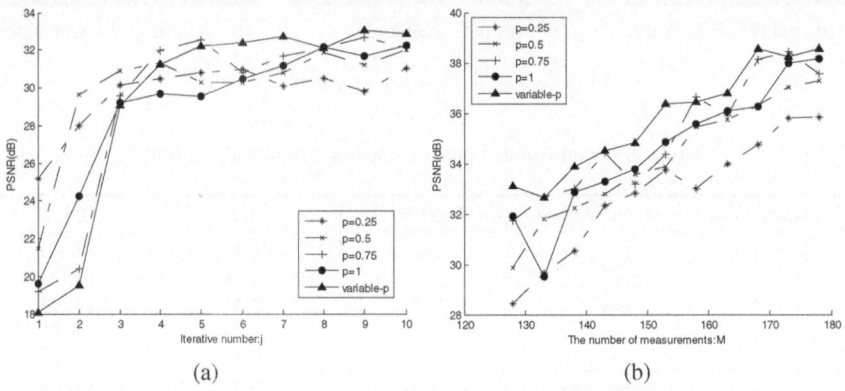

(a)   (b)

Fig. 4. PSNR with the change of maximum iteration number and the number of measurements

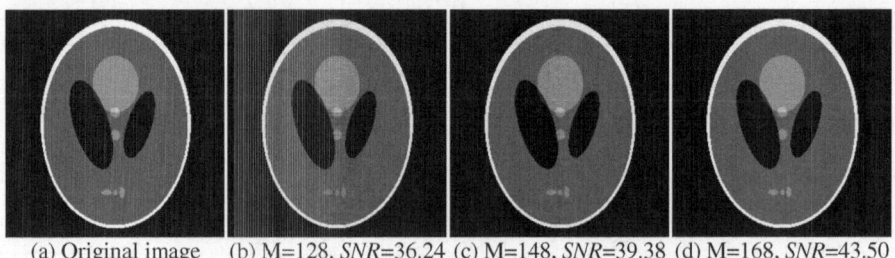

(a) Original image   (b) M=128, SNR=36.24 (c) M=148, SNR=39.38 (d) M=168, SNR=43.50

Fig. 5. PSNR with the change of measurements

Fig. 4 illustrates the performance of the variable-p algorithm and fixed-p algorithms for various values of maximum iteration number, under fixed measurements $M=128$. We observe that the performance of the proposed algorithm is not better than the fixed-p algorithm at the beginning. With the iterative number increasing, its performance is superior to the fixed-p algorithm obviously.

Fig. 5 compares the performance of the two algorithms for various values of measurements. The proposed algorithm outperforms the others both in visual quality and the PSNR measurement.

5 Discussion and Conclusion

Reconstructing signals from very few measurements is a significant in applications when data is expensive or difficult to acquire. Compressed sensing makes this to be possible. In this paper, we combined the ε -regularized iteratively weighted algorithm[4] for $l_p(0<p<1)$ norm optimization and the dynamical adjustment strategy of p parameter to improve the reconstruction performance. Numerical experiments show that the proposed variable-p iteratively weighted algorithm outperforms the fixed-p algorithm in both visual quality and the PSNR measurement, and a low requirement of measurements.

Acknowledgment. This work was financially supported by the National Natural Science Foundation of China under Grant No. 61071170, and Program for New Century Excellent Talents in University.

References

1. Candès, E.: Compressive sampling. In: International Congress of Mathematics, Madrid, Spain, pp. 1433–1452 (2006)
2. Candès, E., Wakin, M.: An Introduction to Compressive Sampling. IEEE Signal Processing Magazine 25(2), 21–30 (2008)
3. Chen, S., Donoho, D., Saunders, M.: Atomic decomposition by basis pursuit. SIAM Review 43(1), 129–159 (2001)
4. Yang, Y., Liu, Z., Lv, F.Y.: Signal recovery based on iterative weighted l1 norm. Computer Engineering and Applications 46(3), 128–130 (2010)
5. Chartrand, R.: Exact reconstructions of sparse signals via nonconvex minimization. IEEE Signal Proc. Lett. 14(10), 707–710 (2007)
6. Chartrand, R., Yin, W.: Iteratively Reweighted Algorithms For Compressive Sensing. In: 33rd International Conference on Acoustics, Speech, and Signal Processing (2008)
7. Chartrand, R., Staneva, V.: Restricted isometry properties and nonconvex compressive sensing. Inverse Problems 24 (2008)
8. Domíngueza, R.J., Cabrerab, S.D., Rosilesb, J.G., Pineda, J.V.: Reconstruction in compressive sensing using affine scaling transformations with variable-p diversity measure. In: Digital Signal Processing Workshop and 5th IEEE Signal Processing Education Workshop (2009)
9. Candès, E., Wakin, M., Boyd, S.: Enhancing Sparsity by Reweighted l1 Minimization. Joural of Fourier Analysis and Applications 14, 877–905 (2008)

Video Frame Quality Assessment Using Points Calculation in High Dimensional Space

Shi-jiao Zhu and Jun Yang

School of Computer and Information Engineering, Shanghai University of Electric Power,
Shanghai 200090, China
zhusj707@hotmail.com, mail_yangjun@hotmail.com

Abstract. Video quality assessment is widely used for signal measure. Classic method is often use algebra method for make a compute model, such as PSNR, which often lead to difficult for alignment of video sequence number and it limit its application in real world. This paper presents a novel method bases on high dimensional space. The method considers a image as a point in high dimensional space and make correspond calculation. Firstly, it use special kernels to covering some image points from original image; then when a noised image is put into space, the method is performed to find the most similar one in high-dimensional space and gives its similarity. Experimental results show that the propose method make the measurement easily and meet the real noised image sequence. The proposed method is constructive and this work can provide a very useful method for video quality assessment model.

Keywords: Visual Quality Assessment, High Dimensional Space, Point Calculation.

1 Introduction

Digital videos are increasing used in our day-to-day lives through the explosion of video applications such as digital television, digital cinema, wireless handset TV. Digital videos typically pass through several processing stages before they reach an end user and often possible being noised [1]. For signal measurement, image quality assessment is an important field in the real practice and the measurement can be using in communication in order to improve network's quality [2].

For the image quality assessment (IQA) problem, there are two different categories: subjective assessment by humans and objective assessment by algorithm automatically [3]. For the human subjectivity assessment, an algorithm is defined by how well it correlates with human perception of quality. Among the algorithms, The Multi-scale Structural Similarity Index performed consistently well using a variety of measures of correlation with the human perception of quality [4]. The Visual Information Fidelity index(VIF) is an alternate approach to IQA[5].. However, these methods are limited for video sequence or required more precise time. Some application is only make a measure between received image and original one. Meanwhile, real image is often chaotic sequence received or image quality is low. These methods are invalid for this kind of real application.

H. Deng et al. (Eds.): AICI 2011, Part II, LNAI 7003, pp. 352–359, 2011.

In this paper, we explore the possibility of measurement in high dimensional space [6]. We first present a study of coving objects in space. Our study includes CMMB video test sequence. The whole produce is constructive dynamically; the framework can generate samples covering objects with small prediction error in practice. In addition, we can propose a new general algorithm for constructing network to cover distributions of samples in feature space.

The paper is organized as follow. Section 2 presents basic definitions and description image calculation in high-dimensional space; section 3 presents an algorithm for coving objects in high-dimensional space. Results of images and measurement with real-noised image are provided in Section 4, with conclusions in Section 5.

2 Image Calculation in High Dimensional Space

Since the main problem about image representation, in this paper we focus our attention on the algorithm of image's itself in high dimensional space. This algorithm requires the relative points of image in a high dimensional space. By introducing this idea to the points-based method, we present a more suitable method which has the advantage of blindness image quality assessment.

For a digital image which size is M×N, we denote is with $f(x,y)$ as a point in high dimensional space, where 0<x<M,0<y<N. It includes original image and noised image. In order to assert the image's quality, we define below scheme as Fig1.

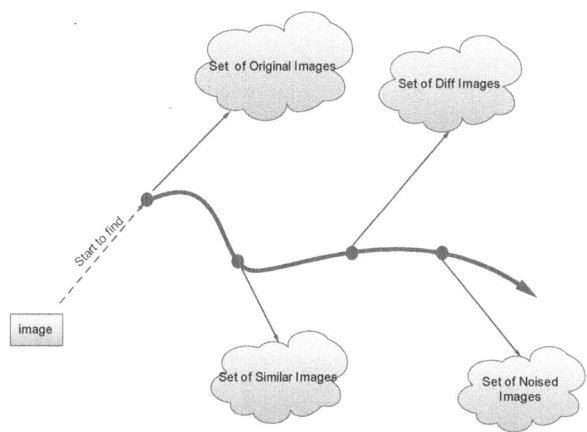

Fig. 1. Scheme of point calculation

For images, it is classified as original, similar, diff and noised images. The main reason is to find sub-set of image in high dimensional space.

Its main idea is to find the points distribution of image in the high dimensional space based on original image. Video quality is decrease when translating in network, such as cable network or wireless network. From the theory of geometrical learning [7], some similar objects in high dimensional space are homeomorphism and can be measured as neighbors [8].

For the different points in hyper-space, covering entity can be made by adjust parameters [9]. For symbols $X_i \in B_i, X_i \neq Xo_i$, measure distance can be calculated by formula 1 and the shortest distance between current point to center point can be computed by formula 2.

$$X_j = \{X_k \mid \min(\rho(X_k, X_j)), X_k \in B_i\}, X_k \neq Xo_i \tag{1}$$

$$r_x = r - \min(\rho(X_i, Xo_i), \rho(X_j, Xo_i)) \tag{2}$$

When this operating is performed in hype-space for covering vectors of X_i, X_j, the result can be got like fingure2. The covering parameters are shown in two-dimensional space. The distance is described in formula 3.

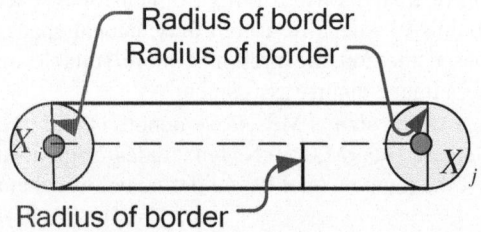

Fig. 2. Covering two neighbor points (2-Dim)

$$d^2(x, x_i, x_j) = \begin{cases} \|x - x_i\|^2, & q(x, x_i, x_j) < 0 \\ \|x - x_i\|^2, & q(x, x_i, x_j) > \|x_j - x_i\| \\ \|x - x_i\|^2 - q(x, x_i, x_j)^2, & \text{others} \end{cases} \tag{3}$$

Among this expression, where $q(x, x_i, x_j)$ is defined as below.

$$q(x, x_i, x_j) = \left\langle x - x_i, \frac{x_j - x_i}{\|x_j - x_i\|} \right\rangle \tag{4}$$

The definition of covering S can be shown in formula 5.

$$S(x; x_i, x_j, r) = \{x \mid d^2(x, x_i, x_j) < r^2\} \tag{5}$$

As for a sample pair, classifier $c: X \to Y$ is defined as the probability according to an unknown distribution D over $X \times Y$.

3 Covering Algorithm

Suppose that in constructive neural network, the whole mapping objects are constructed step by step. Samples covering objects can be generated with different procedure number. The whole architecture is shown in figure 1.

Let's consider the binary classification problem. The input space is X, which is an arbitrary subset of $\mathbb{R}^n$, and the output is $Y=\{0,1\}$ which is a binary classification problem. Therefore a pair of input and output can be symbolized as $z \equiv \{x,y\}$, $x \in X, y \in Y$. The output sequence of the Samples Mapping Objects can be written as $O = \{o_1, o_2, ..., o_p\}$ where $p(p \in Z_+)$ is the produce number which is determined in the process of network construction. The final output of constructive network is Y_i where i class denotation is $Y_i = \min\{i \mid Q(o_i) = 1\}$, Q is a function mapping $y_i \rightarrow \{0,1\}$.

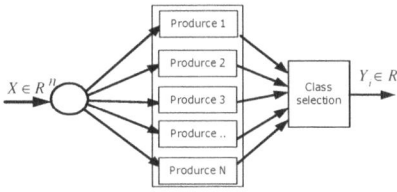

Fig. 3. The architecture of Mapping Ojects

For inside neurons, formula is described as

$$\psi = f\left[\sum_{i=1}^{n}\left(\frac{w_j}{|w_j|}\right)^s \left|w_j(x_j - w_j')\right|^P - \theta\right],$$

Where θ is threshold, S is sign symbol, P is shape symbol, w' is center vector and w is direction vector. For RBF neuron, the parameters are given by $P = 2$, $w_j = 1$, $S = 1$. w_j' is center vector. For hyper-plane neuron, the parameters are given by $P = 1$, $w_j = 1$, $S = 1$. With different parameters, ψ gives different covering shapes in high dimensional space in geometric viewpoint.

For constructive algorithm, let's consider hype-ball neurons in hidden layers where high priority level is characterized by small priority number. The general algorithm can be described as follows:

Input: Feature space data set $X=\{X_1, X_2, ..., X_m\} \subset \mathbb{R}^n$, and the target is $Y \in R$ .Priority number k=1 neuron sets $\{\psi\}, D' = \Phi$

Output: Samples Mapping Objects

Algorithm produce:

```
While  X ≠ φ  do
For each  Xᵢ in  X
```
→get max sub set ($X_{i,sub}$) of X_i and its min Euclid distance (d) of $X_{j,i \neq j}$

→use hype-ball neuron(ψ,d) to cover $X_{i,sub}$,and set
priority k to neuronψ

→add $X_{i,sub}$ to temp set $\grave{D}$

```
End of for
```
→set $X - \grave{D}$ to X , $\grave{D} = \Phi$
```
k = k + 1
End while
For new coming data, the algorithm will update the pro-
durce number of neurons or add new neuron with a
special value. Here is the algorithm:
```
Input: new feature training

set $X'=\{X'_1,X'_2,...,X'_m\} \subset \mathbb{R}^n$, $Y \in R$.

Output: Updated Produrce Number of Mapping Objects

Algorithm Produrce:

```
While  X' ≠ φ  do
For each  X'ᵢ in  X'
```
→Get a consistent subset $X'_{i,sub}$ of X_i randomly and then
do the following produce:
```
If covered( X'ᵢ,ₛᵤᵦ )
do nothing
else
```
   if(misclassified($X'_{i,sub}$))

   Adjust covering space range of hyper-ball neuronψ
and adjust its priority number to lower one.
```
else
   add new neuron with higher priority number k.
end if
end if
```
→add $X'_{i,sub}$ to temp set $\grave{D}$

```
End of for
```
→set $X - \grave{D}$ to X' , $\grave{D} = \Phi$
```
End while.
```

When new samples input into constructive neural network, the priority level of hidden neurons is strengthened or weaken. Using this method, the old information is not destroyed (forgot) after new data learning, but can be partly fetched at any latest priority. This produce is similar to man's learning procedure. As this updating and learning method is only to adjust the special priority level of neurons, therefore, it can process large data set with more effective heuristic algorithm.

For sequence video frames, we will split it into some independent images and transform them into eigenvector in feature space using FFT. An image frame is spitted and transformed by FFT on each sub-block. The ultimate identify formula is written as $O_{AVLI} = \{O_{AVLI(1)}, O_{AVLI(2)}, ..., O_{AVLI(k)}\}$.

Where $O_{AVLI(i)}$ is the i piece time quantum. The last result is written as

$$\max\{count(i) \mid O_{AVLI(i)} = O_{AVLI(j)}, i \neq j\}.$$

Where $count(i)$ is a function of taking sum number of same class in distinguished sequence and the value i gives the similar measure between original image and compared one.

4   Experimental Results

In order to verify the correctness and effectiveness of our proposed solution, a prototype system is developed by Visual C++ and used in a project of CMMB. The test video sequence is collected from CMMB source (TV), which is encoded by H.264 with size 320*240. When transformed sub-block using FFT, an image is split into 8*8 sub-blocks. Noised level is 0 to 5, the smaller is not noised. Video clips are mapping into trends line with different noised level. In Fig. 4, it shows this trend. In Fig. 5, it gives the comparison between real and measurement; the results indicate that the effect of proposed method for measure image based on point calculation in the high dimensional space is coincidence with real condition. In the point calculation method, it calculates some relative image points in high dimensional space which provide

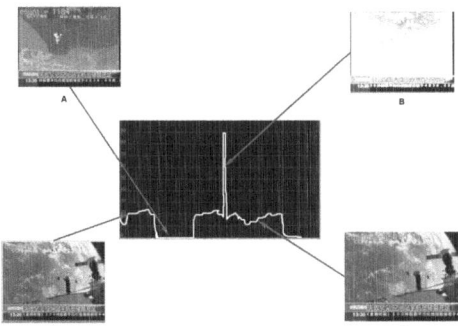

Fig. 4. Noised image mapping to Quality Assessment Trends Line

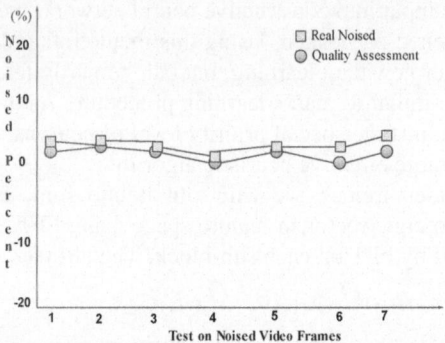

Fig. 5. The comparison between Real and Measurement

more information. On the other side, the sequence of image is not very required and its relation-ship can be covered in high-dimensional space. From relative images, relation-ship of noised image and original image can be mapped into a trend which can gives information of image quality measure. Additionally, the computation FFT complexity of point calculation method is about $O(Nlog_2N)$ and this characteristic can be used in some real-time application.

5 Conclusions

In this paper, we present a new solution for video's image assessment based on high dimensional space. The contributions of this paper can be summarized as follows:

(1) A new idea for image asserts. Testing samples is not sequenced accurately. Based on geometric calculation, it can be used in some real and bad noised environment because it is not rely on time sequence. The proposed method is robust.

(2) The points are computed by referencing image generated form original image based idea of same originate object with same properties, it is easy to implement using geometry method.

Experimental results indicate our method is effective in terms of accuracy, robustness, and stability in video quality assessment. The novelty of this solution is the direct embedding of finding reflecting parameters of image using points in high dimensional space. In addition, the proposed method allows simple and fast implementation for real-time application. More studies in the aspect of basic theory in high-dimensional space inspired by biology should be invested in future.

Acknowledgement. This work is supported by Shanghai Education Commission Research Project under Grant 09YZ344, Shanghai Technology Innovation Project (09160501700, 10110502200) and Shanghai Special Research Fund of Young College Teacher under Grant Z2010-017. The authors are grateful for the anonymous reviewers who made constructive comments.

References

1. Final report from the video quality experts group on the validation of objective quality metrics for video quality assessment,
   `http://www.its.bldrdoc.gov/vqeg/projects/frtv_phaseI`
2. Sheikh, H.R., Wang, Z., Cormack, L., Bovik, A.C.: Live ImageQuality Assessment Database Release 2, `http://live.ece.utexas.edu/research/quality`
3. Sheikh, H.R., Bovik, A.C.: Image information and visual quality. IEEE Trans. Image Process. 15(2), 430–444 (2006)
4. Wang, Z., Simoncelli, E.P., Bovik, A.C.: Multi-scale structural similarity for image quality assessment. In: Proc. IEEE Asilomar Conf. Signals, Syst., Comput., pp. 1398–1402 (2003)
5. Sheikh, H.R., Bovik, A.C.: Image information and visual quality. IEEE Trans. Image Process. 15(2), 430–444 (2006)
6. Ninassi, A., Meur, O.L., Callet, P.L., Barbba, D.: Does where you gaze on an image affect your perception of quality? Applying visual attention to image quality metric. In: Proc. IEEE Int. Conf. Image Process. ICIP 2007, vol. 2, pp. 169–172 (2007)
7. Shoujue, W., Jiangliang, L.: Geometrical Learning, descriptive geometry, and biometric pattern recognition. Neuron Computing 67, 9–28 (2005)
8. Wang, S.J.: Bionic: pattern recognition - A new model of pattern recognition theory and its applications. Acta Electron. Sinica 30(10), 1–4 (2002)
9. Zhu, S., Wang, Z., Liao, M.: Research on K-classification Covering for PONN. Computer Application 27(2), 330–332 (2005) (in chinese)

IGC: An Image Genre Classification System[*]

Joo Hwan Lee[1], Sung Wook Baik[1], Kangseok Kim[2], Changduk Jung[3],
and Wonil Kim[1,**]

[1] College of Electronics and Information Engineering at Sejong University, Seoul, Korea
Tel.: +82-2-3408-3795
twinmoon@sju.ac.kr, sbaik@sejong.ac.kr, wikim@sejong.ac.kr
[2] Department of Knowledge Information Security at Ajou University, Suwon, Korea
kangskim@ajou.ac.kr
[3] Department of Computer and Information Science at Korea University, Korea
jcd1234@korea.ac.kr

Abstract. In this paper, we present image genre classification system, called IGC. The proposed system categorizes images into one of three genres, such as art, photo, or cartoon images. The images features are extracted using standard MPEG-7 visual descriptors, after which they are trained using Neural Networks. The simulation results show that the proposed system successfully classifies images into correct classes with the rate of over 85% depending on the employed features.

Keywords: image genre, photo, cartoon, MPEG-7 visual descriptors, neural networks.

1 Introduction

As the attention and focus of information shift from textual forms to digital multimedia forms, we encounter much more digital images than before. Consequently, now we have a new issue of dealing with these digital contents such as art, photo, or cartoon images. Currently millions of art, photo, and cartoon images are located on the Internet. Digital viewers want to access and choose their favorites more efficiently from the sea of digital contents.

The main purpose of this paper is to apply MPEG-7 standard to digital multimedia images by utilizing MPEG-7 descriptors. By analyzing MPEG-7 descriptors, we create a prototype system that can be used in categorizing digital image genre, such as art, photo, or cartoon images, under visual environments, and introduce effective methodology of image classification via experiments. For example, it will tell that a given image belongs to art, cartoon or photo image with confidence rate from 0.0 to 1.0. The system uses MPEG-7 visual descriptors for image features and the

---

[*] "This research was supported by Basic Science Research Program through the National Research Foundation of Korea(NRF) funded by the Ministry of Education, Science and Technology (No.2010-0028046)".
[**] Corresponding author.

H. Deng et al. (Eds.): AICI 2011, Part II, LNAI 7003, pp. 360–367, 2011.

classification module employs neural network. The usage of this system is enormous. It can be properly fit into the image classification engine in image search system.

We discuss related works on the image genre classification in section 2. In section 3, we propose our Neural Network based image genre classification system, called IGC. The simulation results are presented in section 4. We conclude in section 5.

2   Previous Research

2.1   MPEG-7 Descriptors and Image Description

MPEG-7 is a recent emerging standard used in image classification systems. It is not a standard for encoding and decoding of video and audio, but it is a standard for describing media content. It uses a XML to store metadata and solves the problem of lacking standard to describe visual image content [1].

Ilvesmaki and Iivarinen has applied MPEG-7 standard to defect image retrieval. They tested descriptors by extracting MPEG-7 feature vectors for a pre-classified defect database of more than 1300 images [2].

Verdaguer proposed the system which describe and arrange automatically photos only according to color features. Two color descriptors, the Color Layout Descriptor and the Dominant Color Descriptor, have been employed in his research [3].

Soysal and Alatan combined low-level color descriptor and texture descriptor. Their simulation result shows accuracy improvements between 3.5-6.5%, compared with the best performance of single classifier systems. In the way of combining classifiers and descriptors, they proposed two decision mechanisms, one of which demonstrates significant improvement over the next one [4].

Spyrou et al. proposed a fusing method using various low-level MPEG-7 visual descriptors. Their work is motivated to fuse several descriptors in order to improve the performance of several machine-learning classifiers [5].

Kim et al. proposed a neural network based classification module using MPEG-7 [6, 7]. In this model, inputs for the neural network are fed from the feature values of MPEG-7 descriptors that are extracted from images. Since the various descriptors can represent the specific features of a given image, the proper evaluation process should be required to choose the best one for the adult image classification.

2.2   Image Genre Classification

The automatic classification of web images as photographs or graphics including cartoons is a well-known contents image classification. Examples are the WebSeek search engine J. Smith's research [8] and the systems described in N. Rowe's research [9]. Unfortunately, their features take advantage of some characteristics of web images that do not exist in cartoon images, notably the aspect ratio and the word occurrence in the image URLs. In the same fashion of J. Smith and N. Rowe [8, 9], V. Athitsos emphasizes the basic characteristics of cartoons and implemented nine color descriptors in order to distinguish photos and graphics on a database of 1200 samples [10].

Ianeva et al. proposes an approach for classifying individual video frames as being a cartoon or a photographic image [11]. It introduces descriptors like the ones based on the pattern spectrum of parabolic size distributions and the complexity of the image signal approximated by its compression ratio. It applies the farthest neighbor histogram descriptor suggested by V. Athitsos to the data collection. However this characteristic is expensive to compute without resulting in improved error rates [10].

The photo/graphics classifier of V. Athitsos had been previously implemented as part of the Acoi system [12]. A decision rule classifier (C4.5, [13]) has been trained on the features given in V. Athitsos's research on varying quantities of training data. The implementation has a classification score of 0:9 on a data set of 14,040 photos and 9,512 graphics harvested from the World Wide Web.

Roach et al. presents an approach for the classification of video fragments as cartoons using motion only [14]. Yet, its database consists of only 8 cartoon and 20 non-cartoon sequences, therefore it is difficult to predict how it would perform, and its data set is not publicly available. Truong et al. addresses another effort for the classification of video into seven categories [15]. Two of the features are similar to R. Glasberg's research [16], but the approach is different and the experiments are incomparable.

3   The Proposed Cartoon Image Classification System

3.1   The Proposed Architecture

The sample images of art, cartoon, and photo are illustrated in Figure 1. The proposed system classifies these images as one of three categories, art image, cartoon image, and photo image.

Figure 2 represents the overall architecture of the proposed image genre classification system (IGC). The proposed architecture consists of two modules; feature extraction module and classification module.

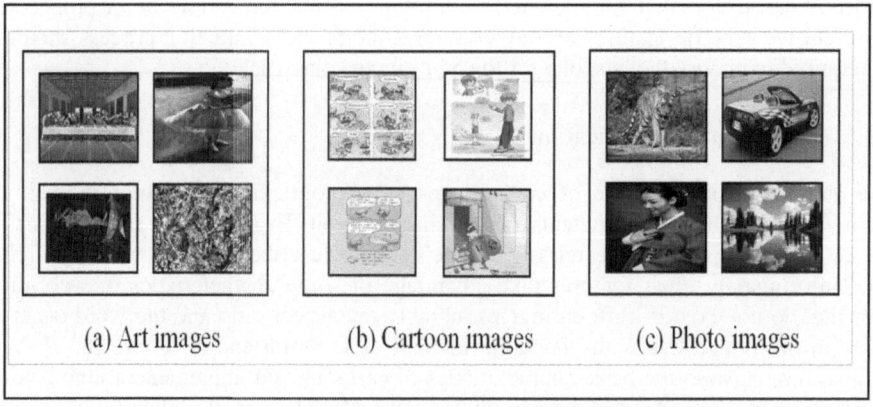

(a) Art images   (b) Cartoon images   (c) Photo images

Fig. 1. Example images from the three genres used for simulation

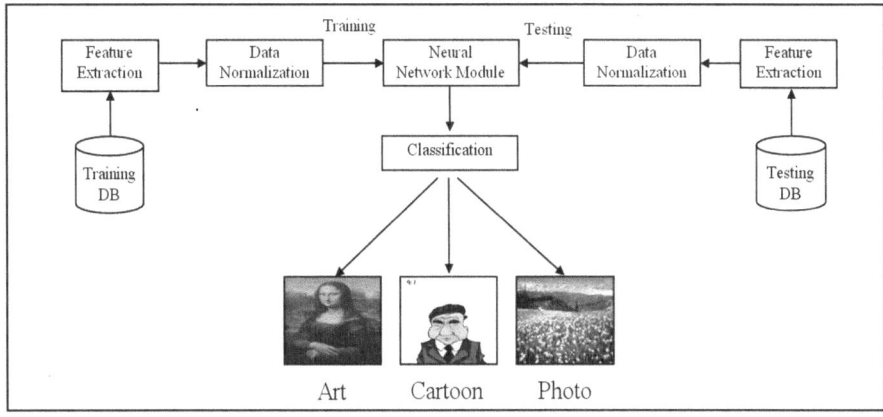

Fig. 2. The overview of the proposed Image Genre Classification System

3.2   Feature Extraction Module

The feature extraction module and the classification modules are connected in serial form, as shown in Figure 3. In the feature extraction module, there are three engines. From the figure, MPEG-7 XM engine extracts the features of images with XML description format. The parsing engine parses the raw descriptions to transform them to numerical values, which are suitable for neural network implementation. The preprocess engine normalizes the numerical values to the 0-1 range. By normalizing the input features, it can avoid that input features with big number scale dominant the output of the neural network classifier (NNC) for the classification of the sports image over input features with small number scale.

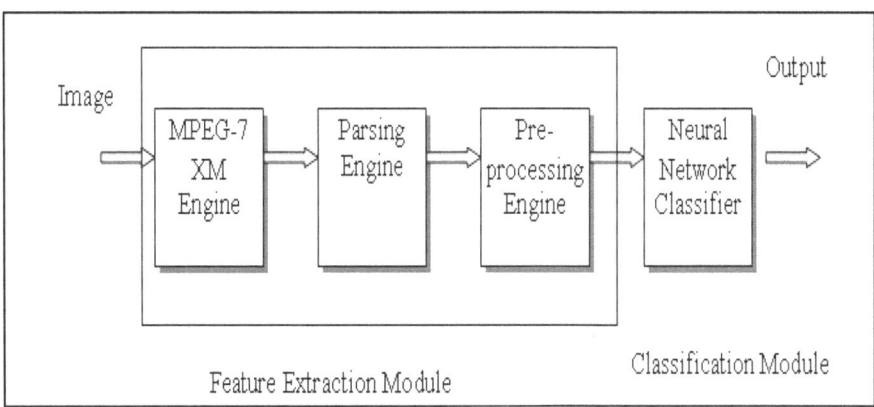

Fig. 3. The Overview of Feature Extraction Module

3.3   Classification Module

Using the data set of the normalized input features and classes of sports, we can model an NNC in the classification module. According to different MPEG-7 descriptors, the number of the input features can be various. Let us denote the input feature vector obtained from the first MPEG-7 descriptor as $X_{D_1} = (x_{D_{1,1}}, x_{D_{1,2}}, \cdots, x_{D_{1,i}}, \cdots, x_{D_{1,n_1}})$, here $x_{D_{1,i}}$ is the ith input feature extracted from MPGE-7 descriptor 1 and the subscript $n1$ is the dimension of the input features from the first MPEG-7 descriptor. With the same way, the input feature vector obtained from the last MPEG-7 descriptor k can be expressed as $X_{D_k} = (x_{D_{k,1}}, x_{D_{k,2}}, \cdots, x_{D_{k,i}}, \cdots, x_{D_{k,n_k}})$. Also, the output vector can be expressed as $Y = (y_1, y_2, \cdots, y_i, \cdots, y_s)$, here yi is the output from the ith output node and the subscript s is the number of classes. By utilizing the hard limit function in the output layer, we can have binary value, 0 or 1, for each output node yi as Equation (1).

$$y_i = f_o(netinput_o) = \begin{pmatrix} 1, & netinput_o \geq 0 \\ 0, & \text{otherwise} \end{pmatrix} \tag{1}$$

where fo is the hard limit function at the output node and $netinput_o$ is the net input of fo. As shown in Equation (2), the net input is can be expressed as the product of the output vector in the hidden layer, denoted as Y_h, and the weight vector Wo at the output layer.

$$netinput_o = W_o^T Y_h \tag{2}$$

With the same way, the hidden layer output vector, Y_h, can also be computed by functioning the product of the input weight vector and the input vector. Thus, the accuracy of the NNC depends on the values of whole weight vectors. To obtain the optimal weight vectors, the NNC is trained using the back-propagation algorithm which is commonly utilized for training neural networks. The training is done after coding each class of sports into s dimension orthogonal vector. For example, since we have two and three classes, the classes are coded to (1, 0), (0 1) or (1, 0, 0), (0 1, 0), (0, 0, 1). Once obtaining an optimal weight vector, we evaluate the performance of NNC using the test data which is unseen during training phase.

4   Simulation and Results

4.1   Environments

For cartoon-photo classification simulation, 1600 images were used for training (800 for each image genre), and 720 for testing (360 for each image genre). For art-cartoon-photo classification simulation, 2400 images were used for training (800 for each image genre), and 1080 for testing (360 for each image genre). In both cases five descriptors were employed for feature values, Color Layout, Color Structure, Homogeneous Texture, Region Shape, and Edge Histogram. In cartoon-photo classification case of simulations, the classification modules were equipped with two hidden layers with 50 nodes each and were trained 100,000 iterations. In art-cartoon-photo classification case of simulations, the classification modules were equipped with two hidden layers with 30 nodes each and were trained 100,000 iterations.

4.2   Result

The simulation result of cartoon-photo classification is shown in Table 1 and that of art-cartoon-photo classification results is shown in Table 2. The cartoon-photo classification task presents good result in Color Layout, Color Structure and Edge Histogram as in Table 1. In Color Structure and Edge Histogram descriptor simulations, the proposed neural network successfully classifies cartoon images with 97.79% and 97.24% respectively. In addition, in the result of Homogeneous Texture, it shows good performance as 93.63 % of photo image classification.

Table 1. Classification Results of Cartoon-Photo Images (%)

		Cartoon	Photo
Cartoon	C.L.	**92.82**	7.18
	C.S	**97.79**	2.21
	R.S.	**78.18**	21.82
	E.H.	**97.24**	2.76
	H.T.	**84.53**	15.47
	Average	**90.12**	9.89
Photo	C.L.	3.87	**96.13**
	C.S	4.14	**95.86**
	R.S.	15.51	**84.49**
	E.H.	6.65	**93.35**
	H.T.	6.37	**93.63**
	average	7.31	**92.70**

Table 2. Classification Results of Art-Cartoon-Photo Images (%)

		Art	Cartoon	Photo
Art	C.L.	**69.71**	8.61	22.22
	E.H.	**79.17**	6.94	13.89
	H.T.	**75.00**	10.28	14.72
	R.S.	**50.56**	17.78	31.67
	C.S.	**82.50**	1.39	16.11
	average	**70.99**	9.00	19.73
Cartoon	C.L.	5.83	**86.94**	7.22
	E.H.	11.39	**84.44**	4.17
	H.T.	8.33	**86.94**	4.72
	R.S.	24.72	**59.72**	15.56
	C.S.	1.11	**98.06**	0.83
	average	10.28	**83.22**	6.50
Photo	C.L.	25.00	2.50	**72.50**
	E.H.	17.22	5.56	**77.22**
	H.T.	20.00	4.72	**75.28**
	R.S.	32.50	15.28	**52.22**
	C.S.	19.72	1.67	**78.61**
	average	22.89	5.95	**71.17**

Art-cartoon-photo image classification shows relatively lower performances than cartoon-photo image classification since it deals with three genres of images. However, the IGC system performs excellent result in case of cartoon image classification. It is reasoned that the cartoon images bear very distinct image features. Generally, the system performs good result in Color Structure descriptor and performs worse result in Region Shape descriptor. The results seem very promising and can be applied to various image processing domains. It can be applied and implemented as the main part of image search engine or image collection engine. For a large image data base, it is very useful tool for image retrieval system.

5   Conclusion

In this paper, we proposed image genre classification system, called IGC. The proposed system categorizes images into one of three genres, such as art, photo, or cartoon images. The classification module of the system learns corresponding classification task according to feature values, which is extracted from MPEG-7 descriptors. The simulation results show that the proposed system successfully classifies images into correct classes with the rate of over 85% depending in the employed features.

References

1. Sikora, T.: The MPEG-7 visual standard for content description – an overview. IEEE Transactions on Circuit and Systems for Video Technology 11(6), 696–702 (2001)
2. Ilvesmaki, A., Iivarinen, J.: Defect image classification with MPEG-7 descriptors. Helsinki University of Technology (2003)
3. Verdaguer, S.L.: Color based image classification and description. Politecnica Universiy, Spain (2009)
4. Soysal, M., Alatan, A.A.: Combining MPEG-7 Based Visual Experts for Reaching Semantics. In: García, N., Salgado, L., Martínez, J.M. (eds.) VLBV 2003. LNCS, vol. 2849, pp. 66–75. Springer, Heidelberg (2003)
5. Spyrou, E., Le Borgne, H., Mailis, T., Cooke, E., Avrithis, Y., O'Connor, N.: Fusing MPEG-7 visual descriptors for image classification. In: International Conference on Artificial Neural Networks (2005)
6. Kim, W., Lee, H.-K., Yoo, S.-J., Baik, S.W.: Neural Network Based Adult Image Classification. In: Duch, W., Kacprzyk, J., Oja, E., Zadrożny, S. (eds.) ICANN 2005. LNCS, vol. 3696, pp. 481–486. Springer, Heidelberg (2005)
7. Kim, W., Lee, H.-K., Park, J., Yoon, K.: Multi Class Adult Image Classification Using Neural Networks. In: Kégl, B., Lee, H.-H. (eds.) Canadian AI 2005. LNCS (LNAI), vol. 3501, pp. 222–226. Springer, Heidelberg (2005)
8. Smith, J.R., Chang, S.-F.: Searching for images and videos on the world wide web. Tech. Rep. 459-96-25, Center for Communications Research, Columbia University (1996)
9. Rowe, N.C., Frew, B.: Automatic caption localization for photographs on word wide web pages. Tech. Rep., Department of Computer Science, Naval Postgraduate School (1997)
10. Athitsos, V., Swain, M.J., Frankel, C.: Distinguishing photographs and graphics on the world wide web. In: IEEE Workshop on Content-Based Access of Image and Video Libraries, Puerto Rico (June 1997)

11. Ianeva, T., de Vries, A., Rohrig, H.: Detecting cartoons: A case study in automatic video-genre classification. In: IEEE International Conference on Multimedia and Expo., vol. 1, pp. 449–452 (2003)
12. Windhouwer, M.A., Schmidt, A.R., Kersten, M.L.: Acoi: A System for Indexing Multimedia Objects. In: International Workshop on Information Integration and Web-based Applications & Services, Yogyakarta, Indonesia (November 1999)
13. Quinlan, J.R.: C4.5: Programs for Machine Learning. Morgan Kaufmann, San Francisco (1993)
14. Roach, M., Mason, J.S., Pawlewski, M.: Motion-based classification of cartoons. In: Int. Symposium on Intelligent Multimedia (2001)
15. Truong, B.T., Dorai, C., Venkatesh, S.: Automatic genre identification for content-based video categorization. In: Proc. 15th International Conference on Pattern Recognition, Barcelona, Spain, vol. II, pp. 230–233 (September 2000)
16. Glasberg, R., Elazouzi, K., Sikora, T.: Cartoon-Recognition Using Visual-Descriptors and a Multilayer-Perceptron. In: WIAMIS, Montreux, April 13-15 (2005)

A Cartoon Image Classification System Using MPEG-7 Descriptors[*]

Junghyun Kim[1], Sung Wook Baik[1], Kangseok Kim[2],
Changduk Jung[3] and Wonil Kim[1,**]

[1] College of Electronics and Information Engineering at Sejong University, Seoul, Korea
Tel.: +82-2-3408-3795
junghyun64@sju.ac.kr, sbaik@sejong.ac.kr, wikim@sejong.ac.kr
[2] Department of Knowledge Information Security at Ajou University, Suwon, Korea
kangskim@ajou.ac.kr
[3] Department of Computer and Information Science at Korea University, Korea
jcd1234@korea.ac.kr

Abstract. Today cartoon images take more portion of digital multimedia than ever as we notice this phenomenon in the entertainment business. With the explosive proliferation of cartoon image contents on the Internet, we seem to need a classification system to categorize these cartoon images. This paper presents a new approach of cartoon image classification based on cartoonists. The proposed cartoon image classification system employs effective MPEG-7 descriptors as image feature values and learns features of particular cartoon images, and classifies the images as multiple classes according to each cartoonist. In the performance simulation we evaluate the effectiveness of the proposed system on a large set of cartoon images and the system successfully classifies images into multiple classes with the rate of over 90%.

Keywords: MPEG-7 visual descriptor, Image Classification, Neural Network, Cartoon.

1   Introduction

With the fast development of digital multimedia, we can access much more digital contents, such as cartoon images, on the Internet and TV than ever. As the volume of cartoon image contents is exponentially increased and they are easy to be accessed, we need to think of another issue: How are these cartoon image contents categorized to be easily accessed? Now millions of cartoon images are residing in people's blogs and cartoon viewers might want to choose their favorite cartoons from the Internet. Thus, to manage a digital library for cartoon image contents, we need an automatic cartoon image classification system.

---

[*] "This research was supported by Basic Science Research Program through the National Research Foundation of Korea(NRF) funded by the Ministry of Education, Science and Technology (No.2010-0028046)".
[**] Corresponding author.

H. Deng et al. (Eds.): AICI 2011, Part II, LNAI 7003, pp. 368–375, 2011.

The main purpose of this paper is to apply MPEG-7 standard to cartoon images for image classification according to the cartoonist. By analyzing MPEG-7 descriptors, we create a prototype system that can be used for cartoon image classification techniques under visual environments, and introduce effective methodology of descriptor fusion via experiments. In this paper, we use neural networks for the image classification. An input value for the network is several values of visual features extracted by MPEG-7.

We discuss several methods of the image classification in section 2. In section 3, we propose our Neural Network based cartoon image classification system. The simulation results are presented in section 4. We conclude in section 5.

2   Previous Research

2.1   MPEG-7 Descriptors and Image Classification Systems

MPEG-7 is a emerging standard that describes media content used in image classification systems. Even though it is not a standard dealing with the actual encoding and decoding of video and audio, it solves the problem of lacking standard to describe visual image content. It uses a XML to store metadata. The aim, scope, and details of MPEG-7 standard are nicely overviewed by Sikora of Technical University Berlin in his paper [1].

Among series of researches that use various MPEG-7 descriptors, Ro et al. [2] shows a study of texture based image description and retrieval method using an adapted version of homogeneous texture descriptor of MPEG-7. Other studies of image classification use descriptors like a contour-based shape descriptor [3], a histogram descriptor [4], and a combination of color structure and homogeneous descriptors [5]. As a part of the EU aceMedia project research, Spyrou et al. propose three image classification techniques based on fusing various low-level MPEG-7 visual descriptors [6]. Since the direct inclusion of descriptors would be inappropriate and incompatible, fusion is required to bridge the semantic gap between the target semantic classes and the low-level visual descriptors.

There is a CBIRS that combines neural network and MPEG-7 standard: researchers of Helsinki University of Technology developed a neural, self-organizing system to retrieve images based on their content, the PicSOM (the Picture + self-organizing map, SOM) [7]. The technique is based on pictorial examples and relevance feedback (RF). The PicSOM system is implemented by using tree structured SOM. The MPEG-7 content descriptor is provided for the system. In the paper, they compare the PicSOM indexing technique with a reference system based on vector quantization (VQ). Their results show the MPEG-7 content descriptor can be used in the PicSOM system despite the fact that Euclidean distance calculation is not optimal for all of them.

Neural network has been used to develop methods for a high accuracy pattern recognition and image classification for a long period of time. Kanellopoulos and Wilkinson perform their experiments of using different neural networks and classifiers to classify images including multi-layer perceptron neural networks and maximum likelihood classifier [8]. The paper examines the best practice in such areas as: network architecture selection, use of optimization algorithms, scaling of input data, avoiding chaos effects, use of enhanced feature sets, and use of hybrid classifier methods. They have recommendations and strategies for effective and efficient use of neural networks in the paper as well.

It is known that the neural network of the image classification system should make different errors to be effective. So Giacinto and Roli propose an approach to ensemble automatic design of neural network [9]. The approach is to target to select the subset of given large set of neural networks to form the most error-independent nets. The approach consists of the overproduction phase and the choice phase, which choose the subset of neural networks. The overproduction phase is studied by Partidge and the choice phase are sub-divided into the unsupervised learning step for identifying subsets and the final ensemble set creation step by selecting subsets from the previous step [10].

Kim et al. proposed a neural network based classification module using MPEG-7 [11, 12]. In this model, inputs for the neural network are fed from the feature values of MPEG-7 descriptors that are extracted from images. Since the various descriptors can represent the specific features of a given image, the proper evaluation process should be required to choose the best one for the adult image classification.

2.2   Cartoon Image Classifications

R. Glasberg et al. proposes a approach for classifying mpeg-2 video sequences as cartoon or non-cartoon by analyzing specific color, texture, and motion features of consecutive frames in real-time [13]. It is a well-known video genre classification problem, where popular TV broadcast genre like cartoon, commercial, music, news, and sports are studied. In the system the extracted features from the visual descriptors are non-linear weighted with a sigmoid-function and afterwards combined using a multilayered perceptron to produce a reliable recognition.

Rama et al. proposed a flexible scheme based on a non-linear classifier called Fuzzy Integral. This operator was supposed to give a relevance measure to all the features involved in the classification as well   to classify the images [14].

Berkels et al. particularly extract cartoon images from 2D aerial images in city areas. These images are mainly characterized by rectangular geometries of locally varying orientation. Their method is based on a joint classification of the shape orientation and a rectangular structure that are preserved before the restoration of image shapes [15].

Humphey implement a system that using low-level descriptors to classify a query as either cartoon or non cartoon. His system employs neural network for training database of ground-truth features. The performance of the system relatively well for training data compared to previous work, but fail to exhibit the same classification accuracy in test case [16].

Bosch et al. used image classification method according to the object categories that they contain in the large number of object cases. To implement this they combine three ingredients as follows, (1) shape and appearance representations that support spatial pyramid matching over a region of interest. (2) an automatic selection of the regions of interest in training phases. (3) the use of random forests as a multi-way classifier. The advantage of such classifiers is the ease of training and testing[17].

3   The Proposed Cartoon Image Classification System

3.1   The Proposed Architecture

The sample images of single cut cartons and multi cut cartoons are illustrated in Figure 1 and Figure 2 respectively. The proposed system classifies these images as one of three categories. The categories are predefined like s1, s2, s3 and m1, m2, m3 with respect to cartoonist.

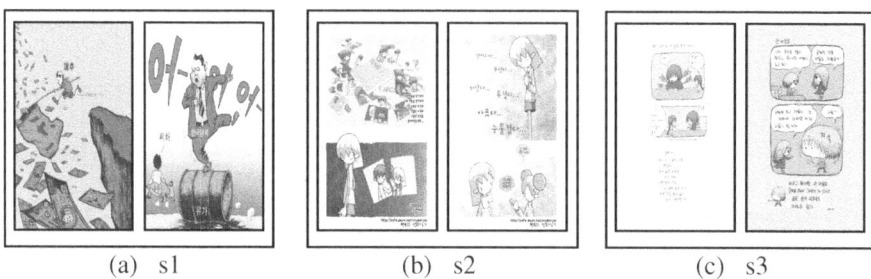

(a) s1   (b) s2   (c) s3

Fig. 1. Example images of single cut cartoon used in simulation

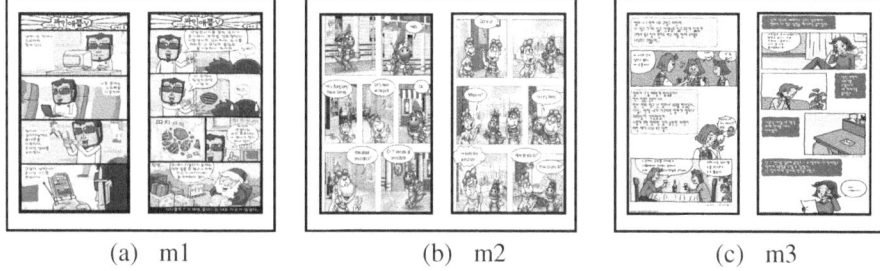

(a) m1   (b) m2   (c) m3

Fig. 2. Example images of multi cut cartoon used in simulation

Figure 3 represents the overall architecture of the proposed cartoon image classification system. The proposed architecture consists of two modules; feature extraction module and classification module. Features defined in the MPEG-7 descriptors for the given query images are extracted, and then used as inputs for the classifier module.

3.2   Feature Extraction

By running the MPEG-7 XM program, features of training images are extracted in XML format. This feature information in XML format is parsed in the next step and is normalized into values between 0 and 1 with respect to values generated by each descriptor. These normalized values are used as inputs for the neural network classifier. The original values are converted into normal values, and followed by the class information. The class information, which is attached to the feature value, is the orthogonal vector value. For example, a category one cartoon image is represented as (1 0 0), whereas category two and three cartoons are (0 1 0) and (0 0 1) respectively.

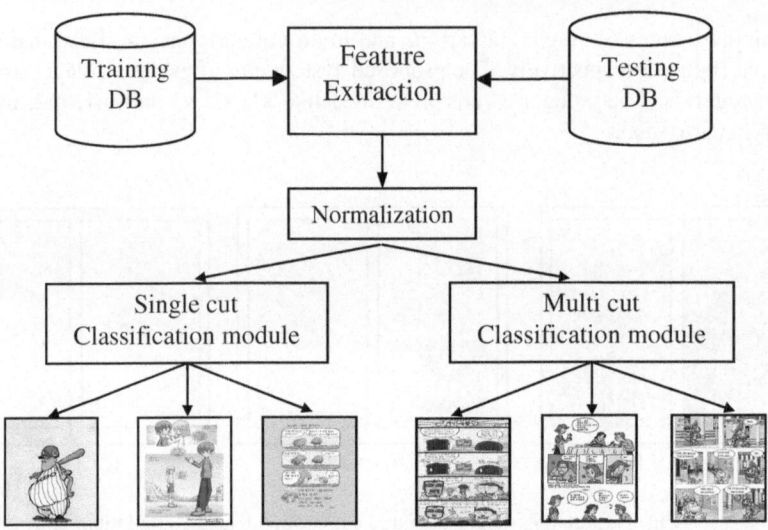

Fig. 3. The overall architecture of cartoon image classification system

3.3   Classification Module

The classification module employs neural network. The neural network classifier learns a relation of the feature values and a corresponding class by modifying the weight values between nodes. We use the backpropagation algorithm to train the network. It consists of input layer, output layer, and multiple hidden layers. The number of input nodes depends on a dimension of each descriptor, whereas the number of output nodes is three. The class information for the three output nodes is represented orthogonally like (1, 0, 0) depending on the classes as mentioned above. In a testing process, similar to the training process, the system extracts features from query images using MPEG-7 descriptors and classifies the images using the neural network that generated by the training process.

4   Simulation and Results

4.1   Environments

The simulation uses a total of 600 images for training (100 for each cartoon images), and 300 for testing (50 for each cartoon images). It employs five descriptors for feature values, Color Layout, Color Structure, Region Shape, Homogeneous Texture, and Edge Histogram. The inputs consist of MPEG7 normalized descriptor values. Two classification modules were evaluated; one for single cut cartoon images and the other for multi cut cartoon images. The both modules were equipped with 2 layer 50 hidden nodes each and trained 100,000 iterations. The output layer consists of 3 nodes, one for each cartoon class.

4.2   Result

The simulation results of five descriptors for single cut cartoon images and multi cut cartoon images are shown in Table 1 and Table 2 respectively. In Table 1, the proposed cartoon image classification system for single cut cartoon images performs excellent result in Color Structure. The average of Color Structure simulation results is 99.34%. The system also shows good performance results in other 4 descriptors. For example, in Edge Histogram and Homogeneous Texture, the average results are 90.67% and 93.98% respectively. In Region Shape, it performs relatively low but reasonable results since the average is over 81%.

Table 1. Classification Results for Single Cut Cartoon Images

Color Layout				Color Structure		
	S1	S2	S3		S1	S2	S3
S1	88.00	12.00	0.00	S1	100.00	0.00	0.00
S2	6.00	84.00	10.00	S2	2.00	98.00	0.00
S3	0.00	18.37	81.63	S3	0.00	0.00	100.00
Region Shape				Edge Histogram		
	S1	S2	S3		S1	S2	S3
S1	82.00	16.00	2.00	S1	86.00	14.00	0.00
S2	10.00	84.00	6.00	S2	14.00	86.00	0.00
S3	14.29	8.16	77.55	S3	0.00	0.00	100.00
Homogeneous Texture				Average		
	S1	S2	S3		S1	S2	S3
S1	92.00	8.00	0.00	S1	**89.60**	10.00	0.40
S2	0.00	94.00	6.00	S2	6.40	**89.20**	4.40
S3	0.00	4.08	95.92	S3	2.86	6.13	**91.02**

Table 2. Classification Results for Multi Cut Cartoon Images

Color Layout				Color Structure		
	M1	M2	M3		M1	M2	M3
M1	96.00	4.00	0.00	M1	96.00	4.00	0.00
M2	8.00	82.00	2.00	M2	0.00	98.00	2.00
M3	1.89	13.21	84.91	M3	0.00	0.00	100.00
Region Shape				Edge Histogram		
	M1	M2	M3		M1	M2	M3
M1	82.00	8.00	10.00	M1	100.00	0.00	0.00
M2	0.00	80.00	20.00	M2	0.00	98.00	0.00
M3	14.29	8.16	77.55	M3	0.00	0.00	100.00
Homogeneous Texture				Average		
	M1	M2	M3		M1	M2	M3
M1	100.00	0.00	0.00	M1	**94.80**	3.20	2.00
M2	0.00	96.00	4.00	M2	1.60	**90.80**	5.60
M3	0.00	4.08	95.92	M3	3.24	5.09	**91.68**

Moreover, in Table 2, the proposed cartoon image classification system for multi cut cartoon images performs excellent result in Color Structure. The average of Color Structure simulation results is 98%. In Edge Histogram and Homogeneous Texture, the average results are 99.34% and 97.31% respectively. However, the result of Region Shape is worse than other descriptors as 79.85%.

Overall, the proposed cartoon image classification system performs excellent result in Color Structure, Homogeneous Texture and Edge histogram than other two descriptors. The results seem very promising and can be applied to various image processing domains. It can be easily extended to medical image processing, in which identifying a particular image belongs to a certain symptom is very critical. Also it can be implemented as the main part of image search engine or image collection engine. For a large image data base, it is very useful tool for image retrieval system.

5   Conclusion

In this paper, we presented cartoon image classification system employing MPEG-7 descriptors as image feature values. The proposed system learns features of particular cartoon images and classifies the images into multiple classes according to the cartoon stylist. In the performance simulation, the proposed system successfully classifies images into multiple classes with the rate of over 90%.

References

1. Sikora, T.: The MPEG-7 visual standard for content description – an overview. IEEE Transactions on Circuit and Systems for Video Technology 11(6), 696–702 (2001)
2. Ro, Y., Kim, M., Kang, H., Manjunath, B., Kim, J.: MPEG-7 homogeneous texture descriptor. ETRI Journal 23(2), 41–51 (2001)
3. Bober, M.: The MPEG-7 visual shape descriptors. IEEE Transactions on Circuit and Systems for Video Technology 11(6), 716–719 (2001)
4. Won, C., Park, D., Park, S.: Efficient use of MPEG-7 edge histogram descriptor. ETRI Journal 24(1), 23–30 (2002)
5. Pakkanen, J., Ilvesmäki, A., Iivarinen, J.: Defect image classification and retrieval with MPEG-7 descriptors. In: Bigun, J., Gustavsson, T. (eds.) SCIA 2003. LNCS, vol. 2749, pp. 349–355. Springer, Heidelberg (2003)
6. Spyrou, E., Borgne, H., Mailis, T., Cooke, E., Arvrithis, Y., O'Connor, H.: Fusing MPEG-7 visual descriptors for image classification. In: Duch, W., Kacprzyk, J., Oja, E., Zadrożny, S. (eds.) ICANN 2005. LNCS, vol. 3697, pp. 847–852. Springer, Heidelberg (2005)
7. Laaksonen, J., Koskela, M., Oja, E.: PicSOM – Self-organizing image retrieval with MPEG-7 content descriptor. IEEE Transactions on Neural Networks: Special Issue on Intelligent Multimedia Processing 13(4), 841–853 (2002)
8. Kanellopoulos, I., Wilkinson, G.: Strategies and best practice for neural network image classification. International Journal of Remote Sensing 18(4), 711–725 (1997)
9. Giacinto, G., Roli, F.: Design of effective neural network ensembles for image classification purposes. Image and Vision Computing 19(9-10), 699–707 (2001)

10. Patridge, D.: Network generalization differences quantified. Neural Networks 9(2), 263–271 (1996)
11. Kim, W., Lee, H.-K., Yoo, S.-J., Baik, S.W.: Neural Network Based Adult Image Classification. In: Duch, W., Kacprzyk, J., Oja, E., Zadrożny, S. (eds.) ICANN 2005. LNCS, vol. 3696, pp. 481–486. Springer, Heidelberg (2005)
12. Kim, W., Lee, H.-K., Park, J., Yoon, K.: Multi Class Adult Image Classification Using Neural Networks. In: Kégl, B., Lee, H.-H. (eds.) Canadian AI 2005. LNCS (LNAI), vol. 3501, pp. 222–226. Springer, Heidelberg (2005)
13. Glasberg, R., Elazouzi, K., Sikora, T.: Cartoon-Recognition Using Visual-Descriptors and a Multilayer-Perceptron. In: WIAMIS, Montreux, April 13-15 (2005)
14. Rama, A., Tarres, F., Sanchez, L.: Cartoon Detection Using Fuzzy Integral. In: WIAMIS 2007 Proceedings of the Eight International Workshop on Image Analysis for Multimedia Interactive Services (2007)
15. Berkels, B., Burger, M., Droske, M., Nemitz, O., Rumpf, M.: Cartoon Extraction Based on Anisotropic Image Classification. In: Modeling and Visualization. Springer, Heidelberg (2006)
16. Humphrey, E.: Cartoon Recognition and Classification. University of Miami (2009)
17. Bosch, A., Zisserman, A., Munoz, X.: Image Classification using Random Forests and Ferns. In: IEEE 11th International Conference on Computer Vision (2007)

Denoising of Coal Flotation Froth Image Using Opening and Closing Filters with Area Reconstruction and Alternating Order Filtering

Jinling Yang[1,2], Jieming Yang[1], and Muling Tian[1,3]

[1] Institute of Mechatronics Engineering, Taiyuan University of Technology,
Taiyuan 030024, China
[2] Shanxi Fenxi Zijin Coal Industry Co., Ltd.,
Linshi 031300, China
[3] College of Electrical and Power Engineering, Taiyuan University of Technology,
Taiyuan 030024, China
yangjinlingjx@163.com,yangjieming@tyut.edu.cn,
tianmuling@tyut.edu.cn

Abstract. Image denoising of coal flotation froth plays an important part in the subsequent image processing such as image segmentation and feature extraction. In traditional image denoising, there exists some inconsistency between removing the noise and preserving the most sharp detail information of object edges. In this paper, a morphological denoising algorithm is proposed for removing the noise of coal flotation froth image. This algorithm combines the opening and closing filters based on area reconstruction with an alternating order filtering method, and the elliptical structuring elements with increasing radius are adopted in the morphological filters. Based on the algorithm, denoise processing of a lot of coal froth images acquired from coal flotation working site was carried out. Denoising results show that many isolated spots on the original bubble images have been obviously eliminated, and no edge blurring appears, instead, the useful detail information in image is preserved.

Keywords: Coal Flotation, Morphology, Area Reconstruction, Opening and Closing Filter, Alternation Order Filtering.

1   Introduction

Flotation froth feature is the important indicator to evaluate whether the flotation state is good or bad because the flotation froth contains a lot of information about the procedure operation variables and product quality. For the past 20 years, many foreign and domestic scholars have studied several methods of extracting the flotation froth characteristics based on machine vision technology, which utilizes imaging techniques to detect froth bubbles features and to evaluate the flotation process performance. Moolman (1995)[1] extracted some significant features such as average bubble size, froth texture, chromatic information, etc. from the copper flotation froth

H. Deng et al. (Eds.): AICI 2011, Part II, LNAI 7003, pp. 376–382, 2011.
© Springer-Verlag Berlin Heidelberg 2011

surface. Giuseppe Bonifazi (2001)[2] collected the digital sample images in a copper industrial flotation plant operating in steady conditions, and the morphological and structure measurements of the froth bubbles were obtained by using image enhancement and segmentation techniques. Wang and Bergholm (2003)[3] described a set of image segmentation algorithms for mineral froth images based on gray-value valley detection. In the flotation froth image processing, one of the key issues is image segmentation by means of which the bubble size, size distribution and other parameters of the physical characteristics of the flotation froth can be obtained.

In the course of processing the coal flotation froth image, it should be considered that the froth image is made up of many bubbles of non-homogeneous composition, and in most industrial flotation cases, the illumination on the bubble surface is uneven and the bubble surface appears uneven reflection point or noise because of light reflection. In addition, the coal flotation froth image includes mainly the gray-scale information and hardly any color information [4]. Moreover, the bubbles touch each other, and there is no void space (background) between bubbles [5]. The specific nature of the coal flotation froth image will affect the subsequent image processing, such as image over-segmentation [6], which will cause the feature extracted from the froth image become meaningless. Therefore, it is necessary to improve the image quality by denoising techniques, which can make the subsequent image processing easier and valid.

The purpose of image denoising is to retain the useful information and eliminate or weaken the useless noise of the image. There are many ways to eliminate noise. One is the low-pass filter in the spatial domain, such as mean filter (a kind of linear smooth filter) and median filter (a kind of nonlinear smooth filter). Another is the low-pass filter in the frequency domain. In essence, when the low-pass filter eliminates the noise of an image, it would also eliminate the useful high-frequency part of the image information. Thus the traditional denoising method will cause a blurred image edge, and the contour information is lost. Wavelet decomposition and reconstruction filtering can lessen the edge blur, but it is difficult to select the suitable wavelet threshold which is related to the processing images. However, the image denoising method based on mathematical morphology can overcome these deficiencies and preserve more image details while removing some kinds of noises. For this reason, a kind of denoising algorithm for the coal flotation froth image based on the gray-scale image morphology is porposed which combines opening and closing filter of area reconstruction with alternating order filtering method. This algorithm adopts the most basic morphological operations, so it's simple and easy to implement in industrial environment.

2   Foundation of Gray Scale Morphology

Morphology is a broad set of image processing operations that process images based on shapes. The gray scale morphology which mainly focuses on the grayscale images is an extension of the binary morphology. Dilation, erosion, opening operation and closing operation are the fundamentals of the gray scale morphology [7].

2.1   Gray Scale Dilation and Erosion

Dilation means adding some pixels to the boundaries of objects in an image, while erosion means removing some pixels from object boundaries.

Assume $f(x, y)$ is the input image and $b(x, y)$ is a structuring element which could be considered as a sub-function. Define $f \oplus b$ as the dilation of the structuring element b onto the image f, as shown in (1).

$$(f \oplus b)(s,t) = \max\{f(s-x,t-y)-b(x,y)$$
$$| (s-x),(t-y)\in D_f;(x,y)\in D_b\} \tag{1}$$

Where, D_f and D_b represent the fields of domain of f and b respectively, and $(s-x,t-y)\in D_f$. Note that b is a function here. This operation is similar to a 2-dimentional convolution operation but the 'sum' is replaced by the 'maximum' and the 'multiplication' is replaced by the 'sum'.

Similarly, the erosion, represented by $f\ominus b$, is defined as (2), where D_f and D_b represent the same as the above and $(s+x,t+y)\in D_f$ must be satisfied.

$$(f\ominus b)(s,t) = \min\{f(s+x,t+y)-b(x,y)$$
$$| (s+x),(t+y)\in D_f;(x,y)\in D_b\} \tag{2}$$

This operation is similar to a 2-dimentional convolution operation, but the 'sum' is replaced by 'minimum' and the 'multiplication' is replaced by 'subtraction'.

2.2   Opening and Closing Operation

The opening operation and the closing operation of a gray-scale image are of the same form with the binary image. An opening operation of a structuring element b onto the image f is defined as $f \circ b$ shown in (3).

$$f \circ b = (f\ominus b) \oplus b \tag{3}$$

And the definition of the closing operation is shown in (4)

$$f \bullet b = (f \oplus b)\ominus b \tag{4}$$

3   Morphological Image Smoothing

For gray scale image, denoising is a process of morphologically smoothing. Morphological filters contain mainly two aspects: the morphological operation and the choice of structuring elements. The image denoising is achieved by the combination of opening and closing operation, which is often used in morphological filter. In common, the bright details whose size is smaller than the structuring element are eliminated by opening operation, and overall gray values as well as big bright regions of the image are unchanged basically. similarly, the dark details whose size is smaller than the structuring element are eliminated by closing operation, and overall gray values as well as big dark regions of the image are unchanged basically. Morphological opening or closing filter has good characteristics of removing noises, and the speckle noise in the light and dark areas of an image can be filtered by combining with the two kinds of operations. But it will cause the filtered image deformed in shape if only considering the size of the structuring elements but neglecting the shape information. In order to get better filtering performance, it is critical to select the size and the shape of the structuring elements reasonably. By morphological opening and closing operation with multiple dimensions and different shapes of structuring elements respectively, or the series-parallel combination form of different shapes and sizes of structuring elements [8, 9], the noises of an image can be removed and the details of the image can be better protected.

3.1   Selection of Structuring Elements

Structuring element is a background image with certain size. The morphological transform will be realized by various morphological operation of the structuring element onto the input image. Structuring elements have no definite shape and size, which can be decided by the final filtering performance. Structuring elements play a key role in all sorts of morphological transform [5, 6]. Generally, the image structure whose size and shape match with those structuring elements can be retained. The role of structuring elements in morphological filtering is similar to the filter window in signal processing. It will directly influence the processing result of the original noisy image that whether the chosen shape and size of structuring elements are appropriate or not. Similarly, the rational size of structuring element is vitally important in the design of the morphological filters, and the choice of structuring element is difficult in the disposal of mathematical morphology. If a bigger structuring element is selected, the details of the image will be lost. Otherwise, the noise won't be removed completely. So the geometry shape and the variation characteristics of input image should be observed to get the basic information of the input image first in image denoising processing, such as overall structure of the image, general shape, then, according to the information, corresponding structuring element is selected. The shape of the structuring element should be as similar as possible to image shape, and the size of structuring element should be larger than that of noise spot but smaller than that of non-noise image. Due to the geometric shapes of input image are complex, some structuring elements combined by several shapes should be chosen to adapt to different geometrical input image. In addition, different available structuring elements are selected respectively in different steps of morphological operation so as to improve matching degree of the structuring elements and the processed image.

In the process of coal flotation, flotation forth image is mainly composed of a large number of bubbles, although whose sizes and shapes are different, their general shapes are similar to elliptic shapes. So the structuring elements with oval shapes have been selected. Meanwhile, a series of structuring elements with increasing radius 2,3,4, sometimes 5 have been used in morphological filtering in order to get better denoising characteristics and edge information.

3.2   Design of Opening and Closing Filter Based on Area Reconstruction

With the connecting area as the criterion of filtering, area reconstruction will reconstruct image morphologically by grayscale information [10]. It can better keep the geometry characteristics of the object when the interference is filtered out.

The algorithm, which combines opening and closing filters based on area reconstruction with alternating order filtering method, uses the results of opening and closing operations by an elliptical structuring element with certain size as markers, and then chooses the original image and the opening reconstruction image as a mask separately, twice reconstructions are carried out and the intermediate result is obtained. Next, another twice reconstructions were repeated for intermediate result using structuring element with bigger size. Finally, the required filtering image was reconstructed. The algorithm schematic diagram shows in Fig.1 and Fig.2.

The concrete realization steps of the algorithm shows as follows:

1. The area opening reconstruction for original image f is carried out by choosing $g_o = f \circ b$ as maker (" $\circ$ "means opening operation), and the result of opening reconstruction f_o is obtained.

2. The area closing reconstruction for image f_o is carried out by choosing the minimum value of $f_o \bullet b$ and f_o as maker g_{oc} (" $\bullet$ "means closing operation), and the output image f_{oci} is obtained as the intermediate result.

3. Enlarging the radius of the structuring element b, repeat the step 1 and step 2 above for intermediate result f_{oci} .

4. Repeat the above steps; the final filtering result image f_e is obtained.

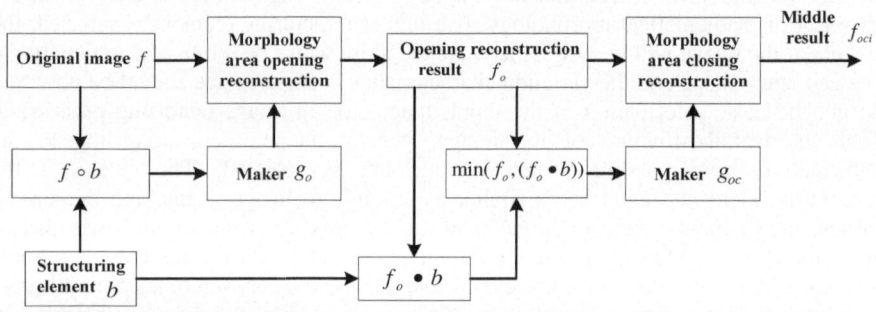

Fig. 1. The mid procedure of opening and closing filter based on area reconstruction

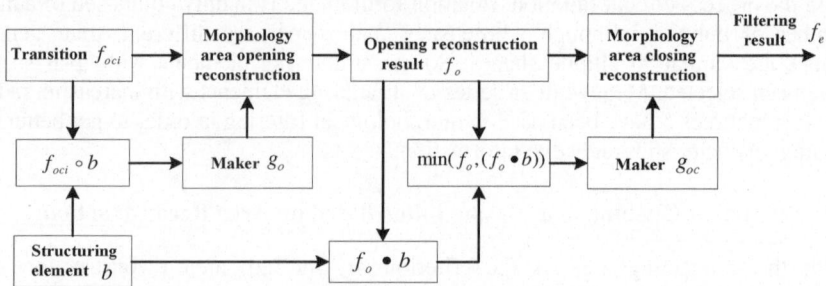

Fig. 2. The final procedure of opening and closing filter based on area reconstruction

3.3   Processing Results of Opening and Closing Filter Based on Area Reconstruction

Three coal flotation froth images acquired from actual production process are taken to be the preparatory processing images, whose dimension is 512×512 pixels.
Elliptical structuring element with radius 2, 3, 4 and 5 are selected respectively to do opening and closing filtering based on area reconstruction. The result images after filtering are illustrated in Fig.3.

Where, images (a), (c) are original coal flotation froth images, images (b), (d) are bubble images after filtering. It can be seen that the bubbles of original froth images contain many isolated spots caused by uneven illumination or reflection, which could cause the over-segmentation problem in the process of image segmentation, and the isolated spots have been effectively eliminated after filtering, and no edge blurring or image distortion was caused.

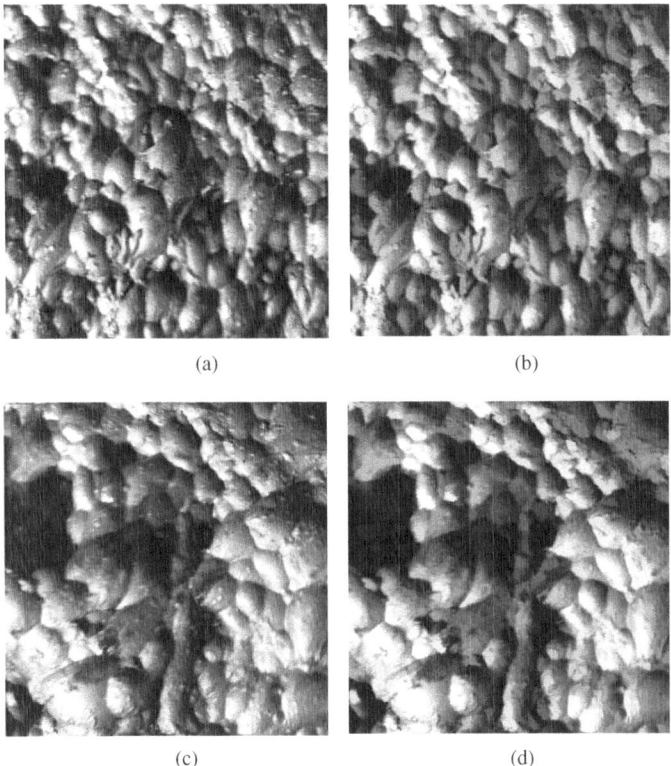

(a)   (b)

(c)   (d)

Fig. 3. Original forth image and forth image after filtering of coal flotation

4   Conclusion

The traditional low-pass denoising method would cause the blurring edge while removing the noise,   and some of the detail information in the image will be lost. The method of opening and closing filter based on mathematical morphology area reconstruction can overcome this defect, and can maintain the distinct object edges and preserve more details of image. Taking the coal flotation froth image as original input image, the denoising algorithm, which combines opening and closing filters based on area reconstruction with alternating order filtering and adopts elliptical structuring elements with increasing radius in turn in morphological filter, is proposed to remove the noise in the original coal froth image. Denoising results show that the isolated spots on the bubble are eliminated effectively, and the froth image becomes distinct and smooth. The morphological filtering method proposed in this paper offers a favorable condition to the subsequent processing of froth image such as image segmentation and feature extraction.

References

1. Moolman, D.W., Aldrich, C., Van Deventer, J.S.J.: The Interpretation of Flotation Froth Surfaces by Using Digital Image Analysis and Neural Networks. Chemical Engineering Science 50, 3501–3513 (1995)
2. Bonifazi, G., Serranti, S., Volpe, F., Zuco, R.: Characterisation of Flotation Froth Colour and Structure by Machine Vision. Computers & Geosciences 27, 1111–1117 (2001)
3. Wang, W., Bergholmb, F., Yanga, B.: Froth Delineation Based on Image Classification. Minerals Engineering 16, 1183–1192 (2003)
4. Liu, W.L., Wang, G., Wang, J., Lu, M.X.: Floating Bubbles Characters and Condition Identification. China Coal 29, 50–54 (2003) (in Chinese)
5. Lu, M.X., Yong, Y., Wang, F., Liu, W.L.: Threshold Segmentation Technology Applied to Get Physical Features of Foam Image From Slime Floatation. Coal Science and Technology 30, 34–37 (2002)
6. Lin, X.Z., Gu, Y.Y., Zhao, G.Q.: Feature Extraction Based on Image Segmentation of Coal Flotation Froth. Journal of China Coal Society 32, 304–308 (2007) (in Chinese)
7. Rafael, C.G., Richard, E.W.: Digital Image Processing Using MATLAB (in Chinese). Publishing House of Electronics Industry, Beijing (2005) (in Chinese)
8. Maragos, P., Schafer, R.W.: Morphological Filters - Part I: Their Set-Theoretic Analysis and Relations to Linear Shift-invariant Filters. IEEE Transactions on Acoustics, Speech, and Signal Processing 35, 1153–1169 (1987)
9. Maragos, P., Schafer, R.W.: Morphological Filters - Part II: Their Relations to Median, Order Statistic, and Stack Filters. IEEE Transactions on Acoustics, Speech, and Signal Processing 35, 1170–1184 (1987)
10. Meijster, A., Michael, H.F.W.: A Comparison of Algorithms for Connected Set Openings and Closings. IEEE Transactions on Pattern Analysis and Machine Intelligence 24, 48–494 (2002)

A Novel Image Coding Method with Visual Cortical Model

Rongchang Zhao and Yide Ma

School of Information Science & Engineering, Lanzhou University
Byrons.zhao@gmail.com, ydma@lzu.edu.cn

Abstract. To attain a high compression ratio and high-quality reconstructed images, an irregular segmented region coding algorithm is developed. An novel segmentation algorithm using spiking cortical model is applied to partition an image into irregular regions and tidy contours, the crucial regions corresponding to objects in scene are retained and a lot of tiny parts are merged. The experimental results show higher quality reconstructed images and less time consuming under higher compression ratio.

Keywords: image compression, irregular segmented region coding, orthogonal basis function, chain code, spiking cortical model.

1 Introduction

Block-oriented image compression technique is widely applied because of its low computation complexity, such as JPEG, H.261 and MPEG. The block-oriented image compression technique disregards the region information, and does not exploit intra-region redundancy, in which the region is corresponding to object in scene.

The second-generation image compression technique [1] can achieve high compression ratio through identifying and using features in the image while still maintaining the image quality. These methods mainly consider the correlation among pixels within regions and the fact that the human perception varies in different parts of images. Therefore, region of interest (ROI) coding [2] is suitable for images which include some significant objects compared with the background, and such ROI can be coded with high-quality methods[3]. The technique can improve the compression ratio, and it is applied to some methods like JPEG 2000. In the core coding system of JPEG 2000, ROI is transformed to certain sub-band of wavelet.

Besides transform coding, the second-generation image coding includes irregular segmented regions coding [4-6]. This technique attempts to separate an image into some irregular regions with slowly varying intensity by boundaries, and then applies appropriate coding methods to regions and contours respectively. Region-oriented compression for image was proposed by Gilge in 1990, and it segments the image into regions depending on the objects in scene.

In this paper, a new kind of image coding method, named as Irregular Segmented Region Coding using SCM (ISRCS), is presented, and the principle of irregular segmented region coding and decoding is mainly investigated in detail. Spiking

H. Deng et al. (Eds.): AICI 2011, Part II, LNAI 7003, pp. 383–389, 2011.

Cortical Model (SCM) [7, 8] is based on Eckhorn's neuron model [9], and is derived from the phenomena of synchronous pulse bursts in mammal's visual cortex. The coding scheme much better matches HVS [1] and will be not only able to achieve higher compression ratio but also obtain reconstructed images with better quality.

2   Region Segmentation Based on SCM

The aim of segmentation is to divide an image into non-overlapping regions with similar contribution and every region corresponds to different object. The basic contribution for segmentation is pixel intensity for gray image. The pixels with slowly varying intensity are partitioned by the contours from scene.

In this section, we propose an irregular region segmentation method based on SCM. The neuron decodes the input signal and exports pulse, all of pulse images contain the object pattern information, then regions and contours could be captured by fusing the spatial-temporal information.

To simplify the paper, the SCM is given directly as $(1) - (5)$:

$$F_{ij}[n] = I_{ij} \tag{1}$$

$$L_{ij}[n] = \sum W_{ijkl} Y_{kl}[n-1] + DIFF_{ij}[n] \tag{2}$$

$$U_{ij}[n] = f U_{ij}[n-1] + F_{ij}[n] L_{ij}[n] + F_{ij}[n] \tag{3}$$

$$Y[n] = 1 \ if \ U_{ij}[n] > E_{ij}[n]; \ otherwise \ 0 \tag{4}$$

$$E_{ij}[n] = g E_{ij}[n-1] + V_E Y_{ij}[n-1] \tag{5}$$

where subscript (i,j) is the identification number of a neuron, I_{ij} is the external stimulation of a neuron, $F_{ij}[n]$ is the feedback input, $L_{ij}[n]$ is the linking input, $U_{ij}[n]$ is the internal activity, and $E_{ij}[n]$ is the dynamic threshold and it decrease exponentially. W is the synaptic weight matrices, f and g are decay consistent constants, V_E is the threshold amplitude constant, n is the iteration, $Y_{ij}[n]$ is the binary pulse output, and $E_{ij}[n-1]$ is the previous dynamic threshold, $DIFF_{ij}[n]$ is the difference between neuron (i,j) and its 8-neighborhood. Each part communicates with its neighboring neurons through the synaptic weights W respectively. Then the neuron combines the feedback input with the linking input as the internal activity, and spike trains will be generated ($Y_{ij}[n]=1$) by SCM when the internal activity $U_{ij}[n]$ is greater than the dynamic threshold $E_{ij}[n]$. The linking input L derives from two parts: one is the coupled information and the other is the difference with its 8-neighborhood. The spikes produced by neighbors participate in the stimulus of this neuron through the multiplication with W. The difference enhances the impact of the rapid change of image pixel value.

A pulsed neuron may result in the synchronous spikes of its neighbors with approximate intensity. The model could catch not only spatial information but also information of similar pixel value. The spikes produced after different iteration contain the temporal information, so pulse images at different time involve spatial-temporal information of object pattern. The output pulse images contain features of stimulus such as edge, texture and regional information and it is the source of the segmented image.

In the model, a pixel in an image corresponds to a neuron in neural network, and the value of I_{ij} is formed by the intensity of corresponding image pixel. After iterations, the output matrix Y is labeled using the number "0" and "1".

3   Representation for Irregular Regions

For regions representation, the basic approach is approximation of a weighted sum of basis functions and the weight coefficients are quantized and coded [10,11]. This section presents an outline of polygonal approximations theory and representation method of irregular regions.

In a linear independences space, any signal $f(x)$ can be expressed as a linear combination of basis functions $\{\psi_n\}_{n\in N}$ for example $f(x) = \sum\limits_{n=0}^{+\infty} c_n \psi_n$. But in the actual application, it is hoped that approximate the signal by the combination of limited parts of basis functions. Obviously, finding a set of optimal basis functions to express the region exactly and fast is the key problem. The other issue is the value of c_n. To calculate the value of c_n easily and exactly using the concept of inner product and to express the signal simply, the orthogonal basis functions are chosen.

Let $f(x, y)$ denotes the intensity of pixel corresponding to coordinate (x, y), $f'(x, y)$ is the approximating function of $f(x, y)$, and it can be represented by weighted sums of N basis functions $\{\varphi_1, \varphi_2 \ldots \ldots \varphi_N\}$ which are parameterized by their corresponding coefficients $\{c_1, c_2 \ldots \ldots c_N\}$,

$$f(x, y) \approx f'(x, y) = \sum_{i=1}^{N} c_i \varphi_i(x, y) \tag{6}$$

The error function can be defined as

$$E = \left\| f' - f \right\|^2 = \sum_y \sum_x (f'(x,y) - f(x,y))^2$$

$$= \sum_y \sum_x \left(\sum_{i=1}^{N} (c_i \varphi_i(x,y) - f(x,y)) \right)^2 \tag{7}$$

If $N \to \infty$, it means $\{\varphi_i(x, y)\}$ is a set of complete orthogonal basis functions, the E is zero, else, to minimize E by c, for $\forall i$, let $\partial E/\partial c_i = 0$, and the value of c_i could be calculated as (8) by means of the orthogonal characteristic.

$$c_i = <f, \varphi_i> = \sum_y \sum_x f(x,y) \varphi_i(x,y), \quad 1 \le i \le N \tag{8}$$

If the basis functions in a given region are orthogonal, the coefficients could be obtained easily and independently. However, initial basises are not orthogonal generally, so the orthogonalization process is necessary.

Suppose that the naturally ordered binomials $1, x, y, x^2, xy, y^2, x^3, x^2y\ldots$ act as the linearly independent initial basis. With the help of orthogonalization method, the orthogonal basis could be gotten for every segmented region and the approximating function can be expressed as (6).

4   Experimental Results and Analysis

In this section, a lot of experimentations are implemented to demonstrate the performance of ISRCS. Algorithm I denotes the image coding method based on ISRCS, algorithm II is JPEG which is based on 2D-DCT, and algorithm III is JPEG2000 (the algorithm is realized by JPEG2000 developer toolkit[12]). The performance of image coding algorithm will be shown with the reconstructed images and two quantitative parameters: Peak Signal to Noise Ratio(PSNR) and Compression Ratio(CR).

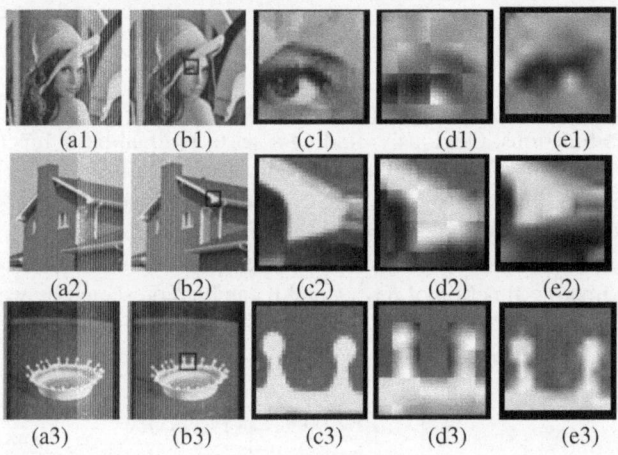

(a1)   (b1)   (c1)   (d1)   (e1)

(a2)   (b2)   (c2)   (d2)   (e2)

(a3)   (b3)   (c3)   (d3)   (e3)

Fig. 1. Reconstructed Image. (a) are the original image, (b1 – b3) are reconstructed images based on algorithm II, (c - e) are zoomed from the reconstructed image based on algorithm I, II and III respectively. (d) are broken by the block distortion and (e) are blurred although it is not block distortion. We would like to express our sincere thanks to the author David Taubman for JPEG2000 developer toolkit named Kakadu Software.

Table 1. PSNR (DB) and CR of the algorithms

Algorithm	Lena		Milkdrop		House	
	CR	PSNR	CR	PSNR	CR	PSNR
I	14.9	32.74	14.11	33.61	21.6	34.31
II	13.6	29.90	10.70	29.10	11.7	28.37
III	15.8	26.87	12.53	32.50	14.4	30.35

As shown in Fig.1(a1) – (a3), "Lena", "House" and "Milkdrop" with 128×128, 8 bits are used as test images. The reconstructed images are shown in Fig.1(c) – (e), at the same time PSNR and CR of the images are shown in Table.1.

The compared results represent that with the approximate CR, the PSNR of Algorithm I is higher than Algorithm II and III. The blocks zoomed to 400% shown in

Fig.1 (d) present serious block distortion that is known as mosaic effect that destroys the natural edges and contours of objects in original image, while Fig.1 (c), (e) contain no such. Compared with the proposed algorithm, reconstructed images based on JPEG 2000 does not reserve block distortion yet but it is blurry for it loses part of high frequency components.

Furthermore, the results of the segmentation algorithm described in Section 2 applied to "cameraman" image are shown. Fig.2 (a) is the original image and Fig.2 (b) is the output pulse image after 8 iterations. Fig.2 (c) shows the segmented image using the proposed algorithm. Fig.2 (d), (e) and (f) show the segmented image based on watershed algorithm, the recursive shortest spanning tree (RSST) technique and the algorithm described in [13].

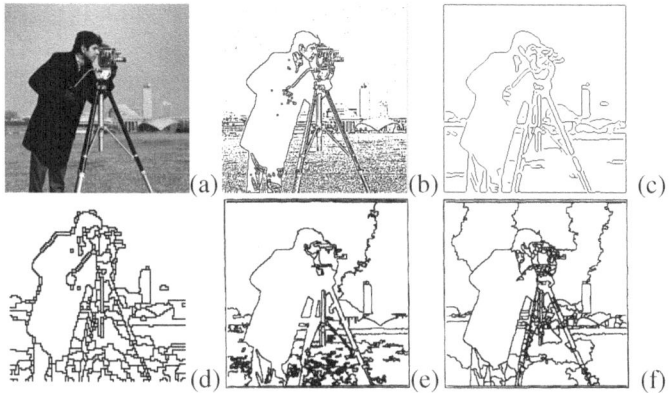

Fig. 2. (a) The original image. (b) The output pulse image of SCM after 8 iterations. (c) The proposed algorithm based on the output pulse image and the region connection method (89 regions, 3012 contour pixels). (d) Image segmented with the watershed algorithm (196 regions, 2659 contour pixels) (e) the RSST algorithm (70 regions, 8031 contour pixels). (f) The algorithm based on [13] (300 regions, 6783 contour pixels).

The proposed segmentation algorithm extracts contours based on the output pulse images of SCM after different iteration. Fig.2 (b) is an example of output images of SCM. It could be observed that the output image series shows the different precision of texture. The suited outputs must be chosen because the expected segmented image not only should catch and segment regions with homogeneous pixels, but also control the number of the smaller regions and contour pixels. The proposed algorithm merges the smaller regions into its neighbors based on region connected method. It could be observed that the shape of the regions is clear. The proposed algorithm catches most regions with lesser contour pixels compared with the two methods shown in Fig.2.

Most experiments have shown that quite a few of bits are spent for coding the contour pixels. Thus the number of contour pixels is crucial in irregular segmented region coding. ISRCS is compared with other algorithms and the results are shown in Fig.3. It could be observed that in this paper the number of contour pixels per region in general accord with the value in method of [13] and the value is steady along with the increase of regions.

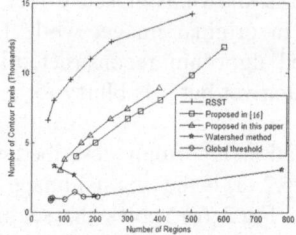 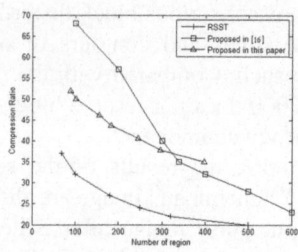

Fig. 3. Relation between Number of Regions and Contours (left), and relation between Compression Ratio and the Number of Regions based on Image 'cameraman' (right).

The relation between compression ratio and the number of regions is depicted in Figure.3 for the "cameraman" image.

5   Conclusion

An efficient irregular segmented image coding method based on spiking cortical model is represented and be named as ISRCS in this paper. In the framework of ISRCS, the mission is divided as two parts: region segmentation and segments coding. This paper proposes a segmentation method based on the output pulse images of SCM. This method obtains homogeneous region and smooth contour because the segmented image not only holds natural contour of objects, but also obtains regions which is mapping to object with homogenous pixels. It is suitable for image coding because of the representation of the region by orthogonal basis functions.

References

1. Kunt, M., Ikonomopoulos, A., Kocher, M.: Second-generation image-coding techniques. Proceedings of the IEEE 73, 549–575 (1985)
2. Bradley, A.P., Stentiford, F.W.M.: JPEG 2000 and Region of Interest Coding. In: Digital Image Computing: Techniques and Applications, Australia, pp. 303–308 (2002)
3. Kunt, M., Benard, M., Leonardi, R.: Recent results in high-compression image coding. IEEE Transctions on Circuits and Systems 34, 1306–1336 (1987)
4. Sikora, T., Makai, B.: Shape-adaptive DCT for generic coding of Video. IEEE Transctions on Circuits System Video Technology 5, 59–62 (1995)
5. Li, S., Li, W.: Shape-adaptive discrete wavelet transforms for arbitrarily shaped visual object coding. IEEE Transctions on Circuits and Systems for Video Technology 10, 725–743 (2000)
6. Gilge, M.: Region-oriented transform coding (ROTC) of images. In: The International Conference on Acoustics, Speech, and Signal Processing, vol. 4, pp. 2245–2248 (1990)
7. Zhan, K., Zhang, H.J., Ma, Y.D.: New Spiking Cortical Model for Invariant Texture Retrieval and Image Processing. IEEE Transactions on Neural Networks 20, 1980–1986 (2009)

8. Ma, Y.D., Zhan, K., Wang, Z.B.: Applications of Pulse-Coupled Neural Networks, pp. 6–8. Higher Education Press, Beijing (2010)
9. Eckhorn, R., Reitboeck, E., Arndt, M., Dicke, P.W.: Feature Linking via synchronisation among distributed assemblies: simulations of results from cat visual cortex. Neural Computation 2, 293–307 (1990)
10. Gilge, M., Engelhardt, T., Mehlan, R.: Coding of arbirearily shaped image segments based on a generalized orthogonal transform. Signal Processing: Image Communication 1, 153–180 (1989)
11. Kwon, O., Chellappa, R.: Segmentation-based image compression. Optical Engineering 32, 1581–1587 (1993)
12. Kakadu Software, http://www.kakadusoftware.com
13. Christopoulos, C.A., Philipsb, W., Skodras, A.N., Cornelis, J.: Segmented image coding: Techniques and experimental results. Signal Processing: Image Communication 11, 63–80 (1997)

Experiments on Automatic Seam Detection for a MIG Welding Robot[*]

Mitchell Dinham, Gu Fang, and Jia Ju Zou

School of Engineering, University of Western Sydney, Australia
15234937@scholar.uws.edu.au

Abstract. To make robotic welding more flexible, vision systems are used to detect the weld seam and plan a path for the robot to follow. In this paper an image processing technique is introduced that can automatically detect the weld seam in a "butt-weld" configuration. This method is an improvement on the existing K-Cosine algorithm. The 3D location of weld points is determined using a robot Hand-in-Eye stereo vision system. This paper will also introduce a practical method for robot and Hand/Eye calibration. The validity of these methods will be verified through experiments using a MIG welding robot.

Keywords: Stereo vision, Arc welding robot, weld seam detection

1 Introduction

Currently, robotic welding is a very rigid and structured process, with systems that are generally purpose-built for mass production. Each new job must be programmed by human operators using teach and playback methods. These assemblies can take considerable amounts of time to program and commission making them inflexible and unsuitable to be used in wider manufacturing processes. This can be attributed to the expense of changing tooling and fixtures as well as the costs associated with the lost production time for reprogramming the welding robot for every new part. In instances of maintenance and repair, a new weld path would need to be reprogrammed as the position of wear and tear is generally unique and therefore pre-programmed paths are not applicable. To make robotic welding in these environments feasible, the robot would need the intelligence and the flexibility to locate the weld seam and then weld the parts automatically. Vision systems can be used as a method for automatically locating weld seams and monitoring weld pool dynamics ([1], [2]).

It can be said that vision guided robotic welding has many unique challenges in terms of image processing. These challenges include low contrast images due to the similarity between the steel weld assemblies and work benches and the uneven surface texture of steel weld assemblies caused by dirt and scratches.

In [3], the image undergoes several pre-processing stages such as sharpening, median filtering and thinning before being converted to a binary image. The initial and final seam points are then determined by searching for corners and edges that are within proximity to each other using a predefined threshold. Similarly in [4] a modified

---

[*] This work is supported by the Australian Research Council under project ID LP0991108 and the Lincoln Electric Company (Australia).

H. Deng et al. (Eds.): AICI 2011, Part II, LNAI 7003, pp. 390–397, 2011.

K-Cosine algorithm [5] is used to determine weld seam points using corner detection from boundary points. These methods have shown they are capable of detecting both straight line and curved seams, however the conditions used in these papers contain highly contrasted images. While it can be argued that this is a valid approach to seam detection in TIG welding which is a process commonly used in aluminium welding, there is often little image contrast when mild steel is used in MIG welding.

Image processing in weld seam detection can be simplified by assuming that the weld seam or work piece is located centrally in the image, as presented in the works by [6] and [7]. If the work piece is assumed to be located centrally, then a predefined search window can be used to narrow down the search for the weld seam and aid in the segmentation of unwanted features in the image.

In this paper a predefined region of interest is used to set a threshold to segment the weld assembly from the background. The intensity information from the region of interest is then used to segment the background using a threshold in red, green, blue (RGB) space. Once the image has been segmented it is converted to binary. The modified K-Cosine method in [5] is then used to calculate the weld seam points.

For the seam points to be useful in a robotic welding system, they must be transformed into 3D co-ordinates using triangulation. To find the matched points in a stereo image pair, a stereo matching algorithm must be used. The epipolar constraint and cross correlation can be used to match a point from one view to the other [8]. Popular methods for cross-correlation of stereo images such as sum of squared difference (SSD), normalised cross-correlation (NCC) and their variants [9],[10] use either fixed or adaptive search windows on rectified stereo images. In this paper, the SSD algorithm is used on non rectified images.

The validity of the work presented in this paper is verified through experimentation on an industrial robot arm fitted with a calibrated Eye-in-Hand stereo vision system.

The paper is organized as follows: Section 2 details the methodology used in image processing and stereo matching, with the experimental results given in Section 3. The conclusions are then given in Section 4.

2   Methodology

2.1   Camera Calibration

The cameras intrinsic and extrinsic parameters were obtained using the calibration toolbox given in [11]. The calibration grid pattern consisted of 30mm x 30mm squares.

2.2   Hand-Eye and Robot Calibration

Hand-Eye and Robot Calibration is achieved using the optimized algorithm in [12]. This algorithm not only provides the optimized hand-eye and robot parameters but also provides an optimized stereo triangulation algorithm based on the work by [8].

Given the 3D co-ordinates of a point $^{w}P=(X_w,Y_w,Z_w)^T$ in the world frame W, these points can then be found relative to the robots' base frame R through:

$$^{R}P = {}^{R}T_W \begin{bmatrix} X_W & Y_W & Z_W \end{bmatrix}^T \tag{1}$$

where ^{R}P is the point P's location in the robot frame, $^{R}T_W$ is the transformation matrix that relates the world coordinate to the robot coordinate. By using Eq. (1) a weld path can be obtained in the robot coordinate frame.

2.3   Seam Detection

The initial boundary detection method used in [4] is based on a highly contrasted foreground and background. In this paper a more realistic setting commonly seen in a MIG welding situation is used.   It is depicted in Figure 1.

To deal with this more realistic situation, the method introduced in [4] is improved. In this paper, the background is segmented from the foreground using a threshold in red, green and blue (RGB) image space.   Assuming that the work piece can be setup to remain centred in the image a sample of the foreground can be obtained by defining a region of interest (ROI) of dimension W × H as shown in Figure 2. From this sample window the intensity of each of the RGB values in the foreground can be obtained.

Given the sample window ROI

$$ROI = \left\{ I_R\left(u_i, v_j\right), I_G\left(u_i, v_j\right), I_B\left(u_i, v_j\right)\right\}$$

$$i = 1, \ldots, W, \ j = 1, \ldots, H$$

(2)

where I_R is the red level intensity at pixel co-ordinates (u_i, v_i), similarly I_G and I_B are the green and blue level intensities respectively.

Fig. 1. The work piece and background used in [5] (a) and the conditions used in this paper (b)

It is assumed that the work piece which is typically raw mild steel will have lower pixel intensity values than the background. Based on this assumption, the background can be segmented by calculating the maximum intensity of the foreground and then thresholding the background. Due to the similarity in intensity values in gray image space, segmentation by intensity thresholding is difficult. It can be argued that RGB space can provide a greater depth of information regarding foreground and background.

The individual threshold values of I_R, I_G and I_B is determined by the mean of the maximum intensity values of each column in ROI and is given by

$$R_{threshold} = mean\{\max I_R(u_i : u_H \mid i = 1, K, W)\}$$

(3)

$$G_{threshold} = mean\{\max I_G(u_i : u_H \mid i = 1, K, W)\}$$

(4)

$$B_{threshold} = mean\{\max I_B(u_i : u_H \mid i = 1, \ldots, W)\}$$

(5)

Using (3) – (5) the original RBG image I_{RBG} can be segmented using the following threshold.

$$I_{RBG}\{R\} = \begin{cases} 0 & I_R \ge R_{threshold} \\ I_R & otherwise \end{cases} \tag{6}$$

$$I_{RBG}\{G\} = \begin{cases} 0 & I_G \ge G_{threshold} \\ I_G & otherwise \end{cases} \tag{7}$$

$$I_{RBG}\{B\} = \begin{cases} 0 & I_B \ge B_{threshold} \\ I_B & otherwise \end{cases} \tag{8}$$

Once the image is segmented, I_{RGB} is converted to gray scale, which is followed by image contrast enhancement using histogram equalization and median filtering before being converted to a binary image. From the binary image, the weld seam co-ordinates are obtained using the methodology introduced in [4].

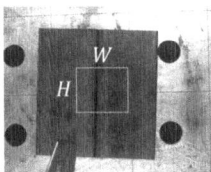

Fig. 2. Sample Window

2.4   Image Matching

Stereo matching using epipolar geometry is known as correspondence. Stereo correspondence is matching a point from one image to the other by searching along the epipolar line. A point in the left image x_1 the corresponding point x_2 must lay somewhere along the epipolar line l_2. A full description of epipolar geometry can be found in [8], however a brief summary is provided below.

The epipolar constraint can be used to determine the matching point using following equations:

$$x_2^T F x_1 = 0 \tag{9}$$

$$l_2 = F x_1 \tag{10}$$

where $x_1 = (u_1, v_1, 1)^T$, $x_2 = (u_2, v_2, 1)^T$ which are the point of interest in the left and right images respectively and F is the fundamental matrix.

For a calibrated stereo vision system, the Fundamental matrix can be calculated using

$$F = \{K_{CL}\}^{-1} S\{R\}^{-1}\{K_{CR}\}^{-1} \tag{11}$$

where K_{CL} and K_{CR} are, respectively, the left and right cameras' intrinsic parameters obtained during camera calibration, R is the rotation matrix between the left and right cameras and S is the skew symmetric matrix of the translation between the two cameras.

However, this calculation only provides the points along the epipolar line, therefore search methods such as Sum of the Squared Difference (SSD) and Normalised Cross Correlation (NCC) have been developed. Cross correlation, like the epipolar constraint, involves searching along the corresponding epipolar line, with the difference being that the matching criteria does not rely on there being a unique minimum as is [8]. The search algorithm uses a fixed or variable search window to find a matching point based on the best matched windows between the two images.

The aim of the SSD algorithm is to match the two windows based on the smallest difference between them; mathematically it can be represented as

$$SSD = \min \sum_{(i,j) \in R} \left(f(i,j) - g(i,j) \right)^2 \tag{14}$$

where R is the size of the search window, and $f(i,j)$ and $g(i,j)$ are the gray scale intensities of each pixel in the search window in the left and right images respectively.

3 Experimental Results

3.1 Experimental Setup

The Experiment was conducted using a Fanuc ArcMate 100iC, six axis industrial welding robot, fitted with a welding torch and a Lincoln Electric Power Wave F355i Welder. The stereo vision system consists of two USB 1280x1024 colour, uEYE CCD cameras. The Cameras are attached to the robot arm as shown in Figure 3. The algorithms were run using the Image Acquisition and Image Processing Toolbox in Matlab.

Fig. 3. Experimental Setup

3.2 Pre-processing

The original RGB image taken from the left camera is shown below in Figure 4(a). The two pieces of steel are butted against each other with no gap. The assembly was placed in a random position in front of the robot.

In this experiment, the dimension of ROI is 400×400. The ROI window is shown in Figure 4(b). In Figure 4(c) the threshold image has been histogram equalized to improve contrast and a 3×3 median filter has been implemented to smooth the image. Lastly in Figure 4(d) the image has been converted to a binary image ready for the seam point detection algorithm.

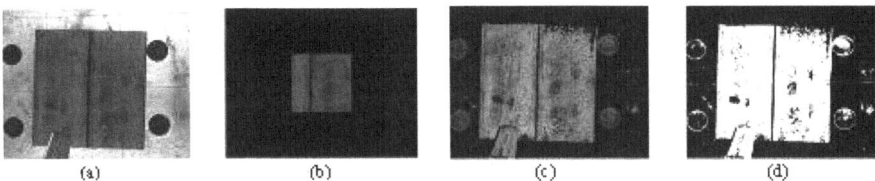

Fig. 4. The original RGB image (a), the ROI window (b), the threshold image (c) and the binary image (d)

3.3 Seam Point Detection

The seam point detection method from [5] is used to detect the seam points and is shown in Figure 5.

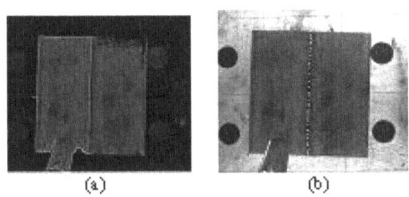

Fig. 5. Boundary image (a) and the seam points (b)

3.4 Stereo Matching

It can be argued that since the weld is a straight line, only the first and last seam points are necessary to perform the weld. In Figure 6(a) and 6(c) the "arc-start" and "arc-end" points are shown. In Figure 6(b) and Figure 6(d) the corresponding point in the image captured from the right camera is shown along with the epipolar line. The correlation window is set at 14×14 pixels. The matching errors are given in Table 1.

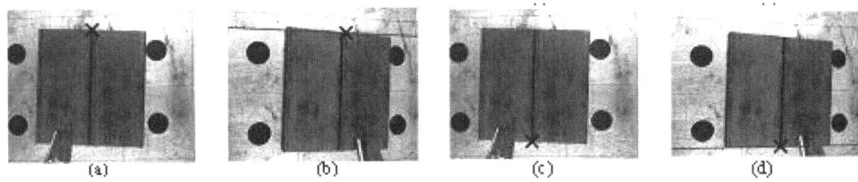

Fig. 6. "Arc start" point in the left image (a) corresponding "arc-start" point in the right image (b), "arc-end" point in left image (c), corresponding "arc-end" point in the right image (d)

Table 1. Stereo matching using SSD with a 14 x 14 window

	Calculated point (u_r,v_r)	Actual point (u_r,v_r)	Error (pixels)
Arc start	(789.5,185.5)	(772.5,184.3)	(17,1.2)
Arc end	(744,954.4)	(746.4,954.3)	(2.4,0.1)

3.5   Welding

Using the co-ordinate points given by the stereo matching algorithm, the 3D co-ordinates of the seam points can be established using the triangulation algorithm given in [12]. The error in the 3D seam co-ordinates are given in Table 2. The Actual MIG welding results are shown Figure 7. It can be seen that the weld start point is not located perfectly in the centre of the seam. The positioning errors are due to the errors in stereo matching. The error in the Z direction which mostly affects the electrode "stick-out" at the arc start point did not significantly decrease the quality of the weld, because the stick-out error decreased as the weld progressed. The desired stick-out for this application is 13mm; the actual stick-out at the start of the weld was approximately 25.8 mm and 11.8mm at the end of the weld.

Table 2. Triangulation Error

	Error (mm)		
	X	Y	Z
Arc start	2.565	0.585	12.768
Arc end	0.284	-0.089	-1.234

The welding parameters were obtained from the standard MIG constant voltage (CV) procedure from the Lincoln Electric GMAW manual [13].

Fig. 7. Welded assembly (a), "arc-start" point (b), "arc-end" point (c)

4   Conclusion

In this paper experimental results on vision guided robotic MIG welding are presented. The method presented in this paper does not rely on the operator to program the robot, as the vision system is capable of detecting the weld seam on a randomly placed weld assembly. The algorithm is also capable of determining the 3D position of the weld seam in relation to the robot through the use of stereo matching and triangulation.

This algorithm is practical and robust and can be used in an industrial setting. Further work needs to be done in the area of stereo matching to improve the triangulation accuracy. At this stage, the algorithm presented here is for "butt-welds", however this will be the basis of further work in more complex welding arrangements such as fillet and lap welds.

References

1. Pachidis, T.P., Lygouras, J.N.: Vision based path generation method for a robot based arc welding system. Journal of Intelligent Robot Systems 48(3), 307–331 (2007)
2. Chen, S.B.: On the key technologies of intelligentized robotic welding. In: Robotic Welding, Intelligence and Automation. LNCIS, vol. 362, pp. 105–115 (2007)
3. Zhou, L., Lin, T., Chen, S.B.: Autonomous acquisition of seam co-ordinates for an arc welding robot based on visual servoing. Journal of Intelligent Robot Systems 47(3), 239–255 (2006)
4. Micallef, K., Fang, G., Dinham, M.: Automatic seam detection and path planning in robotic welding. In: Tarn, T.-J., Chen, S.-B., Fang, G. (eds.) Robotic Welding, Intelligence and Automation. LNEE, vol. 88, pp. 23–32. Springer, Heidelberg (2011)
5. Sun, T.: K-Cosine corner detection. Journal of Computers 3(7), 16–22 (2008)
6. Shi, F., Zhou, L., Lin, T., Chen, S.: Efficient weld seam detection for robotic welding from a single image. In: Robotic Welding, Intelligence and Automation. LNCIS, vol. 362, pp. 289–294 (2007)
7. Ryberg, A., Ericsson, M., Christiansson, A.K., et al.: Stereo vision for path correction in off-line programmed robot welding. In: IEEE International Conference on Industrial Technology, pp. 1700–1705 (2010)
8. Hartley, R.I., Zisserman, A.: Multiple view geometry in computer vision, 2nd edn. Cambridge University Press, Cambridge (2003)
9. Luo, G., Yang, X., Xu, Q.: Fast stereo matching algorithm using adaptive window. In: IEEE International Symposiums on Information Processing, pp. 25–30 (2008)
10. Liang, Z., Gao, H., et al.: 3D reconstruction for telerobotic welding. In: IEEE International Conference on Mechatronics and Automation, pp. 475–479 (2007)
11. Bouget, J.: Camera calibration toolbox for matlab (2010), http://www.vision.caltech.edu/bouguetj/calib_doc/index.html#parameters
12. Dinham, M., Fang, G.: Low cost simultaneous calibration of a stereo vision system and a welding robot. In: 2010 IEEE International Conference on Robotics and Biomimetics (2010) (to appear)
13. Lincoln Electric, Gas metal arc welding (GMAW) guidelines. Lincoln Electric Company Publication (1995)

Spatially Variant Mixtures of Multiscale ARMA Model for SAR Imagery Segmentation

Yan Zhang[1] and Yanwei Ju[2]

[1] Department of Applied Mathematics and Physics, The PLA University of Science
and Technology, Nanjing, 2111101, China
zhangyan12073100@126.com
[2] Nanjing Research Institute of Electronic Technology, Nanjing, 210039, China

Abstract. We propose a new model built on multiscale tree structure, spatially variant mixtures of multiscale autoregressive moving average (SVMMARMA) model, for unsupervised synthetic aperture radar (SAR) imagery segmentation. We derive an expectation maximization (EM) algorithm for learning the pixel labeling as well as the parameters of the component models. We also present the bootstrap sampling technique applied to the parameter estimation, which not only increases estimation precision, but also saves computation time greatly. Finally, we design classifier based on Euclidean distance of multiscale ARMA coefficients. Experiments results show this model gives better results than previous methods.

Keywords: SVMMARMA model, SAR imagery, Bootstrap sampling, Euclidean distance.

1 Introduction

Synthetic aperture radar (SAR) imagery segmentation plays a key role in the subsequent analysis for target detection, recognition, and image compression. However, the speckle appearing on SAR images is a natural phenomenon generated by the coherent processing of radar echoes [1, 2], and speckle seriously degrades segmentation performances. So there are various multiresolution segmentation algorithms, such as multiscale autoregressive (MAR) model, mixture multiscale autoregressive (MMAR) model, have been proposed [3-6]. An acceptable segmentation can be provided by MAR model, but the approach is not precise and is a supervised segmentation method. The segmentation results of MMAR model are precise, however, parameter estimation of MMAR model is very time-consuming and MMAR model can't describe the spatially variant characteristics. Although the spatially variant finite mixture model proposed by Gopal can describe the spatially variant characteristics [7], and Blekas give its improved estimation methodology [8], the segmentation results are sensitive to speckle noise. In this letter, we present a spatially variant mixtures of multiscale autoregressive moving average (SVMMARMA) model. This model not only exploits the multiscale stochastic structure inherent in SAR image, and accurately characterizes the evolution in scale of homogeneous regions of terrain, but also describes spatially variant characteristics and

H. Deng et al. (Eds.): AICI 2011, Part II, LNAI 7003, pp. 398–404, 2011.

complexity of SAR image. We derive a fast iterative EM algorithm for estimating our model. The classifier for our segmentation is based on the Euclidean Distance of multiscale autoregressive moving average coefficients at several scales, which fuses more multiscale inherent structure and information for precise classification. Moreover, the MAR model and MMAR can be considered as a special case of the SVMMMARMA model. Experimental results show that this model gives better results than previous methods whatever segmentation quality or computation time.

2   SVMMARMA Model of SAR Imagery

The starting point for our model development is a multiresolution sequence X_L, $X_{L-1}, \cdots, X_0$ of SAR images [3], where X_L and X_0 correspond to the coarsest and finest resolution images, respectively. The resolution varies dyadically between images at successive scales. More precisely, we assume that the finest scale image X_0 has a resolution of $\delta \times \delta$ and consists of an $N \times N$ array of pixels (with $N = 2^L$ for some L). Hence, each coarser resolution image X_l has $2^{-l}N \times 2^{-l}N$ pixels and resolution $2^l \delta \times 2^l \delta$. Each pixel $X_l(i, j)$ is obtained by taking the coherent sum of complex fine-scale imagery over $2^l \times 2^l$ blocks, performing log-detection (computing 20 times the log-magnitude), and correcting for zero frequency gain variations by subtracting the mean value. Accordingly, each pixel in image X_l corresponds to four "child" pixels in image X_{l-1}. This indicates that quadtree is natural for the mapping. Each node s on the tree is associated with one of the pixels $X_l(i, j)$ corresponding to pixel (i, j) of SAR image X_l. As an example, Fig. 1 illustrates a multiresolution sequence of three SAR images, together with the quadtree mapping. We use the notation $X(s)$ to indicate the pixel mapped to node s. The scale of node s is denoted by $l(s)$.

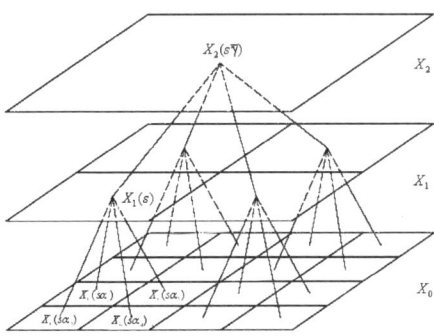

Fig. 1. Sequence of three multiresolution SAR images

The MMAR model [6] is defined as follows:

$$F(X(s)|X_s) = \sum_{k=1}^{K} \pi_k \Phi \left(\frac{X(s) - \sum_{t=0}^{p_k} a_{k,t} X(s\overline{\gamma}^t)}{\sigma_k} \right) \tag{1}$$

where $\sum_{k=1}^{K} \pi_k = 1, \pi_k > 0$, F is the distribution function, K is the number of classes, $\mathfrak{I}_s$ is the set of $X(s\overline{\gamma}),\ldots,X(s\overline{\gamma}^p)(p = \max_k p_k)$, and $\Phi(\cdot)$ is the standard normal distribution function.

The SVMM model [7] is defined as follows:

$$F(X(s)|X_s) = \sum_{k=1}^{K} \pi_k^s f\left(X(s)\right) \tag{2}$$

where π_k^s denote the probability of the pixel at node s belong to the kth calss; $f(\cdot)s$ is density functions; $\sum_{k=1}^{K} \pi_k^s = 1, 0 \le \pi_k^s \le 1$.

Considering the advantages of MMAR model and SVMM model, we propose the SVMMARMA model as follows and derive fast iteration steps in next section:

$$F(X(s)|X_s) = \sum_{k=1}^{K} \pi_k^s f\left(X(s) - \sum_{t=0}^{p_k} a_{k,t} X(s\overline{\gamma}^t) - \sum_{l=0}^{q_k} b_{k,l} w(s\overline{\gamma}^l)\right) \tag{3}$$

p_k and q_k are autoregressive and moving average orders, and other denotations are same as the explanation above.

In fact, the MMAR model can't consider the spatially variant property of image, and the parameter estimation is time-consuming for it is a searching method based on maximization of likelihood function; the SVMM model can't consider the multiscale information, and its segmentation results are sensitive to speckle noise. So we propose the SVMMARMA model and give good parameter estimation method and multiscale classifier for better image segmentation. We can easily notice that MAR model, MMAR model and SVMM model are special cases of SVMMARMA model.

3 Parameter Estimation and EM Algorithm of SVMMARMA Model

Theoretically speaking, finite-order SVMMARMA models are equivalent to infinite-order SVMMAR models. In practice, however, there usually exist finite-order SVMMAR models that are good enough for approximation. Thus, for simplicity, we in fact used SVMMAR models in all our experiments, although the algorithm can be used for general SVMMARMA models.

In addition, many researches have applied a Bootstrap method in pattern classification [10, 11]. Jain [12] showed that bootstrapping was a powerful non-parametric technique to evaluate classifier's performance. Here we employee Bootstrap sampling technique to get Bootstrap sample and sample number [9]. The bootstrap sample size $n_0 = 1000$ at scale 0 is enough to have the representation by the representative criterion, and reader can find the detail in [9]. The parameters of SVMMAR can be obtained by dealing the bootstrap sample based the following derived EM algorithm.

The iterative EM algorithm for estimating parameters consists of an E-step and an M-step. In the context of SVMMAR model for image segmentation, the missing data corresponding to the unknown class of each bootstrap sample pixel $X^*(s)$, the expectation of the complete-data log-likelihood can be expressed as

$$Q(\Theta|\Theta(t)) = \sum_{\{s|l(s)=l\}} \sum_{k=1}^{K} f(\omega_k|X^*(s), \Theta(t)) \ln f(X^*(s)|\omega_k, \Phi_k)$$

$$+ \sum_{\{s|l(s)=l\}} \sum_{k=1}^{K} f(\omega_k|X^*(s), \Theta_k) \ln \pi_k^s \tag{4}$$

where $f(X^*(s)|\omega_k, \Theta_k) = f(e_{sk})$, $e_{sk} = X^*(s) - a_{k,0} - \sum_{u=1}^{p_k} a_{k,u} X^*(s\overline{\gamma}^u)$, the notation $X^*(s\overline{\gamma}^u)$ denotes the pixel mapped to node $s\overline{\gamma}^u$ at scale u.

For E-step, the posterior probabilities $f(\omega_k|X^*(s), \Theta_k)$ can be computed using the Bayes ruls as

$$f(\omega_k|X^*(s), \Theta_k) = \frac{f(X^*(s)|\omega_k, \Phi_k)\pi_k^s}{\sum_{u=1}^{K} f(X^*(s)|\omega_u, \Phi_u)\pi_u^s}, s \in \{s|l(s)=l\}; k=1,2,\cdots,K \tag{5}$$

For M-step, using the Lagrangian multiplier method:

$$\frac{\partial}{\partial \pi_k^s}(Q(\Theta|\Theta(t)) - \lambda(\sum_{k=1}^{K} \pi_k^s - 1)) = 0 \tag{6}$$

to obtain the best estimate as

$$\hat{\pi}_k^s = f(\omega_k|X^*(s), \Theta_k) \tag{7}$$

We can estimate the other parameters by solving equations $\dfrac{\partial Q(\Theta|\Theta_k)}{\partial \sigma_{kt}^2} = 0$ and

$\dfrac{\partial Q(\Theta|\Theta_k)}{\partial a_{k,j}} = 0, j = 0,1,2,\cdots, P; k=1,2,\cdots, K$ to estimate the parameters:

$$\hat{\sigma}_k^2 = \frac{\sum\limits_{\{s|l(s)=l\}} f(\omega_k|X^*(s),\Theta_k)e_{sk}^2}{\sum\limits_{\{s|l(s)=l\}} f(\omega_k|X^*(s),\Theta_k)}, \qquad k=1,2,\cdots,K \tag{8}$$

$$\begin{bmatrix} a_{k,0} \\ a_{k,1} \\ a_{k,2} \\ \vdots \\ a_{k,P_k} \end{bmatrix} = \begin{bmatrix} \sum\limits_{\{s|l(s)=l\}} A_k & \sum\limits_{\{s|l(s)=l\}} A_k X^*(s\overline{\gamma}^{i+1}) & \cdots & \sum\limits_{\{s|l(s)=l\}} A_k X^*(s\overline{\gamma}^{i+P_k}) \\ \sum\limits_{\{s|l(s)=l\}} A_k X^*(s\overline{\gamma}^{i+1}) & \sum\limits_{\{s|l(s)=l\}} A_k X^{*2}(s\overline{\gamma}^{i+1}) & \cdots & \sum\limits_{\{s|l(s)=l\}} A_k X^*(s\overline{\gamma}^{i+1})X^*(s\overline{\gamma}^{i+P_k}) \\ \sum\limits_{\{s|l(s)=l\}} A_k X^{*2}(s\overline{\gamma}^{i+2}) & \sum\limits_{\{s|l(s)=l\}} A_k X^*(s\overline{\gamma}^{i+1})X^*(s\overline{\gamma}^{i+2}) & \cdots & \sum\limits_{\{s|l(s)=l\}} A_k X^*(s\overline{\gamma}^i)X^*(s\overline{\gamma}^{i+2}) \\ \vdots & \vdots & \vdots & \vdots \\ \sum\limits_{\{s|l(s)=l\}} A_k X^*(s\overline{\gamma}^{i+P_k}) & \sum\limits_{\{s|l(s)=l\}} A_k X^*(s\overline{\gamma}^{i+1})X^*(s\overline{\gamma}^{i+P_k}) & \cdots & \sum\limits_{\{s|l(s)=l\}} A_k X^{*2}(s\overline{\gamma}^{i+P_k}) \end{bmatrix}^{-1} \begin{bmatrix} \sum\limits_{\{s|l(s)=l\}} A_k X^*(s\overline{\gamma}^i) \\ \sum\limits_{\{s|l(s)=l\}} A_k X^*(s\overline{\gamma}^i)X^*(s\overline{\gamma}^{i+1}) \\ \sum\limits_{\{s|l(s)=l\}} A_k X^*(s\overline{\gamma}^i)X^*(s\overline{\gamma}^{i+2}) \\ \vdots \\ \sum\limits_{\{s|l(s)=l\}} A_k X^*(s\overline{\gamma}^i)X^*(s\overline{\gamma}^{i+P}) \end{bmatrix} \tag{9}$$

where $A_k = f(\omega_k|X^*(s),\Theta_k)$.

All the parameters can be obtained by iterating (7), (8) and (9) until convergence.

The use of the bootstrap sampling method in image segmentation presents three advantages:

(i) The choice of independence pixel sample which would allows an estimation of the statistical parameters of the image in the best conditions of independence;

(ii) The reduction of redundancy of information connected to the choice of a small representative sample, allows a gain in a factor N/n in times of calculation.

(iii) The bootstrap sample is less possible to include speckle noise, so the parameter estimation procedure based bootstrap sample is less probability to be effected by speckle noise.

4   Classifier for SAR Imagery Segmentation

Unlike previously proposed Bayesian classifier based on posterior distribution of residual part in MMAR model and estimation of pixel labelling in SVMM model, when all the parameters are estimated, we propose a classifier classify each pixel, that is, Euclidean Distance between multiscale autoregressive coefficients of several scales, which fuses more multiscale inherent structure and information and is more robust than the mentioned classifiers. We classify each pixel $X(s)$ into the class k if

$$k(X(s)) = \arg(\min_{1 \le k \le K} \{D(\hat{\boldsymbol{\Phi}}_s, \boldsymbol{\Psi}_k)\}) \tag{10}$$

where $\hat{\boldsymbol{\Phi}}_s = \left(a_{0,1}^s, a_{0,2}^s, \cdots, a_{0,p_k}^s, a_{1,1}^{s\overline{\gamma}}, a_{1,2}^{s\overline{\gamma}}, \cdots, a_{1,p_k}^{s\overline{\gamma}}\right)$, $s \in \{s|l(s)=0\}, s\overline{\gamma} \in \{s\overline{\gamma}|l(s\overline{\gamma})=1\}$

is the coefficients set of a multiscale autoregressive process that is obtained by least square (LS) estimation based on a test window of the classified pixels surrounding it at scale 0 and 1, and $\boldsymbol{\Psi}_k = \left(a_{0k,1}, a_{0k,2}, \cdots, a_{0k,p_k}, a_{1k,1}, a_{1k,2}, \cdots, a_{1k,p_k} \right)$ is the estimated MAR coefficients set of kth class via SVMMAR mode at scale 0 and 1. $D(\hat{\boldsymbol{\Phi}}_s, \boldsymbol{\Psi}_k)$ is Euclidean Distance between $\hat{\boldsymbol{\Phi}}_s$ and $\boldsymbol{\Psi}_k$.

5 Experimental Results and Analysis

To demonstrate the segmentation performance of our proposed model, we apply it to two complex SAR images in Fig. 2a. From the complex images, we generate the previously mentioned quadtree representation and use a second order regression. Because it is found that by increasing the regression order to $P_k = 2$, we can achieve a lower probability of misclassification and a good trade-off between modelling accuracy and computational efficiency. We use the classifier (10) to get the final segmentation results. Figs. 2 and Table 1 show results from applying the SVMMARMA model to two SAR images, as well as results from the MMAR model and SVMM model for comparison. These results show our algorithm performs better than the MMAR model does whatever the segmentation quality or computation time.

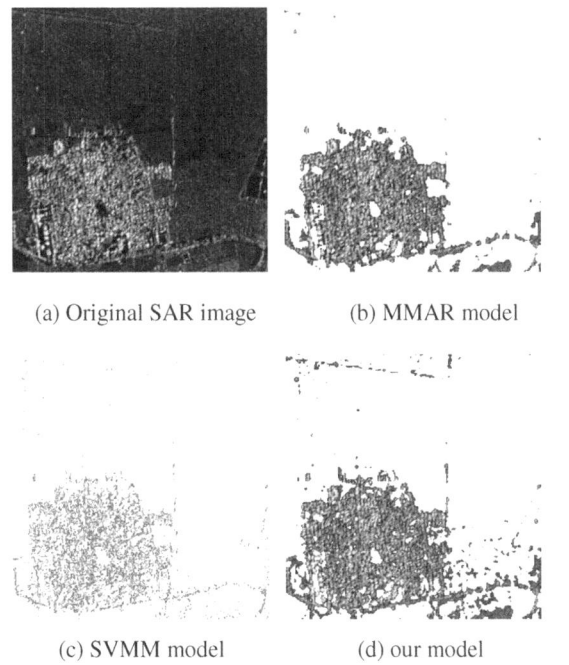

(a) Original SAR image	(b) MMAR model
(c) SVMM model	(d) our model

Fig. 2. segmentation results of different mothds

Table 1. CPU time (sec.) for different model

image method	the SAR image
MMAR model	2867.3
SVMM model	14.8
SVMMAR model	239.8

6 Conclusion

The first contribution of our paper is that we propose a new model for image segmentation; the second contribution is that we give quick and precise parameter estimation for the proposed model; the third contribution is that we design a multiscale classifier for better segmentation and classification. Experimental results support our method.

References

1. Saad, A., El, A.S., Barba, D.: Speckle filtering in SAR images by contrast modification, comparison with a large class of filters. Ann. TelTecommun 51(5–6), 233–244 (1996)
2. Lee, J.S.: Speckle suppression and analysis for SAR images. Opt. Eng. 25(5), 636–643 (1986)
3. Fosgate, C., et al.: Multiscale segmentation and anomaly enhancement of SAR imagery. IEEE Trans. Image Process 6(1), 7–20 (1997)
4. Irving, W., Novak, L., Willsky, A.: A multiresolution approach to discrimination in SAR imagery. IEEE Trans. Aerosp. Electron. Syst. 33(4), 1157–1169 (1997)
5. Kim, A., Kim, H.: Hierarchical stochastic modeling of SAR imagery for segmentation/compression. IEEE Trans. Signal Process. 47(2), 458–468 (1999)
6. Wen, X.-B., Tian, Z.: Mixture multiscale autoregressive modelling of SAR imagery for segmentation. Electronics Letters 39(17), 1272–1274 (2003)
7. Gopal, S.S., Herbert, T.J.: Bayesian pixel classification using spatially variant finite mixtures and the generalized EM algorithm. IEEE Trans. Image Processing 17(7), 1014–1018 (1998)
8. Blekas, K., Likas, A., Galatsanos, N.P., Lagaris, I.E.: A spatially constrained mixture model for image segmentation. IEEE Transactions on Neural Networks 16(2), 494–498 (2005)
9. Zribi, M.: Non-parametric and unsupervised Bayesian classification with Bootstrap sampling. Image and Vision Computing 22(1), 1–8 (2004)
10. Koch, I., Marshall, G.: Bootstrap coverage plots for image segmentation. In: IEEE-ICPR, pp. 447–451 (1996)
11. Vijaya, S.V., Murty, M.N.: Bootstrapping for efficient handwritten digit recognition. Pattern Recognition 34, 1047–1056 (2001)
12. Jain, A.K., Dubes, R.C., Chen, C.C.: Bootstrapping techniques for error estimation. IEEE Trans. Pattern Anal. Mach. Intell. PAMI 9(5), 628–633 (1987)

Study of Image Segmentation for MR Diffusion Weighed Image Based on Active Contour

Guannan Chen[1], Daner Xu[2], Hengyang Hu[1], Tingyin Wang[1], and Rong Chen[1]

[1] Key Laboratory of OptoElectronic Science and Technology for Medicine, Fujian Normal University, Ministry of Education, Fuzhou 350007, China
edado@fjnu.edu.cn
[2] College of Humanities and Social Science, Fujian Agriculture and Forestry University, Fuzhou, 350002

Abstract. MR Diffusion Weighed Image(DWI) is one of many functional magnetic resonance imaging(fMRI) techniques, and could provide complicated spatial and structural information about the tissue. Aiming at segmentation MR diffusion weighed image for real-time application with numerical stability constraints and high efficiency, a method based on the minimization algorithm is developed. Our approach is based on the image segmentation tasks into a global minimization method. The minimization algorithm minimization the energy, avoid the drawback in the level set approach and easy to implement, allows us a fast minimization of the active contour. Experimental results show that the effectiveness for image segmentation with our method is preferable.

Keywords: MR Diffusion Weighed Image, Image segmentation, Minimization algorithm.

1 Introduction

MR Diffusion Weighed Image (DWI) is one of many functional magnetic resonance imaging(fMRI) techniques. It is the only way to conduct water molecule diffusion imaging in vivo. MR diffusion weighed image reflects the diffusion properties of water molecules in an organism and appraises the random motion of the water molecule, providing spatial and structural information about the tissue. However, due to the complexity of human anatomy organization structural information and the irregularities of soft tissue, image segmentation for MR diffusion weighed image turns to be a difficult issue.

At present, several active contour model and Variational Level set method has used to process MRI image [1], and obtains a good result while segmenting some simple objects. To achieve the accurate results and well effectiveness for complex image such as brain MR diffusion weighed image needs to be resolved. In this paper, we propose some modified minimization algorithm for the active counter algorithm to obtain better numerical stability constraints and high efficiency.

H. Deng et al. (Eds.): AICI 2011, Part II, LNAI 7003, pp. 405–410, 2011.
© Springer-Verlag Berlin Heidelberg 2011

2 Minimization Algorithm

Following the model of active contours [2], Caselles, Kimmel and Sapiro in [3] and Kichenassamy, Kumar, Olver, Tannenbaum and Yezzi in [4] proposed a new enhanced version of the snake model called the geometric active contour (GAC) model. This new formulation is said geometrically intrinsic because the proposed snake energy is invariant with respect to the curve parameterization. The model is defined by the following minimization problem:

$$\min_C \left\{ E_{GAC}(C) = \int_0^{L(C)} g\left(\left|\nabla I_0(C(s))\right|\right) ds \right\} \tag{1}$$

where ds is the Euclidean element of length and L(C) is the length of the curve C defined by L(C) = $\int_0^{L(C)} ds$, hence, the energy functional (1) is actually a new length obtained by weighting the Euclidean element of length ds by the function g which contains information concerning the boundaries of objects . The function g is an edge indicator function that canishes at object boundaries such as $g(\left|\nabla I_0\right|) = \dfrac{1}{1 + \beta \left|\nabla I_0\right|^2}$.

The calculus of variations provides us the Euler-Lagrange equation of the functional E_{GAC} and the gradient descent method gives us the flow that minimizes as fast as possible E_{GAC}.

Despite the many good numerical results obtained with this segmentation model and strong theoretical properties [8], the snake/GAC model is highly sensitive to the initial condition. Actually, the quality of the segmentation result depends a lot on the choice of the initial contour, which means that a bad initial contour can give an unsatisfactory result.

In a recent work, Chan, Esedoglu and Nikolova [5] proposed a new approach to deal with global minimum and overcome the limitation of local minima. In their paper, they related image segmentation to image denoising in order to find global minimizers of two denoising and segmentation models. The first model is a binary image denoising model which removes the geometric noise in a given shape and the second model is the active contours without edges (ACWE) model of Chan and Vese [6,7].

In this paper, we develop a minimization models for the active contour model. This model is based on the active contour segmentation model and the piecewise-constant Mumford and Shah's model, which is related to the ACWE model of Chan and Vese to globally minimize the active contour model subject to intensity homogeneity constraints.

The minimization problem of the active contour model use the well-known Mumford and Shah's functional and the Chan and Vese's model of active contours without edges. The MS model is one of the most influential variational model to solve the image segmentation problem. This model determines the optimal piecewise smooth approximation of a given image, which is equivalent to partition an image into distinct homogeneous regions which boundaries are sharp and piecewise regular. The ACWE model is also an important segmentation model based on curve evolution techniques, the level set approach and the MS model. This model detects boundaries of objects based on the detection of homogeneous regions, like in the MS model, and not on the detection of large image gradients such as in the classical snake model. The efficiency of the ACWE model is presented on various experimental results for which the classical snake model, based on the image gradient, is not applicable. The variational model of ACWE, which corresponds to the two-phase piecewise constant approximation of the Mumford and Shah's model, is as follows:

$$\min_{\Omega_{C,c1,c2}} \left\{ E(\Omega) = P(\Omega_{C,c1,c2}, \lambda) + \lambda \int_{\Omega_c} (c_1 - f(x))^2 dx \right.$$
$$\left. + \lambda \int_{\Omega \setminus \Omega_c} (c_2 - f(x))^2 dx \right\}$$

(2)

Where f is the given image, Ω is a closed subset of the image domain Ω, $P(\Omega_c)$ is the perimeter of the set Ω, λ is an arbitrary positive parameter which controls the trade-off between the regularization process and the fidelity of the solution the original image f and c_1, $c_2 \in$ R. The variational model determines the best approximation, in the L sense of the image f as a set of (non-connected) regions with only two different values, c_1 and c_2. If Ω_c is fixed, the values of c_1 and c_2 which minimize the energy E are the mean values inside and outside Ω_c. Finally, the term $P(\Omega)$ imposes a smoothness constraint on the geometry of the set Ω which separates the piecewise constant regions.

The energy E can be written according to a level set function φ:

$$E(\phi, c_1, c_2, \lambda) = \int_{\Omega} |\nabla H(\phi)| +$$
$$\lambda \int_{\Omega} (H(\phi)(c_1 - f(x))^2 + H(-\phi)(c_1 - f(x))^2) dx$$

(3)

The steady state solution of the gradient flow is:

$$\partial_t \phi = div(\frac{\nabla \phi}{|\nabla \phi|}) - \lambda r(x, c_1, c_2)$$

(4)

So, we can carry the minimization of the segmentation task:

$$E(u, c1, c2, \lambda) = TV_g(u) + \lambda \int_{\Omega} r(x, c1, c2) u dx$$

Thus, the minimization algorithm are considered:
We search for u as a solution when v be fixed:

$$\min_{u} \{TV_g(u) + \frac{1}{2\theta} \|u - v\|_{L2}^2\}$$

(5)

we search for v as a solution when u be fixed:

$$\min_{u} \{ \int_{\Omega} \lambda r_1(x, c_1, c_2) v dx + \frac{1}{2\theta} \|u - v\|_{L2}^2\}$$

(6)

3 Solution of Minimization Algorithm

The solution of (5) is given as:

$$u = v - \theta divy$$
$$g(x)\nabla(\theta divy - v) - |\nabla(\theta divy - v)| \, y = 0 \tag{7}$$

And the equation can be fixed by follow:
$y_0 = 0$;

$$y_{n+1} = \frac{y_n + \delta t \nabla(div(y_n) - v/\theta)}{1 + \delta t |\nabla(div(y_n) - v/\theta)| / g(x)} \tag{8}$$

The solution of (6) is given as:

$$v = \min\{\max\{u(x) - \lambda r_1(x, c_1, c_2), 0\}, 1\} \tag{9}$$

The initial values are $u_0 = v_0 = y_0 = 0$. The constants c1 and c2 are updated every 10 to 15 iterations. And the step is equal to $\delta t = 1/4$, and the stopping criteria is $\varepsilon \geq \max\{|u_{n+1} - u_n|, |v_{n+1} - v_n|\}$.

4 Experiments and Results

In order to objectively validate the result of image segmentation based on minimization algorithm in this paper, we choose MR diffusion weighed image, and compare the effect with ACWE algorithm and minimization algorithm.

Fig1(a) is a MR diffusion weighed image, which include gray matter, white matter, cerebrospinal fluid, and Background. Figure 2(b) and Figure 2(c) are the segmentation results of the original ACWE segmentation algorithm with λ=0.001 and λ=0.01. And the segmentation results are not suitable in some slight topological structure. Figure 2(d) is the segmentation results of our algorithm. The ROI has been segmented more better subjectively to cut through the low contrast region of the object. The time of ACWE segmentation algorithm is 30s with λ=0.001 and 35s with λ=0.01, but 25s with λ=0.001 and 29s with λ=0.1 using our algorithm.

Table1 is the accuracy of the results which are statistic analyzed from one hundred MR diffusion weighed image and one hundred MR image. The accuracy of our algorithm is better than the ACWE algorithm objectively.

Table 1. The accuracy of the results

	MR diffusion weighed image	MR image
ACWE algorithm	88.31%	87.85%
Our algorithm	91.45%	92.78%

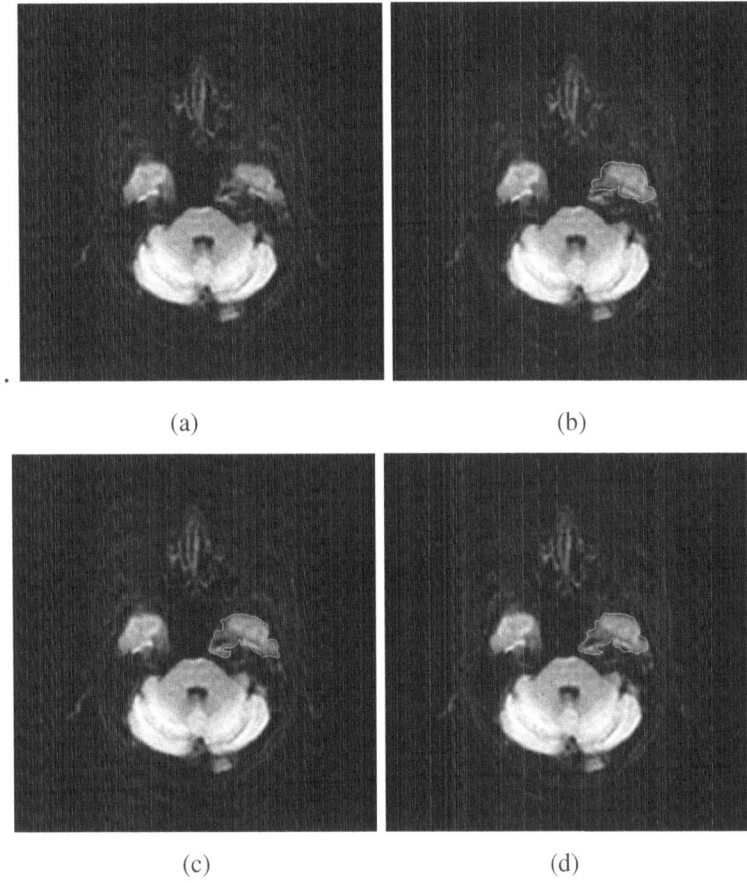

(a)   (b)

(c)   (d)

Fig. 1. Processing a MR diffusion weighed image

5   Conclusion

Some processes based on the original dual level set algorithm are presented, moreover, the principles, and the problem of them are analyzed. A new method based on minimization algorithm for image segmentation is presented for MR diffusion weighed image in this work. The new method can not only obtain the more accuracy result but also shorten the time of computing. Experimental results also show that the effectiveness for MR diffusion weighed image and MR image segmentation with our method is better than the original method's.

Acknowledgments. This work was supported by the Natural Science Foundation of Fujian Province (No. 2010J05130), Development Projects of FUJIAN PROVINCIAL TUMOR HOSPITA & Fujian Normal University (No. DH-571).

References

1. Warach, S., Chien, D., Li, W., Ronthal, M., et al.: Fast magnetic resonance diffusion-weighted imaging of acute human stroke. Neurology 42(9), 1717–1723 (1992)
2. Kass, M., Witkin, A., Terzopoulos, D.: Snakes: Active Contour Models. International Journal of Computer Vision, 321–331 (1987)
3. Caselles, V., Kimmel, R., Sapiro, G.: Geodesic Active Contours. International Journal of Computer Vision 22(1), 61–79 (1997)
4. Kichenassamy, S., Kumar, A., Olver, P., Tannenbaum, A., Yezzi, A.: Conformal Curvature Flows: From Phase Transitions to Active Vision. Archive for Rational Mechanics and Analysis 134, 275–301 (1996)
5. Chan, T., Esedo⁻glu, S., Nikolova, M.: Algorithms for Finding Global Minimizers of Image Segmentation and Denoising Models, UCLA CAM Report 04-54 (2004)
6. Chan, F.T., Vese, L.: Active contours without edges. IEEE Trans. Image Processing 10(2), 266–277 (2001)
7. Li, C.M., Xu, C.Y., Changfen, G.: Level Set Evolution without Re-initialization: a New Varitional Formulation. In: Computer Vision and Pattern Recognition, pp. 430–436. IEEE, New York
8. Vese, L.A., Chan, F.T.: Multiphase Level Set Framework for Image Segmentation Using the Mumford and Shah Model. International Journal of Computer Vision 2002 50, 271–293 (1992)

Image Enhancement of X-Ray Film Base on Mutil-Scale Retinex

Zhishe Wang and Jilin Wei

College of Applied Science,
Taiyuan University of Science & Technology, Taiyuan, China
wzs2003@163.com, jilin_wei@163.com

Abstract. View of film system for medical diagnosis was presented. the system which took the cold cathode fluorescent lamps (CCFL) as the background light source, excluded ambient light impact on the concept of film by a light shell , and realized the digital X-ray film through the CCD camera the image information transferred to the computer. The details of hidden areas on some obscure digital X-ray images were enhanced by multi-scale Retinex (MSR) algorithm. With this method, the image contrast enhancement, sharpening and dynamic range compression was achieved at the same time. The information of hidden areas of X-ray image was obviously enhanced. The enhancement technique was compared with other techniques such as histogram equalization, homomorphism filter. The result of experiment shows that the MSR algorithm can overcome the lack of enhancement of traditional digital X-ray method and satisfy the clinic demand.

Keywords: X-ray film, Retinex, image contrast, image enhancement.

1 Introduction

At present, the radiology images of many hospitals stored a lot of precious information on the traditional X-ray film, these information play a very significant role in clinical diagnosis, teaching and scientific research [1]. But some of material have metamorphism with the passage of time, image information has become blurred and can't be used for medical diagnosis, teaching and scientific research. Therefore, it is necessary to achieve satisfactory results for these x-rays using digital image processing technology.

A medical imaging picture observation device which is named usually view film instrument is essential equipment for doctor to medical observation and diagnosis. The performances of view film instrument which vary degrees of image contrast and definition is influent to the effect of reading image information. Currently, view film instrument have two major problems: One is the influence of backlighting. If the ambient light is stronger, contrast will be reduced in the same background strength lighting, and some important information might be ignored; another problem is that view film instrument can not distinguish some information of X-ray darker areas, and can not reach the medical diagnosis requirements.

H. Deng et al. (Eds.): AICI 2011, Part II, LNAI 7003, pp. 411–417, 2011.

This paper introduces a new kind of medical view film auxiliary diagnostic system. the system which took the cold cathode fluorescent lamps (CCFL) as the background light source, can isolate completely the X-ray film and the ambient light from the outside world by using isolation light shell, and eliminate the influence of ambient light for view film by maximum use of the background lighting. At the same time, this system realizes digital x-rays film through the CCD camera to overcome the current domestic market view film instrument faults. Some poor contrast images which contain dim parts and gloomy details of X-ray film were enhanced by multi-scale Retinex (MSR) algorithm. The Experimental results show that we took to enhance image darker area details information and meet doctors clinical diagnosis, teaching and scientific research of the requirements.

2   Construction of Film System

A new type view of film system for medical diagnosis system was introduced, which mainly composed by the background lighting, dimming control, automatic switch, separated light shell and CCD camera. The construction of film system was shown in Fig.1.

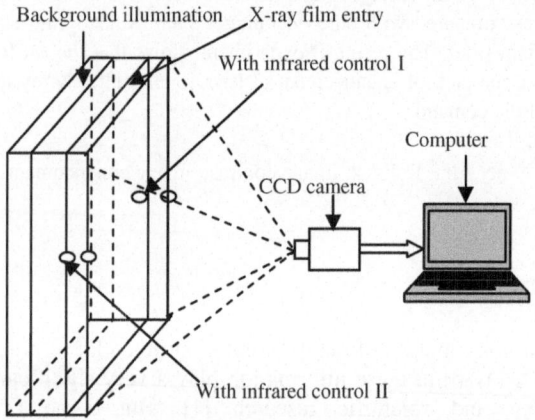

Fig. 1. Construction of film system

When the X-ray film is inserted into separated light shell, the infrared radio control outputs signal after the presence of X-ray film is detected. Starting the CCFL when the signal is detected by dimming control procedure, at the same time, CCFL can dynamically adjust the concept of light intensity to meet the film demand. CCD camera transmits the X-ray image information to the computer to realize digital X-ray film, using computer for further processing and analysis, and then the details of hidden areas on some obscure images was enhanced by multi-scale Retinex.

3   Multi-Scale Retinex (MSR) Algorithm

3.1   The Theory of Algorithm

Multi-scale Retinex algorithm is both a good dynamic range compression of image and a good image enhancement method of ensuring consistency of good and color of image. The algorithm can be described in the following formula [2-6]:

$$R_{MSRi}(x, y) = \sum_{k=1}^{M} w_k (\log I_i(x, y) - \log[F_k(x, y) * I_i(x, y)]) \ \ i=1,\cdots,N \tag{1}$$

Where $I_i(x, y)$ is the input image, Subscript i is the i_{th} spectral band, N is the number of spectral bands, N = 1 is grayscale image, N = 3 is color image, $R_{MSRi}(x, y)$ is output image. $F_k(x, y)$ is the environmental function, w_k is the weight coefficient related to F_k , M is the number of environmental functions, and * is convolution. Environmental functions $F_k(x, y)$ can be expressed as:

$$F_k(x, y) = K \cdot \exp(-(x^2 + y^2)/c^2) \tag{2}$$

Where c is scaling function, and K satisfies the following formula:

$$\iint F_k(x, y)dxdy = 1 \tag{3}$$

F_k selects a different standard deviation c, which used to control the scale of the environment function scope. The effect of MSR algorithm processing mainly depends on the scale factor c of the environment function. When the c is smaller, it is better to complete the dynamic range compression, and then the local feature of image is clearly. When the c is larger, there is a better consistency of color and sense, and a better effect of the overall image. The experiments results show that the selection of large, medium and small scales, for most of the digital X-ray images, the selection of weight of each scale should according to emphasis the dynamic range or focus on consistency of good and color.

3.2   MSR Algorithm

From the expression (1) of MSR algorithm can be seen that the algorithm realizes to enhancement process the image by convolution on the spatial. However, the amount of computation of the convolution on spatial is very large, so it is difficult to ensure the real-time of the algorithm. To improve the real-time, we transmit convolution on spatial into the product on frequency domain by Fourier transform. The algorithm is as follows:

(1) We choose Gaussian function as the environmental function. There,

$$K = \sum\sum \exp(-(x^2 + y^2)/c^2) \cdot \tag{4}$$

Based on the large number of experiments of digital X-ray image processing, we choose three different standard deviation c of 15, 80, and 250 respectively.

(2) On the condition of the three kinds of scales, the convolution of the image was taken through using three different Gaussian environmental functions. Convolution process as the following equation:

$$DFT^{-1}[DFT(F(x, y) \bullet DFT(I(x, y))]$$ (5)

(3) Weighted average of the results are obtained by calculating the three scales with (1), the right is $1 / 3$.

(4) Gain mapping the output gray, the results of display can be obtained. Image pixel will appear a negative value after MSR approached, and it will appear beyond the scope of the display, which needs to be compressed into the pan and display range. Here, using a method of the gain/offset to correct image pixels, Then the display shows gray scale range (0-255), using format (7) which is mapped to the modified gray values of image.

$$R_0(x, y) = G \times R_{MSRi}(x, y) + offset$$ (6)

$$R(x, y) = 255 \times \frac{R_0(x, y) - r_{min}}{r_{max} - r_{min}}$$ (7)

Where $R_{MSRi}(x, y)$ and $R_0(x, y)$ are the image gray value of the input and output respectively. We do a lot of research on the selection of the gain coefficient G and our offset, the results showed that all kinds of image after MSR has a very similar histogram distribution, so most of the images of these two values can take a fixed value, it doesn't effect the image enhancement. In this paper, G=3 and $offset = 50$ are selected, r_{max} and r_{min} are maximum and minimum of gray value of the modified images, $R(x, y)$ is the image gray value of displayable after mapped.

3.3 Processing Results and Analyses

The digital X-ray film is obtained through the view of film system for medical diagnosis. Fig.2 (a), (b), (c) is respectively the original image, Histogram equalization image and MSR image.

In Fig.2 (a), the information of the dim space of the original image is indistinguishable. In Comparison the images processed with histogram equalization enhancement algorithm and MSR image enhancement algorithm with the original image, we can find that histogram equalization method can't obviously enhance the information of dim space and the noise became greater, but the MSR algorithm can effectively enhance the information of dim space and significantly improve the contrast.

The images in Fig.3 are the corresponding gray histogram of images in Fig.2. The grayness of original image collected in the dim space and the whole effect is dimmer; after processing with histogram equalization enhancement algorithm, the details of dim space isn't enhanced and the grayness still collected in the dim space, although the contrast is improved; however, after processing with MSR algorithm, the grayness distribution of image collected in the brighter space, which shows that MSR algorithm can significantly improve the contrast and enhance the details of dim space. Additionally, according to the histogram grayness distribution, the grayness distribution obtained by using MRS algorithm is better than other two, which made the image clearer.

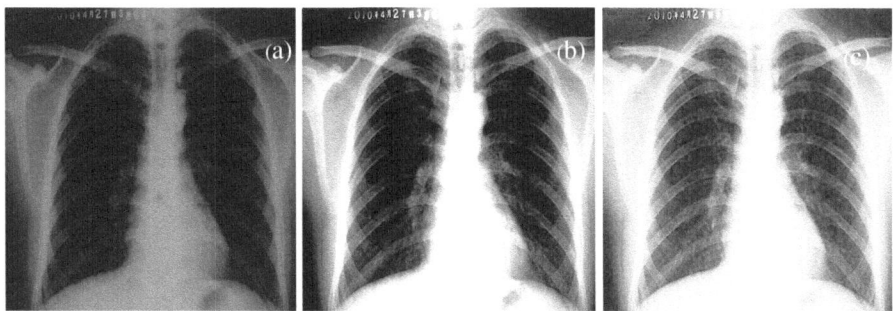

Fig. 2. Comparison of several enhanced processing algorithms. (a) Original image ;(b) Image after histogram equalization; (c) Image after MSR.

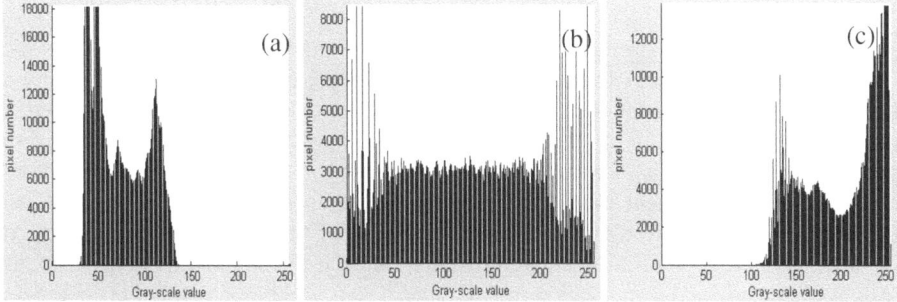

Fig. 3. Histogram comparison of several enhanced processing algorithms. (a) Histogram of original image; (b) Histogram of image after histogram equalization; (c) Histogram of image after MSR.

To analysis the effect of several enhancement methods objectively, quantitatively, using the mean, standard deviation, information entropy and definition as a measure of objective criteria for image quality [7]. Table1 show the several indicators of the results of enhancement in the Fig.2. The result shows that, MSR enhancement algorithm, compared with the histogram equalization method, significantly improve the image for image brightness, suppress the image noise, and increase the amount of information and definition of the image.

Table 1. Indicators table of image processing results

Image	mean	Standard deviation	Entropy	Definition
Fig2.a	69.5021	48.168	6.7790	16.5150
Fig2.b	128.1057	66.919	6.8647	38.1598
Fig2.c	158.9994	85.468	7.0897	40.8954

In table1, the definition is defined as the average 8-D diffusion value of each pixel [8], can be expressed as:

$$DEF = \frac{\sum_{i=1}^{M \times N} \sum_{j=1}^{8} |df / dx|}{M \times N} \tag{8}$$

Where df is the gray value difference and dx is the pixel distance.

4 Conclusions

A view of film system for medical diagnosis was presented, which took CCFL as the background light source, excluded ambient light impact on the concept of film by a light shell, and realized the digitization of X-ray film, overcome the shortcomings of the film apparatus in domestic market. Some poor contrast images which contain dim parts and gloomy details of X-ray film were enhanced by multi-scale Retinex (MSR) algorithm. The experiment shows that not only the satisfactory enhancement effect can be obtained by the MSR algorithm but the efficiency of running program is raised. At the same time, this algorithm can significantly enhance the contrast of X-ray film, as well as the details and visualization of dark space, so it will be favorable for doctors to improve the accuracy of clinical diagnoses with high application value.

Acknowledgments. The project is funded by Youth Foundation of Taiyuan University of Science & Technology (No.20103019) and Science and Technology Development Program of Shanxi Province (No.2007032052).

References

1. Hans, G.: Evaluation of mammographic viewbox luminance,illumininance and color. Med. Phys. 32, 819–821 (1993)
2. Land, E.: An alternative technique for the computation of the design the retinex theory of color vision. Proc. Nat. Acad. Sci. 83(12), 3078–3080 (1986)
3. Rahman, Z., Jobson, D., Woodell, G.A.: Multiscale retinex for color rendition and dynamic range compression. In: Applications of Digital Image Processing XIX, Proc. SPIE, vol. 2847 (1996)

4. Woodell, G.A., Jobson, D.J., Rahman, Z., Hines, G.D.: Enhancement of imagery in poor visibility conditions. In: Sensors, and Command, Control, Communications, and Intelligence (C3I) Technologies for Homeland Security and Homeland Defense IV, Proc. SPIE, vol. 5778 (2005)
5. Jobson, D.J., Rahman, Z., Woodell, G.A.: Retinex processing for automatic image enhancement. Human Vision and Electronic Imaging VII, SPIE Symposium on Electronic Imaging, Porc. SPIE 4662 (2002)
6. Jobson, D.J., Rahman, Z., Woodell, G.A.: Properties and performance of a center/surround retinex. IEEE Trans.on Image Processing: Special Issue on Color Processing 3(6), 451–462 (1996)
7. Wang, Y.C., Li, S.J.: Enhancement of radiography based multi-scale Retinex. Optics and Precision Engineering 14(1), 70–76 (2006)
8. Wang, H.-n., Zhong, W., Wang, J., et al.: Research of Measurement for Digital Image Definition. Journal of Image and Graphics 9(7), 828–831 (2004)

Contourlet-Based Error-Amended Sharp Edge Scheme for Image Zooming

Nian Cai[1], Haiyuan Zhang[1], Nan Zhang[1], and Fangzhen Li[2]

[1] School of Information Engineering, Guangdong University of Technology,
Guangzhou 510006, P.R. China
[2] Department of Computer Science, Shandong Economic University, Ji'nan 250014, China
cainian@gdut.edu.cn

Abstract. A novel image interpolation method is proposed by combining the error-amended sharp edges scheme with the contourlet transformation. The proposed method incorporates the error-amended part into the bilinear interpolation algorithm. Directions of the interpolation points are determined by the Sobel operator, then we get a preliminary zoomed image. A new interpolated image is obtained when the low-frequency components of the preliminary zoomed image are replaced by the enhanced amplitude of the original image. Finally the high-resolution image is achieved by the inverse contourlet transform of the new interpolated image. The experimental results indicate that, compared with traditional image zooming methods, the proposed method can get clearer and sharper edges, especially for the original images having more details.

Keywords: image interpolation, contourlet transform, error-amended sharp edge scheme.

1 Introduction

Image zooming is used to obtained high resolution images from low resolution ones by means of image interpolation in many applications, such as remote sensing, medical imaging, film making, robot vision, military. A neighborhood of pixels is important for interpolation. Three methods in common use are nearest neighbor, which is the fastest, bilinear interpolation, which is more accurate but slower and suffers some loss of high frequency components, and cubic convolution, which is very accurate but slowest [1, 2]. They neglect the orientations of edges and textures so as to blur interpolated images, especially the edges. More and more researchers devote their research to preserving the edge orientation and got some outstanding achievements. Li and Orchard propose a new edge-directed interpolation (NEDI) algorithm based on local covariance coefficients [3]. Cha and Kim put forward a modified bilinear interpolation method named the error-amended sharp edge (EASE) scheme, which is anisotropic and edge-adaptive [4]. It amends the bilinear interpolation error by using the classic interpolation error theorem and proves superior

H. Deng et al. (Eds.): AICI 2011, Part II, LNAI 7003, pp. 418–425, 2011.
© Springer-Verlag Berlin Heidelberg 2011

over traditional methods in edge preservation and similarly efficient as cubic interpolation schemes.

The interpolation methods above pay more attention to the local correlation of the interpolated pixels' neighborhood, which improves the subjective quality of interpolated images, but neglect the global correlation of the images, which results in the loss of the images' high frequency components to some extent. Wavelet transform offers a multiscale and time-frequency-localized image representation and wavelet-based algorithms have proven successful for image interpolation [5, 6]. A wavelet bilinear interpolation iterative algorithm is introduced in [5], which can automatically search the optimal high-resolution image with a maximal signal-to-noise ration. Literature [6] presented a wavelet-domain image resolution enhancement method, which employs linear least-squares regression to estimate the unknown detail coefficients. These wavelet-based methods outperform classic interpolation methods in terms of subjective quality and objective quality. Wavelets, however, can only capture limited directional information and can not "see" the smoothness along the contours, which makes the disadvantages of weak intrinsic geometrical structures for image representation. The contourlet transform, developed by Do et. al, is a flexible multiscale, directional, time-frequency localization decomposition for images, which allows for more flexible number of directions at each scale than the wavelet transform [7-9].

Thus contourlets are employed in this paper to improve the ability in obtaining intrinsic geometrical structures. Then a modified error-amended sharp edge scheme is provided based on the contourlet transform, which is called contourlet-based error-amended sharp edge (CEASE). Firstly, the EASE scheme is introduced to interpolate the low-resolution original image. Then the interpolated image is decomposed by the contourlet transform. The low-frequency components are replaced by the enhanced original image by means of linear transformation, then a new contourlet-transformed image is achieved. At last, the inverse contourlet transform is used to achieve the high-resolution image.

2 EASE Interpolation Scheme

The EASE is an edge-adaptive interpolation method to amend the error of the bilinear method based on the interpolation error theorem. For simplicity, we present an EASE scheme for the (2×2)-magnification of 2D image. In this case, there is an interpolated point between every two pixels, which is called aligned point, and an interpolated point in the center of every four-neighborhood, which is called interior point. That is to say, there are ten aligned points and four interior points in a 3×3 window. Assuming that $f(i, j)$ is the intensity of the pixel (i, j), the $f(i+1/2, j)$ is the intensity of the right aligned point,

$$f(i+1/2, j) = \frac{f(i, j) + f(i+1, j)}{2} + \frac{1}{4} * \min \mod(E_L, E_R)$$ (1)

where E_L and E_R are the forward error and the backward error correspondingly,

$$E_L = f(i,j) - \frac{f(i-1,j) + f(i+1,j)}{2}$$

$$E_R = f(i+1,j) - \frac{f(i,j) + f(i+2,j)}{2} \tag{2}$$

and the minmod function determines the error-amending direction

$$\min\bmod(a,b) = \begin{cases} a, & \text{if } ab > 0 \text{ and } |a| \le |b| \\ b, & \text{if } ab > 0 \text{ and } |a| > |b| \\ 0, & \text{if } ab \le 0 \end{cases} \tag{3}$$

When E_L and E_R have different signs, there is an edge or an inflection point between two pixels. And the linear interpolation method can be accurate enough to estimate $f(i+1/2, j)$. While E_L and E_R have the same sign, the minmod function selects the minimum in modulus. Then we can estimate the values of another nine aligned points in the 3×3 window with this scheme. To estimate the values of the four interior points, interpolation should be implemented along the local edge direction. Four edge-adaptive directional Sobel derivatives at the point $(i+1/2, j+1/2)$ are calculated firstly

$$\begin{aligned}
S_1 &= |f(i+1,j) + 2f(i+1,j+1/2) + f(i+1,j+1) \\
&\quad -f(i,j) - 2f(i,j+1/2) - f(i,j+1)| \\
S_2 &= \sqrt{2}\,|f(i+1/2,j+1) + f(i+1,j+1) + f(i+1,j+1/2) \\
&\quad -f(i,j+1/2) - f(i,j) - f(i+1/2,j)| \\
S_3 &= |f(i,j+1) + 2f(i+1/2,j+1) + f(i+1,j+1) \\
&\quad -f(i,j) - 2f(i+1/2,j) - f(i+1,j)| \\
S_4 &= \sqrt{2}\,|f(i,j+1/2) + f(i,j+1) + f(i+1/2,j+1) \\
&\quad -f(i+1/2,j) - f(i+1,j) - f(i+1,j+1/2)|
\end{aligned} \tag{4}$$

On the assumption that the edges are locally bilinear, the edge direction is between the two directions that estimate the two smallest directional Sobel derivatives, which are adjacent to each other and denote as following:

$$S_p = \min(S_1, S_3), \, S_q = \min(S_2, S_4) \tag{5}$$

where S_p and S_q denote the smallest directional Sobel derivatives in the vertical/horizontal direction and the 45°/135° direction correspondingly. Then the value of the interior point $(i+1/2, j+1/2)$ is derived as following

$$f(i+\frac{1}{2}, j+\frac{1}{2}) = \frac{\sqrt{2}S_q}{S_P + \sqrt{2}S_q} L_p + \frac{S_p}{S_P + \sqrt{2}S_q} L_q \tag{6}$$

where p and q are defined as in Eq. (5) and

$$\begin{aligned}
L_1 &= (f(i,j+1/2) + f(i+1,j+1/2))/2 \\
L_2 &= (f(i,j) + f(i+1,j+1))/2 \\
L_3 &= (f(i+1/2,j) + f(i+1/2,j+1))/2 \\
L_4 &= (f(i+1,j) + f(i,j+1))/2
\end{aligned} \tag{7}$$

Thus we can also estimate another three interior points by the scheme above.

3   Contourlet Transform and CEASE

The contourlet transform proposed by Do et al., named pyramid directional filter bank, is a multiscale image representation method, which can deal effectively with images having smooth contours. It has excellent abilities of multiresolution, time-frequency localization, directionality and anisotropy. The contourlet transform decomposes an image into several directional subbands at multiple scales by combining the Laplacian pyramid (LP) with a directional filter bank (DFB). A LP is used to decompose the image at multiple scales to obtain a bandpass image. Then a DFB is applied to each bandpass channel to capture the high frequency (representing directionality) of the image.

In this paper, a modified EASE scheme is developed by combining the contourlet transform with the EASE scheme. The scheme is summarized as follows.

(1) The low-resolution original image is interpolated with the EASE scheme and zoomed as the image I_1.
(2) The image I_1 is decomposed by the contourlet transform.
(3) A new contourlet-transformed image I_2 is achieved when the low-frequency components of the transformed image above are replaced by the enhanced original image via linear transformation.
(4) The high-resolution image is achieved by the inverse contourlet transform for the image I_2.

4   Results and Discussions

In this paper, the average gradient and the entropy are used to objectively evaluate the interpolation performance. The average gradient T can depict the sharpness of textures and edges in the images and is defined as follows

$$T = \frac{1}{MN} \sum_{i=1}^{M} \sum_{j=1}^{N} \sqrt{(\Delta I_x^2 + \Delta I_y^2)/2} \tag{8}$$

$$\begin{aligned} \Delta I_x &= f(i+1, j) - f(i, j) \\ \Delta I_y &= f(i, j+1) - f(i, j) \end{aligned} \tag{9}$$

where M and N denote the length and width of the image correspondingly. The entropy H can depict the richness of image details and is defined as follows

$$H = -\sum_{i=1}^{n} p(x_i) \log p(x_i) \tag{10}$$

Three original images which have different amount of image details are selected in the experiments. They are the synthetic image, which is smoothest and whose size is 256×256, the Lena image, which has mid-complexity details and whose size is 128×128, and the monkey face image, which has most details and whose size is 128×128 (Fig. 1). The images are zoomed for the (2×2)-magnification by six interpolation methods, which are the bilinear interpolation, the bi-cubic interpolation, the EASE scheme, the NEDI, the wavelet bilinear interpolation, the CEASE. Due to the limitation of the space, these zoomed images are visually displayed in the same sizes of original images (Fig.2-Fig.4). Here Labels denotes the zoomed results obtained by the different methods, which are (a) the bilinear interpolation, (b) the bi-cubic interpolation, (c) the EASE scheme, (d) the NEDI method, (e) the wavelet bilinear interpolation, (f) the CEASE scheme. And their objective evaluation results are shown in Table 1.

(a)   (b)   (c)

Fig. 1. (a) the synthetic image, (b) Lena, (c) the monkey face

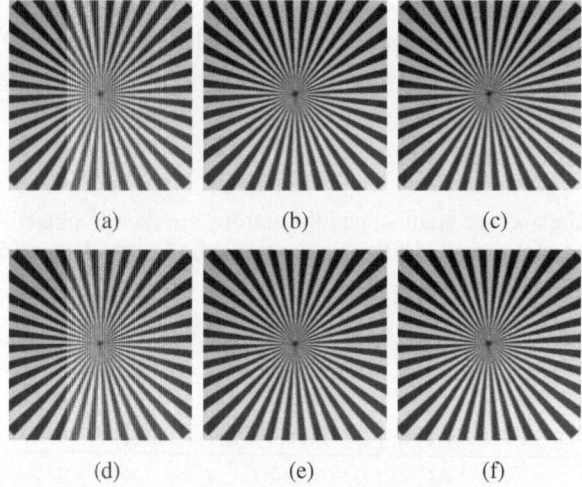

(a)   (b)   (c)

(d)   (e)   (f)

Fig. 2. The zooming results of the synthetic image

Obviously the bilinear interpolation produces the worst performance since less pixels are involved in the interpolation, which results in the loss of high-frequency components. Heavier computation burden and the ring artifacts are two disadvantages of the bi-cubic interpolation, although it could give preferable zooming results. The EASE and NEDI methods result in better performance while they preserve the edges by means of the estimation of the edge orientations. The wavelet bilinear method gives the excellent performance for involving the global correlation. The CEASE method gives the best visual and statistic performance, which indicate that the proposed method can see the smoothness along the contours and preserve the edges at best, especially for the original images having more details.

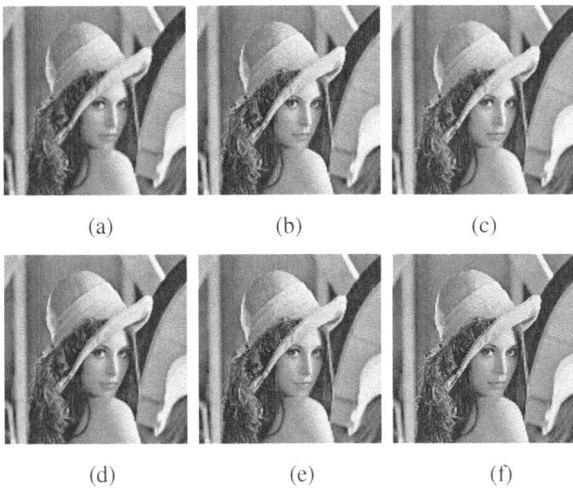

Fig. 3. The zooming results of the Lena image.

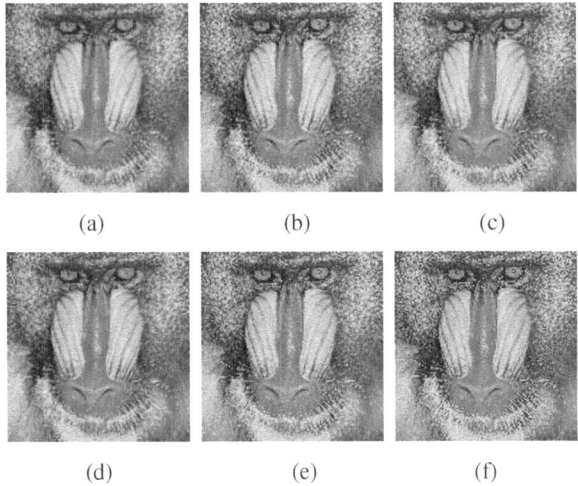

Fig. 4. The zooming results of the monkey face image

Table 1. The objective performance for the zooming methods

Images	methods	T	H
Synthetic	bilinear	7.703	7.289
	bicubic	8.154	7.296
	EASE	8.067	7.291
	NEDI	8.263	7.283
	Wavelet bilinear	8.499	7.297
	CEASE	9.152	7.382

Table 1. (*continued*)

Lena	bilinear	5.575	7.387
	bicubic	6.904	7.445
	EASE	6.834	7.420
	NEDI	7.181	7.430
	Wavelet bilinear	8.400	7.465
	CEASE	9.534	7.474
monkey	bilinear	9.406	7.177
	bicubic	12.877	7.272
	EASE	13.327	7.262
	NEDI	13.478	7.262
	Wavelet bilinear	16.666	7.288
	CEASE	20.288	7.407

5   Conclusions

A novel interpolation method, named CEASE, is proposed by incorporating the contourlet transform into the EASE method. The CEASE method makes an attempt to preserve the edges excellently through the estimation of the edges' orientations. Here the contourlet transform is used to decompose the image interpolated by the EASE method. A new decomposed image is obtained when the low-frequency components of the decomposed image are replaced by the enhanced original image by means of the linear transform. Finally, a zoomed image is achieved when the new decomposed image is transformed by the inverse contourlet transform. The experimental results indicated that the proposed method is superior to the popular interpolation methods, especially for the original images having more details.

Acknowledgements. This work was supported by the National Natural Science Foundation of China (Grant No. 61001179) and the Natural Science Foundation of Guangdong Province, China (Grant No. 07301038).

References

1. Castleman, K.R.: Digital Image Processing. Prentice Hall, Engle Cliffs (1996)
2. Parker, J.A., Kenyon, R.V., Troxel, D.E.: Comparison of interpolating methods for image resampling. IEEE Trans. Medical Imaging 2(1), 31–39 (1983)
3. Li, X., Michacl, T.: New edge directed interpolation. IEEE Trans. Image Processing 10(10), 1521–1527 (2001)
4. Cha, Y., Kim, S.: The Error-Amended Sharp Edge (EASE) Scheme for Image Zooming. IEEE Trans. Image Processing 16(6), 1496–1505 (2007)
5. Bo, L., Youshan, Q., Guilan, F., Xiufang, Y., Bin, X.: Maximal PSNR Wavelet Bi-linear Interpolation Iterative Algorithm in Remote Sensing Image. ACTA Photonica Sinica 35(3), 468–472 (2006)

6. Temizel, A., Vlachos, T.: Wavelet domain image resolution enhancement. IEE Proceedings Vision, and Signal Proceedings 153(2), 25–30 (2006)
7. Po, D.D.Y., Do, M.N.: Directional multiscale modeling of images using the contourlet transform. IEEE Trans. Image Processing 15(6), 1610–1620 (2006)
8. Do, M.N., Contourlets, V.M.: A directional multiresolution image representation. In: Proc. IEEE Int. Conf. Image Processing, Rochester, NY, USA, pp. 357–360 (2002)
9. Do, M.N., Vetterli, M.: The contourlet transform: an efficient directional multiresolution image representation. IEEE Trans. Image Processing 14(12), 2091–2106 (2005)

A Solution of Multiple Targets Tracking for Linear CCD Based Optical Positioning System Applied to Image Guided Surgery

Zuxing Li[1,2] and Jian Wu[1]

[1] Tsinghua University Graduate School at Shenzhen,
Research Centre of Biomedical Engineering, Road Lishui. 2279,
518055 Shenzhen, China
[2] Southeast University, School of Biological Science & Medical Engineering,
Sipailou 210096 Nanjing, China
itisbreezing@hotmail.com, wuj@sz.tsinghua.edu.cn

Abstract. Doctors often need to use several surgery instruments at the same time during Image Guided Surgery (IGS). However, it's hard for linear CCD based Optical Positioning System (OPS) to maintain both a high frequency and efficiency when tracking multiple targets which are often close to each other at the same time during IGS. This paper proposes a grouping algorithm and track prediction algorithm to match the markers and their corresponding linear CCD images. We finally design an efficient solution of multiple targets tracking for linear CCD based OPS applied to IGS, which proves to have a high recognition rate, accuracy and tracking frequency.

Keywords: Linear CCD, Optical Positioning System, Multiple Targets Tracking, Image Guided Surgery, Solution.

1 Introduction

Optical Positioning System (OPS) play an important role in the fields of Image Guided Surgery (IGS) and motion measurement. An OPS uses linear CCD or 2-D CCD for imaging. Compared to 2-D CCD, 1-D CCD has a higher accuracy and frequency, and easier to compute image coordinates. Markers used in OPS can be IR EDs (Infrared-Emitting Diodes) for active tracking or Retro Reflective Spheres (RRS) for passive tracking [1]. Current linear CCD based OPS always use IREDs as the markers. G. Bianchi [2] designed The COSTEL system for human motion measurement and analysis in 1990. Qiuting Wen [3] designed an OPS for IGS that can track one Surgery Instrument (SI) with four markers.

As for IGS, doctors usually need to use several SIs at the same time. Sometimes these SIs are very close to each other. In this case, it's harder for linear CCD based OPS to maintain both a high frequency and high reliability. This paper proposed an efficient solution for multiple SIs tracking in the linear CCD based OPS.

H. Deng et al. (Eds.): AICI 2011, Part II, LNAI 7003, pp. 426–432, 2011.

2   Methods

2.1   Single Surgery Instrument Tracking (SSIT)

F. Gazzani [4] constructed 7 parameters Direct Linear Transformation (DLT) method for linear CCD imaging, and proposed corresponding calibration procedure for Lens Distortion Error (LDE). The Marker P (X, Y, Z)in the world coordinates system and its image λon linear CCD satisfies the equation (1):

$$(\lambda L_5 - L_1, \lambda L_6 - L_2, \lambda L_7 - L_3, \lambda - L_4)[X \quad Y \quad Z \quad 1]^T = 0 \tag{1}$$

Jian Wu [5] rigorously proved the seven DLT parameters can be expressed as functions of the only 7 camera interior and exterior orientation elements, and carefully describe the method of Single Marker Tracking (SMT) that 3 independent CCDs can track one marker.

While, one surgery instrument tracker needs at least 3 markers for positioning its tip (SIT), Jay B. West [6] discussed how Positioning Error (PE) of the Surgery Instrument Tip (SIT) depends on the number and spatial distribution of the markers and the position of the SIT relative to the markers in detail. In our OPS, all markers are light on at the same time to keep the precise positioning of SIT. Qiuting Wen [7] designed an efficient condition called Correspondence Restraint Condition (CRC) for us to sieve out Fake Markers (FM) from all N^4 Possible Markers (PMs), which describes as that the rank of the Coefficient Matrix (CM, constructed form the coefficients of plane equations of the N imaging planes) equal to 3 when N≥3. To use the CRC and keep high positioning accuracy, we use 4 CCDs in our OPS shown in Fig.1.

We replace the condition r(CM)=3 by det|CM|<threshold in our algorithm implementation and get a screening rate of 92.2% on the average.

North Digital Inc [8] provides specific designs of Surgery Instrument Model (SIM). We designed 3 simple SIs referring to the design document, shown as Fig. 1.

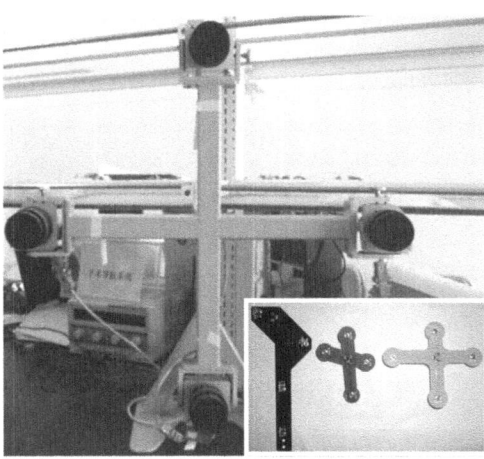

Fig. 1. The left shows our OPS with 4 CCDs. The right down shows three SIs, SI_0, SI_1, SI_2 respectively with 4 markers A, B, C, D.

We can use the Model Restraint Condition (MRC) to further filter the PMs filtered by CRC and indentify RMs. Here we use distance combinations condition as MRC.

2.2 Multiple Surgery Instruments Tracking (MSIT)

Different SI has different SIM and MRC, so we can achieve MSIT on the basis of SSIT. However, the problem becomes more complicated since all SIs are light on at the same time. Supposing we have 3 SIs, that means each CCD has 12 images, generating 20736 PMs, resulting in a poor performance. We design two methods to match SIs with their corresponding CCD images to reduce PMs. Graph.1 illustrates the final solution proposed in this paper.

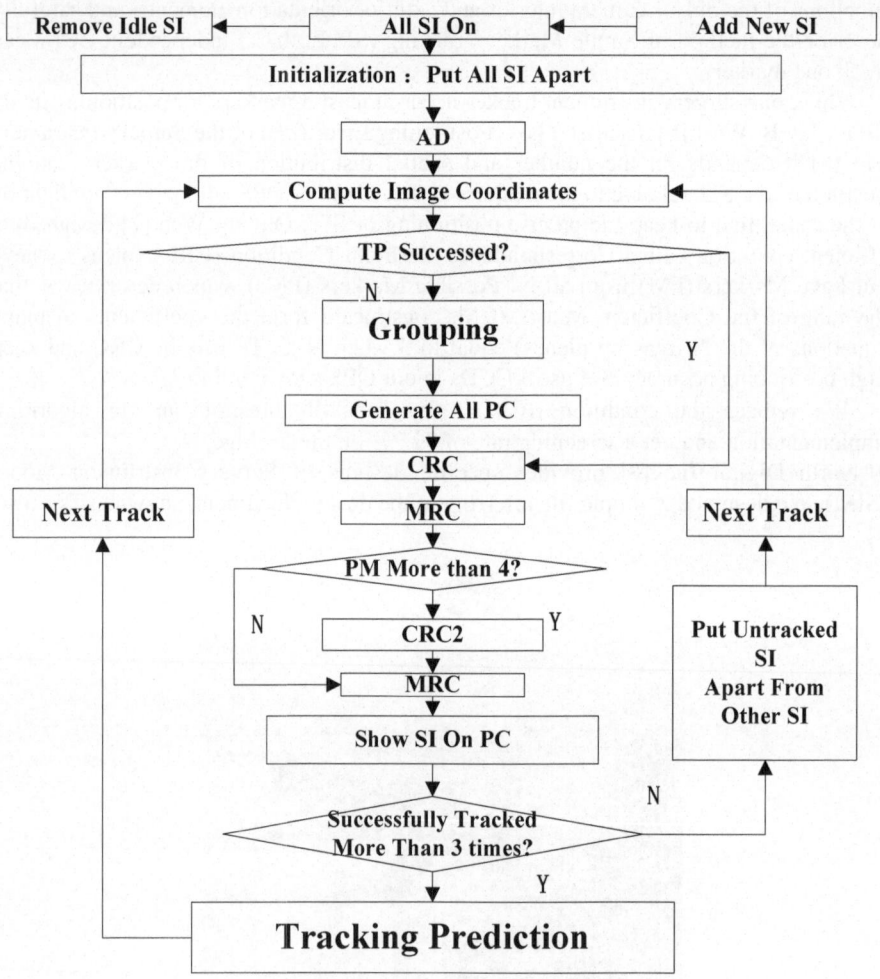

Graph 1. Illustration of our solution

Grouping

Two linear CCDs in our OPS are put approximately horizontally to track the change of the horizontal position of markers. The other two are put approximately vertically for sensing the vertical position change. If all SIs are put apart horizontally and vertically, the corresponding CCD images are separated too. We divide the images into several small groups. All possible combinations composed of horizontal and vertical groups will be used for SSIT.

Track Prediction (TP)

Since the images always have limited moving speed, we use the real-time image's moving track to predict the possible image coordinate of a marker. Only the image coordinates in a possible range will be used for next tracking.

Specifically, supposing SI_0 has been tracked successfully more than 3 times. The image coordinate of marker A on CCD0 is S_1, S_2, S_3, at t_1, t_2, t_3 respectively.

We can compute the average speed and acceleration as:

$$\bar{v}_{12} = \frac{S_2 - S_1}{t_2 - t_1} = \frac{S_2 - S_1}{dt}$$

$$\bar{v}_{23} = \frac{S_3 - S_2}{t_3 - t_2} = \frac{S_3 - S_2}{dt} \tag{2}$$

$$\bar{a}_{13} = \frac{\bar{v}_{23} - \bar{v}_{12}}{dt}$$

We predict the image coordinate at t_4 as:

$$s_4 = s_3 + (\bar{v}_{23} + \bar{a}_{13} * dt)dt = 3(s_3 - s_2) + s_1 \tag{3}$$

We can predict the image coordinates of all markers on each CCD in the same way.

Once some SI are continuously successfully tracked more than 3 times (t_{n-2}, t_{n-1}, t_n). The possible image coordinates range of the SI at t_{n+1} will be predicted. That means the tracking of the SI at t_{n+1} will be faster and have a higher success rate, from which the next tracking at t_{n+2} will further benefit and so on.

3   Experiments Results

We tested performance of the Grouping Algorithm, results shown in Table 1. We can see Grouping Algorithm performance very well statically. However, the efficiency and frequency drop obviously in dynamic case (here we only move SI_2 freely, so the efficiency of SI_2 drops more severely than the other two).

Table 1. Performance of the Grouping Algorithm. Static: all SIs are put apart horizontally and vertically. Dynamic: all SIs can be moved freely. (Here, we start the CRC2.).

SI	Time/s	Efficiency/%	Frequency/HZ	Static or Dynamic
SI_0	120	99.4	8.38	S
SI_0	140	89.9	7.94	D
SI_1	120	99.2	8.38	S
SI_1	140	89.6	7.94	D
SI_2	120	99.4	8.38	S
SI_2	140	40.0	7.94	D

We also tested the performance of the Track Prediction Algorithm, results shown in Table 2. Note that results are obtained in the case that all SIs are close to each other. We can find an obvious improvement due to using TP. Here we freely move SI_2 to get close to the other two, so the efficiency of SI_2 is lowest both in case of Using TP or not. However, the obvious improvement of SI_2 especially proves the efficiency of TP.

Table 2. Performance of TP. (Here, we start the CRC2.)

SI	Time/s	Efficiency/%	Frequency/HZ	Use TP
SI_0	91	86.2	5.35	N
SI_0	130	95.5	8.05	Y
SI_1	91	54.8	5.35	N
SI_1	130	69.4	8.05	Y
SI_2	91	23.6	5.35	N
SI_2	130	62.2	8.05	Y

We use every single SI to test the efficiency of the CRC2, results shown in Table3. We can see the efficiency increases evidently at the cost of a little drop of the update frequency.

Table 3. Effects of CRC2

SI	Time/s	Efficiency/%	Frequency/HZ	Use CRC2
SI_0	139	77.0	56.1	N
SI_0	120	95.2	54.0	Y
SI_1	144	74.9	55.6	N
SI_1	120	90.05	55.1	Y
SI_2	156	69.2	55.6	N
SI_2	144	75.5	55.2	Y

4   Discussions

We can achieve SSIT by lighting markers in order. However, the cable used to drive the markers will disturb the doctors during surgery. If we drive markers wirelessly, the refresh frequency declines due to poor wireless communication frequency, which results in severe motion artifact. Finally, we light on all markers at the same time by portable battery on SI to obtain a high frequency, accuracy, reliability and not disturb surgery operating, although at the cost of algorithm complexity. Similarly, we give up lighting SIs in sequence to achieve MSIT.

In addition, LDE always comes along with optical imaging. We use specially manufactured lens to ignore the LDE [5].

Since we must leave a room for judging distance between PMs, some FMs may also satisfy the threshold. Furthermore, the MRC we used is not the necessary and sufficient condition to judge RMs, so, we sometimes inevitably get more than 4 PMs after MRC filtration. In this case, we use CRC2 to further filter. Specifically, we choose 4 PMs form the N PMs, generating A_N^4 combinations. Choose those combinations with good co-planarity for further MRC filtration. The normalized volume of the tetrahedron constructed from 4 PMs describes the co-planarity. In algorithm implementation, we compute the determinant of the matrix composed of the three base vectors of the tetrahedron to judge the co-planarity. Table 3 shows the effects of CRC2.

5   Conclusion

Here we propose an operating demand for our OPS potential users to maintain a good performance when MSIT. First, try to put all SIs apart horizontally and vertically. After a moment (usually less than one second), all SIs will be continuously successfully tracked several times (due to high recognition rate of the Grouping algorithm). Then SIs can be moved freely (because TP already stated). If some SI is tracked unsuccessfully (hidden from other objects or moved too fast) when IGS, doctors can put the SI apart from the others, and wait a little moment, then he can move the SI to where he wants. (Also see in Graphic.1)

Acknowledgement. We thanks for the support of Chinese National Natural Science Foundation (81000649) as well as the Shenzhen City National 863 project matching funding support.

References

1. West, J.B., Maurer, C.R.: Designing Optically Tracked Instruments for Image-Guided Surgery. IEEE Transactions on Medical Imaging 23(5), 533–545 (2004)
2. Bianchi, G., Gazzani, F., Macellari, V.: The COSTEL system for human motion measurement and analysis. Image Based Motion Measurement 1356, 38–50 (1990)
3. Wen, Q.: A study on Multiple Marker Positioning using Linear CCD based Optical Tracking System: [master degree papers]. Biomedical Engineering, THU, Beijing (2004)

4. Gazzani, F.: Performance of a 7-parameter DLT method for the calibration of stereo photogrammetric systems using 1-D transducers. J. Biomed. Eng. 14, 476–482 (1992)
5. Wu, J., Wang, G., Dingy, H., Luo, W.: Direct linear transformation of linear Charge-coupled device camera s in a 3-D measurement system. J. Tsinghua Univ. (Sci. & Tech.) 44(6), 860–863 (2004)
6. Qiuting, W., Wu, J., Tao, H., Wang, G., Ye, D.: An Approach to the correspondence Problem in the 1-D Optical Transducers Tracking System. In: Proceedings of the SPIE, vol. 7169 (2009)
7. North Digital Inc.: Polaris Vicra Tool Kit Guider (2005)

Research on Tracking Algorithm of Moving Target in Complex Background

Qigui Zhang[*] and Bo Li

Department of Information Engineering,
Taiyuan University of Technology, Taiyuan, 030024, China
zhang_qg63@hotmail.com, labourlibo@126.com

Abstract. To study the video sequences in the complex background, an improved tracking algorithm of moving target is proposed that combining Camshift algorithm and Kalman filter. Use a Kalman filter to predict the target position in the next frame and the Camshift algorithm to find its actual position based on the color characteristics in the prediction area. In addition, other methods are mixed to deal with the color interference and cover problem. The experimental results denote that the improved algorithm completes a real-time and accurate target tracking in the complex dynamic background.

Keywords: Kalman, Camshift, Complex Background, Moving Target Tracking, Color Interference, Cover Problem.

1 Introduction

With the development of computer technology, the system of video target tracking is widely used in various fields. It becomes very difficult to track target in the complex background because of the changes of background and target size. The Camshift algorithm [1, 2] can automatically adjust the window size to fit the tracked target in the image size based on the Meanshift algorithm [3, 4]. However, the algorithm cannot achieve effective tracking, and may produce wrong tracking when the target is in large color interference and occlusion cases. So the estimator should be introduced to predict the motion parameters of the moving target.

This paper proposed an algorithm that combining Camshift algorithm and Kalman filter. The improved algorithm effectively solves the color interference and occlusion problems in the complex background. And it still correctly tracks the moving target with good real-time performance and robustness.

2 Analysis of Existing Algorithm

2.1 The Camshift Algorithm

The Camshift algorithm converts the image from RGB space to HSV space, establishes a histogram of H component, and gets color probability distribution graph [5] after back projection [6]. The algorithm steps are as follows:

---

[*] Corresponding author.

H. Deng et al. (Eds.): AICI 2011, Part II, LNAI 7003, pp. 433–438, 2011.

(1)Select search window in the color probability distribution graph. The Search window size is s.

(2)Calculate center of mass of the search window.

Zero order moment : $M_{00} = \sum_x \sum_y I_c(x, y)$.

First order moment of x: $M_{10} = \sum_x \sum_y x I_c(x, y)$

First order moment of y: $M_{01} = \sum_x \sum_y y I_c(x, y)$

The search window center of mass (x_c, y_c): $x_c = M_{10}/M_{00}$; $y_c = M_{01}/M_{00}$

$I_c(x, y)$ is pixel value of coordinate (x_c, y_c).The ranges of x and y are search window size

(3)Reset search window size s: $s = 2\sqrt{M_{00}/256}$

(4)Repeat (2) (3) until the center of mass convergence

2.2 The Kalman Filter

A Kalman Filter [7] is an algorithm that estimates state sequences of dynamical systems with linear minimum error covariance. Assuming that the system is linear.

State equation: $x_k = Ax_{k-1} + w_{k-1}$

Observation equation: $z_k = Hx_k + v_k$

A is state transition matrix. H is observation matrix. Interference noise w_k and observation noise v_k are the independent zero-mean Gaussian white noise. $w_k \sim N(0, Q_k); v_k \sim N(0, R_k)$.

State vector $X(k) = (x_k, y_k, v_{x,k}, v_{y,k})^T$ is the target center position and velocity components in the XY axis. Observation vector $Z(k) = (x_k, y_k)^T$ is the target center position observed in the current frame.

Use the following five equations to achieve recursive calculation of the filter:

(1) State prediction equation: $\hat{x}(k|k-1) = A\hat{x}(k-1|k-1)$

(2) State covariance prediction equation: $P(k|k-1) = AP(k-1|k-1)A^T + Q$

(3) Kalman gain coefficient equation:

$$K_k = P(k|k-1)H^T \cdot [HP(k|k-1)H^T + R]^{-1}$$

(4) State correction equation: $\hat{x}(k|k) = \hat{x}(k|k-1) + K_k[Z_k - H \cdot \hat{x}(k|k-1)]$

(5) Covariance correction equation: $P(k|k) = (I - K_k H)P(k|k-1)$

3 Algorithm Design

Combine the Camshift algorithm and Kalman filter to track the target in the normal conditions. Use Kalman filter to predict the target position to improve the target tracking effect.

The algorithm steps are as follows:

(1) Manually select the initial window. Make its position and size as the input of the Camshift algorithm. Initialize state vector $X(0) = (x_0, y_0, 0, 0)^T$ as initial value of the Kalman filter

(2) Calculate the center of mass (x_c, y_c) of current frame based on the previous frame window, and reset the window size

(3) Move the center to the center of mass in the search window until convergence, and output the center of mass (x_c, y_c) and window area A

(4) Make $Z(k) = (x_c, y_c)$, update Kalman filter parameters, and get optimal revised estimation $(\hat{x}_c, \hat{y}_c)$

(5) Read the next frame. Make $(\hat{x}_c, \hat{y}_c)$ as the center of current frame, and $\sqrt{2}A$ as the window size. Repeat (2) (3) (4) until the end of tracking.

Tracking process as shown (Dashed part is the core of Camshift algorithm):

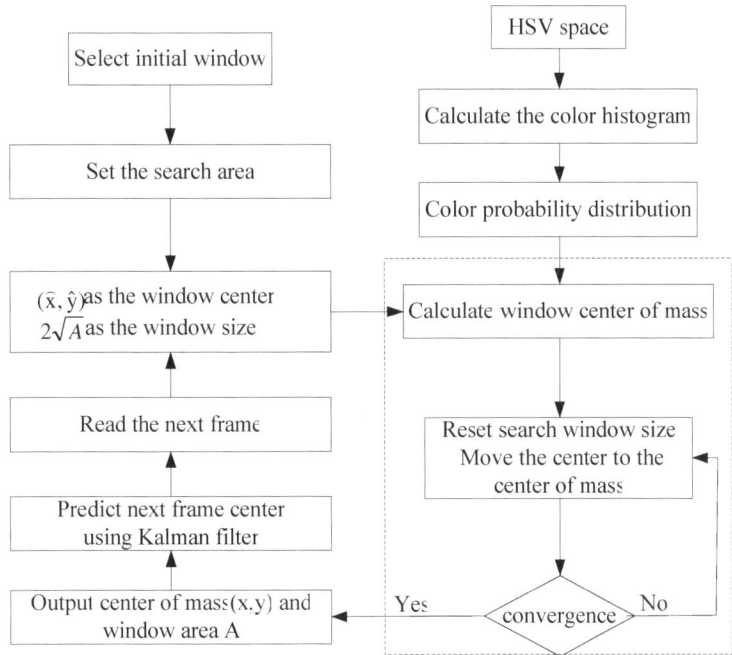

Fig. 1. The improved tracking flowchart

To solve the color interference and cover problems in practice, this paper gives some further specific solutions

(1) The traditional Camshift algorithm needs to manually choose the initial search window. If the initial search window is chosen too large, there must be excessive interference from background pixels. It makes the initial color histogram inaccurate leading to the tracking window is larger than the target. So this paper improves it by running Canny edge detection [8] in the initial window to get the target edge and calculate accurate initial color histogram in closed target outline area.

(2) Close the Camshift matching algorithm during target occlusion. Use Kalman filter to estimate the state of target, keep the former parameters and stop updating. After occlusion, re-open the Camshift matching algorithm, and update the Kalman filter parameters with the observed value. Then recover the former normal algorithm for prediction and correction.

(3) Define D=W/H as target aspect ratio, and D<1. W and H are separately wide and long of the target minimum circumscribed rectangular. If the ratio is out of the range in two consecutive frames, the target is judged suffering interference by the similar color regions. In this case, the Meanshift algorithm shows better anti-interference ability than Camshift algorithm. Enforce the target area limited to the size of previous frame and the center of mass reverted to the position of previous frame. Use the Meanshift algorithm to calculate the optimal matching position. So it does not shift too large as a result of drift to non-target area when suffering interference by the similar color regions.

4   Experiments

The result of experiment which is achieved based on C language programming in the Microsoft Visual C++6.0environment. The actual sequences of images are taken from video, in order to verify the correctness of the improved algorithm combining Camshift algorithm and Kalman filter:

(a)Manual selection   (b) Binary image after Canny   (c) Processed window

Fig. 2. Improved initial window

Fig.2 shows comparison of the target initial windows. Figure (a) is initial window of manual selection. Obviously, there is too much interference of background pixels because of inaccurate selection. Run Canny edge detection in initial window, and get the target binary image as Figure (b). Add window around as Figure (c). The result shows the improved initial window is more close to the human body outline. So we can get more accurate color histogram.

Fig. 3. The original Camshift occlusion algorithm

Fig. 4. The improved occlusion algorithm

Fig. 5. The improved interference algorithm

Fig.3 shows occlusion tracking with the original Camshift algorithm. Target is tracked lost when target occludes. Then when target reappears, the original algorithm can not capture and track the target timely, leading to tracking failure. Fig.4 shows occlusion tracking with the improved algorithm. When target occludes, use Kalman filter to predict the center of mass, and keep window unchanged. Then when target reappears, the improved algorithm can capture and track the target correctly, and improve the stability of the moving target tracking.

Fig.5 shows the improved algorithm can judge whether the target suffers interference. The algorithm can identify tracking target correctly and continue to track. It improves the tracking accuracy.

5 Conclusion

This paper provides a method of target tracking by combining Camshift algorithm and Kalman filter. This method can track the target in complex background. Some further specific solutions are given to solve the color interference and cover problems. First, run Canny edge detection in initial window to get more accurate color histogram. Second, close the Camshift algorithm and only use Kalman filter to predict when target occludes. Finally, use the target aspect ratio to judge whether the target is suffering interference, and use Meanshift algorithm to calculate the optimal matching position instead of Camshift algorithm. The experiment proves that the improved method completes a real-time and accurate target tracking, and solves the color interference and occlusion problems.

References

1. Nummiaro, K., Koller-Meier, E., van Gool, L.: An adaptive Col-or-Based Particle Filter. Image and Vision Computing 21(1), 99–110 (2003)
2. Nouar, O.D., Ali, G., Raphael, C.: Improved object tracking with CamShift algorithm. In: Proceedings of 2006 IEEE International Conference on Acoustics, Speech, and Signal Processing, pp. II657–II660. IEEE, Piscataway (2006)
3. Gang, T., Ruimin, H., Zhongyuan, W.: A meanshift target tracking algorithm based on motion vector analysis. Journal of Image and Graphics 15(1), 85–90 (2010) (in Chinese)
4. Collins, R.T.: Mean-Shift blob tracking through scale space. In: Proc of IEEE Int. Conf. on Computer Vision and Pattern Recognition, pp. 234–240. Victor Graphics, Baltimore (2003)
5. Bradski, G.R.: Computer Vision Face Tracking for Use in a Perceptual User Interface. Intel Technology Journal, (Q2), 1–15 (1998)
6. Cheng, L., Dong-jian, H.: Efficient method for object contour extraction based on probability distribution image. Computer Application 28(10), 2636–2638 (2008)
7. Yu, D., Weiw, Zhang, Y.H.: Dynamic target tracking with Kalman filteras predictor. Opto—Electronic Engineering 36(1), 52–56 (2009)
8. Zhe, L., Fuli, W., Yuqing, C.: An improved canny algorithm for edge detection. Journal of Northeastern University: Natural Science Edition 28(12), 1681–1684 (2007)

An Improved Image Data Hiding Method Using Two-Layer Embedment Strategy

Wien Hong[1], Yeon-Kang Wang[2], Kai-Yung Lin[1], and Mei-Chen Wu[1]

[1] Department of Information Management, Yu Da University, Taiwan
[2] Department of Department of Multimedia and Game Science, Yu Da University, Taiwan
{wienhong,ykwang,linky,97404532}@ydu.edu.tw

Abstract. In this paper, we propose a reversible image embedding method that extends Hong and Chen's work by using a two-layer embedment strategy. Hong and Chen's method uses a set of basic pixels as a guide, and linearly predicts the values of other pixels to create prediction error histogram for data embedment. However, the set of basic pixels provides no embeddable space. The proposed method employs a two-layer embedment strategy and predicts the pixel values of the set of basic pixels by using their neighboring pixels. Embeddable spaces are created by adopting the histogram shifting method. The experimental results revealed that the proposed method provides higher payload than that of prior works under the same visual quality.

Keywords: Histogram shifting, Reversible, Embedding capacity.

1 Introduction

Data embedding is a method that embeds messages into digital media for the purpose of secret transmission [1]. Any digital media can be used as a carrier to carry messages. When a digital image is used for carrying data, this image is called the cover image and the image with data embedded is called the stego image [2]. When data are embedded, the image quality may degrade. In general, the degradation caused by data embedding should be as small as possible while keeping the payload high [3].

Reversible data hiding is a technique that the original image can be recovered after the embedded messages are extracted [4]-[9] and therefore, has many applications such as military or law enforcement. In 2006, Ni et al. [5] proposed a reversible data hiding method based on histogram shifting. In their method, histogram bins of the cover image are shifted to create empty bins for data embedment. However, the payload of Ni et al.'s method is low, and is not suitable for applications demanding high payload. In 2009, Tsai et al. [7] proposed a reversible data hiding method that embedded data using the modification of prediction error histogram. In their method, image is partitioned into blocks of $n \times n$ pixels, and the center pixel of each block is chosen as the basic pixels. The non-basic pixels in each block are predicted by using the values of basic pixels to create a histogram in the prediction error domain. Data are embedded by modifying the prediction errors. Tsai et al.'s method provides significant higher payload than that of Ni et al.'s method under the same image quality.

H. Deng et al. (Eds.): AICI 2011, Part II, LNAI 7003, pp. 439–443, 2011.
© Springer-Verlag Berlin Heidelberg 2011

In 2010, Hong and Chen extent Tsai et al.'s method by using a sophisticate prediction scheme [8]. In their method, the basic pixels of the top, bottom, left and right blocks of the current block are exploited to obtain a better prediction accuracy. Because the peak height of the error histogram produced by Hong and Chen's method is higher than that of Tsai et al.'s method, their method provides higher payload than that of Tsai et al.'s method. However, the based pixels in Hong and Chen's method do not join the embedding process and leave parts of the embeddable space unused. The proposed method adopts two-layer embedding strategy by embedding messages into both basic and non-basic pixels. Because the non-basic pixels that surround the basic pixels provide rich information for prediction, the additional payload is considerable and only introduces an insignificant image distortion.

The rest of this paper is organized as follows. In Section 2, the proposed method is introduced. Section 3 presents the experimental results, and concluding remarks are made in the last section.

2 The Proposed Method

The proposed method extends Hong and Chen's method [8] by embedding additional data bits into the basic pixels. Hong and Chen partition the cover image into blocks of $n \times n$ pixels. In each block B_i, the non-basic pixels $\{B_{i,k}\}_{k=0}^{n \times n - 1}$ are predicted by the corresponding basic CC pixels and four satellite pixels CL, CT, CR and CB. A schematic diagram of Hong and Chen's method for block size 3×3 is shown in Fig. 1.

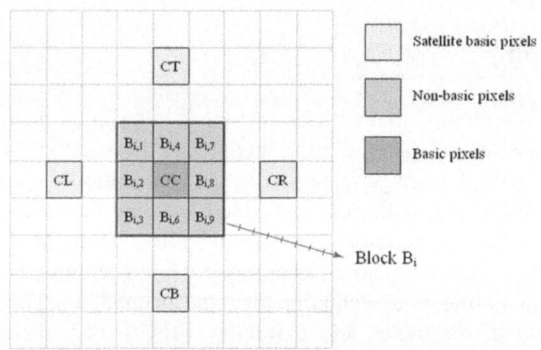

Fig. 1. A Schematic diagram of Hong and Chen's method

After embedding data bits using Hong and Chen's method, those non-basic pixels $\{B_{i,k}\}_{k=0}^{7}$ are modified to $\{B'_{i,k}\}_{k=0}^{7}$ and a stego image S is obtained. Because the pixel values in the same block are highly correlated, the proposed method further predicts the value of basic pixels by averaging the corresponding eight non-basic pixels to create a prediction error histogram. The additional data are then embedded by modifying the prediction errors. Fig. 2 depicts the embedding procedure of the proposed method and the detailed embedding steps are listed as follows.

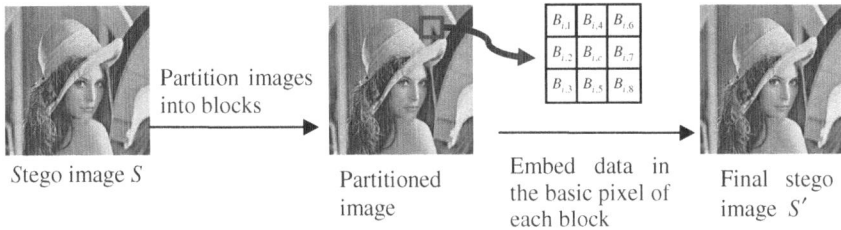

Fig. 2. The embedding procedure of the proposed method

Step 1. Embed data into the cover image I using Hong and Chen's method to obtain the stego image S.

Step 2. Partition S into blocks $\{B'_{i,k}\}_{k=0}^{n \times n-1}$ of size $n \times n$.

Step 3. For each block B'_i, the value of the basic pixel $B'_{i,c}$ is predicted by the mean of its eight neighboring pixels. Let the predicted result be $\hat{B}'_{i,c}$.

Step 4. Calculate the prediction error $e_i = B'_{i,c} - \hat{B}'_{i,c}$ of $B'_{i,c}$.

Step 5. Embed data bits by modifying the prediction errors using the histogram shifting technique to obtain new stego block B''_i, and the final stego image S' is then obtained.

The data extraction process is performed in a reverse order; namely the data embedded in the basic pixels have to be extracted and recover S' to S first. Then, the data embedded in non-basic pixels is extracted and recovers S to the original image I. The detailed extraction and recovering procedure are listed as follows.

Step 1. Partition S' into blocks B''_i of size $n \times n$.

Step 2. For each block B''_i, the value of the basic pixel $B''_{i,c}$ is predicted by averaging of its eight surrounding pixels. Let the predicted results be $\hat{B}''_{i,c}$.

Step 3. Calculate the prediction error $e_i = B''_{i,c} - \hat{B}''_{i,c}$ of $B''_{i,c}$.

Step 4. Recover the original pixel values $B'_{i,c}$ of $B''_{i,c}$, and extract the data bits embedded in the basic pixel of each block.

Step 5. Extract the data bits embedded into the non-basic pixels, and the original cover image I can be restored by using the histogram shifting method.

3 Experimental Results

In this section, we perform several experiments to evaluate the embedding performance of the proposed method. Six images including Lena, Jet, Peppers, Boat, Elaine, and Baboon, are used a test images, as shown in Fig. 3. These 512×512 test images are obtained from USC-SIPI image data base [10].

(a) Lena   (b) Jet   (c) Peppers

(d) Boat   (e) Elaine   (f) Baboon

Fig. 3. Six test images

The data bits to be embedded were generated by using a pseudo random number generator (PRNG). The PSNR was used to measure the stego image quality, which is defined as

$$PSNR = 10\log_{10}\frac{255^2}{MSE},$$

where MSE is the mean square error between the cover and stego image. Table 1 is the comparison results of the proposed method with Tsai et al.'s and Hong and Chen's method. The results revealed that the proposed method offers the highest payload under roughly the same image quality. The averaged maximum payload of the proposed method is 41740 bits, which is significantly higher the Tsai et al. and Hong and Chen's method. Although the PSNR of the proposed method is slightly lower than those of Tsai et al. and Hong and Chen's methods, the difference between the cover and the stego image is imperceptible for PSNR at this level. Therefore, the proposed method is suitable for applications requiring high payload and high image quality.

Table 1. Embedding performance compassion of various methods

Image	Tsai et al.		Hong et al.		Proposed	
	Payload	PSNR	Payload	PSNR	Payload	PSNR
Lena	38950	49.05	46503	49.24	52809	48.74
Jet	58105	49.25	64186	49.44	73056	48.93
Peppers	32186	48.98	36671	49.14	41740	48.63
Boat	25788	48.92	29377	49.06	33404	48.56
Elaine	25462	48.92	28833	49.06	32644	48.58
Baboon	12983	48.80	14034	49.91	16118	48.40
Average	32245	48.99	36600	49.31	41628	48.65

Note that the payload of the proposed method mainly relies on the prediction accuracy. A better prediction result produces higher peak height and subsequently provides higher payload.

4 Conclusions

This paper extends Hong and Chen's work and proposed a reversible data hiding method based on the modification of prediction errors. The propped method employs two-layer embedding strategy by embedding data bits into basic pixels in each image block. Because the neighboring pixels of each basic pixel provides rich information to better predict the basic pixel values, a significant amount of additional data bits can be embedded into basic pixels without introducing significant distortion. The experimental results revealed that the averaged payload of the proposed method is 5,000 and 9,000 bits higher than those of Hong et al.'s and Tsai et al.'s method.

References

1. Provos, N., Honeyman, P.: Hide and Seek: An Introduction to Steganography. IEEE Security and Privacy 3, 32–44 (2003)
2. Petitcolas, F.A.P., Anderson, R.J., Kuhn, M.G.: Information Hiding—A Survey. Proceedings of the IEEE, special issue on protection of multimedia content 87(7), 1062–1078 (1999)
3. Wang, H., Wang, S.: Cyber Warfare: Steganography vs. Steganalysis. Communications of the ACM 47(10), 76–82 (2004)
4. Tian, J.: Reversible Data Embedding Using a Difference Expansion. IEEE Transactions on Circuits and Systems for Video Technology 13(8), 890–896 (2003)
5. Ni, Z., Shi, Y.Q., Ansari, N., Su, W.: Reversible Data Hiding. IEEE Transactions on Circuits and Systems for Video Technology 16(3), 354–362 (2006)
6. Thodi, D.M., Rodríguez, J.J.: Expansion Embedding Techniques for Reversible Watermarking. IEEE Transactions on Image Processing 16(3), 721–730 (2007)
7. Tsai, P.Y., Hu, Y.C., Yeh, H.L.: Reversible Image Hiding Scheme Using Predictive Coding and Histogram Shifting. Signal Processing 89(6), 1129–1143 (2009)
8. Hong, W., Chen, T.S.: A Local Variance-Controlled Reversible Data Hiding Method Using Prediction and Histogram-Shifting. The Journal of Systems and Software 83(12), 2653–2663 (2010)
9. Hong, W., Chen, T.S.: Reversible Data Embedding for High Quality Images Using Interpolation and Reference Pixel Distribution Mechanism. Journal of Visual Communication and Image Representation 22(2), 131–140 (2011)
10. USC-SIPI image database, http://sipi.usc.edu/database

A Hierarchical Situation Assessment Model Based on Fuzzy Bayesian Network[*]

Huimin Chai and Baoshu Wang

School of Computer Science and Technology, Xidain University, Xi'an, China
chaihm@mail.xidian.edu.cn, bswang@xidian.edu.cn

Abstract. A hierarchical fuzzy Bayesian network model for situation assessment is developed in the paper, which includes two layers: the top layer serving as a fusion center, the bottom layer as the continuous data discretization. In this model, Bayesian network (BN) is integrated with the fuzzy theory, which can generalize the continuous variable to fuzzy variable in BN. The fuzzy theory is utilized to partition the value of continuous variable into fuzzy state, which forms the soft evidence for Bayesian network. The inference mechanism of the model is given, through which the continuous and discrete data can be fused. As an example, an air strike scenario is simulated and analyzed to illustrate the functionality of the proposed model.

Keywords: Situation assessment, Bayesian Network, Fuzzy theory.

1 Introduction

In recent years, decision-making in real-time dynamic battlefield is becoming increasingly complex due to the nature and diversity of threats and tactics that may be encountered. Situation assessment (SA) is the ongoing process of inferring relevant information about forces of concern in a battlefield situation to achieve situation awareness, which is needed by the campaign commanders or analysts to support decision-making[1,2,3,4].

There is no universally definition of situation assessment. In the data fusion process model given by the Joint Development Laboratory [1], situation assessment is the level 2 fusion. The analysis is made of data from sensors and other sources in situation assessment for building an accurate and timely picture of the battlefield situation, including location, movements, and deployment and intension of enemy force. The definition suggested by Endsley [2] is widely accepted by the research community in various domains. Endsley defines SA as consisting of three levels: perceiving elements in the environment within a volume of space and time; comprehending what they mean in context; and predicting their status in the future.

However, with the growing number of various information collected from different sensors, determining how best to process and correlate these data to obtain an

---

[*] The research is supported by the Fundamental Research Funds for the Central Universities (No.KS0510030005).

H. Deng et al. (Eds.): AICI 2011, Part II, LNAI 7003, pp. 444–454, 2011.

effective assessment has become a major challenge of situation assessment. To address this issue, many researchers have developed a few of methods and models for situation assessment, which includes fuzzy reasoning and theory [5,6], Bayesian networks [7,8], template matching[9], case-based reasoning[10,11], ontology-based system [12,13], etc. Eric G. Little et al. [13] presented an attempt to reason about situations and threats by building formal ontologies that combined a top-down philosophical perspective with a bottom-up application-based perspective. Katia Sycara, Robin Glinton et al. [14] developed the HiLIFE(High-Level Information Fusion Environment) computational framework for seamless integration of high levels for fusion. A model is given for inferring adversary intent by mapping sensor readings of opponent forces to possible opponent goals and actions. A novel probabilistic approach to intention recognition is proposed for partial-order plans, which is based on dynamic Bayesian networks [15]. A generic approach to threat assessment is given by Justin M. Beaver and etc [16], which includes a threat taxonomy and decision-level information fusion framework. Bayesian networks are selected as the mechanism for the threat assessment engine and implementing the signature taxonomy.

In this paper, we integrated fuzzy theory with Bayesian network and proposed a fuzzy Bayesian network (FBN) model. It can give a more reasonable knowledge representation and more effective inference engine in situation assessment. Moreover, a hierarchical structure for constructing fuzzy Bayesian network to represent and analyze uncertainties and assessing battlefield state is described. The rest of this paper is organized as follows. Section 2 presents the fuzzy Bayesian network model for situation assessment. Section 3 describes a hierarchical structure of FBN model and its inference mechanism. Section 4 illustrates a simple application, and the results are given. Section 5 concludes this paper and presents some prospects for future research.

2 Fuzzy Bayesian Network for Situation Assessment

2.1 Bayesian Networks

Bayesian networks (BNs) are directed, acyclic graphs that encode the cause effect and conditional independence relationships among variables in the probabilistic reasoning system, where nodes of the graphs are the variables of the domain one wants to model [17]. A node in the network is conditionally independent of all non-descendant nodes given its direct parents. Each node stores its probability distribution given its direct parents.

Bayesian networks have been proved to be an effective knowledge representation and inference engine in artificial intelligence and expert systems. According to [20], a BN is expressed as $B(G,P)$:

(1) The graph G is not allowed to have any directed cycles and from this follows that it is a directed acyclic graph(DAG). A set of random variables(either discrete or continuous) that constitutes the nodes of the directed graph. If there is an edge from node X to node Y, then X is called parent to Y.

(2) For every node X_i, there is conditional probability table(ab. CPT) that quantifies the effect that any parent nodes have on the node in question. The CPT is expressed as $p(X_i, pa(X_i))$, which pictures the mutual relationship of each node and its parent nodes. The important concept in BN is the conditional independence between variables. For any variable X_i, the parent variables of X_i is $pa(X_i)$, the X_i is independent of the set $S(X_i)$, which is the set of the variables that are not child variables of $pa(X_i)$. So the probability of X_i can be computed as following:

$$p(X_i / S(X_i), pa(X_i)) = p(X_i / pa(X_i)) \tag{1}$$

This specification implies that a BN consists of two parts: the topology of the network and the conditional probability distributions. The Bayesian network can represent all of the node's joint probability due to the node relationship and the conditional probability table. Applying the conditional independence into the chain rule, we can get the following expression:

$$p(X_1, X_2, ..., X_n) = \prod_{i=1}^{n} p(X_i / pa(X_i)) \tag{2}$$

2.2 Fuzzy Bayesian Network Model

Situation assessment in particular contains a high degree of uncertainty. The basic elements when reasoning under such conditions are random variables. So Bayesian network is one of available methods for situation assessment. However, in practical application, some target features extracted from sensors are continuous. To use the continuous variables in BNs, it requires the discretization of the continuous input. In general, mapping continuous variable to discrete one can be done with a quantizer. This type of discretization does not provide any form of interpolation and the results are crisp division of the input. A smoother discretization way is to use the fuzzy partitioning. Therefore, we integrated fuzzy theory with Bayesian networks and proposed a fuzzy Bayesian network model for situation assessment, which can generalize the continuous variable to fuzzy variable in BNs.

Now suppose $X = (X_1, X_2, ..., X_n)$ be the set of variables in the model. If the variable X_i is a continuous variable and has a definite states set $\{x_{i1}, x_{i2}, ..., x_{iri}\}$, X_i can be transformed into a fuzzy variable μ_i. The corresponding fuzzy set U_i is utilized to map the variable X_i to fuzzy states, which can be defined as:

$$U_i = \{\hat{x}_{i1}, \hat{x}_{i2}, ..., \hat{x}_{iri}\} \tag{3}$$

where $\hat{x}_{ij}$ is the j-th fuzzy state, ri denotes the number of the fuzzy states. The fuzzy state $\hat{x}_{ij}$ can be defined as following

$$\hat{x}_{ij} = \{\mu_{ij}(x) \mid x \in X_i\} \tag{4}$$

where $\mu_{ij}(x)$ is the membership function of fuzzy state $\hat{x}_{ij}$, and x denotes the value of the variable X_i.

It is equivalent to say that given a continuous variable X_i, the condition probability of the node with its parent node can be replaced by $P(\mu_i \mid pa(\mu_i))$:

$$P(X_i \mid pa(X_i)) \rightarrow P(\mu_i \mid pa(\mu_i)) \tag{5}$$

where μ_i is the corresponding fuzzy variable defined by X_i.

The fuzzy Bayesian network here can be defined as:

$$FBN = (X, Y, \hat{Y}, L, P) \tag{6}$$

where X denotes the set of discrete variables in the network, Y is the set of continuous variables, $\hat{Y}$ is the set of fuzzy variables defined by Y, L is the set of directed links, and P is the conditional probability distribution of Bayesian network.

3 Hierarchical FBN Model

Military situation assessment requires reasoning an unknown number of different information observed by various sensors. So a hierarchical model is suitable for situation assessment system capable of fusion various information. As mentioned earlier, the fuzzy Bayesian network (FBN) model is the integration of BN and fuzzy theory. The FBN model is arranged in hierarchical structure in this paper.

3.1 Structure of Hierarchical FBN Model

We present our key ideas of FBN model for situation assessment with a two-layer structure, as shown in Fig.1. It consists of a BN model at the top layer serving as a fusion center, fuzzy mapping at the bottom layer serving as continuous data discretization; the bottom layer can process the sensor information and provide soft evidence to the corresponding BN node.

According to the hierarchical FBN model, we have the following:

(1) The top layer BN model contains N=$n+m$ random variables, which includes discrete variables $\{X_1, X_2, ..., X_n\}$, and fuzzy variables $\{\mu_1, \mu_2, ..., \mu_m\}$. Each random variable has $\{Q_i \mid i = 1, 2, ..., l\}$ number of discrete states. As mentioned earlier, the states of fuzzy variables are partitioned from continuous variables. The conditional probabilities $\{P(V_i \mid pa(V_i)) \mid i = 1, 2, ..., N\}$ constitute the parameters of the model. They correspond to the conditional probability tables(CPTs) in the discrete case. The size of CPTs will increase with the number of parent nodes. In many cases, the parent nodes can be assumed to be marginally independent to the effect node via Noisy-OR logic, which will limit the conditional probabilities to a reasonable size.

(2) The bottom fuzzy mapping layer processes the continuous senor data with fuzzy set theory. It utilizes the fuzzy member function to partition the continuous variable X_i into fuzzy state $\mu_i = \{\hat{x}_{i1}, \hat{x}_{i2}, ..., \hat{x}_{iri}\}$, which forms the soft evidence for fuzzy variable μ_i in BN.

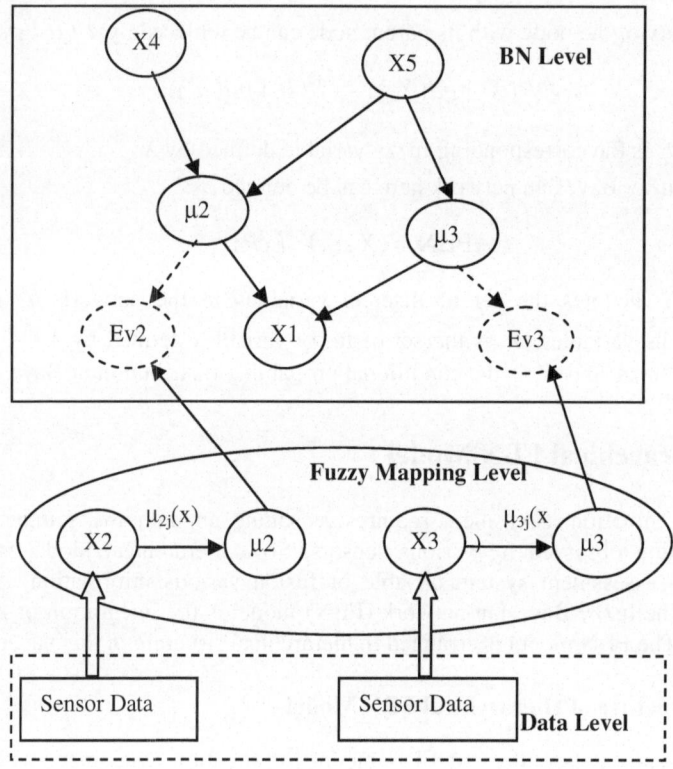

Fig. 1. Hierarchical fuzzy Bayesian network (FBN) model structure

3.2 FBN Model Inference

Evidence is a terminology of BNs. The evidence for a particular BN node can be observed as one of its states, called hard evidence; or the evidence may be observed with uncertainty, called soft evidence. Soft evidence is the most general type of evidence introduced to reflect uncertainty.

For a node without parents, soft evidence is equivalent to modifying the prior probability of that node; otherwise, soft evidence on a variable X_i is represented by a reported   state x_{ij} together   with   its   conditional   probability   vector

$P(X_i = x | H_i)(i = 1, 2, ..., ri)$, where H_i denotes the hypothesis that the true state is the i-th state.

To simplify the process of FBN inference, consider a fuzzy node μ_i with states $(\hat{x}_{i1}, \hat{x}_{i2}, ..., \hat{x}_{iri})$. Define $H_j (j = 1, 2, ..., ri)$ as hypotheses that node μ_i is in state $\hat{x}_{ij}$. The results of fuzzy function member $\mu_{ij}(x)(j = 1, 2, ..., ri)$ form the soft evidence vector:

$$e = \{\mu_{i1}(x), \mu_{i2}(x), ..., \mu_{iri}(x)\} \tag{7}$$

The $\mu_{ij}(x)(j = 1, 2, ..., ri)$ is approximately considered to be equivalent to the condition probability $P(\mu_{ij} | X_i = x)$. Then the soft evidence vector can be defined as:

$$e = \{P(\mu_i = 1/H_1), P(\mu_i = 1/H_2), ..., P(\mu_i = 1/H_{ri})\} \tag{8}$$

where $P(\mu_i = 1/H_j)$ represents that the observed value of μ_i is "1" if the state is $\hat{x}_{ij}$, which is indeed the probability $P(\mu_{ij} | X_i = x)$.

Whenever soft evidence is reported to a BN node, as shown in Fig.1, a dummy node(Ev2 as example) is added to represent the output of the fuzzy mapping layer. The state of the dummy node is "1" or "0". According to (8), the conditional probability distribution of the dummy node can be defined as:

$$\begin{bmatrix} P(\mu_i = 1/H_1), 1 - P(\mu_i = 1/H_1) \\ P(\mu_i = 1/H_2), 1 - P(\mu_i = 1/H_2) \\ ...... \\ P(\mu_i = 1/H_{ri}), 1 - P(\mu_i = 1/H_{ri}) \end{bmatrix} \tag{9}$$

Thus, given the parameters in (9), we can update the belief of fuzzy node μ_i as following:

$$Bel(\mu_i = \hat{x}_{im}) = P(\mu_i = \hat{x}_{im} | Evi = 1)$$
$$= \frac{P(Evi = 1 | \mu_i = \hat{x}_{im}) P(\mu_i = \hat{x}_{im})}{\sum_{j=1}^{ri} P(Evi = 1 | \mu_i = \hat{x}_{ij}) P(\mu_i = \hat{x}_{ij})} \tag{10}$$

where ri denotes the number of the fuzzy states, $m = 1, 2, ..., ri$, the prior probability distribution of fuzzy node μ_i is the probabilistic belief before the new evidence arrives.

4 Experiment and Results

4.1 Example

Let's consider the following scenario: there is a conflict in the sea, and the enemy attempt to attack our target. They send out some aircrafts to access to our base. Our sensors detect the enemy targets depending on the situation firstly, and then the defensive system extracts some events, such as the event of radiant turn on or off, the change of target flying direction or height, across border of important region, and so on. These can be used for prediction of the enemy's tactical intention in such scenario. In the paper, the hierarchical FBN model is utilized to analyze the situation.

The sensor variables are mainly included as following:

(1) Distance: it is a continuous variable, which denotes the distance between enemy target and our base.

(2) Height: a continuous variable, which is the flight height of enemy target.

(3) Speed: a continuous variable, which denote the flying speed of enemy target.

(4) radio silence: it is a discrete variable, which represents radio and radiant of enemy is turned off in a period. It has two discrete states: Yes(Y) and No(N).

(5) electronic interference: the variable denotes whether enemy execute electronic interference while close to our military region. It is a discrete variable which has two states: Yes(Y) and No(N).

(6) across border of base region: it denotes whether enemy get across the border of our base region. It is a discrete variable which has two states: Yes(Y) and No(N).

For the continuous variables including Distance, Height and Speed, it is necessary to partition them by fuzzy mapping. We can divide the value range of continuous variable into several grades (the Distance, Height and Speed continuous variables are divided into three grades). According to the grades of value range, the corresponding fuzzy states of each continuous variable can be defined. For the variable Distance, the fuzzy states include long, medium and near; for the Speed, the fuzzy states have slow, medium and fast; and the fuzzy states of variable Height include high, medium and low.

For the purpose of mapping the continuous variable into fuzzy states, the membership function of each fuzzy state should be given. For example, the membership function of variable Speed can be defined as:

$$\mu_{S(l)}(x) = \begin{cases} 1 & 0 \le x \le v_1 \\ (v_2 - x)/(v_2 - v_1) & v_1 < x \le v_2 \\ 0 & x > v_2 \end{cases} \quad (11)$$

$$\mu_{S(m)}(x) = \begin{cases} 0 & x \le v_2 - v_b \\ (x - v_2 + v_b)/v_b & v_2 - v_b < x \le v_2 \\ (v_2 + v_b - x)/v_b & v_2 < x \le v_2 + v_b \\ 0 & x > v_2 + v_b \end{cases} \quad (12)$$

$$\mu_{S(f)}(x) = \begin{cases} 0 & x \le v_2 \\ (x-v_2)/(v_3-v_2) & v_2 < x \le v_3 \\ 1 & x > v_3 \end{cases} \tag{13}$$

where $v_1 = 0.5Ma$, $v_2 = 1.5Ma$, $v_3 = 2.5Ma$, $v_b = 1Ma$. $\mu_{S(l)}(x)$, $\mu_{S(m)}(x)$, $\mu_{S(f)}(x)$ respectively denote the membership function of fuzzy states: slow, medium and fast, which can be represented by Fig.2.

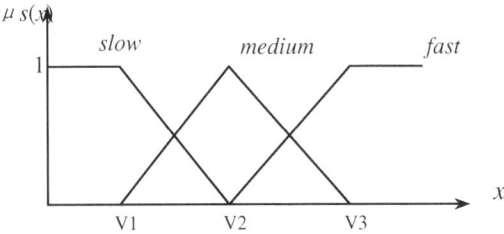

Fig. 2. The fuzzy set of Speed

4.2 Simulation

According to scenario described in section 4.1, the hierarchical FBN model is constructed, which is shown in Fig.3. In the BN level, there are two types of node, which are situation node(round) and sensor node(square). The situation node includes air strike node, scouting node, attack node and concealment node. Air strike node means whether the enemy would have air strike intention. Scouting node means whether the enemy executes the scouting action. Similarly, attack node stands for attack action, and concealment stands for concealment action. The other nodes are sensor nodes described in section 4.1, which include fuzzy nodes transformed from the continuous variables in the fuzzy mapping level.

With the Genie software, we constructed and compiled the fuzzy Bayesian network model of prediction of air strike in Fig.3. When we input different situation evidences including soft evidence and hard evidence, the prediction can be reasoned by FBN inference.

In table 1, the information collected from sensors at time T_1, T_2, T_3 are given while an enemy group of targets are close to our base.

Table 1. The data from sensors

Time	Height (m)	Distance (m)	Speed (Ma)	RS	EI	AB
T1	8000	11000	1.6	Yes		
T2	6000	6500	1.9		Yes	
T3	2000	2000	2.1			Yes

(RS: Radio Silence, EI: Electronic Interference, AB : Across Border).

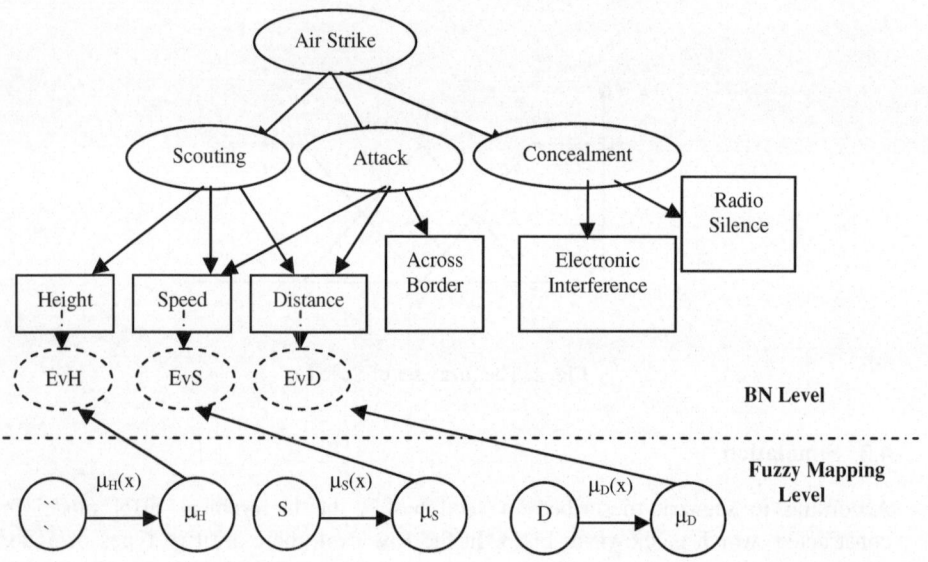

Fig. 3. Hierarchical FBN model for prediction of air strike

Then we can utilize the senor data to predict the enemy's intension based on the FBN model. At time T_1, the reasoning process of FBN is shown in the following. First, the fuzzy member functions in bottom level are utilized to partition the continuous variables H(Height), D(Distance), S(Speed) to their fuzzy states, which form the soft evidence:

$$\text{Height: } e1 = \{\text{High}=0.18, \text{Medium}=0.82, \text{Low}=0\}$$

$$\text{Distance: } e2 = \{\text{Long}=0.24, \text{Medium}=0.76, \text{Near}=0\}$$

$$\text{Speed: } e3 = \{\text{Slow}=0, \text{Midium}=0.9, \text{Fast}=0.1\}$$

According to (9), the conditional probability distribution of the dummy node (EvH as example) can be specified as:

$$\begin{bmatrix} P(\mu_H = 1/H_1 = high) = 0.18, P(\mu_H = 0/H_1 = high) = 0.82 \\ P(\mu_H = 1/H_2 = medium) = 0.82, P(\mu_H = 0/H_2 = medium) = 0.18 \\ P(\mu_H = 1/H_3 = low) = 0, P(\mu_H = 0/H_3 = low) = 1.0 \end{bmatrix}$$

With a hard evidence: Radio Silence $e4 = \{\text{True} = 1, \text{False} = 0\}$, we can obtain the probability of the enemy's air strike intension:0.659. In the process of inference at time T_2, T_3, the hard evidences of the previous time are not removed, but the soft evidences are updated. Then the results of FBN inference at time T_2, T_3 are respectively 0.726, 0.933.

5 Conclusion

In this paper, we proposed a hierarchical fuzzy Bayesian network model which can process continuous data. The simulation results show the model is available for situation assessment. In the future work, we will employ deterministic node, decision node and utility node in the FBN model, which can present the expert's knowledge efficiently. And the problem how to reduce the number of conditional probability will also be discussed.

References

1. Hall, D.L., Llinas, J.: Handbook of Multisensor Data Fusion. CRC Press, Washington (2001)
2. Endsley, M.R.: Toward a Theory of Situation Awareness in Dynamic Systems. Human Factors Journal 37(1), 32–64 (1995)
3. Linas, J., Bowman, C., et al.: Revisiting the JDL Data Fusion Model II. Proceedings of Information Fusion, 1–13 (2004)
4. Salerno, J.J.: Where's Level 2/3 Fusion- a Look Back over the Past 10 Years. In: Proceedings of Information Fusion, pp. 1–4 (2007)
5. Stover, J.A., Hall, D.L., Gibson, R.E.: A Fuzzy-logic Architecture for Autonomous Multisensor Data Fusion. IEEE Transaction on Industrial Electronics 43(3), 403–410 (1996)
6. Huimin, C., Baoshu, W.: A Fuzzy Logic Approach for Force Aggregation and Classification in Situation Assessment. In: Proceedings of the International Conference of Machine Learning and Cybernetics, pp. 1220–1225 (2007)
7. Das, S., Grey, R., Gonsalves, P.: Situation Assessment via Bayesian Belief Networks. In: Proceedings of the Fifth International Conference on Information Fusion, vol. 1, pp. 664–671 (2002)
8. Ji, Q.: Information Fusion for High Level Situation Assessment and Prediction. Report:OMB No.074-0188 (March 2007)
9. Noble, D.F.: Schema-Based Knowledge Elicitation for Planning and Situation Assessment Aids. IEEE Trans. on Systems, Man and Cybernetics, Part A 19(3), 473–482 (1989)
10. Looney, C.G., Liang, L.R.: Cognitive situation and threat assessment of ground battlespaces. Information Fusion 4, 297–308 (2003)
11. Looney, C.G.: Exploring Fusion Architecture for a Common Operational Picture. In: Proceedings of Information Fusion, vol. 2, pp. 251–260 (2001)
12. Kokar, M.M., Matheus, C.J., Baclawski, K.: Ontology-based Situation Awareness. Information Fusion 10, 83–98 (2009)
13. Little, E.G., Rogova, G.L.: Designing ontologies for higher level fusion. Information Fusion 10, 70–82 (2009)

14. Sycara, K., Glinton, R., et al.: An integrated approach to high-level information fusion. Information Fusion 10, 25–50 (2009)
15. Krauthausen, P., et al.: Intension Recognition for Partial-Order Plans Using Dynamic Bayesian Networks. In: Proceedings of Information Fusion, vol. 444–451 (2009)
16. Matheus, C.J., Ulicny, B., et al.: Towards the Formal Representation of Temporal Aspects of Enemy/Threat Courses of Action. In: Proceedings of Information Fusion, vol. 240–247 (2009)
17. Heckerman, D.: A Tutorial on Learning with Bayesian Network. Technical Report MSD-TR-95-06, Microsoft Research (March 1995)

Wavelet Multi-Resolution Analysis Aided Adaptive Kalman Filter for SINS/GPS Integrated Navigation in Guided Munitions[*]

Lei Cai[1], Fancheng Kong[2], Faliang Chang[1], and Xuexia Zhang[3]

[1] College of Control Science and Engineering,Shandong University, Jinan 250061, China
[2] Aviation Ammunition Department, Xu Zhou Air Force College, Xu Zhou 221000, China
[3] College of Animal Science, Henan Institute of Science and Technology, Xinxiang 453003, China
[4] Troops 94569, PLA of China, Jinan 250023, China
cailei1998@sohu.com

Abstract. SINS/GPS integrated navigation requires solving a set of nonlinear equations. In this case, the new method based on wavelet multi-resolution analysis (WMRA) aided adaptive Kalman filter (AKF) for SINS / GPS integration for aircraft navigation are proposed to perform better than the classical. The WMRA is used to compare the SINS and GPS position outputs at different resolution levels. These differences represent, in general, the SINS errors, which are used to correct for the SINS outputs during GPS outages. The proposed scheme combines the estimation capability of AKF and the learning capability of WMRA thus resulting in improved adaptive and estimation performance. The simulations show that good results in SINS/GPS positioning accuracy can be obtained by applying the new method based on WMRA and AKF.

Keywords: Wavelet multi-resolution analysis, integrated navigation, adaptive Kalman filter, GPS/SINS.

1 Introduction

Inertial navigation system can supply not only continuous vehicle position and velocity information but also three axes attitude. Yet, SINS has a great shortcoming. Its navigation errors will dramatically increase with time [1]. So, SINS cannot work for a long time by itself to meet the demand of accurate navigation.

The global positioning system (GPS) has been extensively used in navigation because of its accuracy and worldwide coverage [2]. GPS augmentations such as satellite-based augmentation systems (SBAS) and ground-based augmentation systems (GBAS) allow improving the accuracy of the navigation solution. Indeed, ground stations estimate GPS measurement errors that are then transmitted to the GPS receiver thanks to a satellite constellation. However, many tracking channels can be

---

[*] This work was supported by China Natural Science Foundation Committee (60775023, 60975025), Natural Science Foundation Committee of Shandong Province of China (Z2005G03), and SRF for ROCS, SEM.

H. Deng et al. (Eds.): AICI 2011, Part II, LNAI 7003, pp. 455–462, 2011.
© Springer-Verlag Berlin Heidelberg 2011

affected simultaneously by interferences, which can result in a loss of the GPS signal. In this case, a self-contained system such as a calibrated inertial navigation system (INS) can ensure the continuity of navigation with a good accuracy.

2 The GPS/INS Nonlinear Filtering Model

2.1 State Model

In the proposed framework, the state vector is composed of the INS error that are defined as the deviation between the actual dynamic quantities and the INS computed values $\delta X = X - X_{INS}$. The state model describes the INS error dynamic behavior depending on the instrumentation and initialization errors. It is obtained by linearizing the ideal equations around the INS estimates as follows:

$$\delta \dot{X} = f\left(X, U\right) - f\left(X_{INS}, U_{INS}\right) \tag{1}$$

$$\delta \dot{X} = \nabla f\left(X_{INS}, U_{INS}\right) \delta X \tag{2}$$

The state vector is usually augmented with systematic sensor errors:

$$\delta X = \left(\delta v^{n}, \delta \rho, b_{g}, \delta \lambda, \delta \phi, b, d\right) \tag{3}$$

where v^{n} stands for the velocity relative to the earth centered/earth fixed frame and resolved in the locally level frame; ρ is the vector of attitude angles; $\left(\lambda, \phi, h\right)$ is the geodetic position in latitude, longitude, altitude; b_{a} and b_{g} represent the accelerometers and gyrometers biases; $b = c\tau_{r}$ and d are respectively the GPS clock offset and its drift.

A coarse analysis shows that the errors develop through a variety of sources. Horizontal position and velocity experience a pendulum-like motion called Schuler oscillation. In addition, the earth rotation introduces a cross-coupling between the horizontal dynamic components, hence a modulation of the previous oscillation (Coriolis effect at Foucault frequency). Supposing that the attitude angles are perfectly known, such a behavior is well described by:

$$\delta \ddot{\phi} = -\Omega_{Schuler}^{2} \delta \phi + \Omega_{Foucault} \delta \dot{\lambda} \tag{4}$$

$$\delta \ddot{\lambda} = -\Omega_{schuler}^{2} \delta \lambda \tag{5}$$

As for vertical channel, gravity compensation results in an unstable altitude error propagation of the form:

$$\delta \ddot{\phi} = -\Omega_{Schuler}^{2} \delta \phi + \Omega_{Foucault} \delta \dot{\lambda} \tag{6}$$

where $k = \sqrt{2g/R}$, g being the gravity and R the earth radius. However, this paper assumes that the altitude h is known (thanks to an independent vertical reference such as a barometric altimeter).

Accurate models of the instrument biases are required to achieve a good localization performance. For short-term applications, the accelerometers' and gyrometers can be properly defined as random walk constants $\dot{b}_a = w_a$ and $\dot{b}_g = w_g$. Note that the standard deviations of the white noises w_a and w_g are related to the sensor quality. The navigation solution also depends on the receiver clock parameters b and d modeled as $\dot{b} = d + w_b$ and $\dot{b} = w_d$, where w_b and w_d are mutually independent zero-mean Gaussian random variables (whose variances can be determined by the Allan variance parameters. For simplicity, denote as X (instead of δX) the state vector. The discrete-time state model takes the following form:

$$X_{t+1} = A_t X_t + v_t, v_t \ \square \ N\left(0, \sum{}_v\right) \tag{7}$$

where $t = 1, \cdots, T$ and T is the number of samples. The coupling effects between the components of X_t results in a block diagonal matrix A_t whose elements are detailed in [3].

2.2 Measurement Model

The hybridization filter is driven by the GPS pseudoranges. Consequently, the observation equation associated to the ith satellite can be defined as:

$$\rho_i = \sqrt{\left(X_i - x\right)^2 + \left(Y_i - y\right)^2 + \left(Z_i - z\right)^2} + b + w_i \tag{8}$$

where $i = 1, \cdots, n_s$ (recall that ns is the number of visible satellites). The vectors $\left(x, y, z\right)^T$ and $\left(X_i, Y_i, Z_i\right)^T$ are the positions of the guided munitions and the ith satellite expressed in the rectangular coordinate system WGS-84. However, these observations have to be expressed as functions of the state vector components to make the filtering problem tractable.

Thus, the position is transformed from the geodetic to the rectangular coordinate system as follows:

$$\begin{cases} x = \left(N + h_{INS} + \delta h\right)\cos\left(\lambda_{INS} + \delta\lambda\right)\cos\left(\phi_{INS} + \delta\phi\right) \\ y = \left(N + h_{INS} + \delta h\right)\cos\left(\lambda_{INS} + \delta\lambda\right)\sin\left(\phi_{INS} + \delta\phi\right) \\ z = \left(N + h_{INS} + \delta h\right)\sin\left(\lambda_{INS} + \delta\lambda\right) \end{cases} \tag{9}$$

where $N = \dfrac{a}{\sqrt{1-e^2 \sin^2 \lambda}}$. The parameters a and e denote the semi major axis

length and the eccentricity of the earth's ellipsoid. These expressions have to be substituted in (8) to obtain the highly nonlinear measurement equation:

$$Y_t = h_t(X_t) + CX_t + w_t. \qquad (10)$$

3 Wavelet Multi-Resolution Analysis for SINS /GPS Output Analysis

Wavelet analysis is based on a windowing technique with variable-sized windows. Wavelet transform (WT) allows the use of long time intervals where precise low frequency information is needed, and shorter intervals where high frequency information is considered. In general, the major advantage offered by wavelets is the ability to perform local analysis [4].

Therefore, it will be adopted in this study to analyze both the SINS and GPS output components. As shown in Fig.1, WMRA decomposes the signal into various resolution levels (here supposing 3 levels). The data with coarse resolution contain information about the low frequency components and retain the main features of the original signal. The data with fine resolution retain information about the high frequency components.

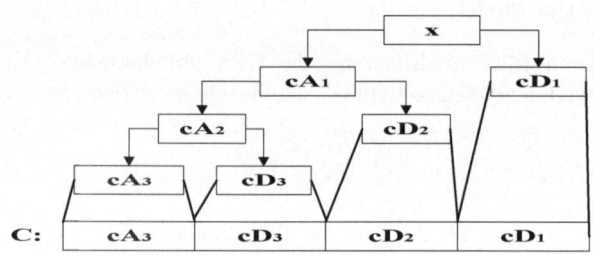

Fig. 1. The structure of applying WMRA

In general, a space V_J can be separated into two subspaces: a subspace V_{J-1} (approximation) and a space W_{J-1} (detail), which is just the difference of these two spaces. If this process is iterated, successive approximations will be decomposed in turn, so that one signal is broken into many fine resolution components. The original signal can then be reconstructed from the sum of the final approximation component and the detail components of all levels.

The mathematical procedure of WMRA for input signals X is as follows:

(1) For an input signal $x(n)$, calculate the approximation coefficient $a_{j,k}$ at the jth resolution level as follows:

$$a_{j,k} = 2^{(-j/2)} \sum_n x(n)\phi(2^{-j}n - k) \tag{11}$$

where $\phi(n)$ is called the scaling function. Scaling functions are similar to wavelet functions except that they have only positive values. They are designed to smooth the input signal (i.e. seeking the signal approximation). They work in the signal in a way similar to averaging the input signal $x(n)$. The scaling function is applied to the input signal to determine the approximation. This operation is equivalent to low pass filtering.

(2) The approximation of $x(n)$ at the jth resolution level is then computed as

$$x_j(t) = \sum_{k=-\infty}^{\infty} a_{j,k}\phi_{j,k}(t) \tag{12}$$

(3) Calculate the detail coefficient $d_{j,k}$ at the j th resolution level:

$$d_{j,k} = \sum_n x(n)\psi_{j,k}(n) \tag{13}$$

Wavelet functions $\psi_{j,k}(n)$ are designed to seek the details of the signals. The detail function will be applied to the input signal to determine the details. This operation is equivalent to high-pass filtering.

(4) The detail of $x(n)$ at the jth resolution level is then computed as follows:

$$g_j(n) = \sum_{k=-\infty}^{\infty} d_{j,k}\psi_{j,k}(n) \tag{14}$$

Hypothetically, the analysis can stop at the j th resolution level and the signal can be reconstructed using the approximation at that level and all the details, starting from the first resolution level until the j th level.

$$x(n) = \sum_{k=-\infty}^{\infty} a_{j,k}\phi_{j,k}(n) + \sum_{j=1}^{j}\sum_{k=-\infty}^{\infty} d_{j,k}\psi_{j,k}(n) \tag{15}$$

The first term represents the approximation at level j and the second term represents the details at resolution level j and lower. In conclusion, WMRA builds a pyramidal structure that requires an iterative application of scaling and wavelet functions as low-pass (LP) and high-pass (HP) filters, respectively. These filters initially act on the entire signal band at the high frequency (lower scale values) first and gradually reduce the signal band at each stage.

The WMRA is applied to both the SINS and GPS longitude λ, latitude ϕ, altitude h and velocity components. In this study, we decided to compare the SINS and GPS outputs components at three resolution levels. Because after some attempts, it can be demonstrated three resolution levels is enough for this analysis. The wavelet coefficients that represent one of the SINS output components in the three decomposition levels are

$$C_{SINS} = \left[\left| cA_{si3} \left| cD_{si3} \right| cD_{si2} \left| cD_{si1} \right| \right| \right] \tag{16}$$

The corresponding wavelet coefficients of the GPS position component is represented as

$$C_{GPS} = \left[\left| cA_{g3} \left| cD_{g3} \right| cD_{g2} \left| cD_{g1} \right| \right| \right] \tag{17}$$

By subtracting the wavelet coefficients of each of the GPS outputs from the corresponding wavelet coefficients of each of the SINS outputs, the wavelet coefficients of the error signals can be extracted as

$$E = \left[\left| cA_{e3} \left| cD_{e3} \right| cD_{e2} \left| cD_{e1} \right| \right| \right] \tag{18}$$

The error signal can then be reconstructed from the wavelet coefficients obtained in (18).

The reconstructed error represents, in general, the SINS errors, which are used to correct for the SINS outputs during GPS outages. This means that the proposed navigation system will rely on the GPS output components until the GPS signal is blocked. Whenever the GPS signal is available, the GPS output component is compared to the corresponding SINS output component and the corresponding output error is computed. Optimal estimation and modeling of this error signal is performed by ANN, which is discussed in the following section. It should be highlighted that separate WMRA is designed for each output component of SINS and GPS.

4 Integrated Navigation System Based on WMRA Aided AKF

4.1 The Concept of WMRA Aided Adaptive Kalman Filter

Research works in the past adopted the approach of incorporating a neural network into the classical Kalman filter [5]. In order to enhance the adaptive capability, WMRA aided adaptive KF approach is proposed in this paper.

The basic concept of the proposed method is shown in Fig. 2, in which WMRA is employed to aid the adaptive KF to reduce the estimation error due to, among other imperfections, highly maneuvering, and model varying effect. The scheme combines the estimation capability of the adaptive KF and the learning capability of the WMRA. The implementation of WMRA aided adaptive KF has three stages, namely, (1) architecture, (2) training and testing, and (3) recall [6]. The WMRA is trained off line to learn the errors in navigation. The complex modeling requirement in the KF is reduced by the WMRA because errors in navigation are eliminated during the recall phase.

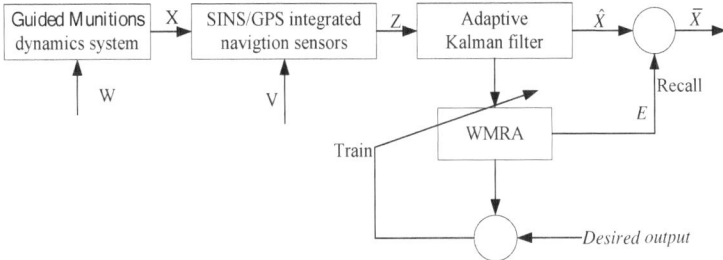

Fig. 2. SINS/GPS fault-tolerant integrated navigation system structure

4.2   The Architecture of SINS/GPS Integrated Navigation System

In this paper, the proposed SINS/GPS fault-tolerant integrated navigation system is based on federated filter structure, as illustrated in Fig. 3. Each local filter is dedicated to a separate sensor subsystem. Before inputting to the master filter, the data of local filters have been detected (and isolated) by WMRA detectors. The global optimal estimation $\hat{X}_k$ from master filter is revised by data fusion WMRA. Then, the navigation parameter relative real value $\hat{X}_k$ is obtained.

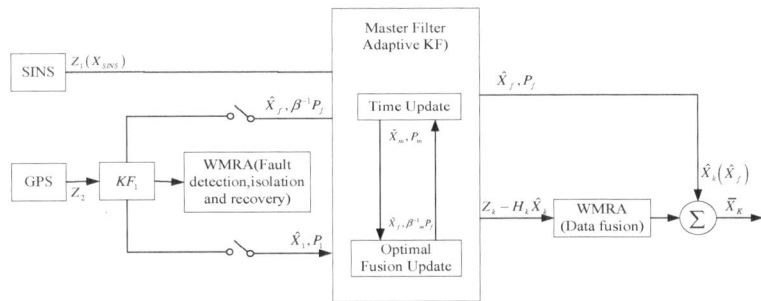

Fig. 3. SINS/GPS fault-tolerant integrated navigation system structure

5   Simulation Results

All the development made in this study was implemented using VC++ and MATLAB7.0 computer-aided design software (MathWorks, Natick, MA) including the wavelets and neural network toolboxes.

The fig.4 and fig.5 show the typical performance of MWWA aided AKF design for SINS/GPS output signal. The reference solution (the blue curve in figures) is provided by GPS signal, and then we have intentionally considered some GPS outages to verify the performance of MWWA aided AKF method.

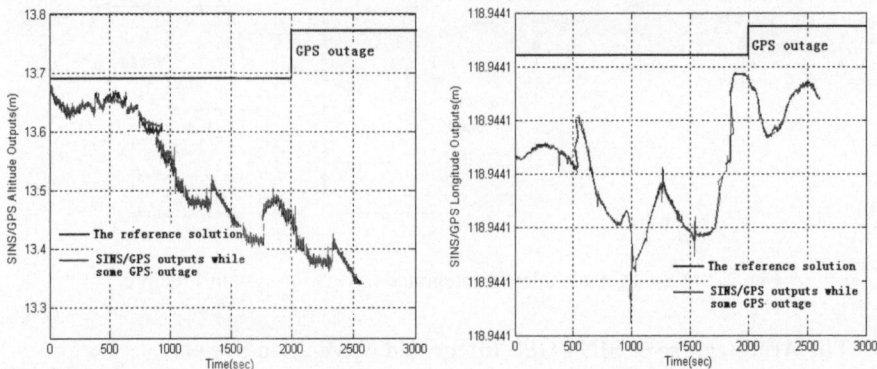

Fig. 4. Altitude comparison   **Fig. 5.** Longitude comparison

6 Simulation Results

The proposed new method based on wavelet multi-resolution analysis Aided Adaptive Kalman Filter for GPS/SINS integration for aircraft navigation is efficient for the accuracy requirement for aircraft. It can provide reliable and accurate position information for the vehicle while sometime GPS outages. However, simulation results conducted in nominal situations (with a good observability) show that quite similar performance is achieved with the different filtering strategies. A comparison in critical situations (such as loss of observability or presence of multipath) is currently under investigation.

References

1. Saulson, B.G.: Nonlinear estimation comparison for ballistic missile tracking. Automatica 43, 1424–1438 (2004)
2. Schei, T.S.: A finite-difference method for linearization in nonlinear estimation algorithms. Automatica 51, 252–260 (2003)
3. Kotecha, J.H., Djuric, P.M.: Gaussian particle filtering. IEEE Transactions on Signal Processing 51, 2592–2601 (2003)
4. Chen, X., Zhu, X., Li, Z.: Application for GPS/SINS loosely-coupled integrated system by a new method based on WMRA and RBFNN. In: Huang, D.-S., Heutte, L., Loog, M. (eds.) ICIC 2007. LNCS, vol. 4681, pp. 394–403. Springer, Heidelberg (2007)
5. Chai, L., Yuan, J., Fang, Q., Kang, Z., Huang, L.: Neural network aided adaptive kalman filter for multi-sensors integrated navigation. In: Yin, F.-L., Wang, J., Guo, C. (eds.) ISNN 2004. LNCS, vol. 3174, pp. 381–386. Springer, Heidelberg (2004)
6. Semeniuk, L., Noureldin, A.: Bridging GPS outages using neural network estimates of INS position and velocity errors. Meas. Sci. Technol. 17(9), 2783–2798 (2006)

Multi-satellite Combined Orbit Determination Parameterized Fusion Model and Weighting Iterative Estimation Algorithm[*]

Deyong Zhao[1] and Hongmei Yu[2]

[1] Department of Management Engineering, Mechanical Engineering College,
Shijiazhuang, 050003, P.R. China
zdy77218@sina.com
[2] Department of Basic Subject, Wuhan Ordnance N.C.O. Academy,
Wuhan, 430075, P.R. China
yuhongmei@sina.com

Abstract. For multi-LEO combined orbit determination (COD) satellite-network based on space-based tracking telemetry and command (STTC) satellites, kinematic orbit information can be obtained only using the method of precise point positioning (PPP) based on observation models, but the orbits results are not very precise because that the precision of observation data and the Geometry Dilution of Precision (GDOP) of STTC constellation cannot meet the demands of high precision application requirements of LEOs. The high precision denotation model of satellite orbit dynamics based on physics parameter model and mathematics model which associates sparse parameter representation with time sequence analysis, nonlinear semi-parametric combined observation model based on system error parameters modeling and non-parametric component denotation of model error, and COD parameterized fusion model are established aiming at multi-satellite high precision COD based on bi-satellite positioning system and low earth orbiters (LEOs). Then parameters estimation algorithms of the former two kinds of models and the combined estimation algorithm of parameterized fusion model are designed. Theoretic analysis and simulated computation results show that the high precision denotation method of sparse parameters model and the optimized modeling method of observation model considering model error can improve modeling precision, and combined estimation algorithm of parameterized fusion model can synchronously ameliorate orbit determination precision ulteriorly.

Keywords: Combined orbit determination, parameterized fusion model, weighting iterative estimation method, optimal weighting algorithm.

1 Introduction

Combined orbit determination is a process to estimate the orbit parameters of two or more space vehicles at the same time by combining inter-satellite measurement and

---

[*] Project supported by the NSFC (No. 60904098).

H. Deng et al. (Eds.): AICI 2011, Part II, LNAI 7003, pp. 463–470, 2011.
© Springer-Verlag Berlin Heidelberg 2011

satellite-earth and unifying fusion processing for space-based measurement system or constellations with inter-satellite links [1]. Precise dynamic model, reliable observation model and reasonable estimation method are three basic elements to obtain high precision COD result. The research on existing COD technique follows the traditional research approach of satellite precise orbit determination (POD), which looks for the precise modeling of dynamic model and accurate estimation of parameters to be estimated. However, for perturbation force parts with indefinable physical model or parameters, experiential processing method is used to compensate or modify the dynamic modeling error, such as experiential acceleration or stochastic process[2,3], which can easily cause model morbidity. For the construction of observation model, the existing method builds a compact fusion model of data processing [4], which does nothing about the model error or the mixed error [5]. The parameter estimation method is limited by the modeling method of dynamics model and observation model, so the existing method is essentially a linear processing algorithm based on least square estimation or its improved type. However, Consideration on nonlinear influencing factors which affect the precision of COD is less.

This paper uses the COD of LEOs based on Bi-satellite Positioning System (BPS) as the research background, and the perturbation characteristic of satellite orbit is deeply analyzed and a high precision denotation method of satellite orbit dynamics based on sparse parameter representation with time sequence analysis is proposed. Through analyzing the observation model error behavior and the nonlinear influencing factors of COD, an error modeling method which combines parametric modeling and non-parametric component representation is proposed and a nonlinear semi-parametric combined observation model is built. On that basis, the parameterized fusion model of COD is built and the nonlinear semi-parametric combined estimation algorithm which combines parametric estimation and nonparametric estimation is designed.

2 Satellite COD Parameterized Fusion Model

The principle of LEO COD based on BPS can be briefly described by the following model:

$$\begin{cases} Y = G(X,t) + \varepsilon \\ \dot{X} = F(X,t) \end{cases}. \tag{1}$$

Wherein: $X = (X_{B1}, X_{B2}, X_U)^T$ stands for the position and speed state vector as well as dynamical parameter to be estimated. Y stands for actual observation vector; G stands for calculative observation vector; ε stands for observation noise; F stands for the acting force.

2.1 Dynamics High Precision Denotation Model

In the inertial coordinate system, the differential equation of satellite motion is:

$$\dot{X} = F(X,t) = \vec{f}_{TB} + \vec{f}_{NB} + \vec{f}_{NS} + \vec{f}_{TD} + \vec{f}_{RL} + \vec{f}_{SR} + \vec{f}_{AL} + \vec{f}_{DG} + \vec{f}_{TH}. \tag{2}$$

According to the orbit perturbation modeling thought above, the high precision denotation method of satellite orbit dynamics model based on physics and mathematics model can be expressed:

$$\dot{X} = F(X,t) = F_0 + F_S + e_F .$$ (3)

Wherein: F_0 stands for the force of which precise modeling can be built, such as low level non-spherical perturbing force; F_S stands for orbit perturbation acting force, which mainly comprises the perturbing force that the model is precise but parameters cannot be precisely determined and the perturbing force that neither model nor parameters can be precisely determined. The sparse parameter model of orbit perturbation is planned to be built through sparse denotation; e_F stands for orbit perturb-bation noise, and its time sequence model is planned to be built through time sequence analysis.

2.2   Sparse Parameter Model of Orbit Deviation

Suppose the perturbation deviation signal caused by orbit perturbation acting force F_S is expressed by X_{F_S}, then we have

$$X_{F_S} = \sum_{r \in \Gamma} \alpha_r \phi_r .$$ (4)

When dictionary D is determined, sparse denotation of perturbation signal X_{F_S} is to solve sparse denotation coefficient α_r, which can be represented by (P_0):

$$(P_0 - \text{noise}) \ \min_\alpha \left\| X_{F_S} - D\alpha \right\|_2^2 + \lambda \|\alpha\|_0, \ X_{F_S} = D\alpha + z .$$ (5)

Wherein: X_{F_S} stands for noised signal($\|z\|_2^2 \le \varepsilon^2$). The regularization parameter λ controls the balance between the permissible error and sparseness. For the noised question of orbit perturbation, if the sparseness condition is met, the sparse parameter model (5) of satellite orbit perturbation deviation signal X_{F_S} can be expressed as:

$$(P_1 - \text{noise}) \ \min_\alpha \|\alpha\|_1 \ \text{meets} \ \left\| X_{F_S} - D\alpha \right\|_2^2 \le \varepsilon^2 .$$ (6)

According to Lagrange multiplier method, the sparse parameter model above will come down to solve the following optimization problem:

$$\arg\min_\alpha \left[\frac{1}{2} \left\| X_{F_S} - D\alpha \right\|_2^2 + \lambda \|\alpha\|_1 \right] .$$ (7)

2.3   Time Sequence Model of Orbit Residual Error

Suppose satellite position and velocity component caused by the orbit perturbations acting force e_F are expressed by X_{e_F}. The statistical characteristics of X_{e_F} can be analyzed through time sequence modeling method. In the actual data processing, for sequence $\Delta E_1, \Delta E_2, \cdots, \Delta E_N$, the estimations of auto-covariance function r_k , autocorrelation function ρ_k and partial correlation function $\varphi_{kk} (k \ge 1)$ are:

$$
\begin{cases}
\hat{\gamma}_k = \dfrac{1}{N}\displaystyle\sum_{i=1}^{N-k}\Delta E_i \cdot \Delta E_{i+k} \\[2mm]
\hat{\rho}_k = \hat{\gamma}_k/\hat{r}_0
\end{cases}
\quad
\begin{cases}
\hat{\varphi}_{11} = \hat{\rho}_1, \quad \hat{\varphi}_{k+1,j} = \hat{\varphi}_{k,j} - \hat{\varphi}_{k+1,k+1}\cdot\hat{\varphi}_{k,k+1-j} \\[2mm]
\hat{\varphi}_{k+1,k+1} = (\hat{\rho}_{k+1} - \displaystyle\sum_{j=1}^{k}\hat{\rho}_{k+1-j}\cdot\hat{\varphi}_{k,j})(1 - \displaystyle\sum_{j=1}^{k}\hat{\rho}_j\cdot\hat{\varphi}_{k,j})^{-1}
\end{cases}
\tag{8}
$$

From the autocorrelation and partial correlation function of orbit perturbation residual error of U obtained from wavelet decomposition, we can know that ρ_k has tailing characteristic while φ_{kk} has truncation characteristic, so the orbit perturbation residual error sequence of LEO can be expressed by low level AR model. For model order determination, the AIC standard is based on the following:

$$
AIC(k) = \log\hat{\sigma}_\varepsilon^2(k) + \frac{2k}{N}, \quad k = 0,1,2,\cdots,p .
\tag{9}
$$

Wherein: $\hat{\sigma}_\varepsilon^2(k)$ is the estimation of σ_ε^2 when the perturbation residual error data $AR(k)$ is fitted. Here suppose $P = 5$, search for the minimum value of $AIC(k)$ of AR model whose order is not more than 5, then the calculation result is shown in Table 1.

Table 1. AR model parameter of different orders

Parameter	(1)	(2)	(3)	(4)	(5)
AIC value	-2.528	-3.899	-3.928	-3.873	-3.787
σ_ε^2 value	0.079	0.021	0.019	0.021	0.022

From Table 1, we can see that the AIC of the model is the least when $p = 3$. As a result, the orbit perturbation position residual error of U is a $AR(3)$ model, which is in accordance with the simulated result.

2.4 COD Parameterized Fusion Model

In the satellite COD data processing based on sky and earth measurement, besides the measurement systematic error and random error whose model can be built, there are other model errors caused by nonlinear influencing factor, for example, colored noise of the observation data and truncation error and so on. The matrix form of combined orbit determination observation model based on systematic error parametric modeling is as follows:

$$
Y = G(X_0) + g(a) + \varepsilon .
\tag{10}
$$

Wherein: a stands for the systematic error coefficient to be estimated. Considering the model error vector s which exists in observed value, the nonlinear semi-parametric combined observation model based on BPS can be expressed as follows:

$$
Y_1 = S_1(X_0) + g_1(a_1) + s_1 + \varepsilon_1, \quad Y_2 = S_2(X_0) + g_2(a_2) + s_2 + \varepsilon_2 .
\tag{11}
$$

Essentially, the satellite COD based on parametric fusion is the fusion process of information provided by sparse parameter model of dynamics and parametric model of tracking measurement system. When the satellite orbit dynamics high precision denotation model based on sparse parameter representation and time sequence analysis and the nonlinear semi-parametric combined observation model of model error modeling are synthesized, the classical COD model (1) can extend to the COD parametric fusion model:

$$\begin{cases} Y_1 = S_1(X_0) + g_1(a_1) + s_1 + \varepsilon_1 \\ Y_2 = S_2(X_0) + g_2(a_2) + s_2 + \varepsilon_2 \end{cases}, \quad \begin{cases} \dot{X}_{B1} = F_{01}(X_{B1},t) + F_{S1}(X_{B1},t) & X_{B1}(t_0) = X_{B1}^0 \\ \dot{X}_{B2} = F_{02}(X_{B2},t) + F_{S2}(X_{B2},t) & X_{B2}(t_0) = X_{B2}^0 \\ \dot{X}_U = F_{0U}(X_U,t) + F_{SU}(X_U,t) + e_{FU}(X_U,t) & X_U(t_0) = X_U^0 \end{cases} \quad (12)$$

3   COD Integrative Fusion Model Optimal Estimation Algorithm

3.1   Weighting Iterative Estimation Method

Based on multi-resolution wavelet analysis, the satellite orbit perturbation deviation signal X_{F_S} can be decomposed into the subspace $V_0, W_0, W_1, \cdots, W_{j-1}$. Here, the subscript $0 \sim j-1$ are corresponding to different resolution spaces from low frequency to high frequency. If the scaling function $\phi(t)$ and wavelet function $\psi(t)$ are given, the satellite orbit perturbation deviation signal X_{F_S} can only be decomposed into (take two-scale wavelet transform for example):

$$\begin{aligned} X_{F_S} &= g_j(t) + g_{j-1}(t) + g_{j-2}(t) + f_{j-2}(t) \\ &= \sum_l d_{j,l} \psi_{j,l}(t) + \sum_l d_{j-1,l} \psi_{j-1,l}(t) + \sum_l d_{j-2,l} \psi_{j-2,l}(t) + \sum_l c_{j-2,l} \phi_{j-2,l}(t) \end{aligned} \quad (13)$$

Under the circumstance of two-scale wavelet transform, for the subspace j : $\alpha_j \propto (2^j)^{1/2+\varepsilon_\alpha}$, then: $\|\alpha_j\|_1 / \|\alpha_{j-1}\|_1 = (2)^{1/2+\varepsilon_\alpha}$, suppose λ_0 is the penalty coefficient of subspace V_0, for the subspace, there is the following relationship: $\lambda_j = (\delta)^{j+1} \cdot \lambda_0, \delta \geq \sqrt{2}$. A sparseness metric function with separability is defined as: $\rho(\alpha) = \|\alpha\|_1 = \sum \rho(\alpha_j) |\alpha|^2 \cdot \rho_0(\alpha)$. Based on wavelet decomposition, the optimization problem can be changed to the following form:

$$\arg\min_\alpha \left[\frac{1}{2} \left\| X_{F_S} - \sum_{j=0}^k \Phi_j \alpha_j \right\|_2^2 + \sum_{j=0}^k \lambda_j \rho(\alpha_j) \right]. \quad (14)$$

The matrix expression of optimization problem (14) is: $\arg\min_\alpha (1/2) \cdot \|X_{F_S} - D\alpha\|_2^2 + \lambda \alpha^T diag\{\rho_0(\alpha)\}\alpha$, wherein, $diag\{\rho_0(\alpha)\}$ is a diagonal weighting matrix. The weighting iteration method based on wavelet decomposition supposes $\rho_0(\alpha)$ remains stationary in the iteration process, let $W(\alpha) = diag\{\rho_0(\alpha)\}$ and $J(\alpha) = (1/2) \cdot (X_{F_S} - D\alpha)^T (X_{F_S} - D\alpha) + \lambda \alpha^T W(\alpha)\alpha$, then, when $\lambda > 0$ and $D^T D > 0$, the above optimization problem can be solved by proximate Newton iteration method. From $\nabla J(\alpha) = 0$, we obtain $(D^T D + 2\lambda W(\alpha))\alpha = D^T X_{F_S}$, then $\alpha = (D^T D + 2\lambda W(\alpha))^{-1} D^T X_{F_S}$, let $Q(\alpha) = (2W(\alpha))^{-1}$, we obtain

$$\alpha = Q(\alpha)D^T \left(\lambda I_{M \times M} + DQ(\alpha)D^T\right)^{-1} X_{F_s}. \tag{15}$$

So the iterative scheme to solve optimization problem (14) is as follows:

$$Giving \ \alpha^{(0)}, D, \ \alpha^{(n+1)} = Q\left(\alpha^{(n)}\right)D^T \left(\lambda I_{M \times M} + DQ\left(\alpha^{(n)}\right)D^T\right)^{-1} X_{F_s}. \tag{16}$$

3.2 The Combined Optimal Estimation Algorithm

For the integrative COD parameterized fusion model (12), it can be respectively expressed as the following forms:

$$Y = S(X_0) + g(a) + s + \varepsilon, \ \dot{X} = F_0(X_0) + F_s(X_s) + e \tag{17}$$

When e is the Gauss white noise sequence, to solve X_0, a, s, X_s is namely to solve the two following minimum questions at the same time:

$$\left\| Y - S(X_0) - g(a) - s \right\|^2 = \min, \ \left\| \dot{X} - F_0(X_0) - F_s(X_s) \right\|^2 = \min. \tag{18}$$

When the variance σ_ε^2 of ε and σ_e^2 of e are known, steps of combined estimation algorithm are as follows:

Step1 The satellite orbit initial value $X_0^{(0)}$, the sparse parameter model coefficient initial value $X_S^{(0)}$ and a constant $\delta > 0$ are given ;

Step2 Substitute them in the model (17), and the instantaneous $X^{(0)}(t_i)$ of all kinds of satellites at any time can be obtained;

Step3 Preset the initial value $a^{(0)}$ and $s^{(0)}$, combine with $X^{(0)}(t_i)$, and substitute it in (17), the minimum problem (9) is solved;

Step4 Substitute $X_0^{(j)}$ in (17) to solve the minimum question (18). Solve the orbit parameter $X_0^{(j+1)}$ and $X_S^{(j+1)}$ through the iterative weighting algorithm based on formula (16);

Step5 Define cost function $P(X_0, a, s) = (Y - S(X_0) - g(a) - s)^T \cdot (Y - S(X_0) - g(a) - s)$ and $Q(X_0, X_S) = (\dot{X} - F_0(X_0) - F_s(X_s))^T \cdot (\dot{X} - F_0(X_0) - F_s(X_s))$, for given δ if $P(X_0^{(j)}) - P(X_0^{(j+1)}) \le \delta$ and $Q(X_0^{(j)}) - Q(X_0^{(j+1)}) \le \delta$, then $X_0 = X_0^{(j+1)}$; else let $X_0^{(0)} = X_0^{(j+1)}$, return to step1 ;

Step6 Repeat above steps until X_0, a, s, X_S are convergent, the result is recorded as $\hat{X}_0$, namely final estimation result in parameterized fusion model.

4   Simulation Application and Precision Analysis

4.1   Simulation condition

The "real" satellite orbit: all perturbation models (JGM2 model, the gravitation between the sun and the moon, the atmospheric drag, and so on) are considered, which respectively form the theoretic "real" orbits of the LEO and BPS;

Range-sum simulation data: according to BPS ephemeris the theoretical range-sum data are calculated, besides, the range error caused by observation residual error system error model and the 10-meter random error are added, and the data switching cycle and the observation area of BPS are considered. Finally, the observable segmental arc are selected; *Satellite physical model parameter*: double star (J4 JGM2 model, the gravitation between the sun and the moon, the solar light pressure); LEO (J20 JGM2 model, the atmospheric drag, the gravitation between the sun and the moon, the solar light pressure); *Satellite sparse parameter model*: model dictionary is structured by wavelet function symmlet-8.

4.2 Results and Explanation of COD Simulation

CASE 1: Simulation data with length of 172800 seconds and one sampling point in each 5 seconds are selected, and actual available data is 2940 seconds. Only the perturbation physical model is used for COD.

CASE 2: Simulation data are as above. The sparse parameter model coefficient, constant systematic error and model error are resolved by parameterized fusion combined estimation algorithm.

The simulation conditions and corresponding COD simulation calculation are as the following Table 2.

Table 2. COD simulation results of different cases

Simulation case	Observation data	COD	Type of satellite	Precision of orbit determination(RMS)			
				X-axis	Y-axis	Z-axis	Position error (m)
1	172800 (2940)	Physical model COD	U1	23.63	10.47	24.24	35.44
			B1	127.3	115.7	19.25	173.1
			B2	46.65	54.33	18.69	74.01
2	172800 (2940)	parameterized fusion model COD	U1	4.08	8.04	4.14	9.92
			B1	23.12	27.03	5.72	36.03
			B2	14.32	11.44	22.26	28.83

4.3 Brief Conclusion

(1) If only the physical model is used for COD, there is relatively big dynamical modeling error between dynamical model implied and the actual model. As a result, the COD precision is hard to improve; especially LEO precision cannot meet application requirements;

(2) When parameterized system error, model error and model parameters are estimated by integrative parameterized fusion COD, the orbit determination precision of LEO can be improved evidently.

5 Conclusions

The paper analyzed the defects of existing COD dynamical model, the observation modeling method and the parametric estimation method, then high precision denotation method of dynamical model based on physical model and mathematic model is proposed; a model error modeling method which combines parameter modeling and nonparametric component denotation is proposed aiming at the observation model. Then, the integrative parameterized fusion models of COD are built and the corresponding combined estimation algorithm is designed. The result of simulation calculation shows that the integrative parameterized fusion models of COD are the fusion of single modeling method and that the combined estimation algorithm can further improve the precision of COD. At the same time, considering the GNSS possible development, the proposed integrative parameterized fusion models of COD can be further extended and improved and used in orbit determination of COD satellite network composed by multiple LEOs based on satellite constellation.

References

1. Yunck, T.P.: First assessment of GPS-based reduced-dynamic orbit determination on Topex/Poseidon. Geophysics research Letters 21(7), 541–544 (1994)
2. Svehla, D., Rothacher, M.: Kinematic and reduced-dynamic precise orbit determination of low earth orbiters. Advances in Geosciences 1(1), 47–56 (2003)
3. Montenbruck, O., van Helleputte, T., Kroes, R.: Reduced Dynamic Orbit Determination using GPS Code and Carrier Measurements. Aerospace Science and Technology 9(3), 261–271 (2005)
4. Zhao, D., Pan Xiaogang, C.: The Model and Algorithm of LEO Satellite COD Based on Bi-satellite Positioning System. In: Progress in Intelligent Computation and Its Application, pp. 619–624. China University of Geosciences Press, WuHan (2005)
5. Yi Dongyun, D.: Research on complicated characteristics of dynamic measurement errors and precision evaluation of data processing results. National University of Defense Technology doctoral dissertation, Changsha (2003)

A Tentative Idea of a Novel Consensus Fusion Method for Multi-sensor

Peng Zhang[1], Wen-jun Xie[1], Jian-ye Zhang[2], and Zhan-lei Wang[1]

[1] The Engineering Institute, Air Force Engineering University, Xi'an, China, 710038
[2] Department of Science Research, Air Force Engineering University, Xi'an, China, 710051
peng1439@163.com

Abstract. In the case of any prior knowledge is unknown, a novel consensus fusion algorithm is put forward. The algorithm takes use of the redundancy information between two consecutive measurements to define the new weight assignment, so the weight coefficient of sensors can be determined dynamically. The algorithm can avoid data saturation when the measurement information increasing, and ensure itself sensitivity when the measurements became changing. The simulation result shows that the weight coefficient assignment in the proposed algorithm is more effective, and the fusion precision can be improved further.

Keywords: Consensus fusion, redundant information, support degree, multi-sensor.

1 Introduction

Measurement values provided by multi-sensor systems can be fused with proper fusion algorithms. So that more reliable detection result can be obtained. At present, the fusion methods can be divided into two categories. One is based upon the prior knowledge of measurement values [1-3], and the other is lack of any prior knowledge of measurement values.

The first kind can achieve perfect effect because of prior knowledge existing. But it would be invalid when the theoretic conditions cannot be satisfied with. So the second kind of algorithm which needn't prior knowledge is proved to be more useful in practice, such as, the method based on fuzzy theory [4], confidence distance [5-6], nearest statistic distance [7], support degree [8-9] and so on. However, there are still some problems in the mentioned methods above. Firstly, since in many domains the recent measurement is more useful than older one, the time dimension in the fusion should also be taken into account to improve sensitivity of the algorithm. Secondly, the amount of data in question is typically so large that the present methods cannot executed efficiently on the entire series, including computation and storage complexity.

In order to solve these problems, a novel multi-sensor fusion algorithm is proposed in this paper. The algorithm takes use of the exponential function to build the support degree matrix, and each sensor's consistency value of different time can be obtained. By which the algorithm can be completely free from the prior knowledge. And in the meantime, the new method just takes use of the redundant information between two

H. Deng et al. (Eds.): AICI 2011, Part II, LNAI 7003, pp. 471–478, 2011.

consecutive measurements to define new weight assignment, and determines the weight coefficient for sensor dynamically. So the data saturation can be avoided when the measurement information increasing and the sensitivity can be ensured when the measurement is changing. The simulation result shows that the weight coefficient assignment in the new algorithm is more effective, and the fusion precision can be improved further.

2 Consistency Value

Sensor array, consists of n sensors, are used to measure static or gradual changing parameter X directly. The measurement equation is denoted as:

$$z_i(k) = X + v_i(k) \quad i = 1, 2, \cdots, n \tag{1}$$

Where $z_i(k)$ is measurement value of the ith sensor at time k, X is the measured truth value, $v_i(k)$ is measurement noise at time k, and $E[v_i], D[v_i]$ are unknown.

2.1 Consistency Value Based on Exponential Function

Any two sensors' support degree at time can be expressed by the support degree matrix $SD(k)$:

$$SD(k) = \begin{bmatrix} 1 & a_{12}(k) & \cdots & a_{1n}(k) \\ a_{21}(k) & 1 & \cdots & a_{2n}(k) \\ \vdots & \vdots & 1 & \vdots \\ a_{n1}(k) & a_{n2}(k) & \cdots & 1 \end{bmatrix} \tag{2}$$

$a_{ij}(k)$ reflects the closeness of the measurement values of two sensors at time k. And support degree of the measurement values of sensor i and j at time k is given by:

$$a_{ij}(k) = \exp(-\alpha(z_i(k) - z_j(k))^2) \tag{3}$$

α is an adjustable parameter. Usually the support degree between measurements is 0 or 1, and using exponential attenuation function to quantize the support degree can avoid absolute quality.

Obviously, if $\sum_{j=1}^{n} a_{ij}(k)$ has a relative large value, the sensor i is more consistent with other sensors, and vice versa [10]. Consistency Value of sensor i with all the other sensors at time k is given by:

$$r_i(k) = \frac{\sum_{j=1}^{n} a_{ij}(k)}{n} \tag{4}$$

$r_i(k)$ reflects the closeness of the measurement values of sensor i with all the other sensors (sensor i included) at time k.

2.2 Weight Assignment

Although $r_i(k)$ is large at a certain time, it doesn't mean that sensor i is always reliable at any time. For example, $r_i(k)$ is relative larger at time k, but become relative smaller at time $k-1$, so we cannot think the measurement of sensor i is reliable. In addition, avoiding data saturation and ensuring sensitivity of the fusion algorithm, we try to find out the redundant information by using of two consecutive measurements which can show the significance to distinguish different factor influence degree.

Definition 1. Considering the influence on the weight coefficient by the proportion of Consistency Value of sensor i, the mean value of $r_i(k)$ and $r_i(k-1)$ should be calculated as fusion basic quotient $P_B(k)$:

$$P_B(k) = \frac{r_i(k-1) + r_i(k)}{2} \tag{5}$$

This weight quotient is based on the fact that we would always believe the new information is more useful than the older information, so the weight for the last two data value should be more important than the old ones. Know from the fusion weight coefficient assignment in [8], $P_B(k)$ just shows itself sensitive than the summation of $r_i(k)$ within the time limit. On the other hand, it can make the reduction of computation and storage complexity at the same time obviously.

Definition 2. Considering the mutual influence on fusion result by the support degree between Consistency Value of sensor i at time k and $k-1$, correlation degree $R_C(k)$ of Consistency Value between two consecutive measurements can be defined as:

$$R_C(k) = 4r_i(k) \cdot r_i(k-1) / [r_i(k) + r_i(k-1)]^2 \tag{6}$$

Where $0 < R_C(k) \le 1$, and if $r_i(k) = r_i(k-1)$, then $R_C(k) = 1$.

Definition 3. Considering the influence of correlation degree on fusion algorithm, the fusion correlation degree quotient can be defined as:

$$P_R(k) = \frac{4r_i(k) \cdot r_i(k-1)}{[r_i(k) + r_i(k-1)]^2} \cdot \frac{r_i(k) + r_i(k-1)}{2} \tag{7}$$

Note that $P_R(k)$ is always less than $P_B(k)$. The intuition behind this may be based on the following fact. We would always believe the $P_R(k)$ should more important than $P_B(k)$. For example, $r_i(k) = r_i(k-1) = 0.3$, $P_B(k) = 0.3$, $R_C(k) = 1$. In this given situation, the fusion basic quotient $P_B(k)$ is relative smaller than any other sensor, but obviously larger than others. The reliable information containing in the measurements of sensor i reflected by the $P_B(k)$ shows that the sensor i is far away from the truth value. So the weight coefficient of the sensor should be smaller even if $R_C(k)=1$.

To ensure the convergence of the fusion algorithm, the sensor should be endowed with larger weight coefficient, where both $P_B(k)$ and $R_C(k)$ are larger at the same time. So we can get convergence weight coefficient $C_S(k)$ by fusion basic quotient and fusion correlation degree quotient as follows:

$$C_S(k) = P_B(k) + P_R(k) \tag{8}$$

The encouragement and punish mechanism are taken use of to enlarge difference among consistency parameter of vary measurements. That is to say, the better sensors should be endowed with much larger weight coefficient further. So consistency parameter of measurement value of sensor i with all the other sensors at time k can be given renewedly by:

$$r_i'(k) = C_S(k) \cdot [P_B(k) + P_R(k)] = [P_B(k) + P_R(k)]^2 \tag{9}$$

After normalizing, the fusion weight coefficient of sensor i at time k if give by

$$q_i(k) = \frac{r_i'(k)}{r_1'(k) + r_2'(k) + \cdots + r_n'(k)} \tag{10}$$

2.3 Fusion Estimation

Through the above analysis we conclude the propose fusion algorithm by the following steps.

Step1. Collection of the measurements of the sensor array.

Step2. Calculation the support degree $SD(k)$ of the sensor i ($i = 1, 2, \cdots, n$) at time k.

Step3. Calculation the Consistency Value of sensor i by (4).

Step4. Calculation the fusion weight coefficient by (5) and (7).

Step5. Standardization and normalization the final weight coefficient by (9) and (10)

Step6. Ultimate fusion expression is given by

$$\hat{X}(k) = \sum_{i=1}^{n} q_i(k) z_i(k) \tag{11}$$

3 Experimental Evaluation

Four thermocouples, with observation noise distribution unknown, are used to detect the temperature of a constant temperature box, whose troth value is 3. After 20 time test, the measurement result is shown as Table 1.

Table 1. Measurement values(unit $^\circ$ C)

Measurement Moment	Measurement values			
	Sensor1	*Sensor2*	*Sensor3*	*Sensor4*
1	2.9783	2.9167	3.0062	3.8630
2	2.9426	3.0595	3.0594	2.8871
3	3.0163	3.0087	2.9906	5.1773
4	2.9705	3.1091	2.9931	3.3417
5	3.0533	3.0029	2.9952	0.5029
6	3.0147	2.9331	3.0357	7.8706
7	2.9654	3.0428	3.0627	1.7811
8	2.9279	3.0285	2.9800	5.0699
9	3.0407	3.0355	3.0645	5.0058
10	3.0595	2.9398	2.999	2.5298
11	2.9197	3.0128	4.9471	7.2454
12	2.9597	3.0264	5.0109	0.2342
13	2.8914	2.9970	4.9494	4.8433
14	3.0253	3.0846	5.0295	1.0692
15	3.0190	2.9495	4.9990	2.8553
16	3.0000	2.9841	3.0547	2.6219
17	3.0214	3.0447	3.0365	4.7335
18	3.0020	3.0338	3.0284	2.2330
19	2.9811	2.9852	2.9262	2.2979
20	3.0059	3.0157	3.0721	1.9470

To comparing the fusion result, three methods described in Table 2 have been used.

Table 2. Fusion Methods Description

Methods	Table column subhead
Method1	Mean value fusion algorithm. The fusion result at time k is the mean value of all the sensors measurement values at time k.
Method2	Fusion algorithm is proposed in [8], where $\alpha = 0.85$, $\lambda = 0.35$
Method3	Fusion algorithm is proposed in this paper, where $\alpha = 0.85$

The entire fusion result is shown as Figure 1, and we use the estimate absolute error to analyze the result.

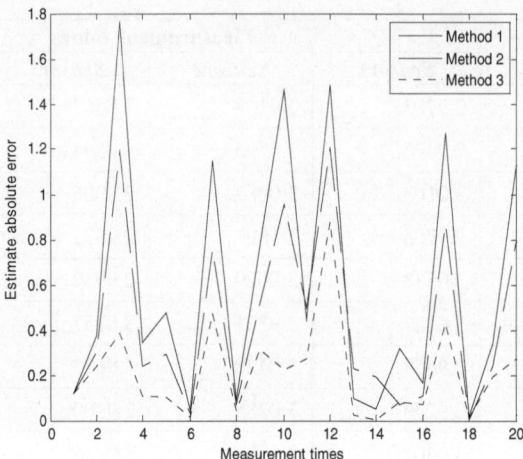

Fig. 1. Curve of estimate absolute error

Judging from the absolute error, by calculating the Standard Mean Square Error of measurement between real value sequence, we can get σ_1=0.6859、 σ_2=0.5286、 σ_3=0.3935(σ_i is the Standard Mean Square Error of method i), method 3 is the most effective as a whole, and this is more obvious after trouble happening.

The fusion weight coefficients of Method 1 are always 1. The fusion weight coefficients assignment of Method 2 and Method 3 are shown as Figure 2 and Figure 3.

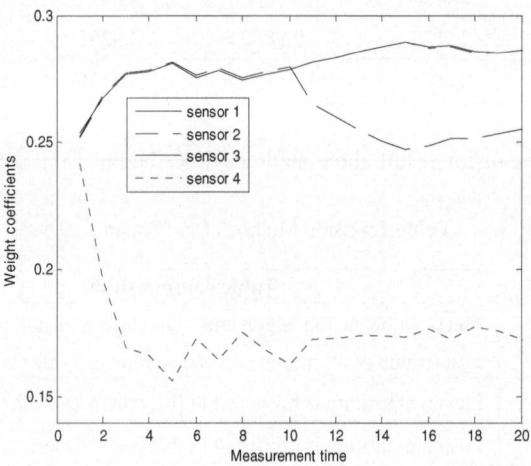

Fig. 2. The fusion weight coefficients of Method 2

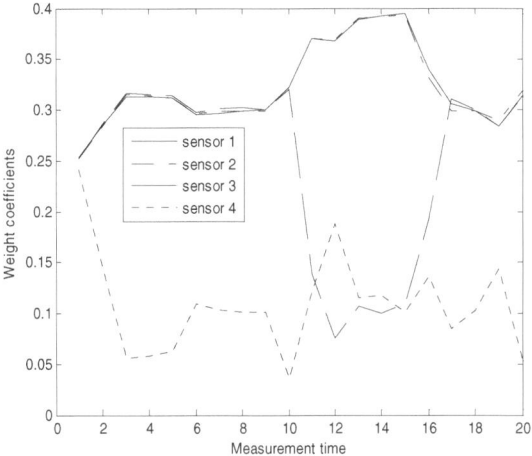

Fig. 3. The fusion weight coefficients of Method 3

From figure 2 and 3, it can be show that the weight coefficients of sensor 4 is little all the time, and the weight coefficients of sensor 2 will minish while the trouble happen. But when the trouble disappeared, the weight coefficients of sensor 2 can be re-assigned in method 3 correctly and quickly. So the weight coefficient assignment in the new algorithm is more effective and the sensitivity can be ensured when the measurement is changing.

4   Conclusion

In this paper we proposed a new multi-sensor consensus fusion algorithm. In the case of any prior knowledge is unknown, it can avoid data saturation when the measurement information increasing, and ensure sensitivity when the measurement is changing. The experimental results show that this method could get a more reliable, accurate fusion result, while we handle with the large continuous generated measurement values.

Acknowledgments. The authors wish to thank support by the Innovation Foundation 2011 of The Engineering Institute, Air Force Engineering University under which the present work was possible. And we also thank Yong Sun for his helpful suggestions for the improvement of this paper.

References

1. John, M.R.: Fusion of multi-sensor data. Journal of Robotics Research 7, 78–96 (1998)
2. Sun, S.-l.: Multi-sensor optimal information fusion Kalman filters with applications. Aerospace Science and Technology, 57–62 (August 2004)

3. Yong, S., Jie, Z., Bo, J.: A new method to improve the distributed inspection data characteristic. Electric Measurement & Instrumentation 41, 8–10 (2004)
4. Feng, H., Zhu, L., X, Z.: Measurement of multi-sensor data fusion method based on fuzzy theory. Journal of Applied Optic. 30, 987–991 (2009)
5. Wang, Z., Cao, Q., Nan, L., Zhang, L.: Precision Location Technology of Pipeline Robot Based on Multi-Sensor Data Fusion. Robot 30, 238–241 (2008)
6. Shuming, H., Xu, D., Xu, H., Zang, G.: Application of the Consistency Check by Using Measurements of the Multi-IMU for Missile. Journal of Astronautic Metrology and Measurement 26, 13–16 (2006)
7. Zhansheng, D., Chongzhao, H., Tangfei, T.: Consistent Multi-sensor Data Fusion Based on Nearest Statistical Distance. Instrument Transaction 26, 478–481 (2005)
8. Sun, Y., Jing, B.: Consistent and Reliable Fusion of Multi-Sensor Based on Support Degree. Chinese Journal of Sensors and actuator 18, 537–539 (2005)
9. Li, J., Li, H.: A Data Fusion Method Based on Improved Consensus Algorithm. Journal of Disaster Prevention and Mitigation Engineering 26, 170–174 (2006)
10. Wang, W., Zhou, J., Wang, R.: A method of multi-sensor data fusion. Journal of Transducer Technology 22, 39–41 (2003)

Melody Recognition System Based on Overtone Series Theory

Jianfeng Yang and Yin Feng[*]

Cognitive Science Department, Xiamen University, 361005, China
yangjfhello@163.com, FengYin@xmu.edu.cn

Abstract. The problems of "humming with wrong pitch" and human capability of pitch proofing are investigated first. A method about pitch proofing based on a human-computer interaction process and a pitch computational model based on overtone series theory are then proposed. Finally, a system named MIHS is developed and the experimental results show that the method is feasible and effective.

Keywords: Automatic melody transcription, humming to MIDI, computer music, human-computer interaction.

1 Introduction

Melody can be inputted into computer using some existing tool (e.g. Composer, etc.) and MIDI keyboard. But, you're required to know the score. Just like a sentence can be inputted into computer now through speech, a melodic score can also be got and recorded in MIDI format by your humming using MIHS proposed in this paper. As we know, the technology on automatic singing/humming transcription is an important issue of QBH (Query by Humming) System. Domestic and foreign scholars studying on QBH System also have conducted a variety of useful explorations on automatic singing/humming transcription and achieved very good results [1].

Although the Automatic Melody Transcription has been extensively studied, the automatic singing/humming transcription technology is still not mature enough for practical use. There are two main reasons. First, the technical reasons of system, leading to the mistaken understanding of humming melody. Second, singers themselves are unable to correctly sing the expected melody. Now, the existing researches on automatic singing/humming transcription mainly focus on the former, such as the automatic extraction of fundamental frequency from a unique note and the way to automatically determine the boundaries corresponding to a unique note [2-4]. However, the latter has been rarely concerned about. Many people can remember and recognize their expected melody through their hearing, but people's humming ability is not as good or universal as language ability. If we use the twelve-tone equal temperament to define the scale between two notes, we will find that not everyone can hum a melody flawlessly. Some people would be completely unaware of the mistakes when humming a melody. Some can also stably hum an entire melody in a tonality, but there may be a deviation of semitone interval or even more which can't be

---

[*] Corresponding author.

H. Deng et al. (Eds.): AICI 2011, Part II, LNAI 7003, pp. 479–486, 2011.

perceived by most people. Therefore, in order to obtain the expected melody from a "not entirely correct" humming melody, a human-computer interaction process of melody pitch and rhythm proofing is necessary. In this paper, we designed a new system based on a human-computer interaction process to resolve humming errors. And the system can help singer obtain the expected melody and reproduce the piano melody with synthetic sounds.

2   Theoretical Analysis

2.1   Human-Computer Interaction of Fixing Pitch and Humming Errors Processing

Humming involves two aspects of music ability. One is the ability of pitch recognition and the other is the ability to imitate singing. Most people can accurately sing the pentatonic scale (Do, Re, Mi, So, La).

Internationally, 440Hz is defined as the pitch frequency issued from the a1 key of the piano keyboard, and we call it intonation. The values that result from the pitch frequency of 440Hz divided (or multiplied) by $21/12 \approx 1.05946$ several times and the pitch frequencies calculated through the twelve-tone equal temperament are also defined as the pitch frequencies which are lower (or higher) in several semitones than the standard note a1 and the standard pitch frequencies respectively. According to this method, we can construct a mapping table between the pitch and the frequency shown in Tab.1.

Table 1. Mapping table between pitch and frequency

Pitch	..	B	c	..	b	c1	..	a1	..
Fre	..	123.5	130.8	..	247	261.6	..	440	..

The tone or music notes we hear in our daily life are mostly based on the twelve-tone equal temperament. However, the ability of pitch recognition and singing imitation varies from person to person. Most people, even some professional singers, may make mistakes when humming a melody. We'll adopt an experiment involving a person's musical hearing to illustrate this problem. For easy description, the following two definitions are introduced.

Definition 1: Ability of basic musical hearing: a person has the ability of basic musical hearing if he or she can judge any two notes played concurrently or played in order satisfied the relations described below:

- Same musical interval
- Discrepancy of semitone or even more and pitch relation between two notes

Definition 2: Ability of singing: we assume that a singer named A has the ability of basic musical hearing and define SH as a unique and monosyllabic singing note which can be recognized by the singer A.

Now, consider the following experiment of humming melody by manual segmentation.

Test1: Let a singer A sings any part of the well-known melody, national anthem of the People's Republic of China, and save it as a wave file using an audio editing tool (such as CoolEdit2001). And we assume that the singer A has the ability of basic musical hearing, so that he or she can judge whether the signal of melody in time domain satisfies the following two demands:

• Single note or several notes exist in any selected part of the melody
• Determine the general boundaries of every single note

Therefore, the singer A will be able to divide the wave file into a number of adjacent notes in time domain manually through his or her aural and visual judgments in audio editing platform. (See Fig.1).

Fig.1 is partial description in time domain of the melody, national anthem of the People's Republic of China. The boundaries of each note forming a single note are separated by a dark blue vertical line, and we call each note a sound block.

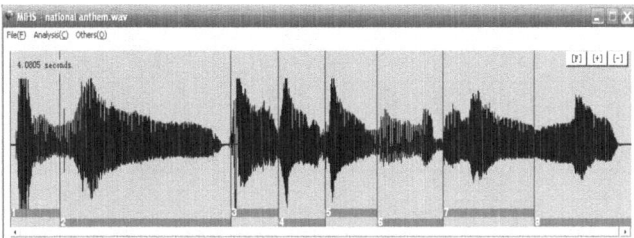

Fig. 1. Divide part of the national anthem into 10 note blocks manually

2.2 Human-Computer Interaction Process

1) Please Choose any standard pitch frequency in Tab.1
2) Play the selected standard pitch using synthetic sound (such as piano sound)
3) Play a single note chosen from any humming waveform signal using an audio editing tool (such as CoolEdit2001)
4) Compare the pitch relation between the sounds played in step 1 and step 2

a) If they are in the same interval, the pitch chosen in step 3 is same with the frequency chosen in step 2 corresponding to the pitch in Tab.1 and process ends

b) If the difference of pitch between the two sounds is the multiple of an octave and the pitch selected in step 2 is higher than that selected in step 3, choose another standard pitch frequency from Tab.1, an octave below the previous one, instead of that selected in step 2 (otherwise choose another standard pitch frequency, an octave above the previous one) and turn to step 2

c) Otherwise, choose another standard pitch frequency from Tab.1, a semitone below the previous one, instead of that selected in step 2 and turn to step 2

The singer A with the basic musical hearing can correctly complete the process of fixing pitch. The process of fixing pitch is just like the way by which the musician adjusts sound. The difference is that singer A is not as professional as the musician. Therefore, singer A can assign each note a right pitch based on the human-computer interaction 1. We identified the pitch sequence adjusted based on the human-computer interaction as "actual pitch sequence". Thus, the "actual pitch sequence" of the fragment of national anthem of the People's Republic of China is available in third line in Tab.2.

Although some of the pitch aren't accurate, most people can recognize the melody when the "actual pitch sequence" is played. This shows that the pitch contour is basically extracted from the melody. Any one has the singing ability of the music score is not difficult to find the two closest tonalities for the actual singing: G and #G. For the purpose of comparison, Tab.2 in the fourth row and fifth row, respectively, lists the pitch sequences of the melody in tonality of G and #G.

Table 2. Part of the humming melody and the corresponding pitch sequences in tonality of G and #G

Sequence number	1	2	3	4	5	6	7	8	9	10
Lyric	起	来	不	愿	做	奴	隶	的	人	们
Actual pitch	#d	g	#f	g	g	d	f	g	g	g
G: pitch	d	g	g	g	g	d	e	#f	g	g
#G: pitch	#d	#g	#g	#g	#g	#d	f	g	#g	#g

Fig. 2. Part of the standard score of National Anthem

Apparently, the Tab.2 shows that there is a deviation between the actual pitch sequence and ideal pitch sequence whatever we choose (G or #G) as the tonality of the melody. And we call this deviation "pitch error".

There are always pitch errors occurring for most people, even some professional singers, because of their limited ability. Reference [6] clearly pointed out that most of 7-year-old children can distinguish the difference of quarter note, and most 12-year-old children are able to identify the difference of eighth note. Therefore, most people have basic musical ability as long as they have accepted musical education in primary and secondary school.

2.3   Pitch Computational Model Based on Overtone Series Theory

Internationally, a variety of extraction methods for fundamental frequency have been proposed. But it's difficult to directly compare the merits of these various methods because of their differences in test method, environmental factor and singer's musical ability. Therefore, in this section we proposed a method based on overtone series theory, without filtering the signal before calculation, to calculate fundamental frequency, and experimental results showed that it has high recognition rate.

According to overtone series theory, musical note with a fixed pitch is complex tone, which is constituted by its fundamental frequency and harmonics. Generally, if the pitch frequency of complex tone T is F_T, we define K times of pitch frequency: $K*F_T$ (K is an integer).

The energy of fundamental frequency is not always largest among the harmonics. In dealing with this issue, we assume that singers with basic musical ability defined in definition 1 can judge that the melody is only constituted by fundamental frequency and K times fundamental frequencies (K is an integer). To simplify the problem, we may assume that the main components of melody are constituted by fundamental frequency and K times fundamental frequencies (K=2,..., 6).

Definition 3: T_D is a set of all the chromatic scale pitch names in a certain compass. P_N: a pitch name in T_D. F_{PN} is the standard frequency corresponding to the pitch name P_N in Tab.3. We define $[F_{PN} \cdot \frac{1}{\sqrt[24]{2}}, F_{PN} \cdot \sqrt[24]{2}]$ as P_N's frequency range based on twelve-tone equal temperament and adopt FFT transform on the humming waveform. The sizes of transform window and overlapping window are 2048 and 1024 respectively. Aw (F) is the amplitude of frequency F in window W and we assume that only one note called S_H exists in humming waveform. So the window W belongs to the signal S_H, denoted as $w \in S_H$. The pitch name S_H belongs to T_D set. C_1 is the pitch name of the musical note T_{C1}, and the corresponding pitch frequency is F_{C1}. Tab.3 presents the first six frequencies named F_K (C_1) of overtone series, the pitch name P_{NK} and the corresponding frequencies F_{12K} (C_1) based on twelve-tone equal temperament. (K=1, 2, 3, 4, 5, 6).

Table 3. First six frequencies of overtone series

Overtone series	1	2	3	4	5	6
$F_K(C_1)$	F_{c1}	$2*F_{c1}$	$3*F_{c1}$	$4*F_{c1}$	$5*F_{c1}$	$6*F_{c1}$
P_{NK}	c1	c_2	g_2	c_3	e_3	g_3
$F_{12K}(C_1)$	F_{c1}	$2 \cdot F_{c1}$	$2^{\frac{7}{12}} \cdot F_{c1}$	$4 \cdot F_{c1}$	$2^{\frac{1}{3}} \cdot F_{c1}$	$2^{\frac{7}{12}} \cdot F_{c1}$

It should be noted that there is a slight difference between overtone series of musical note and the frequencies based on twelve-tone equal temperament. In fact, the resonance of middle ear and inner ear offsets the difference. Generally, for a humming segmentation SH with a unique pitch named P, we define the corresponding pitch name of overtone series as P_k and the corresponding pitch frequency as F_{12} (P_K) (K = 1, 2, 3, 4, 5, 6). Therefore, the frequency range can be obtained by

$$D(F_{12}(P_K)) = [F_{12}(P_K) \times \frac{1}{\sqrt[24]{2}}, F_{12}(P_K) \times \sqrt[24]{2}] \tag{1}$$

Hence, the sum of amplitude of all frequencies defined in the frequency range D (f_{12} (P_K)) can be obtained by

$$S_{AK}(S_H, P) = \sum_{W \in S_H, F \in D(F_{12}(P_K))} Aw(F) \tag{2}$$

Where Aw (F) is the amplitude of frequency F in window W, so the sum of amplitude of the first six standard pitch frequencies of overtone series can be obtained by

$$S_6(S_H, P) = \sum_{K=1}^{6} S_{AK}(S_H, P) \tag{3}$$

We believe that there is a pitch named P in T_D set maximizing the value of S_6 (S_H, P) which is so-called pitch computational model based on overtone series theory. And the results of model testing and evaluation are given in the next section.

3   MIHS

The Fig.3 shows the main interface of the system-MIHS (Melody Input by Humming System) developed in Xiamen University. Click the "Show Tuning Function" button in the right bottom to display the tuning control panel. MIHS system asserts that each user has the basic musical ability defined in definition 1. Next, we will show that how users convert the humming wave file into a sequence only containing pitch and duration and reproduce the piano melody with synthetic sounds.

The whole task involves two processes. First, note block segmentation. Second, pitch adjustment process. Each process will be shown in the following section.

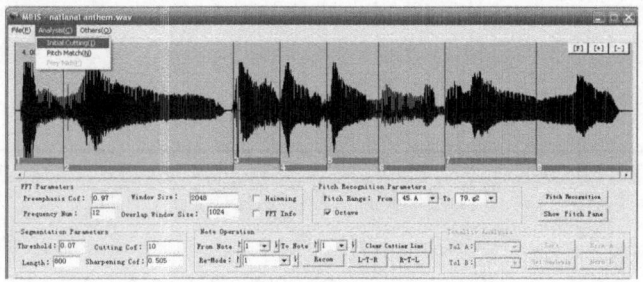

Fig. 3. MIHS system

4   Experimental Results

The evaluation of existing Singing Transcription System usually includes the following three steps:

- Let a singer sings an existing MIDI melody
- System analyzes the MIDI melody and generates result which includes a pitch name sequence and the duration relation of each note block based on frame unit.
- Calculate the pitch error rate through comparing the result with the MIDI melody based on frame unit or pitch unit.

This assessment method has two drawbacks. First, it's unable to judge the pitch error caused by the note block boundaries misjudgment or fundamental frequency misjudgment. Second, this assessment method doesn't examine the pitch errors, duration errors caused by singer or other singing imitation technologies. Therefore, the results of this assessment method largely depend on the singer's singing ability.

In this paper, we proposed an effective method making full use of singer's hearing and optesthesia to check the singing errors and system errors. And let a user with rich score knowledge to perform the evaluation of experimental results. The evaluation includes the following three items:

1) Pitch error rate by singing incorrectly is given by:

$$\frac{No\text{-}Of\text{-}Hum\text{-}Error\text{-}Block}{No\text{-}Of\text{-}Total\text{-}Block} \times 100\% \tag{4}$$

Where No-Of-Hum-Error-Block is the number of actual pitches inconsistent with the right pitches of the expected melody. No-of-Total-Block is the total number of the note blocks of the humming melody.

2) Pitch error rate by system misjudgment is given by:

$$\frac{No\text{-}Of\text{-}Sys\text{-}Error\text{-}Block}{No\text{-}Of\text{-}Total\text{-}Block} \times 100\% \tag{5}$$

Where No-Of-Sys-Error-Block is the number of pitches calculated incorrectly by the MIHS system and it reflects the pitch recognition performance of the pitch computational model based on overtone series theory.

3) Proofreading error rate is given by

$$\frac{No\text{-}Of\text{-}User\text{-}Error\text{-}Block}{No\text{-}Of\text{-}Total\text{-}Block} \cdot 100\% \tag{6}$$

Where No-Of-User-Error-Block is the number of incorrect pitches after performing the note block segmentation and tuning process.

We set the user's proofreading error rate as the final pitch error rate and the basic performance of the system. In order to compare the effects of the system using by users with different musical ability, five users had been invited to test the system. The five users have different musical ability. User A and user B can stably hum a melody in a tonality, user C sometimes may sing out of tune, and user D and user E have stronger pitch recognition ability. Tab.4 lists the evaluation results of the five users' test data. Each user sings 20 familiar melodies and the length of each melody is about 10-30 seconds. The range of all pieces of melodies is $[A, c_2]$, that is, 100 Hz to 523.25 Hz.

Table 4. Experimental results

	Total Length	Pitch error rate-sing	Pitch error rate-sys	Proofreading error rate
User A	286.97 s	9.75%	36.7%	9.55%
User B	240.96 s	6.46%	24.3%	5.89%
User C	284.12 s	24.1%	10.4%	25.6%
User D	252.12 s	3.93%	11.6%	6.07%
User E	252.50 s	1.90%	9.07%	1.90%
Average		9.23%	18.4%	9.80%

5 Conclusion

It can be seen that pitch error rate by singing incorrectly and proofreading error rate basically reflect the user's musical ability and the user's ability to use this system. Compared with user A, user B and user C, user D and user E have lower pitch error recognition rate. This human-computer interaction process is an effective way to perform this task as long as user has basic musical ability.

Apparently, compared with other tools (MIDI keyboard or music software), the MIHS system proposed in this paper can not only be as a tool for melody input, but the front-end processing of QBSH system that can improve the hit rate of humming music retrieval system.

Acknowledgements. The work described in this paper is supported by National Nature Science Foundation of China under grant No. 60975076.

References

1. Wang, X.F.: Content-based music retrieval, Northwest University PhD thesis (June 2008)
2. Lin, C.Y., Roger Jang, J.-S.: Automatic Phonetic Segmentation by Score Predictive Model for the Corpora of Mandarin Singing Voices. IEEE Trans. on Audio, Speech, and Language Processing 15(7), 2151–2159 (2007)
3. Krige, W.A., Niesler, T.R.: An HMM Based Singing Transcription System (2006), http://www.dsp.sun.ac.za/~trn/reports/krige+niesler_prasa06.pdf
4. Ryynanen, M.P., Klapuri, A.P.: Modeling of Note Events for Singing Transcription, (2004), http://www.cs.tut.f/sgn/arg/mattimryynane_final_sapa04.pdf
5. Vutaniemi, T., Klapuri, A., Eronen, A.: A Probabilistic Model for the Transcription of Single Voice Melodies. In: Proc. of 2003 Finnish Signal Processing Symposium, Tampere, Finland, May 19, pp. 59–63 (2003)
6. Zhao, S.G.: Introduction to music education psychology. Shanghai Music Press (April 2003)

Markov Graphic Method for Information Retrieval

Jiali Zuo[1,2], Mingwen Wang[3], and Hao Ye[4]

[1] School of information technology, Jiangxi university of Finance and Economics,
Nanchang, 330032, China
[2] School of advanced Vocation and Technology, Jiangxi Normal University,
Nanchang, 330027, China
[3] School of Computer and Information Engineering, Jiangxi Normal University,
Nanchang, 330022, China
[4] Math and Computer Science Department, Jiangxi Science and Technolocy
Normal University, Nanchang, 330013, China
`August813cn@hotmail.com, mwwang@jxnu.edu.cn,`
`yehao21cn@gmail.com`

Abstract. Information retrieval model is central in information retrieval, which have been studied by many researchers. But over the decade, no single retrieval model has proven to be most effective. One of the reasons is the term independent assumption. Research have shown that adding useful information to retrieval model can improve the performance of retrieval model. As graphical model can model information effectively, we use Markov network to construct the term relationship, and model the term relationship and information retrieval model in a unified framework. Experimental results show that our model can improve the retrieval performance.

Keywords: Information retrieval model, Markov Network, term relationship.

1 Introduction

Information retrieval model is central in information retrieval, which have been studied by many researches. But over the decade, no single retrieval model has proven to be most effective. There are many reasons why most retrieval models cannot achieve satisfactory retrieval performance, one of them is term independent assumption taken by some models, such as vector space model. Vector space model use vector to represent document and query, which assume that the appearance and importance of a term is independent to other terms [1]. Statistical language model defines a distribution over all the possible term sequences. But the simplest and most used unigram language model is still take term independent assumption [6]. However, it is obvious that the conditional independence assumption is rarely true in most real-world applications. Therefore, there are many researches on how to incorporate some useful information into information retrieval model.

Actually, there are two different useful information that can be used, semantic information and statistical information. Semantic information contains syntax, co-reference and named-entities [7],But more and more researches show that only simple

H. Deng et al. (Eds.): AICI 2011, Part II, LNAI 7003, pp. 487–494, 2011.

methods can yield significant improvements, while higher-level processing only yields very small improvements or even a decrease in accuracy [8].

Therefore, a more common way is to use statistical information, such as term relationship mainly expressed using term co-occurrence. Some research add the relevant information into model directly [2,3,9.10], other studies focus on query expansion[11,12,13] or feedback [14,15,16].

So many research have shown that some useful information can improve retrieval performance, and the most useful information is term relationship. But how to model this information and how to incorporate this information with information retrieval model in a unified framework still require more study.

Actually, from the linguistic point of view, we can find that the meaning of a term will be effect by its connection with other terms. As an example, when bank is connected with water, it means sloping land, and when it connected with money, its meaning is different. In information retrieval, a document relevant or not depend on the meaning of query terms. That is to say, the relevant degree of a document is decided by all the terms importance and its connection with each other.

In this paper we use Markov network to model term relationship. Actually, there are some successful applications of Markov network in information retrieval. Meltaz propose a Markov random model for term dependencies [5,15]. Different from these models, we use Markov network to model a document. The reason is although Term relationship not only exists in document but also in query that query is too short to make it hard to measure term relationship in it. Therefore, we just only consider term relationship in document. Using edge in Markov network to represent term relationship, we can model term information and information retrieval model in a unified framework.

The paper is organized as follows. In section 2 we give a brief introduction about Markov network and its application in information retrieval. Section 3 will introduce the information retrieval model we propose. Section 4 is about the experiments results, and the conclusions are given in the final section.

2   Markov Network and Its Application in Information Retrieval

Markov network is a kind of undirected graphical model that can model complex problems especially for those that contains a great deal of variant. A Markov network consists of:

(1) A Markov network can be expressed as $G(V, E)$ where V is a set of nodes of all the collection, and E is a set of edges between nodes representing dependencies between random variables.

(2) A set of functions $\Psi(c)$, each is a non-negative function assigned to a clique on the graph of.

The property of Markov network is any variable in the graph is independent of its non-neighbors given observed values for its neighbors. Therefore, different problems have different Markov network, even though for one problem, different edge configurations impose different node independencies, and then get different joint distribution. The key problem of using Markov network in information retrieval is how to construct a Markov network G and how to estimate the joint distribution P over this graph, and then use its value to measure the relevant of D and Q.

According the Markov property, the joint distribution over the graph G can be factorized over the cliques of graph:

$$P_G(Q,D) = \frac{1}{Z} \prod_{c \in C(G)} \psi(c) \tag{1}$$

Where, $D=\{t1,t2,...,tn\}$ is a set of terms, Q is query node, $C(G)$ is the set of cliques of graph G, and the functions $\Psi(c)$ are referred to as factor potential or clique potentials. Z normalizes the distribution and is hard to compute. For ranking purpose, we can infer that:

$$P_G(D \mid Q) \stackrel{rank}{=} \log P_G(D \mid Q) = \log \frac{P_G(Q,D)}{P_G(Q)} \stackrel{rank}{=} \log P_G(Q,D) \stackrel{rank}{=} \sum_{c \in C(G)} \log \psi(c) \tag{2}$$

3 Markov Graph Method for Information Retrieval Model

3.1 Markov Network Construction

Given a query Q and document D indexed by term, we can represent them as $Q(t_1,t_2,t_3,t_4,t_5,t_6)$ and $D(t_1,t_2,t_3,t_4,t_7,t_8)$, and then we construct Markov network for document D that denoted by d as figure 1 shows. In this graph, Q represent query node, t1,...,tn indicates term nodes, and edge between any two nodes show there exist some relationship between these two nodes.

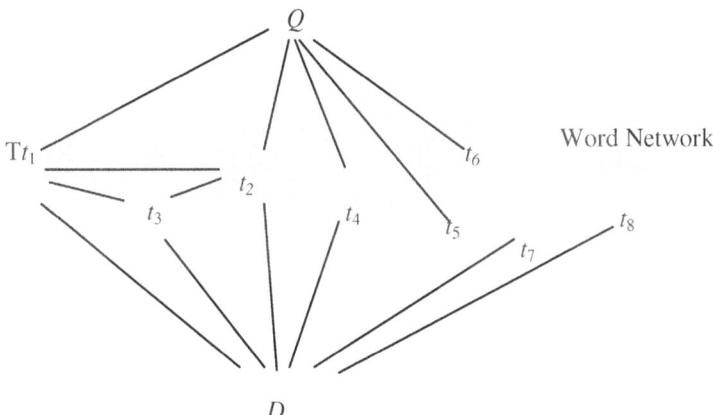

Fig. 1. A simple example of the Markov network construction

To compute joint distribution $P(Q,D)$, we need to alysis the network to get all cliques, and then define a set of potential functions $\Psi(c)$ for each clique. Consider the complexity to analyze graph we just compute cliques that have great influent to retrieval:

C_{QT1}: A clique contains a query node Q and a term node that appear in the document, and there is an edge between query node Q and term node t_i.

C_{QTn}: A clique contains a query node Q and two or more term node $t_1 \ldots t_n$ (number of terms=n), and there are edges between each two term nodes. In this paper, we set n=2, and we can consider n>2 in future work. Actually, analyze different cliques will cause different retrieval result. In this paper we just give the basic framework of our Markov network information retrieval model, and only consider cliques that contain only one single term and two terms.

C_{QT1} is about the contribution of single term t_i to retrieve, and C_{QTn} is about the contribution of term relationship. In our model, if query and document all consist of term t_i, t_j and t_k, there are relationship between t_i and t_j, and t_k have no relationship with other terms, then the graph will have clique $\{ t_i, t_j, Q \}$ to make the contribution of these three terms different. Obviously t_i and t_j is more important than t_k. As we see figure 1, there is an edge between t_1 and t_2, which means the these two terms have relationship, and the relevant degree of t_1 will increase because of the relevance of t_2. Therefore t_1 and t_2 is more important than t_4 for the relevant degree of this document over the query.

3.2 Definition of Term Relationship

In our paper, we use term co-occurrence to measure term relationship:

$$\mathrm{Re}\,l_D(t_i,t_j) = p_D(t_i,t_j)\log\frac{p_D(t_i,t_j)}{p_D(t_i)p_D(t_j)} \tag{3}$$

Equation 3 shows that window of co-occurrence is defined as sentence. Other types of windows, such as paragraph can be used too. Actually, we also consider some other methods using the distance between terms to compute term relationship, which will be discussed in the future work.

3.3 Retrieval Model

From the equation 2, we know that the potential function Ψ is important in the estimate the joint distribution. Actually the general formation of potential function is the form of $exp(\lambda_c f())$, and its definition is decided by the task and cliques we consider. In our model, we defined potential function over C_{QT1} as the matching degree between term t and query Q. This matching degree can also be regarded as the relevant degree between tern t and query Q. As the relevant degree is the term weighting in query and document, so the potential function should consist of this information.

Take figure 1 as example, we can get ranking function:

$$P_G(D \mid Q) \overset{rank}{=} \lambda_1 f_1(t_1, Q) + \lambda_2 f_2(t_1, t_2, Q) + \lambda_3 f_3(t_2, Q) \\ \lambda_4 f_4(t_4, Q) + \lambda_5 f_5(Q)] \tag{4}$$

where every feature function f_i is real-valued feature function over cliques and λ_i is the weight of the feature function. Feature function can take various forms and there also can define multiple potential functions for one clique. To simplify the model, some cliques can take the same feature function, such as f_1, f_3 and f_4. At the same time, f_1, f_2 and f_3 are not appropriate to use same feature function.

If we just consider two kinds of cliques, the general rank function will be :

$$P_G(D \mid Q) \overset{rank}{=} \sum_{c \in QT_1} \lambda_1 f_{T_1}(c) + \sum_{c \in QT_2} \lambda_2 f_{T_2}(c) + \lambda_Q f_{T_Q}(Q) \tag{5}$$

The purpose of information retrieval is to find relevant document, then ranking function turns to be:

$$P_G(D \mid Q) \overset{rank}{=} \sum_{c \in QT_1} \lambda_1 f_{T_1}(c) + \sum_{c \in QT_2} \lambda_2 f_{T_2}(c) \tag{6}$$

Equation 11 show that the ranking function has two units, which are information of QT_1 and information of QT_2. As we discussed in former section, QT_1 is about term relevant degree and QT_2 is contribution of term relationship. And λ_1 represent the weight of two unit separately, where $\lambda_1 + \lambda_2 = 1$. If λ_1 is bigger, model performance mainly influenced by term, and if λ_2 is bigger, model tent to term relationship. In extreme case, if λ_1 is set to 0, the model turn to general retrieval model, and $\lambda_2 = 1$ means that model consider term relationship only.

4 Experiments

The experiments in this section use three standard dataset: (1) Med with1033 and 30 queries. (2) Cran with 1398 documents and 223 queries. In the experiments, we only use title of the queries, title and body of document. As these three dataset are preprocessed as follows: all numbers and stopwords are removed, words are converted into lowercase, and word stemming is performing using the Porter stemmer.

4.1 Feature Selection

As we discussed above that feature selection is of great impact to retrieval performance, we use two most used feature functions in this paper, which is Language models with Drichlet smoothing[5] and BM25[16]. Some other feature functions can also be used.

4.2 Experiment Results

For the evaluation, we use MAP, P@10 and P@20 to measure the retrieval performance, and take BM25 and unigram language model as baseline model. According some relevant research, we set k=2.0, b=0.8[15] in BM25. Parameter in language model is taken 1000.

Table 1. Performance of Markov network model comparing with baseline model

λ_2		Med			Cran	
Model	MAP	P@10	P@20	MAP	P@10	P@20
Baseline(BM25)	0.4485	0.5167	0.4383	0.2850	0.2175	0.1531
MGM(BM25)	**0.4959**	**0.6069**	**0.4897**	**0.3472**	**0.2473**	**0.1727**
Baseline(LM)	0.3825	0.4600	0.3850	0.2205	0.1726	0.1285
MGM(LM)	**0.4550**	**0.5757**	**0.4569**	**0.3047**	**0.2198**	**0.1532**

Table 1 compare the result of our model(noted by MGM) and baseline model. In experiments, result of baseline model is obtained using equation 6 and λ_1 is set to 0. Actually, it is clear that our model works better than baseline model. The optimal parameter settings indicate that the proportion of the term relationship information is very large.

Table 2. Performance of Markov network model with different parameter(MAP)

	Med		Cran	
λ_2	BM25	LM	BM25	LM
0	0.4485	0.3825	0.2850	0.2209
0.1	0.4576	0.3981	0.3085	0.2481
0.2	0.4684	0.4102	0.3229	0.2647
0.3	0.4747	0.4230	0.3308	0.2771
0.4	0.4821	0.4275	0.3388	0.2858
0.5	0.4914	0.4366	0.3431	0.2921
0.6	**0.4945**	0.4460	0.3446	0.2957
0.7	0.4944	0.4513	**0.3467**	0.3001
0.8	0.4924	**0.4536**	0.3447	0.3023
0.9	0.4872	0.4515	0.3463	0.3028
1	0.4685	0.4341	0.3454	**0.3047**

In order to examine show the sensitivity of model to parameters, we do a set of experiments where λ_2 from 0.1 to 1.0, and the result of MAP is shown in table 2. From these tables we find that optimal results are obtained when λ_2 is larger. When λ_2 is 1.0, which means λ_1 is 0, the model only considers term relationship information, the result is still better than the baseline model. Actually, the reason is that potential function of QT_2 contains both term relationship information and term weighting. Although the result is better than baseline model, it is worth than the best performance. Because in this extreme case, model only contains those query term importance that has relationship with other query terms. If a query term has no relationship with other query terms, its contribution to retrieval turns to be 0. However, as a whole, the final results show that there is no other query term without relationship to other terms has little effect on the final result.

All the experiment results indicate that to some extent, document ranking depend on term contributation to retrieval, which comes from not only term weighting, but also contribution from other terms. Then, the accurate definition of the term relationship plays a very important role in retrieval performance and needs more analysis of graph.

5 Conclusion

This paper presents a general information retrieval model of Markov graph method. Different from previous studies, our model use Markov network to represent term relationship to construct a document model. The benefit of using Markov network in information is the model can use any arbitrary text features and provides an intuitive way to express term relationship. Experimental results show that the model can improve retrieval effectiveness.

In this paper, we use term co-occurrence to compute term relationship and we can explore other ways to estimate term relationship in future. Meanwhile, graph structure needs more analysis to explore more kinds of cliques. Therefore, word contribution to the search will be more accurate, which also requires more research follow-up.

Acknowledgement. This work is supported by Project supported by the National Science Foundation of China (No.60963014), the Science Foundation of Jiangxi Province (No.2008GZS0052), the Youth Science Technology Fund of Education Department of Jiangxi Province (No. GJJ10089), and the Jiangxi Normal University Youth Development Foundation (No.2049).

References

1. Salton, G., Wong, A.K.C., Yang, C.S.: A Vector Space Model for Automatic Indexing. Communications of the ACM 18(11), 613–620 (1975)
2. Rijsbergen, C.J.V.: A Theoretical Basis for the Use of Co-occurrence Data in Information Retrieval. Journal of Documentation 33(2), 106–119 (1977)
3. Harper, D.J., Rijsbergen, C.J.V.: An Evaluation of Feedback in Document Retrieval Using Co-occurrence data. Journal of Documentation 34(3), 189–216 (1978)

4. Zhai, C.: Statistical Language Models for Information Retrieval: A Critical Review. 7-Foundation and Trends in Information Retrieval 2(3), 137–215 (2008)
5. Metzler, D.: Beyond Bags of Words: Effectively Modeling Dependence and Features in Information Retrieval. University of Massachusetts Amherst, Amherst (2007)
6. Ponte, J.M., Croft, W.B.: A Language Modeling Approach to Information Retrieval. In: 21st Annual International ACM SIGIR Conference on Research and development in Information Retrieval, pp. 275–281. ACM, New York (1998)
7. Lease, M.: Natural Language Processing for Information Retrieval: the Time is Ripe (again). In: 1st Ph.D. Workshop at ACM Conference on Information and knowledge Management, pp. 1–8. ACM, New York (2007)
8. Brants, T.: Natural Language Processing in Information Retrieval. In: 14th Meeting of Computational Linguistics in the Netherlands, pp. 1–13, University of Anterwep, Anterwep (2003)
9. Gao, J., Nie, J., Wu, G., Cao, G.. Dependence Language Model for Information Retrieval. In: 27th Annual International ACM SIGIR Conference on Research and development in Information Retrieval, pp. 170–177. ACM, New York (2004)
10. Karimzadehgan, M., Zhai, C.: Estimation of Statistical Translation Models Based on Mutual Information for Ad Hoc Information Retrieval. In: 33rd Annual International ACM SIGIR Conference on Research and Development in Information Retrieval, pp. 323–330. ACM, New York (2010)
11. Bai, J., Song, D., Bruza, P., Nie, J., Cao, G.,: Query expansion using term relationships in language models for information retrieval. In: 14th ACM Conference on Information and knowledge Management, pp. 688–695. ACM, New York (2005)
12. Xu, J., Croft, W.B.: Query Expansion Using Local and Global Document Analysis. In: 19th Annual International ACM SIGIR Conference on Research and development in Information Retrieval, pp. 4–11. ACM, New York (1996)
13. Lv, Y., Zhai, C.: Positional Relevance Model for Pseudo-Relevance Feedback. In: 33rd Annual International ACM SIGIR Conference on Research and Development in Information Retrieval, pp. 579–586. ACM, New York (2010)
14. Cao, G., Nie, J., Bai, J.: Integrating Word Relationships into Language Models. In: 28th Annual International ACM SIGIR Conference on Research and development in Information Retrieval, pp. 298–305. ACM, New York (2005)
15. Metzler, D., Croft, W.B.: A Markov Random Field Model for Term Dependencie. In: 28th Annual International ACM SIGIR Conference on Research and development in Information Retrieval, pp. 472–479. ACM, New York (2005)
16. Iwayama, M., Fujii, A., Kando, N., Marukawa, Y.: An Empirical Study on Retrieval Models for Different Document Genres: Patents and Newspaper Ariticles. In: 26th Annual International ACM SIGIR Conference on Research and development in Information Retrieval, pp. 251–258. ACM, New York (2003)

Shot Boundary Detection Based on Distance Separability[*]

Shaoshuai Lei, Xinying Xu, Qian Yang, Gang Xie, and Hao Duan

College of Information Engineering, Taiyuan University of Technology
79 Yingze West Street, Taiyuan, China, 030024
lss0043@link.tyut.edu.cn, xuxinying@tyut.edu.cn ,
yq1351@link.tyut.edu.cn , xiegang@tyut.edu.cn,
dh0399@link.tyut.edu.cn

Abstract. Shot boundary detection is the first important task of content-based video retrieval. In this paper, a new SBD algorithm is proposed aiming to obtain accurate detection, and its performances are evaluated with different types of video. This algorithm computes distance ratio between within-class and between-class of two group frames, rather than the difference between two frames, which can resist light effects and camera/object movements in the same shot. The experimental results show that this universal algorithm can gain higher precision and recall.

Keywords: Shot boundary detection, Distance separability, Adaptive threshold.

1 Introduction

A sequence of frames captured by one camera in a single continuous action in time and space is referred to as a shot. There are high similarities between adjacent frames in the same shot, while low ones in different shots. Shot boundary detection aims to detect the places of shot transitions which can be broadly classified into two types, i.e., cut transitions and gradual transitions [1]. Generally, it is composed of two steps, i.e., computing the difference of adjacent frames, and comparing the difference to a given threshold. Each time the threshold is exceeded, a shot boundary is detected.

The major features computing frame-difference include pixel differences, statistical differences, histogram comparisons, edge differences, mutual information and motion vectors [2-4]. The threshold selection can be broadly classified two types, i.e., fixed and adaptive threshold. The fixed threshold implementation is simple, but it can't adapt to video content changes. In order to further eliminate subjective errors and adapt to different video types, some adaptive threshold methods are emerging [5]. The above method yielded some achievements, but there are still some difficulties [6-7], as follows:

The flash and light changes often increase greatly the differences between adjacent frames. Thus, they often are falsely detected as cut transitions.

---

[*] This paper is funded by Returned students in personnel fund projects in Shanxi Province (2009-31) and International scientific and technological cooperation projects in Shanxi Province (2008081026).

H. Deng et al. (Eds.): AICI 2011, Part II, LNAI 7003, pp. 495–502, 2011.

Motions of camera/object may lead to large differences between adjacent frames, during which, the motions are sometimes detected as gradual transitions by mistake.

The essential reason of above problems is that the difference between two frames is sensitive to light effects and object/camera movements and its anti-interference ability is poor. To solve the defects of frame-difference method, this paper uses the distance-based separability of samples directly to detect the cut and gradual transitions, rather than the differences of adjacent frames, which can effectively resist light effects and objects/camera movements in the same shot and magnify the differences of different shots.

The remainder of this paper is organized as follows. The feature vector is collected in section 2. Then, the innovative algorithm is proposed in Sect. 3, and its performances are evaluated in Sect. 4. Finally, conclusion is given in section 5.

2   Video Feature Selection

The Hue, Saturation and Value are divided into 7, 2 and 2 series respectively in HSV color histogram, and each image is quantified a one-dimensional histogram containing 36 handle according to (1), which is more consistent with the human vision than other colors space. Therefore, This means that column vector of the H, as shown in (2), can denote each frame.

$$L = 4H + 2S + V + 8 \tag{1}$$

$$H = \{H_1, H_2, ..., H_{36}\} \tag{2}$$

3   Detection Algorithm Based on Distance Separability

Establishing the sliding window W_{2L+1} of length 2L+1, set the former L frames as the sample V1, the after L frames as a sample V2, as shown in (3) and (4). And calculate the two samples between-class distance and within-class distance. At the same time, the window is moved to right frame by frame to find the maximum between-class distance and the minimum within-class distance, which can ascertain border frame. The basic principle of this algorithm is that the greater distance of two clusters of samples and the smaller divergence of each sample, the better separability.

$$V_1 = (H_{(i-L)}, H_{(i-L+1)}, ..., H_{(i-1)}) \tag{3}$$

$$V_2 = (H_{(i+1)}, H_{(i+2)}, ..., H_{(i+L)}) \tag{4}$$

3.1   Preparation

Firstly, calculate the mean vector m_i of sample V_i. m_i is the mean of each class.

$$m_i = \frac{1}{L}\sum_{i\in V_i} H_i, i = 1,2. \tag{5}$$

Then, calculate dispersion matrix S1 of sample V1 and dispersion matrix S2 of sample V2. Total dispersion matrixes SW is shown in (6).

$$S_W = S_1 + S_2 \tag{6}$$

Where,

$$S_i = \sum_{i\in V_i}(H - m_i)(H - m_i)^T, i = 1,2. \tag{7}$$

S_b is between-class dispersion matrix of sample V_1 and sample V_2.
Where,

$$S_b = (m_1 - m_2)(m_1 - m_2)^T \tag{8}$$

3.2   Construction of Evaluation Function

The fact that the maximal between-class distance and the minimal within-class distance means that shot starts to change. To ensure that the maximal between-class distance and the minimal within-class distance, it is necessary to ensure that trace(Sb) is maximal and trace(Sw) is minimal according to the distance separability criterion. So the author constructs a new evaluation function. Formula is showed as (9).

$$F = \frac{trace(S_b)}{trace(S_W)} \tag{9}$$

3.3   Calculation of F Value Curve

As the sliding window is moved to right frame by frame, F value is calculated in the meantime. When the sliding window is in the same shot, F value is essentially the same in the ideal situation. Then, the F value increases gradually when the sliding window frame by frame steps into the next shot. Only when the back L frames entirely come into the next shot and the front L frames are still in the previous shot, the F value achieves a local maximum and then decreases gradually until the front L frames entirely come into the next shot. So the frame which maximum point of F value corresponds in is considered as border frame.

Take video senses105 from the video standard library OpenVideo (URL: http://www.open-video.org/index.php) as an example, its F value curve is shown in Fig. 1. As shown in Fig. 1, the F values change little within a single shot, and in the part of potential shot transitions, F values change greatly. The figure can preferably reflect cut and gradual transitions. To further demonstrate the effect of this method, the cut curve and the gradual curve drawn from Fig. 1 are shown respectively in Fig. 2 and Fig. 3.

3.4   Adaptive Threshold Selection

As shown in Fig.1, except of several bigger F values, there are still many burrs, which are due to existence of the object/camera movements in the shots [8-9]. Since the algorithm uses the degree of dispersion between two samples, it can largely inhibit the noise caused by light effects and objects/camera movements. Therefore the values of burrs are very small, and will not affect the cut and gradual detections. We just need to set a simple threshold which can effectively eliminate the impact of these burrs. Here we use the classic double-threshold method. The method can not only remove the burrs, but also can distinguish the cut and the gradual transitions.

We can calculate the double-threshold T_H and T_L according to (10) and (11). m_F is the mean of F, and S_F is the standard deviation of   F.

$$T_H = K(m_F + nS_F) \tag{10}$$

$$T_L = Km_F \tag{11}$$

K and n are empirical tuning parameters which can be adjusted according to difference type of video.

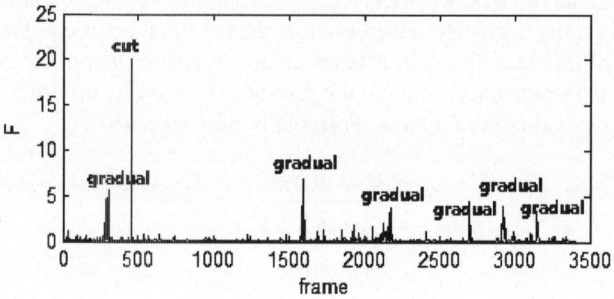

Fig. 1. The F value for processed video senses 105

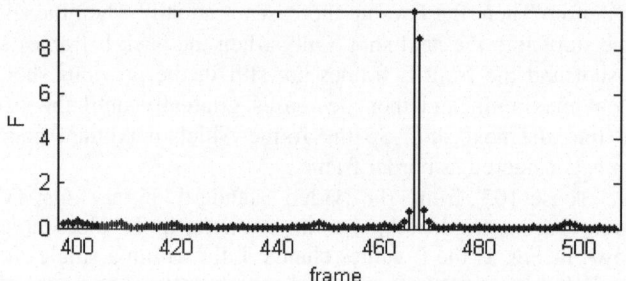

Fig. 2. One of cut boundary change of video senses 105

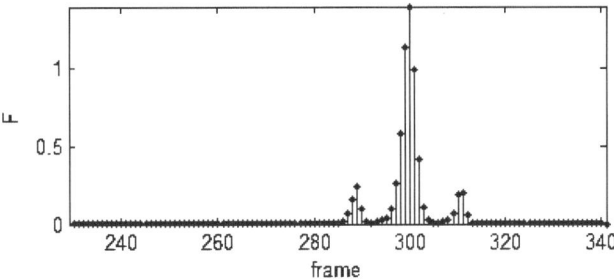

Fig. 3. One of gradual boundary change of video senses 105

To further explore the initial frame of shot boundary, F values are quantified as 0, 0.5 and 1, the result of which is expressed by V. If $F>T_H$, V value is equal to 1, where cut transitions occur. If $T_L<F<T_H$, V value is equal to 0.5, where gradual transitions occur. In the other case, V values are equal to 0. As shown in Fig. 4, the quantization of F value not only distinguishes between cut transitions and gradual transitions, but also effectively detects the region of the cut and gradual transitions. Finally the frame where the F value is maximal in every quantitative region is collected as the border frame of two adjacent shots.

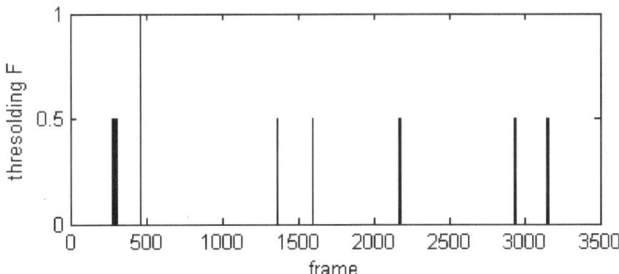

Fig. 4. The processed F value of video senses 105 by the threshold

4   Experiments and Results

To test the robustness of the algorithm, the selected video clips include a large number of flash and object/lens movements. All data are from OpenVideo and TRECVID 2001. Experiment environment is Matlab7.9.0. In these experiments, this paper uses recall and precision to evaluate the algorithm's performances.

Experimental results show that this method can suppress the changes from flashes and object/camera movements. Fig.5 shows a video clip including flashes, and as shown in Fig.6, the F value curve changes little between flash frames (No.3703, 3704 and 3836, due to the limited pages, only part frames are given here) and the contiguous non-flash frames, which ensures the flash frames will not be mistaken for cut frames. Fig.7 shows a video clip (No.1150~1301,ditto.) including object movements and camera movements, as shown in Fig.8, the F value curve is less volatile in the same shot and the motions will not be mistaken for the gradients.

Fig. 5. Clip anni006_4 including flash frames

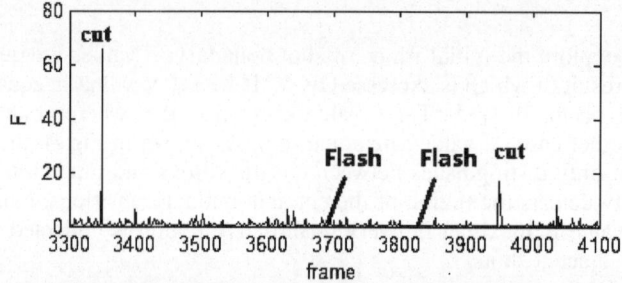

Fig. 6. F value curve of video anni006_4

Fig. 7. Video clip anni006_2 including double movements

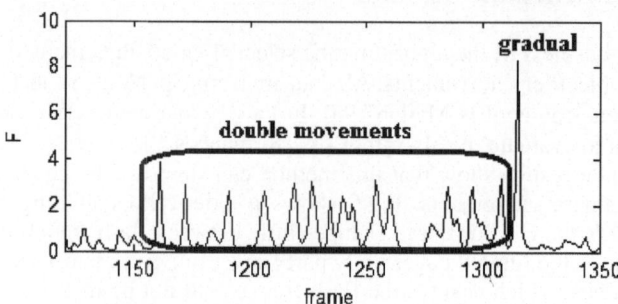

Fig. 8. F value curve of video anni006_2

In addition, there are some error cases in gradual detections for this new algorithm. Due to the fact that the gradual transition usually occurs in many frames, the distance ratio of two group frames is so small that it may not be regarded as a transition.

Table 1. Shot boundary detection results

video	Cut	Gradual	Correct	Missed	False	Recall %	Precision %
anni005_1	21	4	22	3	3	88	88
anni005_3	8	9	14	3	3	82.35	82.35
anni006_1	21	4	21	4	2	85	91.3
anni006_2	15	5	16	4	3	80	84.2
BOR03_1	20	3	22	1	1	95.7	95.7
BOR03_2	20	1	18	3	0	85.7	100
BOR03_3	19	0	18	1	2	94.7	90
BOR03_4	16	0	16	0	5	100	76.2
BOR08_1	20	8	25	3	0	89.3	100
NAD31_1	47	3	47	4	1	92.2	97.9
senses111_1	9	0	9	0	0	100	100

The experimental results are shown in Table 1. According to Table 1, this algorithm has satisfactory recall and precision, and is adaptive even for complex videos.

5   Conclusions and Prospect

This study proposes a universal SBD algorithm which can detect the cut and gradual transitions in a same step. This algorithm can achieve a satisfactory detection rate for cut transitions, and is slightly worse for gradual transitions. However, there are much more cuts than graduals in videos, and the overall accuracy can be kept at a high level.

Of course, there are still some open issues that need to be investigated:

(1) There are many kinds of gradual transitions which are complete different between each other. It is still difficult to detect all of them one by one, especially when they are combined together.

(2) Different parameter sets will be selected for different test videos. It is a challenge to make only one set of parameters suitable for various videos.

(3) There are errors between border frames of adjacent shots extracted by our algorithm and the actual positions.

In the future, we will improve our algorithm and conduct extensive experiments with larger datasets and more video types to achieve better performance.

References

[1] Yuan, J., Wang, H., Xiao, L., Zheng, W., Li, J., Lin, F., Zhang, A.: formal study of shot boundary detection. IEEE Trans. Circ. Syst. Video Technology 17, 168–186 (2007)
[2] Zhang, H., Kankanhalli, Smoliar: Automatic partitioning of full-motion video. Multimed Syst. 1, 10–28 (1993)
[3] Nagasaka, A., Tanaka, Y.: Automatic video indexing and fullvideo search for object appearances. Journal of Information Processing 15, 113–127 (1992)
[4] Zabih, R., Miller, J., Mai, K.: A feature-based algorithm for detecting and classifying scene breaks. In: Proc. of ACM International Conference on Multimedia (MULTIMEDIA 1995), pp. 189–200. IEEE Computer Society Press, Los Alamitos (1995)
[5] Youm, S., Kim, W.: Dynamic threshold method for scene change detection. In: Proc. IEEE International Conference on Multimedia and Expo (ICME 2003), pp. 337–340. IEEE Press, Los Alamitos (2003)
[6] Du, K., Xiao, G., Jiang, J.: Shot Boundary Detection Algorithm Based on Multiple Video Features. Computer Engineering 35, 243–245 (2009)
[7] Lian, S.: Automatic video temporal segmentation based on multiple features. Soft Computing 15, 469–482 (2011)
[8] Sze, K.W., Lam, K.M., Qiu, G.: Scene cut detection using the colored pattern appearance model. In: Proc. IEEE International Conference on Image Processing (ICIP 2003), pp. 1017–1020. IEEE Computer Society Press, Los Alamitos (2003)
[9] Zhu, L., Qu, J., Rahman, Asdur, M., Hong, W.: An integrated method for video shot boundary detection. In: Proc. IEEE SoutheastCon (SoutheastCon 2010), pp. 151–154. IEEE Press, Los Alamitos (2010)

The Research of Sub-domain Color Histogram Based on Weight

Gang Li[*] and Ling Zhang

Taiyuan University of Technology, Taiyuan Shanxi 030024 China
Ligang@tyut.edu.cn

Abstract. The traditional shot-cut detection technology based on block color histogram has many disadvantages: sequential block frame difference computation, block without clear boundary, computing cost and so on. The new shot-cut detection algorithm with Domain Histogram by weight is present and brings up the definition of TK (Threshold Kernel) and VF (Visual Factor). The experiments result shows that the algorithm is superior to the traditional blocked histogram.

Keywords: domain histogram; shot-cut detection; weight; threshold kernel; visual factor.

1 Introduction

It is an information age in the 21st century and multi-media information has become a major source of date. Content-based visual Retrieval(CBVR),obtained intensive attention and being researched inclusively by scientist or technician home and abroad in the field of multi-media information, has come about along with the new information century and quickly become a hot spot in the research of multi-media, especially in the research of image, video and database technology.

Shot conversion detecting is the first step of shot cut and is the basis of Content-based visual Retrieval. Although the traditional histogram algorithm has better adaptation to image rotating and the change of viewpoint, it has lost color location information. Elements in two different images have completely different locations, but may have the same histogram, which can cause wrong judgment. The principle of block histogram matching algorithm is to divide the image into sub-block firstly, than to obtain whole image distance by the accumulation of sub-block distance. In most cases, shot conversion can be determined by one or several sub-block, but it has to be computed sequentially until the end frame block in order to measure the whole image distance. This paper proposed a shot-cut detection algorithm with Domain Histogram by weight which can solve the problem of sequential block frame difference computation, block without clear boundary, computing cost and so on. The validity of the algorithm has been demonstrated by experiments.

---

[*] This work is supported by the Fundamental Project torch-plan projects of Shanxi Province No.20080322008.

H. Deng et al. (Eds.): AICI 2011, Part II, LNAI 7003, pp. 503–508, 2011.

2 Histogram Introductions

The core idea of Color Histogram Method is to statistic the frequencies of any color on an image appearing in a certain color space. Firstly, dividing the color range into n discrete interval, calculating the number of pixels per image frame fell into each interval, and obtaining its color histograms, than calculating the histogram difference between two frames as a distance measure.

Global color histogram matching algorithm uses the statistics of an entire image pixel to calculate the difference between the image frame. If we divide color space into n interval, hi(k) and hj(k) separately represent pixel numbers that the ith and the jth frame fell into the kth color interval, so distance between frames measurement function can be defined as follows:

$$D(x_i, x_j) = \sum_{k=1}^{N} \{ |h_i(k)^R - h_j(k)^R| + |h_i(k)^G - h_j(k)^G| + |h_i(k)^B - h_j(k)^B| \} \tag{1}$$

According to the formula 2 and 3, an image can be divided into several sub-blocks by histogram, and then make histograms for each sub-block respectively, finally make weighted.

$$D(x_i, x_j) = \sum_{k=1}^{N} c_k D_{i,j,k} \tag{2}$$

$$D_{i,j,k} = \sum_{m=1}^{M} |H_{i,k}(m) - H_{j,k}(m)| \tag{3}$$

Where, M is the numbers of divided color intervals, $H_{i,k}(m)$ is pixel numbers that the kth sub-block in the ith frame image fell into the mth color intervals, N is the total numbers of the divided blocks. The traditional method of block dividing is very simple in concept, which can contain certain position information in a certain degree.

3 Basic Idea and Related Definitions

According to the block histogram idea, add weight for each block, and make meaningful integrating.

A typical domain division is shown as follows in figure 1, this domain division has a common feature for many images, that is: the fact that picture is always take in the core domain or around where important contents appear. Divide the video frame into 9 blocks, set them into three domains I, II and III, each block in its domain has the same visual position lever. Obviously, domain visual contribution namely weights will increase in order according to I, II and III.

Divide the 9 blocks in a frame into 3 sets, elements in every set are equal, mainly refers to the position equivalence. Make definitions as follows:

1. core domain—I, define it as set S_I
2. core domain I's neighborhood domain— II_i, define them as set S_{II}
3. core domain I's diagonal domain— III_i, define them as set S_{III}

III_1	II_1	III_2
II_2	I	II_3
III_3	II_4	III_4

Fig. 1. Frame domain division

Then there are S(I)={I}, S(II)={ II_1, II_2, II_3, II_4}, S(III)={ III_1, III_2, III_3, III_4}. Use histogram as block feature in each block, so eigenvectors of these three domain are respectively H_I = (h_I), H_{II}=(h1$_{II}$, h2$_{II}$, h3$_{II}$, h4$_{II}$), H_{III}=(h1$_{III}$, h2$_{III}$, h3$_{III}$, h4$_{III}$), where h is the histogram for each block.

We use normalized absolute value distance for the distance of the ith and the jth frame' corresponding domain eigenvector, the definition is:

$$BD_{S(L)} = \left| H_i - H_j \right| = \frac{1}{|H|} \sum_{k=1}^{|H|} \left| h_i(k) - h_j(k) \right| \tag{4}$$

Where H is domain eigenvector, $h_i(k)$ is block histogram, using normalized RGB color space to calculate histogram.

4 Shot-Cut Detection Algorithm Processes Based the Sub-domain Histogram

According to the fact that picture is always take in the core domain or around where important contents appear, domain II is the most closely domain with core domain I, secondly is domain III, calculation method is as follows:

Step0: Initialize the parameters, i=1, j=2
Step1: calculate eigenvectors of every domain for the ith and the jth frame, HI, H II and H III
Step2: calculate the distance of core domain eigenvector BDS(I)
Step3: if BDS(I)>T1, jump to step8
Step4: calculate the distance of neighborhood domain eigenvector BDS(II)
Step5: if BDS(I)+ BDS(II)>T2, jump to step8
Step6: calculate the distance of diagonal domain eigenvector BDS(III)

Step7: if BDS(I)+ BDS(II)+ BDS(III)≤T3, jump to step9
Step8: existing shot-cut, Counting and Storing the result
Step9: if i>frameSum(the total number of frames), jump to step10, otherwise: i++,
        j++, and jump to step1
Step10: analysis end

It is very difficult to determine threshold T for distance measure between frames. Bibliography [4] proposes that we can compare the distance differences of two adjacent frames or two interval frames, if the former is more than m times the latter, shot boundary can be considered. Bibliography [5] using 5 times average difference of adjacent frames as threshold in experiment, but test results are not very ideal. Bibliography [3] proposes that histogram divides 0-255 color space into 32 sub-intervals, and select 5 times all frames' average difference ADF as shot-cut conversion detection threshold, which can guarantee a high recall and precision and take care of computing time and accuracy.

Define 5×ADF/9 as threshold core, note it as Threshold Kernel (TK). Obviously T1, T2 and T3 in the algorithm can be determined as follows:

T1=VF1×TK,   T2=VF2×4TK+ T1, T3=VF3×4TK+ T2

Define VF1, VF2 and VF3 as correction factor, which can be used to indicate visual contribution of three domains to the whole image, i.e. weight, also VF1, VF2 and VF3 can be defined as the visual factor (VF). Easy to know VF1+VF2+VF3=1, then T3=9TK. Clearly, another intuitive meaning of VF is domain zoom, so we can choose different visual factor according to different types of images.

5 Experimental Results

At present in variety of shot detection evaluational standard systems, Recall and Precision have been recognized by the academic circle and been used widely, we define them respectively as follows:

$$recall = \frac{N_{correct}}{N_{correct} + N_{miss}} \tag{5}$$

$$precision = \frac{N_{correct}}{N_{correct} + N_{false}} \tag{6}$$

Where, $N_{correct}$ are shot numbers which have been detected correctly, N_{falset} are shot numbers which have been detected wrongly, N_{miss} are shot numbers which have not been detected.

Experimental environment is Windows XP, CPU is Intel Core(TM)2 Duo T6500, 2.1GHZ, Computer memory is 3G.

We select six video sections drawn from the CCTV News in the experiment, frame rate is 15 frames per second, and the size of frame image is 320 * 240. we use self-designed experimental system VideoRetrievalPlatForm, the first frame serial number of the cutted shot to represent shot. Parameters of the Video sections are as follows:

Table 1. Experimental video parameter list

Name	length(seconds)	frames	size(M)
Xinwenlianbo-1X.wmv	170.626	2559	4.58
Xinwenlianbo-2X.wmv	238.026	3570	2.99
Xinwenlianbo-4X.wmv	320.026	4800	3.98
Xinwenlianbo-5X.wmv	196.026	2940	2.46
Xinwenlianbo-6X.wmv	221.026	3315	2.78
Xinwenlianbo-8X.wmv	147.026	2205	1.87

Obviously, the fact that important content will generally been displayed by experimental video in the center in this paper, which can exactly satisfy domain division characteristics in figure 1. we should make visual factor meet VF1> VF2> VF3, so we can choose VF1=0.5, VF2=0.3, VF3=0.2 in the experiment.

To experiment respectively according to the algorithm process above and shot –cut detection algorithm of no distinction block color histogram, obtaining the following results as figure 2 and figure 3:

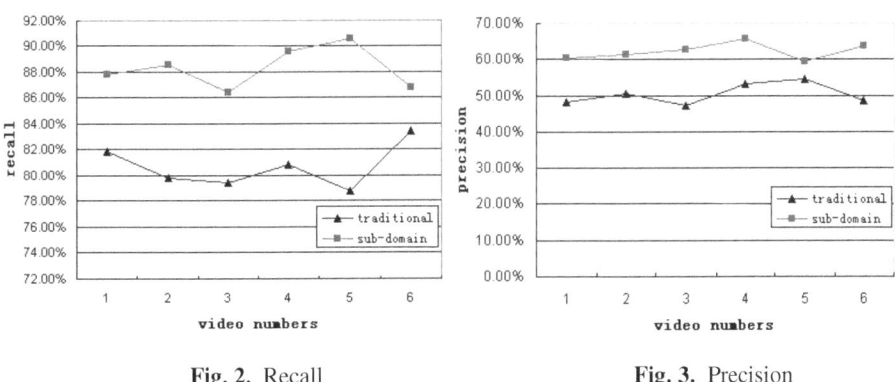

Fig. 2. Recall   **Fig. 3.** Precision

Contrast the results above we can see, compared with the traditional algorithm, algorithm in this paper have make the average recall and precision increase by 7.59% and 11.86%, and have better performance than the traditional shot –cut detection algorithm of no distinction block color histogram. According to the study results of bibliography [3], histogram divides 0-255 color space into 256 sub-intervals, and selecte 1 times all frames' average difference ADF as shot-cut conversion detection threshold, which can guarantee 100% of recall.

6 Conclusion

Algorithm in this paper has only divided the frames into 9 blocks, according to the algorithm idea, domain can be extend, however, it need to be noted that according to relevant definition of 3, the block numbers of divided frame should be the square of an odd, for example a frame can be divided into 25 blocks, in this way core domain can be determined, however at the same time there will be many multilayers of neighborhood domain and diagonal domain, and also there will bring about oblique diagonal domain. No doubt it can improve accuracy and detection efficiency of the algorithm by dividing more blocks which can further refine of each domain weight contribution to the whole image. Criterion of different domains' visual Contribution to the image, namely the determination of domain visual factor VF, is still worth studying.

References

1. Stefan, S., De Witte, V.: Histogram-based fuzzy colour filter for image restoration. Image and Vision Computing 25(11), 1377–1390 (2007)
2. Fang, H., Jiang, J.: A fuzzy logic approach for detection of video shot boundaries. Pattern Recognition 39(9), 2092–2100 (2006)
3. Li, G., et al.: Research on Threshold of Shot Segmentation based on Color Histogram. Computer Development & Applications 16(11), 9–10 (2008)
4. Zhang, Y.J., Kankanhalli, A., Smoliar, S.: Automatic partitioning of video. Multimedia Systems 1(1), 10–28 (1993)
5. Yong, H., Sun, Y.: The Research of the Key Frame-based Video Retrieval, pp. 15–17. Dalian University of Technology, Dalian (2005)

Image Annotation Based on Central Region Features Reduction

Jun Yang[1], Shi-jiao Zhu[1], and Fu Lee Wang[2]

[1] School of Computer and Information Engineering,
Shanghai University of Electric Power, Shanghai, China
mail_yangjun@hotmail.com, zhusj707@hotmail.com
[2] Department of Computer Science, Caritas Institute of Higher Education,
Hong Kong
pwang@cihe.edu.hk

Abstract. Automatic image annotation is an important and useful approach to narrow the semantic gap between visual features and semantics. However, it is time-consuming job since it extracting the visual features from a whole image to learn the relationship between low-level features and high-level semantic. In this paper, an image annotation method based on central region features reduction is proposed. Differ from the traditional annotation approach based on the whole image features, the proposed method analyze the central area which associate with the image semantics and only vision features of the area are extracted, then feature reduction based on Rough Set is used for getting the relationship between image visual features and semantics, lastly image annotation is executed. The experimental results show that the proposed method is effective and useful.

Keywords: Image annotation, Central Region, Feature Reduction.

1 Introduction

With the development of network and multimedia technology, the storage of image information is expanding quickly and image retrieval has become a hotspot of image research field [1-2]. Content-based image retrieval (CBIR) which uses image content such as color and texture to compute the similarity of images have succeeded in fingerprint and logo recognition, etc. However, there is a huge gulf which is called "semantic gap", the lack of coincidence between the low-level features extracted from the visual features and high-level semantics concept, result that CBIR cannot provide meaningful results, and current state-of-art computer vision technology lags far behind the human's ability to assimilate information at a semantic level [3].

In order to reveal image semantics at a higher level, one of the approaches is use different models and machine learning methods to find the relation between image visual features and semantics, then label the image with keywords [4-6], this is image annotation. However, these methods are lacked of considering the time consuming in the process of annotation, so it is unsuitable for the applications of real-time field.

H. Deng et al. (Eds.): AICI 2011, Part II, LNAI 7003, pp. 509–515, 2011.

To address the problems mentioned above, in this work, a fast approach for image annotation based on central area feature reduction is proposed. The consistency and robustness of observations from a great deal of studies, we found that the semantic of an image mostly in the central area instead of edge region. Differ from the traditional annotation approach based on the whole image features, the proposed method analyze the central area which associate with the image semantics and only vision features of the area are extracted, then feature reduction based on Rough Set is used for getting the relationship between image visual features and semantics, lastly image annotation is executed.

The remainder of this paper is organized as follows. The related works are introduced in section 2 and an image annotation method based on central region feature reduction and key issues are discussed in detail in section 3. In section 4, experimentation results are presented and the concluding remarks are given in the last section.

2   Related Works

Using different models and machine learning methods to find the relation between image visual features and keywords for them from labeled images, and propagating keywords to unlabeled images, this is image annotation. There are three main methods for image annotation: annotation based on image segmentation, fixed size block and annotation based on image classification [7]. Annotation based on image segmentation [8, 9] depends on image visual features and precise results of segmentation. The main point is how to correspond features of the regions to keywords. At the ideal condition, every segmented region corresponds to one object. However, the outcome of image segmentation is not satisfied at present. So there exists a big diversity between the expression of image object level part and human vision system. And this problem also exists in fixed size image division, for it may divide one object into several blocks or put several objects into one block. Compared with the two methods, image annotation based on image classification can avoid the low accuracy caused by wrong image division. Cusano et al. [10] categorized images into various groups with Support Vector Machines (SVMs) and counted the frequencies of co-occurrence between the keywords in each group. They then used them to annotate an input image. Gauld et al. [11] treated features separately and trained the optimal classifier for each feature in advance. But these method trains the way annotations are done by using features extracted from whole images and there exists a large number of irrelevant features with image semantics which located the margins of image, it will result in decreasing the accuracy of annotation. To avoid the problem mentioned above, this paper will realize annotation procedure by image classification based on central area feature reduction which indicates the image semantics directly.

3   Annotation Based on Central Region Feature Reduction

Extracting large mounts of visual features and calculating its corresponding similarity values from an image is a time-consuming job for a retrieval system, moreover, vast amounts of visual features is irrelevant to the semantics. The consistency and robustness of observations from a great deal of studies result in that central area can express the semantics of an image adequately instead of edge region. From this point of view, we extract visual features from central area instead of from the whole image, and then acquire decisive features relevant to the semantics based on feature reduction, lastly image annotation can executed automatically based on the mapping relations between low-level visual features and high-level semantics.

3.1 Central Region Feature Exaction

In order to get central region feature, we divide an image into 4×4 blocks and extract central 3×3 blocks visual features. In CBIR technology, similarity of content is measured by low-level feature which is inherent in images. The low-level feature includes color, shape, texture, etc. In our approach, we use a method of combining spatial and neighboring information based on HSV color histogram [12]. For each color, we generate its biggest prominent region area based on HSV color histogram and capture the area's neighboring information by computing its neighboring area's color roughness. By comparing the regional traits and its neighboring information, the similarity is defined as follows.

$$Sim_v(q,p) = 1 - (\sum_{i=0}^{n-1} \frac{\dfrac{|S_{avg}(q_i) - S_{avg}(p_i)|}{1 + S_{avg}(q_i) + S_{avg}(p_i)}}{\times \dfrac{|H_{area}(q_i) - H_{area}(p_i)|}{1 + H_{area}(q_i) + H_{area}(p_i)}}) \tag{1}$$

In formula 3, Harea denotes the pixel numbers of the biggest area of ith color, Savg denotes the average color roughness of the neighboring area of biggest prominent region of the ith color, and n is the number of colors based on HSV histogram.First, confirm that you have the correct template for your paper size.

3.2 Feature Reduction

Stage 1. Discretization of low-level feature values.

The purpose of feature discretization is to bring down the cardinalities in the low-level visual features. Many methods [13] can be used to discretize the low-level features values, In this paper, we adopt Entropy-based discretization method [14], uses the class information entropy of candidate partitions to select interval boundaries for discretization, to divide the continuous feature values into several disjoint sets which use one discrete value to present feature values.

Stage 2. Feature Reduction.

Reduction of Knowledge is a core issue in Rough Set theory. It is well know that not the whole knowledge is necessary to define some categories available in the knowledge considered, in another words, some knowledge is redundant. In reduction of knowledge the basic role is played by tow fundamental concepts- a reduct and the core. Intuitively, a reduct of knowledge is its essential part, which suffices to define all basic concepts occurring in the considered knowledge, whereas the core is in a certain sense its most important part.

Let C be a conditional attribute set, D be a decision set, POS denotes a positive region, U is a universe and A denotes attribute. For $c \in C$, if $POS_{(C-\{c\})}(D) = POS(D)$, we will say that c is indispensable in C, otherwise, c is dispensable. If c is an indispensable attribute, delete it from C will result in inconsistency, if all of c in C are indispensable, call C is dependant. The set of R={C-{c}} is called a reduction of C, the set of all indispensable relation in C will be called the core of C, and will be denote CORE(C). A decision table is a four-ary $T = (U, A, C, D)$ is consistent, if and only if $C \Rightarrow D$.

Based on the definition above, a visual features-semantics decision table is constructed as shown in table 1. In the table, an object set is composed by 6 images $I = \{i_1, i_2, i_3, i_4, i_5, i_6\}$, C is a set of low-level features, in the table, we call C as a conditional attribute set. $D = \{1, 0\}$ is a set of high-level semantics of the image i, it has two values in the set, 1 present semantic relevant, 0 present semantic irrelevant, we call D as a decision set.

For high-level semantics, not the whole low-level visual features is necessary, remove these redundant features will not affect the effect of classification. By reducing on the decision table 1, a mapping relationship between visual features and semantics is acquired.

Table 1. Visual features-semantics decision table

I	C(conditional attribute)				D(decision attribute)
	c_1	c_2	c_3	c_4	
i_1	c_{11}	c_{12}	c_{13}	c_{14}	1
i_1	c_{21}	c_{22}	c_{23}	c_{24}	0
i_1	c_{31}	c_{32}	c_{33}	c_{34}	1
i_1	c_{41}	c_{42}	c_{43}	c_{44}	1
i_1	c_{51}	c_{52}	c_{53}	c_{54}	1
i_1	c_{61}	c_{62}	c_{63}	c_{64}	0

3.3 Image Annotation

A framework for image annotation is given in Fig.1. Firstly, for the images in an image database, the visual features are extracted in advance and the semantics is presented by semantic network [15].The semantic network is represented by a set of keywords links to images in collection. More keywords, more complicated the image semantic is. The degree of relevance of the keyword to the associated image semantic content is represented as the weight on each link. On each link, wij denotes the degree of keyword i associates with image j. The higher the wij, the more accurate the keyword describes the image. Since the weight can be adjusted, so the process of perfecting semantic network is the process of updating keywords and its weights. Then, feature reduction is performed based on the decision table composed by the central region features and semantics, which is introduced in detail above, by doing that, a set of key features decide the image semantic is acquired. Before a new image adding into the database, image annotation can executed automatically based on the mapping of semantic and visual features.

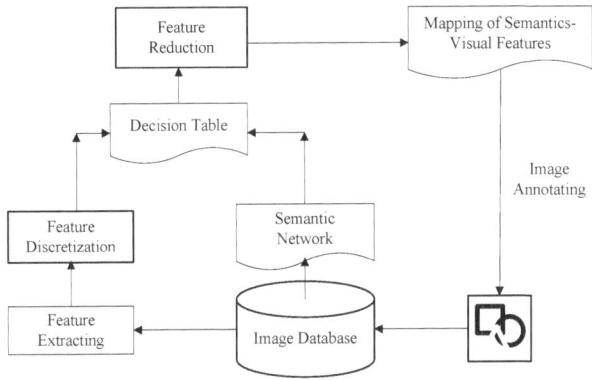

Fig. 1. A Framework for image annotation

4   Experiment

We get 1000 images from internet according to [16] which size if 24 true color. The image size is 384×256 or 256×384 which belong to 10 categories. In this paper, the image database is composed by 5 categories: beach, bus, flower, horse and building, totally 500 images. For each kind of images, 60 images are selected as training set and they are extracted color features based on central region, a decision table is built based on feature discretization. Then feature reduction is performed, from Table 2, we notice that the rate of reduction is above 80% since feature reduction remove large number of redundant features and verify the hypothesis that the visual features which associate with an image semantic only a tiny portion of total visual features.

Table 2. Effect of Feature Reduction

Semantic	Number of Visual Features before Reduction	Number of Visual Features after Reduction	Reduction Rate
Beach	97	12	87.63%
Bus	97	19	80.41%
Flower	97	14	85.57%
Horse	97	16	83.51%
Buildings	97	19	80.41%

Using the features after reduction for annotating the rest of images in the database, 40 images for each kind, the accuracy of annotation is shown in Fig. 2. The accuracy rates of flower, horse and beach are higher than buildings and bus, the reason of it is that whether the foreground or background of horse (flower, beach) is simple, the difference of visual features is small result in that the features after reducting can express the semantic well. On the contrary, the features of bus (buildings) after reducting can not present the semantic since the difference of its visual features is huge.

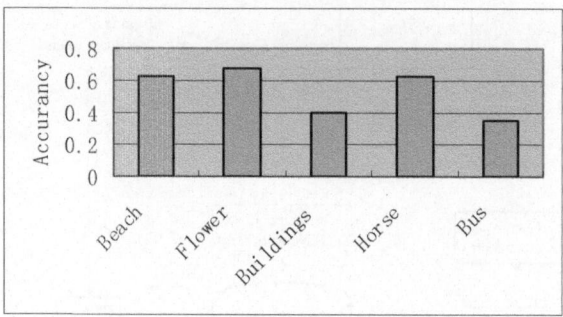

Fig. 2. Accuracy Rate of Annotation

5   Conclusion

In this paper, a method of image annotation based on central region features reduction is proposed. The benefit of the method is threefold:

(1) "Semantic gap" is one of the issues in the field of image retrieval, in this paper, a mapping relationship is established based on the feature reduction. Knowledge Reduction based on Rough Set is used to remove the features irrelevant with the semantic, since the features after reducting can express the semantic fully, it can be used into image classification effectively.

(2) Extracting large mounts of visual features and calculating its corresponding similarity values from an image is a time-consuming job for a retrieval system, in this paper, we only extract the features of the central area since it can express the semantics of an image adequately instead of edge region. By doing that, not only the mount of extracting features is decreased that the speed of calculating will be fast, but also remove a great deal of features from edge region which not helpful to improve accuracy of retrieval effect

Acknowledgment. This work is supported by National Natural Science Fund (61073189), Shanghai Natural Science Fund (09ZR1413400), Shanghai Education Commission Research Project (09YZ344), Shanghai Technology Innovation Project (09160501700, 10110502200), and Leading Academic Discipline Project of Shanghai Municipal Education Commission(J51303). The authors are grateful for the anonymous reviewers who made constructive comments.

References

1. Smeulders, A., et al.: Content-based image retrieval at the end of the early years. IEEE Trans. PAMI 22(12), 1349–1380 (2000)
2. Zhang, R., Zhang, Z.: Effective image retrieval based on hidden concept discovery in image database. IEEE Trans. on Image Processing 16(2), 562–572 (2007)
3. Naphade, M., Huang, T.: Extracting semantics from audiovisual content: The final frontier in multimedia retrieval. IEEE Trans. on Neural Networks 13(4), 793–809 (2002)

4. Peng, H., Bu, J.: Improve Image Annotation by Combining Multiple Models. In: Third International IEEE Conference on Signal-Image Technologies and Internet-Based System, pp. 3–9 (2008)
5. Osman, T., et al.: An Integrative Semantic Framework for Image Annotation and Retrieval. In: 2007 IEEE/WIC/ACM International Conference on Web Intelligence, pp. 366–373 (2007)
6. Jeon, J., Laverenko, V., Manmatha, R.: Automatic image annotation and retrieval using cross-media relevance models. In: SIGIR 2003 Conference, pp. 119–126 (2003)
7. Hu, X., Zhang, Y., Yang, L.: A New Method for Semi-Automatic Image Annotation. In: The Eighth International Conference on Electronic Measurement and Instruments, pp. 866–869 (2007)
8. Jeon, J., Lavrenko, V., Manmatha, R.: Automatic image annotation and retrieval using cross media relevance models. In: Proceedings of the ACM SIGIR Conference on Research and Development in Information Retrieval (2003)
9. Duygulu, P., Barnard, K., de Freitas, J.F.G., Forsyth, D.: Object recognition as machine translation: Learning a lexicon for a fixed image vocabulary. In: Heyden, A., Sparr, G., Nielsen, M., Johansen, P. (eds.) ECCV 2002. LNCS, vol. 2353, pp. 97–112. Springer, Heidelberg (2002)
10. Cusano, C., Ciocca, G., Scettini, R.: Image annotation using SVM. In: Proceedings of Internet Imaging IV (2004)
11. Gauld, M., Thies, C., Fischer, B., Lehmann, T.: Combining global features for content-based retrieval of medical images. In Cross Language Evaluation Forum (2005)
12. Jun, Y., Wang, J.-c., et al.: Color histogram image retrieval based on spatial and neighboring information. Computer Engineering and Applications 43(27), 158–160 (2007)
13. Dougherty, J., et al.: Supervised and unsupervised discretization of continuous features. In: Machine Learning Proceedings of the 12th International Conference, pp. 194–202 (1995)
14. Wang, W., Zhang, A.: Extracting semantic concepts from images: a decisive feature pattern mining approach. Multimedia System 11(4), 352–366 (2006)

Research of Image Retrieval Algorithms Based on Color

Hua Zhang[1,2], Ruimin Hu[1,2], Jun Chang[1,2], Qingming Leng[2], and Yi Chen[2]

[1] Computer School, Wuhan University, Wuhan, Hubei, China
zhanghua@whu.edu.cn, hrm1964@163.com, changmy0@163.com
[2] National Engineering Research Center for Multimedia Software, Wuhan University, Wuhan, Hubei, China
lengqingming@126.com, coolel_yi@hotmail.com

Abstract. With the explosion of multimedia data, the traditional image retrieval method by text couldn't meet people's demand of more accurate retrieval results any longer. Therefore, the content-based image retrieval (CBIR) has been researched to achieve more accurate results. CBIR uses image visual features to represent image and perform retrieval. Color feature is applied most widely in image retrieval systems. In this paper, we choose several common CBIR algorithms based on color to analyze their robustness to the characteristics of images. We test 9 kinds of images for the algorithms. From the experiment performance, we evaluate the adaptability of the algorithms under different kinds of images.

Keywords: Content-based image retrieval, Color histogram, Similarity matching, Evaluation.

1 Introduction

Recent years have witnessed an explosive growth of multimedia data due to higher processor speeds, faster networks, and wider availability of high-capacity mass-storage devices. The most popular traditional method is text-based image retrieval [1]. However, the content of images couldn't be represented by text-based image retrieval adequately. In this case, content-based image retrieval [2] is proposed to meet the demand of more accurate retrieval results. CBIR retrieves images by their visual features, such as color, texture, shape, etc.

A lot of CBIR algorithms have been proposed by researchers [1-4]. Choosing adaptive algorithm is an ultra important step for implementing CBIR system. Color feature is the most widely applied feature in CBIR, because color is generally related to objects in image and insensitive to noise, image degradation, changes in size, resolution or orientation [1, 4]. In this paper, we'll introduce 4 common algorithms used for image retrieval based on color. With different categories of retrieved images, the algorithms might correspond to different retrieval results. Therefore, we test nine categories of images and analyze the final retrieval results to evaluate the adaptability of the algorithms under different kinds of images.

H. Deng et al. (Eds.): AICI 2011, Part II, LNAI 7003, pp. 516–522, 2011.

2   Color Space

2.1   RGB Color Space

RGB color space [5] is defined by the three chromaticities of the red, green, and blue additive primaries. The value ranges of those colors are from 0 to 255. If all the color values are equal to 0, the complex chromaticity is black, and the complex chromaticity would be white while all the color values are 255. RGB is utilized in various applications because of its convenient for computer graphics.

2.2   HSV Color Space

HSV [5] actually is one of the most common cylindrical-coordinate representations of points in an RGB color model. HSV stands for hue, saturation, and value. In each cylinder, the angle around the central vertical axis corresponds to "hue", the distance from the axis corresponds to "saturation", and the distance along the axis corresponds to "value".

Comparing with the RGB Color Space, HSV is more closely to human perspective feeling, therefore we choose HSV to test the retrieval algorithms in this paper.

3   Feature Extraction

3.1   Color Histogram

Color histogram [6-7] represents the color feature properly. For digital images, a color histogram gives the number of pixels that have colors within the same value range, which span the image's color space and the set of all possible colors. In a color histogram, abscissa denotes the color range and ordinate means the number of pixels. The formula is defined as follows:

$$H(i) = \frac{n_i}{N} \quad i = 1, 2, ..., k \tag{1}$$

Where N is the total number of pixels, n_i is the number of pixels with color i, and k is the number of color values in the histogram. The color histogram of image M is a vector as $H(M)=(h_1, h_2, ..., h_k)$.

3.2   Cumulative Color Histogram

Cumulative color histogram [6] improves the traditional color histogram. While we use the traditional one, the color histogram will appear in several regions of zero value if the pixels of the image cannot take all possible color values. And it will affect the accuracy of histogram calculation negatively. The concept of cumulative color histogram is proposed to solve this problem. Cumulative histogram is defined as follows:

$$CH(i) = \sum_{j=1}^{i} h_i \quad i = 1, 2, ..., k \tag{2}$$

Where h_i is the color histogram above, k is the number of color values of the histogram. The cumulative color histogram of image M is a vector as $CH(M)=(ch_1, ch_2, ..., ch_k)$.

3.3 Color Histogram Based on Partitioning

However the retrieval result of color histogram cannot satisfy us as it does not give the distribution of the color. The segmentation-based color histogram [4, 8] can solve the problem. Divide image into several sub-parts, then calculate each sub-parts' local color histogram. After that, calculate the corresponding similarity between the sub-parts at the same position in two images. At last we can get the overall color similarity by cumulating the local similarity of sub-parts with the specified weights.

3.4 Color Histogram Based on Representative Color and Partitioning

Representative color in an image means the color which value number is the most. In most cases, representative color of these images is also similar when two images are similar. Color histogram based on primary color is in view of this thought.

If we combine representative color-based color histogram with the histogram based on partitioning, we can get a new algorithm: color histogram based on representative color and partitioning [3]. Instead of calculate every sub-block's local color histogram, we calculate their representative colors.

4 Similarity Matching

4.1 Histogram Intersection

Histogram intersection [6] is proposed by Swain in 1991, and it suppresses the background effect well. The calculation process of histogram intersection is simple and fast. It is defined as follows:

$$d(A,B) = \sum_{i=1}^{n} \min(a_i, b_i) \tag{3}$$

Where A and B represent feature vectors of image A and image B, and n is the dimension of the vector.

4.2 Euclidean Distance

Euclidean distance [7] calculates the distance between two points which would measure with a ruler. While we can calculate two pixels' distance by using it. The formula is given below:

$$d(A,B) = [\sum_{i=1}^{n} |a_i - b_i|^2]^{\frac{1}{2}}$$ (4)

Where A and B are feature vectors, n is the dimension of the vector. Many image retrieval systems choose the Euclidean distance to measure the image similarity. For example, MARS system calculates the similarity of texture feature by using it; Netra uses it to calculate similarity of color and shape.

4.3 Quadratic Distance

Quadratic distance [7] has proven to be more effective than the Euclidean distance and histogram intersection in similarity measurement, because the similarity between different colors is taken into account in this method. Quadratic distance can be expressed as that:

$$d(A,B) = \sqrt{(A-B)^T M (A-B)}$$ (5)

In this formulation, M=[m_{ij}], m_{ij} means the similarity between two colors which values are i and j in color histogram. This approach consider of the color that are similar but not the same. But the calculation of Quadratic distance is complex.

As Euclidean distance is being widely used and effective, in this paper, we choose Euclidean distance in feature matching.

5 Experiment and Evaluation

5.1 Approach of Evaluation

The evaluation methods have the representative features: precision and recall. They are two popular metrics for evaluating the correctness of a pattern recognition algorithm, and also used in evaluate images' retrieval results recently.

Precision [4] in image retrieval is the fraction of retrieved images that are relevant to the search:

$$P = \frac{\{relevant\_images\} \cap \{retrieved\_images\}}{retrieved\_images}$$ (6)

Recall [4] in image retrieval is the fraction of the images that are relevant to the query which are successfully retrieved.

$$R = \frac{\{relevant\_images\} \cap \{retrieved\_images\}}{relevant\_images}$$ (7)

5.2 Experiment

Image database used in our experiments is Corel Image Gallery. There are over 60,000 images in Corel image database, covering people, natural scenery, animals, plants, buildings and so on. In this experiment, we picked up 9 categories of images from the Corel: bus, elephant, scenery, flower, coastline, beach, horse, waterfall and mountain. The number of image of every image category is around 100, which the number of similar images is 25 or so. We choose 4 algorithms to test (Table 1).

Table 1. Retrieval algorithms

Color Space	Feature extraction	Match	Symbol
HSV	Color Histogram	Euclidean distance	H-CH-E
	Cumulative Color Histogram		H-CCH-E
	Color Histogram based on partitioning		H-PCH-E
	Color Histogram based on representative color and partitioning		H-RPCH-E

During the experiment, we set threshold N, which indicates the maximum number of retrieved images in once retrieval.

Set N = 10,20, ..., 60, calculate each relevant image's precision and recall rate, then use the total number of images to calculate the average precision and the average recall.

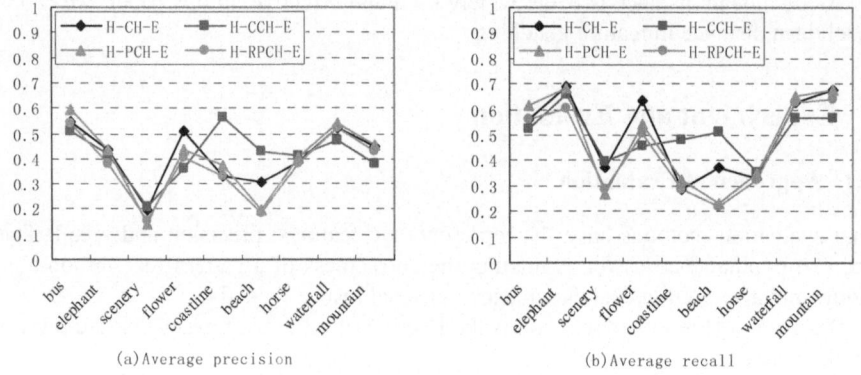

(a)Average precision   (b)Average recall

Fig. 1. Average precision and average recall on the 9 categories of images

Since the similar images' total number of our selected image category are around 25, close to 30, so firstly we take N = 30, calculate the average precision and average recall on the 9 categories of images, then compare algorithms' efficiency with different types of images. The retrieval result is as Fig. 1.

From Fig. 1, we can see that, the retrieval results are significantly different when retrieving different images with same algorithm. For further analysis, we calculate different algorithms' precision and recall with 9 categories of images when N = 10, 20, ..., 60. Based on Fig. 1, we choose two categories of images which retrieval results are typical: Bus and Scenery.

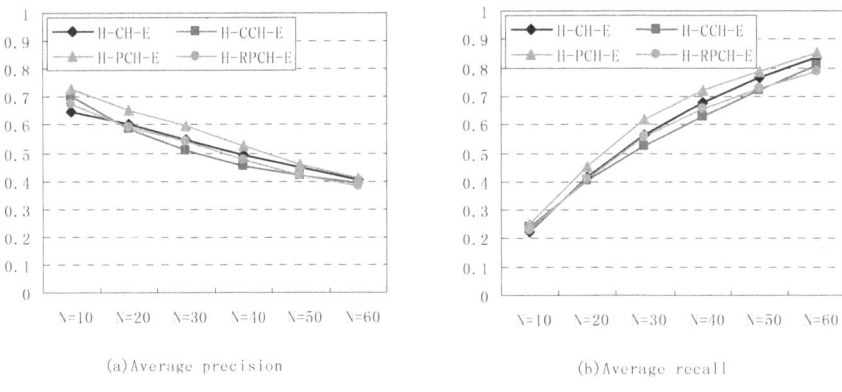

(a)Average precision

(b)Average recall

Fig. 2. Average precision and average recall on Bus image database

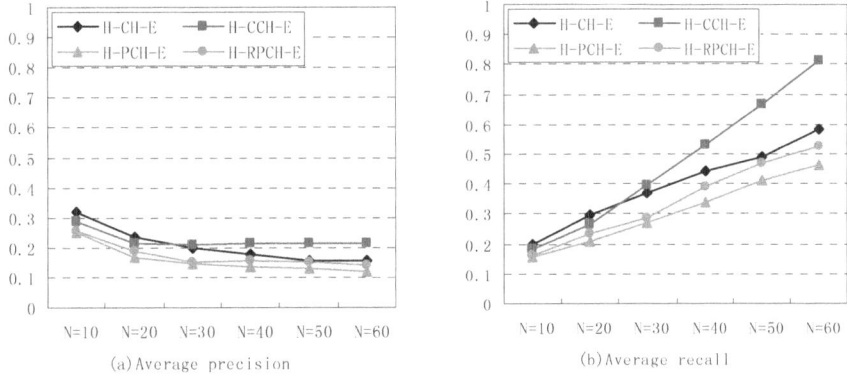

(a)Average precision

(b)Average recall

Fig. 3. Average precision and average recall on Scenery image database

From Fig. 2 and Fig. 3, we can conclude that, H-PCH-E(color histogram based on partitioning) and H-RPCH-E(color histogram based on representative color and partitioning) can get better retrieval results when we retrieve Bus image database. For Bus image, the main part is prominent and there is a big difference between foreground color and background color. When we use the partitioning-based algorithm, the main parts of images will be given relatively large weights to distinguish the main parts and the backgrounds to make the retrieval more accurate.

However, with Scenery image database, the retrieval accuracy of H-CH-E(color histogram) and H-CCH-E(cumulative color histogram) is higher. Images like scenery do not have specific substance, so we cannot distinguish foreground and background well. In that case, raising the main part's weight makes no sense, and global algorithm can get better retrieval results.

6 Conclusion

We introduce 4 algorithms in this paper and have experiment on them with 9 categories of images. When we retrieve images, algorithm's accuracy depends on image's characteristic. Algorithms based on partitioning apply to images having specific main parts while global algorithms are more accurate when retrieve image without clear substance. We can also improve these algorithms with cumulative or representative color histogram.

Acknowledgements. This work is supported by grants from the Major National Science and Technology Special Projects of China (No. 2010ZX03004-003-03), the National Natural Science Foundation of China (No. 60832002, 60970160, 61070080 and 61003184), the National Basic Research Program of China (973 Program) (No. 2009CB320906), and Ph.D Candidates Self-Research Program of Wuhan University of China in 2010 (No. 20102110101000100).

References

1. Rui, Y., Huang, T.S., Chang, S.F.: Image Retrieval: Current Techniques Issues. Journal of Visual Communication and Image Representation 10(3), 39–62 (1999)
2. Aslandogan, Y.A., Yu, C.T.: Techniques and Systems for Image and Video Retrieval. IEEE Trans. on Knowledge and Data Engineering 11(1), 56–60 (1999)
3. Datta, R., Joshi, D., Li, J., Wang, J.Z.: Image Retrieval: Ideas, Influences, and Trends of the New Age. ACM Computing Surveys 40(2), Article 5 (2008)
4. Lee, X., Yin, Q.: Combining color and shape features for image retrieval. In: Stephanidis, C. (ed.) UAHCI 2009. LNCS, vol. 5616, pp. 569–576. Springer, Heidelberg (2009)
5. Wang, J., Yang, W.J., Acharya, R.: Color Space Quantization for Color-Content-Based Query System. Multimedia Tools and Applications 12, 73–91 (2001)
6. Swain, M.J., Ballard, D.H.: Color indexing. International Journal of Computer Vision 7(1), 11–32 (1991)
7. Stricker, M., Orengo, M.: Similarity of Color Images. In: Proceeding of SPIE Storage and Retrieval for Image and Video Databases III, vol. 2420, pp. 381–392 (1995)
8. Qian, R.J., Van Beek, P.J.L., Sezan, M.I.: Image Retrieval Using Blob Histograms. In: Proceeding of IEEE International Conference on Multimedia and Expo. (I), pp. 125–128 (2000)

A Algorithm Based on Adaptive Smoothing and Mixed Probability Model

Xiao-hong Sui and Yan-ying Wang

Electrical & Information Engineering College, Heilongjiang Institute
of Science and Technology, Harbin 150027, China
sui_xiaohong@163.com

Abstract. According to the object surface characteristics effect on sensor signal in the sensor, in order to have the detection with robustness, adaptive smoothing and mixed probability model were adopted. When laser spot played in the complex object surface, the ring image that laser spot form was usually expressed as a strong interference image, there were still some wrong points in the test results, so a detection algorithm with robustness based on adaptive smoothing and mixed probability model is proposed, and the effectiveness of the algorithm is tested by experiment, thus the sensor detection problem in the case of strong interference is solved, and the performance of the sensor is improved.

Keywords: sensor, adaptive smoothing, probability filter, robustness.

1 Introduction

In the main task of the sensor signal processing, the identification of object surface characteristics and detection of ring radius are complementary. Through the identification of object surface characteristics, the targeted algorithm is adopted according to the different characteristics of object surface in the radius, and the radius detection provides the ring location(under the ring center is known),the main area of object surface characteristics identification is gave, the efficiency of the surface characteristics identification is improved.

The identification of surface characteristics is determined on the basis of the sensor imaging, it detects whether the blocked scattered light color had a strong interference on the image signal in the object surface, and instructs the radius detection. Because a variety of object surface characteristics cause complex and unpredictable imaging, the detection algorithm has a higher robustness than the ideal imaging. In order to realize real-time detection, the detection algorithm must be fast, and it is different from the calibration, it need to consider the time cost, which requires the detection algorithm to have some adaptability, the complex surface adopts complex algorithm, and the simple surface adopts rapid and effective method.

Based on the imaging features of the sensor, the paper proposed an algorithm with strong robustness in the complex situation. The algorithm has a good performance and can realize the adaptive selection.

H. Deng et al. (Eds.): AICI 2011, Part II, LNAI 7003, pp. 523–529, 2011.
© Springer-Verlag Berlin Heidelberg 2011

2 According to Strong Interference Detection Algorithm - Adaptive Smoothing

When laser spot plays in the complex object surface, the ring image that laser spot forms is usually expressed as a strong interference image, if such image adopts normal detection algorithm, the test results will deviate the true value to a large extent, and the detection equipment will not have the robustness.

Gaussian smoothing is the method that removes the noise and improves the detection accuracy and robustness of peak, it plays a very good purpose under strong interference does not exist, but when the interference occurs, the wide Gaussian smoothing may make the real peak position canceled. Gaussian smoothing parameter is the variance of peak; it is the average width of the discrete space window in our actual algorithm. Large window width will better remove the noise, but on the other hand, it is more likely to eliminate the real peak.

When the interference is large, an optimal filter width is necessary. In order to establish algorithm to select the best filter width, a cost function is built, the filter width as: $W = [w_1, w_2, \cdots w_N]$, In this formula, w_i is the filter width adopted in the first i scan line. Cost function as:

$$F(W) = A \times \sum_{i=1}^{N} \left(\frac{w_i - w_0}{w_0} \right) + B \times \sigma^2 \tag{1}$$

In this formula, w_0 is the filter width adopted in the sensor calibration, A and B are respectively the weights of width difference and variance. σ^2 is the variance of the scan line detection position:

$$\sigma^2 = \mathrm{var}(l) = E\left[\left(l - \bar{l} \right)^2 \right] \tag{2}$$

In this formula, $l = [l_1, l_i, \cdots l_N]$ is the detection position, l_i is the test result of the first scan line. The purpose of the cost function optimization is that finds the right W_{opt} and makes the final function value be minimal:

$$W_{opt} = \arg\min_{W}(F(W)) \tag{3}$$

The cost function optimization is a discrete multi-variable optimization process:

(1) Initialization: The scan lines adopt all possible filter width to filter, and detect the corresponding peak position, thus the complete mapping from the filter width to detect location is established. The initial filter width is selected as the calibration filter width, when it combines with the appropriate test position, the initial cost function value is given.

(2) The searching and updating process: For the first i scan line, the best filter width is selected on the basis of the filter width and test results of the current other scan lines, and according to the value of cost function. The filter width and the corresponding detection location of the scan line will be also replaced by this value.

Each scan line search and update in turn, after the updating of all the scan lines is finished, the number of iterations will increase by 1, then the first scan line is searched and updated again, which is executed in turn, it is until that the cost function value is less than a certain threshold, or the number of iterations exceeds the maximum number of iterations. The experiments show that the value of the cost function decreases rapidly after one iteration. The method that solves the smoothing problem is known as adaptive smoothing.

3 Filter Method Base on Adaptive Smoothing and Mixed Probability Mode

The width selection problem of smoothing filter is solved better by adaptive smoothing. However, because the presence of strong interference, there are still some wrong points in the test results, the results of adaptive smoothing need to handle again.

A direct removing the wrong points idea is that the threshold is adopted. The points that deviation is greater than a certain threshold are removed, and the remaining points are retained. However, from the adaptive smoothing results, the threshold is difficult to choose, because some errors caused by Gaussian smoothing have the same small deviation as adaptive smoothing, and the threshold method does not take the physical background of the problem into account, it is not a flexible method.

Because the physical background of the interference is decided by the optical system, when the error reflection point is very close to the optical axis of sensor system, it is larger possible that a clear image is appeared on the detector, and the image usually forms an approximate ring, the error points formed by the interference can also be seen as an interference radius in fact, so a removing the interference imaging method is that interference ring is orientated on the basis of the adaptive smoothing, and the detection point of interference ring is removed. However, because the imaging of optical system, the interference ring and the real ring are alternately superposed together, it is difficult to determine whether the detection point is from interference ring, and completely removing the detection point is also not a flexible method.

From the probability view, a flexible and removing error detection point filter method is proposed, the algorithm is mainly based on mixture model and EM algorithm, because the algorithm mainly adopts the idea of probability mode, it is referred to as the probability filter. The ring and true imaging have two classes, they adopt the same Gaussian probability model, the class that uses probability model to express is known as ring type, such as:

$$P = P(x, y | \theta) = \frac{1}{\sqrt{2\pi\sigma}} \exp(-\frac{[d(x, y)]^2}{2\sigma^2}) \tag{4}$$

In this formula, σ^2 is the variance of Gaussian distribution, and d is the distance from (x, y) point to ring center. Obviously, when the distance is near from the point to ring center circle, the ring probability is large, otherwise the probability is small. σ^2 represents the ring width to some extent, when σ^2 is large , there is large corresponding ring width, here, the arithmetic distance (Algebra Distance) from point to circle is approximated as $d(x, y)$,circular equation adopts the following definition, such as:

$$d(x, y) = x^2 + y^2 + Ax + By + C \tag{5}$$

Through considering comprehensively, the parameter θ of ring class is the vector $\theta = [ABC\sigma]$.

The problem of two rings is considered on the basis of building the ring class, so the problem may be considered from the mixed probability model .All the points from the ring can be used the following probability model to express.

$$P(x, y|\Theta) = \sum_{m=1}^{M} a_m P(x, y|\theta_m) \tag{6}$$

In this formula, M is the number of aliasing models, it is equal to 2, a_m is the priori weight, it expresses the proportion that each category is allocated in the total probability distribution, $P(x, y|\theta_i)$ is the probability distribution of the first i ring class, θ_m is respective class parameter. So the problem is transformed well into data loss problem, assuming that the congregation of all the detection points is R , the corresponding log likelihood of complete probability can be expressed as:

$$\lg P(L, Z|\Theta) = \sum_{i}^{N} \sum_{m}^{M} z_{i,m} \log(a_m P(x_i, y_i|\theta_m)) \tag{7}$$

In this formula, Z is missing data, it expresses that the point in the R belongs to a ring class information, $Z_{i,m}$ expresses whether the first i point belongs the first m ring class, it is the binary variable.

EM algorithm is adopted to calculate the probability that the points in the data set belong to a certain ring class. In the E step, Q equation is:

$$Q = E\left[\lg(P(D, Z|\Theta))|D, \Theta'\right] = \lg(P(D, W|\Theta))$$
$$= \sum_{i}^{N} \sum_{m}^{M} w_{i,m} \log(a_m P(x_i, y_i|\theta_m)) \tag{8}$$

In this formula, $w_{i,m}$ is the conditional expectation of parameter $Z_{i,m}$:

$$w_{i,m} = E\left[z_{i,m} \mid (x_i, y_i \theta'_m)\right] \tag{9}$$

In this formula, θ_m' is the estimation value of parameter θ.

In the M step, the parameter that makes the Q equation reach the maximum is used to update the estimation value of log parameter in the front round: $\Theta'(t+1) = \arg\max_{\Theta}(Q)$

Specifically, the derivation of Q function is calculated to obtain the following equation:

$$\frac{dQ}{dA_m} = \sum_{i=1}^{N}\left[-w_{i,m}(x_i^2 + y_i^2 + A_m x_i + B_m y_i + C_m)x_i\right] = 0 \tag{10}$$

$$\frac{dQ}{dB_m} = \sum_{i=1}^{N}\left[-w_{i,m}(x_i^2 + y_i^2 + A_m x_i + B_m y_i + C_m)y_i\right] = 0 \tag{11}$$

$$\frac{dQ}{dC_m} = \sum_{i=1}^{N}\left[-w_{i,m}(x_i^2 + y_i^2 + A_m x_i + B_m y_i + C_m)\right] = 0 \tag{12}$$

$$\frac{dQ}{d\sigma_m^2} = \sum_{i=1}^{N}\left[w_{i,m}(-\sigma_m^2 + (x_i^2 + y_i^2 + A_m x_i + B_m y_i + C_m)^2)\right] = 0 \tag{13}$$

Therefore, the value of parameters A_m, B_m, C_m can be attained   by calculating combined equation, and comparing the value to the least square fitting of calibration circle, find that it is essentially a weighted least squares fitting. Then the result is combined with equation, the solution of parameter σ^2_m can be obtained. E step and M step are repeated, it is until that the change value of Q function is less than a threshold, or when iteration steps are greater than the limited maximum, iteration steps are stopped.

4 Algorithm Testing

The accuracy of the algorithm is tested by measuring the actual object. A V-type groove object is a non-standard diffuse reflected object, so in the bottom of the V-type groove strong interference image will be formed, the object is scanned along V-type groove cross-section, a ring image is caught at intervals of $50\mu m$, the ring image is tested to obtain the radius, and the radius will be map on the distance through the calibration sensor characteristic curve, then 3D shape is obtained on the scanning lines. The results that adopt different algorithms to test shown in the Fig. 1, in the figure horizontal direction is the scanning direction, vertical direction is the distance information, their unit are the entire micron. The solid line is the actual measurement results; dashed line is the results that the scan lines are fitted. From Fig. 1 , It is obvious to see that the effect due to interference on the impact of the basic detection algorithm is better removed after using the adaptive smoothing, and the detection effect is further enhanced due to adopt adaptive smoothing and probability filter at the same.

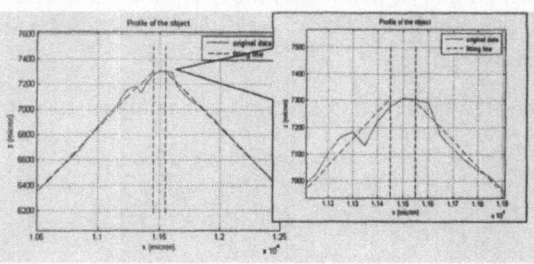

(a) Test result of the basic algorithm

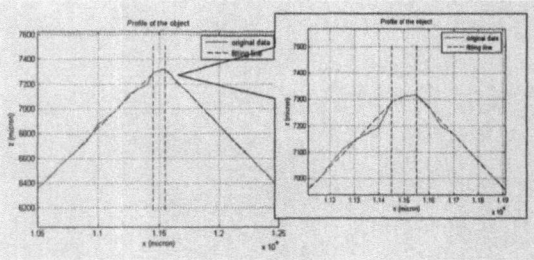

(b) Test result that adaptive smoothing is only adopted

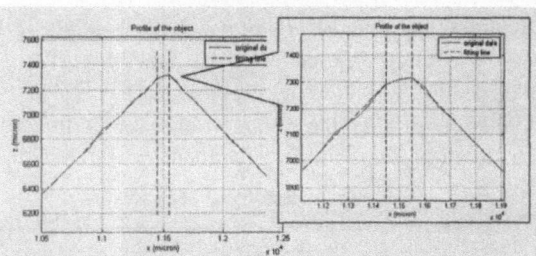

(c) Test result that adaptive smoothing and probability filter are adopted.

Fig. 1. The comparative detection results of adaptive smoothing and probability fitter

The accuracy of the algorithm is considered quantitatively to calculate detection results and the deviation between the fitting lines; the results are shown in table 1. From the table, it can be seen that the detection algorithm due to the strong interference improves the detection accuracy, and enhances the robustness of the sensor in the case of complex surface (strong interference is generated).

Table 1. The detection results of adaptive smoothing and probability fitter in the V-type object

Detection Method	Scanning Section	Fitting Standard Deviation	Fitting Standard Deviation
Basic method	[10500, 11400]	29.347	75.105
	[11550, 12500]	17.126	45.212
Only adaptive	[10500, 11400]	15.4449	39.4979
smoothing is			
adopted	[11550, 12500]	5.7626	19.0335
Adaptive			
smoothing and	[10500, 11400]	10.6929	26.9212
probability filter			
are adopted	[11550, 12500]	4.8900	12.5845

The experiment can be seen that the probability filter obtains good effect; it gives a more accurate probability from the real ring. Naturally, it can be obtained that in the case of strong interference the detection circle radius is equal to the weighted sum of all the detection position, the weight value is the probability that the detection point belongs to the true imaging ring. So the effectiveness of the algorithm is verified, and the detection problem is solved in the case of strong interference, the sensor performance is improved.

5   Conclusion

The probability filter is designed on the basis of the physical background of sensor imaging, for the case that another interference ring is formed in the ring image under there is strong interference in the imaging. Therefore, when the imaging can not satisfy this condition, the algorithm can not be used by ring image, In addition, the probability filter and adaptive smoothing all consume more processing time, so under there is only the strong interference, the treatment is used, which is ensure that the processing time of sensor signal.

References

1. Oike, Y., Ikeda, M., Asada, K.: Smart sensor architecture for real-time high-resolution range finding. In: Proceedings of the 28th European of Solid-State Circuits Conference, ESSCIRC 2002 (2005)
2. Staroswiecki, M.: Intelligent Sensors: A notional View. IEEE Transactions on Industrial Informatics 1(4), 238–249 (2005)
3. Gao, J., Wancg, X., Eckstein, J., Ott, P.: High Precision Ring Location for a New Rotationally Symmetric Triangulation Sensor. International Journal of Information Acquisition 2(4), 279–289 (2005)
4. Forsyth, D.A., Ponce, J.: Computer Vision: A Modem Approach. Prentice-Hall, Englewood Cliffs (2003)
5. Wang, X. J., Jia, Gao, J., Wang, L.: A Survey of Subpixel Object Localization for Image Measurement. In: IEEE Proceedings of 2004 International Conference on Information Acquisition, pp. 398–401 (2004)
6. Chemov, N., Lesort, C.: Statistical efficiency of curve fitting algorithms. Computational Statistics & Data Analysis 47(4), 713–728 (2004)

Discrete HARWHT and Discrete Fractional HARWHT Transforms

Hongqing Zhu

Department of Electronics and Communications Engineering
East China University of Science and Technology
Shanghai 200237, China
Hongqing Zhu, hqzhu@ecust.edu.cn

Abstract. This paper introduces a new transform known as HARWHT. It results from the Kronecker product of the discrete Hartley transform (DHT) and discrete Walsh-Hadamard transform (WHT). The eigenvectors and eigenvalues of the HARWHT transform matrices are presented using Kronecker product. Then, the results of the eigen decomposition of the transform matrices are used to define discrete fractional HARWHT transform. In addition, the study discusses the properties of discrete fractional HARWHT transform, such as angle additivity. Finally, the study investigates the application of the HARWHT and discrete fractional HARWHT in one and two-dimensional signal processing.

Keywords: Fractional, fractional HARWHT transform, HARWHT transform, Kronecker product, eigen decomposition.

1   Introduction

The discrete orthogonal Hartley and Hadamard transform have been used widely in signal processing and image processing due to their simple and efficient implementation with the help of fast algorithm [1-5]. The Hartley transform is a member of the class of orthogonal transforms along with the Fourier transform. It has similar deconvolutional properties as the Fourier transform and also has a fast implementation. It has the additional advantage that its forward and inverse forms are identical, thus simplifying implementation. It has been considered as an alternative to the Fourier transform for spectrum analysis and convolution of real signals [6]. Walsh–Hadamard transforms are highly practical value for representing signals, images and mobile communications for orthogonal code designs [7]. Recently, variations of WHT called center weighted Hadamard transforms (CWHT) [8-9] and Jacket transform have been proposed and their applications to image processing and communications have been reported.

In recent decades, various factional transforms including discrete fractional Fourier transform [10], discrete fractional Hartley transform [10], discrete fractional Sine transform and discrete fractional Cosine transform [11], and discrete fractional Hadamard transform [12] have been introduced and found wide applications in many engineering applications and science. In [12], Pei et al developed a recursive method

H. Deng et al. (Eds.): AICI 2011, Part II, LNAI 7003, pp. 530–537, 2011.

to obtain the Hadamard eigenvectors. Then, the normalized eigenvectors were used to define the discrete fractional Hadamard transform. Instead of the recursive method, Tseng [13] investigated the eigen-structure of discrete Hadamard transform for defining its fractional transform, and found the Kronecker product is more suitable to calculate the eigenvalues and eigenvector of discrete Hadamard transform matrix. Pei et al introduced the fractional Hartley transform using the relationship between fractional Fourier transform kernel and fractional Hartley transform kernel [14]. The eigenvectors of Hartley transforms are same as those of Fourier transform. The eigenvalues of Hartley can be found from the Fourier transforms.

In this paper, motivated by the COSHAR transform [15] and COSHAD transform [16], we propose a hybrid version of the Hartley transform and Hadamard transform called the HARWHT transform. The newly defined HARWHT transform results from the Kronecker product of the discrete Hartley transform and discrete Hadamard transform. The purpose is to compromise between these two transforms considering the implementation, properties and applications. Due to the one-dimensional and two-dimensional discrete HARWHT kernel matrix associated with Kronecker product, thus the discrete fractional HARWHT transform can be defined according to the result of eigen-decomposition of HARWHT kernel matrix. The numerical examples are illustrated to demonstrate the proposed discrete HARWHT transform is more effective.

2 Review of Kronecker Product

Let $A \in \mathbb{R}^{m \times n}$, $B \in \mathbb{R}^{p \times q}$, then the Kronecker product of A and B is defined as the matrix

$$A \otimes B = \begin{bmatrix} a_{11}B & a_{12}B & \cdots & a_{1n}B \\ a_{21}B & a_{22}B & \cdots & a_{2n}B \\ \vdots & \vdots & \ddots & \vdots \\ a_{m1}B & a_{m2}B & \cdots & a_{mn}B \end{bmatrix} \in \mathbb{R}^{mp \times nq} \tag{1}$$

Kronecker product satisfies the following properties:

Property 1: $(A \otimes B)(C \otimes D) = (AC) \otimes (BD)$

Property 2: $(A \otimes B)^{-1} = A^{-1} \otimes B^{-1}$ and $(A \otimes B)^{T} = A^{T} \otimes B^{T}$

Property 3: Let $A \in \mathbb{R}^{m \times n}$ have eigenvalues λ_i, $i \in \underline{n}$ and let $B \in \mathbb{R}^{p \times q}$ have eigenvalues μ_j, $j \in \underline{m}$. Then the mn eigenvalues of $A \otimes B$ are $\lambda_1 \mu_1, \ldots, \lambda_1 \mu_m, \lambda_2 \mu_1, \ldots \lambda_2 \mu_m, \ldots \lambda_n \mu_m$

Proof Property 3: According the property 1, one has

$$(A \otimes B)(x \otimes z) = Ax \otimes Bz = \lambda x \otimes \mu z = \lambda \mu (x \otimes z) \tag{2}$$

Property 4: If $A \in \mathbb{R}^{m \times n}$ and $B \in \mathbb{R}^{p \times q}$ are symmetric, then $A \otimes B$ is symmetric.

Property 5: If $A \in \mathbb{R}^{m \times n}$ and $B \in \mathbb{R}^{p \times q}$ are orthogonal, then $A \otimes B$ is orthogonal.

3 Discrete HARWHT and Fractional HARWHT Transform

3.1 HARWHT Transform

Definition 1: The one-dimension forward HARWHT transform of order m is defined as:

$$Y_m(n) = \frac{1}{\sqrt{N}}[\text{HARWHT}_m(n)]X(n) \tag{3}$$

where, $n = \log_2(N)$. The mth $2^n \times 2^n$ HARWHT transform matrix which is defined as

$$[\text{HARWHT}_m(n)] = [\text{HAR}(m)] \otimes [\text{WHT}(n-m)] \tag{4}$$

and the symbol $\otimes$ represents the Kronecker product.

In the above, $[\text{HAR}(m)]$ and $[\text{WHT}(n\text{-}m)]$ are discrete Hartley transform and Walsh-Hadamard transform of sizes $2^m \times 2^m$ and $2^{n-m} \times 2^{n-m}$, respectively. The defined $\text{HARWHT}_m(n)$ in (4) is a transform matrix, which belongs to a family of discrete orthogonal transformations ranging from the Walsh-Hadamard transform ($m = 0$) to the Hartley transform ($m = n$).

The mth order HARWHT inverse transform is defined as

$$X(n) = \frac{1}{\sqrt{N}}[\text{HARWHT}_m(n)]^T Y_m(n) \tag{5}$$

According to property 5 of Kronecker product, the HARWHT transform is the orthogonal transform.

Two dimensional forward and inverse HARWHT transform of an $N \times N$ matrix (image) are defined by

$$[G] = [\frac{1}{\sqrt{N}}\text{HARWHT}_m(n)][g](\frac{1}{\sqrt{N}}[\text{HARWHT}_m(n)])^T \tag{6}$$

and

$$[g] = [\frac{1}{\sqrt{N}}\text{HARWHT}_m(n)][G](\frac{1}{\sqrt{N}}[\text{HARWHT}_m(n)])^T \tag{7}$$

respectively.

3.2 The Discrete Fractional HARWHT Transform

According to Kronecker product properties and the defining of Walsh-Hadamard transform, one can rewrite the Walsh-Hadamard transform as follows:

$$\begin{aligned}[\text{WHT}(n)] &= [\text{WHT}(1)] \otimes [\text{WHT}(n-1)] \\ &= [\text{WHT}(1)] \otimes [\text{WHT}(1)] \otimes \cdots \otimes [\text{WHT}(1)] \\ &= [\text{WHT}(1)]^{\otimes n}\end{aligned} \tag{8}$$

The lowest orders Walsh-Hadamard transform matrix is expressed as

$$[WHT(1)] = \begin{bmatrix} 1 & 1 \\ 1 & -1 \end{bmatrix} \tag{9}$$

For example, if $m = 2$, the HARWHT transform metrics can be obtained as

$$[HARWHT_2(n)] = [HAR(2)] \otimes [WHT(n-2)] \tag{10}$$

From Eq.(8), the above can be rewritten as

$$\begin{aligned}
[HARWHT_2(n)] &= [HAR(2)] \otimes [WHT(n-2)] \\
&= [HAR(2)] \otimes [WHT(1)] \otimes [WHT(1)] \otimes \cdots \otimes [WHT(1)] \\
&= [HAR(2)] \otimes [WHT(1)]^{\otimes(n-2)}
\end{aligned} \tag{11}$$

If the eigen decomposition of matrices $[HAR(2)]$ and $[WHT(1)]$ are

$$[HAR(2)] = V_1 D_1 V_1^{-1}, \text{ and } [WHT(1)] = V_2 D_2 V_2^{-1} \tag{12}$$

According to the property 3 of Kronecker product, $[HARWHT_2(n)]$ has the following eigen-decomposition:

$$\begin{aligned}
[HARWHT_2(n)] &= (V_1 D_1 V_1^{-1}) \otimes (V_2 D_2 V_2^{-1})^{\otimes(n-2)} \\
&= (V_1 \otimes V_2^{\otimes(n-2)})(D_1 \otimes D_2^{\otimes(n-2)})(V_1 \otimes (V_2)^{\otimes(n-2)})^{-1} \\
&= V_N D_N V_N^{-1}
\end{aligned} \tag{13}$$

After the eigenvalues of the HARWHT are determined, one can easily define the transform kernel of the discrete fractional HARWHT transform by taking the fractional powers p of the eigenvalues:

$$[HARWHT_2(n)]^p = V_N D_N^p V_N^{-1} \tag{14}$$

Similar method can obtain other fractional HARWHT transform matrix if m is other value. Thus, the one-dimensional discrete fractional HARWHT transform matrix with parameter p is described below

$$X = (\frac{1}{\sqrt{N}})^p H_N^{\omega,p} x = (\frac{1}{\sqrt{N}})^p V_N D_N^p V_N^{-1} x \tag{15}$$

One can easy to find that the fractional HARWHT transform will become an identity operation for $p = 0$.

Similarly, the forward and inverse two-dimensional discrete fractional HARWHT transform with order (p, q) is given by

$$[G] = [\frac{1}{\sqrt{N}} HARWHT_m(n)]^p [g]([\frac{1}{\sqrt{N}} HARWHT_m(n)]^q)^T \tag{16}$$

and

$$[g] = [\frac{1}{\sqrt{N}} \text{HARWHT}_m(n)]^{-p}[G]([\frac{1}{\sqrt{N}}\text{HARWHT}_m(n)]^{-q})^T \tag{17}$$

respectively.

3.3 Properties HARWHT

This subsection shall present some properties of the discrete fractional HARWHT.
Properties 1: Additivity:

$$\mathbf{H}_N^{\omega,p_1}\mathbf{H}_N^{\omega,p_2} = \mathbf{H}_N^{\omega,p_1+p_2} \tag{18}$$

Proof: From Eq. (15), we have

$$\mathbf{H}_N^{\omega,p_1}\mathbf{H}_N^{\omega,p_2} = V_N D_N^{p_1} V_N^{-1} V_N D_N^{p_2} V_N^{-1} = V_N D_N^{p_1} D_N^{p_2} V_N^{-1} = V_N D_N^{p_1+p_2} V_N^{-1} = \mathbf{H}_N^{\omega,p_1+p_2}$$

The proof is completed
Properties 2: Unitarity:

$$\mathbf{H}_N^{\omega,-p} = (\mathbf{H}_N^{\omega,p})^{-1} \tag{19}$$

Proof: Using Eq. (15), we have

$$\mathbf{H}_N^{\omega,-p} = V_N D_N^{-p} V_N^{-1} = ((V_N^{-1})^{-1} D_N^p V_N^{-1})^{-1} = (V_N D_N^p V_N^{-1})^{-1} = (\mathbf{H}_N^{\omega,p})^{-1}$$

The proof is completed here.

4 Experimental Results

In this section, we shall use the triangular pulse of width 0.4 to evaluate the performance of the one-dimensional fractional HARWHT transform. Here, we have taken the number of sample points equal to 200 and the sample range is [-1, 1]. The valued of fractional order p are taken from the set $\{0.1, 0.3, 0.4, 0.6, 0.8\}$. We then compute the fractional HARWHT transform of this triangular pulse and draw the output. Table 1 list the transform results with different values of m. We can observe that the last row in Table 1 shows the angle additive, where a fractional HARWHT transform with parameter $p = 0.1$ performed by a fractional HARWHT transform with parameter $p = 0.3$ will be a fractional HARWHT transform with parameter $p = 0.1 + 0.3$. The transformed results have the close output to the transformed results with $p = 0.4$.

In the next example, we consider the two-dimensional case. The numerical results of discrete fractional HARWHT transform of image Lena are depicted in Figs. 1~2. Similar to the one-dimensional fractional HARWHT transform, the angle additivity is also existed in the two-dimensional case (see Figs.1~2). Fig.3 shows the two-dimensional inverse fractional HARWHT transform with different m. It is clearly see that the inverse transformed results are very close the original one. The experiments indicate that the fractional HARWHT transform has the potential for application in a range of areas including signal analysis and image processing.

Table 1. The results of discrete fractional HARWHT of one-dimensional triangle function with different fractional order p

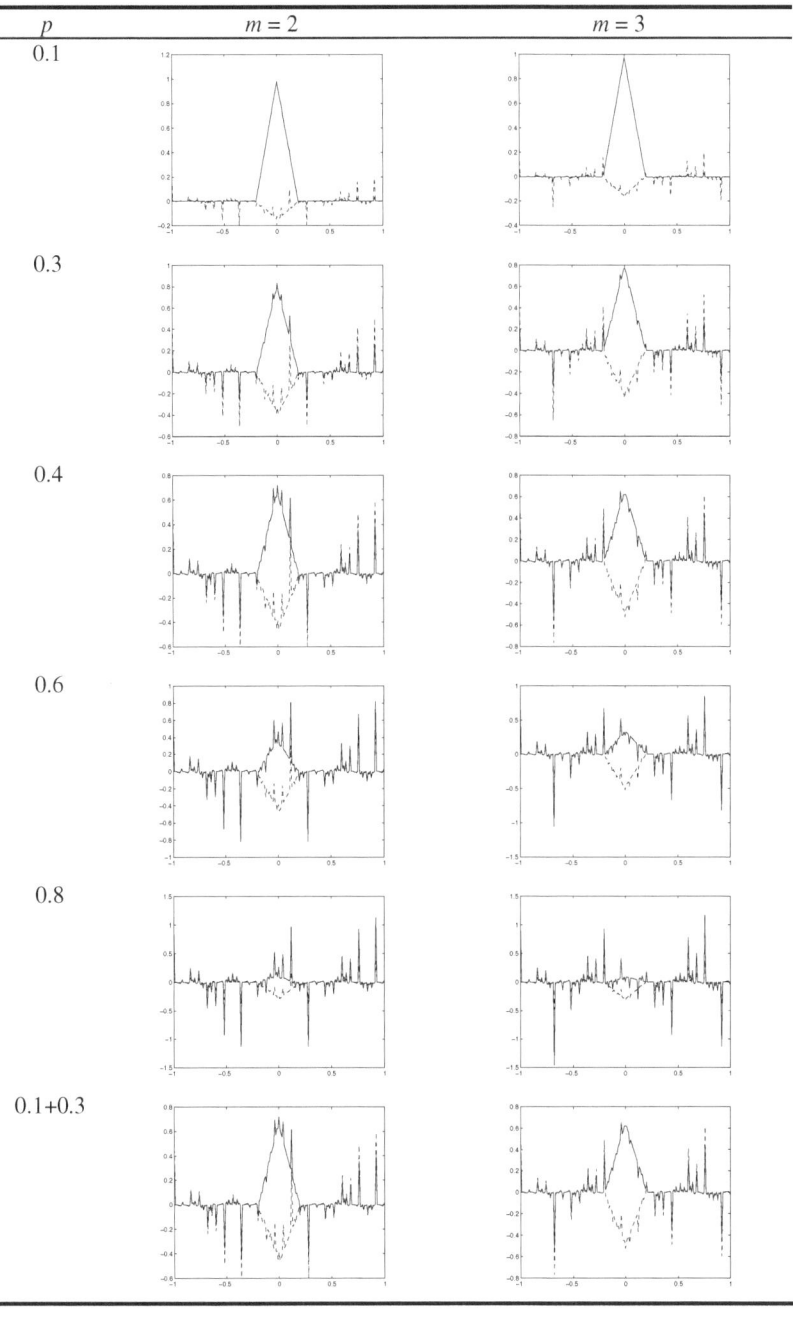

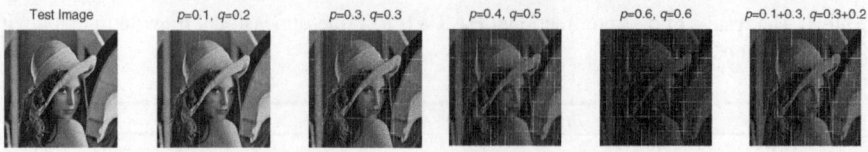

Fig. 1. The results of discrete fractional HARWHT transform of image Lena ($m = 2$)

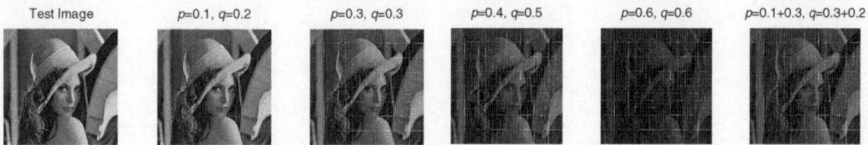

Fig. 2. The results of discrete fractional HARWHT transform of image Lena ($m = 3$)

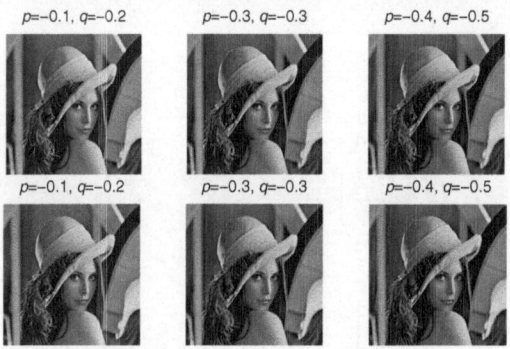

Fig. 3. Inverse fractional HARWHT transform; first row: $m = 2$. Second row: $m = 3$

5 Conclusions

In this paper, the definition of discrete HARWHT and discrete fractional HARWHT transforms had been presented. First, the eigenvector and eigenvalues of HARWHT transform matrix had been investigated using Kronecker product. Then, the eigen decomposition of the transform matrix were used to define the fractional HARWHT kernel matrices. Some mathematical properties had been discussed which were similar to fractional Hartley and fractional Walsh-Hadamard transform. The computations of the fractional HARWHT for one-dimensional triangular pulse signal and image Lena were also implemented. The simulation results demonstrated that the proposed HARWHT and fractional HARWHT transforms would help the signal processing and image processing community.

Acknowledgments. This work has been supported by National Natural Science Foundation of China under Grant No. 60975004.

References

1. Zhu, C., Xiong, B.: Transform-exempted calculation of sum of absolute Hadamard transformed differences. IEEE Trans. Circuits and Systems for Video Technology 19, 1183–1188 (2009)
2. Chen, S.X., Li, F.W.: Fast encoding method for vector quantisation of images using subvector characteristics and Hadamard transform. IET Image Process. 5, 18–24 (2011)
3. Jiang, L., Shu, H., Wu, J., Wang, L., Senhadji, L.: A novel split-radix fast algorithm for 2-D discrete Hartley transform. IEEE Trans. Circuits and Systems-I 57, 911–924 (2010)
4. Bouguezel, S., Ahmad, M.O., Swamy, M.N.S.: New parametric discrete Fourier and Hartley transforms, and algorithms for fast computation. IEEE Trans. Circuits and Systems-I 58, 562–575 (2011)
5. Moreolo, M.S., Muñoz, R., Junyent, G.: Novel power efficient optical OFDM based on Hartley transform for intensity-modulated direct-detection systems. Journal of Lightwave Technology 28, 798–805 (2010)
6. Pei, S.-C., Jaw, S.B.: The analytic signal in the Hartley transform domain. IEEE Trans. Circuits and Systems 31, 1546–1548 (1990)
7. Aung, A., Ng, B.P., Rahardja, S.: Conjugate symmetric sequency-ordered complex Hadamard transform. IEEE Trans. Signal Process. 57, 2582–2593 (2009)
8. Lee, M.H., Zhang, X.-D.: Fast block center weighted Hadamard transform. IEEE Trans. Circuits and Systems—I 54, 2741–2745 (2007)
9. Lee, M.H.: The center weighted Hadamard transform. IEEE Trans. Circuits Syst. 36, 1247–1249 (1989)
10. Pei, S.-C., Tseng, C.-C., Yeh, M.-H., Shyu, J.-J.: Discrete fractional Hartley and Fourier transforms. IEEE Trans. Circuits and Systems—II: Analog and Digital Signal Process. 45, 665–674 (1998)
11. Pei, S.-C., Yeh, M.-H.: The discrete fractional Cosine and Sine transforms. IEEE Trans. Signal Process. 49, 1198–1207 (2001)
12. Pei, S.-C., Yeh, M.-H.: Discrete fractional Hadamard transform. IEEE International Symposium on Circuits and System 3, 179–182 (1999)
13. Tseng, C.C.: Eigenvector and fractionalization of discrete Hadamard transform. In: Proc. IEEE Symp. Circuits and Systems (ISCAS 07), pp. 2307–2310. IEEE Computer Society Press, Los Alamitos (2007)
14. Pei, S.-C., Tsen, C.-C., Yeh, M.-H., Ding, J.-J.: A new definition of continuous fractional Hartley transform. In: Proc. IEEE Int. Conf. Acoustics, Speech, Signal Processing (ICASSP 1998), Seattle, USA, pp. 1485–1488 (1998)
15. Merchant, S.N., Rao, B.V.: COSHAR transform. Information Sciences 54, 131–145 (1991)
16. Merchant, S.N., Rao, B.V.: Signal processing via COSHAD transform. Comput. & Elect. Engng. 12, 3–12 (1986)

An Improved GTS Transmission Algorithm for Marine-Environment Monitoring WSN Systems

Yueheng Li[1], Meiyan Ju[1], Pengfei Ye[1], and Lizhong Xu[1,2]

[1] College of Computer and Information Engineering, Hohai University,
Nanjing, 210098, China
[2] Institute of Communication and Information System Engineering, Hohai University, Nanjing,
210098, China
{Yueheng_li,Jmy,Ypf_raul,Lzhxu}@hhu.edu.cn

Abstract. Wireless sensor network can be applied to large-scale environment surveillance such as marine environment monitoring. In such application case, besides the protocol structure and the energy consumption, the signal's real-time transmission and successfully transmitting rate of critical nodes also play an important role in improving the whole system's performance. In this paper, a new parameter called 'normalized access delay' is introduced into the media access control (MAC) layer of IEEE 802.15.4 to build a novel node time delay category table. Based on this parameter, the so-called Delay-Category- GTS (DCGTS) transmission algorithm is proposed to reduce the transmission delay and to improve the success transmitting rate of critical nodes, enabling the dedicated guaranteed time slot (GTS) can be used for high reliability and real time signal transmission in large-scale marine-environmental monitoring network. NS-2 simulation platform is built to simulate the proposed DCGTS algorithm. The final results demonstrate that the proposed DCGTS algorithm has superior real-time transmission performance and success transmitting rate to the traditional methods.

Keywords: Marine-environment monitoring, wireless sensor network (WSN), guaranteed time slot, normalized time delay.

1 Introduction

With human being's rapid economic developments, more and more attentions have been paid to marine environment monitoring[1]. Timely analysis and evaluation on the marine environment data not only provide for government scientific and rational reference to carry out environment management and decision-making, but also affect the final state strategic policy about marine sustainable development.

Marine environment monitoring oriented WSN is constructed through locating the sensors along seaside. Information can then be sensed and collected from the network within the distributed areas to improve the accuracy and timeliness of the monitoring information, making it easy to release important message like disaster-alarm. Since the working group of IEEE802.15.4 released the standard on physical layer and media access control (MAC) for Low-Rate Wireless Personal Network (LR-WPAN) in 2003

H. Deng et al. (Eds.): AICI 2011, Part II, LNAI 7003, pp. 538–545, 2011.

[2], it has been widely used in WSN for such as environment monitoring, industrial automation and control, etc. In the beacon-enabled [3-6] network of IEEE802.15.4, nodes send data in a competitive or guaranteed time slot (GTS) way during the active period of superframe. Slotted carrier sense multiple access with collision avoidance (CSMA/CA) mechanism enables nodes to transmit data in competitive way. Channel detection will consume some energy. When the network node operates in a GTS way, it is unnecessary to compete with others, so the node can transmit the data during the allocated GTS slot directly. Therefore, when node transmits its data in allocated GTS, it can not only meet the strict time delay requirement of the transmission, but also reduce the energy consumption to some extent. In a time slot within the contention free period (CFP), if the node is allocated a GTS, it transmits the data directly during the specified GTS. So there is no need to compete the transmitting channel with other nodes in a CSMA/CA mechanism. However, the current feature that only up to 7 nodes can be allocated GTS's has limited its application in large-scale network, e.g. the marine-environment monitoring application.

In this paper, we first describe a popular marine environment monitoring WSN system with star topology. In order to overcome its GTS limitations mentioned above, the parameter 'normalized access delay' is introduced, and its main idea is to divide the nodes into many groups in accordance with their different delay requirements. On the basis of the new parameter, a novel Delay-Category-GTS (DCGTS) transmission algorithm was proposed to reduce the whole network's time delay and to improve the success transmitting rate of the node's message. All of these will finally guarantee the real-time transmission and the stability of the marine monitoring WSN.

2   Star Topology WSN Architecture for Marine-Environment Monitoring

Fig.1 shows a star topology WSN architecture for marine-environment monitoring, which consists of sensor nodes, coordinator nodes and data center (DC). Each sensor node is located at the measuring point, and one or more sensors may be equipped according to the actual needs. With the improved MAC protocol of IEEE802.15.4, the sensor nodes will transmit the collected message to the coordinator nodes. After some necessary pre-processing carried out by coordinator nodes, the information will be uploaded via the small satellite station to remote DC. Finally users at different sites can

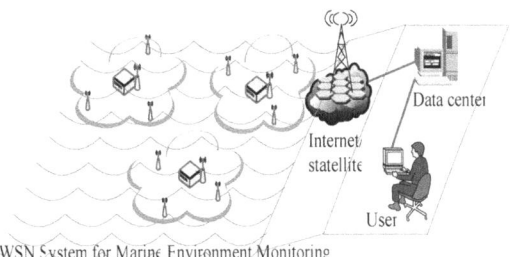

Fig. 1. WSN architecture for marine-environment monitoring

acquire the preprocessed, analyzed, or predicted results from DC. In general, the sensor nodes distributed in WSN collect the required parameters of the marine environments, and complete the data and instructions transmission between the sensor nodes and remote sensing terminals[7].

3   IEEE 802.15.4 Mac Protocol

The architecture of IEEE 802.15.4 protocol [8-12] has been constructed in accordance with the open systems interconnect (OSI) model. IEEE 802.15.4 consists of both physical layer and MAC layer, and has two kinds of operating modes, that is the beacon-enabled and non-beacon enabled modes. Comparatively, the beacon-enabled mode is more widely used in wireless network research and applications, owing to its multicast features and timeslots mechanism. The GTS research and improvement in this paper will be carried out in the beacon-enabled mode.

3.1   The Structure of Superframe

The structure of superframe is defined by the coordinator node. Once the network chooses the beacon enabled mode, the communications between the network devices will be forced to use the superframe.

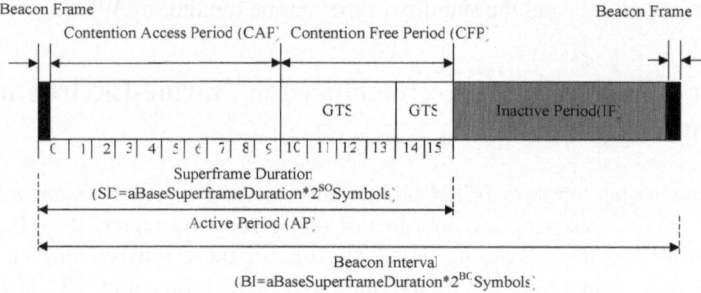

Fig. 2. The superframe structure of IEEE802.15.4

The superframe structure of the beacon enabled mode is depicted in Fig.2. The superframe is composed of the active period and the inactive period. In the inactive period, the devices are in the sleeping mode to save energy because there is no communication between the devices. The active period is further composed of three parts: the Beacon, the Contention Access Period (CAP) and the Contention Free Period (CFP). The beacon interval (BI) and the superframe duration (SD) are determined by two parameters, i.e. the beacon order (BO) and the superframe order (SO). The BI is defined as $BI = aBaseSuperframeDuration \times 2^{BO}$,

where $aBaseSuperframeDuration = 960$ symbols; and SD, which determines the duration of the active period, is defined as: $SD = aBaseSuperframeDuration \times 2^{SO}$

The BO and SO must satisfy the relationship: $0 \le SO \le BO \le 14$.

3.2   GTS Mechanism

A device that wants to allocate a GTS must send a GTS request command to its personal area network (PAN) coordinator to indicate GTS characteristics according to the requirement of the intended application. On receipt of the GTS allocation request, the PAN coordinator sends an acknowledgement message to confirm the receipt and checks if there are available resources in the current superframe based on the remaining length of the CAP and the desired length of the request GTS. The resources are considered to be available if the maximum number of GTS has not been reached, and the allocation of GTS does not reduce the minimum CAP length. The allocation of GTS will be made in an FIFO order by the coordinator provided that sufficient resources are available. The PAN coordinator makes this decision within 4 superframes. Hence, the request-making device, after receiving the acknowledgement of the GTS request command, keeps tracking of the beacon frames for at most 4 superframes. If no GTS descriptor is associated to the device within the time, the GTS request is considered to be failed.

The result of the GTS request is reported by the coordinator in the beacon frames using a GTS descriptor for each request-making device. If the GTS is successfully allocated, the PAN coordinator sets the Start Slot in the GTS descriptor to the superframe slot at which the GTS begins, and the GTS Length in the GTS descriptor to the length of GTS. If the available resources are insufficient for the new requested allocation, the PAN coordinator sets the Start Slot to 0 and the GTS Length to the largest GTS length that can currently be supported.

3.3   Previous Work

Recently, many researches on real-time capability and energy consumption of IEEE 802.15.4 MAC have been reported. Literature [13] proposed an improved scheme with low time-delay in large-scale WSN such as manufacture automation networks; [14] analyzed GTS assignment mechanism and solved the delay and throughput by network calculation, however, the maximum data rate used in his analysis is only 120kbps; an implicit GTS assignment scheduling algorithm based on beacon-enable mode is presented in [15], where the devices were assigned GTS by their required delay deadline and load status in networks, and several devices can share several GTS's on the premise of meeting the requirements of node delay and load. However it did not consider the case that a newly joined node might apply for GTS or share GTS, and the dispatching happened in network layer instead of MAC layer.

4   Proposed Delay-Category-GTS Algorithm

Through the analysis of IEEE802.15.4 MAC and its GTS allocation mechanism, we can find that using GTS instead of CAP to transmit the node message can effectively reduce the maximum access delay and enhance the success ratio of transmission. In order to make the dedicated GTS be suitable for large scale WSN monitoring, we first take a normalization processing to each node delay, and then divide the normalized delays into different categories. Based on these manipulations, we propose a delay category GTS algorithm to improve the whole system's transmission efficiency.

In this paper, the node access delay is defined as the interval between the data generation and its access to final data frame. A useful formula to compute the node access delay has been deduced in [13] as:

$$DC = \frac{SD}{D + n \cdot \lambda \cdot SD} (\frac{b}{T_{date} \cdot C} + 1),$$

(1)

where $\lambda = 1/16$ is a constant; D is the max access delay; b is the traffic amount; n is the number of allocated GTS timeslots; C is the transmission rate; DC is the duty cycle and equals to $SD/BI = 2^{SO-BO}$; T_{date} is the transmission duration in one GTS timeslot. By Equ. (1), we can get the relationship between D and GTS length, SO, DUS(date unit size). Once assign SO a fixed value, we can get the maximum access delays according to different node traffic amounts. It is not difficult to find that, if we set SO, BO, n equally to 1, $T_{date} = SD/16$, and C to 250kbit/s, the maximum node access delays when traffic amount b are 10bits, 75bits and 128bits can be calculated as in Fig.3.

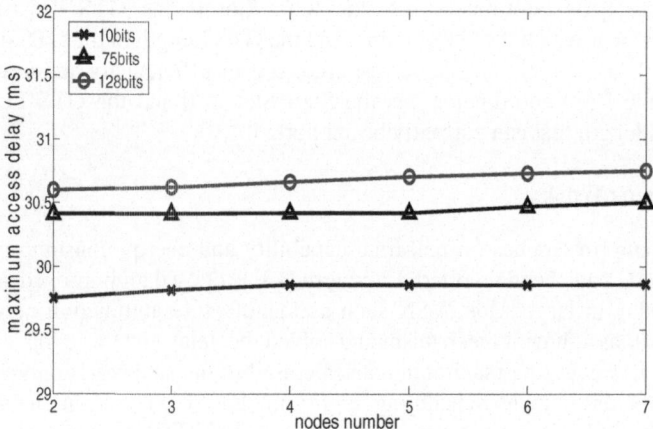

Fig. 3. The maximum access delay

In this paper, we normalize the maximum access delay achieved in Fig. 3 by

$$normDelay = \left\lfloor \frac{D}{BI} \right\rfloor,$$

(2)

where '$normDelay$' means the normalized access delay; operator $\lfloor \cdot \rfloor$ represents the maximum integer less than D/BI. After the normalization to most network nodes, based on these normalized time delays, a Delay-Category-GTS algorithm is presented. This improved GTS algorithm can solve the problem that only up to 7 nodes can be allocated GTS's in a superframe. Moreover, the GTS resource waste caused by static or dedicated GTS channel occupying by one node can also be avoided.

The description of the DCGTS algorithm is as follows:

1) The communication node sends a GTS request frame to the coordinator node. The frame consists of the length, start-end time of GTS, and maximally permitted delay.

2) The maximum delays for different nodes are normalized; then a table is established to describe these normalized values. Nodes with the same normalized value are set in the same row (R_i). The values in different rows are listed in an ascending order.

3) If the coordinator node finds that the GTS of current superframe has enough allocation timeslots, the nodes series with the minimum normalized delay will send their data in the next superframe (SF_j). Meanwhile, the series of nodes assigned to GTS timeslot will be removed from the table.

4) After the first superframe is occupied by a series of nodes, the algorithm will check the table to make sure whether there are rest nodes in the row with the minimum normalized delay. If there is, it means that the GTS scheduling still needs another superframe to allocate GTS's for the rest nodes.

5) If the nodes in the row associated with the minimum normalized delay are empty, while other rows of the table still have nodes to be assigned, the scheduling will continue to allocate GTS's for the rest nodes in the table in the next superframe until the whole table becomes empty. Then the scheduling of nodes is complete[16-18].

5   Simulation Results

5.1   Parameters Setting

In this paper, we use NS2 simulation software [19] to setup a star topology network, which contains several sensor nodes and remote sensing terminals. The mode by which the sensor nodes get access to channel is time slot CSMA/CA. During the data transmission, we also adopt the simplified ad hoc on-demand distance vector routing (AODV). The simulation parameters are set as follows:

Table 1. Some main simulation parameters

Parameters	Setting
Mac head	13 bytes
PHY head	6 bytes
BO	1
SO	1
C	250 bits/s
Data size	128 bits
GTS length	1

5.2   Results and Analysis

Fig. 4 (a) shows the maximum network delay of the nodes in the case of traditional GTS, CSMA/CA and the proposed DCGTS. The maximum network delay in the traditional GTS mechanism is expressed with the dotted line. Due to its inherent limitation, at most 7 GTS's can be allocated in one superframe, and each GTS is exclusive to its respective node.

With an increased number of nodes it can be observed that the network delay of CSMA/CA mechanism also increases. The rapid increasing of the CSMA/CA network delay for an increasing number of nodes is caused by more collisions on the channel due to the increased network loads.

Fig. 4(b) shows that the nodes using DCGTS can transmit their data without any channel competition and the successful transmission ratio may keep nearly 100% even for a large number of nodes, while for CSMA/CA, since the competition of the channel will increase with the growing number of the nodes, the success transmission ratio of CSMA/CA will decrease seriously.

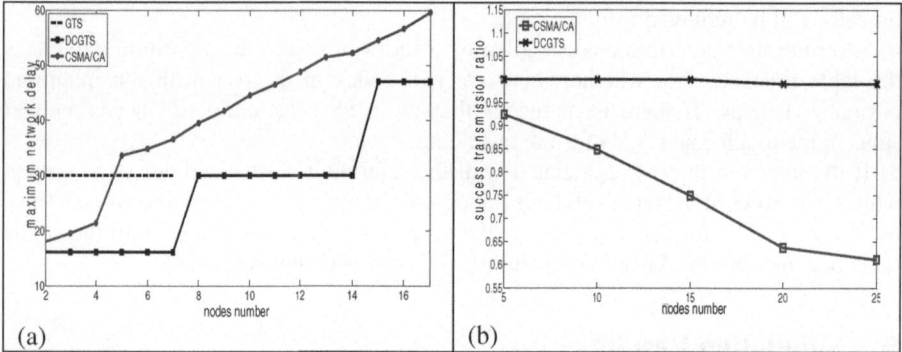

Fig. 4. (a) Maximum network delay of the tradition GTS, CSMA/CA and the proposed DCGTS; (b) Comparative results of the success transmission ratio of CSMA/CA and DCGTS

6   Conclusions

In this paper, an improved GTS transmission algorithm, that is the Delay-Category -GTS (DCGTS) based on normalized maximum access delay is proposed to reduce the WSN node delay and to enhance the success transmitting rate of each node. Since DCGTS can effectively schedule the network node transmission according to the finely designed 'delay category table', and can directly get access to the transmitting channels without experiencing contention procedure by applying to the coordinator node for accessing the dedicated GTS time slots, high real-time communications and system stability can be achieved by the whole WSN systems. The numerical results given by NS-2 simulator show that compared with the traditional GTS transmission and the CSMA/CA method, the proposed DCGTS can achieve nearly 100% success transmission rate and have much less network node time delay.

Acknowledgments. This work was supported by the Natural Science Foundation of Jiangsu Province under the Grant BK2008358; and by the Fundamental Research Funds for the Central Universities (2011B03414).

References

1. Chen, X., Lu, J., Cui, T.: Coupling Remote Sensing Retrieval with Numerical Simulation for SPM Study — Taking Bohai Sea in China as a Case. Int. J. Applied Earth Observ. and Geoinfo. 12, 203–211 (2010)

2. Demirkol, I., Ersoy, C., Alagoz, F.: MAC Protocols for Wireless Sensor Networks: a Survey. IEEE Com. Mag. 44, 115–121 (2006)
3. Retz, G., Shanan, H., Mulvaney, K., Omahony, S., et al.: Radio Transceivers for Wireless Personal Area Networks Using IEEE802.15.4. IEEE Com. Mag. 49, 150–158 (2009)
4. Miller, M.J., Vaidya, N.H.: A MAC Protocol to Reduce Sensor Network Energy Consumption Using a Wakeup Radio. IEEE Trans. Mob. Comput. 4, 228–242 (2005)
5. Ramachandran, I., Das, A.K., Roy, S.: Analysis of the Contention Access Period of IEEE 802.15.4 MAC. ACM Trans. Sensor Net. 3, 1–29 (2007)
6. Tao, Z., Panwar, S., Gu, D., Zhang, J.: Performance Analysis and a Proposed Improvement for the IEEE 802.15.4 Contention Access Period. In: IEEE Wireless Communications and Networking Conference, pp. 1811–1818. IEEE Press, New York (2006)
7. Pirzada, A.A., Portmann, M., Indulska, J.: Performance Analysis of Multi-radio AODV in Hybrid Wireless Mesh Networks. Computer Com. 31, 885–895 (2008)
8. Pollin, S., Ergen, M., Bougard, B.: Performance Analysis of Slotted Carrier Sense IEEE 802.15.4 Medium Access Layer. Wireless Com. 7, 3359–3371 (2008)
9. Koubaa, A., Alves, M., Tovar, E.: Modeling and Worst-Case Dimensioning of Cluster-Tree Wireless Sensor Networks. In: Proceedings of the 27th IEEE Real-Time Systems Symposium, pp. 412–421. IEEE Press, New York (2006)
10. Tubaishat, M., Madria, S.: Sensor Networks: an Overview. IEEE Potentials 22, 20–30 (2003)
11. Chiasserini, C.F., Garetto, M.: An Analytical Model for Wireless Sensor Networks with Sleeping Nodes. IEEE Trans. Mob. Comput. 5, 1706–1718 (2006)
12. Misie, J., Shafi, S., Misie, V.B.: Performance of a Beaeon Enabled IEEE802.15.4 Cluster with Downlink and Uplink Traffic. IEEE Trans. Paral. Distr. Syst. 17, 361–376 (2006)
13. Koubaa, A., Alves, M.: Energy and Delay Trade-off of the GTS Allocation Mechanism in IEEE 802.15.4 for Wireless Sensor Networks. Int. J. Com. Syst. 20, 791–808 (2007)
14. Pirzada, A.A., Portmann, M., Indulska, J.: Performance Analysis of Multi-radio AODV in Hybrid Wireless Mesh Networks. Comput. Com. 31, 885–895 (2008)
15. Pollin, S., Ergen, M., Bougard, B.: Performance Analysis of Slotted Carrier Sense IEEE 802.15.4 Medium Access Layer. Wireless Com. 7, 3359–3371 (2008)
16. Masuno, H., Asahi, K., Watanabe, A.: A Study on Energy-Efficient Protocol Based on the CSMA/CA in Ad-hoc Networks. In: International Symposium on Information Theory and its Applications, pp. 1–6. IEEE Press, New York (2008)
17. Ramach, I., Roy, S.: An Analysis of the Contention Access Period of IEEE 802.15.4 MAC. ACM Trans. Sensor Net. 3, 1–29 (2007)
18. Misic, J., Shafi, S., Misic, V.B.: The Impact of MAC Parameters on the Performance of 802.15.4 PAN. Ad Hoc Net. 3, 509–528 (2005)
19. Ns-2 Simulator, http://www.isi.edu/nsnam/ns

A Multidimensional Scaling Analysis Algorithm of Nodes Localization Based on Steepest Descent in Wireless Sensor Networks

Zhao Qing-Hua[1], Li Liang[2], Li Hua[1], Zhang Kunpeng[1], and Wang Huakui[1]

[1] College of Information Engineering,
Taiyuan University of Technology, Taiyuan, China, 030024
zhaoqinghua218@163.com
[2] Urban and Tourism College, Taiyuan Normal University, Taiyuan, China, 030012

Abstract. This article studies the classical MDS and dwMDS location algorithm.On this basis, steepest descent algorithm is introduced to replace SMACOF algorithm as optimization objective function. The results show that the steepest descent method as the optimization objective function is simple and easy to implement. Compared with the dwMDS method based on SMACOF algorithm, the distributed MDS positioning algorithm with the steepest descent method has increased significantly in accuracy, and it has a relatively good performance in the anti-Error effects, the convergence and convergence speed, even in the uneven performance of the network also performed well.

Keywords: Wireless Sensor Networks, Iterative Optimization, Multidimensional Scaling, steepest descent algorithm, Positioning Accuracy.

1 Introduction

Wireless sensor nodes are usually randomly deployed on a variety of different environments to monitor the implementation of tasks to self-organized coordination between the way. These nodes are usually announced with the aircraft sensor nodes into the specified area. As the sensor nodes are limited by cost, power and size constraints, only a small percentage of nodes randomly laying carry GPS positioning device. These nodes can determine their own position, but others those cannot know the location of the node's own position in advance can only be known under a few nodes according to a positioning system to determine its own location. After determining its own position, the sensor node can be monitored to determine the specific location of the incident. In sensor networks, the location information monitoring events on the premise is the correct positioning of sensor nodes [1-2].

Jose A. Costa [3-4] and others's dwMDS algorithm is based on SMACOF algorithm. The algorithm of distributing localization method is iterative optimization of the local cost function. The algorithm uses Gaussian kernel weighted mechanism to distinguish between neighbor nodes and neighbor nodes and reduces the ranging error associated with the negative deviation by using two-step option. The algorithm is a superior performance of the algorithm that adopted multi-dimensional scaling analysis

H. Deng et al. (Eds.): AICI 2011, Part II, LNAI 7003, pp. 546–553, 2011.

of the algorithm in location technology. But the algorithm generates a better positioning effect only in the relatively small ranging error and the initial estimated location of the node closer to the actual location of the node. The positioning accuracy of the algorithm will be limited when the distance error is large and the initial node position accuracy is low. It is the optimization method of the objective function that the steepest descent algorithm is introduced to replace SMACOF algorithm based on dwMDS algorithm. The positioning accuracy of the steepest descent algorithm is improved obviously and positions the nodes well under the lower connectivity in experiments. The improved algorithm is called the Distributed weighted-multidimensional scaling based on steepest descent method, dwMDSS.

2   Unconstrained Optimization Method

In wireless sensor network, the classical MDS positioning method uses the following global cost function[6]:

$$S = 2 \sum_{1 \le i \le n} \sum_{i < j \le N} \omega_{ij} \left(\delta_{ij} - \|z_i - z_j\| \right)^2 + \sum_{1 \le i \le n} r_i \|z_i - \bar{z}_i\|^2 \tag{1}$$

where the second item in the type (1) does not exist, if it only has the anchor node and the node that the location information is completely unknown. After derivation, $\square$ can be rewritten as follows:

$$S = \sum_{1 \le i \le n} S_i + c \tag{2}$$

where

$$S_i = \sum_{\substack{j=1 \\ j \ne i}}^{n} \omega_{ij} \left(\delta_{ij} - \|z_i - z_j\| \right)^2 + \sum_{j=n+1}^{N} 2\omega_{ij} \left(\delta_{ij} - \|z_i - z_j\| \right)^2 \tag{3}$$

The best estimate location of the node S_i is the local cost function of node i. it can be on every node within the local cost function optimization method of seeking the minimum cost function to the global optimum. We get can be gotten. The objective of all the distributed nodes localization is also achieved.

If $\hat{z}_i$ is estimated coordinates of the node i, and z_i^* is the coordinates of the location closest to the true:

$$z_i^* = \min_{\hat{z}_i} S_i \tag{4}$$

3   A Distributed Node Localization Algorithm Based on Steepest Descent Method

In the numerical analysis, the basic idea of classical function optimization is described as follow. Given initial point $z^{(0)}$, then through the iterative optimization method to optimize the expression of the unconstrained by a series of points { $z^{(k)}$ }, where k is the number of iterations, and as k increases, point $z^{(k)}$ should be able to make the expressions of the unconstrained approach extreme, when $k \rightarrow \infty$, $z^{(k)}$ should be the extreme points of non-binding expressions. In the unconstrained optimization method, the iterative formula usually expressed as follows [7-8]:

$$z^{(k+1)} = z^{(k)} + \alpha_k \mathrm{d}_k \tag{5}$$

In the above formula, k represents the k-iteration, $z^{(k)}$ is the K-times iterations results. d_k is the search direction. When the point moves along the direction, the value of the expression should tend to a minimum, so the direction as the decline direction of expression. α_k is the choice of step in $k+1$ iteration , which is the size along the decent direction on K-th iteration. In the optimization method, the descent direction and step size selection is directly related to computing speed and accuracy of extreme points. In general, the faster processing speed, the greater the computation, such as the Newton method is a optimization method with the very fast calculation speed, whose process can often be one step, but this method involves the solving of Hesse matrix, whose solving needs large computational, especially when there is large number of nodes in the network the matrix will be growing at square growth rate, and the requirements of Hesse matrix is positive definite or positive semi-definite, the general optimization is difficult to meet the requirements. The iteration step size related to the decrease pace and the stability of the algorithm, when the step size is large the rate of decline is faster, but the stability will be worse, which is possible out of extreme range of the solution with bad results. When the step size is smaller, although algorithm stability is better, but the convergence rate will slow down, which would increase the number of iterations to increase the amount of computation, and if step size is too small which may lead the algorithm to converge to local minimum, which cannot achieve better results. The value of the step size generally used to obtain by one-dimensional search method, When determining a direction d_k for the decline direction, send d_k and the results on the iteration step $z^{(k)}$ into (5) formula, when the point z becomes a the step size function, then send the point into the expression which can be obtained the iterative step that get the extreme expression by interpolation method.

Steepest descent method is a classical unconstrained optimization method, which is characterized by computation, although its speed is not as fast as Newton method, but the operation is stable and could make the expression tends to the extreme value smoothly. In the steepest descent method, the expression of the negative gradient direction was chosen as descent direction, this article use the steepest descent method to optimize the local cost function in (3) formula, the function is the non-binding expression, which need the optimization method to optimize solving, whose search direction is the negative gradient direction of the local cost function, the expression is as follows:

$$-\frac{\partial S_i^{(k)}}{\partial z_i^{(k)}} = -[\sum_{\substack{j=1 \\ j\neq i}}^{n} 2w_{i,j}\left(1-\frac{\delta_{i,j}}{\| z_i^{(k)} - z_j^{(k)} \|}\right)(z_i^{(k)} - z_j^{(k)}) +$$

$$\sum_{j=n+1}^{N} 4w_{i,j}\left(1-\frac{\delta_{i,j}}{\| z_i^{(k)} - z_j^{(k)} \|}\right)(z_i^{(k)} - z_j^{(k)})] \tag{6}$$

$$= -(z_i^{(k)} - z_1^{(k)}, z_i^{(k)} - z_2^{(k)}, \ldots z_i^{(k)} - z_N^{(k)})(b_1^{(k)}, b_2^{(k)}, \ldots b_N^{(k)})^T$$

where

$$b_j^{(k)} = \begin{cases} 2w_{i,j}(1-\dfrac{\delta_{i,j}}{\| z_i^{(k)} - z_j^{(k)} \|}), & j \leq n \text{ 且 } j \neq i \\ 0, & j = i \\ 4w_{i,j}(1-\dfrac{\delta_{i,j}}{\| z_i^{(k)} - z_j^{(k)} \|}), & j > n \end{cases} \quad , \quad (j = 1,2,\ldots N) \tag{7}$$

Defining
$$D^{[k]} = (z_i^{(k)} - z_1^{(k)}, z_i^{(k)} - z_2^{(k)}, \ldots z_i^{(k)} - z_N^{(k)}), B^{[k]} = (b_1^{(k)}, b_2^{(k)}, \ldots b_N^{(k)})^T, z_i, \text{the}$$
coordinate of the node i can now be written as:

$$z_i^{(k+1)} = z_i^{(k)} - \alpha^{(k)} \times D^{(k)} \times B^{(k)} \tag{8}$$

The method of choose the iteration step is making the minimize the objective function, as:

$$S_i\left(z_i^{(k)} - \alpha^{(k)} \times D^{(k)} \times B^{(k)}\right) = \min_{\alpha \geq 0} S_i\left(z_i^{(k)} - \alpha \times D^{(k)} \times B^{(k)}\right) \tag{9}$$

Select the step size so that the style is to set up one-dimensional search, it can transformer multi-dimensional cost function into one-dimensional cost function:

$$\varphi(\alpha) = S_i\left(z_i^{(k)} - \alpha \times D^{(k)} \times B^{(k)}\right) \tag{10}$$

4   Simulation and Result Analysis

4.1   Relationship between Connectivity and Positioning Error

4.1.1   Positioning Error Analysis with Changes of Communication Radius in Grid Distribution Scene

Simulation scenario is set as follows, 49 nodes uniformly distributed in the form of grid, ranging error is 20%. With the increase of communication radius, connectivity increases gradually. With the increase of the radius of communication, the connectivity increases as follow: 3.6, 5.9, 8.2, 11, 13.8, 16.8, 19.8, 22.7, and 25.5. Connectivity of each case was carried out 200 Monte Carlo trials.

Figure 1 shows the changing curve of the three algorithms' root mean square error with communication radius. With the communication radius increases, the root mean square errors of three algorithms is significantly reduced. In the radius of communication is between 0.45 and 0.5, dwMDS algorithm and the initial MDS algorithm has upward trend in the error curve, which has a relationship with connectivity, at the time that the corresponding connectivity value is from 16.8 to 19.8, in which case the connectivity value have made the two algorithms tend to saturated.

According to the definition of RMSE, the error is a relative value, so it can't directly reflect the absolute positioning error. Although the root mean square error will decrease with the increase of connectivity, this does not mean absolute error will decrease as the connectivity increases; In order to show the relationship between the position error and the connectivity, the absolute error curve of three algorithms are drawn; Figure 2 shows the absolute error curve of three algorithms as the communication radius changes, from the figure we can show that the error curve of the initial MDS algorithm and dwMDS algorithm fluctuate as the communication radius increases and don't have the significant trend of rise or fall. In this experiment, MDS algorithm assumes that all nodes are connected, In other words, each node is neighbor of all other nodes; therefore, if the ranging error is a constant value, the positioning result of initial positioning algorithm will not change as the connectivity changes. Figure 1 and 2 show that dwMDSS algorithm has good performance in either RMSE values or absolute positioning error, dwMDSS algorithm not only has lower error than MDS algorithm and dwMDS algorithm and error of dwMDSS algorithm decline continuously with the addition of communication radius.

There are three conclusions from the experiment, first, the positioning accuracy of dwMDS algorithm affected serious by the initial position algorithm. Figure 1 and 2 show that although the positioning accuracy of dwMDS algorithm is better than the initial position algorithm but the increment is not much, When the initial position of the error curve rises or falls, dwMDS algorithms error curve show the same trend, this is related to the initial position algorithm used in the experiment, the performance of classical MDS algorithm is good, this also shows that the positioning accuracy of dwMDS algorithm is still limited. Second, in the fixed network topology, the increase of connectivity would improve positioning accuracy. As shown in Figure 2, the absolute error of dwMDSS algorithm continued to decline with the addition of communication radius. But when connectivity reaches a certain value, the error curve of three algorithms no longer drop. At this point the number of neighbors has reached saturation, that is, the error caused by increase of communication radius can offset positive impact caused by the increase in connectivity, this can be shown in the curve from 0.45 to 0.5, dwMDSS location algorithm curve has leveled off, MDS positioning algorithm and dwMDS even upward trend. Third, in the study, connectivity increases by the method of increasing communication radius. However, the improvement of communication radius can cause the intensification of ranging error, because in the RSSI ranging module signal strength attenuates seriously. Therefore the result of positioning error curve is caused by connectivity and ranging error, dwMDSS algorithm shown a downward trend in the error descript that it has good resistance to error performance. In this experiment, the increase in connectivity does not cause the improvement of error of dwMDSS algorithm. So rangding error brings about obvious influence.

4.1.2 Positioning Error Analysis with Changes in the Number of Nodes in Grid Distribution Scene

In order to visually observe how connectivity effects on the localization algorithm without considering the impact of ranging error, we will increase the number of nodes in the network, in other words, the network connectivity improve by the method of increasing the node density, communication radius constant. Nodes are arranged evenly in the 1*1 region. Ranging error is 20%, communication radius is 0.35, the number of nodes in the network increases gradually. They are 25, 36, 49, 64, 81, 100, the corresponding connectivity are4.8, 7.6, 11, 15, 19.6, 24.7. The curve in figure 3 shows that with the increase in the number of nodes in the network, the positioning error of three algorithms decreases significantly, so the size of connectivity is related to location error. However, the method of changes of size of connectivity is not increasing or decreasing the nodes, because it is too time-consuming, the common method is changing communication radius, in this case, positioning error of algorithm is affected not only by the size of connectivity but also ranging error caused by the change of communication radius. If the impact of connectivity is less than the impact of ranging error, then the location error will increases instead of decreases with increasing communication radius, this is the cause of the phenomenon that when communication radius changes from 0.45 to 0.5, the error curve of deMDSS algorithm did not change significantly but the error curve of the other two algorithm which are somewhat less in anti-error capacity have the upward trend. Therefore, the "saturation" in above experiment is not really saturated but caused by the addition of ranging error. At this point, the method of increasing connectivity cannot be increasing communication radius.

4.1.3 Positioning Error Analysis with Changes of Communication Radius in Grid Distribution Scene

100 nodes randomly distributed in the 1 × 1 in the region, ranging error is 20%, and communication radius increases gradually, The corresponding connectivity are:3.05, 6.58, 11.06, 16.43, 22.21, 28.6, 35.3, 42.03. Shown in Figure 4, with the communication radius increases, the root mean square error will be decreased significantly. Based on the comparison of three algorithms, dwMDSS algorithm outperformed dwMDS algorithm, the location error of dwMDSS algorithm is 13 percent lower than initial position and 7 percent lower than dwMDS algorithm when the communication radium is 0.25 and connectivity is about 15.8. Figure 5 shows the absolute error curve of three algorithms, absolute error of dwMDSS algorithm is lower than that of dwMDS algorithm. As the communication radius increases, the error curve leveled off or upward trend, which is the result of ranging error caused by communication radius increases. Moreover, compared figure 4 and figure 5 to figure 1 and figure 2, the error curve in figure 4 and figure 5 is obviously higher than that in figure 1 and figure 2, which is caused by different experimental scenarios. The nodes have fixed position and arrange evenly in the grid network, but the nodes distribute randomly in the randomly distributed scene, the scene of each experiment are randomly deployed in 200 Monte Carlo experiments, each scene is different from others. So positioning accuracy is related to topological structure of network, the localization of uniform network is easier than non-uniform network.

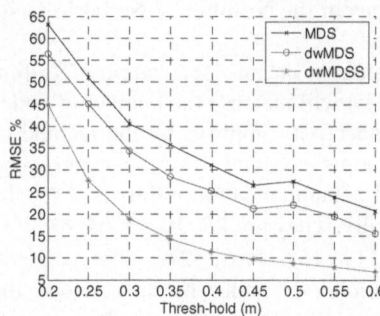

Fig. 1. Change in Location Error with Communication Radius

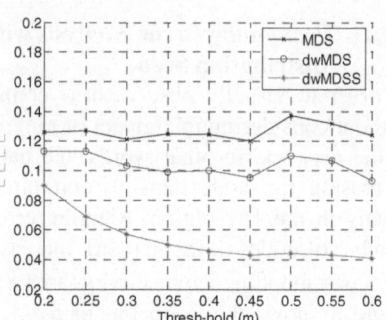

Fig. 2. Change in Absolute Location Error with Communication Radius

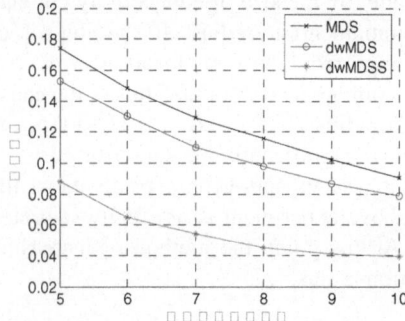

Fig. 3. Change in Location Error with Number of Nodes

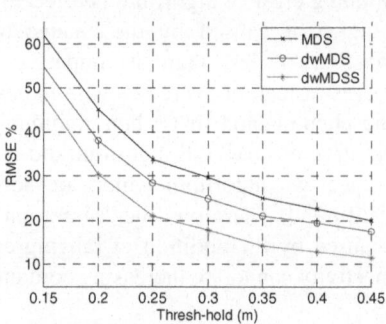

Fig. 4. Change in Location Error with Communication Radius

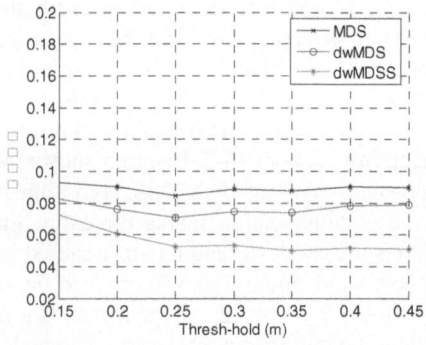

Fig. 5. Change in Absolute Location Error

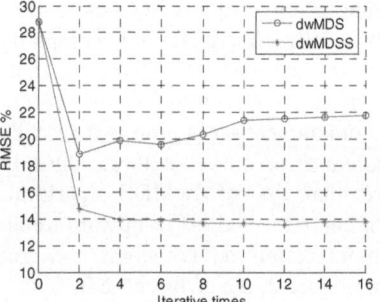

Fig. 6. Convergence of Two Algorithms

4.2   Analysis of Convergence Performance of Algorithm

The algorithm proposed is based on iterative optimization algorithm, in the positioning process; convergence rate of algorithm has a greater impact on communication overhead and energy consumption of nodes. Taking into account that it is difficult to get explicit expression of iterative localization algorithm directly, in the experiment, Software emulation is used to assess the convergence of the algorithm. Simulation condition is set as follows, ranging error is 20 percent, the average connectivity is about 16. Figure 6 shows that dwMDSS algorithm trends to stable after less than 4 iterations and the error of deMDS algorithm drop obviously after 2 iterations but tends to rise after more iteration. When positioning error of two algorithms are in the lowest, positioning error of dwMDSS is 5% percent lower than that of dwMDS.

5   Conclusions

In this paper, the application of gradient optimization method in distributed Localization Algorithm is studied; we also studied the application of steepest descent method in the Positioning and made the simulation. Experimental results show that, as the optimization of objective function, steepest descent method is simpler and easier than SMACOF algorithm and deMDS algorithm, dwMDSS algorithm improves in localization accuracy and has good performance in anti-error effect, the convergence and convergence speed, in addition, it performs well in non-uniform network. Steepest descent method has saw-tooth effect. Although the localization of sensor node is coarse-grained positioning technology, so it does not require the precise location of the node. However, whether saw-tooth effect has a greater impact to location result needs further study.

References

1. Fu-sheng: An Improved DV-Hop algorithm. Ship Electronic Engineering 28(8), 73–76 (2008)
2. Ren, F., Huang, H., Lin, C.: Wireless sensor networks. Journal of Software 14(7), 1282–1291 (2003)
3. Ji, X., Zha, H.: Sensor positioning in wireless ad-hoc sensor networks using multidimensional scaling. In: Proceedings of the 23rd Annual Joint Conference of the IEEE Computer and Communications Societies, pp. 2652–2661. IEEE, Hong Kong (2004)
4. Shang, Y., Ruml, W., Zhang, Y., Fromherz, M.P.J.: Localization from connectivity in sensor networks. IEEE Transactions on Parallel and Distributed Systems 15(11), 961–974 (2004)
5. Groenen, P.: The majorization approach to multidimensional scaling: some problems and extensions. http://Www.springerlink.com/index/Q0G40V3821315035.pdf
6. Costa, J.A., Patwari, N., Hero, A.O.: Distributed weighted-multidimensional scaling for node localization in sensor net-works. ACM Transactions on Sensor Networks 2(1), 39–64 (2006)
7. Cao, H., Chen, G.: Multi-factor dimensionality reduction method - nonlinear mapping in the weather forecast. Atmospheric Science 3(2) (1979)
8. Yuan, Y., Sun, W.: Optimization theory and methods. Science Press, Beijing (1997)
9. Ma, Z., Gu, L., Yang, L., et al.: Modern Applied Mathematics Handbook - Volume calculation and numerical analysis. Tsinghua University Press, Beijing (2005)

A Novel PTS Scheme for PAPR Reduction
in OFDM Systems Using Riemann Sequence

Chen Lin[1,2] and Fang Yong[1]

[1] School of Communication and Information Engineering, Shanghai University,
Shanghai, China
chenlin1008@shu.edu.cn, yfang@staff.shu.edu.cn
[2] School of Computer and Information, Shanghai University of Electronic Power,
Shanghai, China

Abstract. Partial Transmit Sequence technique is one of well-known PAPR reduction techniques for Orthogonal Frequency Division Multiplexing (OFDM). But for data recovery, receivers must have side information, e.g., phase factors from transmitters. It results in a huge amount of computation complexity. In this paper, a novel PTS scheme with the Riemann sequence is proposed. In this scheme, it is not needed to exchange side information between transmitter and receiver. It is shown that better PAPR reduction performance is achieved as compared to the conventional PTS scheme by computer simulations.

Keywords: Orthogonal Frequency Division Multiplexing, Peak-to-Average Power Ratio, Partial Transmit Sequence, Riemann Sequence.

1   Introduction

Orthogonal Frequency Division Multiplexing (OFDM) is an attractive multicarrier technique for wireless communications due to its robustness against severe multipath fading. However, one of the main disadvantages of OFDM is its high Peak-to-Average Power Ratio (PAPR) [1]. When N signals are added with the same phase, they produce a peak power that is N times the average power. A high PAPR brings disadvantages, such as an increased complexity of the A/D and D/A converters, and a reduced efficiency of the RF power amplifier.

In order to reduce the PAPR, several techniques [2] have been proposed in the literature: clipping and filtering, selected mapping (SLM), partial transmit sequences (PTS), tone reservation, tone injection and block coding. Among them, PTS scheme is an attractive solution to reduce PAPR without any distortion of transmitted signals.

In the PTS scheme, input data symbols are divided into disjointed subblocks and the subblocks are separately phase-rotated by individually selected phase factors. These phase factors are also transmitted as side information (SI) when data symbols are sent. Since side information is very critical for successful data recovery, it is protected by channel coding to combat frequency-selective fading. To reduce the search complexity of PTS, various techniques have been suggested in [3-8]. The aim of these methods is to reduce the number of iterations.

H. Deng et al. (Eds.): AICI 2011, Part II, LNAI 7003, pp. 554–560, 2011.

This paper is organized as follows: Section 2 briefly describes the distribution of the PAPR. In Section 3, the conventional PTS scheme for PAPR reduction is reviewed. Then, an improved techniques with the Riemann sequence is proposed, and some performances are achieved by Monte Carlo simulations. Section 4 concludes this paper.

2   Distribution of the PAPR

In OFDM systems, the baseband time domain signal consisting of N subcarriers may be written as [2]

$$x(t) = \frac{1}{\sqrt{N}} \sum_{n=0}^{N-1} X_n \cdot e^{j2\pi n\Delta ft} , 0 \leq t < NT \tag{1}$$

There, Δf is the subcarrier spacing, X_n are the modulating symbols, and NT denotes the useful data block period.

The PAPR of the transmit signal is defined as [2]

$$PAPR = \frac{\max_{0 \leq t < NT} |x(t)|^2}{1/NT \cdot \int_0^{NT} |x(t)|^2 dt} \tag{2}$$

An approximation of $x(t)$ will be made so that only NL equidistant samples of $x(t)$ will be considered where L is an integer that is larger than or equal to 1.

$$x_k = \frac{1}{\sqrt{N}} \sum_{n=0}^{N-1} X_n \cdot e^{j2\pi kn\Delta fT/L} , \quad k = 0,1,\cdots,NL-1 \tag{3}$$

It can be seen that the sequence $\{x_k\}$ can be interpreted as the inverse discrete Fourier transform (IDFT) of data block X with $(L-1)N$ zero padding. The PAPR [2] of the L times oversampled time domain signal samples is given by

$$PAPR = \frac{\max_{0 \leq k \leq NL-1} |x_k|^2}{E\left[|x_k|^2\right]} \tag{4}$$

where $E[\cdot]$ denotes statistical expectation.

From the central limit theorem, it follows that for large values of N ($N>64$), the real and imaginary values of $x(t)$ become Gaussian distributed. Therefore the amplitude of the OFDM signal has a Rayleigh distribution, with a cumulative distribution given by $F(z)=1-e^{-z}$. The probability that the PAPR is below some threshold level can be written as $P(PAPR \leq z) = \left(1-e^{-z}\right)^N$.

In fact, the complementary cumulative distribution function (CCDF) is usually used. The CCDF of the PAPR of a data block with Nyquist sampling rate is expressed as [2]

$$P(PAPR > z) = 1 - (1 - e^{-z})^N$$

(5)

The CCDF of the PAPR denotes the Probability that the PAPR of a data block exceeds a given threshold. With increasing the number of subcarriers N, there was a corresponding increasing in CCDF under a certain PAPR threshold.

3   PTS Techniques for PAPR Reduction

In order to reduce the PAPR of an OFDM signal, PTS technique is proposed. It is one of the initial probabilistic methods for reducing the PAPR problem, with a goal of making occurrence of the peaks less frequency, not to eliminate them. These related techniques are effective and flexible to reduce the PAPR without nonlinear distortion. And they can be used for arbitrary numbers of subcarriers and without restriction on signal constellation.

3.1   The Conventional Partial Transmit Sequence

In the conventional PTS scheme [3], the input data block is partitioned into V non-overlapping subblocks $X^{(v)}$, which are combined to minimize the PAPR. There are three kinds of subblock partitioning schemes: adjacent, interleaved, and pseudo-random partitioning. Among them, pseudo-random partitioning has been found to be the best choice. Each carrier in the subblocks $X^{(v)}$ is multiplied with the phase factor $b^{(v)} = e^{j\varphi^{(v)}}$, $\varphi^{(v)} \in [0, 2\pi)$. The time domain vectors can be composed by the IFFT.

$$y = IFFT\{Y\} = \sum_{v=0}^{V-1} b^{(v)} IFFT\{X^{(v)}\} = \sum_{v=0}^{V-1} b^{(v)} x^{(v)}$$

(6)

Simulation results with 128 subcarriers and QPSK in each carrier are plotted in Fig. 1. It is also advantageous in practice to choose the phase factor $b^{(v)}$ from the set $\{\pm 1, \pm j\}$. With increasing the number of subblocks V, the probability of high PAPR decreases obviously, compared to the original OFDM signal.

However, the receiver must to know which vector had actually been used for recover the data. Therefore, the phase factors must be transmitted as side information, resulting in some loss of band efficiency. W^{V-1} accessorial information sequences is required in the conventional PTS scheme, where V denotes the number of subblocks and W denotes the number of the phase factors. And the redundant bits of side information are as follows: $R_{ap} = (V - 1) \log_2 W$. In order to reduce the search complexity of PTS, the number of phase factors $\{b^{(v)}\}$ may be limited in a certain range.

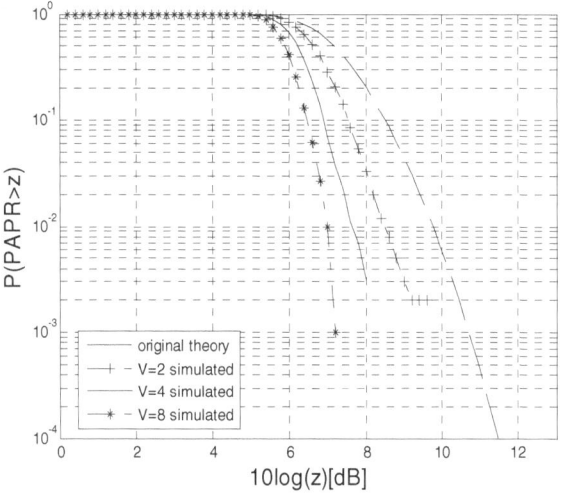

Fig. 1. CCDF of the PAPR by PTS

3.2 Novel PTS Scheme with the Riemann Sequence

The rows of normalized Riemann sequence are firstly selected as phase sequence in SLM scheme in the literature [9]. Riemann sequences are used in SLM scheme along with the thresholding of the power amplifier in the literature [10]. In the literature [11], it was shown that the normalized Riemann sequence used as a phase sequence of SLM can offer very low PAPR than the existing techniques, including Hadamard, Chaotic. In this paper, the Riemann sequences are used in the PTS scheme. And the PAPR and BER performance are obtained compared with the conventional PTS.

The Riemann Matrix is obtained by removing the first row and first column of the matrix B [12], where

$$B(i, j) = \begin{cases} i-1 & if \quad i \quad divides \quad j \\ -1 & otherwise \end{cases} \tag{7}$$

Using Equation (7), Riemann Matrix (B) of order 4 can be written as:

$$B = \begin{bmatrix} 1 & -1 & 1 & -1 \\ -1 & 2 & -1 & -1 \\ -1 & -1 & 3 & -1 \\ -1 & -1 & -1 & 4 \end{bmatrix} \tag{8}$$

The algorithm is as follows:

1) The input data are mapped to constellation points QAM or PSK to produce sequence symbol X .

2) Sequence symbol X is partitioned into disjoint subblocks $\left\{X^{(0)}, X^{(1)}, \cdots, X^{(V-1)}\right\}$. Transform $\left\{X^{(v)}\right\}$ into time domain to get $x^{(v)}$ with the inverse Fast Fourier transform (IFFT).

3) Each block $x^{(v)}$ is multiplied with the different phase sequence vectors $B^{(v)}$, where each row of the normalized Riemann matrix B is taken as $B^{(v)}$, $v = 0, 1, \cdots, V - 1$.

4) The objective is to optimally combine the V subblocks to obtain the time domain OFDM signals with the lowest PAPR for transmission.

$$\tilde{y} = \sum_{v=0}^{V-1} B^{(v)} \cdot x^{(v)}$$

(9)

Block diagram of PTS with the Riemann sequence is given in Fig. 2.

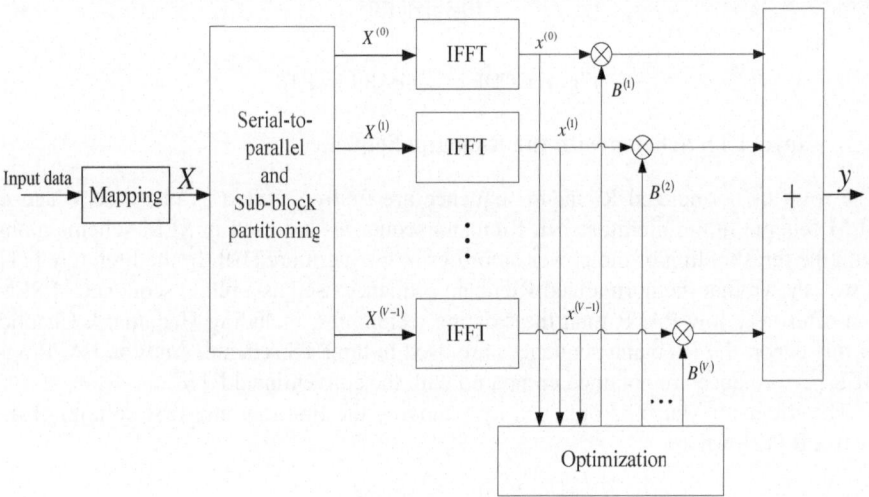

Fig. 2. A block diagram of PTS with the Riemann Sequence

An OFDM system with 128 subcarriers is used in all the simulations. The rows of the normalized Riemann matrix with order 4 are taken as phase vectors. Through MATLAB simulations, a reduction of 4dB in PAPR is achieved for Riemann sequence as compared to the conventional PTS scheme in Fig. 3. The technique of using normalized Riemann sequence as a phase sequence set offer very low PAPR.

In the proposed scheme, a vector $\tilde{B} = \left[\tilde{B}^{(0)}, \tilde{B}^{(1)}, \cdots, \tilde{B}^{(V-1)}\right]$ which contains minimum PAPR values is selected. And the normalized squared sum of error can been utilized as search the index of the phase sequence. The default index is the index with the smallest squared sum of error. The default index of the phase sequence is used to reduce the computational complexity of PTS technique. The bit error rate (BER)

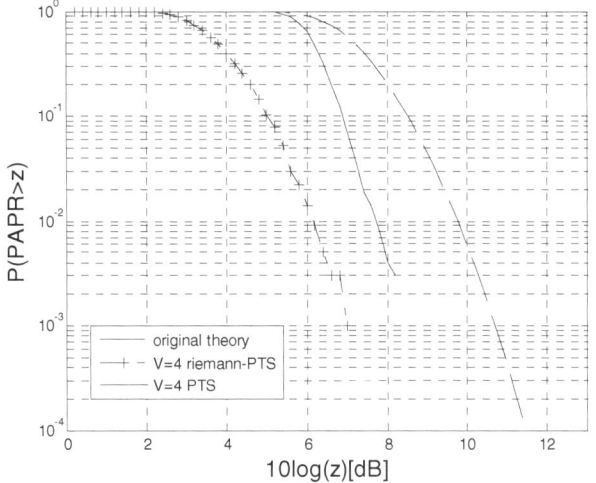

Fig. 3. CCDF of the PAPR by PTS with the Riemann Sequence

performance of the proposed PTS scheme is compared with the conventional PTS scheme in an AWGN channel. As in the Fig. 4, the BER performance is not degraded when using the Riemann sequences.

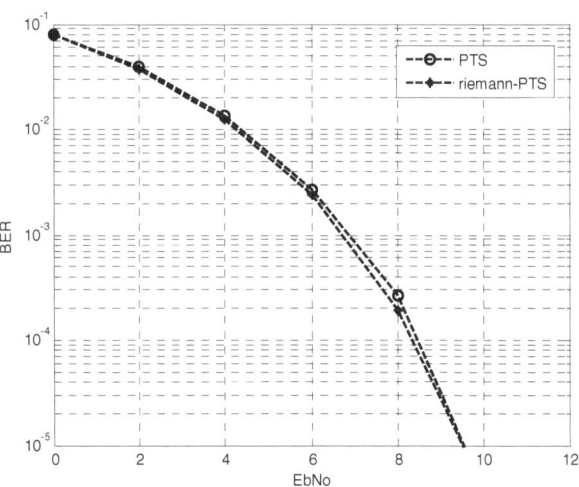

Fig. 4. BER performance in an AWGN channel

4   Conclusions and Future Work

PAPR problem is one of the most important issues to be considered in developing OFDM systems. Several techniques have been proposed for PAPR reduction. But most of them cannot achieve simultaneously a large reduction in PAPR with high frequency efficiency, low complexity and good error correction. Non specific PAPR reduction technique is the best solution for all multicarrier transmission. In this paper, a novel PTS scheme with Riemann sequence is proposed to reduce the PAPR. Simulation results show that the proposed scheme achieves better PAPR and BER performance with low complexity.

Acknowledgments. This work is supported by the Innovation Foundation of the Education Commission of Shanghai Municipality (Grant No.09ZZ89), the Shanghai Leading Academic Discipline Project (Grant No.S30108), and the Science and Technology Commission of Shanghai Municipality (Grant No.08DZ223110).

References

1. Van Nee, R.J., Prasard, R.: OFDM For Wireless Multimedia Communications. Artech House, Boston (2000)
2. Han, S.H., Lee, J.H.: An Overview of Peak-to-Average Power Ratio Reduction Techniques for Multicarrier Transmission. IEEE Wireless Communications, 56–65 (April 2005)
3. Cimini Jr., L.J., Sollenberger, N.R.: Peak-to-average Power Ratio Recuction of an OFDM Signal Using Partial Transmit Sequences. IEEE Commun. Letters 4(3), 86–88 (2000)
4. Jayalath, A.D.S., Tellambura, C., Wu, H.: Reduced complexity PTS and new phase sequences for SLM to reduce PAP of an OFDM signal. In: IEEE VTC 2000, pp. 1914–1917 (2000)
5. Tellambura, C.: Improved Phase Factor Computation for the PAR Reduction of an OFDM Signal Using PTS. IEEE Commun. Letters 5(4), 135–137 (2001)
6. Han, S.H., Lee, J.H.: PAPR Reduction of OFDM Signals Using a Reduced Complexity PTS Technique. IEEE Sig. Proc. Letters 11(11), 887–890 (2004)
7. Yang, L., Chen, R.S., Siu, Y.M., Soo, K.K.: PAPR reduction of an OFDM signal by use of PTS with low computional complexity. IEEE Trans. on Broadcasting 52(1), 83–86 (2006)
8. Shibata, K., Webber, J., Nishimura, T., Ohgane, T., Ogawa, Y.: Blind Detection of Partial Transmit Sequence in a Coded OFDM System. In: 2009 IEEE Global Telecommunications Conference, pp. 1–6 (2009)
9. Irukulapati, N.V., Chakka, V.K., Jain, A.: SLM based PAPR reduction of an OFDM signal using new phase sequence. IEEE Electronica Letters, 1231–1232 (July 2009)
10. Chandwani, M., Singal, A., VishnuKanth, N., Chakka, V.: A Low Complexity SLM Technique for PAPR reduction in OFDM using Riemann Sequence and Thresholding of Power Amplifier. In: 2009 Annual IEEE India Conference, pp. 86–88 (2009)
11. Chen, L., Hu, X.: Improved SLM techniques for PAPR reduction in OFDM system. Journal of Computational Information Systems 6(13), 4427–4434 (2010)
12. Roesler, F.: Riemann's hypothesis as an eigenvalue problem. Linear Algebra Appl. 81, 153–198 (1986)

P300 Feature Extraction for Visual Evoked EEG Based on Wavelet Transform

Xiaoyan Qiao and Na Yan

College of Physical Electronic Engineering, Shanxi University, Taiyuan, China
xyqiao@sxu.edu.cn

Abstract. It is a crucial issue to accurately and quickly extract the feature of visual evoked potentials in the brain-computer interface technology. Based on the non-stationary and nonlinearity of the electroencephalogram (EEG) signal, a method of wavelet analysis is adopted to extract P300 feature from visual evoked EEG. Firstly, the imperative pretreatment for EEG signals is performed. Secondly, the approximate and detail coefficients are gotten by decomposing EEG signals for two layers using wavelet transform. Finally, the approximate coefficients of the second layer are reconstructed to extract P300 feature. The results have shown that the method can accurately extract the P300 feature for visual evoked EEG, and simultaneously, obtain time-frequency information which traditional methods can not do. Therefore, wavelet transform provides an effective method to feature extraction for EEG mental tasks.

Keywords: visual evoked potential, wavelet transform, feature extraction, BCI.

1 Introduction

Visual evoked potential is that imposing appropriate stimulation of the brain on the visual system caused potential changes on cortex. Its amplitude is about $0.5 \sim 50 \mu V$, the frequency range is $0.5 \sim 30 Hz$, signal to noise ratio is $0 \sim 10 dB$. Visual evoked potential is the weak signal of non-stationary and nonlinearity. P300 belongs to event related potentials, and its peak appeared in about 300ms after related events, the most significant area in the head of the parietal bone area [1]. Owing to the shape and the amplitude of the P300 signal, it reflects the brain cognitive function in the decision-making process, and it is also as usual choice for clinical and laboratory tests, which is widely used in brain computer interface (BCI) system as the feature signal to reflect brain activity. At present, methods of feature extraction on evoked potential include coherent average method, power spectrum analysis, high-order spectral analysis, AAR model method, independent component analysis, support vector machines etc. The superposed average technology can effectively extract evoked potential features, but many times stimulus result the subjects' nervous system fatigue. Furthermore, this method ignores the change of evoked potential between each stimulus. Power spectral analysis applies the energy information of the signal in frequency domain, but it loses time domain information. Higher-order spectrum analysis can express signals from higher-level probability statistics, fully suppress the

H. Deng et al. (Eds.): AICI 2011, Part II, LNAI 7003, pp. 561–567, 2011.

gaussian noise signal [2]. But the data from time-domain information under high order spectrum analysis lose useful frequency domain information of signal. AAR model method is more suitable for stationary random signals, but EEG signals are highly non-stationary signals. In addition, AAR model method is very sensitive to the artifact. Independent component analysis from a single (or less times) stimulation extract evoked potential, but inherent physical meaning on the various independent components needs further study. SVM only can extract features and can not extract signals. Wavelet transform is a time-frequency analysis method suitable for non-stationary signal, and its zoom feature makes the difference between sorts outstanding performance. Wavelet analysis decomposes the signal into a series of superposition of wavelet functions, wavelet window size change with frequency. In the low frequency, it has a low time resolution and high frequency resolution, conversely, in the high frequency, high time resolution and low frequency resolution [3]. As the multi-resolution characteristics of wavelet transform it is more suitable for processing non-stationary signals. This paper use wavelet transform is used to extract P300 features of visual evoked EEG in this paper.

2   Basic Algorithm Theories

Wavelet analysis is a local analysis method to time-frequency domain. The wavelet analysis is adaptive for non-stationary signals processing. Based on the multi-resolution analysis, Mallat algorithm uses two theorems through two groups of filter to achieve wavelet transform and inverse transform. Mallat algorithm provides means for wavelet application, particularly in time-frequency signal analysis, only need the relevant data of analyzed signal and the coefficients of two-group filters in two-scale equation.

In the multi-resolution analysis, scaling function is $\varphi(t)$, corresponding wavelet function is $\psi(t$. They meet the two-scale difference equation:

$$\begin{cases} \varphi(t) = \sqrt{2} \sum_{k=-\infty}^{+\infty} h_o(k)\varphi(2t-k) \\ \psi(t) = \sqrt{2} \sum_{k=-\infty}^{+\infty} h_1(k)\varphi(2t-k) \end{cases} \tag{1}$$

Where, $h_o(k)$ is the orthogonal low-pass filter coefficient $\square$ $h_1(k)$ is the orthogonal high-pass filter coefficient.

By the respective orthogonality of $\varphi_{j,k}$ and $\psi_{j,k}$, $h_o(k)$, $h_1(k)$ can be obtained by the following formula:

$$\begin{cases} h_o(k) = <\varphi_{j,0}(t), \varphi_{j-1,k}(t)> \\ h_1(k) = <\psi_{1,0}(t), \varphi_{0,k}(t)> \end{cases} \tag{2}$$

The method based on wavelet transform includes wavelet decomposition and reconstruction. Supposing original signal $f(n)$, if $a_j(k)$ and $d_j(k)$ are the discrete approximation coefficients and discrete detail coefficients in the multi-resolution analysis, $h_o(k)$ and $h_1(k)$ are two orthogonal filters meet to scale equation, then the wavelet decomposition algorithm can be expressed as:

$$\begin{cases} a_o(k) = f(n) \\ a_{j+1}(k) = \sum_k a_j(n)h_o(n-2k) \\ d_{j+1}(k) = \sum_k a_j(n)h_1(n-2k) \end{cases} \tag{3}$$

Wavelet reconstruction algorithm is the reverse process of the decomposition algorithm. It can also be achieved by filter groups. That is:

$$a_j(k) = \sum_n a_{j+1}(k)h_o(k-2n) + \sum_k d_{j+1}(k)h_1(k-2n) \tag{4}$$

Because the wavelet function is not unique, different basic wavelet will produce different results. Daubechies series of wavelet (wavelet series dbN) are the most widely used in engineering as compact supported orthogonal real wavelet function. Its characteristics are: supported length L=2N, order of vanishing moment p=N, with the N increases, the locality of time domain becomes worse, but the locality of frequency domain better. Other compact supported wavelet function, such as Coif wavelet and Sym wavelet are not as good as db wavelet. Therefore, by comparison, the db6 wavelet is selected as the wavelet function of EEG analysis.

3   Experimental Paradigm and Data Description

Experimental paradigm of visual evoked Oddball provided by Donchin, which was selected as the standard data of BCI2005 competition. The user was presented 6×6 matrix of characters (see Figure 1). The testee's task was to focus attention on characters in a word that was prescribed by the investigator. The goal was to evoke EEG features through visual stimulus, recognize the character which user was gazing, and complete the task of spelling words.

For each character, the display was as follows: the matrix was displayed for a 2.5s period. In the first 400ms, character matrix was not highlighted, that is, no display. All rows and lines of the matrix were randomly highlighted at a rate of 5.7Hz, that is, the matrix was highlighted for 100ms and black for 75ms to each row or line. 6×6 character matrix needs to be highlighted for 12 times. Where, containing the target stimulating character (belongs to highlighted row and line) has 2 times. EEG signals evoked by target stimulating were different from those evoked by no-target stimulating. The test was repeated 15 times for each character to ensure the strength of evoked potential. After the 0.1-60Hz band-pass filter and sampling at 240Hz, the recorded data has been converted into Matlab format *. Mat files. The test was performed to A and B subjects, including one training set (85 characters) and one testing set (100 characters) for the A and B subjects. All of the data was stored in single precision. For each *.mat file contains the 64-channel evoked EEG data.

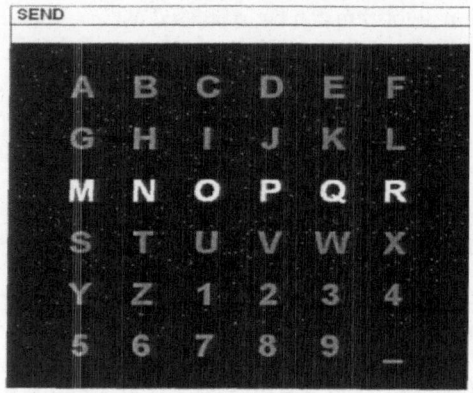

Fig. 1. This figure illustrates the user display for this paradigm

4   Visual Evoked EEG Feature Extractions

Because of EEG belongs to the weak signals, there are various disturbances and noises in the acquired data. Furthermore, measuring the EEG signals is inevitable to be recorded spontaneous EEG signal, EOG artifact and the errors caused by the baseline shifts. Therefore, in order to extract distinct features we need to eliminate the interference and noise without the loss of EEG information. The pre-processing for EEG includes the common average reference (CAR), band-pass filtering, artifact removal, and the superposed average in this paper. Firstly, obtain relatively ideal reference electrode through CAR and select optimal 10 electrodes. Then, smooth the EEG signal through $0.5 \sim 30Hz$ band-pass filter and divide data into segments according to 1s unit after each stimulus starting, rearranged and down-sampled the data, superposed average 15 times on the basis of the above pretreatment. Finally, choosing dB3 wavelet, execute two layers of wavelet decomposition to the pretreated signals and reconstruct approximation coefficient of the second layer to extract the characteristics of evoked EEG. The algorithm is performed in accordance with the principle of multi-resolution analysis described in section 2.

5   Results and Analysis

BCI2000 competition data recorded by 64-channel EEG amplifier were applied for experimental simulation. Only Fz, Fc1, Fc2, C3, Cz, C4, Pz, PO7, PO8, FP1 channels were used in simulation due to obvious P300 response in those channels.

Firstly, the original experimental EEG data was processed in accordance with the above-mentioned pre-processing method. The processed results of the first character about Cz channel are shown as follows. Figure 2 shows the result through common average reference of EEG signal for objective and non-objective characters. Figure 3 shows the result through filtering of EEG signal for objective and non-objective characters. Figure 4 shows the result through 15 times superimposed average of EEG signal for objective and non-objective characters. After the above preprocessing of EEG data, the signal to noise ratio can be improved by 30%. Those data will be used in the subsequent feature extraction.

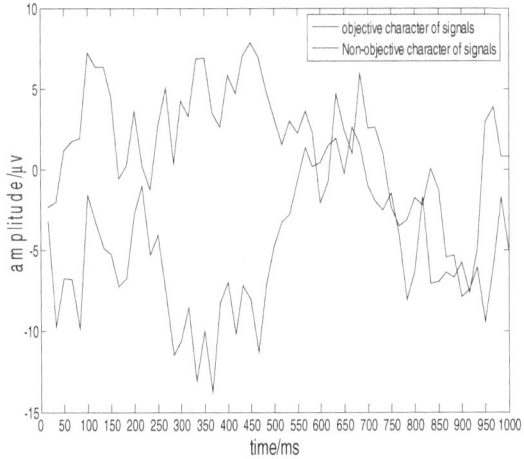

Fig. 2. Results of the EEG signal through common average reference for objective and non-objective characters

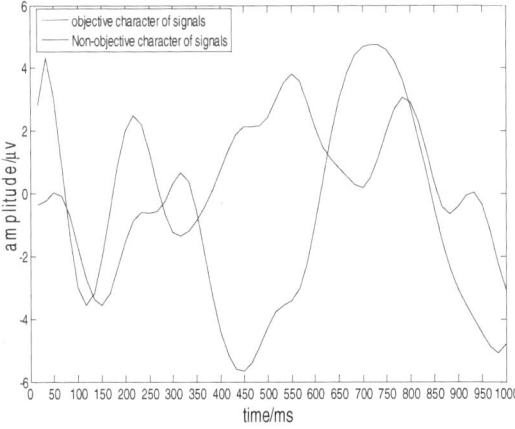

Fig. 3. Results of the EEG signal through filtering for objective and non-objective characters

Secondly, wavelet transform is applied for EEG data about Cz channel. Figure 5 shows the result through reconstructing the second-layer approximation coefficient of wavelet decomposing for objective and non-objective characters. The result has shown that an obvious peak appears at the 266ms after visual evoked stimulating for objective character. However, there is no evoked peak for EEG signal at the 266ms for non-objective characters. Therefore, we can clearly know that P300 feature occurs at 266ms, while we can use the EEG amplitude at 266ms for more classification and identification of evoked EEG signal.

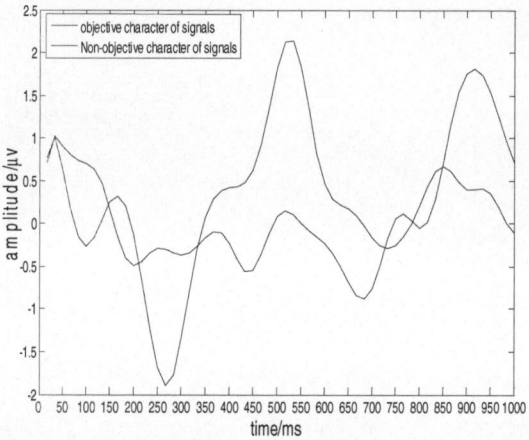

Fig. 4. Results of the EEG signal through 15 times superimposed average for objective and non-objective characters

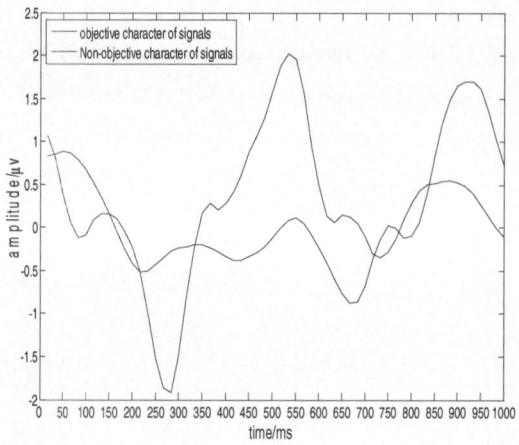

Fig. 5. Results of the EEG signal through reconstructing wavelet coefficients for objective and non-objective characters

6   Conclusions

P300 feature of visual evoked EEG signal is effectively extracted by wavelet transform in this paper. Because wavelet transform takes on the capability of multi-resolution analysis and subtle decomposition for signals, it can express the local information of signals in the time and frequency domain. Furthermore, wavelet transform can be more effective to reveal the non-stationary characteristics of EEG signal and to suppress the interference included in EEG. Therefore, wavelet transform provided an effective method for the feature extraction and automated analysis of evoked EEG signal.

References

1. Zhao, L., Wan, B.: Study on the P300-based brain computer interface. Journal of Tianjin University of Technology and Education 15, 5–9 (2005)
2. Wang, Q., Le, J., Jin, S., Tian, f., Wang, L.: The Study of EEG Higher Oder Spectral Analysis Technology. Chinese Journal of Medical Instrumentation 33, 79–82 (2009)
3. Wang, Y., Qiu, T., Liu, R.: A wavelet analysis method for single channel evoked potential extraction with a few sweeps. Chinese Journal of Biomedical Engineering 30, 34–39 (2011)
4. Eduardo, B.-c.: The Theory and Use of the Quaternion Wavelet Transform. Journal of Mathematical Imaging and Vision 24, 19–35 (2006)

A New Blind Estimation of MIMO Channels Based on HGA

Hua Li, Ju-ming Zhao, Run-fang Hao, and Qing-hua Zhao

College of Information Engineering, Taiyuan University of Technology,
Taiyuan Shanxi 030024, China
hwaerly@163.com

Abstract. new blind estimation of MIMO channels using HGA was proposed for the frequency selective channel. By exploiting the output statistics, an objective function that coming from blind estimation of MIMO channels based on the subspace could be obtained. Then the fitness function based on the objective function is proposed for optimization by a hybrid genetic algorithm (HGA). We have proved this method could be used in channel estimation. Compared with the existing subspace method, this method need not know channel order previously and can estimate the channel parameter and channel order together. The simulation results show the effectiveness of the proposed method.

Keywords: MIMO, Channel estimation, HGA, Fitness function.

1 Introduction

The multiple input multiple output (MIMO) technique represents an efficient method to increase data transmission rate without increasing band-width since different data streams are transmitted from different transmitted antenna[1]. It is the important breakthrough of the intelligent antenna in wireless communication. Channel estimation in a MIMO system is usually a difficult task because the number of channels rapidly increases with the number of antennas and users. In order to alleviate the need for training sequences, achieve a much desired bandwidth gain, blind identification which estimates the channel impulse responses solely using the output statistics, is desirable. Research in this area is very active and many methods have been proposed in recent years.

In this paper, we will propose an objective function that coming from blind estimation of MIMO channels based on the subspace method. Then the fitness function based on the objective function is proposed for optimization by a hybrid genetic algorithm (HGA)-based approach. We proved our method could be used in channel estimation. Compared with the existing subspace method, our method can estimate the channel parameter and channel order together. The efficiency of this approach is demonstrated from computer simulations.

H. Deng et al. (Eds.): AICI 2011, Part II, LNAI 7003, pp. 568–574, 2011.

2   System Model

Let us consider a MIMO system with M_T transmitters and M_R receivers. The channel is FIR frequency selective fading MIMO channel, and the order of the channel is L. The noise at the receiver front end is white Gaussian noise and is assumed to have zero mean and be uncorrelated with the rest of the signals. Under these assumptions, the received signal can be expressed as:

$$x_i(n) = \sum_{j=1}^{M_T} \sum_{l=0}^{L-1} h_{ij}(n,l)s_j(n-l) + b_i(n)$$

$$1 \le i \le M_R, \quad -\infty \le n \le +\infty$$

(1)

In the above model, $h_{ij}(n,l)$ denotes the lth path channel fading coefficient from j transmitter to i receiver at the time n. $s_j(n)$ denotes the transmitted signal from j transmitter at the time n. $b_i(n)$ denotes the additive white Gaussian noise with zero mean and variance σ_b^2 at the time n which is added on i receiver. With Eq.(1), the transmitted and received signals and noise can be expressed as vectors respectively:

$$x(n) = [x_1(n), x_2(n), \cdots, x_{M_R}(n)]^T$$

$$s(n) = [s_1(n), s_2(n), \cdots, s_{M_T}(n)]^T$$

$$b(n) = [b_1(n), b_2(n), \cdots, b_{M_R}(n)]^T$$

the channel matrix can be express as:

$$H(l) = \begin{bmatrix} h_{11}(l) & h_{12}(l) & \cdots & h_{1M_R}(l) \\ h_{21}(l) & h_{22}(l) & \cdots & h_{2M_R}(l) \\ \vdots & \vdots & \ddots & \vdots \\ h_{M_T1}(l) & h_{M_T2}(l) & \cdots & h_{M_TM_R}(l) \end{bmatrix}$$

So the Eq. (1) can be rewrite as:

$$x(n) = \sum_{l=0}^{L-1} H(l)s(n-l) + b(n)$$

(2)

Take $N+1$ as the length of projected window, so the convolution form above can be rewrite as matrix form.

$$X_n = \tilde{H}S_n + B_n$$

$$X_n = [x(n), x(n-1), \cdots, x(n-N)]^T$$

(3)

where

$$S_n = [s(n), s(n-1), \cdots, s(n-N-L)]^T$$

$$B_n = [b(n), b(n-1), \cdots, b(n-N)]^T$$

The channel matrix $\tilde{H}$ is a $(N+1)M_R \times (N+L+1)M_T$ block Teoplitz Sylvester matrix, and $\tilde{H}$ can be expressed as

$$\tilde{H} = \begin{bmatrix} H(0) & \cdots & H(L-1) & 0 & \cdots & 0 \\ 0 & H(0) & \vdots & H(L-1) & \ddots & \vdots \\ \vdots & \ddots & \ddots & \ddots & \ddots & 0 \\ 0 & \cdots & 0 & H(0) & \cdots & H(L-1) \end{bmatrix} \quad (4)$$

There are hypotheses about the model as below

(a) $\tilde{H}$ is column nonsingular, that is $(N+1)M_R > (N+L+1)M_T$. $H(0)$ and $H(M)$ are column nonsingular, that is $M_R > M_T$.
(b) the signal source are independent.
(c) the noise is additive white gaussian noise, that is $E[B_n B_n^T] = \sigma^2 I$. The noise and the signal are independent. That is, for all m and n, there are $E[b(n)s(m)] = 0$.
(d) the order of the channel L is known.

3   Subspace Algorithm for Blind Estimation of MIMO Channels

First, the autocorrelative matrix of the receiving signals should be calculation. Because of the hypothesis above, the noise and the signal are mutual independence, so the autocorrelative matrix can be write as

$$R_{XX} = E[X_n X_n^H] = E[(\tilde{H}S_n + B_n)(S_n^H \tilde{H}^H + B_n^H)]$$
$$= E[\tilde{H}S_n B_n^H] + E[\tilde{H}S_n S_n^H \tilde{H}^H] + E[B_n B_n^H] + E[B_n S_n^H \tilde{H}^H] \quad (5)$$

Decompose R_{XX} eigenvalue. $\lambda_0 \geq \lambda_1 \geq \cdots \geq \lambda_{(N+1)M_R - 1}$ is the eigenvalue of R_{XX}. Because R_{SS} is nonsingular, the first item on right hand of Eq.(6), namely, the rank of the signal is $(N+L+1)M_T$. Therefore, the eigenvalue can be divided as two parts.

$$\lambda_i > \sigma^2, \quad i = 0, \cdots, (N+L+1)M_T - 1$$

$$\lambda_i = \sigma^2, \quad i = (N+L+1)M_T, \cdots, (N+1)M_R - 1$$

The corresponding eigenvector spread as signal subspace and noise subspace respectively. They can expressed as

$$U = \begin{bmatrix} U_0, \cdots, U_{(N+L+1)M_T-1} \end{bmatrix}$$

$$G = \begin{bmatrix} G_0, \cdots, G_{(N+1)M_R-(N+L+1)M_T-1} \end{bmatrix}$$

The dimensions of them are respectively

$$(N+1)M_R \times (N+L+1)M_T$$

$$(N+1)M_R \times ((N+1)M_R - (N+L+1)M_T)$$

Therefore, the autocorrelative matrix can be rewrite as

$$R_{XX} = U diag \left(\lambda_0, \cdots, \lambda_{(N+L+1)M_T-1} \right) U^T + \sigma^2 G G^T \tag{6}$$

Compare with Eq.(5) and Eq.(6), we can see, the column vector of $\tilde{H}$ also spread as the signal subspace. Because of the orthogonality of the signal subspace and the noise subspace, the column vector of $\tilde{H}$ and noise subspace are also orthogonal. So we can have

$$G_i^T \tilde{H} = 0 \tag{7}$$

The channel parameters can be determined uniquely by Eq.(7). The cost function was defined as

$$J(h) = \left\| G_i^T \tilde{H} \right\| \tag{8}$$

The channel order is not a variable In Eq.(8). The estimation of the channel parameters could be achieved by minimize $J(h)$, that is

$$\hat{h} = arg \min_h J(h) \tag{9}$$

where

$$h = \begin{bmatrix} h_{11}(0), \cdots, h_{M_T M_R}(0), h_{11}(1), \cdots, h_{M_T M_R}(1), \cdots, h_{11}(L-i), \cdots, h_{M_T M_R}(L-1) \end{bmatrix} \tag{10}$$

4   Blind Estimation of MIMO Channels Based on HGA

GA is a type of structured "random" search that mimics the process of biological evolution. The algorithm begins with a population of chromosomes (i.e. a collection of parameter estimations). Each chromosome is evaluated for its fitness in solving a given optimization task. At every generation, crossover and mutation are applied to the fittest chromosomes in order to generate new offspring for the next generation. After a number of generations, workable solutions can be evolved for the optimization task. The features of our proposed HGA are described as follows.

Code rule: there are two parts in a single chromosome. The channel parameter and channel order have been coded together to be estimation at same time.

The ith generation jth chromosome expressed as $(c,h)_j^i$, $(j=1,\cdots,Q)$. Q is genus size. c is channel order, adopted binary system coding. h is channel parameter, adopted real number coding. The interior framework is $\{c_1\ c_2\ \cdots\ c_N h_{11}(0)\ \cdots\ h_{M_r M_s}(0)\ h_{11}(1)\ \cdots\ h_{M_r M_s}(L-1)\}$

Original genus and variable genus: In order to prevent the algorithm convergence to zero, the restrict is as follows, $\|h\|=1$, $c_i \neq 0$, $(i=1,2,\cdots,N)$.

Giving birth to random Q chromosomes which meet restricts upwards as original genus. Q is invariable in every generation.

Fitness rule: the fitness function was defined as $f(c,h)_j^i = [c\,J(h)]_j^i$. According to coding rule, the fitness function is positive and is more smaller more better.

Selection: chooses parents for the next generation based on their scaled values from the fitness scaling function

Crossover: consider a pair of chromosomes

$$\left(c_j^i,h_j^i\right)=\left(c_{1,j}^i,c_{2,j}^i,\cdots,c_{N,j}^i,h_{1,j}^i,h_{2,j}^i,\cdots,h_{M,j}^i\right)$$

$$\left(c_k^i,h_k^i\right)=\left(c_{1,k}^i,c_{2,k}^i,\cdots,c_{N,k}^i,h_{1,k}^i,h_{2,k}^i,\cdots,h_{M,k}^i\right)$$

Let $l \in [1,N]$ is a random integer, $l_1,l_2 \in [1,M]$ being two random integers and $[l_1 < l_2]$, $\alpha_{l_1+1},\cdots,\alpha_{l_2}$ are random numbers in interval $(0,1)$, then two corresponding chromosomes of next generation are

$$\left(c_j^{i+1},h_j^{i+1}\right)=\left(c_{1,j}^i,\cdots,c_{1,k}^i,\cdots,c_{N,j}^i,h_{1,j}^i,\cdots,h_{l_1,j}^i,\alpha_{l_1+1}h_{l_1+1,j}^i+(1-\alpha_{l_1+1})h_{l_1+1,k}^i,\cdots,\alpha_{l_2}h_{l_2,j}^i+(1-\alpha_{l_2})h_{l_2,k}^i,h_{l_2+1,j}^i,\cdots,h_{M,j}^i\right)$$

$$\left(c_k^{i+1},h_k^{i+1}\right)=\left(c_{1,k}^i,\cdots,c_{1,j}^i,\cdots,c_{N,k}^i,h_{1,k}^i,\cdots,h_{l_1,k}^i,\alpha_{l_1+1}h_{l_1+1,k}^i+(1-\alpha_{l_1+1})h_{l_1+1,j}^i,\cdots,\alpha_{l_2}h_{l_2,k}^i+(1-\alpha_{l_2})h_{l_2,j}^i,h_{l_2+1,k}^i,\cdots,h_{M,k}^i\right)$$

Mutation: consider a chromosome $h_j^i = (h_1,h_2,\cdots,h_M)_j^i$, generating a random integer d in interval $[1,M]$ and a random real number β in interval $[-1,1]$, then a corresponding chromosome of next generation is

$$h_j^{i+1} = \left(h_1,\cdots,h_{d-1},h_d + \beta/P,h_{d+1},\cdots,h_M\right)$$

P affects the convergence rate. In the beginning, P should be a minor number. After several generations, P should be augmented.

Stopping criteria: determine what causes the algorithm to terminate.
(1) Generation limit - completed the maximum number of iterations the genetic algorithm performs.
(2) Fitness limit one- the best fitness value had not improved in several generations. That is

$$\left|\min_j f(c,h)_j^i - \min_j f(c,h)_j^{i-x}\right| < e\min_j f(c,h)_j^i \tag{11}$$

e is a real number in interval $(0,1)$.

(3) Fitness limit two- the best fitness value approach to even fitness value. That is

$$\min_{j} f(c,h)_{j}^{i} < \frac{1}{Q}\sum_{j=1}^{Q} f(c,h)_{j}^{i} \tag{12}$$

5   Simulation

The simulation MIMO channel is rayleigh fading channel. The order of the channel from the transmitted end to received end is $L = 3$. There are two antennas in the transmitted end and four antennas in the received end. The noise at the receiver front end is white Gaussian noise and is assumed to have zero mean and be uncorrelated with the rest of the signals. The length of every chromosome is 5. There are 600sampling points to be utilized estimating autocorrelative matrix of the received signal. Population size is $Q = 20$. Selection probability is $p_s = 0.2$. Crossover probability is $p_c = 0.25$, Mutation probability is $p_m = 0.01$. Generation limit is 500. $e = 0.1$. In Fig.1, the curve show evolution curve for MIMO channels estimation. In the beginning of this curve, there is relatively larger oscillation, and the gap between best fitness and mean fitness is relatively larger. Following the generation increases, the oscillation and gap decrease gradually.

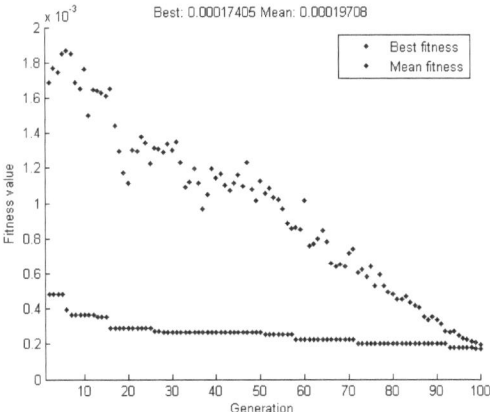

Fig. 1. Evolution curve for MIMO channels estimation

The channel parameter is estimated by using HGA and subspace algorithm. The performance level is weighed by

$$\text{NMSE} = \frac{1}{MV}\sum_{j=1}^{V}\sum_{i=1}^{M}\left\|\hat{H}_{ij} - H_{ij}\right\|^{2} \Big/ H_{ij}^{2} \tag{13}$$

In Fig.2, the curve show the performance level of MIMO channel estimation based on HGA approach to subspace.

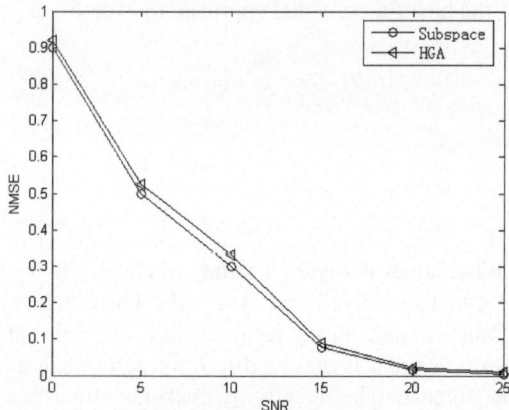

Fig. 2. Performance comparison

6   Conclusion

A blind estimation of MIMO channels using HGA was proposed for the frequency selective channel. This new algorithm can estimate MIMO channel parameter and channel order. Simulation result shows that this new estimation method has high estimation precision. The emphasis of the research for the future will focus on how to increase the convergence speed.

References

1. Telatar, I.E.: Capacity of multi-antenna Gaussian channels. European Trans. on Telecomm., 585–595 (October 1999)
2. Chen, F., Kwong, S., Wei, G., Ku, C.K.W., Man, K.F.: Blind linear channel estimation using genetic algorithm and SIMO model. Signal Processing 83, 2021–2035 (2003)
3. Jeon, H.-G., Serpedin, E.: A novel simplified channel tracking method for MIMO-OFDM systems with null sub-carriers. Signal Processing 88, 1002–1016 (2008)
4. Li, H., Zhang, W., Zhao, Q.-h., Wang, H.-k., Zhang, Z.-x.: Blind Estimation of MIMO Channels Using Genetic Algorithm. In: 2009 Fifth International Conference on Natural Computation (ICNC 2009), vol. (4), pp. 163–166 (2009)
5. Enescu, M., Sirbu, M., Koivunen, V.: Adaptive equalization of time-varying MIMO channels. Signal Processing 85, 81–93 (2005)
6. Zeng, Y., Ng, T.S.: Blind estimation of MIMO channels with an upper bound for channel orders. Signal Processing 86, 212–222 (2006)

The Blind Equalization Algorithm
Based on the Feedback Neural Network

Xiaoqin Zhang and Liyi Zhang[*]

School of Electric Information Engineering, Tianjin University, Tianjin China, 300072
School of Information Engineering, Tianjin University of Commerce, Tianjin China, 300134
`alisoner@sina.com, zhangliyi@tjcu.edu.cn`

Abstract. In this paper, a new blind equalization algorithm based on the feedback neural network is proposed. The feedback is introduced into the neural network to improve control performance, so it can control the step-size variation of blind equalization suitably. That is, the quality of blind equalization is advanced. The structure and state functions of the feedback neural network is provided in this paper. The cost function is proposed, and the iteration formulas of equalization parameters are derived. Results of the simulation verify the effectiveness of the proposed algorithm.

Keywords: fuzzy neural network, blind equalization, feedback, control.

1 Introduction

The adaptive equalizer needs to send the training sequence constantly, so bandwidth is occupied partly. In the broadcast and multi-point communication, the adaptive equalizer can't send the training sequence again to initialize the receiver. So it can't satisfy the development request of the digital communication technology.

Blind equalization technology only utilizes the statistical property of received signals to adjust the parameter adaptively without the assistance of the training sequence. Blind equalizer overcomes the disadvantage of the tradition equalizer. It can compensate for channel characteristics, reduce Inter-symbol Interference (ISI) and improve the communication quality. Blind equalization technology has become one of the hotspot in communication technologies.

Because feedback fuzzy neural network (FFNN) combines the fuzzy systems with neural networks, it has strong mapping ability, self-learning ability and approximation ability of nonlinear systems. In this paper, a feedback is introduced into the neural network to improve control performance, so it can control the step-size variation of blind equalization suitably. That is, the quality of blind equalization is advanced.

This paper is organized into five sections. Sections 2 introduces the principle of CMA blind equalization algorithm. In sections 3 a new feedback neural network is proposed and their learning algorithms are derived. In section 4, computer simulations

---

[*] Corresponding author.

H. Deng et al. (Eds.): AICI 2011, Part II, LNAI 7003, pp. 575–581, 2011.

are performed as compared with the forward neural network algorithm. Finally, section 5 gives the conclusions.

2   The Foundational Principle of Blind Equalization Algorithm

The foundational principle block diagram of CMA blind equalization algorithm as shown in Fig.1.

In Fig.1, $x(n)$ is the transition sequence, $n(n)$ is add noise, $y(n)$ is the accept sequence or the blind equalizer input, $\tilde{x}(n)$ is the equalizer output sequence, $\hat{x}(n)$ is the decision output sequence.

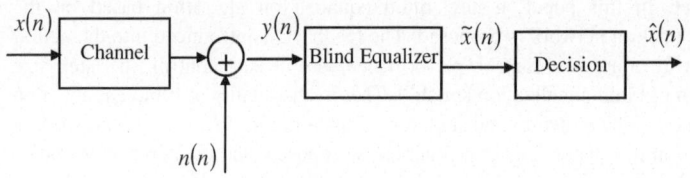

Fig. 1. The principle diagram of CMA blind equalization algorithm

The cost function of CMA is [1]

$$J(n)=\frac{1}{4}E\left[\left[|\tilde{x}(n)|^2 -R_2\right]^2\right]$$ (1)

where

$$R_2 =\frac{E\left[|x(n)|^4\right]}{E\left[|x(n)|^2\right]}$$ (2)

The weight iteration formula of CMA is

$$\mathbf{W}(n+1)= \mathbf{W}(n)+\lambda\tilde{x}(n)\left[R_2 -|\tilde{x}(n)|^2\right]\mathbf{Y}^*(n)$$ (3)

where, λ is step-size.

The fixed step size is used in traditional CMA algorithm, which affects the convergence properties of CMA. If the big step-size is used in CMA, the amplitude of weights adjustment will be big, and the convergence speed and tracking speed will be accelerated. But the bigger steady residual error (SRE) will be produced. On the contrary, if the small step-size is used in CMA, the amplitude of weights adjustment will be small, and the smaller SRE will be produced. But the convergence speed and tracking speed will be decelerated [2].

In order to both quicken algorithm convergence rate and decrease SRE, a new blind equalization algorithm based on FFNN controlling the step-size is proposed. In this paper, the big step-size is used in the beginning of algorithm to quicken the algorithm convergence rate. Then the step-size is decreased gradually along with the degree of convergence to recede the SRE to optimize algorithm.

3   The Blind Equalization Algorithm Based on FFNN

3.1   The Structure and the State Algorithm Based on FFNN Controller

The structure of FFNN is shown in Fig.2. It is consists of four layers: input layer, fuzzification layer, rule layer and output layer.

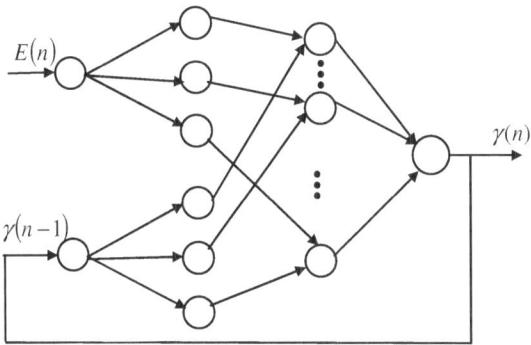

Fig. 2. The structure of   FFNN controller

The input of FFNN are $E(n)$ and $\gamma(n-1)$. The output of FFNN is $\gamma(n)$, which is the variation of the step-size. The fuzzy sets of $E(n)$ are {big, middle, small}, and the fuzzy sets of $\gamma(n-1)$ are {positive, zero, negative}. $E(n)$ is defined as

$$E(n) = MSE(n)$$

$$(4)$$

The state functions of FFNN controller are defined as
(1) The input layer
$$_z I_1^{(1)}(n) = E(n), \quad I_2^{(1)}(n) = \gamma(n-1)$$

$$O_{ij}^{(1)}(n) = I_i^{(1)}(n) \quad (i = 1,2 \quad\quad j = 1,2,3)$$

$$(5)$$

(2) The fuzzification layer
$$I_{ij}^{(2)} = O_{ij}^{(1)}$$

$$O_{jm}^{(2)}(n) = \exp\left[-\left(\frac{I_{ij}^{(2)}(n) - m_{ij}^{(2)}(n)}{\sigma_{ij}^{(2)}(n)}\right)^2\right] \quad (m = 1,2,3) \tag{6}$$

(3) The rule layer
$$I_{jm}^{(3)}(n) = O_{jm}^{(2)}(n)$$

$$O_l^{(3)} = \prod I_{jm}^{(3)} \qquad (l = 1,2,\cdots,9) \tag{7}$$

(4) The output layer
$$I_l^{(4)}(n) = O_l^{(3)}(n)$$

$$\gamma(n) = O^{(4)}(n) = \sum_{l=1}^{9} \rho(n) I_l^{(4)}(n) \tag{8}$$

where, $I_i^{(k)}(n)$ is the i th input node of the k th layer, $O_i^{(k)}(n)$ is the i th output node of the k th layer, $m_{ij}(n)$ is the center of the membership function, $\sigma_{ij}(n)$ is the width of the membership function, $\rho(n)$ is the weight of the output layer.

3.2   The Iteration Formula of FFNN Blind Equalization Algorithm

We define a new cost function [3]

$$J = \frac{1}{2}\left[|\gamma(n)|^2 - R\right]^2 \tag{9}$$

where,

$$R = \frac{E\left[|E(n)|^4\right]}{E\left[|E(n)|^2\right]} \tag{10}$$

Then the steepest descent method is used in FFNN blind equalization algorithm. There are three parameters $m_{ij}^{(2)}$, $\sigma_{ij}^{(2)}$ and ρ will be iterated. They have different parameter iteration formula.

(1) ρ iteration formula

$$\frac{\partial J(n)}{\partial \rho(n)} = 2\left[|\gamma(n)|^2 - R\right]\gamma(n)I_l^{(4)*}(n) \tag{11}$$

So,

$$\rho(n+1) = \rho(n) - \eta_\rho\left[|\gamma(n)|^2 - R\right]\gamma(n)I_l^{(4)*}(n) \tag{12}$$

where, η_ρ is the iteration step-size.

(2) $m_{ij}^{(2)}$ iteration formula

$$\frac{\partial J(n)}{\partial m_{ij}^{(2)}(n)} = 4\left[|\gamma(n)|^2 - R\right]\gamma(n) \cdot \rho^*(n) \cdot O_l^{(3)}(n) \cdot \frac{I_{ij}^{(2)}(n) - m_{ij}^{(2)}(n)}{\left[\sigma_{ij}^{(2)}(n)\right]^2} \tag{13}$$

So,

$$m_{ij}^{(2)}(n+1) = m_{ij}^{(2)}(n) - \eta_m\left[|\gamma(n)|^2 - R\right]\gamma(n) \cdot \rho^*(n) \cdot O_l^{(3)}(n) \cdot \frac{I_{ij}^{(2)}(n) - m_{ij}^{(2)}(n)}{\left[\sigma_{ij}^{(2)}(n)\right]^2} \tag{14}$$

where, η_m is the iteration step-size.

(3) $\sigma_{ij}^{(2)}$ iteration formula

$$\frac{\partial J(n)}{\partial \sigma_{ij}^{(2)}(n)} = 4\left[|\gamma(n)|^2 - R\right]\gamma(n) \cdot \rho^*(n) \cdot O_l^{(3)}(n) \cdot \frac{\left[I_{ij}^{(2)}(n) - m_{ij}^{(2)}(n)\right]^2}{\left[\sigma_{ij}^{(2)}(n)\right]^3} \tag{15}$$

So,

$$\sigma_{ij}^{(2)}(n+1) = \sigma_{ij}^{(2)}(n) - \eta_\sigma\left[|\gamma(n)|^2 - R\right]\gamma(n) \cdot \rho^*(n) \cdot O_l^{(3)}(n) \cdot \frac{\left[I_{ij}^{(2)}(n) - m_{ij}^{(2)}(n)\right]^2}{\left[\sigma_{ij}^{(2)}(n)\right]^3} \tag{16}$$

where, η_σ is the iteration step-size.

So, the weight iteration formula of CMA is

$$\mathbf{W}(n+1) = \mathbf{W}(n) + \lambda(n)\tilde{x}(n)\left[R_2 - |\tilde{x}(n)|^2\right]\mathbf{Y}^*(n) \tag{17}$$

where, $\lambda(n)$ is the variable step-size.

$$\lambda(n+1) = \lambda(n) + \gamma(n) = \lambda(n) + \sum_{l=1}^{9}\rho(n)I_l^{(4)}(n) \tag{18}$$

This is the blind equalization algorithm based on feedback fuzzy neural network.

4   Computer Simulation Results

The input signal in simulation is 16QAM, noise ratio is 20dB, and the filter order is 11. The simulation channel is the common channel [4]. Its z-transform is

$$H(z) = 1 + 0.5z^{-1} + 0.25z^{-2} + 0.125z^{-3} \tag{19}$$

The convergence constellations using FFNN algorithm (a) and using forward neural network (FWNN) algorithm [5] (b) in common channel are shown in Fig.3. Where, $\eta_\rho = 0.003$, $\eta_m = 0.0035$, $\eta_\sigma = -0.005$. The sample number is 4000.

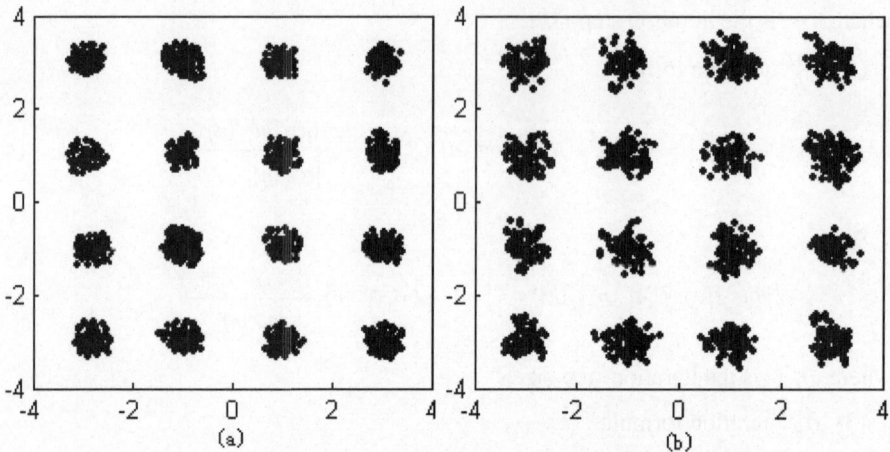

Fig. 3. 16QAM signal convergence constellations

We can see that the constellation based on the new algorithm is more centralized and clearly.

The BER (Bit Error Rate) curves using FFNN algorithm and using FWNN algorithm in common channel are shown in Fig.4.

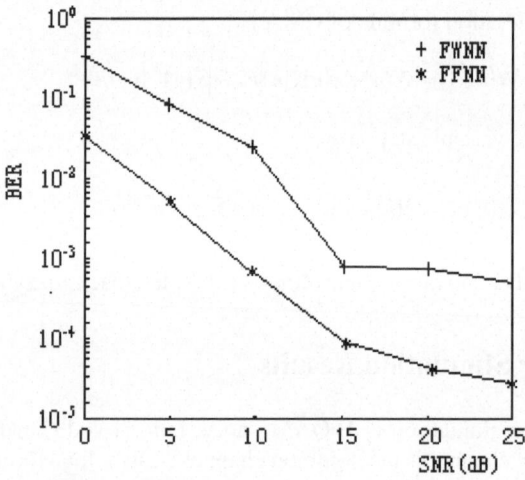

Fig. 4. BER curves of 16QAM in common channel

From the BER curves, we can see that the new algorithm has lower bit error rate than FWNN algorithm.

5   Conclusion

In this paper, the FFNN is used to control the step-size of CMA algorithm. The performance of the blind equalizer is improved. Computer simulation results show that the new algorithm has faster convergence speed, lower bit error rate, smaller SRE than FWNN algorithm.

References

1. Godard, D.N.: Self-recovering equalization and carrier tracking in two-dimensional data communication systems. IEEE Trans. on Communication 28, 1867–1875 (1980)
2. Gu, Y., Tang, K., Cui, H., Du, W.: Novel variable step size NLMS algorithm. Journal of Tsinghua University (Science and Technology) 42(1), 15–18 (2002)
3. Yan, P., Zhang, C.: Artificial Neural Networks and Simulate Devolutionary Computation. Tsinghua University Press, Beijing (2000)
4. Amari, S., et al.: Adaptive Blind Signal Processing–Neural Network Approach. Proc. IEEE 86(12), 2026–(2048)
5. Cheng, H.-q., Zhang, L.-y.: Blind Equalization Algorithm Using Feed-forward Neural Network Based on a Modified Target Function. Journal of Taiyuan University of Technology 37(S1), 39–41 (2006)

Spatial Representation and Reasoning: Integrating Synthetic Character's Visual Perception and Symbolic Representation

Flavio S. Yamamoto and Marcio L. Netto

Polytechnic School of University of São Paulo
PSI: Electronic Systems Department
São Paulo, Brazil
fsy@usp.br, lobonett@lsi.usp.br

Abstract. We propose a framework for handling information about how objects establish relationships with each other in the space. This framework is a model to address systems composed of multiple characters endowed with qualitative spatial reasoning. From the visual perception, each agent constructs its own knowledge representation about the world. These agents use imagery to compose spaces of subsets, their spatial knowledge representation. Such spaces are used as semantic domains to modelling spatial knowledge and reasoning. This kind of representation makes it natural to use constraint programming to implement an engine for spatial reasoning.

Keywords: Hybrid Modal Logic, Multi-Agent System, Qualitative Spatial Reasoning, Constraint Programming, Synthetic Vision.

1 Introduction

In this work we propose a framework for handling information about how objects establish relationships with each other in the space. This framework is a model to address systems composed of multiple agents endowed with qualitative spatial reasoning (QSR). From the visual perception, each agent constructs its own knowledge representation about the world. These agents use imagery to compose spaces of subsets, their spatial knowledge representation. Such spaces are used as semantic domains to modelling spatial knowledge and reasoning. We consider that this type of spatial knowledge representation incorporated to the cognitive framework of an agent improves substantially its abilities related to orientation, positioning and navigation.

In this case, we understand that cognition is something strictly connected to the design of processes related to the information flow between the perception and the intellect, between the beliefs and the knowledge of autonomous agents. Figure 1 shows the general structure of the cognition of the agents.

The literature about spatial logics offers a large number of approaches for symbolic representations (see Aiello [1]). Qualitative Spatial Reasoning (QSR)

H. Deng et al. (Eds.): AICI 2011, Part II, LNAI 7003, pp. 582–593, 2011.
© Springer-Verlag Berlin Heidelberg 2011

is a particular case of these logics. Several texts serve as introduction for the foundations and applications of QSR Forbus [16], Randell [40], Cohn ([14], [13]), Bennett [5], Casati [12], Renz ([41], [42]), Parikh ([37, Chapter 6], Heinemann ([22], [23], [24]). However there are few texts which incorporate to the symbolic language another way of representation, for example, a way which would be expressed by means of images ([29] and [49]).

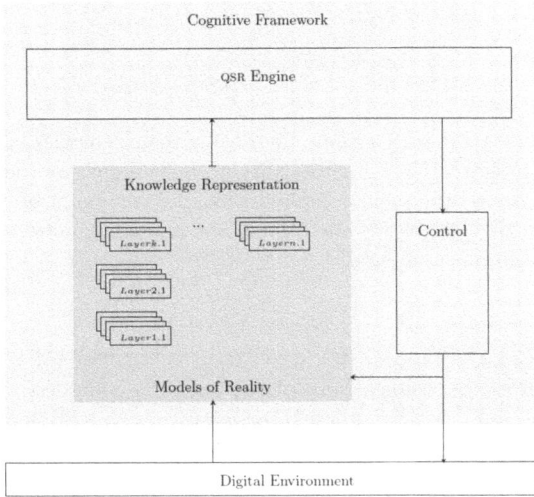

Fig. 1. Outline of the Cognitive Framework. The layers are constructed according to the perception of the agent. Each agent has a set of spatial relations which define the way how it percepts the space. A set of layers constitute a model of reality, the view of the world from the viewpoint of an agent in a given time, which serve as a foundation for the QSR.

The present work is organized as follows: in the next section we introduce the context in which our framework is inserted. In Section 3 we deal with the language of modal logics for spatial knowledge in order to represent and perform the qualitative spatial reasoning in dynamic multi-character systems. In this section we also deal with the usage of imagery in this cognitive structure. In the final section we present our considerations and future work related to the project.

2   Visual Perception, Imagery, and Spatial Representation

Our concern in the present work is not to deal with the perception apparatus of autonomous agents which live in virtual worlds. However, we describe how we use visual perception in our construction. In order to construct the representation of what is percepted by an agent, we use techniques of *synthetic vision*, following Noser ([35], [36]), Kuffner [26], and Peters [38]. Figure 2 shows the use of the concept of *synthetic vision*, extracted from Peters [38].

Fig. 2. Examples of synthetics vision. In the figure on the left, the picture at the bottom right corner shows the character's vision. In the figure on the right, the smaller picture on the left shows the scene rendered from the viewpoint of the character. The smaller picture on the right shows the same scene using the false colouring technique to check proximity between objects.

The technique used in [38] can be described as follows: the *render* generates the scene (128 x 128 area) in flat mode (without texture or other effects) from the viewpoint of each agent; each object of the scene is assigned to one false-color. The rendered image is then scanned in order to extract objects. The frequency of the scanning may vary. In [38] the authors adopted a system similar to the one of Kuffner, [26], replacing *octrees* to store information about the watched objects. In our case, we propose the use of *scene graphs* combined with *binary space partitioning* (BSP) trees.

BSPs allow to represent a spatial array taking into consideration the location of the elements which constitute the space, i.e. they are a good solution to deal visibility problems. The construction of partitions based in the orientation by alignment of polygons chooses a polygon, to be positioned by a partitioning plan, for each cell of the scene. This positioning divides the space in two sets. If an object intercepts this plan (i.e. belongs to more than one sector), then it can be added to both sectors, or be divided until it can be inserted into a cell. This process is repeated until all objects are represented in the structure. There is an empirical test in which there is a scene with 100 polygons and only five of them must be tested by partitioned cell in order to generate a balanced tree, Moller [31].

In the case of 3D environments, the problem of visibility is in how to obtain an adequate sequence of the objects which compound a scene, considering their depth in bi-dimensional projections, selecting only what is in the vision field of an observer. If the position of the observer changes, it is necessary to perform the repositioning of all objects of the scene. However, since the scene objects do not change with time, we can use a pre-processed and static structure for the computations of visibility, Samet [44].

This process is part of *spatial cognition* because it is linked to the information flow between the perception and the knowledge base of autonomous agents. Particularly, it is the information flow between Sensors and Perception, see Figure 4.

In this situation, the visual perception is indirect because it requires *computation* between what it is captures and its representation: *a notation, sign or a set of signs which "re-presents" a thing in the absence of it.*

Our focus is in the next step: in the functioning and in the role of the several memories (symbolic and visual) and in the internal representation and its use by the inference mechanisms (we consider only one inference machine here). More precisely, we are interested in the processing of information related to the abilities of orientation, positioning and navigation.

The construction of our cognitive framework has details inspired by studies about human cognition. For example, we use markers (*objects* or *locations* such as *pivots*) to improve the performance of the agents involved in activities related to spatial orientation. This strategy is inspired in experiments such as the ones described in Presson [39], Richardson [43], and Gunzelmann [20] among many others encountered in the literature.

Other aspect that we use in our construction, inspired in the human cognition, is the codification of spatial information when they are expressed under *egocentric* referentials (defined according to the observer) or *allocentric* ones (defined according to external locations with respect to the observer). For example, an egocentric *proximity* relation is established by the proximity of the object with respect to the observer. An egocentric *orientation* relation expresses, for example, the direction of the object with respect to the face of the observer: *in front of* (north), *to the right* (east), *to the left* (west), *behind* (south). An egocentric *containment* relation can assign to an agent an object (in this case, it is a relation *of possession*), an object *is in* a *location* and *a location is in another location* (*to be in the interior of*).

In the allocentric reference systems, the *referentials* can be objects and locations, Klatzky [25], and Tversky [46]. In our case, information based in allocentric referentials, especially in the situation where the referentials are environmental landmarks, are candidates to the composition of long-term memory.

2.1   Qualitative Spatial Reasoning

Topological definitions and properties concerning neighborhood allow us to deal with regions in space. However, the language of topology do not treat explicitly the process of *spatial reasoning*. On the other hand it is possible to assume as *primitive element* the relation *to be connected* and to build a calculus system such as the *Region Connection Calculus* (RCC), Randel [40] or by using modal operators such that one can read spatial entities, McKinsey [30].

There is a large number of proposals for spatial reasoning systems which explore the concept of location and other various concepts of spatial relations. Among them are: the region calculus such as in Bennett [6], modal logics about space Aiello ([2], [1]), Gabelaia [18], and Kurucz [50]), the topological maps of routes in Kuipers [27] and the use of topological knowledge as in Parikh [37]. These systems are different from each other because of the choice of the types of *primitive elements* and the respective relationships among such elements.

In none of the above mentioned systems it is possible to an agent to *reason about what is happening in a given location*. Formally this is done by adding to the language a special *sort* of syntactic element called *nominal*. Hybrid Modal Logics (HML) have this expression power, Blackburn ([8], [7]). In our case, we use a weak variant of HML which allow us to simulate the behaviour of the *nominals* according to Heinemann ([23] and [24]).

3   QSR and Modal Logics about Spatial Knowledge

In spite of the sensor-percepting mechanism for the capture of information being the same for all agents, theoretically each agent may have its own characteristics according to the way it relates to the space, i.e. spatial relations for a given agent are not necessarily identical to other agent.

In this work, we consider three classes of spatial relations: *proximity*, *orientation* and *containment*. Each agent has a form of relation of each class. The notion of proximity allows us to, for example, to consider the *possibility of an agent to reach an object or location*. This is, relations of proximity can be defined as being *adjacency relations*: *irreflexive* and *symmetric*, Bandini [4].

Relations which deal with orientation assume referentials in space, objects and locations have their positions in space according to direct or indirect relations between objects and objects, objects and locations, and locations and locations. They are *irreflexive*, *asymmetric* and *transitive*, i.e. they are *strict partial order* relations, R_i^o, Bandini [4].

Containment relations are used to express, among other things, *physical inclusions*: a clock in the box, a table at a bar. They are *partial order* relations: *reflexive*, *antisymmetric* and *transitive* R_i^c. In this case, two locations are identical if one is in the other and vice-versa. Yet, if a location has an specific orientation with respect to another location, then every location contained in that will have the same orientation, [4].

The classes of relations described above put objects and locations in a spatial array whose representation is a *relational structure*, namely a *graph*. Let X be a non-empty set, for example, of *locations* and R a relation over X which assigns locations to locations. Then the set $X^R = \{y \mid (x, y) \in R, x \in X\}$ is the set E of edges.

We assign to such graphs a reading which carries the notion of spatial knowledge about a space of subsets in a system with multiple characters. The space of subsets is obtained in the following way: given a graph $G = (X, E)$, each node x of the graph is assigned to a set $U, U \in \mathcal{P}(X)$. Over this structure we can read that the pair (x, U) denotes a location and its adjacencies.

The sensor-perception process is the same for all agents. After the rendering, the objects (or group of objects) and the (spatial) composition of the scenario are extracted and a relational structure (scene graphs combined with BSPs) is built. Each agent i applies one (or more) of its relations over this structure: R_i^p, R_i^o or R_i^c, i.e. the pairs (x, U) are built.

For example, in Figure 3, picture on the left side, we have an agent in a scene with six objects. The tree on the right side is its BSP. Let us suppose that agent

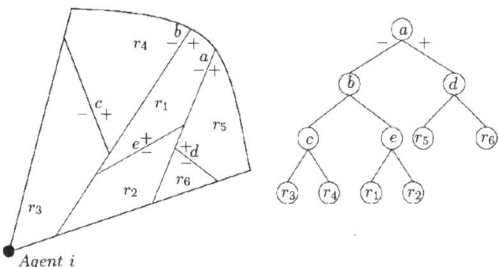

Fig. 3. The figure shows a setting where the verification of visibility via BSP and the construction of a space of subsets via the relation of proximity R_i^p are performed

i wants to establish a relation of proximity, R_i^p, among objects, from the most distant to the closest to it. The run on the tree BSP determines how i will make its construction. It is enough to run the tree from behind to front. The partitioning guarantees which are the leaves which are most distant from the observer, i.e. the projection of regions must be performed in the sequence: r_6, r_5, r_2, r_1, r_4, r_3. Each region r_i refers to an object or *location*: o_i.

More precisely, let us consider $X = \{o_1, o_2, o_3, o_4, o_5, o_6\}$ the set of objects or *names of locations*. We can obtain the relative locations, for example, between objects, i.e. we can determine the pairs (o_i, U) for each o_i, having the relation os proximity with the observer (agent) as a reference. Doing this we have the following pairs (x, U): $(o_3, \{o_4\}), (o_4, \{o_3, o_1\}), (o_1, \{o_2, o_4\}), (o_2, \{o_5, o_1\}),$ $(o_5, \{o_6, o_2\})$.

We can look at the relation of proximity, determined by the pairs (x, U) as a variable (idea originally found in [47]), i.e. it suffices to consider each pair (x, u) with $u \in U$ and $U \in \mathcal{P}(X)$ such that U occurs in the projections as a constant $(\mathbf{x}, \mathbf{u})$. So, a relation that is generally seen as a *restriction* can be considered as a *variable*, in declarative programming view (see Brand [11]). This way of dealing with relations will be useful for the use of the technique of constraint programming (see comments in Section 4).

The partitioning of space minimizes the total number of verifications to know if a given region is visible or not. As the run on the BSP is performed, a general cell is checked, in case the agent can visualize. If it cannot, it is not necessary to check the nodes above.

The relations of orientation on a plane can be established using the four cardinal points as a reference: North, South, East and West. That is, the relations R_i^o are formed by *relations of primitive orientation*: R_i^N, R_i^S, R_i^L and R_i^o. In this fashion, the pair (x, U) obtained through the relation R_i^S reads: for i the object x is to the *south* of the objects (or locations) in U. Other orientations can be derived from the primitive ones, for example, $R_i^{SE} = R_i^S \cap R_i^E$. If each object contains a *face*, then we will be able to use allocentric reference systems with fixed cardinal points and erase the indexes i from the relations of orientation.

The containment relations in terms of sensorial to perception, for objects and locations visible to the agent, can be obtained by scene graphs placing the camera in the region which we want evaluate the *to be in*.

We will build a language which can be interpreted over structures $(X, \mathcal{O})$ with $\mathcal{O} \subseteq \mathcal{P}(X)$ and which allows us to express information and spatial knowledge. Our proposal is inspired in Georgatos [19] and Heinemann [24].

3.1   QSR **Based em Spaces of Subsets**

The procedure of formalization is the usual: let $\mathsf{P} = \{p_0, p_1, \ldots\}$ be the set of *propositional symbols*, $m \in \mathbb{N}$ be the number of agents A_i with $i \in \{1, 2, \ldots, m\}$.

The *well-formed expressions* are given by: $\alpha := p \mid \neg\varphi \mid \varphi \wedge \psi \mid \varphi \vee \psi \mid \varphi \rightarrow \psi \mid K\varphi \mid \Box\varphi \mid [A_i^*]\varphi$ (with $* \in \{o, p, c\}$). The operator K refers to *knowledge*, $\Box$ refers to *refinement* and $[A_i^*]$ *over agent i* (under $*$ point of view, $* \in \{o, p, c\}$). The duals of K, $\Box$ and $[A_i]$ (i.e. $\neg K \neg$, $\neg \Box \neg$ and $\neg[A_i^*]\neg$) are denoted by L, $\Diamond$ and $\langle A_i^* \rangle$ respectively.

For the semantics we consider a non-empty set X and $\mathcal{O} \subseteq \mathcal{P}(X)$. The set $\mathcal{N}_x = \{(x, U) \mid x \in X \ e \ U \in \mathcal{O}\}$ contains the *neighborhoods of x* for each x, $\mathcal{N}_S$ contains the atomic elements of the semantics. The spatial relations of each agent i, $i \in \{1, 2, \ldots, m\}$ constitute the set $\mathcal{R} = \{R \mid R \in \mathcal{P}(\mathcal{N}_x)\}$, i.e. $R_i^o, R_i^p, R_i^c \in \mathcal{R}$. We call $\mathcal{S} = (X, \mathcal{O}, \mathcal{R})$ a *structure of spatial relations* over the space $(X, \mathcal{O})$. If $\nu : \mathsf{P} \rightarrow \mathcal{P}(X)$ is a *valuation function*, then $\mathcal{M} = (X, \mathcal{O}, \mathcal{R}, \nu)$ will be called a multi-agent system over $\mathcal{S}$. Given a $\mathcal{M}$ and $(x, U) \in \mathcal{N}_S$, we have (we omit the case of the classical connectives):

- $x, U \models_{\mathcal{M}} p$ iff $x \in \nu(p)$;
- $x, U \models_{\mathcal{M}} K\varphi$ iff for all $y \in U$ we have that $y, U \models_{\mathcal{M}} \varphi$;
- $x, U \models_{\mathcal{M}} [A_i^*]\varphi$ iff for all $y \in X^{R_i^*}$, $y, U^{R_i^*} \models_{\mathcal{M}} \varphi$, with $* \in \{o, p, c\}$;

The pair (x, U) plays analogous role of a *possible world* in the usual modal logics. In our case, we call (x, U) *Model of Reality* (MR), see Figure1. The reading in this case would be: *U is the vision of the world by the agent when located in x.* The interpretation over egocentric and allocentric referential systems allows the agent to construct different Us from the viewpoint in x.

The operators are interchangeable. The way of using operator K refers to the *knowledge of the agent*, for example, given $\mathcal{M}$, the expression $\mathcal{M} \models [A_i^*]K\varphi \leftrightarrow K[A_i^*]\varphi$ says that *the knowledge of something linked to a given spatial relation depends on the agent if and only if, in fact this something is linked to this spatial knowledge relation of the agent* for $* \in \{o, p, c\}$. In this fashion, the operator K defines what will go to the long-term memories.

For the axiomatization of multi-character systems we have the usual distribution schemes: $K(\varphi \rightarrow \psi) \rightarrow (K\varphi \rightarrow K\psi)$ and $[A_i^*](\varphi \rightarrow \psi) \rightarrow ([A_i^*]\varphi \rightarrow [A_i^*]\psi)$, for all $i \in \{1, 2, \ldots, m\}$ and $* \in \{o, p, c\}$. Yet, $K\varphi \rightarrow \varphi$, $K\varphi \rightarrow K(K\varphi)$, $\varphi \rightarrow K(L\varphi)$, $K[A_i^*]\varphi \rightarrow [A_i^*]K\varphi$ and $\langle A_i^* \rangle K\varphi \rightarrow K[A_i^*]K\varphi$.

Some results about *theorems* of this system are similar to the ones found in [19]. We are working on adaptations to deal with several agents. Studies about models, i.e. the relations between formulas and *accessibility relations* are in progress.

The inclusion of a set of actions Act that the agents could perform completely changes the logics even if it is compared to the one proposed in [19]. The formalization of these concepts are also in progress. In the same situation are the *meta-theorems* about *soundness* and *completeness*. In the case of *decidability*, the system is *decidable* because the *domain* is finite (the set of places and spatial relations is finite). The verification algorithm of the modal formulas satisfiability terminates.

4   Concluding Remarks

The contribution of this work are the individualized formalization given to the agents and the interpretation of this formalism over graphs which capture spatial relations for each agent converting them in an individualized space of subsets. We adopted a weak way of dealing with the nominals, i.e. there is no satisfiability operator as a syntactic element of the language in order to express the agent's own vision inside the language.

As we mentioned, we are evaluating the inclusion of a set Act containing *primitive actions* that the agents would be able to perform. An action in a given action (x, U) would be: let $\mathcal{R}_{\mathsf{Act}} = \{R_a \mid a \in \mathsf{Act}\}$ a set of relations linked to the actions in $\mathcal{O}$. So, given $(X, R_{\mathsf{Act}}, \mathcal{O})$, we have that $x, U \models_{\mathcal{M}} [a]\varphi$ iff for all $y \in X$ with $(x, y) \in R_a$, then $y, U^{R_a} \models_{\mathcal{M}} \varphi$. In these conditions, we have to include one more operator over actions.

The multi-layer structure for the construction of MRs is can be layered. The implementation of the inference machine by contraint programming would process new layers with new restrictions.

We are developing a computational implementation for the described theory. There are two directions: one is a relational structuring of the spatial information flow between the perception and the intellect of the agent (manages the internal representation in a given memory model); the other is the implementation of the inference mechanism based on the language of logics presented in the previous section (QSR).

The implementation which is related to the visual perception and its conversion into scene graphs combined with BSPs follow the models proposed in [38], [26] and [29]. Once the internal representation of the captured image is ready, agent i constructs its MRs extracting other graphs, each one based in one of the spatial relations: R_i^p, R_i^o e R_i^c. In fact, we are dealing with relations R_i^p only. Such graphs stay in the short-term visual memort and are obtained from egocentric referentials.

The long-term visual memory keep graphs obtained from allocentric referentials. One relational structure stay in the long-term memory of each agent, deals with the agent's knowledge: $[A_i^*]$, $* \in \{o, p, c\}$ interchanging with K modal operator.

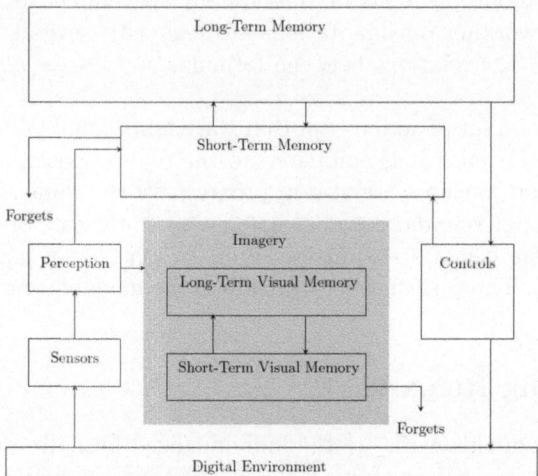

Fig. 4. Scheme for the Memory Model

The short-term memory is in fact a working area. The information contained in the long-term memory and in the visual memories are allocated temporarily in the short-term memory to perform a given inference. The scheme of this structure is on Figure 4.

The implementation of the inference mechanism through CP is dedicated, among other tasks, to solve satisfatibility problems of modal formulas. A MR of each agent is a multi-layer construction where each layer is obtained according to a spatial relation, i.e. relations work as restrictions on a finite search space, ideal scenario to apply CP. The basic ideas of the program are in Brand [10] and Stevenson [45].

The implementation work is being tested in two tools: ECL^{i}PS^e, Wallace [48], and Mozart-Oz, Haridi [21]: in both, the strategy is the same. However, using declarative programming environments allows us to adopt a new vision of the problem: to treat the *relations as variables*, Brand [11]. We are studying this possibility to optimize local searches. Finally, communication interfaces in C++ for integration with Soar, Laird [28], and Act-R, Anderson [3], are being developed.

References

1. Aiello, M., Pratt-Hartmann, I., van Benthem, J. (eds.): Handbook of Spatial Logics. Springer, Heidelberg (2007)
2. Aiello, M., van Benthem, J.: A modal walk through space. Journal of Applied Non-Classical Logics 12(3-4), 319–364 (2002)
3. Anderson, J.R.: How can the Human Mind Occur in the Physical Universe. Oxford University Press, Oxford (2007)
4. Bandini, S., Mosca, A., Palmonari, M.: A hybrid logic for commonsense spatial reasoning. In: AI*IA, pp. 25–37 (2005)

5. Bennett, B.: Modal logics for qualitative spatial reasoning. Bull. of the IGPL 3, 1–22 (1995)
6. Bennett, B., Cohn, A.G., Gooday, J., Gotts, N.M.: Qualitative spatial representation and reasoning with the region connection calculus. Geoinformatica 1, 1–44 (1997)
7. Blackburn, P.: Representation, reasoning, and relational structures: a hybrid logic manifesto. Logic Journal of IGLP 8, 339–365 (2000)
8. Blackburn, P., de Rijke, M., Venema, Y.: Modal Logic, vol. 53. Cambridge University Press, Cambridge (1999) (draft version)
9. Blackburn, P., Seligman, J.: Hybrid languages. Journal of Logic, Language and Information 4(3), 251–272 (1995)
10. Brand, S., Gennari, R., de Rijke, M.: Constraint methods for modal satisfiability. In: Apt, K.R., Fages, F., Rossi, F., Szeredi, P., Váncza, J. (eds.) CSCLP 2003. LNCS (LNAI), vol. 3010, pp. 66–86. Springer, Heidelberg (2004)
11. Brand, S.: Relation Variables in Qualitative Spatial Reasoning. In: Biundo, S., Frühwirth, T., Palm, G. (eds.) KI 2004. LNCS (LNAI), vol. 3238, pp. 337–350. Springer, Heidelberg (2004)
12. Casati, R., Varzi, A.: Spatial entities. In: Stock, O. (ed.) Spatial and Temporal Reasoning, pp. 73–96. Kluwer Academic Publishers, Dordrecht (1997)
13. Cohn, A.G.: Modal and non-modal qualitative spatial logics. In: IJCAI 1993 Workshop on Spatial and Temporal Reasoning (1993)
14. Cohn, A.G., Cui, Z., Randell, D.A.: Qualitative simulation based on a logical formalism of space and time. In: 6th International Workshop on Qualitative Reasoning about Physical Systems, Edinburgh (1992)
15. Dabrowski, A., Moss, L.S., Parikh, R.: Topological reasoning and the logic of knowledge. Annals of Pure and Applied Logic 78(1-3), 73–110 (1996)
16. Forbus, K.D.: Mental Models: Qualitative Reasoning About Space and Motion. LEA Associates (1983)
17. Forbus, K.D.: Qualitative Reasoning. In: The Computer Science and Engineering Handbook, pp. 715–733. CRC Press, Boca Raton (1996)
18. Gabelaia, D.: Modal definability in topology. Master's thesis. ILLC - Universiteit van Amsterdam (2001)
19. Georgatos, K.: Update using subset logic. Analysis (2010)
20. Gunzelmann, G., Anderson, J.R.: Location maters: why target location impacts performance in orientation tasks. Memory and Cognition 34(1), 41–59 (2006)
21. Haridi, S., Van Roy, P.: Concepts, Techniques, and Models of Computer Programming. MIT Press, Cambridge (2004)
22. Heinemann, B.: A hybrid treatment of evolutionary sets. In: Coello Coello, C.A., de Albornoz, Á., Sucar, L.E., Battistutti, O.C. (eds.) MICAI 2002. LNCS (LNAI), vol. 2313, pp. 204–213. Springer, Heidelberg (2002)
23. Heinemann, B.: A hybrid logic of knowledge supporting topological reasoning. In: Rattray, C., Maharaj, S., Shankland, C. (eds.) AMAST 2004. LNCS, vol. 3116, pp. 181–195. Springer, Heidelberg (2004)
24. Heinemann, B.: Topology and knowledge of multiple agents. In: Geffner, H., Prada, R., Machado Alexandre, I., David, N. (eds.) IBERAMIA 2008. LNCS (LNAI), vol. 5290, pp. 1–10. Springer, Heidelberg (2008)
25. Klatzky, R.L.: Allocentric and egocentric spatial representations: Definitions, distinctions, and interconnections. In: Freksa, C., Habel, C., Wender, K.F. (eds.) Spatial Cognition 1998. LNCS (LNAI), vol. 1404, pp. 1–17. Springer, Heidelberg (1998)

26. Kuffner, J., Latombe, J.C.: Perception-based navigation for animated characters in real-time virtual environments. In: The Visual Computer: Real-Time Virtual Worlds (1999)
27. Kuipers, B.: Modelling spatial knowledge. Cognitive Science 2, 129–154 (1978)
28. Laird, J.E., Newell, A., Rosenbloom, P.S.: Soar: an architecture for general intelligence source. AI 33, 1–64 (1987)
29. Lathrop, S.D.: Extending Cognitive Architectures with Spatial adn Visual Imagery Mechanisms. PhD thesis. Computer Science and Engineering in The University of Michigan (2008)
30. McKinsey, J.C., Tarski, A.: The algebra of topology. Annals of Mathematics 45, 141–191 (1944)
31. Moller, T.A., Haines, E.: Real Time Rendering. AK Peter and CRC Press (2008)
32. Montello, D.R.: Spatial Cognition, volume International Encyclopedia of the Social And Behavioral Sciences. In: Smelser, N.J., Baltes, P.B. (eds.), pp. 14771–14775. Pergamon Press, Oxford (2001)
33. Moratz, R., Nebel, B., Freksa, C.: Qualitative spatial reasoning about relative position. In: Freksa, C., Brauer, W., Habel, C., Wender, K.F. (eds.) Spatial Cognition III. LNCS (LNAI), vol. 2685, pp. 385–400. Springer, Heidelberg (2003)
34. Nebel, B., Scivos, A.: Formal properties of constraint calculi for qualittive spatial reasoning. Künstliche Intelligenz Heft 4(02), 14–18 (2002)
35. Noser, N., Renault, O., Thalmann, D., Thalmann, N.M.: Naviagation for digital actors based on synthetic vision, memory and learning. Computer Graphics 19, 7–19 (1995)
36. Noser, N., Thalmann, D.: Synthetic vision and audition for digital actors. In: Proc. Eurographics 1995, Maastricht (1995)
37. Parikh, R., Moss, L.S., Steinsvold, C.: Topology and Epistemic Logic. In: Handbook of Spatial Logics, pp. 299–3141. Springer, Heidelberg (2007)
38. Peters, C., O'Sullivan, C.: Synthetic vision and memory for autonomous virtual humans. Computer Graphics Forum 21(4), 743–752 (2002)
39. Presson, C.C., Mondello, D.R.: Points of reference in spatial cognition: Stalking the elusive landmark. British Journal of Developmental Psychology 6, 378–381 (1988)
40. Randell, D.A., Cui, Z., Cohn, A.G.: A spatial logic based on regions and connections. In: Proc. of the 3rd International Conference on Principles of Knowledge Representation and Reasoning, pp. 165–176 (1992)
41. Renz, J.: Qualitative spatial representation and reasoning. In: Renz, J. (ed.) Qualitative Spatial Reasoning with Topological Information. LNCS (LNAI), vol. 2293, p. 31. Springer, Heidelberg (2002)
42. Renz, J., Nebel, B.: Qualitative Spatial Reasoning using Constraint Calculi. In: Handbook of Spatial Logics, pp. 161–215. Springer, Heidelberg (2007)
43. Richardson, A.E., Mondello, D.R., Hegarty, M.: Spatial knowledge acquisition from maps and from navigation in real and virtual environments. Memory and Cognition 27, 741–750 (1999)
44. Samet, H.: Applications of Spatial Data Structures. Computer Graphics. In: Image Processing, and GIS. Addison Wesley, Reading (1990)
45. Stevenson, L.: Modal Satisfiability in a Constraint Logic Environment. PhD thesis. University of South Africa (2008)
46. Tversky, B.: Structures of mental spaces: how people think about space. Environment and Behaviour 35, 66–88 (2003)

47. Tsang, E.P.K.: The consistent labeling problem in temporal reasoning. In: Proc. of 6th National on Artificial Intelligence, AAAI 1987, pp. 251–255 (1987)

48. Wallace, M.G., Novello, S., Schimpf, J.: ECL^{i}PS^e: A platform for constraint logic programming. ICL System Journal 12(1), 159–200 (1997)

49. Wintermute, S.B.: Abstraction, Imagery, and Control in Cognitive Architecture. PhD thesis. Computer Science and Engineering in The University of Michigan (2010)

50. Wolter, A.K.F., Zakharyaschev, M.: Modal logics for metric spaces: open problems. In: Advances in Modal Logic, vol. 4, pp. 221–242. King's College Publisher (2003)

Dynamic Description Logics Based Semantic Web Services Composition

Hui Peng[1], Limin Chen[2], Weizhong Zeng[3], and Junjian Tang[1]

[1] Education Technology Center,
Beijing International Studies University, 100024, Beijing, China
[2] Key Laboratory of Intelligent Information Processing, Institute of Computing Technology,
Chinese Academy of Sciences, 100190, Beijing, China
[3] Information Engineering School, Nanchang University, 330031, Nanchang, China
penghui@bisu.edu.cn, chenlm@ics.ict.ac.cn, zwzzwz9211@163.com,
tangjunjian@bisu.edu.cn

Abstract. The automatic Web services composition has been a research focus since an ever-increasing numbers of Web services are created and published. In this paper, we present a dynamic description logics (DDLs) based method for automatic Web services composition. DDLs are an extension of description logic with a dynamic dimension. It adds actions expressions into description logic and makes up a set of reasoning mechanism for action expressions. The DDLs reasoner has been built for DDLs formulas. As an Web service can be regarded as an action in Web, its accomplishment changes the state of Web, from original state to aim state, an Web service can be described as an action in DDLs, which this action can be described in terms of formulas in DDLs. Due to these relations between Web service and DDLs actions, our method describes both the goal service and atomic services in terms of DDLs formulas. We proved that if a goal formula can not be satisfied then the services composition can be found. The procedure of checking the satisfiability of the formula is also the procedure of discovering the services composition. Thus the problem of automatic services composition is reduced to the problem of checking the satisfiability of formulas in DDLs. An example of automatic services composition in travel area shows the effectiveness of our method.

Keywords: semantic Web services, services composition, dynamic description logics, action.

1 Introduction

A Web service is a set of related functionalities identified by uniform resource identifier (URI) that can be advertised, located, and triggered by other applications and humans through the Web [1]. If no single available Web service can satisfy the functionality required by a user, there should be a possibility to combine existing services together to fulfill the request. The problem of Web services composition is the process of selecting, combining and executing existing services to achieve a requestor's objective [2].

H. Deng et al. (Eds.): AICI 2011, Part II, LNAI 7003, pp. 594–601, 2011.
© Springer-Verlag Berlin Heidelberg 2011

The semantic Web initiative addresses the problem of Web data lack of semantic by creating a set of XML based language and ontology. After combining semantic Web with Web service, researchers have built service ontology to describe capability information about a Web service and make use of the description and reason function of the ontology to discovery, select and compose Web services automatically. Ontology Web Language for Services (OWL-S) [8] is a prevalent language which formalized by W3C for building service ontology. OWL-S Profile provides methods to describe service capabilities. The function description in the OWL-S Profile describes the capabilities of the service in terms of inputs, outputs, preconditions and effects (IOPE). Thus a Web service can be regarded as an action in Web in function degree. However, the underlying logics for OWL-S, i.e., description logics [8] (DLs for short), are initially designed for representing static knowledge, and cannot be used directly in describing services and also the automatic composition of Web services. To describe dynamic knowledge in Web, the extension of DL in dynamic dimension is a kind of effective method. DDLs have been concerned in this area since 2005 [3].It adds actions expressions into description logic and makes up a set of reasoning mechanism for action expressions.

In this paper, we present a dynamic description logics (DDLs) based method for automatic Web services composition. DDLs are introduced first, then the DDLs based description of Web services and the algorithm of automatic services composition is explained in details.

2   An Overview of Dynamic Description Logics

Description logics are a well-known family of formalisms for representing knowledge about static application domains. They are playing an important role in the semantic Web, acting as the basis of the W3C-recommended Web ontology language for services OWL-S [8]. Because DL is only good at expressing and reasoning about static knowledge, it is not effective to express and reason about dynamic knowledge such as Web services. In this situation, DDLs [3] was proposed to replenish DL. Except all elements of DL, The action expression was added and the union expression and reason about static and dynamic knowledge was proposed in DDLs. Thus, DDLs has become a hopeful way for expressing Web services.

2.1   Syntax and Semantic of DDLs [4]

The basic elements in DDLs are concepts, roles and actions. The complex concepts, roles and actions can be composed of atomic concepts, roles and actions by operators. Operators include alternant which written as ∪, iteration which written as * , choice which written as ? , sequence which written as ; etc. The DDLs which actions are added in logic system ALC is written as D_{ALC}.

Primitive symbols of D_{ALC} are a set N_R of role names, a set N_C of concept names, a set N_I of individual names and a set N_A of atomic action names. Starting with them, concepts, formulas, and actions can be built with the help of a set of operators.

Concepts of D_{ALC} are generated with the following syntax rule:

$$C,C' \rightarrow C_i \mid \{p\} \mid \neg C \mid C \cup C' \mid \forall R.C \mid \exists R.C \mid C \cap C' \mid \perp \mid \top \qquad (1)$$

where the definition of concept is $D \equiv C$, both D and C are concept names.

Formulas in D_{ALC} are generated with the following syntax rule:

$$\varphi, \varphi' \rightarrow C(p) \mid R(p,q) \mid \neg\varphi \mid \varphi \lor \varphi' \mid <\pi>\varphi \mid [\pi]\varphi \mid \varphi \Box \varphi \mid \varphi \rightarrow \varphi \mid true \mid false \qquad (2)$$

An atomic action definition is of the form $\alpha(v_1, ..., v_n) \equiv (P,E)$, where,

- α is an atomic action name;
- P is a finite set of formulas for describing the preconditions of carrying out action α;
- E is a finite set of formulas for describing the effects of carrying out action α;
- $v_1, ..., v_n$ is a finite sequence of all the individual names occurring in P and E;

If $\alpha(v_1, ..., v_n) \equiv (P,E)$ is an atomic action definition and $p_1, ..., p_n$ a sequence of individual names, replacing each occurrence of v_k in P *and* E with p_k $(1 \leq k \leq n)$, then $\alpha(p_1, ..., p_n)$ is called an atomic action which is defined by $(P_{\{p_1/v_1,...,p_n/v_n\}}, E_{\{p_1/v_1,...,p_n/v_n\}})$, for example, an action of buying tickets can be denoted as buyTicket(x,y)°({ person(x) ,ticket(y) ,ØholdTicket(x,y)},{ holdTicket(x,y)})

Actions in D_{ALC} are defined as the following rules:

- atomic action $\alpha(a_1, ..., a_n)$ is an action
- if both α and β are actions, $\alpha;\beta$, $\alpha \cup \beta$, $\alpha*$ are also actions
- if φ is an assertion then φ? Is an action.

For an action $\alpha(x_1,...x_n) \equiv (P\alpha, E\alpha)$, $P\alpha$ stands for the state before action α is executed and $E\alpha$ stands for the state after action α is executed. Action α is executed means that the set of formula $P\alpha$ and $E\alpha$ are satisfiable.

There are four basic parts in a DDLs system: *TBox, ABox, ActionBox* and the reason system on these Boxes. *TBox* is the set of concepts and formulas; *ABox* is the set of assertions; *ActionBox* is the set of action assertions.

All reasoning problems on DDLs can be reduced to the problem of the satisfiability of formulas [4]. The reliability and completeness of the algorithms of solving the reason problems has been proved [4]. The reason machine of DDLs(DDLs reasoner) has been described and fulfilled [5]

3   DDLs and Semantic Web Services

3.1   DDLs Based Semantic Web Service Description

In OWL-S, the function of a semantic service is described by its inputs, outputs, precondition and effects(IOPE), thus, the service can be described as S={I, O, P, E}. Because every semantic service can be regarded as an action, then the IOPE of service can be described by DDLs formulas. If S{I}, S{O}, S{P}, S{E} stand for the set of formulas about inputs, outputs, precondition and effects of service S each. Service S was executed means the state which satisfied the set of formulas about S{I} and S{P} was changed into the state which satisfied the set of formulas about S{O} and S{E}. If S={I, O, P, E} is a atomic service and $\alpha(v_1,\ldots v_n) \equiv (P_\alpha, E_\alpha)$ is a DDLs atomic action, we can describe S with α like this.

α=S   the action name is the service name

$$P_\alpha = S\{I\} \sqcup S\{P\} \qquad (3)$$

The set of precondition formulas of the action is the union set of the formulas set of inputs and preconditions of the service

$$E_\alpha = S\{O\} \sqcup S\{E\} \qquad (4)$$

The set of effect formulas of the action is the union set of the formulas set of outputs and effects of the service

$v_1,\ldots v_n$ are objects which the service are related to

For example, a service about reserving an flight ticket can be described as BookMatcheTicke (v1,v2,v3,v4,v5) ≡ ({MatcheNumber (v1), Person (v2), CreditCard (v3), ownCreditCard (v2,v3)}, {MatcheTicket(v4), Price(v5), hasPrice(v4,v5)}).

In the above description, we assume that the input of the service is the number of flight, the output is the price of flight, the precondition is the consumer owns the credit card.

3.2   The Algorithm of DDLs Based Web Services Composition

The reasoner about D_{ALC} has been fulfilled. It can verify the satisfiability of formulas by construct the abstract model of the formula.

The verification of the satisfiability of a formula φ is like this. First, inconsistent formulas are defined. Then expanding φ according to the expanding rules until no rules can be used or inconsistent occurs. The extending procedure stops when the following two conditions occur. One is the model which satisfies φ has been found. The other is inconsistent occurs that means φ can not be satisfied.

The reason how DDLs reasoner was used in Web services composition is explained in the following two points.

(1) An action sequence plan={ $s_1, s_2, \ldots, s_k$ } ($s_i = (P_i, E_i), 0 \le i \le k$) is a match on ABox $\mathcal{P}$ for a aim state φ if and only if the formula (5) is unsatisfiable . plan={ $s_1, s_2, \ldots, s_k$ } means that executing actions in plan in turn can get to state φ.

$$[(s_1, s_2, \ldots, s_k)^*]\Pi \wedge \text{Conj}(\mathcal{P}) \wedge \neg \text{<plan>}\varphi \qquad (5)$$

In formular(5) Π stands for ($\text{Conj}(P_1) \rightarrow <(P_1,E_1)>true$) $\wedge \ldots \wedge$ ($\text{Conj}(P_k) \rightarrow <(P_k, E_k)>true$) , $\text{Conj}(\mathcal{P})$ stands for conjunction form of all formulas in formula set $\mathcal{P}$.

(2) an action which is not in action sequence of the plan need to extend if formular (6) can not be satisfied.

$$[(s_1, s_2,..., s_k)*]\Pi \wedge \text{Conj}(\mathcal{P}) \wedge \neg \text{<plan>} true \qquad (6)$$

The explanation of formula can not be satisfied is:

The formula Conj(P) $\square$ ¬<plan>> can not be satisfied

⇔ The formula Conj(P)→ <(plan)> φ is true

⇔ The formula Conj(P)→ <(plan)> φ is true

⇔ At the present state Conj($\mathcal{P}$), executing action <plan> can get to aim φ

Formula Π has promised every atomic action can be executed when the precondition is true. Formula $[(s_1, s_2,..., s_k)*]\Pi$ has promised every sequence composed by atomic actions can be executed when the precondition is true.

The atomic services and a goal service can be described according 3.1 for services composition, if the function of the goal service is described as RS={I, O, P, E} and $\mathcal{P}$= RS {I, P}, φ= RS {O, E }, then the service composition which satisfied the goal service $\square$ {$\mathcal{P}$}, {φ}$\square$ is the atomic services sequence which the sequence ($s_1, s_2,..., s_k$) can make the formula $[(s_1, s_2,..., s_k)*]\Pi \wedge \text{Conj}(\mathcal{P}) \wedge \neg \text{<plan>}\varphi$ to be unsatisfied.

If the aim service is G=($\mathcal{P}, \varphi$), the set of atomic services is S={ $s_1, s_2,..., s_k$ }$\square$ with the help of DDLs reasoner, the algorithm which discovery the atomic services composition which satisfied the aim can be described as Table 1.

Table 1. DDLs based algorithm of service composition

Begin

1. Services={ $s_1, s_2,..., s_n$ } // keep all atomic actions
2. QueueOfPlans ={} // the start queue of plan is initialized with empty list
3. QueueOfServices= < $s_1, s_2,..., s_n$ >// the queue of service is initialized with the ordered set of service.
4. While(QueueOfServices is not empty){
5. QueueOfPlans=the head of QueueOfServices;
6. If(the formula (5) in which the atomic service are from QueueOfPlans is unsatisfiable){
7. Return QueueOfPlans as a successful service composition}
8. Else{
9. For(each s_i ∈ Services){
10. If(the formular (6) in which the atomic service are from QueueOfPlans is unsatisfiable){
11. QueueOfPlan= { QueueOfPlans, S_i}}
12. }//end For
13. }//end Else
14. }//end While

End

3.3   An Example

An service composition example from travel area is put forward in this section. The ontology file is saved in http://keg.cs.tsinghua.edu.cn/ontology.travel.

> TBox:
> FlightTicketReserveConfirm ⊑ ReserveConfirm
> TrainTicketReserveConfirm ⊑ ReserveConfirm
> LDBusTicketReserveConfirm ⊑ ReserveConfirm
> AirTicket ⊑ Ticket
> TrainTicket ⊑ Ticket
> LDBusTicket ⊑ Ticket
> The function of the goal service is described as:
> Inputs:
> traveler: Henry
> departure place: beiJin
> arrive place: yunNan
> departure time: 2009/12/13
> traffic tool: flight
> the number of credit card: creditCardNo
> the number of ID: idCardNo
> output: the reserved flight ticket
> according to 3.2, the goal service can be described as G=($\mathcal{P}$, φ),which

$\mathcal{P}$ = {Person (Henry), DeparturePlace (beiJin), ArrivalPlace (yunNan), departureDate (2007-12-13), departureTime (17:00), arrivalDate (2007-12-24), arrivalTime (8:00), IntendVehicle (flight), CreditCardNo (creditCardNo), IDCardNo (idCardNo), knows (agent, Henry), knows (agent, beiJin), knows (agent, yunNan), knows (agent, 2007-12-13), knows(agent, 17:00), knows (agent, 2007-12-24), knows (agent, 8:00), knows (agent, flight), knowsVisacard (agent, creditCardNo), knowsIDcard (agent, idCardNo), VisaValidate (Henry, creditCardNo), AirTicket(y), IDCertify(Henry, idCardNo), ¬SendTicketConfirm (sentTicketConfirm), ¬holds (Henry, y)}

> φ= SendTicketConfirm(sentTicketConfirm) ∧holds (Henry, y)}
> Parts of atomic services in this example are:
> S1: flight checking service: CheckFlight.
> S2: flight ticket reserve service:ReserveFlightTicket
> S3: account transfer service: AccountTransferReserve
> S4: send ticket service: SendTicket.

Replacing plan in formula (5) with any sequence of atomic services and replacing $\mathcal{A}$ φ in formula (5) with $\mathcal{P}$, φ in goal service, run algorithm in table 2, the results is if plan=<S1,S2,S3,S4>, formula (5) is unsatisfiable. So the sequence <S1,S2,S3,S4> is the services composition for the goal. The results which the DDLs reasoner gives out are showed in Fig 1.

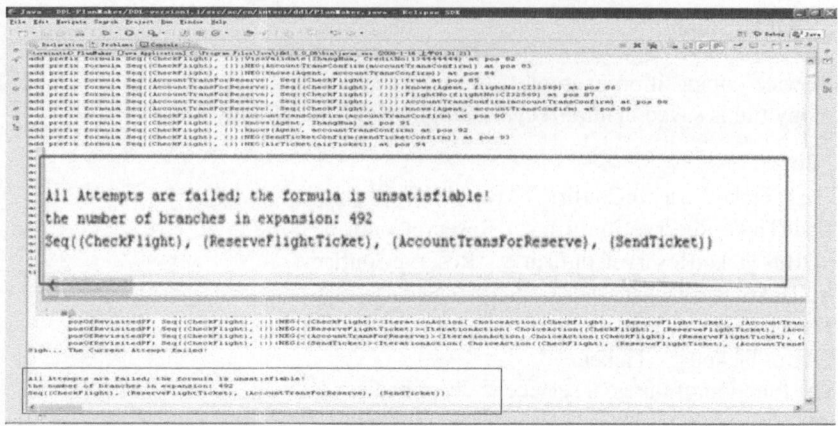

Fig. 1. The results of automatic services composition in travel area

4   Related Works

We care the dynamic knowledge such as semantic Web service more and more with the development of semantic Web [6]. The description and reasoning about semantic Web knowledge is also extending to services or actions too [15]. The extending of DL is also concerned extensively [9, 10, 11]. The noted work in this area includes:

A related work from Baader combines DL with the action theory in situation calculus and describes an atomic action α as $(Pre, occ, post)$[7]. *Pre, occ, post* stands for the precondition before the action is executed, the indefinite part in action executing and the results after the action is executed each. *Pre, occ* and *post* are described with individual assertion, the executability and projection were discussed in the work and the two problem were changed into the consistence checking problem of ABox in DL.

A related work from Hongkai Liu [12] forward the work from Baader [7]. It adopts general concept inclusion axiom when describe actions. It considers the question of executability and projection about actions in this situation. Hongkai Liu researches the refresh problem of knowledge and proposes an algorithm for knowledge refreshment [13].

Another related work from Evren Sirin has developed and optimized DL reasoner Pellet and combines it with plan tool HTN to fulfill services composition [14].

Compared with the DL based method for Web services composition, the three advantages of the method in this paper lies in:

1. The more concise description of Web service. An action is described as $\alpha(v_1,...,v_n) \equiv (P_\alpha, E_\alpha)$ in DDL. A service is matched along with an action.

2. The more complex action can be described in DDL. We can describe atomic action, alternant action, iteration action, choice action, sequence action etc [4]. Only atomic action and sequence action is described in DL [7].

3. The algorithm of service composition is more concise. In DDL, reasoning about action is no longer the part of the algorithm of service composition. It has been a part

of reasoner of DDL. All reason problems have been reduced to checking the satisfiability problem of DDL formulas. In DL based services composition, the reasoning procedure about action is implicated in the composition algorithm, which increases the complexity of the algorithm apparently.

Acknowledgements. This work is supported by the project of designing m-learning terminals for IPv6-basd networking environment ([2008]48 from Technological Bureau of Ministry of Education, China.), the National Science Foundation of China (No. 60775035) and the research project of Beijing international studies university (No. 11Bb014).

References

1. Alonso, G., Casati, F., Kuno, H., Machiraju, V.: Web Services. Springer, Heidelberg (2003)
2. D.Booth, et al.: Web services architecture. Technical report, W3C Working Group Note (2004), http://www.w3.org/TR/ws-arch/
3. Shi, Z., Dong, M., Jiang, Y., Zhang, H.: A Logic Foundation for the Semantic Web. Science in China. Series F 48(2), 161–178 (2005)
4. Chang, L., Lin, F., Shi, Z.: A dynamic description logic for representation and reasoning about actions. In: Zhang, Z., Siekmann, J.H. (eds.) KSEM 2007. LNCS (LNAI), vol. 4798, pp. 115–127. Springer, Heidelberg (2007)
5. Chang, L.: Ph.D thesis Institute of Computer Science of Chinese Academy (2008)
6. Bovykin, A., Zolin, E.: A framework for describing information providing web services. In: Proc. of the 13th Workshop on Automated Reasoning, pp. 3–4 (2006)
7. Baader, F., Lutz, C., Milicic, M., Sattler, U., Wolter, F.: A Description Logic Based Approach to Reasoning about Web Services. In: WWW 2005, Chiba, Japan, May 10-14 (2005)
8. The OWL Services Coalition. OWL-S: Semantic Markup for Web Services (2004), http://www.w3.org/Submission/OWL-S/
9. Giacomo, G.D., et al.: Planning with sensing for a mobile robot. In: Steel, S. (ed.) ECP 1997. LNCS, vol. 1348, pp. 156–168. Springer, Heidelberg (1997)
10. Artale, A., Franconi, E.: A Temporal Description Logic for Reasoning about Actions and Plans. Journal of Artificial Intelligence Research 9, 463–506 (1998)
11. Wolter, F., Zakharyaschev, M.: Dynamic description logic. In: Segerberg, K., et al. (eds.) Advances in Modal Logic, vol. 2, pp. 449–463. CSLI Publications, Stanford (2000)
12. Liu, H., Lutz, C., Milicic, M., Wolter, F.: Reasoning about Actions using Description Logics with general TBoxes. In: Proceedings of the 10th European Conference on Logics in Artificial Intelligence (JELIA 2006), Liverpool, United Kingdom (2006)
13. Liu, H., Lutz, C., Milicic, M., Wolter, F.: Updating Description Logic ABoxes. In: Doherty, P., Mylopoulos, J., Welty, C. (eds.) Proceedings of the Tenth International Conference on Principles of Knowledge Representation and Reasoning (KR 2006), pp. 46–56. AAAI Press, Menlo Park (2006)
14. Sirin, E.: Combining Description Logic Reasoning with AI Planning for Composition of Web Services. Ph.D thesis University of Maryland (2006)
15. Lutz, C., Sattler, U.: A Proposal for Describing Services with DLs. In: Proceedings of the 2002 International Workshop on Description Logics, Toulouse, France (2002)

Blind Source Separation Based on Power Spectral Density

JingHui Wang and YuanChao Zhao

Tianjin Key Laboratory of Intelligence Computing and Novel Software Technology
Tianjin University of Technology
TianJin, China 300191
Csr_dsp@sina.com

Abstract. In this paper, a novel blind separation approach using power spectral density(PSD) is presented. The power spectrum itself is the Fourier transform of the auto-correlation function. Auto-correlation function represents the relationship of long and short-term correlation within the signal itself. This paper using power spectral density and cross power spectral density separate blind mixed source signals. In practice, non-stationary signals always have different PSD. The method is suitable for dealing with non-stationary signal. And simulation results have shown that the method is feasible.

Keywords: Blind Source Separation, Power Spectral Density.

1 Introduction

Blind source separation (BSS) consists of recovering a set of unknown mutually independent source signals from their observed mixtures without knowing the mixing coefficients. It has a variety of signal separation applications of the biomedicine, radar and the sonar, and also has been widely used in the communications, speech and dimensionality reduction in hyperspectral image analysis[1].

BSS problem is an optimization problem. At present, research focuses on blind signal separation, blind deconvolution and blind equalization. Those methods involving statistical signal processing and adaptive signal processing. But the BSS model and the algorithm and is closely related to a specific application and its background, When expansion and migration to other applications, it's difficult work.

For practical and precise characteristics of the application needs, researchers started from the time domain and frequency domain to time-frequency domain and adaptive aspects of BSS analysis. Time-frequency analysis became an important method, because BSS based on time frequency approaches is well-suited to non-stationary signals and set no restriction on the Gaussian property of the sources[2][3]. The time-frequency BSS research has three classes. The first one is still significantly related to classical BSS approach. Adel Belouchrani take advantage explicitly of the non-stationarity of the signals based on a joint diagonalization of a combined set of spatial Time-Frequency Distributions(TFD). A. Holobar presented TFBSS, focusing on identification of single source auto terms which correspond to diagonal spatial

H. Deng et al. (Eds.): AICI 2011, Part II, LNAI 7003, pp. 602–609, 2011.

time-frequency distribution of the sources vector with only one non-zero diagonal element. In this class the correct choice of time-frequency points plays a key role in recovering sources, which is dependent on the correct threshold set by signals and ones experiences. The second class includes several methods based on the ratios of time-frequency transformations of observe signals, some of them require the sources to have no overlap in the time-frequency domain, which is quite restrictive. The third class does not require any localization properties of the sources, or restricting the mixing system to be linear, it is based on the idea that independent signals have independent time-frequency transformation or time frequency distribution(TFD). Some change convolutive mixtures to simply instantaneous mixture at every frequency bins, but the difficult point in these approaches is the ambiguity and permutation. Other approaches are based on a correlation based blind source separation in time domain and time-frequency domain, which also has some restrictions on the source definitions.

A certain extent, the power spectrum is a special time-frequency analysis method. In this paper, we develop a blind signal separation approach based on power spectral density and cross power spectral density. This approach exploits different scale power spectral density and cross spectrum density. This method is also suitable for blind separation of nonstationary signals.

2   Blind Sources Separation Model

Consider m sensors receiving an instantaneous linear mixture of signals emitted from n sources. The $m \times 1$ vector $x(t)$ denotes the output of the sensors at time instant t which may be corrupted by an additive noise n(t). Hence, the linear data model is given by [5][6][7]:

$$x(t) = As(t) + n(t) \tag{1}$$

where the $m \times n$ matrix A is mixing matrix. The n source signals are collected in a $n \times 1$ vector denoted $s(t)$ which is referred to as the source signal vector. The sources are assumed to have different structures and localization properties in the time frequency domain. The mixing matrix A is full column rank but is otherwise unknown. In contrast with traditional parametric methods, no specific structure of the mixture matrix is assumed.

3   Power Spectral Density and Cross-Spectral Density

3.1   Energy Spectral Density and Power Spectral Density

The energy spectral density describes how the energy (or variance) of a signal or a time series is distributed with frequency. If $f(t)$ is a finite-energy (square integrable) signal, the spectral density $\Phi(\omega)$ of the signal is the square of the magnitude of the continuous Fourier transform of the signal[10][12].

$$\Phi(\omega) = \left| \frac{1}{\sqrt{2\pi}} \int_{-\infty}^{\infty} f(t)e^{-i\omega t} dt \right|^2 = \frac{F(\omega)F^*(\omega)}{2\pi} \tag{2}$$

where ω is the angular frequency (2π times the ordinary frequency) and $F(\omega)$ is the continuous Fourier transform of $f(t)$, and $F^*(\omega)$ is its complex conjugate.

If the signal is discrete with values $f(n)$, over an infinite number of elements, we still have an energy spectral density:

$$\Phi(\omega) = \left| \frac{1}{\sqrt{2\pi}} \sum_{n=-\infty}^{\infty} f(n)e^{-j\omega n} \right|^2 = \frac{F(\omega)F^*(\omega)}{2\pi} \tag{3}$$

where $F(\omega)$ is the discrete-time Fourier transform of $f(n)$. If the number of defined values is finite, the sequence does not have an energy spectral density per se, but the sequence can be treated as periodic, using a discrete Fourier transform to make a discrete spectrum, or it can be extended with zeros and a spectral density can be computed as in the infinite-sequence case.

The continuous and discrete spectral densities are often denoted with the same symbols, as above, though their dimensions and units differ; the continuous case has a time-squared factor that the discrete case does not have. They can be made to have equal dimensions and units by measuring time in units of sample intervals or by scaling the discrete case to the desired time units.

The definitions of energy spectral density require that the Fourier transforms of the signals exist. An often more useful alternative is the power spectral density (PSD), which describes how the power of a signal or time series is distributed with frequency. Here power can be the actual physical power, or more often, for convenience with abstract signals, can be defined as the squared value of the signal, that is, as the actual power dissipated in a load if the signal were a voltage applied to it. This instantaneous power (the mean or expected value of which is the average power) is then given by ($s(t)$ is a signal):

$$P(t) = s(t)^2 \tag{4}$$

Since a signal with nonzero average power is not square integrable, the Fourier transforms do not exist in this case. The Wiener-Khinchin theorem provides a simple alternative. The PSD is the Fourier transform of the autocorrelation function, $R(\tau)$, of the signal if the signal can be treated as a wide-sense stationary random process.

This results in the formula

$$S(f) = \int_{-\infty}^{\infty} R(\tau)e^{-2\pi i f \tau} d\tau = F(R(\tau)) \tag{5}$$

The ensemble average of the average periodogram when the averaging time interval $T \to \infty$ can be proved to approach the power spectral density (PSD):

$$E\left[\frac{|F(f_T(t))|^2}{T}\right] \to S(f) \tag{6}$$

The power of the signal in a given frequency band can be calculated by integrating over positive and negative frequencies,

$$P = \int_{F_1}^{F_2} S(f)df + \int_{-F_2}^{-F_1} S(f)df \tag{7}$$

The power spectral density of a signal exists if the signal is a wide-sense stationary process. If the signal is not stationary, then the autocorrelation function must be a function of two variables. In some cases, such as wide-sense cyclostationary processes, a PSD may still exist. More generally, similar techniques may be used to estimate a time-varying spectral density.

3.2   Cross Spectral Density

Just as the Power Spectral Density (PSD) is the Fourier transform of the auto-covariance function we may define the Cross Spectral Density (CSD) as the Fourier transform of the cross-covariance function[11]. The PSD is a special case of the cross spectral density (CPSD) function, defined between two signals X_n and Y_n as

$$P_{xy}(\omega) = \frac{1}{2\pi} \sum_{n=-\infty}^{\infty} R_{xy} e^{-j\omega n} \tag{8}$$

The goal of spectral density estimation is to estimate the spectral density of a random signal from a sequence of time samples. Depending on what is known about the signal, estimation techniques can involve parametric or non-parametric approaches, and may be based on time-domain or frequency domain analysis. For example, a common parametric technique involves fitting the observations to an autoregressive model. A common non-parametric technique is the periodogram.

The spectral density of $f(t)$ and the autocorrelation of $f(t)$ form a Fourier transform pair. One of the results of Fourier analysis is Parseval's theorem which states that the area under the energy spectral density curve is equal to the area under the square of the magnitude of the signal, the total energy:

$$\int_{-\infty}^{\infty} |f(t)|^2 dt = \int_{-\infty}^{\infty} \Phi(\omega)d\omega \tag{9}$$

The above theorem holds true in the discrete cases as well.

4   Power Spectral Density Blind Source Separation

4.1   Time-Frequency Analysis and Wigner-Ville Distribution

In many applications, we are interested in the frequency content of a signal locally in time. Some signals are called nonstationary. The Wigner-Ville distribution function is a powerful time-frequency analysis tool and it can be used to illustrate the time-frequency properties of a signal.

The Wigner-Ville distribution of a function $f(x)$ is defined as [7]:

$$X(t,\omega) = \int_{-\infty}^{\infty} x(t+\frac{\tau}{2})x^*(t-\frac{\tau}{2})e^{-j\omega\tau}d\tau \tag{10}$$

Power spectrum analysis is based on the analysis of time and scale, scale and frequency are closely related, therefore,the power spectral density signal separation method is also timefrequency characteristics of the signal separation.

4.2   The Principles of Power Spectral Density Blind Source Separation

The discrete time form of the Cohen's class of time frequency analysis, for a signal x(t), is given by [8][9]

$$D_{xx}(t,f) = \sum_{l=-\infty}^{\infty}\sum_{k=-\infty}^{\infty} \phi(k,l)x(t+k+l)x^*(t+k-l)e^{-j\,4\pi fl} \tag{11}$$

Where t and f represent the time index and the frequency index. The kernel $\phi(k,l)$ characterizes the distribution and is a function of both the time and lag variables. The cross time frequency distribution of two signals $x_1(t)$ and $x_2(t)$ is defined by

$$D_{x_1x_2}(t,f) = \sum_{l=-\infty}^{\infty}\sum_{k=-\infty}^{\infty} \phi(k,l)x_1(t+k+l)x_2^*(t+k-l)e^{-j\,4\pi fl} \tag{12}$$

We replace D_{xx} and $D_{x_1x_2}$ by equation (5) and (8). Expressions (11) and (12) are used to define the power spectral density distribution matrix $D_{xx}(t,l)$.Where t and l represent the time index and the different scale power spectral density index.

Under the linear data model of equation (1) and assuming noise-free environment. In accordance with the power spectral density matrix defined, the scale power spectral density matrix can be deduced the following structure:

$$D_{xx}(t,l) = AD_{ss}A^H \tag{13}$$

Where D_{SS} is the source different power spectral density matrix. By selecting auto-term power spectral density, D_{SS} will be diagonal. Moreover, since the sources have orthogonal time scale supports, the diagonal entries of D_{SS} are all zero except for one value which corresponds to the particular time scale domain.

4.3 Summary Alogrithm

The separation algorithm is summarized as follows:

1. Decorrelation and data whitening.
2. Compute the observed signal power spectral density as given in (5) and (8).
3. Using a threshhold to keep only the points with sufficient energy.For different scale point,compute the main eigenvector and eigenvalue.
4. Seperate different eigenvector class, each of them containing closely separated vectors,set the number of sources equal to the number of classes.
5. Use an adequate source synthesis procedure to analysis.

5   Simulation and Synthetic Signals

The following experiment was divided into two parts, first part is the random signal mixed and its independent component analysis, the second part is a mixture of time-varying signals. The data for reference only, the different results come from different simulation data.

5.1   Random Signal

The following is a Gaussian random signal generation, using power spectral density independent component analysis can be reconstructed signal. Figure 1 is observed signals and its sources and estimated signals. The mixing matrix is chosen randomly.

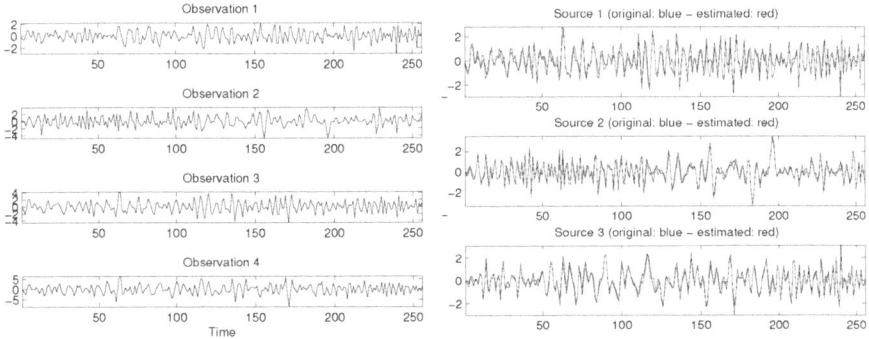

Fig. 1. Observed Signal(left) and its sources and estimated signals(right)

Table 1. Power Spectrual Density Blind Separation(Random Signal)

Method	SDR	SIR	SNR
Power Spectrum	-8.2505	-8.2309	24.0498

5.2   Nonstationary Signal

Figure 2 is observed signals and its.separated signal.Following is a mixed signal. The
mixing matrix is chosen randomly.

$$s_1(t) = \cos(0.0002441 4 t^2 + 0.05 t)$$

$$s_2(t) = \cos(4.13\sin(0.0154\pi t) + 0.25 t)$$

$$s_3(t) = \cos(0.00000178787 t^3 - 0.0014 t^2 + 0.402 7 t)$$

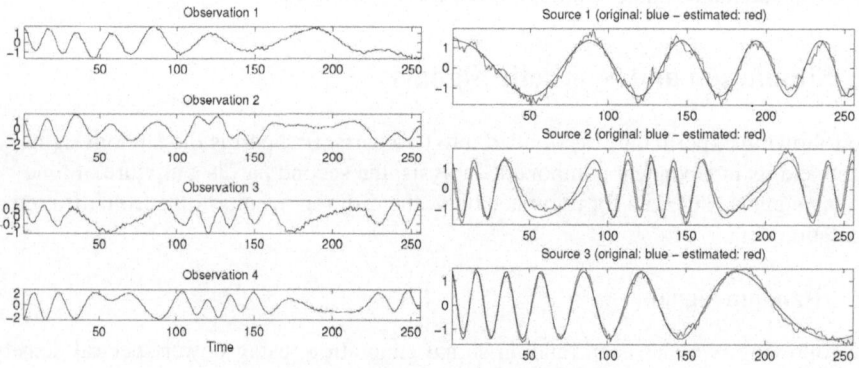

Fig. 2. Observed Signal(left) and Sources and Separated signal(right)

Table 2. Power Spectral Density and JADE Blind Separation(Nonstationary Signal)

Method	SDR	SIR	SNR
Power Spectrum	-3.5417	-3.5113	23.1444
JADE	-3.9275	-3.8785	20.9377

6   Conclusion

In this paper, we have presented blind sources separation algorithms based on power
spectral density. Power spectral density is particularly suitable for different power
spectral density signal. In some cases, the method suited for non-stationary signal.
Simulation results have shown that the method is feasible. The method extends the
relationship between time and frequency to the scale and frequency.

Acknowledgments. This work is supported by National Natural Science Foundation of China (No.61001174), Program for New Century Excellent Talents in University of China (No. NCET-09-0895).

References

1. Nguyen, L.-T., Belouchrani, A., Abed-Meraim, K., Boashash, B.: Separating More Sources then Sensors Using Time-Frequency Distributions. In: Sixth International Signal Processing and its Applications, vol. 2, pp. 583–686 (2001)
2. Belouchrani, A., Amin, M.G.: Blind source separation based on time-frequency signal representations. IEEE Trans. Spch. Aud. Proc. 46, 2888–2897 (1998)
3. Grinsted1, A., Moore1, J.C., Jevrejeva, S.: Application of the cross wavelet transform and wavelet coherence to geophysical time series, Nonlinear Processes in Geophysics. European Geosciences Union, 561–566 (2004)
4. Ding, S.: A power iteration algorithm for ica based on diagonalizations of non-linearized covariance matrix. In: International Conference on Innovative Computing, Information and Control, Beijing (2006)
5. Gikibar, A., Fevotte, C., Doncarli, C., Zazula, D.: Single autoterms selection for blind source separation in time frequency plane. In: Proc. EUSIPCO 2002, Toulouse, France, September 3-6 (2002)
6. Barry, D., Fitzgerald, D., Coyle, E., Lawlor, B.: Single Channel Source Separation using Short-time Independent Component Analysis. AES Audio Engineer Society (October 08, 2007)
7. Shan, Z.: Aviyente Source Separation in the Time-Frequency Domain by Maximizing an Information-Theoretic Criterion. In: 2006 IEEE International Conference on Electro/Information Technology, May 7-10, pp. 43–48 (2006)
8. Reju, V.G., Koh, S.N., Soon, I.Y.: Soon Underdetermined Convolutive Blind Source Separation via Time-Frequency Masking. IEEE Transactions on Audio, Speech, and Language Processing. , 101–116 (2010)
9. Shan, Z., Swary, J., Aviyente, S.: Underdetermined Source Separation in the Time-Frequency Domain. In: International Conference on Acoustics, Speech and Signal Processing, pp. 945–948 (2007)
10. Davenport, W.B., Root, W.L.: An Introduction to the Theory of Random Signals and Noise. IEEE Press, New York (1987) ISBN 0-87942-235-1
11. Brown, R.G., Hwang, P.Y.C.: Introduction to Random Signals and Applied Kalman Filtering. John Wiley & Sons, Chichester, ISBN 0471128392
12. http://en.wikipedia.org

Anomaly Detection in Categorical Datasets Using Bayesian Networks

Lida Rashidi, Sattar Hashemi, and Ali Hamzeh

Department of Computer Science and Engineering, Shiraz University, Shiraz, Iran
lrashidi@cse.shirazu.ac.ir, s_hashemi@shirazu.ac.ir,
ali@cse.shirazu.ac.ir

Abstract. In this paper we present a method for finding anomalous records in categorical or mixed datasets in an unsupervised fashion. Since the data in many problems consist of normal records with a small minority of anomalies, many approaches build a model from the training data and compare the test records against it. But instead of building a model, we keep track of the number of occurrences of different attribute value combinations. We also consider a more meaningful definition of anomalies and incorporate the Bayesian network structure in it. A scoring technique is defined for each test record. In this procedure we combine supports of different rules according to the Bayesian network structure in order to determine the label of the test instances. As it is shown in the results, our proposed method has a higher or similar f-measure and precision compared to a Bayesian network based approach in all cases.

Keywords: Anomaly Detection, Bayesian Network.

1 Introduction

Detection of anomalous records can be quite crucial in many application domains such as network intrusion detection [1], image processing [2], fraud detection [3], and bio-surveillance systems [4]. In Intrusion Detection Systems (IDS), we can prevent theft of sensitive information by producing an alarm whenever an abnormal sequence of requests has been received. In bio-surveillance systems, anomalies may mean that a disease is becoming epidemic in a specific region. Therefore their detection leads to performing precautionary acts such as vaccination which may save lives. Also in astronomical datasets, finding anomalous records may help astronomers to make a new discovery [5].

In anomaly detection methods, we are looking for instances which do not obey from the normal behaviour of the data that we have previously seen. Defining the normal behaviour can be a challenging task, but since the majority of the available data is considered to be normal, we can use the whole train dataset in order to build the normal model. For instance one can build a statistical model of the normal data and calculate the test record likelihood in order to decide whether it is abnormal or not.

H. Deng et al. (Eds.): AICI 2011, Part II, LNAI 7003, pp. 610–619, 2011.

Another challenge in these problems is how to define anomalies. In this paper we employ a definition in which rare attribute values may not lead to anomalous records if there is not enough evidence supporting the fact that they deviate from normal attribute value combinations [6] and we also incorporate the parent-child relationships among attributes in order to find anomalous records.

Finally we have to define a scoring technique for determining the label of test instances. For this purpose we build a rule base for each test instance and combine the support of the rules with minimum overlap. In this process we again take advantage of the Bayesian network structure. We only consider the support of the rules which do not have a relationship with the already considered ones according to the Bayesian network structure.

The remainder of the paper is organized as follows. Section 2 investigates a few methods which have been previously used for anomaly detection in categorical datasets. In Section 3, we define the problem and discuss our approach for solving it in detail. This is followed by Section 4 where we introduce the datasets used and also present our analysis of the experimental results in comparison to the baseline technique. Finally, we draw a conclusion from the discussed method and results and also introduce the possible future work.

2   Related Work

Anomaly detection techniques have been used in a variety of application domains such as network intrusion detection [7], fraud detection [8], image processing [2] and etc. The data in these domains can be a sequence such as time series or in the form of single records. Different methods are employed for each data type. For instance regression models such as Autoregressive Integrated Moving Average (ARIMA) [9] are used for anomaly detection in time series. Another method which has been successfully applied on continuous time series is called HOT SAX [10]. Since the problem we are considering is defined for categorical datasets with high arity and in an unsupervised fashion, we only review some of the unsupervised techniques applied for this type of datasets.

2.1   Association Rule Based Methods

One of the methods that satisfies the requirements mentioned in the Section 2, is association rule mining. In this method, normal patterns are formulated as rules. Therefore in the beginning rules are extracted from the normal data and then these rules are pruned by comparing their support with a threshold and finally test instances which do not conform to these rules are considered anomalous. This method has been used in network intrusion detection [11]. Another way of finding anomalies in a categorical dataset is to generate the frequent itemsets and score the test records based on these itemsets [12].

2.2   Nearest Neighbor Based Methods

Methods based on nearest neighbor can also be used for this type of datasets. In these techniques, a distance metric has to be utilized in order to calculate the anomaly score of an instance. Since we cannot use the same metrics for categorical and continuous attributes, we take advantage of a number of distance measures which are defined for categorical attributes [13]. When there is a mix of attributes in the dataset, we have to find a way to combine the distances among single attribute values [14]. The basic idea in these methods is that the anomalous instances are far from even their nearest neighbors [15].

2.3   Information Theory Based Method

Information theoretic methods are another category of anomaly detection techniques which can also be employed for mixed datasets. These methods calculate information theoretic metrics such as entropy for the whole dataset and find the subset of instances whose elimination from the dataset induces the biggest difference in the metric value. This subset is considered to consist of anomalous records [16].

2.4   Bayesian Network Based Approaches

Since Bayesian networks are popular representations for datasets with categorical attributes, they have been utilized for anomaly detection purposes in them. In this technique, the Bayesian structure is learned from the data [17] and the Bayesian network parameters are estimated. After constructing a Bayesian network for normal records, we can calculate complete record likelihood given the model for test instances in order to decide whether a test record is anomalous or not. The records which do not obey from the normal behaviour tend to have low likelihoods. This method has been successfully used in network intrusion detection [18] and disease outbreak detection [19].

3   Proposed Method

We propose an anomaly detection technique for datasets with categorical or mixed attributes in an unsupervised fashion. The key assumption about the training dataset is that the ratio of anomalous to normal records is very insignificant. The proposed method takes advantage of the Bayesian network structure and stores the counts for different attribute value combinations using a structure called AD Tree [20]. For each test record a scoring technique is executed and according to the calculated score, we can determine whether the record is anomalous or not.

3.1   Anomaly Definition

Our goal is to find meaningful anomalies in the dataset; therefore we have employed the following definition which assigns a high anomaly score to test records only when we have seen enough train records. We consider subsets of size at most k and calculate the r-value for each record. For instance two attribute sets A, B with at most k elements are employed to calculate the r-value for a test record.

$$r(a_t, b_t) = \frac{p(a_t, b_t)}{p(a_t)p(b_t)} \qquad (1)$$

According to the above formula, if probability of an attribute value combination such as $p(a_t)$ or $p(b_t)$ happens to be low in the training dataset, the r-value becomes bigger and the record will have a smaller chance of being considered anomalous. For each test record, all of the appropriate attribute sets are taken into account. Since the probabilities in equation 1 may become zero, we must apply Laplace smoothing and modify it as follows.

$$r(a_t, b_t) = \frac{c(a_t, b_t) + 1}{N + 2} \times \frac{N + 2}{c(a_t) + 1} \times \frac{N + 2}{c(b_t) + 1} \qquad (2)$$

In equation 2, N represents the total number of train instances and $c(a_t, b_t)$ stands for the number of instances in the train dataset which have a_t, b_t as values for attribute sets A, B.

3.2 Bayesian Network Structure

Many datasets have a large number of attributes which makes the calculation of r-values too costly; therefore we have to only consider attribute sets which are related to each other in a meaningful way. Since the definition of r-value was taken from the idea of conditional probability in which one attribute set is considered to be the parent and the other one the child, we tend to incorporate this idea and only consider attribute sets which have a parent-child relationship with each other according to the Bayesian network structure.

The Bayesian network structure demonstrates the relationships among various attributes. Therefore, we can extract the required information for calculating r-values. In order to find the Bayesian network structure we have employed optimal reinsertion algorithm [17] which utilizes an efficient method called ORSearch.

3.3 AD Tree

In order to find the number of occurrences of different attribute value combinations, we have to store the counts in a structure. One of the most efficient structures for this purpose is AD Tree.

We only consider attribute sets of size at most k and also apply some constraints in order to make the computations more efficient [20]. For instance, if the following equations do not hold for each attribute set of A, B; we don't have to calculate r-value for the combination of these attributes sets $r(a_t, b_t)$.

$$c(a_t) > \frac{1}{\alpha} - 1 \qquad c(b_t) > \frac{1}{\alpha} - 1 \qquad (3)$$

In the above formula α is a threshold considered for the r-values. If these two constraints are not satisfied, then $r(a_t, b_t)$ will always be greater than α.

3.4   Scoring Technique

After constructing the AD Tree and using a few speedups [6], we have to calculate the anomaly score for each test instance. In order to assign a score to each record, we have to consider a threshold so that we can order the calculated r-values and prune them according to this threshold.

We look at the problem at hand in a rule-base fashion. Every combination of two attribute sets with r-values smaller than 1 can be considered as a rule or pattern for determining anomalous records. Therefore we have to find a way to combine these rules and come up with a final score for the test records.

We order the rules according to their r-values and assign the minimum r-value to the score. We also add the attribute sets defining the r-value into an empty set U. The next smallest r-value is multiplied by the score and its describing attribute sets are added to U if it satisfies the following three conditions:

1. Attribute sets describing the rule shouldn't be a subset of the set U.
2. Attribute sets describing the rule shouldn't be a superset of the set U.
3. At least one member of the attribute sets must not have a parent-child relationship with any member of set U.

The first constraint states that once we have considered an attribute set with smaller r-value which is a superset of the attribute sets for the rule at hand, we may not consider the rule's attribute sets, i.e. since we have already added the rule which covers the new rule's conditions, there is no necessity for adding the new rule to our rule-base.

The second constraint states that if a rule with fewer conditions results in a smaller r-value than a rule with more conditions, then the latter rule doesn't show any evidence of anomalousness of a record. Since by adding more constraints the probability of low likelihood increases, we expect to see a lower r-value for a rule with more constraints. Therefore we do not consider the r-value of this rule in our scoring procedure.

The third constraint counts for the fact that parent-child relationship among attributes means that there is mutual information among them and we want to prevent our rule-base from having rules with the same information, i.e. once a parent attribute set has a low r-value, it is quite possible that the children also have low r-values. Therefore, before adding a rule into our rule-base we have to make sure that at least one attribute has no parent-child relationship with the attributes already in U.

The final score for each record is calculated according to the described procedure and this score is compared against a threshold which determines whether the test record is anomalous or not. The overall procedure is coded below.

```
Begin
        ∀i : (R_1, {A_1, B_1}),...., (R_n, {A_n, B_n})
            C = {A_i, B_i} - U;
        If  ({A_i, B_i} ⊄ U and U ⊄ {A_i, B_i} and
            {∃j | ∀k : parentChild(C_j, U_k) ≠ 1})
            score = score × R_i;    U = U ∪ {A_i, B_i};
        Else
            ;
End.
```

4   Experimental Evaluation

We have applied the proposed method on two datasets which are described in Section 4.1. The next section contains the information concerning training and testing phases. Finally the results are represented in Section 4.3.

4.1   Datasets

The first dataset is KDD Cup 1999 which consists of network connection records. This dataset has 41 attributes among which only 7 are categorical and the other 34 attributes are continuous. We have discretized the continuous attributes into five levels. In this dataset there are some basic features extracted from individual TCP connections such as duration or protocol type. The other group of features is suggested by domain knowledge and some traffic features are calculated using a two second time frame.

Since we are considering unsupervised anomaly detection, we have removed the label of 500000 training records among which only 1% is anomalous. Since the ratio of anomalous to normal records in the training data is insignificant, we consider the training data to be normal.

There are 24 attack types in the dataset but we have only considered three of them: mailbomb, neptune, and warezmaster. The test dataset for each type of attack consists of 10000 records containing 10% anomalies and 90% normal records.

The second dataset that we are considering in our experiments is Census from UCI Machine Learning Repository. This dataset consists of 14 attributes among which 8 are nominal and the rest is real. We have discretized the real values into 5 levels. We have omitted the labels from the training dataset and considered records with income less than 50 as normal instances. We used 22654 unlabeled records for training and 18868 records for testing containing around 40% anomalous and 60% normal records. The datasets descriptions are summarized in Table 1.

4.2   Training and Testing

We are comparing our method against Bayesian network. For implementing the proposed method AD Tree and the Bayesian structure are constructed from the data as described in Sections 3.2, 3.3.

In the testing phase, we consider combinations of every pair of attribute sets if there exists a parent-child relationship between the attributes of one set with another. After calculating the r-value for the combinations that satisfy the parent-child relationship, we have to build our rule-base system. We have considered k=2 since the number of attributes in KDD dataset is 41.The final score of each test record is calculated according to these rules. The scoring procedure is described in detail in Section 3.4. Finally the test records' scores are compared against a threshold which determines the label of the instance which can be normal or anomalous.

4.3   Results

The baseline method consists of building a Bayesian network and calculating the complete test record likelihood given the model as its anomaly score. In order to compare our method against the baseline, we have taken advantage of F-measure which focuses on both precision and recall. Considering mere accuracy is not an option because the majority of the data consists of normal records, for instance by predicting all records as normal in KDD Cup 1999, the accuracy is 90%. Therefore, we have to employ a measurement which considers both precision and recall.

$$f - measure = \frac{2 * P * R}{P + R} \tag{4}$$

$$P = \frac{TP}{TP + FP}, R = \frac{TP}{TP + FN} \tag{5}$$

Figure 1 depicts the precision and recall for census dataset by varying the threshold for the baseline and the proposed technique. We have considered the best threshold which leads to highest F-measure for each technique and summarized the results in Table 2.

As it is depicted in Table 2, for attack types Mailbomb and Neptune, the F-measure and precision of the proposed technique is significantly higher than that of the baseline and the recall is almost the same in these two cases. For attack type Warezmaster the f-measure of the proposed method and the baseline are very close but the precision of the proposed technique is higher and the recall is lower than that of the baseline. In Census dataset the f-measure, precision and recall are almost the same. As you can notice the precision of the proposed method in all of the datasets is higher or very similar to the baseline. This is due to the fact that rare attribute values do not lead to low r-values when considered in attribute value combinations.

Therefore as we mentioned before, only meaningful anomalies are detected in these dataset. Since the problem at hand is anomaly detection, having a high precision means fewer false alarms which is an important concern in many systems.

In both datasets k=2 is considered because the number of attributes in KDD Cup 1999 is large and we cannot afford the overhead added by a greater number for k. Therefore we are considering rules with at most four conditions in our rule-base system. By using our proposed scoring technique instead of only considering the minimum threshold to be the final score of a test instance, we are actually incorporating all the information in our rules and deducing the score form them. It is shown that even for the rules with few conditions the proposed method has an acceptable result.

Table 1. Dataset Description.

Dataset	Attributes	Train Size	Test Size	% of anomalies	% of normal records
KDD Cup 1999	41	500,000	10,000	10%	90%
Census	14	22654	18868	39.8%	60.2%

Table 2. Results comparing baseline and proposed method

Attack Type	Method	F-measure	Precision	Recall
Mail Bomb	Baseline	83.01 %	71 %	99.9 %
	Proposed	**94.19 %**	**92.82 %**	95.6 %
Warezmaster	Baseline	75.99 %	63.14 %	95.4 %
	Proposed	75.22 %	**68,88 %**	83 %
Neptune	Baseline	74.41 %	58.54 %	96.7 %
	Proposed	**85.15 %**	**76.37 %**	96.3 %

Dataset	Method	F-measure	Precision	Recall
Census	Baseline	56.93 %	100 %	39.79 %
	Proposed	**57.16 %**	99.57 %	**40.08 %**

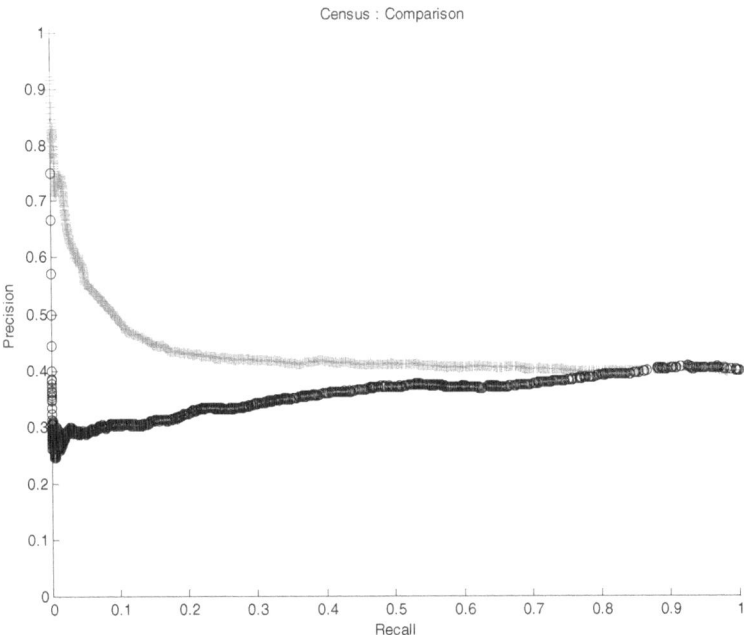

Fig. 2. Black circles and gray pluses indicate proposed method and the baseline.

5   Conclusion and Future Work

In this paper we have presented a method for unsupervised anomaly detection in categorical or mixed datasets. As opposed to Bayesian network we are not building a model for data, we are only storing counts for different attribute value combinations and extracting rules from them in order to determine whether a   single instance is anomalous or not. As it is depicted in the results, our method performs significantly better in two of the attack types and the same or higher than the baseline in other datasets. Besides the precision rate of our method is always higher or close to the baseline which is due to anomaly definition discussed in Section 3.1.

As a future work, we can change the scoring technique in the way that it doesn't only consider the immediate parent-child relationships. We can assign weights to the rules instead of omitting them. Rules which have more mutual information with the already mentioned rules should have lower weights.

References

1. Lakhina, A., Crovella, M., Diot, C.: Mining Anomalies Using Traffic Feature Distributions. In: Proceedings of the 2005 Conference on Applications, Technologies, Architectures, and Protocols for Computer Communications, pp. 217–228. ACM Press, New York (2005)
2. Pokrajac, D., Lazarevic, A., Latecki, L.J.: Incremental Local Outlier Detection for Data Streams. In: Proceedings of IEEE Symposium on Computational Intelligence and Data Mining (2007)
3. Donoho, S.: Early Detection of Insider Trading in Option Markets. In: Proceedings of the Tenth ACM SIGKDD International Conference on Knowledge Discovery and Data Mining, pp. 420–429 (2004)
4. Wong, W.K., Moore, A.W.: Handbook of Biosurveillance. Academic Press, London (2006)
5. Dutta, H., Giannella, C., Borne, K., Kargupta, H.: Distributed Top-k Outlier Detection in Astronomy Catalogs Using the Demac System. In: Proceedings of 7th SIAM International Conference on Data Mining (2007)
6. Das, K., Schneider, J.: Detecting Anomalous Records in Categorical datasets. In: Proceedings of the 13th ACM SIGKDD International Conference on Knowledge Discovery and Data Mining. ACM Press, New York (2007)
7. Gwadera, R., Atallah, M.J., Szpankowski, W.: Markov Models for Identification of Significant Episodes. In: Proceedings of 5th SIAM International Conference on Data Mining (2005)
8. Phua, C., Alahakoon, D., Lee, V.: Minority Report in Fraud Detection: Classification of Skewed Data. In: SIGKDD Explorer Newsletter, pp. 50–59 (2004)
9. Chen, D., Shao, X., Hu, B., Su, Q.: Simultaneous Wavelength Selection and Outlier Detection in Multivariate Regression of Near-infrared Spectra. Analytical Sciences, 61–67 (2005)
10. Keogh, E., Lin, J., Fu, A.: Hot Sax: Efficiently Finding the Most Unusual Time Series Subsequence. In: Proceedings of the Fifth IEEE International Conference on Data Mining, pp. 226–233 (2005)
11. Tandon, G., Chan, P.: Weighting Versus Pruning in Rule Validation for Detecting Network and Host Anomalies. In: Proceedings of the 13th ACM SIGKDD International Conference on Knowledge Discovery and Data Mining (2007)
12. He, Z., Xu, X., Huang, J.Z., Deng, S.: A Frequent Pattern Discovery Method for Outlier Detection. In: Li, Q., Wang, G., Feng, L. (eds.) WAIM 2004. LNCS, vol. 3129, pp. 726–732. Springer, Heidelberg (2004)

13. Chandola, V., Boriah, S., Kumar, V.: Understanding Categorical Similarity Measures for Outlier Detection. Technical Report 08-008. University of Minnesota (2008)
14. Tan, P.N., Steinbach, M., Kumar, V.: Introduction to Data Mining. Addison Wesley, Reading (2005)
15. Chandola, V., Banerjee, A., Kumar, V.: Anomaly Detection: A Survey. ACM Computer Survey, 1–58 (2009)
16. Ando, S.: Clustering Needles in a Haystack: An Information Theoretic Analysis of Minority and Outlier Detection. In: Proceedings of 7th International Conference on Data Mining, pp. 13–22 (2007)
17. Moore, A., Wong, W.K.: Optimal Reinsertion: A New Search Operator for Accelerated and More Accurate Bayesian network Structure Learning. In: Proceedings of the 20th International Conference on Machine Learning, pp. 552–559 (2003)
18. Ye, N., Xu, M.: Probabilistic Networks with Undirected Links for Anomaly Detection. In: IEEE Systems, Man, and Cybernetics Information Assurance and Security Workshop, pp. 175–179 (2000)
19. Wong, W.K., Moore, A., Cooper, G., Wagner, M.: Bayesian network Anomaly Pattern Detection for Disease Outbreaks. In: Proceedings of the Twentieth International Conference on Machine Learning, pp. 808–815 (2003)
20. Moore, A., Lee, M.S.: Cached Sufficient Statistics for Efficient Machine Learning with Large Datasets. Journal of Artificial Intelligence Research, 67–91 (1998)

Detecting Overlapping Communities in Social Networks by Game Theory and Structural Equivalence Concept

Hamidreza Alvari, Sattar Hashemi, and Ali Hamzeh

Department of Electrical and Computer Engineering, Shiraz University,
Shiraz, Iran
alvari@cse.shirazu.ac.ir, s_hashemi@shirazu.ac.ir,
ali@cse.shirazu.ac.ir

Abstract. Most complex networks demonstrate a significant property 'community structure', meaning that the network nodes are often joined together in tightly knit groups or communities, while there are only looser connections between them. Detecting these groups is of great importance and has immediate applications, especially in the popular online social networks like Facebook and Twitter. Many of these networks are divided into overlapping communities, i.e. communities with nodes belonging to more than one community simultaneously. Unfortunately most of the works cannot detect such communities. In this paper, we consider the formation of communities in social networks as an iterative game in a multiagent environment, in which, each node is regarded as an agent trying to be in the communities with members structurally equivalent to her. Remarkable results on the real world and benchmark graphs show efficiency of our approach in detecting overlapping communities compared to the other similar methods.

Keywords: Social networks, community detection, overlapping communities, game theory, structural equivalence.

1 Introduction

The solution to the Königsberg bridges puzzle in 1736 by Leonhard Euler [1] was perhaps the origin of the graph theory. Since 20th century, graph has been extremely used as a representation tool, for a wide range of complex systems in different areas. Nowadays, graphs and their analysis have become a prominent component in studying such systems and their properties, including social, biological, technological, and informational networks. Emergence of huge amount of data and computational resources provided by the computer revolution has made the processing and analysis of data very hard. Recent rapid expansion of real networks to millions or even billions of vertices has produced a deep change in the way graphs are approached [2-4]. These large networks exhibit interesting common properties, such as high network transitivity [5], power-law degree distributions [6], the existence of repeated local motifs [7] and the outstanding property 'community structure' or 'clustering',

H. Deng et al. (Eds.): AICI 2011, Part II, LNAI 7003, pp. 620–630, 2011.

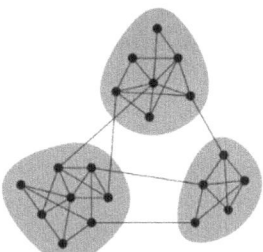

Fig. 1. Shaded sets of vertices show communities of the network, within which there are many edges, with only a smaller number of edges between vertices of different groups [8]

meaning the advent of dense connected groups, modules, clusters or communities of vertices in the graph, and sparser connections between them. The schematic example of a graph with communities is shown in Figure 1.

Because of its high applicability, this property has attracted a lot of researchers from different fields of study. From the important applications of detecting such groups, one can refer to detecting groups within World Wide Web which might correspond to web pages on the related topics [9], groups in social networks like Facebook and Twitter, which often show knit relationships between their members [10], and even groups in a metabolic network which might represent cycles and other functional groupings [11]. In addition, clustering Web clients having similar interests and being geographically near to each other, can improve the performance of services provided on the World Wide Web [12] and Detecting clusters of customers with similar interests in the network of purchase relationships between customers and products of online retailers (e.g. www.amazon.com) can lead to set up efficient recommendation systems and improve business opportunities [13]. As another application, clustering large graphs can help in creating data structures to store the graph more efficiently [14].

Perhaps, one of the most appealing issues which deserves initiating new trend of researches is to address overlapping communities, say, the case in which some nodes in the network belong to more than one community at the same time. An intuitive example of this concept is the membership of each of us in the communities like family, friends, co-workers, etc. Unfortunately only some of the proposed methods (See for example [18-22]) are capable to find these overlapping communities in a given networks.

In this paper, we have proposed a new framework based on game theory and structural equivalence concept to identify the overlapping communities in the networks. To do so, two alternative approaches, named PSGAME and NGGAME, are designed and developed. The former approach incorporates Pearson correlation into game theory, whereas, the later approach makes use of neighborhood relation as similarity measure in the game of concern. In addition, a new similarity measure, neighborhood similarity, established on the neighborhood and adjacency relationships is introduced. This measure, calculates similarities between graph vertices. Experiments show that these methods give more accurate results than the other state of art rival approaches.

The measures taken in the rest of the paper are organized as follows. In Section 2 the community detection problem is defined and a brief review of the history of existing methods on it is given in the section 3. In Section 4, our proposed framework is explained in details and in Section 5 the comparisons between our results and the results of some other popular methods in the literature are mentioned. Finally in Section 6, the conclusions and hints for future works are discussed.

2   Problem Statement

Given an underlying graph G, with $|G| = n$ vertices (nodes) and m edges, the community detection problem is to cluster these vertices into C communities or groups based on some predefined measures such that these communities can have intersections (i.e. overlapping communities) or not. However the community detection problem, intuitive at first sight, is in fact, not well defined, because main elements of it (e.g. the community concept) are not precisely defined and there are often some ambiguities in their definitions. This has resulted in presenting so many interpretations of it in the literature.

The main issue on community detection problem is to look for some quantitative measure and definition of community. Unfortunately no universally accepted definition is in hand, because this definition often depends on the underlying problem and its application. But intuitively we expect more edges inside the community compared to the outside of it and the rest of the graph. This simple concept is the basis of the most definitions of community. However social network analysts have distinguished three main classes of definitions for community: local, global and vertex similarity based. According to the local definition, a community is being evaluated independently of the graph, while in the global definition communities are defined with respect to the graph as a whole. Definitions based on the vertex similarity, assume that communities are groups of vertices most similar to each other.

3   Related Work

Research on the community detection problem has a long history and has been appeared in several forms and applications including sociology and computer science. The first analysis of community structure in the networks dates back to 1927 and the paper written by Stuart Rice, who looked for clusters of people in small political bodies, based on the similarity of their voting patterns [15]. Since then, many works have been done, which can be categorized into two main groups: optimization methods which look for optimizing some measures and methods with no optimization, which search for some predetermined structures.

From these works, one can refer to the works done by Girvan and Newman in 2002 and 2004 that introduced two important concepts 'edge betweenness' [10] and 'modularity' [16], the work done by Brandes and Erlebach which intoroduced the term 'conductance' [17] and the work done by Palla et.al [20]. Recently some works have been done considering overlapping concept. Gregory proposed CONGA [18] and CONGO [19] based on 'split betweenness' to detect overlapping communities in the networks. In 2005, Palla et al. showed that searching for some predetermined structures like fully connected graphs in the network can lead to detecting such communities. Meanwhile very few works are done based on the game theory [21, 23]. These works address the problem of community detection by a game-theoretic framework, in which nodes of a graph are considered as rational agents who want to maximize their payoffs according to some criterion. The game-theoretic methods are grounded with a systematic theory for formation of communities in the networks, as in the real world, which communities are formed based on some purposes, not for optimizing some local or global objectives.

4   Proposed Framework

It is naturally plausible if the problem of community detection in the network is regarded as a play of interactions between humans in the society, where each node of the underlying network is considered as a selfish agent, who wants to maximize her total utility. A little concentration on the problem shows that we as humans always need to make deep social relationships with our friends in the society we belong to, or sometimes need to leave them according to our profits. Based on this intrinsic fact, we often choose between *join*, *leave* and *switch* operations in our social interactions. When we think that joining to a community will be good for us because of some reasons, we will join it. When belonging to one community is pernicious for us, we will leave it. On the other hands when we find another community, more profitable, we leave the community we belong to, in order to join to this community, i.e. we switch from one community to another.

Communities are often defined as the groups of the most similar vertices to each other. Therefore one can compute the similarities between each pair of vertices of the network with respect to some local or global property; no matter whether they are connected directly or not. There are a lot of similarity measures in the literature that are at the basis of traditional methods like hierarchical, partitional and spectral clustering [24]. These measures are mainly divided into two categories: when it is possible to embed the graph vertices in a Euclidean space, the most prominent measures are Euclidean distance, Manhattan distance and cosine similarity, but when a graph can't be embedded in space, adjacency relationships between vertices are used (See for example [25]).

In this work we've used two similarity measures based on adjacency relationships and structural equivalence [26]. Two vertices are called structural equivalent if they have the same neighbors, even if they are not directly connected. The measures we used are Pearson correlation and our novel similarity measure, neighborhood similarity. Here, we formulate the community detection problem as an iterative game, in which each node is a rational agent who plays the community formation game hopefully to maximize her total utility based on structural equivalence (similarity). This game will continue until no agent can improve hers. Considering that the underlying network is given in the form of a graph, our framework is as follows.

Each node of the graph G is considered as an agent that has a personal utility function. Before starting the game, similarities between all agents are calculated by a similarity measure. When starting the game, each agent based on this similarity as her utility, will choose between joining to a new community or existing one, leaving from existing community and switching from existing community to another existing one. A node can also do nothing if these operations don't change her utility. Overlapping community structure of the network will come into the view after agents reach local equilibrium. We used local Nash equilibrium in this game, because reaching global one is not feasible [27].

Naturally when joining to a new community, each of us will be beneficiary, but on the other hands, we must pay some costs (e.g. fees). Therefore, we've used a gain function Q and a loss function L and a utility function U, as their difference for each node:

$$Q_i(S) = \frac{1}{2m} \sum_{\substack{j=1 \\ j \neq i}}^{n} C_{ij} \delta_{ij} \tag{1}$$

$$L_i = \frac{1}{m}(|s_i| - 1) \tag{2}$$

In above equations, S indicates the strategy profile of all agents, i.e. labels of memberships of all agents, m is the number of graph edges, n is the number of nodes or agents, C_{ij} is the similarity between node i and node j, The output of δ function is 0 or 1; when two agents have common labels, i.e. $|s_i \cap s_j| \geq 1$, the output is 1, otherwise 0. Finally $|s_i|$ is the number of labels agent i belongs to.

```
Algorithm 1      PSGAME (NGGAME)

Input   underlying network graph G.
Output  community as a final division of G.

  1. Initializing each node of G as a selfish agent.

  2. Initializing community as a set, indicating final
     communities of G.  Initially each agent is a
     singleton community.

  3. Calculating similarities between each pair of
     agents based on Pearson (neighborhood) similarity.

repeat
     1. Choosing an agent randomly from agents who have
        been seen less.

     2. This agent will choose the best operation among
        join, leave, switch or no operation operations
        based on her utility function.
until local equilibrium is reached
```

We used this framework in two methods PSGAME and NGGAME, based on whether C_{ij} is calculated by Pearson correlation measure or by neighborhood similarity measure. Pseudocode of our proposed framework is shown in below.

4.1 PSGAME

Pearson correlation is a measure related to structural equivalence which calculates correlation between columns or rows of an adjacency matrix. This measure can be used in order to calculate similarities between nodes of a graph. PSGAME is a game based method in which similarity between agents i and j, C_{ij}, is calculated by Pearson correlation. Here A is an adjacency matrix of G, μ_i is an average and σ_i is a variance:

$$C_{ij} = \frac{1}{n\sigma_i\sigma_j}\Sigma_k(A_{ik} - \mu_i)(A_{jk} - \mu_j) \tag{3}$$

$$\mu_i = \frac{1}{n}\Sigma_j A_{ij} \tag{4}$$

$$\sigma_i = \sqrt{\frac{1}{n}\Sigma_j(A_{ij} - \mu_i)^2} \tag{5}$$

In fact, this metric quantifies how similar are two nodes and is measured from -1 to +1. Score 1 indicates that they are perfectly similar and a score of -1 means that they are dissimilar. In other words, the Pearson correlation score, quantifies how well two data objects fit a line.

4.2 NGGAME

Two nodes are most likely to be in one community, if they have common neighbors and are connected directly by an edge. Therefore we proposed a new similarity measure, neighborhood similarity, based on the number of common neighbors, adjacency matrix of the graph and degrees of the nodes. This similarity measurement is in the range [-1, +1]. NGGAME is a game based method that uses neighborhood similarity to calculate similarity C_{ij} between agents i and j. Let ω_{ij} be $|\Gamma(i) \cap \Gamma(j)|$ and $\Gamma(i)$ indicates the set of neighbors of node i. Assume A is adjacency matrix of G, m is the number of edges, n is the number of vertices and d_i is the degree of node i.

$$C_{ij} = \begin{cases} \begin{cases} \omega_{ij}(1 - \frac{d_id_j}{2m}) & A_{ij} = 1 \\ \frac{\omega_{ij}}{n} & A_{ij} = 0 \end{cases} & \omega_{ij} \geq 1 \\ \begin{cases} \frac{d_id_j}{4m} & A_{ij} = 1 \\ -\frac{d_id_j}{4m} & A_{ij} = 0 \end{cases} & \omega_{ij} = 0 \end{cases} \tag{6}$$

When nodes i and j have common neighbors, i.e. $\omega_{ij} \geq 1$ and they are themselves connected directly, i.e. $A_{ij} = 1$, C_{ij} gets its largest value, because it seems that these nodes are very similar. As long as they have no common neighbors and they are

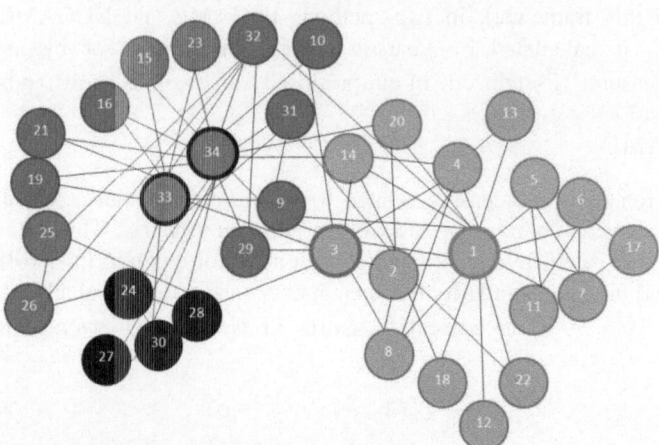

Fig. 2. Communities found by NGGAME on the Zachary network. Nodes with thick colored margins show overlapping communities.

not connected themselves, C_{ij} gets its worst value. These cases and two other cases are shown in above formula.

5   Experiments

We conducted our experiments on both real world and benchmark graphs. To evaluate our work, from different metrics used in literature [24], we used recent version of *normalized mutual information* [28] that can support overlapping communities.

5.1   Real World Graphs

We have evaluated our work on real world graphs, Dolphin network [29] and Zachary Karate Club network [30], two well-known networks in the literature with known community structure.

In Dolphin network, the network of bottlenose dolphins living in Doubtful Sound (New Zealand) analyzed by biologist David Lusseau, there are 62 dolphins and edges were set between animals that were seen together more often than expected by chance. On the other hands, Zachary network consists of 34 vertices, the members of a karate club in the United States, who were observed during a period of three years. Edges connect individuals who were observed to interact outside the activities of the club. At some point, a conflict between the club president and the instructor led to the fission of the club in two separate groups, supporting the instructor and the president, respectively [24]. The communities of the Zachary network found by NGGAME method is shown in Figure 2.

5.2   Benchmark Graphs

In addition we ran our method on a set of benchmark graphs recently proposed by Lancichinetti and Fortunato [31]. Briefly speaking, the graphs are constructed in the following steps: (1) generate the number of communities that each node will belong to; assign the degrees to the nodes based on a power law distribution with exponent τ_1; (2) assign the community sizes from another power law distribution with exponent τ_2 for a fixed number of communities; (3) generate the bipartite graph between the nodes and the communities with the configuration model; (4) for each node, assign the cross-community degree and internal degrees within each community based on μ (mixing parameter); (5) build the graphs for each community and the cross-community edges with the configuration model.

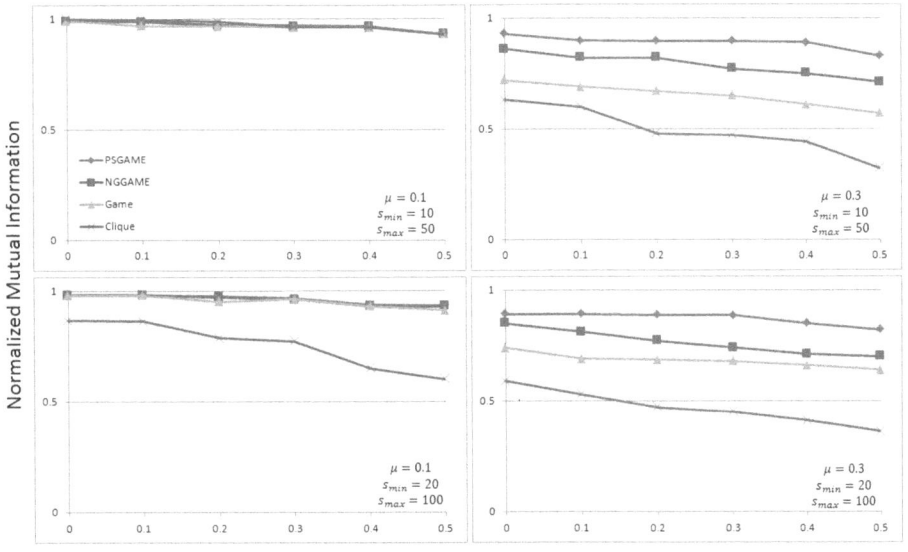

Fig. 3. Comparison between results on the benchmarks with 1000 nodes

The comparative evaluation between different algorithms are shown in Figure 3 where the y axis is the *normalized mutual information* (NMI) and x axis shows different fractions of overlapping nodes of benchmarks from 0 to 0.5. The numbers s_{min} and s_{max} refer to the limits of communities sizes. We set the other parameters of the benchmarks as $\tau_1 = 2$, $\tau_2 = 1$, $k_{avg} = 20$, $k_{max} = 50$, $om=2$ and two numbers 0.1 and 0.3 for μ or mixing parameter (i.e. proportion of crossing edges). Results on the benchmarks demonstrate that our approach is superior with respect to the methods that can detect overlapping communities, such as Clique [20] and Game [21]. It is noticeable that Clique algorithm needs the size of cliques as input. In this work we examined clique sizes of 3 to 8.

Finally as a toy example, a very simple synthetic graph and its communities found by NGGAME and Game are depicted in Figure 4. This example shows that NGGAME can give more reasonable division of underlying graph compared to the Game method.

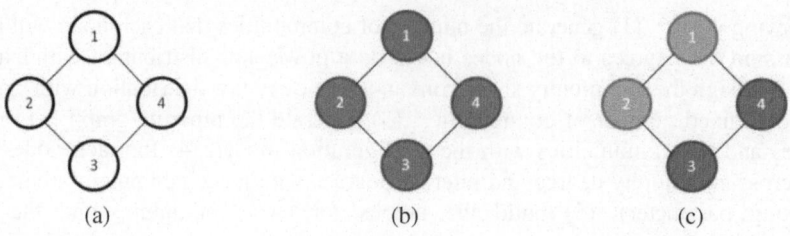

Fig. 4. (a) A toy (synthetic) example. Communities found by (b) NGGAME, (c) Game

6   Conclusion and Future Work

In this work, inspired from social life, we presented a novel framework for detecting overlapping communities in social networks, based on game theory and structural equivalence (similarity) concept. Furthermore we proposed a new similarity measure, neighborhood similarity measure which calculates similarity of graph nodes based on neighborhood relations.

We used this framework in two methods, PSGAME and NGGAME. The first method embeds Pearson correlation measure while the other one uses neighborhood similarity as similarity measure. The motivation behind these methods is that nodes in one community are obviously among the most similar ones to each other compared to the other nodes outside this community. Therefore if we consider each node as a selfish agent who plays the game in order to maximize her sheer goal, this goal will be joining to the most similar nodes to her.

Results show that we have reached to more reasonable divisions of underlying graphs compared to the other existing methods. From two proposed methods, PSGAME presents better results on very large graphs, while NGGAME has reasonable results on the small graphs.

For future works, one can provide another similarity measure or use another existing one instead of Pearson in order to use in this framework. Similarly, loss function used here, can be replaced by a new one. On the other hands, one can embed joint decision concept into this framework. This may have better results at the expense of the high running time. Finally, an extension of this framework to the weighted and directed graphs is straightforward.

References

1. Euler, L.: Commentarii Academiae Petropolitanae 8, 128 (1736)
2. Albert, R., Barabási, A.-L.: Rev. Mod. Phys. 74(1), 47 (2002)
3. Newman, M.E.J.: SIAM Rev. 45(2), 167 (2003)

4. Barrat, A., Barthélémy, M., Vespignani, A.: Dynamical processes on complex networks. Cambridge University Press, Cambridge (2008)
5. Watts, D.J., Strogatz, S.H.: Nature. 393, 440–442 (1998)
6. Barabási, A.-L., Albert, R.: Science 286, 509–512 (1999)
7. Milo, R., Shen-Orr, S., Itzkovitz, S., Kashtan, N., Chklovskii, D., Alon, U.: Science 298, 824–827 (2002)
8. Newman, M.E.J.: Proc. Natl. Acad. Sci. USA 103, 8577–8582 (2006)
9. Flake, G.W., Lawrence, S.R., Giles, C.L., Coetzee, F.M.: IEEE Computer 35, 66–71 (2002)
10. Girvan, M., Newman, M.E.J.: Proc. Natl. Acad. Sci. USA 99, 7821–7826 (2002)
11. Chen, J., Yuan, B.: Bioinformatics 22(18), 2283 (2006)
12. Krishnamurthy, B., Wang, J.: SIGCOMM Comput. Commun. Rev. 30(4), 97 (2000)
13. Reddy, P.K., Kitsuregawa, M., Sreekanth, P., Rao, S.S.: A Graph Based Approach to Extract a Neighborhood Customer Community for Collaborative Filtering. In: Bhalla, S. (ed.) DNIS 2002. LNCS, vol. 2544, pp. 188–200. Springer, Heidelberg (2002)
14. Wu, A.Y., Garland, M., Han, J.: In: KDD 2004: Proceedings of the Tenth ACM SIGKDD international conference on Knowledge Discovery and Data Mining, pp. 719–724. ACM Press, New York, NY, USA (2004)
15. Rice, S.A.: Am. Polit. Sci. Rev. 21, 619 (1927)
16. Newman, M.E.J., Girvan, M.: Phys. Rev. E 69(2), 26113 (2004)
17. Brandes, U., Erlebach, T.: Network analysis: methodological foundations. Springer, Berlin (2005)
18. Gregory, S.: An Algorithm to Find Overlapping Community Structure in Networks. In: Kok, J.N., Koronacki, J., Lopez de Mantaras, R., Matwin, S., Mladenič, D., Skowron, A. (eds.) PKDD 2007. LNCS (LNAI), vol. 4702, pp. 91–102. Springer, Heidelberg (2007)
19. Gregory, S.: A Fast Algorithm to Find Overlapping Communities in Networks. In: Daelemans, W., Goethals, B., Morik, K. (eds.) ECML PKDD 2008, Part I. LNCS (LNAI), vol. 5211, pp. 408–423. Springer, Heidelberg (2008)
20. Palla, G., Derényi, I., Farkas, I., Vicsek, T.: Uncovering the Overlapping Community Structure of Complex Networks in Nature and Society. Nature 435, 814–818 (2005)
21. Chen, W., Liu, Z., Sun, X., Wang, Y.: A game-theoretic framework to identify overlapping communities in social networks. Data Min. Knowl. Disc. 21, 224–240 (2010)
22. Zhang, S., Wang, R., Zhang, X.: Identification of Overlapping Community Structure in Complex Networks Using Fuzzy C-means Clustering. Physica A: Statistical Mechanics and its Applications 374(1), 483–490 (2007)
23. Adjeroh, D., Kandaswamy, U.: Game-Theoretic Analysis of Network Community Structure 3(4), 313–325 (2007), doi:10.5019/j.ijcir.2007.112
24. Fortunato, S.: Community detection in graphs. arXiv:0906.0612 (2009)
25. Wasserman, S., Faust, K.: Social Network Analysis: Methods and applications. Cambridge University Press, Cambridge (1994)
26. Lorrain, F., White, H.: J. Math. Sociol 1, 49 (1971)
27. Aiós-Ferrer, C., Ania, A.: Local equilibria in economic games. Econ. Lett. 70(2), 165–173 (2001)
28. Lancichinetti, A., et al.: Detecting the overlapping and hierarchical community structure in complex networks. Andrea, New J. Phys. 11, 33015 (2009)

29. Lusseau, D.: The emergent properties of a dolphin social network. Proc. Bio.1. Sci. 270, S186–S188 (2003)
30. Zachary, W.W.: An information flow model for conflict and fission in small groups. J. Anthropol Res. 33(4), 452–473 (1977)
31. Lancichinetti, A., Fortunato, S.: Benchmarks for testing community detection algorithms on directed and weighted graphs with overlapping communities. Phys. Rev. E 80(1), 16118 (2009)

A New Metric for Greedy Ensemble Pruning*

Huaping Guo, Weimei Zhi, Xiao Han, and Ming Fan

School of Information Engineering, ZhengZhou University, P.R. China
hpguo.gm@gmail.com, iewmzhi@zzu.edu.cn, iexhan.gm@gmail.com,
mfan@zzu.edu.cn

Abstract. Ensemble pruning is a technique to reduce ensemble size and increase its accuracy by selecting an optimal or suboptimal subset as subensemble for prediction. Many ensemble pruning algorithms via greedy search policy have been recently proposed. The key to the success of these algorithms is to construct an effective metric to supervise the search process. In this paper, we contribute a new metric called DBM for greedy ensemble pruning. This metric is related not only to the diversity of base classifiers, but also to the prediction details of current ensemble. Our experiments show that, compared with greedy ensemble pruning algorithms based on other advanced metrics, DBM based algorithm induces ensembles with much better generalization ability.

Keywords: Ensemble Pruning, Greedy Search Policy, Diversity based Metric.

1 Introduction

Ensemble of multiple learning machines, i.e. a group of learners that work together as a committee, has been a very popular research topic during the last decade in machine learning and data mining. The main discovery is that an ensemble is potential to increase classification accuracy beyond the level reached by an individual classifier alone. The key to the success of ensembles is to create a collection of diverse and accurate base classifiers [1].

Many approaches can be used to create accurate and diverse ensemble members, for example, by manipulating the training set to create diverse data training for base classifiers (e.g. bagging [2] and boosting [3]), by manipulating the input features to map the training set into different feature spaces so that diverse training sets are constructed for base classifiers (e.g. random forest [4] and COPEN [5]) and by manipulating the parameters or the structure of corresponding learning algorithm to create accurate and diverse ensembles.

One problem existing in these methods is that they tend to train a very large number of classifiers which increase the response time for prediction. The minimization of run-time overhead is crucial in some applications, such as stream mining. Equally important is that they tend to construct an ensemble with both high and low accurate classifiers. Intuitively, the latter may affect the expected

---

* The work is supported by the National Science Foundation of China (No. 60901078).

H. Deng et al. (Eds.): AICI 2011, Part II, LNAI 7003, pp. 631–639, 2011.

performance of the ensemble. Ensemble pruning [6,7,8], also called ensemble selection or ensemble thinning, is a technique to tackle these problems by selecting an optimal or suboptimal subset as subensemble for prediction.

In principle, there are exponentially many combination candidates of ensemble members. While some of the candidates performs better than others on a given data information, finding the best candidate is computational infeasible because of the exponential size of the search space. Several efficient ensemble pruning methods [9,10,11,12,13,14,15] via a greedy search policy have been proposed: given a subensemble S which is initialized to be empty (or full), searching for the space of different combination candidates by iteratively adding into (or removing from) S the classifier $h \in H \backslash S$ (or $h \in S$) that optimizes a cost function. The major issue in this approach is to design an effective metric to guild the search process.

In this paper, we contribute a new metric called DBM (diversity based metric) to guild the search of greedy ensemble pruning methods. This metric is related not only to the diversity of base classifiers, but also to the prediction details of the current ensemble. The experimental results show that, compared with the greedy ensemble pruning algorithms based on other metrics, DBM based algorithm induces subensembles with significantly better performance.

The remainder of this paper is structured as follows: after reviewing the related work in section 2, section 3 introduces the proposed metric. Section 4 presents the experimental results, and finally, Section 5 concludes this work.

2   Related Work

Let h be a classifier and let S be an ensemble. Partalas et al. identified that the prediction of h and S on an instance $\mathbf{x}_j$ can be categorized into four cases: (1) $e_{tf}{:}h(\mathbf{x}_j){=}y_j{\wedge}S(\mathbf{x}_j){\neq}y_j$, (2) $e_{tt}{:}h(\mathbf{x}_j){=}y_j{\wedge}S(\mathbf{x}_j){=}y_j$, (3) $e_{ft}{:}h(\mathbf{x}_j){\neq}y_j{\wedge}S(\mathbf{x}_j){=}y_j$, and (4) $e_{ff}{:}h(\mathbf{x}_j){\neq}y_j \wedge S(\mathbf{x}_j){\neq}y_j$. They concluded that considering all four cases is crucial to design ensemble diversity metrics [12].

Many diversity metrics are designed by considering some or all four cases. Examples include the complementariness [10] and concurrency [11]. The complementariness of h with respect to S and a pruning set D is calculated by

$$COM(h, S) = \sum_{\mathbf{x}_i \in D} I(\mathbf{x}_i \in e_{tf}) \tag{1}$$

where $I(true) = 1, I(false) = 0$. The complementariness is exactly the number of examples that are correctly classified by the classifier h and incorrectly classified by the ensemble S. The concurrency is defined by

$$CON(h, S) = \sum_{\mathbf{x}_i \in D} (2I(\mathbf{x}_i \in e_{tf}) + I(\mathbf{x}_i \in e_{tt}) - 2I(\mathbf{x}_i \in e_{ff})) \tag{2}$$

which is similar to the complementariness, with the difference that it considers two more cases and weights them.

Both complementariness and concurrency consider only part of the four cases aforementioned. To take into account all four cases reasonably, Partalas et al. [12,14] introduces a metric called Uncertainty Weighted Accuracy (UWA) which is defined as

$$CON(h, S) = \sum_{\mathbf{x}_i \in D} (NT_i * I(\mathbf{x}_i \in e_{tf}) + NF_i * I(\mathbf{x}_i \in e_{tt})$$
$$- NF_i * I(\mathbf{x}_i \in e_{ft}) - NT_i * I(\mathbf{x}_i \in e_{ff})) \tag{3}$$

where NT_i is the proportion of classifiers in the current ensemble S that predict $\mathbf{x}_i$ correctly, and $NF_i = 1 - NT_i$ is the proportion of classifiers in S that predict $\mathbf{x}_i$ incorrectly.

Although UWA considers all four cases, it is not very reasonable for multi-class problem since it falls short in considering the specification of ensemble prediction on each class. This is illustrated by the following extreme example. Let the votes of S on examples $\mathbf{x}_i$ and $\mathbf{x}_j$ be $v_i = v_j = [34, 34, 34]$. Suppose the prediction of S on $\mathbf{x}_i$ and $\mathbf{x}_j$ are $S(\mathbf{x}_i) = S(\mathbf{x}_j) = 1$, and suppose the predictions of h on them are $h(\mathbf{x}_i) = y_i = 1$ and $h(\mathbf{x}_j) = y_j = 2$ respectively. Then, $UWA(h, S, \mathbf{x}_i) = NF_i = (34 + 34)/(34 + 34 + 34) = 0.6666$ and $UWA(h, s, \mathbf{x}_j) = NT_j = 34/(34+34+34) = 0.3333$. This results is contradictory to our intuition: $UWA(h, S, \mathbf{x}_i) = UWA(h, S, \mathbf{x}_j)$.

In this paper, we designed a new metric by considering both the four cases and the specification of the ensemble prediction on each class to explicitly evaluate the contribution of a classifier to an ensemble.

3   Proposed Metric

In this section, we design a new metric which considers both the four cases aforementioned and the specification of ensemble predictions. For simplicity of presentation, this section focuses on forward ensemble pruning: given an ensemble subset S which is initialized to be empty, we iteratively add into S the classifier $h \in H \setminus S$ that optimizes a cost function.

Based on the diversity of the prediction of h and S on examples, we category the pruning set D_{pr} into the following four groups

$$\begin{aligned}
e_{tf} &= \{\mathbf{x}_j | \mathbf{x}_j \in D_{pr} \wedge h(\mathbf{x}_j) = y_j \wedge S(\mathbf{x}_j) \neq y_j\} \\
e_{tt} &= \{\mathbf{x}_j | \mathbf{x}_j \in D_{pr} \wedge h(\mathbf{x}_j) = y_j \wedge S(\mathbf{x}_j) = y_j\} \\
e_{ft} &= \{\mathbf{x}_j | \mathbf{x}_j \in D_{pr} \wedge h(\mathbf{x}_j) \neq y_j \wedge S(\mathbf{x}_j) = y_j\} \\
e_{ff} &= \{\mathbf{x}_j | \mathbf{x}_j \in D_{pr} \wedge h(\mathbf{x}_j) \neq y_j \wedge S(\mathbf{x}_j) \neq y_j\}
\end{aligned} \tag{4}$$

Let each member h_t in ensemble S map an example $\mathbf{x}_i$ to a label y, $h_t(\mathbf{x}_i) = y \in [1, L]$. Let $V = \{v^{(\mathbf{x}_1)}, v^{(\mathbf{x}_2)}, ..., v^{(\mathbf{x}_N)} \mid v^{(\mathbf{x}_i)} = [v_1^{(\mathbf{x}_i)}, ..., v_L^{(\mathbf{x}_i)}], i \in [1, N]\}$ be a set of vectors where $v_j^{(\mathbf{x}_i)}$ is the number of votes on label j of example $\mathbf{x}_i$ of the ensemble S combined by majority voting. Denote $v_{max}^{(\mathbf{x}_i)}$ and $v_{sec}^{(\mathbf{x}_i)}$ as the number of majority votes and second largest votes of S on the example $\mathbf{x}_i$ respectively. Let $v_{h(\mathbf{x}_i)}^{(\mathbf{x}_i)}$ be the number of votes of S on label $h(\mathbf{x}_i)$. The DBM (Diversity based

Metric), the proposed metric, of a classifier h with respect to ensemble S and pruning set D_{pr} is defined as

$$DBM_{D_{pr}}(h, S) = \sum_{x_i \in D_{pr}} ConDBM(h, S, \mathbf{x}_i) \tag{5}$$

where

$$ConDBM(h, S, \mathbf{x}_i) = \frac{I(\mathbf{x}_i \in e_{tf})}{v_{max}^{(\mathbf{x}_i)} - v_{y_i}^{(\mathbf{x}_i)} + 1} + \frac{I(\mathbf{x}_i \in e_{tt})}{v_{y_i}^{(\mathbf{x}_i)} - v_{sec}^{(\mathbf{x}_i)} + 1} \\ - \frac{I(\mathbf{x}_i \in e_{ft})}{v_{y_i}^{(\mathbf{x}_i)} - v_{h(\mathbf{x}_i)}^{(\mathbf{x}_i)} + 1} - \frac{I(\mathbf{x}_i \in e_{ff})}{v_{max}^{(\mathbf{x}_i)} - v_{y_i}^{(\mathbf{x}_i)} + 1} \tag{6}$$

If $\mathbf{x}_i \in e_{tf}$ or $\mathbf{x}_i \in e_{tt}$, then $Con(h, S, \mathbf{x}_i) \geq 0$, since h correctly classifies $\mathbf{x}_i$. Otherwise, $Con(h, S, \mathbf{x}_i) \leq 0$, since h incorrectly classifies $\mathbf{x}_i$. The specific analysis is as follows.

- For $\mathbf{x}_i \in e_{tf}$, where $h(\mathbf{x}_i) = y_i$ and $S(\mathbf{x}_i) \neq y_i$, $(v_{max}^{(\mathbf{x}_i)} - v_{y_i}^{(\mathbf{x}_i)})$ is the estimation of the difficulty that ensemble S correctly classify the example $\mathbf{x}_i$. It is small when $v_{y_i}^{(\mathbf{x}_i)}$ is large and thus $\frac{1}{v_{max}^{(\mathbf{x}_i)} - v_{y_i}^{(\mathbf{x}_i)}}$, the reward estimation of the addition of a correct classifier, is large when $v_{y_i}^{(\mathbf{x}_i)}$ is large (refer to Eq. 6). The rationale is as follows. If the number of correct classifiers in the ensemble S is large, i.e., $v_{y_i}^{(\mathbf{x}_i)}$ is large, then the example $\mathbf{x}_i$ is near the boundary that S correctly and incorrectly classifies $\mathbf{x}_i$, and thus the addition of a correct classifier may change the decision of ensemble S from incorrect to correct. Therefore, the impact of the addition of the classifier h is significant. On the other hand, if the number of correct classifiers in the ensemble S is small, i.e., $v_{y_i}^{(\mathbf{x}_i)}$ is small, then it is difficult for S to correctly predict the example and thus the impact of the addiction of the classifier h is not significant. The extra number 1 is to avoid $v_{max}^{(\mathbf{x}_i)} - v_{y_i}^{(\mathbf{x}_i)} = 0$. For instance, Let $\mathbf{x}_j$ and $\mathbf{x}_k$ be two examples. Suppose the votes of the ensemble S on $\mathbf{x}_j$ and $\mathbf{x}_k$ are [12, 7, 11] and [17, 2, 11] respectively. Let $y_j = y_k = 3$. Although $v_{y_j}^{(\mathbf{x}_j)} = v_{y_k}^{(\mathbf{x}_k)} = 11$, it is easier to correct S's prediction on $\mathbf{x}_j$ than on $\mathbf{x}_k$, since the difference between $v_{max}^{(\mathbf{x}_j)}$ and $v_{y_j}^{(\mathbf{x}_j)}$ is smaller than the difference between $v_{max}^{(\mathbf{x}_k)}$ and $v_{y_k}^{(\mathbf{x}_k)}$. Therefore, $ConDBM(h, S, \mathbf{x}_j) = \frac{1}{12-11+1} = \frac{1}{2} > ConDBM(h, S, \mathbf{x}_j) = \frac{1}{17-11+1} = \frac{1}{7}$.

- For $\mathbf{x}_i \in e_{tt}$, where $h(\mathbf{x}_i) = S(\mathbf{x}_i) = y_i$, $(v_{y_i}^{(\mathbf{x}_i)} - v_{sec}^{(\mathbf{x}_i)})$ is the estimation of the easiness that the ensemble S correctly classifies example $\mathbf{x}_i$. It is large when $v_{y_i}^{(\mathbf{x}_i)}$ is large and thus $\frac{1}{v_{y_i}^{(\mathbf{x}_i)} - v_{sec}^{(\mathbf{x}_i)}}$, the reward estimation of the addition of a correct classifier, is small when $v_{y_i}^{(\mathbf{x}_i)}$ is large. The rationale is as follows. If the number of classifiers in S that correctly classify $\mathbf{x}_i$ is large, i.e., $v_{y_i}^{(\mathbf{x}_i)}$ is large, then S correctly predict $\mathbf{x}_i$ with high confidence and thus the addition of a correct classifier is not really very useful. The lower the number of correct classifiers, the more important is the addition of this candidate. Eq. 6 avoids the issue of UWA mentioned in section 2, that is illustrated by the following example. Suppose the votes of the ensemble S on examples $\mathbf{x}_i$ and $\mathbf{x}_j$ are both $[34, 34, 34]$. let $y_i = 1$ and let $y_j = 2$. Assume $S(\mathbf{x}_i) = S(\mathbf{x}_j) = 1$, $h(\mathbf{x}_i) = 1$ and $h(\mathbf{x}_j) = 2$. Then $ConDBM(h, S, \mathbf{x}_i) = ConDBM(h, S, \mathbf{x}_j) = 1/(34 - 34 + 1) = 1$ that follows our intuition.

- For $\mathbf{x}_i \in e_{ft}$, where $h(\mathbf{x}_i) \neq y_i$ and $S(\mathbf{x}_i) = y_i$, $(v_{y_i}^{(\mathbf{x}_i)} - v_{h(\mathbf{x}_i)}^{(\mathbf{x}_i)})$ is the estimation of the easiness of example $\mathbf{x}_i$ to be correctly predicted by the ensemble S. Since h incorrectly predicts $\mathbf{x}_i$, h contributes a penalty to S, and the penalty, $\frac{1}{v_{y_i}^{(\mathbf{x}_i)} - v_{h(\mathbf{x}_i)}^{(\mathbf{x}_i)}}$, is large when the difference between $p_{y_i}^{(\mathbf{x}_i)}$ and $p_{h(\mathbf{x}_i)}^{(\mathbf{x}_i)}$ is small. Intuitively, if the number of erring classifiers is large, then $\mathbf{x}_i$ is near the boundary that S correctly and incorrectly classifies $\mathbf{x}_i$, and thus the addition of incorrect classifier h may change the S's decision from correct to incorrect. Therefore, the impact of the addition of classifier h is large.

- For $\mathbf{x}_i \in e_{ff}$, where $h(\mathbf{x}_i) \neq y_i$ and $S(\mathbf{x}_i) \neq y_i$, $(v_{max}^{(\mathbf{x}_i)} - v_{y_i}^{(\mathbf{x}_i)})$ represents the difficulty that ensemble S correctly predict $\mathbf{x}_i$, and its decrease will lead to the increase of the penalty $\frac{1}{v_{max}^{(\mathbf{x}_i)} - v_{y_i}^{(\mathbf{x}_i)}}$. The rational is that if $(v_{max}^{(\mathbf{x}_i)} - v_{y_i}^{(\mathbf{x}_i)})$ is large, it is hard for S to correctly predict $\mathbf{x}_i$ and thus the addition of h will not affect a lot on S's prediction. The smaller the difference between $p_{max}^{(\mathbf{x}_i)}$ and $p_{y_i}^{(\mathbf{x}_i)}$, the larger penalty is the addition of this candidate.

In addition, it is easy to prove $-1 \leq ConDBM(h, S, \mathbf{x}_i) \leq 1$. In this way, ConDBM, and thus DBM (the proposed metric), considers both the diversity of base classifiers and the specification of ensemble predictions.

4   Experiments

4.1   Data Sets and Experimental Setup

19 data sets, of which the characteristics are not shown due to space limit, are randomly selected from the UCI repository [16]. Each data set is randomly divided into three subsets with equal sizes, where one is used for training model, one for pruning model, and the other one for testing model. There are six permutations of the three subsets and thus experiments on each set consist of six sub-experiments. We repeat 10 independent trials on each data set. Therefore a total of 60 trials of experiments are conducted on each data set.

We evaluate the performance of DBM using forward ensemble selection, where complementariness (COM) [10], concurrency (CON) [11] and uncertainty weighted accuracy (UWA) [14] are used as the compared metrics. In each trial, a bagging is trained. The base classifier is J48, which is a Java implementation of C4.5 [17] from Weka [18]. In all experiments, the ensemble size is 200. For simplicity, we denote DBM, COM, CON and UWA as the corresponding pruning algorithms supervised by these metrics respectively.

4.2   Experimental Results

The experimental results of the 19 tested data sets are reported both in figures and a table. The figures show the curves of average accuracy with regard to the

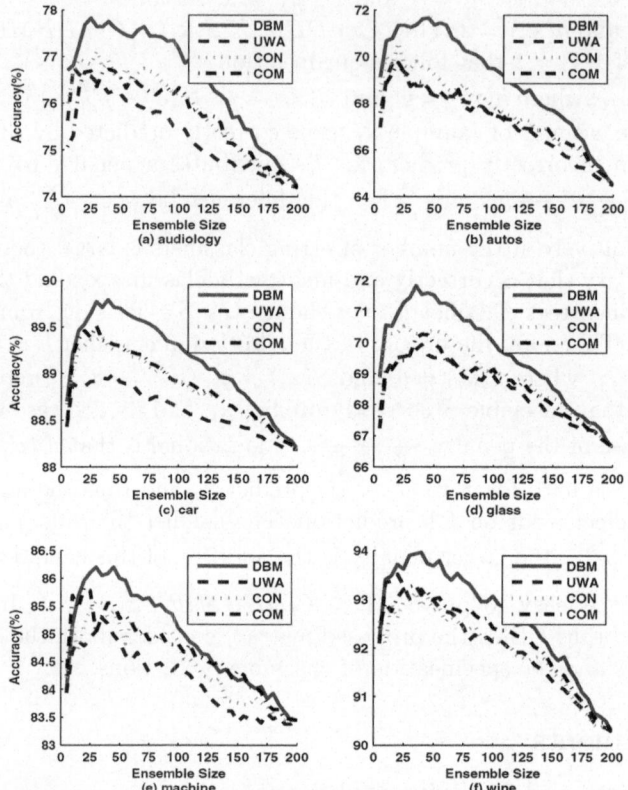

Fig. 1. Comparative results for six data sets in the first case

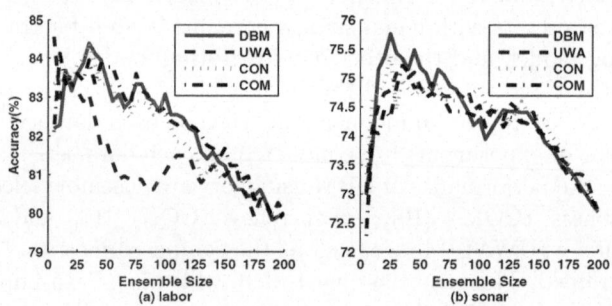

Fig. 2. Comparative results for two data sets in the second case

size of subensembles, where the results of these dada sets are grouped into three categories: (1) DBM outperforms UWA, CON and COM; (2) DBM performs comparable to one of them at least, and outperforms others; and (3) DBM is outperformed by at least one of them. 13 data sets fall into the first category, 3

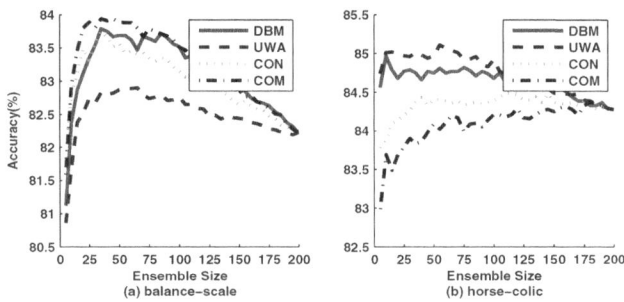

Fig. 3. Comparative results for two data sets in the third case

data sets fall into the second category, and 3 data sets fall into the third category. The table is the comparison summary between DBM and other metrics on all data sets. The more details about this table will be introduced when describing the table.

Fig. 1 reports the accuracy curves of the four compared metrics for six representative data sets that fall into the first category. The corresponding standard deviations are not shown in the figures for clarity reason. The accuracy curves for data set "audiology" are reported in Fig. 1(a). As shown in Fig. 1(a), with the increase of the number of aggregated classifiers, the accuracy curve of subensembles selected by DBM, UWA, CON and COM increases rapidly, reaches the maximum accuracy in the intermediate steps of aggregation which is higher than the accuracy of the whole original ensemble, and then drops until the accuracy is the same as the whole ensemble. Fig. 1 also shows that the accuracy curve of DBM is always above the accuracy curve of UWA, CON and COM. The remainder five data sets "autos", "car", "glass", "machine" and "wine" have similar results to "audiology".

Fig. 2 reports the accuracy results for two representative data sets from the second group, where DBM performs similar to at least one of UWA, CON and COM, and outperforms others. The accuracy curves for "labor" and "sonar" are reported in Fig. 2(a) and Fig. 2(b) respectively. Fig. 2(a) shows that DBM outperforms UWA, and performs comparable to the others. Fig. 2(b) shows that the four compared methods performs similar to each other.

Fig. 3 reports the accuracy curves for two data sets in the third group, where DBM is outperformed by at least one of UWA, CON and COM. Fig. 3(a) and Fig. 3(b) shows that, although DBM is outperformed by one of other metrics on "balance-scale" and "horse-colic" respectively, the goodness is not significant. In addition, DBM outperform the other metrics, especially on "horse-colic".

Table 1 summarizes the mean and standard deviation of 60 trials for each data set. For reference, we display the accuracy of bagging (the whole ensembles) as well. Experimental results in this paper empirically show that these pruning methods generally reach minimum errors when the size of the subensembles are between 20 and 50 (10%-25% of the original ensemble size). Therefore, the subensembles formed by DBM with 30 original ensemble members are compared

Table 1. The mean accuracy and standard deviation of DBM, UWA, CON, COM and Bagging.

Dataset	DBM	UMA	CON	COM	Bagging
anneal	98.22±0.85	98.20±0.81	98.06±0.97 •	97.95±0.97 •	97.23±1.23 •
audiology	77.64±4.30	76.45±4.78 •	77.11±4.16 •	76.36±4.84 •	74.19±5.49 •
autos	71.26±5.50	69.12±5.60 •	69.49±5.40 •	68.73±5.39 •	64.49±5.85 •
balance-scale	83.55±2.12	82.68±2.43 •	83.59±2.20	83.81±2.20	82.22±2.57 •
car	89.77±1.33	88.92±1.50 •	89.36±1.47 •	89.51±1.46 •	88.19±1.30 •
ecoli	82.90±3.55	82.20±3.51 •	82.62±3.44	82.34±3.51 •	81.49±3.78 •
flags	58.96±5.64	58.47±5.70	59.75±4.94	59.31±4.86	57.97±5.22
Glass	71.45±5.37	69.60±5.08 •	70.40±4.82 •	69.60±4.95 •	66.64±5.52 •
horse-colic	84.79±2.80	84.96±2.72	84.26±2.49	83.90±2.59 •	84.28±2.45
hypothyroid	99.45±0.30	99.43±0.30	99.43±0.30	99.41±0.28 •	99.33±0.28 •
irish	98.54±0.88	98.54±0.88	98.54±0.88	98.51±0.85	98.53±0.93
kr-vs-kp	99.14±0.34	99.10±0.35	99.02±0.36 •	98.83±0.51 •	98.56±0.69 •
labor	83.86±7.24	82.89±7.16	83.95±7.41	83.42±7.98	80.00±9.43 •
cpu	86.20±3.70	85.05±3.96 •	85.59±4.23	85.02±4.52 •	83.45±4.48 •
page-blocks	97.11±0.36	97.09±0.39	97.08±0.36	97.07±0.35 •	96.93±0.40 •
segment	95.94±0.86	95.83±0.82 •	95.82±0.93 •	95.87±0.91	95.29±0.90 •
sick	98.47±0.37	98.45±0.39	98.41±0.40 •	98.35±0.43 •	98.19±0.41 •
sonar	75.43±5.31	75.07±4.88	74.44±5.64	74.83±4.78	72.69±5.66 •
wine	93.90±4.23	93.01±4.73 •	93.00±4.75 •	93.26±3.65 •	90.28±4.44 •
win/tie/loss		9/9/0	11/8/0	13/6/0	16/3/0

• *represents that DBM outperforms the comparing method in pair-wise t-tests at 95% significance level, and* ○ *suggests that DBM is outperformed by comparing method.*

with subensembles formed by UWA, CON and COM with the same size using pair-wise t-tests at the 95% significance level. A bullet next to a result indicates that DBM is significantly better than the respective method (column) for the respective data set (row). An open circle next to a result indicates that DBM is significantly worse than the respective method.

As shown in table 1, DBM outperforms bagging on 16 out of 19 data sets, which indicates that DBM efficiently performs pruning by achieving better predictive accuracies with small subensembles. In addition, DBM is also shown to significantly outperform UWA, CON and COM in 9, 11 and 13 out of 19 data sets respectively. This fact indicates that DBM is a useful metric to supervise greedy ensemble pruning algorithms.

Combining the results all above, we conclude that DBM is a rather ideal metric to supervise greedy ensemble pruning algorithms to prune ensembles.

5   Conclusion

This paper contributes a new diversity based metric called DBM for greedy ensemble selection. This metric is related to the diversity of base classifiers as well as to the prediction details of the current ensemble.

Our experiments show that, compared with the greedy ensemble pruning methods based on other advanced diversity metrics, DBM based method has significantly better generalization capability in most of data sets.

The proposed metric in this paper can apply not only to forward ensemble pruning methods, but also to other diversity based greedy ensemble pruning methods. Therefore, more experiments will be conducted to evaluate the performance of the proposed metric.

References

1. Kuncheva, L.I.: Combining Pattern Classifiers: Methods and Algorithms. John Wiley and Sons, Chichester (2004)
2. Breiman, L.: Bagging predictors. Machine Learning, 123–140 (1996)
3. Freund, Y., Schapire, R.F.: A decision-theoretic generalization of on-line learning and an application to boosting. Journal of Computer and System Sciences 55, 119–139 (1997)
4. Breiman, L.: Random forests. Machine learning 45, 5–32 (2001)
5. Zhang, D., Chen, S., Zhou, Z., Yang, Q.: Constraint projections for ensemble learning. In: 23rd AAAI Conference on Artificial Intelligence (AAAI 2008), pp. 758–763 (2008)
6. Zhou, Z.H., Wu, J., Tang, W.: Ensembling neural networks: Many could be better than all. Artificial intelligence 137, 239–263 (2002)
7. Zhang, Y., Burer, S., Street, W.N.: Ensemble pruning via semi-definite programming. The Journal of Machine Learning Research, 1315–1338 (2006)
8. Chen, H., Tino, P., Yao, X.: Predictive ensemble pruning by expectation propagation. IEEE Transactions on Knowledge and Data Engineering, 999–1013 (2009)
9. Caruana, R., Niculescu-Mizil, A., Crew, G., Ksikes, A.: Ensemble Selection from Librariries of Models. In: 21st International Conference on Machine Learning (2004)
10. Martinez-Muverbnoz, G., Suarez, A.: Aggregation ordering in bagging. In: International Conference on Artificial Intelligence and Applications (IASTED), pp. 258–263. Acta press, Calgary (2004)
11. Banfield, R.E., Hall, L.O., Bowyer, K.W., Kegelmeyer, W.P.: Ensemble diversity measures and their application to thinning. Information Fusion, 49–62 (2005)
12. Partalas, I., Tsoumakas, G., Vlahavas, I.P.: Focused Ensemble Selection: A Diversity-Based Method for Greedy Ensemble Selection. In: 18th European Conference on Artificial Intelligence, Patras, Greece, July 21-25, pp. 117–121 (2008)
13. Martínez-Munoz, G., Hernández-Lobato, D., Suárez, A.: An analysis of ensemble pruning techniques based on ordered aggregation. IEEE Transactions on Pattern Analysis and Machine Intelligence 31, 245–259 (2009)
14. Partalas, I., Tsoumakas, G., Vlahavas, I.P.: An ensemble uncertainty aware measure for directed hill climbing ensemble pruning. Machine Learning, 257–282 (2010)
15. Lu, Z.Y., Wu, X.D., Zhu, X.Q., Bongard, J.: Ensemble Pruning via Individual Contribution Ordering. In: 16th ACM SIGKDD Conference on Knowledge Discovery and Data Mining (2010)
16. Asuncion, D.N.A.: UCI machine learning repository (2007)
17. Quinlan, J.R.: C4.5: programs for machine learning. Morgan Kaufmann, San Francisco (1993)
18. Witten, I.H., Frank, E.: Data Mining: Practical Machine Learning Tools and Techniques, 2nd edn. Morgan Kaufmann, San Francisco (2005)

Fuzzy Clustering Based on Generalized Entropy and Its Application to Image Segmentation

Kai Li and Yu Wang

School of Mathematics and Computer,
Hebei University, Baoding 071002, China
{likai_njtu,wangyu}@163.com

Abstract. Fuzzy clustering based on generalized entropy is studied. By introducing the generalized entropy into objective function of fuzzy clustering, a unified model is given for fuzzy clustering in this paper. Then fuzzy clustering algorithm based on the generalized entropy is presented. At the same time, by introducing the spatial information of image into the generalized entropy fuzzy clustering algorithm, an image segmentation algorithm is presented. Finally, experiments are conducted to show effectiveness of both clustering algorithm based on generalized entropy and image segmentation algorithm.

Keywords: Generalized entropy, unified model, fuzzy clustering, image segmentation.

1 Introduction

Clustering is an important tool for data analysis. It groups data objects into multiple classes or clusters, wherein data have much high similarity in same cluster whereas they have great difference in different cluster. One of the most commonly used methods is k-means clustering algorithm[1].Since Zadeh proposed the concept of fuzzy in 1965, people began to study fuzzy clustering algorithm. Ruspin first proposed Fuzzy C partition in 1969. In 1974, Dunn proposed a weighted index of m = 2 fuzzy C-means algorithm. And Bezdek extended to m> 1 of the fuzzy C-means algorithm in 1981. In reality, fuzzy clustering has been widely studied and applied in various fields, for example, image processing, pattern recognition, medical, etc. However, the fuzzy clustering algorithm (FCM) only deal with the points of the data set which have the same weight, number of data points in each cluster with no difference, and the loss of anti-noise properties, etc. In order to solve these problems, the researchers proposed many clustering algorithms. In 1979, Gustafson and Kessel proposed the clustering algorithm for clusters of different shapes by using the Mahalanobis distance. Dave extended the FCM by proposing the FCS algorithm which is used for the detection curve boundary in 1990; in 1991, Borowski and Bezdek introduced different norms to the FCM algorithm. In 1993, Yang put forward a kind of punished FCM (PFCM) based on fuzzy classification of maximum likelihood. In 1994, Karayiannis proposed the maximum entropy clustering algorithm

H. Deng et al. (Eds.): AICI 2011, Part II, LNAI 7003, pp. 640–647, 2011.

[2]; In 1995, aiming at the uncertainty problem, Li and others introduced the maximum entropy inference method and proposed the maximum entropy clustering algorithm by combining the loss function of the point to the center [3]; Krishnapuram and Keller proposed possibilistic C-means algorithm by relaxing the constraint that the sum of fuzzy C partition is equal to 1, to overcome the flaw of FCM under the noisy environment. In 2000, Tran and Wagner proposed the fuzzy entropy clustering algorithm using the objective function proposed by Li; In 2002, Wei and Fahn proposed a fuzzy bidirectional associative clustering network which solves the problem of fuzzy clustering [4]; In the same year, Wu and Yang proposed AFCM by using the index distance; in 2004, Wang and others developed a feature weighted FCM based on the feature selection methods; In 2005, Yu and Yang studied FCM and its expanded algorithm, and established a unified model of GFCM; In 2010 Graves and Pedrycz made a comparative experimental study of fuzzy C-means and kernel-based fuzzy C-means clustering algorithm, and obtained the conclusion that kernel-based clustering algorithm is sensitive to the kernel parameters. As for the image segmentation, spatial information is introduced into the clustering algorithm to improve the performance of image segmentation and the anti-noise performance of the algorithm. In 2002, Ahmed and others proposed BCFCM algorithm and successfully applied to the segmentation of MRI data by adjusting the objective function of FCM. Later, in order to reduce the spending time, Chen and Zhang proposed an improved BCFCM algorithm which is applied the kernel theory in BCFCM in 2004 and then they proposed the KFCM algorithm with spatial constraints. In the same year, Zhang and Chen proposed a new kernel-based fuzzy C-means algorithm which is applied to the medical image segmentation; in 2008, Yang and Tsai proposed the GKFCM algorithm which is successfully applied to image segmentation by further studying kernel-based clustering algorithm with a spatial bias correction [6]. In 2010, Kannan and others proposed fuzzy C-means based kernel function in segmenting medical images [7]. In this year, Swagatam and others researched Kernel-induced fuzzy clustering of image segmentation [8]. Fuzzy clustering based on entropy is mainly studied in this paper. We present a unified objective function based on generalized entropy in FCM. At the same time, fuzzy clustering algorithm based on generalized entropy is obtained, and they are applied to image segmentation.

This paper is organized as follows. In section 2, we describe the proposed unified model in detail. In the following section, fuzzy clustering algorithm and image segmentation algorithm based on generalized entropy are given. We evaluate our method on IRIS data set and some chosed images. At the same time, we compare it with the classical FCM in section 4. Some conclusions are given in the final section.

2   The Unified Model Based on Generalized Entropy

Fuzzy clustering algorithm is common method. It has widely been applied to many real problems. However, as it exist some problems, researchers present some clustering algorithm by revising objective function. In 1994, Karayiannis proposed the Maximum entropy clustering algorithm, which makes the clustering of data points from the maximum uncertainty gradually transformed into a deterministic process by the introduction of the entropy of the membership and the distance to the center point in the clustering process. The objective function is defined as

$$J(\mu,a) = \alpha \sum_{j=1}^{n} \sum_{i=1}^{c} \mu_{ij} \log \mu_{ij} + \frac{1-\alpha}{n} \sum_{j=1}^{n} \sum_{i=1}^{c} \mu_{ij} \parallel x_j - a_i \parallel^2. \tag{1}$$

Now, by reducing the objective function (1) and let $\beta = \dfrac{1-\alpha}{n\alpha}, 0 < \alpha < 1$, above equation is written as

$$J(\mu,a) = \sum_{j=1}^{n} \sum_{i=1}^{c} \mu_{ij} \log \mu_{ij} + \beta \sum_{j=1}^{n} \sum_{i=1}^{c} \mu_{ij} \parallel x_j - a_i \parallel^2. \tag{2}$$

In 1995, aiming at the uncertainty problem, Li and others introduced the maximum entropy inference method and proposed the maximum entropy clustering algorithm by combining the loss function of the point to the center. Its objective function is defined as

$$J(\mu,a) = \beta^{-1} \sum_{j=1}^{n} \sum_{i=1}^{c} \mu_{ij} \log \mu_{ij} + \sum_{j=1}^{n} \sum_{i=1}^{c} \mu_{ij} \parallel x_j - a_i \parallel^2. \tag{3}$$

Actually, the objective function (2) and (3) above is consistent.

In 2000, Tran and Wagner proposed the fuzzy entropy clustering algorithm by using the objective function proposed by Li. In 2002, Wei and Fahn proposed a fuzzy bidirectional associative clustering network to solve the problem of fuzzy clustering with the objective function as follows

$$J(\mu,a) = \beta \sum_{j=1}^{n} \sum_{i=1}^{c} \mu_{ij} \log \mu_{ij} + \sum_{j=1}^{n} \sum_{i=1}^{c} \mu_{ij}^{m} \parallel x_j - a_i \parallel^2. \tag{4}$$

Above objective functions are shown that they are basically similar each other in different clustering algorithms. In the following, we give a unified objective function

$$J_G(\mu_{ij},v) = \sum_{j=1}^{n} \sum_{i=1}^{c} \mu_{ij}^{m} \parallel x_j - v_i \parallel^2 + \delta \sum_{j=1}^{n} \sum_{i=1}^{c} (2^{1-\alpha} - 1)^{-1} (\mu_{ij}^{\alpha} - 1)$$
$$\alpha > 0, \alpha \neq 1 \tag{5}$$

It is seen that when $m = 1$ and $\alpha \to 1$, objective function above is become that proposed by Karayiannis, Li, Tran and Wagner. When $\alpha \to 1$, objective function above is become that proposed by Wei and Fahn.

We can see that main difference in the two cases above is the second term of the unified model, written it as $H(\mu,\alpha)$ and named it as the generalized entropy. It can be proved when $\alpha \to 1$, $H(\mu,\alpha)$ is Shannon entropy.

3 Fuzzy Clustering and Image Segmentation Based on Generalized Entropy

From the unified objective function (5) we know that m and α can take the different value. When $m \neq \alpha$, its analytic solution was very difficult to obtain. Here, we mainly consider the objective function with m$= \alpha$, namely

$$J_G(\mu_{ij}, v) = \sum_{j=1}^{n} \sum_{i=1}^{c} \mu_{ij}^{m} \parallel x_j - v_i \parallel^2 + \delta \sum_{j=1}^{n} \sum_{i=1}^{c} (2^{1-m} - 1)^{-1} (\mu_{ij}^{m} - 1) \qquad (6)$$

3.1 Fuzzy Clustering Based on the Generalized Entropy

The problem of fuzzy clustering based on the generalized entropy is as follows:

$$min \; J_G(\mu_{ij}, v)$$
$$s.t. \quad \sum_{i=1}^{c} \mu_{ij} = 1, \; j = 1, 2, \cdots, n \qquad (7)$$

Now we use the Lagrange method to obtain the fuzzy degree of membership and the cluster center. The Lagrange function for optimization problem (7) is

$$L(\mu_{ij}, v, \lambda_1, \cdots, \lambda_n) = \sum_{j=1}^{n} \sum_{i=1}^{c} \mu_{ij}^{m} \parallel x_j - v_i \parallel^2 + \delta \sum_{j=1}^{n} \sum_{i=1}^{c} (2^{1-m} - 1)^{-1} (\mu_{ij}^{m} - 1)$$
$$+ \lambda_1 (\sum_{i=1}^{c} \mu_{i1} - 1) + \cdots + \lambda_n (\sum_{i=1}^{c} \mu_{in} - 1)$$

Using $\dfrac{\partial L}{\partial \mu_{ik}} = 0$ and $\dfrac{\partial L}{\partial v_i} = 0$, we obtain

$$\mu_{ik} = \frac{1}{\displaystyle\sum_{j=1}^{c} \left(\frac{\parallel x_k - v_i \parallel^2 + \delta(2^{1-m} - 1)^{-1}}{\parallel x_k - v_j \parallel^2 + \delta(2^{1-m} - 1)^{-1}} \right)^{\frac{1}{m-1}}},$$
$$i = 1, 2, \cdots, c; k = 1, 2, \cdots, n \qquad (8)$$

$$v_i = \frac{\displaystyle\sum_{j=1}^{n} \mu_{ij}^{m} x_j}{\displaystyle\sum_{j=1}^{n} \mu_{ij}^{m}}, i = 1, 2, \cdots, c \qquad (9)$$

The generalized entropy fuzzy clustering algorithm (GEFCM) is as follows:

Step 1   Fix the number of Clusters c, assign proper m, δ, ε and the maximum iterations *maxIter*

Step 2   Initialize the cluster centers $v_i (i = 1, 2, \cdots, c)$.

Step 3   *while j<maxIter*

  Update degree of membership using (8) ;

   Update the cluster centers using (9) ;

  Calculate $Err = \| v^j - v^{j-1} \|$, break if $Err < \varepsilon$, or else let $j=j+1$;

  end

3.2   Image Segmentation Based on Generalized Entropy

By introducing the spatial information of image into the generalized entropy fuzzy clustering algorithm, we can use it for the segmentation of image, the specific objective functions is as follows:

$$J_{GS}(\mu_{ij}, v) = \sum_{j=1}^{n} \sum_{i=1}^{c} \mu_{ij}^{m} \| x_j - v_i \|^2 + \delta \sum_{j=1}^{n} \sum_{i=1}^{c} (2^{1-m} - 1)^{-1} (\mu_{ij}^{m} - 1)$$

$$+ \beta \sum_{j=1}^{n} \sum_{i=1}^{c} \mu_{ij}^{m} \| \overline{x}_j - v_i \|^2$$

$$s.t. \quad \sum_{i=1}^{c} \mu_{ij} = 1, j = 1, 2, \cdots, n$$

Where $\overline{x}_j$ is the mean of samples in $x_j's$ window. The Lagrange function is as follows:

$$L(\mu_{ij}, v, \lambda_1, \cdots, \lambda_n) = \sum_{j=1}^{n} \sum_{i=1}^{c} \mu_{ij}^{m} \| x_j - v_i \|^2 + \delta \sum_{j=1}^{n} \sum_{i=1}^{c} (2^{1-m} - 1)^{-1} (\mu_{ij}^{m} - 1)$$

$$+ \beta \sum_{j=1}^{n} \sum_{i=1}^{c} \mu_{ij}^{m} \| \overline{x}_j - v_i \|^2 + \lambda_1 (\sum_{i=1}^{c} \mu_{i1} - 1) + \cdots + \lambda_n (\sum_{i=1}^{c} \mu_{in} - 1)$$

Let $\dfrac{\partial L}{\partial \mu_{ik}} = 0$ and $\dfrac{\partial L}{\partial v_i} = 0$, then

$$\mu_{ik} = \cfrac{1}{\sum_{j=1}^{c} \left(\cfrac{\| x_k - v_i \|^2 + \delta(2^{1-m} - 1)^{-1} + \beta \| \overline{x}_k - v_i \|}{\| x_k - v_j \|^2 + \delta(2^{1-m} - 1)^{-1} + \beta \| \overline{x}_k - v_j \|} \right)^{\frac{1}{m-1}}}, \tag{10}$$

$$i = 1, 2, \cdots, c; k = 1, 2, \cdots, n$$

$$v_i = \cfrac{\sum_{j=1}^{n} \mu_{ij}^{m} (x_j + \beta \overline{x}_j)}{(1 + \beta) \sum_{j=1}^{n} \mu_{ij}^{m}}, i = 1, 2, \cdots, c. \tag{11}$$

In this paper, the method for image segmentation using (10) and (11) is named as GEFCMS.

4   Experimental Study

In following experiments, we study two groups of experiments to test and verify the effectiveness of the generalized entropy clustering algorithm: (i) we mainly select the IRIS data set in UCI; (ii) we mainly selected the Coin, BinImage, Lena and MRI images and some images were added salt-and-pepper noise. The fixed algorithm [7] was used to select the initial center in both groups.

In unsupervised learning, IRIS data set is often used to evaluate the performance of learning algorithm, there are 150 points and four characteristics in the data set that can be divided into three categories. One of the categories and the other two are completely separated, the data points of remaining two categories have some overlap. The study showed that the best performance of the existing clustering algorithm is with approximately 15 error clustering points [9]. Table 1 shows results of experiment on Iris data based on generalized entropy fuzzy clustering algorithm (GEFCM). NofErr is expressed as the number of error data point in clustering algorithm. The experimental results show that presented algorithm GEFCM has better performance and the number of error clustering are smaller than 15. At the same time, in the experimental study, we obtained better clustering results by selecting randomly initial center, where the number of error clustering data is only 7. Unfortunately the experimental results are not steady.

Table 1. The performance of using different value m with GEFCM

m	δ	NofErr
4	5	14
6	5	13
11	5	12
13	5	11

In the experimental study of image segmentation, BinImage image is artificially generated binary image, Coin and MRI images are from Matlab itself and Lena image is chose from network. In the experiment, most images are added salt-and-pepper noises, the size of window is 3×3, and xj itself is not included when we calculate the sample mean $\bar{x}_j$ in the window. The results are shown from Fig. 2 to Fig. 5. In the experimental results below, (a) is the original image or it is added salt-and-pepper noises. Figures with (b) and (c) are the results of image segmentation with fuzzy clustering algorithm and GEFCMS algorithm, respectively.

The results of experiment show that we can obtain more satisfactory results for noisy images and noise-free images by using either GEFCMS, but noise cannot be removed by using FCM algorithm. Of course, the method in this paper involves some parameter setting, and different parameter may have different influence to the results.

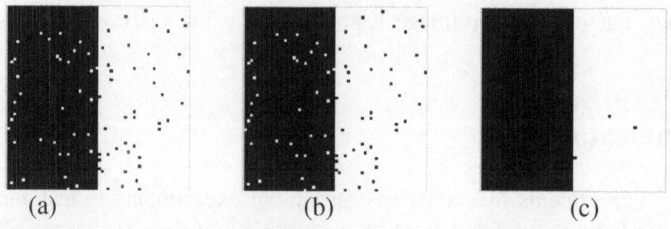

Fig. 2. Results of the segmentation of BinImage using different methods

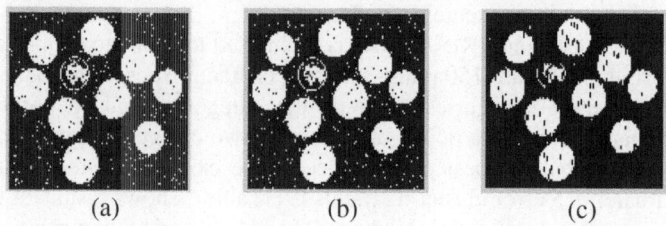

Fig. 3. Results of the segmentation of Coin image using different methods

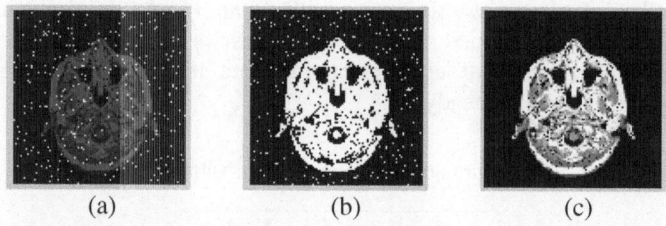

Fig. 4. Results of the segmentation of MRI image using different methods

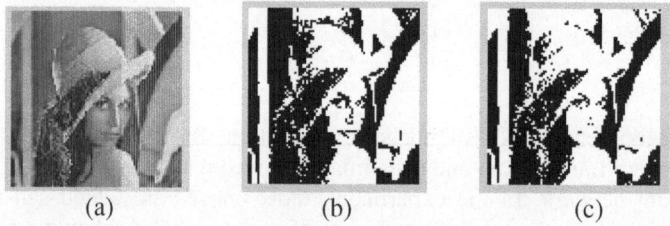

Fig. 5. Results of the segmentation of Lena image using different methods

5   Conclusions

In this paper, we mainly propose the unified objective function of fuzzy clustering algorithm based on generalized entropy and present the generalized entropy fuzzy clustering algorithm. At the same time, we obtain image segmentation algorithm GEFCMS based on generalized entropy by introducing the spatial information of image into GEFCM. We study with experiment the effectiveness of clustering algorithm and image segmentation algorithm based on generalized entropy, and obtain satisfactory results. In the future, we need to further study generalized clustering algorithm in order to get some better results by choosing suitable parameters.

Acknowledgments. This work is support by Natural Science Foundation of China (61073121) and Nature Science Foundation of Hebei Province (F2009000236).

References

1. Anil, K.J.: Data clustering: 50 years beyond K-means. Pattern Recognition Letters 31, 651–666 (2010)
2. Karayiannis, N.B.: MECA : maximum entropy clustering algorithm. In: Third IEEE Conference On Fuzzy Systems, pp. 630–635. IEEE Press, New York (1994)
3. Li, R.P., Mukaidon, M.: A maximum entropy approach to fuzzy clustering. In: Proceedings of Fourth IEEE International Conference on Fuzzy System, Yokohama, Japan, pp. 2227–2232 (1995)
4. Wei, C., Fahn, C.: The multisynapse neural network and its application to fuzzy clustering. Transactions on Neural Networks 13, 600–618 (2002)
5. Daniel, G., Witold, P.: Kernel-based fuzzy clustering and fuzzy clustering: A comparative experimental study. Fuzzy Sets and Systems 161, 522–543 (2010)
6. Yang, M.S., Tsai, H.S.: A gaussian kernel-based fuzzy c-means algorithm with a spatial bias correction. Pattern Recognition Letters 29, 1713–1725 (2008)
7. Kannan, S.R., Ramathilagam, S., Sathya, A., et al.: Effective fuzzyc-means based kernel function in segmenting medical images. Computers in Biology and Medicine 40, 572–579 (2010)
8. Swagatam, D., Sudeshna, S.: Kernel-induced fuzzy clustering of image pixels with an improved differential evolution algorithm. Information Sciences 180, 1237–1256 (2010)
9. Pal, N.R., Bezdek, J.C., Tsao, E.C.K.: Generalized clustering networks and kohonen's selforganizing scheme. IEEE Trans. on Neural Networks 4, 549–557 (1993)

Study on Multi-objective Dynamic Job Shop Scheduling

Lixin Qi[1] and Xiaoxia Liu[2]

[1] School of Automobile & Transportation, Shenyang Ligong University, Shenyang, China
syqlxyy@126.com
[2] School of Mechanical & Electrical Engineering, Henan University of Technology,
Zhengzhou, China
liuxiaoxia001@163.com

Abstract. A multi-objective scheduling method based on the controlled Petri net and GA is proposed to the dynamic job-shop scheduling problem (JSP) constrained by machines, workers. Firstly, the multi-objective flexible JSP optimization model was built. Then, a controller designed method for Petri net based on Parikh vector is introduced, and the Petri net model is constructed for urgent jobs. The genetic algorithm (GA) and the Pareto set is applied based on the controlled Petri net model. The set of Pareto optimum solutions can be obtained. Finally, a simulation experiment is employed to show that the proposed method could solve multi-objective FJSP problem effectively.

Keywords: Parikh vector, Petri net controller, multi-objective optimization, dynamic job shop scheduling, genetic algorithm.

1 Introduction

As one class of typical production scheduling problems, job shop scheduling with flexible processing considered as a particular hard combinatorial optimization problem in scheduling area. Due to its importance and wide applications in flexible manufacturing system, the flexible JSP was widely concerned by many researchers in industrial engineering and operational research. Methods exist for the JSP, for example, queuing system, mathematical programming, system simulation and control theory and so on; however, these methods have limited description. So it is necessary to look for efficient method. The intuitive graphical representation and the powerful algebraic formulation of Petri nets has lead to their use for modeling, analyzing and controlling in a number of practical fields[1-5]. Most of the literature on scheduling problems has considered single objective optimization. However, Many, or even most, real engineering problems actually do have multiple objectives, i.e., minimize cost, maximize performance, maximize reliability, etc. The ultimate goal of a multi-objective optimization algorithm is to identify solutions in the Pareto optimal set. However, identifying the entire Pareto optimal set, for many multi-objective problems, is practically impossible. Therefore, a practical approach to multi-objective optimization is to investigate a set of solutions that represent the Pareto optimal set as well as possible. Hence, the need arises in JSP for powerful graphical and analytical tools such as Petri net (PN) [1-3] and search techniques such as genetic algorithm (GA).

H. Deng et al. (Eds.): AICI 2011, Part II, LNAI 7003, pp. 648–655, 2011.

In this paper, firstly, designing the controllers with a method for Petri net based on Parikh vector and the flexible manufacturing system modeled with Petri net. Then based on the Petri net model, a genetic algorithm based on Pareto was applied to flexible JSP with multi-objective modeled. Finally, a scheduling example is employed to show that the method proposed in this paper is effective and feasible.

2 Description of Dual-Resource JSP

2.1 Problem Description

The problem may be described as follows:

n jobs are to be scheduled on m machines with p workers. Each job involves a set of feasible processing routings, which are performed on the machines in a pre-specified order. Each processing involves one or more working operations. Each operation is specified by the required machines and the fixed processing time. The objective is to plot a processing routing for each job, and to find a permutation of jobs that minimizes the maximum completion time, the maximum load of machines and the total expense of machines and workers. Suppose the following conditions are applied based on benchmark supposition in order to satisfy a scheduling objective during modeling: (a) a job does not visit the same machines twice; (b) all the jobs are available at time 0; (c) an operation cannot be interrupted; (d) one job is immediately delivered to the next machine after processing on one machine, and transporting time is neglected; (e) assistant processing time for different operations is added to processing time.

2.2 Objective Function

$$f_1 = \min(\max C_i) \tag{1}$$

$$f_2 = \min G \tag{2}$$

$$f_3 = \min(\max \sum_{i=1}^{n} \sum_{j=1}^{n_i} t_{ijk} X_{ijk}) \tag{3}$$

$$G = \sum_{i=1}^{n} \sum_{j=1}^{n_i} \sum_{k=1}^{m} (c_k + w_{q_k}) t_{ijk} \tag{4}$$

Where f_1 、 f_2 、 f_3 is completing time, operating cost and load of machines respectively; i is job number; j is machining operations number of job i; k is machine number, O_{ij} is operation number j of job i; C_i is completion time of job i; t_{ijk} is processing time of operation O_{ij} on machine k, q_k is the worker processing operation O_{ij} on machine k; c_k is hourly rate of machine k; w_{q_k} is hourly wage rate of worker q_k , G is expense of all machines and workers.

3   Petri Net Model

3.1   Parikh Vector Constraints

In DES Petri net model, the logical conjunction of separate linear constraints involving Parikh vector only, which have the following form:

$$cv < b \qquad (5)$$

Where $C \in Z^{m_c \times n}$, $b \in Z^{+m_c}$, Z is the set of integers, Z^+ is the set of non-negative, n is the number of transitions in the plant, m is the number of places, m_c is the number of constraints.

According to [5], for the linear inequality constraint (5), each place can be described with a inequality. Consider the place p_1 in Fig. 1: when transition t_1 fires once, then decreasing one token in place p_1. When transition t_2 fires once, then increasing one token in place p_1. Since gaining is greater than the losing, so the inequality is obtained:

$3 + v_2 \geq v_1$

Formalizing:

$v_1 - v_2 \leq 3$

The places p_2, p_3, p_4, p_5 in the figure 1 can be represented respectively:

$v_3 - v_1 - v_2 \leq 0$

$v_2 - v_3 \leq 1$

$v_4 - v_5 \leq 0$

$v_5 - v_6 \leq 0$

If the constraints can be described with inequality (5), then the controller place can be obtained correspondence to each constraint. The incidence matrix and initial markings of controller place is:

$D_{pc} = -c$; $\mu_c = b$

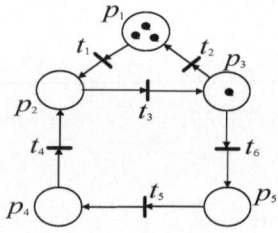

Fig. 1. Petri net model

3.2   Controller Design of Petri Nets with Uncontrollable Transitions

A transition is uncontrollable if the controllers are not given the ability to directly inhibit it. The freedom of an uncontrollable transition to fire is limited solely by the structure and state of the plant. Uncontrollable transitions in a plant may not receive any arcs from the places which make up the external Petri net controller.

In linear inequalities (5), if the transitions related to the Parikh vectors are uncontrollable, then the method taken is shown as follows:

Examining if the constraints are admissible. A set of constraints is admissible if $C_{uc} \leq 0$ is true, in spite of the inability to detect or control certain transitions. (C_{uc} is the coefficient matrix corresponds to the uncontrollable transitions in coefficient matrix C), then constructing controller; otherwise, carrying through constraints transformation.

Theorem 1: Let $R \in Z^{m_c \times m_{uc}}$ (m_{uc} is number of places related to uncontrollable transitions), $C' = RD + C$, $b' = b - R\mu_0$, where $R \geq 0$, $b' \geq 0$, if $C'v \leq b'$ is true, then $Cv \leq b$ is true.

Proof $C'v \leq b'$, namely $(RD + C)v \leq b - R\mu_0$, then $R(Dv + \mu_0) + Cv \leq b$, since $\mu = Dv + \mu_0 \geq 0$, therefore $Cv \leq b$.

Theorem 2: Let $R \in Z^{m_c \times m_{uc}}$, if

$$
\begin{cases}
R \geq 0 \\
b - R\mu_0 \geq 0 \\
RD_{uc} + C_{uc} \leq 0
\end{cases}
$$

Let $C' = RD + C$, $b' = b - R\mu_0$, then $C'v \leq b'$ 为 is a set of admissible constraints.

Proof: $C'_{uc} = RD_{uc} + C_{uc} \leq 0$, namely the quality of uncontrollable transitions is satisfied for the Parikh vector constraints (C', b') , so $C'v \leq b'$ is a set of admissible constraints.

The method of transforming inadmissible constraints into admissible constraints is given according to theorem 1 and theorem 2.

R in theorem 2 can be obtained according to matrix transformation:

$$
\text{Let } M = \begin{bmatrix} D_{uc} & \mu_0 & I \\ C_{uc} & -b & 0 \end{bmatrix}
$$

where $M \in Z^{(m_{uc} + m_c) \times (n_{uc} + m_c)}$, $D_{uc} \in Z^{m_{uc} \times n_{uc}}$, $C_{uc} \in Z^{m_c \times n_{uc}}$, $I \in Z^{m_{uc} \times m_{uc}}$, $0 \in Z^{m_c \times m_{uc}}$. $M(i, j)$ denotes the $(i, j)^{th}$ element of the matrix M , and let $j = 1$.

①. If $M(p, j) > 0$ in the $M(m_{uc} + 1 \cdots m_{uc} + m_c, j)$, then go to ②; otherwise $j = j+1$, carrying out① again.

②. If $M(q, j) < 0$ is not true in the $M(1 \cdots m_{uc}, j)$, then the admissible controller can not be designed, otherwise finding out $\min(|M(m_{uc} + 1 \cdots m_{uc} + m_c, j)|)$, and it satisfy $M(q, j) < 0$, then go to ③。

③. If $|M(q, j)| \geq M(p, j)$ is true, then go to (a); otherwise go to (b):

(a) $M(p, \bullet) = M(p, \bullet) + M(q, \bullet)$;

(b) $d = floor(M(p, j) / |M(q, j)|)$,

If $mod(M(p, j), M(q, j)) = 0$

Then $M(p, \bullet) = M(p, \bullet) + dM(q, \bullet)$;

Otherwise $M(p, \bullet) = M(p, \bullet) + (d + 1)M(q, \bullet)$.

④ . Carrying out ① again until $M(p, j) > 0$ is not true in $M(m_{uc} + 1 \cdots m_{uc} + m_c, j)$; and now matrix M is transformed into matrix

$$M' = \begin{bmatrix} D_{uc} & \mu_0 & I \\ C'_{uc} & R\mu_0 - b & R \end{bmatrix}, \text{so } C' = RD + C \text{ can be found.}$$

The new admissible controller can by designed according to the new constraints: $C'v \leq b'$. Since it only considers the places related to uncontrollable transitions and the transitions related to above places, so it reduces the matrix dimension. The superiority is more remarkable especially for systems with large scale.

4   GA Algorithm Based on Pareto

The essential difference between single objective and multi-objective optimization is that the optimal solution of multi-objective optimization problems is a set [6]. The ideology based on Pareto optimal solutions accords with actual situation relatively when the decision-maker has no clear preference of the objectives relative to each other beforehand. Therefore, this paper studies the flexible job shop scheduling problem (FJSP) with multi-objective by GA and Pareto optimal solutions ideology. The details are as follows:

- Permutation representation represents a solution of a problem as chromosome.
- Create initial population and fitness function.
- Crossover operation: Before the operation, divide population into K sub-populations (4 sub-populations in this paper simulation): select the optimum individual in each sub-population and crossover with other individuals. Adopt PPX, GOX, GPMX1, and GPMX2 (see Byung et al. [7]) in simulation, which can make the population have obvious diversity.
- Mutation: Mutation operation is used to maintain the variety of populations, and it is operated on some genes of a chromosome. Mutation operation can renovate and make up genes that are lost in the selection and crossover operation. In this paper, INV mutation is used to produce small perturbations on chromosomes.
- Pareto-ranking approach. Pareto-ranking approaches explicitly utilize the concept of Pareto dominance in evaluating fitness or assigning selection probability to solutions. Before selection, each individual in current population is ranked by means of their Pareto optimal relation. All objectives are assumed to be minimized. Therefore, a lower rank corresponds to a better solution in the following discussions. All Pareto optimal individuals in current population are ranked by 0, then delete them from the population, all Pareto optimal ones in remaining population are ranked 1, and so on, until all individuals are determined. This kind of Pareto-ranking approach can make the same class individual have the same selection probability.
- Selection. Select high-ranking chromosome between offspring chromosome produced by crossover in different sub-population and parent..

- Pareto Filter: In order to avoid losing the current optimum solution in the search process, save the current optimum solution through adding Pareto filter. In every generation, the individuals ranked 0 are all put into Pareto filter. The size of Pareto optimal set can be set randomly. When new individuals' amount exceeds the size, some similar individuals should be deleted.
- Criterion of algorithm termination: Given the iterations T, in the optimizing process, if the searching iterations are equal to T then stop searching, and the optimum value set in the Pareto Filter are the solutions.

5 Case Study

Consider the following FMS system. The resource demand and expense on workers and machines are listed in table 1- table 4.The algorithm parameters are that population size is 30, crossover rate is 0.85, mutation rate is 0.01.

Table 1. Working table of workers and machines

Machine	1	2	3	4	5	6
Labor	1	1/2	2	3	3/4	4

Table 2. Processing time of machines

Job	Operation	Time	Machine	Job	Operation	time	Machine
1	1	10	3	4	1	4	1/2
	2	8	1/2		2	6	4/5/6
	3	5	4/5/6		3	10	1/2
2	1	8	3	5	1	7	3
	2	6	4/5/6		2	10	4/5/6
	3	8	1/2		3	10	1/2
3	1	4	1/2	6	1	8	4/5/6
	2	9	3		2	6	3

Table 3. Machine cost rate (yuan per hour)

Machine	1	2	3	4	5	6
Cost Rate	13	10	11	8	12	9

Table 4. Worker cost rate (yuan per hour)

Labor	1	2	3	4
Cost Rate	20	15	15	18

Table 5. Tasks table of urgent jobs

Job	Operation	Time	Machine
7	1	6	1/2
	2	10	3
	3	5	4/5/6
8	1	9	3
	2	7	4/5/6
	3	10	1/2

5.1 Petri Net Model

Due to the characteristic of operation for emergent jobs operation, they can be seen uncontrollable. The Petri net model of an emergent job is show in Fig.2(real line part), where t_2 and t_3 are uncontrollable transitions.

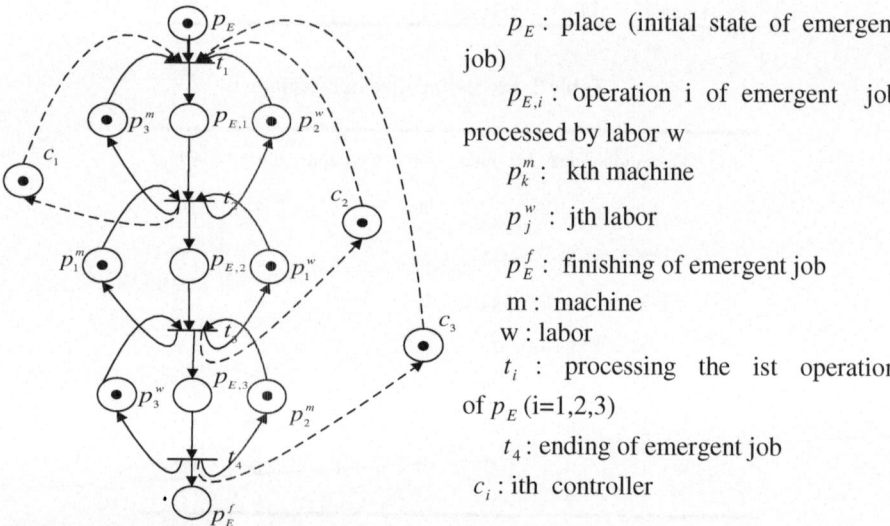

p_E : place (initial state of emergent job)

$p_{E,i}$: operation i of emergent job processed by labor w

p_k^m : kth machine

p_j^w : jth labor

p_E^f : finishing of emergent job

m : machine

w : labor

t_i : processing the ist operation of p_E (i=1,2,3)

t_4 : ending of emergent job

c_i : ith controller

Fig. 2. The controlled Petri net model of an emergent job

5.2 Simulation Results

In the Pareto optimal set obtained from this algorithm, there are several solutions, one of whose three objectives' values is optimum. If an urgent order comes at time t=20 (table5), then one of the new optimal scheduling results as shown in Fig.3(the makespan is 71; the maximum load of machine is 41; and the total expense is 3224).

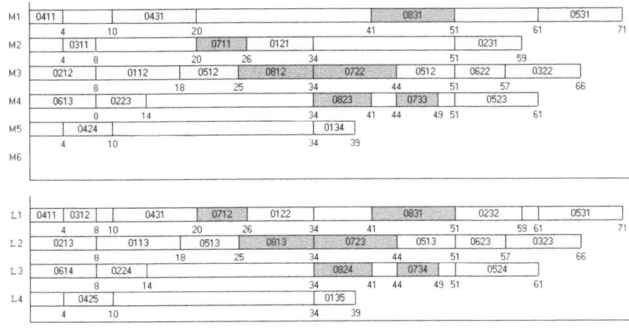

Fig. 3. The Gantt chart of urgent jobs

6 Conclusion

The FJSP with multiple objectives are closer to the reality and play an important role in directing practice. A new scheduling method based on the controlled Petri net with uncontrollable transitions and GA based on Pareto is proposed to the job-shop scheduling problem (JSP) with urgent jobs constrained by machines, workers. The simulation results illustrate that the proposed method could solve multi-objective job shop scheduling problem effectively, and it is capable of generating alternative schedule after an uncertain disturbance takes place on a job shop.

References

1. Hu, H., Li, Z.: Synthesis of liveness enforcing supervisor for automated manufacturing systems using insufficiently marked siphons. Journal of Intelligent Manufacturing 21, 555–567 (2010)
2. Frantisek, C.: Automated Solving of the DEDS Control Problems. In: Imam, I., Kodratoff, Y., El-Dessouki, A., Ali, M. (eds.) IEA/AIE 1999. LNCS (LNAI), vol. 1611, pp. 735–746. Springer, Heidelberg (1999)
3. Wang, S.G., Yan, G.F.: A Method for the Design of Petri Net Controller Enforcing General Linear Constraints. Journal of Software 16(3), 419–4261 (2005)
4. Tao, Z., Xiao, T.Y., Hao, C.Z.: Controller Study of DES Petri Net with Mixed Constraint. Computer Integrated Manufacturing System 13(8), 1603–1607 (2007)
5. Marian, V., Iordache, P.J.: Antsaklis. Synthesis of supervisors enforcing general linear vector constraints in Petri nets. In: Proceeding of the American Control Conference, Anchorage, pp. 154–159 (2002)
6. Cui, X.: Multiobjective Evolutionary Algorithms and their Applications. National Defense Industry Press, Beijing (2006) (in Chinese)
7. Byung, J., Hyung, R., Hyun, S.: A hybrid genetic algorithm for the job shop scheduling problems. Computers & Industrial Engineering 45, 597–613 (2003)

Automatic Discovery of Subgoals Based on Improved FCM Clustering

Kun Hu, Xue-Li Yu, and Zhi Li

Department of Computer Science and Technology
Taiyuan University of Technology
Taiyuan, Shanxi
hkl206@sina.com, yugroup@126.com, lizhi_tyut@hotmail.com

Abstract. This paper proposes a learning method which can discover the subgoals on the different state subspaces. It uses the improved fuzzy c-means clustering algorithm to classify the state spaces firstly, and then uses the unique direction value to find the set of subgoals, and finally creates the set of options. The experimental result shows that it can discover the subgoals automatically and quickly. This method can be adapted to the learning tasks under the dynamic audio-visual environment.

Keywords: Hierarchical Reinforcement Learning; Fuzzy C-Means Clustering, Subgoals, Option.

1 Introduction

Hierarchical Reinforcement Learning (HRL) [1] is a kind of learning method which includes Option, HAM, MAXQ and so on. This kind of method need decompose the primitive task into the smaller and simpler subtask sequence, and then uses the learning algorithms to find the optimal sub-policy on the constrained subspace. In this process the subtask is the important part for the earning task and the algorithm implementation. How to discover the subtask automatically during learning process is a problem worthy of studying. This paper discusses it based on Option.

Option uses the subgoals to found the subtask sequence. It can be applied to the task decomposition for the task having partition features. The subgoals can be the state regions of high frequency accessing [2], or the state set between the regions of high dense connection [3], or the state regions having funnel characteristics [4], or the path data by k-cluster [5], or the least edge set at the status transfer diagram [6], and so on. Those methods need the successful experiences to find the subgoals and filter the bottleneck states according to the prior knowledge. At the same time, those algorithms are sensitive relatively for the parameters, so they have certain limitation when they apply to some domains. Based on those methods, the paper proposes a convenient and robustness method of subgoals discovering under the dynamic audio-visual environment. This method uses the improved fuzzy c-means clustering algorithm to classify the state spaces firstly, and then uses the unique direction value to find the set of subgoals, and creates the set of options finally. The experimental

H. Deng et al. (Eds.): AICI 2011, Part II, LNAI 7003, pp. 656–663, 2011.

result shows that it can discover the subgoals automatically and quickly, and it can adapt to the learning tasks under the dynamic audio-visual environment.

2 Option Method and Analysis

Option is a kind of macro action which adds the action execution process into the primitive action. And every option corresponds to a subtask. Option is expressed by a triple-tuple <I, π, β> which I is a initial state of the option, π is a internal strategy and β is a judgment conditions for the terminated state. An option will be activated if and only if its current states s belongs to the set of initial conditions I. The strategy π, $\pi : S \times \bigcup_{y \in S} A_y \to [0,1]$, decides the selected actions when the option be executed, that is to say agent selects the action a to feedback the environment according to the strategy $\pi(s,a)$ and the environment state s will be translated to the state s'. If the state s' is the terminated state, which means agent arrives the subgoals and $\beta(s')=1$, then the current option will be finished and agent will select the other option to execute. Because the learning system can select any option to execute at any state, then every primitive action also can be regard as an option. In the set of option, there are two kinds of option, one can be executed in the single step time, and the other can be executed and finished after multistep time.

The value function, which is the concept in the classic Markov decision model, can be applied on the option spontaneously. And it will be updated after every option finished. Given the option o be executed at the state s and finished at the state s' after the τ step, if using the Q-Learning algorithm to learn the optimal policy, then the iterative formula of value function for Option method as following [2]:

$$Q_{k+1}(s,o) \leftarrow (1-\alpha)Q_k(s,o) + \alpha\left[r + \gamma^\tau \max_{o' \in O_{s'}} Q_k(s',o')\right] \tag{1}$$

In this formula r is the cumulative discount reward values, τ is the continuous running time of the option o, α is learning factor and o' is the next selected option at the state s'. Q(s, o) also converges to the optimal value function of state-action under the convergence condition of Q-Learning algorithm [5].

According to the above description we have known that every option has the action policy which can convert the initial state into the terminated state effectively. During the option creating, we can use the subgoals as the terminated states, use the neighboring state of subgoals as the initial state, and then execute the certain algorithm to make sure the internal strategy. After those processes we can get the optimal result for the whole state space through running the iterative formula. So the subgoals are the important hardcore to produce the appropriate option.

Under the dynamic audio-visual environment, agent identifies itself states through apperceiving environmental information including picture, voice and some unknown information, and it can complete learning task according to the correlative algorithm. The whole optimal policy can be acquired through decomposing the policy into the state subspace instead of the whole state space. So we can discover some subgoals on the different state subspaces, produce the appropriate option, and then acquire the optimal policy by running option algorithm.

At present, those HRL methods based on the clustering algorithms also need make sure the number of clustering firstly and then partition the unidentifiable objects strictly [5,7,8]. The initial clustering center affects the final result seriously. Fuzzy C-Means (FCM) is a kind of fuzzy clustering algorithm which is a kind of flexible fuzzy partition algorithm based on c-means algorithm and fuzzy data set. In FCM method, the sample data are ascribed to the different clustering according to itself uncertainty description. The membership degree of sample can be acquired through optimizing the objective function. Based on the sample's membership degree and nonlinear multiple objective function, FCM transforms the clustering problem into the nonlinear programming problem, that is to say that the optimal fuzzy partition results can be acquired through optimizing the objective function automatically.

But FCM cannot make sure the number of clustering automatically and it need give the several initial centers randomly before FCM algorithm execute. It can drop into the local optimal value easily and it is sensitive for the noise data at the most cases. The paper adopts FCM algorithm based on the grid and density weights [9] to assort the state space under the dynamic audio-visual environment, and then discover the subgoals on the state subspaces. This method can overcome the FCM's problems effectively, acquire the better clustering result and realizes the subgoals discover.

3   Subgoal Discovering Method

The basic idea of this method is that the sample data on the dynamic audio-visual environment will be partition into the several grid cells firstly, and then the system calculates and selects the condensation points, and uses condensation points to initialize the clustering centers, and then running the fuzzy clustering for sample data. When the sample data have been clustered we can adopt the unique direction value to find the set of subgoal on the state subspaces. Finally we give the whole algorithm.

3.1   State Space Clustering

Given the set of sample data is $X = (x_1, x_2, ...x_n)$ which n is the number of elements and c is the number of sample clustering. The u_{ij} expresses the membership degree between the i-th sample and the j-th clustering. The algorithm as following:

Function StateCluster(k, d)

1   Partitions the sample space into the k and forms the k^d grid units;
2   Maps the n elements into the k^d grid units and calculates density weight and the condensation points for every grid unit;
3   Selects the condensation point p which has the max density weight, and adds into the set of clustering centers;
4   Searches the condensation point p' which affiliates to the same cluster with the point p, and deletes p' and p from the set of condensation point; If the density weight of the grid unit for the point p is greater than the point p then finishes this searching process else continues to search from p';

5   If the set of condensation point is empty then the process of selecting condensation point finishes else return to the step 3

6   Uses the condensation points to initialize the set of center point z_0;

7   Initializes the number of fuzzy clustering c using the number of center point;

8   Sets the iterative counter t=0;

9    $w_i = \dfrac{z_i}{\displaystyle\sum_{j=1}^{n} z_j}, 1 \le i \le n$;

10   $u_{ij} = \dfrac{1}{\displaystyle\sum_{k=1}^{c} (\dfrac{d_{ij}}{d_{kj}})^{\frac{2}{m-1}}}, 1 \le i \le c, 1 \le j \le n$;

11   Updates the set of center point z_{t+1};

12   If $z_t \ne z_{t+1}$ then return to the step 9 else output u_{ij};

End StateCluster

The function's output is the set of membership degree u_{ij}. In this process, density weight is the number of samples in the grid unit, and the condensation point is the average value point for all samples in the grid unit. The adjacent units are those units which have adjacent boundary or points with the current point.

3.2 Discover Subgoals

Because the actions at the subgoals are restricted but the other are arbitrary in the grid environment, so it can be used to distinguish the subgoals with other states according to the limited characteristics of action in the grid unit. The unique direction value can express this character, the subgoals can be discovered through finding the grid units which have the max unique direction value. On the clustering state space, the successful path from start point to end point be decomposed on the different subspaces, and it reduces the state space for calculating the subgoals effectively.

The every state at the successful path has also the horizontal and vertical direction value. At the certain successful path, s_{ij} expresses the agent's current state at the i-th row and j-th column, if the access order of the state s_{ij} is the average value of the access order for the adjacent sides then the horizontal or vertical direction value equals 1 otherwise equals 0. It is well known that the unique direction value of the subgoals also equals 1 and the subgoals have only the horizontal or vertical direction value, because the subgoals is the only state which must be passed at the successful path. For the all successful path, the vertical direction value of state s_{ij} equals the absolute value of the difference value between horizontal vertical direction value and the vertical direction value. Because the subgoals have greater access frequency, then the vertical direction value of subgoal is greater than others, and it can distinguish the subgoals with other states easily. The discovering algorithm as following.

Function SubgoalsDiscover(u_{ij}, c)

1   Forms the set of path $L = (l_1, l_2, ..., l_m)$;

2   Partitions the state space according to u_{ij} ;

3    $HorDirVal(s) = \sum_{l \in L} IsHorDir(sl)$

4    $VerDirVal(s) = \sum_{l \in L} IsVerDir(sl)$

5    $UniDirVal(s) = |VerDirVal(s) - HorDirVal(s)|$;

6   Find and output the former c of the max unique direction value.

End SubgoalsDiscover.

3.3 Options Create

After agent discovered the set of subgoals, we can use every subgoal to create option correspondingly and form the set of option. During this creation process, we can use experience replay [10] to produce the internal strategy π, and use some states between the former subgoal and the latter subgoal to regard as the input set I, which meets the condition that the distance between the subgoal and those state is less than λ, and use the subgoal to regard as the terminated state. This algorithm as following:

Process CreateOptoin()

1   Save successful trajectories to TrajSet;

2   If number of trajectories > threshold T then

3   Set the number of dimensions d and partition k;

4   u_{ij} = **StateCluster(k, d)**;

5   SubgoalList $\leftarrow$ **SubgoalsDiscover(**u_{ij}**, c)**;

6   Clear redundancy from SubgoalList by examining adjacent states;

7   For each $g \in subgoalList$

8   Create an option o=< I , π , β > of reaching g;

9   Init I by examing trajectories in TrajSet;

10   Set $\beta(subgoal)=1$, $\beta(S-I)=1$, $\beta(*)=0$;

11   Init policy π using experience replay;

12   Endfor

13   EndIf

End CreateOptoin;

This creation process is a dynamic process. After collecting some successful paths, we can use the improved FCM algorithm to extract the subgoals and update option.

4   Experiment Result and Analysis

In order to verify the efficiency for the above algorithm, this section give a experiment that an agent tries to avoid some obstacles and audio-visual information, and navigates from start point S to end point G according to some policy in the dynamic environment, such as Figure 1.

Fig. 1. The dynamic audio-visual environment

This environment is a two-dimension grid space and the scale is 25☐25. The start point S located on the top-left corner and the end point G located the top-right corner. White area represents the reachable pathway, orange regional means obstacles and gray area represents the audio-visual information. Agent has four optional actions such as move forward, backward, left and right. Every action can acquire the reward, and agent moves toward a fixed direction by probability 0.9 and moves toward stochastic direction by probability 0.1. If agent meets obstacles or boundary then the reward is 0. If agent meets the audio-visual information then the reward is -0.2. The reward is 1 until agent meets end point. There are two aims for this experiment: one is to judge whether the algorithm can cluster the state space effectively or not, the other is to validate whether the subgoals can be discovered automatically or not.

Fig. 2. The result of state clustering

Experiment has been executed 20 times independently and the path at every time which agent attempted to arrive at end point has been recorded. The result shows at the figure 2 in which the grid units having the same letter expresses the same state cluster and the units having asterisk are the discovered subgoals.

From figure 2 we can find that the whole state space has been partitioned into the 5 subspaces, and every state space is about the 1/25 of the whole state space. The discovered subgoals are also the state which must be passed at the successful path. So this method can find the optimal policy on the subspaces, and the convergent speed of leaning algorithm has been improved too.

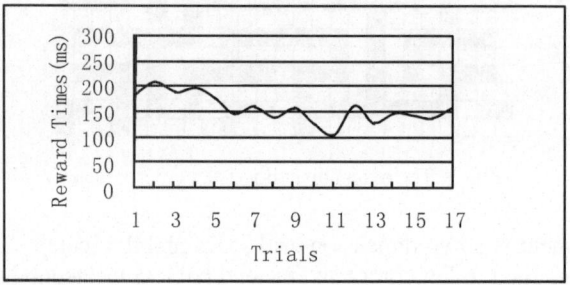

Fig. 3. The reward times of trials

The reward time's result of the experiment likes the Figure 3. The reward time denotes the consumable time which agent spend the time to go to the target. From the figure we can find that the average reward time is about 154ms and the reward time is steady and faster comparatively. This shows that the hierarchical structure of subtasks has achieved automatically, and the system can receive the optimal sequence of output states. And the convergence speed of the algorithm is quickly, because of the state space clustering can further partition for subtasks in larger state space. This way can reduce the dimensionality of subtask and expedite the convergence speed.

5 Conclusions

The paper presents an improved HRL method based on Option. This method uses the improved fuzzy c-means clustering algorithm to classify the state spaces firstly, and then uses the unique direction value to find the set of subgoals. Experiment result shows that this method acquires the better clustering results and it can make agent discover the subgoals automatically and quickly. It can be adapted to the learning tasks under the dynamic audio-visual environment. The following work is that analyses algorithm complexity and gives the proof in theory and optimizes it.

Acknowledgment. This paper was supported by the National Natural Science Foundation of China under Grant No.60873139, which title is the Research on Synergic Learning Algorithm of Audio-vision Cross-modal Coherence. And it was supported by Open Fund of the State Key Laboratory of Virtual Reality Technology and Systems (Grant No. SKVR-KF-09-04). It is also partially supported by the

Provincial Natural Science Foundation of China under Grant No.2008011040. Acknowledges all persons supported this work, especially thanks to professor YU for taking time to review the details of the paper and giving her insightful comments.

References

[1] Shi, C., Shi, Z., Wang, M.: Online Hierarchical Reinforcement Learning Based on Path-matching. Journal of Computer Research and Development 45(9), 1470–1476 (2008)

[2] Martin, S., Doina, P.: Learning Options in Reinforcement Learning. In: Proceedings of the 5th International Symposium on Abstraction. Reformulation and Approximation, Kananaskis, Alberta, Canada, pp. 212–223 (2002)

[3] McGovern, A., Barto, A.G.: Automatic Discovery of Subgoals in Reinforcement Learning using Diverse Density. In: Proceedings of the 18th International Conference on Machine Learning (ICML 2001), pp. 361–368 (2001)

[4] Goel, S., Huber, M.: Subgoal Discovery for Hierarchical Reinforcement Learning Using Learned Policies. In: Proceedings of the 16th International FLAIRS Conference (FLAIRS 2003), pp. 346–350 (2003)

[5] Wang, B., Gao, Y., Chen, Z., Xie, J., Chen, S.: K-Cluster Subgoal Discovery Algorithm for Option. Journal of Computer Research and Development 855, 851–855 (2006)

[6] Menache, I., Mannor, S., Shimkin, N.: Q-cut - dynamic discovery of sub-goals in reinforcement learning. In: Elomaa, T., Mannila, H., Toivonen, H. (eds.) ECML 2002. LNCS (LNAI), vol. 2430, p. 295. Springer, Heidelberg (2002)

[7] Mannor, S., Menache, I., Hoze, A., Klein, U.: Dynamic Abstraction in Reinforcement Learning via Clustering. In: Proceedings of the 21st International Conference on Machine Learning, pp. 560–567. ACM Press, New York (2004)

[8] Simsek, O., Wolfe, A.P., Barto, A.G.: Identifying Useful Subgoals in Reinforcement Learning by Local Graph Partitioning. In: Proceedings of the 22th International Conference on Machine Learning, pp. 816–823. ACM Press, New York (2005)

[9] Li, S., Kaiqi, Z., Guannan, D.: An Initialization Method for Fuzzy C-Means Clustering Algorithm Based on Grid and Density Weight. Computer Applications and Software 25(3), 22–23 (2008)

[10] Lin, L.-j.: Self-improving agents based on reinforcement learning, planning and teaching. Machine Learning 321, 293–321 (1992)

Manifold Ranking-Based Locality Preserving Projections

Jia Wei, Zewei Chen, Pingyang Niu, Yishun Chen, and Wenhui Chen

School of Computer Science and Engineering, South China University of Technology,
Guangzhou 510006, Guangdong, China
csjwei@scut.edu.cn

Abstract. As a widely used linear dimensionality reduction technique, Locality Preserving Projections (LPP) preserves the neighborhood structure of the dataset by finding the optimal linear approximations to the eigenfunctions of the Laplace-Beltrami operator on the manifold, which makes it have several advantages of both linear and nonlinear methods. However, its neighborhood graph is generated by adopting the Euclidean distance as the similarity metric of different samples which leads to the unsatisfying effectiveness of LPP. To address the limitation of Euclidean distance we propose an improved LPP called Manifold Ranking-based LPP (MRLPP) which can effectively preserve the neighborhood structure of the dataset, either globular or non-globular. Experimental results on several datasets demonstrate the effectiveness of our method.

Keywords: locality preserving projections, manifold ranking, neighborhood graph.

1 Introduction

In recent years, researchers have paid more and more attention on the techniques of dimensionality reduction with the aim of transforming high dimensional data into a meaningful representation of reduced dimensionality [1]. This has led to the proposal of various dimensionality reduction methods which can be divided into two classes: linear methods and nonlinear methods.

Classical linear dimensionality reduction methods such as the Principal Component Analysis [2], Linear Discriminate Analysis [3] have better performance to deal with the linear datasets while nonlinear methods such as Laplacian Eigenmaps (LE) [4] and Locally Linear Embedding(LLE) [5] are more efficient at revealing the manifold structure of nonlinear datasets. Due to the limitation of the linear assumption, the linear methods fail to uncover the geometry structure of the datasets in real word which are often highly nonlinear. However, nonlinear methods have their disadvantages either. The nonlinear methods are often sensitive to the parameters and have higher computational complexity compared to linear methods. Besides, most of them cannot deal with out-of-sample situation. Locality Preserving Projections (LPP) [6] is a linear dimensionality reduction technique which is different from traditional linear methods. It builds the graph Laplacian matrix of the neighborhood graph

H. Deng et al. (Eds.): AICI 2011, Part II, LNAI 7003, pp. 664–671, 2011.

incorporating neighborhood information of the datasets and then the optimal linear transformation matrix is computed which maps the data points to a low dimensional subspace. LPP can be seen as an alternative to PCA, which makes it fast and suitable for practical application. What's more, because it is a linear approximation of the nonlinear method LE so it can preserve effectively the intrinsic nonlinear manifold structure of the datasets in nonlinear space.

However, the neighborhood graph in LPP is generated by adopting the Euclidean distance as the similarity metric of samples which leads to the unsatisfying effectiveness of LPP. That's because Euclidean distance cannot describe well the intrinsic construct of the data samples with non-globular distributions or manifold structure in real word. To address this problem, we propose an improved algorithm of LPP called Manifold Ranking-based LPP (MRLPP). MRLPP utilizes the manifold ranking [7] to construct the neighborhood graph, which can effectively preserve the neighborhood structure of data samples , either globular or non-globular. Therefore, MRLPP has higher performance than original LPP and is more robust to noise and outliers as well. We will show these advantages in section 4.

The paper is organized as follows. Section 2 presents a brief description of original LPP. The theory about manifold ranking is given in section 3. In addition, we also provide a detail about MRLPP. The experimental results on different datasets are shown in section 4. Finally, we give the conclusions and future work in section 5.

2 Locality Preserving Projections

In this section, we give a brief description of LPP. Firstly, we will give a generic form of linear dimensionality reduction. Let $X = \{x_1, x_2, \ldots, x_n\}$, $x_i \in R^D$ and x_i is the i-th sample in dataset X. The goal of LPP is to find a transformation matrix A ($A \in R^{D \times d}$) which can map these n points to a set of points $Y = \{y_1, y_2, \ldots, y_n\}$, $y_i \in R^d$, $d \ll D$, such that y_i is the d dimensional representation of x_i, where $y_i = A^T x_i$. The procedure of LPP is formally stated below:

(1) Construct a neighborhood graph G whose k-nearest neighborhood matrix S is as follow:

$$S_{ij} = \begin{cases} 1 & if\ i(j)\ is\ among\ the\ k-NN\ of\ j(i) \\ 0 & otherwise \end{cases} \tag{1}$$

Where node i and j correspond to sample x_i and x_j, respectively.

(2) Endow the weights to the edges of graph G. Apply Gaussian heat kernel weight w_{ij} to encode the similarity between i and j of G. Gaussian heat kernel is as follow:

$$w_{ij} = \begin{cases} \exp(-d_{ij}\big/\sigma^2) & if\ S_{ij} = 1 \\ 0 & otherwise \end{cases} \tag{2}$$

Where d_{ij} is the Euclidean distance between i and j.

(3) Compute the eigenvectors and eigenvalues for the generalized eigenvector problems:

$$XLX^T a = \lambda XDX^T a \qquad (3)$$

Where D is a diagonal matrix, $D_{ii} = \sum_j W_{ji}$, and L is a graph Laplacian matrix, $L = D - W$.

Let the column vectors $a_0, a_1 \cdots, a_{d-1}$ be the solutions of equation (3), ordered according to their eigenvalues in ascending. Thus, the d-dimensional embedding y_i of x_i is $y_i = A^T x_i$, $A = (a_0, a_1, \cdots, a_{d-1})$. A is a $D \times d$ matrix. Further details of LPP can be found in [6].

From the procedure of LPP described above, we notice that the construction of neighborhood graph is crucial to LPP. In other words, different neighborhood graph may lead to different transformation matrix A. The main reason is that the graph is constructed based on Euclidean distance, which may fail to reveal the real relationship of the data samples. As shown in Fig.1, the 4-nearest neighbors of point 'a' ranked by Euclidean distance is {b, c, f, g} circled by dotted line, which is not suitable obviously. To solve this problem, we propose MRLPP in which the neighborhood graph is constructed based on manifold ranking. We can see that in Fig.1 the 4-nearest neighbors of point 'a' based on manifold ranking are {b, c, d, e} circled by chain line. By comparison, we find that manifold ranking is more proper to uncover the intrinsic structure of the nonlinear data space than Euclidean distance. We will give the details of manifold ranking in section 3.

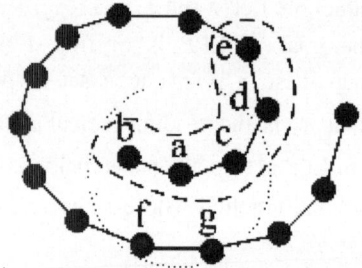

Fig. 1. The different neighborhoods based on Euclidean distance and manifold ranking

3 Manifold Ranking-Based LPP (MRLPP)

3.1 Manifold Ranking

The core idea of manifold ranking is to rank the data with respect to the intrinsic manifold structure collectively revealed by a great amount of sampled input data. Given a set of points $X = \{x_1, \ldots, x_q, x_{q+1}, \ldots, x_n\} \subset R^D$, the first q points are the queries and the rest are the points that we want to rank according to their similarity to the queries. Let $d(x_i, x_j)$ denote a similarity metric of each pair of points x_i and x_j, such as Euclidean distance. Let $f : X \rightarrow R$ denote a ranking function which assigns each point x_i a ranking value f_i which can be viewed as a vector $f = [f_1, \ldots, f_n]^T$. We also define a vector $y = [y_1, \ldots, y_n]^T$, in which $y_i = 1$ if x_i is a query, and $y_i = 0$ otherwise. The procedure of manifold ranking is as follows:

(1) Sort the pairwise distances among points in ascending order. Repeat connecting the two points with an edge according the order until a connected graph is obtained.

(2) Form the affinity matrix defined by $W_{ij} = \exp[-d^2(x_i, x_j)/2\sigma^2]$ if there is an edge linking x_i and x_j. Because there are no loops in the graph, we set $W_{ii} = 0$.

(3) Symmetrically normalize W by $S = D^{-1/2}WD^{-1/2}$ in which D is the diagonal matrix, $D_{ii} = \sum_{j=1}^{n} W_{ij}$.

4) Rank each point x_i according its ranking score f^*_i:

$$f^* = (1-\alpha)(I - \alpha S)^{-1} y \tag{4}$$

Where α is a parameter in $[0,1)$ and I is the unit matrix. The point with largest score is ranked first. For more details please refer to [7].

We use the algorithm above to select the k-nearest neighbors of all points. For each point $x_i \in X$, we set $y_i = 1$ and set other elements of vector y to 0. The ranking scores of each point x_i is attained by using equation 4 and then select the points which have the k-largest ranking scores as the k-nearest neighbors of x_i.

3.2 MRLPP

We propose an improved LPP, MRLPP which uses manifold ranking to construct the neighborhood graph G to the original LPP. Different from the original LPP, in the first step of its procedure, MRLPP constructs the neighborhood graph G by manifold ranking not by Euclidean distance. That means if i is among the k-largest ranking scores of j computed by the method of manifold ranking, then i is the k-NN of j in graph G. The rest steps of MRLPP are the same with the original LPP.

4 Experimental Results and Analyses

In this section we perform the experiments to evaluate the effectiveness of MRLPP on three different databases by comparing with the original LPP, PCA and the baseline method which don't make dimensionality reduction. Also, we take the error rates of classification with the nearest neighbor classifier on the testing samples as the comparison criterion. On each dataset, randomly select sixty percent from samples of each category as training set, others as testing set and repeatedly run all experiments for five times. For the sake of accuracy, we make a preprocessing on each dataset with the 95% principal components preserved before the dimensionality techniques applied. What's more, the first 30 dimensionality results of each dataset are shown in our experiments. Since the error rates of all methods on every dimensionality is obtained in the best cases respectively, the values of parameters like k are different according to the dimensionality of each method.

4.1 Yale Face Database

The Yale face database [8] includes 165 grayscale images of 15 individuals. Each image is different with respects of lighting condition, facial expression and with/without glasses. Fig.2 shows a group of images of one person. The original dimensionality of each image is 1024. The experimental result on this database is shown in Fig.3.

Fig. 2. Sample images of Yale

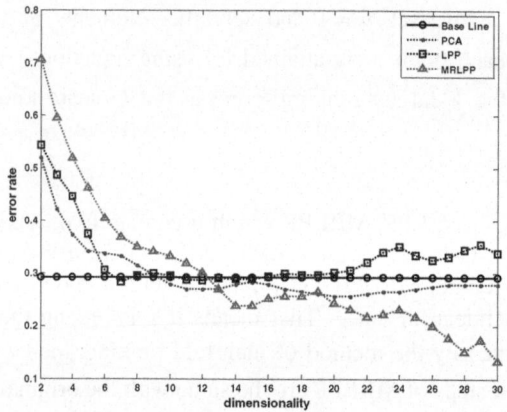

Fig. 3. Classification error rates of the methods on Yale

4.2 WANG Database

This database[1] is a subset of 1,000 images of the Corel Stock Photo database which includes 10 classes of 100 images for each class. Nature images (lakes, mountains) and synthetic images (buildings, cars) are contained. Each image is represented as

---

[1] http://wang.ist.psu.edu/docs/related.shtml

144-dimensional vector by the color and edge directivity descriptor [9]. Fig.4 is the experimental result on WANG database.

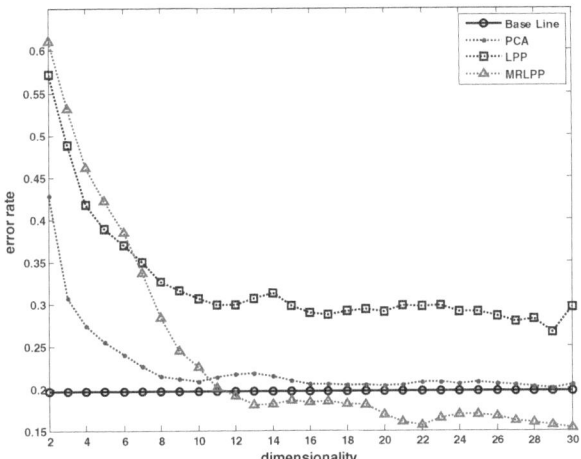

Fig. 4. Classification error rates of the methods on WANG

4.3 Multiple Features Database

This dataset [10] consists of features of handwritten digits ('0'-'9') which has 200 samples per class for a total of 2,000 samples. Digits are represented in terms of multi features such as Fourier coefficients, profile correlations, Karhunen-Love coefficients, etc. Each image is represented by a 649-dimensional vector. The result is shown in Fig.5.

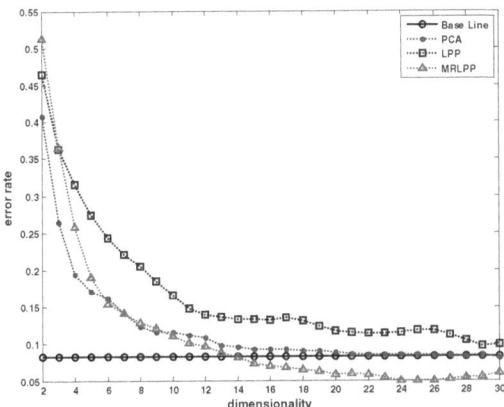

Fig. 5. Classification error rates of the methods on multiple features

4.4 Experimental Analyses

From Fig.3, Fig.4 and Fig.5, some conclusions can be drawn. Firstly, MRLPP can achieve much better performance than the original LPP and PCA on the three datasets, which confirms that MRLPP can describe the intrinsic geometric distribution of the samples much better than other two methods. Secondly, as the target dimensionality increases, the error rate of MRLPP decreases rapidly while others in a low speed. The error rate of MRLPP is as low as 0.05 in Fig.5 particularly. Thirdly, the error rate of the baseline method in Fig.3 is higher than that of in other two figures. We assume that is because Yale has more noises than other datasets, which also can be confirmed from Fig.2. Further, in Fig.3 PCA and MRLPP keep lower error rate than baseline method which confirms that both methods are robust to the noises and can promote the performance of classification to some extent. MRLPP has lower error rate than baseline method in Fig.4 and Fig.5 as well.

5 Conclusions and Future Work

In this paper, we propose an improved LPP, MRLPP which properly incorporates manifold ranking to the original LPP. Compared with the Euclidean distance, manifold ranking can effectively uncover the neighborhood structure of the data manifold. The experimental results on three different datasets have shown the effectiveness of MRLPP.

However, MRLPP is unsupervised so that it cannot make use of the labeled samples. Our future work is to join the information of labeled samples to MRLPP.

Acknowledgment. This project is supported by the Undergraduate Free Research Project of Fundamental Research Funds for the Central Universities, SCUT and the Fundamental Research Funds for the Central Universities, SCUT (No. 2009ZM0189, 2009ZM0175).

References

1. van der Maaten, L.J.P., Postma, E.O., van den Herik, H.J.: Dimension Reduction: A Comparative Review. Technical Report, TiCC-TR 2009-005. Tilburg University (2009)
2. Jolliffe, I.T.: Principal Component Analysis, 2nd edn. Springer, Heidelberg (2002)
3. Duda, R.O., Hart, P.E., Stork, D.G.: Pattern Classification, 2nd edn. Wiley & Sons, Chichester (2001)
4. Belkin, M., Niyogi, P.: Laplacian Eigenmaps for Dimensionality Reduction and Data Representation. Neural Computation 15(6), 1373–1396 (2003)
5. Roweis, S., Saul, L.: Nonlinear dimensionality reduction by locally linear embedding. Science 290(5500), 2323–2326 (2000)
6. He, X., Niyogi, P.: Locality Preserving Projections. In: Advances in Neural Information Processing Systems, vol. 16, pp. 153–160. MIT Press, Cambridge (2004)
7. Zhou, D., Weston, J., Gretton, A., et al.: Ranking on Data Manifolds. In: Advances in Neural Information Processing Systems, vol. 16, pp. 169–176. MIT Press, Cambridge (2004)

8. Georghiades, A.S., Belhumeur, P.N., Kriegman, D.J.: From Few to Many: Illumination Cone Models for Face Recognition under Variable Lighting and Pose. IEEE Transactions on Pattern Analysis and Machine Intelligence 23(6), 643–660 (2001)

9. Chatzichristofis, S.A., Boutalis, Y.S.: CEDD: Color and edge directivity descriptor: A compact descriptor for image indexing and retrieval. In: Gasteratos, A., Vincze, M., Tsotsos, J.K. (eds.) ICVS 2008. LNCS, vol. 5008, pp. 312–322. Springer, Heidelberg (2008)

10. Asuncion, A., Newman, D.J.: UCI Machine Learning Repository. School of Information and Computer Science. University of California, Irvine (2007),
http://mlearn.ics.uci.edu/MLRepository.html

Active Learning for Sparse Least Squares Support Vector Machines[*]

Junjie Zou, Zhengtao Yu, Huanyun Zong, and Xing Zhao

School of Information Engineering and Automation, Kunming University of Science
and Technology, Kunming 650051, China
Key Laboratory of Intelligent Information Processing, Kunming University of Science
and Technology, Kunming 650051, China
dilzjj@msn.com, ztyu@hotmail.com, zonghuanyun@sina.com,
zhaoxing2011@163.com

Abstract. For least squares support vector machine (LSSVM) the lack of sparse, while the standard sparse algorithm exist a problem that it need to mark all of training data. We propose an active learning algorithm based on LSSVM to solve sparse problem. This method first construct a minimum classification LSSVM, and then calculate the uncertainty of the sample, select the closest category to mark the sample surface, and finally joined the training set of labeled samples and the establishment of a new classifier, repeat the process until the model accuracy to meet Requirements. 6 provided in the UCI data sets on the experimental results show that the proposed method can effectively improve the sparsity of LSSVM, and can reduce the cost labeled samples.

Keywords: LSSVM, Square, Active Learning.

1 Introduction

In statistical learning theory, Support Vector Machine (SVM), which was first proposed by Vapnik based on structural risk minimization principle [1-4], has revealed extensive application vistas and significance of research because of its excellent generalization ability under the premise of the ample learning. But model of SVM requires solving the quadratic programming problems with nonlinear inequalities constraints, and the solution costs high. Focusing on this issue, a method of Least Squares Support Vector Machines was presented by Suykens [5], which solved by converting nonlinear inequalities constraints into equation, it reduced the complexity of computing greatly. However, this method possessed all samples involved in the training as the support vector; there may be many redundant samples, namely, the collection of LSSVM lack of sparse. First, the pruning strategy needs to

---

[*] This paper is supported by National Nature Science Foundation (60863011), Yunnan Nature Science Foundation (2008CC023), Yunnan young and middle-aged science and technology leaders Foundation (2007PY01-11).

H. Deng et al. (Eds.): AICI 2011, Part II, LNAI 7003, pp. 672–679, 2011.

be implemented after the completion of normal solving. Second, it modeled after the completion of all training samples labeled.

Active learning algorithm is a learning method which selects the optimal samples from sample space by evaluating function for building a learning model [6, 7]. It is an iteration process, each iteration uses evaluating function to evaluate the samples, and select the best samples to obtain a model that contains the most effective samples. Evaluation function is the key to active learning algorithm. Lewis [8] and Freund [9] put forward Query by Committee (QBC) which process is similar to bagging algorithm, so it requires high performance of "voters". Kenji [10] and Lindenbaum [11] proposed the neural network active learning algorithm and nearest neighbor active learning algorithm in view of generation ability of the model respectively.

In this paper, following the thought of active learning, we proposed a new method of Sparse Least Squares Support Vector Machine in view of uncertainty of information and the characteristics of LSSVM hyper-plane. This method selects the training samples which are most beneficial for building classification surface to be labeled and trained, so as to improve the sparseness of LSSVM by the use of active learning method.

Section 2 mainly deduced the least squares support vector machines, section 3 described the least squares support vector machines based on active learning in detail. The experimental results are given in Section 4, Section 5 summarizes the thesis.

2 Least Squares Support Vector Machines

SVM is the most important statistical learning model in the field of machine learning, its core idea is to find support vector to build the optimal classification surface. Building classifier by the use of support vector is essentially the process of sparse training samples; therefore SVM has a certain sparse ability.

Although SVM has good sparsely, solving formula (1) is still very time-consuming. Therefore to simplify the solution process, Suykens [5] had made the improvement of basic support vector machines from the distortion and the generalized perspective, and proposed the Least Squares Support Vector Machines (LSSVM)。 The basic method of this thought is as follows: Least Squares for fuzzy terms of target function $J_p(w)$ is introduced   in formula (1), namely, $J_p(W) = \frac{1}{2}W^TW + (C\sum_{K=1}^{N}\xi_K)^2$.

Due to dealt fuzzy terms with least square, the constraints in formula (1) has also changed. Let $\gamma = 2 \cdot c^2$, the constrained optimization model of least squares support vector machine [5] can be expressed as equation (2)

$$\begin{cases} \min_{w,b} J_p(w) = \frac{1}{2}w^Tw + \frac{r}{2}\sum_{K}^{N}e_k^2 \\ s.t. y_k \left[w^T\varphi(x_k) + b \right] = 1 - e_k \, k = 1,...,N \end{cases} \quad (2)$$

Where e_k is slack variable. γ is penalty factor. y_k denotes the classification results, for example, in the binary classification, $y_k \in \{+1,-1\}$. x_k is the vector of input samples. N is number of training samples. W is the weight vector, $\varphi(x_k)$ as a mapping function, mapped x_k to high dimensional space.

Then, use the Lagrange multiplier method to solve (2), and then let each partial differential equation of gradients to be zero, next, gradients are then converted into the equivalent matrix expression, so that the equation (3) can be obtained.

$$
\begin{pmatrix} 0 & y^T \\ y & \Omega + \dfrac{E}{\gamma} \end{pmatrix} \cdot \begin{pmatrix} b \\ \alpha \end{pmatrix} = \begin{pmatrix} 0 \\ 1_v \end{pmatrix}
\tag{3}
$$

Where E is identity matrix. y denotes $[y_1 \ y_2 \ ... \ y_n]^T$. 1_v is $n \times 1$ matrix with all entries equal to one. α denotes $[\alpha_1 \ \alpha_2 \ ... \ \alpha_n]^T$. γ is relaxation factor, usually set based on training samples. Ω is the kernel function matrix with class information.

To obtain Lagrange multipliers α and parameter b by solving the equation (3) and construct the final classification function.

From the above analysis, LSSVM converts the quadratic programming problems with inequalities constraints into solving matrix form of formula (3). There is apparent superior in performance and speed, but it has also brought new problems. That is no support vector for LSSVM, all the samples were to participate in the classification, so LSSVM have lost the sparsely of SVM while improving the solution efficiency. Several questions are involved here: First, all samples involved in the training, which reduce the efficiency of the model to a certain extent. Second, the training set mixed noise samples may cause some loss of LSSVM accuracy. Third, LSSVM requires labeling all the training samples, which is a very time-consuming job. Therefore sparse LSSVM has become a research [5, 12, 13] . However, his filtering method of all these methods is so complex, or needs to label all samples that can be sparse. By analysis, this paper proposed active learning for sparsity to solve the above problems.

3 Active Learning and LSSVM

3.1 Active Learning

classifier In the field of machine learning, learning process can be divided into active learning and passive learning according to the different ways of sample selection. Active learning queries the samples, evaluates the learning samples automatically by using evaluating function, and selects the samples beneficial to improve performance for training. While passive learning just passive accepting samples, not question about the validation of sample information. The main advantage of active learning is chiefly embodied in following three aspects: First, reduce the labeling work of training samples. Second, minimize the overall collection of training samples and decrease the model internal friction. Third, improve the model performance and reduce the noise samples to participate in learning.

Active learning algorithm [6] is usually expressed as a model for 5 unit group $M_{AL}=\{C, L, U, F, S\}$.Where C denotes decision maker (expressed as a for classification problem).L represents labeled training set. U said the unlabeled sample set. F is the evaluation function, to access whether the sample u_i in U sample set should be added to L for decision maker learning. S stand for marker, label the new sample u_i by supervision or semi-supervised way.

In the above active learning algorithm, the evaluation function F is constructed based on the uncertainty theory, its basic idea is to label the most uncertain class samples which the classifier C cannot determine the classification currently. Information entropy values can often be used to measure the uncertainty, the higher entropy values, the more classifier C cannot determine the samples' classification, therefore, so the more it should be singled out for study. In the view of geometry, the samples with maximal entropy are usually located near the surface, so it can be called samples selection algorithm based on nearest neighbor boundaries. For example, the Posterior probability $p(y_i|u_j)$ of u_j in the unlabeled samples collection U is computed as shown below according to the information entropy theory.

Submit the top-k samples with maximum entropy to label, and then add the labeled samples to collection L.

$$L = \{L \bigcup u_j \mid u_j = \arg Rank_j(H(p_j)), j = 1...k\} \tag{4}$$

Where $H(p_j)$ is information entropy. $Rank_j(x)$ denotes the jth sample arranged in ascending order. u_j is the jth sample vector in the unlabeled samples collection U. It is easy to prove that for any i, u_j is chosen when $p(y_i|u_j)=1/n$.

3.2   Active Learning for Sparse LSSVM Algorithm

At present, there are many studies on sparse LSSVM [14] and active learning algorithms of traditional SVM [15, 16]. But a few works have been done about active learning algorithm for sparse LSSVM, this paper will discuss this question. Section 3.1 has already pointed out that it needs to build evaluation function F on the basis of uncertainty theory. Starting from the principle of SVM, the most uncertain sample is refers to the nearest sample to class plane in the classification process.

According to the above derivation combined with the definition of the uncertainty, the evaluation function of samples can be obtained:

$$F'(u_j) = \arg \min_{u_j}\{\sum_{x_i \in L} |\alpha_i^* y_i K(x_i, u_j) + b^*|\} \tag{5}$$

Where sign t represents the number of iterations. uj is the jth sample in the unlabeled samples collection. α^*, b^* are the parameters for the current classifier. $K(\cdot)$ is kernel function.$F(u_j)$ is defined as: select the sample $u_i \in U$ that is closest to classification hyper-plane H constructed by Ct as a new instance to be labeled.

Active learning algorithm for sparse LSSVM will be given in the following:

If you have more than one surname, please make sure that the Volume Editor knows how you are to be listed in the author index.

Algorithm 1: Active learning for sparse LSSVM algorithm

Input : Labeled corpus $L=\{l_1, l_2, ..., l_m\}$, unlabeled corpus $U=\{u_1, u_{\cdot}, ..., u_n\}$, where $m<<n$. T is the maximum number of iterations. P is the accuracy of classifier C. e_t is the expected accuracy

Output : Classifier C^t, where t denotes the established classifier in the tth iterations

---

Process :
1. Initialize:Construct the initial labeled collection L, in which there is at least one instance for each type of samples, and then use LSSVM training the initial collection L to obtain the initial classifier C^0
2. For (t=1 to T) or (P<e_t) do
   a. Calculate $F^t(u_j)$, get the top m samples collection U', $U'=\{u_1', u_2', ..., u_m'\}$
   b. Submit U' to the labeler and Add U' to L,$L'=\{L \cup U'\}$,let L= L'.
   c. Train the LSSVM by use of L^t samples to get C^t
   d. Use C^t to label testing samples automatically, and judge its accuracy P
   End For

---

4   Experiment and Result Analysis

4.1   Data Set

In order to evaluate the performance of sparse LSSVM based on active learning algorithm, this paper adopt 6 classification data sets provided by UCI[1]. In the field of image, we use image segmentation data of Massachusetts University to classify 7 different scenarios. In the field of biology, we use Kenta's ecoli dataset (Protein Localization Sites) and yeast data set to identify proteins. In the field of medicine, we apply heart dataset to judge the status of the heart. In the manufacturing industry, the car dataset is adopted to evaluate the automobile quality. In physics filed, we employ ionosphere database provided by Johns Hopkins University to assess the ionosphere conditions. Datasets shown in Table 1.

Table 1. Sample division, class number and feature dimension of classification dataset. One of the sample denoted "Training Samples/ Testing Sample/ Class Number/ Feature Dimension".

dataset	Car	Image seg.	Ecoli.	heart	yeast	ionosphere
sample	206/120/ 8/8	2150/160/7 /19	160/110/ 2/13	250/101/ 2/34	1300/428/4 /10	979/500/10 /9

4.2   Metrics and Test Methods

The sparse rate is used as a measure of the proportion that the actual training samples of total samples, it can be expressed as $u=(n-n_{real})/n$, where n denotes the training samples space, n_{real} represents the actual samples space involved in the training, the higher the value, the greater degree of sparsely. Accuracy indicates the test samples

---

[1] http://archive.ics.uci.edu/ml/index.html

were correctly classified, expressed as the ratio of correct classification samples of total samples.

4.3 Comparison of Active Learning and Random Sampling Experiment

Initiative to select valid samples is the most important function of active learning, this paper carried out the LSSVM performance comparison experiment between random sampling(Random-LSSVM) and active learning sampling (AL-LSSVM).Simultaneously, we experiment on the effect of m value(m denotes the number of chosen samples to be labeled in each time).

Experimental results are shown in Figure 1, where the horizontal axis represents the number of training samples, the vertical axis stands for the precision, the blue solid line represents AL-LSSVM, the red dotted line denotes Random-LSSVM. It can be seen from Figure 1 in the initial stage, the accuracy of AL-LSSVM method fluctuated and even lower than the Random-LSSVM. However, with the gradual increase of the sample space, the effect of AL-LSSVM method will immediately apparent and ahead of Random-LSSVM method. By analysis, the volatility of the initial phase is due to the most uncertain samples derived from the new samples, it has a deep influence on small samples of model, thus prone to fluctuated in the initial phase. But later achievements verify the efficiency of AL-LSSVM algorithm.

By comparing different m influenced on the model from Figure 1, we can see that AL-LSSVM and Random-LSSVM will be gradually equivalent with the increase of m size. Therefore, it is necessary to test and select the appropriate m value in different application systems. In this paper, because the chosen training samples is relatively small, so we choose m=1 as a benchmark for the follow-up experiments.

4.4 Experiments on Accuracy and Sparse Rate of AL-LSSVM

For the sake of comparison, this paper also adopts SVM and standard LSSVM for testing the above-mentioned 6 data sets. SVM use SMO algorithm of Weka [2] to experiment, while LSSVM apply LSSVMLab[3] tools to conduct the experiment. The experimental results shown in table 2.From the result in Table 2,the accuracy of standard LSSVM and AL-LSSVM are all increased compared with SVM model. From the perspective of accuracy, AL-LSSVM has not been a great improvement than the standard LSSVM; this could be less noise data in the training samples, which warrant the performance of standard LSSVM. However, due to AL-LSSVM has higher sparsely than LSSVM, so AL-LSSVM has already achieved very good results showed as the experimental results in this paper.

Table 2. Comparisons of average classification accuracy

Precision	Car	Image seg.	Ecoli.	heart	yeast	ionosphere
SVM	82.3±1.0	85.0±2.4	82.3±1.3	82.0±1.1	52.7±1.2	87.2±1.2
LSSVM	89.8±2.3	89.3±0.0	86.0±1.0	84.5±6.0	53.3±0.4	91.0±2.0
ALLSSVM	90.0±0.3	90.4±0.9	87.4±0.5	86.1±0.3	56.1±1.2	95.0±0.2

[2] http://www.cs.waikato.ac.nz/ml/weka/
[3] http://www.esat.kuleuven.be/sista/lssvmlab/

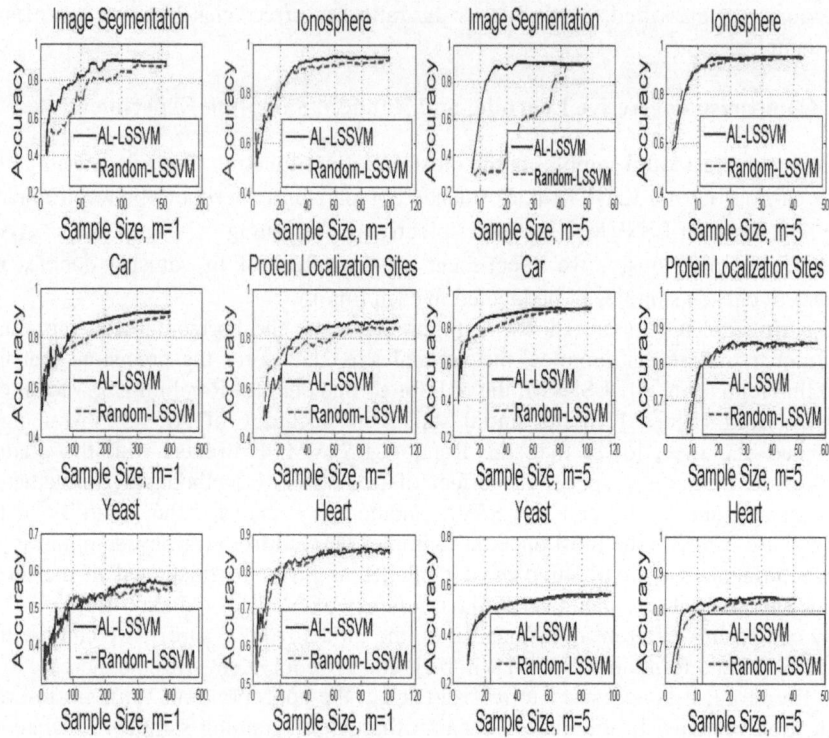

Fig. 1. Comparison of AL-LSSVM and Random-LSSVM

Table 3 illustrates the experimental results for sparse performance of AL-LSSVM. Because the sparsely of standard LSSVM is zero, therefore not be listed. As can be seen from Table 3, except for Car dataset, the experiment on the remaining data sets show that AL-LSSVM algorithm has greatly improved on sparsely compared with SVM.

Table 3. Comparisons sparsely of SVM with AL-LSSVM

Spare Ratio	Car	Image seg.	Ecoli.	heart	yeast	ionosphere
SVM	49.0±5.0	15.0±2.4	25.5±6.8	20.5±1.1	12.7±1.2	47.2±2.9
LSSVM	43.5±2.0	63.9±1.0	70.2±1.1	54.1±1.5	49.5±2.3	79.1±3.3
V.S.	-5.5±7.0	48.9±3.4	44.7±7.9	33.6±2.6	36.8±3.5	31.9±6.2

5   Preparation

Sparsely is one of the keys to improve least squares support vector (LSSVM).The proposed method of active learning strategies to sparse LSSVM not only greatly improves the sparse nature of LSSVM, but also reduce the annotation cost, the standard data sets in the experiment also illustrates this point. Further study will combines the initial cluster technologies to optimize the process of constructing classifier for LSSVM, and solve the problem of fluctuations in the initial stage

References

1. Vapnik, V.N.: The Nature of Statistical Learning Theory. Springer, N.Y (1995)
2. Dong, J.X., Krzyzak, A., Suen, C.: Fast SVM training algorithm with decomposition on very large data sets. IEEE Transaction on Pattern Analysis and Machine Intelligence 27(4), 603–618 (2005)
3. Joachims, T.: Making large scale SVM learning practical, pp. 169–184. MIT Press, Cambridge (1999)
4. Cortes, C., Vapnik, V.: Support vector networks. Machine Learning 20(3), 273–297 (1995)
5. Suykens, J.A.K., Vandewalle, J.: Least Squares Support Vector Machine Classifiers. Neural Processing Letters 9(3), 293–300 (1998)
6. Li, M., Sethi, I.K.: Confidence-based active learning. IEEE Transaction on Pattern Analysis and Machine Intelligence 28(8), 1251–1261 (2006)
7. Simon, H.A., Lea, G.: Problem solving and rule education: a unified view knowledge and organization. Erbuam. 15(2), 63–73 (1974)
8. Lewis, D.D., Gale, W.A.: sequential algorithm for training text classifiers. In: Croft, W.B., Rijsbergen, C.J. (eds.) Proc. of Annual SIGIR Conf. on Research and Development in Information Retrieval SIGIR 1994, vol. 15(2), pp. 3–12. Springer, London (1994)
9. Freund, Y., Seung, H., Shamir, E., et al.: Selective sampling using the query by committee algorithm. Machine Learning 28(2), 133–168 (1997)
10. Kenji, F.Z.: Statistical active learning in multilayer perceptrons. IEEE Transaction on Neural Networks, 17–26 (2000)
11. LindenBaum, M., Markovitch, S., RusaKov, D.: selective sampling for nearest neighbor classifiers. Machine Learning 54(2), 125–152 (2004)
12. Mitchell, T.: Generalization as search. Artificial Intelligence 18(2), 203–226 (1982)
13. Hoegaerts, L., Suykens, J.A.K., Vandewalle, J., De Moor, B.: A comparison of pruning algorithms for sparse least squares support vector machines. In: Pal, N.R., Kasabov, N., Mudi, R.K., Pal, S., Parui, S.K. (eds.) ICONIP 2004. LNCS, vol. 3316, pp. 1247–1253. Springer, Heidelberg (2004)
14. Tao, S., Chen, D., Hu, W., et al.: CCA sparse least squares support vector machine classifiers. Journal of Zhejiang University (Engineering Science) 41(7), 1093–1096 (2007)
15. Tong, S.: Chang. E: Support vector machine active learning for image retrieval. In: Proceedings of the 9th ACM International Conference on Multimedia, Ottawa, Canada, pp. 107–118 (2001)
16. Michael, I.M., Graham, E.P., Daniel, P.E.: Support Vector Machine Active Learning for Music Retrieval. Multimedia Systems 12(1), 3–13 (2006)

Naïve Bayes vs. Support Vector Machine: Resilience to Missing Data

Hongbo Shi and Yaqin Liu

School of Information Management, Shanxi University of Finance and Economics
030031 Taiyuan, China
shb710@163.com, liuyaqin2003@126.com

Abstract. The naïve Bayes and support vector machine are the typical generative and discriminative classification models respectively, which are two popular classification approaches. Few studies have been done comparing their resilience to missing data. This paper provides an experimental comparison of the naïve Bayes and support vector machine regarding the resilience to missing data on 24 UCI data sets. The experimental results show that when the missing rate is very small (e.g. 1%), the resilience of the naïve Bayes classifiers to missing data are approximately similar to that of support vector machine classifiers. With the increase of the missing rate, however, the resilience of the naïve Bayes classifiers to missing data are slowly decreased and that of support vector machine classifiers to missing data are rapidly decreased. This demonstrates that the naïve Bayes classifiers have better resilience to missing data than support vector machine classifiers.

Keywords: missing data, the naïve Bayes, SVM, resilience.

1 Introduction

Missing data is a common problem that appears in many real world situations. For example, sensor failures in industrial control processes, omitted entries in databases and non-response in questionnaires [1]. Many scientific, industrial, business and economic decisions are related to the information available at the time of making decisions. In these applications, if we merely ignore the incomplete instance or handle inappropriately missing values, it may lead to biased results in statistical modeling. Therefore, it is essential to research on the problem of missing data.

Many researchers engaged in a serious study of missing data. In order to identify the reason why data are missing, Little and Rubin define three different types of missing data mechanisms [2]: missing completely at random, missing at random and not missing at random. To take advantage of missing data, some common methods handling missing data, which used before learning algorithms, are proposed, for example, case deletion, attribute deletion, mean imputation, multiple imputation and so on. The most representative classification algorithms which are able to deal with missing values were investigated, such as decision trees[3], fuzzy approaches[4], Bayes approaches[5] and support vector machines[6]. In addition, [7] examined the

H. Deng et al. (Eds.): AICI 2011, Part II, LNAI 7003, pp. 680–687, 2011.

effect of missing data to different classification algorithms, including two rule inducers, a nearest neighbor method, two decision tree inducers, a naïve Bayes inducer, and linear discriminant analysis. They found that the naïve Bayes method was by far most resilient to missing data.

Generative and discriminative approaches are two different paradigms for solving classification problems, which have different thoughts and frameworks. The discriminative approaches look for an optimal decision function $f(x)$ or the probability $p(y|x)$ of x being the class y to separate the data from data with the other class label, whereas a generative model often captures the generation process of x by modeling $p(x|y)$ and tries to represent the true density of the data. The naïve Bayes classifier and support vector machine (SVM) are the typical generative and discriminative models, respectively. In this paper, we compare the naïve Bayes with support vector machine for examining their reliance to missing data. We select these two particular algorithms for several reasons. First, they are popular with data analysts, machine learning researchers, and statisticians. Second, the naïve Bayes and support vector machine are the generative and discriminative approach, respectively. Third, they often are applied to handle higher dimension data, for instance, text data.

2 Naïve Bayes Classifier vs. Support Vector Machine Classifier

2.1 Naive Bayes Classifier

The naïve Bayes classifier is a typical generative classifier, which can be regarded as a special case of Bayesian network classifiers [8]. In general, Bayesian network classifier models first the joint distribution $p(x,y)$ of the measured attributes x and the class labels y factorized in the form $p(x|y)p(y)$, and then learns the parameters of the model through maximization of the likelihood given by $p(x|y)p(y)$. Due to there is a fundamental assumption that the attributes are conditionally independent given a target class, the naïve Bayes classifier in fact learns the parameters of the model through maximization of the likelihood given by $p(y)\prod_j p(x_j|y)$.

Since the naïve Bayes classifiers optimize the model over the whole dimensionality, and are capable of learning even in the presence of some missing values. Furthermore, the naïve Bayes classifier is a stable, and its classification result is not significant changed due to noises or corrupted data.

2.2 SVM Classifier

The SVM [9] classifier is a typical discriminative classifier. Different from generative classifier, it mainly focuses on how well they can separate the positives from the negatives, and does not try to understand the basic information of the individual classes. The SVM classifier maps first the instance x in a training set into a high dimensional space via a function Φ, then computes a decision function of the form $f(x) = <w, \Phi(x)> + b$ by maximizing the distance between the set of points $\Phi(x)$ to the hyperplane or set of hyperplanes parameterized by (w, b) while being consistent on the training set.

The SVM classifier builds a single model for all classes and hence it requires simultaneous consideration of all other classes. Moreover, the SVM classifier performs well on data sets that have many attributes, even if there are very few cases on which to train the model.

3 Missing Data Mechanisms

For data sets with missing values $X=\{x^{(i)}, y^{(i)}|\ i=1,\ldots,n\}$, all attribute values can be partitioned into two categories: observed values and missing values, and hence each instance $x^{(i)}$ is composed of two parts: the observed attribute values $x_{o_i}^{(i)}=\{x_j^{(i)}\ |\ j\in o_i\}$ and the missing attribute values $x_{m_i}^{(i)}=\{x_j^{(i)}\ |\ j\in m_i\}$, where o_i and m_i are the set of indices for observed and missing attributes, respectively. Each instance $x^{(i)}$ has its own observed set o_i and missing set m_i.

Let $M=\{M_j^{(i)}\ |\ i=1,\ldots,n,\ j\in o_i\cup m_i\}$ be a missing data indicator matrix. If $x_j^{(i)}$ is observed, then $M_j^{(i)}=1$, otherwise, $M_j^{(i)}=0$. We refer to M as the *missingness*. The parameters of characterizing the distribution of *missingness* is usually called the missing data mechanism ξ, therefore the missing data mechanism is characterized by the conditional distribution of M given the input data set $X=(X_m, X_o)$,

$$p(M\mid X,\xi)=p(M\mid X_m,X_o,\xi) \tag{1}$$

where X_o and X_m are the observed input set and the unknown input set, respectively.

According to whether there is the dependence relationship between the *missingness* and data, [2] defines three types of the missing data mechanisms: missing completely at random (MCAR), missing at random (MAR) and not missing at random (NMAR).

- MCAR

In MCAR situation, there are no constraints to the relationship between the *missingness* and data, and the missing values are randomly distributed across all observations, and the probability of *missingness* does not depend on the values of other covariates. The MCAR condition can be expressed by the relation

$$p(M\mid X_m,X_o,\xi)=p(M\mid\xi) \tag{2}$$

Since there are not dependence between missing values and other data values in MCAR situation, the basic way of handing missing data, e.g. mean imputation or special values imputation, may be valid.

- MAR

For MAR, the missing values are not randomly distributed across all observations, the probability of the *missingness* is conditional on the values of other covariates, and the missing values are therefore randomly distributed within subsets of observations.

The *missingness* is independent of the missing variables but the pattern of data *missingness* is traceable or predictable from other variables in the database. The MAR condition can be expressed by the relation

$$p(M\mid X_m,X_o,\xi)=p(M\mid X_o,\xi) \tag{3}$$

- NMAR

In NMAR situation, the missing values are not distributed randomly. In contrast to the MAR and MCAR situation, the probability of the *missingness* cannot be predicted from the values of other covariates and may depend on the values of the missing data. If the probability of the *missingness* can not be modeled, it is likely to lead to biased model estimates. There is a no general method of handling missing data properly.

When data are MCAR or MAR, the missing data mechanism is known as ignorable. Ignorable mechanisms are important, because when they occur, a researcher can ignore the reasons for missing data in the analysis of the data, and thus simplify the methods used for missing data analysis [10]. Therefore, the majority of research works focuses on the MAR or the MCAR situation.

4   Experimental Setup and Results

4.1   Data Sets

In order to investigate the properties of the Naïve Bayes and support vector machine classifier with respect to missing values, we chose 24 data sets from the UCI machine learning repository [11]. Since the main goal of the experiments is to explore the impact of missing rate on different classification algorithms, all of data sets have not missing values.

The MCAR was chose as the missing data mechanism of the experiments. To simulate the missing completely at random setting, we randomly replaced a fraction of attribute values with '?' ('?' represents missing values) according to a uniform distribution, and assumed the rest are observed. Following the method of [7], the proportion of missing data ranges from 1% to 40%, i.e. 1%, 5%, 10%, 15%, 20%, 25%, 30%, 35% and 40%. On each original data set, nine data sets with different missing rate were generated by our data generating algorithm.

4.2   Evaluation Metrics

Before starting all of the experiments, we need to define a performance measure that is appropriate for measuring the impact of missing data. The classification accuracy has been the standard comparison metric used in studies of classifier induction in the machine learning literature, which is the number of correct predictions on the test data divided by the number of test data instances. Since accuracy can be affected by the data structure and by the missing data, and our focus is to compare the resilience of various classification algorithms to missing data, we need to define a measure called resilience of missing data (*ResMiss*), calculated as

$$ResMiss = \frac{Accuracy_{missing} - Accuracy_{original}}{Accuracy_{original}} \times 100\% \qquad (4)$$

where $Accuracy_{missing}$ and $Accuracy_{original}$ represent accuracy with missing data and original full data, respectively. The *ResMiss* measures the difference between the accuracy achievable with missing values and achievable with the original full data relative to that achievable with the original full data. The smaller the *ResMiss* is, the better the resilience of an algorithm to missing data is. If *ResMiss* of an algorithm is equal to 0, the algorithm will not affected by the existing missing values in the data set.

4.3 Workbench and Methodology

All the experiments were performed in the Weka system [12], which provides a workbench that includes full and working implementations of many popular learning schemes. To compare the resilience of the naïve Bayes to missing data with that of support vector machine, we need first to obtain their classification accuracy on different data sets. We use "weka.classifiers.bayes.NaiveBayes" as the naïve Bayes classifier (simply called NB) and "weka. classifiers.functions.SMO" as the support vector machine classifier (simple called SVM) implemented in Weka system.

The classification accuracy is observed via 10 runs of 10-folds stratified cross validation on data sets. $Accuracy_{missing}$ and $Accuracy_{original}$ are obtained on missing data sets and the original data sets, respectively. Then, we compute $ResMiss$ of the naïve Bayes classifier and SVM classifier by using the equation (4).

4.4 Result and Analysis

Fig. 1 shows that the comparison of the average $ResMiss$ of the naïve Bayes and support vector machine to missing data on 24 data sets. The X axis is the percentage of missing values with respect to the original data set, and the Y axis is the measure $ResMiss$ of the resilience of missing data.

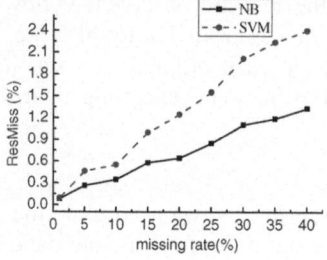

Fig. 1. Comparison of the average ResMiss of the naïve Bayes classifier with that of the SVM classifier with repect to missing data on 24 data sets

From Fig. 1, we can obviously observe that when the missing rate is about 1%, the average $ResMiss$ of the naïve Bayes and the SVM are approximately the same. With the increase of the missing rate, the average $ResMiss$ of the naïve Bayes classifier goes up in relatively slow speed and the average $ResMiss$ of the SVM goes rapidly up. When the missing rate is up to 40%, the average $ResMiss$ of the naïve Bayes is 1.2% lower than that of SVM. That is to say, only when the missing rate is very small, the resilience of the naïve Bayes and the SVM are approximately the same. In general, the resilience of the naïve Bayes classifier to missing data is superior to that of the SVM classifier to missing data, especially in the case that the missing rate is higher.

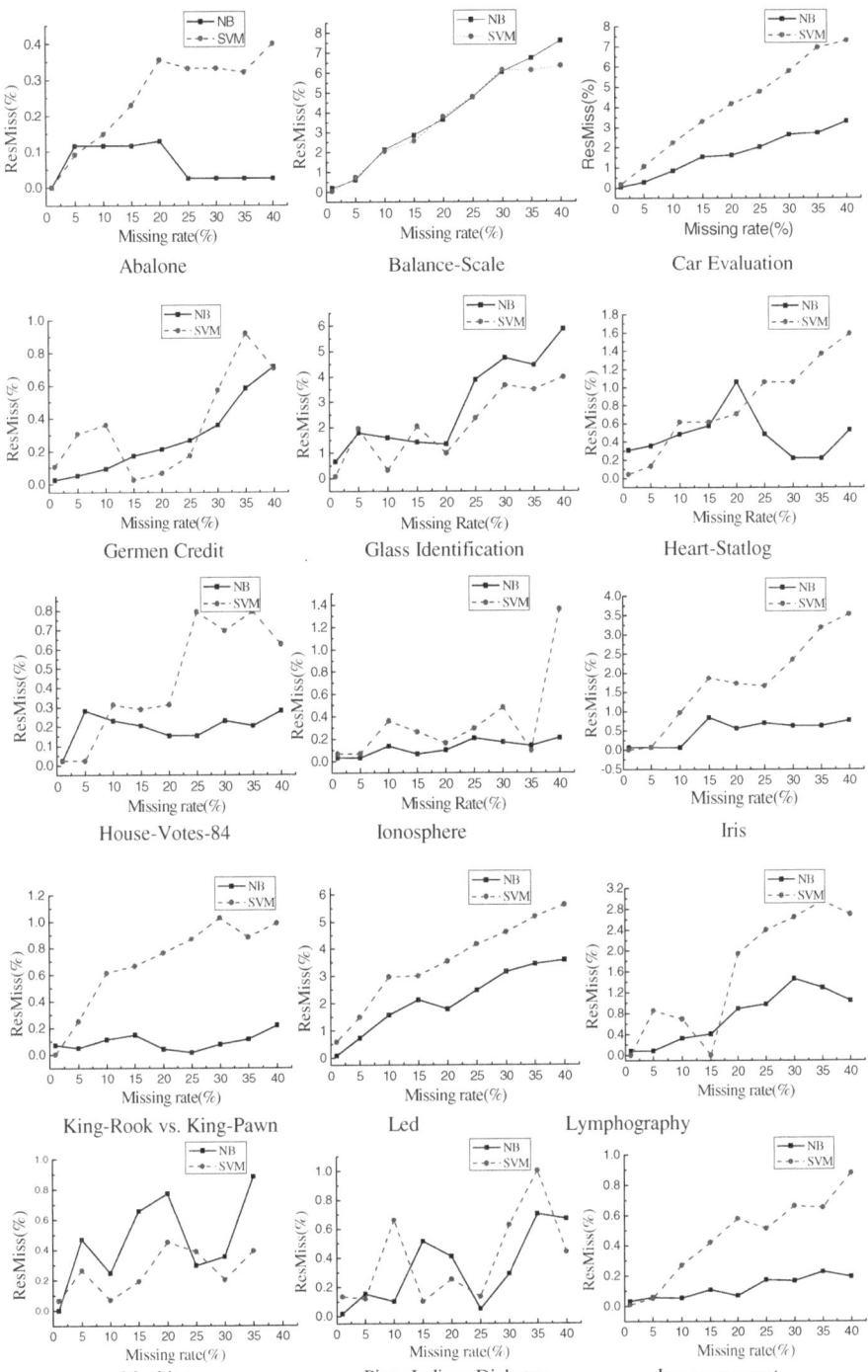

Fig. 2. Comparison of the resilience of the naïve Bayes classifier and the SVM classifier to missing data on 24 data sets

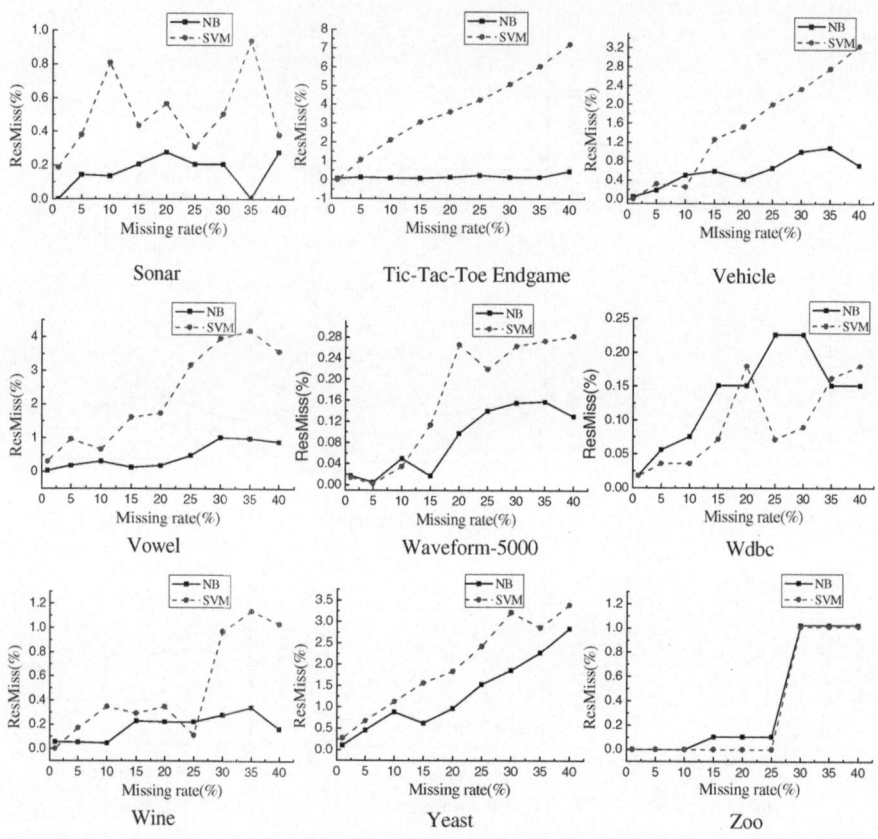

Fig. 2. (*continued*)

To compare clearly the resilience of the naïve Bayes with that of the SVM on each data set, Fig. 2 shows *ResMiss* comparison of the naïve Bayes and the SVM on 24 data sets. From Fig. 2, some results can be observed:

- For most data sets, the resilience of the Naïve Bayes classifier to missing data is superior to that of the SVM.
- Merely for individual data sets, the above conclusion is not true. For wdbc, machine and glass, the resilience of the Naïve Bayes classifier to missing data is inferior to that of the SVM; for blance-scale and zoo, the resilience of the Naïve Bayes classifier to missing data is very similar to that of the SVM.
- For all of data sets, when the missing rate is very small, the naïve Bayes and the SVM are almost same resilient to missing data. With the increase of the the missing rate, however, the gap of the resilience to missing data between the naïve Bayes and the SVM is significantly increased.

5 Conclusions

The naïve Bayes and support vector machine are the typical generative and discriminative classification model, respectively. To understand the effect of missing data to two classification approaches, this paper conducted an experimental comparison of the naïve Bayes classifiers and the support vector machine classifiers regarding their resilience to missing data. The experiments were performed on 24 UCI data sets. The experimental results show that the naïve Bayes classifiers have better resilience to missing data than the support vector machine classifiers.

Our experimental results are obtained in MCAR situation, and whether these conclusions are true in MAR and NMAR situation need further to investigate.

Acknowledgments. This paper is funded by the National Natural Science Foundation of China under Grant No. 60873100 and the Natural Science Foundation of Shanxi Province of China under Grant No. 2009011017-4 and No. 2010011022-1.

References

1. García-Laencina, P.J., Sancho-Gómez, J.L., Figueiras-Vidal, A.R.: Pattern classification with missing data: a review. Neural Computation & Applications 9, 1–12 (2010)
2. Little, R.J.A., Rubin, D.B.: Statistical Analysis with Missing Data, 2nd edn. John Wiley & Sons, New York (2002)
3. Webb, G.I.: The problem of missing values in decision tree grafting. In: 10th Australian Joint Conference on Artificial Intelligence, pp. 273–283. Springer, London (1998)
4. Ichihashi, H., Honda, K.: Fuzzy c-means classifier for incomplete data sets with outliers and missing values. In: International Conference on Computational Intelligence for Modeling, Control and Automation, pp. 457–464. IEEE Computer Society, Washington, DC (2005)
5. Ramoni, M., Sebastiani, P.: Robust Bayes classifier. Artificial Intelligence 125, 209–226 (2001)
6. Pelckmans, K., Brabanter, J.D., Suykens, J.A.K., Moor, B.D.: Handling missing values in support vector machine classifiers. Neural Network 18, 684–692 (2005)
7. Kalousis, A., Hilario, M.: Supervised knowledge discovery from incomplete data. In: 2nd International Conference on Data Mining. WIT Press, Cambridge (2000)
8. Friedman, N., Geiger, D., Goldszmidt, M.: Bayesian network classifiers. Machine Learning 29, 131–163 (1997)
9. Vapnik, V.: Statistical learning theory. John Wiley & Sons, New York (1998)
10. Schafer, J.L.: Analysis of incomplete multivariate data. Chapman & Hall, Florida (1997)
11. Frank, A., Asuncion, A.: UCI Machine Learning Repository. University of California, School of Information and Computer Science, Irvine, CA (2010),
    http://archive.ics.uci.edu/ml
12. Witten, I.H., Frank, E.: Data Mining: Practical Machine Learning Tools and Techniques with Java Implementations. Morgan Kaufmann Publishers, Seattle (2000)

Mining at Most Top-K% Spatio-temporal Outlier Based Context: A Summary of Results

Zhanquan Wang, Chunhua Gu, Tong Ruan, and Chao Duan

Department of Computer Science and Engineering,
East China University of Science and Technology, Shanghai, China
{zhqwang,chgu,ruan.tong}@ecust.edu.cn,duanchaoaa@126.com

Abstract. Discovering STCOD is an important problem with many applications such as geological disaster monitoring, geophysical exploration, public safety and health etc. However, determining suitable interest measure thresholds is a difficult task. In the paper, we define the problem of mining at most top-K% STCOD patterns without using user-defined thresholds and propose a novel at most top-K% STCOD mining algorithm by using a graph based random walk model. Analytical and experimental results show that the proposed algorithm is correct and complete. Results show the proposed method is computationally more efficient than naive algorithms. The effectiveness of our methods is justified by empirical results on real data sets. It shows that the algorithms are effective and validate.

Keywords: Spatio-Temporal Outliers, Top-K%.

1 Introduction

Spatio-temporal outlier detection, called anomaly detection in space and time, is an important branch of the data mining research [1][2][3]. At most top-K% spatial-temporal context outlier detection (TopSTCOD) represents some special objects that have some anomalous behavior without composite interesting measures in the space and time. Formally, given a collection of objects over a common Spatio-temporal framework, and a neighborhood relation over neighbors, a TopSTCOD mining algorithm aims to discover correct and complete sets of interesting and non-trivial TopSTCODs. A TopSTCOD represents a pattern set whose interest measures are in the top-K% of the complete set of objects and have higher values than patterns which are not found in STCOD method. Discovering TopSTCODs is important for many spatio-temporal application domains. For example. In the Masai Mara national reserve (MMNR) in Kenya[10], there are many species, such as wildebeest and zebra, they are gregarious species, but two groups often lives nearby. The existing methods can't find the patterns without composite interesting measures, and these thresholds values are mostly domain-specific and without domain knowledge, it is very difficult to set up suitable interest measure thresholds to mine the STCODs. If the user-defined threshold is too small to mine the patterns, it is highly likely that too many patterns will be generated. If the threshold values are too large, it is also possible to discover

H. Deng et al. (Eds.): AICI 2011, Part II, LNAI 7003, pp. 688–695, 2011.

too few patterns and miss possible significant ones. So it is very important and interesting for biologists to research their behavior and habit without interesting measure thresholds. There are other applications are such as military, ecology, and homeland defense [2][4][5].

To the best of our knowledge, this is the first work to discover top-K% spatio-temporal contextual outliers detection at spatio-temporal dataset; It includes the statement which are applicable to the real applications; A new and computationally efficient TopSTCOD mining method is presented; It includes comparisons of approaches and experimental designs. This paper focuses on TopSTCODs by statement of top K%. The rest of the paper is organized as follows. Section 2 reviews some background and related works in outlier detection data mining. Section 3 proposes basic concepts to provide a formal model of TopSTCOD. TopSTCOD and fast TopSTCOD mining algorithms are presented in section 4. The experimental results are proposed in section 5 and section 6 presents conclusions and future work.

2   Related Work

The quality of identified contextual outliers heavily relies on the meaningfulness of the specified context [2][6][8][9][12][19]. However a STCOD mining algorithm proposed in author's previous work which requires user-defined thresholds: a spatial contextual outlier measure and the time prevalence measure. The spatial contextual outlier is used to determine if the pattern is spatially anomalous. The time prevalence measure is used to determine if the pattern is frequent. These thresholds values are mostly domain-specific and without domain knowledge, it is very difficult to set up suitable interest measure thresholds to mine STCODs. If the user-defined threshold is too small to mine the STCODs, it is highly likely that too many patterns will be generated. If the threshold values are too large, it is also possible to discover too few patterns and miss possible significant ones. This study aims to discover TopSTCODs with no need for user-defined spatial threshold and time prevalence threshold by using a random walk graph and spectral analysis[2][11] which is a powerful tool to study the structure of a graph at each timeslot, where we use transition matrix to study how to get unknown contextual information for spatio-temporal data.

3   Basic Concepts and Statement of Modeling

The random walk graph and contextual outliers is omitted due to space limit [6]. The focus of this study is to discover at most top K% spatio-temporal context detection objects (TopSTCODs) over a spatio-temporal framework and a neighborhood relation R (or relation of social network). First we introduce basic concepts, and then explain the modeling of at most top-K% STCODs. Fig.1 shows an example of spatio-temporal contextual outlier. In spatio-temporal data, we proposed a spatiao-temporal framework. The context-based spatio-temporal outlier detection is different from the general outlier detection, which does not only consider spatial attributes and time attributes, but also consider the contextual information. The framework is as follow: a framework of spatio-temporal framework STF, an object (node) set:

$O = \{o_1,...o_i,...,o_n\}(1 \leqslant i \leqslant n)$, n is number of nodes at each timeslot. $T = \{t_1,...,t_j,...,t_m\}(1 \leqslant j \leqslant m)$, m is the number of timeslot. So we can define $STF = \{O_1,...,O_m\}$, $STF = OXT$, O_i is the object set at the timeslot t_i.

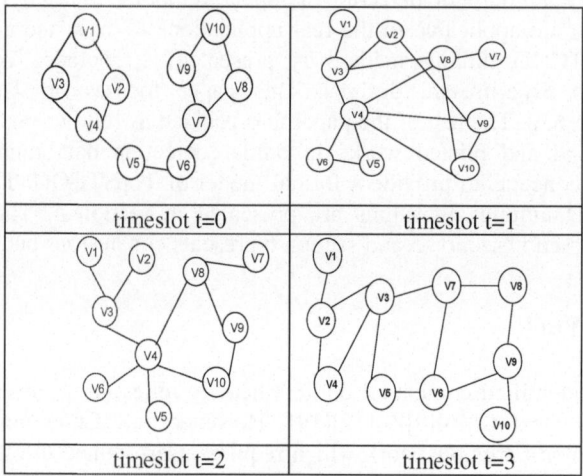

Fig. 1. An example for TopSTCOD

3.1 Modeling of at Most Top K% Spatio-Temporal Context Detection

A method that can detect the contextual outlier for spatio-temporal dataset with the non-main eigenvector is proposed. In the model, every non-main eigenvector of the transitional matrix defines a unique graph of 2-labeling/2-coloring. Intuitively, given a 2-coloring graph, each sub-graph could be regard as a context. Assume S^+ is a sub-graph and S^- is another, we can get the probability of a node be visited from the beginning of S^+ or S^-. There are some nodes called contextual outliers if the probability of they are visited by S^+ or S^- is equal.

Definition 1: Assume (S^+, S^-) is a 2-coloring of G, S^+ is a index set of the node marked +, and S^- is a index set of the node marked -. They are satisfied the follow condition: $S^+ \neq \varphi, S^- \neq \varphi, S^+ \cup S^- = \{1,...,n\}$. Then we can call (S^+, S^-) a pair of contexts of G. And the random walk in G can be called a contextual random.

Definition 2: (fixed expectation): Assuming G is a random walk graph , W a transitional matrix, μ_i is the expectation of random variable[8], if μ_i satisfies the follow condition: $\mu_i = c \sum_{j=1}^{n} \mu_j w_{ij}, \forall i, 1 \leqslant i \leqslant n$, where c is a constant of time-independent, then we call $\mu = (\mu_1,...,\mu_n)^T$ is the fixed expectation corresponding the contextual random walk of S^+ and S^-.

If W is a transitional matrix of positive, then every non-main eigenvector of W can uniquely determine a pair of contexts and the corresponding fixed expectation. Particularly, assume v is a eigenvector which corresponding to the eigenvalue $\lambda < 1$ of W. So we can regard v as a non-main eigenvector of W and get the follow lemma:

Lemma 1: Given a non-main eigenvector v of a positive transitional matrix, then

$$\sum_{i=1}^{n} v(i) = 0,$$ where $v(i)$ is an item of v.

According to lemma 1, we can define a 2-coloring of G with v, it can provide a pair of contexts: $S^+ = \{i : \mathbf{v}(i) > 0\}, S = \{i : \mathbf{v}(i) < 0\}$.

Now considering the contextual random walk with (S^+, S^-) in G, we can get follow theorems:

Theorem 1 (the fixed expectation of a contextual random walk): If assuming

$$\mu = (\mu_1,...,\mu_n)^T \quad , \quad \mu_i = \frac{\mathbf{v}(i)}{\sum_{j=1}^{n}|\mathbf{v}(j)|}, \forall i, 1 \leqslant i \leqslant n \text{ ,where } v \text{ is non-main}$$

eigenvector corresponding to the eigenvalue λ of W, so definition 4 is satisfied. Therefore, μ is a fixed expectation of contextual random walk graph. Theorem 1 indicates that every non-main eigenvector uniquely determines a 2-coloring graph (S^+, S^-) and its fixed expectation μ. According to the theorem 1, we can define the contextual outlier with fixed expectation.

Definition 3 (contextual outlier value): Assume G is a random walk graph, W a positive transitional matrix, then the contextual outlier value (COV) of node i is $|\mu_i|$, and μ_i is the fixed expectation which defined according to Theorem 1.

According to the definition above, we can know that the contextual outlier value of any node is between 0 to 1. A small value indicates that the node is a contextual outlier.

We compute its contextual outlier value for all nodes in time slot t=0,1,2,3.

$\mu =$	$\mu =$	$\mu =$	$\mu =$
0.1168	0.0652	−0.1307	0.1228
0.1096	0.0845	−0.0452	0.0318
0.1096	0.1664	−0.2766	0.1903
0.1332	−0.1467	−0.0956	0.1232
0.0309	−0.1766	−0.0271	0.0318
−0.0309	−0.1766	−0.0271	−0.0858
−0.1332	0.0364	0.0749	−0.0448
−0.1096	0.0931	0.1585	−0.1389
−0.1096	0.0370	0.1120	−0.1176
−0.1168	0.0175	0.0523	−0.1129
timeslot t=0	timeslot t=1	timeslot t=2	timeslot t=3

Given a set of spatio-temporal objects with a neighborhood relation R (or relation of social network), an at most top-K% STCOD is a subset of spatio-temporal object which are neighbors in space and time.

Definition 6: Given a spatio-temporal dataset, and a set T of time slots, a pattern is in the top-K% STCOD list if it is in the first K% of the number of all objects based on the lowest value of in the spatial contextual measures at each timeslot $(ascend(fixexpecation_{ti})/n \leqslant K\%)$ and the highest values in the time measures for all timeslots$(descend_{timeslots}((c\_ascend(fixedexpectation_{ti})/n \leqslant)K\%) \leqslant K\%)$, where ascend is count of sorting ascend for the contextual outlier value at each timeslot. descend is value of sorting descend time prevalence index values.

Table 1. Valuse of the contextual outlier

nodes	t=0	t=1	t=2	t=3	Time prevalence index values
v1	0. 1168	0. 0652	0. 1307	0. 1228	0
v2	0. 1096	0. 0845	0. 0452	0. 0318	1/4
v3	0. 1096	0. 1664	0. 2766	0. 1903	0
v4	0. 1332	0. 1467	0. 0956	0. 1232	0
v5	0. 0309	0. 1766	0. 0271	0. 0318	3/4
v6	0. 0309	0. 1766	0. 0271	0. 0858	2/4
v7	0. 1332	0. 0364	0. 0749	0. 0448	1/4
v8	0. 1096	0. 0931	0. 1585	0. 1389	0
v9	0. 1096	0. 037	0. 112	0. 1176	0
v10	0. 1168	0. 0175	0. 0523	0. 1129	1/4

Fox example, in fig.1. there are ten objects. A top-20% STCOD will include two objects (v5,v6) which are the top-20% of ten objects which are at most 20% spatio-temporal outlier based context. Table.1 shows the detailed part.

3.2 Analysis for Model

At most top-K% spatio-temporal contextual outliers which are produced from our methods are correct because the patterns satisfy threshold pairs. The patterns are complete because our algorithms can find any STCODs as long as it satisfies our definitions and rules. The model average time complexity is $O(n^2 m)$. We omit the detail analysis due to space limit.

4 Mining TopSTCODs

In the section, we discuss the implementation of our spatio-temporal contextual outlier values in practice. We propose a hierarchical algorithm which iteratively partitions the data set for each time slots until the size of the sub graph is smaller than a user specified threshold pairs. In every time slots, we acquire the contextual outlier value of spatial object with the method of contextual outlier detection mentioned above. Set a K%. The naïve algorithm1 of context-based spatio-temporal outlier detection is omitted due to space limit, We only describe the fast algorithm for spatio-temporal contextual outlier which is more efficient than naïve method.

Algorithm2: top K% spatial-temporal contextual outlier detection

---

Inputs: spatial-temporal data set STD, number of timeslot m, K;

Output: at most top K% spatial-temporal contextual outliers

1: TopSTO ← φ,

2: foreach $t_i \in$ T   do

3:     foreach i∈ TopSTO do

4:       Tr(t_i,i)=0;

5:     end;

6:   creat random walk graph G and transition matrix W;

7:   TopSTO (G, W,K) ;

8:     foreach i∈ L do

9:           if   i(score)$_{PERCENT}$ > K then

10:               Tr(t_i,i)=1;

11:         end;

12:     end;

13: end

14: foreach i∈ TopSTO do

15:   TOS(i)= $\sum_{j=1}^{m} Tr(t_j,i) / m$;

16:     if   TOS(i) $_{PERCENT}$ > K   then

17:             TopSTO = TopSTO ∪ {i};

18:     end

19: end

The time complexity of our algorithm is a time polynomial. The algorithm involves calculating the first and second largest eigenvalue and eigenvector of an n × n matrix, where n is the number of nodes. So its complexity is mainly determined by the complexity of eigen-decomposition. Second time cost is sorting data by outlier values, and the average time complexity is $O(n^2 m)$, the time cost for judging outlier is $O(nm)$. Therefore, we would adopt a efficient method to calculate eigenvalue and eigenvector. As a characteristic of outliers is that they are composed by minority objects, so we don't necessarily to consider all the objects in the process of calculation. We can set a K%, only put the object whose outlier value is smaller than threshold K% into the sort list L. It can keep the most normal data without any unnecessary operation in order to improve algorithm. When calculating outlier in the time series, we don't need to deal with all objects, but only a minority objects, so the size of the sort list will be greatly reduced. When judging spatial contextual outlier, we can set number set a K%, the object whose outlier value is smaller than K% will regard as outlier, this is the first modified part.

The second modified part is: when judging outlier in the time slots, some nodes have satisfied the judging condition before deal with all the times, so it is unnecessary to deal with the later times. The improved algorithm is described as the fast algorithm.

5 Experimental Evaluation

In this section, we present our experimental evaluations of several design decisions and workload parameters on our TopSTCOD mining algorithms. We used two real-world training dataset,(mail log for users and vehicle data set). We evaluated the behavior of two algorithms. Fig.2 shows the experimental setup to evaluate the impact of design decisions on the performance on these methods. Table.2 shows real dataset in vehicles. Experiments were conducted on a Windows XP, 2.0GHz Inter Pentium 4 with 1.5GB of RAM.

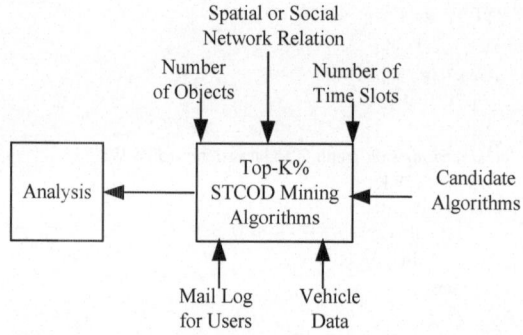

Fig. 2. Experimental setup

5.1 Effect of Number of Time Slots

According to the location information of the vehicle we establish transition matrix with spatial relation R(R=100). Experiment analysis would be done according to number of time slots. We evaluated the effect of number of timeslots on the execution time of both algorithms by mining at most top-10% STCOPs. The parameter K parameter was set at 10. The execution time of both algorithms increase, as the number of timeslots is increased (Fig.3). The TopSTCOD-Miner is computationally more efficient than the naïve approach because of its early pruning strategy (Fig.3). As the number of time slots increases, the ratio of the increase in execution time is smaller for TopSTCOD -Miner than with the naïve approach.

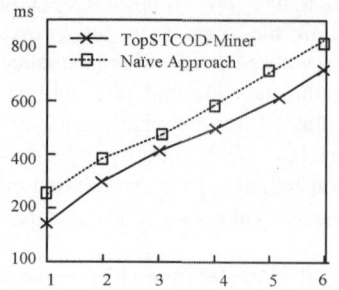 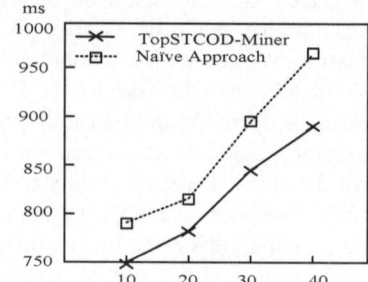

Fig. 3. The relationship between the number of timeslots and time

Fig. 4. The relationship between K and running time

5.2 Effect of Parameter K

In the third experiment we evaluated the effect of number of K on the execution times of algorithms. The neighborhood distance and number of timeslots are 100m and 10. Fig. 4 shows that the execution time of both algorithms increases and the TopSTCOD-Miner outperforms the naïve approach as the parameter K increases.

From the experiment analysis above, we can draw a conclusion that the improved algorithm is more efficient than the original algorithm.

6 Conclusion

We defined at most top-K% spatio-temporal contextual outlier detection and its mining problem. We also presented a novel and computationally efficient algorithm for mining these patterns and its improved method, and proved that the model is correct and complete in finding at most -K% spatio-temporal contextual outliers. Our experimental results using the vehicle dataset from the real world provide further evidence of the viability of our approach. For future work, we would like to explore the relationship between the proposed composite interest measures and spatio-temporal statistical measures of interaction[2]. We plan to develop other new computationally efficient algorithms for mining TopSTCODs; further study variation of transition matrix due to multi-scale of space or time, and space and time.

Acknowledgement. The authors are very grateful to the financial support from the National Natural Science Foundation of China under Grant No. 60703026

References

1. Han, J.W., Kamber, M.: Data mining concepts and techniques. Morgan Kaufmann Publishers, San Francisco (2001)
2. Shekhar, S., Chawla, S.: Spatial databases: a tour. Prentice Hall, Englewood Cliffs (2003)
3. Breunig, M.M., Kriegel, H.-P., Ng, R.T., Sander, J.: Lof: Identifying density-based local outliers. In: SIGMOD Conference (2000)
4. Moonesinghe, H.D.K., Tan, P.N.: Outlier detection using random walks. In: ICTAI (2006)
5. Kou, Y., Lu, C.T., Chen, D.: Spatial weighted outlier detection. In: SDM (2006)
6. Wang, X., Davidson, I.: Discovering contexts and contextual outliers using random walks in graphs. In: ICDM 2009 (2009)
7. Chandola, V., Banerjee, A., Kumar, V.: Anomaly detection: a survey. ACM Comput. Surv. 41(3) (2009)
8. Skillicorn, D.B.: Detecting anomalies in graphs. In: ISI (2007)
9. Liu, F.T., Ting, K.M., Zhou, Z.H.: Isolation forest. In: ICDM, pp. 413–422 (2008)
10. Barnet, V., Lewis, T.: Outlier in statistical data. John Wiley&Sons, New York (1994)
11. Chung, F.: Spectral graph theory. American Mathematical Society, Providence (1997)
12. Song, X., Wu, M., Jermaine, C.M., Ranka, S.: Conditional anomaly detection. IEEE Trans. Knowl. Data Eng. 19(5) (2007)

SD-Q: Selective Discount
Q Learning Based on New Results of
Intertemporal Choice Theory

Fengfei Zhao and Zheng Qin

Department of Computer Science and Technology
Tsinghua University, Beijing, China
zhaofengfei@gmail.com, qingzheng@mail.tsinghua.edu.cn

Abstract. We discuss the reinforcement learning from an intertemporal choice perspective. Different from previous research, this paper wants to emphasize the importance of deeper understanding the psychological mechanism of human decision-making. In what follows we aim to improve the previous Q learning algorithm according to the new results of intertemporal choice experiments. We start with a brief introduction to new findings of intertemporal choice theory and reinforcement learning. Then we propose a new reinforcement learning algorithm with selective discount (SD-Q). Experiments show that, SD-Q is superior to both the traditional Q learning algorithm and the reinforcement learning method without considering the discount.

Keywords: reinforcement learning, selective discount, SD-Q learning, Q learning, intertemporal choice.

1 Introduction

Deeper understanding the physiological and psychological mechanism of human decision-making will help us to improve our existing artificial intelligence methods[1]. Intertemporal choice is an economic term describing how an individual's current decisions affect the future. Traditional intertemporal choice researchers believe that the individual makes decisions based on the expectation-maximization rule, that is, to calculate the total utility of all the results of each option and select the option with the maximum total utility. This idea is based on the two assumptions that are "independence" and "additive" [2]. Once a decision theory requires "independence" and "additive", it tacitly approves "cancellation axiom", which means people's preferences are not affected by the common elements in alternative options.

Nobel laureate in economics, Allais, questioned expected utility maximization in risky choice and put forward the famous "Allais Paradox" [3]. Allais Paradox shook the dominance of expected utility theory and made the risky choice researchers aware of the mishap of expectation maximization.

Reinforcement learning is an important branch of machine learning, and it also involves the intertemporal reward problem. Reinforcement Learning formulas also

H. Deng et al. (Eds.): AICI 2011, Part II, LNAI 7003, pp. 696–702, 2011.
© Springer-Verlag Berlin Heidelberg 2011

assume that the relationship between current reward and future reward meets the assumption of "independence" and "additive". To improve the previous reinforcement learning algorithm according to the new results of intertemporal experiments is an exciting and challenging attempt. Q learning is one of the most widely used reinforcement learning algorithms, and we improve it based on the analysis of psychological experiments. Our experiments prove that the improved algorithm has a clear advantage over the original one.

The rest of the paper is organized as follows: section 2 shows an interesting finding in intertemporal choice experiments. Section 3 gives an overview of reinforcement learning. In section 4, we introduce our algorithm, SD-Q learning. Section 5 describes our results of experiments. We conclude in section 6.

2 Findings of Intertemporal Experiments

Inspired by "Allais paradox", the researchers of Institute of Psychology, Chinese Academy of Sciences speculate: If the mainstream theory of intertemporal choice still follows the cancellation axiom, there should be an intertemporal choice version's the Allais paradox in intertemporal choice [4]. The paradox is found by them as follows:

Question 1
A:Get ￥1000,000 now, and lose ￥2000,000 in 1 year.
B: Lose ￥2000,000 in 1 year, and get ￥5000,000 in 10 years.

Question 2
C: Now get ￥ 1,000,000
D: 10 years later received ￥ 5,000,000

The researchers found that in question 1, 71.1% chose the option B, but in question 2, 76.7% chose the option C. It should be noted that Question 2 is got by eliminating the common elements "after 1 year loss of ￥ 2,000,000" in Question 1. Facing the two options which are removed the common component, people made a decision which is completely different from the decision they made before deleting the common elements. This is contrary to the "cancellation axiom".

3 Overview of Reinforcement Learning

3.1 Reinforcement Learning

Reinforcement learning (RL) is derived from the conditioned reflex theory in biology, whose basic idea is to reward the desired results and punish the undesired results, to form conditioned reflex gradually which trend to good results ([5], [6], [7]). Reinforcement learning is a method to get maximum reward by learning how to map the state to action. Different from most other machine learning methods, in reinforcement learning algorithm, agents are not told which action should be taken, but have to find which action will bring the greatest reward by constantly trying.

In reinforcement learning, the learning agent is in the environment which is described as a finite set S and all actions which learning agent can perform form a finite set A. When in some state s_t implementation of an action a_t will let the agent receive a reward r_t which is a real number. This process produces a series of states, actions and immediate rewards. Agent's task is to learn a set of strategies π : It maximize the sum of the expected rewards $r_0 + \gamma r_1 + \gamma^2 r_2 + \ldots$, $0 \le \gamma < 1$, in which the following reward r value decreases with their delay factor γ, that is to say, it maximizes $V^\pi(S_t)$, which is defined as : $V^\pi(S_t) \equiv r_t + \gamma r_{t+1} + \gamma^2 r_{t+2} + \ldots \equiv \sum_{i=0}^{\infty} \gamma^i r_{t+i}$.

Then the optimal policy can be expressed as:

$$\pi^* \equiv \arg\max_\pi V^\pi(s), (\forall s) \tag{1}$$

3.2 Q Learning

Q learning algorithm is proposed by Watkins [8]. It is easy to know that, the best action a in the state s is the one which can maximize the sum of immediate reward r (s, a) and the value V of successor state, which can be expressed as:

$$\pi^*(s) \equiv \arg\max_a [r(s,a) + \gamma V^*(\delta(s,a))] \tag{2}$$

In this expression, $\delta(s, a)$ denotes the successor state of s after executing action a. However, in many practical problems, it is unrealistic to learn the V value directly, so the Q function has been proposed, which is defined as:

$$Q(s,a) \equiv r(s,a) + \gamma V^*(\delta(s,a)) \tag{3}$$

The optimal policy can be expressed as:

$$\pi^*(s) \equiv \arg\max_a Q(s,a) \tag{4}$$

Learning agent gets immediate rewards by continuing exploring and updates the Q values with the formula:

$$Q(s,a) \leftarrow Q(s,a) + \alpha[r + \gamma \max_{a'} Q(s',a') - Q(s,a)]$$
$$s \leftarrow s' \tag{5}$$

Where α is the learning rate. The above steps complete the whole process of Q learning.

Because it is independent from existing environment, Q learning is considered as one of the most effective reinforcement learning algorithm, is also one of the most widely used algorithms.

4 SD-Q Learning Based on New Results of Intertemporal Choice Theory

In original Q-learning formula, reward value and punishment value are assumed to meet cancellation axiom. However, according to new findings of intertemporal choice, this assumption is unreasonable. So in this work we propose a new reinforcement learning method called SD-Q learning (selective discount Q learning), and we do not assume that the proposed model meets the assumption of "independence" and "additive". In SD-Q learning, we rewrite the Q learning formula as:

$$Q(s,a) \equiv f(r(s,a), \ V^*(\delta(s,a)))$$ (6)

$f(a, b)$ is defined as follows: a denotes immediate reward value and b denotes reward value in the future. Q value is calculated from the function $f(a, b)$, rather than the simple weighted sum of a and b. The specific form of $f(a, b)$ can be determined according to the need of the practical problems. In this paper, we give a simple definition of $f(a, b)$, and more complex forms of $f(a, b)$ can be derived by learning from samples.

From the result of Question 2 in section 2, we can see that, people still consider the discount while they are choosing the recently rewards and long-term rewards. Therefore, f can be defined as: $f(a, b) = a + \gamma*b$ when both a and b are greater than or equal to 0 . However, in Question 2, when we replace reward with loss, we find that people do not consider delay factor obviously as they did before. That is to say, there is no obvious discount when one considers the loss. Hence, when both a and b are less than 0, we define f as: $f(a, b) = a + b$. When a and b have different symbols, according to Question 1 and other related experiments, most people think it is more important that the overall effect is a loss or a reward. Hence, if the sum of a and b is negative, we calculate the f value without any discount as what we do when both a and b are greater than or equal to 0. At this time, we define f as: $f(a, b) = a + b$. If the sum is positive, we consider the sum as a single reward and we define f as: $f(a, b) = \gamma*(a + b)$.

To sum up, f can be written as:

$$f = \begin{cases} a + \gamma * b & \text{when } a \geq 0, b \geq 0 \\ a + b & \text{wh en } a + b < 0 \\ \gamma * (a + b) & \text{others} \end{cases}$$ (7)

By this new definition, we can get a reasonable explanation for previously mentioned intertemporal choice problem. However, it will be verified by experiment whether the SD-Q reinforcement learning method which is modified according to human behavior would get good results.

5 Experiments

Let us validate our SD-Q reinforcement learning method by a classic and simple example ([9], [10]). Figure 1 shows a 5*5 grid world containing a taxi agent, in which there are 4 landmarks that are labeled as R (ed), B (lue), G (reen), and Y (ellow). The problem is episodic. In each episode, the taxi chooses a random location as a starting point. A passenger randomly emerges at one of the four landmarks. The passenger wants to reach one of the four landmarks (also randomly selected). The taxi must go to the place where the passenger stays and pick up the passenger. Then the taxi drives to the passenger's destination and put down the passenger to terminate the episode. In order to unify, even if the passenger is already in the destination, the taxi also needs a process of uploading (pick up) and unloading (put down).

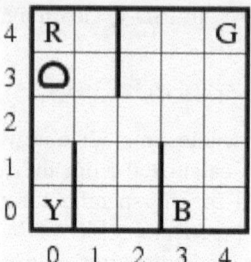

Fig. 1. The taxi domain

Throughout the process, the taxi can execute a total of six optional actions, namely, the navigation actions, east, west, south, and north, together with pickup and putdown actions. There is a -1 reward for every action. A reward of +20 will be given to the learning agent when the passenger is put down at the right destination successfully. Wrong pickup action or putdown action will bring a reward of -10. Navigation operations which make the taxi hit a wall lead to no practical action, but bring a -1 reward. To simplify the situation, results of the implementation of all actions are deterministic.

We use experiments to compare Q learning, Q learning completely without discount and the new proposed SD-Q learning method. In the experiments of the taxi domain, we first let the learning agent totally learns 500 episodes every experiment (learning rate $\alpha=0.2$ and discount factor $\gamma=0.95$), and we perform the experiment 100 times to get the average value. Figure 2 shows the statistical results of the experiments. The abscissa represents the number of periods and the ordinate represents the total number of steps (actions). We can see SD-Q is superior to the other two.

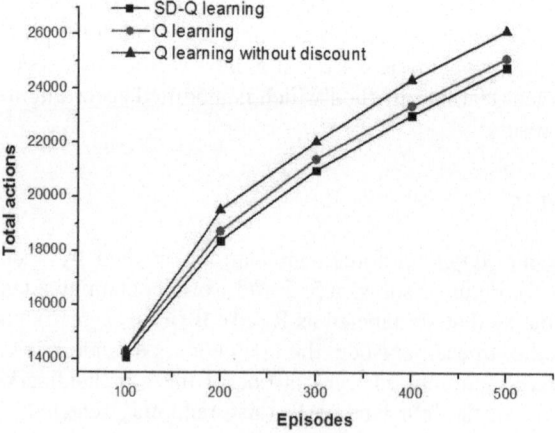

Fig. 2. Experiments result (500 episodes)

Now that SD-Q learning method of 500 episodes has been proved effective, we will interest in the situation with more episodes. We let the learning agent totally learns 5000 episodes every experiment (learning rate α=0.2 and discount factor γ=0.95), and we still perform the experiment 100 times to get the average value. Table 1 shows the statistical results of the experiments and the values in the table represent the average number of steps (actions). As episodes increases, SD-Q is always better than the other two.

Table 1. Experiments Result (5000 episodes)

Episodes	SD-Q	Q	Q(no discount)
500	24816.30	25148.17	26163.01
1000	32038.41	32435.56	33131.62
1500	38753.02	39145.96	39893.09
2000	45277.55	45560.03	46286.59
2500	51938.34	52215.16	52840.55
3000	58238.27	58726.30	59569.58
3500	64841.66	65259.00	65878.84
4000	71358.87	71875.48	72351.35
4500	77974.12	78241.89	78649.02
5000	84535.60	84922.98	85525.45

5 Conclusions

Deeper understanding of psychology and physiology will help us get a better perspective on the nature of intelligence. Improving reinforcement learning method by researching and imitating the decision-making way of human beings, would make the reinforcement learning method more effective, so that the machine has the ability to think more like humans. In this paper, we introduce the new findings of intertemporal choice into the classic Q reinforcement learning method, and propose SD-Q method which is a new reinforcement learning algorithm. Experiments prove that, in some cases, neither completely using discount nor no discount at all is the best choice; selective discount will get better results.

References

1. Weber, B.J., Chapman, G.B.: The combined effects of risk and time on choice: Does uncertainty eliminate the immediacy effect? Does delay eliminate the certainty effect? Organizational Behavior and Human Decision Processes 96, 104–118 (2005)
2. Loewenstein, G., Prelec, D.: Preferences for sequences of outcomes. Psychological Review 100, 91–108 (1993)

3. Allais, M.: Le comportement de l'homme rationel devant le risque: Critique des postulats et axioms del'école americaine (Rational man's behavior in face of risk: Critique of the American School's postulates and axioms). Econometrica 21, 503–546 (1953)
4. Rao, L.-L., Li, S.: New paradoxes in intertemporal choice. Judgment and Decision Making 6(2), 122–129 (2011)
5. Kearns, M., Singh, S.: Near-optimal reinforcement learning in polynomial time. In: Proceedings of the Fifteenth International Conference on Machine Learning, pp. 260–268 (1998)
6. Singh, S.P.: Transfer of learning by composing solutions of elemental sequential tasks. Machine Learning 8, 323–339 (1992)
7. Moriarty, D., Schultz, A., Grefenstette, J.: Evolutionary algorithms for reforcement learning. Journal of Artficial Intelligence Research 11(1), 241–276 (1999)
8. Watkins, C., Dayan, P.: Q-Learning. Machine Learning 8(3), 279–292 (1992)
9. Dietterich, T.G.: Hierarchical reinforcement learning with the MAXQ value function decomposition. Journal of Artificial Intelligence Research 13, 227–303 (2000)
10. Dietterich, T.G.: The MAXQ method for hierarchical reinforcement learning. In: Fifteenth International Conference on Machine Learning, pp. 118–126. Morgan Kaufmann, San Francisco (1998)

Principled Methods for Biasing Reinforcement Learning Agents

Zhi Li, Kun Hu, Zengrong Liu, and Xueli Yu

College of Computer Science and Technology, Taiyuan University of Technology
79 Yingze West Street, Taiyuan City, Shanxi Province, China
lizhi_tyut@hotmail.com, hkl206@sina.com,
NZr_liu@sxinfo.net, xueli13287@263.net

Abstract. Reinforcement learning (RL) is a powerful technique for learning in domains where there is no instructive feedback but only evaluative feedback and is rapidly expanding in industrial and research fields. One of the main limitations of RL is the slowness in convergence. Thus, several methods have been proposed to speed up RL. They involve the incorporation of prior knowledge or bias into RL. In this paper, we present a new method for incorporating bias into RL. This method extends the choosing initial Q-values method proposed by Hailu G. and Sommer G. and one kind of learning mechanism is introduced into agent. This allows for much more specific information to guide the agent which action to choose and meanwhile it is helpful to reduce the state research space. So it improves the learning performance and speed up the convergence of the learning process greatly.

Keywords: Reinforcement learning, prior knowledge, bias, Q-learning, biasing Q-learning.

1 Introduction

Agent technologies for virtual agents and physical robots are rapidly expanding in industrial and research fields. The ability to acquire new behaviors through learning is fundamentally important for the development of agent technologies. Reinforcement learning (RL) [1] is a common approach to agent learning from experience.

All reinforcement learning methods share the same goal: to solve sequential decision tasks through trial and error interactions with the environment [2, 3]. A learning agent repeatedly observes the state of its environment, and then chooses and performs an action. Performing the action changes the state of the world, and the agent also obtains an immediate numeric payoff as a result. The agent must learn to choose actions so as to maximize a long term sum or average of the future payoffs it will receive.

One of the main limitations of RL is the slowness in convergence. This is because it is often studied under the assumption that there is little or no prior information about the task at hand. This assumption, however, is not the defining characteristic of learning. Humans rarely approach a new task without presumptions on what type of

H. Deng et al. (Eds.): AICI 2011, Part II, LNAI 7003, pp. 703–709, 2011.
© Springer-Verlag Berlin Heidelberg 2011

behaviors are likely to be effective. This bias is a necessary component to how we quickly learn effective behavior across various domains. Without such presumptions, it would take a very long time to stumble upon effective solutions.

Bias, in the context of learning, is a term used to describe a learning system's predisposition for learning something at the expense of others. Incorporating bias or advice into reinforcement learning takes many forms. Thus, several methods have been proposed to speed up RL through the incorporation of prior knowledge or bias into RL.

A brief study to mitigate the dimensionality problem by crafting key states by hand can be found in Hailu and Sommer [4].A method for incorporating an arbitrary number of external policies into an agent's policy can be found in Malak and Kholsa [5]. Their system uses an elaborate policy weighting scheme to determine when following an external policy is no longer beneficial. If reliable advice on which actions are safe and effective is known, one can restrict the agent's available actions to these. Deriving such expert knowledge has been heavily studied in the control literature and has been applied to reinforcement learning by Eric Wiewiora and by Perkins and Barto [6, 7].

2 Maze World

The system is represented by an agent or robot going around a maze shown in Fig.1. The maze world is grid world consisting of 10×10 states, one of which is identified as a goal state G and any of the state can be chosen as a start state S. It is assumed that all the states are discrete, distinct and completely distinguishable.

The robot chooses from four actions, representing an intention to move in one of the four cardinal directions (N, E, S, W). Any movement moves the robot in the intended direction, except for those into the wall (black grid) or the world boundary. Attempting an action against world boundary or a wall does not change the state. None of this structure and dynamics is known to the unbiased learning system a priori.

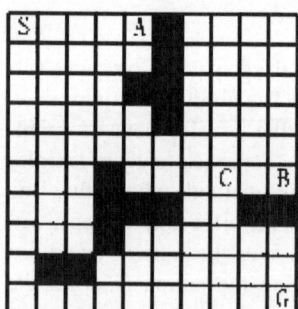

Fig. 1. Maze World

In this domain, the task of the robot is to reach the goal state through the shortest steps. Reward is -1 for all transitions except for those into the goal state, in which case it is +1.

3   Bias Design

Our maze world experiments extend the methodology found in Hailu G. and Sommer G. [8]. An belief matrix B, a version of reflex for discrete state-action space, is used to restricts the set of possible hypothesis by putting a strong belief on each hypothesis, so that strong negative belief is needed to eliminate an hypothesis from consideration. An hypothesis is a pairing of any state with any action and it is associated with a belief value that represents the appropriateness of the pairing. In short, belief values either eliminate or put preference on the set of possible actions that can be tried at each state by encoding prior knowledge in the belief matrix (equation 1),

$$
B = \begin{bmatrix} b_{11} & b_{12} & \cdots & b_{1p} \\ b_{21} & b_{22} & \cdots & b_{2p} \\ \vdots & \vdots & \vdots & \vdots \\ b_{n1} & b_{n2} & \cdots & b_{np} \end{bmatrix},
\tag{1}
$$

where $i \in \{1,2,\cdots,n\}$ represents state, $j \in \{1,2,\cdots,p\}$ represents action.

For the task described above, we consider mainly environment bias and goal bias. Environment bias: a part of the environment knowledge that informs the agent to stay away from collision with the boundary of the world or other obstacles is encoded in the belief matrix. Referring to figure 1, the actions of *up* (N) and *right* (E) should be forbidden at state A, for example.

Goal bias: is a goal directed bias. Since the destination is known, it is possible to bias the learner in someway to the goal. For example, a positive number are supplied only for those states that are near to the goal and the remaining states are negative number for the agent to discover the positive number through RL. These numbers are semantic meanings that represent the *reachability* of a state. The reachability of a state is defined as the minimum sequence of actions required to reach a specified goal starting from that state. It is difficult to describe the relation between states with spatial distance. An agent can be near to the goal spatially, however, it may require a series of actions before it reaches that goal. Referring to figure 1, state B is spatially nearer to the goal than state C, obviously, an agent that starts from state B requires more steps to reach the goal than it starts from state C.

The choice of these biases is primary guided by the particular task at hand. For the case of tasks requiring reaching a given destination, goal biases are useful and available. But environment bias is more generic and also can be applied across tasks.

4   Q-Learning

The framework of most of RL algorithms is a Markov Decision Process (MDP) .An MDP is defined as a five tuple $M = <S, A, T, R, \gamma>$, where S is a finite set of states, A is a finite set of actions, $T: S \times A \times S \rightarrow R$ is a transition function, $R: S \times A \rightarrow R$ is a bounded reward function and $0 \leq \gamma < 1$ is a discount factor on the summed sequence of rewards. The agent's goal is to learn an optimal policy, $\pi^* : S \rightarrow A$, which maps states to actions, that will produces the greatest cumulative reward over all states s.

The RL algorithm that we use in this work is based on Q-learning [9]. The Q-learning optimal action-value function is:

$$Q^*(s,a) = E[R(s,a,s') + \gamma \max_{a'} Q^*(s',a')] \; . \tag{2}$$

This represents the expected value of the reward for taking action a from state s, ending up in state s', and then acting optimally. $\gamma \in [0,1]$ is the discount factor. Q-values are typically stored in a tabular representation. Q-learning is an off-policy method, that is to say, the optimal action value function Q^* is directly approximated, independently of the policy being followed. Its updating rule is:

$$Q(s,a) \leftarrow Q(s,a) + \alpha[r + \gamma \max_{a'} Q(s',a') - Q(s,a)] \; , \tag{3}$$

where r is the reward received for the transition from the state s to the new state s' by executing the action a. $\alpha \in [0,1]$ is the learning-rate parameter. Under some conditions [10], Q-learning algorithm is guaranteed to converge to the optimal value function Q^*. The method, we called biasing Q-learning, is embedding the bias (here is belief matrix B) in the initial action value function of the standard Q-learning algorithm.

5 Learning Model

Q-learning learns about the optimal policy regardless of the policy that is being followed. For this reason Q-learning is called off-policy and this can be useful to control learning polices for agent. So our work is based on Q-learning. On the other hand, the convergence of Q-learning needs that in every state every action is eventually selected an infinite amount of times. Although in many cases the optimal policy is learned long before the action values are highly accurate. If the action space is stationary, the size of state space is an important factor in Q-learning convergence rate.

Biasing Q-learning can give the agent a hint on whether a particular state is good or bad, but it cannot provide the same sort of effects about various states. The main thought of our method is to introduce an knowledge base which includes the prior knowledge about tasks. It can be used to bias Q-learning and also be used to reduce the size of the agent research space.

We now describe our framework of this method. Showing in fig2, reinforcement learning model includes three modules and their functions are described as following:

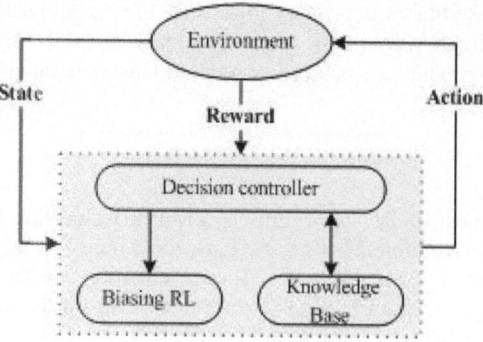

Fig. 2. Learning Model

(1) Biasing RL module: In this module biasing Q-learning algorithm is being used but it is different from the biasing Q-learning method discussed above. Their action selection part is separated out and controlled by decision control module, they only accomplishes the other calculations. That is to say, in every discrete time step t_i, biasing RL module perform action a_t which is selected by decision control module and get an experience sample consisting of the tuple $\{s_t, a_t, r_{t+1}, s_{t+1}\}$, then use it to update Q values.

(2) Decision control module: This module mainly decides which action will be selected. Using the information from knowledge base, this module selects action and sent to biasing RL module. When exploration of the agent can not be directed by knowledge, decision control module introduces the exploration police in the standard Q-learning, such as ϵ-greedy or Boltzmann exploration.

(3) Knowledge base module: This module contains the prior knowledge about tasks and knowledge getting from agent learning process. Using this knowledge the module gives advice to decision control module according to the current state the agent is. This module also produces the belief matrix B which is used to initial Q-values. Referring to figure 1, agent is in state B and the module gives advice action *down* according to the prior goal knowledge. This action *down* has an immediate consequence of collision with a wall, so a learning mechanism should be set up to learn new knowledge.

5.1 Learning Mechanism

The main thought of learning mechanism is: during agent learning process, error action can be decided from the prior knowledge. Whenever this happens, the mistake can be corrected and store in knowledge base.

Fist, we have following definitions:

(1) Using MDP M= (S, A, R, T) to show the process of agent learning, where S is a finite set of states, A is a finite set of actions, T: $S \times A \times S \to R$ is a transition function and R: $S \times A \to R$ is a bounded reward function.

(2) S_r is a set of sate which includes all the states whose action can be decided by knowledge. S_r is changeable on amount and quality of knowledge. A_r is a set of actions which decided by knowledge and $A_r \subset A$.

(3) S_e is a set of sate which includes all the states whose action can not be decided by knowledge or the decision is a mistake (such as collision with a wall or the world boundary). S_e is also changeable. A_e is a set of actions which can be selected on S_e and $A_e \subseteq A$.

With these definitions we have our learning mechanism: At state s, there is an action decided by knowledge and this decision is a mistake, then $s \in S_e$ and marked with a tag $e(s)$ =true. If there exist a path $s_i \xrightarrow{a_i} s_{i+1} \xrightarrow{a_{i+1}} \cdots \xrightarrow{a_{n-1}} s_n$ and e (s_n) =true, then $s_i \in S_e$.

5.2 Learning Algorithms

According to the discussion above, we have our learning algorithms shown in table1.

Table 1. Learning Algorithms

1: Initialize Q with Matrix B;
2: **Repeat** (for each episode):
3:   Initialize s, t=0, e=0;
4:   **Repeat** (for each episode):
5:   **If** e(s_t) = true **then**
6:     $A_r(s_{t-1}) = A_r(s_{t-1}) - \{ s_{t-1} \}$;
7:     Choose a_t from s_t using policy derived from Q (Boltzmann exploration);
8:     Take action a_t, observe r , s';

9:   $$Q(s,a_t) \leftarrow Q(s,a_t) + \alpha[r + \gamma \max_{a'} (s',a') - Q(s,a_t)];$$

10:   $s_{t+1} \leftarrow s'$;

11:     t ← t+1 ;
12:   **else** a_t = Ask_Action(KB, s_t);
13:     **If** a_t = null **then goto** 7 ;
14:       **else** Take action a_t, observe r , s';

15:   $$Q(s,a_t) \leftarrow Q(s,a_t) + \alpha[r + \gamma \max_{a'} (s',a') - Q(s,a_t)]$$

16:   $s_{t+1} \leftarrow s'$;

17:     t ← t+1 ;
18: **Until** termination condition is met

6 Conclusions

Through discussing and comparing we find that our method allows for much more specific information to guide the agent which action to choose and meanwhile it is helpful to reduce the state research space. So our method improves the learning performance and speed up the convergence of the learning process greatly.

Acknowledgments. We gratefully acknowledge the support from National Natural Science Foundation of China (No.60873139), Shanxi Natural Science Foundation (2008011040) and Open Fund of the State Key Laboratory of Virtual Reality Technology and Systems (SKVR-KF-09-04).

References

1. Sutton, R.S., Barto, A.G.: Reinforcement Learning: An Introduction. The MIT Press, Cambridge (1998)
2. Gabriel, M., Moore, J.W. (eds.): Learning and Computational Neuroscience. MIT Press, Cambridge; Mam, Y.: The Technical Writer's Handbook. University Science, Mill Valley (1989)
3. Barto, A.G., Sutton, R.S., Watkins, C.J.C.H.: Learning and sequential decision making. In: Gabriel, M., Moore, J.W. (eds.) Learning and Computational Neuroscience. The MIT Press, Cambridge (1990)

4. Hailu, G., Sommer, G.: Embedding knowledge in reinforcement learning. In: International Conference on Artificial Neural Network (ICANN), Sweden, pp. 1133–1138 (1998)
5. Malak, R.J., Kholsa, P.K.: A framework for the adaptive transfer of robot skill knowledge among reinforcement learning agents. In: IEEE International Conference on Robotic Automation (2001)
6. Wiewiora, E., Cottrell, G., Elkan, C.: Principled Methods for Advising Reinforcement Learning Agents. In: Proceedings of the Twentieth International Conference on Machine Learning (ICML 2003), Washington DC (2003)
7. Perkins, T., Barto, A.: Lyapunov design for safe reinforcement learning control. In: Machine Learning, Proceedings of the Sixteenth International Conference. Morgan Kaufmann, San Francisco (2001)
8. Hailu, G., Sommer, G.: On Amount and Quality of Bias in Reinforcement Learning. In: IEEE International Conference on Systems, Man and Cybernetics (IEEE SMC 1999), Tokyo, Japan, pp. 1491–1495 (1999)
9. Watkins, C.: Learning from delayed rewards. Ph.D. dissertation. Cambridge University, Cambridge, England (1989)
10. Watkins, C., Dayan, P.: Technical note: Q-learning. Machine Learning 8, 279–292 (1992)

Author Index